Gift to U.N.I. Library Fund drive
of 1992.
From Ruth I. (Erickson) Purtle,
now Schroeder.
Graduate of Iowa State Teachers 1938.
One of several blind students of
the 1930's.

National Center for the Blind
Baltimore, Maryland

Walking Alone
and Marching Together:

A History of the Organized Blind Movement in the United States, 1940-1990

by Floyd Matson

National Federation of the Blind
Baltimore, Maryland

Copyright © 1990 by The National Federation of
the Blind

All rights reserved. No part of this book may be
reproduced or utilized in any form or by any
means, electronic or mechanical, including
photocopying, recording, or by any information
storage and retrieval system, without permission in
writing from the publisher.

Inquiries should be addressed to
National Federation of the Blind, 1800 Johnson
Street, Baltimore, Maryland 21230

Printed in the United States of America

Library of Congress Cataloging in Publication Data

Main entry under title:
Walking Alone and Marching Together

Includes indexes.
ISBN 0-9624122-1-X

10 9 8 7 6 5 4 3 2 1

First Edition

Table of Contents

Floyd Matson: "Bio-bibliography."

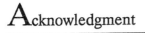Acknowledgment

I wish to express my thanks to Anthony D. Cobb and the entire staff at the National Center for the Blind in Baltimore for their indispensable assistance in the tedious process of collecting data, assembling materials, and scanning the manuscript of this book for factual errors.

It is also a particular pleasure to acknowledge the cooperation of the present generation of leaders in the organized blind movement—who are too numerous to single out by name but who gave freely and often extensively of their time, memory, and wisdom in the interest not merely of building a historical record— that was part of it, of course—but of telling a story (as true as it is remarkable) that has never been told before.

The narration of that story, however, is entirely my responsibility. No one in the organized blind movement with whom I have talked tried to tell me how to write it, or sought to influence its point of view. I have had full access to the files of the National Federation of the Blind and free rein in developing my historical reconstruction of salient events. In the writing of that history I have attempted to present the facts (and the drama) in the context of the time in which they occurred, not in the light of later developments. I have done this even though in some instances relationships have evidently somewhat altered in recent years— the most notable example being, perhaps, the relationship between the NFB and the American Foundation for the Blind. This is only to say that I have tried not to rewrite history to conform to present attitudes or agendas. To the best of my ability I have sought to tell it as it was—and as it must have felt to all those blind Americans who, through half a century of pain and progress, were forming a more perfect union of their own.

Floyd Matson
Honolulu, Hawaii
April, 1990

A Story Never Told

There is no lack of books about blindness and the blind. They are about evenly divided in number between what might be called the generic and the personal—the former ordinarily purporting to be scientific and objective, and the latter being generally literary and impressionistic. The so-called objective studies are usually specialized and rather abstruse, bearing titles like *Blindness as a Socio-Psychological Problem* or *A Stress Analysis of a Blind Nonwhite Caneless Traveler*. The personal and impressionistic volumes are typically inspirational in nature, with names like *My Eyes Have a Cold Nose; Keep Your Head Up, Mr. Putnam; To Race the Wind*; and so on.

Among the generic books many undertake to deal with one aspect or another of "blindness and the blind"—that is, with the background and evolution of various things done to the blind or for the blind, such as charities and corrections, poor laws and public assistance, special education, vocational rehabilitation, sheltered workshops, white canes, guide dogs, vending facilities, psychological adjustment, and the like. Most of these books, for all their claims of scientific discovery and objective information, tell us little about the blind themselves—except for those blind persons who work professionally in the field. What they do tell us about is the "blindness system"—that far-flung network of agencies, institutions, and charities dispensing services to the blind. And even then such studies are mostly of limited and temporary value—yielding place successively to newer texts with fresher studies and reports and brighter graphics.

These historical and sociological studies of blindness and the blind are, so to speak, like *Hamlet* without the prince—like a his-

tory of modern industry without mention of the labor movement—like India without Nehru or Ghandi. Even Richard S.
French's classic study of sixty years ago, *From Homer to Helen
Keller,* tells us more about the achievements of sighted benefactors like Samuel Gridley Howe or blind professionals in the blindness field like Robert Irwin than about the deeds and thoughts
of blind persons themselves and their elected leaders. In short,
the blindness system has, quite understandably, written and
reflected and biographized largely about itself.

During the past generation the three books dealing with
blindness that have probably received the most attention and discussion are Thomas J. Carroll's *Blindness: What It Is, What It
Does, and How to Live With It* (1961), Robert A. Scott's *The
Making of Blind Men* (1969), and Frances Koestler's *The Unseen
Minority: A Social History of Blindness in the United States* (1976).
The first two of these books almost entirely ignore the existence
of the organized blind movement (despite the impression of exhaustive coverage of the field); and the third, by far the most
comprehensive and highly touted, gives only scant and slighting
reference to organizations *of* the blind while attending in
scrupulous detail to the story of the largest of all American agencies *for* the blind. It is true that the title of Koestler's book
promises to give us a history of the blind in America. But the
promise remains a promise, and the very title takes on unintended
irony; for when we have finished this long treatise, the blind—the
"unseen minority"—remain unseen. They also remain unheard.
Although we learn a great deal about the establishment of the
American Foundation for the Blind and its appointed leaders—
the professional elite of the blindness system—we learn next to
nothing about the democratic movement founded by the blind
themselves and built by leaders of their own choosing.

Let it be emphatically said that the roster of leaders in the
institutional history of the American Foundation for the Blind
and its sister agencies—embracing (among others) such well
known names in the field as Major M. C. Migel, Robert Irwin,
M. Robert Barnett, Peter Salmon, Louis Rives, and William Gallagher—carries a freight of substantial impact upon the lives of
blind Americans. Theirs is, indeed, an important story—and appropriately it is one that has been well and thoroughly told.

But it is only part of the story. What has been lacking is a
history of what blind people have done for themselves, what they
have accomplished together, what they have thought and felt and
said and aspired to be and do. This book seeks to correct that

omission and to provide that history—to relate a story never told. In order to give the most accurate account possible and to provide a public file for future reference, the narrative relies extensively upon spoken and written landmarks—the original texts and documents left upon the record by those who made the history, carried the struggle, and fought the fight—the very good fight of the organized blind movement in America.

Theirs is a roster of distinction—one that balances, by any standard which can be imagined, the honor roll of agency luminaries already cited. Accordingly, it is to these statesmen in the American democracy of the blind—leaders like Newel Perry, Jacobus tenBroek, Raymond Henderson, Perry Sundquist, Lawrence Marcelino, Isabelle Grant, Kenneth Jernigan, Donald Capps, and Marc Maurer (to name only a few among many)—that this book is properly and gratefully dedicated.

The Dark Ages— and the Dawn of Organization

The year 1990 holds extraordinary significance for blind Americans. It marks the golden anniversary of the National Federation of the Blind—and so memorializes the first half-century of collective self-organization by the blind people of the United States. This book is the story of those fifty years of Federationism in America: the history of a unique social revolution, democratic and nonviolent but not always peaceful; the drama of an irresistible force—some call it "blind force"—colliding again and again with the seemingly immovable objects of supervision and superstition; and the narrative of a minority group— once powerless, scattered, and impoverished—coming together as a people and forging an independent movement, gaining self-expression and learning self-direction, proclaiming normality and demanding equality.

The story begins, officially, with the establishment of the National Federation of the Blind in 1940. But the historic significance of that event can be fully understood only against the background of earlier attempts to improve the dependent status of the blind through self-organization and self-help. It is a little-known fact that organizations of the blind have existed in one form or another for many hundreds, possibly thousands, of years. The earliest record of their existence comes, perhaps surprisingly, from China—where blind paupers (most of them apparently beggars like others of the disabled) banded together for mutual protection nearly a millennium ago, giving rise to numbers of guilds and associations (composed entirely of blind people) which were able in time to achieve full legal and social status. The extraordinary self-determining and self-sufficient character of these pre-modern Chinese associations has been described by a blind sociologist, C. Edwin Vaughan, writing in the National Federation of the Blind's *Braille Monitor* (April, 1988):

> In Medieval China for at least 1,000 years guilds of craftsmen, workers, and merchants were common. Their purpose was to prevent exploitation from government officials and to provide internal regulation of trade and craft areas of employment. There was in Beijing, formerly Peking, a guild comprised of blind persons who made a career of singing, entertaining, and storytelling. Parents would seek to place a young blind son into this guild so that he might learn a trade for his future lifelong employment. As he succeeded in the required skills, he would rise in status in the guild to the level of master.
>
> Blind guild members in China were self-governing. The guild was governed by a board of forty-eight members of whom forty-seven were blind. The secretary was the only sighted person. The guild governed itself with regard to membership, including the discipline of members, the charges for services, and the recruitment of new members into the guild. The guild met twice each year, and the meetings lasted until 5:00 a.m.

But it was in Europe, during the Middle Ages, that independent guilds and brotherhoods of the blind came to be most highly organized and successful in their purpose. One of the most impressive of these self-contained groups was known as the "Congregation and House of the Three Hundred," which flourished in Paris in the thirteenth century. In this remarkable congregation lived several hundred blind men and women who successfully governed themselves through a popular assembly and were, within the severe monastic limits of the enterprise, entirely self-sufficient. In time, however, the suspicions and stereotypes of the wider society worked against this extraordinary experiment in self-government by the sightless. "Both the administration and the statutes of the congregation," as a historian tells us, "underwent in the course of time a number of changes, with a considerable loss to the blind of their original rights and a corresponding increase of the influence of the sighted."[1]

Still other "free brotherhoods of the blind," as they were called, flourished throughout Europe during medieval times. Most of them were in the form of guilds, and it is worth noting briefly the character and function which these voluntary associations embodied. First of all, of course, they were a means of mutual protection—at a time when blindness was regarded either as a communicable disease or as punishment for sins, and when the sightless might be cruelly punished or put to death with impunity. But the blind brotherhoods also had a positive role to play; they were a vehicle of self-expression and representation for the blind in the affairs of the community. In that respect they were a force, not for segregation, but for integration of the blind into the carefully articulated society of the period. For these guilds of the blind were not unique in the age of feudalism; they coexisted with a wide variety of other specialized associations, each with its particular rights and status, which together made up the medieval community. Through such groups, largely voluntary, the blind and others of the disabled gained a collective identity and a degree of security which was otherwise denied them. Indeed, group membership was essential to all men and women as a source of recognition and identification. "The unattached person during the Middle Ages," as the historian Lewis Mumford has written, "was one either condemned to exile or doomed to death; if alive, he immediately sought to attach himself, at least to a band of robbers. To exist, one had to belong to an association: a household, a manor, a monastery, a guild; there was no security except in association, and no freedom that did not recognize the obligations of a corporate life."

What was true for the prosperous and able-bodied—"there was no security except in association"—was more profoundly true for the blind; and it is likely that they enjoyed a greater measure of physical and economic security within the corporative, guild-oriented society of the Middle Ages than in any previous period of history—certainly more than in the so-called "golden age" of classical antiquity, when the common fate of blind males was to be sold into galley slavery and that of blind females to be sold into "white slavery." Nor would the first centuries of the modern era compare favorably with the medieval situation. For the blind, as for others of the disabled, the breakup of the feudal order and the emergence of the modern world were in crucial respects not progress but retreat. The movement from group status to individual contract—and more specifically the enactment of the infamous Elizabethan Poor Laws—not merely deprived the blind of their fraternal guilds but left them scattered, alienated, and utterly dependent upon the charitable impulses of a new society indifferent at best and frequently cruel in its treatment of the handicapped. In this atmosphere it is not surprising that organizations of the blind, like trade unions and other independent associations of the poor, were actively discouraged and discredited. Within the various separate institutions that grew up to take care of them—the almshouses and workhouses and subsequently the schools, homes, lighthouses, and sheltered workshops—the blind were in effect segregated not only from normal society but also from each other.

It was not until the last quarter of the nineteenth century that voluntary associations of blind people began again to take shape, initially in the form of local and specialized groups. One of the first on record was the Friedlander Union of Philadelphia, organized in 1871; six years later came the New York Blind Aid Association, also composed predominantly of sightless members. By the 1890s there were a number of such groups across the country, many of them composed of alumni of the state schools for the blind. These alumni associations, representing as they did the educated minority of the blind population, tended to take a limited view of their responsibilities and interests, rather than seeking to represent the blind generally. They were the forerunners, but not yet the pathfinders or trailblazers, of the twentieth-century movement of the organized blind. Like the medieval blind guilds, the early alumni associations were largely defensive in character, for the primary stimulus to their organization came from the tragic failure of the special schools for the blind to attain the great objective which had been the dream of the pioneer educators (such men as Valentin Hauy of France, Johann Klein of Austria, and America's Samuel Gridley Howe), namely, the goal of economic integration of the educated blind into the mainstream of society. Before resuming our narrative of self-organization, it is worth recalling this misadventure of the schools and the shock of recognition which it provided. From their beginnings toward the middle of the nineteenth century, American residential schools for the blind followed the model of the

European schools in placing their main curricular emphasis upon vocational training—which chiefly meant instruction in the skills of weaving, knitting, basketry, and chair caning, plus music and other arts. It was the conviction of the early schoolmasters that once their blind wards had shown the ability to master these trades they would be embraced forthwith by a tolerant and receptive society. "It is confidently believed," said one school official in 1854, "that the blind, with proper instruction, will be able to maintain themselves free of charge from their friends or the state. There will be as few exceptions among this class, according to their numbers, as among those who have sight."[2]

In their idealism, these early schoolmen showed themselves to be true heirs of the Enlightenment. Like their counterparts in general education, as well as in social and penal reform, they believed that it was necessary only to strike the chains from their wards in order to make them at once free and self-sufficient. But it was not long before they discovered their error—which was that while the blind were being prepared to enter society, nothing was being done to prepare *society* to receive them. The old prejudices and aversions of employers and the general public remained intact; the newly trained graduates of the schools were given little or no chance to prove their abilities, but instead found all doors closed against them. "Our graduates began to return to us," according to a school official, "representing the embarrassment of their condition abroad, and soliciting employment at our hands."[3]

The response of the schools to this rebuff was perhaps only natural, but it was also unfortunately defeatist. Instead of undertaking programs of public education, selective placement and the like in order to break down the occupational barriers against their blind students, the schoolmasters simply abandoned the goal of normal competitive employment altogether. As a blind leader of a later era, Jacobus tenBroek, was to write of this episode: "At the first signs of public resistance, the optimistic philosophy of the school men crumbled; they conceded in effect that they had been wrong in believing the blind capable of competition and self-support; they were prepared to accept as irremovable the prohibitive stereotypes against which they had formerly ranged themselves, and to assist in reinforcing the ancient walls of segregation and dependency."[4] TenBroek's critical words were appropriate to the fact; instead of a place in the sun, the blind students were offered a shelter in the shade of the school yard, where they might safely practice what were already known as the "blind trades" without fear of competition or contamination from the seeing world. As one report of the period sadly concluded: "The proper preventive is the establishment of a retreat where their bread can be earned, their morals protected, and a just estimate put upon their talents."[5]

That statement might stand as a prophetic description of the sheltered workshop movement which arose as a result of the bitter experience of the schools for the blind with vocational training and employment. The role of the workshops will be discussed in later pages; but it is pertinent here to note that the blind alumni associations came into being in the wake of this episode, providing something of a buffer against the total loss of confidence and self-respect among the educated blind. One such alumni group was that which was formed in 1895 by graduates of the Missouri School; within a year of its founding the Missouri group opened its ranks to graduates of other schools and took on the name of the American Blind People's Higher Education and General Improvement Association. It drew support promptly from blind individuals and groups in a dozen states across the country, and before the turn of the century had held conventions in Missouri and Kansas. In 1903 the character of the group as an organization *of* the blind was abruptly transformed when representatives of several school administrations appeared at its convention bearing a plan for a wholly different kind of association to include not only the blind but also school and program administrators. In 1905 the Association formally abandoned its old identity altogether and became the American Association of Workers *for* the Blind (AAWB)—thus ending the first tentative attempt on the part of blind Americans to organize independently on a nationwide basis.

This denouement was not, however, quite as destructive a blow to the principle of self-organization and self-expression as it would seem. For one thing the impulse to organize on local and state levels, once set in motion by the alumni of the schools, grew steadily and soon embraced other groups of blind persons.

At the same time the development of general-purpose national agencies combining all areas of work for the blind—agencies such as the AAWB and (later) the American Foundation for the Blind—represented a forward step toward the professionalization and modernization of this special (and traditionally backward) field of services to the blind.

Following its reorganization to include sighted professionals in 1905, the AAWB soon became what one observer has described as "the N.A.M. (National Association of Manufacturers) of work for the blind." During the next decade and a half, the AAWB consolidated its position until it became the recognized voice of the numerous professional agencies about the country, not limited to one or two functions but speaking to the needs of the blind population generally. In 1921 the American Foundation for the Blind was established, primarily as a research and coordinating arm of the agencies for the blind; in effect, if the AAWB filled the role of an "N.A.M." in work with the blind, the Foundation took on the stature of a combined Dupont-General Motors in the blindness system.

The American Foundation for the Blind provided the framework for the organizational pattern of the service agencies which was to prevail undisturbed until the advent of the National Federation of the Blind in 1940. This pattern, carried out by a host of agencies at the state and community levels, often under the guidance of the AFB, embraced four distinct areas of endeavor: those of *research, resources, services,* and *representation.* All four of these functions—including even that of representing, or speaking for, the blind—were, for their time, entirely legitimate and constructive; indeed, the AFB made great progress over the years with regard to the first three functions. It initiated the first substantial and systematic research into blindness and its problems; it developed and made available for the first time a variety of significant resources, and it greatly expanded the range and quality of services to the blind—educational and economic as well as recreational and social. As for its role in those years as spokesman for the blind, the American Foundation for the Blind at its worst was better than no spokesman at all and at best was an effective champion for modernized policies and much-needed legislation. As Jacobus tenBroek, Kenneth Jernigan, and other leaders of the organized blind have repeatedly maintained, the agency structure of work for the blind during the decades prior to 1940—controlled at the top as it was by the AFB and the AAWB—resembled nothing so much as a colonial regime of the nineteenth-century variety imposed, with benevolent purpose and some constructive effect, upon a dependent and inarticulate people. Like other colonial administrations, furthermore, the agency system was destined to give way to a democratic form of self-government when its blind wards should come to find their own voice and to declare their independence.

That critical turning point was to come in 1940 as the natural and almost inevitable climax of the spontaneous urge toward association on the part of blind people in state after state. Many of these groups were outcroppings of the school alumni combinations, such as the Alumni Association of California School for the Blind—formed by the legendary Newel Perry and a handful of hardy colleagues before the turn of the century for the announced purpose of helping blind people (as Dr. Perry declared) "to escape defeatism and to achieve normal membership in society." Although it cannot be said that these early associations among the blind were yet prepared to demand the full rights of equality and normality, Newel Perry's declaration set the precedent and pointed the direction in which they were to evolve. Over the next three decades local organizations of blind men and women within half a dozen states came together to form statewide associations. Among them were the Central Committee of the Blind of Illinois; the Badger Association of the Blind in Wisconsin; the Pennsylvania Federation of the Blind; the Mutual Federation of the Blind in Ohio; and the California Council for (later *of*) the Blind.

The fundamental purposes of the multiplying local and state associations of the blind during these years were no different from those which had animated the "free brotherhoods" of the Middle Ages: mutual protection, group identity, and a measure of self-expression. To these must be added the more modern urge to demonstrate to the seeing world the capacity of blind men and women to lead their own lives and govern their own affairs. Moreover, within these organizations were incubating the more practical objectives which were to find expression in the national movement of the blind. Among them were the vision of full and open employment of blind persons in the mainstream of competitive pursuits, programs of public aid providing the incentives needed to enable the blind to achieve self-support, and vocational rehabilitation programs geared to individual talent and ability rather than to the stereotyped trades of the workhouse and the workshop.

These were, of course, barely imagined vistas of possibility in the period prior to the Great Depression and the New Deal of the 1930s. Social provisions for the blind were traditionally limited to state and county programs, in accordance with the ancient customs of the Poor Law. But with the vast increase of poverty and unemployment during the Depression—and notably with the passage of the Social Security Act of 1935—public welfare and job opportunity became a national concern, and with it the particular needs and problems of blind Americans.

The growth of a national consciousness and a sense of solidarity on the part of blind Americans corresponded with this broader public awareness of the need for national (or federal) solutions to the problems of disadvantaged groups. But the assumption of federal responsibility for public welfare and Social Security was far from being an unmixed blessing. While the Social Security Act injected new energies and revenues into the old aid programs, it also introduced a battery of conditions and requirements which often bound the blind recipient more tightly than ever in dependency and red tape. In short, as Jacobus tenBroek pointed out, the expansion of public aid from the states to the national level did not eliminate the evils of the traditional system—it only made them national.

The negative side of the federal assumption of responsibility for welfare came to be felt most sharply under the 1939 amendments to the Social Security Act. These changes required that under any state program for the blind to which federal funds were contributed all the income and resources of the blind recipient must be counted in fixing the amount of the aid grant, if any. What this meant, in fact, was that a basic goal for which the blind had been striving—the exemption of reasonable amounts of income as an incentive to self-support—was to be eliminated by federal edict.

In various ways during the Depression years the center of gravity in public welfare was shifting rapidly from the state capitals to Washington. It was now Congress, along with the White House, which took the decisive steps forward or backward in the fields of welfare aid, vocational rehabilitation, public health, disability insurance, sheltered workshops, and a host of related services directly affecting the lives and livelihoods of blind men and women.

Inevitably, the nationalizing of welfare led to the nationalizing of the organized blind movement. Various factors, internal and external to the movement, combined in this preliminary period to nourish a growing sense of brotherhood, of common needs and aspirations, both among blind students mingling in their residential state schools and among blind workers meeting and sharing grievances in their all-too-sheltered workshops. A powerful rallying cry emerged during the course of the Depression decade in the form of the struggle to "save Social Security from the Social Security Board"—that is, to protect blind recipients of aid from the means test and other onerous conditions newly imposed by the federal agency. The campaign to salvage and reform the program of aid to the blind, and in so doing to transform relief into rehabilitation, was to dominate the agenda of the National Federation of the Blind at its founding convention and to remain a guiding theme through its first decade.

Newel Perry summed up the nature and trend of the evolving national movement in a 1940 editorial. "During the last forty years," he wrote, "a growing group consciousness has been noticeable among the blind of our country. Practically every state and large city now has an active organization with a membership composed exclusively of blind persons. These clubs seek to improve the economic conditions of the blind through the enactment of legislation and through other means. The dream of a national organization is now to be realized."

FOOTNOTES

1. Richard S. French in *From Homer to Helen Keller* (New York: American Foundation for the Blind, 1932).

2. Quoted in Harry Best, *Blindness and the Blind in the United States* (New York: Macmillan, 1934), p. 474.

3. *Ibid.*, p. 476.

4. Jacobus tenBroek and Floyd Matson, *Hope Deferred: Public Welfare and the Blind* (Berkeley: University of California, 1959), p. 251.

5. Quoted in Best, *op. cit.*, p. 476.

Chapter 1

Mobilization and Momentum: The Founding

"To the Blind of the Nation: The time has come to organize on a national basis!"

So declared the first President of the National Federation of the Blind, in an appeal broadcast to blind Americans from the site of the organizing convention at Wilkes-Barre, Pennsylvania, in mid-November of 1940. The speaker was a 29-year-old Californian, Jacobus tenBroek, who had lost his sight in childhood and went on undeterred to earn no less than five college degrees, three of them postgraduate diplomas in law. He would go on further to become a distinguished constitutional scholar, chairman of the California Social Welfare Board, chairman of his department at the University of California, and author of award-winning books (among them a definitive study of public welfare programs for the blind, *Hope Deferred*). But at the time he spoke in 1940, tenBroek was a junior instructor at the University of Chicago Law School, just beginning his twin careers as university professor and leader of the organized blind. This is what he said to his fellow blind in that first year of mobilization:

> In dealing with the public, especially in its many governmental forms, we, as handicapped persons, have long known the advantage and even the necessity of collective action. Individually, we are scattered, ineffective and inarticulate, subject alike to the oppression of the social worker and the arrogance of the

governmental administrator. Collectively, we are the masters of our own future and the successful guardian of our own common interests. Let one speak in the name of many who are prepared to act in his support, let the democratically elected blind representatives of the blind act as spokesmen for all, let the machinery be created to unify the action and concentrate the energies of the blind of the nation. The inherent justice of our cause and the good will of the public will do the rest.

When the problems of the blind first began to be regarded as a proper subject of public concern, they fell within the jurisdiction of the county or township authorities. At that time, local organizations of the blind were adequate. But when, in the course of time, our problems were taken over by the state legislative and executive authorities, the local organizations of the blind had to be associated in a larger group capable of statewide action. Now that the national government has entered the field of assistance to the blind we must again adjust our organizational structure to the area of the governmental unit with which we must deal. The time has come to join our state and local blind organizations in a national federation. Only by this method can the blind hope to cope with the nationwide difficulties at present besetting us.

There are many goals upon which we can unite: the ultimate establishment of a national insurance program which will eliminate the diversities of treatment of the blind among the states and insure an adequate support to all; the correction of the vices that have crept into the administration of the Social Security Act by seeking its amendment in Congress; the proper and reasonable definition of the blind persons who should receive public assistance; governmental recognition of the fact that the blind are not to be classified as paupers and that they have needs peculiar to and arising out of their blindness; the proper type of statutory standards by which eligibility for public assistance should be determined; adequate methods for restraining the influence and defining the place of the social worker in the administration of aid laws; proper safeguards to prevent administrative abuse and misinterpretation of statutes designed for our benefit; legislative and administrative encouragement of the blind who are striving to render themselves self-supporting; legal recognition of the right of a blind aid recipient to own a little, earn a little, accept a little; governmental recognition of our inalienable right to receive public assistance and still retain our economic, social, and political independence, our intellectual integrity, and our spiritual self-respect—these are but a few of the problems that are common to the blind throughout the nation. But the mere listing of them shows the imperative need for organization upon a national basis, for creating the machinery which will unify the action and concentrate the energies of the blind, for an instrument through which the blind of the nation can speak to Congress and the public in a voice that will be heard and command attention. Until the blind become group-conscious and support such an organization, they will continue to live out their lives in material poverty, in social isolation, and in the atrophy of their productive powers.

With that call to action and to mobilization, tenBroek captured the sense of urgency with which the new movement of the blind was imbued in the year of its birth. In 1940 the condition of blind people in America was a barren landscape of impoverishment and frustration, and an inner state of desolation and despair. In one of the largest states, California, no more than 200 blind men and women were (by official estimate) actually at work in normal occupations. Thousands upon thousands who were able and willing to work were without jobs, forced to live on public aid grants which in most states were beneath the level of minimum subsistence. Of those lucky enough to be employed at all, most eked out a starvation wage—as low as five cents an hour—laboring in sheltered workshops at ancient trades (commonly known as "blind trades") such as chair caning and broom making, with little hope of moving outward and upward into regular jobs. The very few sightless persons who held decent positions then were typically either teachers at the schools for the blind or employees of agencies in the blindness system. Only a token number had been able to secure vending stands under the Randolph-Sheppard Act of 1936, which had been enacted to give preference to blind persons in the establishment of these modest "business enterprises" within federal buildings.

Vocational rehabilitation service for the blind was even more ineffective and rudimentary. In fact, although there were limited state and local efforts at rehabilitating the blind, and even an occasional gesture in that direction from the national government, the blind did not become officially "feasible" for services under the federal-state rehabilitation program until the enactment of the Barden-LaFollette Act in 1943. As for education, in 1940 only a handful of blind youth were attending colleges and universities while for the vast majority of students who graduated from schools for the blind the prospects of a normal life and livelihood were virtually as dismal as they had been a century before—when the annual report of one such school had lamented that "our graduates have begun to return to us,...soliciting employment at our hands."

This was the bleak climate in which a scattering of blind men and women from seven states assembled at Wilkes-Barre, late in 1940, for the purpose of realizing a dream of national unity and self-expression. To be precise, there were sixteen delegates present at the founding convention of the NFB, representing these states: California, Illinois, Minnesota, Missouri, Ohio, Pennsylvania, and Wisconsin. The sixteen men and women who were the delegates "in at the creation"—the founding fathers and mothers of the National Federation of the Blind—were Jacobus and Hazel tenBroek of California; Gayle and Evelyn Burlingame of Pennsylvania; David Treatman, Robert Brown, Enoch Kester, Harold Alexander, and Frank Rennard, all of Pennsylvania; Ellis Forshee and Marlo Howell of Missouri; Mary McCann and Ed Collins of Illinois; Emil Arndt of Wisconsin; Frank Hall of Minnesota, accompanied by Lucille deBeer; and Glenn Hoffman of Ohio.

In an early order of convention business, the delegates elected tenBroek as the first President of the National Federation of the Blind, and chose a slate of officers to serve with him which included Robert Brown, First Vice President; Frank Hall, Second Vice President; and Emil Arndt, Treasurer. The first meeting of the National Federation of the Blind was also a constitutional convention; in one of their most significant actions the delegates drafted and adopted a constitution, which announced in its second article that "the purpose of the National Federation of the Blind is to promote the economic and social welfare of the blind." This original constitution, which was to be amended in details over the years but never altered in spirit or purpose, was brief enough to be typed on a single page. (The complete text of the original constitution is reprinted as Appendix C to this volume, together with the constitution as last amended in 1986 as Appendix D.)

Of all the memorable events of this inaugural convention of the organized blind, the most impressive to many delegates was the powerful and brilliantly argued address delivered at the banquet by their young President. Confronting the question "Have Our Blind Social Security?", tenBroek answered no in thunder—and proceeded to enunciate a vigorous, sweeping attack on the actions of the federal Social Security Board in betraying the principles and the promise of the Social Security Act. For all its rhetorical power and unmistakable passion, this "maiden" speech by the newly chosen leader of the movement was also an expert demonstration of his prowess as a constitutional scholar; and it remains significant after fifty years as a ringing declaration of the Federation's dominant concern during the first decade with the bedrock issues of economic and social security. Beyond that, the speech was a striking demonstration of the new tone and manner of the organized blind leadership in its dialogue with the world (and in particular with the custodial agencies). Here was no trace of the supplicant, let alone of the mendicant; no appeals to pity; no talk of the tragedy of blindness or the permanent dependence of its victims. Nor—perhaps even more astonishing—was there any echo of the traditional genuflection and ritual praising of the agency authorities (such as the Social Security Board) who then held over the blind the power of life or death. The note that was struck by President tenBroek at the outset of his first convention speech—that of independence, aggressiveness, and determination—set the tone for the body of presidential speeches to come in the years and decades ahead, those not only of Jacobus ten-Broek but of his successors Kenneth Jernigan and Marc Maurer as well.

The full text of the 1940 presidential address follows:

HAVE OUR BLIND SOCIAL SECURITY?
by Jacobus tenBroek

Five years ago, in 1935, the Congress of the United States passed and the President of the United States signed what was widely regarded as the most progressive and humanitarian social legislation since the Thirteenth Amendment to the Constitution emancipated the slaves. Two years later, in 1937, the Supreme Court of the United States sustained this enactment against a charge of constitutional invalidity. Because the primary aim of this liberal legislation was security against certain of the major social and economic hazards of life, it was called the Social Security Act. It aspired to nothing less than protection against the pennilessness of unemployment, security against the destitution of age, and mitigation of the desolation of blindness. In its passage, the worker found release from apprehension, the aged found physical comfort, and the blind found hope.

After five years of experience with the Social Security Act, what has become of these lofty purposes that were thus expressed by the nation's Legislature, approved by its Chief Executive, and sanctified by its highest Court?

Ladies and gentlemen, I come before you tonight, in the first place, to say that so far as the blind are concerned the Social Security Act has not only failed to attain its plainly expressed goals but it has been used as a weapon to compel the states to treat their blind in a more niggardly fashion; and I come before you in the second place to proclaim to the wide world that the reason for this failure and the wielder of this weapon against you has been the Social Security Board at Washington. Proceeding in profound ignorance of the problems of the class with which it has dealt, moved by an intolerable authoritarian arrogance, the Social Security Board at Washington has constituted itself a supreme tribunal to judge whether the states are treating their blind badly enough. If they are not, these administrative despots in the nation's Capital apply compulsion by way of open threat and subversive action. So damaging have the activities of this Board become that it represents the greatest single menace to the welfare of the blind now in existence. Our salvation depends upon our ability to confine its operations within the limits of the law. Its unauthorized exercise of discretionary power must be terminated. This can only be accomplished by a militant, aggressive, group-conscious national organization of the blind. By this means we may diminish the Board's arrogance if we cannot reduce its ignorance.

To speak now more particularly, I levy three specific charges against the Social Security Board at Washington: First, it has unlawfully arrogated to itself the power to define the expression "needy individuals who are blind" as used in the Social Security Act; second, having illegally usurped this power, the Social Security Board has exercised it in a narrow, restrictive, and untenable way; third, the Social Security Board has arbitrarily, unlawfully, and oppressively insisted that the states, in order to gain or retain federal participation in their plans for aid to the blind, must determine need on an individual basis and not on a basis of legislatively fixed general standards.

(1)—The illegality of the Board's assumed power to define the expression "needy individuals who are blind" in the Social Security Act can easily be demonstrated by a resort to the Congressional record. Title X of the Social Security Act which deals with the blind was amended into the Act by the Senate Finance Committee of which Senator Harrison was chairman. The report of the committee to the Senate and the statements of this chairman when introducing the Act were very emphatic as to the location of the authority to define the term "needy individuals who are blind." Senator Harrison said, "We have laid down the conditions (in the Act)...and we leave to the states to say who shall be the persons selected to receive the federal assistance." As if to place the matter beyond all controversy or doubt as to the intention of Congress, Chairman Harrison made the following carefully worded statement: "It must be recalled that when this proposal was first made to the Senate Finance Committee it gave much more power to officials in Washington, so far as pensions were concerned. The authorities were to pass on state plans with respect to amount of pensions, who should get pensions and so forth...but we subsequently effected a complete change. I know it was the opinion of the Committee on Finance that the whole order should be changed and that the authority should be vested in the states...." It is hard to imagine how the power of speech could be more accurately employed in describing what was within the mind of Congress.

Equally forceful is the procedural history. Under Section 1002 (a) of that Act a state plan for the blind must, in order to gain participation by the federal government, provide for seven specifically set forth conditions. In the Senate, Senator Wagner moved to amend Section 1001 (a) by adding two additional requirements which must be present in a state plan if it is to have federal approval. They were "(8) provide that money payments to any permanently blind individual will be granted in direct proportion to his need; and (9) contain a definition of needy individuals which will meet the approval of the Social Security Board." The amendments were accepted by the Senate without discussion. However, when the Social Security Act reached the conference committee of the House and Senate for a resolution of their differences, these amendments were stricken out at the insistence of the House, and the Senatorial conferees readily concurred in the omission when attention was called to their significance. Is it possible that anything more illuminating could have been done? This procedural history indicates that amendments were framed and proposed for the purpose of compelling states to provide a definition of need which was satisfactory to the Social Security Board, and upon reflection these amendments were deliberately withdrawn from the Act. Hence it is not possible to have any doubt that Congress intended that the Social Security Board should not have the specific power which it now claims.

(2)—The definition of a needy blind person which the Social Security Board has foisted upon a number of reluctant states and upon the outraged blind of the nation has been that he is one who lacks the physical necessities of life, one whose needs will be satisfied by the provision of a bare animal minimum in food, shelter, and clothes. Thus, according to the Social Security Board a needy blind person is one whose need is the same as that of paupers, indigents, and the aged, for concerning these latter the state intends only to relieve material poverty.

This definition must be rejected by anyone having even the slightest acquaintance with the needs of the blind. A needy blind person has a greater need than paupers, indigents, and the aged, because there are additional elements comprising it. Besides the physical necessities of life, his need consists in some fair utilization of his productive capacity. This can only be obtained by restoring him to economic competence in a competitive world. Without it his need will never have been terminated. With it he is a normal, useful, self-respecting citizen. Hence his need is as broad as the effects of his blindness. It can only be met by a rehabilitation that is social, economic, and psychological, and these are the objectives within the intentions of the legislatures of many of our states in their statutory schemes providing aid to the blind.

In order that the blind recipients of aid may enlarge their economic opportunities and may be rehabilitated into independent livelihood these statutory schemes provide that the blind may possess a certain amount of tangible and intangible assets and may accumulate a certain amount of earnings without penalty. These statutory schemes recognize that one of the purposes of aid to needy blind persons is to remove them from the class of needy blind persons and one of the means of enabling them to so remove themselves is to permit them a reasonable sum of personal property. They acknowledge that this, in the last analysis, must be the distinction between aid and relief. These state plans were well designed and deliberately worked out to fulfill the demands of these comprehensive purposes. That a cry should now be heard from Washington that these plans should be dedicated to less than this is only explained by the famous remark of Justice Brandeis about the zealots who even if well-meaning are without understanding.

(3)—In providing that needy blind persons should be afforded financial assistance two courses were open to the legislatures of the states: They might have left the welfare departments to determine who were needy persons within the meaning of the word "needy" as generally used, or the legislature might have defined the word "needy" with particularity, setting up definite tests, and leaving the welfare authorities no function but to determine whether each particular applicant complied with those tests. As between these two alternatives some of the legislatures had no real choice in view of the extensive rehabilitative objectives they wished to accomplish. If these were to be realized it was apparent to the legislatures that a system would have to be created in which there was a minimum of administrative interference with the conduct and funds of the recipients. Administrative personnel, whether by reasons of training or native ineptitude, were notoriously considered to be unqualified as discretionary agents in such matters. Furthermore, if the blind were to be given a chance to enlarge their economic opportunities, and if their efforts to render themselves self-supporting were to mean anything, they would have to be given complete freedom of choice as to the direction of the rehabilitative effort, and entire flexibility within prescribed limits, as to their economic arrangements and position.

Accordingly, the legislatures of such states as Pennsylvania, Illinois, and California set up in the aid statutes themselves a complete system of standards on the crucial issue of what "need" is and what blind persons should receive assistance. Thus, under these statutes, the sole function of the welfare authorities is to find out whether an applicant falls within the categories specified by the legislatures. Senator Wagner's proposed amendment (8) would have given the Board some discretionary power to determine whether the state plan made payments in direct proportion to the blind person's need, and that amendment was also stricken out. The fact of this deliberate omission is proof of the absolute intention of Congress to leave the matter as to who was needy and as to what blind persons should receive assistance to the judgment of the states. It is further proof that Congress intended that the judgment of the states in that matter should be so free that it could set up a statutory system with a complete set of standards for the payment of aid and thus obviate the fettering restrictions of a social service budgetary system which would interfere with rehabilitative efforts. It is proof that state plans in order to gain Social Security Board approval do not have to grant aid to blind persons in direct proportion to their need and may make flat payments to all persons who come within the classification. Consequently, the expressed attitude of the Social Security Board that it may refuse to approve state plans because they grant aid not in accordance with individual need is utterly and palpably untenable and is an assumption of the power which Congress, by omitting the proposed amendment (8), specifically aimed to prevent.

In this discussion, I have concentrated attention chiefly upon the Social Security Act and the Social Security Board's interpretation of it. I have done so because that subject represents one of the primary problems now confronting the blind and because that subject shows, in an acute form, the need for unified action and national organization on the part of the blind. It is a problem of vital importance both to those states now receiving federal funds and to those which have been denied the participation of the federal government. It is not a problem that can be handled by one state or by a small group of states. All the blind in all the states must combine and concentrate their energies upon it in order to reach a workable and satisfactory solution.

Another reason for spending so much time and attention upon the Social Security Act and the Social Security Board's interpretation of it is that that subject points to a number of other problems that are common to the blind throughout the nation. The proper definition of blind persons who should receive state assistance is one such problem; the proper type of standards to be set up in the state statutory schemes is a second; the proper function and place of the social worker in the administration of the state and national legislation is still a third. Finally, the whole idea of a national pension or annuity is involved in this discussion. The problems arising in connection with the administration of the Social Security Act will undoubtedly recur in connection with the administration of a national pension when that is obtained. It is important for us to build up a national body of common and transmissible experience upon these subjects in order to avoid the errors of the past and make secure our future. Upon all of these problems it is necessary for the blind to organize themselves and their ideas upon a national basis, so that blind men the nation over may live in physical comfort, social dignity, and spiritual self-respect.

So spoke Jacobus tenBroek, in the first of a long series of presidential addresses delivered at the Federation's yearly conventions (his last was to be in 1967 at Los Angeles). In a letter written only days after the 1940 inaugural convention, tenBroek further clarified the purpose of his speech and spelled out the intimate connection between the rise of the organized blind movement and the issues of security facing the nation's blind. "The National Federation of the Blind is intended," he wrote to a correspondent, "to be a permanent organization devoted to the advancement of the social and economic welfare of the blind; but the immediate impulse in its creation arose out of the necessity to bring concerted pressure to bear on Congress and the Social Security Board on behalf of the blind of the nation."

TenBroek pointed out in his letter that the National Federation of the Blind convention at Wilkes-Barre had passed two closely related resolutions: the first calling for a national pension for the blind, and the second seeking congressional action to block the Social Security Board from obstructing the purposes of the Social Security Act. On both subjects "the delegates were unanimous and emphatic," he wrote. "Practically all of the delegates present at Wilkes-Barre felt that the ultimate solution to many of these difficulties lay in the establishment of a federal pension act which would contain adequate safeguards against the type of thing we have experienced under the Social Security Act, but they all agreed that for immediate and practical purposes we should concentrate our energies upon the passage of an amendment to the Social Security Act reserving to the states the right to define "need" and the right to determine what should result from a consideration of an aid recipient's other resources and income." He concluded with these positive words: "Without being unduly optimistic, I personally feel that we are now striking out along the right lines, and I can assure you that the new organization is in the hands of energetic blind persons who thoroughly understand the problems of the blind."

Jacobus tenBroek's exuberant confidence in the durability and mission of the fledgling Federation found expression in a letter he sent in early January, 1941, to his California mentor and senior colleague, Dr. Newel Perry. "With the National Federation of the Blind not yet two months old," he wrote, "its permanence is definitely assured. The factor guaranteeing that permanence is the closely knit nucleus composed of Minnesota, Pennsylvania, and California." What tenBroek might well have said, but of course did not, was that the main factor guaranteeing that permanence was his own tireless organizing efforts throughout the states—which embraced not only finding and recruiting new members but galvanizing the leaders of existing local groups. What he did say was that several states, among them Washington and Colorado, were then on the point of joining the Federation while others still stubbornly resisted his continuous efforts to bring them into the fold. "The Utah-Idaho group," he told Dr. Perry, "has been confoundedly slow about answering my letters, as has been the case with an organization in Omaha, Nebraska." In the same letter tenBroek singled out half a dozen other groups and individuals with whom he was in regular contact. He barely mentioned in passing that all of this activity was taking place at the same moment that his own teaching career at the University of Chicago Law School was just resuming. "The Christmas holidays," he said in closing, "ended with the second of January, and I am again deeply immersed in the problems of legal research and writing with students with whom I have been unable to teach very much of either as yet."

Barely two months later, tenBroek reported to Dr. Perry on the results of a week's intensive lobbying in Washington—only the first half of a campaign (in which he was joined by Gayle Burlingame) to change the hearts and minds of officials in the Roosevelt administration regarding the needs of blind recipients of public assistance under the Social Security program. "Gradually working our way upwards," he wrote, "Burlingame and I first presented our case to Jane Hoey, director of the Bureau of Public Assistance, and her associate, a lawyer named Cassius. Next we went to Oscar Powell, executive director of the Social Security Board; and finally to Paul V. McNutt, administrator of the Social Security Agency." TenBroek then added these terse characterizations: "Hoey," he said, "is simply another social worker of the familiar type but with a higher salary than most. Cassius has lost none of his qualities since Shakespeare described him, except that his wit has been sharpened by a little legal training. Powell is a very high-caliber man with a fine sense of argumentative values, a considerable store of good nature, and unusual perception. He simply is not a believer in our fundamental assumptions."

TenBroek then turned his attention to the top man in the agency hierarchy. "McNutt, on the other hand," he said, "is a lesser Hitler by disposition and makes our California social workers look like angels by comparison." However, tenBroek was not intimidated by this authoritarian personality and persisted in pressing him for a clear-cut statement of the agency's position. "Are you saying to us," he asked McNutt at one point, "that blind men should have their grants reduced no matter how small their private income and no matter how great their actual need?" McNutt's answer was that he was saying precisely that. "I formulated the question in several other ways only to get the same reply," tenBroek wrote. "I can't say that I wasn't glad to get this declaration from McNutt since it provides us with an official declaration by the highest administrator of them all that ought to be of immense propagandistic value to us. "Moreover," he added sharply, "McNutt's conduct during the conference has provided us with the most perfect example of the arbitrary and tyrannical methods of the Board that we could hope to have."

Nor was tenBroek content to end his petitioning at the top of the agency hierarchy. "In the remaining week that I shall stay in Washington," he wrote, "we shall attempt to carry our appeal the last administrative step. Senator Downey of California and Senator Hughes of Delaware are attempting to secure for us appointments with President and Mrs. Roosevelt." Unfortunately, those White House appointments were not forthcoming; and no meeting was ever held between the vigorous President of the United States, who was disabled but scarcely handicapped by polio, and the equally vigorous President of the National Federation of the Blind, who was disabled but scarcely handicapped by blindness. It is fruitless, of course, to speculate on the possible results of such a meeting between the two national leaders, each of whom was then the champion of a "new deal" for the people whom he served. But it is plausible at the least to suppose that there would have been between these two men an unusual degree of mutual regard born out of their shared experience of triumph over physical afflictions of a severity that in their day, shattered the lives of ordinary people.

The efforts of tenBroek and his fellow Federationists to reform the policies of the Social Security Board were unsuccessful in the short run. But not in the longer run. During the next two decades virtually all of their demands for the improvement of aid to the blind were to become law, and by the mid-sixties the program was so broadly liberalized as to represent a model for other public assistance programs—such as aid to the aged and aid to the disabled—to strive to emulate. The Federation's early campaign had greater success on another front: as a rallying cry for the blind of the nation. During the months following the inaugural convention, the word spread widely of a new organization in the field of blindness unlike any other—a national organization *of* the blind rather than *for* the blind, a democratic association made up of blind persons rather than an appointive agency made up (despite its occasional blind showpieces) mostly of sighted specialists—in short, a blind people's movement.

By the time of the National Federation of the Blind's second annual convention, held in August of 1941 at Milwaukee, the atmosphere had begun to change—most notably the climate of opinion among the blind themselves. Where there had been a total of sixteen delegates from seven states at the Wilkes-Barre convention the year before, there were 104 persons from eleven states in attendance at Milwaukee. The prevailing mood of the delegates was conveyed in a post-convention bulletin by the president of the Michigan Federation of the Blind, Wayne Dickens, who wrote: "A lively interest among the delegates in the progress of the blind and particularly their enthusiasm for the legislative program of the Federation carried the business of the convention through to completion with thoroughness and dispatch;...and the volume as well as the quality of the work accomplished was a source of general satisfaction."

Dickens pointed to a social interlude during the convention to illustrate his observation: "Late Friday afternoon, just before the banquet," he wrote, "the delegates mingled on the mezzanine. Leaders in blind affairs in their home states, and well informed on all phases of blind welfare, the delegates readily began that exchange of ideas, plans, and suggestions which characterized the convention both on the floor and behind the scenes and which supplied the delegates with a wealth of information with which to direct their respective state programs for the coming months. An observer would have readily perceived that people of ability and intelligence had rallied to the support of the Federation."

An observer at the next year's convention at Des Moines would have noted that even more people of ability and intelligence were rallying to the Federation's support. In 1942 (at the third convention) no fewer than 150 delegates representing fifteen states were in attendance. The convention featured a banquet address by Dr. Newel Perry and a crowded agenda of committee reports, resolutions, and speeches followed by spirited debate. After Raymond Henderson, newly elected executive director, spoke on future legislative policy, the delegates were provoked to extended discussion. "It was generally agreed," wrote Wayne Dickens in his convention report, "that some deliverance from the pauper's oath should be attained if the blind are to receive adequate help. Some members wanted this deliverance to be carried to such a point that eligibility for the pension would be judged by the fact of blindness alone." (It may be noted here that deliverance from the "pauper's oath," which under Social Security took the form of a means test based on "individual need individually determined," would become the major plank in the Federation's legislative program during the next few years, and that the idea of a flat grant or pension based on blindness alone would become the preferred formulation.)

Although the issue of public assistance remained at the forefront of attention at the 1942 convention, other concerns which were to gain importance in later years began to be apparent. As Raymond Henderson was to write in a post-convention bulletin: "The delegates decided that the time had come when the Federation should no longer limit its activities to improvement in the Social Security situation." Problems of employment, and more especially of job discrimination, surfaced at least mildly in resolutions dealing with such matters as civil service barriers and sheltered workshop maneuvers to exploit blind workers through exemptions from the Fair Labor Standards Act. (Again, it should be noted that these issues of employment opportunity and discrimination would eventually supersede the problems of Social Security on the Federation's agenda, and in one case at least—that of exclusion from the civil service—the organized blind would, in barely more than a decade, begin to break down the barriers and end the discrimination.) The growing spread of interest in the cause of Federationism among blind people everywhere in the land was illustrated during the 1942 convention by a host of reports of new organizing activities on the community and statewide levels. Wayne Dickens told of his own efforts in Michigan to mount a statewide membership drive, which had already netted 170 members. In Connecticut, three local blind groups were reportedly seeking to establish a statewide association for the purpose of joining the National Federation. And a social club in Birmingham, Alabama, was said to have "redefined its purposes and organized upon a statewide basis with the intention of entering the Federation as soon as the assessment can be raised." The convention delegates, however, were not content with these encouraging signs of activity and interest. They enthusiastically endorsed a motion by Dr. Newel Perry, the venerable dean of the movement in California, to the effect that (as the convention bulletin put it) "every delegate present assume that it is his obligation to make a definite, personal, active effort to induce in any way all non-member states to join the Federation as soon as possible," and that "we make ourselves each a committee of one to enlarge the organization as rapidly as possible."

"The decade of the forties," as Jacobus tenBroek was to recall in later years, "was a time of building: and build we did, from a scattering of seven state affiliates at our first convention to more than four times that number in 1950. In the decade of the forties we proved our organizational capacity, established our representative character, initiated legislative programs on the state and national levels, and spoke with the authority and voice of the blind speaking for themselves."

Early in that inaugural decade tenBroek and his handful of fellow founders had formulated the basic principles underlying the organized blind movement. In their essence these principles were to endure unscathed through half a century of change and growth; but of necessity, their felt priority and degree of emphasis shifted over time. As the presidential speech delivered by ten-Broek at the 1944 convention banquet serves to demonstrate, the attention of the organized blind in that early period was still mainly focused on "subsistence" centering upon public assistance—in the face of the stark reality that the vast majority of blind men and women were still regarded as unemployable (other than in sheltered workshops) and were therefore dependent upon the public aid provisions of the Social Security Act. The issue of security—one of the classic trinity of Federation goals (Security, Opportunity, Equality)—would gradually yield the high ground of attention to other needs, notably those of employment and opportunity, as blind men and women through the inspiration and momentum of the Federation came to move by the thousands off the public assistance rolls into the competitive job market. But in the war-torn forties President tenBroek and his colleagues felt compelled to devote as much emphasis to bedrock security and survival as to the other urgent imperatives of early Federationism; those of organization and expression. His convention address of 1944 follows:

THE WORK OF THE NATIONAL FEDERATION OF THE BLIND
by Jacobus tenBroek

It is somewhat less than four years ago since a small group of us met at Wilkes-Barre, Pennsylvania, and organized the National Federation of the Blind. The years that lie between that original meeting and this convention have been marked by arduous labor and by what I think are many successful accomplishments. They have been marked also by many new and increasingly difficult problems, by temporarily increased economic opportunities for the blind, and by tremendous changes in the world to which we must adjust ourselves.

It is a pretty safe guess that the world and this nation will not return after the war to conditions as we knew them before 1941. It therefore behooves us as an organization to review our work, re-examine our program, and consider what modifications, if any, need to be made to meet the new world that is to come.

In thinking over the activities of the National Federation of the Blind, a considerable number of highly diverse and varying projects come to mind. We have, of course, had a prolonged struggle with the Social Security Board and the Federal Security

Administrator, Paul V. McNutt. We have had our squabbles with
the Civil Service Commission. We have had our squabbles with
the Administrator of the Fair Labor Standards Act. We have put
forth extended efforts before the Congress of the United States
and before the legislatures of some of the states. We have had
problems with respect to sheltered shops and replacement and
rehabilitation and stands. We have had personal problems and
general problems, we have had problems of every sort and variety,
and at one time or another, we have turned some of our time and
energy to their attempted solution.

The problems of the National Federation of the Blind are as
numerous and diverse as the total problem of blindness, and consequently they reach into every phase of the life of our people
and the life of our community and of the nation. But in looking
over these different activities, it seems to me that underlying them
have been a relatively small number of important principles which
can be more or less simply stated.

The first of these guiding precepts has been the principle of organization. We have come to realize that we must organize. We
know now that we cannot solve our problems on an individual
basis. We cannot face the power of government single-handed,
nor the tyranny of unthinking, groundless discrimination, nor the
desolation and frustration of enforced idleness, nor the absence
of organized opportunity to earn a livelihood and to become self-
respecting, active participants in the life of our communities. We
cannot face these things single-handed if we hope to overcome
them. Individually, we are scattered, ineffective and inarticulate.
We have come to realize that we must organize, that we must act
collectively, that we must supply ourselves with the machinery to
unify the action and concentrate and direct the energies of the
blind for a common goal.

Once we have this basic organizational faculty in mind, certain
other things follow more or less automatically. Since the blind,
because of their experience, know their problems better than
anyone else, better than social workers or teachers or government
administrators, since they alone fully understand the problems of
blindness, their organization must be democratic. There must be
general participation by the blind in the determination of policies
and in all major decisions, and the officers of the organizations
must be subject periodically to removal if they do not perform
their duties satisfactorily.

The second fundamental thing that follows, once we have fully grasped the meaning of the organizational principle, is that the organization must be as large and as broad as the problems with which we must deal. There was a time when local organizations were sufficient because the problems of the blind were handled locally. There was a time when state organizations were adequate. But the problems of the blind are now national in character, and the organization of the blind must also be national in character.

I think it is now possible for us to say without possibility of contradiction that we are national in character. When we met at Wilkes-Barre to form the organization, seven states were represented: Minnesota, Wisconsin, Illinois, Missouri, Ohio, Pennsylvania, and California. We now number eighteen. In addition to the original seven charter members there are Iowa, Nebraska, Colorado, Michigan, South Dakota, Washington, and Alabama. They constituted fourteen at the time of our Des Moines convention. Since that time, we have added four other members: Delaware, New Jersey, North Dakota, and Oregon.

Besides these members, every active organization of the blind themselves in the United States is either a member or affirmatively supports our program. It is therefore possible for us to say that the National Federation of the Blind is the organization through which the blind of the nation, through collective action and unified, articulate self-expression, can improve the conditions under which they live. The National Federation of the Blind is not an organization speaking for the blind; it is the blind speaking for themselves.

The second of the fundamental principles underlying our program and guiding our activities substantially is our demand for equality. Now, the idea of equality lies at the basis of modern democratic organization and is commonly thought to apply to all groups except such minority groups as the blind. It does not mean, of course, that all men are equal in physical, mental, or moral qualities. In modern society, the idea that men are created equal and that they should be treated equally is simply this:

Every man should be given an opportunity to fit himself into the economic organization of the country in a way which his qualities and his training provide for. It is the opportunity to be tested on our merits. This is the idea of the United States Supreme Court, which has often said that the idea of equality is the idea that men should be treated equally unless there is a sufficient difference between them which is related to social purposes and bears upon the objective then in contemplation; that is to say, that the color of hair is utterly a matter of no concern whatsoever if you want a man to drive a railroad locomotive. If what you want is a man to use a typewriter, you don't need to worry how many feet he has. Likewise, visual acuity is not the basis upon which any man should be employed who has to use his head or his hands. This is the principle upon which we have conducted our fight to secure for the workers in the sheltered shops the same protection with respect to minimum wages that other workers are guaranteed by the Fair Labor Standards Act.

Labor should be compensated according to its value or its skill or something else. It does not depend on the amount of sight you have. It is on this principle that we have introduced our amendment to the Civil Service Act of the United States, by which we prohibit discrimination on account of blindness, and it is on this principle that we are fighting a new vicious form of discrimination because of blindness which has recently arisen in California, and which will likely spread to other states.

The Board of Chiropractors of that state recently provided that no person with less than fifty per cent of visual acuity would be allowed to take the examinations or to enter the profession. This utterly crude, arbitrary, and unreasonable action was taken despite the fact we have many successful chiropractors and despite the fact also that lack of sight is in many ways an asset in the profession, because that profession depends on manipulation, which depends on dexterity, which is a quality that the blind must cultivate.

Therefore, our second fundamental principle is the principle of equality, and it underlies practically all of the claims that we make, because it is not based upon any notion that all men are physically or mentally equal, but that they have an equal right to insist upon opportunities for which they are properly qualified.

The third of the principles has to do with public assistance. It is the proposition that public assistance should be granted upon a blanket grant basis to all the members of a class, that is to say, that the statutes granting public assistance should simply provide general categories and all blind persons falling within those categories should receive as automatically as possible the uniform amount of assistance which is provided for in the law. We have favored this system for very important reasons.

One of them is this: that blind people are normal, intelligent persons, who have the problem of adjusting themselves physically, spiritually, and mentally to a handicap which is permanent. In the process of readjustment, there are no general formulae, no regularly established procedures. It is an individual process, and any method of assistance which puts the blind under guardianship, which places them at the discretion of social workers for their guidance, is a system which destroys that individual personal process of reconstruction. It is for these reasons that we oppose a system of relief which insists upon the means test, budgeting, individual need individually determined, and large social worker discretion, which in our experience have been veritable instruments of oppression.

The fourth of the principles which underlie our work and guide our activities also relates to public assistance. It is this: that the statutes providing public assistance for the blind should contain an exempt earnings clause; that is to say, they should provide that the earnings of a blind person, at least up to a certain point, should be his, and his pension, his grant, his public aid should not be reduced by the amount of those earnings. Generally speaking, we favor this proposal because other systems, particularly the present ones, encourage idleness with all the evils that attend idleness.

A man is not going to work to earn a penny if he knows that that penny will be taken from him in terms of a reduction of his pension and if he knows that penny will not in any way increase his total income. It is only by permitting a man to accumulate a certain amount of money, preferably through encouraging earnings, that the blind will be able to get themselves off the relief rolls through rehabilitation, investment in stands or professional education, or any other of similar ways.

The final principle about which I would like to make a few remarks has to do with our relationship to other organizations in the nation. Naturally, we are happy to invite any group to help us and assist us if they believe in our program and the principles for which we are fighting, but as our program has gone forward, we have come to realize that there is one segment of the community which, more than any other, has responded generously to our appeal. That segment is organized labor. The reason for this is not far to seek.

In organizational structure and in purpose, we have many things in common. The blind have organized their local organizations and their state organizations into a National Federation which is modeled in many ways after the national organizations of organized labor. Through forces over which we have no control, we are forced to extend to each other a good deal of mutual aid and to ask society for protection and to some extent for assistance. That is exactly what organized labor must do. In modern industrial conditions, the individual worker is helpless without the cooperation of his fellow workers.

Therefore, because of these reasons, because we are trying to do for our people what organized labor is trying to do for its people, because of the similarity in organizational structure, in purpose and in work, and because of the laboring man's inherent sympathy for the underprivileged and the conditions under which they live, organized labor has responded more than generously, materially, morally, and with political support.

These are the principles underlying all the diverse, various activities which we have undertaken. Whether we should now adhere to them will depend upon our estimate of the world that is to come, and will depend upon decisions of this organization which will be democratically arrived at. Those decisions will be reached tomorrow and on the next day. Thank you!

The 1944 convention of the National Federation of the Blind may be regarded as typical of the annual meetings held during the organization's first decade. Attending the three-day sessions in Cleveland, Ohio, were fewer than 200 delegates from 18 states—a sizable gain from the prior convention two years before (none was held in 1943 due to wartime travel bans) but still a small enough group to hear the banquet oratory without the aid of loudspeakers. For reasons of economy, the Federation's National Convention was held jointly with the state convention of the Ohio affiliate—a situation that misled several guest speakers into supposing that they were merely at a state meeting. (One of them called it a "party" and others expressed surprise at the presence of blind persons from out of state.) Even more discouraging was the substitution of alternative speakers (at least four times) in place of the invited luminaries—graphic evidence of the unimportance, not to say irrelevance, of the organized blind in the eyes of most politicians and public figures of the time.

Few of the guest speakers at that wartime convention appeared to be aware at all of the Federation's objectives or philosophy; most spoke of matters entirely unrelated to the concerns of the blind, or failed to perceive the relationship where it did exist. At one point a representative of the Navy women's auxiliary, the WAVES, spoke at length about the great diversity of skills and characteristics among the "girls" recruited into military service but made no reference to the conspicuous absence (through exclusion) of blind women in either the WAVES or the WACS. Another speaker, representing the Red Cross, spoke glowingly of the contributions of blind people to the war effort; but his reference was merely to giving blood and making donations, not to participation in war-related occupations—from which in fact blind workers, however well trained, were still largely excluded even in the wartime absence of "able-bodied" males.

More curious even than the indifference and ignorance of these convention guests—viewed from the standpoint of a later generation—is the appearance of passivity and acquiescence on the part of the National Federation of the Blind delegates themselves in the face of such patronizing oratory. The convention proceedings reveal not a single retort or rebuke, nor even a polite question, from the assemblage of delegates at the banquet. Their prevailing silence might be variously interpreted; but it would seem evident that these early Federationists, with few exceptions, had come to the convention not to educate but to be educated. (Indeed that is what one of their own officers told them they were there for.) They were still new at self-organization, not altogether comfortable with self-expression, not even sure yet of their worthiness and dignity—let alone of their equality. But, with each passing year and each annual convention, these members of the National Federation of the Blind would become more confident of themselves and of their movement, and less willing to be seen but not heard. Even in that early year of 1944, in the incipient phase of the organized blind movement, the leadership of the Federation was speaking out and talking back; before much longer, an increasingly active and involved membership would be doing the same.

Again in 1945, because of the dislocations caused by the Second World War and its conclusion, the Federation did not hold a convention. The 1946 convention was held in St. Louis, Missouri, and the 1947 meeting was convened in Minneapolis, Minnesota. And the Federation increasingly continued to speak out and talk back.

Even the leaders of the Federation, however, were still relatively restrained in their declaration of the movement's goals and objectives. As late as 1948 President Jacobus tenBroek stated that the Federation "proposes to enable blind men and women of this country to live as near normal lives as possible," and that it is "dedicated to the proposition that the blind can become productive members of society." That restraint was only realistic, to be sure; at a time when only a fraction of blind people were employed at all, it was sufficient to aim at being simply productive rather than fully competitive and to hope for lives as near normal as possible. Yet the same spokesman felt confident enough, at the 1948 convention in Baltimore, to proclaim "A Bill of Rights for the Blind" containing an ambitious roster of new demands for recognition and respect. In addition to its eloquent appeal for equality and "normality," this convention address by President tenBroek represents a turning-point in its unusual emphasis on employment opportunity and transformation of relief into rehabilitation. The text follows:

A BILL OF RIGHTS FOR THE BLIND
by Jacobus tenBroek

I have a serious question to ask the sighted persons present—would you swap vision for a good chicken dinner? On the face of it this is an absurd question, for no one who has vision would swap it for anything. But for those of us who are blind, this question is not necessarily absurd. It is not that we prefer to have lost our eyesight, but having been deprived of it, we have discovered it is dispensable. There are even some blind among us who assert that blindness is a joy; for, as they point out, those who lose their heads are decapitated; those who lose their clothes are denuded; does it not follow, therefore, that those who lose their eyesight are delighted?

Let us suppose that as we leave this meeting our sighted guests were to be involved in an accident which destroyed their vision. This is not an idle supposition. Every year, without regard for social or economic background, color or creed, through accident and illness, blindness is forced on thirty thousand men and women in the United States. What problems would you face as a newly blinded person? What needs would be yours? You would probably spend months or years consulting doctors and eye specialists in futile efforts to regain your precious vision. But after your patience and certainly your pocketbook had been exhausted, you probably would wish for death. The world we live in is a visually oriented world, and for the sighted eternal darkness seems unthinkable. You probably would resign yourself to be set aside from ordinary pleasures and accustomed pursuits. But if you were lucky enough to know something about blindness or were properly guided in the early days of your sightlessness, your adjustment would be swift. After initial orientation to self-locomotion and self-care, the world would become familiar through the auditory and tactual senses.

There are a quarter of a million blind persons in the United States, but this statistic fails to tells us that the blind man or woman has the same feelings and desires, the same sorrows and joys as sighted persons. You would probably be no different after adjustment to blindness from what you had been before you became blind. To be sure, there are physical limitations to blindness, but most of these are of no more than nuisance value. You bump into things; you occasionally lose your way home; you even, in the mistaken notion that you are following the clicking of high heels out of a crowded railroad station, wind up in the ladies' rest room. But with proper orientation you would develop techniques for overcoming this physical limitation in blindness. The Braille system would replace script in your books, tape measures, thermometers, carpenters' levels, and speech notes.

What I have said so far will illustrate the wide-spread misconceptions about the nature of the physical handicap of blindness. If sighted people find it hard to get an accurate notion of what blindness is in its relatively obvious physical aspects, how much more must they misapprehend its subtler psychological, social, and economic ramifications? It may, therefore, be worthwhile to try to clear up some of these misconceptions; for us to say what the principal problems of blindness are; for us to tell the story of blindness as we live it daily. Since we do it without bitterness or malice and knowing full well that the sighted community bears

basis, quite regardless of individual need—to farmers by price support and parity payments, to industrialists by tariffs, to laborers by minimum wage and maximum hours provisions, to youth by public education. Blind persons as a class, no less than these other groups, require the helping hand of government to carry them to a healthy life embodied in active contribution to their communities.

The third right that we would seek to establish in our great charter of liberties is one that is not peculiar to the blind, but one which is common to all—equality; but the special circumstances of blindness, particularly the lack of understanding about it, make it desirable to re-assert the right and show its relevance. The idea of equality has been associated with all the great struggles of the masses of mankind to better their lot in the history of Western civilization. It is viewed by the philosophers of democracy as the most enduring impulse and authentic demand of the human spirit. It has been established by our own national experience as the indispensable condition of liberty. It was placed at the base of our constitutional system from Lockean and Jeffersonian sources and placed in the Constitution as the culmination of the greatest humanitarian movement in our history, namely, abolitionism. It reaches back deeply into ethical, religious, humanistic, and libertarian origins.

Yet this fundamental part of our system and our heritage is daily denied to the blind. We are denied equal treatment under the rule of law, equal right to the self-respect which derives from a sense of usefulness, and equal opportunity to compete for the normal means of livelihood. More often than not a denial of equality involves a denial of opportunity, and this, the right to equality of opportunity is the fourth and the last of the rights we should seek to have included in our Bill of Rights.

"Full and equal membership in society entitles the individual," says the report of the President's Committee on Civil Rights, "to the right to enjoy the benefits of society and to contribute to its progress....Without this equality of opportunity the individual is deprived of a chance to develop his potentialities and to share in the fruits of society. The group also suffers through the loss of the contributions which might have been made by persons excluded from the main channels of social and economic activity."

Exclusion from the main channels of social and economic activity and thereby a lack of opportunity for self-support—these constitute the real handicap of blindness, far surpassing its physical limitations. The government service is frequently closed to us through groundless discrimination on account of blindness. In some states this has been ameliorated by corrective legislation—not so, incidentally, in the federal government—but even in those states enforcement is spotty, difficult, and almost non-existent. In some professions, at which the blind have excelled, such as osteopathy and chiropractic, there have been persistent efforts to exclude the blind by administrative ruling. Teaching, especially in junior colleges and universities, where blindness is not a factor in performing the work, has as yet opened up only to a relatively few. In private employment the same story is to be told; the usual experience is for the blind man to be brushed aside as incompetent, as unable, as the fellow you could never expect to perform that job unless he could see. With respect to self-employment, which almost always involves some capital, the investor regards the blind man as a bad financial risk.

The absence of economic opportunity is more than the absence of economic security. It is the disintegration of the personality. It is men living out their lives in social isolation and the atrophy of their productive powers. The curse of blindness is idleness—idleness which confines the blind to the sidelines of life, players warming the bench in the game that all should play.

For equality of opportunity to be a reality to the blind, competent blind persons must be admitted without discrimination to the common callings and professions as well as to positions in the Civil Service. We do not ask that blind men should be given jobs because they are blind; we do not ask that they be given preferential treatment or handicap allowances. We ask only that when a blind man has the training, the qualifications, the dependability, and the aptitude, he be given an equal chance with the sighted—that the bars to public and private employment interposed by legislative enactment, administrative whim, and managerial prejudice and misunderstanding be removed.

These problems too have a significant and an immediate application to the public assistance laws. Those laws, once again, are not geared to meet the real needs of blindness. It should follow from what has been said that every effort needs to be made to rehabilitate the blind into active endeavor, social contribution, and remunerative employment. Far from achieving these ends, or even from permitting them, the public assistance acts generally tend to perpetuate the blind permanently on the relief rolls. Earnings and other income are automatically deducted from the amount of the grant made, and thus much of the motive for rehabilitation, self-improvement, and active endeavor is removed. If the blind recipients of relief were permitted to retain a reasonable portion of their earnings and to accumulate a small amount of capital, they would have incentive to be active, to do something; their rehabilitation and productive effort would be encouraged; and the ultimate goals of self-support and independence of the public assistance rolls would open up to the realistic vision of men who cannot see.

Nor is this hope a dream of the future. The Congress of the United States unanimously passed a measure, unfortunately vetoed by the President, allowing the states, without loss of federal funds, to exempt forty dollars of the monthly earnings of blind aid recipients. For this measure we do honor to Congressman Reed of New York, Senator Martin of Pennsylvania, and Senator Ives of New York. They took the lead and put it across. They deserve and do receive the eternal gratitude of the blind. As Senator Ives explained on the floor of the United States Senate, this was but a short step in the right direction; but of all the steps, it is the most important, for it establishes a principle—a principle whose ultimate fulfillment will drive to the shambles the soul-stifling conception of the needs basis—a principle which, with public understanding, with security, equality, and opportunity, will convert blindness into a mere physical nuisance and blind men into social assets.

So, with the ringing words "Security; Equality; Opportunity" President tenBroek at once coined the famous motto of the Federation and prepared the way for new goals and commitments. The objective of security has since found expression and partial realization in improved programs of Social Security; but the goals of opportunity and equality have had their focus on another front—that of productive employment in the full range of normal occupations and professions. The drive for jobs—for more and better jobs—had been foreseen from the birth of Federationism; as early as 1941 a speaker at the National Convention declared that "before further progress can be made toward a solution of our employment difficulties, our attitude and standard in this field will have to undergo complete revamping." He predicted that "we shall have to ascertain whether or not blind people's capacity is limited to a few standard occupations such as chair caning, broom and mop making, piano tuning and music, and news dealing. In short, we shall have to ask ourselves the question, 'Is the blind man a producer or a permanent dependent?'"

The answer which the Federation gave to that question was direct and unequivocal: the organized blind were to be committed to the task of dissolving all barriers to the acceptance of blind persons in private industry, in the professions (notably including teaching), and the skilled trades. From the outset the National Federation of the Blind repudiated the traditional and widespread stereotype of blind persons as permanent dependents and natural inferiors limited to the routine "blind trades" of the sheltered workshops—those twentieth-century relics of the infamous Victorian workhouses exposed and excoriated in the novels of Charles Dickens. During the Federation's second decade, in the 1950s, the battle against the sheltered workshops and custodial agencies (themselves no less organized and determined than the National Federation of the Blind) was to take on the proportions of a mortal struggle perceived by the agencies as a struggle for survival and by the blind as a struggle for liberation.

Underlying this conflict was a profound difference of philosophy, and of psychology, regarding the nature of blindness itself. Until the advent of the organized blind movement, there had been little or no dispute about that; the entire world appeared agreed that blindness was a total and tragic blight which left its victim mentally incompetent and physically immobilized—in short, a permanent dependent. Virtually all of the institutions created by society to care for its blind wards—institutions which by the mid-twentieth century numbered in the hundreds and extended their supervision literally from cradle to grave—were based on that negative stereotype and had acquired a vested interest in its perpetuation. Plainly put, what this meant was that if the blind should ever come to be redefined as normal human beings, with the full range of ordinary abilities and possibilities, these custodial agencies would become irrelevant and obsolete. It was as simple, and critical, as that. The battle lines were drawn, then, not merely around specific practices and policies of the agencies but upon fundamental assumptions of philosophy bearing on the meaning of blindness and the character of the blind.

Nowhere were these issues more deeply explored or eloquently articulated than in a 1951 convention address by President Jacobus tenBroek entitled "The Neurotic Blind and the
Neurotic Sighted—Twin Psychological Fallacies." In this
landmark speech, tenBroek departed from his customary style of
public address to launch an incisive scholarly attack upon the
psychological theories and assumptions supporting the structures
of custodialism. His address follows:

THE NEUROTIC BLIND AND THE NEUROTIC SIGHTED—
TWIN PSYCHOLOGICAL FALLACIES
by Jacobus tenBroek

Long and significant strides have been taken by the nation's blind
in the eleven years since the first convention of the National
Federation of the Blind. Through successive advances in public
assistance and social welfare, by improvements in vocational
guidance and placement, and with increasing gains in economic
opportunity and cultural participation, the blind are moving
steadily closer to the ultimate goal of full and equal membership
in American society. A very great deal, of course, remains to be
done; and it may be well to remind ourselves, on this anniversary,
of the several dominant features of the Federation program with
which we are today most actively and immediately concerned.

Perhaps first in any listing of the ends to which our organization
is pledged, is the goal of *understanding*—which, in negative terms,
means nothing less than the total eradication of the ancient
stereotype of the "helpless blind man," that age-old equation of
disability with inability which remains today, as ever, the real affliction of blindness. Second, and closely dependent upon the first,
is the assertion of our *normality*: the elementary truth that the
blind are ordinary people, and more exactly that they are *persons*—unique individuals each with his own particular as well as
his general human needs. Third among our objectives is *security*,
representing a normal human striving which is only accentuated—
not transformed—by the fact of blindness, and to which the
programs of public assistance are especially addressed. But
security remains a static and even a stultifying concept without
the further element of *opportunity*, which is the fourth of our objectives: opportunity to participate and to develop, to become useful and productive citizens. Fifth in line (but not in importance)
is the goal of *equality*, which is both a precedent and a product
of all the rest: equality which flows from the sense of belonging,

from the frank acceptance of the community, and which entails equal treatment under the law, equal opportunity to employment, and equal rights within society. Sixth is the objective of *education*: education of the blind in terms of social adjustment and vocational rehabilitation; and education of the sighted—parents, teachers, employers, and the community—in terms of the several goals already mentioned. Seventh and last is the platform of adequate *legislation*, permanent safeguards based on rational and systematic evaluation of our needs and erasing once and for all the restrictive barriers of legal discrimination and institutionalized ignorance.

These are only the most general and conspicuous of the goals to which we are committed. Within each area, of course, there are concrete problems and particular emphases. In public assistance, for example, the overriding need is to secure adequate protection while actively encouraging the efforts of recipients to surmount the relief rolls by way of self-sufficiency; and in the field of rehabilitation, the objective is to improve the services of training and placement while retaining administration by those qualified to understand the distinct needs and problems of the sightless. On every level the accent varies; but when all parts work together in harmony under skilled direction, they express the underlying theme of Integration—social, psychological, and economic. And the dominant note that emerges is one of hope; for if it is true that we are a long way still from equal partnership with the sighted in the continuing experiment of democracy, it is also true that by contrast with our status only eleven years ago we are a long way toward it.

In this brief summation of goals and achievements, there is however an implicit assumption which is so generally taken for granted that it is only rarely recognized. The assumption is that the blind are fit to participate in society on a basis of equality; that there is nothing inherent in their handicap, or invariable in their psychology, which renders them incapable of successful adjustment and adaptation to their society. And the corollary of this assumption is that there is nothing fixed or immutable about the obstacles encountered by the blind in their progress toward integration; that social attitudes and opinions are essentially on our side, and that where they appear otherwise they are based on ignorance and error and can be changed.

These are large assumptions; and they carry an immense responsibility. For upon them rests the entire structure of social programming and welfare services to which this organization is dedicated. But suppose, for a moment, that these assumptions are false. Suppose that the blind are not just ordinary people with a physical handicap, but psychological cripples; and suppose, further, that the complex of attitudes and beliefs about the blind entertained by the general public are at bottom completely hostile and immune to change. If these suppositions should somehow receive scientific sanction—or even if they should become widely accepted among the public and among the blind—it is easy to see that the consequences for programs of education, assistance, rehabilitation, and employment (to name only the most conspicuous) would be profoundly different from those we now pursue. The long campaign to integrate the blind into society on a basis of equality would have to be discarded as naive and utopian; the effort to enlighten public opinion and to erase its gross discriminations would have to be abandoned as illusory and futile. The blind would become again, as they have been so often in the past, a caste apart, a pariah class; and our efforts on their behalf would be reduced to the administration of palliatives designed to make their social prison as comfortable as possible—but not to help them escape.

To all this it may be replied that there is after all no danger of such reactionary suppositions gaining credence in informed circles; that the weight of scientific and theoretical opinion is altogether on the other side. And so in fact it has appeared; as recently as last year's convention I should have agreed wholeheartedly with this belief. Today, however, I am compelled to announce that this confidence is no longer justified. For the suppositions I have outlined are precisely those avowed and put forward by two recent writings that lay serious claim to scientific status: one of which asserts that the conditions of blindness invariably impose a neurotic personality structure—a psychological crippling; and the other of which declares that social attitudes toward the blind are fundamentally a sublimation (a deflection) of aggressive instinctual drives, carrying an inescapable undercurrent of hostility. The first of these may be called the thesis of the "neurotic blind"; the second, the thesis of the "neurotic public."

What is most surprising about these theories, at first glance, is that they are the work of two outstanding individuals who are themselves blind, and whose sympathetic and generous contributions in the field have earned distinguished reputations for both. One of these gentlemen, Dr. Thomas Cutsforth, is a prominent psychologist and authority on problems of the blind, whose classic work *The Blind in School and Society*, published over fifteen years ago, has been credited with greatly modernizing the fundamental concepts of the psychology of blindness. The other, Mr. Hector Chevigny, is the author of two notable books on blindness, besides being a reputable historian and a skilled professional writer. About the complete integrity and considerable ability of both these men there can be no question; but about the truth and value of their respective theories there can be and there is a very large question indeed.

The first of the two views—as expressed by Dr. Cutsforth in a symposium on blindness published last year[1]—maintains that the response to blindness under modern conditions results invariably in a pattern of behavior indistinguishable from that of neurotics. To his credit, Dr. Cutsforth does not say, as so many psychologists have said in the past, that it is the physical defect which created the disturbance; rather he says what amounts to much the same thing, that the conditions imposed by blindness make such personality distortion inevitable. The blind person, we are told, comes to evaluate himself as society in its ignorance evaluates him; and as a result he soon feels inferior and alone. In his effort to regain both self-respect and social esteem, he reacts in either of two ways—and two ways only—the way of "compulsive" compensation, or the way of "hysterical" withdrawal. Both responses, according to Cutsforth, are "fundamentally neurotic"—which means, among other things, that they hinder rather than assist the individual to adjust to his handicap and to society.

Such terms as "compulsive" and "hysterical," of course, plainly beg the question; they are neurotic by definition. Most of us, however, would probably agree that the ostrich reaction of withdrawing from reality and retreating into infantile dependence is no solution to the problem of adjustment; but the author's attitude toward the familiar adjustive mechanism known as "compensation" is less easily accepted. We shall say more about compensation later on; for the moment it is enough to point out that even the psychoanalyst Alfred Adler, whose rigid theory of "organ inferiority" made neurosis a virtually inevitable accompaniment of physical handicap, nevertheless maintained that the defect could be overcome and complete adjustment achieved through compensatory activity.[2] Not so, however, Dr. Cutsforth. "In following this pattern [of compensation]," he asserts, "the individual develops along the lines of the compulsive personality....Therapeutic or educational emphasis upon compulsive symptoms leads in the dangerous direction of creating lopsided personalities, monstrosities, or geniuses as the case may be...compensations are

as much evidence of personality pathology as the less approved
and more baffling hysterical reactions."[3]

Clearly, there is little hope for the blind person within the terms
of this analysis. He is committed to behaving either compulsively
or hysterically—and both ways are equally neurotic. What is more,
any attempt to combine the two mechanisms only makes matters
worse. Nor is there much hope to be derived from clinical treatment of this "blind neurotic"; for "it is obvious," says Cutsforth,
"that any therapeutic program for the adjustment of the blind personality that concerns itself only with the correction of either or
both of these personality malformations is doomed to failure."[4]
Since these malformations are the only ones allowed, it is a bit
difficult to know what else a therapeutic program might be concerned with. But it may be supposed that what the author has in
mind is a broader program aimed at the modification of unsympathetic social attitudes, which are admitted to lie at the root of
what he calls "the neurosis involved in blindness." This is, however, very far from his purpose. Observing that "until recently the
blind and those interested in them have insisted that society revise
and modify its attitude toward this specific group," he continues:
"Obviously, for many reasons, this is an impossibility, and effort
spent on such a program is as futile as spitting into the wind."[5]

Only two of the "many reasons," evidently the most clinching, are
vouchsafed to us. The first is that "society has formulated its emotional attitudes not toward blindness itself, but toward the reaction pattern of the blind toward themselves and their own
condition."[6] But since the reaction of the blind to their own condition has already been defined as a reflection of social attitudes,
this amounts to saying that the social attitudes are formed in
terms of something which itself is formed by social attitudes—a
neat bit of circular reasoning which avoids coming out anywhere.
The second reason advanced against this "spitting into the
wind"—that is, trying to change social attitudes—should be of particular interest to members of the National Federation of the
Blind: "...it is extremely doubtful," claims Dr. Cutsforth, "whether
the degree of emotional maturity and social adaptability of the
blind would long support and sustain any social change of attitude,
if it were possible to achieve it."[7] And finally, he declares: "It is
dodging the issue to place the responsibility on the unbelieving
and non-receptive popular attitudes. The only true answer lies in
the unfortunate circumstance that the blind share with other
neurotics the nonaggressive personality and the inability to participate fully in society."[8]

The implications of this extremist theory for the broad field of social programming are not difficult to make out. In its assignment of the primary responsibility for maladjustment to the blind individual alone, it discourages attention to the home and community environment in which character is formed and personality develops; and, even more specifically, in its emphasis on the immutability of social attitudes, it disparages all attempts to modify or revise them as futile and even dangerous. Indeed, Dr. Cutsforth labels as "hypocritical distortions" all efforts to, as he puts it, "propagandize society with the rational concept that the blind are normal individuals without vision."[9] If the blind are not normal, there is obviously little point in attempting to educate or prepare them for a normal life. If they are compulsive and hysterics, far from seeking equal treatment and full participation in society they should be content with the exiled status of the misfit and the deranged. There is no need to spell out in specific terms the numerous ways in which this verdict would operate to undermine the progress of the blind toward equality and integration. The only one of our programs which might in some sense survive its test is that of public assistance—but it would be an assistance shorn of opportunity and bereft of dignity, an empty charity without faith and without hope. The Cutsforth thesis of the "neurotic blind," in short, would seem to rule out any and all solutions to the problems of rehabilitation and adjustment other than that of prolonged psychotherapeutic treatment on the individual level—and even here, as we have seen, it is not at all clear what there is to be treated.

Fortunately, there is an answer—a scientific answer—to this defeatist theory. But before turning to that it is necessary to consider the other recent theory which by implication supports the reactionary suppositions we have outlined: namely, Hector Chevigny's thesis of the "neurotic public." (This viewpoint, as set forth in a book called *The Adjustment of the Blind*,[10] is the joint property of Chevigny and his co-author, Sydell Braverman; but because he is the senior author and because his name is most widely associated with the ideas in the book, we shall refer to the formulation as Chevigny's.) Observing that the emotion which is most commonly encountered in attitudes toward the blind is that of pity, Chevigny subjects the "pity concept" to a psychoanalytic examination along the lines of classical Freudian theory, coming to the conclusion that pity "derives from an original cruelty impulse through either sublimation or reaction formation."[11] This original impulse is variously and ambiguously defined as fear, guilt, and sadism; but the implication is plain throughout that expressions of pity always represent a deflection of deep-seated feelings of hostility. Chevigny next attempts to distinguish between pity and kindness, maintaining that kindness has a "different origin in the psyche" and represents beneficent rather than hostile feelings. Curiously, however, kindness itself is later conceded to be "a sublimation of the aggression toward one another present in all children, [and] it may also be the end product of a less sound defense system against the same drives."[12] In short, kindness, like pity, is essentially a sublimation of aggressive drives; from which it would appear that the distinction between the two emotions, if any, is one of degree rather than kind. Far from distinguishing pity from kindness, Chevigny has succeeded only in making the point that all attitudes toward the blind, however apparently well-meaning, are founded on a subterranean rock of antipathy and aggression.

The inconsistency of this psychoanalysis of attitudes becomes understandable when it is seen as a particular instance of the paradox inherent in the whole system of Freudian instinctivism: the paradox that, as Freud himself expressed it, "the things of highest value to human culture are intelligible as a consequence of frustrated instincts."[13] The most virtuous emotions—love and affection, toleration, sympathy, and compassion—all are explainable in terms of the sublimation of innate aggressive drives; even the sense of justice, as Erich Fromm has pointed out, was traced by Freud to the envy of the child for any one who possesses more than he.[14] Freud's psychological determinism does not consist however, as popular writers often suppose, in the reduction of all behavior to the sex drive, but rather in the conception of a dialectical struggle between the forces representative of life and death—a struggle underlying all human history, individual and cultural. "The tendency to aggression," he insisted, "is an innate, independent, instinctual disposition in man and...constitutes the most powerful obstacle to culture."[15] But if the existence of culture depends on the suppression of natural instincts—if, as Freud put it, "the core of our being consists of wishes that are unattainable, yet cannot be checked"[16]—then cultural equilibrium is at best precarious, if not foredoomed to destruction. Indeed Freud came to wonder whether civilization might not be leading to "the extinction of mankind, since it encroaches on the sexual function in more than one way...."[17] "As he saw it," observes a prominent modern psychoanalyst, "man is doomed to dissatisfaction whichever way he turns. He cannot live out satisfactorily his primitive instinctual drives without wrecking himself and civilization. He cannot be happy alone or with others. He has but the alternative of suffering himself or making others suffer."[18] Short of destruction of the species, then, the conflict of man and society must remain forever unresolved. Whenever the inhibiting social forces are for a moment relaxed, we see "men as savage beasts to whom the thought of sparing their own kind is alien."[19] But on the other hand, whenever the inhibitions become too severe, or the frustrated instincts pile up against the blocks—as periodically they must—then, says Freud, the organized explosion known as war becomes inevitable. "A period of general unleashing of man's animal nature must appear, wear itself out, and peace is once more restored."[20]

So much for the Freudian theory of instincts, and the extreme cultural pessimism to which it gives rise. It is relevant to our present purpose insofar as it illuminates the consequences for social programming which might be expected to follow its application to the psychology of social attitudes. For if Chevigny is correct, and all social attitudes toward the blind, antagonistic, or benevolent, are explainable as the consequence of frustrated instincts, then by Freudian standards two conclusions may be said to follow: First, that the services and programs based upon these attitudes, like all cultural products, are achieved only at the cost of general neurosis and are therefore unhealthy and precarious; and second, that the submerged hostile feelings toward the blind must periodically erupt over the barriers in outbreaks of persecution and aggression. It would seem evident that this thesis—the thesis of the "neurotic public"—affords little hope of any rational and sustained progress in the social welfare of the blind; at least until such time as the general population may be induced to undergo extended psychoanalytic therapy. In the face of universal hostility, however well-disguised, there can be no serious thought of achieving recognition and integration; and the solution to the problems of the blind must perforce be sought in the reinforcement, rather than the removal, of the medieval barriers of isolation and segregation.

It may however be flatly stated that the Chevigny thesis of the "neurotic public" is not widely entertained by serious students. The validity of its Freudian assumptions has been sharply and effectively challenged by major developments over the past ten years within psychology and the social sciences—most notably, perhaps, in the sphere of the cultural anthropologists. An impressive number of psychiatrists and psychoanalysts as well, concluding that man's biological nature need not condemn him to conflict with society, declare that in fact anxiety and conflict are largely the

Dr. Cutsforth's assertion that "it is dodging the issue to place the blame on social attitudes," and that these are somehow out of bounds to investigators, receives even shorter shrift from the findings of research psychologists and social scientists working with the handicapped. Instead there is general agreement that, in the words of Lee Myerson, "the problem of adjustment to physical disability is as much or more a problem of the non-handicapped majority as it is of the disabled minority"[29]; and, unlike Dr. Cutsforth, the data uniformly indicate the practicability, as well as the need, of changing the attitudes of parents, teachers, employers, and the community generally. Some students, such as Roger Barker, emphasize the similarity between the "minority status" of the blind and that of racial and religious subgroups, and suggest that the solutions found to problems of prejudice in general—through such means as education, psychology, propaganda, learning, and politics—may be equally applicable to the physically handicapped.[30] An opinion area of primary importance, of course, is the home environment. Sommers, among others, asserts that "parental attitudes and actions constitute the most significant factors in setting the fundamental habit patterns of the blind child"; but, since parents themselves reflect the attitudes of the community, she concludes that "our main concern in dealing with the problems of personality development in such an individual must be an effort to shape the reactions of his environment. The training of the handicapped and the education of those with whom he is most closely associated and of society at large must take place simultaneously."[31] Her concluding words are especially worthy of quotation: "The ultimate results will depend on the extent to which the home, the school, the community, and society at large coordinate and direct their efforts toward giving [the blind child] sympathetic understanding but not undue pity, encouraging independence and initiative, and helping him to achieve success and happiness as a contributing member of the family group and as an adult member of society."[32]

In summary, it may be said that this view of the relation of blindness to personality development, espoused by the great majority of research psychologists and workers with the blind, denies that any single personality pattern is invariably associated with blindness, holding rather that individual responses depend primarily upon such variable, and modifiable, factors in the environment as the attitudes of parents and the community. The practical implications of this more "optimistic explanation lie definitely in the direction of encouraging the modification of public attitudes and relationships toward the blind, and of fostering programs directed toward the greater all-around participation of the blind in society. The great objective of public understanding—first among our seven organizational goals—emerges in the light of this empirical evidence as not only necessary but eminently practicable; and along with it the erasure of false stereotypes and the establishment of our normality. The various specific programs of education and legislation, of rehabilitation and social security, are similarly supported by these findings as indispensable means toward achievement of the ends we have set for ourselves—the ends of full equality, of unlimited opportunity and of total integration.

This, then, is the scientific evidence that underlies the growing structure of programs and services supported by the National Federation of the Blind. It is this evidence that finally gives the lie to the antique notions of inferiority and incapability which have surrounded the blind from earliest times. And it is this evidence that effectively refutes the reactionary thesis of the "neurotic blind" and its corollary of the "neurotic public"; for it asserts that there is nothing in the psychology of the blind which miscasts them for the role of equal partners with the sighted and that there is nothing in the psychology of the sighted which prevents their recognition of this demand. It would of course be premature—as in scientific matters it is always premature—to claim either that present knowledge is complete or that the achievement of integration will follow automatically from its publication. But it is not too much or too soon to declare, with all the conviction at our command, that the blind are capable of fulfilling the equalitarian destiny they have assigned themselves—and that society is capable of welcoming them.

FOOTNOTES

1. Paul A. Zahl, ed., *Blindness: Modern Approaches to the Unseen Environment* (Princeton University Press, 1950).

2. See Rudolf A. Dreikurs, "The Social- Psychological Dynamics of Physical Disability." *Journal of Social Issues*, Vol. 4, No. 4 (1948), p. 42.

3. *Op. cit. supra* note 1, pp. 176-177.

4. *Id.* at p. 176.

5. *Id.* at p. 179.

6. *Ibid.*

7. *Ibid.*

8. *Id.* at p. 183.

9. *Id.* at p. 179.

10. Hector Chevigny and Sydell Braverman, *The Adjustment of the Blind* (New Haven: Yale University Press, 1950).

11. *Id.* at p. 148.

12. *Id.* at p. 149.

13. Quoted in Joseph Jastrow, *Freud: His Dream and Sex Theories* (Cleveland: World Publishing Co., 1932), p. 290.

14. Erich Fromm, *Escape from Freedom* (New York Norton Co., 1941), p. 294.

15. Sigmund Freud, *Civilization and Its Discontents* (London: Hogarth Press, 1946), p. 102.

16. Quoted in Jastrow, *op. cit. supra* note 13, p. 290.

17. Quoted in Franz Alexander, *Fundamentals of Psychoanalysis* (New York: Norton Co., 1948) p. 323.

18. Karen Horney, *Neurosis and Human Growth* (New York: Norton Co., 1950), p. 377.

19. Freud, *op. cit. supra* note 15, p. 86.

20. Clara Thompson, *Psychoanalysis: Its Evolution and Development* (New York: Hermitage, 1950), p. 140.

21. H. S. Sullivan, *Conceptions of Modern Psychiatry* (Washington, D.C.: William Alanson White Psychiatric Foundation, 1947), p. 87.

22. Hans von Hentig, "Physical Disability, Mental Conflict and Social Crisis," *Journal of Social Issues*, Vol. 4, No. 4 (1948), p. 27.

23. Vita Stein Sommers, *The Influence of Parental Attitudes And Social Environment on the Personality Development of The Adolescent Blind* (New York: American Foundation for the Blind, 1944), p. 65.

24. *Ibid.*

25. Alfred Adler, *Problems of Neurosis* (New York: Cosmopolitan Book Company, 1930), p. 44.

26. R. G. Barker, Beatrice A. Wright, and Mollie Gonick, "Adjustment to Physical Handicap and Illness" (New York: Social Science Research Council, *Bulletin 55*, 1946), p. 84.

27. *Id.* at p. 85.

28. B. L. Diamond and A. Ross, "Emotional Adjustment of Newly Blinded Soldiers," *American Journal of Psychiatry*, (1945), vol. 102, pp. 367-371.

29. Lee Myerson, "Physical Disability as a Social Psychological Problem," *Journal of Social Issues*, Vol. 4, No. 4, (1948), p. 6.

30. Roger G. Barker, "The Social Psychology of Physical Disability," *Id.* at p. 31.

31. Sommers, *op. cit. supra* note 23 p. 104. See also Stella E. Plants, "Blind People are Individuals," *The Family*, Vol. 24, No. 1 (March, 1943), pp. 8, 16.

32. Sommers, *Id.* at p. 106.

Chapter 2

Growth, Harmony, and the Fight to Organize

The decade of the 1950s was, for the organized blind movement in the United States, almost to the end a period of sustained development, of internal harmony and cooperation, and of broad new visions expressed in campaigns of unprecedented daring. Measured in terms of growth alone, the principle of self-organization by the blind was thoroughly vindicated in this decade and the National Federation of the Blind proven to be successful beyond question—even by its foes. The 1949 convention had been held in Denver, the 1950 convention in Chicago, and the 1951 convention in Oklahoma City. During these years the Federation continued to expand and mature.

By 1952 some 150 delegates from 31 states were in attendance at the Nashville convention which was organized, as it happened, by a young Tennessee state president named Kenneth Jernigan, attending his first National Convention. At the San Francisco convention four years later, the total climbed to 42 state affiliates with more than 700 delegates. When the National Federation of the Blind convened in Miami for its twentieth anniversary convention in 1960, no fewer than 47 states sent a total of 900 delegates to the scene.

The fifties were also a decade of successive precedents and breakthroughs on a variety of fronts. The 1952 convention featured the first address by a state governor as well as the National

Federation of the Blind's first nationwide broadcast (a fifteen-minute address by President tenBroek carried live on NBC). The year 1953, when the convention met in Milwaukee, witnessed the inauguration of the Federation's first substantial fund-raising campaign (which would bear mixed fruit in subsequent years with results both economically productive and internally disruptive). In 1954 at Louisville the first copies appeared of "Who Are the Blind Who Lead the Blind" and "What is the National Federation of the Blind"—both of them written by Kenneth Jernigan (the first is reprinted in updated form in Appendix B to this volume). The next year saw the first of many National Federation of the Blind surveys of state programs for the blind carried out at gubernatorial request—those of Colorado and Arkansas, authored jointly by Jernigan and First Vice President George Card. In 1953 as well, the Newel Perry Award for distinguished service to the blind was presented for the first time; it went to Governor Ed Johnson of Colorado for his courage in inviting the blind into his state to perform the unheard-of function of judging the agency for the blind. Another precedent of much greater significance which was achieved in the course of the decade was the breakthrough in Civil Service employment—a slow and arduous process of persistent challenges to the entrance tests in all categories of the Civil Service. The first limited victory came in 1953 when the Civil Service Commission capitulated to mounting pressure and opened just one of its examinations, at that time known as the Junior Management Assistant Examination (reputedly the toughest of the lot), to blind candidates. The result was one of triumph and vindication; across the country, spurred by the National Federation of the Blind, twice as many blind applicants proportionally passed the examination as those possessing sight. (Some six percent of the blind, as opposed to three percent of the sighted, passed the examination.) By the early sixties, as a chastened Commission began to work cooperatively with the Federation, most of the civil service barriers came tumbling down, with the result that today blind men and women are at work for the federal government in ever-increasing numbers as attorneys, chemists, switchboard operators, transcribers, skilled workers, and much more.

Of all the campaigns of reform launched by the National Federation of the Blind during the dynamic decade of the fifties, none was more sweeping in ambition or momentous in significance than the struggle for the "right to organize," which centered around embattled legislation known then and ever since as the "Kennedy Bill"—after its co-sponsor, Senator (and future President) John F. Kennedy. The need for such legislation, protecting the right of blind organizations to exist without harassment from hostile agencies, became urgent early in the decade as the remarkable success of the Federation in recruiting blind persons to its cause—and carrying out independent surveys of state programs—began to draw alarmed resistance and opposition from major elements of what was to become known as the "Blindness System." As the word of Federationism was carried to the cities and towns of America, new and independent associations of blind people sprang up while old organizations that had grown dormant were given a new lease on life. In state after state these local groups formed themselves into statewide bodies, which in turn sought affiliation with the National Federation of the Blind. Each level of organization gained strength and confidence from the other—and together they exerted mounting pressure upon the public agencies.

The response of the agencies to this independent activity and spirit was not wholly negative, to be sure. In some states the organized blind were regarded not as a threat to existing policies but as an invaluable source of information and advice in the mutual effort to improve state programs and services. In these cooperative relationships the National Federation of the Blind typically lent a hand in such areas as public relations, funding, and the pursuit of progressive legislation. But if many public and voluntary agencies greeted the rise of the organized blind movement in a spirit of cooperation, there were as many others—both within the states and nationally—which reacted with bitter hostility. Their opposition had various causes, of course, among them the simple disbelief that blind persons might be capable of managing their own lives and exercising the normal rights of other citizens.

But there was a more immediate and practical—not to say vengeful—motive behind the opposition of numerous elements in the blindness system; it was the perceived threat to various of their programs and institutions, notably the sheltered workshops and the blind-oriented federal vending stand program, which represented a formidable stake in the continued dependency of the blind. Managerial groups tended not unnaturally to look upon independent organizations of their blind workers as trade unions seeking to improve their rights and working conditions; and indeed the two were related, as the National Federation of the Blind state affiliates pressed for a variety of reforms in the agency programs and supported the affiliation of shop workers with actual labor unions.

By the time of the NFB's 1956 convention in San Francisco, the agency attacks upon the organized blind movement were no longer merely scattered but concerted and orchestrated; and not merely critical but bitterly hostile and frequently vicious. In a classic convention address, "Within the Grace of God," which combined satirical humor with moral urgency, President Jacobus tenBroek undertook to counter these attacks and to answer the questions they were raising: "Whence come these attacks? What is the motivation behind them? Is such conflict unavoidable? To what degree is reconciliation possible?" The full text of his memorable speech follows:

WITHIN THE GRACE OF GOD
by Jacobus tenBroek

It is a privilege of a very special order, and one to which I have long looked forward, to address you here tonight in the unique and wonderful city of San Francisco. For all of us who are native Californians (which means as you know that we have moved at least six months ago from Iowa or Oklahoma) this occasion marks the fulfillment of a cherished ambition; and we feel something of the pardonable pride of hosts who know that their hospitality has been as graciously accepted as it has been warmly given.

But there is something else that is special about the present occasion. Our city and our state are blessed in this year of grace with not one but two history-making conventions, each of which is appearing on the local stage for the first time: our own and that of the Republican Party. There can be no question, of course, which is the more important and far-reaching in its consequences—but let us admit that the Republicans too have an objective of some scope.

During our regular convention sessions today we have had a fairly full review of the work of the National Federation of the Blind. We have seen the accelerated growth of the organization marked by the accession of nine state affiliates in the year since our last National Convention, lifting us from a beginning of seven states in 1940 to a grand total of forty-two states today and with a clear view of affiliates in forty-eight states in the foreseeable future. We have seen an organization with purposes as irrepressible as the aspiration of men to be free, with far-flung activities and accomplishments, with the solid adherence and participation of rank and file members, and with the selfless devotion of an ever-increasing array of able and distinguished leaders. We have seen the action and the forces of action. We have also seen the reaction and the forces of reaction. There is perhaps no stronger testimony to our developing prestige and influence as the nationwide movement and organization of the blind than the scope and intensity of the attacks upon us. These attacks are not new. They have persisted from the very beginning. They have ranged from unspeakable, whispering campaigns against the character and integrity of the leaders of the Federation to public disparagement of its goals and structure. Now, however, the attacks have taken on a new bitterness and violence. They include open avowals of a determination to wipe several of our affiliates out of existence and every step possible has been taken to bring about this result.

Whence come these attacks? What is the motivation behind them? Are they personal? Are they institutional? Are they based on policy differences as to ends as well as to means? What is the pattern of action and reaction for the future? Is such conflict unavoidable? To what degree is reconciliation possible?

It is to an analysis of these problems and to an answer to these questions that I should like to direct your attention tonight.

Let me begin by giving you a purely hypothetical and very fanciful situation. Imagine that somewhere in the world there exists a civilization in which the people without hair—that is the bald—are looked down upon and rigidly set apart from everyone else by virtue of their distinguishing physical characteristic. If you can accept this fantasy for a moment, it is clear that at least two kinds of organization would come into being dedicated to serve the interests of these unfortunate folk. First, I suggest, there would appear a group of non-bald persons drawn together out of sympathy for the sorry condition of this rejected minority: in short, a benevolent society with a charitable purpose and a protective role.

At first, all of the members of this society would be volunteers, doing the work on their free time and out of the goodness of their hearts. Later, paid employees would be added who would earn their livelihood out of the work and who would gradually assume a position of dominance. This society would, I believe, have the field pretty much to itself for a rather long time. In the course of years, it would virtually eliminate cruel and unusual punishment of the bald, furnish them many services, and finally create enclaves and retreats within which the hairless might escape embarrassing contact with normal society and even find a measure of satisfaction and spiritual reward in the performance of simple tasks not seriously competitive with the ordinary pursuits of the larger community.

The consequence of this good work would, I venture to say, be a regular flow of contributions by the community, an acceptance by the community of the charitable foundation as the authentic interpreter of the needs of those unfortunate and inarticulate souls afflicted with baldness, an increasing veneration for the charitable foundation, and a general endorsement of its principles, and— gradually but irresistibly—the growth of a humanitarian awareness that the bald suffer their condition through no fault of their own and accordingly that they should be sponsored, protected, tolerated, and permitted to practice, under suitable supervision and control, what few uncomplicated trades patient training may reveal them able to perform.

Eventually, a great number of charitable organizations would be established in the field of work for the bald. They or some of them would join together in a common association which might well be entitled the American Association of Workers for the Bald. Step by step, upon the published "Proceedings" of their annual meetings, carefully edited to eliminate the views of the outspoken bald, they would aspire to climb to professional status. As a part of their self-assigned roles as interpreters and protectors of the bald, they or some of them, would sooner or later undertake to lay down "criteria" and "standards" for all service programs for the bald to be "a manual of guidance for those responsible for operating the programs...."

These, then, would be the assumptions and the ends to which the charitable organizations for the bald would tirelessly and successfully exert themselves. They would petition the community through both public and private enterprise to support these purposes, and their appeals would dramatize them through a subtle invocation of the sympathetic and compassionate traits of human nature. Sooner or later, some of them—in order to drive competitors out of business, garner favor with the public, and give color of legitimacy to their own methods—would issue what they would unabashedly call a code of fund-raising ethics.

All this presumably would take much time; but before too many generations had passed I expect that most if not all of these objectives would have come to fruition, and there would appear to be an end to the problem of the bald.

Unfortunately, however, there seem always to be those who persist in questioning established institutions and revered traditions; and in my improbable fable, at some point well along in the story, there would appear a small band of irascible individuals—a little group of willful men—bent on exposing and tearing down the whole laborious and impressive structure of humanitarianism and progress. Incredibly and ironically, these malcontents would emerge from the very ranks of the bald themselves. At first I suspect that they would pass unheard and almost unnoticed; but eventually their numbers would increase and their dissent become too insistent to be easily ignored. What they would be saying, as I make it out, is something like this:

> You have said that we are different because we are bald, and that this difference marks us as inferior. But we do not agree with certain Biblical parables that possession of hair is an index of strength, certainly not that it is a measure either of virtue or of ability. Owing to your prejudice and perhaps your guilt—because you do not like to look upon us—you have barred us from the normal affairs of the community and shunted us aside as if we were pariahs. But we carry no contagion and present no danger, except as you define our condition as unclean and make of our physical defect a stigma. In your misguided benevolence you have taken us off the streets and provided shelters where we might avoid the pitiless gaze of the non-bald and the embarrassment of their contact. But what we wish chiefly is to be back *on* the streets, with access to all the avenues of ordinary commerce and activity. We do not want your pity, since there need be no occasion for it; and it is not we who suffer embarrassment in company with those whom we deem our fellows and our equals. You have been kind to us, and if we were

animals we should perhaps be content with that; but our
road to hell has been paved with your good intentions.

One of the leaders of the bald doubtless would rise to say:

> We do not want compassion, we want understanding; we
> do not want tolerance, we want acceptance; we do not
> want charity, we want opportunity; we do not want de-
> pendency, we want independence. You have given us
> much, but you have withheld more; you have withheld
> those values which we prize above all else, exactly as you
> do: personal liberty, dignity, privacy, opportunity, and—
> most of all—equality. But if it is not in your power, or
> consistent with your premises, to see these things as our
> goals, be assured that it is within our power and consis-
> tent with our self-knowledge to demand them and to
> press for their attainment. For we know by hard ex-
> perience what you do not know, or have not wished to
> recognize: that given the opportunity we are your equals;
> that as a group we are no better and no worse than you—
> being in fact a random sample of yourselves. We are your
> doubles, whether the yardstick be intellectual or physical
> or psychological or occupational. Our goals, in short, are
> these: we wish to be liberated, not out of society but into
> it; we covet independence, not in order to be distinct but
> in order to be equal. We are aware that these goals, like
> the humane objectives you have labored so long to ac-
> complish, will require much time and effort and wisdom
> to bring into being. But the painful truth must be
> proclaimed that your purposes are not our purposes; we
> do not share your cherished assumptions of the nature
> of baldness, and will not endure the handicap you have
> placed upon it.

> And so we have formed our own organization, in order
> to speak for ourselves from the experience which we
> alone have known and can interpret. We bear no malice
> and seek no special favors, beyond the right and oppor-
> tunity to join society as equal partners and members in
> good standing of the great enterprise that is our nation
> and our common cause.

End of quotation—end of fable. Is this fable simply a fanciful
story or is it a parable? Some will say, I have no doubt, that I
have not presented the case of the blind—that there is no parallel
and therefore no parable. For one thing, is it not surely ridiculous

to imagine that any civilized society could so baldly misinterpret the character of those who are not blessed with hair on their heads? It may be! But civilized society has always so misinterpreted the character of those who lack sight in their eyes; and on a basis of that misinterpretation has created the handicap of blindness. You and I know that blind people are simply people who cannot see; society believes that they are people shorn of the capacity to live normal, useful, productive lives, and that belief has largely tended to make them so.

For another thing, did the fable accurately portray the attitudes of at least some of the agencies for the blind? Are their goals really so different from the goals of the blind themselves? Do they actually arrogate to themselves the roles of interpreter and protector, ascribing to their clients characteristics of abnormality and dependency? To answer these questions and to demonstrate the *bona fides* of the parable, I shall let some agency leaders speak for themselves in the form of seven recent quotations:

Quotation number one uttered by an agency psychiatrist: "All visible deformities require special study. Blindness is a visible deformity and all blind persons follow a pattern of dependency." That one hardly requires any elucidation to make its meaning plain.

Quotation number two uttered by the author of a well-known volume upon the blind for which the American Association of Workers for the Blind conferred upon him a well-known award: "With many persons, there was an expectation in the establishment of the early schools...that the blind in general would thereby be rendered capable of earning their own support—a view that even at the present is shared in some quarters. It would have been much better if such a hope had never been entertained, or if it had existed in a greatly modified form. A limited acquaintance of a practical nature with the blind as a whole and their capabilities has usually been sufficient to demonstrate the weakness of this conception." That one also speaks adequately for itself.

Quotation number three uttered by a well-known blind agency head: "After he is once trained and placed, the average disabled person can fend for himself. In the case of the blind, it has been found necessary to set up a special state service agency which will supply them not only rehabilitation training but other services for the rest of their lives." The agencies "keep in constant contact with them as long as they live." So the blind are unique among the handicapped in that, no matter how well-adjusted, trained, and placed, they require lifelong supervision by the agencies.

Quotation number four uttered by another well-known blind agency head: "The operation of the vending stand program, we feel, necessitates maintaining a close control by the Federal Government through the licensing agency with respect to both equipment and stock, as well as the actual supervision of the operation of each individual stand. It is therefore our belief that the program would fail if the blind stand managers were permitted to operate without control." This is, of course, just the specific application of the general doctrine of the incompetence of the blind expressed in the previous quotation. Blind businessmen are incapable of operating an independent business. The agencies must supervise and control the stock, equipment, and the business operation.

Quotation number five, first sentence of the Code of Ethics (so-called) of the American Association of Workers for the Blind: "The operations of all agencies for the blind entail a high degree of responsibility because of the element of public trusteeship and protection of the blind involved in services to the blind." The use of the word "protection" makes it plain that the trusteeship here referred to is of the same kind as that existing under the United Nations Trusteeship Council—that is, custody and control of underprivileged, backward, and dependent peoples.

Quotation number six uttered by still another well-known blind agency head: "To dance and sing, to play and act, to swim, bowl, and roller skate, to work creatively in clay, wood, aluminum, or tin, to make dresses, to join in group readings or discussions, to have entertainments and parties, to engage in many other activities of one's choosing—this is to fill the life of anyone with the things that make life worth living." Are these the things that make life worth living for you? Only the benevolent keeper of an asylum could make this remark—only a person who views blindness as a tragedy which can be somewhat mitigated by little touches of kindness and service to help pass the idle hours but which cannot be overcome. Some of these things may be accessories to a life well filled with other things—a home, a job, and the rights and responsibilities of citizenship, for example.

Quotation number seven uttered by still another head of a blind agency: "A job, a home, and the right to be a citizen, will come to the blind in that generation when each and every blind person is a living advertisement of his ability and capacity to accept the privileges and responsibilities of citizenship. Then we professionals will have no problem of interpretation because the blind will no longer need us to speak for them, and we, like primitive segregation, will die away as an instrument which society will include only in its historical records." "A job, a home, and the right to be a citizen," are not now either the possessions or the rights of the blind—they will only come to the blind in a future generation! A generation, moreover, which will never come to the sighted since it is one in which "each and every blind person" will live up to some golden rule far beyond the human potential. In that never-to-be-expected age, the leaders of the agencies for the blind will no longer discharge their present function of "interpretation," because the blind will then be able to speak for themselves.

Whatever else can be said about these quotations, no one can say that these agency leaders lack candor. They have stated their views with the utmost explicitness. Moreover, these are not isolated instances of a disappearing attitude, a vestigial remainder of a forgotten era. Such expressions are not confined to those here quoted. Many other statements of the same force and character could be produced; and the evidence that the deed has been suited to the word is abundant. At long last, we now know that we must finally lay at rest the pious platitude and the hopeful conjecture that the blind themselves and the agencies for the blind are really all working towards the same objectives and differ only as to means for achieving them. I would that it were so. We are not in agreement as to objectives although we frequently disagree as to means as well.

The frankly avowed purposes and the practices of the agencies tend in the direction of continued segregation along vocational and other lines. The blind would move vigorously in the direction of increasing integration, of orienting, counseling, and training the blind towards competitive occupations and placing them therein, towards a job, a home, and normal community activities and relations. The agencies, by their words and their acts, tend to sanctify and reinforce those semi-conscious stereotypes and prejudicial attitudes which have always plagued the condition of the physically disabled and the socially deprived. We, by our words and acts, would weaken them and gradually blot them out altogether. Their statements assert and their operations presuppose a need for continuous, hovering surveillance of the sightless—in recreation, occupation, and congregation—virtually from cradle to grave. We deny that any such need exists and refute the premise of necessary dependency and incompetence on which it is based. Their philosophy derives from and still reflects the philanthropic outlook and ethical uplift of those Friendly Visitors of a previous century whose self-appointed mission was to guide their less fortunate neighbors to personal salvation through a combination of material charity and moral edification. We believe that the problems of the blind are at least as much social as personal and that a broad frontal attack on public misconceptions and existing program arrangements for the blind is best calculated to achieve desirable results. We believe, moreover, that it is worthwhile inquiring into the rationale of any activity which takes as its psychological premise the double-barreled dogma that those deprived of sight are deprived also of judgment and common sense, and that therefore what they need above all else is to be adjusted to their inferior station through the wise ministrations of an elite corps of neurosis-free custodians.

The agency leaders say, and apparently believe, that the blind are not entitled to the privileges and responsibilities of citizenship or to full membership in society betokened by such attributes of normal life as a home and a job. This can only be predicated on the proposition that the blind are not only abnormal and inferior but they are so abnormal and inferior that they are not even persons. We believe that blind people are precisely as normal as other people are, being in fact a cross section of the rest of the community in every respect except that they cannot see. But were this not so, their abnormality would not strip them of their personality. The Constitution of the United States declares that all persons born in the United States or naturalized are citizens. There is nothing in the Constitution or in the gloss upon it which says that this section shall not apply to persons who are blind. If born in the United States or naturalized, whether before or after blindness, blind persons are citizens of the United States *now* and are *now*, not merely in some future generation, possessed of the right to be citizens and share the privileges, immunities, and responsibilities of that status. Moreover, the bounty of the Constitution extends to all persons, whether citizens or not, rights to freedom, equality, and individuality. As citizens, then, or as persons, who happen to be deprived of one of their physical senses, we claim, under the broad protection of the Constitution, the right to life, personal freedom, personal security; the right to marry, to have and rear children, and to maintain a home; and the right, so far as government can assure it, to that fair opportunity to earn a livelihood which will make these other rights possible and significant. We have the right freely to choose our fields of endeavor, unhindered by arbitrary, artificial, or manmade impediments. All limitations on our opportunity, all restrictions on us based on irrelevant considerations of physical disability, are in conflict with our Constitutional right of equality and must be removed. Our access to the mainstreams of community life, the aspirations and achievements of each of us, are to be limited only by the skills, energy, talents, and abilities we individually bring to the opportunities equally open to all Americans.

Finally, we claim as our birthright, as our Constitutional guarantee, and as an indivestible aspect of our nature the fundamental human right of self-expression, the right to speak for ourselves individually and collectively. Inseparably connected with this right is the right of common association. The principle of self-organization means self-guidance and self-control. To say that the blind can, should, and do lead the blind is only to say that they are their own counselors, that they stand on their own feet. In the control of their own lives, in the responsibility for their own programs, in the organized and consistent pursuit of objectives of their own choosing—in these alone lies the hope of the blind for economic independence, social integration, and emotional security.

You may think that what I have said exaggerates the error and the danger to be expected from those whose only interest is to serve the welfare of the blind. I think it does not. No one could ask, it is true, for any more conscientious and devoted public servants than those who serve in the rank and file of the agencies for the blind, public and private. The leaders of many agencies, too, must be given commendation for enlightened policies and worthwhile programs. We have heard from some of these agency leaders yesterday at our convention and we will hear from more before our convention is over. No one can doubt either that the agencies when so manned and so led may be of immense and constructive assistance in a multitude of ways, during the onward movement of the blind into full membership in society. As to some of the agencies not headed by leaders of the character just described, credit must be given for sincerity and good intentions. This, however, but serves to raise the question whether, in social terms, sincere and upright folly is better or worse than knavery. This discussion I forbear to enter.

What should the posture of the National Federation of the Blind be in the midst of these attacks and struggles? As the possessors of power, we must exercise it responsibly, impersonally, and with self-restraint. As a people's movement, we cannot allow others to deflect us from our course. We must apply our power and influence to achieve our legitimate goals. To this end, we must all exert ourselves to the utmost. Our opponents have history and outmoded concepts on their side. We have democracy and the future on ours. For the sake of those who are now blind and those who hereafter will be blind—and for the sake of society at large—we cannot fail. If the National Federation of the Blind continues to be representative in its character, democratic in its procedures, open in its purposes, and loyal in its commitments—so long, that is, as the faith of the blind does not become blind faith—we have nothing to fear, no cause for apology, and only achievement to look forward to. We may carry our program to the public with confidence and conviction—choosing the means of our expression with proper care but without calculation, and appearing before the jury of all our peers not as salesmen but as spokesmen, not as hucksters but as petitioners for simple justice and the redress of unmerited grievances. We will have no need to substitute the advertisement for the article itself nor to prefer a dramatic act to an undramatic fact. If this is group pressure, it is group pressure in the right direction. If this involves playing politics, it is a game as old as democracy, with the stakes as high as human aspiration.

In the sixteenth century, John Bradford made a famous remark which has ever since been held up to us as a model of Christian humility and correct charity and which you saw reflected in the agency quotations I presented. Seeing a beggar in his rags creeping along a wall through a flash of lightning in a stormy night Bradford said: "But for the Grace of God, there go I." Compassion was shown; pity was shown; charity was shown; humility was shown; there was even an acknowledgement that the relative positions of the two could and might have been switched. Yet despite the compassion, despite the pity, despite the charity, despite the humility, how insufferably arrogant! There was still an unbridgeable gulf between Bradford and the beggar. They were not one but two. Whatever might have been, Bradford thought himself Bradford and the beggar a beggar—one high, the other low; one wise, the other misguided; one strong, the other weak; one virtuous, the other depraved.

We do not and cannot take the Bradford approach. It is not just that beggary is the badge of our past and is still all too often the present symbol of social attitudes towards us; although that is at least part of it. But in the broader sense, we are that beggar and he is each of us. We are made in the same image and out of the same ingredients. We have the same weaknesses and strengths, the same feelings, emotions, and drives; and we are the product of the same social, economic, and other environmental forces. How much more consonant with the facts of individual and social life, how much more a part of a true humanity, to say instead: "There, *within* the Grace of God, *do* go I." Thank you.

That convention address of 1956 by President tenBroek did not, of course, for all its reasoned argument and good humor, bring an end to the strife brought on by the coalition of hostile agencies in the blindness system. On the contrary, in the next few years the agency forces retaliated in more areas and in new ways. Blind workers in the sheltered shops, and blind operators of vending stands in state-controlled programs, were fired out of hand or threatened with dismissal if they dared to join or support the National Federation of the Blind. Blind employees of state agencies and commissions were subjected to a wide variety of pressures. Confidential case records of blind persons active in the National Federation of the Blind, who were receiving public aid or services, were opened and their contents exploited in an effort to discredit them and their group affiliations. At one desperate point, a combination of state agencies created a special committee, a kind of strike force, to seek ways of counteracting and undermining the Federation. President Jacobus tenBroek put the case squarely and simply when he declared at the 1957 convention in New Orleans: "The National Federation of the Blind stands today an embattled organization. Our motives have been impugned; our purposes reviled; our integrity aspersed; our representative character denied. Plans have been laid, activities undertaken, and concerted actions set in motion for the clear and unmistakable purpose of bringing about our destruction. Nothing less is sought than our extinction as an organization."

The response of the Federation to these attacks constitutes one of the most dramatic chapters of its history: namely, the campaign to gain protection for the right of the blind to organize, to speak for themselves, and to be heard. In effect there were three distinctive rights involved in this struggle: the right to organize invoked the constitutional guarantee of free association and assembly; the right of the blind to speak for themselves involved not only free-speech guarantees but the very principles of representative democracy; and the right to be *heard*, perhaps the most controversial of all, implied the development of regular channels of consultation and participation of the blind in the broad range of public programs affecting their lives. On the face of it these were far-reaching demands; in the context of blind affairs, hitherto a history of the inarticulate, the demands were nothing short of revolutionary.

In a compelling speech delivered at the 1957 convention in New Orleans, President tenBroek definitively portrayed the three rights of the blind revolution—and the 300,000 wronged by their denial. He made clear the interconnections between the right to organize, the right to speak, and the right to be heard; and he laid down a challenge to the hostile agencies of the blindness system to cease their destructive attacks and join the cause in which, officially and ostensibly, they served—the cause of security, opportunity, and equality for blind Americans. Here is what he said to the convention:

THREE RIGHTS—AND THREE HUNDRED THOUSAND WRONGED
by Jacobus tenBroek

"When bad men combine, the good must associate; else they will fall, one by one, an unpitied sacrifice in a contemptible struggle."

So said the Great Commoner, Edmund Burke, nearly 300 years ago. And speaking of those who had organized the political associations of Great Britain, he declared: "They believed that no men could act with effect who did not act in concert; that no men could act in concert who did not act with confidence; that no men could act with confidence who were not bound together by common opinions, common affections, and common interests."

No luster has been lost from these words over the intervening centuries. Their meaning, if anything, is magnified today, in our modern age of mass organization and mass communication, of vast diversity of interests and differences of opinion. But if the argument for association still holds good for the generality of men, it has a special urgency for the blind men and women of America.

For if we cannot say that "bad men" have combined against us, we can and do say that men of bad philosophy and little faith have done so—sighted and sightless men whose vision is short, whose ears are stopped, and whose minds are closed by institutional and occupational self-interest, whose banner is the wretched patchwork of medieval charity and poor relief.

When such as these combine, the blind indeed must associate: else we shall fall, as we have fallen in the past, one by one, a merely pitied sacrifice in a contemptible struggle.

And if it is also true, as Burke believed, that no men can act with effect who do not act in concert, how much more profoundly true is this of men who cannot act at all as individuals because they are deprived of every normal avenue of opportunity and expression. The rejected, the declassified, the disfranchised, the custodialized, are compelled in sheer self-defense to organize—to act in concert in order to act with effect—to act with confidence in order to act in concert—and to bind themselves together on the basis of their common opinions, common affections, and common interests.

The blind of America have bound themselves together primarily in order to *unbind* themselves of the arbitrary shackles which throughout all history have confined their movement and smothered their self-expression. Their emancipation from this social straitjacket requires the achievement of three essential and inseparable rights: three rights which constitute the fountainhead of American democracy and the recognized birthright of ordinary citizens: three rights withheld from our 300,000 blind.

They are the right to organize, the right to speak, and the right to be heard.

These rights comprise a trinity related as closely to one another as the points of a triangle. Each gains its meaning in the presence of the others; each loses its significance in the absence of the others. To paraphrase the language of Burke, no men can act effectively who do not have the right to organize; no men can organize at all who do not have the right to self-expression; and no men can achieve self-expression who do not have the right to be heard.

That these three rights are indeed inseparable—that each is the touchstone of the others—was fully recognized by those who framed our Constitution, and who placed them side by side in the First Amendment, identified as the rights of free speech, assembly, and petition—essential liberties beyond the control of Congress but not beyond its protection.

In modern terms, the right of free speech is the right of self-expression; the right of assembly is the right to organize; and the right of petition is the right to be heard.

The blind of America are today in the throes of an historic struggle to secure for themselves these rights which the Constitution guarantees to all Americans. In two bills now before Congress—S. 2411, sponsored by Senator Kennedy, and H.R. 8609, sponsored by Congressman Baring—are incorporated the safeguards which for the first time in history would gain for the blind the rights to self-organization, to self-expression, and to consultation in the public conduct of their affairs.

Before turning to that legislation, let us take a closer look at this trinity of rights—the struggle for which has plunged us into the most bitterly contested battle of our organized existence.

First of all, what is the right to organize? At bottom, it is only the recognition, in law and common sense, that man is a social animal—and that, in particular, men of common interests and a common purpose gain satisfaction and support from each other's company. But there is more to it than that. In a self-governing democracy the right to organize is virtually synonymous with the right of self-expression—that freedom of speech which is the foundation of all our liberties. Our theory of government is an attempt to capture the values of a diverse society; to seek the truth through open competition in the marketplace of ideas. It is essential to this principle that all legitimate demands be heard, that no body of citizens be silenced or suppressed. The great value of voluntary groups and associations to democracy is that they give a voice to citizens who, in Burke's words, "are bound together by common opinions, common affections, and common interests." Without the right to organize, the right to speak would remain for millions a cruel mockery of their mute condition. For these groups it is organization alone which makes the right to speak articulate.

If the blind are to speak for themselves, if they are to be heard in public forum and the councils of government, let us be certain that they will speak forcefully, and with a single voice. Let us guard our organized structure from collapse into a Tower of

Babel—a confusion of tongues. Let us remember that to act in concert means to take concerted action; that the hallmark of a functioning democracy is not anarchy but unity; and that when all of us are faithful to our responsibilities as members, we may be sure that we shall act in concert and with confidence—that the voice of the blind will be heard in the land and that it will carry the ring of truth.

But what is this "right to be heard," and why is it so closely linked to the right to speak and the right to organize? The answer is of course that no degree of organization, and no amount of speech, is of any value if no one is listening. The right to be heard is the right to be consulted in matters of direct and vital concern. It is the right to have access to the agencies of government, the right to an audience at the seats of the mighty, the right of petition, the right of fair hearing. The right to be heard, for the organized blind, means in particular the right of consultation with the administrators of federal-state programs of public assistance, of vocational rehabilitation, of vending stands, and of other aids and services. But the right to be heard extends equally to consultation with those so-called private agencies which in effect are quasi-public in their structure, in the character of their programs, and in the source of their funds. These large foundations and charitable institutions, often the recipients of public aid and always the advisor of public programs, bear an obligation equal to that of government to consult with the clients of their services— who must otherwise become the victims of their arbitrary authority.

Until such agencies as these, both public and quasi-public, recognize the right of the blind to be heard, our cause may endure but it can never prevail. For no constitution, no law, no formal regulation, can compel anyone to listen. There are none so deaf as those who will not hear—no minds so closed as those resistant to new ideas and to the appeals of newly vocal groups. But it is the right to be heard, through the means of consultation, which we are seeking to establish in the two bills now before Congress. I might add that our immediate task is to establish the right of these bills to be heard: to get them before the proper committees and to give them a public hearing. Once this right has been recognized and implemented by Congress, our voice will no longer cry in a wilderness. Our words will then fall upon the ears of government, not always perhaps like music, but like the serious speech of reasonable men acting in concert and with confidence, and bound together by common opinions, common affections, and common interests.

But is there really a need for protection of the right to be heard? Do not the blind already possess the full sympathy and good wishes of society? Are not their problems clearly recognized and their demands understood and carried out by a benevolent government and a kindly community?

The answer, to put it bluntly, is that the blind have indeed gained sympathy, but they have not gained understanding. They have won compassion without comprehension. Over the centuries they have progressed from the status of outcasts to that of social wards—but not yet to that of free citizens. The goals of protection—of adequate shelter, of minimum security, are presently within their grasp; but the goals of dignity, of opportunity, of independence, of total integration into normal society, are still placed beyond their reach. In short, the blind have been given the right to life; it remains for them to secure the right to liberty and the pursuit of happiness.

The present halfway house in which the blind live results from the fact that, until a very short time ago, the blind remained silent while others spoke for them—sighted benefactors who wished them well but neither knew nor understood the reality of loss of sight. These good neighbors and well-meaning friends contributed unwittingly to the development of a crippling stereotype, a two-sided image of the nature of blindness which is equally in error on both sides: it has been too *pessimistic* on the one hand and too *optimistic* on the other.

The apparent paradox of this popular stereotype is the product of society's failure to distinguish clearly between the two different kinds of limitation which accompany blindness: the *physical* limitation and the *social* limitation. On the one hand, the physical effects of loss of sight have been drastically exaggerated in all societies. "The blind man," intoned an ancient saying, "is as one dead!"

If that view is no longer current, it is still commonly believed that the blind man is as one immobilized. This conviction of the "total immobilization" of the blind person has persisted stubbornly in the face of massive scientific and factual evidence to the contrary. Nor is it a view usually held toward others of the physically handicapped. Surely there are few who imagine that loss of hearing, for example, carries with it the loss of all mental faculties; or that the lack of taste, or of the sense of smell, must render a man incapable of normal activity and enterprise. Nevertheless, it is widely felt that loss of sight involves a total personality transformation which leaves its victims mentally incompetent, psychologically abnormal, socially inept, and physically helpless.

That is one side of the stereotype: a thoroughly pessimistic and defeatist picture of the *physical* effects of loss of sight. On the other side, no less significant and no less wrong, is an attitude of casual optimism if not unconcern toward the *social* limitations imposed by the sighted community upon the blind. These social limitations include discrimination in employment; segregation in and from ordinary social relations; exclusion from living accommodations, public and private; rejection from many of the normal activities of the community; and relations with government in which they are viewed as wards rather than citizens, or as patients rather than clients. They have not yet been fully emancipated and are very far from being accepted on a basis of social equality and individual capacity. Their inferior and deprived status is thought to be their normal, natural, and inevitable lot.

Fortunately today there are increasing signs of a basic change in this traditional perspective. The blind themselves are organized and steadily winning the right to self-expression and to consultation in the public conduct of their affairs. No less important, growing numbers of welfare and service groups are coming to recognize and support the competence of the blind in the management of their own affairs.

Among the most striking and heartening examples of this new spirit of cooperation and understanding—as opposed to condescension and pity—is that developing in the Lions Clubs of America. I could take a good deal of your time this evening illustrating the ways in which Lions in many parts of the country are participating with us today in our movement toward equality and self-expression. But I know of no better statement of this new spirit of Lionism, than that which was made before our National Convention this summer by Tim Seward, himself a prominent Lion and administrative assistant to Congressman Walter S. Baring of Nevada. In the past, said Mr. Seward, the Lions who have always felt a particular closeness to their blind neighbors have done things for them rather than with them.

I believe we are on the threshold of a new era....I know that there are some of us in Lionism [he goes on to say] who feel that the blind are infringing on our right by conducting their own white cane drives, because the Lions for the past 25 years have honored White Cane Day. But the white cane is a symbol of blindness, and what more understanding and true spirit of Lionism could there be than to return the symbol of blindness to the blind and thank God they are able to carry their own banner....

I believe [he continued] that it is time we better understand our relationship with the blind, and to do that we must better understand the blind. We should understand that you not only seek but are entitled to both social and economic equality; that you are normal people and as such you have the right of self-expression as individuals and through your organizations; that both federal and state agencies should consult with your representatives in formulating programs that concern your welfare, or further your opportunities....To this end I believe we can work together as a team, and lend a hand when it is needed. I believe that it is far better that we learn the purposes and objectives of your organization and help you accomplish them rather than try to steer you on a different course. In short, I believe we should work *with* you rather than *for* you, and this I believe is true Lionism.

This clear affirmation is representative of a spirit rapidly spreading today among welfare and service organizations. This new spirit has been translated into practical administration by many public officials including some who administer programs for the blind. We have received from blind agency personnel in a substantial number of states correspondence testifying to the value of close consultation with organizations of the blind. Listen to these quotations:

1. From the organized blind of the state, "the state has received sound advice concerning the problems and needs of the blind, thus enabling us to draft policies and procedures which are not only realistic but are also geared to helping blind persons in their efforts to decrease dependency."

2. "The organizations of the blind have undertaken an interpretative program among their members with respect to the responsibilities, as well as the rights, of recipients of aid to the blind.

This in turn has contributed greatly to the smooth functioning administration of the program."

3. "As an administrator, I have found the State Federation of the Blind a valued source of assistance in administering services for the blind. Its activities have been a key factor in the growth and improvement of our programs during the past few years."

4. "From the first, the Federation has provided helpful counsel and advice to the department. One means has been through its representation on the State Aid to the Blind Advisory Committee."

5. "I feel that it is of the utmost importance to know how the persons served feel about the services provided, how such services can be improved. The Federation of the Blind has been an excellent vehicle for this purpose."

6. "Please be assured of this agency's willingness and intention of always and in every way possible carrying out the thesis that we can progress in the interest of the blind only by close cooperation, and we certainly believe that when blind people organize together to help themselves it certainly is helpful to any group or agency interested in the same ultimate goals."

7. "The values derived from close consultation with the blind cannot be obtained from any other source."

Who are the state administrators who have made these and similar statements? Are they unknowns in the field? Are they minor officials without position, influence, or opportunity to observe the overall picture? Quite the contrary! They are the top administrators of their programs, thoroughly in possession of the facts and responsible not only for what they say but for the conduct of their agencies. They are: Harry L. Hines, Director, Services for the Blind, Nebraska; Clifford A. Stocker, Administrator, Commission for the Blind, Oregon; Malcolm Jasper, Director, Iowa Commission for the Blind; Perry Sundquist, Chief, Division for the Blind, California; Merle Kidder, State Director, Division of Vocational Rehabilitation, North Dakota; Harry E. Hayes, Director, Services for the Blind, Kansas; T. V. Cranmer, Supervisor, Services for the Blind, Kentucky; Thomas J. Lucas, Director, Division of Public Assistance, Wisconsin; Howard H. Hanson, Director, Services to the Blind, South Dakota; Barbara Coughlan,

Director, State Department of Public Welfare, Nevada; John F. Mungovan, Director, State Division of the Blind, Massachusetts.

To confer the benefits which these administrators have listed on all administrators of programs for the blind through Congressional implementation of the rights of organization, speech, and consultation is the very purpose of the Kennedy and Baring bills. That purpose has seemed so obvious to many people that they have wondered why such legislation should be needed at all—or, at least, have felt confident that no one could wish to stand in the way of so reasonable an object.

In case there are any among you who still feel such confidence, allow me to remind you of the resolution condemning the Kennedy bill which was railroaded through their convention this summer by a controlling faction of the American Association of Workers for the Blind. In this official diatribe the "little group of willful men" placed squarely on the record its considered judgment of the competence of blind people generally, the irresponsible character of their organizations, and the dictatorial function of such groups as the AAWB. In their sweeping denunciation of the bill and all it stands for, these agency spokesmen made four distinct and definite points:

First, the blind are second-class citizens, undeserving of the normal responsibilities and privileges accorded as a birthright to other Americans. Do I exaggerate? Here are their exact words: the bill "embodies a completely unsound and retrogressive concept of the responsibilities and privileges of blind persons as citizens." What clearer statement could there be of the view that loss of sight is tantamount to loss of citizenship—in particular, of the right to speak and the right to be heard?

Second, the organized blind lack even the maturity and simple competence to participate on normal terms in the conduct of programs affecting them. Do I distort their meaning? Now hear this: "the proposed legislation, if enacted, would create an *arbitrary* and unwieldy system of review and supervision of all federally-financed benefits or services on behalf of blind persons by *professionally unqualified* groups; and...such reviews would in effect *make these blind persons supervisors* of the federal agencies and programs...and such administrative procedure would *impair the efficiency* of federal programs...." These statements leave no room for doubt as to the utter contempt with which the dominant elements in the AAWB regard the abilities of their blind clients; in a word, they regard these abilities as nonexistent.

Third, only the AAWB and its fellow custodians possess the rights and competence to consult on programs for the blind—in fact, to dictate what these programs are to be—and this vested interest must be protected at all costs against the unwarranted intrusion of the blind themselves. Am I unfair to them? Look at the resolution: in contrast to its rejection of the organized blind from consultation, it declares that one of the "principal functions" of the AAWB "is to provide the benefits of its extensive knowledge about the problems of blindness to those leaders in our American society who are responsible for the reflection in legislation of sound social thinking"—in other words, to advise and supervise the programs for the blind. The resolution is replete with such odious contrasts: where the blind are "professionally unqualified," the agencies are "professionally responsible" and moreover possess the "professional processes" and "authentic information" to counteract the errors and evils perpetrated by the unprofessional blind.

Fourth, although the Kennedy bill is here condemned as "completely unsound and retrogressive," all of its provisions are said to be contained in the Constitution and in the laws! Does this spurning of the Constitution seem unlikely? Listen:"...[A]ll of the provisions of this bill are already guaranteed in the Constitution of the U.S. and furthermore, most federally authorized programs of benefits already provide through statutes or regulations opportunities for fair hearings." If this is true, then all the preceding statements damning the bill are flagrant attacks upon the Constitution! But what is even more amazing is the incredible constitutional doctrine here set forth that it is unnecessary and improper to give legislative enforcement to any right. This lack of understanding of American government and institutions on the part of a group most of whom are in the employ of government is appalling. Might we observe that the leaders of the AAWB are "professionally unqualified" when it comes to questions of constitutional law.

By this reasoning we should do away with all our laws against murder because the Constitution guarantees the right to life. By this reasoning we should throw out all our laws protecting property—because the Constitution guarantees the right to property. By this reasoning we should discard all our laws protecting persons against unlawful imprisonment—because the Constitution guarantees the right to liberty. By this reasoning we should eliminate all our laws protecting individuals against violence to their persons or invasion of their rights of privacy—because the Constitution guarantees the right of the people to be secure in their persons, houses, papers, and effects. By this reasoning we should repeal all those legislative enactments maintaining the rights of citizens—because the Constitution forbids abridgment of the privileges and immunities of citizens. By this reasoning we should destroy all those legislative provisions requiring that persons similarly situated be treated alike—because the Constitution guarantees to all persons the equal protection of the laws. By this reasoning we should strike down one by one, section by section, clause by clause, those statutes which prohibit the peonage and chattelage of man—because the Constitution abolishes slavery and involuntary servitude.

In most of its provisions the Constitution is not a self-executing document. Virtually all of its provisions require the support of special laws in order to gain enforcement. Even the 13th Amendment—sometimes cited as one of the few examples of a self-executing provision—has been implemented by particular legislation, and indeed the Amendment itself calls for just such implementation.

To these four planks in the anti-blind platform of the AAWB, some others have recently been added by their once-silent partner, the American Foundation for the Blind. In a July bulletin of the Foundation, the Kennedy bill was also condemned as "administratively unsound" because it would, in some unspecified way, "injure the spread" of services for the blind. More important, however, said the Foundation, passage of the measure "would tend to further the segregation of blind persons, and coerce them into added identification with selected organized groups if they wished to have any voice in affairs affecting their welfare."

Note the logic of that assertion. The bill would strengthen and assist organizations of the blind—therefore it would further the segregation of the blind. In other words there must be no legislation to support the farmers, because it could only serve to further their segregation. There must be no legislation to advance the cause of private enterprise, because it could only serve to further the segregation of businessmen. There must be no legislation on behalf of organized labor, because to strengthen the unions is only to further their segregation. There must be no aid to needy children or the totally and permanently disabled because such aid will further the segregation of these groups. By this logic, there must be no legislation of any kind for any group of citizens—except, presumably, that legislation aiding the AFB and the AAWB. That alone may be encouraged without the danger of segregation.

But we may also agree that successful self-organization by the blind would tend to further their segregation from the grip of custodial agencies. As for the charge of "coercion," it need only be said that the primary purpose of the Kennedy and Baring bills is to afford the blind protection from the degree of coercion which now exists by virtue of the denial of their rights to organize, to speak for themselves, and to be heard in the councils of government.

One more declaration of the American Foundation against the Kennedy bill deserves our attention. In a separate release the executive director, Mr. M. Robert Barnett, characterized the introduction of the bill as "a regrettable incident" because it is "likely to cause one of the most serious philosophical debates yet experienced in our field." We may all agree that the bill is likely to produce such a result: but why should such a "serious philosophical debate" be regrettable? Why, on the contrary, is it not welcomed as a golden opportunity to be eagerly embraced by all who are sincerely interested in the welfare of the blind and therefore in the solution of their problems? One might suppose that no greater contribution could be made in our field than the production of serious philosophical debate. But Mr. Barnett considers it "regrettable." Are there now those who would deny to the blind not only the rights of free speech and organization but even the right of free thought and philosophical reflection? Such serious discussion should, it would seem, prove regrettable only to those whose philosophy cannot stand the rigors of the contest.

On the basis of the assertions in the AAWB resolution and the Foundation release it is hard to imagine any wider and more unbridgeable gulf of thought and principle than exist between our philosophy and theirs. We believe the blind to be normal individuals lacking only the sense of sight. They believe the blind to be abnormal individuals lacking maturity, responsibility, and mentality. We believe the organized blind to be the best interpreters of their own needs and aspirations. They believe the organized blind to be entirely—indeed, dangerously— unqualified and instead assert their own claim to act in the name of the blind without the approval of the blind. We believe the role of the agencies, whether public or quasi-public, to be that of servants of their blind clients, responsible to their interests, and responsive to their needs. They believe the role of the agencies to be that not of public servants but of private dictators, members of an elite corps of self-designated experts beyond the reach or consultation of the people. Finally, we believe these bulletins and resolutions to be a shocking revelation of backwardness and prejudice among the dominant agency. They believe—but wait! Do they really believe? Is it possible that these specious arguments are not really their beliefs but only the outpouring of propaganda in a ruthless campaign to stamp out the competition of the organized blind and to perpetuate their own unchallenged dominance? With the publication of these revealing resolutions whatever trust and confidence the blind may once have had in the integrity and wisdom of those who dominate the AAWB has been forever swept away. They are shown to be among those who have been dragged protesting into the 20th century—but still have one foot in the grave of medieval charity and custodialism and the other foot in the pit of their own institutional and occupational vested interests.

Their belief is that the blind should be overseen and not heard; that the blind have no right of self-expression because the blind are not full-fledged citizens and, besides, are not capable of "sound social thinking"; and that the organized blind, if they cannot be dismissed as a handful of eccentrics, must be dispersed as a mob of delinquents.

Once upon another time a somewhat different group of deprived people—only slightly more numerous than we are today—rose up against their own protectors on this very issue of the right of men and citizens particularly to the rights of self-expression and representation. In terms of material strength they were no match for their adversary—at that time the world's greatest power. But the rebels were united in their dedication to certain unalienable rights—among these were life, liberty, and the pursuit of happiness in their own way—and they were determined to make good their declaration of independence. Their power was not so much physical as spiritual. It lay in their collective will, their unity of purpose, and their faith in themselves. Armed with these weapons, their cause proved invincible 180 years ago.

God helping us, that cause will prevail today. The good have associated and will not fall, one by one, an unpitied sacrifice in a contemptible struggle.

In the summer of 1957 two identical bills were introduced into Congress—one by Senator John Kennedy of Massachusetts and the other by Congressman Walter S. Baring of Nevada—expressly "to protect the right of the blind to self-expression through organizations of the blind." When he rose in the Senate to introduce and speak for his bill, the future President went directly to the heart of the matter in forceful words which clearly reflected his commitment to the political and civil rights of disadvantaged Americans. This is what he had to say:

> Organizations of blind persons exist today in many cities and communities throughout the country....In most of our states today, organizations of the blind have formed one or more statewide organizations. Forty-three of these statewide organizations of the blind are now federated into a single nationwide organization, the National Federation of the Blind.

> Organizations of this kind [Senator Kennedy continued] have been formed by the blind to advance their own welfare and common interests. These organizations provide to our blind citizens the opportunity for collective self-expression. Through these organizations, these citizens are able to formulate democratically and voice effectively their views on the programs that our national government and our state governments are financing for their aid and rehabilitation. It is important that these views be expressed freely and without interference. It is important that these views be heard and considered by persons charged with responsibility for determining and carrying out our programs for the blind.

> In some communities [he said] this freedom that each of our blind citizens should have to join, or not to join, organizations of the blind has been prejudiced by a few professional workers in programs for the blind who have allowed their personal views to be expressed in official action for or against particular organizations of the blind. Administrators and workers in welfare programs for the blind possess unusual power to control the lives and influence the conduct of their clients. It is important that our blind citizens be protected against any exercise of this kind of influence or authority to interfere with their freedom of self-expression through organizations of the blind.

The Kennedy bill was designed to do two complementary things: to insure to the blind the right to organize without in-

timidation or interference and to guarantee their right to speak
for them-selves and to be heard through meaningful consultation
with the agencies responsible for services affecting their welfare.
Literally as well as symbolically it was a blow for participatory
democracy, establishing the principle of representation by the
clients of the services—the consumers—in the decision-making
councils of government.

For a three-week period at Christmas of 1957, Kenneth Jernigan made an extensive swing through much of the country writing testimony for Federationists to give during anticipated
upcoming hearings on the bill. One such undertaking resulted in
an eloquent analysis of the need for the bill and for checks and
balances to curb the power of the agencies. This testimony, which
was given by Walter McDonald of Georgia, was printed in the
March, 1958, *Braille Monitor*.

CHECKS AND BALANCES

We are asking Congress to enact legislation requiring that the
blind be consulted about programs affecting them and protecting
the right of the blind to organize. Why are we doing this? Is it
really conceivable that there are times when the best interests of
the blind and of the agencies established to serve the blind are
different, even antagonistic? If there are such times, then the need
for the legislation we are proposing is obvious.

Let me create for you a rather fanciful and purely hypothetical
situation. Suppose the year is not 1958, but 1940 instead. Suppose
further that you are not in your present circumstances but are in
work for the blind. You may be a social caseworker, a home
teacher, or the manager of a sheltered workshop. You may be
sighted or blind. It makes no difference for the purposes of our
story.

In 1940 the Depression was just beginning to ease and the
lifeblood of commerce to flow through the nation again. It was a
year of hope—a time to dream dreams and have ambition. Like
the rest, you have your dream and your ambition, but it is not a
selfish dream, not an unworthy ambition. You have in mind the
launching of a project which will benefit blind people, not only
those with whom you have been working but others throughout
your state and region.

You have observed that one of the greatest problems confronting the blind is their difficulty in traveling independently. In the past, when you have tried to help a blind person get a job, almost the first question you have always been asked by the prospective employer has been, "But how can he get to and from work?" You have given a great deal of thought to the matter and have concluded that the best answer to the problem is the guide dog. Guide dogs cannot be procured in your part of the country, and the local blind person who wants one must travel many hundreds of miles at great trouble and expense. Besides, there is usually a long waiting list. You decide to do something about the situation. In short, you decide to establish a guide dog school.

You quit your job and put your whole time and energy into the project. You talk to local business people and begin to raise money. Soon you have a building, and you are collecting a staff of guide dog trainers and beginning to bring in dogs and students. You work day and night, and you pay yourself a salary of, let us say, ten thousand dollars a year—which is not unreasonable and certainly not too high for the amount of time and effort you are putting in.

Your school prospers. Blind people who have learned to travel by using your dogs are working in competitive industry and the professions throughout the country, and you have letters of gratitude and appreciation from them as well as many newspaper clippings and magazine articles telling of their success.

Your happiness is complete. You are doing a worthwhile job, and you are respected and honored throughout your entire state. In your own community you have become quite a figure and have more prestige than anyone else doing work for the blind. Yearly fund drives, complete with picture displays of guide dogs leading their masters, touch the hearts of thousands of donors and insure plenty of money for the growth and expansion of the school.

Time rushes by, and the year is now 1960. One day I come into your office, and I tell you of the perfection of a new travel aid for the blind. Perhaps I say something to this effect:

> Scientists at the Massachusetts Institute of Technology have, as you probably know, been working for several years to perfect an electronic travel aid for the blind. They have now achieved success. The instrument is perfect. It is light, compact, inexpensive, and able to scan

for at least thirty feet in all directions and to give the blind person all of the information his eyes would give him if he were sighted. I have one of the instruments here with me, and since I know that you have devoted the greater part of your life to the improvement of the lot of the blind and that you are sincerely interested in their welfare, I am certain you will (after looking at the instrument and verifying my statement about it) rejoice with me that the blind no longer need canes or dogs. I am sure that you will close up your school, discharge your staff, cease your fundraising, stop paying yourself your salary of ten thousand dollars a year, and tell the public that the guide dog is no longer needed.

If this were a true instead of a hypothetical situation, what would you do? I submit that you would rationalize and say to yourself and to others, "These people are doing real harm to the blind. It may be a good instrument, but nothing will ever replace the guide dog, at least not in our lifetime." You would not admit to yourself that you were merely protecting your own vested interests. You would rationalize. The alternative would be to give up your position, your prestige, your feeling of importance, your established program, and last but not least your ten thousand dollars a year.

As I have said, this is purely a hypothetical situation. Nineteen-sixty has not yet arrived, and the people at the Massachusetts Institute of Technology have not, so far, perfected their travel aid. Besides, as any guide dog school official will tell you, nothing will ever replace the guide dog, at least not in our lifetime.

The situation I have created for you is purely hypothetical, but its real-life counterpart is occurring every day in literally hundreds of agencies for the blind in this country. It occurs every time the manager of a sheltered workshop for the blind has to decide whether to encourage his best and most skilled workers to leave the sheltered workshop and seek employment in competitive industry or to discourage them from seeking such employment so that they will stay in the shop. If they go, they will be finding normal lives and better pay, but the efficiency of the shop will be lowered, and more subsidies will have to be found. On the other hand, if the best workers are kept in the sheltered workshop, over-all efficiency rises, and the workshop manager looks good as an administrator. He is getting skilled labor at substandard wages to help offset the inefficiency of his poorer workers. What is he to do, consider the welfare of the blind worker who might be placed in private industry or defend the interests of the overall workshop program? The answer is that many workshop managers rationalize and tell themselves that it is really to the best interests of all the workers to be kept in sheltered employment.

The same basic situation occurs every time the administrator of a vending stand program for the blind has to decide what kind of system he will have. If he advocates the philosophy of independence for the blind and admits to himself and others that many blind are capable of operating vending stands without constant care and supervision on the part of the agency, he needs fewer vending stand supervisors, and his agency will not expand as rapidly as it would under what has come to be known as the "controlled" system. The result is that most vending stand agencies have "controlled" rather than "independent" programs.

In reality the counterpart of my hypothetical situation occurs every time the blind set up an independent organization of their own in a community where a well-established agency doing work for the blind exists. The agency has a monopoly on fundraising in the name of the blind. Its officials have unchallenged prestige and are considered to be the authorities in the field. If the blind organize, the empire is challenged; the monopoly is threatened.

The agency leaders not only rationalize to themselves; they also propagandize the public in an attempt to perpetuate their programs and defend their vested interests. The first sentence of the Code of Ethics (so-called) of the American Association of Workers for the Blind reads as follows: "The operations of all agencies for the blind entail a high degree of responsibility because of the element of public trusteeship and protection of the blind involved in services to the blind."

As our national President, Dr. tenBroek, has so aptly put it, "The use of the word 'protection' makes it plain that the trusteeship here referred to is of the same kind as that existing under the United Nations Trusteeship Council—that is, custody and control of underprivileged, backward, and dependent peoples."

Mr. M. Robert Barnett, executive director of the American Foundation for the Blind, says on page 12, of the *Pinebrook Report*, an official publication of the Foundation: "A job, a home, and the right to be a citizen will come to the blind in that generation when each and every blind person is a living advertisement of his ability and capacity to accept the privileges and responsibilities of citizenship. Then we professionals will have no problem of interpretation because the blind will no longer need us to speak for them, and we, like primitive segregation, will die away as an instrument which society will include only in its historical records."

No statements could be clearer than these and none could be more unsound or more harmful to the best interests of the blind and to public understanding of our problems. The matter is as simple as this. Most agency workers are basically good people, but they are also human. They tend to defend their own vested interests, and those interests are not always identical with the interests of the blind they are supposedly serving. We need agencies for the blind, and we need independent organizations of the blind. In the best American tradition the two forces serve as checks and balances. Both have duties; both have rights; both have responsibilities. The existence of one need not, and should not, constitute a threat to the proper activities of the other. No agency should claim to "represent the blind" or set itself up as a "spokesman for the blind." No organization of the blind nor any individual member should indulge in sweeping condemnation of all agencies and all agency activities. When each recognizes that the other has a necessary and appropriate role, mutual jealousy and antagonism should give way to an attitude of mutual respect and to a spirit of cooperation.

Against the right-to-organize bill during that epochal struggle were the Federal Department of Health, Education, and Welfare and various of its subdivisions such as the Office of Vocational Rehabilitation, along with such powerful professional organizations as the American Foundation for the Blind and the American Association of Workers for the Blind. The major arguments advanced by these agency interests were, first, that the legislation was not needed because everyone has the right to free association, and, second, that the bill would give the organized blind a degree of authority and influence over public programs sufficient to outweigh the combined power of the professional agencies.

In the end, that combined power was enough to defeat the Kennedy bill in the Congress. But it was a Pyrrhic victory for the agencies. In 1959, extensive public hearings were held on the issue by a subcommittee of the House Committee on Education and

Labor; the National Federation of the Blind's testimony alone took up three full days and ran to several volumes of transcript. The impact of the hearings was felt at various levels and by all groups involved. "Little Kennedy Bills," as they came to be called, were introduced in a number of states and passed by several. More important, the objectives of the bill—to protect the rights of assembly and petition, the right to organize, and the right to be heard—came to be at least partially achieved in practice where they were not formally granted in law. Like the trade union movement a generation before, the organized blind movement came to be granted a kind of tacit legitimacy by the agencies of the blindness system; the overt attacks upon National Federation of the Blind members and leaders ceased (although not the covert hostility), and an era bearing the semblance of peaceful coexistence was ushered in.

As it turned out, however, the withdrawal of the agencies from the battlefield was in reality a strategic retreat—a temporary cease-fire—rather than a genuine peace-making effort. There was little serious recognition yet of the rights of the blind to self-expression and self-direction, whether individually or collectively. At the end of the embattled decade of the fifties, the prevailing attitude of the custodial agencies was still essentially that proclaimed a few years before, with casual confidence and ill-disguised contempt, by one of their representative spokesmen: "The fact," he wrote, "that so few workers or organizations are doing anything appreciable to [improve the condition of the blind] cannot be explained entirely on the grounds that they are not in the vanguard of social thinking. It is rather because they are realistic enough to recognize that the rank and file of blind people have neither the exceptional urge for independence nor the personal qualifications necessary to satisfactory adjustment in the sighted world."

It was just such misguided notions as those—plus the appalling fact of their confession by the administrator of one of the nation's largest private agencies for the blind—that prompted Jacobus tenBroek to address, at the 1957 convention of the National Federation of the Blind in New Orleans, what he termed "The Cross of Blindness." The symbolic cross he saw the blind to be bearing was the burden of social stigmas, stereotypes, and superstitions—the dead weight of public prejudice and misunderstanding. In a masterful speech which has since become one of his most famous, tenBroek spelled out in equally vivid terms both the case for and the case against self-organization by the blind. His address, delivered before a banquet audience of 700, stands as a memorial to the high ground—the peak of unity and confidence—which was attained by the National Federation of the Blind in that watershed year. That high ground was soon to be lost, in the turmoil of civil war, and not to be reached again for years to come. But in 1957 the national movement of the organized blind, not yet a score of years old, appeared as firm in its solidarity as it was irresistible in its force. And no one who heard the leader of the movement speak that day could doubt that these newly independent and self-assertive people would forever refuse to bear the stigmatizing cross of blindness.

Here is the full text of that speech:

CROSS OF BLINDNESS
by Jacobus tenBroek

In the short seventeen years since our founding of the National Federation of the Blind, we have grown from a handful of men and women scattered over seven states to a Federation of forty-three state affiliates. The first convention of the NFB in 1940 was attended by twelve or fifteen persons—our convention last year had a registration of seven hundred and five from every corner of the Union.

That is rapid organizational growth by any yardstick considering the total blind population of the country and the difficulties in organization. Who are these people of the National Federation of the Blind? What is the purpose that has led them to self-organization in such numbers and unites them now with such apparent dedication and enthusiasm?

It is not enough, I think, to answer that the members of the NFB are drawn together by their common interest in the welfare of the blind; for many of the sighted share that, too. Nor is it sufficient to say that we are united only because we are blind; many who are affiliated with agencies for the blind have that characteristic also. It is fundamental to the uniqueness of our group that we are the only nationwide organization *for* the blind which is also *of* the blind. The composition of the NFB, indeed, is living testimony to the fact—unfortunately not yet accepted by society as a whole—that the blind are capable of self-organization: which is to say, of leading themselves, of directing their own destiny.

Yet this is still only half the truth, only a part of the characteristic which defines our Federation and provides its reason for being. Our real distinction from other organizations in the field of blind welfare lies in the social precept and personal conviction which are the motive source of our activity and the wellspring of our faith. The belief that we who are blind are normal human beings sets us sharply apart from other groups designed to aid the blind. We have all the typical and ordinary range of talents and tech-niques, attitudes, and aspirations. Our underlying assumption is not—as it is with some other groups—the intrinsic helplessness and everlasting dependency of those who happen to lack sight, but rather their innate capacity to nullify and overrule this disability—to find their place in the community—with the same degree of success and failure to be found among the general population.

Perhaps I can best document this thesis of the normality of the blind with a random sample of the occupations represented at our National Convention a year ago in San Francisco. Among the blind delegates in attendance, there were three blind physicists engaged in experimental work for the United States Government. There was one blind chemist also doing experimental work for the national government. There were two university instructors of the rank of full professor, a number of other college instructors of various ranks, and several blind teachers of sighted students in primary and secondary grades in the public schools. There were thirteen lawyers, most in private practice, two employed as attor-neys by the United States Government, one serving as the chair-man of a state public service commission, one serving as a clerk to a state chief justice. There were three chiropractors, one os-teopath, ten secretaries, seventeen factory workers, one shoemaker, one cab dispatcher, one book mender, one appliance repairman, four telephone switchboard operators, numerous businessmen in various businesses, five musicians, thirty students, many directors and workers in programs for the blind, and sixty-one housewives.

At any other convention there would be nothing at all remarkable about this broad cross section of achievement and ability; it is exactly what you would expect to find at a gathering of the American Legion or the Exalted Order of Elks, or at a town meeting in your community. Anywhere else, that is, but at a convention of the blind. It never ceases to surprise the public that a blind man may be able to hold his own in business, operate a farm successfully, argue a brief in a court of law, teach a class of sighted students, or conduct experiments in a chemistry lab. It comes as a shock to the average person to discover that the blind not only can but *do* perform as well as the next man in all the normal and varied callings of the community.

But this "shock of recognition," on the part of many people, too easily gives way to a mood of satisfaction and an attitude of complacency. After all, if the blind are so capable, so successful, and so independent, what is all the fuss about? Where is the need for all this organization and militant activity? Why can't the blind let well enough alone?

These are reasonable questions, surely, and deserve a reasoned answer. I believe that the answer may best be given by reciting a list of sixteen specific events which have taken place recently in various parts of the country. The events are:

1. A blind man (incidentally a distinguished educator and citizen of his community) was denied a room in a well-known YMCA in New York City—*not* on the ground that his appearance betokened inability to pay, which it did not; *not* on the ground that he had an unsavory reputation, which he did not; *not* on the ground that his behavior was or was likely to be disorderly, which it was not— but on the ground that he was blind.

2. A blind man was rejected as a donor by the blood bank in his city—*not* on the ground that his blood was not red; *not* on the ground that his blood was watery, defective in corpuscles, or diseased; *not* on the ground that he would be physically harmed by the loss of the blood—but on the ground that he was blind.

3. A blind man (in this case a successful lawyer with an established reputation in his community) was denied the rental of a safety-deposit box by his bank—*not* on the ground that he was a well-known bank robber; *not* on the ground that he had nothing to put in it; *not* on the ground that he couldn't pay the rental price—but on the ground that he was blind.

4. A blind man was rejected for jury duty in a California city—*not* on the ground of mental incompetence; *not* on the ground of

moral irresponsibility; *not* on the ground that he would not weigh the evidence impartially and come to a just verdict—but on the ground that he was blind.

5. A blind college student majoring in education was denied permission to perform practice teaching by a state university—*not* on the ground that her academic record was poor; *not* on the ground that she had not satisfied the prerequisites; *not* on the ground that she lacked the educational or personal qualifications—but on the ground that she was blind.

6. A blind applicant for public employment was denied consideration by a state civil service commission—*not* on the ground that he lacked the education or experience specifications; *not* on the ground that he was not of good moral character; *not* on the ground that he lacked the residence or citizenship requirements—but on the ground that he was blind.

7. A blind woman was refused a plane ticket by an airline—*not* on the ground that she couldn't pay for her ticket; *not* on the ground that her heart was weak and couldn't stand the excitement; *not* on the ground that she was a carrier of contagion—but on the ground that she was blind.

8. A blind machinist was declared ineligible for a position he had already held for five years. This declaration was the result of a routine medical examination. It came on the heels of his complete clearance and reinstatement on the job following a similar medical finding the year before. These determinations were made—*not* on the ground of new medical evidence showing that he was blind, for that was known all along; *not* on the ground that he could not do the job which he had successfully performed for five years with high ratings; *not* on the ground of any factor related to his employment—they were made on the ground that he was blind.

9. A blind high school student who was a duly qualified candidate for student body president was removed from the list of candidates by authority of the principal and faculty of the school—*not* on the ground that he was an outside infiltrator from some other school; *not* on the ground that he was on probation; *not* on the ground that he was not loyal to the principles of the United States Constitution—but on the ground that he was blind.

10. A well-known insurance company, in its standard policy issued to cover trips on railroads, expressly exempts the blind from coverage—*not* on the ground that there is statistical or actuarial evidence that blind travelers are more prone to accident than sighted travelers are; *not* on the ground that suitcases or fellow passengers fall on them more often; *not* on the ground that trains carrying blind passengers are more likely to be wrecked unless it is the engineer who is blind—but solely on the ground of blindness. Many, if not most, other insurance companies selling other forms of insurance either increase the premium or will not cover the blind.

11. A blind man, who had been a successful justice court and police court judge in his community for eleven years, ran for the position of superior court judge in the general election of 1956. During the campaign his opponents did not argue that he was ignorant of the law and therefore incompetent; or that he had been guilty of bilking widows and orphans; or that he lacked the quality of mercy. Almost the only argument that they used against him was that he was blind. The voters, however, elected him handily. At the next session of the state legislature a bill was introduced disqualifying blind persons as judges. The organized blind of the state were able to modify this bill but not to defeat it.

12. More than sixty blind men and women—among them doctors, teachers, businessmen and members of various professions—were recently ordered by the building and safety authority of a large city to move out of their hotel-type living quarters. This was *not* on the ground that they were pyromaniacs and likely to start fires; *not* on the ground that they were delinquent in their rent; *not* on the ground that they disturbed their neighbors with riotous living—but on the ground that as blind people they were subject to the code provisions regarding the "bed-ridden, ambulatory, and helpless," that anyone who is legally blind must live in an institution-type building—with all the rooms on the ground floor, with no stairs at the end of halls, with hard, fire-proof furniture, with chairs and smoking-stands lined up along the wall "so they won't fall over them."

13. The education code of one of our states provides that deaf, dumb, and blind children may be sent at state expense to a school for the deaf, dumb, or blind outside of the state, if they possess the following qualifications: (1) they are free from offensive or contagious diseases; (2) they have no parent, relative, guardian, or nearest friend able to pay for their education; (3) that by

reason of deafness, dumbness, or blindness, they are disqualified from being taught by the ordinary process of instruction or education.

14. In a recent opinion the supreme court of one of the states held that a blind person who sought compensation for an injury due to an accident which he claimed arose out of and in the course of his employment by the state board of industries for the blind, was a ward of the state and therefore not entitled to compensation. The conception that blind shop workers are wards of the state was only overcome in another state by a recent legislative enactment.

15. A blind person, duly convicted of a felony and sentenced to a state penitentiary, was denied parole when he became eligible therefor—*not* on the ground that he had not served the required time; *not* on the ground that his prison behavior had been bad; *not* on the ground that he had not been rehabilitated—but on the ground that he was blind.

16. A blind man, incidentally a member of this organization, who sat down at a gambling table in Reno, where such things are legal, was denied an opportunity to play—*not* on the ground that he didn't know the rules of the game; *not* on the ground that he might cheat the dealer or the other players; *not* on the ground that he didn't have any money to lose, which they proved, incidentally—but on the ground that he was blind.

These last two cases show that the blind are normal in every respect.

What emerges from this set of events, is the age-old stereotype of blindness as witlessness and helplessness. By virtue of this pervasive impression, a blind man is held to be incapable of weighing the evidence presented at a trial or performing the duties of a teacher. He cannot take care of himself in a room of his own and is not to be trusted on a plane. A sightless person would not know what he has put into or removed from a safety deposit box; and he has no right to employment in the public service. He must not even be permitted to continue on a job he has performed successfully for years. Even his blood cannot be given voluntarily for the common cause.

Contrast these two lists—the one of the occupations represented at the NFB convention, the other of the discriminatory activities. The first is a list of accomplishments of what the blind have done and therefore can do; the second is a list of prohibitions of what the blind are thought incompetent to do and therefore are debarred from attempting. The first list refers to the physical disability of blindness. It demonstrates in graphic fashion how slight a disadvantage is the mere loss of sight to the mental capacity and vocational talent of the individual. The second list refers not to the disability but to the *handicap* which is imposed upon the blind by others. The origin of the disability is plainly inside the blind person. The origin and responsibility for the handicap are just as plainly outside him—in the attitudes and preconceptions of the community.

Let me be very clear about this. I have no wish to minimize the character and extent of blindness as a disability. It is for all of us a constant nuisance and a serious inconvenience. To overcome it requires effort and patience and initiative and guts. It is not compensated for, despite the fairy tales to the contrary, by the spontaneous emergence of a miraculous "sixth sense" or any other magical powers. It means nothing more or less than the loss of one of the five senses and a corresponding greater reliance upon the four that remain—as well as upon the brain, the heart, and the spirit.

It may be said that the discriminatory acts which I have cited, and others like them which are occurring all the time, simply do not reflect informed thought. They are occasional happenings, unpremeditated, irrational, or accidental. Surely no one would justify them; no one would say that they represent an accurate appraisal of the blind and of blindness.

Well, let us see. Let us look at some pronouncements of presumably thoughtful and informed persons writing about the blind—agency heads, educators, administrators, social workers, historians, psychologists, and public officials. What do they have to say about the potentialities of the blind in terms of intellectual capacity, vocational talent, and psychological condition? What do they report concerning the prospects for social integration on the basis of normality and economic advancement on the basis of talent?

First, an educator. Here are the words of a prominent authority on the education of the blind, himself for thirty years a superintendent of a school for the blind. "It is wrong to start with the school," this authority writes, "and to teach there a number of occupations that the blind can do, but to teach them out of relation to their practical and relative values. This is equivalent to attempting to create trades for the blind and then more or less angrily to demand that the world recognize the work and buy the product, whether useful or useless." More than this, it is necessary to recognize the unfitness of the blind "as a class" for any sort of competition and therefore to afford them not only protection but monopoly wherever possible. Declaring that "it must be unqualifiedly conceded that there is little in an industrial way that a blind person can do at all that cannot be done better and more expeditiously by people with sight," this expert considers that there are only two ways out, one being the extension of concessions and monopolies and the other the designation of certain "preferred" occupations for the blind—"leaving the battle of wits only to those select few that may be considered, and determined to be, specially fit."

The conclusion that employment possibilities for the blind are confined, with only negligible exceptions, to the purview of sheltered workshops is contained in this set of "facts" about the blind which the same authority asserts are "generally conceded by those who have given the subject much thought:... that the handcrafts in which the blind can do first-class work are very limited in number, with basketry, weaving, knitting, broom and brush making, and chair caning as the most promising and most thoroughly tried out...that in these crafts the blind cannot enter into direct competition with the seeing either in the quality of product or the amount turned out in a given time...that the crafts pursued by the blind may best be carried on in special workshops under the charge of government officials or trained officers of certain benevolent associations...that among the "higher" callings piano tuning and massage are, under favoring conditions such as prevail for masseurs in Japan, the fields offering the greatest chance of success, while the learned professions, including teaching, are on the whole only for those of very superior talent and, more particularly, very superior courage and determination to win at all costs."

Second, an historian. The basis for this assessment, and its justification, have been presented in blunt and explicit language by a well-known historian of blindness and the blind in the United States. He says, "[T]here exists in the community a body of men who, by reason of a physical defect, namely, the loss of sight, are disqualified from engaging in the regular pursuits of men and who are thus largely rendered incapable of providing for themselves independently." They are to be regarded as a "disabled and infirm fraction of the people" or, more specifically, as "sighted men in a dark room." "Rather than let them drift into absolute dependence and become a distinct burden, society is to lend an appropriate helping hand" through the creation of sheltered, publicly subsidized employment.

Third, administrators. That this pessimistic appraisal of the range of talent among the blind has not been limited to the schoolmen and historians may be shown by two succinct statements from wartime pamphlets produced by the Civil Service Commission in an effort to broaden employment opportunities for the physically disabled. "The blind," it was found, "are especially proficient in manual occupations requiring a delicate sense of touch. They are well suited to jobs which are repetitious in nature." Again: "The placement of persons who are blind presents various special problems. Small groups of positions in sheltered environment, involving repetitive work, were surveyed in government establishments and were found to have placement potentialities for the blind." Such findings as these were doubtless at the base of a remark of a certain public official who wrote that: "Helping the blind has its strong appeal to the sensibilities of everyone; on the other hand, we should avoid making the public service an eleemosynary institution."

Fourth, a blind agency head. The executive director of one of the largest private agencies for the blind justifies the failure of the philanthropic groups in these blunt terms: "The fact that so few workers or organizations are doing anything appreciable to [improve the condition of the blind] cannot be explained entirely on the grounds that they are not in the vanguard of social thinking. It is rather because they are realistic enough to recognize that the rank and file of blind persons have neither the exceptional urge for independence nor the personal qualifications necessary to satisfactory adjustment in the sighted world....It is very difficult and exceptional for a blind person to be as productive as a sighted person."

Fifth, a psychologist. Even plainer language—as well as more impressive jargon—has been used by another authority who is widely considered the pre-eminent expert in the field of blind psychology. "Until recently," he writes, "the blind and those interested in them have insisted that society revise and modify its attitude toward this specific group. Obviously, for many reasons, this is an impossibility, and effort spent on such a program is as futile as spitting into the wind...it is extremely doubtful whether the degree of emotional maturity and social adaptability of the blind would long support and sustain any social change of attitude, if it were possible to achieve it." If this is not plain enough, the writer continues: "A further confusion of attitude is found in educators and workers for the blind who try to propagandize society with the rational concept that the blind are normal individuals without vision. This desperate whistling in the dark does more damage than good. The blind perceive it as a hypocritical distortion of actual facts....It is dodging the issue to place the responsibility on the unbelieving and nonreceptive popular attitudes....The only true answer lies in the unfortunate circumstance that the blind share with other neurotics the nonaggressive personality and the inability to participate fully in society [Get this now, they are talking about you and me]....There are two general directions for attacking such a problem, either to adjust the individual to his environment, or to rearrange the environment so that it ceases to be a difficulty to the individual. It is quite obvious that the latter program is not only inadvisable, but also impossible. However, it is the attack that nearly every frustrated, maladjusted person futilely attempts."

Sixth, a social worker. This sweeping negation of all attempts to modify the prejudicial attitudes of society toward the blind, however eccentric and extreme it may sound, finds strong support in the field of social casework. In areas where "such ideas remain steadfast," reads a typical report, "it is the function of the social caseworker to assist the blind person to work within these preconceived ideas. Since handicapped persons are a minority group in society, there is greater possibility of bringing about a change in an individual within a stated length of time than there is in reversing accepted concepts within the culture." The "well-adjusted blind person," it is argued, should be able to get along in this restrictive social setting, and the caseworker must concentrate on his personal adjustment since it is easier to reform the client than to reform society.

Seventh, a blind philanthropist. Let me close my list of testimonials with one final citation. I think it must already be sufficiently obvious that, granting the assumptions contained in all these statements, the blind have no business organizing themselves apart from sighted supervision; that a social movement of the blind and by the blind is doomed to futility, frustration, and failure. But just in case the point is not clear enough, I offer the considered opinion of a well-known figure in the history of blind philanthropy: "It cannot, then, be through the all-blind society that the blind person finds adequate opportunity for the exercise of his leadership. The wise leader will know that the best interests of each blind person lie within the keeping of the nine hundred and ninety-nine sighted people who, with himself, make up each one thousand of any average population. He will know, further, that if he wishes to promote the interests of the blind, he must become a leader of the sighted upon whose understanding and patronage the fulfillment of these interests depends....There is...no advantage accruing from membership in an all-blind organization which might not be acquired in greater measure through membership in a society of sighted people."

What is the substance of all these damning commentaries? What are the common assumptions which underlie the attitudes of the leaders of blind philanthropy and the authorities on blind welfare? The fundamental concepts can, I think, be simply stated. First, the blind are by virtue of their defect emotionally immature if not psychologically abnormal; they are mentally inferior and narrowly circumscribed in the range of their ability—and therefore inevitably doomed to vocational monotony, economic dependence, and social isolation. Second, even if their capabilities were different they are necessarily bound to the fixed status and subordinate role ordained by "society," whose attitudes toward them are permanent and unalterable. Third, they must place their faith and trust, not in themselves and in their own organizations, but in the sighted public and most particularly in those who have appointed themselves the protectors and custodians of the blind.

A few simple observations are in order. First, as to the immutability of social attitudes and discriminatory actions towards the blind, we know from intimate experience that the sighted public wishes well for the blind and that its misconceptions are rather the result of innocence and superstition than of deliberate cruelty and malice aforethought. There was a time, in the days of Rome, when blind infants were thrown to the wolves or sold into slavery. That time is no more. There was a time, in the Middle Ages, when blind beggars were the butts of amusement at country fairs, decked out in paper spectacles and donkeys' ears. That time is no more. There was a time, which still exists to a surprising extent, when the parents of a blind child regarded his disability as a divine judgment upon their own sins. But that time is now beginning to disappear, at least in the civilized world.

The blind are no longer greeted by society with open hostility and frantic avoidance, but with compassion and sympathy. It is true that an open heart is no guarantee of an open mind. It is true that good intentions are not enough. It is true that tolerance is a far cry from brotherhood, and that protection and trusteeship are not the synonyms of equality and freedom. But the remarkable progress already made in the civilizing of brute impulses and the humanizing of social attitudes towards the blind is compelling evidence that there is nothing fixed or immutable about the social status quo for the blind and that, if the blind themselves are capable of independence and inter-dependence within society, society is capable of welcoming them.

Our own experience as individuals and as members of the National Federation of the Blind gives support at short range to what long-range history already makes plain. We have observed and experienced the gradual breakdown of legal obstacles and prejudicial acts; we have participated in the expansion of opportunities for the blind in virtually every phase of social life and economic livelihood—in federal, state, and local civil service; in teaching and other professions; in the addition of a constructive element to public welfare. Let anyone who thinks social attitudes cannot be changed read this statement contained in a recent pamphlet of the Federal Civil Service Commission:

> Sometimes a mistaken notion is held that...the blind can do work only where keenness of vision is not important in the job. The truth appears to be that the blind can do work demanding different degrees of keenness of vision on the part of the sighted. If there is any difference in job proficiency related to a degree of keenness of vision required for the sighted, it is this: the blind appear to work with greater proficiency at jobs where the element is present to a noticeable extent in the sighted job than where vision is only generally useful.

Second, are the blind mentally inferior, emotionally adolescent, and psychologically disturbed; or on the contrary, are they normal and capable of social and economic integration? The evidence that they are the latter can be drawn from many quarters: scientific, medical, historical, and theoretical. But the evidence which is most persuasive is that which I have already presented: it is the evidence displayed in the lives and performance of such average and ordinary blind men and women as those who attended our National Convention last summer. It is the evidence of their vocational accomplishments, their personal achievements, the plain normality of their daily lives. To me their record is more than an impressive demonstration: it is a clinching rebuttal.

It would, of course, be a gross exaggeration to maintain that all blind persons have surmounted their physical disability and conquered their social handicap.

It is not the education of the sighted only which is needed to establish the right of the blind to equality and integration. Just as necessary is the education of the blind themselves. For the process of their rehabilitation is not ended with physical and vocational training; it is complete only when they have driven the last vestige of the public stereotype of the blind from their own minds. In this sense, and to this extent only, is it true that the blind person must "adjust" to his handicap and to society. His adjustment need not—indeed must not—mean his submission to all prevailing social norms and values. His goal is not conformity but autonomy: not acquiescence, but self-determination and self-control.

From all of this it should be clear that it is a long way yet from the blind alleys of dependency and segregation to the main thoroughfares of personal independence and social integration which we have set as our goal. And I believe it is equally plain that our progress toward that goal will demand the most forceful and skillful application of all the means at our command: that is, the means of education, persuasion, demonstration, and legislation.

We need the means of *education* to bring the public and the blind themselves to a true recognition of the nature of blindness—to tear away the fossil layers of mythology and prejudice. We need *persuasion* to induce employers to try us out and convince society to take us in. We need *demonstration* to prove our capacity and normality in every act of living and of making a living. And finally we need *legislation* to reform the statute books and obliterate the legal barriers which stand in the way of normal life and equal opportunity—replacing them with laws which accurately reflect the accumulated knowledge of modern science and the ethics of democratic society.

This final platform in our program of equality—the platform of adequate legislation—is in many respects the most crucial and pressing of all. For until the blind are guaranteed freedom of opportunity and endeavor within the law there can be little demonstration of their ability and little prospect of persuasion. What is needed is nothing less than a new spirit of the laws, which will uproot the discriminatory clauses and prejudicial assumptions that presently hinder the efforts of the blind toward self-advancement and self-support. The new philosophy requires that programs for the blind be founded upon the social conception of their normality and the social purpose of their reintegration into the community, with aids and services adjusted to these conceptions.

These then are the objectives of the self-organized blind; goals freely chosen for them by themselves. And this is the true significance of an organization of the blind, by the blind, for the blind. For the blind the age of charity, like that of chivalry, is dead; but this is not to say that there is no place for either of these virtues. In order to achieve the equality that is their right, in order to gain the opportunity that is their due, and in order to attain the position of full membership in the community that is their goal, the blind have continuing need for the understanding and sympathy and liberality of their sighted neighbors and fellow citizens. But their overriding need is first of all for recognition— recognition of themselves as normal and of their purposes as legitimate. The greatest hope of the blind is that they may be seen as they *are*, not as they have been portrayed; and since they are neither wards nor children, their hope is to be not only seen but also heard—in their own accents and for whatever their cause may be worth.

During the decade of the fifties—at least until the outbreak of the civil war in the closing years—the organized blind movement enjoyed rapid and steady growth not only in membership but also in public reputation and influence. With the launching of a successful fund-raising program early in the decade, it became possible to spread the word of Federationism more widely and effectively than ever—through the new *Braille Monitor*, which was now published in both Braille and inkprint editions, as well as through a profusion of speeches, articles, and special publications such as *The Blind and the Right to Organize: A Report to the Nation*, a compilation of key documents relating to that struggle by the National Federation of the Blind.

With increased information and publicity came enhanced recognition and stature for the Federation and its leadership—notably its founder and chief executive, Jacobus tenBroek. In the course of the struggle for the Kennedy bill, tenBroek and others of his colleagues in the movement found themselves rather suddenly in the limelight of public attention—repeatedly interviewed on radio and television, reported on in the press, and even (in the case of one California newspaper) editorialized about. One of the most significant and widely read examples of this newly favorable press appeared in the *New Yorker* magazine on January 11, 1958, in the form of a prose "profile" of President tenBroek, which vividly conveyed both his forceful personality and his back-breaking schedule of travels on behalf of the organized blind. For its expression of the human and personal dimensions of leadership, the *New Yorker* sketch remains a valuable memento of both the man and the movement. Here is the article as it appeared in the magazine:

NEW YORKER MAGAZINE FEATURES NFB PRESIDENT

Jacobus tenBroek, a hearty, vigorous man of forty-six with aquiline features, a ruddy complexion, and a carefully groomed reddish goatee, is an authority on government and constitutional law, a field in which he has published a number of highly regarded books and monographs; the chairman of the Speech Department of the University of California at Berkeley; a member of California's Social Welfare Board; and the country's leading lobbyist and campaigner against an adage that he deems mistaken, mischievous, and far too commonly accepted—the one that goes "When the blind lead the blind, they all fall into the ditch." As President and one of the founders of the National Federation of the Blind, Professor tenBroek, who lost his sight when he was a boy, has a formidable spare-time schedule of speeches, conferences, and caucuses, through which he seeks to spread his organization's belief that the blind are much more capable than is generally realized of holding down normal jobs and running their own affairs. "I've had to make ten flying trips throughout the country on the last twelve weekends," he told us when he called on us at our office during a stopover of a few hours in New York, in route from Washington, D.C., where he had been talking with congressmen about legislation that his organization is advocating, to Springfield, Massachusetts, where he was scheduled to make a speech before one of the Federation's local chapters.

"As a rule, I board the plane Friday evening, right after my last class," he said. "I prepare my speeches during the trip and usually manage to pick up a return flight that gets me to Berkeley just in time for my Monday-morning eight-o'clock class." He laughed. "My children—I have three—are getting fed up with this routine. They say they're beginning to forget what I look like."

One of Professor tenBroek's chief ambitions as he flies about the country is to persuade people he meets that he is not exceptional in either talent or character but pretty much an ordinary man who has simply refused to accept the widespread assumption that a blind person must live a dependent and sheltered life. "I've got a neighbor in Berkeley—a blind man I've known since we were classmates at school—who built his house entirely with his own hands," he said. "It's quite a good-sized house, too—about twenty-seven hundred square feet. He built the forms, poured the cement, put in the plumbing, did the wiring—everything. The place is on a fairly steep hillside, and before he could start he had to make himself a large power-operated boom, for hauling his materials up to the site. Now, *there's* a man that someone like me—someone who has no aptitude for that sort of thing—would call an exceptional person, but he doesn't seem to think he is. He says he just happens to be handy with tools." The Professor shook his head in admiration.

"As things are now," he went on, "most of the country's three hundred and twenty-five thousand blind people who work are employed in the special sheltered shops that society—with the best and most charitable intentions—has set up for us, where we can make baskets and such, and come to no harm. Only about two or three per cent of us are holding normal jobs out in the world. My organization is convinced at least twenty times that many could be doing so if they had the chance. What we seek for the blind is the right to compete on equal terms. In this, the Federation—the only national organization in this field whose membership and officers are all blind—is very much at odds with most of the traditional organizations and agencies set up to help us, which are sure they know better than we do what is good for us. But we've been making considerable progress. In the last few years, we've succeeded in persuading the Civil Service to let blind people try out for many categories of jobs from which they used to be excluded."

We asked Professor tenBroek what jobs he himself thinks are impossible for the blind to hold. He laughed, stroked his goatee professorially, and said, "Well, airplane pilot, I suppose—though, for that matter, planes fly most of the time nowadays on automatic controls, don't they, and someday may be completely automatic. Actually, I can't say what the limits are. Every time I think I have hit on some job that a blind man couldn't conceivably hold, I find a blind man holding it. One of my friends in the Federation is an experimental nuclear physicist, and you wouldn't think of that as a promising field for a blind man to be in. Dr. Bradley Burson is his name, and he's at the Argonne National Laboratory, near Chicago. When he was working on problems involving the decay of radioactive matter, he invented some devices for himself that measured the decay in terms of audible and tactile signals, rather than the commonly employed visual signals. Some of the devices turned out to be more accurate than the standard ones, and are now widely used at the lab. I'd always assumed that being an electrician would be impossible for a blind man, but not long ago I found a blind electrician—a fellow named Jack Polston. I went and talked to his boss, and he told me that Polston does everything any other electrician can do—wiring, soldering, and all the rest. While I was there, Polston was doing the complete wiring for a service station, which I'm told is a particularly complicated job. To be sure, he had been an electrician before he became blind, but don't ask me how he solders without setting the place on fire. I couldn't, even if I had my sight. Anyway, now that I've found him I'm pestering the Civil Service not to disqualify blind people automatically from trying out for electricians' jobs."

Professor tenBroek paused for a moment, and then said, "Don't let me give you the idea that it isn't a nuisance to be blind. To bump your head on an overhanging sign as you walk down the street or to fall into a hole that anybody else can see—it's a nuisance, I can assure you, but it isn't a catastrophe." He stood up, buttoning his coat, and picked up his cane and his briefcase. "Well," he said briskly, "it's after two o'clock, and I'll have to step lively if I'm going to make it out to LaGuardia in time to catch the three-fifteen for Springfield. If you'll be so kind as to see me to the elevator, I'll carry on from there."

Among the leaders of the organized blind, Jacobus tenBroek was clearly pre-eminent in this first generation of Federationists; and he remained so until his death in 1968. But from the start of the movement he gathered around him the ablest men and women he could find—the best and the brightest—among the blind of the nation. Among them were lawyers like Raymond Henderson of California; businessmen like George Card of Michigan; social workers like Perry Sundquist of California; and philosophers like Kingsley Price of Johns Hopkins University. Specialized talents aside, the primary characteristic which tenBroek sought in his circle of colleagues was energetic devotion to the cause of the organized blind; and as a teacher and mentor of youth he was particularly intent upon seeking out this leadership potential among the younger members of the movement. (One of his greatest disappointments over the years was the reluctance of many successful blind persons of the professional middle class to be identified with a movement of rank-and-file blind people who not only were often unemployed but were categorized as "unemployable.")

During the course of the fifties, year after year, the name of one younger leader in the movement came increasingly to be heard in the conventions, discussed in the meetings, pronounced in the *Braille Monitor*, and recognized among the organized blind everywhere. Kenneth Jernigan first sprang into national prominence in 1952 when he organized the National Federation of the Blind convention and was elected to the Board of Directors. From that time on he was in the thick of it; by 1958, when Jernigan accepted an appointment as director of the Iowa Commission for the Blind, he also became the Second Vice President of the National Federation of the Blind, and the following year became the First Vice President. The full scope and impact of Jernigan's participation in the movement to that point was set forth in a 1958 *Braille Monitor* article by the man who knew the most about it: Dr. tenBroek. Ostensibly the article was an announcement to the membership of Jernigan's Iowa appointment; in truth it was a tribute from the Federation's leader and senior statesman to the younger man who had become his chief lieutenant. In retrospect this testimonial takes on a prophetic quality; for of all the confidantes and colleagues who surrounded President tenBroek in that era, the one who was to remain longest by his side, and ultimately to receive from his hands the mantle of leadership, was the young man of whom he was writing then.

This is what Jacobus tenBroek said about Kenneth Jernigan in 1958:

FEDERATION LEADER APPOINTED DIRECTOR
OF IOWA COMMISSION FOR THE BLIND
by Jacobus tenBroek

Last month Kenneth Jernigan, a member of the Board of Directors of the National Federation of the Blind, was appointed director of the Iowa Commission for the Blind. This appointment was not only appropriate—it was significant.

In his new position Mr. Jernigan has charge of all Iowa programs for the blind with the exception of public assistance and the state school for the blind. Among the services under his direction are: vocational rehabilitation, vending stands, home industries, home teaching, the distribution of talking books, and registration of blind persons in the state.

There are, of course, many Federationists who hold positions in state and other administrative agencies. Some of these are the directors of their agencies. There are, in addition, numerous agency heads who are favorably disposed toward the organized blind. They did not go from the movement to their administrative positions; they came to, or at least towards, the movement from an intelligent discharge of their administrative responsibilities. The distinctive factor in the Jernigan appointment is that now a National Federation leader and member of its Board of Directors has been selected to serve as the head of a state agency for the blind. Mr. Jernigan's appointment is indeed a tribute to the independent and enlightened judgment of the Iowa Commission.

There is a good deal of loose and self-adulatory talk among certain AAWB leaders about their professional status and an alleged lack of "professionalism" among the organized blind. This talk may be examined from two sides: how "professional" are the agency leaders and workers; how "unprofessional" are the organized blind. Whatever answer may be given to the first question, there are many in the organized blind movement whose knowledge about blindness and the substance of administration of programs for the blind can only be described as professional. So too as to their attitudes, their caliber, their bearing, and, in many cases, their careers and duties. In the present case, Kenneth Jernigan has been a "professional," in all these senses of the term for many years.

The honor and the responsibility have especially fittingly gone to Kenneth Jernigan. Few readers of the *Braille Monitor* and fewer members of the Federation need to be reminded of the character of this man and of the quality of his achievements. Since his entrance into the movement nearly a decade ago—and especially since his election to the NFB Board of Directors in 1952—no one of us has labored more unstintingly or battled more courageously for the advancement of our common cause.

To enumerate all of Kenneth's contributions would be to trespass upon space limitations. I might recount a few of the highlights of his career as a Federationist leader. He is, first of all, the only member who has served on all the NFB's survey teams—those which canvassed the state programs for the blind of Colorado and Arkansas in 1955 and of Nevada in 1956, at the request of their respective governors, and set in motion a chain reaction of liberalization and reform whose effects will be felt for years to come. Kenneth also was the chairman of two of our most thoroughly successful National Conventions—those of Nashville in 1952 and San Francisco in 1956. He has given selflessly of his time and inexhaustible energy to cross and recross the country in the interests of Federation unity, harmony, and democracy—and has performed miracles of diplomacy and arbitration in situations which might best be described as those of peacemaking, problem solving, and troubleshooting. More lastingly important even than this has been his consistent contribution to the over-all leadership, expansion, and sustained course of the movement.

Much of Kenneth's most valuable activity on our behalf, indeed, has been carried on behind the scenes. It is not widely known, for example, that he is the author of those indispensable guidebooks of our movement: "What is the National Federation of the Blind" and "Who Are the Blind Who Lead the Blind." He is, additionally, the author of many Federation documents that have gone "unbylined." He has represented the NFB, informally as well as formally, at numerous outside conventions and gatherings throughout the country. His speeches and reports on the floor of the National Convention, year in and year out, have been both widely anticipated events and uniformly applauded successes. One of these in particular requires special mention: his address before the 1957 convention on "Programs for Local Chapters of the Federation." Few statements have more correctly portrayed and deeply instilled the conception of the Federation—made up as it is of local clubs, state affiliates, conventions, officers, and headquarters—as a single unified entity each part of which is the concern, responsibility, and local benefit of every individual member. By popular demand this analysis has been Brailled, taped, mimeographed, and distributed to Federationists throughout the length and breadth of the land. His 1955 study, "Employment of the Blind in the Teaching Profession," carried out for the California affiliate of the Federation, has been eagerly and broadly applied throughout the country in the increasingly successful campaign to break down the barriers to the hiring of blind teachers in the public schools. In fact, there is scarcely any aspect of our national movement over the past half-dozen years which has not benefited from the alert counsel and untiring devotion of time and talent which Ken has so willingly given.

I have said that his appointment to the directorship of the Iowa Commission is a tribute to the members of that enlightened agency. It is no less a tribute to the membership of the Iowa Association of the Blind, under the able leadership of Dr. H. F. Schluntz of Keystone, Iowa.

But in the end, of course, the credit for the appointment must go mainly to Ken Jernigan. His objective qualifications include upwards of a decade of counseling, administering, coordinating, teaching, and public relations, first with the School for the Blind in Nashville, Tennessee, and after 1953 with the Orientation Center for the Adult Blind in Oakland, California. But to these formal qualifications must be added such vital statistics as the following:

Totally blind from birth, raised on a rural farm in Tennessee, and educated in the Nashville School for the Blind, Kenneth went on to take a bachelor's degree in social science from the Tennessee Polytechnic Institute—graduating with the highest grades ever made by any student enrolled at the institution. In addition he somehow found time to become president of the Speech Activities Club, president of the Social Science Club, member of Cabinet Tech Christian Association, member of Pi Kappa Delta fraternity, winner of first prizes in Extemporaneous Speaking and Original Oratory at a Southeastern conference of the fraternity; to get a poem published in a nationwide anthology of college poetry; and to be elected to "Who's Who Among Students in Colleges and Universities of America."

Following his graduation from Tennessee Polytechnic, Ken went on to take a master's degree in English from Peabody College in Nashville, plus an additional year of graduate study. Once again he found enough time aside from his studies to head various societies and win a variety of awards, including the Capt. Charles W. Browne Award in 1949.

I shall pass over lightly his brief career as a professional wrestler during the summer of 1945; his operation of a furniture shop the summer before, where he built all the furniture and managed the entire business; and his two-year livelihood as an insurance salesman prior to joining the staff of the Tennessee School for the Blind. But these diverse adventures and apprenticeships of his early career do serve graphically to illustrate Ken Jernigan's extraordinary vitality of personality and equally extraordinary drive and determination.

This appointment poses a critical question and gives the proper answer to it. Will the NFB give orders to Jernigan the administrator or, alternatively, will Jernigan the administrator change his role in the Federation?

To pose this question at all presupposes some basic fallacies. It presupposes that the organized blind are on one side of the line and the agencies are on the other. It presupposes that the function of the agencies is to rule and that of the blind to obey. It presupposes that the agencies are professional and that the blind are unprofessional; that the agencies know what is best for the blind and the blind should accept it without question; that the agencies are custodians and caretakers and the blind are wards and charitable beneficiaries; that the agencies are the interpreters of the blind to the sighted community and the blind are incapable of speaking for themselves; that agencies exist because the blind are not full-fledged citizens with the right to compete for a home, a job, and to discharge the privileges and responsibilities of citizenship. These are basic fallacies.

The basic truth is that there is no disharmony, conflict, or incompatibility between the two posts. The basic truth is that the blind are citizens, that they are not wards, that they are capable of speaking for themselves, and that they should and must be integrated into the governmental processes which evolve, structure, and administer programs bearing upon their welfare. The basic truth is that agencies administering these programs, committed to the democratic view of clients as human beings and as citizens and joining them in the full expression of their capabilities, have a vital role to play.

There is thus no matter of choosing between two "masters" moving in different directions. The common object can best be achieved through a close collaboration between the blind and the agencies serving them. The object cannot be achieved without that collaboration. Separate sources of authority, organizational patterns, and particular responsibilities do not necessarily, and in this case do not properly, entail conflicting commitments. Jernigan the Federation leader and Jernigan the administrator of programs in Iowa are therefore at one.

Chapter 3

Civil War: Disunity and the Road to Recovery

"A house divided against itself cannot stand." These words of Abraham Lincoln—forever resonant with the echoes of civil war—rang in the ears of blind Americans during a critical four-and-a-half-year period in the history of the organized blind movement extending roughly from mid-1957 to early 1962. For in those years their own house, self-built and self-designed, was divided against itself—and there was serious reason to doubt whether it could any longer stand.

The reasons for this protracted civil war among the organized blind were various but not fundamentally complicated. The troubles within the movement were related in part to the troubles without; for at least a few active members came to resent and resist the "hard line" adopted by the National Federation toward the hostile agencies of the blindness system in the struggle for the right to organize. (That difference of philosophy and attitude was to become more evident in later years when the splinter group formed by dissident ex-Federationists, under the name of the American Council of the Blind, consistently opposed the NFB in its struggles with industries and agencies engaged in acts of discrimination against the blind.)

A deeper source of division, however, sprang from the very success of the Federation—its rapid rise in affluence and influence. Whereas in the lean years of the movement there had been a scarcity of office-seekers and volunteer workers, during the prosperous fifties aspiring leaders sprang up on all sides—some of whom won national office and responsibility while others failed in their bids for recognition and accordingly came to feel neglected and ill-used. Reinforcing this source of friction in the movement were marked differences of personality and temperament among some of the more prominent members, which in a few cases became so deep as to become irreconcilable. Clearly—as the bitterness and hysteria of many personal attacks upon Federation leaders demonstrated—there were elements of envy and jealousy, as well as ambition, involved in the campaign of disruption. Added to these feelings of personal grievance, furthermore, were the common frustrations and suspicions aroused in many blind persons by the very real inequities encountered daily and habitually in a world geared to vision and the visual.

Although signs of disgruntlement had surfaced earlier, the first substantial outbreak of civil war occurred in the summer of 1957 with the firing of A. L. Archibald, the Federation's Washington representative. Archibald had tried to achieve political power by making alliances with various members of the Federation's leadership, but these efforts had been unsuccessful except in the case of Board Member Durward McDaniel of Oklahoma. Increasingly Archibald refused to accept supervision or follow instructions from President tenBroek. Finally (in August of 1957) tenBroek fired Archibald, but the full story of the events leading to the dismissal was not told until almost two years later.

In the spring of 1959 (at the height of the Federation's civil war) a special supplement of the *Braille Monitor* was issued. It carried, among other things, the details of the Archibald episode. Written by Kenneth Jernigan, the Archibald article played an important part in charting the course for the organization during the remainder of the internal struggle.

THE ARCHIBALD STORY
by Kenneth Jernigan

In August of 1957 A. L. Archibald was fired from the staff of the National Federation of the Blind. This event ushered in a new era in Federation affairs. It became the focal point of an internal conflict, which was already getting underway. It was the beginning of a civil war.

Throughout all of the strife which has plagued the Federation ever since, one figure, A. L. Archibald, has been ever present. In whatever part of the country the conflict has flared, wherever there have been unrest and dissension, wherever there have been charges made—there has A. L. Archibald been. He has lurked in the background as a principal agitator and emissary of hate and suspicion.

Unlike McDaniel and Boring [Durward McDaniel of Oklahoma and Marie Boring of North Carolina], he has not, until recently, made public statements or circulated letters through the mail. He has kept himself in the background. Many of the delegates at Boston did not even know that he was present at the convention. Yet, he was always at Durward McDaniel's side.

The time has now come when A. L. Archibald must be brought forth from the shadows. His story must be told so that Federationists everywhere may know the real reasons for his dismissal—the facts about his performance as a Federation staff member.

The McDaniel faction has sought to make Archibald a hero. In general the story they tell is this: Archibald was a tireless worker for the Federation. He was brilliant and shrewd, a lobbyist without equal. He was loyal to the organization that hired him. He worked both day and night to advance its interests. Because he would not bow to the whims of the "dictator" who was and is the President of the Federation, he was suddenly fired without warning or cause. He was not even given an opportunity to resign or told why he was being dismissed. Emissaries from the dictatorial President simply came to his hotel room one night and gave him a letter saying that he was fired.

What are the facts? Is this a true account of what happened? Was Archibald really a hard worker? Did he win friends for the Federation? What were his attitudes toward the elected officers of the organization? Were there specific reasons for his dismissal, or was it simply based on whim? Let Federationists everywhere read the record and judge for themselves. Let them read Archibald's own letters. Let him speak for himself. This is the Archibald story.

When the Federation was established in 1940, there was little money to hire staff or do anything else. The first thought of paid employees came in 1942 at the Des Moines convention. At that time the delegates unanimously decided that the *President*, not the Executive Committee [the name "Executive Committee" was later changed to "Board of Directors"], should do the hiring. The nominating committee was also serving as a resolutions committee. The exact wording of the motion establishing the first Federation staff position was as follows:

Mr. President:

Your nominating committee formally recommends that the Federation authorize its *President* to appoint a person to act as his assistant and to be officially designated as Executive Director of the National Federation of the Blind.

Passed Unanimously.

The first Executive Director of the Federation, Mr. Raymond Henderson, was selected and appointed by the President. He served brilliantly and efficiently from 1942 until his death in 1945. The President then selected and appointed Mr. Leslie Schlingheyde. Mr. Schlingheyde, however, did not get his work done, and he was dismissed by the President. In 1946 Mr. Archibald was hired as a part-time employee. In 1952 he was employed on a full-time basis.

It was hardly a year after his full-time employment that the trouble started. He began to refuse to carry out assignments given him by the President of the Federation. He insisted upon his right to decide whether specific articles or other printed material sent him by Dr. tenBroek should be distributed in Washington. In one instance he categorically refused to circulate a particular article concerning public assistance because he thought the wording was not quite what it should be—this despite the fact that he was a hired staff member and Dr. tenBroek was the elected *President* of the organization with responsibility for supervising his work.

From 1952 to 1956 there was a gradual deterioration in Archibald's performance and attitude. He tried more than once (unsuccessfully) to form political alliances with individual members of the Executive Committee, always with complaints against Dr. tenBroek and the fact that he, Archibald, was under Dr. tenBroek's supervision. He became increasingly sulky and insubordinate, and there were long periods of time when he did (and moreover seemed incapable of doing) little if any work at all.

Throughout all this nonperformance and insubordination, Dr. ten-Broek was patient in the extreme. As he later said, he kept hoping that if he were patient long enough, "Archie would come to his senses." In the meantime Dr. tenBroek was careful to make no statement which would injure Archibald's relation with the affiliates. He had only words of kindness and friendliness for him.

It may well be that the 1956 convention at San Francisco, that meeting which seemed so harmonious and full of promise for the Federation, was the real turning point in the Archibald story. Archibald's earlier attempts at forming alliances with members of the Executive Committee in opposition to the President had been unsuccessful. At the 1956 convention the name of Durward McDaniel was placed in nomination for the Second Vice Presidency of the Federation. He was defeated in the nominating committee. It was then that McDaniel went to Dr. tenBroek's room and angrily talked to him and other leaders of the Federation about "the presidential succession." It was soon after the San Francisco convention that Archibald's insubordination increased markedly and that carbons of almost all of his letters began to be sent to McDaniel, but not to other members of the Executive Committee.

The extent of Archibald's nonperformance and insubordination is so great that it should be shown by his own letters. Otherwise it could hardly be believed.

On August 6, 1956, Dr. tenBroek wrote to Archibald requesting him to prepare a draft of proposed federal rules and regulations implementing the new self-care and self-support provisions of the 1956 Social Security Act Amendments. This was simply a routine assignment.

On August 15, 1956, Mr. Archibald replied in perhaps one of the strangest letters ever written by an employee to an employer. Among other things, he said that while he appreciated the honor of it all, he felt forced to decline to carry out the assignment. He was not content merely to send this letter to the President of the Federation but sent it to others as well, among them, of course, Durward McDaniel. The letter says:

> Dear Chick: [Dr. tenBroek was called "Chick" by some of his close associates.]

My vacation plans and reservations have all been canceled. I don't know how much good this will do the Federation; for I can't cancel my secretary's plans. She is scheduled to give birth to a baby this week. Tomorrow, in fact, is the due date. Having had the forethought to time the arrival of this infant for some time after the close of the congressional session, these plans can be changed by no one. She has, in fact, pressed her luck a bit by staying on as long as she has. But this is her final day with me. I have thus far had no luck in finding a temporary replacement. Were it not for her kindness in volunteering to come in for a few hours now and again until she goes to the hospital, my prospects for getting anything done would indeed be slight. I have set these facts forth in order that you and others may understand fully my situation here with respect to the project outlined in your letter of August 6th.

My first comment with respect to that project is that you do me entirely too much honor to believe that I can, like Athena sprang from the head of Zeus, single-handedly come forth with a complete plan in all its refinements whereby the Social Security Administration will have to do no work to adopt regulations putting into effect the new self-support purpose of state public assistance plans. I am sure that there are many ideas which would never occur to me; nor do I have any long administrative experience to think of all the details. Therefore, while I appreciate the honor of it all, I am compelled to decline the full responsibility for developing a set of regulations to submit to Schottland. [He refers to Charles Schottland, the head of the Social Security Administration.] I am in consequence calling upon a group of Federation leaders, including yourself, to concentrate upon this project with virtually the same attention that I shall be giving to it. Without their help and yours the project will amount to very little. Having deleted the last paragraph of your letter from the copies I have made of it (the paragraph is not relevant to the project), I am accordingly sending copies of your letter and this one to the people who are listed below in an earnest appeal for ideas from them and with the full knowledge on my part that if they do not make contributions we will probably not have very much to suggest to Schottland.

Cordially,
A. L. Archibald
Executive Director

On August 20, 1956, Dr. tenBroek replied:

Dear Archie:

This will reply to the tone and substance of your letter of August 15.

In my letter to you of August 6, I asked that you set to work immediately preparing a draft of proposed federal rules and regulations implementing the relevant provisions of the 1956 Social Security Act Amendments. In so doing, I had no idea that I was conferring an honor upon you. I was sending you an assignment, which I now repeat.

The task is not at all formidable. This is the sort of thing that staff people are doing in welfare departments all around the country every day and in voluntary agencies and organizations. I expected that the product would need some refinement and that it would not spring full-grown from your head, making unnecessary any further work either on our part or that of Schottland. There is no need to worry about refinement, however, until a primary draft is in hand.

As I view the picture, it is urgent that we prepare our proposals as soon as possible. We are under the gun. The federal people are already hard at work on such rules. Moreover, the people in the state departments are also getting their ideas together. Our proposals will have their maximum impact if presented while a relatively fluid condition still exists in the minds of federal and state directors. Progressively as their ideas jell, the possibility of getting our ideas accepted diminishes.

Let me say two things about your distribution of this assignment to other Federation leaders. The first is that if I had wanted them to work on the matter at this stage, I would have written them myself. The second is that this is the wrong stage of the matter at which to call on them for their contribution. They are all extremely busy and overburdened with Federation work. They should, therefore, be asked to contribute only when they can do so with maximum advantage and minimum effort. That stage would be to make their comments and suggestions when the primary draft has been prepared and the pick and shovel work done. Doing that pick and shovel work and getting the primary draft ready should be performed by staff.

You should, therefore, understand that these are instructions to you and that I expect them to be treated as such. When you have completed your draft, please send it directly to me....

Cordially yours,
Jacobus tenBroek
President

Despite continued urging on the part of Dr. tenBroek, the proposed draft of the federal rules and regulations was not forthcoming.

On November 21, 1956, Dr. tenBroek wrote as follows:

Dear Archie:

On October 9 I sent you a copy of a rough draft of proposed Social Security rules and regulations prepared by Perry Sundquist. In the covering letter to you and a number of other people, I requested comments and suggestions preparatory to the working out of a final draft, which I indicated I would try to do in a couple of weeks from that time when I returned from Ohio. Subsequent events have prevented my completing the draft. Meanwhile, much valuable time has gone by and valuable opportunity has been lost to present a set of well worked out proposals to the state and federal agencies.

I now re-assign this task to you. From August 6 to October 9 you were supposed to have been working on this job anyway. During most of that time you had very little else to do. Surely you had ample chance to do the thinking required. Assuming that you did not do it, however, you now have before you Perry's rough draft to aid you in the process. A very few days of concentrated work should produce the finished product. I expect you to get at it immediately and to complete it quickly. You are to send your final draft to me for review and distribution.

Cordially,
Jacobus tenBroek
President

Let Federationists everywhere read and marvel at the reply of November 26, 1956.

Dear Chick:

You expressed an interest in learning what progress is being made on the proposed revisions of federal public assistance regulations to carry out the new self-care provisions added to Title X this year.

I am happy to say that work on these proposals has been underway for a long time past. I believe that, if there are no further serious interruptions such as have occurred frequently since the project was first undertaken, the job will be completed in the fairly near future....

I am happy to say (he refers here to Dr. tenBroek's appendectomy) that you have come out of your recent surgery in apparent good shape. We *all* seem to be subject to interruptions which are not of our own choosing.

Cordially,
Archie

One need hardly add that the inevitable copy was sent—to Durward K. McDaniel.

On December 5, 1956, Dr. tenBroek replied in a letter which most administrators would consider mild indeed under the circumstances:

Dear Archie:

In your letter of November 26 you begin with the sentence: "You have expressed an interest in learning what progress is being made on the proposed revisions of federal public assistance regulations to carry out the new self-support and self-care provisions added to Title X this year." This is a most amazing sentence. Yet, it expresses an attitude which you persist in clinging to. As the person in the organization responsible for supervising your work and determining what it will be, I gave you a work assignment. After numerous dilatory tactics, delays, and procrastinations, you now write me describing this work assignment as a mere expression of interest on my part just as you would reply to an outsider who had asked about this or that.

In the past when you have attempted to force an issue on this score, I have systematically followed the practice of deliberately avoiding it, hoping that if I were patient long enough you would gradually find your proper niche in the Federation and come to your senses. It is obvious now that my excessive patience has not been helpful. It is time, therefore, that we straighten this matter out once and for all.

You have simply got to face the fact, and moreover accept it fully, that your position in the Federation is not that of an independent constitutional officer. You are not free to decide what work you will do and what work you will not do and when and how you will do it. You are not free to select your own duties. Your duties are to be carried out under the supervision and direction of the President of the Federation. The tasks you will perform, your overall work load, and how and when you will perform assigned tasks are to be determined by him unless in the circumstances of particular cases he tells you that you are free to decide for yourself.

It is absolutely preposterous that at this late day I should have to say these things to you. You know full well that this has been the mode of operation in the Federation as long as you have been in it. The letter of appointment which I sent you when you were raised to your present salary was very explicit on this point. In addition, you were present at the Executive Committee meeting at the Omaha convention in 1955 at which a resolution was formally passed confirming the long-standing mode of operation on this point, i.e., assigning to the President the authority and responsibility of determining the duties and supervising the work of all employees of the Federation. That resolution reads:

"WHEREAS, there is now every reason to believe that the income of the National Federation of the Blind will continue to increase and that, as a result, our organization will soon be in a position to make long overdue and desperately needed additions to its paid staff; and

"WHEREAS, it seems desirable that there is a restatement and clarification of our established policies with respect to the hiring, supervision, direction, and if necessary, the dismissal of staff members:

"THEREFORE, be it resolved in the future, as in the past, the President of the National Federation of the Blind shall have the exclusive authority to negotiate with, hire, supervise, direct, and when necessary, dismiss any and all members of the staff of this organization."

There are some intimations in your letter that you have not had time to get this assignment done and that you have been subject to distractions beyond your control. This assignment was originally given you some four months ago. Let us assume that you spent a month working on Dave Cobb's Post Office report, which is an extravagant assumption. [Dave Cobb was the Federation's Washington attorney.] Let us assume further that other work claimed your attention, or that you were sick for another month. I have had no evidence that either of these assumptions is correct. Since August you have done very little Federation work. Still this would leave approximately two months in which to do a job that at the very outside would take a week of concentrated effort.

You are receiving a very substantial salary. Including full maintenance in a Washington hotel, it totals between $9,000 and $10,000 a year. [This salary must be seen in the context of the value of the dollar in 1956.] For that amount of money, the Federation has a right to expect a substantial amount of work, and beyond that, a substantial amount of cooperative compliance with those responsible for the executive direction of the operations of the Federation. There are several people in the Federation who are more productive than you are despite the fact that they carry on full-time jobs in addition to their work for the Federation.

This may seem to you like a tough letter. After so many years of patience and putting up with your refusal or inability to comply with work assignments and of your maneuvers to carve out a different position in the Federation from that assigned to you, it is intended to be just that. It may also seem to you like an angry letter. If so, it is based on an attitude that I have had for a long time and will continue to have for a long time.

So far as I am concerned, Archie, you have only one course open to you and that is at long last to face and to accept the role assigned to you in the Federation and to carry out with a greater show of willingness and deliberate effort the tasks you are asked to perform.

Cordially yours,
Jacobus tenBroek
President

It has been said by some that Archibald was given no intimation of the fact that his attitudes and work performance were not satisfactory. He was fired in August of 1957. The foregoing letter from Dr. tenBroek was written December 5, 1956. Let the record speak for itself.

These are by no means the only instances of insubordination on the part of Archibald during 1956. During the early part of the greeting card difficulties with the Post Office, our then Washington attorney David Cobb, suggested that Dr. tenBroek should secure from him and other employees of the Federation, including Archibald, an exact accounting of the way they spent their time working for the Federation. This would permit the distribution of expenditures in accordance with the various headings in the Federation's books. On June 13, 1956, Dr. tenBroek wrote to Archibald requesting that he keep a daily work log. On October 5, 1956, it was necessary to write again:

Dear Archie:

On June 13 I wrote you a letter asking you to keep a daily work log indicating the allocation of your time to the various projects on which you are engaged. I asked you to send me copies of this daily work log near the end of each month. It is now October 5, and in none of the intervening months have I received any work logs from you.

I now call your attention to this matter again. You are herewith instructed to begin keeping such daily work logs starting with the 1st of October and to send them to me at the end of each month.

Cordially,
Jacobus tenBroek
President

On November 21, 1956, Dr. tenBroek wrote once again:

Dear Archie:

On June 13 I wrote you asking that you keep a daily work log. On October 5 I reminded you of my earlier communication, pointed out that you had not complied with it in any of the intervening months, and repeated the instruction that you were to send me copies of your daily work logs near the end of each month. You still have not complied with these instructions.

I reiterate to you once again that you are to keep a daily work log indicating what time is spent on what projects and that these daily work logs are to be sent to me near the end of each month.

Cordially,
Jacobus tenBroek
President

Perhaps the only comment needed is this: Archibald never complied with the request. Was he really a dutiful and hard-working employee of the Federation, laboring diligently to advance its cause? What does the record say?

The year 1957 brought many new things, but it did not bring a new Archibald. He was back at the same old stand. Note the following letter from Dr. tenBroek dated April 10, 1957:

Dear Archie:

Last year I had occasion to write you several times to inform you with such emphasis as I could muster that some of your attitudes, methods, and procedures were decidedly unsatisfactory to the Federation. One of the points I discussed explicitly was the procedure by which you distribute to a number of people a request to submit ideas and judgments to you. In the case of the Switzer letter [he refers to Mary Switzer, head of the federal rehabilitation program] you indulged in this same procedure—modifying it, however, to the extent of at least sending out your preliminary evaluation along with the request. The method is still completely unsatisfactory.

The procedure implies and your letter to Bill Taylor makes quite explicit that you will pick and choose among the comments submitted and decide what policy the

Federation will follow. [Bill Taylor was a Federationist from Pennsylvania who was an attorney.] It is a basic principle of the Federation, as you well know, from public documents of the Federation as well as from instructions from me, that staff members of the Federation shall not decide important issues of policy.

I do not expect to go over this same territory with you two or three times every year....

Yours sincerely,
Jacobus tenBroek
President

To those who feel that the Archibald story reveals a new technique in employee-employer relationships, it can only be said that more novel experiments were yet to come.

In April of 1957 Archibald sent to Dr. tenBroek a bulletin concerning bills affecting the blind which had been introduced into Congress. He requested that the bulletin be mailed immediately to all of the membership. Dr. tenBroek felt that the bulletin was not well written, that it was entirely too long, and that it emphasized rather starkly the poverty of the Federation's legislative efforts for the past few months. He so informed Archibald. On May 10, 1957, Archibald wrote:

Dear Chick:

I have your letter of May 7, 1957, commenting upon my letter of April 29, which responded to your letter of April 25, describing the bulletin I sent you for release as emphasizing "starkly the poverty of" the Federation's legislative program. You re-assert your description. I again reject it.

I further herewith reiterate my request that the bulletin as submitted to you except for one paragraph be put on the mimeograph machine and mailed out to the general mailing list without delay.

You will receive this Monday, May 13. Unless I hear from you by letter, wire, or telephone before noon on Wednesday, May 15, that the bulletin is in the course of publication to be mailed, I shall proceed at my personal expense to order it mimeographed here and mailed out to the limited and incomplete mailing list of this office. It can be decided later whether the National Federation of the Blind will reimburse me for the expense. Needless to say, I shall disregard any directive from you ordering me to refrain from this course of action....

Cordially,
A. L. Archibald
Executive Director

Again the inevitable carbon. To whom? *Durward K. McDaniel.*

At this stage surely most administrators would have felt that Archibald's usefulness to the organization had ended. A paid staff member announces that a particular piece of material must be mailed out immediately. If the elected President does not comply with his wish, then he, the paid staff member, will "order" the mailing to be done from the Washington office. Moreover, he will disregard any directive to the contrary.

Apparently McDaniel felt that his friend had gone too far and had perhaps put himself in an untenable position. Accordingly, Mc-Daniel, in a telephone conversation with Dr. tenBroek on May 13, 1957, suggested that he, McDaniel, would negotiate with "Archie" and get him to "back down" on his demand. Dr. tenBroek said that there was no negotiating to be done. In a few days the Archibald bulletin was mailed out from Washington. It contained no spectacular material or information, and is probably not remembered by most Federationists.

Despite the fact that Archibald had said in his letter of May 10 with regard to the mailing of his bulletin, "It can be decided later whether the National Federation will reimburse me for the expense," he sent a bill to Dr. tenBroek on July 16, 1957, in the amount of $328.50. It will be noted from Dr. tenBroek's reply dated July 31, 1957, that still other instances of insubordination had occurred in the meantime. Archibald had asked whether he could take his secretary to the New Orleans convention. Dr. ten-Broek had told him that he should not do this, that it would be cheaper to hire local secretarial help than to pay all of the travel expenses involved. Note Dr. tenBroek's letter concerning the Archibald bulletin and the secretarial incident:

July 31, 1959

Dear Archie:

I have your letter of July 16 containing a number of suggestions and attaching two bills, one from Ginn's and one from the City Duplicating Center. The bill from Ginn's has been forwarded to Emil for payment. [Emil Arndt of Illinois was the Federation's Treasurer.] The bill from City Duplicating Center (the firm that had printed the Archibald bulletin), since it is a personal one, is herewith being returned to you....

I cannot agree with your suggestion that a Washington bank account be established from which you could make payments on your own authorization. Such an independent account would facilitate the development of staff positions into the positions of constitutional officers.

You are authorized to incur Federation bills prior to approval from Federation headquarters only if the bills are small and of a routine nature. For all other bills you must secure headquarters approval in advance. This applies not only to supplies and equipment, but also to trips for the Federation.

When I was in Washington in June, you expressly raised the question with me of taking your secretary to the New Orleans convention. At that time I told you not to do so since arrangements were being made to procure secretarial help locally. Yet, you did take your secretary and submitted a bill for her travel expenses to the Federation. That bill was paid by Emil before he secured my approval. Emil has been alerted not to allow such a slip to occur again.

Cordially yours,
Jacobus tenBroek
President

P. S. Your bill from Ginn's is not accompanied by any invoice. You should secure invoices in triplicate along with all bills so that Emil and I will have a permanent record of what the expenditures were for and the third invoice can be returned with the paid bill so that the supplier knows what was covered in the payment.

On August 15, 1957, the real character of Archibald was clearly revealed—if, indeed, there had been any doubt about the matter before. He announced to Dr. tenBroek that he, Archibald, intended to incur expenses in the name of the Federation for any item or service that he considered necessary and reasonable. He said that it was unreasonable of Dr. tenBroek to ask him to send invoices in triplicate, that Dr. tenBroek had a photographing machine in his office, and could make his own copies. Finally, he said that the bill for the mailing of his bulletin *must* and *would* be paid by the Federation. He said that if it were not paid, he would advise the creditors to *sue* the Federation, and that he would give testimony in their behalf. This was the *responsible, loyal, and hard-working Archibald!* These are his exact words:

August 15, 1957

Dear Chick:

I have deliberately permitted a considerable time to elapse before reacting to your letter of July 31. Surely you realize that I will not agree to accept a Federation expense as a personal bill. I am, therefore, returning to you herewith for prompt payment the bill from City Duplicating Center, Inc. in the amount of $328.50. Since you have delayed payment of this bill into the third month, there is no difficulty in supplying you with copies in triplicate.

I need not recount here the facts surrounding the incurring of the bill. They are known in detail to you, to Durward McDaniel, and to me. When Durward was in Washington during the last week of May, I confirmed with him my understanding of the agreement reached by telephone between you and him on May 14, following your receipt of my letter of May 10. I can say with confidence that both Durward and I understood that I was to mail the legislative bulletin from here and forward the bill to you in the normal procedure.

My actions were taken in good faith. I am sure Durward acted in good faith also. I directed City Duplicating Center to bill the National Federation. They accepted the job in good faith, and billed the Federation in good faith. They expect to be paid in good faith. In addition to repeated billings, they have telephoned to inquire why they have not been paid and reimbursed.

You may rest assured that under the circumstances I shall not pay from my personal funds any bill made out to the National Federation. [It might be inserted here that Archibald made the bill in the name of the Federation utterly without authorization.] *Even if the Federation's creditor should find it necessary to sue for payment, I shall take no action except to give testimony to the facts as I know them.* If I am again contacted by City Duplicating Center on the subject of this bill, I shall have no alternative but to *advise* them regarding their course of action. Before raising any question about the bill, you permitted two months to pass [this statement is not true, of course, since the bill was not even sent until July 16, and Dr. tenBroek answered on July 31] during which there was ample time and opportunity to straighten out any misunderstanding which might have existed, and to take action to avoid embarrassment for the Federation. I can only be very forthright and honest with the Federation's creditor if questioned again....

Your request for bills and invoices in triplicate will seem demanding to business establishments supplying us with small assortments of items. You have a photographic reproducing machine in your office. You can easily make as many copies for record as you desire.

Your recollection of our conversation on June 13 about taking my secretary to New Orleans is obviously hazy. I regret the necessity of directly contradicting your statement that you "told" me not to take her to the convention. I did not "expressly" raise with you the question of taking her along. After some questions about how she was working out as my secretary, you commented that you were attempting to make some arrangements in New Orleans for secretarial help. When I had heard nothing more regarding the subject of secretarial help in New Orleans, I made the decision on Friday before leaving for the convention to secure reservations for my secretary in order to assure myself of competent help in the difficult and arduous task of drafting, re-drafting, and putting in final form the very large number of resolutions presented....

My practice generally in respect to incurring expenses for which I ask reimbursement from the Federation has always been to exercise great care to determine that they were reasonable, under the circumstances. For me to operate under any other rule would be to make my work impossible of accomplishment in a variety of situations. There have been occasions which have required me to reach a decision on my own that a hurried trip was necessary, and there have been occasions when I have had to hire people to get urgent work for the Federation done.

There have also been other instances which could be enumerated. The only practicable way for me to function is to continue the exercise of the rule of reason in making outlays for which I expect to gain reimbursement.

Very truly yours,
A. L. Archibald
Executive Director

Once more the inevitable carbon. To whom? To all members of the Executive Committee? No! To *Durward K. McDaniel.*

It was at this stage that Dr. tenBroek paid the bill for Archibald's bulletin and fired him. He did not further negotiate with him or plead or persuade. He simply fired him.

In view of all of the past circumstances, however, the letter of dismissal and the financial conditions allowed can hardly be called other than generous. The First Vice President [George Card] personally delivered Dr. tenBroek's letter to Archibald in Washington. The letter reads:

August 20, 1957

Dear Archie:

Effective immediately upon receipt of this notice your services as Executive Director of the Federation are terminated.

You are directed to turn over to George Card the keys to the Federation's Washington office and all files and other Federation property in your custody.

Your salary will continue for four months as separation pay.

Your reasonable travel and removal expenses to California, if you desire to return there, will be met by the Federation. Other expenses incurred by you after receipt of this notice will not be paid by the Federation.

Your maintenance expenses incurred prior to the receipt of this notice but not yet paid will be processed and paid by the Federation in the usual way.

Very truly yours,
Jacobus tenBroek
President

In his letter of August 23, 1957, to the Executive Committee Dr. tenBroek said in part:

Dear Colleague:

On behalf of the Federation I have today carried out the personally very unpleasant duty of firing Mr. A. L. Archibald as the Federation's Washington representative. The separation has been made immediately effective....

Archie has been a full-time employee of the Federation since 1952. Prior to that, beginning in 1946, he was a part-time employee. He was originally hired as an Executive Director. However, I soon discovered Archie was not cut out to be an executive. He was very slow and inefficient in handling routine matters. He failed to allocate time in accordance with the importance of items. He went to pieces under pressure. I therefore assigned him to duties in connection with the Washington work of the Federation. These increased gradually until in the past two or three years he has spent full time, practically the year round, in Washington. Despite this reassignment of duties, the title of Executive Director has not been changed.

At the present time Archie's salary is $10,000 per year. He received $5,000 in cash plus full maintenance. Full maintenance during the past 12 months has amounted to $5,235.00. If Archie maintained a home in California, his living expenses in Washington could not properly be considered salary. In that event they would be properly treated as costs of travel. However, Archie does not have to maintain a residence elsewhere and does not maintain one. Since he is in Washington practically the year round and that is the almost exclusive location of his work for the Federation, the payment of the ordinary living expenses such as rent and food must be regarded as part of his salary.

There are two major reasons for Archie's separation at this time. The first has to do with the level of his performance; the second with the conception of his position....

Throughout the remainder of this letter Archibald's performance and lack of performance are discussed in detail. Since much of the discussion would be repetitious to those who have read the foregoing letters, it will be omitted.

However, perhaps the final paragraph dealing with the relations between hired staff and elected officers should be quoted. It reads:

> The theory and even necessity behind this policy and practice (that is, that hired staff members all be under the supervision of *elected* officers) is of utmost importance to the future of the Federation. If the policies of the Federation are to be carried out and its purposes accomplished, the Federation must have a strong executive. Because of the Federation's democratic and representative make-up, that executive must be elected. The difficulties I have had with Archie during the past several years illustrate what can be seen without such illustration: Either the staff will govern the officers, or the officers will govern the staff. All of the advantages in the struggle are on the side of the staff. They are permanent; they are full-time; they are paid; they become knowledgeable. Even without a deliberate purpose to do so, the whole tendency of the operation is for them to become the governing forces. In the Federation, the President must have authority to hire, fire, and supervise the staff. If the President's administration is not a good one, if he is weak, ineffective, or otherwise incapable of discharging his duties, then the delegates at the convention should elect another person. No such safeguards exist in the case of the staff. If the organization is to remain democratic, then all major policies must be handled by persons who are responsible to the convention by election. Once the staff is in control, then the Federation simply becomes another agency. It loses its democratic and representative character. Elected officers simply become the fronts for the activities of paid employees.

Cordially yours,
Jacobus tenBroek
President

Even though Archibald's conduct had been of the character described, Dr. tenBroek permitted him on August 24, 1957, to submit a letter of resignation for the record. This was done in order to increase his chances of employment elsewhere. The same consideration (namely, the wish to do nothing which would damage Archibald's chances of finding employment) has been largely responsible for the fact that the entire story has never been fully told before. Such a consideration can no longer be taken into account.

McDaniel's reaction to the Archibald firing was immediate and violent. With Archibald's firing, McDaniel saw for a second time the ruin of his hopes and ambitions. The first setback had come in 1956 when he had failed to get the nomination for Second Vice President. Now the alternative means of achieving power and influence, an alliance with the Washington staff representative of the Federation, was also gone. In a bitter letter to the members of the Federation's Board of Directors dated August 29, 1957, McDaniel railed against the President and demanded an immediate meeting of the Executive Committee. He said concerning the Archibald firing:

> In closing I would like to make a statement about the President's letter of August 23rd, 1957. I am one of the few members of the executive committee who has been intimately acquainted with this episode as it developed. This letter of August 23rd is an inadequate revelation of the facts. I know A. L. Archibald very well. I know that he has had no desire to exert an improper influence upon the organization which has employed him. This superficial and erroneous issue of staff versus elected officials must not confuse and conceal the real problems confronting us. I can think of many major achievements to add to Mr. Archibald's credit. I was shocked to receive such a letter about a loyal Federationist who apparently was not given a chance to resign. I note in today's mail an effort to mitigate this injustice by accepting a resignation which was voluntarily submitted....

> Sincerely and fraternally,
> Durward

As Federationists will remember, the meeting of the Executive Committee demanded by McDaniel was held in Chicago early in September of 1957. At that Executive Committee meeting, despite all of his threats and railings, McDaniel had no case to make and he and Marie Boring stood alone as a disgruntled twosome. McDaniel went away from that Executive Committee meeting a bitter and a disappointed man. Ever since that time his actions have seemed to say, "If I cannot rule the Federation, I will *ruin* it...."

The foregoing series of letters and statements has been called "The Archibald Story." But it might also be called "The Story of

Frustrated and Twisted Ambition," "The Story of Rule or Ruin," "The Story of Distortion and Suspicion," or it might simply be called: "THE MCDANIEL STORY."

At the Federation's Boston convention in 1958 a small minority (soon to be known as the McDaniel-Boring faction) sought to gain control of the convention, or failing that, to disrupt it. After a long and embittered debate, the dissident group was decisively put down by a vote of the delegates, and order was at least temporarily restored. But it was plain to most conventioneers that the internal strife had just begun and that it was threatening to consume the Federation. Thus one veteran observer of NFB conventions—*Braille Monitor* editor George Card of Wisconsin—reported despairingly on the scene at Boston:

"There has never been a National Convention like this one," he wrote, "and it is my fervent hope that there will never be another like it in the future." He went on to declare: "For the first time in our history, there seemed to be real dissension among us. Feelings ran higher and higher as the time for the showdown approached....When it was all over, there was little evidence of any real reconciliation. Some degree of tension and grimness was apparent right through to adjournment on Monday....Whether or not the National Federation can ever again become the united, consecrated organization that it always has been is now in the balance."

Those grim sentiments came to be even more widely shared among Federationists in the months that followed the Boston convention. In May of 1959 (as has already been said) the NFB published a special edition of the *Braille Monitor* devoted expressly to "a full account of the internal warfare which threatens to destroy the National Federation of the Blind." The special issue featured a report from the President, Jacobus tenBroek, entitled "The Crisis in the Federation." His narrative began with these words:

Two years ago I reported to you that the National Federation was faced with a concerted and serious attack from without—from a number of powerful agencies which had pooled their resources to oppose our right to organize.

Today I am obligated to report to you that the Federation is faced with an equally concerted and no less serious attack from a different source: an attack from within.

The assault upon the Federation by the agencies was principally characterized then—as it is still characterized—by defamation of the character of our elected leadership, by ridicule of the achievements of our movement, and by systematic attempts to disrupt or dominate our national, state, and local organizations.

The present attack upon the Federation from within is characterized by the same strategy and tactics: by defamation of the character of our elected leadership, by ridicule of the achievements of our movement, and by systematic attempts to disrupt or dominate our national, state, and local organizations.

Declaring that "one thesis above all has been repeated again and again with mounting clamor and bitterness by a small group of members"—the thesis that "tenBroek must go"—the Federation's President maintained that the effort to oust him from elective leadership did not stand by itself but was part of a larger scheme to destroy the democratic character of the Federation—if not the Federation itself. He went on:

The drive for the elimination of the present administration has been accompanied, as thousands of our members and much of the public are now aware, by such depths of vituperation and divisive action as to bring the National Federation of the Blind to the brink of ruin. Whether such total destruction of our movement is within the purpose of the minority faction may still be a matter of speculation; but that the disruption of the Federation has been deliberately threatened as the alternative to resignation of the President is now plainly part of the record.

The bitter division within the National Federation, which this special edition of the *Monitor* documented in comprehensive detail, raged on unabated into the 1959 convention at Santa Fe, where the issue was finally formulated in terms on which the entire convention could vote (the so-called "Georgia Compromise"). The steps leading up to the decisive action, and the mood of the delegates during the strife-torn convention, formed the substance of an illuminating *Monitor* report by editor George Card. His article, simply entitled "Convention Notes," follows:

CONVENTION NOTES

A Year of Travail: A great many of us left Boston at the end of our National Convention a year ago rather depressed and full of forebodings for the future of our beloved organization. The 1958 convention had been a disillusioning experience. From all previous annual meetings we had gone home inspired and with rekindled enthusiasm for our cause. At Boston, for the first time, we had found ourselves torn by internal dissension. Old comrades-in-arms, veterans of many battles with our traditional foes, hurled bitter recriminations at each other.

The year that followed was surely the darkest in our history. The internecine bitterness intensified as each month passed. Our mail-boxes were clogged with voluminous documents, full of charges and countercharges, until many of our members became utterly bewildered. Those on the outside who hate and fear us looked on with deep satisfaction, confidently and joyously predicting to each other that the end of the National Federation, as a united and powerful movement, was in sight.

But when the hour for adjournment came at five last Monday afternoon, most of us started for home with a feeling that per-haps, after all, the good ship NFB had ridden out the storm, had righted herself and was once more on course. Not that the 1959 convention was a peaceful one. Not by any means. But the decision of the delegates—when it finally came—bespoke such an overwhelming vote of confidence in the tenBroek administration that no doubt can any longer exist as to the sentiments of the democratic majority. Since both sides on innumerable occasions had sworn eternal fealty to the democratic process, there is now at least reasonable ground for hope that the verdict, freely and democratically arrived at, will this time be accepted in good faith.

A Day of Decision: The showdown came late Saturday night, after thirteen and a half hours of debate. Everyone was given a chance to express his views. Dr. tenBroek, as always, leaned over back-ward in an effort to be absolutely fair. There was plenty of ap-plause but no boos or catcalls, and all speakers were given respectful attention. I have listened to many debates in state legis-latures and in the halls of Congress, but I have never seen an audience display a more mature attitude throughout. In all can-dor, however, I doubt whether a single vote was changed by what the speakers had to say. Nearly everyone had come to Santa Fe with his mind grimly made up; and if there were any switches after the convention began, I suspect they were brought about in smoke-filled rooms.

The Georgia Compromise: Many of us have been racking our brains all year in a desperate effort to find a face-saving compromise formula. We had not found one. Yet, the Santa Fe delegates were offered such a compromise, and it came from a most unexpected quarter. The delegation from Georgia worked it out and presented it to us. It was just a bit startling at first, but it was beautifully simple and entirely workable. As it was finally voted on, after the thirteen and a half hours, it contained three parts: 1. All officers and members of the Executive Committee were to resign immediately, the nominating committee (one member nominated by each state) was then to bring in a complete slate, and those elected by the convention delegates would serve out all unexpired terms. If one resigned, all were to be considered recalled—providing the motion to adopt the Georgia compromise passed by a two-thirds vote. 2. All incumbent officers and members of the Executive Committee were to be eligible for re-election. 3. After this convention, anyone who persists in reckless and irresponsible charges against any other member, or members, without substantial evidence, may be given a fair hearing before the Executive Committee and, if found guilty, deprived of the rights and privileges of membership in the National Federation.

The Executive Committee is made up of the five constitutional officers and eight directors. All officers are elected every two years. Four of the directors are elected each two years and normally serve for four years. The numerical strength of the Executive Committee is, therefore, under ordinary conditions, thirteen. This time there were only ten. During the past year I had resigned as First Vice President while John Nagle and Walter McDonald had resigned as directors. During the course of the debate all four remaining officers declared their willingness to resign, and Clyde Ross and Jesse Anderson did the same with respect to their memberships on the Executive Committee. Three of the four officers— Dr. tenBroek, Kenneth Jernigan, and Alma Murphey—spoke in favor of the Georgia compromise. When the vote came, it was a resounding thirty-four to twelve in favor of adoption.

When President tenBroek arose and uttered the terrifying words, "I hereby resign as President of the National Federation of the Blind," the assembly sat stunned. I felt my body temperature drop about thirty degrees. He was immediately elected temporary chairman of the meeting by acclamation; and when he took back the gavel, the delegates stood up and cheered wildly. It was one of the most dramatic and emotion-fraught moments I have ever lived through. The temporary chairman ruled that the vote on the Georgia compromise had constituted a recall of all ten members of the Executive Committee. This ruling was challenged and appealed to the floor. It was upheld by a vote of forty to five.

Late as it was, the nominating committee went into immediate session. The Wisconsin delegation had nominated me as its representative on this committee. The nominating session lasted about three hours, and on the whole the atmosphere was one of friendliness and cooperation. George Burke of New Jersey acted as chairman and did a superb job. When he finished, it was well after three a.m.

The election was held immediately after the Sunday morning session began so that we would not be without officers. The nominating committee recommended the following slate: President, Dr. Jacobus tenBroek; First Vice President, Kenneth Jernigan, Iowa; Second Vice President, Donald Capps, South Carolina; Secretary, Alma Murphey, Missouri; Treasurer, Emil Arndt, Illinois; Directors (unexpired three-year terms): Jesse Anderson, Utah; Clyde Ross, Ohio; David Krause, Virginia; Victor Buttram, Illinois; Directors (unexpired one-year terms): Eleanor Harrison, Minnesota; Don Cameron, Florida; William Hogan, Connecticut; Dean Sumner, South Dakota. In some instances other candidates were nominated from the floor, but the committee's slate was elected—with a single exception. Russell Kletzing of California was nominated against Dean Sumner, and the vote twice resulted in a tie. Then, Connecticut switched from Sumner to Kletzing—and that did it.

The hopes of the vast majority of Federation members for an end to the factional plotting and disruption which had led to the decisive actions of the "Georgia Compromise" at the 1959 convention were dashed, however, as the disgruntled losers continued to maneuver for power at the next National Convention—the twentieth anniversary convention to be held in Miami in 1960. On the other side the Federation's elected officers, led by President tenBroek and First Vice President Kenneth Jernigan, had become determined both to settle the internal conflict once and for all and to restore the convention to its normal agenda of positive programs, undertakings, and accomplishments.

The first sign of this deepened determination on the part of the leadership came with startling surprise on the opening day of the Miami convention. What the President was to term "a severe blow to the National Federation and all its members" occurred with the unexpected withdrawal of Kenneth Jernigan as First Vice President and member of the Board of Directors. In a dramatic address to the convention, Jernigan announced his refusal to permit his name to be placed in nomination for any future office. He attributed his decision to two principal factors: the mounting responsibilities of his job as director of the Iowa Commission for the Blind, and, of course, "of more compelling importance," the factional warfare within the Federation which had recently come to concentrate its campaign of character assassination in large part upon him.

Jernigan provided in his address the most complete and detailed account yet available to Federationists of the origins and ambitions of the dissident faction within their midst, as well as an assessment of the destructive effects of the continuing civil war.

The text of his speech follows:

For the past eight years I have been a member of the Board of Directors of the National Federation of the Blind. For the past year and a half I have been First Vice President of the organization. With this convention my membership on the Board comes to an end. Under present circumstances I feel that I cannot be a candidate for re-election to the Vice Presidency or any other Board position. In short, I will be unable to permit my name to be placed in nomination for any elective office in the Federation this year.

When I reached this decision several months ago, I quite naturally discussed the matter at some length with Dr. tenBroek. It was his opinion and also mine that the reasons involved in my withdrawal from office were of such a nature that they should be discussed with the convention. Accordingly, I am now on the platform for that purpose....

To summarize my first reason for withdrawing from Federation office this year, let me say that the time needed to make the program of the Iowa Commission for the Blind a complete success makes it difficult for me to carry the full responsibilities of Federation First Vice President. It is as important for the Federation as for the blind of Iowa that the program succeed. The withdrawal from office does not mean that I intend to become in any way inactive in the movement, and it certainly does not mean that I feel that there is any conflict of interest involved. I would be a strange Federationist, indeed, if such were the case.

The second reason for not allowing my name to be placed in nomination for Federation office this year—admittedly in some ways more compelling than the first—has to do with the present internal situation which faces us. In order to explain I must talk a bit about history and background.

My first Federation convention was at Nashville in 1952. That convention is still talked about and remembered by many as one of the best we have ever had. In more ways than one it was a milestone and a turning point in my life. I found a united, dedicated, aggressive organization working toward the achievement of goals which I could believe in wholeheartedly and support without reservation. Merely to be in the meeting hall and listen was an inspiration and a challenge. Many of you will remember that I was president of the Tennessee affiliate in 1952 and that I had charge of arrangements and planning. I made up my mind at that convention that the Federation was the greatest and most promising force in existence for the betterment of the blind and that I would give to it all that I possessed in the way of effort, ability, and talent. I have never regretted the decision. It was in 1952 that I was elected to membership on the Board.

Nineteen-fifty-two was a good year for the Federation, as were '53, '54, and '55. The greeting card program was launched and made successful. Whereas in 1952 the national office of the Federation had less than $30,000 to work with, our income was five times as much by 1955. For the first time in the history of the organization money was also being pumped into the state affiliates. New members were coming in. New growth was being achieved. Everywhere there was expansion. And above all there was unity—the kind of unity and devotion to purpose which made the Federation unique. There was virtually no politics in the Federation and comparatively little striving for position. Leadership was based not on influence peddling or the holding of office, but upon the ability to work and the willingness to work. The conventions at Milwaukee, Louisville, and Omaha were climaxes for successive years of growth. They were not political battlefields

where contending majorities and minorities monopolized the sessions with charge and countercharge and little else. Instead, they
were meetings of inspiration and substantial program items, of
friends and comrades gathered to exchange ideas, of organizational renewal and preparation for the year to come. They were not
like Boston or Santa Fe.

By 1956 at San Francisco the progress was phenomenal. The first
state surveys had been made. Nine new affiliates had come into
the Federation in a single year. The *Monitor* was a going concern
with a regular staff and a monthly publication.

As important as any of these things, our enemies had taken alarm
and were desperately trying to crush us—a sure token of growing
prestige. It seemed that the achievement of our goals was near at
hand.

But such was not to be the case. By the 1957 convention at New
Orleans—still a tremendous success—a subtle change was beginning to come over the organization. A small group of people from
within our own midst began, for reasons best known to them-selves, to sow dissension and to foment civil war. They began to write
letters and to go from state to state systematically destroying the
unity and feeling of oneness which had always been the principal
asset and distinguishing feature of the Federation. They began to
say that the Federation, where any blind person had always been
able to make his voice heard, was not truly democratic—that we
had simply believed that it was—that in reality it was controlled
by a sinister dictator and his small clique of followers who had
somehow hoodwinked the gullible, unsuspecting members into
thinking the Federation was representative and democratic. In
short, the blind were told that there had been a colossal "fix" and
that they had, for eighteen years, been too stupid to see it—a
"fix" which this enlightened minority had just discovered and was
bent upon exposing. There were half-truths, innuendoes, twisted
facts, and outright falsifications.

By the time of the Boston convention the Federation that we all
had known and loved, the old Federation of unity and oneness,
of constructive achievement, and substantive, inspiring conventions was dead—killed by the very people who had said they had
come to save it. In the year between New Orleans and Boston the
Federation was transformed from a dedicated crusade to a bickering, political movement.

During that year many things changed. Perhaps the most important of these changes occurred in the activities and direction of effort which took place. My own personal role was altered substantially. Before New Orleans virtually none of my time or attention was given to internal political matters. Between 1952 and 1957 I traveled more than 530,000 miles organizing and building chapters in state affiliates; wrote "What Is The National Federation of the Blind" and "Who Are the Blind Who Lead the Blind," and "Local Organizations of the Blind—How to Build and Strengthen Them"; conducted a study for the Federation concerning the employment of the blind in the teaching profession; and took part in three state surveys of programs affecting the blind. These were happy years. The work was challenging and rewarding. Even the hostility and opposition of the agency administrators in Arkansas and the bitter accusations of having ruined the lives of some of the rehabilitation officials dismissed in Colorado and Nevada did not diminish the keen pleasure. The brotherhood and mutual support which characterized our movement were at the heart of the joy of accomplishment. It was a time of unparalleled growth and progress.

After New Orleans all of this changed. For the first time in Federation history a group from within our own ranks organized itself and pounded away at the very foundations of our movement with sledge-hammer blows. It coordinated its efforts and embarked upon a systematic campaign of vindictive destruction and sabotage of the elected officers and leaders. If the majority was to survive, if indeed the very structure of the organization was to be preserved, speedy action and counter-measures had to be taken.

The situation can, perhaps, best be summarized in the words of Edmund Burke, the English political philosopher, who championed the fight of the American colonies for independence. Burke said, "When bad men combine, the good must associate. If the good do not associate, then they fall one by one, useless sacrifices in a contemptible struggle." To paraphrase these words, we might say, "When a minority of disgruntled dissenters combine to achieve destruction and to subvert the will of the majority, then the members of that majority must associate and bestir themselves to militant action. If the majority does not so associate and bestir itself, then its members will fall one by one, useless sacrifices in a contemptible struggle—not to mention which the minority dominates and controls the society."

This sort of thing was new to us. We had long been accustomed to fighting our external enemies, but never before had we been forced to repel slander and false charges from those who had been our comrades-in-arms and still proclaim themselves to be Federationists. With sorrow and reluctance—and, perhaps, too slowly and with too much kindness—the great overwhelming majority of Federation members, officers, and leaders organized for battle and took up the challenge of the civil war.

The majority was at a disadvantage, however, in defending itself because it could not devote its full time to the struggle. It had the responsibility of carrying on the constructive work and programs of the Federation, of repelling our external enemies, and of keeping the organization afloat, while the minority, on the other hand, could and did divorce itself completely from such responsibility, spending virtually all of its time and energy in subversive attack and destruction. The minority would be hard put to point to a single legislative or other constructive proposition which it has advanced or been responsible for since the New Orleans convention. In the interest of promoting the basic objectives of our movement the external work of the Federation could not be allowed to come to a standstill.

Therefore, between New Orleans and Boston the effort of the officers and leaders had to be divided and redoubled. Legislative and other program work had to be continued and at the same time the affiliates had to be alerted to what was happening internally. This had to be done in such a way as not to give our external enemies aid and comfort or knowledge of our growing problems. State and local leaders all over the country had to be shown the documentary evidence of what was occurring and warned of what was to come at Boston. They needed indisputable and provable facts as ammunition against the propaganda of half-truths being spread.

With the same energy which I had always tried to give to promoting the welfare of the Federation, I along with other leaders and members of the movement entered into this grim, new task. As I went from state to state late in 1957 and early 1958 collecting evidence and writing testimony for the right to organize bill, I also talked to the members about what was happening to us internally. For the first time in my life I found myself working for the Federation without pleasure or zest. I knew beforehand that I would earn the hatred and bitter attack of the dissenters in exact proportion to the effectiveness of my work. Dr. tenBroek and the other leaders were, of course, in the same situation.

In this connection the minority showed how badly it had misassessed matters when at the Santa Fe convention last year several of its members said from the platform (as if they thought it was an accusation, and one which I would feel called upon to deny) that I had gone from state to state organizing the majority and showing the documentary evidence of what the dissenters were doing. They should have known than I have never yet apologized for or been ashamed of any work that I have ever done in behalf of the Federation. They should also have known that I would not have denied but rather would have insisted that I had done all that I could to expose their tactics and subversion.

At the Boston convention in 1958 the Federation became acquainted for the first time with political hauling and maneuvering. The minority came organized as a bloc, and the majority found itself forced to close ranks and counter-organize in self-defense. Votes were taken not on the merit of issues but along party lines. Slates of candidates were selected, and the spirit of crusade and dedication died a painful death.

After Boston a new vocabulary came into being in the Federation. The minority taught us that when they attacked any of the rest of us or made charges, it was "democracy in action" or "the right of free speech." When these attacks were answered, however, it was "character assassination" or "defamation" and "slander." If they won an issue (a rare occurrence) it was "the will of the people" or "democracy." When they lost on an issue, it was "dictatorship" and "tyranny." When they combined to try to elect candidates or to defeat or pass motions, it was "freedom of association" and "the democratic process." When the majority combined for the same purposes, it was "dirty politics" and "tyrannical dictatorship."

Despite the fact that the will of the convention was made clear at Boston, the civil war continued. By the time of Santa Fe the days of unity and dedication were only a memory, and even the memory was beginning to fade. Again, the convention made clear its will and by a majority even larger than the one at Boston.

By Santa Fe, however, the real beginnings of chaos were commencing to set in. The political alliances and arrangements which had been made during the preceding two years were bearing their inevitable fruit. It had become accepted practice that the way to achieve recognition was not by the difficult method of doing hard work for the Federation and forwarding programs. There was a quicker and an easier way. Form alliances. Circulate resolutions, make personal attacks, rise in defense of a popular leader, and, above all—yes, above all!—come up with suggestions for change— any change, so long as it would bring notoriety and publicity.

Another year has now gone by, and we are at Miami. The civil war has continued and, if possible, has even further degenerated. There is now scarcely a person in our movement who is not under attack by someone or disliked by this or that group. Our legislative and other programs have largely become secondary to internal politics. Witness, for example, last year at Santa Fe when even the right-to-organize bills were publicly attacked on the floor of the convention by the minority faction.

Or consider the fact that letters which I now have in my possession were written into Iowa by the dissenters attempting to destroy the expanding work of rehabilitation and job placement being put into effect by the Commission for the Blind. In order to hurt me personally as administrator of the Commission, certain members of the dissenting faction were willing to destroy the program of rehabilitation and job placement for the entire blind population of the state. The same thing occurred in California when Dr. ten-Broek came up for reappointment to another term on the Social Welfare Board. Regardless of the effect on the blind of the state, letters of vindictive, personal attack were sent to the Governor. As you know, Dr. tenBroek was reappointed anyway—and made chairman of the board into the bargain. Again the dissenters were defeated in their efforts at destruction, but the next Federationist anywhere in the country who comes up for appointment to an advisory or policy-making board and who has not capitulated to the minority may expect to be treated to the same type of vicious and unprincipled attack.

Also consider the letters opposing Federation legislation recently sent by the dissenters to Congressman Baring and others. Is this the so-called constructive activity to which the dissenters point with pride? Is this their positive new program? Is this the brave new democracy they would bring us?

Our fund-raising programs have been endangered, and the very existence of the Federation as a continuing organizational entity is now threatened. Yet, there are those who at this present convention and even at this late date in our civil war will tell us that the past three years of destruction and strife have been a wonderful thing for the Federation, that we are now stronger than ever. I doubt that many of us will be taken in by that line. Certainly our external enemies are not taken in by it. If what we have had for the past three years has been success and progress, I would to God we had been less successful and less progressive.

The attacks on me personally have increased steadily since the New Orleans convention. For the reasons I have already given it was inevitable that this would be so. I knew what the cost would be when the civil war began and accepted it as an unpleasant but necessary by-product of the work which had to be done. During the past three years, especially since Santa Fe, I have been accused of every possible vice—of being unscrupulous and ruthless, without principle, morally dishonest, and above all of being desperately and wildly ambitious. These charges have been made not only by the recognized members of the minority faction, but also by some whose principal claim to recognition is the fact that they have previously held themselves out to the general membership as friends and supporters of the administration.

Again I say that such charges and attacks were inevitable in the climate of continuing civil war and political maneuvering. Such a climate encourages petty politicians and office seekers to attempt to bargain for position and to seek notoriety by slick maneuver and slanderous attack. Always as civil war continues, it degenerates into chaos and anarchy. Factions splinter and beget new factions, which in turn divide and further splinter. As dissolution and ruin approach, stability becomes harder and harder to maintain.

Leadership in the Federation does not depend upon the holding of office. It has never so depended. To the extent that the organization is worthwhile, leadership as always will continue to depend upon willingness to work and ability to work.

Very soon after the Santa Fe convention I told Dr. tenBroek that I felt I could serve the Federation and the administration better if I did not allow my name to be placed in nomination for office at Miami. Such a decision would certainly set the record straight with respect to the whispered charges of reckless ambition and desire for presidential succession. It would also rob the enemies of the administration of one of their principal issues—an issue in fact upon which they have based more and more of their campaign in recent months. It would utterly destroy one of the main arguments upon which the case of the dissenters has been built and by which they have sought to justify their actions. Then, too, it must be admitted frankly that the continuing torrent of personal abuse and vilification made the prospect of Federation office seem somewhat less than attractive.

The decision was made, but not announced. Why? The answer is surely obvious. What now of the charges of reckless ambition and desire for office which the opponents of the administration have so laboriously put together? During the remainder of this convention the delegates will undoubtedly be subjected (from the platform, but principally in the corridors and bedrooms) to hurried and desperate verbal gymnastics in an attempt to explain away the utter deflation of what has been charged. It will be interesting, indeed, to see how the dissenters attempt to explain away their calumny and misrepresentation.

In leaving Federation office to become a rank-and-file member I would like to make these final remarks. By ceasing to be an Executive Committeeman I do not cease to be an active Federationist. Nor do I cease to be a part of the administration. I shall continue to defend and support it actively.

Moreover, I shall continue to give whatever organizational help I can to any local or state affiliate in the nation. When I am invited to do so (and as time permits), I shall attend state conventions, write articles and testimony for the Federation, attend meetings, or do anything else which I may be asked to do.

I have already said that the Federation has very nearly been destroyed by the past three years of political bickering and civil war. It may already be too late to reverse the trend and forestall the final descent into chaos and utter destruction. However, I believe that this is not necessarily the case. It is not on a note of despair but of hope that I should like to conclude. It is no game we play—this business of organization. It is as serious and important as the lives and destinies of us all. The formula for solving our problems and saving our organization is simple. It is also painful and hard to face. It is this. One way or another, once and for all, now and forever, we absolutely must put a stop to the disgraceful internal strife and warfare which is destroying the Federation. It is as simple as that. We must make it unmistakably clear to all concerned that this organization will no longer tolerate the

continued wrecking and destruction of its goals and purposes—
whether the wrecking and destruction be in the name of free
speech, democratic procedures, rights of the minority, freedom of
association, will of the people, or any other high-sounding and
respectable phraseology used to cloak real purposes. We must
refuse to be intimidated or bamboozled by pious words. We must
have the courage to put down the demagogue, even if he makes
his appeal in the name of the very virtues in our organization
which he would destroy. If it requires taking stern action, then
stern action must be taken. If it requires losing some of the dissenters, then they must be lost. Whatever the cost, it is cheaper
than the alternative of absolute ruin which faces us. We cannot
delay, and we cannot equivocate. By not choosing one course of
action, we automatically take the other.

Perhaps the old Federation was too idealistic. If so, I can only say
that I believe most of its members wanted it that way, and loved
and respected it for what it was. The traditional goals and objectives of the Federation are still the most compelling reason for
our existence as an organization. To open new fields of opportunity to the blind, to secure the passage of needed legislation, to
exchange ideas and give encouragement to each other, to labor
in a common cause against discrimination and denial of acceptance as normal people, to establish the right of the blind to compete for regular jobs in public or private employment—these are
the things for which the Federation was created. These are the
things which continue to make it worthwhile. Surely the National
Federation of the Blind means enough in the lives of the blind
people of this nation that a way will be found to save it from
destruction and, even more important, to save it from becoming
merely a hollow shell and an empty mockery of the great crusade
of former days.

With those solemn words, Kenneth Jernigan left the convention rostrum and gave up his elective office. But he continued,
side by side with President tenBroek, to lead the fight on the
convention floor in defense of the National Federation and its
democracy. During the next four days, decisions of major consequence were taken on several fronts. The Constitution of the NFB
was substantially amended; six state affiliates were suspended for
activities destructive of the Federation; all national officers and
Board Members found themselves facing election; and important
commitments were made in various program areas. When the
Miami convention was finally adjourned the National Federation

of the Blind, while still a house divided, was not merely standing but was more firmly grounded than before the convention. The amendments to its Constitution, all adopted overwhelmingly, spelled out rights and responsibilities in terms not readily twisted or evaded. And the convention's decisive action in suspending from membership the six state affiliates (those of Georgia, Louisiana, Maryland, North Carolina, Oklahoma, and South Dakota) that had been at the heart of the insurrection proved to be the most effective step yet adopted toward a solution of the protracted civil war.

It should be noted that the action taken against these state groups was not that of expulsion—they were not permanently thrown out of the Federation but only suspended as affiliates until such time as they might furnish evidence in good faith of a willingness to abide by the responsibilities as well as the rights of membership. In a post-convention *Monitor* article reviewing the suspensions, President tenBroek repeated the main points of the motion he submitted to the convention:

> Through calculated activities on various fronts, these states have critically endangered our vital source of fundraising; they have opposed our basic legislative programs, and thus have jeopardized our warmest relationships with Congress; they have obstructed and fought against our organizational efforts within the states themselves; they have plotted assiduously to impugn the reputations of our elected officers and to block their appointments to positions in public service; and they have cast suspicion upon our integrity and fundamental purposes as an organization of the blind. They have done these things deliberately, actively, and vigorously. Moreover, they have formed the spearhead of a permanent hostile organization within the National Federation—the so-called "Free Press Association," openly dedicated to a policy of rule or ruin. All six states have contributed through specific actions and concerted agitation to the condition of alarming instability which has come to characterize our organization in the eyes of growing numbers of friends, foes, and the public alike. The harm which has already been done to the Federation and its cause is incalculable. The harm which would be done in the future if this condition were permitted to continue is, however, not incalculable. It would, quite simply, be fatal.

The eventual consequence of the Federation's action in suspending the six state affiliates was to lead to the permanent separation of these factional groups, the closing of the Federation ranks around its leadership, and the formation of a splinter organization known as the American Council of the Blind as a haven for the disgruntled and a willing ally of anti-Federation forces in the blindness system. But in the short run the civil strife continued unabated within the National Federation during the period leading up to the 1961 convention in Kansas City.

At the time of the firing of A. L. Archibald in the summer of 1957 the Federation was a united movement with harmony among its leaders and members and a clear-cut purpose to achieve its goals. But as the civil war got underway and continued month after month and year after year, the unity and viability of the movement began to disintegrate. The strains were such that friend began to attack friend, and total chaos seemed likely.

No better example of the destructive disintegration can be given than the conduct of George Card of Wisconsin. At the beginning of the civil war in 1957 he was First Vice President of the organization, as well as the Editor of the *Braille Monitor*. During 1958 and 1959 the minority faction (calling itself the Free Press Association) made prolonged and vicious attacks upon Card, impugning his morals and motives and accusing him of a variety of derelictions. In 1959 he resigned as First Vice President but continued as a paid staff member, serving as Editor of the *Braille Monitor*.

By 1960 the internal strife had become so bitter that war weariness was almost universal. The unity of purpose which had once characterized the movement was gone, and almost every day someone else came forward with a different scheme to end the fighting. Even George Card (*Monitor* Editor and long-time stalwart) was apparently not immune. Shortly after the conclusion of the 1960 Miami convention, he openly joined the minority faction and began a nationwide campaign, going from state to state to attack President tenBroek. Apparently his level of dissatisfaction had been rising for months, but he now openly changed sides and fought with the same vigor against the administration which he had formerly shown in its behalf.

In September of 1960 he was replaced as *Monitor* Editor by Kenneth Jernigan. This was four months before the *Monitor* suspended publication—December, 1960, being the last edition for the next four years. The October, 1960, *Braille Monitor* carried an article about Card's defection to the minority. The text of that article follows:

GEORGE CARD RESIGNS FROM NFB STAFF

The resignation of George Card from his position as a staff member of the National Federation of the Blind became effective in mid-September as the result of a letter to the President reaffirming his defection from the administration and his adherence to the McDaniel "Free Press" faction.

Card's defection, although long in the making, was first openly announced two weeks earlier in a letter to Dr. tenBroek setting forth his "plans for the immediate future"—plans which were indicated to be permanent and unalterable, and which included joining the McDaniel faction in its Nashville meeting and embarking upon a countrywide tour of agitation against the national administration and the policy of the National Convention. At that time Card stated: "I am going to campaign to the best of my abilities in an effort to persuade the states which voted against the suspensions to stand their ground next year and to persuade at least twelve other states to join with them and to vote for reinstatement at Kansas City. I shall write many letters (always on my personal stationery), and I shall make as many personal contacts as I can....I am going to Nashville the latter part of this week."

Card's defection and resignation constitute the latest links in a chain of events set in motion over a year ago when he inaugurated a series of attacks upon the President, the First Vice President, other staff members, and close associates of the Federation. As the evidence and destructive consequences of Card's activities became unmistakable, the President ordered him as a staff employee to cease carrying them on. Instead of complying with this elementary condition of staff employment, Card broadened his attacks and redoubled his political activities. During recent months, and most conspicuously following the Miami convention, the scope of his campaign has been still further extended.

On August 20 the President informed George Card that due to the deterioration of his health and effectiveness, as well as of his personal relationships, he was to be relieved of several of his staff duties (notably the editorship of the *Monitor* and the supervision of greeting card mail) and placed on semi-retirement at reduced salary. Card's reply was to challenge the President's authority to carry out the transfer of staff functions, to level an attack upon him personally and upon the convention for its action in suspending six affiliates, and to disclose his plan to tour the country as the agent of the McDaniel faction's purposes. As detailed elsewhere in this issue (see article entitled "Round-Up of Free Press Agitation"), Card has since begun his tour and has visited numerous states with the now openly avowed objective of eliminating the President of the Federation and overthrowing the policy democratically adopted by the National Convention.

On September 10 President tenBroek wrote to George Card answering various of his charges and clarifying his status as a staff member of the Federation. In view of Card's subsequent resignation and political itinerary, the President's letter is herewith reprinted in full:

Dear George:

Let me try to make a few things crystal clear. I made a similar effort last spring which apparently failed. In personal terms you cannot afford to misunderstand now.

You tell me in your letter of August 29 that I may wish to withdraw my offer to you of a changed job in the light of your avowed intention to carry on a campaign against the administration for the unconditional reinstatement of the suspended affiliates. I made no offer. I shall not withdraw any offer. In my function as President, I altered your status as an employee of the Federation. You were placed on semi-retirement; your duties were adjusted. If because of this change of status and assignment of tasks or because of any other reason you wish to resign, that is entirely up to you. You are free to remain as a staff member only if you comply with the established policies of the organization regarding the staff. You may not carry on a political campaign regarding the duties assigned to you as a staff member; you may not carry on a political campaign regarding the policies of the organization; you may not carry on a political campaign affecting the officers or members of the Executive Committee. All three of these things you are quite patently carrying on at present. Only one of them is frankly avowed in your letter to me of August 29. You must cease all such activity and cease it immediately. If you do not, you will have automatically resigned your position as a staff member.

I still adhere to what I said in Omaha in 1955. Federation members who have genuine moral scruples on any point should not be subject to moral pressure. There is quite a difference, however, between a moral scruple and political shenanigans, and between a staff employee and a member or officer. I see no moral or other scruple in what you are now doing; you are simply joining a political campaign which, if it is successful, will eventually destroy the Federation.

The renewal of your campaign against the administration includes an outright fabrication. I did not, in our June 30 meeting in Miami, request you to make a statement in my support. You volunteered to make it. Moreover, you did so in the presence of a third person, so that you knew that you could not get by with your present misrepresentation. Or is this, after all, as I am convinced it is, another lapse of memory accompanying your deterioration of health? These lapses have occurred frequently in the past couple of years, and at times have been virtually complete.

You seem, indeed, to be strangely ambivalent on the subject of your own health. When the purpose is to show that you can carry on all your staff functions, you claim that your health is not a factor. At other times, you are willing to portray it in the direst terms. At Miami you asked your wife to leave the room in order to inform Bernie Gerchen and me that you felt the end to be very near, that you were in incessant pain, and that the symptoms were occurring which the doctors had warned you to watch for. Whatever you may now wish to say about it, the objective evidences concerning the state of your health cannot be disregarded.

Your defection to the McDaniel camp is reflected not only in your personal attacks but in your faithful echo of the McDaniel doctrine concerning the suspensions. That argument holds that it is only the minority which has rights, and that those rights are unlimited, whatever the degree of internal or external wreckage they may cause. When, after years of this bickering warfare, the majority at last rose at Miami to assert its own rights and protect the Federation from further destruction, its democratic decision is held out by you to be a "mockery of fair play" and a "monstrous miscarriage of justice." There is nothing unjust or unfair in requiring members to fulfill the minimum responsibilities of their membership, and holding them to account for flagrant refusal to do so. There is no need to repeat (to you of all people) what the grounds of suspension were; they were not only recited at length in my presentation of the motions at Miami, but they have been thoroughly and painfully thrashed out for three years at our conventions and meetings, in the *Monitor* and *Free Press*, in public bulletins, open correspondence, and continuous discussion throughout the country. Most Federationists now know them by heart.

Furthermore, as you well know, the suspension decision was not a punitive action or courtroom prosecution, to be regarded in legal terms of crime and punishment. It was simply an effort on the part of the majority to save the Federation from future destruction. It was preventive and protective rather than punitive and retributory. It was not expulsion which was voted, but only suspension. The proper judicial analogy is that of a restraining order or preliminary injunction from which the defendants are released if they can show that they are complying with proper standards. Any or all of the suspended members may be swiftly and readily readmitted to full standing whenever they are willing to abide by the indispensable conditions of membership in any democratic society. If they cannot bring themselves to do so, they are free to disaffiliate. The choice is clear, and it is theirs to make.

What choice they are making is also quite clear from their post-convention conduct. The Georgia convention refused to budge an inch from the activities which had led to their suspension. Moreover, they then and there voted a $300 contribution to the Free Press Association and authorized delegates to attend its forthcoming meeting with power to join. Oklahoma voted a $500 contribution to the Free Press. The Louisiana executive committee voted to surrender the national charter. The first vice president of the Georgia Federation dispatched a letter to Congressman Baring doing everything possible to alienate him from the Federation. A Free Press meeting was called for Nashville on the Labor Day weekend. The six suspended states and one or two others were present. They voted not to comply with any conditions of readmission that may be laid down by the Federation. They made a pact that no one of them would seek or accept readmission unless all were readmitted. They voted to establish another national organization. George Card traveled to Nashville to attend the Free Press meeting and has since projected a long tour of states in league with the Free Press and to achieve their objectives.

It would be instructive to know how you explain and justify these latest factional maneuvers. Are these maneuvers "fair play" or are they such unmistakably vicious blows at the very existence of the Federation that suspension (if it were not already in effect) must seem only the gentlest of possible sanctions?

We both know that the actions and attitudes which you now see fit to disclose have long been in the making. For many months prior to the convention you were engaged in attacking the Federation's fund raiser, in attacking its then First Vice President as a ruthless and unscrupulous schemer, and in attacking me as the accomplice or dupe of both of them. These charges which you knew to be altogether false when you spread them, were merely the weapons of a personal political campaign designed to destroy the First Vice President, to bolster your own position as finance director, and to foster an image of the President as an impractical and idealistic professor utterly dependent upon the practical common sense of the finance director.

Early in 1960 I was forced to call you to task for this agitation, and to direct you as a staff employee to bring it to a halt. Instead of complying, you offered to resign from the paying part of your position. Out of consideration for your years of service, as well as for your failing health, I declined the offer. You then promptly took up the affair with a member of the Executive Committee and formed your league with Dave Krause, with the result that problems of staff were made the principal issue of the March meeting of the Executive Committee. Since then you have not only refused to discontinue your political activity but have vastly increased it and broadened the scope of your attacks.

You state in your letter that I should not have informed the convention of my decision not to remain either as President or as a member if the Federation was unable to defend itself against these attacks. That decision was a fact. Obviously it should be considered among other facts. If it is not a fact of importance to you, it is not unimportant in the minds of others. To have kept the members in the dark about it would have been the height of deception. It had the same relevance to the discussion as the other factual consequences of this destructive campaign bearing upon our relations with Congress, our fundraising, and our effectiveness as an organization.

In another phase of your attack on me, you speak of a "myth" of my indispensability. I have never contributed to such a myth or believed anything of the kind; on the contrary, I shall be most happy to be relieved of the Presidency whenever the majority believes that it has found a better man for the job. But in the meantime I assure you that I shall not be driven from that office by the harassment of a minority, even though you have now seen fit to join its cause.

But if I have done nothing to encourage the "myth" you mention, I confess that I have done much to build another one: the myth of George Card. Unlike you I do not now regret that action. There was then a great deal of justification for it. I would not now seek to rewrite history as it then stood. That you have ceased to be the George Card you once were makes of the earlier portrayal a myth of today or of any time since Boston.

I have, despite everything, been willing to retain you as a member of the Federation staff with the adjusted responsibilities indicated in my letter. Let me repeat, however, unequivocally that if you continue to flout the constitutional policy governing staff employment, and to carry on the further agitation you have outlined and already initiated, you will forthwith have resigned from your position.

Jacobus tenBroek
President

As 1960 drew to a close, the level of discord seemed (if this were possible) to increase. The minority (calling itself the Free Press) met in Nashville, Tennessee, over the Labor Day weekend and followed the meeting with a series of blasts at the Federation and its leaders. The *Braille Monitor* no longer attempted to stand "above the battle" but openly came into the fray to defend the democratic character of the Federation and the right of the majority to set policy. Editor Kenneth Jernigan set the tone in an open letter to the members in the November, 1960, issue of the magazine, saying that he believed the Federation to be democratic and worthwhile and that he would defend it from the destructive elements that were trying to tear it down.

Jernigan was as good as his word, for in that same November, 1960, issue of the *Braille Monitor* he published a satirical commentary on the lack of democracy in the Free Press Association. Here, in part, is what he said:

Everyone knows that the Free Press Association [later the American Council of the Blind] is made up of dedicated reformers. The Free Press would never have been established if its members could have received fair play and just treatment in the Federation. Despite slander and vilification by the tenBroek administration and others, the Free Press and its adherents practice democracy in its purest form. Let those who doubt the truth of this statement consider the following comparisons between the National Federation of the Blind (which everybody knows to be a notorious dictatorship) and the Free Press group.

The National Federation conventions are open meetings. Anyone may attend. Anyone may make tape recordings. Anyone may take notes. Anyone may speak on any issue, subject only to time limitations voted by the majority after discussion and debate. At the Miami convention of the Federation and at the Santa Fe convention in 1959 members of the Free Press group made tapes of the entire proceedings.

Compare with this the meetings of the Free Press Association. At Nashville this year during the Labor Day weekend the Free Press leaders stopped people at the door and demanded to know what their sentiments were before they could enter the room. Now, wait! I know what you're thinking! Don't jump to conclusions. You can't call this undemocratic. You see, this was not a "meeting." It was simply a "session" of the Free Press held as a committee of the whole. Yes, I know that meetings of the resolutions committee and other committees of the Federation are open to all who wish to attend, but you just don't understand. A new organization has to protect itself against spies and tyrannical majorities. As I was saying, at the Free Press meeting in Nashville people were questioned at the door as to their loyalties and sentiments before they could enter. Permission was denied for anyone to make tape recordings. The President of the Federation requested the right to attend, either personally or by representative, but permission was denied.

During the Free Press meeting one person was caught taking notes. Mr. McDaniel immediately explained that no one could take notes except "the official note takers." Of course, these "official note takers" had not been elected by the group. One person who managed to get into the meeting and who said, when asked about her loyalties, that she hadn't made up her mind but had come to observe, was asked to leave the meeting. She did leave. In other words, the Free Press proved that it certainly practices what it preaches.

Perhaps the greatest testimonial to the Federation's basic soundness and deep significance to the blind of the nation was the fact that through all of this pulling and hauling the overwhelming majority of the state and local leaders and the rank-and-file members remained unwavering in their support of the tenBroek administration and their wish to leave the civil war behind them. The 1961 convention in Kansas City was to see the climax of the hostilities and the beginning of the end of the strife.

The Kansas City convention represented a watershed in the history of the movement; for it was then that a symbolic thunderclap struck the Federation and its members—an occurrence which none anticipated and few were prepared to accept. Here is how that event was described in a subsequent convention report by John Taylor:

After 21 years as founder and as the continuously elected President of the National Federation, Dr. Jacobus tenBroek surprised and dismayed the convention by announcing his resignation from office on the first morning of the sessions. Dr. tenBroek's resignation, which came in the middle of his current two-year term in office, was prompted solely by the bitter factional strife which has gripped its activities during the past 12 months. As the new President of the organization, I cannot fully describe my own feelings. Dr. tenBroek brought this organization into being and has nurtured it through a score of years. We have lost in Dr. tenBroek the greatest leader the organized blind movement has ever had or will ever have. His announcement struck dismay into the hearts of hundreds in the audience; at its conclusion there were few among us with eyes entirely dry. As founder of the Federation, as its only President for 21 years, as its leader and leading spirit, he built the Federation (against persistent external opposition during the whole life of the Federation and internal disruption in recent years) into an organization that is democratic, representative, and national. In a unique way, and to a striking degree, its philosophy is his philosophy; its character is his character; its accomplishments are his. In the hearts and gratitude of his fellows, he stands as the blind man of the century.

The stunning announcement by Jacobus tenBroek of his resignation from the presidency, catastrophic as it appeared to most of the delegates, served to inspirit the convention to the task of putting its house in order. The key decision was a vote against readmitting unconditionally the four state affiliates still under suspension (two had been re-accepted). The result of this vote was that the suspended affiliates, while they did not formally withdraw from the NFB, walked out of the convention and met in a neighboring hotel, where they formed themselves into the opposition American Council of the Blind—taking with them a handful of other disgruntled Federationists, and by so doing effectively bringing to an end the organized insurrection within the NFB.

The American Council of the Blind, being composed as it was of people who had not succeeded in the mainstream of the organized blind movement, grew slowly and sporadically through the years. After a full generation it remained comparatively small. During the first twenty years of its existence the Council spent much of its time reliving the Federation's civil war and attacking the Federation and its leaders. The 1980s saw some mellowing of this attitude, but at the end of the decade bitterness against the Federation still constituted a significant element of the Council's rationale. As it developed, the organization moved closer to the more reactionary agencies in the field and was often used by them as a counter to the Federation's advocacy role. It is fair to say that the American Council of the Blind has never played a major part in the affairs of the blind.

The struggle within the Federation, the events surrounding the 1961 convention, and the establishment of the American Council of the Blind were assessed by Jacobus tenBroek in 1962, when the organized blind movement was recovering from its self-inflicted wounds. His speech said in part:

> The last of the threats to the welfare of the blind is by no means the least. In many ways it is the gravest of all. It is the self-challenge of our own division and dissension—the internal peril of palsy and paralysis. Movements, too, have their diseases. And the worst of these, the one most often fatal, is the virus of creeping anarchy—the blight of disunity and discord which gnaws at the vitals of a stricken movement until its will is sapped, its strength drained away, and its moral fiber shattered. The movement of the organized blind—we all know to our sorrow—has been so afflicted. If our movement is to rise again, there must be among us a massive recovery of the will to live: a revival of the sense of purpose and mission, indeed of manifest destiny, which once infused this Federation and fired its forward advance.
>
> If we fail in that, more than a movement dies. The Federation has been, above all things, a repository of faith—the faith of tens of thousands without sight and otherwise without a voice. It has become a symbol, a living proof, of the collective rationality and responsibility of blind men and women—of their capacity to think and move and speak for themselves, to be self-activated, self-disciplined, and self-governing: In a word, to be *normal*. Our failure is the death of that idea. Our success is the vindication of that faith.

Chapter 4

Democracy in Transition: The Second Generation

“ “The decade of the sixties,” said Kenneth Jernigan many years later, “was almost the exact reverse of the fifties for the organized blind. It began in despair and ended in triumph.” And he went on to recall: “The Federation drew itself together, shook off the civil war, and began to rebuild. It was during the sixties that we lost our great leader, Dr. tenBroek, but he had done his work well. The progress continued. By the end of the decade we were bigger, stronger, better financed, and more united than we had ever been.”

In truth the National Federation of the Blind during this decade underwent not only a recovery and revival but a renaissance. Out of the protracted struggle against the dissidents and enemies within—in the crucible of civil war—was forged a leaner movement with a sharper edge, a tougher hide, and a fiercer will. At times—on the march, in the streets, on the picket lines—it took on the appearance of an army. At the end of the decade, in a stirring speech at the 1969 convention banquet, Kenneth Jernigan evoked the spirit not just of reform but of revolution. “The challenge is ours,” he said, “and the time is now. Our revolution will not wait, and it will succeed—but only if we take the lead and take the risks. It is for us to persuade, to participate, to persevere, and to prevail—and prevail we will....The time is now, and the challenge is real. I ask you, with all that the question implies: Will you join me on the barricades?”

The forceful message which those words conveyed was the inspiration for a new generation of the organized blind—the second National Federation of the Blind generation—which in the course of the sixties, borne on the shoulders of their pioneering elders, came into maturity and authority within the movement. As the leader and spokesman of the first generation had been Jacobus tenBroek, so the leader and spokesman of the second generation was Kenneth Jernigan. (And for the third generation, not yet on the horizon, the leader and spokesman would be Marc Maurer.) Each of these blind leaders of the blind placed his stamp and left his mark, indelibly, upon the period and the movement; and while those imprints were closely akin and much alike in character, each bore distinguishing traits of personality and style, as well as of the time and the generation.

In an important sense, the new decade might be said to have begun not in 1960 but with the ending of the civil war and with the resignation (temporary, as it turned out) of President ten-Broek in favor of a younger set of leaders. The first of these was John Taylor, who as First Vice President at the time of tenBroek's resignation in 1961 succeeded automatically to the presidency. (Perry Sundquist, a veteran leader in the movement, assumed the presidency briefly in 1962 after Taylor resigned for career reasons in the spring of that year.) The second of the "youth brigade" was Russell Kletzing, a California attorney who was elected President at the Detroit convention in 1962 and served until 1966—the landmark year in which Dr. tenBroek was restored to the helm of the movement he had founded (and was now fated to serve for just two more years before his death).

The third member of the generation of "young Turks" who were moving into positions of leadership during the early sixties was Kenneth Jernigan, then First Vice President of the National Federation of the Blind as well as director of the Iowa Commission for the Blind. By the end of the decade Jernigan was to succeed Dr. tenBroek as President and to retain the official leadership for a score of years. The future prominence could not have been foreseen in February, 1963, when the *Blind American* (temporary successor to the *Braille Monitor*) published a vivid biographical sketch of Jernigan under the title "Profile of a Trailblazer." The article was authored by Anthony Mannino, executive secretary of the American Brotherhood for the Blind and a leader of the organized blind movement in California. In the light of later events which catapulted Jernigan into national and global leadership in the blindness field, Mannino's early profile takes on the added interest of a prophetical assessment of character and personality. Here is the text of the article:

PROFILE OF A TRAILBLAZER
by Anthony Mannino

(Editor's note: Mr. Mannino is the executive secretary of the American Brotherhood for the Blind.)

Late in 1962, at the Iowa state budget hearings held by the newly-elected governor, one agency head presented the reports and estimates of his department so convincingly that on the following day his presentation was prominently featured by news reporters who had attended the hearings. The official who had so impressed his listeners was Kenneth Jernigan, director of the Iowa Commission for the Blind, delivering the annual report and budget proposals of the commission. The achievements and plans to which he had given such forceful expression were the climax of a concentrated effort in accomplishing the formidable task accepted by this blind leader in the field of rehabilitation.

On May 6, 1958, a blind man was asked to assume direction of the programs for the blind of an entire state. After many years of efforts by the organized blind to gain consultation and a voice in programs for the blind, it fell to Ken Jernigan to face the double test of proving his own ability as well as the soundness of the philosophy of the organized blind with respect to rehabilitation and related services.

When Ken stepped into the job, Iowa was dead last in the nation in rehabilitation of the blind. Today it stands in the front ranks of the states in this essential work—a leap forward accomplished in just four years under Ken's direction. His philosophy proclaims that the real problem of blindness is not loss of eyesight, but rather the misunderstanding and lack of information which accompany it. If a blind person has proper training and an opportunity to make use of it, blindness for him is only a physical nuisance. On the basis of his firm belief in these guiding precepts, Jernigan has rapidly built a state program geared to independence rather than dependency, to rehabilitation rather than resignation—and dedicated to the proposition that blind people are inherently normal, potentially equal, and thoroughly competent to lead their own lives and make their own way in competitive society. And he has proved his case, with resounding success.

To understand the success of this bold program, and the man responsible for it, we must go back a generation—into the hills of Tennessee. The Jernigan family had lived in Tennessee for years; but the time came in the 1920s when economic pressures drove many of the back-country farmers into the cities. Kenneth's father was one of those who sought work in the factories in order to earn enough to return to his farm. He chose the automobile industry of Detroit; and it was there Ken was born in 1926.

The new baby had scarcely been made comfortable in his crib when the family moved back to the farm in Tennessee. Somehow, modern conveniences and motorized farm machinery had not found their way to this edge of the Cumberland plateau, which was only fifty miles southeast of Nashville and almost completely inhabited by Anglo-Saxon people. They still clung to their ancient culture and their more or less primitive dwellings. Even today, the mule-drawn plow has not entirely left the scene. Corn, hay, and milk were the chief agricultural products which gave this industrious folk their livelihood. Generation followed generation in the same pattern of life and endeavor.

But little Kenneth was different from the other folk. He had been born blind. However, this did not seem to create any great problem or concern in the Jernigan household. The child received a typical upbringing, and as he grew older he assumed a few of the many chores which had to be done about the farm. Some of the heavier tasks he shared with his older brother; but bringing in wood for the stove and fireplaces, and stacking board-lumber which his father had shaped, were among his earliest prideful accomplishments. Playmates were few, besides his brother, but they all included Kenneth in their games. He recalls that some of the games were modified a little so that he could join the fun.

In January, 1933, at six years of age, Kenneth was taken to Nashville to be enrolled at the Tennessee School for the Blind. It was like going into another world—suddenly faced with what seemed gigantic buildings, strange foods, mysterious steam heat, and electricity. Accustomed to getting up early, the youngster wandered away from the sleeping quarters on the very first morning and proceeded to get utterly lost. Unable to find his way back to the dormitory, he finally gave up and stretched out on the floor of one of the rooms he had wandered into—to wait until someone found him. It was a miserable beginning for a boy fresh from a comfortable home environment.

But Ken liked school and the world it opened up for his growing mind. Now he could read books, books, and more books, all by himself. In preschool years, he had always enjoyed having books read to him; and his first expressed desire at the school was to learn to read and write. He was not aware that it would have to be in Braille, and his first efforts to cope with the strange system were discouraging. In spite of his intense eagerness for reading and writing, Ken failed both of these subjects that first year. After that, he never failed either of them again. Today he is one of the fastest Braille readers in the country; and his love for books and reading burns as brightly as ever.

There is one phase of Ken's education at the T. S. B. which he now wishes might have been different—or might not have been at all. That was the emphasis placed on the study of music. From his own experience as well as his adult observation, he holds the firm opinion that musical training should not be imposed upon students who show little interest or talent for it. But the tradition at the school in his day, as at most other schools for the blind even today, demanded that every student be drilled in some form of music, whatever his lack of talent or interest.

Tradition must be served; and Ken found himself spending long hours of tedious study with the violin, beginning with the second grade. After three years, he "graduated" into the band with a trombone; and yet was stuck with the violin for another two years. In the band he soon forsook the "tailgate" (trombone) in favor of the alto horn, then (in desperate hope) the cornet, then the baritone horn—and finally a disastrous fling at the drums. He was quickly relegated back to the brass section—on the assumption, apparently, that he might have little talent but possessed plenty of brass. At long last, recognizing his profound lack of aptitude, Kenneth resigned from the band. As he recalls the event today, it was a great relief not only to him but also to B. P. "Gap" Rice, the bandleader!

Meanwhile, he had dropped the violin lessons and shifted to the piano. Here, again, the effort turned out to be a waste of time because he was more interested in the mechanics of the piano than in its musical potential. When he resorted to taking the big instrument apart instead of playing it, the teacher was truly convinced that Ken would never be a musician.

The world had lost another hornblower—but it gained a craftsman. In 1944, while still in high school, Ken started to make and sell furniture. Using the money he earned on his father's farm during the summers, he bought tools and hardware. The logs were on the farm and the sawmill nearby, so this was a practical venture for an ambitious young man. He proceeded to manufacture tables, smoking-stands, and floor lamps of original design. But he dared not attempt to do the staining and varnishing, because he had been led to believe that a blind person could not manage such delicate work. Only later did Ken learn that he could indeed do this work himself, and do it well.

This experience furnished further proof to Ken Jernigan that the blind individual must avoid the pitfalls of premature acceptance of "realistic" advice as to the limitations of his abilities and capabilities. He firmly believes that orientation centers for the blind can render a most important service if they will teach and practice the basic truth that, given the opportunity, the average blind person can hold the average job in the average business or industry.

Young Mr. Jernigan graduated from high school in 1945 and immediately petitioned the state rehabilitation service for the chance to prepare himself for a career in law. He was advised against it. That fall, after a rugged six-week bout with appendicitis, he matriculated at Tennessee Polytechnic Institute in Cookesville. He did not find there all the encouragement he needed and hoped for; but the now strong and independent young man who had already taken a whirl at professional wrestling was not to be talked into negative horizons or limited objectives. His hunger for knowledge was altogether too compelling and his love of books too deep. His scholastic ability soon produced high grades, and the pattern of his college life was formed.

But it was not all study and lessons. Throwing himself into campus activities from the outset, Ken was soon elected to office in his class organization and to important positions in other student clubs. The college debating team especially attracted his attention, and he took part in some 25 inter-collegiate debates. He became president of the Speech Activities Club and a member of Pi Kappa Delta speech fraternity. In 1948, at the Southeastern Conference of the Pi Kappa Delta competition held at the University of South

Carolina, Ken won first prize in extemporaneous speaking and original oratory.

In his junior year he was nominated as one of two candidates for student-body president. He lost in a very close election, but the very next year regained his political prestige by backing his room-mate for a campus-wide office and winning. In his senior year at Tennessee Tech, he was named to the honored list of "Who's Who in Colleges and Universities."

During his undergraduate days Ken started a vending business by selling candy, cigarettes, and chewing-gum out of his room. Later on he purchased a vending machine and, with permission gained from the college president, installed it in the science building. Before finishing college he had expanded the business to an impressive string of vending machines placed in other buildings. Upon graduation, Ken sold this profitable business to a fellow student, an ambitious sophomore named John Taylor—today the director of rehabilitation with the Iowa Commission for the Blind and a past President of the National Federation of the Blind.

After receiving his B. A. in social science, with a minor in English, from T.P.I., Ken went directly for graduate work to the Peabody College for Teachers in Nashville. There he majored in English and minored in history. This time his campus activities were centered upon the literary magazines. He accomplished a great deal of writing of articles and editorials, and became editor of a new literary publication. Meanwhile, he received his Master of Arts degree in the winter quarter of 1949, but remained to finish the school year with further studies.

The following fall young Jernigan returned to the Tennessee School for the Blind, this time as a teacher in the high school English department. The renewed personal contact with blind students, their aspirations and problems, stirred his determination to give them counseling to the best of his ability—and toward bringing out the best of *their* abilities. Although he had achieved success with his own education, it was not in the field he really wanted to pursue. He could not forget that before entering college his deep desire to become an attorney had been smashed as not "feasible" by a traditionally-minded rehabilitation officer. Ken discovered later—too late—that the rehabilitation man had been far from correct in his stand. Blind persons were then studying law, others were already lawyers, and the field of law was not closed but wide open to trained blind individuals.

Ken vows today that he will never make this mistake in giving counsel to blind students. "We in rehabilitation have no right to make the choice for anybody as to what his vocation should be, when that person is eager and motivated to try in a field of his choice," he maintains.

After he had mastered the routines of teaching and settled into various school activities, Ken became interested in organizational work with the blind. He joined the Nashville chapter of the then Tennessee Association for the Blind (which later became the Tennessee Federation of the Blind). He was elected to the vice presidency of the state affiliate in 1950, and to the presidency in 1951. Though he was extremely busy, Ken found time for several courses at summer school and later branched out into selling life insurance. This latter endeavor proved to be as profitable as teaching and soon became a rewarding part-time job. Meanwhile, through his participation in organizations of the blind, Ken began to have his first contacts with national figures in the organized blind movement. Outstanding among these was Dr. Jacobus tenBroek, founder and President of the National Federation of the Blind.

While Ken enjoyed teaching at the Tennessee School, he wanted to do more in this expanding field. In 1953 he left the school to accept a position at the Oakland Orientation Center in California. His work, especially in counseling and guidance, became more intensified through the closer contact with persons trying to regain their rightful place in society. His interest in the National Federation was also sharpened by the many projects undertaken for that organization. One of the major projects in which he played an important role while in California was the campaign to gain recognition and the right to credentials for blind teachers in that state. Stemming from this great initial effort, there are now almost 50 blind teachers employed in California through the teachings, guidance, advice, and encouragement received from Kenneth Jernigan. When he left Oakland to accept the leadership of the Iowa Commission for the Blind, the people who knew him were confident that he would fulfill that challenging assignment with outstanding success.

With the zest of a crusader, Ken plunged into the task of building up the Iowa programs for the blind. He found the commission housed in small and poorly equipped quarters, with a budget of only twenty thousand dollars. The entire staff consisted of six people. It was in all respects a dismal picture and a bleak prospect.

But it did not remain so for long. Step by step, Ken skillfully planned and expanded the program, services, staff, and budget of the Commission. He argued up and down the state and won growing support for his programs. Today the Commission is housed in a fully equipped six-story building, serving more than four thousand blind Iowans. A budget of $400,000 is financing programs of rehabilitation, orientation, home teaching, home industries, vending stands, Braille library, and many other related services. Each of these programs is characterized by the dynamic director.

In a way, with each year of experience in work for the blind, Ken gained as much as he gave. With each passing year he has become more convinced that blindness need not serve as a hindrance in virtually any vocation. Admitting that sight is an advantage, he hastens to point out that there are numerous alternative techniques which, learned and utilized properly, provide the blind person with the "equalizer."

Kenneth Jernigan has worked for what he believes in—and his preachment has been practiced with driving energy. Speaking with firm conviction, he declares: "If I were asked to sum up my philosophy of blindness in one sentence, I would say—*It is respectable to be blind.* Few people would deny this in the abstract; but when we analyze what they really believe, we find that most of them are at first ashamed of blindness."

This blind leader is convinced that the dominant attitudes of society toward blindness place unwarranted limitations upon the blind person. Since social attitudes, unlike the physical fact of blindness, are open to change, he maintains that one of our principal functions should be to encourage proper attitudes toward blindness and the blind. Adequate knowledge, understanding, and recognition of talents must be brought to supplant traditional preconceptions, prejudices, and generalizations about the blind. From a climate of healthy social attitudes will emerge the opportunities and full rights of citizenship which should be the birthright of the blind. And they, in turn, will then carry their full and proper share of the responsibility of free and independent citizens in our democratic society.

At the 1963 National Convention in Philadelphia—attended by some 600 Federationists—an unprecedented event took place which served to underline the rising stature of Kenneth Jernigan in the movement. Although it was the custom then and later for the Federation's President to deliver the banquet address—given the symbolic and ceremonial significance of that annual oration—in this year the honor was bestowed upon the First Vice President. Rising to the occasion, Jernigan presented a deeply considered philosophical statement which was to remain after a quarter of a century among the most decisive formulations on record of the profound difference between the affirmative creed of the organized blind and the custodial doctrines of the blindness system. Following is the text of Jernigan's address, "Blindness: Handicap or Characteristic," which was first delivered at the banquet of the 1963 National Convention in Philadelphia.

BLINDNESS—HANDICAP OR CHARACTERISTIC
by Kenneth Jernigan

It has been wisely observed that philosophy bakes no bread. It has, with equal wisdom, been observed that without a philosophy no bread is baked. Let me talk to you, then of philosophy—my philosophy concerning blindness—and, in a broader sense, my philosophy concerning handicaps in general.

One prominent authority recently said, "Loss of sight is a dying. When, in the full current of his sighted life, blindness comes on a man, it is the end, the death, of that sighted life....It is superficial, if not naive, to think of blindness as a blow to the eyes only, to sight only. It is a destructive blow to the self-image of a man...a blow almost to his being itself!"

This is one view, a view held by a substantial number of people in the world today. But it is not the only view. In my opinion it is not the correct view. What is blindness? Is it a "dying"?

No one is likely to disagree with me if I say that blindness, first of all, is a characteristic. But a great many people will disagree when I go on to say that blindness is *only* a characteristic. It is nothing more or less than that. It is nothing more special, or more peculiar, or more terrible than that suggests. When we understand the nature of blindness as a characteristic—a normal characteristic like hundreds of others with which each of us must live—we shall better understand the real need to be met by services to the blind, as well as the false needs which should not be met.

By definition a characteristic—any characteristic—is a limitation. A white house, for example, is a limited house; it cannot be green or blue or red; it is limited to being white. Likewise every characteristic—those we regard as strengths as well as those we regard as weaknesses—is a limitation. Each one freezes us to some extent into a mold; each restricts to some degree the range of possibility, of flexibility, and very often of opportunity as well.

Blindness is such a limitation. Are blind people more limited than others?

Let us make a simple comparison. Take a sighted person with an average mind (something not too hard to locate); take a blind person with a superior mind (something not impossible to locate)—and then make all the other characteristics of these two persons equal (something which certainly is impossible). Now, which of the two is more limited? It depends, of course, entirely on what you wish them to do. If you are choosing up sides for baseball, then the blind man is more limited—that is, he is "handicapped." If you are hiring someone to teach history or science or to figure out your income tax, then the sighted person is more limited or "handicapped."

Many human characteristics are obvious limitations; others are not so obvious. Poverty (the lack of material means) is one of the most obvious. Ignorance (the lack of knowledge or education) is another. Old age (the lack of youth and vigor) is yet another. Blindness (the lack of eyesight) is still another. In all these cases the limitations are apparent, or seem to be. But let us look at some other common characteristics which do not seem limiting. Take the very opposite of old age—youth. Is age a limitation in the case of a youth of twenty? Indeed it is, for a person who is twenty will not be considered for most responsible positions, especially supervisory and leadership positions. He may be entirely mature, fully capable, in every way the best qualified applicant for the job. Even so, his age will bar him from employment; he will be classified as too green and immature to handle the responsibility. And even if he were to land the position, others on the job would almost certainly resent being supervised by one so young. The characteristic of being twenty is definitely a limitation.

The same holds true for any other age. Take age fifty, which many regard as the prime of life. The man of fifty does not have the physical vigor he possessed at twenty; and, indeed, most companies will not start a new employee at that age. The Bell

Telephone System, for example, has a general prohibition against hiring anyone over the age of thirty-five. But it is interesting to note that the United States Constitution has a prohibition against having anyone under thirty-five running for President. The moral is plain: any age carries its built-in limitations.

Let us take another unlikely handicap—not that of ignorance, but its exact opposite. Can it be said that education is ever a handicap? The answer is definitely yes. In the agency which I head I would not hire Albert Einstein under any circumstances if he were today alive and available. His fame (other people would continually flock to the agency and prevent us from doing our work) and his intelligence (he would be bored to madness by the routine of most of our jobs) would both be too severe as limitations.

Here is an actual case in point. Some time ago a vacancy occurred on the library staff at the Iowa Commission for the Blind. Someone was needed to perform certain clerical duties and take charge of shelving and checking talking book records. After all applicants had been screened, the final choice came down to two. Applicant A had a college degree, was seemingly alert, and clearly of more than average intelligence. Applicant B had a high school diploma (no college), was of average intelligence, and possessed only moderate initiative. I hired applicant B. Why? Because I suspected that applicant A would regard the work as beneath him, would soon become bored with its undemanding assignments, and would leave as soon as something better came along. I would then have to find and train another employee. On the other hand I felt that applicant B would consider the work interesting and even challenging, that he was thoroughly capable of handling the job, and that he would be not only an excellent but a permanent employee. In fact, he has worked out extremely well.

In other words, in that situation the characteristic of education—the possession of a college degree—was a limitation and a handicap. Even above-average intelligence was a limitation; and so was a high level of initiative. There is a familiar bureaucratic label for this unusual disadvantage: it is the term "overqualified." Even the overqualified, it appears, can be underprivileged.

This should be enough to make the point—which is that if blindness is a limitation (and, indeed, it is), it is so in quite the same way as innumerable other characteristics to which human flesh is heir. I believe that blindness has no more importance than any of a hundred other characteristics and that the average blind person is able to perform the average job in the average career or calling, provided (and it is a large proviso) he is given training and opportunity.

Often when I have advanced this proposition, I have been met with the response, "But you can't look at it that way. Just consider what you might have done if you had been sighted and still had all the other capacities you now possess."

"Not so," I reply. "We do not compete against what we might have been, but only against other people as they are, with their combinations of strengths and weaknesses, handicaps and limitations." If we are going down that track, why not ask me what I might have done if I had been born with Rockefeller's money, the brains of Einstein, the physique of the young Joe Louis, and the persuasive abilities of Franklin Roosevelt? (And do I need to remind anyone, in passing, that FDR was severely handicapped physically?) I wonder if anyone ever said to him:

"Mr. President, just consider what you might have done if you had not had polio!"

Others have said to me, "But I formerly had my sight, so I know what I am missing."

To which one might reply, "And I was formerly twenty, so I know what I am missing." Our characteristics are constantly changing, and we are forever acquiring new experiences, limitations, and assets. We do not compete against what we formerly were but against other people as they now are.

In a recent issue of a well-known professional journal in the field of work with the blind, a blinded veteran who is now a college professor, puts forward a notion of blindness radically different from this. He sets the limitations of blindness apart from all others and makes them unique. Having done this, he can say that all other human characteristics, strengths, and weaknesses, belong in one category—and that with regard to them the blind and the sighted individual are just about equal. But the blind person also has the additional and unique limitation of his blindness. Therefore, there is really nothing he can do quite as well as the sighted person, and he can continue to hold his job only because there are charity and goodness in the world.

What this blind professor does not observe is that the same distinction he has made regarding blindness could be made with equal plausibility with respect to any of a dozen—perhaps a hundred—other characteristics. For example, suppose we distinguish intelligence from all other traits as uniquely different. Then the man with above one hundred twenty-five IQ is just about the same as the man with below one hundred twenty-five IQ—except for intelligence. Therefore, the college professor with less than one hundred twenty-five IQ cannot really do anything as well as the man with more than one hundred twenty-five IQ—and can continue to hold his job only because there are charity and goodness in the world.

"Are we going to assume," says this blind professor, "that all blind people are so wonderful in all other areas that they easily make up for any limitations imposed by loss of sight? I think not." But why, one asks, single out the particular characteristic of blindness? We might just as well specify some other. For instance, are we going to assume that all people with less than one hundred twenty-five IQ are so wonderful in all other areas that they easily make up for any limitations imposed by lack of intelligence? I think not.

This consideration brings us to the problem of terminology and semantics—and therewith to the heart of the matter of blindness as a handicap. The assumption that the limitation of blindness is so much more severe than others that it warrants being singled out for special definition is built into the very warp and woof of our language and psychology. Blindness conjures up a condition of unrelieved disaster—something much more terrible and dramatic than other limitations. Moreover, blindness is a conspicuously visible limitation; and there are not so many blind people around that there is any danger of becoming accustomed to it or taking it for granted. If all of those in our midst who possess an IQ under one hundred twenty-five exhibited, say, green stripes on their faces, I suspect that they would begin to be regarded as inferior to the non-striped—and that there would be immediate and tremendous discrimination.

When someone says to a blind person, "You do things so well that I forget you are blind—I simply think of you as being like anybody else," is that really a compliment? Suppose one of us went to France, and someone said: "You do things so well that I forget you are an American and simply think of you as being like anyone else"—would it be a compliment? Of course, the blind person must not wear a chip on his shoulder or allow himself to become angry or emotionally upset. He should be courteous, and he should accept the statement as the compliment it is meant to be. But he should understand that it is really not complimentary. In reality it says: "It is normal for blind people to be inferior and limited, different and much less able than the rest of us. Of course, you are still a blind person and still much more limited than I, but you have compensated for it so well that I almost forget that you are inferior to me."

The social attitudes about blindness are all pervasive. Not only do they affect the sighted but also the blind as well. This is one of the most troublesome problems which we have to face. Public attitudes about the blind too often become the attitudes of the blind. The blind tend to see themselves as others see them. They too often accept the public view of their limitations and thereby do much to make those limitations a reality.

Several years ago Dr. Jacob Freid, at that time a young teacher of sociology and now head of the Jewish Braille Institute of America, performed an interesting experiment. He gave a test in photograph identification to Negro and white students at the university where he was teaching. There was one photograph of a Negro woman in a living room of a home of culture—well furnished with paintings, sculpture, books, and flowers. Asked to identify the person in the photograph, the students said she was a "cleaning woman," "housekeeper," "cook," "laundress," "servant," "domestic," and "mammy." The revealing insight is that the Negro students made the same identifications as the white students. The woman was Mary McLeod Bethune, the most famous Negro woman of her time, founder and president of Bethune-Cookman College, who held a top post during Franklin D. Roosevelt's administration, and a person of brilliance and prestige in the world of higher education. What this incident tells us is that education, like nature, abhors a vacuum, and that when members of a minority group do not have correct and complete information about themselves, they accept the stereotypes of the majority group even when they are false and unjust. Even today, in the midst of the great civil rights debate and protest, one wonders how many Negroes would make the traditional and stereotyped identification of the photograph.

Similarly with the blind the public image is everywhere dominant. This is the explanation for the attitude of those blind persons who are ashamed to carry a white cane or who try to bluff sight which they do not possess. Although great progress is now being made, there are still many people (sighted as well as blind) who believe that blindness is not altogether respectable.

The blind person must devise alternative techniques to do many things which he would do with sight if he had normal vision. It will be observed that I say *alternative* not *substitute* techniques, for the word *substitute* connotes inferiority, and the alternative techniques employed by the blind person need not be inferior to visual techniques. In fact, some are superior. Of course, some are inferior, and some are equal.

In this connection it is interesting to consider the matter of flying. In comparison with the birds, man begins at a disadvantage. He cannot fly. He has no wings. He is "handicapped." But he sees the birds flying, and he longs to do likewise. He cannot use the "normal," bird-like method, so he begins to devise alternative techniques. In his jet airplanes he now flies higher, farther, and faster than any bird which has ever existed. If he had possessed wings, the airplane would probably never have been devised, and the inferior wing-flapping method would still be in general use.

This matter of our irrational images and stereotypes with regard to blindness was brought sharply home to me some time ago during the course of a rehabilitation conference in Little Rock, Arkansas. I found myself engaged in a discussion with a well-known leader in the field of work with the blind who holds quite different views from those I have been advancing. The error in my argument about blindness as a characteristic, he advised me, was that blindness is not in the range of "normal" characteristics; and, therefore, its limitations are radically different from those of other characteristics falling within the normal range. If a normal characteristic is simply one possessed by the majority in a group, then it is not normal to have a black skin in America or, for that matter, white skin in the world at large.

It is not normal to have red hair or be over six feet tall. If, on the other hand, a normal characteristic is simply what this authority or someone else defines as being normal, then we have a circular argument—one that gets us nowhere.

In this same discussion I put forward the theory that a man who was sighted and of average means and who had all other characteristics in common with a blind man of considerable wealth would be less mobile than the blind man. I had been arguing that there were alternative techniques (not substitute) for doing those things which one would do with sight if he had normal vision. The authority I have already mentioned, as well as several others, had been contending that there was no real, adequate substitute for sight in traveling about. I told the story of a wealthy blind man I know who goes to Hawaii or some other place every year and who hires sighted attendants and is much more mobile than any sighted person I know of ordinary means. After all of the discussion and the fact that I thought I had conveyed some understanding of what I was saying, a participant in the conference said—as if he thought he was really making a telling point, "Wouldn't you admit that the wealthy man in question would be even more mobile if he had his sight?"

Which brings us to the subject of services to the blind and more exactly of their proper scope and direction. There are, as I see it, four basic types of services now being provided for blind persons by public and private agencies and volunteer groups in this country today. They are:

1. Services based on the theory that blindness is uniquely different from other characteristics and that it carries with it permanent inferiority and severe limitations upon activity.

2. Services aimed at teaching the blind person a new and constructive set of attitudes about blindness—based on the premise that the prevailing social attitudes, assimilated voluntarily by the blind person, are mistaken in content and destructive in effect.

3. Services aimed at teaching alternative techniques and skills related to blindness.

4. Services not specifically related to blindness but to other characteristics (such as old age and lack of education), which are nevertheless labeled as "services to the blind" and included under the generous umbrella of the service program.

An illustration of the assumptions underlying the first of these four types of services is the statement quoted earlier which begins, "Loss of sight is a dying." At the Little Rock conference already mentioned the man who made this statement elaborated on the tragic metaphor by pointing out that "the eye is a sexual symbol" and that, accordingly, the man who has not eyes is not a "whole man." He cited the play *Oedipus Rex* as proof of his contention that the eye is a sexual symbol. I believe that this misses the whole point of the classic tragedy. Like many moderns, the Greeks considered the severest possible punishment to be the loss of sight. Oedipus committed a mortal sin (unknowingly he had killed his father and married his mother); therefore, his punishment must be correspondingly great. But that is just what his self-imposed blindness was—a punishment, not a sexual symbol.

But this view not only misses the point of *Oedipus Rex*—it misses the point of blindness. And in so doing it misses the point of services intended to aid the blind. For according to this view what the blind person needs most desperately is the help of a psychiatrist—of the kind so prominently in evidence at several of the orientation and adjustment centers for the blind throughout the country. According to this view what the blind person needs most is not travel training but therapy. He will be taught to accept his limitations as insurmountable and his difference from others as unbridgeable. He will be encouraged to adjust to his painful station as a second-class citizen and discouraged from any thought of breaking and entering the first-class compartment. Moreover, all of this will be done in the name of teaching him "independence" and a "realistic" approach to his blindness.

The two competing types of services for the blind—categories one and two on my list of four types—with their underlying conflict of philosophy may perhaps be clarified by a rather fanciful analogy. All of us recall the case of the Jews in Nazi Germany. Suddenly, in the 1930s, the German Jew was told by his society that he was a "handicapped" person—that he was inferior to other Germans simply by virtue of being a Jew. Given this social fact, what sort of adjustment services might we have offered to the victim of Jewishness? I suggest that there are two alternatives— matching categories one and two on my list of services.

First, since he has been a "normal" individual until quite recently, it is, of course, quite a shock (or "trauma," as modern lingo has it) for him to learn that he is permanently and constitutionally inferior to others and can engage only in a limited range of activities. He will, therefore, require a psychiatrist to give him counseling and therapy and to reconcile him to his lot. He must "adjust" to his handicap and "learn to live" with the fact that he is not a "whole man." If he is realistic, he may even manage to be happy. He can be taken to an adjustment center or put into a workshop, where he may learn a variety of simple crafts and curious occupations suitable to Jews. Again, it should be noted that all of this will be done in the name of teaching him how to live "independently" as a Jew. That is one form of adjustment training: category one of the four types of services outlined earlier.

On the other hand, if there are those around who reject the premise that Jewishness equals inferiority, another sort of "adjustment" service may be undertaken. We might begin by firing the psychiatrist. His services will be available in his own private office, for Jews as for other members of the public, whenever they develop emotional or mental troubles. We will not want the psychiatrist because the Nazi psychiatrist likely has the same misconceptions about Jews as the rest of his society. We might continue then by scrapping the "Jew trades"—the menial routines which offer no competition to the normal world outside. We will take the emphasis off of resignation or of fun and games. We will not work to make the Jew happy in his isolation and servitude, but rather to make him discontent with them. We will make of him not a conformist but a rebel.

And so it is with the blind. There are vast differences in the services offered by various agencies and volunteer groups doing work with the blind throughout the country today. At the Little Rock conference this came up repeatedly. When a blind person comes to a training center, what kind of tests do you give him, and why? In Iowa and some other centers the contention is that he is a responsible individual and that the emphasis should be on *his* knowing what he can do. Some of the centers represented at the Little Rock conference contended that he needed psychiatric help and counseling (regardless of the circumstances and merely by virtue of his blindness) and that the emphasis should be on the *center personnel's* knowing what he can do. I asked them whether they thought services in a center were more like those given by a hospital or like those given by a law school. In a hospital the person is a "patient." (This is, by the way, a term coming to be used more and more in rehabilitation today.) The doctors decide whether the patient needs an operation and what medication he should have. In reality the "patient" makes few of his own decisions. Will the doctor "let" him do this or that? In a law school, on the other hand, the "student" assumes responsibility for getting to his own classes and organizing his own work. He plans his own career, seeking advice to the extent that he feels the need for it. If he plans unwisely, he pays the price for it, but it is his life. This does not mean that he does not need the services of the law school. He probably will become friends with the professors and will dis-

cuss legal matters with them and socialize with them. From some
he will seek counsel and advice concerning personal matters. More
and more he will come to be treated as a colleague. Not so the
"patient." What does he know of drugs and medications? Some
of the centers represented at the Little Rock conference were
shocked that we at the Iowa Commission for the Blind "socialize"
with our students and have them to our homes. They believed
that this threatened what they took to be the "professional
relationship."

Our society has so steeped itself in false notions concerning blindness that it is most difficult for people to understand the concept
of blindness as a characteristic and for them to understand the
services needed by the blind. As a matter of fact, in one way or
another, the whole point of all I have been saying is just this:
Blindness is neither a dying nor a psychological crippling—it need
not cause a disintegration of personality—and the stereotype
which underlies this view is no less destructive when it presents
itself in the garb of modern science than it was when it appeared
in the ancient raiment of superstition and witchcraft.

Throughout the world, but especially in this country, we are today
in the midst of a vast transition with respect to our attitudes about
blindness and the whole concept of what handicaps are. We are
reassessing and reshaping our ideas. In this process the professionals in the field cannot play a lone hand. It is a cardinal principle of our free society that the citizen public will hold the
balance of decision. In my opinion, it is fortunate that this is so,
for professionals can become limited in their thinking and committed to outworn programs and ideas. The general public must
be the balance staff, the ultimate weigher of values and setter of
standards. In order that the public may perform this function with
reason and wisdom, it is the duty of each of us to see that the
new ideas receive the broadest possible dissemination. But even
more important, we must examine ourselves to see that our own
minds are free from prejudices and preconception.

   The final years of the tenBroek era—years in which Kenneth
Jernigan, as First Vice President, came to play an increasingly
vital role—were characterized by innovation and progress in a
number of program areas. It was in 1964 that the National
Federation of the Blind moved conspicuously onto the world
stage through its inauguration of the International Federation of
the Blind, and during this decade the numbers and participation

of foreign delegates at the National Federation's conventions began to increase significantly. (The international role of the National Federation of the Blind will be discussed in Chapter Nine.)

One of the truly extraordinary events in all of Federation history—still wondrous to recall a quarter of a century later—was the silver anniversary convention of 1965, which was held (as luck and good planning would have it) in Washington, D.C. That significant site permitted the Federation's leaders to line up over 100 members of Congress, both senators and representatives, as banquet guests—and for Kenneth Jernigan, as master of ceremonies, to draw a thirty-second speech from every one of them. The Vice President of the United States, Hubert Humphrey, was among those who addressed this most glittering of conventions; so was Robert F. Kennedy, then a junior senator from New York; and so too was John McCormack, the venerable Speaker of the House of Representatives and one of the most powerful men in government of his generation.

Something of the splendor of this twenty-fifth annual convention was conveyed by an article the following month in the *Braille Monitor*, which appeared under the heading "'The Week That Was.'"

"THE WEEK THAT WAS"

For nearly one thousand blind Americans and their families, the week of July 4, 1965, will long be a time to remember—with pleasure, with purpose, and with pride.

For "that was the week that was": the week of the Washington convention, magnificently commemorating the Silver Anniversary of the National Federation of the Blind....

The week of Vice President Hubert H. Humphrey, announcing to delegates in ringing tones that "The proof of your achievement is that what once had been private goals—your goals—have now become public official goals, *our* goals as a nation...."

The week of Senator Robert F. Kennedy, the Federation's gift volume in his hands, pledging to carry on the profound commitment of his brother John F. Kennedy to the rights of the blind to speak for themselves and to be heard....

The week of Speaker of the House John W. McCormack, delivering the convention's keynote address, commending Federationists for their spirit of independence, their implementation of the constitutional right to organize, and the effectiveness of their advice to Congress on legislation affecting the blind....

The week of our own President Russell Kletzing, presiding over historic events and helping to make them so by his own performance and speeches....

The week of Senator Vance Hartke, Senator Frank Moss, Congressman Walter S. Baring, and Congressman Phillip Burton, one by one narrating their personal hopes and collective efforts to raise the standards of aid and opportunity for the nation's blind.

That was the week that was: the week of television cameras pointed like howitzers at the speaker's stand from both sides of the packed auditorium, of news reporters and photographers circling about the platform, scribbling notes and popping flashbulbs...of microphones clustered like a metal bouquet on the rostrum... of radio interviews and TV broadcasts beamed to all parts of the country.

That was the week that was: the week of the "Hartke demonstration," a spontaneous migration of hundreds of Federationists to the Capitol in order to lend graphic support to the fight for the Hartke bill then in contest on the Senate floor...a fight which was rewarded with overwhelming Senate passage of the historic measure on July 9.

That was the week that was: the week of the "banquet of banquets"—the monumental convention dinner which brought together 600 Federationists and 103 members of Congress in a single room for a single purpose...with Representatives and Senators rising in turn for an impromptu 30-second speech...each one commanded, clocked, and congratulated by a masterly if unceremonious Master of Ceremonies, First Vice President Kenneth Jernigan...a stirring occasion made still more memorable by the address of President Emeritus Jacobus tenBroek, which was hailed by one Congressman present as "the best speech I have ever heard bar none."

That was the week of social commingling and reunion: of community sings around the piano in the vast Hospitality Room...of bus loads of conventioneers complete with children, dogs, and television cameramen touring the Washington and Lincoln monuments, the Jefferson Memorial, and the Kennedy grave at Arlington...a week of gatherings by the fountain in the Mayflower Hotel lobby, of convivial tables in the Presidential Room and smaller groups consorting in the Rib Room, and of expeditions to Scholl's Colonial Cafeteria...of exhibits in the Cabinet Room, open house in the National Convention suite, and private parties everywhere...a week of festivity, fellowship, and Federationism.

That was the week of international federation: of speeches and panel discussions featuring overseas leaders of the worldwide blind movement—from Germany, Equador, Saudi Arabia, England, and Korea—along with our own famed internationalists, Dr. tenBroek and Isabelle Grant.

That was the week of the Leadership Seminar: a two-day conclave following the convention of some 60 stalwart Federationists from numerous states, living and studying together at the University of Maryland's Center for Adult Education—reviewing, debating, and absorbing an array of programs and procedures looking toward leadership and democratic organization among the blind.

That was the week of action and accomplishment: of the President's Report, the White Cane report, the Washington congressional report, and the state reports on the progress of legislation...of important resolutions on a dozen political and social fronts...of meetings general and special: meetings of blind merchants, of teachers, of various national committees...the week of succession of speeches and discussions tackling concrete problems and programs, bringing the issues into the open, closing the ranks on policy decisions and initiatives, moving the Federation onward....

That was the week that was...the week that is a landmark in the history of the organized blind...the week that will be remembered by all who were there with pleasure, with purpose, and with pride.

Another report on the Washington convention of 1965—this one in the form of a prose poem capturing the highlights of the memorable week through a succession of striking images—appeared in the *Monitor* under the by-line of Floyd S. Field, a veteran New York Federationist with the soul of an artist. His narrative ode, "All's Quiet Tonight Along the Potomac," follows:

ALL'S QUIET TONIGHT ALONG THE POTOMAC
by Floyd S. Field, President, Niagara Chapter,
Empire State Association of the Blind

All's quiet tonight along the Potomac!

Where Generals McClellan and Mead reviewed their troops: where General Grant marched his victorious army past the White House: where the Drummer Boy of the Rappahannock played his dirge as President Andrew Johnson bade farewell to the martyred Lincoln when his body left the railroad station on the first Pullman on his sad trip back to Illinois.

"All this a century ago: one hundred years of winter's snow on Lincoln's grave, as all heroes of Blue and Gray are now laid peacefully away."

All's quiet tonight along the Potomac!

Where five-score and no years later another President Johnson seeks rest in Texas as the twenty-fifth annual convention of the National Federation of the Blind concludes its conclave at the Mayflower: where for one hour Toastmaster Ken Jernigan ruled members of Congress with an iron hand, allowing each the unheard- of cloture time of thirty seconds—and bringing out humor most of us thought impossible. "I yield you thirty seconds, Mr. Congressman"—and one replied: "With Ken as Speaker, the House would be in adjournment by March." Where founder Jacobus tenBroek told in a masterful speech of the first twenty-five years of the National Federation of the Blind: of its establishment and battles, its victories and defeats, its progress and firm foundation.

All's quiet tonight along the Potomac!

In the ballroom where President Russell Kletzing presided; and where Convention Chairman Ken Jernigan gave daily prizes to those present at the right time; and where International President tenBroek and our General of the Foreign Armies, Isabelle Grant, told of progress of the independent blind around the world, of Fatima Shah, in Pakistan, too busy serving her fellow blind to hold her new grandchild on her lap, and of how we may assist her and others.

All's quiet tonight along the Potomac!

Where the featured tour brought busloads of blind people and guides to visit the Lincoln Memorial; the Arlington National Cemetery, where they saw the "Changing of the Guard" and with special permission used the path of the Kennedy family in visiting the grave of the martyred President, standing there in reverence; and the 555-foot monument to the Father of Our Country while others toured the Capitol, the Senate chambers, the Smithsonian Institution, and even tried to converse with life-size dummies in the famous wax museum.

All's quiet along the Potomac!

Where the annual financial report was distributed and made less dry by the distribution of water by members of a chapter named for another mighty river—to NFB officials, foreign visitors, and presidents of state affiliates—even putting a few drops in the Mayflower fountain.

And thus concluded the twenty-fifth anniversary convention of the Federation—said to have had the very highest esprit de corps—its delegates returning to resume their work for the blind in Hawaii and Alaska, in Maine and Texas, in California and West Virginia, and in a total of 36 sovereign states—but with many taking time to attend a seminar on problems of the sightless at the University of Maryland. And as the honor guard is changed regularly at Arlington; and the eternal flame, kindled by Jackie, burns steadily on the grave of the late President; and until hordes of Shriners take over our nation's Capital:

All's quiet tonight along the Potomac!

The silver anniversary convention of 1965—with its parade of statesmen, its congressional chorus, its week-long flow of rhetoric—was above all a symphony of words. In this regard the leaders of the National Federation of the Blind—notably Jacobus tenBroek, Kenneth Jernigan, and Russell Kletzing—found themselves addressing the convention, not in competition but in concert with some of the most illustrious public figures of the age: Hubert Humphrey, Bobby Kennedy, John McCormack, and many others. Yet, by common consensus of the delegates and convention guests, none who spoke during those memorable sessions was quite as impressive in appearance, as eloquent in delivery, or as powerful in impact as their founder and President Emeritus, Dr. tenBroek. Something of the effect which his banquet address had upon the audience (at least a hundred of whom were hardened politicians) may be gleaned from the response of one Congressman, Edward R. Royball of California, who attended the dinner: "This was the most outstanding speech I have ever heard," he said. "May I suggest that it be written up and sent to every member of Congress, both House and Senate, to every member of every state legislature, and to every member of our city councils throughout the country. I want them all to be proud of whatever contribution they have made to this magnificent movement."

Dr. tenBroek's speech, "The Federation at Twenty-Five: Postview and Preview," clearly represented the summation of his career as leader of the organized blind movement. While it was not formally a valedictory (he would deliver two more banquet addresses in succeeding years), there was about this oration an air of finality and the reflective quality of a testament. In assessing the quarter century of collective achievement and struggle—in placing the work of the Federation in historical perspective—Jacobus tenBroek was at the same time putting his own house in order.

Viewed in that context, "The Federation at Twenty-Five" stands as a symbolic watershed—an emblem of transition—between the generation of the pioneers, embodied in tenBroek himself, and the oncoming generation of builders and planners represented on that platform by the long-time disciple who introduced him to the banquet audience, Kenneth Jernigan. (And Jernigan's own speech of introduction conveyed a similar message in its reference to the "spiritual" side of the movement and of the incarnation of that spirit in the person of Dr. tenBroek.)

Here is the complete text of the banquet speech delivered by Dr. tenBroek at the 25th annual convention of the National Federation of the Blind held in Washington, D.C., in July, 1965:

THE FEDERATION AT TWENTY-FIVE:
POSTVIEW AND PREVIEW
by Jacobus tenBroek

Oscar Wilde tells us: "Most modern calendars mar the sweet simplicity of our lives by reminding us that each day that passes is the anniversary of some perfectly uninteresting event." We must approach the task of celebration and review with some pause and some humility, neither exaggerating our importance nor underestimating it. It is my task in this spirit to capsulize our history, convey our purposes, and contemplate our future.

The career of our movement has not been a tranquil one. It has grown to maturity the hard way. The external pressures have been unremitting. It has been counseled by well-wishers that all would be well—and it has learned to resist. It has been attacked by agencies and administrators—and learned to fight back. It has been scolded by guardians and caretakers—and learned to talk back. It has cut its eyeteeth on legal and political struggle, sharpened its wits through countless debates, broadened its mind and deepened its voice by incessant contest. Most important of all, it has never stopped moving, never stopped battling, never stopped marching toward the goals of security, equality, and opportunity for all the nation's blind. It has risen from poverty to substance, from obscurity to global reputation.

It is fitting that the anniversary of our own independence movement should coincide with that of the nation itself. The two revolutions were vastly different in scope but identical in principle. We too memorialize a day of independence—independence from a wardship not unlike that of the American colonists. Until the advent of the National Federation of the Blind, the blind people of America were taken care of but not represented; protected but not emancipated; seen but rarely heard.

Like Patrick Henry on the eve of revolution, we who are blind knew in 1940 that if we wished to be free, if we meant to gain those inestimable privileges of participation for which we had so long yearned, then we must organize for purposes of self-expression and collective action; then we must concert to engage in a noble struggle.

In that spirit the National Federation of the Blind was founded. In that spirit it has persevered. In that spirit it will prevail.

When the founding fathers of the Federation came together at Wilkes-Barre, to form a union, they labored in a climate of skepticism and scorn. The experts said it couldn't be done; the agencies for the blind said it shouldn't be done. "When the blind lead the blind," declared the prophets of doom, "all shall fall into the ditch."

But the Federation was born without outside assistance. It stood upright without a helping hand. It is still on its feet today.

At the outset we *declared* our independence. In the past 25 years we have *established* it Today we may say that the National Federation of the Blind has arrived in America—and is here to stay. That is truly the "new outlook for the blind."

We have not reached our present standing, as all of you know, by inertia and idleness. The long road of our upward movement is divided into three phases—corresponding to the first decade, the second decade, and the third half-decade of our existence as an organization. Each of these three periods, though a part of a continuum, has had a different emphasis and a different character. Let us look at each of them.

The Federation was not born with a silver spoon in its mouth—but, like the nation itself, it was born with the parchment of its principles in its hand. Our basic philosophy and purposes—even most of our long-range programs—existed full-panoplied at our origin. We were dedicated to the principles of security with freedom; of opportunity without prejudice; of equality in the law and on the job. We have never needed to alter or modify those goals, let alone compromise them. We have never faltered in our confidence that they are within our reach. We have never failed to labor for their implementation in political, legal, and economic terms.

The paramount problems of our first decade, the 1940s, were not so much qualitative as quantitative; we had the philosophy and the programs, but we lacked the membership and the means. The workers were few and the cupboard was bare.

Each month as we received our none too bountiful salary as a young instructor at the University of Chicago Law School, Hazel and I would distribute it among the necessities of life: food, clothing, rent, Federation stamps, mimeograph paper and ink, other supplies. So did we share our one-room apartment. The mimeograph paper took far more space in our closet than did our clothes. We had to move the mimeograph machine before we could let down the wall bed to retire at night. If on a Sunday we walked along Chicago's lake front for an hour, four or five fewer letters were written, dropping our output for that day to fewer than twenty-five.

The decade of the forties was a time of building: and build we did, from a scattering of seven state affiliates at our first convention to more than four times that number in 1950. It was a time of pioneering: and pioneer we did, by searching out new paths of opportunity and blazing organizational trails where no blind man had before set foot. It was a time of collective self-discovery and self-reliance: of rising confidence in our joint capacity to do the job—to hitch up our own wagon train, and hitch it up we did.

In the decade of the forties we proved our organizational capacity, established our representative character, initiated legislative programs on the state and national levels, and spoke with the authority and voice of the blind speaking for themselves. In these very terms the decade of the fifties was a time both of triumph and travail. The triumph was not unmixed but the travail was passing.

Our numbers escalated to a peak of forty-seven statewide affiliates with membership running to the tens of thousands. Our resources multiplied through a campaign of fundraising. Our voice was amplified with the inauguration of the *Braille Monitor* as a regular publication in print, Braille, and tape, which carried the word of Federationism to the farthest parts of the Nation and many distant lands.

With the funds to back us up, with a broad base of membership behind us, with constructive programs of opportunity and enlargement, with growing public recognition and understanding, the Federation in the fifties galvanized its energies along an expanding front. We sent teams of blind experts into various states, on request of the governors, to prepare master plans for the reform of their welfare services to the blind. We aided our state affiliates in broad programs of legislative and administrative improvement in welfare and rehabilitation. We participated in opening the teaching profession to qualified blind teachers in a number of states. We assisted in bringing to completion the campaign to secure white cane laws in all of the states so that blind men might walk abroad anywhere in the land sustained "by a faith justified by law." We shared with others the credit for infusing into federal welfare the constructive objective of self-care and self-support, progressive improvements in the aid grant and matching formula, and the addition of disability insurance. Over the unflagging opposition of the Social Security Administration, we secured the acceptance by Congress, in progressive amounts, of the principle of exempt income for blind aid recipients; at first temporary, and finally permanent permission for Pennsylvania and Missouri to retain their separate and rehabilitative systems of public assistance; and we began to lay the groundwork by which our blind workers in the sheltered shops might secure the status and rights of employees. We pushed, pulled, and persuaded the civil service into first modifying, then relaxing, and finally scrapping its policy of discrimination against blind applicants for the public service.

In these enterprises, as against the doctrinaire, aloof resistance of administration, we had the cordial good will, practical understanding, and humane regard of an ever-growing number of Congressmen.

All of a sudden, in the furious fifties, the National Federation of the Blind was very much noticed. Our organizations became the objects of intense attention—if rarely of affection—on the part of the agencies, administrators, and their satellite groups which had dominated the field.

As the organized blind movement grew in affluence and in influence, as affiliates sprang up in state after state, county after county, across the land, as a groundswell of protest rose against the dead ends of sheltered employment and segregated training, of welfare programs tied to the poor law and social workers bound up in red tape, the forces of custodialism and control looked down from their lighthouses and fought back.

"The National Federation of the Blind," said its President in 1957, "stands today an embattled organization. Our motives have been impugned; our purposes reviled; our integrity aspersed; our representative character denied. Plans have been laid, activities undertaken, and concerted actions set in motion for the clear and unmistakable purpose of bringing about our destruction. Nothing less is sought than our extinction as an organization."

No Federationist who lived through that decade can forget how the battle was joined—in the historic struggle for the right of self-expression and free association. The single most famous piece of legislation our movement has produced—one which was never passed by Congress but which made its full weight felt and its message known throughout the world of welfare and the country of the blind—was the Kennedy-Baring Bill.

It is fitting that John F. Kennedy, then the junior senator from Massachusetts, was a sponsor of that bill of rights for the blind, who gave his name and voice to the defense of our right to organize.

Eight years ago he rose in the Senate to introduce and speak for his bill "to protect the right of the blind to self-expression." He told how some 43 state associations of blind persons had become "federated into a single nationwide organization, the National Federation of the Blind." He declared: "It is important that these views be expressed freely and without interference. It is important that these views be heard and considered by persons charged with responsibility...." He pointed out that in various communities this freedom had "been prejudiced by a few professional workers in programs for the blind." He urged that "our blind citizens be protected against any exercise of this kind of influence or authority to interfere with their freedom of self-expression through organizations of the blind."

The Kennedy Bill was simple and sweeping in its purposes: to insure to the blind the right to organize without intimidation; and to insure to the blind the right to speak and to be heard through systematic means of consultation with the responsible agencies of government.

That bill of rights was not enacted; but it gained its ends in other ways. Lengthy and dramatic public hearings were held by a committee of Congress, at which dozens of blind witnesses both expert and rank-and-file testified to the extent of coercion and pressure brought against them by the forces hostile to their independence. "Little Kennedy bills" were introduced in a number of state legislatures and enacted by some. The forces of opposition called off their attack upon the organized blind and beat a strategic retreat.

Meanwhile, in that second decade, the Federation faced another bitter struggle within its own house. Not all Federationists were happy with the way the movement was going. There were a few who were decidedly "soft on custodialism," over friendly to the agencies which opposed us. There were others with a burning passion for leadership and office, an ambition which burned the deeper as it burned in vain. There were still others whose grievances were personal; real enough to them if not substantial in fact. All of these factors combined in the fifties to form a temporary crisis of confidence and collaboration.

But then, as suddenly as it had begun, the civil turmoil ended. Those who had desired power for their own ends or for itself, who had sought to change the character and officers of the movement, departed to form their own organizations. Shaken in its unity, depleted in resources, diminished in membership, the Federation began the hard task of rebuilding and rededication.

That task has been the primary assignment of the sixties, and today, at the halfway point, we may report that it has been accomplished. During the five years past we have regained stability, recovered unity, and preserved democracy.

We have found new and dynamic leadership, in the person of a President imbued with youth and creative vigor. We have regained our fund raiser and with him has come the prospect of renewed resources. We have restored and rejuvenated the *Braille Monitor*, as not only the voice but the clarion call of the federated blind. We have reached across the seas, extending the hand of brotherhood and the vision of Federationism to blind people the world over—through the International Federation of the Blind.

We have made new friends—yes, and found new champions—in the Congress of the United States and in the legislatures of the states. And in so doing we have brightened the vistas of hope and opportunity not only for half a million blind Americans but for all the handicapped and deprived who rely upon their government for a hand up rather than a handout.

And in this new decade of the sixties, we of the Federation are reaching toward another base of understanding and support. We intend to carry our case and our cause, not only to the lawmakers in Congress but to the judges in the courts as well: for it is in their tribunals that new pathways of progress are being cleared, as the result of a happily evolving concept which holds that the great principles of the Constitution—among them liberty, dignity, privacy, and equality—must be brought down off the wall and made real in the lives of all our citizens with all deliberate speed.

The organized blind have traveled far in the past quarter century. The road ahead will not be easy. But the road is never easy for the blind traveler; every step is a challenge, every independent advance is a conquest. The movement of the organized blind in society is like the movement of the blind person in traffic: in both cases the gain is proportionate to the risk. Let us adventure together.

It was Theodore Roosevelt who said that the sign of real strength in a nation is that it can speak softly and carry a big stick. The sign of strength in our movement is that we speak vigorously and carry a white cane.

Whatever may be the challenges to come—whatever the opposition to be converted or defeated, whatever the problems of maintaining internal democracy and external drive, whatever the difficulties of activating successful but indifferent blind, whatever the slow progress and temporary setbacks in achieving our ultimate goals—our experience and accomplishments of a quarter of a century tell us one thing: we can prevail!

And we shall prevail!

We *have* prevailed over the limitations of blindness, in our lives and in our movement. We *shall* prevail over the handicap of blindness in all its forms: not the physical disability, which is an act of nature that may not be repealed, but the social handicap which is an act of men that men may counteract.

We *have* prevailed, in our movement and our minds, over the myth of the "helpless blind man." We *shall* prevail over that myth of helplessness in the minds of all who have sight but not vision.

We *have* prevailed over the foredooming conclusion that the blind are ineducable, that lack of sight means loss of mind, and over the only slightly less foredooming conclusion that the blind can be taught but only the rudiments of academe and rudest of crafts. We *shall* prevail over every arbitrary restriction and exclusion inhibiting the fullest development of mind and skill of every blind person.

We *have* prevailed over the legal stricture that the blind should not mix and mingle with the public in public places but should confine their movement to the rocking chair. We *shall* prevail over the lingering concept in the law of torts that the white cane and white cane laws should not be given full credence and that blind persons are automatically guilty of contributory negligence whenever an accident befalls them.

We *have* prevailed over some of the myriad social discriminations against the blind in hotels, in renting rooms, houses, and safety deposit boxes, in traveling alone, in blood banks, in playing at gambling tables, in jury duty, and serving as a judge, in purchasing insurance, in release from the penitentiary on parole, in holding student body offices, in marriage laws and customs. We *shall* prevail over the whole sorry pattern which is no less vicious because it is sustained by the best of motives.

We *have* prevailed over the notion that the blind are capable only of sheltered employment. We *shall* prevail over the institution of the sheltered workshop itself as a proper place for any blind person capable of competitive employment.

We *have* prevailed against the exclusion of qualified blind workers in a number of fields of competitive employment. We *shall* prevail over such discrimination in every calling and career.

We *have* prevailed over the principle of welfare aid as a mere palliative for those in distress, without built-in incentives to help them out of that distress. We *shall* prevail over the stubborn remnants of the poor-law creed—the means test, the liens pest, the requirement of residence, the concept of relatives' responsibility—wherever they rear their Elizabethan heads in the statutes of the states and nation.

We *have* prevailed over the obstacles to communication and communion among the blind of America—the physical distances, the psychological differences, the lack of devices for writing and talking—which have isolated us from one another. We *shall* prevail over the greater obstacles to communication and affiliation among the blind people of the world—we shall carry Federationism to all the nations.

We *shall* prevail because we have demonstrated to the world and to ourselves that the blind possess the strength to stand together and to walk alone; the capacity to speak for themselves and to be heard with respect; the resolute determination of a common purpose and a democratic cause; the faith that can move mountains—and mount movements!

Twenty-five years—a quarter of a century—how much time is that? In the perspective of eternity, it is an incalculable and imperceptible fraction. In the chronology of the universe, it is less than an instant. In the eye of God, it is no more than a flash. In the biography of a social movement, based on justice and equality, it is a measurable segment. In the life of a man—say from his thirtieth to his fifty-fifth year—it encompasses the best years, the very prime, when experience, energy, and intelligence mingle in their most favorable proportions, before which he is too young, and after which he is too old. As a man who spent those twenty-five best years of life in and with the Federation, I have few regrets, immense pride, and boundless hope for the future.

Thus spoke Dr. tenBroek in summation of the first quarter century of the organized blind movement in America, and of his own career as its founder and prime mover. His speech was the capstone of a convention singularly graced by the presence of public figures, many of whom were of national prominence and a few of whom were already of historic stature. One of the latter was Robert Kennedy, younger brother of the slain President, who in turn would be assassinated three years later during his own campaign for the presidency. Then a junior senator from New York, Kennedy was at the National Federation of the Blind convention to receive for the Kennedy Memorial Library a special award and other memorabilia honoring the late President for his role as a champion of the organized blind in their struggle for the right to organize. This is how the *Braille Monitor* reported the younger Kennedy's appearance before the convention and his brief acceptance speech:

When he had received the plaque and books from the Federation's President, Senator Kennedy stood silently for what seemed a long moment, opening one volume after another and swiftly scanning the contents while the warm applause from the audience of around 1,000 persons rose and then slowly died away. When he spoke it was obviously without the aid of notes or text; he spoke deliberately, softly, but with the familiar Kennedy inflection—and the unmistakable Kennedy grace.

"I want to just tell you," the Senator began, "how appreciative and how grateful I am to you for this presentation to the John F. Kennedy Memorial Library. As I look over these books with your names in them—the documents on the right of the blind to organize, and then the correspondence that President Kennedy had with some of your officers—it brings back to my mind once again the strong feeling of affection and admiration that President Kennedy had for you and for your efforts—both after he became President, and prior to that time when he was a senator from the state of Massachusetts....

"A Greek philosopher once wrote; 'What joy is there in day that follows day, some swift, some slow, with death the only goal?' What we are interested in—those of you that are here, and those of us who are in the Senate of the United States, who feel strongly about this problem—is to make sure that you can live out your lives making a contribution to society, and live your lives in dignity.

"I think back to the time when I was Attorney General," he went on. "Two of the best lawyers in the Civil Rights Division, two of the lawyers who did almost more than anyone else to bring rights to all of our citizens, were persons who were blind. It might come as a surprise to many people in the United States that the man in charge of surveying and studying the records within the Civil Rights Division—records that have to be so carefully appraised— that all this was done under the direction and control of a man who is blind.

"So I know from personal experience what kind of a contribution those who are blind can make—what a difference they can make in a department of the government, what a difference they can make in an agency, what a difference they can really make in industry and labor.

"So I join with you," the Senator concluded, "first in thanking you for your recognition of President Kennedy's interest in you and your organization. And I also say that that interest is not ended: that this is a recognition of the past because of what we intend to accomplish in the future.

"And in that effort, in what you are trying to do—both as individuals and as officers of this organization—I want to pledge to you the help and assistance of the junior senator from the state of New York. Thank you very much."

Another memorable moment in the course of the historic 1965 convention occurred when Hubert Humphrey, then Vice President of the United States, was honored in a special ceremony as recipient of the Federation's Newel Perry Award. In receiving the award Humphrey reminded the delegates that this was his third meeting with the organized blind: "Eighteen years ago, as mayor of Minneapolis, I welcomed your members to that great city for your seventh annual convention. Five years ago, as a U.S. Senator from Minnesota, I attended another very enthusiastic convention—your state convention in Minnesota. And today I am proud to meet with you again, proud to receive your plaque, to greet so many old, dear friends, and I hope to make new ones."

Vice President Humphrey then said: "Today the nation is fulfilling many of the hopes, yes, the visions, of your own Federation and of other pioneering organizations. Your great founder Jacobus tenBroek had this vision. He had a gift of foresight—which others who had the blessing of physical sight did not possess....Your Federation has compiled a remarkable and fruitful record—nationally, in the states, cities, and rural areas. You have brought hope to countless thousands of the blind, where before there had been so much hopelessness. You have encouraged self-help by the blind in place of dependency. Your Federation has taken many steps forward. You have come a long way. And I regard it as a great honor to have walked with you and worked with you. Long may the Federation flourish in its service, in its leadership. Long may the courageous blind help to lead a courageous America to a better life for all."

With those words, and waving aloft his Newel Perry plaque, Hubert Humphrey took leave of the Washington convention—giving way to a parade of other orators and luminaries. Among them was the Federation's own First Vice President, Kenneth Jernigan, who took full advantage of the massive turnout of congressmen and politicians in the audience to deliver a major address on a subject of perennial importance (and one to which he would return frequently at future conventions): that of the needless social handicap imposed upon the blind, not by their own physical condition but by the misconceptions of the public. In effect Jernigan turned his speech into a seminar on blindness, proclaiming the Federationist doctrine that blind persons are only normal people who can't see—not abnormal people who can't function. But he demonstrated that the very words we use—starting with the word *blind*—and the very concepts we form out of these words, like the concept of the "helpless blind," carry a freight of unacknowledged connotations which become stumbling blocks on the road to independence.

Here is the text of that speech:

BLINDNESS—CONCEPTS AND MISCONCEPTIONS
by Kenneth Jernigan

When an individual becomes blind, he faces two major problems: First, he must learn the skills and techniques which will enable him to carry on as a normal, productive citizen in the community; and second, he must become aware of and learn to cope with public attitudes and misconceptions about blindness—attitudes and misconceptions which go to the very roots of our culture and permeate every aspect of social behavior and thinking.

The first of these problems is far easier to solve than the second. For it is no longer theory but established fact that, with proper training and opportunity, the *average* blind person can do the *average* job in the *average* place of business—and do it as well as his sighted neighbor. The blind can function as scientists, farmers, electricians, factory workers, and skilled technicians. They can perform as housewives, lawyers, teachers, or laborers. The skills of independent mobility, communication, and the activities of daily living are known, available, and acquirable. Likewise, the achievement of vocational competence poses no insurmountable barrier.

In other words the real problem of blindness is not the blindness itself—not the acquisition of skills or techniques or competence. The real problem is the lack of understanding and the misconceptions which exist. It is no accident that the word *blind* carries with it connotations of inferiority and helplessness. The concept undoubtedly goes back to primitive times when existence was at an extremely elemental level. Eyesight and the power to see were equated with light, and light (whether daylight or firelight) meant security and safety. Blindness was equated with darkness, and darkness meant danger and evil. The blind person could not hunt effectively or dodge a spear. In our day, society and social values have changed. In civilized countries there is now no great premium on dodging a spear, and hunting has dwindled to the status of an occasional pastime. The blind are able to compete on terms of equality in the full current of active life. The primitive conditions of jungle and cave are gone, but the primitive attitudes about blindness remain. The blind are thought to live in a world of "darkness," and darkness is equated with evil, stupidity, sin, and inferiority.

Do I exaggerate? I would that it were so. Consider the very definition of the word *blind,* the reflection of what it means in the language, its subtle shades and connotations. The 1962 printing of the World Publishing Company's college edition of *Webster's New World Dictionary of the American Language* defines *blind* as follows: "without the power of sight; sightless; eyeless; lacking insight or understanding; done without adequate directions or knowledge; as, blind search. Reckless; unreasonable; not controlled by intelligence; as, blind destiny; insensible; drunk; illegible; indistinct. In *architecture*, false, walled up, as, a *blind* window." The 1960 edition of *Webster's New Collegiate Dictionary* says: "blind. Sightless. Lacking discernment; unable or unwilling to understand or judge; as, a *blind* choice. Apart from intelligent direction or control; as, *blind* chance. Insensible; as, a *blind* stupor; hence, drunk. For sightless persons; as, a *blind* asylum. Unintelligible; illegible; as, *blind* writing."

There are a number of reasons why it is extremely difficult to change public attitudes about blindness. For one thing, despite the fact that many achievements are being made by the blind and that a good deal of constructive publicity is being given to these achievements, there are strong countercurrents of uninformed and regressive publicity and propaganda. It is hard to realize, for instance, that anyone still exists who actually believes the blind are especially gifted in music or that they are particularly suited to weaving or wickerwork. It is hard to realize that any well-educated person today believes that blind people are compensated for their loss of sight by special gifts and talents. Yet, I call your attention to a section on blindness appearing in a book on government and citizenship which is in current use in many public high schools throughout our country. Not in some bygone generation, but today, hundreds of thousands of ninth-grade students will study this passage:

Caring for the Handicapped

The blind, the deaf, the dumb, the crippled, and the insane and the feeble-minded are sometimes known collectively as the *defective*—people who are lacking some
normal faculty or power. Such people often need to be
placed in some special institution in order to receive
proper attention.

Many blind, deaf, and crippled people can do a considerable amount of work. The blind have remarkable talent
in piano tuning, weaving, wickerwork, and the like. The
deaf and dumb are still less handicapped because they
can engage in anything that does not require taking or
giving orders by voice.[1]

I confess to being surprised when I learned that the book containing the foregoing passage was in general use. It occurred to
me to wonder whether the text was unique or whether its "enlightened" views were held by other authors in the field. The
results of my investigation were not reassuring. I call your attention to the selection on blindness appearing in another text in
common use throughout the high schools of our nation.

The blind may receive aid from the states and the federal
government, if their families are not able to keep them
from want. There are over one hundred institutions for
the blind in the United States, many of which are supported wholly or partly by taxes. Sometimes it seems as
if blind people are partly compensated for their misfortune by having some of their other talents developed with
exceptional keenness. Blind people can play musical instruments as well as most of those who can see, and many
activities where a keen touch of the fingers is needed can
be done by blind people wonderfully well. Schools for the
blind teach their pupils music and encourage them to
take part in some of the outdoor sports that other pupils
enjoy.[2]

If this is not enough to make the point, let me give you a quotation from still another high school text in current use:

Kinds of Dependents

There are many persons who do not take a regular part
in community life and its affairs, either because they cannot or will not. Those who cannot may be divided into

the following classes—(1) *"The physically handicapped"*: the blind, the deaf, and the crippled; (2) *the mentally handicapped*: the feeble-minded and the insane; (3) *the unemployed*: those incapable of work, the misfits, and the victims of depression; and (4) *the orphaned*: those children left in the care of the state or in private institutions. The community should care for these people or help them to care for themselves as much as possible.

Those who will not play their part in community life are the criminals. Schools have been established where the blind are taught to read by the use of raised letters called the Braille system. They are also taught to do other things such as to weave, make brushes, tune pianos, mend and repair furniture, and to play musical instruments. It is far better for the blind to attend these institutions than to remain at home because here they can learn to contribute to their own happiness.[3]

In attempting to change public attitudes, not only must we overcome the effects of Webster's dictionary and a host of textbooks, but we must take into account another factor as well. Several years ago the agency that I head was attempting to help a young woman find employment as a secretary. She was a good typist, could fill out forms, handle erasures, take dictation, and otherwise perform competently. She was neat in her person and could travel independently anywhere she wanted to go. She was also totally blind. I called the manager of a firm which I knew had a secretarial opening and asked him if he would consider interviewing the blind person in question. He told me that he knew of the "wonderful work" which blind persons were doing and that he was most "sympathetic" to our cause but that his particular setup would not be suitable. As he put it, "Our work is very demanding. Carbons must be used and forms must be filled out. Speed is at a premium, and a great deal of work must be done each day. Then, there is the fact that our typewriters are quite a ways from the bathroom, and we cannot afford to use the time of another girl to take the blind person to the toilet."

At this stage I interrupted to tell him that during the past few years new travel techniques had been developed and that the girl I had in mind was quite expert in getting about, that she was able to go anywhere she wished with ease and independence. He came back with an interruption of his own.

"Oh, I know what a *wonderful* job the blind do in traveling about and accomplishing things for themselves. You see I know a blind person. I know Miss X, and I know what a good traveler she is and how competent." I continued to try to persuade him, but I knew my case was lost. For, you see, I also know Miss X, and she is one of the poorest travelers and one of the most helpless blind people I have ever known. There is a common joke among many blind persons that she gets lost in her own bedroom, and I guess maybe she does.

The man with whom I was talking was not being insincere; far from it. He thought that the ordinary blind person, by all reason and common sense, should be completely helpless and unable to travel at all. He thought that it was wonderful and remarkable that the woman he knew could do as well as she did. When compared with what he thought could normally be expected of the blind, her performance was outstanding. Therefore, when I told him that the person that I had in mind could travel independently, he thought that I meant the kind of travel he had seen from Miss X. We were using the same words, and we were both sincere, but our words meant different things to each of us. I tremble to think what he thought I meant by "good typing" and "all-around competence."

When I go into a community to speak to a group and someone says to me, "Oh I know exactly what you mean; I know what blind people can do, because I know a blind person," I often cringe. I say to myself, "And what kind of blind person do you know?"

This gives emphasis (if, indeed, emphasis is needed) to the constantly observed truth that all blind people are judged by one. If a person has known a blind man who is especially gifted as a musician, he is likely to believe that all of the blind are good at music. Many of us are living examples of the fallacy of that misconception. Some years ago I knew a man who had hired a blind person in his place of business. The blind man was, incidentally, fond of the bottle and was (after, no doubt, a great deal of soul searching on the part of the employer) fired. The employer still refuses to consider hiring another blind person. As he puts it, "They simply drink too much."

Once I was attending a national convention made up largely of blind people, and a waitress in the hotel dining room said to me, "I just think it is wonderful how happy blind people are. I have been observing you folks, and you all seem to be having such a good time!"

I said to the waitress, "But did you ever observe a group of sighted conventioneers! When they get away from their homes and the routine of daily life, they usually let their hair down and relax a bit. Blind people are about as happy and about as unhappy as anybody else."

Not only is there a tendency to judge all blind people by one, but there is also a tendency to judge all blind people by the least effective and least competent members of the larger, sighted population. In other words, if it can't be done by a person with sight, a "normal person," then, how can it possibly be done by a blind person? One of the best illustrations of this point that I have ever seen occurred some time ago when an attempt was being made to secure employment for a blind man in a corn oil factory. The job involved the operation of a press into which a large screw-type plunger fed corn. Occasionally the press would jam, and it was necessary for the operator to shut it off and clean it out before resuming the operation. The employer had tentatively agreed to hire the blind man, but when we showed up to finalize the arrangements, the deal was off. The employer explained that since our last visit, one of his sighted employees had got his hand caught in the press, and the press had chewed it off. It developed that the sighted employee had been careless. When the press had jammed, he had not shut it off, but had tried to clean it while it was still running. The employer said, "This operation is dangerous! Why, even a sighted man got hurt doing it! I simply couldn't think of hiring a blind man in this position!" It was to no avail that we urged and reasoned. We might have told him (but didn't) that if he intended to follow logic, perhaps he should have refused to hire any more sighted people on the operation. After all it wasn't a blind man who had made the mistake.

There is still another factor which makes it difficult to change the public attitudes about blindness. All of us need to feel superior, and the problem is compounded by the fact that almost everyone secretly feels a good deal of insecurity and inadequacy—a good deal of doubt regarding status and position. On more than one occasion people have come to the door of a blind man to collect for the heart fund, cancer research, or some other charity, and have then turned away in embarrassment when they have found they were dealing with a blind person. Their comment is usually to the effect, "Oh, I am sorry! I didn't know! I couldn't take the money from a blind person!" In many instances, I am happy to say, the blind person has insisted on making a contribution. The implication is clear and should not be allowed to go unchallenged. It is that the blind are unable to participate in regular community life, that they should not be expected to assume responsibilities, that they should receive but not give as others do.

More than once I have seen confusion and embarrassment in a restaurant when it came the blind person's turn to treat for coffee or similar items. At the cash register there was an obvious feeling of inappropriateness and shame on the part of the sighted members of the group at having restaurant employees and others see a blind person pay for their food. Something turns, of course, on the question of means; and the blind person should certainly not pay all of the time; but he should do his part like any other member of the group.

Recently I registered at a hotel, and the bellboy carried my bags to my room. When I started to tip him (and it was a fairly generous tip), he moved back out of the way with some embarrassment. He said, "Oh, no, I couldn't! I am a gentleman!" When I persisted he said, "I am simply not that hard up!"

It is of significance to note that he had an amputated hand and that he was quite short of stature. What kind of salary he made I do not know, but I would doubt that it was comparatively very high. His manner and tone and the implication of his words said very clearly, "I may be in a bad way and have it rough, but at least I am more fortunate than you. I am grateful that my situation is not worse than it is." There was certainly no ill intent. In fact, there were both charity and kindness. But charity and kindness are sometimes misplaced, and they are not always constructive forces.

Let me now say something about the agencies and organizations doing work with the blind. Employees and administrators of such agencies are members of the public, too, and are conditioned by the same forces that affect other people in the total population. Some of them (in fact, many) are enlightened individuals who thoroughly understand the problems to be met and who work with vigor and imagination to erase the stereotypes and propagate a new way of thought concerning blindness and its problems; but some of them (unfortunately, far too many) have all the misconceptions and erroneous ideas which characterize the public at large. Regrettably there are still people who go into work with the blind because they cannot be dominant in their homes or social or business lives, and they feel (whether they verbalize it or not) that at least they can dominate and patronize the blind. This urge often expresses itself in charitable works and dedicated sincerity, but this does not mitigate its unhealthy nature or make it any less misguided or inappropriate.

Such agencies are usually characterized by a great deal of talk about "professionalism" and by much high-flown jargon. They believe that blindness is more than the loss of eyesight; that it involves multiple and mysterious personality alterations. Many of them believe that the newly blinded person requires the assistance of a psychiatrist in making the adjustment to blindness, and, indeed, that the psychiatrist and psychotherapy should play an important part in the training programs for the blind. They believe that the blind are a dependent class and that the agencies must take care of them throughout their entire lives. But let some of these people speak for themselves. One agency administrator has said: "After he is once trained and placed, the average disabled person can fend for himself. In the case of the blind, it has been found necessary to set up a special state service agency which will supply them not only rehabilitation training but other services for the rest of their lives." The agencies "keep in constant contact with them as long as they live."

This is not an isolated comment. An agency psychiatrist has this to say: "All visible deformities require special study. Blindness is a visible deformity and all blind persons follow a pattern of dependency."

Or consider this by the author of a well-known book on blindness: "With many persons, there was an expectation in the establishment of the early schools that the blind in general would thereby be rendered capable of earning their own support—a view that even at the present is shared in some quarters. It would have been much better if such a hope had never been entertained, or if it had existed in a greatly modified form. A limited acquaintance of a practical nature with the blind as a whole and their capabilities has usually been sufficient to demonstrate the weakness of this conception."[4]

It cannot be too strongly emphasized that the foregoing quotations represent individual instances and not the total judgment of the agencies and organizations doing work with the blind. Opinions and approaches vary as much with the agencies as with the general public. I would merely make the point here that being a professional worker in the field does not insure one against the false notions and erroneous stereotypes which characterize the public at large.

For that matter, being a blind person is no passport to infallibility either. Public attitudes about the blind too often become the attitudes of the blind. The blind are part of the general public. They tend to see themselves as others see them. They too often accept the public view of their limitations and thus do much to make those limitations a reality. There is probably not a single blind person in the world today (present company included) who has not sold himself short at one time or another.

At one time in my life I ran a furniture shop, making and selling the furniture myself. I designed and put together tables, smoke stands, lamps, and similar items. I sawed and planed, drilled and measured, fitted and sanded. I did every single operation except the final finish work, the staining and varnishing. After all, as I thought, one must be reasonable and realistic. If anyone had come to me at that time and said that I was selling myself short, that I should not automatically assume that a blind person could not do varnishing, I think I would have resented it very much. I think I would have said something to this effect: "I have been blind all my life, and I think I know what a blind person can do; you have to use common sense. You can't expect a blind person to drive a truck, and you can't expect him to varnish furniture either."

Later when I went to California to teach in the state's Orientation Center for the Blind, I saw blind people doing varnishing as a matter of course. By and by I did it myself. I can tell you that the experience caused me to do a great deal of serious thinking. It was not the fact that I had hired someone else to do the varnishing in those earlier days in my shop. Perhaps it would have been more efficient, under any circumstances, for me to have hired this particular operation done so that I could spend my time more profitably. It was the fact that I had automatically assumed that a blind person could not do the work, that I had sold myself short without realizing it, all the while believing myself to be a living exemplification of progressive faith in the competence of the blind—a most deflating experience. It made me wonder then, as it does today: How many things that I take for granted as being beyond the competence of the blind are easily within reach? How many things that I now regard as requiring eyesight really require only insight, an insight which I do not possess because of the conditioning I have received from my culture, and because of the limitations of my imagination?

There is also the temptation to have our cake and eat it too, the temptation to accept the special privileges or shirk the responsibility when it suits us and then to demand equal treatment when we want it.

Some years ago when Boss Ed Crump was supreme in Memphis, an interesting event occurred each year. There was an annual football game, which was called the "ball game for the blind." Incidentally, Mr. Crump also conducted an annual watermelon-slicing for the Negro. With respect to the "ball game for the blind," Mr. Crump's friends went about contacting the general public and all of the businesses of the area soliciting donations and purchases of tickets. Probably a good deal of arm-twisting and shaming were done when necessary. The total take was truly impressive. In the neighborhood of one hundred thousand dollars was raised each year. The money was then equally divided among all known blind persons in the county, and a check was sent to each. It usually amounted to about one hundred dollars and was known as the "Christmas bonus for the blind."

Most of the blind whom I knew from Shelby County gladly received these checks, and most of the rest of us in the state (either secretly or openly) envied them their great good fortune. How short-sighted we all were! The blind people of Memphis were not being done a favor! They were being robbed of a birthright. As they gave their money and bought their tickets, how many businessmen closed their minds (although without conscious thought) to the possibility of a blind employee? How many blind people traded equal status in the community, social and civic acceptance, and productive and remunerative employment for one hundred dollars a year? What a bargain!

As I said in the beginning, the real problem of blindness is not the loss of eyesight but the misconceptions and misunderstandings which exist. The public (whether it be the general public, the agencies, or the blind themselves) has created the problem and must accept the responsibility for solving it. In fact, great strides are being made in this direction.

First must come awareness, awareness on the part of the blind themselves, and a thorough consistency of philosophy and dedication of purpose; an increasing program of public education must be waged; vigilance must be maintained to see that the agencies for the blind are staffed with the right kind of people; with the right kind of philosophy; and the movement of self-organization of the blind must be encouraged and strengthened. This last is a cardinal point, for any disadvantaged group must be heard with its own voice, must lead in the achievement of its own salvation.

Accomplishments are made of dreams and drudgeries, of hope and hard work. The blind of the nation are now moving toward a destiny, a destiny of full equality and full participation in community life.

That destiny will be achieved when the day comes on which we can say with pleasure and satisfaction what we must now say with concern and consternation: "Public attitudes about the blind become the attitudes of the blind. The blind see themselves as others see them."

FOOTNOTES

1. McCrocklin, James, *Building Citizenship* (1961, Allyn and Bacon, Inc., pub.; Boston), p. 244.

2. Hughes, R. O., *Good Citizenship* (1949, Allyn and Bacon, pub.; Boston), p. 55.

3. Blough, G. L., and David S. Switzer, and Jack T. Johnson, *Fundamentals of Citizenship* (Laidlow Brothers, pub.; Chicago), pp. 164-167.

4. From an address entitled "Within the Grace of God" by Professor Jacobus tenBroek, delivered at the 1956 convention of the National Federation of the Blind in San Francisco.

If the silver anniversary convention of 1965 was a high point on the Federation's road to revival and reconstruction, the next year's convention held in Louisville provided the decisive confirmation of the movement's full recovery. It came with the restoration to the presidency of the man who had held that office for 21 years before relinquishing it in 1963. That dramatic and unanticipated event followed the decision of Russell Kletzing, the incumbent National Federation of the Blind President, to step down. Following his formal announcement to that effect at the close of the presidential report, the convention hall buzzed with speculation and wonderment. Here is how the *Braille Monitor* reported the episode:

CONVENTION ACCLAIMS tenBROEK AS PRESIDENT

"Because of my unbounded faith in you, I am gratified to find that you have some faith in me."

With these words, Professor Jacobus tenBroek resumed the office of President of the National Federation of the Blind which he had previously held for 21 years after the organization's founding in 1940.

Thus occurred the high point of the 1966 convention and one of the highlights of 26 years of Federation history. This dramatic and wholly unexpected event followed the decision of Russell Kletzing, the Federation's President for the past four years, not to be a candidate for re-election—a decision reached earlier and informally made known to many delegates as they arrived at the convention. It thus came as no surprise when Russ declared at the conclusion of his President's Report on the first afternoon of the convention that because of the growing requirements of his professional career and of his family he would not run again.

Ken Jernigan, as the man whom informal discussion among the delegates had generally singled out as the obvious successor to the office, then took the floor in an atmosphere of mounting suspense.

"Mr. President," he began, "I wish to make a brief statement and a motion." As the tension in the audience rose still further, Ken went on to say that at the urging of other Federation leaders he himself had given serious consideration to permitting his own name to be placed in nomination for the presidency but "I have never felt right about it." For him it was proper to be Dr. tenBroek's "chief lieutenant but not his chief."

"During the last few days," Jernigan continued, "and again this morning, in this hotel, I discussed with Dr. tenBroek the reasons why he, our founder and leader, ought to run for the presidency at this time. Those shattering and best forgotten days of the civil war are over; and his spirit, his integrity, his value are now needed more than ever to carry us to new heights of unity and accomplishment—but not as President Emeritus—rather, as President."

Observing that Dr. tenBroek "this morning gave me a decision that permits this motion now," Ken went on to say "again that I will do everything that I can to assist Dr. tenBroek in the years ahead and that if the time comes when he cannot or will not allow his name to be placed in nomination for the presidency, I will definitely be a candidate for that office."

He then moved that the convention "unanimously, by acclamation, elect as its President Jacobus tenBroek."

There followed a demonstration the like of which Federationists had not experienced before—unless it was on that other memorable occasion five years earlier when Professor tenBroek announced his resignation and retirement from the presidency. On both occasions the response of the delegates was not one merely of volume but of the expression of intense feelings. It was one of those rare times about which one can say truly that there was not a dry eye in the assemblage.

"There is no doubt of the sense of this convention," exclaimed Russ Kletzing after some minutes of demonstration. "President tenBroek, will you please come up here?"

The first extemporaneous words of the newly acclaimed leader of the National Federation reflected the mood of the gathering; "A man ought not to come to these conventions unless he has a strong heart.

"We have lived together and worked together for a long time now, and most of you know that I'm a sentimental fellow. Because of my unbounded faith in you, I'm gratified to find that you have some faith in me.

"I saw Don Capps a little while ago and he said, as he has regularly for the past five years; 'You wouldn't be interested in being President, would you?' I replied. 'Do you think I'm mad?' And he said, 'Well, I suspect that you've had that kind of madness all the time I've known you.'

"It is a kind of madness," Dr. tenBroek continued. "A man, having once undertaken the burdens and responsibilities of this office, ought really in good sense not to be eager to shoulder them again.

"But as is true of you, so also it is true of me that the Federation gets in one's blood. In this movement we have a great cause to carry forward and to work for. It is not just a matter of our personal feelings and our private lives, if we have some sense of responsibility to others, some sense of obligation to contribute whatever we can to improve the lot of our fellows."

President tenBroek went on to speak of the work of Jernigan and Kletzing and of fruitful collaboration with them over the years.

He gaveled his first presidential session to adjournment with the request that the delegates give Russ Kletzing a standing ovation for his performance as President during the past four years.

The session ended with the delegates on their feet, applauding and cheering.

Shortly after the 1966 convention, Dr. tenBroek learned that he had cancer; and it was not much longer before it would prove to be incurable. Nevertheless, as Kenneth Jernigan was to say of him later: "He came to the 1967 convention in Los Angeles in high good humor and tranquillity. It was his last. There are many who say it was his greatest. When he rose to make the banquet address, it seemed a fitting climax and valedictory."

That valedictory speech of President tenBroek was sharply focused and pointedly addressed. Whereas, two years before, at the silver anniversary convention, he had reviewed the full sweep of the movement's history and accomplishments, now he concentrated upon a single troubled phase of its career: namely, the present state of its relations with the agencies in the field. Dr. tenBroek's address left no doubt of his conviction that the conflict of the organized blind with the agencies claiming dominion over them was the paramount issue of the period—the outcome of which would decide the fate of blind Americans, individually and collectively, for many years to come.

"The blind have a right to live in the world," he declared. "That right is as deep as human nature; as pervasive as the need for social existence; as ubiquitous as the human race; as invincible as the human spirit. As their souls are their own, so their destiny must be their own." But Dr. tenBroek went on to assert that "this bedrock right is challenged directly by many agencies...not only by their actions but by their words." He therefore posed the fundamental issue in the form of a blunt question to the organized blind: "Are We Equal to the Challenge?"

Following is the text of President tenBroek's final banquet address as delivered before that 1967 convention at Los Angeles:

ARE WE EQUAL TO THE CHALLENGE?
by Jacobus tenBroek

When last we met together in this Golden State—eleven years ago, in that "other California" whose unofficial capital is San Francisco—I delivered another banquet address which I dare say some of our grizzled members still remember. It was entitled "Within the Grace of God." It was frankly a fighting speech, and I'd like for a moment to recall to your minds and memories what the fight was all about.

That 1956 speech was principally concerned with the development of our movement—the organized blind movement of the United States—and with the relations of that movement with the private voluntary agencies, and combinations of agencies, in the field of work for the blind.

The state of our relations with the agencies, at that turbulent point of our history, can be briefly characterized. It was a state of war. We were in fact the targets of concerted opposition—both nationally and within many of our affiliated states. The purpose of that attack was to break up the organized blind movement and return its members to the alienation, dependency, and disorganization of the status quo ante bellum—that is, the good old days before the blind were organized.

Among other things, that agency opposition took the form of a verbal campaign directed against the basic premises and pillars of our movement. In editorials, speeches, books and broadsides, authoritative spokesmen for major agencies reminded the blind over and over of their legendary "lacks and losses"—their irremediable dependency, their emotional imbalance, their obvious inequality, their desperate need for professional guidance and custodial care until their dying day—or, alternatively, until that future golden age, as one agency director expressed it, "when each and every blind person is a living advertisement of his ability and capacity to accept the privileges and responsibilities of citizenship."

Now we are together again in California—eleven years after. How goes the battle today? How do we stand now in relation to the agencies?

Before confronting those questions, let it be understood that our embattled relationship with the agencies is only one phase of a many-sided movement of the blind reaching toward integration, equality, and independence. It goes hand in hand with our struggle to improve life and livelihood through legislative action—national, state, and local. It has its counterpart also in the arena of the courtroom, where dramatic struggles against discrimination and exclusion continue to be fought—alternately won and lost and won again. On still another front we are engaged in positive relationships with other groups and associations, in particular those of the disabled, the disadvantaged and the deprived. Our concern must always be with the lame and the halt as well as with the blind! And then there is our own domestic front: the internal order of the Federation, with its constantly renewed challenges of diversity and democracy.

On all these fronts and more, we are called upon to devote our fullest energies and creative efforts toward the discovery of new solutions to changing issues and evolving needs. But in each of these areas, the agencies loom as both a fact of our lives and a factor in our planning. Nor is this a peculiar problem of blind Americans. Elsewhere in the world—everywhere else in the world—much the same tense and tortuous relationship exists. It exists, to be sure, at different stages and in various forms. In many countries of Europe, although rear-guard battles are still being fought, the course of the struggle has long since been determined. The pattern has been one, not of extinction of the agencies, but of their conquest and assimilation. The blind people of Europe have organized themselves and have taken over the agencies.

In England, on the other hand, almost alone of the principal European nations, the battle continues to rage unabated. There a large national organization of the blind stands on the battle line against an entrenched and powerful agency and its satellites. It is an unequal struggle, though far from one-sided; and the organized blind of Great Britain have no early hope of carrying out the continental pattern. Rather they seek to secure their goals through increasing governmentalization, thereby gradually superseding the voluntary societies by having the government take over their vested interests.

In Canada the story is perhaps the saddest and sorriest of all. In that northern clime an agency colossus bestrides the world of the blind from coast to coast, making free use of company-union tactics wherever any independent sentiment dares to express itself among the disorganized blind. Only a handful of undaunted spirits remain to hold the banner aloft in the deserted battlefield. Still a different pattern exists in some European countries, and especially those beyond the Iron Curtain, where large national organizations of the blind exist, apparently dominant in their field. There, for the most part, private agencies and voluntary societies are virtually nonexistent but the question remains whether the blind organizations are genuinely self-determined and self-directing or only the passive instruments of governmental policy and action. If the flow of communication is truly from the blind to the government, as well as the other way around, if there is genuine dialogue and not just authoritarian monologue, then in those lands the three-cornered struggle among the blind, the agencies, and the government has been resolved into a two-sided partnership. Let us hope that this is indeed the case.

In the United States, meanwhile, the wheel of fortune has not yet turned so far. The private agencies and voluntary societies are very much in evidence, as powerful as they are visible. Are they our collaborators or our calumniators? When the agency official passes by, who goes there: friend or foe?

The answer today, no less than eleven years ago, must be qualified and doubtful. There are agencies aplenty marching with us, fully attuned to our aspirations and activities, alert to our petitions, admiring of our programs. Doubtless too, their numbers have grown since 1956. But there are also large and powerful agencies abroad in the land, considerable in number and vast in influence, which remain hostile to our movement in thought, in speech, and in action.

And the worst of these, it may well be, is the newest: namely, COMSTAC. For COMSTAC seeks to impose upon the blind not less but more authority and custody than ever before. Under the guise of professionalism, it would perpetuate colonialism. Its philosophy is a throwback to the age of the silent client, before the revolution in welfare and civil rights which converted the client into an active and vocal partner in the programming and dispensing of services. In its lofty disregard of the organized blind as the voice of those to be served, COMSTAC betrays its bureaucratic bias—that is, its distorted image of the blind client not as a *person* to be *served* but as a defective mechanism to be *serviced*.

Nowhere is the relationship between blind Americans and the social agencies more distressing or scandalizing than in the sheltered workshops where the relationship is one of pervasive exploitation on the one hand and an elemental struggle for survival on the other. Here the normal dignity of worker-management relations is not to be found; on the contrary, blind shop workers find themselves regarded not as workers but as wards, not as visually disabled simply, but as emotionally disturbed as well. They have been denied the status of organized labor, denied the right to strike, denied even the protection of minimum wage standards given as a matter of course to other workers.

The inmates of the St. Louis Lighthouse have been out on strike since last March, in spite of these deprivations—just for the right to sit down and talk with the lighthouse-keepers. Other strikes have broken out across the country as blind shop workers have decided to stand up and speak out. Because of this rebellious spirit, this show of backbone, they are beginning to make progress. But their gains are coming, step by painful step, against the bitter-end opposition of the overseers in what must still be designated the sheltered *sweatshops* of America.

This condition of cold war between agencies and the organized blind is being waged with particular force and fury within the World Council for the Welfare of the Blind at whose gates the organized blind of nation after nation have come knocking and have either been turned away or relegated to second-class membership. The American blind, through the NFB, have battled for years to occupy the seat that is rightfully theirs upon the World Council's executive board and to gain equal representation with the agencies, but have been spurned, insulted, and ignored. The effort of the organized blind of Australia to gain a single place in that country's delegation to the World Council, long opposed by the controlling agencies within Australia, has now been blocked by a ruling of the World Council that the organized blind need not be represented at all.

The rationalization for this action and this attitude is contained in a 1964 resolution enacted by the World Council as a compromise to stave off a motion by the NFB. That resolution states that "where in any country there exists a substantial group of blind persons organized into associations and where there are blind *persons* occupying leading positions in agencies for the blind, adequate provision should be made for their representation in the national delegation." The emphasis is upon blind persons, wherever they may be, and not upon the difference between elective associations of blind people, on the one hand, and professional agencies on the other. The lack of distinction is significant; for it treats alike the roles of the agency professional and the elected representative of a democratic group. If the confusion of roles is honest, it reflects a profound ignorance of democracy; if it is disingenuous, it reflects a shocking contempt for democracy.

What is the difference between the two roles? I have been informed by many earnest persons, all of them agency officials, to be sure, that the difference is negligible, but that what little difference there is favors the agency professional. For if he is blind himself, then does he not know the experience of blindness as well as any elected leader? And since he is a trained professional, does he not know social policies and programs better? And, finally, cannot the professional administrator consult his clients as much as any elective fellow and having spoken *with* them qualify to speak *for* them?

These seem plausible arguments on the surface but they convey an astonishing misconception of the democratic process and its meaning. Put aside the fact that there are elected blind leaders who possess at least a modicum of knowledge of the welfare field, and appointed agency officials who possess little. That is beside the real point which is that in a democracy the proper role of the expert and the professional is not to govern, not to rule, but to advise the governors; it is not to make policy decisions but only to implement them. An engineer may tell us how to build a highway; what he cannot do is to make the decision for us whether we should build the highway or whether we should build instead a college, a ball park, or a civic center. The sharpest lesson of democracy is that no professional elite or caste, administrative or military or scientific, must be permitted to usurp the power of the people and their elected representatives to make the decisions of life and liberty, or of life and death.

That the agencies all too often have failed to subordinate the role of the expert is one thing; that they all too often have misconstrued the proper role of the blind is a second thing. But more important than these mistakes is their persisting refusal to acknowledge and accept the elementary principles of humanity and democracy.

The blind have a right to live in the world. That right is as deep as human nature; as pervasive as the need for social existence; as ubiquitous as the human race; as invincible as the human spirit. As their souls are their own, so their destiny must be their own. Their salvation or failure lies within their own choice and responsibility. That choice cannot be precluded or prejudged; those lives cannot be predetermined or controlled. In a democracy the blind have a right to share in the fruits and obligations of the community. They have a right to participate in the decisions that affect their lives and fortunes. And beneath and beyond these democratic rights there is a further one: the right to organize for collective self-expression, and to be represented through their own associations. This, if it does not go without saying, surely goes without disputing.

But no: that basic and bedrock right is challenged directly by many agencies—no less today than a decade ago. Not only by their actions, but by their words, do they stand condemned of throwing stumbling blocks in the path of the blind. I call to your attention an editorial published last September in the *Matilda Ziegler Magazine*, written by its managing editor, Howard M. Liechty, who is also the longtime managing editor of the *New Outlook for the Blind*, the official journal of the American Foundation.

Editor Liechty's editorial is a straightforward, unequivocal, and sweeping attack upon the notion of equality as having any present application to the blind and also upon the effort to move toward *equality* by organized action and legislative reform. "Any attempt to force social equality," writes Editor Liechty, "would mean legislating it, and any thinking man must know that you cannot legislate such a thing of the heart, and force men to accept their fellow men as social equals." And he goes on to quote with favor the words of a former Supreme Court Justice, Charles E. Whittaker, to the effect that no minority group has ever achieved acceptance in America until, "by long years of exemplary conduct, a majority of its members have earned the respect and liking of the people generally."

Well, there you have it. To Editor Liechty today, as to his colleagues a decade ago, the hope of the blind for such peculiar values as full citizenship, individual rights, social acceptance, and human dignity, must continue to be a hope deferred. If anyone should ask how long, oh lords, how long must we be kept waiting, the answer comes back: until by exemplary conduct you have proved your worthiness—all of you together, and each one of you individually.

This requirement so righteously imposed upon the blind, this test of exemplary conduct or good behavior, has a strangely familiar ring. It is the echo of the ancient Poor Law, that separate but unequal body of legal demands and strictures enforced upon the poor, the indigent, and the disabled as the precondition of eligibility for public aid. In scarcely diluted form, these requirements of exemplary conduct are now to be the conditions of eligibility for citizenship itself, not for others, but only for the blind.

To assert, as Editor Liechty does, that the rights of equal opportunity, of equal treatment, and equal access, of participation and expression, cannot be legislatively secured and judicially enforced is to fly in the face of our entire constitutional and political history. It is also to disregard the not inconsiderable history of the organized blind movement from the Kletzing case to the Model White Cane Law.

Of course we cannot be required to love one another; but we can be prevented from expressing our hates, our superstitions, and our prejudices in terms of public law and social policy. We cannot require the sighted to embrace the blind as brothers; but we can stop them from placing obstacles in their path.

We need not suppose that the end of discrimination against the blind will bring an automatic end to prejudice; but we can choose to be guided by the sense of justice, the voice of reason, the commitment to equality, and the passion for freedom which together make up the ancestral faith of American democracy.

Why is it always the defenders of injustice and inequality who cry out against the use of force to bring about change? For it is force they are themselves defending: the force of habit, the force of custom, the force of poor laws and of corrupt institutions. Against this combination of forces there must be brought another and opposing set of forces: the force of conviction, the force of aroused public opinion, the force of responsible government, the force of law.

And why is it, finally, that the means test of "exemplary conduct" always falls upon the *victims* of oppression, exclusion, and discrimination rather than upon the perpetrators? Whose conduct is it that most needs to be challenged and examined? Who is it that should be placed on trial in this case? Is it the blind or is it the men of short vision and little faith, the obsolete custodians of the lighthouse and the sheltered shop, who seek to defend their vested interest by subsidizing the ghost of the helpless blind man?

Through all the years and decades of our existence as an organized movement, for all our splendid success in gaining allies and winning public support, we have faced the persistent opposition of those whom we may call the "hard-core" custodians. The main thrust of their attack upon us has always been that blind people are not ready for equality—not prepared for the burden of freedom—not strong enough to stand upright and walk alone down the main streets of society.

To this denial of equality by the agencies, the organized blind reply: we are not only equal to you—we are equal to your challenge.

Jacobus tenBroek died on March 27, 1968, in Presbyterian Hospital, San Francisco. He was buried in the gently rolling hills not far from Berkeley, overlooking San Francisco Bay and with a lovely view of Mount Tamalpais, a prospect of which he was very fond.

On May 5 of that year a memorial service was held in Berkeley, on the campus of the University of California where Dr. tenBroek had taught for the greater part of his distinguished academic career. The chairman of that memorial assembly was Kenneth Jernigan, who also delivered a eulogy that has come to be generally regarded as the definitive assessment of "the man and the movement." Here is the text of his eulogy:

JACOBUS tenBROEK:
THE MAN AND THE MOVEMENT
by Kenneth Jernigan

If my remarks today were to have a title, it might well be: "Jacobus tenBroek—The Man and the Movement." For the relationship of this man to the organized blind movement, which he brought into being in the United States and around the world, was such that it would be equally accurate to say that the man was the embodiment of the movement or that the movement was the expression of the man.

For tens of thousands of blind Americans over more than a quarter of a century he was leader, mentor, spokesman, and philosopher. He gave to the organized blind movement the force of his intellect and the shape of his dreams. He made it the symbol of a cause barely imagined before his coming: the cause of self-expression, self-direction, and self-sufficiency on the part of blind people. Step by step, year by year, action by action, he made that cause succeed.

There are those who will tell you it all started in Wilkes-Barre, Pennsylvania, in 1940 when the blind of seven states came together to organize. But they are wrong. It started much earlier in the age-old discriminations against the blind, in the social ostracism, the second-class citizenship, and the denial of opportunity—it started in primitive times before the first recorded history, in the feelings of the community at large and the restiveness of the blind, the wish for improvement, the resistance to a system.

Its seeds were there when the first schools for the blind were founded in America in the 1800s, when the first feeble beginnings of rehabilitation occurred in the present century—in the increasing numbers of blind college students, in the ever-expanding agencies established to serve the blind, in the custodialism, the hope, the frustration, the despair, and the courage.

But it also started on July 6, 1911, on the prairies of Alberta, Canada. On that date and in that place was born Jacobus ten-Broek. His father was a strong-willed "renegade" Dutchman who first asserted his own independence by running away from home at seven to become a cabin boy. Over the next thirty years he literally sailed the seven seas and roamed most of the world, but at the ripe age of forty he felt a hankering to settle down. Through devious negotiations with the Dutch community in California he arranged a marriage with a girl whom he met for the first time on their wedding day—and promptly took up homesteading in the rugged Canadian prairies of Alberta. Like his fellow "sodbusters" of that era, Nicolaas tenBroek earned the right to own his section (640 acres) of hard ground through arduous years of clearing and breaking it. But unlike the other homesteaders, who customarily constructed their huts out of the native sod, the elder tenBroek chose to build his home of logs chopped from the tall Alberta timber.

In that primitive, dirt-floor cabin, both Jacobus and his older brother Nicolaas were born. Some years later when the worst edge of grinding poverty had been turned, their father set about erecting the first frame house to be seen in that part of the province. But the rustic log cabin still stands today, hardly the worse for more than a half-century of wear—as a monument to Dutch craftsmanship and North American timber.

One day, seven-year-old Jacobus and a boyhood friend were playing at bows and arrows, taking turns aiming at a roughly constructed bull's eye cut out of a large piece of canvas. On a sudden whim, young tenBroek darted behind the cloth to peer through the hole at his companion. At that moment the other boy released an arrow from his bow—and for once that day the missile was perfectly on target.

The sight of one eye was irrevocably lost to Jacobus tenBroek on that afternoon. Even then, however, had he received prompt and expert medical attention he would have retained the full sight of the other eye. But in rural Alberta in those days, such care was not to be had. Before many years had gone by Jacobus was totally blind.

Perhaps it required the challenge of blindness to get his "Dutch" up. At any rate, the stubborn streak of independence he had inherited from both parents, coupled with a spartan upbringing on a prairie homestead prevented any lapse into helplessness or self-pity. The family decided to move back to California so that Jacobus could enroll in the California School for the Blind. Following this schooling he enrolled in the University of California, where he graduated with highest honors and went on to win the Order of the Coif at the University Law School.

In 1937 he won what he was to consider his greatest triumph: the hand of his wife Hazel. The three children and the happy life which followed gave evidence to the wisdom of that judgment.

The question has been put before: What if that fateful arrow had never flown? But the arrow did fly and the results are a matter of history. Jacobus tenBroek went on to earn five college degrees, including a doctorate from Harvard and another from the University of California. He became a brilliant teacher and scholar, a renowned author, and a prominent authority in the field of social welfare. He also became the founder and leader of the National Federation of the Blind. From the very beginning the organization was active, tumultuous, dynamic, inspiring. It struggled, prospered, had civil war, and rebuilt. And through it all, one man was a central figure—Jacobus tenBroek. His enemies called him a tyrant and hated him. His friends called him Chick and loved him.

I first met Chick in 1952, when the Federation was twelve years old. From that time until his death he was my closest friend—my teacher, companion, counselor, colleague, and brother. I worked with him in good times and in bad, and had occasion to know him in every conceivable kind of situation. He could be harsh and quick of temper, but he could also be gentle, considerate, and generous. He was the greatest man I have ever known.

When he began the Federation in 1940 the plight of the blind was sorry, indeed. To start any organization at all was a monumental effort. It involved finding and stimulating blind people, licking stamps and cranking the mimeograph machine, finding funds and resources, and doing battle with the agencies bent on perpetuating custodialism.

When I came on the scene in 1952, the Federation was a growing concern. The convention was held in New York that year, and we had our first nationwide coverage—a fifteen minute tenBroek speech. The early and mid-fifties were a time of growth and harmony for the organized blind movement. New states were joining the Federation; money was coming into the treasury; and we established our magazine, the *Braille Monitor*. By 1956 the organization had reached full maturity. Almost a thousand delegates gathered at San Francisco to hear a classic statement of the hopes, purposes and problems of the blind. It was Dr. tenBroek's banquet address, "Within the Grace of God." His addresses the following year at New Orleans—"The Cross of Blindness" and "The Right of the Blind to Organize"—were equally cogent.

Shortly after the New Orleans convention smoldering sparks of conflict within the Federation flamed into open civil war. The three succeeding conventions—Boston in 1958, Santa Fe in 1959, and Miami in 1960—left the organization in virtual ruin. What had been a great crusade had now become a bickering political movement. Unity was gone; and although the overwhelming majority of the members still believed in the leadership of Dr. tenBroek, they seemed unable to mobilize themselves to meet this new type of challenge. The opposition established a magazine, calling it the "Free Press." There were character assassinations, charges and counter-charges. When Dr. tenBroek rose to speak to the delegates at the Kansas City convention in 1961, his voice was weary, and his words carried sorrow and defeat. He cited two lists of occurrences during the preceding year—things the Federation had done, and things that had been done to the Federation—by its own disruptive faction from within. He said that he had undergone extreme and bitter personal attack, aimed at destroying his career and his reputation. "They have called me a Hitler," he said, "a Stalin, and a Mussolini. They have compared me to Caesar." He then told the audience that he felt that he had no choice but to resign. As he talked, the dissenters shifted uneasily in their seats, the majority wept. When he finished, I walked off of that stage with him and it seemed to me as if the organized blind movement might be finished.

But the Federation did not die. From those dark days of 1961 it rallied. The resignation of Dr. tenBroek seemed to galvanize the members into action. The dissenters were expelled. Renewal and rebirth began. The 1962 convention at Detroit was a welcome contrast to the four which had preceded it. Although Dr. tenBroek was not the President, he was still the spiritual leader of the movement. This fact was made clear by his reception throughout the meeting and, particularly, at the banquet, where he delivered the principal address.

In 1965 the Federation met in the nation's Capitol. The convention was tumultuous, enthusiastic. The Vice President of the United States spoke, as did the Speaker of the House and numerous others. The climax came at the banquet when more than one hundred congressmen and senators came to the packed hotel ballroom to hear one of the truly great tenBroek speeches.

In the history of every movement there are crucial events and landmark years. 1966 was such for the Federation. When the delegates met at Louisville, there was an air of expectancy. On the afternoon of the first day, President Russell Kletzing rose to make his report. He summarized the past four years of organizational development and concluded by saying that he would not be a candidate for re-election. Then it was moved that Dr. tenBroek be elected to the presidency by acclamation. There was pandemonium. As on that other day in Kansas City, the majority wept. It was a day of complete rededication and renewal.

This was in July. In August Dr. tenBroek learned that he had cancer. The surgery which followed brought hope, waiting, and ultimate disappointment. As the year progressed and the pain grew, the end seemed inevitable. He came to the 1967 convention at Los Angeles in high good humor and tranquillity. It was his last. There are many who say it was his greatest. When he rose to make the banquet address, it seemed a fitting climax and valedictory.

In the fall of 1967 surgery was again necessary. The cancer was widespread and incurable. On March 27, 1968, Jacobus tenBroek died. During his years he lived more and accomplished more than most men ever can or do. He was the source of love for his family, joy for his friends, consternation for his opponents, and hope for the disadvantaged. He moved the blind from immobility to action, from silence to expression, from degradation to dignity—and through that movement he moved a nation.

No greater summation of his philosophy can be given than his own concluding words in his speech "Within the Grace of God."

> In the sixteenth century John Bradford made a famous remark which has ever since been held up to us as a model of Christian humility and great charity. Seeing a beggar in his rags, creeping along a wall through a flash of lightening in a stormy night, Bradford said: "But for the Grace of God, there go I." Compassion was shown; pity was shown; charity was shown; humility was shown; there was even an acknowledgment that the relative positions of the two could and might have been switched. Yet despite the compassion, despite the pity, despite the charity, despite the humility, how insufferably arrogant! There was still an unbridgeable gulf between Bradford and the beggar. They were not one but two. Whatever

might have been, Bradford thought himself Bradford and the beggar a beggar—one high, the other low; one wise, the other misguided; one strong, the other weak; one virtuous, the other depraved.

We do not and we cannot take the Bradford approach. It is not just that beggary is the badge of our past and is still all too often the present symbol of social attitudes towards us; although that is at least part of it. But in the broader sense, we are that beggar, and he is each of us. We are made in the same image and of the same ingredients. We have the same weaknesses and strengths, the same feelings, emotions, and drives; and we are products of the same social, economic, and other environmental forces. How much more consonant with the facts of individual and social life, how much more a part of true humanity, to say instead: "There, within the Grace of God, do go I."

So Chick spoke in a graphic pronouncement. On another occasion he said: "Movements are built of principles and of men. Movements without principles should not exist. Movements with principles—but without men of energy, intelligence, and training to give them life cannot exist."

He was such a man. He gave to the movement all that he had—his time, his energy, and his love. The only thing he took in return was such satisfaction as he derived from his labors. In the hearts of blind men and women throughout America and the world, his memory lives, and will live. In the life and work of Jacobus tenBroek can be read the story of a man and a movement.

The White Cane

A significant episode in that story had begun much earlier. It was in 1964—on October 15—that America, for the first time, officially observed White Cane Safety Day. In issuing his formal proclamation, President Lyndon B. Johnson emphasized the significance of the action and of the visible symbol: "A white cane in our society has become one of the symbols of a blind person's ability to come and go on his own. Its use has promoted courtesy and opportunity for mobility for the blind on our streets and highways. To make the American people more fully aware of the meaning of the white cane, and of the need for motorists to exercise special care for the blind persons who carry it, Congress, by a joint resolution approved October 6, 1964, authorized the President to proclaim October 15 of each year as White Cane Safety Day."

That Presidential proclamation marked a climactic moment in the long campaign by the organized blind to gain national as well as state recognition of the rights of blind pedestrians. Starting in the thirties, early leaders of the blind like William Taylor of Pennsylvania had traveled the country over persuading legislature after legislature to adopt a White Cane Traffic Law for the protection of blind persons on the streets and highways. These pioneer lobbyists were the Johnny Appleseeds of the organized blind movement, scattering the seeds of white cane consciousness among the states.

By 1960, Jacobus tenBroek was able to announce—in one of the most important and influential speeches of his career—that these sustained efforts on behalf of white cane laws had borne fruit everywhere in the land. "It was exactly thirty years ago," he wrote, "that the first legislative step was taken to free the blind from the rocking-chair in which the law still kept them shackled....This year we are celebrating, not only the thirtieth anniversary of that first step onto the highway, but the virtual completion of the campaign which it inaugurated. Today, White Cane Laws are on the books of every state in the union—and for the first time in modern history, everywhere in the land, the blind person truly 'walks by a faith justified by law.'"

The text of that 1960 address—entitled "He Walks By a Faith Justified by Law"—was to be reprinted several times by the *Braille Monitor* over the years and has been widely quoted, cited, and praised elsewhere. In eloquent but informal language, free from jargon, tenBroek summed up the full significance of the white cane, as both a "symbol of equality" and a "sign of mobility." The text of his speech follows:

HE WALKS BY A FAITH JUSTIFIED BY LAW
by Jacobus tenBroek

Nearly a century ago, in a case that has become a landmark, the chief justice of a New York Court wrote as follows:

> The streets and sidewalks are for the benefit of all conditions of people, and all have the right, in using them, to assume that they are in good condition, and to regulate their conduct upon that assumption. A person may walk or drive in the darkness of the night, relying upon the belief that the corporation has performed its duty and that the street or the walk is in a safe condition. *He walks by a faith justified by law*, and if his faith is unfounded, and he suffers an injury, the party in fault must respond in damages. So, one whose sight is dimmed by age, or a nearsighted person whose range of vision was always imperfect, or one whose sight has been injured by disease, is each entitled to the same rights, and may act upon the same assumption. Each is, however, bound to know that prudence and care in turn are required of him, and that, if he fails in this respect, any injury he may suffer is without redress. *The blind have means of protection and sources of knowledge of which all are not aware.*

This resounding opinion is notable today for two oddly different reasons. On the one side it stands as a monumental expression of the modern view that the infirm and the disabled have a right, like any others, freely to travel the public streets and sidewalks. On the other side it is a rather startling revelation of that pervasive prejudice of earlier times that the sightless are different from others not just in degree but in kind—different even from those whose vision is "imperfect" or "injured." It must have been a comforting thought in those not-so-innocent days of charity—a thought not unlike that of the "nobility of poverty"—that the blind were gifted by a kindly Providence with wondrous powers which somehow magically balanced the ledger and made it unnecessary to be greatly concerned about their welfare.

But while this curious residue of unconscious prejudice blurs its message, the real significance of this judicial opinion lies in its straightforward rejection of an age-old discrimination against the visually handicapped. This was the assumption that the blind man's place is in the home or in the asylum, that he takes to the streets and public places at his own risk and peril, and that—in the common legal parlance of the day before yesterday—he is automatically guilty of contributory negligence in any accident involving travel.

In effect, it was held by the courts that the blind were not only sightless but legally without legs to stand on. If they could not see, then they should not attempt to walk. In the eyes of the law, they were immobilized. Their right to be in public places, often conceded as a matter of doctrine, was stillborn.

That was not only the case a century ago; it was also very generally the case, despite the judicial opinion quoted above, as recently as a generation ago. It was exactly 30 years ago, in 1930, that the first legislative step was taken to free the blind from the rocking-chair in which the law still kept them shackled. For while the New York jurist of 1867 had granted the blind the right to walk abroad with the expectation that the streets and sidewalks would be kept in shape, nothing had been done since the advent of the automobile to enable the blind to leave those sidewalks and to cross those streets. It was expressly to provide a new right to be abroad in the new conditions of modern motorized traffic, that the white cane was inaugurated as a travel aid for the blind. This year we are celebrating, not only the 30th anniversary of that first step onto the highway, but the virtual completion of the campaign which it inaugurated. Today White Cane Laws are on the books of every state in the Union—and for the first time in modern history, everywhere in the land, the blind person truly "walks by a faith justified by law." The great and unique achievement of the White Cane Laws has been virtually to wipe out the automatic assumption of contributory negligence on the part of the blind pedestrian, and so to afford him a legal status in traffic, a protection not hitherto conferred.

The white cane is therefore a symbol of equality—and still more clearly a sign of *mobility*. Nothing characterizes our streamlined modern civilization so much as its atmosphere of rapid transit and jet propulsion. More than ever, in urbanized and automobilized America, the race is to the swift—until it almost seems that even the pursuit of happiness takes place on wheels. In the routines of daily living, as at a deeper social level, the keynote of our way of life is *mobility*: the capacity to get around, to move at a normal pace in step with the passing parade. In this race, until very recently, the blind were clearly lagging and falling ever farther behind. In terms of their physical mobility, as in the broader terms of economic and social mobility, this lag was long regarded as the permanent and inescapable handicap of blindness. But today the blind of America are catching up. Just as they are gaining social and economic mobility through the expansion of vocational horizons, so they are achieving a new freedom of physical mobility through the expansion of legal opportunities centering around the White Cane Laws.

For blind people everywhere, the white cane is not a badge of difference—but a token of their equality and integration. For those who know its history and associations, the white cane is also something more: it is the tangible expression not only of mobility, but of a *movement*. It is indeed peculiarly appropriate that the organized movement of the National Federation of the Blind should have as its hallmark this symbol of the white cane. Nor does this take away in any degree from the vital and continuing contributions to the White Cane Laws of the Lions Clubs of America. The Lions have been, and are, staunch allies in the movement of the blind and companions on the march which began a generation ago. During the decade following the introduction of the white cane, statewide organizations of the blind began to emerge in numbers across the country, in the first wave of a movement which was climaxed by the founding of the National Federation in 1940. Through the adoption of the White Cane Laws, the blind have gained the legal right to travel, the right of physical mobility. And at the same time, through the organization of their own national and state associations, the blind have gained the social right of movement and the rights of a social movement.

This is a striking parallel, and an instructive one. For the right to move about independently *within* the states, which the White Cane Laws have steadily won for the blind in the courts, is intimately bound up with the right of free movement *across* state boundaries, which the organized blind are steadily achieving through the reduction or outright abolishment of the residence requirements governing state programs of aid to the blind. In short, it is no empty phrase of rhetoric to say that the blind are "on the move." Thanks to the White Cane Laws, they now move freely and confidently not just on the sidewalks but across the streets. Thanks to the legislative reforms instigated by the Federation, they are moving also more freely than ever from state to state, as need and opportunity dictate; they are moving *upward*, into new careers and callings; and they are moving *forward*, into the main channels and thoroughfares of community life. The blind of America walk by a faith ever more justified by law.

I have said that the White Cane Laws enhance the freedom and confidence of the blind person by affording him a status of legal equality. But it is not, of course, the laws alone but the white cane itself which contributes to his confidence and self-sufficiency. This distinctive cane is several things at once: It is a tangible assist to the blind person in making his way; it is a visual signal to the sighted of the user's condition; and it is a symbol for all of a legal status and protection. Let us immediately concede, however, that the white cane is no magic wand or dowsing-rod, no substitute for sight, and no guarantee of immunity against disaster. The cane cannot read signs or distinguish lights; it cannot traverse all areas immediately ahead and above, and even where it does, it cannot make judgments for its user. In short, it is only a cane—not a brain. And finally it is, of course, not always and universally recognized by the sighted as the legal device of a blind person, although such recognition is already wide and rapidly increasing.

Despite all these necessary and obvious reservations, it is or *should* be indisputable that the white cane is an extremely effective aid to blind people in their daily movements. In fact, however, this conclusion is still disputed and not by the sighted only but even by a few who are blind. No less a personage than General Melvin Maas, president of the Blinded Veterans Association and head of the National Committee on Employment of the Physically Handicapped, has now seen fit to speak out sweepingly against the white cane and all its works—including the White Cane Laws and the whole principle of White Cane Week. The white cane, says the general, is utterly valueless as a signaling device unless it is "elevated at least to the *horizontal* level," which "would present a real hazard to oncoming pedestrians." Apparently General Maas is suggesting that the blind person must point his cane horizontally ahead of him like a swordsman. What the laws provide, in terms of elevation, is rather that the cane be *vertically* raised and extended as far as arm's length. Again, according to the general, "the cane would need to be of such size and shape as to be readily discernible by drivers of vehicles." But this is surely no objection; obviously the cane ought to be as visible as possible, consistent with its portability and convenience. General Maas indeed goes so far in his opposition as to argue that "many cane users do not now use white canes, but use collapsible metallic ones." What he does not say is that there is nothing about collapsible metal canes which prevents them from being colored white (like that which I am carrying today). Finally, the general "clinches" his case with the contention that "the volume and speed of traffic now makes dependence on the cane most hazardous."

There is no doubt, certainly, that traffic hazards are greater today, for everyone, than ever before. But what is the inference? Should the blind then retreat once more to the rocking chair and never venture forth? This is, to be sure, a viewpoint not yet dead among us; as witness the opinion of a Milwaukee district judge, just two years ago, that blind people should stay at home because they only endanger traffic by moving around by themselves. Would General Maas subscribe to that retrogressive doctrine? If, on the other hand, the blind are to be permitted to retain their hard-won right of independent travel, should they now be stripped of the paramount aid and legal protection they have gained?

There are two different questions to be settled here: one of fact and the other of right. The factual question is simply whether the white cane and White Cane Laws are, or are not, a genuine help to blind pedestrians and sighted motorists. On this score the evidence is clear and overwhelming. When, for example, the New York legislature was considering enactment of a state White Cane Law a few years ago, a questionnaire on the merits of the proposal was dispatched to several hundred chiefs of police, attorneys general and safety officers in other states. A very high proportion took the trouble to answer, and the verdict was that White Cane Laws, when properly publicized and administered, are a definite and powerful help to blind and sighted alike. No one, of course, proposed them as a substitute for prudence and common sense on either side; but all agreed that in the presence of ordinary caution and in the service of judgment the white cane is unmistakably a good thing.

Some of the efforts to improve the usefulness and efficiency of the white cane, and to define its proper handling, are fascinating (if not always edifying) to recount.

A Milwaukee city attorney, for example, has proposed that all white canes should fly a flag in traffic—whether at full or half-mast is not revealed. A still more colorful suggestion has been made by a policeman who investigated the most recent traffic death involving a white cane. The carrier, he said, should be enabled upon entering traffic to press a button releasing a set of dangles, whose glitter would presumably attract the eye of the most inattentive motorist; when not in use, the dangles would politely recede into the shell of the cane. Still others have suggested that the white cane ought properly to be at least one and one-half inches thick to improve its visibility—a suggestion which will, no doubt, be happily received by all sightless weight-lifters.

Meanwhile legal minds have labored long and hard over the meaning of the term "raised or extended position" set forth as a requirement by the White Cane Laws of most states. Does "raised" mean, as one city attorney has proclaimed, "pointing upwards"? Does "extended" mean, as General Maas appears to suggest, pointing forward? And does the requirement involve both raising *and* extending the cane, simultaneously or alternately, in the manner of a drum-major? (If the cane in these circumstances also flies a flag and trails dangles, nearly all the elements of a one-man parade would appear to be present.)

There has been no less argument concerning the sanctions most profitably to be included in the White Cane Laws. Some states impose only civil sanctions, thus making it easier to secure the conviction of sighted offenders. Others make allowance for penal sanctions, including jail sentences; but this approach, while apparently more effective, automatically grants to defendants all the protections of criminal law, and by its very severity renders juries reluctant to bring in convictions against negligent drivers. Then, too, there is the question of the right of way to be accorded the blind user of a white cane. In at least one state his rights would appear to be virtually unlimited—even by such normal barriers as traffic signals. Illinois provides that "Any blind person who is carrying in a raised or extended position a cane or walking stick which is white in color or white tipped with red, or who is being guided by a dog, shall have the right of way in crossing any street or highway, whether or not traffic on such street or highway is controlled by traffic signals. The driver of every vehicle approaching the place where a blind person, so carrying such a cane or walking stick or being so guided, is crossing a street or highway shall bring his vehicle to a full stop and proceeding shall take such precautions as may be necessary to avoid injury to the blind person."

At least six other states impose the full-stop requirement, universally insisting that non-blind pedestrians, as well as drivers, must heed the approach of a blind white caner and come to a stop when approaching or coming into contact with him. Such provisions as these would seem to make the blind pedestrian virtually all-conquering.

It should be clear that the legal symbol and physical helpmate of the white cane has not magically solved all the ambulatory problems of the blind. It cannot at a gesture convert a crazed motorist into a sane one; it cannot make the sea of traffic part at its command; above all, it cannot absolve the blind pedestrian from his civilized responsibility to move with prudence and ordinary caution: to "speak politely, while carrying a big stick." Let us claim no more for the white cane and the White Cane Laws than is their due. The paramount right which they confer upon the blind pedestrian is not so much a right-of-way (for that is limited and contingent), nor even a guarantee of safe conduct, but simply a right of *passage*—the right to travel independently in public places, to move in the thick of things, with the confidence of legal status and the reasonable assurance of recognition. Before the era of the white cane, the blind man everywhere ventured forth at his peril and proceeded at his own risk; today "he walks by a faith justified by law."

Nearly a hundred years ago an American writer, Obadiah Milton Conover, composed a short poem which no blind person could then have read with conviction. This year, as we celebrate the anniversary of the white cane and the newly found independence which it signifies, each of us may affirm the poet's boast:

> Alone I walk the peopled city,
> Where each seems happy with his own;
> O friends, I ask not for your pity—
> I walk alone.

With those words of confidence, Jacobus tenBroek looked forward in the first year of the sixties to a future of continuous progress in the social sphere symbolized by the white cane. But by the mid-decade it was apparent to him and his fellow leaders that, in terms of real mobility and the rights of travel, the blind were no longer catching up but falling behind. In the words of a 1966 convention resolution, the existing white cane laws were inadequate to meet the greatly changed traffic and traveling conditions of the freeway era. Moreover, it was maintained that "some court decisions have had the effect of stripping blind pedestrians of their right of free and unhampered movement, and almost made of them trespassers upon the public ways; and state motor vehicle enforcement officials have failed to act positively in upholding and enforcing the spirit of White Cane Laws."

The result was the development by the National Federation of the Blind of a landmark legal innovation—the Model White Cane Law—which was to be one of the most important legislative achievements of the era. The conceptual and research basis of the model law was provided in a major article by Dr. tenBroek, "The Right to Live in the World: The Disabled in the Law of Torts," published in the *California Law Review* in April, 1966. This meticulously researched study represented a survey and analysis of legal doctrines and provisions governing the right of the blind and the otherwise physically disabled "to full and equal access to places of public accommodation, resort, and amusement; to use the streets and highways with reasonable safety in automobile traffic and amid the normal sidewalk hazards; to ride upon buses, trains, airplanes, taxis, and other public conveyances and common carriers; to have entry to and use of public buildings and other public places free from architectural barriers that especially interfere with the physically disabled; to have the benefit in their travels of guide dogs and white canes."

The tenBroek article constituted a reinterpretation of conventional legal concepts in the light of modern conditions, especially the policy of integrating the blind and physically disabled into the normal life of the community. More to the point, it defined the "right to live in the world" and still more specifically the right of free movement and access—as a *civil right* deserving of the same equal protection as the right to vote, the right to privacy, and the right to education. The keynote of tenBroek's study was struck in its opening paragraph:

> Movement, we are told, is a law of animal life. As to man, in any event, nothing could be more essential to personality, social existence, economic opportunity—in short, to individual well-being and integration into the life of the community—than the physical capacity, the public approval, and the legal right to be abroad in the land.

Of special interest to many readers of the tenBroek article was an "Author's Note" which appeared as a footnote as the bottom of the first page:

> Author's Note: If the blind appear in these pages more than other disabled, it may be because the author is blind and has a special interest in his kind. He thinks not, however. The fact is that the blind individually and collectively are a very active group of the disabled, if not the most active. If the National Federation of the Blind appears in these pages more than other organizations and

agencies composed of the blind or dealing with their problems, it may be because the author founded that organization in 1940, served as its President for 21 years, and is still an active leader in it. He thinks not, however. The National Federation of the Blind is an aggressive, militant, activist organization of the blind themselves which in a quarter of a century has achieved a great deal, legislatively and otherwise, and has always been in the thick of the fight. If the *Braille Monitor* is cited more often than other magazines, it may be because the author is editor of that journal. He thinks not, however. That journal specializes in information and coverage which have a special relevance to the issues here discussed.

This article is amply flexed with footnotes, citing a wide range of formal materials. The views expressed, the author believes, are verified by his personal experience as a disabled individual far more than by all the footnote references put together.

The Model White Cane Law which was derived from that law review article first appeared as a proposal, drafted by Dr. ten-Broek and Russell Kletzing, presented to the Federation's 1966 convention in Louisville. Following the presentation, a convention resolution was unanimously adopted endorsing the model legislation and urging members to lobby for its enactment in their respective states.

Following is the text of the Model White Cane Law as it was originally presented.

MODEL WHITE CANE LAW

1. It is the policy of this state to encourage and enable the blind, the visually handicapped, and the otherwise physically disabled to participate fully in the social and economic life of the state and to engage in remunerative employment.

2. (a) The blind, the visually handicapped, and the otherwise physically disabled have the same right as the able-bodied to the full and free use of the streets, highways, sidewalks, walkways, public buildings, public facilities, and other public places;

(b) The blind, the visually handicapped, and the otherwise physically disabled are entitled to full and equal accommodations, advantages, facilities, and privileges of all common carriers, airplanes, motor vehicles, railroad trains, motor buses, street cars, boats, or any other public conveyances or modes of transportation, hotels, lodging places, places of public accommodation, amusement or resort, and other places to which the general public is invited, subject only to the conditions and limitations established by law and applicable alike to all persons;

(c) Every totally or partially blind person shall have the right to be accompanied by a guide dog, especially trained for the purpose, in any of the places listed in section 2(b) without being required to pay an extra charge for the guide dog; provided that he shall be liable for any damage done to the premises or facilities by such dog.

3. The driver of a vehicle approaching a totally or partially blind pedestrian who is carrying a cane predominantly white or metallic in color (with or without a red tip) or using a guide dog shall take all necessary precautions to avoid injury to such blind pedestrian, and any driver who fails to take such precautions shall be liable in damages for any injury caused such pedestrian; provided that a totally or partially blind pedestrian not carrying such a cane or using a guide dog in any of the places, accommodations, or conveyances listed in section 2, shall have all of the rights and privileges conferred by law upon other persons, and the failure of a totally or partially blind pedestrian to carry such a cane or to use a guide dog in any such places, accommodations, or conveyances shall not be held to constitute nor be evidence of contributory negligence.

4. Any person or persons, firm or corporation, or the agent of any person or persons, firm or corporation who denies or interferes with admittance to or enjoyment of the public facilities enumerated in section 2 or otherwise interferes with the rights of a totally or partially blind, or otherwise disabled person under section 2 shall be guilty of a misdemeanor.

5. Each year, the Governor shall take suitable public notice of October 15 as "White Cane Safety Day." He shall issue a proclamation in which:

(a) he comments upon the significance of the white cane;

(b) he calls upon the citizens of the state to observe the provisions of the White Cane Law and to take precautions necessary to the safety of the disabled;

(c) he reminds the citizens of the state of the policies with respect to the disabled herein declared and urges the citizens to cooperate in giving effect to them;

(d) he emphasizes the need of the citizens to be aware of the presence of disabled persons in the community and to keep safe and functional for the disabled the streets, highways, sidewalks, walkways, public buildings, public facilities, other public places, places of public accommodation, amusement, and resort—and other places to which the public is invited, and to offer assistance to disabled persons upon appropriate occasions.

6. It is the policy of this state that the blind, the visually handicapped, and the otherwise physically disabled shall be employed in the State Service, the service of the political subdivisions of the state, in the public schools, and in all other employment supported in whole or in part by public funds on the same terms and conditions as the able-bodied, unless it is shown that the particular disability prevents the performance of the work involved.

The history of the Model White Cane Law over the years since its formulation in 1966, both in the legislatures and in the court, was active and for the most part progressive. By 1972 some 24 states and the District of Columbia had enacted versions of the model law; but in several cases there was a conspicuous omission—that of the section on contributory negligence. The significance of this omission—the motives behind it and its damaging effects upon the rights of blind pedestrians—were emphasized by Kenneth Jernigan in a letter of 1974 responding to a Federationist's appeal for guidance in the matter. This is what President Jernigan wrote in his letter:

NATIONAL FEDERATION OF THE BLIND
OFFICE OF THE PRESIDENT
Des Moines, Iowa, October 3, 1974

Dear Shirley:

I have your letter of September 25, 1974, and I thank you for writing me. The section of the Model White Cane Law which you underlined reads, "...and the failure of a totally or partially blind pedestrian to carry such a cane or to use a guide dog in any such places, accommodations, or conveyances shall not be held to constitute nor be evidence of contributory negligence." I can understand how insurance companies might oppose this section, but for the life of me I cannot understand why any blind person would. In the past, insurance companies have sometimes argued that blind persons have no business traveling on the streets at all and that (even if the blind person is obeying every law and is in the crosswalk) he should not receive any insurance payment if he is hit by a car—the driver of which may be drunk, speeding, or just plain careless. The argument is that the blind person is negligent by being on the street at all.

A modification of this argument says that a blind person is negligent unless he has a clear identification (cane or dog) that he is blind. For my part, I carry a cane when I am on the streets or roads. However, I do not wish to be penalized by law or deprived of my rights if I do not have a cane in my hand or am not accompanied by a dog.

According to our Model White Cane Law, a blind person would still be guilty of contributory negligence if he is careless or if he is not abiding by the law—that is, if he is jaywalking or going against the light or doing any other such thing. Our Model Law simply provides that he cannot be deprived of his legal rights simply because he does not have a cane in his hand or a dog by his side.

Consider the following possibilities: (a) I am walking with a sighted friend and holding his arm. We cross the street at a crosswalk, properly obeying the traffic signal. A drunk driver runs us down, and we are both injured. If our contributory negligence section is not enacted, my friend can collect, but I may be deprived of any insurance payment on the grounds that I am guilty of contributory negligence because I do not have a cane or dog.

(b) I am walking on the streets of Chicago and (as once happened to me) my cane falls through a grating, and I am without it. Suppose I had been hit by a car as I crossed the next street. If I am crossing properly, should I lose all of my legal rights because I do not have a cane?

I carry a cane, and I think I should alert drivers to the fact that I am blind. I believe I should abide by the law. However, I do not wish to be required (under penalty of losing all of my rights) to carry a cane or use a dog.

Perhaps I should say one more thing. Some blind people do not carry a cane because they are ashamed of blindness and think it is not altogether respectable. They have not verbalized it in this manner, but that is how they feel. They say with real pride, "I behave so normally that my friends tell me they forget I'm blind." They also make much of the fact that they associate with sighted people and think and act like sighted people, whatever that may mean. I think this sort of attitude is pathetic.

In other words, I think it makes good sense (all other things being equal) to use cane or dog when one is walking alone—or, for that matter, when one is walking with a sighted person. I also think it is quite respectable and acceptable to take the arm of a sighted person when walking down the street.

We should not be so emotionally uptight that we make an international incident out of every triviality in our life. It is all a matter of balance. I think it makes good sense to carry the cane or use the dog, but I don't want somebody discriminating against me if I don't do it.

Cordially,
Kenneth Jernigan
President
National Federation of the Blind

Chapter 5

Progress and Power: The First Jernigan Presidency

On Easter Sunday, in the year 1980, Kenneth Jernigan sat down to write an informal "Report to the Members" on the state of their Federation, over which he had presided for more than a decade. Looking backward through the years he was struck both by the scale of progress in the movement and by the profusion of forms it had taken. "If you consider the Federation of 1960 and compare it with the Federation of 1980," he wrote, "the ad-vancement is almost unbelievable. In 1960 we customarily had three or four hundred people at our annual convention banquets. We now have in the neighborhood of four times that many! Then, we had no recorded issue of the *Braille Monitor*, no presidential releases on cassette, no seminars, no nationwide distribution of television and radio public service announcements, no Pre-Authorized Check plan, no members-at-large and Associates program, and no affiliates in several of the states."

The Federation's President continued:

Today, what a difference! The *Monitor* is the most influential publication in the field of the blind. Whether they admit it or not, our opponents know it as well as we do. Our public service spots cover the airwaves of the nation, and the presidential releases bind us together in a family of unity and a common bond of shared information and interest. We have our own national headquarters building; and our Braille, print, and recorded materials go out by the hundreds of thousands each year. Our leadership seminars are strengthening our ties as nothing else could. Each year our March on Washington and our continuing NAC demonstrations bring hundreds of us together from throughout the nation to give testimony to our ongoing strength and commitment. What other group (either *of* or *for* the blind) could muster the numbers we bring together to carry out our projects? Everybody knows the answer: None.

So wrote the leader of the world's largest organization of blind people, reviewing the accomplishments and setbacks of the era just past—an era that constituted, during most of its span of years, what has come to be known as the "first Jernigan presidency." That tenure in office had begun in 1968, following the death of the Federation's founder and first President, Jacobus tenBroek. It came to an end in 1977, when mounting health problems forced Jernigan (temporarily, as it turned out) to resign his office. During those nine years most of the advances and innovations he was later to enumerate, in his "Easter Report" to the members, came into being—along with others which were largely taken for granted, such as the steady but phenomenal growth of Federation membership and attendance at National Conventions. Even in the late sixties the sheer numbers of participating members seemed remarkable to old-timers in the movement; at the Des Moines convention in 1968 there were nearly a thousand people on the floor at peak periods. Some 730 of them attended the banquet that year to applaud their newly installed President as he delivered an inspirational address—entitled "Blindness: Milestones and Millstones"—in which he memorialized the passing of the torch from one generation of leaders to the next.

This year [he said] is a time of mourning, and a time of dedication. It is a time to look back, not in anger but in sorrow; and it is a time to look forward, not in complacency but in confidence. It is a time for continuity, and a time for change.

With the death of our beloved President, Dr. tenBroek, we have lost a leader—but we have not lost direction. We mourn the passing of a man, but not the end of a movement. On the contrary; he has shown us the way; he has set our feet on the path; he has fired our minds and fueled our resolution. He has passed the torch to us; let us march with it, and hold it high.

And President Jernigan concluded his address—to a standing ovation—with these resonant words:

> Let the word go out from this place and this moment that the torch has been passed to a new generation of blind Americans, a generation born in this century and fully belonging to it, a generation committed to the belief that all men (seeing or blind) are capable of independence and self-direction, of attaining equality and pursuing happiness in their own way, of serving each other and helping themselves—of walking alone and marching together.

Between that overture and that conclusion, the new chief executive of the movement defined both the milestones of progress and the millstones of resistance which together marked the pathway of the organized blind into the mainstream of society. His address was an artful blend of the abstract and the concrete—of philosophical discussion and practical illustration—alternating in tone and substance between the rhetoric of high purpose and the immediacy of the telling example. With his homespun manner and the trace of a rural Tennessee accent, Jernigan wore his learning lightly; he made his points often through anecdote, and nearly as often the anecdote was personal, drawn from his own life and expressive of his inner feelings. If his language was frequently poetic, it could also be blunt and earthy; as he himself once put it (alluding to a favored "blind trade" of the sheltered shops), "Let us call a spade a spade, and a broom a broom—and let the broomcorn fall where it may."

When Kenneth Jernigan rose in Des Moines to give his maiden speech as NFB President, he was scarcely an unknown quantity to the audience of Federationists; he had been a national leader of the movement for over fifteen years and second in command for a decade. Moreover, he was thoroughly familiar to the members as a speaker and writer, much in demand at state conventions and frequently on display in the pages of the *Braille Monitor*. But this time it was different; now it was the presidency, and this was the banquet address. There was a new authority in the speaker's voice on this night, a new dimension to his presence; and the audience was quick to respond to it. Here was not merely a new hand at the helm but a new voice on the rostrum, a distinctive personality and style which rang out through the phrases of this noteworthy speech—the first one in a distinguished series of presidential addresses which would epitomize the movement of the organized blind for nearly a score of years to come.

Here is the text of that address as given at the 1968 convention banquet:

BLINDNESS—MILESTONES AND MILLSTONES
by Kenneth Jernigan

Twenty-eight is an awkward age in the life of a man or a movement. It is inbetween the more impressive signposts of a quarter-century and a full generation. But for members of the National Federation of the Blind, the number twenty-eight is a landmark; and the year 1968 will be long remembered as a milestone.

This year is a time of mourning, and a time of dedication. It is a time to look back, not in anger but in sorrow; and it is a time to look forward, not in complacency but in confidence. It is a time for continuity, and a time for change.

With the death of our beloved President, Dr. tenBroek, we have lost a leader—but we have not lost direction. We mourn the passing of a man, but not the end of a movement. On the contrary: he has shown us the way; he has set our feet on the path; he has fired our minds and fueled our resolution. He has passed the torch to us: let us march with it, and hold it high.

In this year of decision, then, as we reassess our movement and our course, what major problems and challenges loom before us? What mountains must we now move? What rivers must we cross? What trails must we blaze?

Of all the stumbling-blocks which (as the Bible reminds us) are forever placed in the path of the blind, there is one which I believe to be more formidable and fundamental than any of the rest. Indeed, it is more than just a stumbling block—it is the very cornerstone of the whole vast structure of laws and institutions, customs and practices, which have kept the blind from time immemorial in sheltered custody and confinement.

That cornerstone—which is also a millstone around the necks of those without sight—is the complex of social attitudes traditionally held toward blindness and the blind. It is these attitudes which are most damning and damaging to our hopes for opportunity and equality, for integration and independence. It is concepts—to be specific—such as this, taken from the letter of an insurance company official to an employer about to hire a trained and qualified machinist who happened to be blind:

> Duane, your letter states that there are two or three production jobs available for a person having this particular handicap. I think it is good that anyone would hire handicapped people—however, I think that extreme good judgment should be used in hiring a person who is totally blind, especially for a manufacturing plant.
>
> I cannot imagine that this person would be put on a job where there is machinery having moving parts where this person might possibly get their hands involved. Neither can I imagine them hiring a person and placing him on a job where he would have to walk through the plant, with the possibility of him running into machinery or stepping off into areas where he could be severely injured. However, a manufacturing plant has many areas which are hazardous. One important point of safety is to always be alert and watching for the unexpected. I would assume that this person would be guided when entering or leaving the plant so that he would not run into something.

What an exemplary attitude!—exemplary in its ignorance and blighting consequences. Today there are literally thousands of blind persons successfully at work on power machines of all types (by the way, did you ever see any machinery without moving parts?); and their safety record, as insurance men, above all, ought to know, is superior to that of their fellow-workers. And yet the old attitudes and assumptions—the damning image of the helpless blind man—drive all sense and reason from the head of this insurance executive, and threaten to drive a perfectly good machinist out of a job and very possibly out of a career.

It provides an illustration of a tendency, long familiar in welfare and charity work, to make moral and behavioral demands upon blind persons of a kind not imposed upon the general populace. Some years ago I asked a publisher of technical books for permission to have a volume of his transcribed into Braille for the use of a particular blind student. This is how his lawyer replied to me:

> We suggest that you give us the name of the blind student and her age, and let us know whether you consider her

character and integrity to be above reproach. Assuming a favorable reply, we would prepare a letter of agreement for the blind student to sign, in which she would promise and agree to keep the work confidential to herself and her teacher, and not to sell it or reproduce it in any manner.

This is how I replied:

The young lady in question is a blind person receiving services from our agency. Whether she will be able to become self-supporting may well depend upon the training and help we can give her and upon her background preparation to take advantage of opportunities when they become available. For these reasons we have felt it quite vital that we have the book in question in Braille for her. Even so, there are certain ethical principles which we feel we cannot violate. Personal information about this young lady is, and ought to be, strictly confidential. Whether she is a model of purity and virtue or an utter wretch has nothing to do, so far as we are concerned, with whether she ought to have the right to earn her daily bread. In fact, if one wants to be philosophical about the matter, there might be more justification for making her earn her own living if she were a 'bad' girl than if she were a 'good' girl. Therefore, your request that we give you information about her character seems singularly irrelevant.

It is attitudes such as this which dog our footsteps as we move out of the sheltered past, out of the long night of custodialism and dependency, into the future of equality. And attitudes like *this*—from the manager of a factory in Iowa, rejecting the request of students at the Iowa Orientation and Adjustment Center to make a tour of his mill:

We are certainly sorry [he wrote] to hear that you feel you have been discriminated against by not being granted permission to tour the mill. Our only concern was for your safety, for which we would be solely responsible during the tour. We certainly would not want any individual in your group to risk the possibility of a fall or getting too close to any mill machinery....The refusal of the tour perhaps sounded unfair to you, but if you will reconsider and put yourselves in our position, you know we would have been severely criticized if anyone in your group would have been injured during such a tour. We are sure that if you will give this matter fair reconsideration you will find no discrimination, only thoughtful consideration, on our part.

There is a fair and considerate attitude—courteous, helpful, wishing only to be of service. How often have blind persons been stopped cold in their progress by the classic phrase: "Our only concern was for your safety." Our milestones of progress have been reached despite such millstones of concern placed around our necks.

The answer to that attitude of the mill manager is twofold: first, blind student groups had actually toured his mill twice before, without a mishap; the presumption ought to be that they could tour it again with the same safety. Second, discrimination is almost never a matter of intention or motive; it is a matter of action and the consequences of action. If a drunk is refused admittance to a restaurant on the grounds of drunkenness, that does not constitute discrimination; for he meets the standard test of an undesirable customer. If a blind man is refused admittance to a restaurant on the grounds of blindness, that does constitute discrimination; for blindness does not relate to any reasonable standard of discrimination. When the blind students of a training center—all of them, by the way, well-schooled in the use of machinery and in plant safety measures—are turned away at the door of the mill, it would serve the manager right if they staged a mill-in!

It might be added as a kind of happy ending to this episode, that all such discriminatory exclusions and rejections are hopefully at an end in Iowa—with the passage by the state legislature in 1967 of the Model White Cane Law. Unfortunately, such attitudes of misconception and discrimination are not limited to the public at large.

The crippling and defeating assumptions which even today keep the blind down and keep them out are to be found, not one bit less frequently or less shockingly, among the very professionals upon whom falls the responsibility for the education of the blind and the enlightenment of the public.

An agency professional once raised with me the question of how best to give counsel to a mother with a newborn blind child. My response was that I might send a blind girl of college age, who had been without sight since childhood and who therefore could demonstrate to the woman that blindness is not the end of the road. Or, I said, I might send along a blind mother, with a child or two of her own, who could present a contrasting but equally successful case of adjustment.

To all this my agency friend shook his head in disagreement and disbelief. It wouldn't do, he said, to assign a blind person to the case—whether a mother, a college girl, or any one else—because she would not be able to perceive the visual cues revealing whether the woman was embracing the blind child or giving it affection. In fact, he lectured me at some length concerning the tendency of parents to resent and reject their blind infants, and not pet or caress them. Therefore, he argued, a sighted professional was called for who could observe visually the facial expressions of resentment and rejection, and provide appropriate therapy for the mother.

My reply to this line of reasoning was that the surest way to create and reinforce such negative attitudes on the part of the parent would be to dispatch his type of professional worker, bent on discovering hostility and dispensing therapy at all costs. Where there is no hostility to begin with, such a worker is likely to create it— and where hostility already exists, she is likely to reinforce it. On the other hand, the well-adjusted blind mother or college girl is a living demonstration of how to get along with blindness regarding it as a mere inconvenience, not as a tragedy. Such a blind person has many ways of observing the attitudes and behavior of the new mother; but more important, after a few hours with her, the mother is likely to see blindness in a new light and her normal maternal instincts will do the rest. In other words, the problem raised by my professional friend was not with the mother but with his own misconceptions about blindness.

Indeed, these false notions are to be detected among the very experts who took part in a workshop on "Attitudes and Blindness," a four-day seminar conducted expressly to educate the staff of the Office for the Blind of the Pennsylvania Department of Public Welfare—a meeting held not ten years ago, or five years ago, but in 1967.

Listen to the views of a rehabilitation specialist employed by the American Foundation for the Blind, as he explains to the assembled professionals what blind people are like:

"Many of the blind," he says, "look at the seeing as people from whom to get something. Just because they're sighted, they owe blind people something."

Is that an accurate diagnosis of common attitudes among the blind? What is the basis for such a sweeping and belittling generalization? And what is likely to be the reaction of a newly hired sighted staff worker to this characterization of the blind people with whom he is preparing to work?

In this connection I would ask you to remember that this specialist is speaking to professional workers at a conference called for the express purpose of dealing with attitudes—attitudes of the blind toward the sighted and of the professional worker toward the blind client. There is hardly an effort made to disguise the condescension and contempt which he feels. The fact that this "specialist" happens to be blind himself does nothing to mitigate the tone of his remarks, and perhaps tells us more about his own personal inadequacies and cynical motivations than about the subject under discussion.

But let us hear him out. He goes on to state that one of the best examples of exploitation of the sighted by the blind "is using them purely for their vision in volunteer activities serving the blind. I know of one organization," he says, "where blind people join as regular, full participating members. But there is another class of membership known as associate membership; this classification is set up only for sighted people. Associate members do not have the right to vote, do not have the right to hold office (except for the office of treasurer, of course, which requires sight) [blind treasurers, take note!] and may not serve on committees except the entertainment, hospitality, and refreshment committees. I'm afraid this attitude even pervades the individual thinking of some blind people to a great degree," he says, as he quotes the thinking of an imaginary blind person thus: "You'd better be just nice enough to them so that you can use them when you want to use them, and deal with them when you want to deal with them, and call on them when you can get something from them for nothing." Our rehab specialist then concludes: "I've seen this attitude over the years, and I've not seen it change much."

The first response one is tempted to make is: If that is the attitude he has seen over the years, he must truly be blind—blind to the presence of other and better relationships, of other and better motives. But there is more to it than that. The speaker is also attacking organizations of the blind—such as the National Federation of the Blind and the state affiliates—attacking them on the one hand as *exclusive* and on the other hand as *exploitative.* To be more blunt about it, he is saying that we are prejudiced and discriminatory: we judge ourselves to be superior to the poor nonblind population, and let them into our society only as second-class citizens, unable to vote or hold office. Then we compound the felony by treating them as a minority class of servants and social inferiors, fit only to perform the menial chores of washing up, dishing out the food, and keeping the books. What a picture of snobbery, condescension, and exploitation—and also, what a falsehood!

We are, to be sure, organizations *of the blind*—not organizations of workers for the blind, or friends of the blind, or of persons charitably disposed toward the blind. Our chief distinction and reason for being is that we are blind people who have come together to solve common problems, to make our own decisions and to speak for ourselves. It follows that while we are happy to have seeing people join with us, we would surely abandon our distinctive identity if we should turn authority and decision-making over to them.

Therefore, just as other clubs and lodges have their auxiliaries, so our federations of the blind make a place for interested persons who are not blind. To make something prejudicial out of this—let alone to concoct a sinister declaration of hostility and contempt toward the seeing—is simply nonsense. Again, one wonders what effect this kind of attribution of motives to blind people must have upon the agency staff worker who is preparing to work with the blind.

But let us move on. We have not yet done with this distinguished "specialist" from the American Foundation for the Blind, whose contribution to the workshop discussion on attitudes is much too rich with meaning to put aside lightly. Listen to this:

> Conversely, [he says] there are blind people who look at sighted people as competitors. "I, as a blind person," they say, "must compete with this individual, not because of any spirit of sportsmanship, or not because of any drive to improve my personal position, but to prove myself as a blind person. I must prove not only that I can do it, but that I can do it better." [he goes on] A friend of mine out in the Midwest, totally blind, lives in a very lovely

community on a rather large tract of land, and every morning, winter or summer, he goes out and runs around the block, just to prove to his neighbors that he is physically fit. This same individual also has a bicycle, and he rides this around the yard, particularly when his neighbors are coming home from work. He's got to prove himself.

What an aggressive ogre is that midwestern blind man, sitting there on his tract of land, morning after evening, winter and summer, waiting for his neighbors to come out so that he can ride his bicycle noisily about the yard, or perhaps trot around the block a few times "just to prove that he is physically fit." In order to get at the true character of this analysis of motives, let us suppose a different scene. Let us suppose that the midwestern blind man does not ride a bicycle at all, or run around the block, or do any other outdoor exercise—but simply sits quietly inside his house, encountering no one except his professional friend from the East. What then would be the analysis? May it not be that this would strike our expert on attitudes as a sad situation indeed? Can you not hear him, or someone like him, lamenting the "social isolation" and morbid withdrawal of this poor fellow?

No?—Then consider this piece of jargon:

There are innumerable things one could say about the isolating factors which directly arise from blindness and what can be done about them. First, to a blind person the social use of the eye is impossible....But we believe nonetheless that we have some of the essentials to prevent isolation. One of the most important is the impetus we have lately given to mobility training. It has been estimated that ninety per cent of the blind population is essentially immobile. That alone tells us how isolating blindness can be.

That is not the same rehabilitation specialist I have been quoting, but it is one very much like him. It is the voice of the Chief of Services to the Blind of the Federal Vocational Rehabilitation Administration. And the gist of his commentary is that the common condition of the blind is that of social isolation—from which they can to some extent be rescued by means of increased *mobility*: such as, getting out into the world, riding bicycles, and going around the block.

This flat contradiction between the testimony of two eminent experts in rehabilitation of the blind is a good example of what we might call the "false dilemma" logic all too often encountered in this field. To put it bluntly: the blind are damned if they do, and damned if they don't. In the present instance, our midwestern blind man finds himself damned by one specialist if he stays indoors in "social isolation"—and damned by another if he ventures outside for a bit of healthy exercise—which somehow gets converted into unhealthy exhibitionism.

That point, by the way, is worth considering for a moment. If a blind man takes to running around the block, or riding a bicycle, or doing any of the little behavioral things that normal people do all the time, must he be doing them for some deep, dark impulse of competition, or of "proving himself"—rather than just *im*proving himself? Why is it that other people's behavior can be taken at face value, but the behavior of blind persons cannot—even where it is the same? Instead, it must be subjected to intricate investigation in psychiatric depth. Does not this devious and suspicious approach to the attitudes and motives of the blind reveal much about the attitudes of the investigators themselves? Does it not betray a remarkable lack of faith in the rationality, responsibility, and simple normality of their blind clients? Much is made of the fact that the blind midwesterner waits to ride his bicycle until his neighbors come home from work. It apparently never occurs to the rehabilitation expert that the reason for this timing might be that the blind man also works and so returns home at about the same time as others in the neighborhood. One is tempted to exclaim: Counselor, heal thine own attitudes!

Before leaving this informative workshop conference of rehabilitation experts, let us turn to another illustration of the point we are making. Here is another expert from the Federal Vocational Rehabilitation Administration, remarking on the curious and morbid characteristic of many blind persons that they like to get together with others who are blind.

> The more the individual has a sense of inferiority as a blind person, [he says] the more he is likely to enjoy the company of other people purely and simply because they are blind. I do not mean that there is anything wrong with two blind people enjoying each other's company, but the tendency to group together, in clubs or organizations, in social groups, is partially based on the desire for equality.

In other words, there is nothing wrong with this socializing and organizing on the part of the blind people; but on the other hand, there is. If we look closely at it, all kinds of subterranean and vaguely disreputable motives become apparent; it is all a matter of inferiority, or some sort of urge to be equal when one is not, or something else discovered by Freud or by Freudian social workers. It cannot be because blind persons are people, and people like each other's company. It cannot be because blind persons wish to join hands to solve common problems, and find voluntary association the natural and democratic way of going about it. No! These are the normal, healthy, and obvious motives of *ordinary* people; they will not do for a professional analysis of the sub-ordinary and subordinate.

So much for that publication on attitudes about blindness, the result of a conference of specialists on rehabilitation. Let us consider another publication circulated by a different group of specialists getting ready to hold a rehabilitation conference of their own. What we have here is a questionnaire sent out across the country to instructors working in orientation and training centers for the blind, who were invited to participate in a three-day national workshop on personal management services, under the sponsorship of the American Foundation for the Blind with the collaboration of the Federal Department of Health, Education, and Welfare. The questionnaire asked each instructor to state whether he had or had not developed "a specific organized method or technique" for the teaching of grooming and living activities to blind people—and, furthermore, whether the instructor found it necessary "to *frequently* make changes," or only "*rarely* make changes," in these specific organized techniques. Now, here are some of the activities for which it was expected that instructors would have specific organized techniques and methods: brushing hair, combing hair, tying shoes, lacing shoes, tying necktie, putting dentifrice on brush, brushing teeth, tweezing eyebrows, bathing with soap, using deodorants, shaking hands, asking for help, refusing help, using the telephone and, under the heading "Art of Attraction," *flirting* and *dating*. (One is forced to wonder what "specific organized method or technique" the agency professionals reported in *that* field of personal activity!)

What is to be thought of this high-level national conference of rehabilitation experts and its preoccupation with such earthshaking matters as these? Surely the first thought that comes to one's mind is: Have they nothing more serious to do? Is this the kind of problem that should be occupying the collective attention of the nation's specialists on blindness—problems like how (in a specific organized way) to put the toothpaste on the brush, the necktie on the neck, the soap on the body, or the shoe on the foot? Perhaps the shoe should be on the other foot; perhaps blind people ought to get together in a conference of their own and work out specific organized techniques or methods for instructing specialists in rehabilitation on such urgent matters of personal hygiene as clearing cobwebs from the mind, stringing serious thoughts together, and (under the heading of "Mental Attraction") flirting with new ideas!

What a commentary on the attitudes *toward* the blind held by the very people assigned to improving and educating the attitudes *of* the blind. Certainly if a blind person is defective mentally, or disturbed emotionally, or handicapped multiply, there may be need for attention to such elementary and superficial learning tasks. But if not, then not! How many real and serious problems of social relationship and participation go untreated and unattended while these people play their frivolous and superfluous games.

We could go on—and on and on—with still more examples of demeaning and destructive attitudes on the part of professional workers and administrators in the vineyards of blind welfare and rehabilitation. Their name is legion; their sins are manifest; their mischief is widespread. But there is one more thing to say about them: they no longer hold the field alone. Their attitudes, their teachings, their prejudices, their arrogance—all are being challenged by a new generation of professionals, a new spirit among the blind, a new understanding on the part of the public at large, and a new philosophy of rehabilitation.

The name of the new professionals is not "workers *for* the blind" but "workers *with* the blind." Many of them, in steadily growing numbers, are blind themselves. But, blind or sighted, they base their entire approach on an assumption of responsibility and an attitude of respect toward the people with whom they work. Their injunction to the blind trainee or client is not "you cannot do it," but "do it!" Their doctrine, to borrow from the field of economics, is that of *laissez-faire*—let the blind person *be*—let him become— let him *go*!

One of the basic principles of a democracy is the notion that the balance of power shall be held by the non-professional, by the public at large. In this connection the blind are fortunate, for the professionals in the field (weighed down by vested interest and accumulated doctrine) have often been slower to accept the new ideas than the well-informed man-in-the-street. When faced with the evidence of blind people living and working as normal human beings, the average citizen has usually been able to accept the fact for what it is without looking for hidden meanings or Freudian explanations. The professionals are sometimes not so flexible in their thinking.

The very symbol and substance of the new ideas, and the challenge to the old attitudes, can be found in the organized blind movement. We are determined to speak for ourselves, and with our own voice. The time is now, and the responsibility is ours. No one will give it to us. We must take it for ourselves. And take it we will!

In this time of transition, in this changing of the guard in the affairs of the blind, we might articulate our prospect and our vision by paraphrasing some words from the inaugural address of a recent President of the United States:

Let the word go out from this place and this moment that the torch has been passed to a new generation of blind Americans, a generation born in this century and fully belonging to it, a generation committed to the belief that all men (seeing or blind) are capable of independence and self-direction, of attaining equality and pursuing happiness in their own way, of serving each other and helping themselves—of walking alone and marching together.

The presidential succession which took place in 1968—when the convention chose Kenneth Jernigan to assume the chair left vacant by the death of Jacobus tenBroek—symbolized more than a ceremonial changing of the guard. It represented, as we have already noted, a transition of the generations from the era of the founders—the pathfinders who blazed the trail and laid the foundations of the movement—to their successors of the second generation, who in turn were to build upon that bedrock an expanding institutional structure that in time would tower over the field of work with the blind and cast a lengthening shadow of authority and influence across the land.

That symbolic structure—the National Federation of the Blind—had its original epicenter in California: the state where Jacobus tenBroek lived and taught, where Newel Perry presided as mentor and godfather to the movement, and where such early leaders as Raymond Henderson, Perry Sundquist, and Muzzy Marcelino formed a nucleus around which the Federation grew and flourished in the forties and fifties. California also could claim in that period one of the few training and orientation centers for the blind in the nation; and it was the magnet of that center which, combined with the opportunity to work directly with Dr. tenBroek, attracted a young teacher of the blind named Kenneth Jernigan to the Bay Area in the early fifties, where he and Dr. tenBroek commenced the close working relationship that was to endure until the latter's death. During these years it could be said, with considerable truth, that "as California goes, so goes the Federation."

The epicenter of Federationism as a national movement began gradually to shift following the transfer of Kenneth Jernigan to Des Moines in 1958 to become director of the Iowa Commission for the Blind. During the sixties the Iowa Commission was transformed from possibly the worst rehabilitation agency in the nation (in 1957 it was the lowest of all in job placements) to arguably the best in the nation, by every measure of accomplishment; and in the process of its phenomenal growth it spread Federationism and spawned Federationists. Among the "brightest and best" who graduated from the Commission's Des Moines orientation center in this period and went forth as leaders of the movement were Marc Maurer, Ramona Walhof, Peggy Pinder, James Omvig, and James Gashel. And, as had occurred earlier in California, the Federation's state affiliate in Iowa grew rapidly to become one of the largest and most effective in the country.

It is believed by many who have observed the Federation closely over the last three decades that Jernigan's years in Iowa contributed more to the current status of the National Federation of the Blind, as well as to the field of work with the blind as a whole, than has generally been recognized. One such person (a former staff member) capsulized the experience as follows:

> In 1958 Kenneth Jernigan became director of the Iowa Commission for the Blind. In 1978 he left Iowa. The coming to Iowa, the twenty years there, and the leaving—all three had a significance in the history of the organized blind movement far beyond the simply stated facts. Jernigan's decision to seek out and accept the

Iowa position set the focus for the succeeding decades not only for his own career, but, to a large extent, for the Federation as well. Had Jernigan in 1958 chosen to concentrate his monumental youthful energy along the alternate path which he and Dr. ten-Broek seriously considered for him—a career in national politics—the Federation at fifty would hardly resemble the organization as it is today. And of Jernigan himself? Who knows. But the road taken *was* Iowa—and to understand the Federation today, one must explore thoroughly the multiple levels of Jernigan's twenty years as director of the Iowa Commission for the Blind—for those years and what has come to be known in broad sweep as the "Iowa Experience" forever changed the world for the blind—even for those who didn't know then and who don't know now anything about Iowa.

The tangibles—the huge library with its "books-on-demand" transcription program, the Orientation Center, the thoroughly modern headquarters building, the state-of-the-art equipment, the salary schedules above those for other state workers—and the intangibles—the gleaming corridor floors, the invitations to the Governors' Balls, the Presidential Citation, the international visitors, the upbeat media attention, the crisp "yes sirs" and "no ma'ams"—all proclaimed in ringing tones that which was the central core of the "Iowa Experience": It is respectable to be blind. To be in Iowa meant total immersion in that philosophical precept which shaped and permeated it all—from the inconsequential to the bedrock.

Some saw in Iowa a state rehabilitation agency, giving solid service to the blind of the state and enabling them to become part of the economic, social, and cultural fabric of their communities. And they were right. Thousands of blind Iowans are living testimony.

Some saw a model, a working embodiment of Federation philosophy in action which could be duplicated. And they, too, were right. Over the years they came, and looked. They learned and believed and went away and built elsewhere. In varying degrees, with surges forward amid steps backward, from the Southeast to the Northwest tens of thousands were touched.

Some saw a threat to an entrenched system of blindness agencies which denied the capacity of the blind to live normal lives and earn competitive wages. And The National Accreditation Council for Agencies Serving the Blind and Visually Handicapped was born.

For some—clients, staff, and observers (both blind and sighted)—it was a training ground, in a sense the Federation's West Point. The finer points of philosophy were argued for hours on end; public officials were managed with carrots and sticks; alternative skills and techniques of blindness were honed to perfection; and the mind was stretched with exercises in logical reasoning—a familiar sound being a student roaming the halls muttering, "If a squirrel and a half ate a nut and a half in a day and a half, how many nuts could nine squirrels eat in nine days?"

In many these experiences forged a lifelong and unshakable commitment to the National Federation of the Blind. During the three decades (1960-1990) those who had the benefit of the intensity of the Iowa training during the Jernigan years (1958-1978)—that unique mixture of skills training, mental discipline, attitude examination, love, compassion, determination, and hope—which were the heart of Kenneth Jernigan's Iowa program—fanned out across the country assuming leadership positions at the local, state, and national levels. One need only make a cursory review of the leadership roles of the organized blind movement to assess the impact of the Iowa years.

Jernigan's establishment of the Iowa Commission for the Blind program in 1958 had been a necessary and logical step in the Federation's long-term strategy to build full first-class status for the blind. The tangible success of the program in proving that the average blind person could, indeed, hold the average job in the average place of business vindicated Federation philosophy and set the pace for others to emulate.

Equally necessary and logical in the Federation's long-term strategy was Jernigan's move in 1978 to Baltimore to establish the National Center for the Blind. The National Federation of the Blind had become so central a factor in the entire "blindness system" that its principal leader could no longer (or ever again) be constrained by ties to any governmental entity. With the move to Baltimore and the establishment and expansion of the National Center for the Blind, Jernigan was freed to concentrate his full attention on building in depth—from the grass roots up—the far-flung yet focused mechanism which by the end of the decade of the 1980s had become the powerful force of the National Federation of the Blind.

During the seventies there was to be yet another shift in the movement's center of gravity; this time, however, it would not be concentrated in a particular state but distributed throughout the country. The movement was to become, in a word, *national* in character—genuinely a "National Federation" rather than a confederation of autonomous states, with one or another temporarily predominant. There were various reasons for this new nationalism in the organized blind movement—among them the vibrant role of the National Convention; the spread of the *Braille Monitor*; the development of leadership seminars; and the initiation of recorded presidential releases, which were sent each month to state affiliates and local chapters. But the underlying impetus for the trend derived from a powerful inner force which was transforming the character of the National Federation from that of an ordinary association to that of a special kind of *community*.

The Convention and the Community

The National Federation of the Blind had been founded on twin premises—one theoretical and the other practical. From the very outset its leaders knew that a set of principles, well-understood and carefully applied, was essential to its success. Equally important to success was the building of a strong, effectively run organization to implement the basic principles. The prudent marriage of philosophy and activism issued, over the years, into the unique community of Federationism.

Before the founding of the National Federation, there had been little community among the blind, in America or elsewhere. There were hundreds of thousands of blind individuals who composed a distinguishable population; but they were rarely aware of anything in common other than the lack of sight. It was Jacobus tenBroek, educator and theorist, who gave to this scattered collection of blind Americans a set of guiding principles and a solid structure through which to nurture and actualize them. In turn it was the special genius of Kenneth Jernigan to turn the structure into a community.

The notion of a blind community evolved gradually within the structure of the National Federation of the Blind. Through the early years recruitment into the ranks of the Federation was slow and sporadic, and growth was further hampered by the civil war of the late fifties. But the years of battle, internal and external alike, not only tested and tempered the mettle of the Federationists who endured; it also made of them kindred spirits, co-participants in a movement, brothers and sisters of an extended family—in short, members of a close-knit community. By the end of the sixties, there was evolving in the ranks of the Federation an almost palpable spirit of joint venture and common purpose—what one member called "sharing and caring"—defined by the proven capacity of the members to achieve together what none could do alone. This was a community forged by an act of will, a collective act, on the part of a once-scattered people traditionally discouraged from organizing or associating. They had been brought together in 1940 by a common need; now they were beginning to come together through a common bond. Such a bond was far from customary among the blind.

It should be remembered that blindness itself has always been isolating in multiple ways. First of all, it was commonly assumed by blind persons and those about them that independent mobility—the simple act of getting around on one's own—was impossible for the blind. Second, attitudes about blindness often contained an element of social embarrassment and discomfort occasioned by the very presence of a blind person—making everyone feel relieved when he stayed home "where he belonged." Third, many people both sighted and blind associated blindness with helplessness; hence, a blind person (one not acquainted with the Federation and its philosophy) often attempted to cover a lack of self-confidence by assuring himself that he was better than other blind people—the rest of whom were clearly more helpless than he was. Accordingly all contact with other blind people was to be rigorously avoided. While Jacobus tenBroek had recognized these isolating factors from the outset of the movement, it was

Kenneth Jernigan who took it upon himself in the early fifties—as a teacher and counselor—to work directly with blind persons to overcome this isolation and turn around the defeatist attitudes. First in California and later in Iowa, Jernigan worked in orientation and adjustment centers for the adult blind, bringing blind people together from geographically scattered locations into a single setting. There he concentrated upon instilling into them a sense of independence and self-reliance, grounded in the recognition that they could be proud of their own accomplishments— and that they might share this pride with others. Hundreds of blind persons, through the years, learned the meaning of independence from Dr. Jernigan and returned as self-confident citizens to find careers and establish families in their home communities. Many of them thereafter made a point of retaining their contacts with Dr. Jernigan and his colleagues—and of reaching out in their turn to other blind men and women open to the new ideas. As one of these former students put it: "Recruitment into the Federation is still a matter of one person telling another." And the rate of transmission of the message was accelerated, year by year, as more and more students learned independence and moved confidently out into the world, spreading the word as they went.

But independence alone was never sufficient; there were still the stumbling-blocks of public disbelief and rejection. For these blind men and women of the new generation found that while they might now find a competitive job, raise a family, pay taxes, get about in the world, and generally take pride in themselves, they could still be ejected from a restaurant if the owner deemed their presence disturbing to other patrons. Jernigan's students (and those that they in turn recruited) discovered that there were problems to be solved and changes to be made that no blind individual alone could manage; only collective action could do the job. Like the members of the organized labor movement before them, they learned that "in union there is strength." But there was an added dimension—the closeness of a shared crusade, which touched every aspect of the lives of its participants. In particular, the annual convention of the National Federation of the Blind more and more took on the qualities of a giant meeting of the clan, or the reunion of a vast extended family, while also retaining its practical function as a forum for concerted action. By the end of the sixties the outlines of a genuine community were becoming visible within the structure of the organized blind movement.

The Seminars

As the decade of the seventies got under way, the Federation was growing and flourishing on all fronts. The days of the civil war were nearly a decade in the past—no longer within the experience or even the memory of many current members. States never previously organized were now joining the national movement—and states once torn by civil strife were rejoining—in a campaign led by President Jernigan to establish beachheads, in the form of affiliates, in all fifty states. Local chapters were proliferating and individual membership, in all parts of the country, was rapidly expanding. Every year the National Convention broke existing attendance records (in 1969 the number officially registered was 770; in 1971 it was 1,001; and in 1973 it was 1,506). No one was heard complaining about this trend; nevertheless it began to be recognized that growth itself, for all its virtues, could generate problems of its own if not carefully channeled: problems of complexity, enormity, and anonymity. These "growing pains," of course, were unknown to the previous generation. Through the early decades of the movement, leaders of talent had emerged infrequently and were then swiftly brought into the circle of leadership—where everyone knew everyone else and worked closely together. But with the growth and geographic spread of the Federation, the possibility arose of individual leaders in various parts of the country becoming isolated from one another and working in different directions, thus sowing the seeds of future discord. With this situation in mind, President Jernigan in 1973 instituted a series of leadership training seminars which were to become a permanent fixture in the movement. The object of the seminars, then and later, was to bring together in the setting of the national headquarters a number of members (averaging about 25) from throughout the country who had demonstrated leadership and commitment to the goals of the Federation. From their inception the seminars were held two or three times yearly, at first in Des Moines and later in Baltimore. By 1990 not a single state remained unrepresented by at least a few seminar participants over the years—and there was no state which was not stronger for the experience.

The special value of these seminars, for those who took part in them, stemmed in large part from the intensity of the experience. The seminarians lived and learned and worked together for four active days, at close quarters with one another and with the national President (first Kenneth Jernigan and later Marc Maurer). They came to know the institutional workings of the national headquarters; they learned the history of the movement from the people who made it; they mastered the structure of the basic laws governing work with the blind, and they reasoned through (and talked and argued through) the handling of hundreds of problematic situations—drawn from actual experience—which were posed to them by the President. These contingencies gave the new leaders an opportunity to ponder issues of administration, of policy-making, of finance, and of the routine daily tasks of keeping a movement composed mainly of volunteers working happily along toward its goals. The outcome of each of these seminars was—and remained—a disciplined body of Federationists, schooled in history and relevant law, skilled in the arts of leadership, and welded together through the bonds of friendship and camaraderie. Whenever these seminarians attended a National Convention, they found a ready-made group of companions to whom to turn—for advice, for assistance, and for association.

For over a decade and a half these national seminars produced a substantial corps of Federation leaders, dispersed widely through the country yet held together by the ties of comradeship. Largely because of this informal network of seminarians, the Federation's National Convention during the course of the seventies ceased to be a collection of separate state delegations and took on the character of a true distillation of the national blind community—what one Federationist called a "secular society of friends." The NFB convention—traditionally held each year in the week surrounding Independence Day—afforded a panoply of illustrations of this communal spirit in action. Blind people from all walks of life willingly took on a variety of tasks that might have nothing to do with their backgrounds but everything to do with helping the convention run smoothly. Some of them stood for hours at a stretch, directing traffic or assisting at microphones; others worked at an array of tables, demonstrating new devices or handing out literature. But it was more than the mechanics of the convention for which these members tended to feel responsible; it was the well-being and high spirits of others as well. Should a member turn up with a new baby, for example, what seemed like half the convention might drop by to meet the child. And if a family had suffered a loss, hundreds of Federationists were likely to come around to express their sympathy.

In 1989, a much-loved member—who happened to be the spouse of the Nebraska state president—suddenly died just before the National Convention. The most poignant moment of that year's convention came during the roll call of states on Thursday morning, July 6, when Nebraska was called. After giving the detailed information required of each official delegate, Barbara Walker—who was attending the convention with her two young children—spoke these words to the three thousand people in the auditorium:

> I want to say to everyone here that our Federation family does many things for many people. At this particular time I want to thank everyone for the support that has been shown to my family as we go through the most difficult time I have ever known. I want in particular to thank Fred Schroeder for the eulogy he delivered on behalf of this organization at the services for Jim. It reached many people. I have received calls from people who have opposed our organization on many occasions who, I believe, were reached (and reached deeply) by the message. As we continue in the various struggles which we have to face, I will pledge to do my best to do the work which Jim faithfully honored all the years of his life. I need our Federation family very much right now, and everyone here is responding in a way that is unbelievable to me. Thank you very much.

The National Convention meant many things to many different people. Sometimes it was very personal. One year, a member had found a job in another town but lacked the money to move; his fellow Federationists reached into their pockets and made the move possible. Another year a member was running for elective office; conventioneers from all over the country contributed to the campaign of this blind person who was venturing forth into elective politics. Sometimes it was a small matter that spoke of trust and caring—such as the time when a blind machinist brought her own tools to the convention to show other blind people how she did it. She described her job and then asked that the tools be passed around. They were valuable implements, and someone worried aloud that she might not get them back from the two thousand-plus people in the room. Over the microphone she laughed and said she was not concerned; her fellow Federationists would see to that. She was right, of course.

The Federation's soaring rate of internal growth—which only a few years before had been halted and reversed under the stress of civil war—was surpassing expectations even before the eventful decade of the sixties had come to an end. At the 1969 convention held in Columbia, South Carolina, the number of delegates in attendance approached 1,000. It was at the Columbia convention that President Jernigan seized upon and adapted to new purposes the favorite catchword of the sixties: *"revolution."* He spoke in his banquet address of "a revolution that had just begun to happen—a revolution of the future as well as of the present"—a revolution in the field of blindness that "will replace old outlooks with new insights." In sounding the thematic note that more than any other seemed to epitomize the decade of the sixties in America, Jernigan was also striking a chord for the seventies which would resound throughout his first presidency: a new spirit of aggressive self-confidence and determination on the part of the organized blind. Other Jernigan speeches before this one—and many more to follow—would also emphasize this theme of forceful resolution, of the sense of a new identity ("we know who we are")—and of refusal to turn back or be turned around. But in 1969, in a strongly worded address entitled "Blindness: New Insights on Old Outlooks," the Federation's President expressed these concepts with unsurpassed cogency and flair.

The full text of that speech follows:

BLINDNESS: NEW INSIGHTS ON OLD OUTLOOKS
by Kenneth Jernigan

We are accustomed, in our day, to talk and hear about revolutions: revolutions past and revolutions present; revolutions violent and revolutions nonviolent; revolutions political, economic, technological, racial, social, cultural, and generational. They are of many varieties, these revolutions; but they have at least one thing in common—namely, their historical reality. Either they happened in the past, or they have happened in our own time.

I wish to speak to you, however, about a revolution that has just begun to happen—a revolution of the future as well as of the present. This revolution is one that should have run its course already; and it is one that will, irresistibly, come to fruition and make good its promise in the years ahead. Moreover, it is a revolution which I intend to stir, foment, and agitate; and I hope to solicit your active support in fanning the flames. In fact, if we can get enough people to join us on the barricades, we will not only have set the revolution on its course, but we will have won it.

For the revolution that has just begun to happen is a revolution in the public mind—in the minds of us all—a revolution in our attitudes and assumptions, our deepest premises and prejudices, concerning blindness. It is a revolution to replace old outlooks with new insights.

In a world of many revolutions—of constant novelty and change, of experiment and originality, of new thoughts and fresh ideas—in such a world it is astonishing that we can still be ruled, in any sphere, by superstitions that date to the caveman and images more appropriate to the ice age than the space age. Yet that is still in simple fact the state of our thinking (and, therefore, of our teaching, planning, and programming) about the blind.

This is not to say that there has been no progress. On the contrary, the revolution is well begun; it is on the right track; and it is steadily gathering force and gaining ground. Ever since the National Federation of the Blind came on the scene a generation ago, bringing with it the nerve of independence and the shock of recognition, there has been a shaking of the foundations throughout the field of work with the blind—and in the world beyond. But in view of the immensity of the task before us—even in its preliminary phase of ground-breaking, mind-clearing, and institutional renewal—it is clear that the revolution has barely been launched. To paraphrase Winston Churchill, it is not yet the beginning of the end; it is not even the end of the beginning; but it is the beginning of the beginning. Our revolution is under way. It cannot now be stopped or pacified until it has achieved its goal of overthrowing the graven image which looms as a stumbling block in the path of the blind—that image of their nature and limitations which is graven in stone upon the public mind, stamped upon the yellowing pages of the statute books, and nestled in the dusty corners of custodial institutions.

What then are the outlines and features of this graven image? First, it is an image of *helplessness*—not just of visual disability but of total inability. Second, it is an image of *abnormality*—not just loss of sight but loss of mental and emotional stability. (The blind man, in short, is thought to be not just affected in the eyes but touched in the head.) Third, it is a *"broken image"*—an image of impairment, of imbalance, and disharmony rather than of wholeness and symmetry—an image that calls attention to what is missing rather than what is present, to lacks and losses rather than strengths and talents. Helplessness, abnormality, incompleteness: these are the essential ingredients of a bitter and explosive brew—thoroughly aged and definitely sour—which flows like bile through the veins and capillaries of the body politic.

It is no surprise to find the old stereotype, the graven image of blindness, surviving among the ignorant and innocent. It is another matter to find it flourishing in the gardens of supposed enlightenment and knowledge, among the very people who pride themselves upon their liberal minds and generous hearts—such people, for instance, as those who run the Peace Corps and the VISTA program of the War on Poverty. I would remind you that the poverty program came into existence proclaiming itself to be in the very forefront of progressive thought and modern sophistication. It talked, and talks, of such advanced ideas as "maximum feasible participation" on the part of its clients, the poor. It will be well to bear in mind those protestations and pretensions, in light of the tale I am about to unfold.

Listen now to a true adventure, or misadventure, involving both the Peace Corps and VISTA, which occurred to one of our own active members of the National Federation of the Blind, a leader in her state affiliate. Let me say first that this woman, besides her prominent role in the Federation, has made her living as a physical fitness instructor for fifteen years, has served two terms as president of a statewide public speaking group, and during a recent political campaign covered some fifty precincts by herself, much of the time on foot.

Now on with the story. It began with her application to join the Peace Corps as a volunteer—an application which was turned down, *two years* after its submission, on the ground that a blind person could not conceivably get along alone in a foreign country (this despite the fact which was duly noted in her application, that she had *twice* wandered the length and breadth of Mexico unaccompanied). The Peace Corps asked no further questions, made no other inquiry, sought no additional data. She was blind; that was enough to bury the application and kill the dream.

Then came VISTA—which launched a recruiting drive in her home town. Again she applied. Her references were promptly investigated; a physical examination followed, and soon there came a two-page telegram stating, "You are considered for immediate placement—Wire us collect—Phone us collect." She wired that she was instantly available, and sat back to await further instructions. It was a long wait. Nearly a full year later she received a lengthy questionnaire from VISTA—one which is so remarkable in its method and assumptions that it deserves detailed attention.

Under the heading of "Mobility," the questionnaire sets forth the following queries: "Do you use a wheel chair?" ("No," she replied.) "How far can you wheel?" (Not more than ten miles between coffee breaks," was her answer.)

"Can you move alone from wheel chair to car? Can you move alone from wheel chair to bed? Can you move alone from wheel chair to seat? Can you move alone from wheel chair to bath? Can you move alone from wheel chair to toilet? Do you use crutches?" (Her answers were: Yes, yes, yes, yes, yes—and no.)

"Do you climb steps?" (Yes.)

"Do you use public transportation?" (Yes.)

"Do you open and close doors in getting around?" (Yes.)

"To what extent can you get around in ice, snow, rain, mud, heat, and other weather conditions?" (She answered: "To any extent necessary.")

All of this appeared on the form under the heading of "Mobility." The second category of questions bore the title "Self Care," and included the following: "Have you ever lived alone, away from home before?" (Answer: "Yes: my home is where I make it; I have lived alone for thirty years.")

Then: "Are you able to live alone?" "Would you prefer to live alone?" "Do you dress yourself alone?" "Do you handle your own toileting?" "Can you prepare your own meals?" "Do you feed yourself?" (To this last, instead of merely repeating her standard "yes" answer, our Federationist replied: "I have never suffered from malnutrition from inability to find my mouth.")

The questions continue: "Do you go around unaccompanied to work?" "Do you go around unaccompanied to meetings?" "Do you go around unaccompanied to shop?" And then this: "What daily living situations are difficult for you to handle?" (Her answer: "Dealing with people who ask questions like these.")

Nestled among the forest of questions, by the way—lest it be supposed that our Federationist had somehow received the wrong application form—was this: "Do you use a seeing eye dog?" She answered "No."

Under the heading of "Special Care," the question was asked: "What physical therapy will you continue while in VISTA service?" (Her reply was: "Swimming, judo, and weight-lifting, if possible—they are not essential.")

Under the category "Use of Special Services," there were three questions—to which the respondent made three answers befitting a true Federationist. The dialogue went as follows:

Question: "Have you received physical therapy?" *Answer:* "During some fifteen years of instructing others in physical fitness, I have had to take much of my own advice."

Question: "Have you received speech therapy?" *Answer:* "I have been vice-president and program director of Republican Speakerettes, a public speaking group."

Question: "What contacts have you had with your Vocational Rehabilitation Division, or State Department of Education?" (Please explain in detail.) *Answer:* "Poor: it would seem that I remain un-rehabilitated."

Thus ended the encounter of the blind Federationist with the forward-looking, people-serving, modern-minded agencies of VISTA and the Peace Corps. Of course she never heard again from VISTA. If she had, and if somehow she had been accepted as a

"Volunteer in Service to America," her response would have been predictable; for in her letter to me, she concluded the narrative of her misadventure with this sentence: "Of course all this is merely a matter of curiosity, since I no longer have the slightest interest in VISTA or anything remotely connected with it."

What then of "maximum feasible participation" in the Poverty Program? Here is an agency, self-proclaimed as the most progressive in the land, dedicated to ending prejudice and bringing equality, dignity, and full participation to all who are socially deprived or disadvantaged. What "vistas" does it open for the blind? How much respect does it confer upon the vigorous and enterprising blind applicant? The answer is self-evident. The questionnaire speaks grossly for itself—and I think all of us read and reject its message loud and clear. In only one small corner, tucked away at the very end of the three-page document, is there any effort to determine the skills or abilities of the candidate. That effort is contained in a single question—one out of a total of thirty-eight!

It is not as if the Peace Corps or VISTA had never had experience with a blind applicant since in a few scattered instances blind persons have actually been accepted for service both here and abroad—service well-performed, incidentally, by all accounts and records. It is, rather, that these successes were apparently dismissed as isolated instances, and that the image of the helpless, hopeless blind man remained intact with all of its defeatist presumptions and insulting implications.

So much, then, for the new and modern agencies of social conscience and enlightenment. Let us turn to the older, more experienced institutions of public service. Can it be that the blind fare better here? Is the graven image of the helpless blind man more, or is it less, apparent among such stalwart public institutions as, for example, the city fire department?

For an insight into this question, consider an incident which occurred recently in a midwestern city of moderate size. In that city is a rooming house in which there happen to reside, among others, a number of persons who are blind. One day the owner of the rooming house was startled to observe a number of firemen on her front lawn in the act, apparently, of putting up a large illuminated sign of some kind. Asked what they were doing, and why, the men replied that they were, indeed, installing a sign—one that bore the single luminous letter "I." That letter, they told the landlady, stands for "invalid," and therefore would serve to notify all and sundry that the rooming house harbored invalids—an item of information presumably of value in case of fire or other disaster, since "invalids" (in this case, blind people) are helpless and would need assistance in time of peril. Moreover, said the firemen, when they had finished installing the sign on the lawn, they intended to come inside and affix smaller signs, also bearing the luminous letter "I," upon the doors of each and every one of the blind tenants.

(It is not clear, incidentally, whether the insignia on the doors, and at the entrance of the rooming house, were to be scarlet letters. But surely they would carry much the same stigma, contempt, and condemnation as the famous scarlet letter—"A" for adultery—which was forcibly worn by the ill-fated Hester Prynne of Hawthorne's novel.)

Understandably, the landlady was distressed at the prospect of an illuminated sign at the front of her house, advertising the presence of "invalids" within. She called upon the firemen to cease and desist; and eventually, after some threat and bluster, these public servants did back down. But only part way. They still insisted upon fastening the "I" signs on the doors of the rooms occupied by blind tenants. Indeed, they gained the reluctant permission of the landlady to do so; and the conspicuous little plaques with the single glittering letter would doubtless be there today, were it not for the staunch resistance of the blind tenants—who showed themselves ready to stand in the doorway if necessary in order to protect their rooms and their characters from being thus marked and maligned.

I am pleased to report that the blind residents won the day, and preserved their integrity unmarked, but it is noteworthy that the firemen gave way not because they were converted or persuaded—not because they saw the error of their ways—but only because they were effectively resisted. No doubt the fire chief and his minions in that city (as in many others) still believe that blindness is equivalent to helplessness, and that blind persons are immobilized incompetents, unable to fend for themselves in the event of fire, crisis, or calamity.

This story again illustrates the tendency, as common among public officials as among the public at large, to attribute incompetence (both physical and mental) to persons who are blind. To the firemen in question the blind person is literally a dead weight, a burden to be carried like a piece of furniture from the scene of danger. To the Peace Corps and the Poverty Program, he is at best chair-borne and at worst bed-ridden.

If these two sets of public institutions, national and municipal, are thus dominated by the graven image of blindness, where can we turn for more realistic, reasonable, and respectable assumptions? Surely, one might suppose, there is at least one safe place, one institution secure from prejudice and ignorance, and immunized against the subtle poisons of condescension and contempt—namely, the institutions and agencies actually concerned with the education and rehabilitation of blind persons and with the dissemination of the facts about blindness to the public. There at least, it would seem certain, we should find a new image of the blind man and of his true needs and abilities—one that does not strain at gnats or suffer foolishness gladly, one that rises above the trivial and superficial in order to concentrate upon the paramount problems that block the way to full equality and independence for all blind people.

Let us see. Here is a promising professional publication, produced by the Institute of Blind Rehabilitation of Western Michigan University, at Kalamazoo, in cooperation with the Rehabilitation Services Administration of the U.S. Department of Health, Education, and Welfare. Do we find, here, the sense of importance and the urgency of commitment that are lacking elsewhere, along with recognition of the intellectual and physical capability—the plain normality—of the blind person?

The title of this exhaustive ten-page treatise is *Techniques for Eating—A Guide for Blind Persons.*[1] These are the opening words of the preface: "After a cursory glance at the title of this manual, many people would dismiss it as relatively unimportant, or surely as something that does not present problems to blind persons. Nothing could be further from the truth." Methinks the authors do protest too much; as the Biblical admonition has it, the wicked flee when no man pursueth. For at the very outset the tone is so defensive as to suggest a lack of confidence in the topic.

However that may be, the next words betray a striking lack of belief in the general capacities of blind persons; for it develops that these authors are not addressing the blind person at all, but rather the people around him (families, counselors, guides, and other nursemaids) who are there to take care of him and be responsible to him.

"This manual does not pretend to have all the solutions to the problems presented to the blind individual when eating. At best, it is only intended to serve as guidelines for those who will be working with the blind individual in this specific area. It should be helpful to families or rehabilitation personnel who are in direct contact with the blind individual. Above all, it must be remembered that the acquisition of these skills and techniques require constant practice under close supervision." (I must interrupt here to say—as an old-time grammarian—that the subject-verb disagreement in the foregoing sentence comes from the treatise, not from me!)

What are these intricate "skills and techniques" which require such constant practice under such close supervision? The table of contents tells us, under the general heading of "Techniques:"

"To Approach Table
Exploration of Place Setting
Orientation to Contents of Plate
To Cut Meat With Fork
To Cut Meat With Knife...
To Butter Bread or Roll...
To Pour Salt and/or Pepper
To Put Sugar Into Beverage...
To Pour Cream...
To Pass Foods... (and)
To Eat on Tray."

Here are some examples of the intricacy and complexity of the problems dealt with in this scientific exposition by the authors—both of them, as we are told, experts in education and rehabilitation of the blind:

"During the course of eating, it is advisable to bend the trunk forward, bringing the face above the plate, should something fall from the fork....

"In the process of eating, foods may be picked up by the 'stab' method which involves inserting the tines of the fork into the food and lifting. This is used for such solids as string beans, fruit salad, etc.; or foods may be picked up by the 'scoop' method, which involves dipping the forward part of the fork down into the food, leveling the fork, and then bringing it up."

"In situations where it is difficult to pick up the food, a 'pusher' may be used. This might be a piece of bread or roll, or another utensil such as a spoon or a knife, which holds the food in position to be picked up with the fork."

Now for some concrete techniques, skills, and scientific methods:

"To approach table: (1) Place one hand on back of chair; (2) With free hand, scan arms and/or seat of chair to ascertain shape and whether or not the chair is occupied." (One wonders, in the context of all this frivolous nonsense, whether the authors would also advocate, should the chair be occupied, scanning the occupant to ascertain shape.)

Under the heading "Exploration of place setting," we find the following:

"To locate plate, with flexed arms and curled fingers, lift hands to top edge of table and move gently toward center of table until contact is made." And a little later on: "With arms flexed, and fingers curled, follow right edge of plate, and extending arm and fingers gradually, angle to the right to locate tea cup and/or glass."

Here is an especially complicated maneuver, apparently modeled after jungle-warfare instructions in an army field manual:

"Using edge of plate as point of reference, approach contents of plate from above with tines of fork in perpendicular position. Insert fork into food at positions of 6 o'clock, 9 o'clock, 12 o'clock, and 3 o'clock, identifying food by texture and/or taste. (Fork may be brought to mouth as desired.)"

In the detailed discussion of how "to butter bread or roll," consisting of seven steps or operational phases, there is one I find particularly fascinating. It is "Number 4. Break the roll."

Let me quote just three more specific techniques which appear in the course of these illuminating instructions:

"To eat pie, begin at the tip and, either stabbing or scooping, work toward the back of the pie."

"To take a roll or cookie, locate edge of plate and gently move in to find item." And finally:

"The sensation of hot and cold indicates where hot and cold foods are located." I was glad to learn that; aren't you?

Something of the condescension of this pompous parade of the obvious and the trivial may be observed in the quotation which serves as frontispiece to the publication. It is attributed to Emil Javal, and reads as follows: "Meals being for the blind the pleasantest moments of life, it is very important for him to train himself to eat properly, so that he may feel in a position to accept an invitation out."

Now, why are meals "the pleasantest moments of life" *for the blind*? Can it be because (as some people appear to believe) the blind, in their helpless condition, knowing themselves to be incompetent and irrelevant if not quite immaterial, can have few joys other than eating? "What is a man," asked Hamlet, "if his chief good and market of his time be but to sleep and feed? A beast, no more."

And what about that crack about being in "a position to accept an invitation out." Out of what—the almshouse? Solitary confinement? Why must the blind person wait for "an invitation out," unless he is in truth not capable of sallying forth on his own or of "inviting people in"? Such an archaic attitude might have been suitable in, say, 1905; but we are far removed today from the conditions of social isolation and enforced idleness which this quotation conjures up. The real value of the quotation is the very opposite of that intended by the authors of this tiresome treatise on table topography, this god-awful guide to gracious gourmandering, this moronic manual on meal-time mastication, this oddball odyssey for outlandish oenologists, this poor man's primer on polite pantry protocol and perpendicular pie-pushing. The frontispiece quotation, and indeed the whole sad tract, is graphically illustrative of the demeaning and dispiriting image of blindness and the blind which still controls the thoughts of far too many agency professionals, and so controls the lives of the blind.

And what does all of this mean? What is the significance of these acts and attitudes on the part of government officials and workers with the blind? It is not merely that these several isolated incidents occurred. It is not even that they are symptomatic of a broader pattern of thought and deed, and therefore not isolated at all. It is rather that they bespeak the dominant theme of public and official opinion which everywhere characterizes the image of blindness.

That is the dark and threatening significance of the events which I have laid before you. But such events as these, however common, however destructive, no longer stand alone. Of still greater significance is the positive fact that we have come to recognize these sordid myths and misconceptions for the lies which they are; that we have organized; that we have *mobilized* ourselves into a powerful movement to change the total landscape of the country of the blind; that we have not only won friends and influenced people in our cause but have won battles and influenced the course of public policy.

It is significant, too, that more and more professionals in the field of work with the blind—in the private agencies, in government, in the foundations and universities—are receiving our message and rallying to our cause. It is significant that more and more blind persons are employed, in better and better careers. It is significant, most of all, that despite the heritage of old outlooks, despite the deep hold of the graven image upon their minds, the general public is beginning to show itself ready to listen, to learn, and to understand.

The challenge is ours, and the time is now. Our revolution will not wait, and it will succeed—but only if we take the lead and take the risks. It is for us to persuade, to participate, to persevere—and to prevail—and prevail we will!

The words of Abraham Lincoln, spoken a hundred years ago, are no less applicable to us today: "We cannot escape history. No personal significance or insignificance will spare one or another of us. This fiery trial through which we pass will light us down in honor or dishonor to the last generation. We, even we here, hold the power and bear the responsibility."

The time is now, and the challenge is real. I ask you, with all that the question implies: will you join me on the barricades?

FOOTNOTE

1. *Techniques of Eating: A Guide for Blind Persons.* Prepared by Lloyd C. Widenberg and Ruth Kaartela. Published by School of Graduate Studies, Western Michigan University, Kalamazoo, Michigan 49001.

Increasingly Jernigan was asked to address official gatherings concerned with broad issues of education and the general welfare. One such occasion was a Governor's Conference on the Future of Education held in Des Moines during October, 1969, and attended by over 800 educators and other professionals. Dr. Jernigan was invited, as an educator himself, to speak on the then-controversial subject of innovation in education. His response, although it did not deal directly with blindness and the blind, was infused with the philosophy and outlook he had acquired through two decades of association with both the organized blind and the service agencies of the blindness system. This is what he had to say:

THE FUTURE OF EDUCATION INNOVATION: PANACEA OR PANDEMONIUM?
by Kenneth Jernigan

The question before us on this panel is: Educational Innovation—Panacea or Pandemonium. My response to that question is, summarily, that innovation cannot be a panacea, and need not become pandemonium. At the least it is a palliative, and at best it may be a progression. Nothing is more evident today, to the layman as well as to the expert, than our "systems for the delivery of learning"—that is, our schools—are in trouble. Not only in Iowa, but all over the land—and at all levels from elementary to university—we seem to be going "up the down staircase."

At the college level, students in significant proportions, if not in alarming numbers, militantly confront and sometimes defy their professors and administrators. The common denominator of their various demands is, however, not revolution—at least not yet—but innovation. The cliche most commonly employed to express this demand is "relevance"; and that tiresome term (if it means anything at all) means new departures both in the substance and procedure, the goals and the methods, of academic experience. But that is not all there is to the theme of innovation in higher education. Two recent and broadly influential studies of the college crisis, neither of them concerned primarily with student protest—and both of them the work of sociologists—illustrate in their titles the centrality of the principle of innovation. One is *The Academic Revolution*, by Christopher Jencks and David Riesman; the other is *The Reform of General Education*, by Daniel Bell. Let me, for the moment, simply take note of this pervasive and persistent emphasis on innovation in the current literature on the higher learning in America.

At the secondary level the issues are not quite the same but are no less caught up in considerations of reform and experimental change. Here the problem is more commonly one of drop-outs than of sit-ins (although Students for a Democratic Society, as you know, has begun a campaign to organize the high schools); and questions of contemporary relevance, immediacy, and cogency, are the burning issues in social studies, if not everywhere else in the curriculum.

At the elementary level, where creativity has its native stronghold, the theme of innovation has been a constant—perhaps the only constant—for more generations than any one now living can remember. Whatever may be said in criticism of our primary schools today, they are a far cry from the Dotheboys Halls of Dickens's time, where Nicholas Nickleby and his fellow scholars carried on their rote learning and ritual recitations in constant terror and discomfort—under pain of daily floggings designed to correct that constitutional flaw in the disposition of all children known to the devout as "infant depravity."

Innovation in the shape of humanitarian reform and child-centered learning entered the American schoolhouse with John Dewey and his progressive philosophy even before the turn of the century. It has since been revitalized through successive theoretical transfusions, notably the self-motivating methods of the Montessori school; and today, after many backings and fillings, innovation is again a conspicuous feature of learning theory and methodology in elementary education. But the tide, of course, does not flow all one way. The innovative spirit, with its passion for change and its impatience toward convention, never proceeds very far in any community without encountering resistance; and in the present conservative climate of opinion across the country (brought on in large part, as I believe, by excessive demands for change), it is unlikely that innovators will have their way entirely at any stage of the educational ladder.

No doubt this is as it should be. The history of American education may well be read as a dialectical process of alternating challenge and response between the forces of innovation and those of tradition. But it should not be supposed that this competition of viewpoints is unhealthy in principle or destructive in tendency. On the contrary, it is the educational analogue of the democratic political process on one hand and of the competitive enterprise system on the other. For the debate I am talking about is not over ends and basic values, but rather over means and interpretations. The real enemy of innovation, it should be understood, is not tradition but inertia. Tradition, wherever it is viable and valuable, welcomes change and progress; innovation, wherever it is sensible and successful, soon turns into tradition. The relationship between innovation and tradition, in the school as in society, is properly not one of conflict but of continuity. Each perspective in fact needs the other. Without regular injections of innovative energy, tradition deteriorates into dogma; without the sober and corrective prudence of traditional wisdom, innovation becomes mere novelty, hovering on the edge of chaos.

I hope that I have said enough to demonstrate my own partiality for innovation, disciplined by a respect for the past, in the curriculum and the classroom at all levels of the educational system. Indeed, it would be a betrayal of my own professional career and commitment were I to suggest otherwise. As director of the Iowa Commission for the Blind over the past dozen years, I have been at the storm center (some might say I have been the storm center) of full-fledged revolution in the education of blind people—away from conventional indoctrination in the sheltered blind trades and from adjustment to lives of quiet desperation toward the higher ground of complete equality, independence, and participation. The blind students who pass through our rehabilitation center here in Des Moines emerge not as dependent conformists ready for the broom shop and the rocking chair, but as self-sufficient citizens ready to lead their own lives, to go their own way and to grow their own way—rebels against the "establishment," no doubt, but rebels with a cause. That cause, that sense of mission, may be defined as faith in their own capacity, individually and collectively, to assume the active role of "change agents" in the uncomprehending world around them: more specifically, to reconstruct the social landscape of the country of the blind. Our commitment in the programs of the Iowa Commission is therefore to innovation in the fullest sense, both in ends and means; and in the exercise of this commitment we are continuously experimenting and improvising, remaking and revamping, branching out and breaking through, in every phase of our operation.

Having said that much for innovation, let me reverse direction and say a few words against it. It is a truism that we live in an age more accustomed to change, more comfortable with abrupt transitions and large-scale alterations, than any previous age in history. Moreover, we Americans are geared toward the future, almost obsessively forward-looking, utterly fascinated with the shape of things to come. Planning, forecasting, prognosticating, predicting, projecting, extrapolating—these are our characteristic national pastimes. Witness, as a case in point, the structure and focus of the present conference. Its subject is education, yes; but it is not "education today," let alone "education in retrospect or in historical perspective." No; it is "The Future of Education." And the opening panel this morning was appropriately entitled "2001: An Education Odyssey."

Well and good. As an avid science-fiction reader and amateur futurist myself, it would come with ill grace from me to scorn this forward-oriented posture. My concern is only that, in our haste to get to tomorrowland, in our absorption with the themes of change and innovation, we may overlook the stubborn realities of today and disdain the crucial lessons of yesterday. In the field of education, as in that of government, we cannot afford to break precipitously with what Walter Lippmann has termed the "traditions of civility" and what Edmund Burke called the "prudential wisdom of the past." For to break away from that usable past is to break away from the moorings of civilization itself—and to drift unpiloted not toward the good society of our dreams but toward the "Brave New World" of our nightmares.

It is not only innovation which cannot be regarded as a panacea for our problems. Education itself must not be burdened with unreasonable demands and expectations. It would be difficult to overemphasize the importance of the schools, and especially of the universities, in the future conduct of our civilization; but it would not be at all difficult to overestimate their capacities and resources. As far back as a decade ago Dr. John W. Gardner, the president of the Carnegie Corporation and since Secretary of Health, Education, and Welfare in the Johnson Administration, could declare: "The role of the universities is undergoing a remarkable change. They are thrust into a position of great responsibility in our society—a position more central, more prominent, more crucial to the life of the society than academic people ever dreamed possible...." Indeed, it is this explosive growth of the American college system which Professors Jencks and Riesman have designated the "academic revolution"—and which they describe in their magisterial volume in tones fraught at least as much with concern and apprehension as with optimism and affirmation. Just as the lower schools cannot be all things to all children, so the universities cannot be all things to all men. In short, to avoid falling into pandemonium we must avoid falling back upon panaceas. In the allocation of roles and values to the educational enterprise, we shall need to keep our heads and maintain our balance—in more ways than the one under discussion in this panel. If it is important to strike a balance between the forces of innovation and those of tradition, it is equally vital to balance the values of a general or liberal education against those of vocational and professional training. And most crucial of all may be the need to balance the esthetic and moral persuasions of the "soft" humanities against the aggressive imperatives of the "hard" sciences. Let us admit that there is no imminent danger of our neglecting or disparaging the latter. Between Sputnik I and Apollo II, little more than a decade apart, we have thoroughly redirected and rededicated our educational investment toward the advancement of science and the nurture of its technological progeny. I have no desire to minimize the magnificent accomplishments which have resulted from that national decision. The proof, after all, is in the pudding—or, rather, the proof is written on the moon and stars. But possibly the time has arrived for a reassessment of educational priorities and of the social values that undergird them. As we rocket down the skyways and spaceways of the future, let us not forget what the year 1984 conjured up in the mind of one sensitive futurologist—the British author George Orwell. It was a vision of hell in the shape of a technological paradise. It was the anticipation of a future society which had lost its head, its nerve, and its soul. That imaginary civilization failed, not for lack of innovation or of information—not for lack of scientific and technical skills or of psychological knowledge—but for lack of belief in the values and requirements of free men. Its failure, in a word, was educational.

I cannot leave this issue without a brief extension of my remarks in a particular direction. In all that I have said thus far I have, perhaps, been guilty of perpetuating the favored illusion of schoolmasters, that education is a strictly formal affair confined to primary, secondary, and tertiary institutions—and to the span of years between five and twenty-one—after which it vanishes like the Cheshire Cat, leaving only a bad taste and a wry grin behind. That assumption is, of course, pedantic poppycock. Education is merely learning, intellectual or cognitive growth, and it proceeds continuously in one form or another from cradle to grave. Much of this lifelong process is, to be sure, what Paul Goodman has labeled "mis-education" and others have termed "negative learning"—a good deal of which takes place in unstructured settings (such as watching TV) and even in unwitting or unconscious circumstances (such as watching TV commercials). Learning of a more active kind occurs in other situations, which are wholly or partially non-academic and extra-curricular, but which function as extensions of the academy—"classrooms without walls," as it were. Many of these settings are sufficiently well known to need no mention; but there are others, close to my own experience, which are germane to our theme of educational innovation. Perhaps the most far-reaching example of informal education today, involving millions of Americans, is to be found in the vast array of public aids and services aimed at the disabled, disadvantaged, and deprived. Not all of these services of course entail the transmission of new learning; but it is remarkable how many of them do, and in how many ways. Here are a few: vocational rehabilitation, vocational education, compensatory education, counseling and guidance, self-support and self-care, group therapy and sensitivity training, apprenticeship and internship programs, VISTA, Manpower Development and Training, Youth Corps, Head Start, Upward Bound, orientation and adjustment services, and so on and on.

In these proliferating programs of quasi-educational impact, already almost more in number than anyone can tabulate, there is continuous innovation—and that is doubtless to the good. But there is also continuous indoctrination—and that is presumably to the bad. If the millions of citizen-clients are not being enlightened by these services, they are unquestionably being influenced; and I wish only to suggest that we might do well to ponder the quality and direction of that educative influence.

As someone has surely said before me: when tyranny comes to America, it is likely to come in the guise of "services."

I can do no better, in bringing my remarks to an end, than to offer you a quotation from a small book which has meant much to me, and perhaps also to some of you—*The Prophet*, by Kahlil Gibran:

> Then said a teacher, Speak to us of Teaching.
>
> And he said:
>
> No man can reveal to you aught but that which already lies half asleep in the dawning of your knowledge.
>
> The teacher who walks in the shadow of the temple, among his followers, gives not of his wisdom but rather of his faith and his lovingness.

If he is indeed wise he does not bid you enter the house
of his wisdom, but rather leads you to the threshold of
your own mind.

In 1970, at the Federation's thirtieth anniversary convention,
President Jernigan delivered a banquet address which many
veteran members of the movement were later to regard as among
the most eloquent of his long career in the leadership of the organized blind. Speaking on the topic, "Blindness—The Myth and
the Image," Jernigan exposed the hidden dimension of mythology
and superstition which still conditioned social attitudes toward
the blind. In particular he struck at the "disaster" concept of
blindness with its melodramatic insistence upon regarding every
blind person as a tragic figure; and he demonstrated in graphic
detail that this mythical image was prevalent not merely in public
opinion but in professional policy and practice.

Here in full is the text of that speech:

BLINDNESS—THE MYTH AND THE IMAGE
by Kenneth Jernigan

It is not only individual human beings who suffer from what the
psychologists call an "identity crisis"—that is, a confusion and
doubt as to who and what they are. So do groups of human
beings—communities, associations, minorities, even whole nations. And so it is—in this year of space if not of grace—with the
blind, organized and unorganized. We are, as I believe, in the
midst of our own full-fledged identity crisis. For the first time in
centuries—perhaps in a millennium—our collective identity is in
question. For the first time in modern history there are anguish
and argument, not only as to what we are, but as to what we may
become. The traditional images and myths of blindness, which had
been taken for granted and for gospel throughout the ages, both
by the seeing and by the blind themselves, are now abruptly and
astonishingly under attack.

Who is it that dares thus to disturb the peace and upset the apple
cart of traditional definitions? The aggressors are here in this
room. They are you and I. They are the organized blind of the
National Federation. It is we who have brought on our own identity crisis—by renouncing and repudiating our old mistaken identity as the "helpless blind." It is we who are demanding that we

be called by our rightful and true names: names such as *competent, normal, and equal.* We do not object to being known as *blind*, for that is what we are. What we protest is that we are not also known as *people*, for we are that, too. What we ask of society is not a change of heart (our road to shelter has always been paved with good intentions), but a change of *image*—an exchange of old myths for new perspectives.

Of all the roadblocks in the path of the blind today, one rises up more formidably and threateningly than all others. It is the invisible barrier of ingrained social attitudes toward blindness and the blind—attitudes based on suspicion and superstition, on ignorance and error, which continue to hold sway in men's minds and to keep the blind in bondage.

But new attitudes about the blind have come into being. They exist side by side with the old and compete with them for public acceptance and belief. Between the two there is vast distance and no quarter. As an example consider the following quotation: "The real problem of blindness is not the loss of eyesight. The real problem is the misunderstanding and lack of information which exist. If a blind person has proper training and if he has opportunity, blindness is only a physical nuisance."[1]

That is a quotation from an administrator in the field of work with the blind. Here is another quotation from another official: "We must not perpetuate the myth that blindness is not a tragedy. For each person who has learned to live an active, fruitful life despite blindness, there are thousands whose lives have lost all meaning....A blind person can't be rehabilitated as a crippled person may be. You can give a [crippled] man mobility, but there is no substitute for sight."[2]

Those two quotations represent the considered judgments of two professionals in the field of services to the blind. The statements are squarely contradictory. If one of them is true, the other must be false. Which are we to believe? There is no doubt as to which of the two would win a public opinion poll. The more popular by far is the second—the one that repudiates as a shocking fiction the very idea that blindness is anything less than a total tragedy.

Let us take note in passing of the peculiar tone of finality and conviction in which this second statement—the "hard line" on blindness—is expressed. I believe there is a striking irony in it which all of us would do well to recognize, for it conveys the distinct impression that there is something cruel and unfair to blind people in the mere-nuisance concept of blindness, as opposed to the evidently kinder and fairer portrayal of the condition as an overwhelming disaster.

The difference between these two perspectives on blindness is not merely that one is optimistic and the other pessimistic. There is more to it than that. The crucial difference is that one view minimizes the consequences of the physical disability and actively rejects the notion that blind persons are somehow "different." Its emphasis is upon the normality of the blind, their similarity and common identity with others, their potential equality, and their right to free and full participation in all the regular pursuits and pastimes of their society. The accent here, in a word, is *affirmative*: it is upbeat, dynamic, rehabilitative. It makes much of opportunity and capacity and does not dwell on deprivation and disability.

By contrast the other point of view—which we might call the "disaster" concept—deliberately maximizes the effects of blindness: physically, psychologically, emotionally, and socially. Its emphasis is upon what is missing rather than what can be done—upon lacks and losses rather than upon capacities and strengths. Blindness, these spokesmen are inclined to tell us, is a kind of "dying";[3] and those who are blind (so we are repeatedly informed) are *abnormal*—they are *different*—they are *dependent*—they are *deprived*—they are *inferior*—and above all, they are *unfortunate*. The accent here, in a word, is *negative*. It is downbeat, pessimistic, professionally condescending, frequently sanctimonious, and ultimately defeatist.

I submit that this disaster concept of blindness is not only a popular opinion among professionals and the public today. It is, with only a little updating and streamlining, the ancient myth of blindness—the classic image of the blind man as a *tragic figure*. Let me be clear about this use of the term "tragic." In its classical sense, tragedy is not mere unhappiness. It does not refer to accidental misfortune or limited harm, which can sensibly be overcome. Tragedy involves a sentence of doom, a dire destiny, which one can only confront in all its unalterable terror but can never hope to transcend. The sense of tragedy, in short, is the sense of calamity—to which the only appropriate response is resignation and despair. These words of Bertrand Russell convey the mood exactly: "On such a firm foundation of unyielding despair must the soul's habitation henceforth securely be built."

How does the tragic view of blindness find expression in modern society? I would answer that it takes two forms: among the public it takes one form, and among professionals another. On the public and popular side, it tends to be conveyed through images of total dependency and deprivation—images, that is, of the "helpless blind man." A typical recent example occurred on the well-known TV program, "Password," in which a number of contestants take turns guessing at secret words through synonyms and verbal associations. On one such show the key word to be guessed was "cup." The first cue word offered was "tin"; but the guesser failed to make the connection. The next cue word given was "blind"— which immediately brought the response "cup." There you have it: for all our rehabilitation, all our education, and all our progress, what comes to the mind of the man in the street when he thinks of a blind person is the tin cup of the beggar!

Not only to the man in the street—it also comes, with a slight twist, to the mind of the lady in the newspaper advice column. "Dear Ann Landers," read a recent letter to the well-known oracle and advisor by that name: "I lost my sight when I was eight and I have a wife and three children. It's very hard for a blind man to make a living because nobody wants to hire me. So I do the next best thing. I sit on the corner with a cup and sell pencils. We have moved to several different cities and have done all right. In this town two cops have told me that begging is against the law and to get moving. Why should there be a law against a man trying to make a living? My wife is writing this for me and we need a fast answer so please hurry. Signed, Tough Luck."

To which Ann Landers says: "No one needs to beg in America. There are countless *welfare organizations* who will help you. Write to American Foundation for the Blind...."

That seems at first glance to be a hopeful and constructive suggestion. But take another look: what the lady is suggesting is that the blind man go on welfare—that the only organizations that can help him are welfare agencies! Here is a man who, by his own word, is only trying to make a living. His problem is that no one has hired him and that he had apparently not had adequate training, encouragement, and orientation; so he is making a living the hard way. But, to the lady columnist, his blindness is the problem. It rules him out of the job market and onto the charity rolls. It never even occurs to her that he might seek rehabilitation, or that it might be available to him.

Ann Landers, of course, is not a professional counseling psychologist or social-work specialist. But she might as well be. As it happens, there is no clear line of demarcation between the popular stereotypes about blindness and the supposedly more learned conceptions of many professionals in work with the blind. A remarkable illustration of assumptions shared in both worlds is to be found in the unbelievable shenanigans of a fascinating philanthropic organization called the Stevens Brothers Foundation of St. Paul, Minnesota. In a circular letter sent to "all State Supervisors of the Blind" (note that wording), under recent date, the director of the Foundation wrote as follows:

> Our activities for aid to the Blind for next year will consist of sending samples of some of the following items for which we have made application for Patents, Registered Copyrights and Trademarks:
>
> Templet-Giant Embossed Telephone Dial for the Blind
>
> E-Z-I Dropper and Washer for the Blind
>
> Goldlettering-Silverlettering on Dark Background for the Industrial Blind
>
> Emergency Whistle for the Blind (and to protect women in emergencies)
>
> Nonskid Barrosette Icegrips for the Blind
>
> Koffeemugg for the Blind
>
> Solesatisfier for Aching Feet of the Blind
>
> National Uniform for the Blind
>
> Organization to Investigate the Attributes and Skills of Blind Flying Bats Insofar as they may be applicable to the Blind
>
> Rockerwheel Krutch for the Crippled, Lame and Blind
>
> My Lord and Ladyships Personal Mechanical Valet for the Blind
>
> Eskeymo Bonnet
>
> Buttonon Necktie for the Blind

Children's Fabrique for Finger Etching—Entertainment—Commercial Toymakers for the Blind

Wraparound Overcoat Tails—Leg Warmers for the Blind [and]

Wraparound and Fastenup Muffler Warmer for the Blind.

Pervading this ludicrous, if well-intentioned catalog of artificial aids and fantastic gimmicks is the assumption that the tragic plight of the blind leaves them helpless to do anything at all for themselves without a battery of gadgets—not even tie their ties, handle the telephone, lift an ordinary coffee cup, appear in public without a special identifying uniform, walk on icy surfaces or without aching feet—or even walk without a "krutch," such as needed by the crippled and lame!

If any doubt remains concerning the attitude of the Stevens Brothers toward those whom they seek to help, it is set at rest by the concluding paragraph of their letter: "Our experience has been that we have found those *patients* who use their Signature and Envelope Addresser Cards *learn very quickly* how to use the Letteriter and we hope that you have the same success in training *your Blind* in using these Cards." Blind persons, it would seem, are to be regarded as "patients"—who, despite their dreadful infirmity, "learn very quickly" to operate simple gadgets—that is, *"our* blind" do so, and it is hoped that *"your* blind" may be trained to do likewise.

There may be those who would dismiss this rigmarole as merely the work of a harmless crank, not to be taken seriously by anyone in a position of authority or respectability. Would that it were so. But the most astonishing thing about the exploits of the Stevens Brothers of St. Paul is that they have been found acceptable by a high official of the Federal Department of Health, Education, and Welfare. In fact, he recommends that the philanthropists send their materials to the American Foundation for the Blind and the American Printing House for the Blind. And this same official, coincidentally, has maintained on more than one occasion that blindness can not be regarded as an inconvenience but must be faced up to as an unmitigated disaster.

Yet, is it only coincidence that the man who rejects the nuisance-concept in favor of the disaster-concept of blindness should also be the man who finds acceptable the frivolous gimmicks of the

Stevens Brothers? Perhaps; but I think not. I believe there is a direct connection between the philosophy and the practice, between the theory and the behavior. Feeling as he does that the blind are truly different—that they are, in the words of a recent article "socially isolated" from others and trapped forever in the tragedy of their dark fate—feeling this, what could be more natural than the idea of filling their empty and separate world with toys and games, with wraparound tails, and funny uniforms?

Nor does this government official stand alone in his acceptance of the work of the Stevens Brothers. A veritable flood of congratulatory letters came to the St. Paul philanthropists both from here and abroad in response to their overtures, and were immediately circulated by the hundreds and thousands to public agencies and government officials throughout the world to add respectability to what otherwise would have appeared as sheer nonsense or fantastic lunacy. Here is a typical letter from a state director of services to the blind:

"We shall be very honored, indeed, to act as your agent in distributing these aids to the blind persons in schools and institutions....Congratulations on your exploration into other possible aids and areas where some aid or benefit could result to lessen the handicap of blindness. Best wishes to you for continued success in your efforts, and may health and happiness be yours in great abundance."

Here is another, from the head of services to the blind in a different state: "We will be happy to participate in the distribution of the material for the blind which you have been sending us....We feel the material which you so generously are providing will be very beneficial to the blind."

Here is another, from a workshop for the blind in Bombay, India: "Words are inadequate to express our deep sense of gratitude for your generosity and willing assistance in promoting the cause of the welfare of the blind."

Here is yet another, from the director of the Nak-Tong Revival Home in Pusan, Korea: "Once again the Thanksgiving Season ushered out the Autumn and brings in the Winter, with the turkey steps forward. Furthermore, it's most richest season for us mankind, with poverty averting her head and will not spoil the feast of harvest....While we who lost touch love again and workers pause to pray, the children and adult patients of the Nak-Tong Revival Home should like to extend their sincere greetings to the benefactors like yourself for their goodwill during the past year."

There are many other letters besides; but none of them, I feel, can top that! Surely all of these professionals, who take such delight in the toys and gadgets of the Stevens Brothers, would subscribe to the philosophy of one of their colleagues, as uttered some years ago! "To dance and sing, to play and act, to swim, bowl and roller-skate, to work creatively in clay, wood, aluminum or tin, to make dresses, to join in group readings or discussions, to have entertainments and parties, to engage in many other activities of one's own choosing—this is to fill the life of any one with the things that make life worth living."[4]

Let me remind you of the way in which Dr. Jacobus tenBroek, then in his prime as President of the National Federation of the Blind, responded to that statement. In one of his great convention speeches, "Within the Grace of God," he quoted the passage and went on to say this: "Are these the things that make life worth living for you? Only the benevolent keeper of an asylum could make this remark—only a person who views blindness as a tragedy which can be somewhat mitigated by little touches of kindness and service to help pass the idle hours but which cannot be overcome. Some of these things may be suitable accessories to a life well filled with other things—a home, a job, and the rights and responsibilities of citizenship, for example."[5]

The point I am seeking to make now is the very same point that Dr. tenBroek was seeking to make then. There are two opposing conceptions of the nature of blindness at large in the world. One of them holds that it is a nuisance, and the other that it is a disaster. I think it is clear that the disaster concept is widespread alike in popular culture and in the learned culture of the professionals. Moreover, I would submit that the concept itself is the *real* disaster—the only real disaster that we as blind people have to live with—and that when we can overcome this monstrous misconception, we shall ring down the curtain forever on the fictional drama entitled "The Tragedy of Blindness."

In order to emphasize still further the full extent to which the disaster concept—the tragic sense of blindness—prevails among the professionals in our field, let me introduce in evidence another exhibit. It is a comment from overseas by an official of the National Council for the Blind of Ireland. This is what he says of the blind people of his country: "Although the exceptional and stubborn can learn a trade or pursue an education up to university level [note that "up to"] and follow successful careers, such cases are unusual. Since unemployment has always been a factor in our economy, there are not many posts available. We lack the industries with the necessary repetitive machinery on which the blind can safely work."

All that needs to be remarked about that dreary pronouncement is that it heavily reinforces the defeatist notion that blind persons in general (those who are not peculiarly stubborn and exceptional) should give up any idea of pursuing a normal trade or even of attaining an ordinary education, and should resign themselves to the prospect (itself not too likely) that society in its kindness may be willing to set aside enough repetitive and mechanical chores to take care of most of them, in penury and penitence.

If you think this dark picture reflects only the bogs and mists of old Ireland, consider this letter from the Dean of Admissions of Oral Roberts University, of Tulsa, Oklahoma, written not in the last century or even ten years ago but on May 27, 1970, to a blind applicant for admission:

> Dear ————:
>
> We have received your application for admission and are very impressed with the academic record you have established in high school.
>
> In checking your application I notice that you are blind. At this time, ORU does not have the facilities to accommodate blind students. There is a possibility that some type of program will be initiated in future years; however, at this time, I regret that we will be unable to admit you.
>
> If you have any questions, please let me know. We will be praying with you that the Lord will guide and direct you.
>
> Cordially yours,...

There it is again. One's academic record is impressive, says the Dean; ordinarily it would constitute the sole and sufficient evidence of capability. But unfortunately it appears that one is blind; therefore the academic record, however impressive, is suddenly irrelevant, incompetent, and immaterial. For the university, says the Dean, does not have the "facilities" to accommodate blind students—whatever those facilities might be. Never mind that there are not, should not, and need not be any such facilities, any special aids or instruments, anywhere that blind college students matriculate. Someday, says the Dean, there might be "some type of program"; in the meantime, we shall pray that others may possess more faith, hope, and charity than we at Oral Roberts Christian University.

The life of a blind person, in this considered spiritual view, is therefore a life without meaning—just as it is in the secular view of the Stevens Brothers. Fill it with whistles and tricks, wraparound tails and funny uniforms, but do not undertake to enrich it with higher education or imbue it with serious purpose.

To the deans of small faith and their like-minded ilk, to the Landers sisters and the Stevens brothers and their relatives everywhere, we have not progressed at all beyond the outlook of the primitive Mediterranean society, thousands of years ago, among whom it was a common saying that "the blind man is as one dead."

How are we to reply to these prophets of gloom and doom, who cry havoc and have nothing to offer us but whistles in the dark? We might use logic or theory. We might use history or precept. But the simplest and most effective argument comes from our own experience as blind people. Everything which we are and which we have become rises up to give the lie to the disaster concept of blindness. We, the blind people of this country, are *now* working as farmers, lawyers, scientists, and laborers; as teachers, mechanics, engineers, and businessmen. We are *now* functioning in all of the various professions, trades, and callings of the regular community. We do not regard our lives, as we live them on a day-to-day basis, as tragic or disastrous—and no amount of professional jargon or trumped-up theory can make us do so. We know that with training and opportunity we can compete on terms of equality with our sighted neighbors—and that blindness is merely a physical nuisance.

The blind people of yesterday, and the day before yesterday, had little choice but to accept the tragic view of the gloom-and-doom mongers—the prophets of despair. Their horizons were limited to the bounty of charity, and their world was bounded by the sheltered workhouse. At every turn they were reminded of their infirmity; on every occasion they were coaxed into immobility and dependency. It is no wonder that they fulfilled the prophecy of despair; believing it themselves, they made it come true.

But that was another time, another era, another world. We the blind people of today have carried out a revolution, and have won our independence. We have won it by finding our own voice, finding our own direction, and finding our own doctrine. That doctrine may be simply stated: it is that the blind are normal people who can not see. It is that blindness is not a dying, but a challenge to make a new life. It is also that there are none so blind as those who will not see this simple truth.

The blind people of today, in a word, were not born yesterday. We who are blind do not accept the tragic prophecies of a dire fate. We have a rendezvous with a different destiny. The destiny we go to meet is that of integration and equality—of high achievement and full participation—of free movement and unrestricted opportunity in a friendly land which is already beginning to accept us for what we are.

That is where the blind are leading the blind. Let those who would resist or deny that destiny remain behind, imprisoned in their own antique myths and images—while the rest of us move on to new adventure and higher ground.

FOOTNOTES

1. Iowa Commission for the Blind, *What Is the Iowa Commission for the Blind?* Published by the State of Iowa, Des Moines, n.d.

2. Dr. Jules Stein, "Blindness Study Urged by Doctor," *New York Times*, November 19, 1967, p. 19.

3. Reverend Thomas J. Carroll, *Blindness—What It Is, What It Does and How to Live with It* (Boston: Little Brown and Company, 1961).

4. Philip S. Platt, "Challenges of Voluntary Agencies for the Blind." Paper read at convention of the American Association of Workers for the Blind, June 26, 1951, p. 8.

5. Dr. Jacobus tenBroek, "Within the Grace of God," An Address Delivered at the Banquet of the Annual Convention of the National Federation of the Blind held in San Francisco, July 1, 1956.

Leadership and the Barricades

From its beginning the Federation was concerned with the nature of leadership and the relation of that leadership to the individual members throughout the organization. Philosophical questions dealing with the principles of leadership commonly alternated in conventions and conferences with pragmatic issues dealing with the tactics of leadership. Oncoming leaders of the younger generation exchanged views with grizzled veterans of the first generation; elective officers and rank-and-file members parleyed at meetings and collaborated on resolutions—defining, amending, and fine-tuning the functions of leadership. And successive Presidents, like Kenneth Jernigan at the 1971 convention in Houston, shared their thoughts and convictions with the throng of attending members in annual presidential reports as well as in the more ceremonial banquet addresses.

"There is a kind of covenant in this organization between the membership in convention and the Executive," said President Jernigan in the course of his 1971 report. "I've tried to keep the faith with you, and I believe you have kept it with me. The President of this organization is not simply an impartial chairman presiding over a group of disjointed affiliates. I believe that you elect a President to conduct an administration; that you elect him to take stands on issues; and that you expect him to lead. I believe that if he doesn't lead the way you want him to lead, that you can and will rise up and throw him out. And that's what democracy means."

The President continued: "I think you ought to throw me out of office just as much for inaction or for over-caution, for not leading, for not doing things to help blind people, as you would for rash or precipitous actions and for ill-timed judgments. In other words, I believe that you elected me to lead a movement to try to improve the conditions of the blind, and as long as I'm President, so help me God, I'm going to lead.

"We are a cohesive, spiritual movement," he concluded. "We are an army of liberation for blind people. We are a tough, fighting force. We are a responsible organization. We are a call to conscience and I think, incidentally, that we are unstoppable and unbeatable."

In his banquet address at the 1971 convention Jernigan linked the theme of leadership with that of relationship—more particularly, the various and shifting relationships between the organized blind and elements of the blindness system. In a rousing speech received with waves of applause and a final standing ovation, the NFB President warned all who still clung to the old ways of condescension and caretaking that a day of reckoning was at hand. "We don't want strife or dissension," he said, "but the time is absolutely at an end when we will passively tolerate second-class citizenship and custodial treatment. We are free men, and we intend to act like it. We are free men, and we intend to stay that way. We are free men, and we intend to defend ourselves. Let those who truly have the best interest of the blind at heart join with us as we move into the new era of equality and integration. Let those who call our conduct negative or destructive make the most of it."

The full text of his speech—tersely and aptly entitled "To Man the Barricades"—follows:

TO MAN THE BARRICADES
by Kenneth Jernigan

Some of you may remember the story Will Rogers liked to tell about his early career as a comedian in vaudeville. "I used to play a song called 'Casey Jones' on the harmonica with one hand," he said, "and spin a rope with the other, and then whine into the old empty rain barrel...and then in between the verses I used to tell jokes about the Senate of the United States. If I needed any new jokes that night, I used to just get the late afternoon papers and read what Congress had done that day, and the audience would die laughing."

This story reminds me of my own activities over the past twenty years. I have gone all over the country as the guest of blind groups and civic associations; and, like Will Rogers, I tell stories about the Government of the United States—particularly the Department of Health, Education, and Welfare, and the other "professionals" doing work with the blind. And when I need any new jokes, I just get the latest reports from the agencies and foundations and read what they have been doing recently—and the audience dies laughing. Unless, of course, there are people in the audience who are blind, or friends of the blind—and they die crying.

Which is a roundabout way of saying that much of what goes on in the journals and laboratories and workshops of the agencies for the blind these days is a cruel joke. It is a mockery of social science and a travesty on social service. Far from advancing the welfare and well-being of blind people, it sets our cause back and does us harm.

The blind, along with some other groups in our society, have become the victims of a malady known as "R and D"—that is, Research and Demonstration. The R and D projects are largely financed by the Federal Department of Health, Education, and Welfare and account for an ever-increasing chunk of its budget. The whole tone and direction of programs for the blind in the country—rehabilitation, education, social services, and the rest—have been altered as a result. The art of writing grant applications, the tens of millions of dollars available to fund the approved R and D projects, the resulting build-up of staff in universities and agencies for the blind, the need to produce some sort of seemingly scientific results in the form of books and pamphlets to justify the staff salaries and the field trips and conferences, and the wish for so-called "professional" status have all had their effect. Blind people have become the *objects* of research and the *subjects* of demonstration. They are quizzed, queried, and quantified; they are diagnosed, defined, and dissected; and when the R and D people get through with them, there is nothing left at all—at any rate, nothing of dignity or rationality or responsibility. Despite all of their talk about improving the quality of services to blind people (and there is a lot of such talk these days), the research and demonstration people see the blind as inferiors. They see us as infantile, dependent wards. The signs of this creeping condescension—of this misapplied science, this false notion of what blind people are, and of what blindness means—are all about us. Some things are big, and some are little; but the pattern is conclusive and the trend unmistakable.

Consider, for instance, what has happened to the talking book. From the very beginning of the service from the Library of Congess back in the 1930s, the first side of each talking-book record has concluded with these words: "This book is continued on the other side of this record." The flip side has always ended with:

"This book is continued on the next record." Surely no one can have any serious quarrel with this language. It serves a purpose. The reader, absorbed in the narrative, may well not remember whether he is on the first or second side of a record, and the reminder is useful and saves time.

In the last three or four years, however, something new has been added. After the familiar "This book is continued on the next record," the statement now appears: "Please replace this record in its envelope and container." That one, I must confess, crept up on me gradually. Although from the very beginning I found the statement annoying, it took some time for its full significance to hit me.

Here I was, let us say, reading a learned treatise on French history—a book on Gallic statesmanship—one which presupposes a certain amount of understanding and mental competence. The narrative is interrupted by a voice saying "Please replace this record in its envelope and container." Then it strikes me: These are the words one addresses to a moron or a lazy lout. These words do not appear on records intended for the use of sighted library borrowers. They are intended for the blind. To be sure, they are not an overwhelming or unbearable insult. They are only one more small evidence of the new custodialism, the additional input of contempt for the blind recipient of services which is in the air these days.

I have heard that the words were added at the request of some of the regional librarians because certain blind borrowers were careless with the records. Are sighted people never careless with books or records? Are such words at the end of the record really likely to make the slob less slobby? The ordinary, normal human being (blind or sighted) will, as a matter of course, put the record back into the envelope and container. What else, one wonders, would he do with it?

Regardless of all this, one thing is fairly certain: My remarks on the subject will undoubtedly bring forth angry comments from library officials and others that I am quibbling and grasping at straws, that I am reading meanings that aren't there into innocent words. To which I reply: I am sure that no harm was meant and that the author of the words did not sit down to reason out their significance, but all of this is beside the point. *We* have reasoned out the significance, and we are no longer willing for our road to hell to be paved with other people's good intentions, their failure to comprehend, or their insistence that we not quibble.

Here is another illustration—again, a slight and almost trivial affair. I had occasion recently to visit a public school where there was a resource class for blind and partially seeing children. The teacher moved about with me among the students. "This little girl can read print," she said. "This little girl *has* to read Braille." Now, that language is not oppressively bad. Its prejudice is a subtle thing. But just imagine, if you will, a teacher saying of a pair of children: "This little girl *can* read Braille; this little girl *has* to read print." The supposition is that the child possessing some sight, no matter how little, is closer to being a normal and full-fledged human being; the one without sight can't cut it and has to make do with inferior substitutes.

Confront that teacher with her words, and she will be hurt. She will say, "But that is not how I meant it. It was simply the way I said it." It is true that she was not consciously aware of the significance of her statement and that she did not mean to say what she said; but she said exactly what she meant, and how she felt. And her students, as well as visitors to her classroom, will be conditioned accordingly. I don't wish to make too much of the teacher's terminology, or the words on the talking-book record. Neither exemplifies any great cruelty or tragedy. They are, however, straws in the wind; and either of them could be the final straw—the straw that breaks the blind man's back, or spirit. Far too many backs and spirits have been broken in that way, and the breaking must stop.

As I have said, some of the recent incidents in our field are small, and some are big; but they fit together to make a pattern, and the pattern is conclusive. During the past decade, for instance, the vocational employment objective of rehabilitation has steadily receded before the advancing tide of "social services" and "research and development," and the Division for the Blind in the Federal Rehabilitation Service has diminished accordingly in prominence and importance. By 1967 rehabilitation had taken such a back seat that it became submerged in a comprehensive pot of Mulligan stew set up by the Department of Health, Education, and Welfare called "Social and Rehabilitation Service," with the emphasis clearly on the "social." A new public-information brochure turned out by HEW, listing all the department's branches and programs, placed rehabilitation—where do you suppose?—dead last.

As far as the blind were concerned, the ultimate blow fell late last year. *Federal Register* document 70-17447, dated December 28, 1970, announced the abolition of the Division for the Blind altogether, and its inclusion in the new Division of Special Populations! And who are these "special populations"? They include, and I quote, "alcoholics, drug addicts, arthritics, epileptics, the blind, heart, cancer, and stroke victims, those suffering communication disorders, et cetera." (I leave the specifics of that "et cetera" to your imagination.) Therefore, half a century after the establishment of the federal vocational rehabilitation program, and almost as long after the development of a special division of services for the blind (and still longer since the creation of separate agencies or commissions for the blind in most of the states) the blind of America were to lose their identity and return to the almshouse for the sick and indigent.

This was too much, and every major national organization and agency (both *of* and *for* the blind) combined to resist it. By February of 1971 the HEW officials had made a strategic withdrawal. They announced that they had never intended to downgrade or de-emphasize services to the blind; but that in order to clear up any possible misunderstanding they were establishing a new "Office for the Blind," to be on a par with the "Division of Special Populations," and in no way connected with it. Thus (for the moment) the tide was reversed and the power of united action demonstrated; but the tide is still the tide, and the trend is still the trend.

It is not difficult to find the evidence. For example, under date of February 4, 1971, the Federal Rehabilitation Services Administration issued an information memorandum entitled "Subminimum Wage Certificates for Handicapped Workers." The document is self-explanatory; it is damning; and it is all too indicative of what is happening to the blind in America today. "A recent revision to the wage and hour regulations," the memorandum begins, "broadens State vocational rehabilitation agencies' certification responsibility with respect to employment of handicapped workers at subminimum wages. The responsibility was previously limited by regulation to certain categories of handicapped persons employed *by sheltered workshops*."

"The revision to the wage and hour regulations, effective February 4, 1971," the memorandum continues, "authorizes State rehabilitation agencies to certify certain disabled persons for work *in competitive employment* at less than fifty percent of the statutory minimum wage but not less than twenty-five percent."

So said HEW in February of this year! No longer must the pay be even fifty percent of the minimum wage! No longer is it limited to the sheltered shop! It may now be extended to private industry, to so-called "competitive" employment! And this, we are told, is *rehabilitation*. We are not to quibble. We are not to read meanings into things which are not there. We are not to find patterns or trends or hidden significance. No! We are to take our twenty-five percent "competitive" employment, and be grateful for it. That is what we are *expected* to do, but I doubt that we will do it.

I have already spoken about R and D—the so-called "research and demonstration" financed ever more heavily and lovingly by the Department of Health, Education, and Welfare. I have at hand a typical product of "R and D"—a comprehensive 239-page publication of the American Foundation for the Blind, entitled *A Step-by-Step Guide to Personal Management for Blind Persons*.[1] I invite you now to accompany me on a step-by-step guided tour through its pages and mazes. But let me warn you: It may be a bad trip.

"One of the areas," we are told at the outset of this guidebook, "where independence is valued most highly by a broad spectrum of blind persons...is personal management." I myself would put that a little differently. I would say that the blind person should, and commonly does, take for granted that independence begins at home—that self-care comes before self-support—but that what he values most highly in life is not his ability to master the simple rituals of daily living, such as are detailed in this manual. It is not his ability to wash his face, take a shower, clean his nails, brush his hair, sit down on a chair, rise from a chair, stand upright, wash his socks, light a cigarette, shake hands, nod his head "yes," shake his head "no," and so on and so on through two hundred-plus pages of instruction. No, these are not the supreme attainments and values in the life of the blind person, or of any other civilized person. They are merely the elementary motor and mechanical skills which represent the foundation on which more meaningful and significant achievements rest. The skills of personal management are rudimentary, not remarkable.

However, the American Foundation's guide to personal management for blind persons does not put the matter in such modest perspective. Rather, it is blown up to majestic proportions, as if it were not the beginning but the end of self-realization and independence. Most of all, it is presented as a very difficult and complicated subject—this business of grooming and shaving, bathing and dressing—virtually as the source of a new science. Much is made of the "need for an organized body of realistic and practical personal management techniques." The American Foundation, out of a deep sense of professional obligation and the excitement of pioneering on new scientific horizons, agreed as long ago as 1965 (in its own words) "to undertake the responsibility for developing, over a period of years, workable personal management techniques for blind persons." To begin with, an AFB staff specialist was assigned to coordinate the project, and he proceeded immediately to carry out a massive survey of agencies throughout this country and Canada—on such life-and-death questions and critical issues as how to teach blind persons to shake hands correctly and put the right sock on the right foot.

But surveys at a distance, no matter how thorough and scientific, were not good enough for such profound subject matter. No. What was needed was (to quote the report) "the pooled thinking and experience of a fairly large number of persons from diverse backgrounds and programs." In short, what was needed was a conference, or better yet, a series of conferences—in big hotels in major cities, complete with workshops, round-tables, lunches, dinners, social hours, and sensitivity sessions. In the words of the report: "For three years, 1967, 1968, and 1969, national meetings were held in New York, Chicago, and New Orleans at which key personnel from representative agencies met both to develop techniques and methods and to refine and improve already existing ones."

Here, to illustrate, is a typical technique—developed and refined over the years in New York, Chicago, and New Orleans, representing the distilled wisdom (if that is the proper expression) of key personnel from diverse backgrounds and specialized programs. Here, under the broad classification "Bathing," is the sixteen-step procedure for the "Sponge Bath." I quote in full:

> *Orientation*: Discuss how equipment can be most efficiently used when taking a sponge bath.
>
> *Equipment*: Water, two containers, soap, cloth, towel, bath mat.
>
> *Technique*:

1. Disrobe.

2. Put water of desired temperature in sink or container.

3. Thoroughly wet washcloth and gently squeeze cloth together.

4. Take one corner in right hand, the other in left hand, bring corners together and grasp in whole hand.

5. With other hand grasp remaining cloth. Hold washcloth in closed fist.

6. Hold one hand stationary while turning other hand to squeeze excess water.

7. Unfold cloth and drape over palm of one hand. With other hand pick up soap and dip into water, then rub back and forth from wrist to tips of fingers on cloth.

8. Place soap back in dish.

9. Place soaped cloth in dominant hand.

10. Starting with face and neck, rub soaped cloth over skin portion.

11. Place soaped cloth in water and wring as described above several times until soap has been removed.

12. Use same motion as step 10 to rinse soap from face and neck.

13. Unfold towel. Using either or both hands, dry using a vigorous rubbing motion.

14. Continue to each section of body-washing, rinsing, and drying.

15. As towel gets damp, shift to a dry section.

16. For drying back, put bath towel over right shoulder, grasp lower end hanging in back with left hand and grasp end hanging in front with right hand. While holding towel pull up and down alternately changing position of towel until entire area of back is dry.

Immediately following this highly developed and refined technique—the product of five years of national conferences and international surveys—is the step-by-step guide to taking a "tub bath." I feel that you will want to know that this affair of the tub represents a more advanced and elaborate enterprise in personal management. The greater complexity is evident at the outset. You will recall that the first step in the sponge bath technique was: "Disrobe." But the first step in the tub bath exercise is: *"Disrobe and place clothing where it will not get wet."* That is, of course, a substantial increase in subtlety over the sponge bath.

Let us pause here for a moment and contemplate the significance of that instruction:

"Disrobe and place clothing where it will not get wet." What does it tell us about the intelligence—the *presumed* intelligence—of the blind person under instruction? It tells us that he has not the sense to come in out of the rain; or, more exactly, that he has not the sense to bring his clothes in out of the shower. He is presumed to be either a mental case or a recent immigrant from the jungle, who has never taken a bath before. This latter possibility is given additional credence by instruction number fifteen: "As towel gets damp, shift to a dry section." If the trainee has ever bathed before, he will know about that. Only if he is a babbling idiot or Bomba, the Jungle Boy, does he need to be given that extraordinary advice. This presumption of incompetence or newborn innocence on the part of the blind person is, indeed, pervasive of the entire 239-page guidebook.

What else can it mean to say, with regard to the technique for shaking hands: "If desired, the hands may be moved in an up and down motion?" What else can it mean to say, with regard to the technique for nodding the head: "The head is held facing the person to whom you wish to communicate....With the head held in this position, move the chin down towards the floor about two inches then raise it again to the original position. Make this movement twice in quick succession."

One last quotation, before we leave this magisterial work of applied domestic science. Under the general heading of "Hand Gestures," we find, the technique for "Applauding." It goes like this:

> a. With elbows close to the body, raise both hands until the forearms are approximately parallel to the floor.

> b. Move each hand towards the other so that they come in contact with one another towards the center of the body.

c. The thumb of both hands is held slightly apart from the other four fingers which are held straight and close together.

d. The fingers of the right hand point slightly toward the ceiling and the fingers of the left hand slightly toward the floor so that when the hands come in contact with each other the palms touch but the fingers do not.

e. The thumb of the right hand rests on the knuckle of the left thumb, the fingers of the right hand being above the fingers of the left hand.

f. The hands are brought back to a position about eight to twelve inches apart then brought together in a quick slapping motion.

g. Polite applause would require slapping the hands together about twice each second. More feeling would be expressed by the rapidity, rather than the volume or loudness of the individual's applause.

2. *Hands Inactive*: When the hands are not being used for some specific purpose, the most common position is resting the hands in the lap. For example, the back of the left hand might rest on the left or right leg, or in between, with the palm turned up; the right hand with the palm turned down over the left hand and the fingers of each hand slightly curled around each other.

I cannot leave this great book and its truly vital subject without reading to you the "Foreword" as written by Mr. M. Robert Barnett, executive director of the American Foundation for the Blind: "We would like to take this opportunity," he writes, "to express our appreciation to the many persons professionally involved in work for the blind across the country whose five years of hard work, creativity, and experience have made *A Step-by-Step Guide to Personal Management for Blind Persons* a reality. For many years, countless persons have expressed a need for such a manual and we hope that this publication will help to fill that need."

I would like to know who those "countless persons" are who have expressed a need for such a manual, wouldn't you? Are they blind persons—and if so have they been waiting all these years without being able to test the water, clap the hands, lift the bale, tote the barge, nod, shake, shimmy, rattle, and roll? How have they managed their lives all these years without this personal guide from the American Foundation and its cohorts?

But maybe they are not the ones who have expressed a need for such a manual. Perhaps it is not the blind at all but—as the Foundation puts it—those "professionally involved in work for the blind" to whom this definitive guidebook is addressed. Not our blind brothers, but our blind brothers' keepers. Presumably they are the ones who are to conduct the "orientation" sessions which precede each of the various procedures and techniques—such as: "Discuss types of ties and materials from which ties are made (silk, linen, leather, knit, synthetic, and wool)." And: "Discuss reasons for brushing hair regularly and the suitability of different types of brushes" (scrub brushes, toothbrushes, horse brushes, sagebrushes, brushes with the law, et cetera). Well, admittedly, I added the last part of that sentence myself; but I maintain that it is no different in character, and no more foolish, than the trivial and vacuous material set forth in most of the 239 pages.

Indeed, the very triviality and vacuity of this misguided guidebook may deceive some readers into dismissing it as an unfortunate exception, not characteristic of the main body of work turned out today by serious scholars and professionals in the field of work with the blind. Let me emphasize, therefore, as strongly as I can, the typical and conventional character of this manual. It is not the exception. Its name is legion; its approach, its philosophy, and its superficial contents have been duplicated many times over in the research and demonstration projects of the American Foundation for the Blind, the Department of Health, Education, and Welfare, the college institutes, and the State agencies caught up in the profitable cycle of grants, surveys, tests, and questionnaires.

There is another potential objection to dispose of. That is the supposition that this set of instructions, simple-minded as it is, is not really intended for the ordinary, capable blind person but only for a minority. Moreover, it is true that the book itself makes a verbal nod in this direction, admitting modestly that its techniques are not the only ones possible and that there may be other ways to approach the same goals. But the book also contains an opposite disclaimer, to the effect that the proposed techniques may be too complicated and advanced for some blind persons to handle without preliminary instruction. However that may be, it is clear that this lengthy five-year report is meant to be circulated generally to agencies and schools, to parents and counselors, to guides and custodians, without reservation or qualification.

The best evidence of how this book is intended to be read is to be found in its title. It does not say that it is a step-by-step guide to personal management for mentally retarded or extremely backward blind persons. It does not say it is a guide for tiny children. It says what it means, and means what it says—namely, that it is *A Step-by-Step Guide to Personal Management for Blind Persons.*

And we can do no less than that ourselves; we must also say what *we* mean. As long as such insulting drivel about us continues to be issued in the name of science by agencies doing work with the blind—as long as federal money continues to be available to support it—as long as the climate of general public opinion continues to tolerate it—as long as blind persons continue to be found who can be coaxed or hoodwinked into participating in it—then, for just so long must we of the National Federation of the Blind raise our voices to resist it, denounce it, and expose it for the pseudo-science and the fraud which it is.

The federal research and demonstration projects, the wording on the talking-book records, the attempt to abolish the Division for the Blind in federal rehabilitation, the payment of subminimum wages in sheltered shops and private industry, and the guidebooks to tell us how to run our daily lives are all straws in the wind, signs of the times. But there are other, more hopeful signs. Though the Library of Congress tells us to replace our records in the envelopes and containers, its book selection policies have been refreshingly updated. More and better books are now available to the blind than ever before, including bestsellers and popular magazines. Likewise, though the Division for the Blind was abolished at the federal level, the move was successfully resisted and reversed. And although teachers still talk of blind people who *have* to read Braille and can't read print, although subminimum wages are still allowed in sheltered shops and private industry, and although the Foundation's guidebook is still distributed by the hundreds and thousands to slow our progress, we (the organized blind) are abroad in the land in growing numbers—aware of the peril and prepared to fight it. It is just that simple: We are prepared to fight, and we will fight. We don't want conflict or trouble with anyone; we don't want to quibble or be aggressive or militant; we don't want strife or dissension; but the time is absolutely at an end when we will passively tolerate second-class citizenship and custodial treatment. We are free men, and we intend to act like it. We are free men, and we intend to stay that way. We are free men, and we intend to defend ourselves. Let those who truly have the best interests of the blind at heart join with us as we move into the new era of equality and integration. Let those who call our conduct negative or destructive make the most of it!

I want to say a few words now to those agencies doing work with the blind who march with us in the cause of freedom, who are glad to see the blind emancipated, and who work with us as human beings—not as statistics or case histories or inferior wards. To such agencies I say this: You have nothing to fear from the organized blind movement. Your battles are our battles. Your cause is our cause. Your friends are our friends. Your enemies are our enemies. We will go with you to the legislatures and the federal government to secure funds for your operation. We will urge the public to contribute to your support. We will defend you from attack and work with you in a partnership of progress.

Now, let me say something to those agencies who still look back to yesterday, who condescend to the blind, who custodialize and patronize. To them I say this: Your days are numbered. Once men have tasted freedom, they will not willingly or easily return to bondage. You have told us as blind people and you have told the community at large that we are not capable of managing our own affairs, that you are responsible for our lives and our destinies, that we as blind people must be sheltered and segregated—and that even then, we are not capable of earning our own keep. You have told us that we as blind people do not really have anything in common and that we, therefore do not need an organization— that there is no such thing as an "organized blind movement." But you have not spoken the truth.

If you tell us that you are important and necessary to our lives, we reply: It is true. But tear down every agency for the blind in the nation, destroy every workshop, and burn every professional journal; and we can build them all back if they are needed. But take away the blind, and your journals will go dusty on the shelves. Your counselors will walk the streets for work, and your broomcorn will mold and rot in your sheltered shops. Yes, we need you; but you need us, too. We intend to have a voice in your operation and your decisions since what you do affects our lives. We intend to have representation on your boards, and we intend for you to recognize our organizations and treat us as equals. We are not your wards, and there is no way for you to make us your wards. The only question left to be settled is whether you will accept the new conditions and work with us in peace and partnership or

whether we must drag you kicking and screaming into the new
era. But enter the new era you will, like it or not.

Next, I want to say something to those blind persons who are
aware of our movement and who have had an opportunity to join
it but who have not seen fit to do so. In this category I also place
those blind persons who are *among* us but not really *of* us, who
(technically speaking) hold membership in the Federation but are
not really part of the movement. The non-Federation and the non-
committed blind are a strange phenomenon. Some of them are
successful in business or the professions. I have heard them say,
"I really don't need the Federation. Of course, if I could do anything to help you people, I would be glad to do it, but I am independent. I have made it on my own." I have heard them say:
"You really can't expect me to go down to that local meeting of
the blind. Nobody goes there except a few old people, who sit
around and drink coffee and plan Christmas parties. I am a successful lawyer, or businessman, or judge; and I am busy. Besides,
they never get anything done. They just talk and argue." I have
heard them say: "I don't know that I necessarily have anything in
common with other blind people just because I'm blind. Almost
all my friends are sighted. My life is busy with bowling, hiking,
reading, or my business or profession." I have heard them say:
"You people in the Federation are too aggressive. You are always
in a fight with somebody, or bickering among yourselves. I am an
individualist and never was much of a joiner."

I have heard some of them say: "I am an employee of a
governmental or private agency doing work with the blind, and I
think it would destroy my professional relationship with my clients
if I were to work actively in the Federation. Anyway, we all have
a common concern, the betterment of blind people; so I'll make
my contribution by working as a 'professional' in the field. Besides, not all blind people agree with you or want to join your
organization, and as a 'professional' I have to represent and work
with all blind people."

I have heard them say all of these things, and to such blind persons I say this: You are patsies! Not only that but you are also
deceiving yourselves and failing to act in your own best interest.
Further, you are profiting from the labor and sacrifice, and are
riding on the backs of the blind who have joined the movement
and worked to make it possible for you to have what you have.
Some of you feel superior to many of the blind who belong to the
Federation (especially those who work in the sheltered shops or

draw welfare), but your feelings of superiority are misplaced; for collectively these people have clothed you and fed you. They have made it possible for you to have such equality in society and such opportunity as you now enjoy. Resent what I say if you will, but it is the truth, whether you like it or not and whether you admit it or not. It is true for those of you who work in the agencies as well as for those of you who work in private endeavor.

If you think this movement should be better or that it should be of higher caliber, then join us and help make it that way. If you think the local meetings or the state conventions are dull or uninspiring, then do your part to make them different. Even animals in the jungle have sense enough to hunt in packs. The blind ought to be at least as intelligent.

We need you, and we want you as active participants in the movement; but until you will join, we must do the best we can without you. We must carry you on our backs and do your work for you, and we will do it. The fact that we say you are patsies does not mean that we resent you. Far from it. You are our brothers, and we will continue to look upon you as such, regardless of how irresponsibly you behave. We are trying to get you to think about the implications of your actions. We are trying to get you to join with us to help make things better for other blind people and for yourselves. We are trying to get you to stop being patsies.

Finally, I want to address myself to the active members of the NFB—to the blind, and to our sighted brothers who have made our cause their cause. To the active Federationists I say this: We are not helpless, and we are not children. We know our problems, and we know how to solve them. The challenge which faces us is clear, and the means of meeting that challenge are equally clear. If we fail in courage or nerve or dedication, we have only ourselves to blame.

But, of course, we will not fail. The stakes are too high and the need too great to permit it. To paraphrase the Biblical statement: Upon the rock of Federationism we have built our movement, and the gates of hell shall not prevail against it! Since 1969 we have talked a great deal about joining each other on the barricades. If there was ever a time, that time is now. What we in the Federation do during the next decade may well determine the fate of the blind for a hundred years to come. To win through to success will require all that we have in the way of purpose, dedication, loyalty, good sense, and guts. Above all, we need front-line soldiers, who

are willing to make sacrifices and work for the cause. Therefore,
I ask you again today (as I did last year and the year before): Will
you join me on the barricades?

FOOTNOTE

1. American Foundation for the Blind, *A Step-by-Step Guide to
   Personal Management for Blind Persons,* New York, New
   York, 1970.

When the delegates gathered in Chicago for the 1972 convention, their numbers and enthusiasm gave tangible evidence of
the growing impact which the Federation was having on the lives
of the blind of the nation. Themes of leadership and relationship—of what role the blind should play in determining their own
destiny and in their interaction with the governmental and private
agencies established to give them service, as well as with the
general public—were again major focal points of attention and
discussion. By 1972 the ranks of the first generation had thinned.
This was the second generation (the new generation) taking up
the banner and carrying it forward in the Federation's struggle
for equal treatment and first-class status in society. In this banquet address President Jernigan captured the mood of the convention and charted the course for the years ahead.

"We must never forget the historic and social significance
of our movement or lose perspective in the momentary triumph
of victory or sadness of defeat," he told the banquet audience.
"The course is well-marked and clear. It has been from the beginning; and, unless we lose our nerve or betray our ideals, there
can be absolutely no question that the future is ours."

He went on to declare that, more than ever in matters affecting the blind, "the choice is fundamentally one of competing
philosophies. On one side is the philosophy which regards the
blind as innately different and inferior to the sighted. On the
other side is the philosophy which regards us as innately normal
and equal to the sighted. These two conceptions compete with
one another in virtually every area of life—from occupation to
recreation, and from cradle to grave. One of them regards blindness as a dead end; the other regards it as a live option."

Here is the text of the 1972 banquet address:

BLINDNESS—THE NEW GENERATION
by Kenneth Jernigan

When I was a schoolboy taking literature classes, there was a helpful formula which told something of the development of the short story in America. It went like this: "Poe standardized it; Bret Harte localized it; Hawthorne moralized it; O'Henry humanized it; and Mark Twain humorized it."

It seems to me that this formula, with a little rearrangement, might well apply to the problem of blindness as it has come to be defined and dealt with by various social groups and interests. Thus we might say of blindness that many of the professional agencies tend to dehumanize it; the experts jargonize it; the counselors psychoanalyze it; the journalists sentimentalize it; the fund raisers melodramatize it; and the organized blind—what do we do?—we recognize it, naturalize it, and seek to de-mythicize it.

In the face of all these "izers" and "izings," it might seem there is no end of attitudes and approaches to the problem of blindness. But I believe that underlying all the variations there are two fundamentally opposing viewpoints: One of which is positive, still believed only by a minority, and true; the other of which is negative, widely accepted as fact, and thoroughly false. In one way or another everything we of the National Federation of the Blind do or say recognizes this philosophical conflict. It has been so since our founding in 1940.

We must never forget the historic and social significance of our movement or lose perspective in the momentary triumph of victory or sadness of defeat. The course is well marked and clear. It has been from the beginning; and, unless we lose our nerve or betray our ideals, there can be absolutely no question that the future is ours.

The first 32 years constituted a generation of growth: From infancy to maturity, from weakness to strength, from innocence to experience. It was also a generation of struggle, against alien forces from without and dissident forces from within—a struggle for survival and a test of endurance. That baptismal generation is now over and finished. The struggle has been won: The tasks of early growth completed. We are now well into our second generation.

At first glance it might seem that today we find ourselves on a new battlefield, facing new issues: As—in fact, to some extent—we do. The problems of the future, which even now press upon us, might initially seem to be quite different from the problems of the past—but this is more appearance than reality.

During the first generation of the Federation, Dr. tenBroek, our beloved leader, talked to us year after year about the misconceptions and stereotypes of blindness, the false images and ancient superstitions which dog our steps and are believed by a majority of the worker in governmental and private agencies, as well as by the public at large. These misconceptions and stereotypes, these false myths and images, still dog our steps and are still our principal problem. The thing that has changed is our strength and our numbers, and particularly, the momentum of our impact and our sense of purpose. The problem is the old problem—but we are not the old we—let there be no mistake about that. We are a new breed, the organized blind; and we are abroad in the land. We have come of age—with united action, organizational experience, resources, self-awareness, self-belief, and unshakable determination.

In the justice of our cause (and regardless of the costs) we are absolutely unstoppable and unbeatable. An increasing percentage of the public is beginning to understand, and even the agencies and foundations (some gladly and some with mulish bad temper) are coming to recognize the facts of life.

Therefore, I come to you tonight—as I have done on previous occasions and as Dr. tenBroek did before me—to talk to you about our problems as individuals and as a movement, and to plan with you the concerted action we must take.

As I have said, the choice is fundamentally one of competing philosophies. On one side is the philosophy which regards the blind as innately different and inferior to the sighted. On the other side is the philosophy which regards us as innately normal and equal to the sighted. These two conceptions compete with one another in virtually every area of life—from occupation to recreation, and from cradle to grave. One of them regards blindness as a dead end; the other regards it as a live option.

Let me offer you an illustration from what may seem the relatively unimportant area of recreation. I would not mention it at all if it were unique or exceptional. But it is not. It is the typical and standard thinking which pervades the field of work with the blind today—which fills the journals, saturates the conferences, and motivates the actions of the so-called "professionals." It is the very heart and soul of what we as blind people must change if we are to be free citizens instead of wards—and change it we will.

A short time ago I received a book from Brigham Young University, accompanied by a letter which read: "Dear Sir: If you believe that the blind person needs to enlarge his narrowed horizons and keep himself physically strong and toned, you will be interested in the first edition of one of our newer books *Swimming for the Blind*, by Gloria R. Seamons." The letter continued: "Exercise may be more important for the blind than it is for the sighted, and swimming may well be the best kind of exercise a blind person can perform."

This communication, like the book it accompanied, fairly radiates the dead end philosophy of blindness. It begins by assuming that the blind person, any blind person, has "narrowed horizons," which need to be enlarged—and that swimming is the best available means of doing it. Poor blind fellow, he must lack the ability to handle more serious or complicated methods of broadening his experience or enlarging his horizons. Nor is that all: "Exercise may be more important for the blind than it is for the sighted." Why? Is it because blind people are presumed to be immobile and passive creatures, who must be stirred and prodded into vacating the rocking chair for a little exercise?

Now, I myself happen to believe that swimming is an excellent form of recreation and exercise, *for anyone*. It is good for baldheaded men, red-headed women, gifted children, and persons who are blind—but neither more nor less for any of them than for the rest of them. To suppose otherwise is to impute a form of inferiority (of peculiar weakness) to the group singled out. This is, however, precisely the imputation of the book to which I refer, *Swimming for the Blind*. Thus, the introduction contains such statements as the following:

"The activities of the sightless...'are limited, and there are not many occasions when they will have an opportunity to call upon such qualities as strength, speed and endurance....'" Or try this one: "Shall they be handicapped with feebleness, awkwardness, and helplessness in addition to blindness?..." Or try this: "It is lack of energy and determination, not the want of sight that causes so many failures among the blind."

"In swimming alone," the book goes on to tell us, "can the average person without sight leap freely into the air without fear of injury. In swimming alone can they move freely alone while using a large number of the 'big muscle' groups of the body...."

"Sterling states," the book points out, that "it offers a creative life to replace the destructive one....Swimming is more of a social asset to the blind than the general public. A blind person fits well into a swimming party, but he often feels out of place in other activities."[1]

So says this typical bit of would-be research produced at Brigham Young University, but the blind person might well feel out of place even in a swimming party if he should practice the method devised by a scientific instructor named Belenky—who, we are told, "divided his beginning skills into eight phases. One of these phases included a 'whomping' movement in which the student was on 'all fours' in the shallow water. It was accomplished by a jump in which both hands were lifted out of the water."[2]

Despite the adventurousness of the "whomping" movement, Belenky (as it turns out) is far from adventurous concerning the abilities and general competence of the blind. "Any person," he is quoted as writing, "but particularly a blind child, should at all times be aware not only of his abilities in the water, but his limitations as well. He should strive to overcome these limitations, but never can he be permitted to be foolhardy."[3]

Another expert named Sterling carries this prudence and caution even farther. He recommends that the blind swimmer use "a sponge taped to the top of the swim cap or head to avoid injury and lessen tension in learning to swim on the back."[4]

If the sponge on the head doesn't relieve all the tension of the swimmer, there is always the therapy of music—which we are told, "has been found to be beneficial for relaxing the students before the class begins or during the play period. It also provides a rhythm to which a swimmer may match his strokes. When piped underwater, music can make inviting the practice of rhythmic breathing."[5]

With a sponge on top, and music underneath, what more could the blind swimmer desire? Well, perhaps, he could be coddled, comforted, and controlled in the course of his training as exemplified by the following five-step set of instructions under the heading, "Health and Safety Measures":

1. The instructor must be the eyes for the visually impaired swimmer. Students should be met at the dressing room door and led to the pool at the shallow end....

2. The teacher must work in the water with the swimmer. The student should not be overprotected, however, but should be encouraged to become as independent as possible.

3. The instructor must be aware of danger signals such as chilling or over exertion and should allow the student to leave when necessary.

4. If it is found necessary to leave the student, he should be placed in contact with the side of the pool, the deck, or a chair.

5. The blind often have a discharge from the eyes and nose. Facial tissues should be kept handy.[6]

And one final warning from this expert to the teacher: "Each student should be allowed to work at his own rate, for rushing may impede learning. Generally the sightless progress more slowly than their seeing peers. Repetition, therefore, is important."[7]

If I may sum up the essential points of these various instructions, they would seem to be as follows: The blind are dumber than other people. They are weepers and snifflers. They cannot be trusted to find their own way to the pool or be left alone, even in shallow water. Even more briefly, I might sum up what they are saying like this: You can lead the blind to water, but you can't let them think.

To these would-be scientists, with their insulting drivel, we the blind have something to say: You claim to be experts about blindness, and you say you are professionals; but in reality you are neither. You are witch doctors and fakes. In the name of helping us you hurt us, and you call it "professionalism." You even do it with our own tax money. We are here to tell you that we have had enough, and we are also here to tell you that we are going to put a stop to what you are doing. Call us radicals and militants if you will, but heed what we say. We have the will and the means to give force to our words, and your days are numbered!

If what I have been describing were unique, we might pass over it with amusement and even perhaps with tolerance. But it is, as I have already indicated, far from isolated. It runs like a polluted stream through most of the professional and technical literature of rehabilitation, and it bespeaks a deeply held assumption of the innate and ineradicable difference—the essential inferiority—of those of us who are blind.

Here, for a similar example, is Irwin M. Siegel, M.D., speaking on "The Biomechanics of Posture" in a symposium on Parameters of Posture and Mobility in the Blind, held at the Illinois Visually Handicapped Institute not long ago. "Much postural divergency," Dr. Siegel says, "is particular to the fact of blindness." What he means by that is—but let him say it in his own words: "A rapidly growing blind child is awkward in his movements because he has a poor discriminative appreciation of spatial relationship and is, therefore, totally oblivious of grossly faulty posture. He does not have the vocabulary or the experience."[8]

Now, let us play a little trick on Dr. Siegel. Let us repeat his statement, word for word, put with one slight change. Let us leave out the word "blind." Now, the statement reads: "A rapidly growing child is awkward in his movements because he has a poor discriminative appreciation of spatial relationship and is, therefore, totally oblivious of grossly faulty posture. He does not have the vocabulary or the experience." I ask you, is that statement any less acceptable—any less factual or plausible—than the original, which referred exclusively to the blind child? If you agree with me that it is not, then I have made my central point: It is not only *beauty* that is in the eye of the beholder; it is also *inferiority*.

We are not yet through with Dr. Siegel and his syndrome of postural divergency on the part of the blind. "Some of the problems commonly seen," he says on the same page, "are as follows: (1) Dorsal round back (kyphosis), often due to a structural problem that cannot be helped by exercise. Sometimes bracing may be necessary. (2) Twisted back (scoliosis), yet another structural problem which may occasionally require operative correction. (3) Flat feet, often correctible through proper foot wear."[9]

Now, let me just say about all this that it is not only nonsense but dangerous nonsense. In its correlation of blindness with flat feet, twisted back, and round back, the statement takes leave of all scientific sense and sanity and enters the realm of superstition. It may be that some people who are blind have flat feet; many, very many, do not, and never have had. It may be that some people who were raised in Canada have round back or twisted back; that does not make it a "Canadian condition." To say that *blind* people have flat feet, or that fast-growing *blind* children (not just children) are awkward in their movements, is to imply a cause-effect relationship in which blindness is the cause of a host of secondary disabilities and problems. It never ceases to amaze me that would-be scientists, when they are in pursuit of a generalization or a federal grant, can be more unscientific and downright stupid than ordinary, illogical laymen. In other words, as far as I am concerned, Dr. Siegel has not caught the blind flat-footed, even if he should happen to have dorsal round back.

It is surely the case that the main trouble with the treatment of blind people is not that we have been overlooked but that we have been over*seen*. We have been over-surveyed, over-classified, and over-studied, as well as overprotected. We have been subjected both to *in*tensive examination and to *ex*tensive treatment. We have been aided and comforted, attended and supervised, virtually from cradle to grave. We have been transformed from people into clients, and from clients into patients; and, as I have already said, we are tired of it and intend to put a stop to it. Let those who resent this make the most of it. After all, it is *our* lives that are involved, and we mean to act accordingly.

Is it any wonder, in view of these prejudices and misconceptions on the part of self-proclaimed "professionals," that the general public should be confused and undecided in its attitudes toward blindness? The extent of this confusion is documented every day in terms of wild attributions, arbitrary exclusions, and discriminatory practices directed against blind persons. Recently in Iowa, for example, the head of the State University's Institute of Agricultural Medicine made headlines with a dire warning about the results of the misuse of ammonia as a farm fertilizer:

"We're greatly concerned," he said, "with ammonia accidents because the penalty for a mistake could be so severe—blindness. How can a farmer farm without eyesight? We're concerned with all kinds of agricultural accidents...but even if a farmer loses a finger in a machine accident he can still farm, but not if he's blind."[10]

So said the university official. Such statements help us keep perspective. With all the massive publicity we have carried on in Iowa—radio, television, newspaper, public speaking, and the rest—a prominent spokesman of our State University can unqualifiedly declare (and the newspapers are willing to print his declaration without editorial challenge) that a blind person cannot farm. Yet, there are many blind farmers throughout the nation. Several of them are in the State of Iowa. One of them (totally blind and quite successful) is a member of the policy board of the Iowa Commission for the Blind. He is in the audience tonight.

As this episode suggests, great reinforcement of negative images and superstitions concerning blindness comes from the popular mass media of communication—the press, TV, radio, movies, even comic strips and comic books. As a vivid example in the latter domain, a recent issue of *Batman* grossly exploited public doubts and fears about the blind, disguising an army of "crooks" as blind men—complete with tin cups, pencils, heavy wooden canes, dark glasses, and signs reading, "I AM BLIND." Upon first discovering these hoods tapping along the sidewalk, Batman exclaims to his sidekick: "Odd, Robin! So many blind men out this late after midnight. Almost looks like they're holding a convention in town!" "Not odd at all, Batman," replies Robin. "They are! The 'U.S. Sightless Society' is meeting here in Gotham." "Then," says Batman, "it's *doubly* odd!" At which point the text reads: "What has Batman noticed that escapes even the trained eyes of his veteran junior aide, Robin? And possibly you, reader?" What do you suppose it is? Simple. In Batman's words: "Why would a convention of 'sightless' persons be out on the town—sightseeing?" They couldn't be, of course; so they must be fakes and crooks. Now I wonder what that makes of you and me? And what does it make of our own "U.S. Sightless Society"—the National Federation of the Blind? We, too, have tours, and some of us (I suppose) are fakes and crooks; but the two things are not necessarily related.

A short time ago tragedy struck a famous personage who is near and dear to us all—the great detective of the comic page, Dick Tracy. He was totally blinded (or so we were led to believe) by a fire which consumed his home and left only Tess Trueheart intact and able-bodied. What happened to Tracy was what happens to blind people almost invariably in fiction and the funnies: He dropped out of all public activity ("A blind detective?" hooted the chief of police: "Don't make me laugh!"), and Tracy took to shuffling about the city with dark glasses and an old-fashioned, heavy cane, accompanied in every drawing by the words "tap-tap." There was much weeping and wailing down at the police station and great celebration among the criminal element—until one day, a few weeks later, it was revealed that his blindness was only a hoax; and Dick Tracy could emerge from darkness and oblivion and once again take up his career as the scourge of the underworld. The comic strip has not only sentimentalized his blindness but had fictionalized and melodramatized it as well, playing on the ancient myth and exploiting it for all it was worth.

Insulting and humiliating as all these items from the professional literature and the mass media are, they might be tolerated except for the fact that they translate into acts of discrimination against individual blind persons and into second-class citizenship for all of us who are blind. This is what I have repeatedly tried so unsuccessfully to communicate to the members of the National Accreditation Council for Agencies Serving the Blind and Visually Handicapped. It is what other minority groups have said concerning their problems to government and the public at large. Harriet Beecher Stowe, for instance, could not write *Uncle Tom's Cabin* today, nor could *Amos 'n' Andy* find a radio audience in the present climate of public opinion. The reason is obvious, and we as blind persons must understand that reason thoroughly and act accordingly.

Let me give you an example, a very recent example, of what happens to blind people in the climate of public opinion which permits the sort of professional literature and popular comics we have been discussing.

My example is drawn from correspondence which took place not long ago between a blind college student and a college administrator. The story began when Pat Wright, a scholarship winner at Occidental College in California, made application, along with two of her sighted classmates, to transfer to Howard University as an exchange student. It should be borne in mind as the narrative unfolds, that Howard is regarded by many as the nation's foremost black college with a high reputation for courage and leadership in the struggle for civil rights.

In his formal reply to the application of the three Occidental College students, Howard's vice president for Student Affairs indicated his acceptance of the two sighted applicants and went on to state: "I do have reservations with respect to Miss Pat Wright, the young lady who is blind. Given the nature of racial conflicts and concerns operative today, I would strongly advise against Miss Wright's coming to Howard. Many people today are extremely insensitive and bent on causing problems for others. It is my feeling that Miss Wright would find the experience to be less than rewarding."

There you have the logical result of the attitudes inherent in the professional literature and the comics. Miss Wright, the so-called "young lady who is blind," brought the matter into focus in her letter of reply:

"In examining your most polite and proper refusal," she wrote, "I find that without doubt your rejection of me is discriminatory, infringing upon my human right to live in the world in a place and manner of my own choosing....I resent most strongly the prejudicial implications of that statement. You seem to be operating under stereotyped notions that people who are blind are by nature passive, incapable of adapting to new situations; inadequate to handle emergencies; physically immobile; physically incapable of functioning 'normally' in the 'sighted world'; and particularly vulnerable to the physical, verbal, and emotional abuses of 'normal' people."

There is more to Miss Wright's reply—including a reference to the apparent likelihood that she was being discriminated against on grounds of race and sex as well as of blindness. As it turns out, that was unfair; for in a second letter addressed to her, the university administrator took pains to point out that no such multiple prejudice or discrimination was intended. "I regret," he wrote, "that your interpretation of my letter was so at variance with its intent and wish to assure you that my decision was based largely on the absence of any special facilities and services in any campus building, for the blind, and not because of your race or sex. I would make the same decision in the case of a black male applicant."

There it is again. There is no consciousness whatever of any prejudice or discrimination in this act of blunt rejection. The applicant for admission, it is clear, might be almost anything or anybody, and still be quite acceptable—anybody, that is, other than a blind person, whose condition allegedly necessitates "special facilities and services."

I have chosen this particular illustration, out of many similar cases which turn up every year, because it is especially rich in irony. What would this black official of a black university make, one wonders, of a rejection issued to a black applicant by any school on grounds that there were no special facilities or services available for students with black skins? He would, of course, cry "Jim Crow." He would protest that segregation and separate treatment are relics of a bygone prejudiced past, violating alike civil rights and constitutional commands.

As with the professional literature and the mass media, so with Pat Wright. The story is typical, not unique. Variations of her experience are enacted hundreds of times every day throughout the nation. Not only do they occur in major events but in the small incidents so familiar to us all. How often, when a blind person and a sighted person are together in a restaurant, does the waitress say: "Does he want cream in his coffee?" How often, in fact, (regardless of the setting) is the conversation concerning the needs, wishes, actions, or abilities of the blind person directed to a sighted associate, as if the blind person were not there at all? Of even more significance, how often does the blind person fail utterly to grasp the implications of the situation and show his conditioning to the stereotype by laughing at the whole thing, exhibiting his so-called "sense of humor?" It is not necessary to be deadly serious and never smile, but fat people who make jokes about themselves for being fat or black people who poke fun at the Negro stereotypes are usually more pathetic than humorous. We as blind people should not be defensive or have chips on our shoulders. Neither should we fail to understand what these things really mean and what actions must be taken.

In the small incidents and the gut issues of existence the stereotype confronts us every day. It confronts us in the sheltered shops which pay subminimum wages; it confronts us in the agencies which fear the justice of our cause and seek to dismiss us as militants and radicals; it confronts us in the distortions and jargon of the professional journals; it confronts us in the colleges and universities which deny admission; it confronts us in the insurance companies which refuse equal coverage; it confronts us in the landlords who hesitate to rent; it confronts us in the factories and offices which find reasons for exclusion and denial; it confronts us in the pity we constantly receive from the general public; it confronts us in the pathetic pride of those blind individuals who try to shun other blind people and our movement and who say, "I am independent—I am uniquely talented—I am not like other

blind people—I have made it on my own with sighted people";
and finally, it confronts us in the lack of self-respect and the scraping and bowing of those blind persons who fawn on the agencies
and their sighted neighbors and who are ashamed of their blindness and behave like the "Uncle Toms" they are. It confronts us,
in short, in all of the activities and aspirations which go to make
up life itself.

By any standard one cares to set, the challenge is formidable. The
government and private agencies, established to assist the blind,
more often than not serve as stumbling blocks to keep us down
and keep us out. The mass media, while well-intentioned and willing to help, reinforce the worst and most destructive of the misconceptions. The American Council of the Blind, that small group
of bitter dissidents who splintered away from our movement a
decade ago, is widely regarded as nothing but a front for the worst
of the agencies—a company union, and a force for disunity. The
National Accreditation Council for Agencies Serving the Blind and
Visually Handicapped, the self-appointed custodian and keeper of
the blind, is working diligently to gain power and respectability.
Partly because of all these things and partly because of long-standing tradition, the thinking of the general public is still largely controlled by superstition, prejudice, and ignorance about what we
are and what we hope to become.

This is the picture, but it is only part of the picture. All I have
said is true; yet, the future has never looked as bright as it does
today. The reason is simple. We the blind are organized, and on
the move. We have faith in ourselves and belief in the justice of
our cause, and we have the determination and the resources to
translate our faith and belief into action and accomplishment.
Above all, we have found (in the National Federation of the
Blind) the unifying force, the vehicle for success.

I want to make it clear that we are not condemning all agencies
doing work with the blind. Far from it. We would not be where
we are today had it not been for the help and understanding of
progressive agencies. As I have said many times before, such agencies have nothing to fear from us. We work with them in partnership and harmony.

In fact, our purpose is not to condemn at all but to bring change—
to be seen for what we are and heard with our own voice. The
truth is as basic and elemental as this: We are simply no longer
willing to live as second-class citizens. Regardless of the cost or

hostility, we won't do it. If our choice is to have confrontation or to lie down and be walked on like rugs, then the choice is painful, but it is also inescapable. It must be confrontation.

In the struggle we do not stand alone. More and more of the blind are rallying to the cause, and many of the sighted are as dedicated to the movement as we are. An increasing number of the agencies are working with us, and there is noticeable improvement in the public attitude. Even so, the days ahead will be a time of serious challenge and conflict.

In stating our position perhaps we can do no better than paraphrase the words of William Lloyd Garrison, spoken over a century ago: We have determined, at every hazard, to lift up the standard of emancipation in the eyes of the nation. That standard is now unfurled; and long may it float—till every chain be broken, and every blind person set free.

We are aware that many object to the severity of our language, but is there not cause for severity? We will be as harsh as the truth, and as uncompromising as justice. We are in earnest. We will not equivocate. We will not excuse. We will not retreat a single inch. And *we will be heard*!

This is the watchword and the message of the new generation, the new breed of the blind. It is the force of Federationism. It is the spirit of the movement. I say to every blind person who hears these words and to every sighted person who is truly a friend of the blind that the need is great and the time is now. The issues are drawn.

As I conclude, I am sure you know what question I will ask you. Think carefully and don't respond unless you mean it—unless you are willing to give of your time, your money, your strength, and your spirit. I ask you now, as I have done before: Will you join me on the barricades?

FOOTNOTES

1. Gloria R. Seamons, *Swimming for the Blind* (Provo, Utah: Brigham Young University Press, 1966), pp. 1-3.

2. *Ibid.*, p. 6.

3. *Ibid.*,p. 12.

4. *Ibid.*

5. *Ibid.*, p. 13.

6. *Ibid.*, p. 17.

7. *Ibid.*

8. Irwin M. Siegel, M.D., "The Biomechanics of Posture: Applications to Mobility in the Blind," *Parameters of Posture and Mobility in the Blind*, Illinois Visually Handicapped Institute and Western Michigan University (Kalamazoo: Western Michigan University, 1969), p. 50.

9. *Ibid.*

10. *Des Moines Sunday Register*, August 8, 1971, Section T, p. 1.

Marching on Washington

One of the more tangible signs of the new mood of exuberant confidence which characterized the organized blind movement during the first Jernigan presidency (roughly corresponding to the decade of the seventies) was the singular annual pilgrimage that came to be known as the "March on Washington" and later as the "Washington Seminar." Beginning in 1973, the National Federation of the Blind organized these enthusiastic gatherings of members from across the country—typically numbering in the hundreds—who trekked to the nation's capital for visits with their congressmen to talk about matters of concern to the blind. James Gashel, the Federation's Director of Governmental Affairs, described a typical three-day gathering in an article in the July-August, 1979, *Braille Monitor*. His authoritative account makes clear both the political impact and the educational value—not to mention the inspirational effect—of this yearly mobilization of blind people in the capital city. Gashel's report also offers an insight into the complexities of the legislative process at the top level of government—with all its formal hearings, informal meetings, and still more informal maneuvers and compromises. Finally, this story reveals something about its author, the Federation's ingenious and indefatigable "man in Washington." Here is the text of his report:

MARCH ON WASHINGTON 1979
by James Gashel

Since 1973 when Federationists first turned out in numbers to visit the members of the Congress in their Washington offices, we have developed and refined the technique and come to refer to these gatherings as "Marches on Washington." The issues have varied from time to time; the first Marches dealt almost exclusively with NAC and our effort to block further federal funding of this disgraceful AFB power grab maneuver, but by 1976 our voices had been heard sufficiently, and no more federal money went to NAC.

This done, the 1977 March focused on improving services to blind persons through legislation aimed at authorizing special federal funding to separate agencies for the blind which offer comprehensive rehabilitation and related services. We also gathered support for our Disability Insurance bill as the 95th Congress settled in to consider Social Security legislation. Again, the effort and the participation of nearly 200 Federationists who came from across the country at personal expense proved worthwhile, for during the 95th Congress we made progress by securing new authority for specialized services for the blind through the Rehabilitation Act, and we succeeded in obtaining an increase in the amount which blind Social Security Disability Insurance beneficiaries can earn before losing benefits. Above all, of course, we also renewed our relationships with the law-makers who represent us in Washington, and where we have not had contacts before, we were able to establish them.

The March in 1979 maintained the fine traditions we have built for large turnouts and hard work. The agenda for the three days beginning April 30th and ending May 2nd was packed, but the Federation representatives, who traveled from as far as Utah and Idaho, had enough enthusiasm and stamina to keep pace with the rigorous schedule. Well over one hundred assembled for the advance briefing at 9 p.m. Sunday, April 29th, and by Tuesday, with a fresh contingent of troops from Pennsylvania, our numbers had nearly doubled. President Jernigan opened the Sunday evening meeting by bringing all of us up to date on the most recent national developments, and he outlined the challenge of the three days just ahead. Dr. Jernigan also announced that remodeling of our new national headquarters building was complete, so that visiting Federationists would be able to see the facility fully occupied and operational on Tuesday, May 1st. This was truly the high point of the trip to Washington this time, seeing our own National Office close to the nation's capital and realizing the great potential it offers us for growth.

As for our work on Capitol Hill, the kick-off event was a Senate hearing to review the progress made to date in implementing the Randolph-Sheppard Act Amendments of 1974. Senator Randolph presided over the hearing in the beginning, receiving testimony from a panel of NFB leaders and government witnesses. The full text of the NFB testimony will appear elsewhere in this issue. While our spokesmen were Arthur Segal, president of the Blind Merchants Division; James Sofka, president of the NFB of New Jersey; Victor Gonzalez, chairman, Agency Relations Committee, NFB of West Virginia; and James Gashel, the voice of the NFB was also heard in numbers, over 150 strong as we crowded into the packed hearing room, filling every chair and lining the walls.

This was known as an "oversight" hearing which Congressional committees conduct from time to time to see what steps should or can be taken to better enforce the laws. NFB Resolution 78-19 expressed the Federation's outrage at the statements and diversionary tactics of some of the major federal agencies which have been maneuvering to avoid providing business opportunities for blind vendors on federal property. The resolution called for oversight hearings, so we set to work on this by asking Senator Randolph to place this item on the top of the agenda for the Subcommittee on the Handicapped during the 96th Congress, and the Senator responded positively. In fact, this was the first hearing conducted by the Subcommittee, and it generated a great deal of attention.

Although oversight hearings rarely solve anything, they help to get issues and evidence on the record, and the data uncovered by this hearing will be of real value as we seek improved business opportunities through the vending facilities program. At this writing, the record is not fully developed (much is done in writing before and after the hearing), but we learned a number of interesting things. For example, we were told that there are presently 291 cafeterias which could be operated by blind persons on Department of Defense property, but only one (located on a military base in Ohio) is currently in the Randolph-Sheppard program. Upon hearing this, Federation representatives from that state sent word to the front that the base served by this cafeteria will be closed in two years—a fact which certainly dims the military's shining example. It was obvious to everyone that especially the

Department of Defense was having a hard go at finding good things to say about their responsiveness to the Randolph-Sheppard Act, for although it had nothing whatsoever to do with the subject of the hearing, the representative from the Defense Department made a point of explaining how much the military is actually doing to help the blind, helping us, that is, by doing business with the sheltered workshops through National Industries for the Blind. Apparently this man has not been reading the *Wall Street Journal*, and the Subcommittee was not impressed.

The hearing proceeded somewhat in this vein with the federal government witnesses trying to explain to Senator Randolph how much they supported the blind vendor program and with the Senator probing each of them with specific questions regarding their agency's lack of compliance with the law. Senator Randolph had heard our message, and he did his best to help bring out the issues. Later, he made his commitment clear as some of us met with him during lunch in the Senate dining room while the Subcommittee staff took testimony from other witnesses, including the American Council of the Blind. Specifically, we discussed how best to use the results of this hearing to improve the situation for blind vendors, and we agreed on the approach of establishing an action agenda for solving specific issues. Already we have initiated this process with an on-the-spot investigation of some problems in the blind vending program in West Virginia, but much more remains to be done.

With the oversight hearing concluded, we set to work on other legislative concerns; high among them, of course, our continued drive for minimum wage protection for blind people. In the March issue of the *Braille Monitor* we described a rule-making petition which the NFB has filed with the U.S. Department of Labor, but this does not spell an end to our efforts to achieve the same goal legislatively. In fact, the work in the Congress on this is very much in high gear. On April 26, Congressman Phillip Burton introduced the Minimum Wage for the Blind bill once again; the number for this Congress is H.R. 3764, and the bill is identical to H.R. 8104, which Mr. Burton introduced in the 95th Congress and which stirred up much interest, including attracting the *Wall Street Journal*'s awareness through the hearing which was held.

Elsewhere in this issue we will reprint the fact sheet used by Federation representatives to explain the current law and its negative impact on the earning power and the personal dignity of productive blind workers. This fact sheet should be helpful to all

Federationists in asking for support and co-sponsorship of H.R. 3764 by the members of the House of Representatives. In fact, all members of the House should be asked to co-sponsor the Minimum Wage for the Blind bill, and they should inform Phillip Burton of their desire to do so. Soon we hope to announce some action on a Senate version of this bill, but for now our attention must be focused on the House.

With respect to minimum wage, it is important to note that the new chairman of the Labor Standards Subcommittee (the Subcommittee in the House to which H.R. 3764 has been assigned) is Congressman Edward Beard of Rhode Island (a real friend of the Federation) and a co-sponsor of Mr. Burton's minimum wage bill in the 95th Congress. During the March we met with Mr. Beard to discuss plans for this legislation in the present Congress, since he is now in the position of scheduling Subcommittee action. While at this stage there are no specific target dates for Subcommittee consideration of the bill, there is every reason to believe that H.R. 3764 will not sit idle during Mr. Beard's tenure as chairman of the Labor Standards Subcommittee, and yet much, of course, will depend on what we do to gather support for the bill.

As we made the rounds on Capitol Hill, we also called attention to the continuing problem of discrimination against the blind in employment. On February 22, Senator Harrison Williams, chairman of the Senate Committee on Labor and Human Resources introduced a bill known as the "Equal Employment Opportunity for the Handicapped Act," which promises substantially increased civil rights protection for persons having "handicapping conditions" as defined in the Rehabilitation Act of 1973. The number of Senator William's bill is S. 446, and we are currently working to enlist Senate co-sponsors. The fact sheet which can be used to explain the employment discrimination against blind people which occurs and the potential advantages of S. 446 appears elsewhere. Our efforts in generating interest for this legislation were highly successful, and Senate hearings are now scheduled for June 20th and 21st. Meanwhile, in the House of Representatives we met with Carl Perkins, chairman of the House Education and Labor Committee, who agreed to support this legislation actively through his leadership position in the House, and we assembled a long list of Representatives who indicated their desire to co-sponsor the companion bill to S. 446 when it is introduced in the House. At this writing, it is too early to announce the number of the House bill, but members of the House of Representatives who wish to co-sponsor the Equal Employment Opportunity for the Handicapped Act should be advised to inform Mr. Perkins of their support. This will help the legislation get underway in the House with a long list of sponsors.

Passage of S. 446 can be seen as the next phase of civil rights protection for blind and handicapped persons which began with our work on the model white cane laws at the state level over the past decade. Also, with the help of Federation support, several states have included the disabled in the state civil rights laws, and it has long been our objective (confirmed in resolution 78-24) to expand our civil rights protection into federal law. Senator William's bill (and the companion bill to be introduced in the House) offers hope that this may now be achieved.

Of course, we must never visit Capitol Hill without continuing to talk about the need for improvements in the Social Security Disability Insurance program. At the end of the 95th Congress, James Burke, who had sponsored our Disability Insurance bills and helped us achieve some progress, retired, leaving the chairmanship of the Social Security Subcommittee in the House of Representatives to Congressman J.J. Pickle of Texas. Unfortunately, Mr. Pickle is not yet of the same persuasion regarding our plans for changing the Social Security Disability Insurance program, so chances for favorable action at the Subcommittee or Committee level (that is, the House Ways and Means Committee) have dimmed.

Nonetheless, our efforts to attract supporters to the concept of improved Disability Insurance for the blind must continue. The fact sheet which explains the history of the proposed legislation and the need for it will also be found elsewhere in this issue, along with Dr. Jernigan's article, "Why Should the Blind Receive Disability Insurance?" (revised and updated to reflect the 1977 Amendments to the Social Security Act).

At least ten members of the House have introduced identical Disability Insurance for the Blind bills in the 96th Congress. The first of these is H.R. 1037, by Congressman Henry B. Gonzalez of Texas. Other members who support this legislation should also be encouraged to introduce identical bills. Although it is too early to announce the number yet, Senator Dennis DeConcini of Arizona will soon be introducing a Senate version of this bill, and Senators should be urged to co-sponsor by contacting Senator DeConcini.

At this stage in the 96th Congress it appears that there may be a serious effort to enact legislation making a number of changes in the Social Security Disability Insurance program, but many of these would merely aggravate the problems which now exist in the system rather than solving them. For this reason, we must continue to inform our Senators and Representatives that the Social Security Disability Insurance program fails to meet our needs and helps to keep blind people out of the workforce.

While the foregoing legislative concerns represent longstanding commitments of the Federation to improve the lives of blind people, it also became necessary for us to deal spontaneously with a problem related to our public image as represented by the statement of Joseph Hendrie, chairman of the Nuclear Regulatory Commission, comparing the confusion at the Three Mile Island Nuclear Plant in Pennsylvania to "a couple of blind men staggering around making decisions." This statement of Dr. Hendrie's was quoted in the national news media only a few days in advance of our March on Washington, and it was clear to everyone that we ought to make a response. This we did in the form of a resolution, which read:

> WHEREAS, the official transcript of the Nuclear Regulatory Commission (NRC) held on March 30, 1979, quotes NRC Chairman, Joseph M. Hendrie, as saying: "It's like a couple of blind men staggering around making decisions," in describing the actions of officials in dealing with problems at the Three Mile Island Nuclear Power Generating Facility; and
>
> WHEREAS, Chairman Hendrie's statement demonstrates his personal ignorance and represents the traditional false stereotypes about the helpless and incompetent blind; and
>
> WHEREAS, the principle problem faced by blind men and women not actively participating in the mainstream of American life is the lack of understanding about blindness which exists resulting in widespread discrimination against the blind; and
>
> WHEREAS, Chairman Hendrie's statement can only serve to erode further the public attitude about blindness with the result that it will reduce the chances of full participation in the social and economic life of this country; and

> WHEREAS, Chairman Hendrie's gross insensitivity is amplified by his high public office: NOW, THEREFORE,
>
> BE IT RESOLVED by the representatives of the National Federation of the Blind assembled in Washington, D.C., April 29, 1979, that we demand a public apology by Chairman Joseph M. Hendrie, accompanied by a public commitment to off-set the negative impact of his remarks by establishing the goal of making the Nuclear Regulatory Commission a model employer of blind persons at all levels.

During the March this resolution was hand-carried to Dr. Hendrie's office, and so far the response has been a great deal of hand-wringing and some stumbling words of apology, but no commitment yet to do it publicly. It seems that Dr. Hendrie is a bit skittish about facing the television cameras these days.

From all of this, it is clear that despite the beautiful spring weather which graced Washington during the first week of May, the Federationists who assembled for this year's March had little time to enjoy the scenery. While we had hoped to visit in the office of every member of Congress, we fell just a little short of this goal, hitting nearly 500, which is not too bad considering that there are 535 in all. Of course, the work was hard, but already the results show that it was well done and a worthwhile investment. And speaking of investments, once again we were able to conduct this March on Washington without draining funds from our precious Federation reserves, for those who came realized the necessity to finance the effort and in the end contributed nearly $2,000, which met the inevitable expenses in sponsoring such a gathering. This, along with the hours of dedicated labor which went into making the 1979 March on Washington one of our best, shows the true depth of commitment which characterizes the NFB and distinguishes us as a movement. Often those who would like to keep us from speaking and thinking for ourselves wonder why it is that we continue to surmount the many obstacles they try to erect in our path, but there is no need to wonder, for the Federation is sound and growing in strength, numbers, and commitment every day. Let anyone who wonders about this check the record of our 1979 March, for therein lies the evidence of a viable and vibrant movement, which, over the long haul and the short run is absolutely unstoppable.

The Spirit of '73

For each decade in the life of the National Federation of the Blind, there has been one year in particular that seems to represent a hallmark, somehow capturing and symbolizing the spirit of the age. For the seventies, although each successive year reflected new achievements in the organized blind movement, there was none quite like the year 1973. It was then, as we have noted, that the annual March on Washington was initiated. It was in that year that the national leadership seminars—one of the most significant innovations of the first Jernigan presidency—got underway. It was in 1973 that the registration of delegates at the annual convention first went over 1,500. And it was in 1973 that the "NAC Attack" (the demonstrations by the organized blind at top-level NAC meetings) mustered over 1,500 picketers in New York City.

Moreover, it was in 1973, at the New York convention, that President Kenneth Jernigan delivered the first in a series of three annual banquet addresses that represented a distinct departure from his customary style and method—though not from his basic philosophy and doctrine. Each of these interconnected speeches presented, in its title, a pertinent and perplexing question about blindness and the blind—and then answered it, not merely thoughtfully but on the basis of extensive research. In 1973 the banquet speech was entitled "Blindness: Is History Against Us." The following year the President's address bore the title, "Blindness: Is Literature Against Us" and in 1975 it was "Blindness: Is the Public Against Us."

The distinctive tone of all of these public addresses was established at the outset. To the question "Is history against us?" Jernigan answered with both a yes and a no. "We all know what the historical record tells us," he said. "It tells us that, until only yesterday, blind people were completely excluded from the ranks of the normal community....Only lately, it would seem, have blind people begun stealthily to emerge from the shadows and to move in the direction of independence and self-sufficiency."

From what histories and historians have told us, said Jernigan, "it would seem that the blind have moved through time and the world not only sightless but faceless—a people without distinguishing features, anonymous and insignificant—not so much as rippling the stream of history.

"Nonsense!" he exclaimed. "That is not fact but fable. That is not truth but a lie. In reality the accomplishments of blind people through the centuries have been out of all proportion to their numbers. There are genius, and fame, and adventure, and enormous versatility of achievement—not just once in a great while but again and again, over and over."

Now, said Jernigan, "we are at a point in time when the story of the blind (the true and real story) must be told. For too long the blind have been (not un*wept*, for there has been too much of that) but unhonored and unsung. Let us, at long last, redress the balance and right the wrong. Let us now praise our famous men and celebrate the exploits of blind heroes. Rediscovering our true history, we shall, in our turn, be better able to *make* history; for when people (seeing or blind) come to know the truth, the truth will set them free."

President Jernigan went on, in this 1973 address, to relate a history of blindness never told before in quite this way, a story not of gloom and doom but of genuine progress and quickening prospect—although he pointed out that the history remained unfinished and that the next chapters must be written by the blind themselves. "Napoleon is supposed to have said that history is a legend agreed upon. If this is true, then we the blind are in the process of negotiating a new agreement, with a legend conforming more nearly to the truth and the spirit of the dignity of man."

This Jernigan speech presented at the 1973 convention had (not only on the banquet audience who heard it that night but on the blind of the nation) an impact which changed lives and remained undiminished through the years. It gave to blind people a new and unexpected source of pride in themselves—the pride that comes from having a history—and more importantly it gave them a sense of their own capacity to make a difference: to steer their own lives and to shape their own destiny. In the years that followed this landmark address, more and more historical writings began to appear in the *Braille Monitor* and other periodicals, telling of remarkable deeds and contributions by blind persons and groups. It might indeed be said that, in a genuine sense, the 1973 speech not only presented a new history of blindness but opened up a new future as well.

The text of the speech follows:

BLINDNESS: IS HISTORY AGAINST US
by Kenneth Jernigan

Experts in the field, as well as members of the general public, have differed greatly as to what the future may hold for the blind. Some, seeking to tell it like it is, see us blundering on forever in roles of economic dependency and second-class citizenship. Others, more hopefully, predict a slow but steady progress toward independence, equality, and full membership in society. My own view is that this is not a matter for prediction at all, but for *decision*. I believe that neither of these possible outcomes is certain or foreseeable, for the simple reason that the choices we make and the actions we take are themselves factors in the determination of the future. In short, we the blind (like all people) confront *alternative* futures: one future in which we will live our own lives, or another future in which our lives will be lived for us.

But if the future is open and contingent, surely the *past* is closed and final. Whatever disputes men may have about the shape of things to come, there can be no doubt about the shape of things gone by—the permanent record of history. Or can there? Is there such a thing as an alternative *past*?

We all know what the historical record tells us. It tells us that, until only yesterday, blind people were completely excluded from the ranks of the normal community. In early societies they were reputedly abandoned, exterminated, or left to fend for themselves as beggars on the lunatic fringe of the community. In the late Middle Ages, so we are told, provision began to be made for their care and protection in almshouses and other sheltered institutions. Only lately, it would seem, have blind people begun stealthily to emerge from the shadows, and to move in the direction of independence and self-sufficiency.

That is what history tells us—or, rather, that is what histories and the historians have told us. And the lesson commonly derived from these histories is that the blind have always been dependent upon the wills and the mercies of others. We have been the people things were done *to*—and, occasionally, the people things were done *for*—but never the people who *did for themselves*. In effect, according to this account, we have no history of our own—no record of active participation or adventure or accomplishment, but only (until almost our own day) an empty and unbroken continuum of desolation and dependency. It would seem that the blind have moved through time and the world not only sightless but faceless—a people without distinguishing features, anonymous and insignificant—not so much as rippling the stream of history.

Nonsense! That is not fact but fable. That is not truth but a lie. In reality the accomplishments of blind people through the centuries have been out of all proportion to their numbers. There are genius, and fame, and adventure, and enormous versatility of achievement—not just once in a great while but again and again, over and over. To be sure, there is misery also—poverty and suffering and misfortune aplenty—just as there is in the general history of mankind. But this truth is only a half-truth—and, therefore, not really a truth at all. The real truth, the whole truth, reveals a chronicle of courage and conquest, of greatness, and even glory on the part of blind people, which has been suppressed and misrepresented by sighted historians—not because these historians have been people of bad faith or malicious intent but because they have been people, with run-of-the-mill prejudice and ordinary misunderstandings. Historians, too, are human; and when facts violate their preconceptions, they tend to ignore those facts.

Now, we are at a point in time when the story of the blind (the true and real story) must be told. For too long the blind have been (not un*wept*, for there has been much too much of that) but unhonored and unsung. Let us, at long last, redress the balance and right the wrong. let us now praise our famous men and celebrate the exploits of blind heroes. Rediscovering our true history, we shall, in our turn, be better able to *make* history; for when people (seeing or blind) come to know the truth, the truth will set them free.

Let us begin with Zisca: patriotic leader of Bohemia in the early fifteenth century, one of history's military geniuses, who defended his homeland in a brilliant campaign against invading armies of overwhelming numerical superiority. Zisca was, in the hour of his triumph, totally blind. The chronicle of his magnificent military effort—which preserved the political independence and religious freedom of his country, and which led to his being offered the crown of Bohemia—is worth relating in some detail. Need I add that this episode is not to be found, except in barest outline, in the standard histories? Fortunately it has been recorded by two historians of the last century—James Wilson, an Englishman writing in 1820, and William Artman, an American writing seventy years later. What do you suppose these two historians have in common, apart from their occupation? You are right: Both were blind. The account of the career of Zisca which follows has been drawn substantially from their eloquent and forceful narratives.

The Council of Constance, which was convened by the Pope in the year 1414 for the purpose of rooting out heresy in the Church—and which commanded John Huss and Jerome of Prague to be burned at the stake—"sent terror and consternation throughout Bohemia...."[1] In self-defense the Bohemian people took up arms against the Pope and the emperor. They chose as their commanding general the professional soldier John de Turcznow—better known as Zisca, meaning "one-eyed," for he had lost the sight of an eye in the course of earlier battles. At the head of a force of 40,000 citizen-soldiers—a force not unlike the ragged army that would follow General Washington in another patriotic struggle three centuries later—Zisca marched into combat, only to be suddenly blinded in his remaining eye by an arrow from the enemy.

Here is where our story properly begins. For Zisca, upon his recovery from the injury, flatly refused to play the role of the helpless blind man. "...His friends were surprised to hear him talk of setting out for the army, and did what was in their power to dissuade him from it, but he continued resolute. 'I have yet,' said he, 'to shed my blood for the liberties of Bohemia. She is enslaved; her sons are deprived of their natural rights, and are the victims of a system of spiritual tyranny as degrading to the character of man as it is destructive of every moral principle; therefore, Bohemia must and shall be free.'"[2]

And so the blind general resumed his command, to the great joy of his troops. When the news came to the Emperor Sigismund "he called a convention of all the states in his empire...and entreated them, for the sake of their sovereign, for the honor of their empire, and for the cause of their religion, to put themselves in arms....The news came to Zisca that two large armies were in readiness to march against him....The former was to invade

Bohemia on the west, the latter on the east; they were to meet in the center, and as they expressed it, crush this [rebel] between them."[3]

By all the rules of warfare, by all conventional standards of armament and power, that should have been the end of Zisca and his rabble army. "After some delay the emperor entered Bohemia at the head of his army, the flower of which was fifteen thousand Hungarians, deemed at that time the best cavalry in Europe....The infantry, which consisted of 25,000 men, were equally fine, and well commanded. This force spread terror throughout all the east of Bohemia."[4] The stage was set for the fateful climax—the final confrontation and certain obliteration of the upstart rebel forces. "On the 11th of January, 1422, the two armies met on a large plain....Zisca appeared in the center of his front line [accompanied] by a horseman on each side, armed with a poleax. His troops, having sung a hymn,...drew their swords and waited for the signal. Zisca stood not long in view of the enemy, and when his officers had informed him that the ranks were well closed, waved his saber over his head, which was the signal of battle, and never was there an onset more mighty and irresistible. As dash a thousand waves against the rock-bound shore, so Zisca rolled his steel-fronted legions upon the foe. The imperial infantry hardly made a stand, and in the space of a few minutes they were disordered beyond the possibility of being rallied. The cavalry made a desperate effort to maintain the field, but finding themselves unsupported, wheeled round and fled...toward...Moravia....[5]

It was a total rout and an unconditional victory, *but,*...Zisca's labors were not yet ended. The emperor, exasperated by his defeat, raised new armies, which he sent against Zisca the following spring....But the blind general, determined that his country should not be enslaved while he had strength to wield a sword, gathered his brave army "and met the enemy yet again, despite fearsome disadvantages in numbers and equipment. "An engagement ensued, in which the [enemy] were utterly routed, leaving no less than nine thousand of their number dead on the field."[6]

The remaining branch of the grand imperial army, under the command of Sigismund himself, next met a similar fate, and the mighty emperor was compelled to sue for peace at the hands of the blind general. Then there occurred the final magnificent gesture of this extraordinary human being. As the historian Wilson recounts the episode: "Our blind hero, having taken up arms only to secure peace, was glad for an opportunity to lay them down.

When his grateful countrymen requested him to accept the crown of Bohemia, as a reward for his eminent services, he respectfully declined."[7] And this is what Zisca said: "While you find me of service to your designs, you may freely command both my counsels and my sword, but I will never accept any established authority; on the contrary, my most earnest advice to you is, when the perverseness of your enemies allows you peace, to trust yourselves no longer in the hands of kings, but to form yourselves into a republic, which species of government only can secure your liberties."[8]

That is the true story of Zisca—military genius, patriot, freedom fighter, statesman, and blind man. Extraordinary as his heroism was, it exceeds only in degree the story of yet another blind Bohemian—King John, the blind monarch who fell in the historic Battle of Cressy, which engaged the energies and cost the lives of many of Europe's nobility. This king had been blind- for many years. When he heard the clang of arms, he turned to his lords and said: "I only now desire this last piece of service from you, that you would bring me forward so near to these Englishmen that I may deal among them one good stroke with my sword." In order not to be separated, the king and his attendants tied the reins of their horses one to another, and went into battle. There this valiant old hero had his desire, and came boldly up to the Prince of Wales, and gave more than "one good stroke" with his sword. He fought courageously, as did all his lords, and others about him; but they engaged themselves so far that all were slain, and next day found dead, their horses' bridles still tied together.

In the country of the blind, it has foolishly been said, the one-eyed man will inevitably be king. This, of course, is nonsense. In fact, the very opposite has often been true. History reveals that in the realm of the sighted it is not at all remarkable for a blind man to be king. Thus, in 1851, George Frederick, Duke of Cumberland, first cousin to Queen Victoria, ascended the throne of Hanover under the royal title of George the Fifth. That this blind king of Hanover was no incompetent, but distinctly superior to the ordinary run of monarchs, is shown by the words of a contemporary historian, who said: "Though laboring under the deprivation of sight, this Prince is as efficient in his public, as he is beloved in his private, character; a patron of the arts and sciences, and a promoter of agricultural interests...he has acquired a perfect knowledge of six different languages."[9]

A strikingly similar account has been handed down to us of the blind Prince Hitoyasu, who reigned as a provincial governor in Japan over a thousand years ago and "whose influence set a pattern for the sightless which differed from that in any other country and saved his land from the scourge of beggary."[10] Thoroughly trained in both Japanese and Chinese literature, Prince Hitoyasu introduced blind people into society and the life of the court. In ninth century Japan, when the blind led the blind, they did not fall into a ditch, but rose out of it together.

Let us turn now from the records of royalty to the annals of adventure. Perhaps the most persistent and destructive myth concerning the blind is the assumption of our relative inactivity and immobility—the image of the blind person glued to his rocking chair and, at best, sadly dependent on others to guide or transport him on his routine daily rounds. "Mobility," we are led to believe, is a modern term, which has just begun to have meaning for the blind. To be sure, many blind persons have been cowed by the myth of helplessness into remaining in their sheltered corners. But there have always been others—like James Holman, Esquire, a solitary traveler of a century and a half ago, who gained the great distinction of being labeled by the Russians as "*the blind spy.*" Yes, it really happened! This intrepid Englishman, traveling alone across the steppes of Greater Russia all the way to Siberia, was so close an observer of all about him that he was arrested as a spy by the Czar's police and conducted to the borders of Austria, where he was ceremoniously expelled.

Here is how it happened. Holman lost his sight at the age of twenty-five, after a brief career as a lieutenant in the Royal Navy; but his urge to travel, instead of declining, grew stronger. He soon embarked upon a series of voyages—first through France and Italy, then (at one fell swoop) through Poland, Austria, Saxony, Prussia, Hanover, Russia, and Siberia. His real intention, as he later wrote, was to "make a circuit of the whole world," entirely on his own and unaccompanied—an ambition he might well have fulfilled had it not been for the Czar's police and the Russian spy charges. He later published a two-volume account of his travels and observations, and his own reflections upon his Russian adventure are worth repeating: "My situation," he wrote, "was now one of extreme novelty and my feelings corresponded with its peculiarity. I was engaged...in a solitary journey of a thousand miles, through a country, perhaps the wildest on the face of the earth, whose inhabitants were scarcely yet accounted within the pale of civilization, with no other attendant than a rude Tartar postillion, to whose language my ear was wholly unaccustomed; and yet, I was supported by a feeling of happy confidence...."[11]

As Federationists know, there have been other blind travelers in our own time quite as intrepid as James Hólman. Yet Holman's story—the case of the "blind spy"—is important for its demonstration that blind people could wear such seven-league boots almost two centuries ago—before Braille or the long cane, before residential schools or vocational rehabilitation, before even the American Foundation for the Blind and its 239-page book on personal management for the blind.

But there is a more basic side to mobility, of course, than the opportunity and capacity for long-distance traveling. There is the simple ability to get about, to walk and run, to mount a horse or ride a bicycle—in short, to be physically independent. The number of blind persons who have mastered these skills of travel is countless, but no one has ever proved the point or shown the way with more flair than a stalwart Englishman of the eighteenth century named John Metcalf. Indeed, this brash fellow not only defied convention, but the world. Totally blind from childhood, he was (among other things) a successful builder of roads and bridges; racehorse rider; bare-knuckle fighter; card shark; stagecoach driver; and, on occasion, guide to sighted tourists through the local countryside. Here is an account of some of his many enterprises:

> In 1751 he commenced a new employment; he set up a stage wagon betwixt York and Knaresborough, being the first on the road, and drove it himself, twice a week in summer, and once in winter. This business, with the occasional conveyance of army baggage, employed his attention till the period of his first contracting for the making of roads, which engagement suiting him better, he relinquished every other pursuit....The first piece of road he made was about three miles,...and the materials for the whole were to be produced from one gravel pit; he therefore provided deal boards, and erected a temporary house at the pit; took a dozen horses to the place; fixed racks and mangers, and hired a house for his men, at Minskip. He often walked to Knaresborough in the morning, with four or five stones of meal on his shoulders, and joined his men by six o'clock. He completed the road much sooner than was expected, to the entire satisfaction of the surveyor and trustees.[12]

The story of "Blind Jack" Metcalf, for all its individuality, is far from unique. Rather, it underscores what even we as Federationists sometimes forget, and what most of the sighted have never learned at all—namely, that the blind can compete on terms of absolute equality with others—that we are really, literally, the equals of the sighted. We have been kept down by the myths and false beliefs about our inferiority, by the self-fulfilling prophecies of the custodial system which has conditioned the sighted and the blind alike to believe we are helpless, but not by any innate lacks or losses inherent in our blindness.

Metcalf's accomplishments in applied science were probably matched by those of a French army officer more than a century before. Blaise Francoise, Comte de Pagan, was blinded in the course of military service, shortly before he was to be promoted to the rank of field marshal. He then turned his attention to the science of fortifications, wrote the definitive work on the subject, and subsequently published a variety of scientific works, among which was one entitled *An Historical and Geographical Account of the River of the Amazons* (which included a chart drawn up by this military genius after he became blind)!

Like the sighted, the blind have had their share of solid citizens, namby-pambies, strong-minded individualists, squares, oddballs, eggheads, and eccentrics. The sixteenth-century German scholar James Shegkins, for instance, refused to undergo an operation which was virtually guaranteed to restore his sight: "In order," as he said, "not to be obliged to see many things that might appear odious and ridiculous."[13] Shegkins, a truly absent-minded professor, taught philosophy and medicine over many years with great success, and left behind him influential monographs on a dozen scientific subjects.

The success story of Dr. Nicholas Bacon, a blind lawyer of eighteenth century France, somewhat resembles that of our own beloved founder, Dr. Jacobus tenBroek. Both were blinded in childhood by bow-and-arrow accidents, and both went on to high academic achievement in law and related studies. The strenuous exertions which Bacon was forced to go through at each stage of his climb are indicated by the following account:

"When he recovered his health, which had suffered from the accident, he continued the same plan of education which he had before commenced....But his friends treated his intention with ridicule, and even the professors themselves were not far from the same sentiment; for they admitted him into their schools, rather under an impression that he might amuse them, than that they should be able to communicate much information to him." However, he obtained "the first place among his fellow students. They then said that such rapid advances might be made in the preliminary branches of education, but not...in studies of a more profound nature; and when...it became necessary to study the art of poetry, it was declared by the general voice that all was over....But here he likewise disproved their prejudices....He applied himself to law, and took his degree in that science at Brussels."[14]

Years earlier—in the fourth century after Christ—another blind man made an even steeper ascent to learning. He was Didymus of Alexandria, who became one of the celebrated scholars of the early church. He carved out of wood an alphabet of letters and laboriously taught himself to form them into words, and shape the words into sentences. Later, when he could afford to hire readers, he is said to have worn them out one after another in his insatiable quest for knowledge. He became the greatest teacher of his age. He mastered philosophy and theology, and then went on to geometry and astrology. He was regarded by his students, some of whom like St. Jerome became church fathers, with "a touch of awe" because of his vast learning and intellect.

Didymus was not the only blind theologian to gain eminence within the church. In the middle of the seventeenth century, at almost the same moment Milton was composing *Paradise Lost*, a blind priest named Prospero Fagnani was writing a commentary on church law, which was to bring him fame as one of the outstanding theorists of the Roman faith. At the precocious age of 21, Fagnani had already earned the degree of doctor of civil and canon law, and in the very next year, he was appointed Secretary of the Congregation of the Council. His celebrated *Commentary*, published in six quarto volumes, won high praise from Pope Benedict XIV and caused its author to become identified throughout Europe by a Latin title which in translation signifies "the blind yet farseeing doctor."

These few biographical sketches plucked from the annals of the blind are no more than samples. They are not even the most illustrious instances I could have given. I have said nothing at all about the best known of history's blind celebrities—Homer, Milton, and Helen Keller. There is good reason for that omission. Not only are those resounding names well enough known already but they have come to represent—each in its own sentimentalized, storybook form—not the abilities and possibilities of people who are blind but the exact opposite. Supposedly these giants are the exceptions that prove the rule—the rule, that is, that the blind are incompetent. Each celebrated case is explained away to keep the stereotype intact: Thus, Homer (we are repeatedly told) probably never existed at all—being not a man but a committee! As for Milton, he is dismissed as a sighted poet, who happened to become blind in later life. And Helen Keller, they say, was the peculiarly gifted and just plain lucky beneficiary of a lot of money and a "miracle worker" (her tutor and companion, Anne Sullivan).

Don't you believe it! These justly famous cases of accomplishment are not mysterious, unexplainable exceptions—they are only *remarkable*. Homer, who almost certainly did exist and who was clearly blind, accomplished just a little better what other blind persons after him have accomplished by the thousands: that is, he was a good writer. Milton composed great works while he was sighted, and *greater* ones (including *Paradise Lost*) after he became blind. His example, if it proves anything, proves only that blindness makes no difference in ability. As for Helen Keller, her life demonstrates dramatically what great resources of character and will and intellect may live in a human being beyond the faculties of sight and sound—which is not to take anything at all away from Anne Sullivan.

In the modern world it is not the poets or the humanists, but the scientists, who have held the center of the stage. As would be expected, the stereotyped view has consistently been that the blind cannot compete in these areas. How does this square with the truth?

Consider the case of Nicholas Saunderson—totally blind from infancy—who succeeded Sir Isaac Newton in the chair of mathematics at Cambridge University, despite the fact that he had earlier been refused admission to the same university and was never permitted to earn a degree! It was the great Newton himself who pressed Saunderson's appointment upon the reluctant Cambridge dons; and it was no less a personage than Queen Anne of England who made it possible by conferring the necessary degree upon Saunderson. Later he received a Doctor of Laws degree from King George II, a symbol of the renown he had gained as a mathematician. Among Saunderson's best subjects, by the way, was the science of optics—at which he was so successful that the eminent Lord Chesterfield was led to remark on "the miracle of a man who had not the use of his own sight teaching others how to use theirs."[15]

For another example, consider John Gough, a blind English biologist of the eighteenth century, who became a master at classification of plants and animals by substituting the sense of touch for that of sight. Or consider Leonard Euler, a great mathematician of the same century, who (after becoming blind) won two research prizes from the Parisian Academy of Sciences, wrote a major work translated into every European language, and devised an astronomical theory which "has been deemed by astronomers, in exactness of computation, one of the most remarkable achievements of the human intellect."[16] Or, for a final illustration, consider Francois Huber, blind Swiss zoologist, who gained recognition as the pre-eminent authority of the eighteenth century on the behavior of bees. The famous writer Maurice Maeterlinck said of Huber that he was "the master and classic of contemporary apiarian science."[17]

Even after all of this evidence, there will be many (some of them, regrettably, our own blind Uncle Toms) who will try to deny and explain it all away—who will attempt to keep intact their outworn notions about the helplessness of the blind as a class. So let me nail down a couple of points: In the first place, is all of this talk about history and the success of blind individuals really valid? Isn't it true that most blind people throughout the ages have lived humdrum lives, achieving neither fame nor glory, and soon forgotten? Yes, it is true—but for the sighted as well as for the blind. For the overwhelming majority of mankind (the blind and the sighted alike) life has been squalor and hard knocks and anonymity from as far back as anybody knows. There were doubtless blind peasants, blind housewives, blind shoemakers, blind businessmen, blind thieves, blind prostitutes, and blind holy men who performed as competently or as incompetently (and are now as forgotten) as their sighted contemporaries.

"Even so," the doubter may say, "I'm still not convinced. Don't you think the track record for the blind is worse than the track record for the sighted? Don't you think a larger percentage of the blind have failed?"

Again, the answer is yes—just as with other minorities. That's what it's all about. Year after year, decade after decade, century after century, age after age we the blind were told that we were helpless—that we were inferior—and we believed it and acted accordingly. But no more! As with other minorities, we have tended to see ourselves as others have seen us. We have accepted the public view of our limitations, and thus have done much to make those limitations a reality. When our true history conflicted with popular prejudice, the truth was altered or conveniently forgotten. We have been ashamed of our blindness and ignorant of our heritage, but never again! We will never go back to the ward status of second-class citizens. There is simply no way. There are blind people aplenty—and sighted allies, too—(many of them in this room tonight) who will take to the streets and fight with their bare hands if they must before they will let it happen.

And this, too, is history—our meeting, our movement, our new spirit of self-awareness and self-realization. In our own time and in our own day we have found leaders as courageous as Zisca, and as willing to go into battle to resist tyranny. But we are no longer to be counted by ones and twos, or by handfuls or hundreds. We are now a movement, with tens of thousands in the ranks. Napoleon is supposed to have said that history is a legend agreed upon. If this is true, then we the blind are in the process of negotiating a new agreement, with a legend conforming more nearly to the truth and the spirit of the dignity of man.

And what do you think future historians will say of us—of you and me? What legends will they agree upon concerning the blind of the mid-twentieth century? How will they deal with our movement—with the National Federation of the Blind? Will they record that we fell back into the faceless anonymity of the ages, or that we met the challenges and survived as a free people? It all depends on what we do and how we act; for future historians will write the record, but we will make it. Our lives will provide the raw materials from which their legends will emerge to be agreed upon.

And, while no man can predict the future, I feel absolute confidence as to what the historians will say. They will tell of a system of governmental and private agencies established to serve the blind, which became so custodial and so repressive that reaction was inevitable. They will tell that the blind ("their time come round at last") began to acquire a new self-image, along with rising expectations, and that they determined to organize and speak for themselves. And they will tell of Jacobus tenBroek—how he, as a young college professor, (blind and brilliant) stood forth to lead the movement like Zisca of old.

They will tell how the agencies first tried to ignore us, then resented us, then feared us, and finally came to hate us—with the emotion and false logic and cruel desperation which dying systems always feel toward the new about to replace them.

They will tell of the growth of our movement through the forties and fifties, and of our civil war—which resulted in the small group that splintered away to become puppets of the most reactionary of the agencies, a company union: our counterfeit dwarf image, the American Council of the Blind. They will tell how we emerged from our civil war into the sixties, stronger and more vital than we had ever been; and how more and more of the agencies began to make common cause with us for the betterment of the blind. They will tell of our court cases, our legislative efforts, and our organizational struggles—and they will record the sorrow and mourning of the blind at the death of their great leader, Jacobus tenBroek.

They will also record the events of today—of the 1970s—when the reactionaries among the agencies became even more so, and the blind of the second generation of the NFB stood forth to meet them. They will talk of the American Foundation for the Blind and its attempt (through its tool, NAC) to control all work with the blind, and our lives. They will tell how NAC and the American Foundation and the other reactionary agencies gradually lost ground and gave way before us. They will tell of new and better agencies rising to work in partnership with the blind, and of harmony and progress as the century draws to an end. They will relate how the blind passed from second-class citizenship through a period of hostility to equality and first-class status in society.

But future historians will only record these events if we make them come true. They can help us be remembered, but they cannot help us dream. That we must do for ourselves. They can give us acclaim, but not guts and courage. They can give us recognition and appreciation, but not determination or compassion or good judgment. We must either find those things for ourselves, or not have them at all.

We have come a long way together in this movement. Some of us are veterans, going back to the forties; others are new recruits, fresh to the ranks. Some are young; some are old. Some are educated, others not. It makes no difference. In everything that matters we are one; we are the movement; we are the blind.

Just as in 1940, when the National Federation of the Blind was formed, the fog rolls in through the Golden Gate. The eucalyptus trees give forth their pungent smell, and the Berkeley hills look down at the bay. The house still stands in those hills, and the planes still rise from San Francisco to span the world. But Jacobus tenBroek comes from the house no more, nor rides the planes to carry the word.

But the word is carried, and his spirit goes with it. He it was who founded this movement, and he it is whose dreams are still entwined in the depths of its being. Likewise, *our* dreams (our hopes and our visions) are part of the fabric, going forward to the next generation as a heritage and a challenge. History is not against us: the past proclaims it; the present confirms it; and the future demands it. If we falter or dishonor our heritage, we will betray not only ourselves but those who went before us and those who come after. But, of course, we will not fail. Whatever the cost, we shall pay it. Whatever the sacrifice, we shall make it. We cannot turn back, or stand still. Instead, we must go forward. We shall prevail—and history will record it. The future is ours. Come! Join me on the barricades, and we will make it come true.

FOOTNOTES

1. Wilham Artman, *Beauties and Achievements of the Blind* (Auburn: Published for the Author, 1890), p. 265.

2. James Wilson, *Biography of the Blind* (Birmingham, England: Printed by J.W. Showell, Fourth Edition, 1838), p. 110.

3. Artman, *op. cit.*, p. 265.

4. *Ibid.*, p. 266.

5. *Ibid.*, p. 267.

6. *Ibid.*, p. 268.

7. *Ibid.*, pp. 268-269.

8. Wilson, *op.cit.*, p. 115.

9. Mrs. Hippolyte Van Landeghem, *Exile and Home: Advantages of the Social Education of the Blind* (London: Printed by W. Clowes & Sons, 1865), p. 95.

10. Gabriel Farrell, *The Story of Blindness* (Cambridge: Harvard University Press, 1956), p. 7.

11. Wilson, *op.cit.*, p. 262.

12. *Ibid.*, pp. 100-101

13. Artman, *op.cit.*, p. 220.

14. Wilson, *op.cit.*, p. 243.

15. Farrell, *op.cit.*, p. 11.

16. Artman, *op.cit.*, p. 226.

17. Farrell, *op.cit.*, pp. 12-13.

In 1974, at the Federation's convention in Chicago, Kenneth Jernigan undertook a significant variation on the theme of his earlier speech on history and the blind. "Last year," he said in his banquet address, "I examined with you the place of the blind in history—not just what we have done but what the historians have remembered and said we have done. The two, as we found, are vastly different. This year I would like to talk with you about the place of the blind in literature. How have we been perceived? What has been our role? How have the poets and novelists, the essayists and dramatists, seen us? Have they 'told it like it is,' or merely liked it as they told it?"

In addressing his topic question—"Blindness: Is Literature Against Us"—Jernigan noted that the literary record reveals no single theme or viewpoint regarding the blind but instead displays a bewildering variety of images. Yet he claimed to find, upon closer examination of the world of fiction and poetry, of myth and fairy tale, a set of nine separate themes or motifs that recurred again and again. These themes were summarized in a graphic list:

> ...blindness as compensatory or miraculous power; blindness as total tragedy; blindness as foolishness and helplessness; blindness as unrelieved wickedness and evil; blindness as perfect virtue; blindness as punishment for sin; blindness as abnormality or dehumanization; blindness as purification; and blindness as symbol or parable.

Each of these recurrent themes was traced to its sources and varied expressions in literature—and each one in turn was then exposed as false, fraudulent, or (at best) "fictitious" in the full sense of the term. In its multitudinous parade of authors and its array of illustrations and examples—as well as in the scholarship which lay behind the writing—this 1974 address was an effective counterpart to the previous speech on history and historiography—and, like that one, its answer to the key question was complicated. Here is how it was summed up:

> To the question "Is literature against us?", there can be no unqualified response. If we consider only the past, the answer is certainly yes. We have had a bad press....If we consider the present, the answer is mixed. There are signs of change, but the old stereotypes and false images still predominate....If we turn to the future, the answer is that the future—in literature as in life—is not predetermined but self-determined. As we shape our lives, singly and collectively, so will we shape our literature.

The full text follows:

BLINDNESS: IS LITERATURE AGAINST US
by Kenneth Jernigan

History, we are told, is the record of what human beings have *done*; literature, the record of what they have *thought*. Last year I examined with you the place of the blind in history—not just what we have done but what the historians have remembered and said we have done. The two, as we found, are vastly different.

This year I would like to talk with you about the place of the blind in literature. How have we been perceived? What has been our role? How have the poets and novelists, the essayists and dramatists seen us? Have they "told it like it is," or merely liked it as they've told it?

With history there is at least a supposed foundation of fact. Whatever the twisting or omission or misinterpretation or downright falsehood, that foundation presumably remains a tether and a touchstone, always subject to reexamination and new proof. Not so with literature. The author is free to cut through facts to the essence, to dream and soar and surmise. Going deeper than history, the myths and feelings of a people are enshrined in its literature. Literary culture in all its forms constitutes possibly the main transmission belt of our society's beliefs and values—more important even than the schools, the churches, the news media, or the family. How, then, have we fared in literature?

The literary record reveals no single theme or unitary view of the life of the blind. Instead, it displays a bewildering variety of images—often conflicting and contradictory, not only as between different ages or cultures, or among the works of various writers, but even within the pages of a single book.

Yet, upon closer examination the principal themes and motifs of literature and popular culture are nine in number and may be summarized as follows: *blindness as compensatory or miraculous power; blindness as total tragedy; blindness as foolishness and helplessness; blindness as unrelieved wickedness and evil; blindness as perfect virtue; blindness as punishment for sin; blindness as abnormality or dehumanization; blindness as purification; and blindness as symbol or parable.*

Let us begin with blindness and compensatory powers. Suppose one of you should ask me whether I think there is any advantage in being blind; and suppose I should answer like this: "Not an advantage perhaps: still it has compensations that one might not think of. A new world to explore, new experiences, new powers awakening; strange new perceptions; life in the fourth dimension."[1] How would you react to that? You would, I suspect, laugh me out of the room. I doubt that a single person here would buy such stereotyped stupidity. You and I know from firsthand experience that there is no "fourth dimension" to blindness—no miraculous new powers awakening, no strange new perceptions, no brave new worlds to explore. Yet, the words I have quoted are those of a blind character in a popular novel of some time back. (I don't know whether the term has significance, but a blind "private eye," no less.)

The association of blindness with compensatory powers, illustrated by the blind detective I have just mentioned, represents a venerable tradition, reaching back to classical mythology. A favorite method of punishment among the gods of ancient Greece was blinding—regarded apparently as a fate worse than death—following which, more often than not, the gods so pitied the blinded victim that they relented and conferred upon him extraordinary gifts, usually the power of prophecy or some other exceptional skill. Thus, Homer was widely regarded as having been compensated by the gift of poetry. In the same way Tiresias, who wandered through the plays of Sophocles, received for his blindness the gift of prophecy.

The theme of divine compensation following divine retribution survived the passage of the ages and the decline of the pagan religions. Sir Arthur Conan Doyle (one of the most eminent novelists of the last century, and the creator of Sherlock Holmes) conjured up a blind character with something of Holmes' sleuthing talents, in a book entitled *Sir Nigel*. This figure is introduced as one who has the mysterious ability to detect by hearing a hidden tunnel, which runs beneath the besieged castle. His compensatory powers are described in a conversation between two other people in the novel:

"This man was once rich and of good repute [says one], but he was beggared by this robber lord who afterwards put out his eyes, so that he has lived for many years in darkness at the charity of others."

"How can he help in our enterprise if he be indeed blind?" [asks his companion.]

"It is for that very reason, fair Lord, that he can be of greater service than any other man. For it often happens that when a man has lost a sense, the good God will strengthen those that remain. Hence it is that Andreas has such ears that he can hear the sap in the trees or the cheep of the mouse in its burrow."[2]

The great nineteenth-century novelist Victor Hugo, in *The Man Who Laughs*, reflected the view of a host of modern writers that blindness carries with it a certain purity and ecstasy, which somehow makes up for the loss of sight. His blind heroine, Dea, is portrayed as "absorbed by that kind of ecstasy peculiar to the blind, which seems at times to give them a song to listen to in their souls and to make up to them for the light which they lack by some strain of ideal music. "Blindness," says Hugo, "is a cavern to which reaches the deep harmony of the Eternal."[3]

Probably it is this mystical notion of a "sixth sense" accompanying blindness that accounts for the rash of blind detectives and investigators in popular fiction. Max Carrados, the man who talked of living in the "fourth dimension," first appeared in 1914 and went on to survive a number of superhuman escapades through the nineteen twenties. In 1915 came another sightless sleuth—the remarkable Damon Gaunt, who "never lost a case."[4] So it is with "Thornley Colton, Blind Detective," the brainchild of Clinton H. Stagg; and so it is with the most illustrious of all the private eyes without eyes, Captain Duncan Maclain, whose special qualities are set forth in the deathless prose of a dust jacket: "Shooting to kill by sound, playing chess with fantastic precision, and, of course, quickening the hearts of the opposite sex, Captain Maclain has won the unreserved admiration of reviewers."[5]

Even the author is carried away with the genius of his hero: "There were moments," he writes, "when powers slightly greater than those possessed by ordinary mortals seemed bestowed on Duncan Maclain. Such moments worried him."[6]

They might worry us, as well; for all of this mumbo jumbo about abnormal or supernatural powers doesn't lessen the stereotype of the blind person as alien and different, unnatural and peculiar. It makes it worse.

Not only is it untrue, but it is also a profound disservice to the blind; for it suggests that whatever a blind person may accomplish is not due to his own ability but to some magic inherent in blindness itself. This assumption of compensatory powers removes the blind person at a stroke of the pen from the realm of the normal—the ordinary, everyday world of plain people—and places him in a limbo of abnormality. Whether supernormal or subnormal does not matter—he is without responsibility, without rights, and without society. We have been conned into this view of second-class status long enough. The play is over. We want no more of magic powers and compensations. We want our rights as citizens and human beings—and we intend to have them!

It is significant that, for all his supposed charm and talent, Maclain never gets the girl—or any girl. The author plainly regards him as ineligible for such normal human relationships as love, sex, and marriage. Max Carrados put it this way in replying to an acquaintance who expressed great comfort in his presence: "Blindness invites confidence," he says. "We are out of the running—for us human rivalry ceases to exist."[7]

This notion of compensatory powers—the doctrine that blindness is its own reward—is no compliment but an insult. It robs us of all credit for our achievements and all responsibility for our failings. It neatly relieves society of any obligation to equalize conditions or provide opportunities or help us help ourselves. It leaves us in the end without the capacity to lead a regular, competitive, and participating life in the community around us. The blind, in short, may (according to this view) be extraordinary, but we can never be ordinary. Don't you believe it! We are normal people—neither especially blessed nor especially cursed—and the fiction to the contrary must come to an end! It is not mumbo jumbo we want, or magical powers—but our rights as free people, our responsibilities as citizens, and our dignity as human beings.

Negative as it is, this image of compensatory powers is less vicious and destructive than some others which run through the literature of fiction and fantasy. The most damaging of all is also the oldest and most persistent: namely, the theme of blindness as total tragedy, the image summed up in the ancient Hebrew saying, "The blind man is as one dead." The Oedipus cycle of Greek tragic plays pressed the death-in-life stereotype to its farthest extreme. Thus, in *Oedipus Rex*, in which the king puts out his own eyes, the statement occurs: "Thou art better off dead than living blind." It remained, however, for an Englishman, blind himself, to write the last word (what today would be called "the bottom line") on blindness as total disaster. John Milton says in *Samson Agonistes*:

> Blind among enemies,
> O worse than chains,
> Dungeon, or beggary, or decrepit age!...
> Inferior to the vilest now become
> Of man or worm; the vilest here excel me,
> They creep, yet see; I, dark in light, exposed
> To daily fraud, contempt, abuse, and wrong,
> Within doors, or without, still as a fool,
> In power of others, never in my own;
> Scarce half I seem to live,
> Dead more than half....a moving grave,[8]

What is most striking about this epic poem is not the presence of the disaster concept (that might have been expected) but the fact that Milton of all people was the author. His greatest writing (including *Paradise Lost*) was done after his blindness. Then why did he do it? The answer is simple: We the blind tend to see ourselves as others see us. Even when we know to the contrary, we tend to accept the public view of our limitations. Thus, we help make those limitations a reality. Betrayed by the forces of literature and tradition, Milton (in his turn) betrayed himself and all others who are blind. In fact, he actually strengthened and reinforced the stereotype—and he did it in spite of his own personal experience to the contrary. The force of literature is strong, indeed!

The disaster concept of blindness did not stop with Milton. *William Tell*, the eighteenth-century play by Schiller, shows us an old man, blinded and forced to become a beggar. His son says:

> Oh, the eye's light, of all the gifts of Heaven the dearest, best!...And he must drag on through all his days in endless darkness!...To die is nothing. But to have life, and not have sight—Oh, that is misery indeed![9]

A century later the disaster concept was as popular as ever. In Kipling's book, *The Light That Failed*, no opportunity is lost to tell us that blindness is worse than death. The hero, Dick Heldar, upon learning that he is to become blind, remarks: "It's the living death....We're to be shut up in the dark...and we shan't see anybody, and we shall never have anything we want, not though we live to be a hundred."[10] Later in the book, he rages against the whole world "because it was alive and could see, while he, Dick, was dead in the death of the blind, who, at the best, are only burdens upon their associates."[11] And when this self-pitying character finally manages to get himself killed (to the relief of all concerned), the best Kipling can say of him is that "his luck had held till the last, even to the crowning mercy of a kindly bullet through his head." [12]

Joseph Conrad, in *The End of the Tether*, kills off Captain Whalley by drowning, as a fate much preferable to remaining alive without sight. In D.H. Lawrence's *The Blind Man*, there is a war-blinded casualty named Maurice, whose total despair and misery are unrelieved by any hint of future hope; and Rosamond Lehmann, in her novel *Invitation to the Waltz*, goes Lawrence one better—or, rather, one worse. Her war-blinded hero, although he appears to be living a respectable life, is portrayed as if for all practical purposes he were a walking corpse. He leads, we are told, "a counterfeit of life bred from his murdered youth." And when he brings himself somehow to dance with a former sweetheart, it is a sorry spectacle: "She danced with him," says the author, "in love and sorrow. He held her close to him, and he was far away from her, far from the music, buried and indifferent. She danced with his youth and his death." [13]

For writers such as these, the supposed tragedy of blindness is so unbearable that only two solutions can be imagined: either the victim must be cured or he must be killed. A typical illustration is Susan Glaspell's *The Glory of the Conquered*, of which an unkind critic has written: "It is a rather easy solution of the problem to make her hero die at the end of the book, but probably the author did not know what else to do with him."[14]

Let us now leave tragedy and move to foolishness and helplessness. The blind man as a figure of fun and the butt of ridicule is no doubt as old as farce and slapstick. In the Middle Ages the role was regularly acted out on festive holidays when blind beggars were rounded up and outfitted in donkey's ears, than made to gibber and gesticulate to the delight of country bumpkins. Reflecting this general hilarity, Chaucer (in "The Merchant's Tale") presents a young wife, married to an old blind man, who deceives him by meeting her lover in a tree while taking the husband for a walk. The Chaucerian twist is that the old man suddenly regains his sight as the couple are making love in the branches— whereupon the quick-witted girl explains that her amorous behavior was solely for the purpose of restoring his sight. Shakespeare is just as bad. He makes the blinded Gloucester in *King Lear* so thoroughly confused and helpless that he can be persuaded of anything and deceived by any trick. Isaac, in the Old Testament, is duped by his son Jacob, who masquerades as Esau, disguising himself in goatskins, and substituting kid meat for the venison his father craves—all without a glimmer of recognition on the part of the old man, who must have taken leave of the rest of his senses as well as his sense of sight.

An unusually harsh example of the duping of blind people is found in the sixteenth-century play *Der Eulenspiegel mit den Blinden.* The hero meets three blind beggars and promises them a valuable coin to pay for their food and lodging at a nearby inn; but when they all reach out for the money, he gives it to none of them, and each supposes that the others have received it. You can imagine the so-called "funny ending." After they go to the inn and dine lavishly, the innkeeper demands his payment; and each of the blind beggars thereupon accuses the others of lying, thievery, and assorted crimes. The innkeeper—shouting "You people defraud everyone!"—drives the three into his pigsty and locks the gate, lamenting to his wife: "What shall we do with them, let them go without punishment after they have eaten and drunk so much, for nothing? But if we keep them, they will spread lice and fleas and we will have to feed them. I wish they were on the gallows."[15] The play has a "happy ending," but what an image persists of the character of those who are blind: criminal and corrupt, contagious and contaminated, confounded and confused, wandering homeless and helpless in an alien landscape. Their book of life might well be called "Gullible's Travels."

So it goes with the saccharine sweet that has robbed us of humanity and made the legend and hurt our cause. There is Caleb, the "little blind seer" of James Ludlow's awful novel, *Deborah*. There is Bertha, Dickens's ineffably sweet and noble blind heroine of *The Cricket on the Hearth*, who comes off almost as an imbecile. There is the self-sacrificing Nydia, in *The Last Days of Pompeii*; and there is Naomi, in Hall Caine's novel, *Scapegoat*. But enough! It is sweetness without light, and literature without enlightenment.

One of the oldest and cruelest themes in the archives of fiction is the notion of blindness as a punishment for sin. Thus, Oedipus was blinded as a punishment for incest, and Shakespeare's Gloucester for adultery. The theme often goes hand in hand with the stereotype of blindness as a kind of purification rite—an act which wipes the slate clean and transforms human character into purity and goodness. So Amyas Leigh, in Kingsley's *Westward Ho*, having been blinded by a stroke of lightning, is instantly converted from a crook to a saint.

Running like an ugly stain through many of these master plots—and, perhaps, in a subtle way underlying all of them—is the image of blindness as *dehumanization*, a kind of banishment from the world of normal life and relationships. Neither Dickens's blind Bertha, nor Bulwer-Lytton's Nydia, when they find themselves in love, have the slightest idea that anybody could ever love them back—nor does the reader; nor, for that matter, do the other characters in the novels. Kipling, in a story entitled "They," tells of a charming and apparently competent blind woman, Miss Florence, who loves children but "of course" cannot have any of her own. Kipling doesn't say why she can't, but it's plain that she is unable to imagine a blind person either married or raising children. Miss Florence, however, is magically compensated. She is surrounded on her estate by the ghosts of little children who have died in the neighborhood and have thereupon rushed to her in spirit. We are not meant to infer that she is as crazy as a hoot owl—only that she is *blind*, and therefore entitled to her spooky fantasies.

The last of the popular literary themes is that which deals with blindness not literally but symbolically, for purposes of satire or parable. From folklore to film the image recurs of blindness as a form of death or damnation, or as a symbol of other kinds of unseeing (as in the maxim, "where there is no vision, the people perish)." In this category would come H.G. Well's classic "The

Country of the Blind"; also, *The Planet of the Blind*, by Paul Corey; and Maeterlinck's *The Blind*. In the short story by Conrad Aiken, "Silent Snow, Secret Snow," blindness becomes a metaphor for schizophrenia.

In virtually all of these symbolic treatments, there is an implied acceptance of blindness as a state of ignorance and confusion, of the inversion of normal perceptions and values, and of a condition equal to if not worse than death. The havoc wrought upon the lives of blind people in ages past by these literary traditions is done, and it cannot be undone; but the future is yet to be determined. And that future, shaped by the instrument of truth, will be determined by us. Self-aware and self-reliant—neither unreasonably belligerent nor unduly self-effacing—we must, in a matter-of-fact way, take up the challenge of determining our own destiny. We know who we are; we know what we can do; and we know how to act in concert.

And what can we learn from this study of literature? What does it all mean? For one thing, it places in totally new perspective the pronouncements and writings of many of the so-called "experts" who today hold forth in the field of work with the blind. They tell us (these would-be "professionals," these hirelings of the American Foundation for the Blind and HEW, these pseudoscientists with their government grants and lofty titles and impressive papers) that blindness is not just the loss of sight, but a total transformation of the person. They tell us that blindness is not merely a loss to the eyes, but to the personality as well—that it is a death, a blow to the very being of the individual. They tell us that the eye is a sex symbol, and that the blind person cannot be a "whole man"—or, for that matter, presumably a whole woman either. They tell us that we have multiple "lacks and losses."[21]

The American Foundation for the Blind devises a 239-page guidebook[22] for our "personal management," with sixteen steps to help us take a bath, and specific techniques for clapping our hands and shaking our heads. We are given detailed instructions for buttering our bread, tying our shoes, and even understanding the meaning of the words "up and down." And all of this is done with federal grants, and much insistence that it is new discovery and modern thought.

But our study of literature gives it the lie. These are not new concepts. They are as unenlightened as the Middle Ages. They are as old as Oedipus Rex. As for science, they have about as

3. Victor Hugo, *The Man Who Laughs*, p. 316.

4. Isabel Ostrander, *At One-Thirty: A Mystery*, p. 6.

5. Baynard Kendrick, *Make Mine Maclain*, dust jacket.

6. *Ibid.*, p. 43.

7. Bramah, *op. cit.*, p. 7.

8. John Milton, *The Portable Milton*, pp. 615-616.

9. Friedrich Schiller, *Complete Works of Friedrich Schiller*, p. 447.

10. Rudyard Kipling, *Selected Prose and Poetry of Rudyard Kipling*, p. 131.

11. *Ibid.*, p. 156.

12. *Ibid.*, p. 185.

13. Rosamond Lehmann, *Invitation to the Waltz*, p. 48, quoted in Jacob Twersky, *Blindness in Literature*.

14. Jessica L. Langworthy, "Blindness in Fiction: A Study of the Attitude of Authors Towards Their Blind Characters," *Journal of Applied Psychology*, 14:282, 1930.

15. Twersky, *op. cit.*, p. 15.

16. *Ibid.*, p. 47

17. Robert Louis Stevenson, *Treasure Island*, p. 36.

18. *The Life of Lazarillo de Tormes*, summarized in *Magill's Masterplots*, p. 2573.

19. Laura E. Richards, *Melody*, pp. 47-48.

20. John G. Morris, *The Blind Girl of Wittenberg*, p. 103.

21. Reverend Thomas J. Carroll, *Blindness: What It Is, What It Does, and How to Live With It*. This entire book deals with the concept of blindness as a "dying," and with the multiple "lacks and losses" of blindness.

22. American Foundation for the Blind, Inc., *A Step-by-Step Guide to Personal Management for Blind People*. This entire book is taken up with lists of so-called "how to" details about the routines of daily living for blind persons.

23. There is a *tenth* theme to be found here and there on the shelves of literature—a rare and fugitive image that stands out in the literary gloom like a light at the end of a tunnel. This image of truth is at least as old as Charles Lamb's tale

of *Rosamund Gray*, which presents an elderly blind woman who is not only normally competent but normally cantankerous. The image is prominent in two of Sir Walter Scott's novels, *Old Mortality* and *The Bride of Lammamoor*, in both of which blind persons are depicted realistically and unsentimentally. It is evident again, to the extent at least of the author's knowledge and ability, in Wilkie Collins's *Poor Miss Finch*, written after Collins had made a serious study of Diderot's *Letter on the Blind* (a scientific treatise not without its errors but remarkable for its understanding). The image is manifest in Charles D. Stewart's *Valley Waters*, in which there is an important character who is blind—and yet there is about him no aura of miracle nor even of mystery, no brooding or mischief, no special powers, nothing in fact but naturalness and normality. Similarly, in a novel entitled *Far in the Forest*, H. Weir Mitchell has drawn from life (so he tells us) a formidable but entirely recognizable character named Philetus Richmond "who had lost his sight at the age of fifty but could still swing an axe with the best of the woodsmen."

BIBLIOGRAPHY

American Foundation for the Blind, Inc., *A Step-by-Step Guide to Personal Management for Blind People*, New York, 1970.

Barreyre, Gene, *The Blind Ship*, New York, Dial, 1926.

Bramah, Ernest, *Best Max Carrados Detective Stories*, New York, Dover, 1972.

Bronte, Charlotte, *Jane Eyre*, New York, Dutton, 1963.

Caine, Hall, *The Scapegoat*, New York, D. Appleton and Company, 1879.

Carroll, Reverend Thomas J., *Blindness: What It Is, What It Does, and How To Live With It*, Boston, Toronto, Little, Brown and Company, 1961.

Chaucer, Geoffrey, *Canterbury Tales*, Garden City, translated by J.U. Nicolson, 1936.

Collins, Wilkie, *Poor Miss Finch*, New York, Harper and Brothers, 1902.

Conrad, Joseph, *The End of the Tether*, Garden City, Doubleday, 1951.

Stevenson, Robert Louis, *Treasure Island*, Keith Jennison large-type edition, New York, Watt, nd.

Stevenson, Robert Louis, *Kidnapped*, New York, A.L. Burt, 1883.

Stewart, Charles D., *Valley Waters*, New York, E.P. Dutton and Company, 1922.

Twersky, Jacob, *Blindness in Literature*, New York, American Foundation for the Blind, 1955.

Wells, H.G. "The Country of the Blind," *Strand Magazine*, London, 1904.

West, V. Sackville, *The Dragon in Shallow Waters*, New York, G.P. Putnam's Sons, 1922.

Kenneth Jernigan's more or less "extra-curricular" talents as a scholar of history and a critic of culture—notably displayed in the successive banquet speeches dealing with blindness in history and in literature—became increasingly familiar to Federationists and other readers of the *Braille Monitor* during the seventies through the publication of a number of informal essays addressed not to the day-to-day problems of the movement but to more theoretical, and occasionally playful, matters of thought and learning. One such essay, which appeared in the *Braille Monitor* in 1973, was entitled "A Left-Handed Dissertation." Its satirical use of analogy served the purpose of underlining the status of the blind as a minority group, subject to much the same differential treatment and suspicious regard as other minorities. The analogy of blindness with left-handedness was on the order of a parable or cautionary fable, pointing a moral which did not lose its cogency with the passing of the years.

A LEFT-HANDED DISSERTATION:
OPEN LETTER TO A FEDERATIONIST
by Kenneth Jernigan

DEAR COLLEAGUE: You have asked me to comment on a seeming contradiction in the philosophy of the National Federation of the Blind. You tell me that, on the one hand, we say the ordinary blind person can compete on terms of equality with the ordinary sighted person—if he gets proper training and opportunity. You call to my attention our statement that the average blind person can do the average job in the average place of business, and do it as well as his sighted neighbor. You remind me that we tell the world (with great insistence) that the blind person can be as happy and lead as full a life as anybody else.

You tell me that, on the other hand, we say blindness need not be the great tragedy it has always been considered but that it can be reduced to the level of a mere physical nuisance. You say these two propositions seem contradictory and that, if you are to buy the one, you do not see how you can buy the other. You tell me you are prepared to accept the fact that the blind can compete and, therefore, that you are not prepared (unless I can trot out valid reasons to the contrary) to concede that blindness is a nuisance at all—that is, any more than any other characteristic is a nuisance to any other person in normal living.

Let me begin by saying that you have put me in an unusual position. Ordinarily people want to argue the other way. Most of them say that it is ridiculous to pretend that blindness can be reduced to the level of a nuisance since it is obviously a major tragedy, involving severe problems and extreme limitations, not to mention emotional distress and psychological disturbance. You, however, deny that it is even a nuisance and ask me to come up to the line and prove that it is. Fair enough. I shall try. The very fact that you can seriously raise such a question shows how much progress we have made. I doubt that anybody could have done it, even as recently as twenty years ago.

To begin with, even if we were to concede (and I don't concede it, as I will shortly indicate) that there is absolutely nothing which can be done with sight which cannot be done just as easily and just as well without it, blindness would still be a nuisance, as the world is now constituted. Why? Because the world is planned and structured for the sighted. This does not mean that blindness need be a terrible tragedy or that the blind are inferior or that they cannot compete on terms of equality with the sighted.

For an exact analogy, consider the situation of those who are left-handed. The world is planned and structured for the right-handed. Thus, left-handedness is a nuisance and is recognized as such, especially by the left-handed. Even so, the left-handed can compete on terms of equality with the right-handed since their handicap can be reduced to the level of a mere physical nuisance.

If you are not left-handed (I am not. I am a "normal."), you may not have thought of the problems. A left-handed person ordinarily wears his wristwatch on his right arm. Not to do so is awkward and causes problems. But the watch is made for the right-handed. Therefore, when it is worn on the right arm, the stem is toward the elbow, not the fingers. The watch is inconvenient to wind, a veritable nuisance.

Then there are butter knives. Many of them are so constructed that the left-handed must either spread the butter with the back of the knife, awkwardly use the right hand, or turn the wrist in a most uncomfortable way—nuisances all. But not of the sort to ruin one's psyche or cause nightmares, just annoying. The garden variety can opener (the one you grip in your left hand and turn with your right—that is, if you are "normal") is made for "normals." If you hold it in your right hand and turn it with your left (as any respectable left-hander is tempted to do), you must either clumsily reach across it to get at the handle or turn it upside down so that the handle is conveniently located, in which case it won't work at all. Likewise, steak knives are usually serrated to favor the right-handed. Scissors, egg beaters, ice cream dippers, and other utensils are also made for the same group.

So are ordinary school desk classroom chairs. How many have you seen with the arms on the left side? Of course, a few enlightened schools and colleges (with proper, present-day concern for the well-being of minorities) have two or three left-handed chairs in each of their classrooms, but this is the exception rather than the rule. It succeeds only in earning the ill will of chauvinist right-handers, who must use the desks when the room is full and the left-handed are absent. Of course, these occasional left-handed desks are the most blatant form of tokenism, the groveling gratitude of occasional left-handed Uncle Toms to the contrary notwithstanding.

In at least one case, it would seem, the problem of the left-handed is not just a side effect of the fact that the world is constructed for the right-handed but a real, inherent weakness. When the left-handed person writes with ink (the ballpoint pen was a blessing, indeed), his hand tends to smear the ink as it drags over what he has written. Of course, he can hold his hand up as he writes, but this is an inferior technique, not to mention being tiresome. Upon closer examination even this apparently inherent weakness is not really inherent at all but simply another problem created by society in its catering to the right-handed. There is no real reason why it is better to begin reading or writing at the left side of the page and move to the right, except that it is more efficient and comfortable for the majority, the right-handed. In fact, it would be just as easy to read or write from the right to the left (more so for the left-handed), and thus the shoe would be on the other foot—or, more precisely, the pen would be in the other hand.

The left-handed have always been considered inferior by the right-handed. Formerly (in primitive times—twenty or thirty years ago) parents tried to make their left-handed children behave normally—that is, use their right hands. Thereby, they often created trauma and psychiatric problems—causing complexes, psychoses, and emotional disturbances. Today (in the age of enlightenment) while parents do not exactly say, "left is beautiful," they recognize the rights of minorities and leave their left-handed progeny to do their own thing.

(Parenthetically, I might say here that those who work with the blind are not always so progressive. Parents—and especially educators—still try to make the blind child with a little sight read large type, even when Braille would serve him better and be more efficient. They put great stress on reading in the "normal" manner and not being "conspicuous." They make him ashamed of his blindness and often cause permanent damage.)

But back to the left-handed. Regardless of the enlightenment of parents and teachers, the ancient myth of the inferiority of the left-handed still lingers to bedevil the lives of that unfortunate minority. To say that someone has given you a "left-handed compliment" is not a compliment to the left-handed. It is usually the left hand that doesn't know what the right hand is doing, rarely the other way around; and it is the right hand that is raised, or placed on the Bible, to take an oath. Salutes and the Pledge of Allegiance are given with the right hand. Divine Scripture tells us that the good and the evil shall be divided and that, at the day of judgment, the sheep shall be on the right hand and the goats on the left, from whence they shall be cast into outer darkness forever and ever. The guest of honor sits on the right hand of the host, and in an argument one always wants to be right. No one ever wants to be left behind. Whether these uses of the words "left" and "right" are subtleties of language—reinforcing the stereotype and bespeaking deeply ingrained, subconscious prejudice—or whether they are accidental, as the "normals" allege, who can say? It may simply be that the left-handed are supersensitive, wearing chips on their shoulders and looking for insult where none is intended.

It is hard to make this case, however, when one considers the word *gauche*. The 1971 edition of *Webster's Third New International Dictionary of the English Language, Unabridged*, says: "**gauche**...left, on the left, French...lacking in social graces or ease, tact, and familiarity with polite usage; likely or inclined to commit social blunders especially from lack of experience or training...lacking finish or exhibiting crudity as in of style, form or technique)...being or designed for use with the left hand: LEFT-HAND. Synonym see AWKWARD; **gauchely** adverb : in a gauche manner AWKWARDLY, CLUMSILY, CRUDELY."

Whatever else may be said, there is nothing subtle about all of that; nor is there anything subtle about the term *bar sinister,* which comes from the Latin *sinistral*, meaning "left-handed." The 1971 edition of *Webster's Third New International Dictionary of the English Language, Unabridged*, says: "**bar sinister**...the fact or condition of being of illegitimate birth...an enduring stigma, stain, or reproach (as of improper conduct or irregular status)." Supersensitive? Quibbling? Not on your life. Left-handers, arise! You have nothing to lose but your chains. They probably don't fit you anyway, being made for the right-handed. Look for the new slogans any day: "Left is lovely," and "Get righty!"

As with other oppressed minorities, the subtleties of language and prejudice carry over into the job market. I know of a woman, for instance, who lives in Kansas and who sought employment in a factory in that state. She was interviewed and passed every test with flying colors. The prospective employer terminated the interview by telling her, "You are in every way qualified for the job, and I would hire you immediately, except for your handicap." In outrage and indignation she demanded to know what he meant. "Why," he said, "it's obvious! You are left-handed. The machines on our assembly line are made for the right-handed. You would slow down the entire operation." This is not fantasy but fact. The company makes greeting cards. The woman did not get the job.

If, in truth and in fact, the left-handed woman would have slowed the assembly line, it is hard to see how the action of the employer can be called discriminatory. He could not be expected to buy new machinery simply to give her a job, nor could he be expected to redesign the entire factory. The "normal" person is right-handed, and it is reasonable for the factory to be designed accordingly.

Or does all of this miss the whole point? Is this not exactly the way employers and the general public think and talk about the blind? How did he know she was less efficient? Perhaps she had alternative techniques. Perhaps, in fact, she could have done the job better than most of the other people he had on the line. He decided (based on what he doubtless called "obvious" and "common sense" reasons) that she couldn't do the work. Accordingly, she was never even given the opportunity to try. Beware the "obvious," and look very carefully at so-called "common sense."

Do you still say there is no discrimination against the left-handed? Probably you do—unless you begin to think about it, until you get the facts—and even then, some people will say you are quibbling, that you are exaggerating. How very like the case of the blind. How easy to make quick judgments and have all of the answers, especially when you are not confronted with the problem or compelled to look at reality.

From all of this, you can see that the life of the left-hander is not easy. Nevertheless, his infirmity can be reduced to the level of a mere nuisance. It need not mean helplessness or inferiority. It does not necessarily cripple him psychologically. With reasonable opportunity he can compete on terms of equality with his right-handed neighbor. The average left-hander can do the average job in the average place of business and do it as well as the average right-hander. So far as I can tell, there is no inherent weakness in left-handedness at all. The problems arise from the fact that society is structured for the right-handed. But these problems (annoying though they be) do not keep the left-handed from leading normal lives or competing with others. They are at the nuisance level.

Therefore, even if blindness (like left-handedness) had no inherent problems, it would still be a nuisance since society is structured and planned for the sighted—sometimes when it could be arranged more efficiently otherwise. For instance, most windows in modern buildings are not there for ventilation. They are sealed. They are there only so that the sighted may look out of them. The building loses heat in winter and coolness in summer, but the sighted (the majority) will have their windows.

I think, however, that blindness is not exactly like left-handedness. I think there are some things that are inherently easier to do with sight than without it. For instance, you can glance down the street and see who is coming. You can look across a crowded room and tell who is there.

But here, it seems to me, most people go astray. They assume that, because you cannot look across the room and see who is there or enjoy the sunset or look down the street and recognize a friend, you are confronted with a major tragedy—that you are psychologically crippled, sociologically inferior, and economically unable to compete. Regardless of the words they use, they feel (deep down at the gut level) that the blind are necessarily less fortunate than the sighted. They think that blindness means lack of ability. Such views are held not only by most of the sighted but by many of the blind as well. They are also held by many, if not most, of the professionals in the field of work with the blind. In the *Journal of Rehabilitation* for January-February, 1966, an article appeared entitled: "Social Isolation of the Blind: An Underrated Aspect of Disability and Dependency." This article was written by none other than Dr. D. C. MacFarland, Chief of the Office for the Blind, Social and Rehabilitation Service, Department of Health, Education, and Welfare. Dr. MacFarland says:

> Let me repeat a statement which I violently oppose. There is a slowly evolving fiction which can be summed up in the generalization, "Blindness is a mere inconvenience." I do not agree with this, and I do not know what to call such exaggeration in reverse. I think it has done its share of harm, throwing some very well-intentioned people off the track about what blindness really amounts to in people's lives.

It seems to me that Dr. MacFarland is as far off the track as the people who contend that blindness is not even important enough to be considered a nuisance. I think it would be pleasant to look at a sunset. I think it would be helpful to look across a room and see who is there, or glance down the street and recognize a friend. But I know that these things are peripheral to the major concerns of life. It is true that it is sometimes a nuisance to devise alternative techniques to get the same results I could have without effort if I were sighted, but it is just that (a nuisance), not a tragedy or a psychological crisis or an international incident.

It seems to me that many of the problems which are regarded as inherent in blindness are more like those of the left-handed—in other words, created as a natural side effect of the structuring of society for the sighted. It seems to me that the remaining problems (those that are truly indigenous to blindness) are usually vastly overrated and overdramatized.

Blindness can, indeed, be a tragedy and a veritable hell, but this is not because of the blindness or anything inherent in it. It is because of what people have thought about blindness and because of the deprivations and the denials which result. It is because of the destructive myths which have existed from the time of the caveman—myths which have equated eyesight with ability, and light with intelligence and purity. It is because the blind, being part of the general culture, have tended to accept the public attitudes and thus have done much to make those attitudes reality.

As far as I am concerned, all that I have been saying is tied up with the why and wherefore of the National Federation of the Blind. If our principal problem is the physical fact of blindness, I think there is little purpose in organizing. However, the real problem is not the blindness but the mistaken attitudes about it. These attitudes can be changed, and we are changing them. The sighted can also change. They can be shown that we are in no way inferior to them and that the old ideas were wrong—that we are able to compete with the sighted, play with the sighted, work with the sighted, and live with the sighted on terms of complete equality. We the blind can also come to recognize these truths, and we can live by them.

For all these reasons I say to you that the blind are able to compete on terms of absolute equality with the sighted, but I go on to say that blindness (even when properly dealt with) is still a physical nuisance. We must avoid the sin and the fallacy of either extreme. Blindness need not be a tragic hell. It cannot be a total nullity, lacking all inconvenience. It can, as we of the National Federation of the Blind say at every opportunity, be reduced to the level of a mere annoyance. Right on! And let us neither cop out by selling ourselves short with self-pity and myths of tragic deprivation, nor lie to ourselves by denying the existence of a problem. There is no place in our movement for the philosophy of the self-effacing Uncle Tom, but there is also no place for unreasonable and unrealistic belligerence. We are not out to "get sighty."

The 1975 convention of the National Federation of the Blind was again held in Chicago, where the 1972 and 1974 conventions had been so dynamic and successful. The mood of the delegates was confident, enthusiastic, and upbeat—as President Jernigan reflected that mood in his banquet address, "Blindness: Is the Public Against Us."

"Despite the exclusions and denials," he said, "we are better off now than we have ever been. It is not that conditions are worse today than they were ten or twenty years ago, but only that we are more aware of them. In the past we wouldn't have known of their existence, and even if we had, we wouldn't have been able to do anything about it. Today we are organized, and actively in the field. The sound in the land is the march of the blind to freedom. The song is a song of gladness."

The situation of the blind, Jernigan said, had to be viewed in perspective—and the behavior of the blind must be flexible enough to meet the need. "We must use both love and a club," he said, "and we must have sense enough to know when to do which—long on compassion, short on hatred; and, above all, not using our philosophy as a cop out for cowardice or inaction or rationalization."

As to the question posed in the title of his speech, Jernigan gave a resounding answer of affirmation and buoyant belief in the future. "The public is not against us," he said. "Our determination proclaims it; our gains confirm it; our humanity demands it."

This address received a great deal of attention from the media throughout the nation and led to an invitation to Jernigan to speak at a National Press Club luncheon in Washington. The luncheon occurred shortly after the convention, and Jernigan's Press Club speech (which was a variant of the banquet address) was carried nationwide on National Public Radio. The complete text of the banquet address follows:

BLINDNESS: IS THE PUBLIC AGAINST US
by Kenneth Jernigan

When the orange-billed seagull scares from my shadow and flees from my pass, I look up and see the sun laughing a smile on the water.

When mothers and fathers shout and hit their children for discipline, I look up and see the sun lure transient clouds to cover her face.

And when the blind man, dogless, loses his homeward path, I have seen the stranger straighten his solo way while the sun sets.

I have wondered: Is there a land where the birds are unafraid, where the little children are uncried, and the blind
people see—

Where the sun won't laugh at the seagulls and hide from
the children and leave when the blind man is lonely.

That poem—which appears on the wall of a California coffee
house—portrays to a remarkable degree (even if only in
microcosm) both the best and the worst traits of humanity: compassion, bigotry, sensitivity, obtuseness, concern, arrogance, perceptive awareness, and a total lack of understanding. Certainly
with respect to blindness it exemplifies every misconception of the
darkest Middle Ages. When the blind man (dogless or otherwise)
is lonelier than others—when he has it so bad that the sun itself
must flee from his plight, it is not the blindness which should be
mourned but the social attitudes and the cultural heritage—the
root causes of the broken spirit and the blighted soul. Second-
class status and deep despair come not from lack of sight but from
lack of opportunity, lack of acceptance, lack of equal treatment
under the law, and (above all) lack of understanding.

Not only does the coffee house poet speak about blindness but
also (doubtless without knowing it) he speaks about our reason
for organizing; for if the principal problem we face is the blindness
itself (the physical loss of sight and its alleged inherent limitations) there is little purpose in collective action. If, as the poem
puts it, the only solution is, "a land where the birds are unafraid,
where the little children are uncried, and the blind people see,"
we had better pack it in and leave it to the experts. And even
then, there will be no real solution; for, (with present knowledge
and foreseeable technology) most of us who are blind today are
going to stay that way, and that is that. If this is truly the way of
it, let us take such comfort as we can from the doctor, the
preacher, and the psychiatrist—and let us square our shoulders
and take it alone, not seeking the company of others with similar
affliction, who (at the very best) can only remind us of what we
are not, and what we can never become.

But, of course, this is not the way of it—not at all. Everything in
us rejects it. All of our experience denies it. We know that with
training and opportunity we can compete on terms of absolute
equality with the sighted, and we also know that the sighted (with
education and correct information) can come to accept us for
what we are—ordinary human beings, neither especially blessed

nor especially cursed—able to make our own way and pay our own tab.

This is why the National Federation of the Blind came into being. In 1940 a small band of blind people from seven states met at Wilkes-Barre, Pennsylvania, to begin the movement. At first it was mostly faith and dreams, but that was over a generation ago. Today (with more than 50,000 members) we are a nationwide crusade with local chapters in every state and the District of Columbia. At an accelerating pace we have become aware of our needs, our potential, and our identity. An increasing number of the sighted have also become aware and now march with us; but the mass of the public, a majority of the media, and most of the social service agencies still think in pre-Federation terms.

Deep down (at the gut level) they regard us as inferior, incompetent, unable to lead an everyday life of joy and sorrow, and necessarily less fortunate than they. In the past we have tended to see ourselves as others have seen us. We have accepted the public view of our limitations and, thus, have done much to make those limitations a reality. But no more! That day is at an end.

Our problem is so different from what most people imagine, that it is hard for them even to comprehend its existence. It is not the blindness, nor is it that we have lacked sympathy or goodwill or widespread charity and kindness. We have had plenty of that—too much, in fact.

Rather, it is that we have not (in present day parlance) been perceived as a minority. Yet, that is exactly what we are—a minority, with all that the term implies.

Do I exaggerate? In the summer of 1972 the National Federation of the Blind held its convention in Chicago. A local television station sent a black reporter to do coverage. She went directly to the exhibit room and used most of her film on various mechanical aids and gadgets. To round out her story, she came to me and asked that I comment on the value and benefit of it all.

I responded obliquely, asking her how she would feel if she were at a national meeting of the NAACP or the Urban League and a reporter came and said he was there to film the shoe shining and the watermelon eating contest. She said she wouldn't like it. "Well," I said, "suppose the reporter took another tack. Suppose he wanted to spend all of his time and film on an exhibit of gadgets and devices incidentally on display as a sidelight of the meeting, ignoring the real problems which brought the group together in the first place." She said she wouldn't like that either. In fact, she said, it would be worse since the question about the shoe shining and the watermelons could be easily discredited, while the other approach was just as bad but far less apparent and, therefore, probably more restrictive.

I then told her about a reporter who came to one of our meetings and said, "I'd like to get pictures of blind persons bowling and of some of the members with their dogs." I tried to explain to him that such a story would be a distortion—that we were there to discuss refusal by employers to let us work, refusal by airlines to let us ride, refusal by hotels to let us stay, refusal by society to let us in, and refusal by social service agencies to let us out. He said he was glad I had told him and that it had been very helpful and enlightening. Then he added, "Now, could I see the dogs and the bowlers? I am in quite a rush."

As I told this story, the black reporter was obviously uncomfortable. She seemed truly to understand, but when I asked her if she still intended to feature the exhibits and the gadgets, she stuck to her guns. "In the first place," she said, "I've already used all of my film. In the second place my editor told me to do it, so that's the way it has to be." The television coverage appeared on schedule—usual image, usual distortion. There is nothing wrong with bowling or dogs or canes or exhibits, but it was a bad scene.

A year later (in June of 1973) the blind were again in Chicago—this time for a different reason. The National Accreditation Council for Agencies Serving the Blind and Visually Handicapped (NAC) was meeting, and the blind were demonstrating and picketing. Formed in the mid-1960s by the American Foundation for the Blind, NAC symbolized (as it still does) everything odious and repulsive in our long and painful tradition—custodialism by governmental and private social service agencies, ward status, vested interest, intimidation, exclusion, and second-class citizenship. Our attempts to gain representation on NAC's Board were answered by double-talk and tokenism, by Uncle Toms representing nobody but themselves and their masters, and by threats and reprisals. Finally, we had had enough.

So when (without warning and in violation of its own bylaws and policies) NAC tried to hide from us by changing its meeting from

Cleveland, Ohio, to an out-of-the-way motel in Chicago (a motel in the midst of construction and remodeling), we came to confront them. And not just a few of us, but the blind of the nation. It was short notice and difficult doing, but we came—hundreds of us, from all over the country: California, New England, the deep South, and the Midwest.

It was a day of dramatic importance. It was the first time in history that the blind as a people (not just a local group or a given segment but the blind as a people) had mobilized to take to the streets for collective action. There were state delegations, placards and signs, marches in downtown Chicago, and a rally at Civic Center Plaza. Was it newsworthy? By every test known to journalism, the answer would have to be yes.

Yet, the *Chicago Tribune* for Thursday, June 21, 1973, carried not a single line about the demonstrations. It was not that the *Tribune* forgot us. Far from it. There was not just one, but two stories about the blind. And what were these stories that were of such importance as to be more newsworthy than the first national demonstration by the blind in history? One was headlined "Busy blind man finds time to help children." The other was captioned "Blind, he directs music in city school."

What a commentary! It was all there. The blind are especially talented in music. They are also burdened and deprived. Therefore, when one of them (instead of just doing the normal thing and receiving) turns it around and gives to others (particularly, children), it has human interest and news value. What would have happened if Martin Luther King had been leading the first black demonstrations in Chicago and the papers had ignored it—printing, instead, "Busy black man finds time to help children" and "Black, he directs music in city school"? I think you know what would have happened, and so do I. There would have been a furor of massive proportions. Yet, the incidents I have related passed without notice or ripple, almost as a matter of routine.

What I have said must be seen in perspective. The *Tribune* writers and the other members of the Chicago press were not trying to put us down or conspire against us. They were calling it as they saw it, writing what tradition had taught them to write. Like any other cross section of society, they doubtless were (and are) people of integrity and goodwill. It was not a matter of morals or motives, but of comprehension. It was all tied up with their notions about blindness. Pathos, compensatory talents, musical ability, inspiration, bravery against odds, world of darkness, heartrending tragedy—these they (and even their editors) could understand: run-of-the-mill, good human interest, no sweat. But the blind as a minority? Discrimination? Marches? Confrontation with the social service agencies, the very people who were trying to help the blind? Ridiculous! The reporters couldn't understand it, and (at least, at the emotional level) they didn't believe it. So how could they write it? And even if they did, how could their editors approve it, or the public buy it? Forget it. Don't think about it. Let it alone.

Of course, the attitudes of the press are representative of the broader society, and the situation is certainly not unique. It is exactly the way the blacks were treated 50 years ago. They were lumped together and seen as a single caricature—good natured, irresponsible, rhythmic, shiftless, and a mite dishonest, second-class all the way. A black person was never shown in a straight role on the stage or in the movies but only as a foot-shuffling, jolly simpleton. It was Amos and Andy and Uncle Remus and Aunt Jemima; and not only the blacks but all of us will bear the scars for generations to come because of the failure to understand, the lack of concern to care, and the absence of the courage to act. Fifty years ago it was the blacks. Today it is the blind. But we are organized, and we are on the move. We want no strife or confrontation, but we will do what we have to do. We are simply no longer willing to be second-class citizens. They tell us that there is no discrimination—that the blind are not a minority. But we know who we are, and we will never go back.

Lest you think I am picking on Chicago, let me say that New York was about the same. In July of 1973 (only a month after the NAC demonstration in Chicago) the largest group of blind people ever to assemble anywhere in the world up to that time met in New York. For almost a week we discussed our hopes and our problems—planned and dreamed. Some 2,000 of us marched on NAC headquarters. There was a considerable amount of local radio and television coverage, and a little in the papers. Nationally there was hardly a ripple. I can only explain it as before.

It was not conspiracy or deliberate put-down. In some ways it was worse, for an individual can be made ashamed of prejudice and repression—but rarely of charity and kindness. They didn't understand it; they didn't believe it; and (above all) they didn't know how to write it. It didn't fit the image and the preconception.

two incidents coming together that she called to ask what the Federation could do about it.

Of course, this negative behavior is not surprising from small children, or even from the public at large; but surely we have the right to expect better from the social service agencies, the very people who are supposedly knowledgeable and established to help us. Yet, an outfit in Seattle calling itself Community Services for the Blind (ultrarespectable and approved by the United Way) decided this spring to make Mr. Magoo the principal focus of its pubic relations and funding. The leaders of our Washington affiliate protested, but to no avail. A blind man on the Community Services board (Uncle Toms are, indeed, pathetic; and we have our full quota) thought it was funny, and even constructive. But the board's sighted president put it all in perspective:

> The advertising message [he said in a letter to one of our members] is especially directed at people who are *responsible* for the blind—not the blind themselves. We don't feel the blind person will tend to identify himself with Mr. Magoo, necessarily; in fact, many may not even know who he is. If there is any kind of a negative aspect in the fact that Mr. Magoo has poor eyesight, it is all the more effective, just as a crippled child on a muscular dystrophy poster is more effective than a normal child. [Emphasis added.]

What a damning self-indictment! What an ironic commentary on the end of an era and the death of a system. Yet, they tell us that there is no discrimination—that the blind are not a minority. But we know who we are, and we will never go back.

To round out the picture of the public mind, consider the following recent examples: A man wrote to me a few months ago saying that he would like to buy a cat or dog for every blind person in Colorado Springs. "I saw a young blind boy," he said, "with a white cane and a puppy dog. He seemed so happy. If you think it would help I would be glad to see every blind person in Colorado Springs has a pet. Cat or dog."

A dental hygiene student wrote to me from Fresno, California: "I am working on a research paper," she said, "concerning the special needs of visually handicapped or blind people with regard to dental care. I hope to determine: (1) how the dental procedure needs to be altered to accommodate them, and (2) special dental problems of these patients."

Recently a blind woman was in the hospital for gall bladder surgery. A tape on the foot of her bed was inscribed in large letters: "Patient is blind but self-sufficient." It's all tied up in the word *"but."* Am I quibbling? Not really. Is it subtle? Not very.

An expert on penology and social reform wrote to me to say that, in his opinion, the blind (regardless of their misdeeds) should not be put in the penitentiary. "If the seriousness of their offense merits incarceration," he said, "they should be dealt with in a special manner." In other words, even in the "big house" we should be second-class and segregated.

The author of a book on the teaching of medical transcribing wanted her work put into Braille. "I wrote you," she said, "because I have watched the teaching of this subject to the blind over a period of years and it is unnecessarily painful and lengthy. They do make first-rate transcribers and always seem so pathetically grateful for a chance to learn."

A religious organization circulates a card called "Courtesies of Gentleness for the Sighted in Contacts with the Blind." It says:

> A handshake to a blind person is like a smile to a sighted person. So shake hands on greeting and on leaving your blind acquaintance....Never fill to the brim a cup given to a blind person; it is too hard to keep on an even keel. Give him a refill instead....Don't express sympathy for a blind person in front of him....In motoring, guard against slamming the car door on the blind person's hands. Also see that he doesn't extend his arm or hand outside the car....Never force an approaching blind person to give you the right-of-way, for every time he has to deviate from his course, he loses his bearings....

In other words the blind can't plan or do for themselves. Do it *for* them, and think for them, too. And don't express pity for them—at least, not to their faces. Gentle and courteous all of the way.

Incidentally, the Federationist who sent me this card said: "I find it demeaning and offensive."

A doctor at the Mayo Clinic wrote: "I am sorry to say she is blind and cannot be helped. Anything you can do to make her life easier would he greatly appreciated."

From Pennsylvania comes this:

> Today I was advised by the Department of Labor Inspections Division that under the new life safety measures, which will emanate from the Department of Health, Education, and Welfare, it will not be possible to allow a blind person to live on the second floor of a boarding house having more than three guests unless the building totally conforms with the federal specifications and standards.

Southern College, located in Orlando, Florida, announces: "Tuition for all students is basically $417 per quarter. There is an additional quarterly fee of $125 for visually-impaired students."

In 1972, James Reston, the well-known syndicated columnist, commented on Senator Eagleton's forced withdrawal from the Democratic vice-presidential nomination: "This is not primarily Eagleton's fault," Reston said, "but the system's. That system is very compassionate to human beings whose age and health interfere with the efficient execution of their work. It tolerates Supreme Court justices who are in serious ill health or who are even almost blind."[1]

The key word (as I am sure I don't have to tell you) is *even*. That "even" is at the center of our problem as blind people. It takes for granted (as an obvious commonplace, needing no argument) that the blind are unable to perform competently as Supreme Court justices; in fact, that it is ridiculous even to assume that they might; and that any system which tolerates such manifest irrationality can only be explained on the basis of compassion.

Compassion, indeed! The compassion is often misplaced. Recently, for instance, we held a luncheon for employers so that they could get acquainted with blind job applicants, and the East Moline, Illinois, Metal Products Company saw no reason to come.

"Because of the type of business we are in," their letter said, "metal stampings and weldments involving punch presses, shears, brakes, and welders, we feel that we have nothing to offer the blind inasmuch as we have nothing in a counting or packaging type of work."

The irony is that one of the people attending the luncheon (totally blind from childhood) works every day shearing steel and operating presses. He has done it for 15 years and is considered the best in the plant.

In Michigan in 1970 Tom Munn (a blind man) took a State Civil Service examination for the position of mechanic. He passed with a score of 96, and his name was placed on the register. He was not offered employment; others (with lower scores) were hired. In 1972 the Civil Service Commission created a separate list for the handicapped. Munn's name was transferred from the open register to the separate list, and his score was reduced from 96 to 70—which (regardless of performance) was the grade to be given to all so-called "successful" future blind applicants. Munn requested that his performance be evaluated. The request was refused. In 1974 (acting on his own) he secured a work trial evaluation with the Motor Transport Division of the Department of Management and Budget. He did the job without difficulty. The results were ignored. In 1975 (his patience finally exhausted) he contemplated a lawsuit. Officials of the state agency for the blind (the very people charged by law with the duty to help him) allegedly tried to coerce him into silence. Tom Munn and the National Federation of the Blind have now brought action in the federal courts against both the state agency and the Civil Service Commission. Yet, they call it compassion and say we are incompetent. They tell us that there is no discrimination—that the blind are not a minority. But we know who we are, and we will never go back.

Surely all of this is sufficient, but it is only illustrative. Southern Illinois University plans to make a study of the dating and mating selection patterns of the blind; the Minnesota Braille and Sight Saving School plans a course in sex education and wants specialized materials and techniques; and the *National Enquirer* puts it all together in a November 11, 1973, article entitled "Finds Blindness Upsets Sexual Functioning."

> The sex drives of the blind, [the article says] are upset by their inability to see light, states a West German researcher. Dr. H. J. von Schumann, of Dusseldorfs, said he found that irregular menstrual cycles in blind women and loss of sexual ability in blind men seem related to

their inability to see light. The hormone-producing system controlled by the pituitary gland appears to need
stimulation by light if sex hormones it produces are to be
kept at adequate levels.

Hardened as I am to ignorance and superstition, I still find it difficult to know exactly what to do with that one. I confess that I
was reluctant even to bring it to you at all for fear some of the
sighted (lacking firsthand experience) might be tempted to believe
it. The demands of modesty and the wish to be seemly would seem
to rule out any attempted refutation by personal laboratory performance, and the customs and laws of the day make it inadvisable
to stage mass exhibitions to place the matter in perspective. So I
guess the best I can do is this: Pick any random hundred of us,
and put them alongside any random hundred of them; and I
believe we will acquit ourselves with credit and pleasure—probably with volunteers to spare. Ask the sighted with the background
to know.

What a dreary picture! We are dogless and lonely; we can't enjoy
smoking; we are Mr. Magoo; we need pets to keep us company;
we have different dental needs; we must be segregated, even in
the penitentiary; we should be pitied, but not to our faces; we
cannot live on the second floor of a boarding house; our college
tuition is higher; we cannot shear steel or operate presses; we
cannot compete in the Civil Service but must be content with a
separate list and a score of 70; and, finally, we are even inadequate for the joys of sex. It would seem that all that is left is to
pack it in; and even that is taken care of in an article on the right
to death by choice appearing in the January, 1974, *Atlantic*: "I
do not wish," the author says, "to survive any accident or disease
resulting in vision too impaired to see or read. A world without
beauty seen is no world for me. A life without freedom and movement is no life for me. If age and illness deny me these, I choose
death."[2]

So where does all of this leave us? In the first place it leaves us
with the need for perspective; for as the saying goes, we have
never had it so good. Despite the exclusions and the denials, we
are better off now than we have ever been. It is not that conditions are worse today than they were ten or twenty years ago, but
only that we are more aware of them. In the past we wouldn't
have known of their existence, and even if we had, we wouldn't
have been able to do anything about it.

Today we are organized, and actively in the field. The sound in the land is the march of the blind to freedom. The song is a song of gladness. Yes, there are discriminations and misconceptions; but there are also joy and promise. The old is dying, and the new is at hand.

It is true that not all sighted people have goodwill toward us, but most do. As we begin to move toward first-class citizenship (especially, as we insist upon our rights), we will inevitably provoke hostility; but we will also inspire understanding and respect.

If we simply go forth with chips on our shoulders and bitterness in our hearts, we will lose. We must have greater flexibility and more positive belief in ourselves than that. There is a time to fight and a time to refrain from fighting; a time to persuade; a time to take legal action; a time to make speeches; a time to educate; a time to be humble; a time to examine ourselves to root out arrogance, self-deception, and phony excuses for failure; a time to comfort our fellow blind; and a time to stand unflinchingly and uncompromisingly with the fury of hell against impossible odds. Above all, we must understand ourselves and have compassion in our hearts, for the sighted as well as for our fellow blind—and, yes, even for ourselves. We must have perspective and patience and the long view; and we must have the ability and the willingness to make sacrifice, and the courage to refuse to wait.

We must destroy a system which has kept us in bondage, but we must not have hatred in our souls for that system or that bondage—for the bitterness will destroy, not our enemies but us. We must recognize that the system was an indispensable element in making us what we are, and, therefore, that its chains (properly seen) are part of our emerging freedom—not to be hated or despised but to be put aside as outdated and no longer to be borne.

As we look ahead, the world holds more hope than gloom for us—and, best of all, the future is in our own hands. For the first time in history we can be our own masters and do with our lives what we will; and the sighted (as they learn who we are and what we are) can and will work with us as equals and partners. In other words we are capable of full membership in society, and the sighted are capable of accepting us as such—and, for the most part, they want to.

We want no Uncle Toms—no sellouts, no apologists, no rationalizers; but we also want no militant hellraisers or unbudging radicals. One will hurt our cause as much as the other. We must win true equality in society, but we must not dehumanize ourselves in the process; and we must not forget the graces and amenities, the compassions and courtesies which comprise civilization itself and distinguish people from animals and life from existence.

Let people call us what they will and say what they please about our motives and our movement. There is only one way for the blind to achieve first-class citizenship and true equality. It must be done through collective action and concerted effort; and that means the National Federation of the Blind. There is no other way, and those who say otherwise are either uninformed or unwilling to face the facts. We are the strongest force in the affairs of the blind today, and we are only at the threshold. We must operate from a base of power—yes; but we must also recognize the responsibilities of power and the fact that we must build a world that is worth living in when the war is over—and, for that matter, while we are fighting it. In short, we must use both love and a club, and we must have sense enough to know when to do which—long on compassion, short on hatred; and, above all, not using our philosophy as a cop out for cowardice or inaction or rationalization. We know who we are and what we must do—and we will never go back. The public is not against us. Our determination proclaims it; our gains confirm it; our humanity demands it. My brothers and my sisters, the future is ours. Come! Join me on the barricades, and we will make it come true.

FOOTNOTES

1. Reston, James, "System at Fault in Eagleton Case," *The Kansas City Star*, Kansas City (Mo.), July 31, 1972.

2. Maguire, Daniel C., "Death by Chance, Death by Choice," *Atlantic*, Boston (Mass.), Jan., 1974.

When the delegates assembled in Los Angeles for the 1976 National Federation of the Blind convention, they had much to celebrate. Andrew Adams, the commissioner of the Rehabilitation Services Administration, had responded affirmatively to their request that federal funds no longer be used to support the regressive National Accreditation Council for Agencies Serving the Blind and Visually Handicapped (NAC); the Federation's radio and television announcements were blanketing the nation; all fifty states and the District of Columbia were now represented in the organization; and Federation influence and prestige had never been greater. It was in this context and setting that the Federation's President delivered one of his most stirring banquet addresses, "Blindness: Of Visions and Vultures."

He began with a parable concerning a vulture sitting in the branches of a dead tree, and there were many in the audience who thought it referred to some of the more custodial agencies in the blindness system. Repeatedly during the speech President Jernigan returned to a central theme. "We know who we are," he said, "and we will never go back. The vulture sits in the branches of a dead tree, and we see where the wings join the body."

Again in 1976 (as he had done in 1975) Jernigan sounded a note of optimism and hope. "It is not," he said, "that our situation is worse or our problems greater today than in former times. Far from it. It is only that we have become aware and that our level of expectation has risen. In other days we would hardly have noticed, and even if we had, we would not have been organized to communicate or prepared to resist. We have it better now than we have ever had it before, and tomorrow is bright with promise."

The text of the 1976 banquet address follows:

BLINDNESS: OF VISIONS AND VULTURES
by Kenneth Jernigan

Behold a king took forth his three sons to judge their fitness to govern the kingdom, and they stopped by a field, where a vulture sat in the branches of a dead tree. And the king said to the oldest son, "Shoot—but first tell me what you see."

And the son replied: "I see the earth and the grass and the sky...."

And the king said, "Stop! Enough!" and he said to the next son, "Shoot—but first tell me what you see."

And the son replied, "I see the ground and a dead tree with a vulture sitting in the branches...."

And the king said, "Stop! Enough!" and he said to his youngest son, "Shoot—but first tell me what you see."

And the young man replied, his gaze never wavering, "I see the place where the wings join the body." And the shaft went straight—and the vulture fell.

Yes, a fable. But also a moral—a reminder—a commitment.

Last year on July first (ironically, the very day of the opening of our convention) the news commentator Paul Harvey made a national radio broadcast. Entitled "Not All Equal," it said:

> When are we going to stop deluding ourselves about "equality"? A pitiful problem has developed where our Federal and state governments try to enforce equal job opportunities for the handicapped. Of course it can't be done. Frequently the handicapped are turned down for jobs without being told why. The why may involve higher insurance rates, or installation of special signals for the deaf or blind.

> Let me confide, he continued, that politicians and the news media—where a concern is humanitarian—rarely dare speak out against the poor, the deprived, the unlovely, or the imperfect. However impractical the pretense, these thought leaders must continue to pretend that we are all equal. When, in fact, of course, no two of us are.

Harvey rested his case with a quotation from the British author C. S. Lewis:

> No man who says, "I'm as good as you are" believes it. He wouldn't say it if he did. The St. Bernard never says it to the toy dog, nor the scholar to the dunce, nor the employable to the bum, nor the pretty woman to the plain. The claim to equality is made only by those who feel themselves to be in some way inferior. What it expresses is precisely the itching, smarting, writhing awareness of an inferiority which the patient refuses to accept.

So declared Paul Harvey, and the network carried his message to millions. If the problem we confront comes not from misconceptions and discrimination but from the very nature of our condition—from our blindness—then we should not fight it but face it.

It will do us no good to complain or whimper, nor will it help to be bitter. Facts are facts, and they should be dealt with as such—straightforward and to the point.

If the Harvey thesis is right, we have made a tragic mistake in organizing at all. From a handful in 1940, the National Federation of the Blind has grown to its present size of more than fifty thousand members. The reason for the growth is simple. It is our philosophy, and what that philosophy promises. The Federation is based on the proposition that the principal problem of blindness is not the blindness itself, but the mistaken notions and ideas about blindness which are held by the general public. We of the Federation believe that the blind (being part of the broader culture) tend to see themselves as others see them. Accepting the mistaken public attitudes, we help those attitudes become reality. Moreover, we believe that the governmental and private service agencies are also victims of the same misconceptions and stereotypes and that they make their voluminous studies, plan their programs, and custodialize their clients, not (as they claim) from professional expertise and knowledge but from ignorance and prejudice, absorbed from general culture. Finally, we believe that when we as blind people accept the second-class role assigned to us by the agencies and the public, we do it because of social conditioning, not because of correct information or necessity. We do it because of fable, not fact.

This is what the National Federation of the Blind is all about. It is why we organized. It is why we continue. It explains our actions and our behavior—why we intend to speak for ourselves, why we demand a voice in the programs affecting us, and why we insist that only persons chosen by us presume to speak for us. Others cannot do it—even if they are employees or administrators of agencies, even if they claim to be professional experts, and (for that matter) even if they are blind. We speak for ourselves; we do it with our own voice; and we will permit no one else to do it for us. We have always said (and we say today) that we are able to work with the sighted, play with the sighted, and live with the sighted on terms of full equality; and the sighted are capable of accepting us as equals and partners.

Yet, if the Paul Harvey thesis is true, our whole philosophy is a lie. The National Federation of the Blind is not only useless—it is downright destructive; for it promises a future which is impossible to realize and beckons with a dream which can never come true. If the Harvey thesis "tells it like it is," let us repent of our

folly, disband our movement, and apologize for the trouble we
have caused. Let us take whatever charity and kindness society
offers. Let us go our way in acceptance and resignation—and let
us do it alone; for there will be no need for concerted action, no
purpose in pretending we are equals.

But, of course, the Paul Harvey thesis is not true. Everything in
us rejects it. All of our experience denies it. The facts refute it.
It is the very kind of blatant ignorance which called the Federation
into being in the first place and which still continues to poison
the public mind. We want no strife or confrontation, but we will
do what we have to do. We are simply no longer willing to be
second-class citizens. They tell us that there is no discrimination—
that the blind are not a minority. But we know who we are, and
we will never go back. The vulture sits in the branches of a dead
tree, and we see where the wings join the body.

As has always been the case, our principal problem is still lack of
understanding on the part of the public. Some of the misconceptions we confront are overt; some are subtle. Some are deadly;
others simply ridiculous. Several months ago I received a letter
from a man in Missouri:

"Dear Sir," he said. "There is a case of a blind girl around twenty
years of age who has been awfully mistreated. I am only a friend
to her and her mother. I couldn't be yellow dog enough to make
love to a Blind and then try to lie out of it and blame somebody
else."

Beneath the crudity, that letter speaks with terrible eloquence,
calling up the anguish of the centuries. It spotlights the problem
which we the blind must face. That problem is not, as Paul Harvey
seems to think, centered in questions such as our need for special
signals or the inability of employers to hire us because their insurance rates might go up. Rather, it deals with such basics as the
refusal to let us compete (with no favors asked) for jobs we are
perfectly well able to fill, denial of our right to equal treatment
under the law, arbitrary rejection (without reason) of the notion
that we can function as competent human beings, and abridgment
of our dignity as persons.

The discriminations against us are not imaginary, but real—not
exceptional but commonplace. The proof is overwhelming and irrefutable. It is illustrated, for instance, in two recent court cases.

In one a mother was threatened with the loss of her child, on the grounds that, as the judge put it, she is "industrially blind, and does not have the ability to care for the child." In the other case a married couple was declared unfit to adopt a male child because, in the words of the husband, it was "felt that a boy could not relate to me because of my blindness." It need only be added that hundreds of blind mothers are successfully caring for their offspring every day and that adoption of children by blind parents has occurred repeatedly with no problem. In fact, when the adoption case in question was successfully concluded (after considerable conflict with the judge), the boy had no trouble at all relating to his blind father. Yet, they tell us that the problem is in us, not society—that there is no discrimination and that the blind are not a minority. But we know who we are, and we will never go back. The vulture sits in the branches of a dead tree, and we see where the wings join the body.

Last year the American Legion Auxiliary of Oregon prohibited a blind girl (Donna Bell by name) from taking her place as a duly elected delegate to the annual Oregon Girls State observance. The rejection was made on grounds that (as a blind girl) she could not be "physically fit." This arbitrary ruling was subsequently reversed at the insistence of Governor Tom McCall, who said of Donna that "her leadership, character, honesty, scholarship, cooperativeness, *and her physical fitness* qualify her to be here." She attended; she was accepted by her peers; and she performed without problem or incident.

In September of 1975 the New Orleans *Times Picayune* featured the headline: "Blind Children Hate Food, Must Be Force Fed." The article which followed quoted a staff member of a Louisiana institution for the blind and handicapped as saying: "A blind child would starve to death if you didn't force him to eat...they hate food." Those of you attending this banquet can judge that one for yourselves. It has been my experience that we who are blind stow away about as much food with about as much gusto as anybody else. But Paul Harvey would probably tell us that our objection to such ignorance about our eating habits, only proves that we are "patients," expressing the "itching, smarting, writhing awareness of our inferiority which we refuse to accept." Yet, they tell us that there is no discrimination—that the blind are not a minority. But we know who we are, and we will never go back. The vulture sits in the branches of a dead tree, and we see where the wings join the body.

The exclusions and discriminations are, of course, not limited to any geographic area, any age group, or any particular type of situation. They occur anywhere and everywhere. Witness the episode of the drugstore proprietor in Matawan, New Jersey, who informed the blind customer that he should use the back door since the front of the building is mostly glass. When the customer persisted in entering through the front door like any other first-class citizen, he was bluntly ordered to go around to the back door or never come to the store again. In other words knuckle under or stay out.

To be sure this is an extreme case. We are not so often thrown out as put down. Recently I received a letter from Junerose Killian, one of our leaders from Connecticut, in which she related the following:

> The other day, when I was picked up for my class in Transactional Analysis,...the priest whom we also picked up inquired of the minister who was driving the car: "What clinic are we taking her to?" Of course, he automatically assumed that I must be a charity case, and he was astonished to find that I was one of his colleagues in the class.

This letter from Connecticut (this drama in microcosm) symbolizes the attitude of the ages. It refutes Paul Harvey. It says in graphic and unequivocal terms who we are, why we have organized, what we must accomplish, what the public-at-large must learn, and what those who knowingly and deliberately obstruct our path are invited to do—and where they can go. It is a sermon in miniature, a blueprint for Federationism.

Shortly after our convention last year Patti Jacobson, who is one of the Federation's student leaders, responded to a want ad which appeared in the Lakewood, Colorado, *Sentinel.* She tells it this way:

> I called to inquire about the job and was told to come on Tuesday for an interview. The ad indicated that the job was for telephone ticket sales, but no other information was given. I arrived at the office and was told to speak with Joe Chapman. Upon noticing that I was blind, he immediately said that I could not take this job because there were cards with names and addresses on them, which I could not read. I offered to get the cards Brailled. I offered to have a reader come and read the cards. Each

suggestion I made was either ignored, or answered rudely. When he began to see that my suggestions were valid,
he started making irrelevant excuses such as: "Many
times these businessmen make excuses, and you have to
know what to say to them," and "I give directions at the
beginning of each day. and you would have to digest
them." I ask you, what does blindness or sight have to
do with following directions—using one's ears and mind
to listen and think? He later said that he didn't have time
to spend with me individually. He never did say what he
would have to do for me that he does not have to do for
the other employees. When I asked him what he does for
the others (I was going to point out that he would do
just the same for me, no more, no less), he rudely said,
"That isn't any of your business."

He was even further demeaning by saying, "Believe me,
I understand; I've been down and out, too." He still
clings to the old notion that all blind persons are down
and out. After some discussion (I was trying to find out
more about the job, explain my qualifications and
capabilities, and make suggestions, and Mr. Chapman was
interrupting), he finally told me to leave. When I would
not, because I still had not been interviewed, he
threatened to call the police. I had come down there for
an interview, and he would not grant me that right.

That is what happened to Patti Jacobson—not in another century
or another decade but less than a year ago. It was occurring in
the same month that Paul Harvey was making his broadcast. Did
her demand for equal treatment prove, as Harvey would apparently contend, that she was inferior and knew it—that she was only
feeling the "itching, smarting, writhing awareness" of second-class
status which she (the patient) refused to accept? Or did her
demand prove the exact opposite? She was not asking for special
equipment or special concessions. She was only asking for the opportunity to try, the chance to fail or succeed on her own merit:
equal treatment, no favors asked. Yet, they tell us that there is
no discrimination—that the blind are not a minority. But we know
who we are, and we will never go back. The vulture sits in the
branches of a dead tree, and we see where the wings join the
body.

It is bad enough when the uncomprehending public believes we
are children or patients, but it is pitifully worse when we believe

it ourselves—conditioned by the old assumptions and brainwashed by the ancient myths. Listen to this self-description by a blind man in Japan, taken from a Japanese book entitled *How Can I Make What I Cannot See?*

"If you lose something as big as your eyes," he says, "then you're not so greedy about the rest of the world anymore. If you're not greedy, if you have very few desires, then don't you think that in the end you have become much richer? Since I've lost my eyesight, I have found I want very little. My wife guides me around hand in hand. I don't spend much money. I hear lots of music I never heard before, and I don't have to witness horrible incidents. Thus, I have great peace of mind. Doesn't my life sound richer?"

"This," he concludes, "is what we call the blind man's heaven." The worst of it is that these remarks were made in the course of a lecture to young blind students on what the speaker called the "positive virtues of blindness."

He is, indeed, a cripple; and he will probably bring his students to the same condition—not because of blindness but because of society and what it has taught him to believe and become. The tragedy cries out for justice. Yet, Paul Harvey tells us (and the network carries his message) that the problem is not in society, but in us.

Barbara Pierce is one of the leaders of our movement in Ohio. She is in this audience tonight. She is an attractive, capable, busy, normal woman—married to a college professor, raising a family, and minding her own business. She works to change misconceptions where she finds them and recognizes the value of united action on the part of the blind.

A few months ago the Public Relations Committee of the National Federation of the Blind held a seminar, and Barbara attended.

"The PR seminar was very useful." she said, "and raised the level of Federation spirit in the group. I thought you would be interested in a little piece of public education I managed during a cab ride on Sunday. Inspired by the conference, I decided to engage in some spreading of the word. I learned to my consternation that the cab driver had always assumed that blind girls, as he put it, 'got fixed by doctors so that they would have nothing to worry about in that way.' I didn't feel equal to inquiring whether the

and when he does, praise is grossly out of proportion. *Rejection*: the child is ignored or avoided.

Jim and I have experienced a mixture of all these. Friday night, Jim and I had some people over for a cookout. I was in the kitchen fixing baked beans and deviled eggs. Jim came in and asked if there was something he could do. I asked him to slice the tomatoes. (I never meant to start a riot. I only wanted the stupid tomatoes cut up.) One of the other men came in the kitchen and said, "But, he might cut his finger." Jim told him that he had cut tomatoes before and was sure he could do it again. He did so and soon had a nice plateful. The other man, who stayed to watch, then took Jim by one arm and the plate of tomatoes in the other to show everybody what he had done. (A cerebral palsied child who has just learned to walk doesn't get that much praise.)

Jim then proceeded to walk out back and light the charcoal. The same man said, "Are you going to let him do that?" I shrugged and said, "Why not?" The man jumped up and ran out back. When he came back, all he could talk about was how remarkable Jim was.

Everyone calmed down, and we began to eat. Then it started to rain. Jim got up and said to me, "Are the car windows down?" They were, so Jim proceeded to run outside to roll them up—without his cane. The other man jumped up and grabbed Jim's cane. He said, "Does Jim need this?" I said, "No. Don't worry so about him. He's fine." Jim came back and we started to eat again. Jim wanted some more beans, so he went to the stove and got them. The comment then was, "That is just wonderful." What is so wonderful about dipping beans? Jim told me later (after they left) that he felt like taking a bow after everything he had done. I don't think he did anything out of the ordinary, and neither does he. The whole night he felt as if he were on exhibit, and I was experiencing a strong desire to stand up and scream, "He's not stupid, and he's not a child. He's not doing anything terrific, so shut up!"

It didn't end there. Later on that night, Jim and I made a trip to the hospital emergency room. He had got into some poison ivy, and it had spread to his eyes. The nurse on duty was horrible. She didn't think he was remarkable—she thought him to be blind, deaf, mute, stupid, and incapable of doing anything. She asked me, "What is his name? Where does he live? Do his eyes itch?" I was offended and said, "I think he can answer his own questions." Jim calmly told her what she wanted to know, but I could tell he was mad.

When he went in for treatment, a man came over to me and said, "You are so wonderful to be kind to that poor man." I tried to explain that I felt lucky to have a man like Jim. (And I am. He's the best thing that ever happened to me. When we're together, I feel happy and secure and protected. I love him.) After I finished trying to explain to this man our relationship, he said, "You mean you're dating him? Why would a pretty little thing like you want him? He's blind." Then I said something I should not have said. "Yes, he is blind, but he's more of a man than you'll ever be." Jim came out of treatment then, and we left.

Saturday afternoon some more friends came over, and we all went roller skating. It was fun and we all had a good time. When we got back to Jim's apartment, one of the girls said to me, "You really are good to Jim. He needs somebody like you." I told her that I needed him, too. She then asked me if when we were alone was he able to do all the things that other men do. You can imagine my shock at such a question. I assured her that he was.

By Sunday, I was so overwhelmed with all that had happened I couldn't even think. Jim knew something was wrong. I told him that I was okay. He had some cans that needed to be labeled, so I started doing that on his Brailler. I was putting a label on a can of pineapple juice. I spelled it wrong. Jim said he had never seen it written that way. So I cried. He looked utterly shocked that I was crying over pineapple juice. So he said, "I'm going to ask you one time what's wrong, and if you don't want to tell me that's okay, but I'd like to be able to help you with it." So I told him.

I told him that I didn't think it was fair, and that I loved him too much to watch him put up with all that mess. Jim is a sweet, loving, compassionate, intelligent, sexy, desirable man; and I love him, and it hurts for everybody else to treat him like some kind of freak. He's got such a good self-image. And I don't want that changed. He said, "Honey, take it easy. You'll get used to it." No, I won't. I am not going to get used to seeing him insulted.

I just can't understand what difference it makes whether he sees or not. One of our friends recently said to me, "You really are an exceptional person that you can accept Jim." I said that I really wasn't, and that I just didn't think about it. She said, "Oh, it must be hard to forget a thing like that." I told her that I didn't try to forget it, I just didn't think about it—the same as you don't think about the fact that someone has brown hair. It really makes very little difference what color his hair is, and it's the same way with Jim. I know he can't see, and I don't try to forget about it, but I don't really think about it. She couldn't understand. She said, "But it is so obvious." I told her that she stopped looking when she saw the glasses—and that she couldn't see the man behind them, and that she was "blinder" than Jim is. One friend—gone.

The real killer comes when people find out that I'm a special education teacher. I don't think I need to tell you what they say, then.

Jim stayed with me half of the night. He talked to me and listened to me cry. I hope you understand that I wasn't crying because I feel sorry for him but because I love him, and it hurts me when people do such horrible things.

If you have any suggestions as to what to say to these people, I would appreciate hearing them.

Sincerely yours,

How could I respond to such a letter! Its poignant feeling and depth of understanding left nothing to be added—no room for elaboration. It said all there was to say. I called the writer and told her she had strengthened my faith in humanity. I told her the Federation would never quit until the put-downs and denials were finished. I said I felt honored to walk by her side in the march to freedom.

That march has been long, and the end is not yet in sight. The road stretches on for decades ahead, and it stretches backward to the nightmare past of slavery and pain. Yes, I say slavery, and I mean exactly what I say. I use the word deliberately, for no black was ever forced with more absolute finality to the sweat of the cane fields or driven with more terrible rigor to the heat of the cotton rows than we have been forced to the broom shops and backwaters and driven to the rocking chairs and asylums. Never mind that the custody was kindly meant and that more often than not the lash was pity instead of a whip. It was still a lash, and it still broke the heart and bruised the spirit. It shriveled the soul and killed the hope and destroyed the dream. Make no mistake! It was slavery—cruel, degrading, unmitigated slavery. It cut as deep as the overseer's whip and ground as hard as the owner's boot.

But that was the past—another time and another era. This is a new day. It is true that the vestiges of slavery still linger. The drugstore owner still sends us to the back door, and the courts still tell our women that they cannot keep their children and our men that they cannot be suitable fathers. We are told that we hate food, that we cannot go to Girls State, and that we cannot be interviewed for a job. It is automatically assumed that we are headed for the clinic instead of the classroom; the cab driver thinks that all blind girls must be "fixed"; and the sighted woman weeps for the pain and humiliation of the man she loves. Some of our own people grovel and simper about "the positive virtues of blindness," and Paul Harvey sums it up by telling us that our claim to equality is simply the "itching, smarting, writhing awareness" of the inferiority which we (as patients) know we have but refuse to accept. Doubtless there is not one of us (sighted or blind) who has totally escaped unscarred from the conditioning. We must wait until at least the next generation for that. Many of the blind have not yet fully understood and have, thus, not joined the movement. Some of our local affiliates are chapters in name only, waiting for the touch of a leader and the sound of the call to awaken. Much of our work is still ahead—yearning, challenging, needing, and waiting to be done.

All of this is true, but we must see it in perspective. It is not that our situation is worse or our problems greater today than in former times. Far from it. It is only that we have become aware and that our level of expectation has risen. In other days we would hardly have noticed, and even if we had, we would not have been organized to communicate or prepared to resist. We have it better now than we have ever had it before, and tomorrow is bright with promise.

As we make our advance and set our daily skirmish lines we come to the fight with gladness—not with cringing or fear. We come with a song on our lips and joy in our hearts, for we have seen the vision of hope and felt the power of concerted action and self-belief. In the conflict ahead we will take casualties. We know it, and we are prepared for it. Whatever the price, we will pay it. Whatever the cost, we will bear it. The stakes are too high and the promise too certain to let it be otherwise. We are organized and moving forward. We will be free—and the sighted will accept us as partners and equals. We know who we are, and we will never go back. The vulture sits in the branches of a dead tree, and we see where the wings join the body. Our gaze will not waver. Our shaft will go straight to the mark, and the vulture will fall. My brothers and my sisters, the future is ours. Come! Join me on the barricades, and we will make it come true!

The termination of the nine-year tenure in office which would come to be known as the First Jernigan Presidency came with shocking abruptness in New Orleans in 1977 through the unexpected resignation of the movement's leader for reasons of health. Jernigan's resignation, announced at the end of his annual presidential report to the National Convention, left the delegates no choice but to agree on a successor to the highest office. They selected the Federation's Second Vice President, Ralph Sanders, to fill the vacancy; but, as the *Braille Monitor* was to report, the voting was unenthusiastic and reluctant. Here is part of what the *Monitor* had to say about the event:

> When President Jernigan announced his resignation at the conclusion of the first day of the convention, the room was filled with cries of "No!"—expressing the unwillingness of Federationists to hear and accept what was being said. As President Jernigan went on to say that—were his health to improve—he might one day again seek the presidency, he was interrupted once more, this time by a prolonged and tumultuous ovation. This was the first of many outpourings of the intense affection and loyalty to this man felt by the members of the Federation. Both responses recalled the events of a decade earlier when the movement lost the leadership of another giant in the affairs of the blind.

Thus ended the period of unparalleled peace and prosperity within the organized blind movement—a period already coming to be known as the "democratic decade"—which had begun with the arrival of Kenneth Jernigan in the presidency and was closing with his unsought and unwanted departure. There was one thing more for him to do before he took his leave: to rise before the largest banquet audience in Federation history (well over 1,700) and deliver what was then regarded as his valedictory address. He made the most of the occasion, as everyone there knew he would—taking as his text the Biblical passage which proclaims "To everything there is a season." President Jernigan began by observing: "There was a time for me to be President of this organization. That time is no more. A new President now comes to the stage; a new era now begins in the movement."

He went on: "What, then, (at this final banquet on this last night of my presidency) shall I say to you—what that we have not already jointly discussed and collectively experienced during the past quarter of a century? In articles and speeches, in public pronouncements, and in literally thousands of letters I have set forth my beliefs and declared my faith in the capacity of the blind and the need for collective action...

"As President of the Federation, I have always tried to see our movement in broad context—attempting to ease the losses and temper the victories with a sense of perspective. So, on this night, let us talk of history and look to the future—assessing where we are by where we have been and where we are going."

The attentive audiences at convention banquets through the democratic decade had often been touched by the eloquence of their President; but on this warm New Orleans evening, sharing an historic moment and dreading its inevitable end, they were moved as rarely before on these significant annual occasions. For they knew, every man and woman in the throng of Federationists, that they were not just talking of history here with their leader and mentor—they were making it. This is the speech they heard:

TO EVERY THING THERE IS A SEASON
by Kenneth Jernigan

To every thing there is a season, and a time to every purpose under the heaven. A time to be born, and a time to die; a time to plant, and a time to pluck up that which is planted; a time to kill, and a time to heal; a time to break down, and a time to build up; a time to weep, and a time to laugh; a time to mourn, and a time to dance;

a time to cast away stones, and a time to gather stones together; a time to embrace, and a time to refrain from embracing; a time to get, and a time to lose; a time to keep, and a time to cast away; a time to rend, and a time to sew; a time to keep silence, and a time to speak; a time to love, and a time to hate; a time of war, and a time of peace.

Thus it is written in the Scriptures, and thus also it is written in the experience of our daily lives. To every thing there is a season. There was a time for me to be President of this organization. That time is no more. A new President now comes to the stage; a new era now begins in the movement. It remains for me to help with the transition and then assume my new role in the organization.

What, then, (at this final banquet on this last night of my Presidency) shall I say to you—what that we have not already jointly discussed and collectively experienced during the past quarter of a century? In articles and speeches, in public pronouncements, and in literally thousands of letters I have set forth my beliefs and declared my faith in the capacity of the blind and the need for collective action. I have said that what we must have is not pity but understanding, not custody but opportunity, not care but acceptance. I say it still—and this, too: I have tried as best I could to match deeds to words—to be not merely an armchair strategist but a frontline soldier as well. There are scars to prove it; enemies to resent it; and friends to confirm it. Nothing I can say tonight will change the record. In the words of the poet:

The moving finger writes; and, having writ,
Moves on: nor all your piety nor wit
Shall lure it back to cancel half a line,
Nor all your tears wash out a word of it.

As President of the Federation I have always tried to see our movement in broad context—attempting to ease the losses and temper the victories with a sense of perspective. So, on this night, let us talk of history, and look to the future—assessing where we are by where we have been and where we are going.

In 1940, when the blind came to organize, the situation was as bleak as it could possibly be. It was bright enough to create hope and dark enough to make that hope seem impossible. Barely a handful from seven states met on that day in Wilkes-Barre, Pennsylvania, to establish the National Federation of the Blind.

In the climate of growing agency control and custodialism they felt that freedom would not wait—that they must either act then (regardless of their numbers) or risk losing the opportunity forever. The majority they sought (the powerful movement of the organized blind) might never come unless they had the courage to create it and the dream to believe it. They had that courage— they created that dream—and thirty-seven years later we meet here tonight in our thousands, the strongest force in the affairs of the blind in the nation.

It is only when we look back that we realize how far we have come. In 1940 there was virtually nothing by today's standards: no rehabilitation, no libraries, no opportunity for higher education, no rights for sheltered shop employees, no training for the newly blinded, no money for the elderly, no help for the needy, no jobs in Federal Civil Service, no chance in business, no hope in the professions, no state or federal civil rights protection, no encouragement to venture, and no recognition of dignity or worth. There were only the put-downs and exclusions, which made of the blind virtually a subhuman species. It was an atmosphere which broke the spirit and quenched the hope and killed the dream. But that was another time, another generation. Whatever else the National Federation of the Blind may have done, one thing is certain: It has helped us understand and made us believe in ourselves, in each other, and in our collective strength. It has also taught us to fight. In short, it has brought us to see that we are (in every modern sense of the word) a minority.

Through painful experience we have learned that our problems come not from our blindness but from the misconceptions and misunderstandings of society, not from inferiority but public attitudes—attitudes which we ourselves still too often unwittingly accept and thus do much to make reality. With equally painful experience we have learned that the "professionals" in the very public and private agencies established to aid us frequently (instead of helping solve our difficulties) contribute to them. If (and, of course, there has been much more) the Federation had done nothing else but give us these understandings, it would have more than justified its promise. We are now organized, informed, and on the move. We want no strife or confrontation, but we will do what we have to do. We are simply no longer willing to be second-class citizens. They tell us that there is no discrimination—that the blind are not a minority. But we know who we are, and we will never go back.

With all our advances, we still face serious problems. Let anyone who doubts it look at the Gallup Poll taken in January of 1976. It shows that, next to cancer, blindness is the most feared of all human ailments—more than deafness, more than heart disease, more than mental illness, more than any other possible problem. This contrasts sharply with our personal experience. We know that, with training and opportunity, we can reduce blindness to the level of a mere inconvenience; but we also know that custodialism, discrimination, denial of opportunity, and put-downs can make of our blindness a veritable hell—as terrible as it has ever been thought to be. This is why we have organized. It is why the National Federation of the Blind exists—to eliminate the fears, disseminate the truth, and bring new hope: to the sighted and the blind alike.

With the expanding hoard of "professionals" in the field—who must write papers, think up additional services, and find something to do to occupy their time so as to keep their jobs, enhance their prestige, and raise their salaries—it is not surprising that traditional fears and misconceptions are reinforced. The ancient myths and prejudices are absorbed by the "professionals" from the public and then fed back again in the name of science and expertise—bolstered by computers, sanctified by technology, and financed by government grants. It is a formidable array, but it is the same old lie it has always been. We are not inferiors, and we prove it every day through our personal lives and individual experience.

The public attitudes about blindness manifest themselves in every facet of daily existence. Consider, for instance, an item as simple as a mail-order catalogue. Such a catalogue (called *Mail-Order USA*) recently came to me with this cover letter:

> I am sure that your members would appreciate learning more about this book which will help make shopping less of an ordeal. The families of a blind person can send for catalogues of articles the person needs, and in the leisure and quiet of his home decide what he wants to buy—no more being stampeded by impatient sales clerks.

A lot of food for thought is packed into that brief statement. Are the blind so frail that they are more likely than others to find shopping an "ordeal" or be "stampeded" by salesclerks? And observe that it is not the blind person who is expected to order the catalogue but his family, who will decide for him what he wants to buy, and you will notice, in restful circumstances: "in the quiet of his home."

When it comes to cooking and matters related to the kitchen, both the public and the professionals have a field day. An article entitled "Arizona Volunteers and Blind Homemakers" in *Food and Home Notes*, a publication issued by the United States Department of Agriculture, says: "Ever wondered what it's like to be blind? How would you boil water safely?" Where, one might ask, did the Agriculture Department get such ideas? We are not left in doubt. The article goes on to say: "Arrangements worked out through the American Foundation for the Blind provided expert trainees. Every trainee practiced skills both as a blind learner and as a teacher."

The Arizona episode is not the only experience of the American Foundation for the Blind with kitchens. The January 24, 1973, *Miami Herald* reported that the Foundation would sponsor six workshops "for sighted rehabilitation personnel, public health nurses, and county home demonstration agents to teach homemaking techniques to blind persons." Presumably these Foundation-taught personnel would then go into the homes of the blind to teach skills and proper attitudes about blindness. Judge for yourself the level of expectation, the image of blindness, and the probable results from the following statement by Evelyn Berger, home economist, who (according to the article) "introduced local women rehabilitation workers to the challenge of darkness":

"A blind person's kitchen should be simplified as much as possible," she said. "High storage areas should be avoided. Pans used most frequently should be at an accessible level. If the teacher must leave the room for a minute, leave the person with his hand on something, such as a chair back, for security. When you return, announce your arrival with a 'Hi, I'm back.'"

Yes, of course, pans should be at an "accessible level," and "high storage areas should be avoided"—but no more for the blind than for anybody else. As for the talk about putting the hand of the blind person on the back of the chair for security and cheerfully announcing the teacher's return, that is pure drivel—the sort of thing that makes sensational newspaper reading, perpetuates public misconceptions, and creates high-paying jobs for dull-witted custodians.

Under the circumstances is it any wonder that the following passage appears in the standard advertising literature for the Mirro-Matic pressure cooker:

> Braille books for use by sightless people are available through Mirro. These books include the cooking charts, instructions, and 32 recipes. Cooking procedure is not given and must be taught by a sighted person.

Yet, they tell us that there is no discrimination—that the blind are not a minority. But we know who we are, and we will never go back.

Kitchens, with their supposed dangers, seem to hold a special fascination for those concerned with our welfare. Graduate students at the Illinois Institute of Technology recently designed a special kitchen for the blind to (as they put it) help "the sightless achieve greater independence in a vital area of day-to-day living." The September 16, 1976, *Los Angeles Times* quoted the designers as follows:

> Using the ordinary kitchen can be a disaster for a blind person....All unnecessary kitchen and outside noise [should] be eliminated or reduced through soundproofing since blind people use sound to judge their cooking. The ventilation system [should] be designed to provide sounds necessary for a blind person's awareness and control. The kitchen design [should] allow the user's hands to be as independent of each other as possible to allow better preparation for emergencies. A rest area [should] be provided to combat fatigue. The telephone, doorbell, and radio [should] be located in one area of the kitchen. Work areas [should] have different textures and raised edges to provide clues for identification of reference points. Floors [should] have varied textural surfaces to give blind people awareness of location. Varied shaped or textured handles [should] be used for ease of identification. Sinks [should] have a raised edge with small counter area in front. In addition, the sink might have different depths and/or shapes helpful in food preparation and washing. Burners [should] be placed at rear of [the] stove to provide a safe distance between the user and the heating surface. Storage units [should] be made vertically mobile eliminating bending and stretching. Electrical outlets [should] be placed at waist level with large metal plates for ease of locating. The blind person

should be encouraged to maintain close body contact with
his work area to provide an additional clue to his
location.

What a kitchen! It would be ludicrously funny if it were not so
miserably pathetic and if it had not been seen by millions of
readers to confirm and reinforce their notions of our helplessness.
And where do you suppose it all came from! Where do you think
these graduate students from the Illinois Institute of Technology
got their ideas about blindness? How did they learn what we need,
what we can do, and who we are? Did they come to the blind
themselves (to the largest organization of blind people in the
country) to the National Federation of the Blind with its more
than 50,000 members? No. As the newspaper tells us, they went
to the Chicago Lighthouse for the Blind and the Illinois Institute
for the Visually Handicapped. Yet, these institutions (the Chicago
Lighthouse and its like) sometimes express surprise that the blind
resent them and seek to reform them.

We stand at the gates and demand to be heard. The hour is late,
and we will not be turned away. We will speak, and they will listen—in peace if we can, in war if we must. We are simply no
longer willing to be second-class citizens. We know who we are,
and we will never go back.

Not only are the blind thought to need specially designed kitchens
but special apartments as well. Earlier this year, the *New York
Times* carried the headline "Apartment Building for the Blind Is
Planned for Site in Manhattan." The article said:

> The first apartment building in New York City designed
> for the exclusive use of the blind will be built on a vacant
> site on West Twenty-third Street, officials of the As-
> sociated Blind, Inc., said yesterday."

> The nonprofit group is planning a 12-story structure with
> 205 apartments. It will include textured doorknobs so
> that each resident will know which room he is entering,
> an emergency call system in each apartment connected to
> a central security office, and specially designed kitchens
> and bathrooms....

> New York City is taking the lead in accommodations spe-
> cially designed and equipped for the blind, said the chair-
> man of the City Planning Commission....

The apartments will be designed in accordance with new national HUD standards for the blind and handicapped.

To add insult to injury all of this mumbo jumbo and segregation is done in the name of independence and self-expression. The article ends with a quote from the head of the agency involved: "We believe blind people should have the right to express themselves," he said.

Yes, we reply, but what does self-expression have to do with segregated housing? That is the very ghetto from which we are trying to escape.

As with other minorities segregation of the blind, once begun, does not end with housing. Tom Bozikis recently wrote me as follows:

> In the city of Hammond where I reside, we have what is reported to be the world's largest Sunday School. What disturbs me is that this church, the First Baptist Church of Hammond, segregates those with physical and mental limitations from the rest of the parishioners.
>
> There is a Sunday School class for the blind, the deaf, the crippled, and the mentally retarded. They also have a separate area in church for the blind, deaf, etc. For example, the blind have a special section where they sit which is clearly marked and no one else is allowed to sit there. Even in the area of religion we are second-class citizens. Does this mean that the blind will be placed in a special area before the judgment seat?

Whatever the answer to Tom's question may be, at least one person believes the blind are especially blessed: "Dear Sir," a teacher wrote me a few months ago, "I can find no criminal statistics in the Annual Uniform Crime Report in which blind people are a part. I have assumed for 25 years that blind people cannot become criminals due to this sight limitation.

"I teach a course in the correction and prevention of delinquency and crime....

"A 26-year investigation of criminal phenomena has confirmed the Bible's statement that 'if ye were blind ye should have no sin (crime):....(John 9:41)'....

"If you have any statistics relative to either delinquent or criminal behavior among the blind, I shall greatly appreciate a review of it."

By way of answer I sent him a newspaper headlined "Blind Man Kills Landlady." I don't know what his reaction was.

Speaking of crime, I recently received the following letter:

Reasonably healthy and handsome and sterile caucasian widower and prison inmate with at least three more years to serve before parole and who is five feet, ten inches tall and who weighs 150 pounds and who was born on 7 November 1934 would like to make the acquaintance of a blind lady of virtually any age who has never been divorced and who is reasonably secure financially. Objects: matrimony and the mutual happiness of two losers.

If I cannot please you, blind lady, no man can. The need for your being reasonably secure financially is in line with my intention of having a full-time job keeping you happy. We can teach each other much. My sanity and intelligence are matters of public record. What have we to lose?

With a different twist I received a letter from India not long ago:

Dear Sir:

I inquired here through the United States International Services that your Federation deals with blind females in the U.S.A. Please send me some details and photos of the blind females which are unmarried and between age 15 and 25. If some unmarried blind females want to marry with the young Indians (not blind) then I can help them. Some few young Indians want to marry with the blind American ladies. They want to settle themselves in the United States after their marriage."

To be sure, not all of the attitudes about the blind are bad, but the incidents I have mentioned are not isolated exceptions. They occur with monotonous frequency. Consider the following examples:

Mala Rubinstein (of the famous cosmetics Firm) after working with the American Foundation for the Blind to (as she put it) "teach unsighted women how to use a simple collection of cosmetics to heighten their self-sense of beauty and psychic security" said:

> Nature compensates the blind by giving them a highly developed sense of touch, knowledge of the contours and planes of their faces, and a supremely sensitive sense of smell that easily distinguishes between delicate nuances of fragrance.

A release from the Division for the Blind and Physically Handicapped of the Library of Congress last fall said:

> Surely no one would dispute the idea that the one music library in the nation serving the entire blind and physically handicapped community should be as good as the best music libraries serving everyone else. There is even some justification for saying that this library should provide *better* music library services than that available to others. It is a well-recognized fact that music tends to have a greater importance to the blind than to the sighted.

When asked by the newspapers why he found it necessary to make demeaning rules for blind vending stand operators. "stipulating that they bathe twice daily, obtain dental care at least twice a year, eat a balanced diet, and shampoo frequently," Cleo Dolan (the much-publicized head of the Cleveland Society for the Blind) defended himself by saying: "A blind person has to be almost overly cautious, so we set these guidelines." Mr. Dolan's rules covered everything from when the blind should change their underwear to the requirement that they give eight percent of their monthly gross sales to his agency. The federal courts thought so little of the civil rights of the blind that they refused to take jurisdiction. The case (with National Federation of the Blind backing) is now on appeal.

Rowe International, Inc., (a company that sells vending machines) apparently saw no impropriety in the following language in one of its brochures:

> Rowe International, Inc., and our network of over 40 distributor service centers across the country can provide—

> (1) Guidance in developing a profitable vending program.

(2) Training of nonhandicapped supervisors in administering the program.

(3) Training of the blind operators to serve and maintain the equipment (by specialists in training the blind)."

Not long ago I received the following inquiry from a student:

Dear Sir: I am doing a research paper for a class. I would like to know, how many or what percentage of the blind marry and if any steps are taken to prepare them for this part of life. Also what might be the difficulties or advantages of these marriages?

I received the following letter from a blind woman in Connecticut:

I am tired of feeling like a second-class citizen! My most recent frustration occurred when I visited a U.S. Post Office to apply for a passport. I produced my birth certificate, passport pictures, and completed application. Then the crushing blow: "Please put your driver's license number on this line." I replied, "I'm, sorry, I don't have one; I am legally blind."

Though I had numerous credit cards, professional organizations, a Social Security card as well as bank identification card with my picture on it, none would suffice. Finally, my friend, who had accompanied me, was asked to fill out an affidavit swearing to my identity which required her name, driver's license, and passport information.

An article[1] published by the American Foundation for the Blind discusses what is called a severity rating scale for multiply impaired children, in which different conditions are given a numerical value according to their severity. Light perception, total blindness, or blindness before age three is given a severity rating of ten. Mental disorders and retardation are regarded as less severe. In the language of the chart:

An IQ of 49 or below, observed functioning—at a level of one half or less of chronological age, trainable, not educable—add eight. Psychotic. Extreme disorder resulting in a loss of contact with reality. Common symptoms are hallucinations and distorted behavior—add eight.

In other words it is 25 percent worse to be blind than to have an IQ of 49 or be psychotic—not to mention that we have a keener sense of touch and smell than others, that music is more important to us, that we must be told when to change our underwear, that we must have nonhandicapped people to supervise us, that our marriage habits are so peculiar as to warrant special study, and that we must have a driver's license or do without a passport. Yet, because of our protests, some people call us militant. In the face of such prejudice, ignorance, discrimination, gross insensitivity, and what can only be called downright insanity the wonder is that we have behaved with such restraint as we have. In the circumstances our conduct has been mild to a fault, and a model of propriety—but let them wait; we are learning.

Not all misconceptions and discriminations are as overt as the ones I have just mentioned. In fact, the majority cloak themselves in glib generalities about how independent and capable we are. Al Fisher, one of our members who runs a center for the blind in Spokane, recently sent me a perfect example:

> We were asked [he said] to speak to a high school class on child development here. Very early in our discussion we asked how they felt about blindness and what they thought blind people could do. Their reaction was that blind people were no different from anybody else and that a blind person could do about anything he wanted. Then we started getting into specifics and they were skeptical about a number of areas. I asked them if they would be willing to hire a blind person as a babysitter. Not one, including the teacher, said they would. I'm wondering if they aren't expressing what they think is a popular position, something with form but no substance.

I would say Mr. Fisher sizes it up pretty well. Deep down at the gut level (at the place where people feel and live) most of the "professionals" and the general public still believe we are helpless. It is that simple and that compelling. Some of them don't know it; most would deny it; and a few just plain don't care and don't want to be bothered. But the feeling is there, and it is our biggest problem. Change is occurring, but it is occurring slowly; and it does not happen by itself. It happens only if we make it happen, and that is exactly what we are doing, making it happen—often to the anger and consternation of the professionals, and sometimes to the confusion and bewilderment of the public. But we are doing it. Regardless of the consequences, we are doing it—and we are going to keep on doing it. That is what the National Federation of the Blind is all about. There was a time when we did not know our identity, when we settled for second-class citizenship, but that time is finished. Never again! There are blind people in this room (and sighted allies, too) who will take to the streets and fight with their bare hands if they must to prevent it. We know who we are, and we will never go back.

On this last night of my Presidency, as I recall the past and look to the future, I think of a letter which symbolizes the spirit of what we are as a movement and speaks to the special relationship we have developed through the years. It was 1974, and we were going to Cincinnati to demonstrate against NAC. Some of the Kentuckians were troubled about the thought of picketing and wrote to ask exactly what they would be expected to do. I wrote to them as follows:

> You say that there "seems to be somewhat of a reaction to the word: demonstration." As you know, I grew up in the hills of Tennessee, where the waters ran clear and the loyalties deep. I doubt that any member of the Federation (either in Kentucky or anywhere else) had a more conservative upbringing than I. Picketing, demonstrating, and everything associated with those words were foreign to me. As I said in Chicago in 1972, I had never participated in a demonstration in my life— never, that is, before NAC.
>
> For that matter, I still regard myself as a conservative citizen, but I cannot stand by and do nothing while NAC remains unreformed and while I have life and strength. NAC represents tyranny to the blind. That means tyranny to the blind of Kentucky, as well as to the blind of other places. It is that simple, and we cannot avoid our responsibility by telling ourselves it does not exist.
>
> In the days of the youth of our nation a man named Andrew Jackson went down the Mississippi to fight the British at New Orleans. The backbone of his army consisted of Kentucky riflemen straight from the edge of the frontier. They were not radicals or irresponsible hellraisers, but they would die and be double damned before they would give up their freedom to the British. I am not Andrew Jackson, and today's Kentuckians are not the frontiersmen of the 1800s; but if we meekly bow to NAC, we deserve the second-class status we will surely get.

You ask me what is expected of those attending the NAC demonstration, and I reply that we need every man, woman, and child we can get to go to the Barkley Americana May 30 to serve as a visible reminder to the NAC board members that we are free people and not inferiors—that we are not indifferent, not unconcerned, and not afraid to stand up for our rights. This is what is needed, but I would not want a single person to go to that meeting who is unwilling in his heart to go. We need front-line soldiers; but the army we need must be an army of volunteers, not draftees. We want no person there in body only, he must bring his heart with him, or stay at home.

You ask what is expected of Kentucky, and I answer that I want you to come as your fathers came—with the spirit that crossed the mountains, settled the wilderness, and fought the British. Do it, and the gates of hell shall not prevail against us.

The Kentuckians came to that demonstration, and so did hundreds of others from throughout the country. So it has been over the years, and so it will continue to be until we achieve our goals. When NAC arrives in Portland this summer and in Phoenix this fall, we will be there to meet them. We will also be wherever else there is injustice and discrimination against the blind or an opportunity to make new achievements—in the halls of Congress, in the state capitol buildings, in the television studios, in the newspaper offices, in the board rooms of the agencies, in the establishments of commerce, in the classrooms of the universities, in the luncheons of the civic groups, and on the streets and sidewalks. We are the blind speaking for ourselves, and no force on earth will stay our progress.

And now I come to the hardest part of all, to my final words as President. For 25 years I have held office in the Federation. Tomorrow night that comes to an end. I believe the new President we have elected will lead strongly and with purpose.

As I leave the Presidency, I go with the knowledge that our future is bright. It is true that there are problems to be solved and challenges to be met—that the public must be enlightened and the agencies reformed; but we are on the road, and we have already come far on the journey. We must see it in perspective. As I said last year, it is not that our situation is worse or our problems greater today than in former times. Far from it. It is only that we have become aware and that our level of expectation has risen. In other days we would hardly have noticed, and even if we had, we would not have been organized to communicate or prepared to resist. We have it better now than we have ever had it before, and tomorrow yearns with promise.

As we make our advance and set our daily skirmish lines, we come to the fight with gladness—not with cringing or fear. We come with a song on our lips and joy in our hearts, for we have seen the vision of hope and felt the power of Federationism and self-belief. We are organized and moving forward. We will be free—and the sighted will accept us as partners and equals.

On this note I leave the Presidency. You have supported and comforted and loved me in a way that few people have ever experienced, and, in turn, I have loved you—and have sought with all the wisdom and capacity I possess to lead wisely and well. Together we have built dreams and marched to the battlefield. Together we have constructed a mighty movement and brought better lives to the blind. My brothers and my sisters, the future is ours. Come! Let us join our new President on the barricades, and we will make it all come true!

FOOTNOTE

1. Graham, Milton D., "Multiply Impaired Children: An Experimental Rating Scale," *The New Outlook*, March, 1968, pp. 73-81.

Chapter 6

Restoration: The Beginning Years of the Second Jernigan Presidency

A National Convention which would later be designated by its key figure as "one of the finest episodes in our history" took place in the sunshine of Miami Beach during the summer of 1979—when over one thousand members of the National Federation of the Blind gathered in a mood compounded of excitement and determination to dispatch the sowers of internal discord, to map the strategies of a dozen external campaigns, to celebrate a return to solvency, and to reassure each other that old acquaintances were not forgot.

Kenneth Jernigan, who had been restored to the presidency by acclamation only the year before, was to say of this Miami convention that "it was one of our very best. There was a mood of closeness and harmony which probably surpassed anything we have ever had." And Ramona Walhof, the national leader who wrote the Monitor's convention roundup, called it "a tremendous experience—exciting, informative, uplifting, and spiritually rewarding."

What was remarkable about these accolades, in retrospect, was that they were uttered in reference to a convention which was compelled to deal with an organized campaign by dissident members to take over the Federation and reduce it to the impotence of a loose confederation of autonomous state groups. It might

425

have been an ugly scene; but as it turned out the threat was summarily dispatched by the delegates through a series of decisive actions (to be described below) which left no doubt as to the feelings of the membership and the direction of the movement.

Scarcely less remarkable than the convention's dispatch of the internal quarrel was its general equanimity in the face of greater and more concerted attacks from without than the organized blind movement had known since the distant days of the civil war in the late fifties. That prevailing mood of confidence and quiet strength found eloquent expression in the banquet speech which President Jernigan delivered at the Miami convention. Addressing the theme "That's How It Is At The Top of the Stairs," Jernigan pointed out that the Federation's rapid growth in power and stature had brought with it, as a natural consequence, a rising tide of opposition amounting to a backlash: "No group ever goes from second-class status to first-class citizenship without passing through a period of hostility," he said. "Several years ago I made the statement that we had not even come far enough up the staircase of independence for anybody to hate us. I believe I can safely say that that problem has now been solved. We have enemies enough to satisfy even the most militant among us. We have actually progressed to the point of creating a backlash."

He went on to point out that the hardening of opposition and the widening of attacks upon the organized blind movement were cause not for dismay but for satisfaction as graphic evidence of the Federation's ascent to the higher reaches of the stairway: "This is our challenge and our confrontation. It is also the strongest possible proof of how far we have come. For the first time in history, the choice is ours. As other minorities have discovered, the final steps are the hardest."

Here is the complete text of the Miami address:

BLINDNESS: THAT'S HOW IT IS
AT THE TOP OF THE STAIRS
by Kenneth Jernigan

The noted British historian Arnold Toynbee has a sweeping theory of human development called "The Cycle of Challenge and

Response." According to this theory every civilization faces a constant succession of challenges and confrontations, and its viability and soundness can be measured by the vigor and nature of the response. It may meet the challenge head on, emerging stronger and healthier for the encounter; it may react defensively, desperately, leaving the struggle exhausted; or it may, at the first sign of threat, simply lie down and die. As it is with civilizations, so it may be with movements. For that matter, so it may be with individuals. Our vitality, our spirit, and our very capacity for survival can likely be measured not only by the vigor of our response to challenge and confrontation but also by the pattern and the nature of that response.

When the National Federation of the Blind came into being in 1940, there were certainly both challenge and confrontation; but neither the professionals in the field nor the public-at-large understood the full implications of the challenge or anticipated the ultimate fury of the coming confrontation. 1940 was another time and a different climate. Barely a scattering had the faith to believe and the courage to hope. They were the founders of the National Federation of the Blind. Those original Federationists were not the powerful force of concerted action which we know today, not the united voice of the nation's blind. All of that was still a generation ahead, in the promise of the future and the fullness of the years.

It is only when we look back that we realize how far we have come. In 1940 the blind were universally regarded as inferiors, and there was a general feeling that it was inappropriate for them to organize and take a hand in their own affairs. It was an atmosphere which broke the spirit and quenched the hope and killed the dream. But the resistance to the notion that the blind should organize (the challenges and the confrontations) did not, for the most part, come from hatred or viciousness or a wish to hurt. It came, instead, from pity, misunderstanding, misplaced kindness, or (at worst) apathy and a desire to maintain the status quo.

That was 1940. This is 1979. What has happened to us in the intervening years? What challenges and confrontations do we face today? How do these challenges and confrontations differ from those of 1940? In short, as a movement and a people, where are we—and where are we going?

In broad outline the story of the past four decades is easy to read and quickly told. At first the Federation was small and largely ignored. It had few members and little influence. The governmental and private agencies tried to treat it as if it were not unique at all but simply another provider of services (one among many), a miniature duplicate of what already was—in other words, a newcomer but one of themselves. The public (to the extent that the public knew about the Federation at all) took its lead from the professionals.

But the blind knew otherwise. They knew of the need which only the Federation could fill. They knew it in the yearning for freedom, in the lack of opportunity, in the rejection by society, and in the exclusion from the rights and privileges of full participation and equal status. They knew that the Federation was theirs. For whatever successes it might achieve or whatever failures it might make, it was theirs. Its primary purpose was not to provide services but to monitor and hold to account those who did provide services. And there were other purposes: to change social attitudes, fight discrimination, eliminate prejudice, create self-awareness, instill hope, touch the conscience, and (above all) establish a means by which the blind could discuss common problems, reach decisions, and make their voices heard. The Federation was unique. It was (and is) the collective voice of the nation's blind—the blind thinking for themselves, speaking for themselves, and acting for themselves.

Our battle for freedom and recognition parallels to a striking degree that experienced by the blacks, for we are (in every modern sense of that term) a minority. We have our ghettos, our unemployment, our underemployment, and our Uncle Toms. We have our establishment (composed of society as a whole and, particularly, of many of the professionals in the governmental and private agencies). That establishment condescendingly loves us if we stay in our places, and bitterly resents us if we strive for equality. Above all (through our own organization, the National Federation of the Blind) we have discovered our collective conscience and found our true identity. We have learned that it is not our blindness which has put us down and kept us out, but what we and others have *thought* about our blindness. Yet, they tell us that there is no discrimination and that we are not a minority. We want no strife or confrontation, but we will do what we have to do. We are simply no longer willing to be second-class citizens. We have said it before, and we say it again: We know who we are, and we will never go back!

No group ever goes from second-class status to first-class citizenship without passing through a period of hostility. Several years ago I made the statement that we had not even come far enough up the stairway of independence for anybody to hate us. I believe I can safely say that that problem has now been solved. We have enemies enough to satisfy even the most militant among us. We have actually progressed to the point of creating a backlash.

However, we must see the situation in perspective. The hostility and backlash which we are experiencing are not due to mistakes on our part or to radical behavior or to over aggressiveness or to any of the other trumped-up charges which have been made against us. Just as with the black civil rights movement and Martin Luther King, the hostile reactions and backlash are an inevitable step on the stairs which lead from the depths of rejection and custody to the upper level of freedom and first-class status. The bottom steps of that stairway are often paved with condescension and pity; the middle steps are sometimes paved with goodwill and the beginnings of acceptance; but the top steps are always paved with resentment and fear. We have come a long way up. We are approaching the top of the stairs, and we are experiencing our full measure of fear and resentment.

The fear and resentment come from those who have a vested interest in keeping us down: the sheltered shops, with their subminimum wages, which were the subject of the recent *Wall Street Journal* articles[1]; the New York agencies, which we have helped expose through damning audits; the National Accreditation Council for Agencies Serving the Blind and Visually Handicapped (NAC), which we oppose for its phony standards, its meaningless accreditation, its lust to manage our lives, and its desperate effort to gain public support and respectability; the Cleveland Society for the Blind, which we have taken to court because of its wrongful seizure of the earnings of blind food service operators and its attempt to control the smallest details of their daily existence; the American Foundation for the Blind, which we call to task for its drippy publicity and pseudo-professionalism; the insurance companies, which (by court action and administrative regulation) we seek to prevent from charging us extra rates and denying us coverage; the airlines, against whom we demonstrate for trying to tell us where we can sit, that we cannot keep our canes during flight, that we must travel with an attendant, and sometimes that we cannot even board the plane at all; and all of those other public officials and private individuals who have an economic interest in keeping us from achieving independence or who boost their egos and show their insecurity by the need to feel superior, to custodialize, to condescend, and to treat us as wards.

Whether we finish the climb up the stairway to freedom and social acceptance (leaving behind the hostility and backlash) will be determined not by the actions of others but by our own behavior. This is our challenge and our confrontation. It is also the strongest possible proof of how far we have come. For the first time in history, the choice is ours. As other minorities have discovered, the final steps are the hardest.

There are several reasons why this is so: For one thing, the degradations and deprivations at the bottom of the stairs are (once they are pointed out and clearly delineated) so obvious and unjust that they are easily understood; and large groups of the general public can be touched in their conscience and enlisted to help, still keeping intact their sense of superior worth and special status. The minority is a long way down and poses no apparent threat, even by climbing a few steps up. At the top of the stairs things are different. The discrimination is more complex and subtle, the prejudice less obvious, the threat to vested interest more real, and the violations of tradition more imminent.

There is also the fact that the members of the minority group are part of the larger society. They tend to see themselves as others see them. They tend to accept the false views of their limitations and, thus, do much to make those limitations a reality.

I can offer a personal example. On February 11, 1979, an article written by R. H. Gardner appeared in the *Baltimore Sun*. It was headlined: "'Ice Castles' a little hard to swallow," and this is what it said:

> Several years ago, I was at a party when a friend, for reasons I cannot recall, bet me I could not stand on one foot 15 seconds with my eyes closed. I had been quite an athlete in my youth (10 years old), during which period I could stand on practically any part of my anatomy— head, hands, ears or toes—for an indefinite length of time. I accepted the bet.

> To my astonishment, at the count of five I began to waver. At seven, the waver turned into a stagger; and at ten I was lost. It was a great shock for a former athlete (even a 10-year-old one), and I have never forgotten it. For something happens to your balance when you close

your eyes. And how much worse it must be if you're blind!

Being blind, a scientist-friend once pointed out to me, cannot be compared to closing your eyes. When you close your eyes, you still see. You see the undersides of the lids with the light behind them. But what you see when you're blind is what you see out of the back of your head. There is neither light nor sight of any kind. I was reminded of all this while watching 'Ice Castles,' a film about a blind figureskater. I'm told there is a blind figureskater upon whose career the film is loosely based. But it's hard to believe, in view of my experience trying to stand on one leg.

When I read that article I pooh-poohed it and laughed it to scorn. So did one of my sighted associates. Then, just to show how silly it was, she closed her eyes and stood on one foot. But the laughter stopped, for she wobbled and fell. Then, she opened her eyes and tried it again. There was no problem. She kept her balance without difficulty.

"Nonsense!" I said. "Let me show you"—whereupon, I stood on one foot—and immediately lost my balance. That was three months ago. Was I shaken? I certainly was.

Then, I began doing some thinking. We know that the tests which are made by blindfolding sighted people to determine what the blind can do are totally invalid. I have been among the most vocal in pointing that out. I knew (or, at least I thought I knew) that balance is a matter of the inner ear, not the eye. Why, then, did my associate fall when her eyes were closed but keep her balance when they were open? Perhaps the fact that she was accustomed to seeing things around her as part of her daily life made the difference, or perhaps (even though she is well versed in our philosophy) the matter went deeper. Perhaps (reacting to social conditioning) she subconsciously expected to fall and was tense. I suggested that she practice a few times with her eyes closed. And what do you know? It worked. In four or five times she could stand on one foot as easily with her eyes closed as open.

But what about me? I have never had any problem with balance. So I tried it again—and I could do it with perfect ease. If anybody doubts it, I will be glad to demonstrate. Then why did I fall the first time? I reluctantly conclude that (despite all of my philosophy and knowledge to the contrary, despite all of my experience with this very sort of situation dressed out in other forms) I fell into the trap of social conditioning. I hope I won't do it again, but I can't be sure. There is probably not a blind person alive in the world today who has not, at one time or another, sold himself or herself short and accepted the public misconceptions, usually without ever knowing it. Prejudice is subtle, and tradition runs deep. That's how it is at the top of the stairs.

Which brings me back to Mr. Gardner and his newspaper article. He was not trying to hurt us, but just make a living. Nevertheless, based on his single, false experience as a simulated blind man, he makes sweeping generalizations about our lacks and losses. Do you think he would believe we are capable of equality—that we can travel alone, get off an airplane in time of emergency, or compete with others for a regular job—that we deserve insurance at the same rate as the sighted—that we are capable of full and normal lives? Of course not. And his opinions count. He is a member of the press, a molder of thought. And how do you think he will react if one of us brings all of this to his attention?

Probably with defensiveness and resentment—probably as part of the backlash. Perhaps he will even help stimulate unfavorable publicity against us, not realizing or admitting why he is doing it—or even, for that matter, that he *is* doing it. But we have no choice. The alternative is to slide back toward the bottom of the stairs. We will say it as gently and as courteously as we can—but we will say it. We want no strife or confrontation, but we are simply no longer willing to be second-class citizens. We will do what we have to do. We intend to take the final step on the stairs.

You will remember that Ralph Sanders in his banquet speech[2] last year quoted as follows from a gimmicky ad by a company employing blind persons to smell its perfumes: "Why," the ad asks, "do people close their eyes when they kiss? Because by cutting off one sense, they heighten the other four. They are completely immersed in the taste, smell, sound, and touch of the kiss."

Blind people have the "most highly attuned sense of smell possessed by man." What an ad! Such beliefs are widely held, but even a moment's reflection will demonstrate their absolute insanity. If a kiss is really made better by closing the eyes, think what a charge you could get if you put corks in your nose and plugs in your ears. The taste would go all the way to your toes, and the touch would drive you right up the wall. I would not expect the perfume company to appreciate our objection to its ad, but that will not keep us from objecting. That's how it is at the top of the stairs.

Sometimes the public misconceptions about blindness are used as a shield to avoid responsibility or hide from punishment. Consider, for instance, an article which appeared in the March 8, 1979, *Minneapolis Star*. It reads:

> Jerome M. Bach, Minneapolis psychiatrist and a founder of the Bach Institute, a psychotherapy center, has been placed on probation by the Minnesota Board of Medical Examiners for engaging in sexual activities with four of his female patients....
>
> The board's ruling reversed the finding of a state hearing examiner, Howard L. Kaibel, Jr. Kaibel recommended no action be taken against the doctor.
>
> Bach, who suffers from tunnel vision from a degenerative condition of the retina, is legally blind. Because of this, Kaibel said, Bach "depends on physical contact as an additional means of communication and of obtaining information about his patients."...
>
> Bach had become widely known among patients and other therapists for an unusual ability to diagnose emotional problems and for his use of physical contact in therapy.
>
> According to Kaibel's findings, Bach's use of "physical psychotherapeutic intervention is widely known, accepted by literally hundreds of his colleagues and even coveted by some who...are unable to utilize them as effectively."

That is what the article says—and the mind is boggled at the madness. Did Dr. Kaibel really mean it? Dr. Bach had never identified with the blind before, and so far as anybody knows, he has never done so since; but when the heat was on, he tried to hide behind the stereotypes. For once, we did not speak out alone. The medical profession, the women's movement, and others joined with us. We did what we could to make something positive out of the situation—attempting to educate the public and show unaligned blind persons why they should join us. Constant vigil, battle, hostility, and backlash—but also growing efforts to inform the public, achieve concerted action, and heighten self awareness. That's how it is at the top of the stairs.

Blind vendors and food service operators constitute one of the largest groups of the employed blind. They work for their money and earn what they get, but some of them fail to recognize their common bond with the rest of us, their need for the organized blind movement. Those who have such attitudes should read a novel[3] about the CIA published in 1978. It is called *Ballet!*, and it is written by Tom Murphy. Although it speaks directly to blind vendors, it speaks just as falsely and just as insultingly to all of the rest of us. The following passage occurs on page 51 and introduces chapter three:

> Dave Loughlin had the rough bulk of a longshoreman and the ambling shuffle of a geriatric bear. Dave was thirty pounds heavier and more than thirty years older than he'd been in the Army OSS days, the last happy time he could remember. And now, as Dave made his way down the long green-asphalt-tiled corridor that always reminded him of a hospital, of death, he felt every minute of those years, and every extra ounce weighing on him like an unserved sentence. And he felt the effects of last night's boozing, which didn't help any either. He passed the blind lunch counter and shuddered, even though he'd known it would be there, creepy as ever, even if it was the Old Man's idea, even if it did make some kind of perverted sense.
>
> Where else in the world would you have blind men and women cheerfully handing out wrapped sandwiches and cartons of coffee so bad it could have been made only by the blind? Where else but in the ever-vigilant atmosphere of CIA headquarters out in dear old Langley, Virginia?

That book is circulating by the tens of thousands throughout the nation. It approaches genius in its ability to malign and misstate. It manages to lump almost all of the stereotypes into a couple of sentences. The blind are cheerful. We are creepy. It's perverted to have us about. We can't make sandwiches but must get them prewrapped. We can't even make a decent cup of coffee. Here is no kindness (or even condescending pity)—only meanness and contemptuous dismissal. Each one of us (vendor and non-vendor alike) should think carefully about this book and the others like it which blight our opportunities and poison the public mind. We have no choice. The alternative is to slide back toward the bottom of the stairs. We will say it as gently and as courteously as we can—but we will say it. We intend to take the final step on the stairs, and we must take it together. We know who we are, and we will never go back!

The meanness of the Murphy novel is by no means universal, but it is certainly a sign of the times—an evidence of backlash and a proof that we are close to the top of the stairs. Southwest Airlines, which proudly proclaims that it spreads "love around Texas," recently initiated a policy of refusing to transport the blind or the mentally retarded unless they are accompanied by an attendant; and a Southwest official a few months ago wrote the following bit of disgusting gibberish to our Texas president, Glenn Crosby: "In regard to your question about canes being taken away from passengers, this is a security measure. Obviously, we have no way of knowing what a passenger will do with such an object; therefore, as a precaution, all such articles are taken away during flight."

Not much love in that, is there? Nor are the Southwest officials likely to feel any kindness toward the Federation—especially since we are picketing their counters and exposing their behavior to the public. Backlash, yes. But also (hopefully) breakthroughs to reason and public understanding. That's how it is at the top of the stairs, and (regardless of the cost) we intend to take those final steps.

In Iowa (where the progress has probably been greatest and the backlash strongest) not only have we suffered sustained, vicious, unfounded, and unscrupulous attacks from the Des Moines newspaper; but we are also engaged in a battle in the courts. As the blind of the nation know, Herbert Anderson (Iowa's enlightened Insurance Commissioner) ruled a couple of years ago that insurance companies could not discriminate against the blind in rates or coverage. As could have been predicted, the insurance companies (even those which had always claimed that they were, as they put it, most "sympathetic to the blind") suddenly turned hostile. When one of them (Federal Kemper) was fined a thousand dollars and ordered to mend its ways, it decided that the blind were ungrateful and unreasonable and took the matter to court.

On March 23, 1979, Judge Theodore Miller, who will not be remembered as one of the more enlightened spirits of the age, stated as follows in his "Findings of Fact":

> 9. The Court takes *judicial* notice of the fact that the blind have only four of the five senses, consisting of sight,

hearing, taste, smell and touch. Common knowledge provides that one with less than all the common senses operates at a disadvantage and is more susceptible to be unable to function as an able-bodied person than one with all his senses. Federal statutes recognize by implication the disabilities which blind people suffer and have provided tax exemptions for them.

When you sort out the garbled language, the Judge is clearly saying that no proof is necessary—that the blind can't "cut-it" on terms of equality with others. It is a matter of "common knowledge." In number 17 of his "conclusions" Judge Miller takes the astounding position that if blind persons are denied insurance, no discrimination has occurred since they have all been denied to the same degree and, therefore, have received equal treatment. Not much love in that—and not much intelligence either. But that's how it is when you deal with vested interest, threats to tradition, and backlash. Commissioner Anderson and we are appealing this case to the Iowa Supreme Court. Whatever the cost or the backlash, we intend to take those final steps. That's how it is at the top of the stairs.

Today I have said very little about the professionals in the field of work with the blind, but the picture would not be complete without their inclusion. Increasing numbers of them are working with us and taking joy in our progress. But there are others: NAC[4], the American Foundation for the Blind, and their allies have tremendous wealth and broad contacts. They could do much, if they chose, to hasten the day of the liberation of the blind, but they seem to feel that they have a vested interest in our continued dependence and subjugation. Perhaps Louis Rives (blind himself and the President of the National Accreditation Council for Agencies Serving the Blind and Visually Handicapped) has summed up the philosophy of inferiority and defeatism as well as it has ever been put. It is certainly the opposite of everything we believe and have experienced. Last year at the NAC meeting he said that there are only two ways of making the blind and the sighted equal: either the blind can regain their sight, or the sighted can have their eyes plucked out. With such "professionals" in the field is it any wonder that the public is not yet informed? But (with or without the NAC professionals) we will take the final steps. We will reach the top of the stairs.

As President of the Federation I receive many letters. Some are encouraging; others heart-rending. But I think I have never received a more expressive and revealing letter than the one I am about to share with you. It was written by Edgar Sammons, who lives in Mountain City, Tennessee, and speaks with the language and the clarity of Elizabethan prose. I have never met Edgar Sammons, but I have thought long about his letter and have come to feel a deep affection and a high respect for him. He is not a complainer, not a whiner—but he has known custody, terrible loneliness, blighted hope, and real deprivation. Yet, he has made a life for himself. His letter is as significant for what it does not say as for what it says. I have his permission to use it. Otherwise, I would not do it. Here it is:

> I thought I would try to give you a little history of my life. I was born October 30, 1913. They said I lost my sight at three weeks old. I grew just like the rest of them. I think a blind person should be brought up just like a sighted person but most of them are not. Most of them would learn a lot more if they would let them. We just had an old boat house and a little land. Not enough to make a living on. My father always rented corn ground for half of it. My mother put up a lot of stuff, and we always had plenty to eat.

> My father worked on the first highway that came through here. They blacktopped it in 1924. [I interrupt the letter to point out that he is now eleven years old, and this is the first thing that has happened to him that he feels worth noting. But let me continue]:

> My father rented a little farm, and we moved to it. It was not very far from here. We lived there a year and moved back. My mother always wanted to send me to school, but my father never would give up for it. My grandmother and my mother and little baby sister all died in 1924. There were five of us children left. Some people wanted to put us in a home. We had a hard time, but we made out. If the family could have had their way I don't guess I would have been allowed to get off of the place without some of them with me. They couldn't watch me all of the time.

> My grandmother Sammons was still living and they would send me down there when they would go to work in the corn. That suited me just fine. My grandmother would be doing her housework, and I would go down the road about half a mile to my aunt's and stay a while. Sometimes some of them would find it out and tell on me, but

I didn't care what they done about it. I would run off
every chance I got. There was just mud roads, but I got
along. They would take me places with them at night.
They went a lot of places at that that I would have like
to have went, but they left me at my grandmother's. I
think the blind should be allowed to get out and learn to
get around just like the sighted when they are growing
up. A lot of us don't have that chance. My brother and
father went to work in a cotton mill at Johnson City, and
we moved down there in 1927. [He was born in 1913, so
he is now fourteen years old.] The mill closed down in
1928, and we moved back. [Now, he's fifteen.] In 1933
[He's now twenty.] all of the children got off over at
Asheville, North Carolina, and got jobs. [You notice that
he didn't get a job.] My father married again in 1933. I
stayed at home most of the time. After that my job in
the summertime was pasturing the cows in the road. I
had bells on them so I could tell where they was at. I set
on the banks with the cows, wondering how I could get
a little money to get me some tobacco. I was a young
man then.

The welfare started in 1937. [He's now twenty-four.] I
got a little. A lot of the blind didn't get any. There wasn't
very much work for the blind then. I would go to
Asheville and stay a while and come back here and stay
a while.

In 1944 [He's now thirty-one.] I went to Asheville and
got me a job sorting mica. [Remember: This is his first
job. It was the Second World War, and manpower was
scarce. But back to his letter]: They said we could do that
job better than the sighted people. I just got to work nine
weeks, and our part of the job closed down. I stayed a
while longer over there to see if it would start back up,
but it never did.

That was a good job, but in one way I didn't like it. I
stayed with my sister and her husband. They was as good
to me as they could be, but they wanted me with them
all the time. They would come after me at night and take
me to work in the morning. I didn't want that. I wanted
out on my own like other people. I wanted to get out and
get me a girl just like other people.

Well, I come back home and stayed around here most of
the time. My stepmother died in 1951. [Now, he's thirty-

eight.] Grady Weaver started teaching me to read and write Braille—in 1951. I can't spell very good, but that helped some. I stayed at home with my father until 1957. [His life is passing. He's now forty-four.] My father got so bad sick that they had to put him in a rest home, and I went to Morristown and got me a job in the sheltered workshop. Mattie Ruth was working there at that time. She told someone, "the Sammons has come; the bass will be here next." Sure enough in a few days a man did come by the name of Bass. Just a little while after I went to work, Mattie Ruth got sick and went home. She like to have died. She didn't come back any more for about three years. She worked for a while, and her father got sick and she went home to take care of him. He died in 1962. [Now, he's forty-nine.]

After that, I went up and got Mattie Ruth. Her mother said she ought to have run me off the first time I ever come up there. She said I took the last girl she had.

I was forty-three years old before I got out on my own, but it has been the best part of my life. If I had stayed with my people, I don't guess I would have been living by now. I didn't have anything to live for.

That is the letter. It requires no comment, and it tells us what we have to do. In a very real sense Edgar Sammons speaks for us all. The imprisonment and lack of opportunity were just as cruel as if they had been deliberately imposed. They were just as degrading, just as blighting, and just as painful.

We must see that it never happens again. That is why we have to strengthen the Federation, why we have to speak out, and why we have to disregard the hostility and backlash.

Our climb up the stairs to freedom has been slow and difficult, but we are nearing the top. We carry with us a trust—for Dr. tenBroek, for Edgar Sammons, and for all of the others who went before us. We also carry a trust for those who will follow—for the blind of the decades ahead. Yesterday and tomorrow meet in this present time, and we are the ones who have the responsibility. Our final climb up the stairs will not be easy, but we must make it. The stakes are too high and the alternatives too terrible to allow it to be otherwise. If we fail to meet the challenge or dishonor our trust, we will fall far down the stairs, and the journey

back up will be long and painful—probably as much as another
generation.

But, of course, we will not fail. We will continue to climb. Our
heritage demands it; our faith confirms it; our humanity requires
it. Whatever the sacrifice, we will make it. Whatever the price, we
will pay it. Seen from this perspective, the hostility and backlash
(the challenges and confrontations) are hardly worth noticing.
They are only an irritant.

My brothers and my sisters, the future is ours. Come! Join me on
the stairs, and we will finish the journey.

FOOTNOTES

1. Jonathan Kwitny and Jerry Landauer, "Sheltered Shops: Pay of
   the Blind Often Trails Minimum Wage At Charity
   Workrooms," *The Wall Street Journal*, January 24, 1979, pp.
   1 and 35 and "Sheltered Shops: How a Blind Worker Gets
   $1.85 an Hour After 20 Years on Job," *The Wall Street Jour-
   nal*, January 25, 1979, pp. 1 and 31.

2. Ralph Sanders, "The Continuing Challenge of Change," *Braille
   Monitor*, October, 1978.

3. Tom Murphy, *Ballet!* (A Signet Book, New American Library,
   1978), p. 51.

4. National Accreditation Council for Agencies Serving the Blind
   and Visually Handicapped. NAC was the successor to and was
   appointed by the Commission on Standards and Accreditation. COMSTAC, in turn, was appointed by the American
   Foundation for the Blind, which has always provided more
   than one-half the budget—first for COMSTAC and now for
   NAC. In other words the so-called objective "Accreditation
   Council" is owned by the American Foundation for the Blind.

The Civil War That Wasn't

A second "time of troubles" for the organized blind—
reminiscent on a minor scale of the internal struggle that had
wracked the movement two decades before—descended upon the
National Federation in the waning years of the seventies. Like
the earlier episode, the new push for power by a dissident faction
of the membership—which was quickly to prove abortive—grew
out of a combination of adverse factors and events, some inter-

connected and others merely coincidental. But, unlike the earlier episode, this mini-rebellion barely rippled the surface of a united organization and left it stronger, closer-knit, and more mature than ever.

There were other differences between the two periods of stress. The civil war of the fifties had been fought over issues of some consequence (as well as others of merely personal ambition and spite); its effect was to settle in principle the question of NFB's identity and character, establishing the fact that it was not a loose confederation but a unitary national organization with authority to supervise its constituent local and state affiliates. Unfortunately what was established *de facto* was not reinforced and nailed down *de jure*, in the formalities of legal and constitutional procedure; the Federation's members had neither the stomach nor the energy, after their years of civil ordeal, to fight on further in the courts and the convention for what seemed already plainly settled and agreed upon. It was precisely that legal-procedural imprimatur, however, which was the significant achievement of the attempted mutiny of the late seventies. The issue was conclusively resolved in two venues: it was decided in the courts with victorious lawsuits against the dissidents in California, Washington, and Iowa respectively; and it was settled in the convention through constitutional amendments, resolutions, and other democratic decisions.

The most conspicuous difference between the two internal episodes was one of scale. The earlier episode of the fifties deserved the title of civil war, in terms of both size and duration; it involved real numbers, it spread through much of the country, and it sustained heavy casualties—in the form of fallen chapters and split affiliates. The later insurrection broke out in two states—California and Washington—and when it had done its worst and played itself out it could claim but a handful of defectors in a single additional state, that of Iowa. It was for this reason that, for years thereafter, the entire episode would be widely known in the movement as "the civil war that wasn't."

The first of the factors which combined to precipitate the new squabble was the 1977 resignation of President Jernigan for reasons of ill health. Inadvertently, but perhaps inevitably, that development sent a signal to anti-Federationists without—and to dissident members within—that a "window of vulnerability" had been opened and with it an opportunity for mischief and maneuver. To understand the internal side of this scenario it is important to recall the extraordinary growth enjoyed by the Federation during the seventies, which brought new members and chapters into the movement in numbers too great to be easily or quickly assimilated into the Federation community. Added to this, not incidentally, were the economic factors which had transformed the movement in a decade or two from a comfortable "primary group" in which everyone knew everyone into a far-flung network of affiliated groups and individuals. Despite this expansion there was, as we have seen, a countervailing force of community and family bonding; but not everyone in the nationwide network could be readily brought into the family circle. There were bound to be some who still felt alienated and at odds with the mainstream of the organized blind movement; and there would also be others who, alienated or not, misperceived the Federation community as a competitive scramble no different from the cut-throat enterprises of their own experience. In the two far western states of California and Washington—encouraged by their geographic distance from the center, emboldened by the strength of their two affiliates, and enticed by the size of their state treasuries—two overambitious leaders in particular (Robert Acosta and Sue Ammeter) conspired to carve out independent territories of their own, without regard for the limitations and constraints imposed by membership in the National Federation.

It should be noted that, while these internal power plays were going on, parallel forces outside the movement—in particular some elements in the professional blindness system long opposed to the Federation—had also been stirred into renewed agitation by the resignation of President Jernigan and the impression of weakness which that conveyed. The main journalistic conduit for their efforts to sabotage the NFB and its leadership became the *Des Moines Register*, a newspaper whose statewide circulation could be deployed to discredit Jernigan as Director of the Iowa Commission for the Blind as well as to malign the Federation itself with its national headquarters situated in Des Moines. Significantly the same paper had for nearly twenty years supported Jernigan and the Commission with uniform enthusiasm—an attitude exemplified by a 1968 editorial on Jernigan, typical of numerous other articles over the years.

Here is the *Register*'s editorial:

If a person must be blind, it is better to be blind in Iowa than anywhere else in the nation or the world." So said Harold Russell, chairman of the President's Committee on the Handicapped in awarding a presidential citation to Kenneth Jernigan—and it's true.

More than that, the major reason it is true is that for ten years Kenneth Jernigan has been director of the Iowa Commission for the Blind.

Before coming here, Jernigan had sold insurance, taught in a teachers college, worked in a rehabilitation program for the blind in Tennessee, and then been psychologist and counselor at the California Rehabilitation Center for the Blind at Oakland.

He was brought here by Mrs. Alvin Kirsner, who had known him for years. She headed a volunteer group at B'nai Jeshurun's Temple Sisterhood which had turned a needed textbook into Braille—the raised type which blind can read by touch—for Jernigan when he was teaching in Nashville. By 1958 she was chairman of the Iowa Commission for the Blind, which at long last had a program and had talked the Iowa legislature into putting up some money for it.

Bringing Jernigan here to head it was a brilliant stroke. Jernigan is a dynamo. From one of the worst in the country, Iowa's rehabilitation program for the blind became one of the best in the country.

The money was essential, but even more important was the spirit Jernigan managed to infuse into it.

You can see it in the spirited swing of those long fiberglass canes the blind trainees use around Des Moines as they begin to acquire some confidence in the newly learned skill of "traveling"—making their way around without help.

You can see it in the record his trainees have made, and in the growing acceptance of his work by the legislature and the public.

By public, we mean not just the people of Iowa. Among the center's trainees was a woman physician from Pakistan, who went back there to start a similar center. The Iowa program attracts visitors from all over the U.S. and the world.

The presidential award to Jernigan was richly deserved. All Iowans can be proud they have him in their midst.

That sweepingly positive attitude on the part of the *Des Moines Register* shifted abruptly to one of implacable hostility shortly after the Jernigan resignation from the NFB presidency. Various plausible explanations might be offered for this precipitous editorial mood swing. One was that the newspaper, afflicted with falling circulation and reduced revenues, needed a scapegoat and a burning cause around which to rebuild its reputation for "investigative journalism"—a concept which had lately come into great popularity with the daily press and its readers as a result of the famous Woodward-Bernstein exposes during what were known as the Watergate scandals. Here in the newspaper's own back yard, in the person of Kenneth Jernigan, was a local figure with the highest name-recognition quotient across the state of any public official possibly excepting the governor.

The *Register*'s campaign was also evidently linked (through personal connections) to a recent legal victory of the Federation and its Minnesota affiliate over the Minneapolis Society for the Blind in a landmark case which had featured key testimony by Kenneth Jernigan. "Certain facts are known," as Jernigan himself was later to write. "We know, for instance, that Jesse Rosten became head of the Minneapolis Society for the Blind in the early 1970s and that the blind of Minnesota have been engaged in a bitter struggle with the Society for a decade. We know that Gil Cranberg is now head of the editorial section of the *Des Moines Register* and that he has been a power at the newspaper for more than twenty years. Rosten has bragged that Cranberg was his college roommate and that he could get at Jernigan through Cranberg."

Whatever the source of its motivation, the *Register* launched a flurry of attacks against the Iowa Commission and its director which, before the campaign finally subsided two years later, amounted to a total of more than 200 separate articles. All that needs to be said about these attacks by the Des Moines newspaper is that despite all of the headlines, the hype, and the promises of juicy exposure, no formal charges were ever brought, no accusations ever substantiated, and in fact the *Register's* allegations were discredited one after the other until nothing was left of the affair but the disgust of the thinking public in Iowa—who had rightly felt pride in the programs for the blind administered through two decades by Kenneth Jernigan. (Officials of the Minneapolis Star and Tribune, which was part of the corporate structure that owned the *Des Moines Register*, were on the board of the Minneapolis Society for the Blind and apparently deeply resented Jernigan's involvement in the case that exposed the Minneapolis Society's violation of state law and attempted the suppression of rights of the blind of Minnesota. It was widely felt that the attacks by the *Des Moines Register* were at least in part, the result of corporate pique.) There was also evidence that the National Accreditation Council for Agencies Serving the Blind and Visually Handicapped and other regressive agencies in the country made a concerted effort to plant stories in the *Register*, which they could then circulate to divert attention from their poor performance when Federationists called them to account for their program deficiencies and custodialism.

Many if not most of these journalistic assaults had been inspired or fed by the custodial agencies, both national and local, which had persistently warred with the organized blind—among them the American Foundation for the Blind and its notorious offspring, NAC, and a number of state and municipal agencies which had been targeted by the NFB for exploitive labor practices (e.g., the Societies for the Blind in Minneapolis and Cleveland). There was also the "company union" of blindness, the American Council of the Blind, which had become almost abjectly dependent upon NAC and the American Foundation for financial support and accordingly toed the company line and carried out company wishes with respect to the independent blind of the National Federation (although as a dissident splinter group from an earlier era the ACB bore its own bitter grudge against its parent Federation). These and other agency-oriented groups were clearly instrumental in fomenting and sustaining the two-year vendetta waged by the *Des Moines Register*—thereby providing what one blind person called "immoral support" to the new dissidents from California and Washington within the NFB.

In the aftermath of Kenneth Jernigan's resignation from the presidency in 1977—and at the same time as the newspaper attacks commenced in Iowa—a dissident faction began to take shape in two of the Federation's state affiliates: those of California and Washington. The coincidence of these three events suggests that the dissidents thought to see a weakness in the structure of the Federation enabling them to exploit the situation for their own personal ambitions—or at the least to spread confusion and disrupt the movement.

In these purposes, however, they were to be thoroughly disappointed. As indicated earlier, the membership of the Federation closed ranks swiftly behind its elective leaders at the 1979 convention in Miami Beach—following repeated futile efforts to settle the issue by discussion and negotiation, notably at a special meeting in California of the National Board of Directors in September, 1978, during which a full hearing was afforded the dissident faction. The 1979 convention voted overwhelmingly (46 to 3) to expel the faction and proceeded to bestow new charters upon reorganized state affiliates in California and Washington. (It might be added that both of these reconstructed groups were shortly to become among the most vigorous and effective in the movement.)

Despite the decisive action of the convention and the unmistakable repudiation by the membership as a whole, the frustrated dissidents continued to agitate and to insist on their right to be called Federationists. That issue was not finally settled in the courts until January of 1983, when the California Court of Appeal "dismissed with prejudice" the last appeal of the California dissidents and brought an end to the entire episode of misguided ambition and personal spite. (Parallel court cases in Washington and Iowa were also settled in favor of the NFB, as was a peripheral episode in Hawaii which resulted in a reorganized affiliate.)

In the end the mini-rebellion was a sadly abortive affair which reminded some observers of a question asked in a different context: "What if they gave a war and nobody came?" The small band of dissidents in California and Washington, when they left in disgrace, took no affiliates with them—not even their own. They had failed to shake the movement or stir the membership. One member said of them that they were like Shakespearean characters who strut and fret their hour upon the stage and then are heard no more—their play only a tale full of sound and fury, signifying nothing.

The long-range effect of the abortive civil war was summarized by Kenneth Jernigan in a 1983 *Monitor* report on the episode:

> Whereas the NFB Civil War in the late 1950s divided and weakened us, the California situation drew us closer together and brought harmony and increased determination. We are now stronger than we have ever been. We have more momentum, more legislative influence, more sense of organizational purpose, more dedicated members, more love and understanding, and more care and concern for each other. The future looks better than it has ever looked, and tomorrow is bright with promise.

Back to the Future

In the year of its fortieth anniversary, 1980, the movement of the organized blind found itself embarked upon a new and portentous phase of its career. It had successfully maneuvered the difficult physical transition from the Middle West (Des Moines) to the Eastern Seaboard (Baltimore)—in the process purchasing a vast complex of buildings, creating the National Center for the Blind, and multiplying its output of materials. It had also defended itself successfully—not to say spectacularly—against the journalistic assault in Iowa with the publication and mass statewide distribution of an extraordinary "Special Edition" of the *Braille Monitor* (February, 1980) labeled *The Bizarre World of the Des Moines Register: Malicious and Reckless Disregard of the Truth.* (Following that publication, for whatever reason, the *Register* suddenly ceased its drumbeat of critical attacks against Jernigan and the Commission.) At the same time the Federation was launching new campaigns and reinvigorating older ones in a host of areas where blind people were ill-used and poorly treated—in the "unfriendly skies" of major airlines, in the under-

paid and oversheltered workshops, in the conclaves and machina-
tions of the "NAC Pack"—and everywhere that their civil rights
were denied or their dignity assailed.

The sense of motion and change, of transition amounting to
transformation, and above all of renewed commitment to the objectives of Federationism pervaded the atmosphere of the
Leamington Hotel in Minneapolis during convention week, 1980,
where some two thousand blind Americans were assembled for
the anniversary occasion. Apart from being the largest convention
in Federation history, the event epitomized the spirit and character of the NFB's annual meetings during this volatile era; something was happening at every moment day or night throughout
the week—something epochal, edifying, or at least engaging. A
subsequent report in the *Monitor* summarized:

> The tone, the incredibly vast amount of information, the timeli-
> ness and variety of the resolutions, the enthusiasm, the Monday
> press conference, the march to the Minneapolis Society for the
> Blind, the events surrounding the meeting of the Kiwanis Club,
> the panels, the reports, the speakers, and the give-and-take of the
> jammed convention hall made this occasion what it was—a vital,
> dynamic, action-packed, dramatic experience: one which will have
> a lasting and unforgettable impact upon those who were there,
> and, indeed, upon all of the blind everywhere.

The reference in that report to the march on the Minneapolis Society for the Blind points to a remarkable action taken
by the convention as a whole to demonstrate—peaceably but unmistakably—the discontent of the organized blind with the exploitive labor practices of the Society's sheltered workshop, in which
blind employees were forced to work at less (sometimes much
less) than the minimum wage. The NFB's dispute with this
workshop agency had persisted for nearly a decade, both in the
press and in the courts. Convening in Minneapolis—the home of
the Society and its workshop—the Federation decided to adjourn
the convention for several hours one day in order to demonstrate
its case en masse against the Minneapolis Society. This is how
the *Monitor* later described the "Minneapolis March":

> More than 2,000 conventioneers left the hall in an orderly fashion,
> collected signs outside the hotel, and began to march through the

streets toward the Minneapolis Society for the Blind chanting and singing as they went:

"50,000 blind guys can't be wrong!"
"We'll speak for ourselves!"
"NAC, NAC get off our back!"
"MSB hurts the blind!"

Federationists who could not walk traveled to the Minneapolis Society on the bus and joined in the demonstration. Marchers traveled along Hennepin Avenue for several blocks before reaching the Minneapolis Society building. Windows along the way were crowded with curious onlookers. Pedestrians in the streets seemed surprised and interested in reading the signs.

When we reached the Minneapolis Society for the Blind headquarters, the press was waiting to meet us. Some of the reporters were standing with cameras on the roof; others held microphones in the streets; all were anxious to talk to Federationists, anyone who would answer questions. Of course, some of the reporters marched the entire route with us. As the marchers arrived, Dr. Jernigan and Joyce Scanlan began to tell our story once again—only this time to the public in the city of Minneapolis over the loud speaker.

Dr. Jernigan said: "We're here to speak to the Minneapolis Society for the Blind. Since they won't speak to us around the conference table, we have to speak to them in the great outdoors before the public and everybody. By the thousands and the tens of thousands the blind of this nation have rejected what the Minneapolis Society for the Blind stands for. Remember the workshop song. It is truly a folk song that comes from the people: "I've been workin' in the workshop all the livelong day, and with the wages that they pay me it's just to pass my time away."

"Here, look out of your doors, see from behind your walls what the blind of the nation think of you. Look at us and see if you think there are just a few of us as you have said. We're going to show you what the blind are like in our thousands and remember there are tens of thousands of us back in our home communities throughout this country. The days of exploitation are coming to an end.

"The public of this nation will not stand for what you have done once they know it, and we're going to let them know it! Our line of march stretches back for blocks. We'll be here, all of us to see you."

The crowd chanted together, "NAC, NAC get off our back. NAC, NAC get off our back." And we sang the workshop song, thousands of people singing together.

Joyce Scanlan came to the microphone and said: "Hello, Minneapolis Society for the Blind. The blind of the nation have come here *en masse* today to speak to you, to tell you that we are fed up with your paternalism, your custodialism, your lies, your hypocrisy, and the arrogant, aristocratic way in which you have treated the blind so condescendingly. We will no longer tolerate it. We are here to tell you and the public that we will no longer put up with it. We will go back to court to see the proxies that you have not allowed us to see up to this point. We will fight you for violating the court order. We will gain our freedom. We will no longer be slaves of the Minneapolis Society for the Blind and the National Accreditation Council."

The crowd chanted: "We speak for ourselves. We speak for ourselves."

Dr. Jernigan: "Minneapolis Society, in the name of the blind of the nation, I speak to you. We have come to the outer walls of the Minneapolis Society for the Blind. We have come from our farms, our businesses, our workshops, and our agencies. We have come so that we might demonstrate our determination to be free. For four long decades we have struggled to throw off the yoke of bondage which has made us slaves to subminimum wages and substandard lives. We have battled the broom shops, mastered the mattress shops, and rejected the sweat shops. Through our sacrifices, our turmoil, and our scars, we have climbed close to the final plateau on the stairway to freedom. We have rejected the workshop tyranny, repudiated the workshop system, and refused to obey our workshop bosses. We are confident, self-reliant individuals—willing to give as well as receive.

"Through our trials we have learned the value of freedom. We have paid the price for first-class citizenship, and we're not willing to settle for second-class status under control of third-class masters. We have come today from throughout this nation to sustain our march toward freedom, to renew our climb up the stair-way to first-class citizenship. We are here by the thousands representing the tens of thousands and the hundreds of thousands, to reject the custodial, repressive attitudes and programs of the Minneapolis Society for the Blind.

"Our message is clear and unmistakable. It is directed to the Minneapolis Society for the Blind. It is intended as a response to the National Accreditation Council (NAC)- American Foundation for the Blind (AFB)-American Council of the Blind (ACB) combine. You have declared war on the blind of this nation. You have rejected reason. You have determined that character assassination is your only alternative to partnership and participation with the blind in society. Your time is past; your present is perplexed; and our future is not in your hands.

"The top level of the stairway to freedom is just ahead of us. We say to the Minneapolis Society for the Blind: You can neither stop us nor dull our momentum. We have come to your gates to tell you this: We are simply no longer willing to *be* second-class citizens. We have said it to you before. You wouldn't listen to us. We tried to talk to you. You wouldn't talk to us. We are now here today to tell you as forcefully as we can: We do know who we are, and we will never go back. This is the message we leave with you, Minneapolis Society. Think about it, and see where you get with the public in this community from now on. Also talk to your colleagues in NAC throughout the country and the American Foundation for the Blind, and let us know how you fare in the war you have declared on the blind. We would've chosen peace, but you wouldn't have it that way. Very well, we are prepared on your terms to come forth and tell you we stand forth to meet you. We want good will, and we want no strife and confrontation, but we're not going to be second-class, and you can't make us be. That is the message we have to bring to you and the only message we have to bring to you."

This statement was interrupted repeatedly and loudly with prolonged cheers.

As Federationists returned to the meeting hall, we were tired, hot, and hungry. We knew we had accomplished something very important and very worthwhile and hardly noticed how we felt. President Jernigan and Ralph Sanders told the convention that all four TV stations had covered the march and many radio stations had been there as well. Joyce Scanlan said that she hoped we had taught the Society something of the truth of our statements about blindness.

She said: "Jesse Rosten expresses his philosophy on blindness something like this: They say that blindness is only a characteristic, well here are the keys to my car, now give me a ride home." President Jernigan asked if he is sighted, and Joyce answered that he is. Apparently Jesse Rosten thinks driving is the only way to get anywhere.

President Jernigan said: "My answer to that is: Here's my Braillewriter, write me a speech. (Loud cheering from the audience.) It may be easier to get a driver for the car than a writer for a speech."

Joyce Scanlan continued: "I want to tell you about something that the Minneapolis Society brags about that I think you'll like to hear. The State Services for the Blind here contracts with the Society for the rehab services that we all get. State rehab pays 75% of the cost of those programs. The Society has to make up the rest of the cost from some other program. They brag that in the workshop they have between 26 and 27% profit, and they boast that that profit is used for subsidizing the rehab program. Yet, they cannot pay their blind workers the minimum wage."

The fortieth annual convention of the National Federation of the Blind will be remembered by those who attended for the demonstration at the Minneapolis Society for the Blind. Someone raised the question: How can it be militant to do something so productive and really constructive? We knew we were fighting, but no blood was shed. We knew we had won the battle in Minneapolis on July 1 and 2. If what we did was militant, so be it. It was necessary, and victory sounded in the voices of the marchers.

The marchers in that purposeful parade felt that they were making history; the Federationists attending the fortieth anniversary convention felt that they were witnessing history; and the delegates and guests at the convention banquet felt that they were a part of history. Their President—himself a figure of historic proportions, a mover and shaker of such undeniable impact as to have become a legend in his time—fully understood the historicity of the moment and made it the subject of his banquet address: "Blindness: The Lessons of History." As he had done in other presidential orations, Jernigan recalled the background of powerlessness and poverty from which the movement had sprung forty years before, and compared it with the affluence and influence of the present day—emphasizing that the history of the organized blind was not something that happened to them but something that they *made* happen. But he also pointed out that their positive action upon the world was bringing about an equal and opposite reaction of negativity—in the form of a concerted combination of hostile agency forces dedicated to the sabotage and ultimate demolition of the organized blind movement. "Led by the American Foundation for the Blind," he said, "this alliance consists of NAC; our breakaway splinter group, the American Council of the Blind; the Affiliated Leadership League of and for the Blind; and a handful of other would-be custodians and keepers. They have interlocked their boards, concerted their actions, pooled their hundreds of millions of dollars of publicly contributed funds and tax money, and undertaken the deliberate and calculated destruction of independent organization and self-expression on the part of the blind."

But Jernigan expressed confidence that the organized blind would prevail again as they had overcome before against the massed hosts of repression, reaction, and regression: "We shall prevail against NAC and the other custodial agencies; we shall prevail against social exclusion and discrimination; and we shall prevail against those few in our own movement who would destroy it with bitterness and strife. We are stronger and more determined than we have ever been, and we have learned well the lessons of history."

The full text of the 1980 banquet address follows:

BLINDNESS: THE LESSONS OF HISTORY
by Kenneth Jernigan

Napoleon, in one of his more expansive moments, is said to have quipped: "History is merely a legend agreed upon." Queen Elizabeth I, reportedly squelched Mary Queen of Scots with the regal comment: "No, history will *not* vindicate you, for I will write it." In other words, according to this view, history is only a myth and a fable.

But there are those who think otherwise. A time-honored cliche proclaims, with almost mystic authority: "History repeats itself, and those who do not learn it are doomed to relive it." The very qualities which make this pronouncement so attractive are also the ones which make it so dangerous as a standard of conduct. Its slick phraseology and apparent logic divert attention from its oversimplification. History does, indeed, repeat itself—but never precisely, and never exactly. There is always a new twist, a different nuance, an added element. For one thing, the past event itself (the one which is currently in the process of being repeated) is now a factor. Its former occurrence is part of the pattern. It has left its mark and skewed the picture. Those who fail to recognize this truth can never effectively learn the lessons of history. History can give us a sense of heritage and broaden our perspective; it can help us understand and cope with the present; and it can assist us in predicting the future.

Tonight (in July of 1980) we stand at the threshold of the fifth decade of our organization. As we look back to the past and call up our heritage so that we may deal with the present and plan for the future, let us bear in mind what the poet Tennyson said in the middle of the nineteenth century: "I am a part of all that I have met." Let us also remember that history has its cycles, its not quite repetitions, and its patterns and lessons for those who can read and understand.

When the blind came to organize in 1940, the situation was as bleak as it could possibly be. It was bright enough to create hope and dark enough to make that hope seem impossible. Dr. Jacobus tenBroek, the brilliant scholar and constitutional lawyer who founded our movement and led it for the first quarter century, summed up the early years as only he could have done it:

> The paramount problems of our first decade, the 1940s, [he said] were not so much qualitative as quantitative: we had the philosophy and the programs, but we lacked the membership and the means. The workers were few and the cupboard was bare.

> Each month as we received our none-too-bountiful salary as a young instructor at the University of Chicago Law School, Hazel and I would distribute it among the necessaries of life: food, clothing, rent, Federation stamps, mimeograph paper, ink, and other supplies. So did we share our one-room apartment. The mimeograph paper took far more space in our closet than did our clothes.

We had to move the mimeograph machine before we could let down the wall bed to retire at night. If on a Sunday we walked along Chicago's lake front for an hour, four or five fewer letters were written, dropping our output for that day to fewer than twenty-five.

The decade of the forties was a time of building: and build we did, from a scattering of seven state affiliates at our first convention to more than four times that number in 1950. In the decade of the forties we proved our organizational capacity, established our representative character, initiated legislative programs on the state and national levels, and spoke with the authority and voice of the blind speaking for themselves.[1]

This is the way Dr. tenBroek summed up the first decade. The second decade, the 1950s, was a time of both triumph and trouble. It began with hope and momentum. It ended with internal strife and a civil war. By the mid-fifties we had forty- seven state affiliates, money in the treasury, and power in the halls of Congress. In the fifties we established our magazine, the *Braille Monitor*, and began to outline to ourselves and to others the distinctive nature of what we were and what we intended to be. By the end of the decade we were so divided and demoralized that our very existence as a continuing and viable movement seemed highly doubtful.

Dr. tenBroek recognized, as did the rest of us in that corps of leaders he trained in the fifties, that it was no mere accident or coincidence that our growing independence and influence were followed by furious attacks from without by the agencies, and defections and strife from within by people who had been our colleagues in the movement. The governmental and private agencies (the American Foundation for the Blind, the sheltered shops, and the rehabilitation and social work establishment) had money and position and prestige. They used these resources lavishly not as instruments to aid the blind but as weapons to fight us and to protect their vested interests. They intimidated, offered jobs and positions to our potential leaders, promised services and rewards, threatened reprisals, and did everything else in their power to break our spirit and crush our determination. They complained to the post office and tried to discredit our mailings and fund appeals. They exploited the vulnerability of blind vendors and sheltered shop workers. They coerced and promised and rewarded. The purpose was clear: It was nothing less than the complete and total destruction of the National Federation of the

Blind. In the face of such pressure it is not surprising that strains developed from within—that what might, in normal times, have been minor problems of thwarted ambition or temperamental difference became major conflict and civil war.

That first tide of Federationism and independence (which, during the fifties, lapped higher and higher up the walls of the agency establishment and the bastions of custodialism and exclusion) fell back upon itself at the end of the decade, spent and exhausted.

But the Federation did not die. The movement did not disintegrate. Too much was at stake. Too many lives had been touched. The blind had, for the first time in their existence, sensed the possibility of first-class status—and they would simply not be denied. We knew (all of us—not just the leaders but also the rank-and-file: the old, the young; the educated, the uneducated—every one of us) that what we had so painfully achieved must not be surrendered, that self-organization (once lost) might not come again for a generation or a century. Those of us who were left in the movement closed ranks, fought where we could, encouraged each other, remembered our heritage, and marched toward the future. We understood from first-hand experience what the black demonstrators meant when they surrounded the factory gates and shouted with mingled hope and desperation:

I go to my grave
Before I be a slave.

The decade of the sixties was almost the exact reverse of the fifties. It began in despair and ended in triumph. The Federation drew itself together, shook off the civil war, and began to rebuild. It was during the sixties that we lost our great leader, Dr. tenBroek, but he had done his work well. The progress continued. By the end of the decade we were bigger, stronger, better financed, and more united than we had ever been.

Perhaps the sixties can best be capsulized by the opening verse of our "Battle Song," which was composed in 1964. It is known by every Federationist:

Blind eyes have seen the vision of the Federation way;
New White Cane legislation brings the dawn of a new day;
Right of the blind to organize is truly here to stay;
Our cause goes marching on.

And our cause did go marching on, swinging into the seventies. And what a decade it was! At the beginning of the seventies we were saying to the world, "We know who we are"; and by the end we were confidently adding, "And we will never go back!" In the seventies the tide of Federationism rose higher than it had ever reached before—far beyond the peak of the fifties. It was during this decade that we completed the transition from a scattered confederacy to a single, united national movement—powerful, self-assured, and full of destiny. We knew that whatever happened to the blind in the years ahead, the responsibility was ours. Our future, for the first time in history, was in our own hands. Despite the odds, we could do with it what we would. If we had the intelligence and the guts, we could win first-class status and the full rights of citizenship. We did not shrink from the challenge. We welcomed it. In fact, we demanded it. Our declaration of independence and purpose left no doubt as to the course we intended to follow. "We want no strife or confrontation," we said, "but we will do what we have to do. We are simply no longer willing to be second-class citizens. They tell us that there is no discrimination and that the blind are not a minority; but we know who we are, and we will never go back!"

More and more in the seventies we discovered the truth about our heritage and history, and drew strength and pride from what we learned. Our annual conventions were the largest meetings of blind persons ever held anywhere in the world, and (with affiliates in every state in the nation) we came universally to be recognized as the strongest force in the field of work with the blind.

Then, the cycles of history began to assume familiar patterns. Superficially viewed, it was a second run of the 1950s. As our voice grew louder and our strength increased, so did the antagonism and fear on the part of the custodial agencies. As early as the mid-1960s, there were hints and signs of what was to come. The American Foundation for the Blind, seeing its influence diminishing, undertook a new tactic to tighten its loosening grip on the lives of the blind. It announced that it was establishing a so-called "independent" accrediting system for all groups doing work with the blind. As a first step, the Foundation appointed what it called the Commission on Standards and Accreditation of Services for the Blind (COMSTAC). The Commission was to hold meetings, appoint subcommittees, and arrive at a "consensus" for the entire field. Certain blind people (mostly agency officials or persons who were, as the saying goes, "unaffiliated" and, therefore, largely uninformed) were brought to the meetings; but tight control was carefully maintained.

When COMSTAC had finished its work and written its documents, it appointed NAC (the National Accreditation Council for Agencies Serving the Blind and Visually Handicapped). The accreditation was, of course, to be purely voluntary and altogether impartial. The American Foundation for the Blind provided NAC's first executive director, gave most of the money, prepared to control our lives for at least the rest of the century, declared the whole process democratic, and said it was all very "professional"—as, indeed, in a way it was.

By the middle of the seventies it was clear that the principal issues of the fifties were again to be put to the test. It was the old question: Did we have the right to run our own lives, or did the agencies have the right to do it for us? As the decade advanced, the struggle exceeded in bitterness anything which had ever before been seen in the field of work with the blind. Many of the agencies worked with us and shared our aspirations, but others (the reactionary custodians in the American Foundation-NAC combine) abandoned all but the shallowest pretense of dignity and so-called "professionalism" and tried by brute force to beat the blind into line. Especially did they concentrate their hatred upon the National Federation of the Blind and its leaders.

But the 1970s were not the 1950s, and 1980 is not 1960. The custodial agencies we face today are not the agencies of twenty years ago, nor are we the blind of that generation. We are stronger and more knowledgeable than we were then, and the agencies which oppose us (of course, many do not) are more desperate, more frightened, and more shaken in their confidence. Even the most reactionary are now forced to give at least lip service to consumer participation and the rights of the blind.

1960 and 1980 have many similarities, but they also have distinct and significant differences. For one thing, the forces which oppose us today have (probably because of our greater strength and their greater desperation) combined in a closer alliance than was the case twenty years ago. Led by the American Foundation for the Blind, this alliance consists of NAC; our break-away splinter group, the American Council of the Blind; the Affiliated Leadership League of and for the Blind; and a handful of other would-be custodians and keepers. They have interlocked their boards, concerted their actions, pooled their hundreds of millions of dollars of publicly contributed funds and tax money, and undertaken the deliberate and calculated destruction of *independent* organization and self- expression on the part of the blind.

If what I say seems exaggerated, consider a prime example right here in this city where we are meeting. Consider the Minneapolis Society for the Blind and its president, Dick Johnstone. The Minneapolis Society for the Blind accepts federal and state funds and solicits charitable contributions from the public-at-large—all in the name of helping the blind. Mr. Johnstone (the Society's president) supposedly serves without any compensation whatsoever, purely as a matter of public service and civic duty. Yet, last fall at the NAC meeting in Oklahoma City Mr. Johnstone made a speech about the National Federation of the Blind (the largest organization of blind people in this country—a group one would think he would particularly love and cherish since his purpose is to help the blind and promote our interests). Here are some of the things Mr. Johnstone said:

> All NAC needs now is a few more teeth—and the money to apply them. Money can come to NAC—the same way it was lost: with *pressure!* NAC has a policy right now, in hand, ready to go. They can help you in any problems with the NFB without board action. Dr. Bleeker [NAC's executive director] has that authority, right now, unlike other agencies who have had to fiddle around and go to their boards. Believe me, the Minneapolis Society for the Blind is going to have a policy the same way: any help you need, you'll get it out of us. Anything we needed [from NAC] we got. One thing we did learn, and we have researched this a little; and I hope you will, too, to prove it to yourselves: fight!...Negotiate? Never!...The only thing the National Federation of the Blind respects is strength. The power is with us right now, if we will use our heads and use it. If we unite and help one another, as you united to help us, we can't lose....It's time we go on the offensive, quit hiding our heads in the sand....Programs and agencies banding together in strength can only secure success for NAC and all other legitimate agencies....The National Federation of the Blind is going to come back and fight harder than ever, now. The pressure is on us, the legitimate blind, to counter the new attacks that are sure to come.

How does one account for this bitter tirade? Is this the talk of a dedicated volunteer working devotedly for a "professional" service agency, which has only the well-being of the blind at heart? And what does he mean by the "legitimate blind?" Is Mr. Johnstone (in addition to damning our morals and denying our right to exist) also questioning our paternity? This is not the language of service and love, but of slander and war. It smacks of dark alleys, black-jacks, and hoodlumism. Why?

Perhaps the answer is not so difficult after all. Possibly there is a perfectly plausible explanation, one which may explain not only the conduct of Mr. Johnstone and the Minneapolis Society for the Blind but also the behavior of many of the others who attack and condemn us with such spleen and irrational hatred.

First, let us consider Mr. Johnstone personally—this dedicated, unpaid volunteer. He has been president of the Minneapolis Society for the Blind for many years. The *Minneapolis Daily American* in its June 2, 1972, edition carried an article headlined: "Charity Group Refuses To Talk/Blind Are Being Kept In The Dark/President Of Non-Profit Society Given Whopping Contract." The article says in part:

> The Minneapolis Society for the Blind has refused to answer questions regarding bids on a federally assisted construction project.

> The question arose when the *Daily American* learned that Richard Johnstone, president of the Society, also is president of the South Side Plumbing and Heating Company, which has the mechanical contract on the project. Frank A. Church, a U.S. official in the Chicago office of the Department of Health, Education and Welfare said that "special problems" are raised if a member of the board bids on such a contract.

Perhaps the fact that we of the National Federation of the Blind exposed and publicized this situation helps explain Mr. Johnstone's attitude toward us. Some professionalism! Some volunteer! It may also help explain the attitude of the Minneapolis Society in general. But there is more: In the early 1970s the Minneapolis Society for the Blind had a thirty-member board of directors, none of whom was blind. According to the by-laws anybody who made a cash contribution was, thereby, a member. When the blind tried to become members, the Board of the Society declared that *all* members were expelled and that, in the future, nobody would be considered a member except those on the Board. As Federationists know, we took the matter to court in the early 1970s; and after some seven years of battle and delay, we forced the Minneapolis Society to abide by the state law and honor the provisions of its own articles of incorporation. The courts made the Society accept blind members and hold an election. The issue is still not finished and awaits further action by the courts. Is it surprising that Mr. Johnstone and the Minneapolis Society hate us and wish we would cease to exist? Not really.

But there is still more. There is the Kettner case. Lawrence Kettner was "evaluated" so that the Society could get an exemption and wiggle out of paying him the federal minimum wage. To say the least, the "evaluation" was unusual. Kettner was evaluated over a period of fourteen days, but the studies of his work were made only on the third, fourth, sixth, and eighth days. His duties were changed; the equipment was faulty; and there were delays in bringing him supplies. Even so, Kettner's productivity increased markedly (from 49% of normal production to 79%), showing the unfairness of not giving him time studies after the eighth day of the fourteen day period. He says he was called into the director's office and badgered into signing a statement that he was capable of only 75% of normal production. He says he was told he would not be paid for the work he had done if he did not sign. He needed the money. He signed. Even as this was happening, he secured a job in private industry at a rate above the minimum wage.

We publicized the Kettner case far and wide, and we told the Department of Labor about it. Yes, I think I can understand why Mr. Johnstone and the Minneapolis Society for the Blind hate the organized blind movement—and it has nothing to do with so-called high-toned "professionalism." It is a matter of money and cover-up and exploitation. It is as simple and as despicable as that.

As to Mr. Johnstone's statement concerning the "legitimate blind," I would say this: He is not blind, so I do not see how that part applies; and as to the question of legitimacy, I would think (in the circumstances) the Minneapolis Society for the Blind would not want to discuss it. The matter of unblemished paternity is a sensitive issue. So much, then, for Mr. Johnstone and his talk about the "legitimate blind."

But what about the others who attack us, the others in the American Foundation for the Blind-NAC combine? Are their reasons for hating us similar to those of Mr. Johnstone and his

Minneapolis Society? Let us call them off and examine their "legitimacy." First, the Cleveland Society for the Blind. It is locked in a battle with blind snack bar operators. In 1972 the director of the Society told the blind operators that they must contribute specified amounts to the United Torch Campaign or face dismissal. Under the Federal Randolph-Sheppard Program, Ohio was authorized to take as a service charge no more than three percent from the gross earnings of operators, but the Cleveland Society was taking eight percent. This could amount to as much as half of the net earnings of an operator. Moreover, as a condition of employment each blind operator was forced to sign an agreement giving the Cleveland Society unbelievable power over his or her personal life. The operator had to agree (and I quote) to: "have an annual physical check-up; eat a balanced diet; obtain adequate rest commensurate with the hours to be worked at a snack bar; bathe daily; shampoo frequently; use appropriate deodorants; wear clean underclothing; and wear comfortable shoes."

We in the Federation (at least, most of us do) believe in regular bathing and good personal hygiene, but we are not willing (as a condition of employment) to have somebody cram it down our throats—tell us how much rest to get, what kind of food to eat, what kind of deodorants to use, and when to change our underwear. In the newspapers the director of the Cleveland Society defended his rules by saying that "Blind people have to be especially careful."

And, of course, he is right. We do have to be careful—of people like him. We (you and I, the National Federation of the Blind) took this director and his custodial agency to court and publicized what he was doing. The battle still continues. Is it any wonder that the Cleveland Society for the Blind and its director hate the organized blind movement and wish we would cease to exist? Not really. Yet, they tell us that there is no discrimination and that the blind are not a minority; but we know who we are, and we will never go back.

The Cincinnati Association for the Blind and the Houston Lighthouse for the Blind have refused to comply with orders from the National Labor Relations Board that they permit their blind workers to organize. We stimulated those organizing efforts and are now fighting these two agencies in the Federal courts. Is it surprising that they hate us and brand us as "militants" and "trouble-makers?" Not at all. How could it be otherwise?

The Chicago Lighthouse for the Blind used every tactic it could (including the firing of blind organizers) to prevent blind employees from forming a union. We took the matter to the National Labor Relations Board, and we picketed. It is hardly necessary to add that the Chicago Lighthouse is a principal leader in the combine which attacks us. We picketed the Evansville Association for the Blind and told the public what the Association was doing (all in the name of charity, and with publicly contributed funds) to exploit and hurt blind people. We picketed the Columbia Lighthouse for the Blind in Washington, D.C., when it was having a gala charity ball attended by leading socialites. We told these socialites and the public-at-large how the Lighthouse *really* operates, and what it is doing to the lives of blind people. Agency officials in Florida and Alabama have been criminally indicted. All of these groups (the Minneapolis Society for the Blind, the Cleveland Society, the Cincinnati Association, the Houston Lighthouse, the Chicago Lighthouse, the Association, the Columbia Lighthouse, and the Alabama and Florida agencies) have two things in common: They exploit the blind, and they are all accredited by NAC.

Then there is New York—New York, the home territory and the special turf of the American Foundation for the Blind and NAC. In 1978 there was a state audit of Industries for the Blind of New York, Inc. The audit showed that this organization (which was the principal governmental procurement agency for blind-made products in the state) spent its money on liquor and lavish parties and expensive cars and high salaries and God knows what else which the average human being would consider to be totally unrelated to the welfare of the blind. And what is Industries for the Blind of New York, Inc.? Well, it is a board consisting of the representatives of ten agencies, *seven of which are accredited by NAC.* They are flagships in the NAC fleet. Wesley Sprague, director of the New York Association for the Blind, is (of all things) the long-time chairman of NAC's Commission on Standards. Joseph Larkin, director of the Industrial Home for the Blind of Brooklyn, is a NAC board member. Peter Salmon, the Industrial Home's former director, is NAC's past president.

There are some five hundred organizations and groups in this country which might conceivably choose to be accredited by NAC. Yet, by January of 1980 (a decade and a half after its formation) NAC was forced to admit that it had only seventy-nine agencies in its fold. But let me hasten to add that these are very special agencies. Our best information indicates that they probably have a total combined wealth of somewhere in the neighborhood of a half a *billion* dollars. Think about it!—half a *billion* dollars! A few of them may truly be service-oriented and dedicated to high standards and the best interests of the blind—but there are the others, the ones that Mr. Johnstone would presumably call the "legitimate blind." I have detailed for you the conduct of sixteen of these. Sixteen! More than twenty percent of NAC's entire membership. And there is evidence which could be brought against many of the rest.

NAC: What a sorry, miserable spectacle! It is not a concern for "professionalism" which is the bur under the saddle of some of these people. It is the fear that we may expose their real concerns: the making of money, the lapping of liquor, the lust for luxury, and the push for power.

No, it is not surprising that the American Foundation for the Blind-NAC combine hates us and that they are determined to destroy the National Federation of the Blind. We are the principal threat to their master plan—their effort to gain complete control over the lives of every blind man, woman, and child in this nation—their hope to live happily in luxury ever after. To speak of "legitimacy" in the same breath with NAC is reminiscent of what Franklin Roosevelt said in 1936 about mentioning the Depression in the presence of the Republican Party. It is like showing a rope to the family of a man who has been hanged.

As I have already said, there are both similarities and differences between the 1950s and the 1970s—between 1960 and 1980. In the fifties the external attacks brought severe internal conflict. In the late seventies we saw some of the same tendencies—but even though the pressures have been greater this time around, the dissension among us has been minimal, giving testimony to our increased strength and maturity as a movement. We are a part of all that we met in the 1950s. We learned—and history does not quite repeat itself.

There is also a new element, one which was not present twenty years ago. In the fifties we had not yet become strong enough to get very many of our own people appointed to positions of leadership in the agencies. By the seventies the situation was different. In 1976 and 1977 we came within a vote or two of having a majority in the National Council of State Agencies for the Blind. A number of our own members had been named as state directors, and many of the other state directors were and are supportive of our cause.

However, there was a problem, one from which we must learn. Just because an individual calls himself or herself a Federationist, that does not necessarily mean that he or she is immune to the temptations of agency power—the ability to control lives and the urge to equate one's own interests with those of the blind consumers. Increasingly in the seventies we became strong enough to bring reform to a growing number of agencies and to play a deciding role in determining who their directors would be. Quite naturally, our people (having suffered so grievously from the poor service and custodial treatment dished out by the agencies) wanted to have Federationists as directors. Sometimes we made bad choices. It was almost as if, out of reaction to the miserable service we had received, we said: "Give us a Federationist—any Federationist—just so long as we can throw off the yoke of what we have had." It was a mistake—one for which we are now paying.

Some of these so-called Federationists had hardly been appointed to office before they tried to take over the affiliates in their states and make them mere auxiliaries and fronts for their own vested interests. They put aside their loyalties and principles and seemed to forget that they had obtained their jobs as part of a national movement—the overall struggle of the blind as a people to be free. They forgot (if, indeed, they had ever truly believed) what it is that has brought us as far as we have come on the road to first-class status and the full rights of citizenship. No individual or state organization—no local group or single person—could have done it alone. It required the combined effort of us all. It still requires that combined effort if we are to finish the journey. In its absence none of us (not a single blind human being) will go the rest of the way to equality and freedom. We should have been more selective in supporting candidates for agency leadership—but we are a part of all that we have met. We have learned. Fortunately we are strong enough to absorb the shock of the lesson.

We will not make the same mistake again. In the future the primary test of whether we will support an individual for a position of leadership in an agency will not be whether that person is called a Federationist but what kind of philosophy and commitment the individual demonstrates. Of course, this has always been our concern, but the emphasis is now different and the care more thorough. Better a neutral (one with the basics of a good philosophy, who is willing to work with us in partnership to win our support) than a Federationist in name only (one who takes it for granted that, because of his or her reputation as a Federationist—even a strong Federationist—we will automatically be supportive, regardless of the agency's conduct or behavior). We have come too far on the road of liberation to turn back now. We are not willing to exchange one master for another, even if the new would-be custodian has been our colleague or uses the name "Federationist." We will say it as often as we must: We want no strife or confrontation, but we will do what we have to do. They tell us that the blind are not a minority and that there is no discrimination; but we know who we are, and we will never go back.

As Federationists know, I get a constant stream of letters from blind people from all over the country. Some of these letters are highly literate. Others are not. Taken together, they show the pattern and give the details of what it is like to be blind in America today. They tell of the hopes and aspirations and problems which the blind confront. I want to share with you a brief passage from one of these letters. It is from a woman in her early fifties. In page after page she cries out with the heartache of a life of frustration. Here is part of what she says:

> I went to the state rehabilitation agency because I was seeking employment. I believe I was referred there by the employment service. I couldn't understand why no one wanted to hire me. The reason given most frequently was lack of experience. But I was young. "How does one get that experience?" I kept asking myself. And the rehabilitation agency could do nothing to help me. I am sure that each employer I saw felt that I should get my experience some place else.

This part of her letter refers to her early twenties. When she comes to the present (the time of her early fifties) she says:

> The rehabilitation agency can still do nothing to help me. My efforts to obtain employment are the same continuing story. I won't drag it out any further except to say that I have met with repeated failure. I haven't enough skill to get a typing job, and apparently I haven't the training or skill (or is it that I can't get the opportunity?) to do anything else. I never have enough experience to compete, but as was the case when I was young, how can I get that experience if no one will give me a chance to

try? And (now that I am in my fifties) who is going to give me the chance to try with my lack of experience?

I feel already as though I am in forced retirement. I shudder to think how the actual retirement years will be. I am not sure where to go from here—whether I should try to change my life, or merely be resigned to the fact that this is probably how it will be from now on.

I am sure that my story is not new to you. You must hear something like it almost every day. Perhaps you can measure my despair by the number of pages in this letter. I see my life ebbing away and I have yet to find my niche to occupy. This inactivity and lack of a life's work is not how I would choose to spend what is left of my productive years. I dreamed of the future when I was young. Now, I look around me sometimes and say, "Dear God, this is the future." I'm living it now. Perhaps it is the only future I will ever have.

How can I answer such a letter? What can I say to ease the burden or lighten the load? Day by day the hope has been killed, the spirit has been crushed, and the dream destroyed. Yet, NAC and Mr. Johnstone tell us that all will be well if we will only leave it to them and their agencies. All they need, they say, is a few more teeth—and enough money to crush the NFB. How twisted! How pathetic! In their luxury and so-called "professionalism" they do not even know of the existence of the deprivation and the misery—of the daily struggles and problems of the ordinary blind individual.

As we stand at the door of the fifth decade of our organization, we must thoroughly understand the lessons of history, for the eighties will be a time of trial and decision. They will require all that we have in the way of ability and devotion and courage. We must work not only for ourselves but also for the blind of the next generation, for they are our children. If not biologically, they are surely morally our children, and we must make certain that they have the chance for better lives and fuller opportunities than we have had.

When we talk of history, we usually think of the past—but what will future historians say of us—of you and me—of the National Federation of the Blind in 1980? What will they say of our struggle for freedom and our battle with NAC, the American Foundation for the Blind, and the other custodial agencies? As I said in

1973, future historians can only record the events which we make come true.

They can help us be remembered, but they cannot help us dream. That we must do for ourselves. They can give us acclaim, but not guts and courage. They can give us recognition and appreciation, but not determination or compassion or good judgment. We must either find those things for ourselves or not have them at all.

We have come a long way together in this movement. Some of us are veterans, going back to the forties; others are new recruits, fresh to the ranks. Some are young; some are old. Some are edu-cated, others not. It makes no difference. In everything that mat-ters we are one; we are the movement; we are the blind....

If we falter or dishonor our heritage, we will betray not only our-selves but those who went before us and those who come after. But, of course, we will not fail. Whatever the cost, we shall pay it. Whatever the sacrifice, we shall make it. We cannot turn back or stand still. Instead, we must go forward.[2]

We shall prevail against NAC and the other custodial agencies; we shall prevail against social exclusion and discrimination; and we shall prevail against those few in our own movement who would destroy it with bitterness and strife. We are stronger and more determined now than we have ever been, and we have learned well the lessons of history. My brothers and my sisters, the future is ours. Come! Join me in the battle line, and we will make it all come true.

FOOTNOTES

1. Dr. Jacobus tenBroek, "The Federation at Twenty-Five: Postview and Preview," August, 1965, *Braille Monitor*, pp. 87 and 88.

2. Dr. Kenneth Jernigan, "Blindness: Is History Against Us?" Sep-tember, 1973, *Braille Monitor*, pp. 10 and 11.

Turning the Corner

The opening years of the decade of the eighties, which were also the early years of the second Jernigan presidency, might be characterized as the "Era of Rising Expectations" among the blind of the country. No longer was it sufficient merely to have a job—if that job was in a sheltered workshop. No longer was it good enough just to receive vocational training—if that training was in "blind trades" like basket weaving, chair caning, and broom making. No longer could the airlines arbitrarily prohibit blind passengers from sitting in the designated rows; the blind would not be moved. No longer could the entertainment media casually portray blind persons as bungling, confused, and ridiculous; they could try, but they would regret it. These were only a few of the practices whose prejudicial character had been exposed and their practitioners called to account. But it was not the agencies and professional elites of the blindness system who had rung the bell and sent the message. It was the organized blind, the members of the National Federation, who dared to disturb the universe—dared to talk plainly in polite company (such as conventions, government hearings, and NAC meetings)—dared to risk displeasure, verbal abuse, and physical intimidation—dared, in short, to take the heat. Only the organized blind had the nerve (the unmitigated gall) to picket and march and demonstrate on the public streets, to shout their grievances from the housetops, to say again and again, in one idiom or another: "We know who we are, and we will never go back!" or: "We *are* the blind. We *are* the people. We speak for ourselves!"

It was not that way always, of course. In fact it had not been that way very long. Even after the founding of the National Federation in 1940, the lives of blind men and women were still ringed around with insecurity, their movements tentative, their brains washed. But the coming of the NFB had opened the door and let in the air of freedom—the breath of opportunity—the impossible dream of equality. The new age had begun, as Kenneth Jernigan was to say, and the blind had turned a corner of time. After that they would never turn back.

That was part of the message President Jernigan delivered to the Federation and to the world in 1981 at the National Convention in Baltimore. He called his speech "Blindness: The Corner of Time," and he spoke of critical junctures and turning points in the history of the organized blind. "At first the Federation was small and ignored," he said. "Most of the agencies tried to deny its difference, pretending that it was simply another of themselves, one among many. In some parts of the country our chapters were weak and our purpose blurred. Sometimes the agencies took control of our affiliates, bought off the leaders or bribed and threatened.

"But the direction was certain and the trend unmistakable," Jernigan declared. "The blind kept joining—first by the thousands, then by the tens of thousands. In the beginning we were weak and divided. Then came accelerating power and unity. Ultimately we were fifty thousand members—clear in our mission, sure in our purpose, and firm in our unity: the strongest force in the affairs of the blind."

The organized blind, he said, had turned the corner of time. But the problem was that not many others in the field had kept pace with them in their progress and transition; the most reactionary of the agencies (those that turned back at the corner of time) even joined forces and pooled their efforts back in the fifties to resist the organizing efforts of the blind: "Hard though it is to comprehend or believe, their purpose (which became a veritable obsession and a principal endeavor) was to make war upon the blind, the very people they were pledged to serve. Not all of the blind—not the meek or the passive or the ones they could control: these were needed for show and fundraising. Only the troublemakers—the independents—the members of the National Federation of the Blind. Above everything else, they wanted to destroy the National Federation of the Blind and its leaders."

The NFB's President went on to observe that, when those destructive efforts failed and the organized blind grew too powerful to crush, attitudes softened in the blindness system and numbers of agencies summoned the will and the sensibility to approach the present and turn the corner of time. These had become partners and allies of the organized blind, prepared to walk with them (if not to march with them) and to turn the next corner of time without looking back. Lagging behind them, he said, were other agencies with good intentions but poor understanding of the new reality and the new world; for these there was hope, and toward these there should be toleration. "But what about the others?" he went on. "What about...NAC and its principal allies? They are not misinformed or confused, and they are not motivated by good intentions. They know exactly what they are doing. They have deliberately and cold-bloodedly set out to ruin our movement and destroy the reputations and careers of our leaders."

Jernigan thereupon proceeded to document and itemize an incredible succession of accusations, insults, physical assaults, break-ins, and other episodes of "hooliganism and harassment" directed against leaders of the organized blind movement at various levels throughout the country during the years just past—incidents which he charged had all the earmarks of an orchestrated campaign. But he leveled a blunt warning to all those still filled with hate and still dwelling mentally amid the straw and broomcorn of the workhouse, that their time was fast running out: "They will either learn to respect us and treat us as equal human beings, or they will go out of business. It is that simple, that definite, and that final." And he concluded with these ringing words:

Upon the rock of Federationism we have built our movement, and the gates of hell shall not prevail against it! For the first time in history we can play a decisive role in determining our own destiny....What we in the Federation do during the next decade may well determine the fate of the blind for a century to come....We have turned the corner of time, and we live in a newness. My brothers and my sisters, the future is ours! Come! Join me on the barricades and we will make it all come true.

Following is the complete text of the 1981 convention banquet speech:

BLINDNESS: THE CORNER OF TIME
by Kenneth Jernigan

The man was old and senile, and he ate without manners or grace. His daughter was ashamed and ordered him to eat in a corner apart from the others. There came a day when he broke his plate, and the daughter was angry. "My son shall not see such disgusting behavior," she said. "Since you eat like a pig, you shall be treated like a pig. In the future you shall eat in the yard from a trough." Her son was five, the thing in life she loved most. He asked for a hammer and boards.

"For what purpose?" she asked.

"To build you a trough," he said, "so that I may feed you when you are old."

So it has been through the generations, each teaching the next and then doubling back on itself for reinforcement—change coming slow and learning difficult. Yet, there come bends in the road, shifts in direction. It is not inevitable that each generation take hammer and boards to build troughs for the next. Among times there is a time that turns a corner, and everything this side of it is new. Times do not go backward.[1] For the blind the corner has been turned, and the time is now.

When the National Federation of the Blind came into being in 1940, its means were limited, but its mission was clear. There were already many organizations and groups in the field (residential schools, Braille and talking book libraries, sheltered shops, and governmental and private agencies)—and some of them had blind directors. But their mission was not our mission; their purpose was not our purpose.

The National Federation of the Blind was altogether different. It did not operate service programs or provide training. It served as a monitor for those who did. It was a check and balance, a watchdog. And it was something more: It was a means whereby the blind could come together in local chapters, state assemblies, and National Convention to discuss problems and take concerted action. Underlying everything else was a single, overriding article of faith and belief, so compelling as to focus our purpose and cement our unity. It was this: We as blind people have the right (even if we make mistakes) to speak for ourselves; and no other group or individual—no governmental agency, no private service organization, no charitable foundation—has the right to do it for us.

The founders of our movement recognized that our principal problem was not the loss of eyesight—not blindness but what people *thought* about blindness. In other words, the problem was not physical but social. It manifested itself in the misconceptions and mistaken ideas of the general public, and since the professionals in the agencies were part of the public, it manifested itself in their behavior, as well. The blind, also, were part of the public; and they, too, were affected. They saw themselves as others saw them, They tended to accept the public view of their limitations, and thus did much to make those limitations a reality. The problems envisioned by the founders of our movement are still very much with us. But we have turned a corner of time, and there is a newness.

Last year the California Franchise Tax Board (the arm of government which deals with state income tax filings) rejected the forms of many blind taxpayers. Sharon Gold, our California president, demanded an explanation. She was first told that the form had been changed and that many sighted people had checked the wrong box. The blind of California (as is true in many parts of the country) receive an extra state income tax exemption. Whether this is good or bad, it is the law, and there is a box on the form for appropriate checking. The Tax Board officials said that the boxes had been shifted and that the sighted had not been observant.

As Sharon probed further, the explanations became less and less satisfying. When she told the Board that it did not seem reasonable to reject the tax forms of the blind because of the carelessness of the sighted, the officials explained that they had done nothing of the sort. They had, as they put it, used care and "logic." They had examined the face sheet of each tax form on which blindness was checked and had rejected only those showing an occupation or profession which would obviously be impossible for the blind. In cases of doubt (and presumably these were few) they had applied still further "logic." They had, as a board official put it, checked the signature to see "if it appeared to have been signed by a blind person"—whatever that may mean.

Whether Sharon's form was rejected because she is a teacher (one of the impossible professions) or because she cannot legibly write her name, the board did not say. Whichever it was, it had about the same effect. Although we who are blind do not insist on having our cake and eating it too, we are not willing to go to the other extreme and pay for our cake and then not have it. If we must suffer damage to our image (and many feel that we do) because of the millions of tax forms which proclaim that we need an extra exemption simply because we are blind, that should be enough. We should not have to go further and be illegally denied the right to take the exemption, be charged interest for claiming it, and then have to submit to false and demeaning statements about us in the press into the bargain.

Sharon protested to the Tax Board and the newspapers, and we took the matter to court, where it is still being litigated and is now on appeal. Some will say that we are "quibbling"; others that we are overreacting; and still others that we are militant and radical. Well, let them. If it is true that the road to hell is paved with good intentions, it is equally true that the beginning of that road is usually paved with what are called quibbly incidents. The big ones come later when the direction is clear, the pattern well established, and the highway broad and irreversible. We have turned the corner of time, and we are simply no longer willing for our road to hell to be paved with other people's good intentions. The days of second-class status are behind us.

The California Tax Board's notion that the signature of a blind person is different from the signature of a sighted person (and presumably less legible) is widely held. Probably most people (including many in this room) would accept it without question, simply as a matter of common sense. Not long ago I stood at a counter in a bank. I signed a document. My sighted associate said to the teller, "Maybe I had better print his name below the signature, so that you can read it." Then, my associate put her signature on the document. After a moment of embarrassed hesitation, the teller said, "Perhaps you wouldn't mind printing your name, too. I can't read your signature any better than his." My associate has perfect eyesight. If she had been blind, her unreadable signature would have been attributed to blindness. Mine might have been due to haste, lack of attention, poor training, or any of a dozen other things, but it was automatically chalked up to blindness. Moreover, the bank teller probably surrounded the incident with connotations of inferiority, and I doubt that she changed her opinion because of the actions of my associate—or, for that matter, even remarked or remembered them. Blind people cannot write legibly. Sighted people must print their names for them. She has proof.

Under date of May 22, 1980, the *Des Moines Register* printed an article captioned, "Woman Opens Cut, Bleeds to Death." The article says: "A 59-year-old woman bled to death in her home Wednesday after she accidentally reopened an incision she received while undergoing kidney dialysis. Polk County Medical Examiner Dr. R.C. Wooters said she did not realize how much blood she was losing because she was nearly blind." The human body contains several quarts of blood. Do you really think an individual (sighted or blind) would bleed quart after quart and not know it because of blindness?

Mike Cramer is the president of our Chicago Chapter. On September 2nd, 1980, he went to work for the Chicago Transit

Authority as a Customer Assistance Coordinator, handling calls and complaints from the public. On September 4, he received a call from a woman who said she had a complaint. That morning, while she was riding the bus, she had observed a blind man standing up. The driver had not made any of the other passengers get up and give him a seat. Mike listened until she had finished. Then he told her that he was the blind man—that as a company employee he rode to work on a pass and could only sit if all of the paying passengers had seats. This was standard policy and posed no problem for him. The woman was at first surprised, then indignant. She had no intention of giving up her image of blindness or her preconceptions. "All right," she said. "Then I want to speak to your supervisor."

In January of this year the *Christian Science Monitor* News Service sent out a release deploring the evils of gambling. The headline was a grabber. Calculated to capture the fancy and stir the imagination, it read: "Now, Braille Slot Machines for Blind Gamblers." The article (complete with facts and statistics) is a rather standard piece, indicating that the nation in general and gamblers in particular are going to hell in a hand basket. Despite the titillating headline, the only mention of blindness comes in the last two sentences, which read: "At one Atlantic City casino, slot machines are coded in Braille for the blind gambler. Is there a dreadful symbolism here for all of us?" Yes, there is a "dreadful symbolism," but it is not in the slot machines. It is in the mistaken notions and false assumptions of the author and his readers.

On May 13, 1980, the *National Enquirer* carried the headline: "Because Both Mom and Dad are Blind, Five-Year-Old Angel Is Raising Her Baby Brother." The article is a drippy account of a brave and wonderful little girl who gives up normal play and almost all other activities of childhood life to raise baby brother— everything from diapers to feeding. Mommy and Daddy are blind. The blind couple (who, incidentally, are members of this organization) were furious. The article, they say, was a total distortion and a misrepresentation. With devastating logic, they ask: "Who the hell do they think raised the five-year-old?"

And where does all of this nonsense come from—this drivel about angel sisters, rejected tax forms, Braille slot machines, blind bus passengers, and the rest? Of course, much of it comes from the primitive past when light meant safety and dark meant danger. Eyesight and light were equated, as were blindness and darkness. Light was pure and good. Darkness was evil and fear.

But there is something more, an added element which skews the picture and poisons the public mind. I speak of the governmental and private rehabilitation and social service agencies, the libraries and schools, the lighthouses, the workshops, the dog guide facilities, and the various other institutions established to give service to the blind. Not all of them, to be sure, are negative and bad. In fact, a growing number are turning the corner of time and working with us in the newness, espousing our cause and marching with us to freedom and progress. They stand by our sides as partners and equals.

Unfortunately such agencies are not in the majority, nor are they the most powerful or wealthy. Contrary to public belief, most of the agencies do us more harm than good. Some are a mixed bag, providing certain helpful services while, at the same time, doing things which hurt us and hold us back. Others (and it may as well be bluntly and directly said) are so bad and so destructive that, regardless of the occasional good they do, the blind would be better off if they were closed down and put out of business.

This is hard for the average person to accept or understand. How can it be? Why? The answer requires perspective. At first the agencies were few and scattered. They saw their role as one of benevolence and charity—taking care of people who could not do for themselves—giving meager subsistence and a ray of sunshine, adding a little cheer.

Then, in the 1930s, the agencies proliferated. They became big business. The casual volunteer and the friendly visitor began to be replaced by a burgeoning army of so-called "professionals"— rehabilitation counselors, social workers, directors of development (a high-toned term for fundraisers), peripatologists, evaluators, and other such. There were also administrators and a hierarchy of supervisors. As the staffs and the budgets mushroomed, so did the feeling of something to protect, the defensiveness about criticism, the sense of self-importance, and the rationalization of whatever it took to keep the blind in their places so as to justify the elaborate bureaucracy, the ballooning expenditures, and the growing myth of special knowledge and mysterious "professionalism." The second-class status and dependency of the blind were absolutely indispensable to the survival and continued expansion of the system. It is not hard to see why. If the blind need only correct information, a brief period of training in techniques, an initial boost, and a reasonable chance to compete, the agencies (while performing a useful service) cannot be the center of existence. Their role is diminished. On the other hand, if blindness is an unmitigated tragedy (fraught with psychological disturbance and requiring complex and long- term professional care) the agencies necessarily become the dominant element in the life of every person who becomes blind—not for just a day or a month or a year, but forever—from the cradle to the grave.

Seen in this context, the establishment of the National Federation of the Blind in 1940 was a threat of total disaster. If the organization flourished and the contagion spread, if the blind began to act independently and plan their own lives, if they convinced the public and themselves that they could function as equals and compete with others, the custodial agencies would be held in check and viewed without mystery or awe. Their role would be important, but not godlike. Their power would be limited, not infinite.

Real life is not like a textbook, and most events are not clear-cut or immediate. At first the Federation was small and ignored. Most of the agencies tried to deny its difference, pretending that it was simply another of themselves, one among many. In some parts of the country our chapters were weak and our purpose blurred. Sometimes the agencies took control of an affiliate, bought off the leaders or bribed or threatened. There were partnerships, alliances, joint efforts, confrontations, maneuverings, and realignments.

But the direction was certain and the trend unmistakable. The blind kept joining—first by the thousands, then by the tens of thousands. In the beginning we were weak and divided. Then came accelerating power and unity. Ultimately we were fifty thousand members—clear in our mission, sure in our purpose, and firm in our unity: the strongest force in the affairs of the blind.

Likewise, there was change in the agencies. They began as a scattering, local in purpose and differing in view. They constituted no national force. Then, the most reactionary of them (led by the American Foundation for the Blind and its creature the National Accreditation Council for Agencies Serving the Blind and Visually Handicapped, NAC) sought to join forces and pool effort. Hard though it is to comprehend or believe, their purpose (which became a veritable obsession and a principal endeavor) was to make war upon the blind, the very people they were pledged to serve. Not all of the blind—not the meek or the passive or the ones they could control: these were needed for show and fundraising. Only the trouble makers—the independents—the members of the National Federation of the Blind. Above everything else, they wanted to destroy the National Federation of the Blind and its leaders.

Through the years the agencies have become wealthy—tremendously wealthy. Our best information indicates that the top fifteen or twenty of them have combined resources of more than half a billion dollars. There are several hundred of them in the country, and (despite the efforts of NAC and the American Foundation for the Blind), they are not a monolithic force with a single purpose. They are diverse and varied in goals, attitudes, effectiveness, and behavior.

This brings us to the present, to 1981. As I have already said, a growing number of the agencies have turned the corner of time and are sensitively working with us to achieve better lives. They are partners and allies. Some of the others are not vicious but only shackled by old ideas.

Consider, for instance, the Christian Record Braille Foundation. Many of its projects are worthwhile, and (so far as I know) its motives are good. Yet, recently it produced a brochure which (though it may be well-intentioned and excellent for fundraising) hurts our image and slows our progress. Entitled "At Ease With A Blind Person," the brochure says:

> IN TAKING LEAVE: End your conversation in such a manner that the blind person knows you are leaving. Ask if he needs assistance to get to his destination, and take him there if possible.

> IN GETTING INTO A CAR: "Susan we're taking you for a drive into the country. This is the back seat of the car, and you'll be sitting behind the driver."

> As you approach the car, tell her whether she will be sitting in the front or back, or give a choice. When you reach the car, open the door, place her hand on top of it, allowing her to sit down by her own efforts. Make sure she is comfortable, with everything she needs in reach. Make sure your blind passenger is sitting far enough away from the door so that when you close it, it will not bump her in any way.

> IN PARTICIPATING IN CHURCH OR COMMUNITY PROJECTS: Give the blind person some project that will help him feel important such as being a member of the

program committee, or phoning members to alert them to the next meeting.

The problem with the brochure is not meanness but condescension. The blind person is treated like a child or a pet, not an equal human being. The blind are perceived as passive, with things being done to them or for them—not active or participating—not giving, but only taking.

Then, there is the newsletter put out last year by the St. Louis Society for the Blind.[2] Again, it is not meant to be harmful or destructive. Quite the contrary. But it does us real damage and lessens our opportunities. It says:

> The spring of the year can be extremely depressing and threatening to those who cannot see.
>
> This is so because the weather is breaking, travel conditions are improving, and the people who can see, who have been "locked in" for the winter with those who cannot see, are now getting out and moving about independently. This springtime freedom for them leaves you alone once again. Now you must fend for yourself. It's no wonder that depression can set in when the spring of the year can be seen in this light.
>
> The important thing to bear in mind is that you can and will make it through this depression. There are those of us out there who want to see you enjoying the freedom, the warmth and the loveliness of Springtime in a way that is meaningful to you.
>
> If you feel a little "down" or "blue" please don't hesitate to call me so that we can talk over your feelings. Remember, I'm here if you need me.

What a distortion! What condescension and misapplied charity! It is enough to make you ill—but it is not vicious or said with malice. It is meant to be helpful and constructive, but it blights our chances and limits our opportunities just as much as if it sprang from evil motives.

So much for those agencies which have turned the corner of time and work with us, and for those which mean well but are misinformed. What about the others? What about the National Accreditation Council for Agencies Serving the Blind and Visually Handicapped (NAC) and its principal allies? They are not misinformed or confused, and they are not motivated by good intentions. They know exactly what they are doing. They have deliberately and cold-bloodedly set out to ruin our movement and destroy the reputations and careers of our leaders—and if they can get the job done, they will do it.

I know something about this firsthand, for as far back as 1975 a blind lawyer told me (in the presence of a witness) that he had been called to New York and offered money by leading agency officials to embark on a campaign to destroy my reputation and ruin my career. He repeated the story to Jim Gashel, our Director of Governmental Affairs. Jim tells me that a sighted lawyer told him that he had received the same offer. These things are a matter of public record in testimony before a committee of Congress.

There is more! As Federationists know, I was director of Iowa's agency for the blind for twenty years, establishing programs which brought a special citation from President Lyndon Johnson, appointments to national committees from President Ford, and a host of other awards and recognitions: Advisor on matters affecting blindness to the Federal Commissioner of Rehabilitation, Special Consultant to the Chairman of the White House Conference on the Handicapped, Consultant on Blindness to the Smithsonian, recipient of an award from the American Library Association for building and directing the biggest and best library for the blind in the nation, honorary doctorates from Drake and Seton Hall Universities, and a variety of others.

Yet, in 1978 and 1979 I found myself under such vicious and unreasonable attack as to boggle the mind. The *Des Moines Register*, which had always been uniformly supportive, suddenly started a massive campaign of personal vilification, innuendo, and downright falsehood, which continued day after day. There were literally hundreds of articles. The National Federation of the Blind as an organization and I as an individual were put under investigation by the federal district attorney. Every record and paper was subpoenaed and studied, probably at hundreds of thousands of dollars of cost to the taxpayers. There were no charges from the federal attorney—only hints and silence, followed by scurrilous articles of innuendo and suggestion in the newspaper. Yet, the federal attorney did not give back our papers or admit that she had acted on false information. She simply waited. All of this started in the spring of 1978. By the fall of 1980 it had long since been clear that there was nothing to investigate, no basis for charges, and no possibility of further delay without extreme embarrassment to the federal officials. The federal attorney quietly wrote a letter saying that she was closing her file and returning all of our papers—no accusation, no attempt to indict, no slightest suggestion of any wrongdoing or inappropriate action. Also, of course, no expression of regret for any damage to reputation or career. Did the *Des Moines Register* report it all and apologize for its defamation? Not on your life! It did not make a peep.

And why do I bring all of this up? We know that NAC was in contact with the Des Moines newspaper. We know that NAC (using publicly contributed funds) reprinted the articles and circulated them by the thousands throughout the country. We know that Dr. Bleecker, the executive director of NAC, was in touch with the newspaper when he went to the Federal Department of Labor in his unsuccessful attempt to destroy our program of Job Opportunities for the Blind. We know that Dick Johnstone, the president of the Minneapolis Society for the Blind, publicly boasted that the NAC forces had participated in the Iowa campaign to try to destroy me and the Federation—only regretting, as he said, that they had "let the matter die on the vine." Did NAC and its allies attempt to incite the federal attorney with false information? We are not currently prepared to surmise, but under the Freedom of Information Act we have wrested all relevant documents from the files of the FBI and other appropriate federal departments. The emerging pattern is not pleasant.

If I were the only Federation leader to receive such treatment, I might chalk it up to fluke or coincidence, but I am not. Don Capps, our First Vice President, is a respected citizen in his community. He is a high official at the Colonial Life Insurance Company, a past president of Rotary, a prominent member of his church, and a civic leader of statewide note and importance. Yet, he was subjected to the humiliation of publicly being called a "paranoid son of a bitch" by the director of the agency for the blind in his state. When a reporter asked the director if he had said it, there was no retraction or apology, only the comment that he believed that he had not called him a "paranoid son of a bitch" but a "paranoid bastard." The director in question had concerted his efforts with the NAC supporters in a variety of battles against our movement.

Our Second Vice President, Rami Rabby, is a man of culture and learning. He holds a graduate degree with honors from Oxford University. Because he dared express himself at a public meeting, the director of the American Foundation for the Blind and the head of NAC wrote letters to Citibank of New York (where he was employed) and tried to jeopardize his job.

There is more! Last year there was a break-in at my home. Silver and other valuables were thrown on the floor and not taken. Papers had obviously been rifled. Mrs. Anderson, my assistant, visited her parents in Des Moines last year. That very day there was a break-in at their home—little taken, papers rifled, same pattern. Ralph Sanders, our immediate past President, has had at least three break-ins during the past year—a suitcase taken on one occasion and nothing on the others—papers rifled, same pattern. Duane Gerstenberger, our Director of Job Opportunities for the Blind, and Ramona Walhof, the Assistant Director, have both had break-ins during the past few months—papers rifled, same pattern. John Cheadle, while doing a tour of duty in the National Office, and Marc Maurer (another of our leaders) have both had the same experience. Our Denver office was recently rifled—nothing apparently taken. Harold Snider, who has repeatedly gone to NAC meetings as our observer, has had two break-ins during the past few months. Cassettes of NAC meetings and similar items were taken. Our headquarters building in Baltimore has been broken into, and a bottle of gasoline containing a wick was found by our boiler room door. During the past year both Harold Snider and Rami Rabby have had acid thrown at them on the streets. Recently Rami received in his mail box a cardboard with his initials formed in Braille dots made of eight live rifle bullets.

Is all of this coincidence? Perhaps—but I don't think so. Does that mean that I am accusing NAC or its allies of the illegal break-ins and the hooliganism? Not at all. But I do say that the climate of hate and bitterness which they have created can inspire such actions, and I also say that the rate of attack and harassment upon Federation leaders far exceeds any reasonable possibility of happenstance.

While we are exploring these matters, another question presents itself. Why would certain agency officials hate the Federation and wish to destroy us? The answer is not difficult. In Cleveland we helped blind food service operators bring a lawsuit for a million dollars against the Cleveland Society for the Blind and its director for illegally withholding money from the blind operators and for other acts of repression. In Minnesota we brought a suit against the Minneapolis Society for the Blind for illegally excluding blind persons from membership and participation. I personally testified in that case. We also exposed and publicized the fact that Dick

Johnstone, the so-called volunteer head of the Society (and the chairman of its Building Committee) was the owner of a company which received a lucrative plumbing contract for remodeling the Society's building. In Alabama the former head of rehabilitation recently went to the federal penitentiary for extorting public money and automobiles from those receiving grants from his agency. We helped expose him. A workshop official in Alabama was also convicted of theft. We helped in that one, too. The Alabama Institute for the Deaf and Blind (a NAC-accredited agency) had a psychologist, one Tandy Culpepper, who double dipped in his travel expenses early this year and was about to be permitted quietly to resign. We sniffed the matter out and brought it to the newspapers. He is now likely on the road to prosecution and conviction.

In February of this year our magazine, the *Monitor*, exposed irregularities in the audit of the Utah State Agency for the Blind. A janitor at the Agency, accompanied by one of the top officials, came to our Salt Lake City president (who is employed in the agency workshop) and publicly cursed and abused him. Later that day the janitor attacked and physically beat him. This was in February. We immediately sent representatives to protest to the Governor, and we took the matter to the press. Neither the janitor nor the official was fired. In March our Salt Lake president (Premo Foianini, who is in this room tonight) was struck in the back by the janitor with a broom handle with such force that the handle was broken. He was compelled to be off work and take treatments for contusions of the spine. The janitor was brought to court by the Salt Lake City Attorney and convicted of criminal assault. So far as I know, he has not been fired but is still employed by the Utah Agency for the Blind.

We encouraged the investigative reporting which led to the *Wall Street Journal* articles exposing abuses of blind employees in sheltered workshops, and we played the same part in the program carried by Sixty Minutes. In May of last year at the meeting of workshops for the blind held in San Diego, Joseph Larkin (one of the powers in the workshop establishment and a principal leader of NAC) laid it on the line, whistling to keep up his courage and belligerently expressing his fear and desperation. Much can be read between the lines of what he said.

> Can our values ever really flourish, [he asked,] in an arena where we continue to fight with rear guard actions?...The NFB could become the most powerful force.

What can we do to move toward a reassessment and
reassertion of our traditional position? The first step is
to acknowledge that we do not have the same ability to
influence or control events that we once had. There is a
new set of circumstances; and friends, foes, and neutrals
are all more powerful than they used to be.

But that does not mean that we must remain deprived of
a fully effective intelligence mechanism or the will to
move aggressively when the need arises or that the NFB
must be allowed to become a dominant power....

We and our allies still make up the mightiest assembly
of technological, professional, and economic resources in
the delivery of human services within our field. The idea
that we cannot afford a given amount of defense to meet
NFB activity is simply hokum.

So spoke Joseph Larkin. This is the much vaunted "professionalism" of the NAC agencies, the dedication to service, the accountability for the use of publicly contributed funds, and the
concern for the dignity and rights of the blind.

Yes, I think I know why NAC and certain agencies in the field
hate the Federation and try to discredit its leaders. Yet, some
people tell me that they don't see why we can't all get together.
After all, they say, you are all dealing with blindness, and you are
all working for the same thing. To which I emphatically answer:
No, we are not!

Whenever our representatives go to a state legislature or appear
in the halls of Congress, they can almost invariably expect to be
met by agency-inspired attempts at character assassination and
wholesale distribution of the outdated and discredited articles
from the *Des Moines Register*. Apparently, this is the only way the
agency officials know to try to divert attention from their
shortcomings and hide their failures. It has happened here in
Maryland. (Ask the Governor and the members of the Legislature.
They can tell you.) We must expect it to happen every time we
speak out—and not just here but everywhere in the country. But
it is beginning to wear thin. It is having a reverse effect.

Where do we go from here? In the climate of block grants, budget
cuts, and pleas from the agencies that (strictly in our own self-interest, of course) we unconditionally support them, we must avoid
ill-considered actions, hasty judgments, and unwise commitments.

The agencies know our power, so (in their time of need) they are urging us to make an alliance with them and present a common front. Regarding this matter, our course is clear. When the interests of the blind coincide with the interests of the agencies, we should support them. Otherwise, we should not.

Some of the agencies have tried to bring us into line by scare tactics and false information. For instance, when the present Administration took office, the story circulated that the mailing of free reading matter for the blind was about to be lost and that, therefore, we were going to lose our library service. A lot of blind people were stampeded into writing letters supporting the agencies. It is now clear that no such thing was ever contemplated, either by President Reagan or anybody else in a position to count. On the other hand, there are budget cuts and administrative changes which can cause harm and do damage.

We must avoid simplistic solutions. We do not want (and I doubt that the Administration wants) to eliminate needed services to the blind or any meaningful program; but more money for an agency does not necessarily mean more help or a better life for those who are supposed to be served by that agency. Witness Alabama, Cleveland, Minneapolis, Utah, and NAC. We should seek sufficient funding for services to the blind, but we should also take advantage of the present opportunity to reform, improve, and restructure the agencies. With a revamped and diminished bureaucracy (one with enough personnel to carry out legitimate duties but not enough to conduct wars against the blind) we might actually get more and better programs with less expenditure.

Most important of all, we must see our present situation in perspective. We have come a long way since 1940. We are now united and powerful, but we are also mature enough to use our power selectively and responsibly.

When dealing with the public, we can show muscle when necessary. Last year, for instance, when a blind mother in Washington was told that she must give up her children because she was blind, and this year in Florida when the same thing occurred, we had the resources and the know-how to put a stop to it. We went to the courts. Both mothers now have their children and can raise them in peace.

But more and more frequently we do not need to use muscle. Persuasion and discussion are sufficient. The public has great goodwill toward us, and as they learn of our capacity and normality, they are not only willing but glad to accept us as partners and equals. Of course, some are not. But most are—and the number is growing daily.

As to the agencies, many of them have already turned the corner of time and are with us in the newness. They believe as strongly as we that their proper role is partner, not custodian. They are friends and allies.

With respect to those other agencies, the ones who still try to custodialize and control us, their time is fast running out. They will either learn to respect us and treat us as equal human beings, or they will go out of business. It is that simple, that definite, and that final. If they cannot turn the corner of time and share the newness, they will cease to exist.

I want to address my final words to the active members of this organization—to the blind, and to our sighted brothers and sisters who have made our cause their cause. I also want to speak to those of you who are new to our movement, perhaps with us for the first time. To all of you I say this: We are not helpless, and we are not children. We know our problems, and we know how to solve those problems. The challenge we face is clear, and the means of meeting that challenge are equally clear. If we fail in courage or nerve or dedication, we have only ourselves to blame.

But, of course, we will not fail. The stakes are too high and the need too great to permit it. To paraphrase the Biblical statement: Upon the rock of Federationism we have built our movement, and the gates of hell shall not prevail against it. For the first time in history we can play a decisive role in determining our own destiny. If there was ever a time for dedication and commitment, that time is now. What we in the Federation do during the next decade may well determine the fate of the blind for a century to come. To win through to success will require all that we have in the way of purpose, dedication, loyalty, good sense, and guts. It will also require love and an absence of bitterness. We have turned the corner of time, and we live in a newness. My brothers and my sisters, the future is ours! Come! Join me on the barricades and we will make it all come true.

FOOTNOTES

1. C. S. Lewis, *Perelandra*, (Macmillan Publishing Co., Inc., 1944), p. 62.

2. *Highlights*, (St. Louis Society for the Blind, February, March, April, 1980), p. 7.

An underlying theme of Federationist literature and doctrine, evident from the very outset of the movement and increasingly prominent over the decades, was that the fundamental problem of blindness was to be found not in the physical condition but in the social environment—not in anatomy but in attitude. For Kenneth Jernigan in particular this theme, and variations on the theme, resounded and re-echoed in his speeches and writings—all the way from, for example, "Blindness: Concepts and Misconceptions" (a convention address delivered in 1965) through "Blindness: The Myth and the Image" (1970 banquet address) to "Blindness: Simplicity, Complexity, and the Public Mind" (1982 banquet address)—and beyond.

"The real problem of blindness," he said in 1965, "is not the blindness itself—not the acquisition of skills or techniques or competence. The real problem is the lack of understanding and the misconceptions which exist....The primitive conditions of jungle and cave are gone, but the primitive attitudes about blindness remain." And five years later he sounded the warning note again: "Of all the roadblocks in the path of the blind today, one rises up more formidably and threateningly than all others. It is the invisible barrier of ingrained social attitudes about blindness—attitudes based on suspicion and superstition, on ignorance and error, which continue to hold sway in men's minds and to keep the blind in bondage."

In 1982, speaking before a banquet audience at the Minneapolis convention, President Jernigan again struck the same major chord: "Our basic problem in 1940 was society's misconceptions and misunderstandings," he said. "That is still our problem today." But then he noted a significant difference between the early days and the present hour:

"In 1940 we were not organized and had not yet developed our philosophy, planned our public education campaigns, worked to eliminate our own false beliefs and misconceptions, or started the slow process of bringing society to new ways of perceiving and understanding. For the blind of the country, the greatest single difference between 1940 and today (and it is a tremendous difference) is the fact of the National Federation of the Blind—our concerted effort, our carefully thought out philosophy, our mutual encouragement and assistance, and our absolute determination to achieve first-class citizenship. Yes, we have learned it the hard way—but we have learned it. We know who we are, and we will never go back."

The President's theme was a new iteration of one which had been treated before—the public mind and its misconceptions—and that provided him with both a subtheme, "Simplicity," and a contrapuntal theme, "Complexity." For the unchanged patterns of the public mind, the permanence of social attitudes, suggested an underlying simplicity and sameness; but the changes in the lives of blind people through four decades, the impact of self-organization, and the evolution of competence and confidence, was making for a new complexity in the field of blindness and the affairs of the blind. All of these were elements (unresolved and mixed together) in the title of his speech—but not without the hope of future synthesis and balance. The 1982 banquet address—one of the best-remembered of the second Jernigan presidency—was entitled "Blindness: Simplicity, Complexity, and the Public Mind."

The full text follows:

BLINDNESS: SIMPLICITY, COMPLEXITY, AND THE PUBLIC MIND
by Kenneth Jernigan

Not long ago I read a science fiction story which began like this: The ambassador from the 22nd to the 21st century stood on the balcony and surveyed the city. His expression seemed to say, "All things are simple and likely to become more so."

The story ended like this: The ambassador from the 23rd to the 22nd century stood on the balcony and surveyed the city. His expression seemed to say, "All things are complex and likely to become more so."

Tonight the National Federation of the Blind is forty-two years old. That is a considerable time in the life of a person or a movement. It is more than a generation—almost half a century. In the world at large it has brought unbelievable change. In the lives of the blind it has been the turning point, the pivotal period of all history. The principal reason (the new element—the crucial factor) has been the National Federation of the Blind.

When we organized in 1940, our problems were comparatively simple. Very few blind people had jobs or the means of getting jobs, and most thought it was fate, not mistaken public attitudes or lack of opportunity or social conditioning. After all, the thinking went, common sense is common sense. A blind person (any blind person) cannot expect to compete for a job (any job) on terms of equality (real equality) with a sighted person (any sighted person). It was that inclusive and that bad.

And as it was with employment so it was with everything else. We could not participate socially, could not have regular family life, could not raise children, could not manage our own homes, could not live alone, could not engage in normal recreation, could not travel unaccompanied, could not handle money (such of it as we had), could not eat with grace, could not take part in civic affairs, could not plan our own activities, and could not govern our own lives. Things were done to the blind and sometimes for the blind—but rarely ever by the blind. It was not expected or allowed. The blind, being part of the broader society, tended to see themselves as others saw them. We tended to accept the public view of our limitations, and thus did much to make those limitations a reality.

When the average member of the public thought about blindness at all, it was usually with sympathy and pity. Society's communication link with the blind was the network of governmental and private sheltered workshops, social service agencies, and charitable institutions established (as the ordinary person would have put it) "to take care of the blind." Neither the federal nor the state rehabilitation programs regarded us as employable; the public assistance features of the Social Security Act were still new and relatively insignificant; and the army of psychologists, social workers, and technocrats was yet to be created. There were a few libraries for the blind, a limited number of state-operated sheltered workshops, and a scattering of private charitable foundations; but almost without exception these institutions were custodial in nature, limited in scope, and lacking in concepts of freedom and human dignity.

In this atmosphere (in the world of 1940) the prospects were bleak and uncomplicated; and the problems faced by the founders of our movement (though monumental in nature) were equally bleak and uncomplicated: try to get enough for the blind to eat, get people to recognize us as human beings, and reform the agencies. So it was in 1940! But never again! No more! We are beyond that! That was another time and another era. We have learned who we are, and we will never go back.

Today (forty-two years later) the world is a different place. We have organized and are a force in the land, but our problems (far from being diminished) are multiplied and magnified—a sure sign of our growth and progress. All things are complex and likely to become more so. The agencies have grown to such numbers and bigness that they threaten to control not only every aspect of our lives but also of our thoughts as well. As the National Federation of the Blind has become more powerful, many of our own have infiltrated the agency establishment and now often find themselves tempted to dilute their commitment and avoid the call of conscience. How much for the freedom of the blind, and how much for personal advancement and the weekly paycheck? Even more difficult, how to be certain that the decision is totally honest and free from rationalization?

Once the agencies were simple—minimal in service and few in staff. They gave us little: a broom and a brush-off, a sandwich and a sermon. But that little was at least easy to understand. It was the handout of the master to the slave.

The bigness has brought complexity. Many of the agencies have now acquired vast wealth and have changed their focus from service (even if only charitable and condescending service) to the protection of their own vested interests, and growth for the sake of growth. Whereas, in 1940 they ignored us as unimportant, they now regard us as dangerous and act accordingly. They try to buy our most promising leaders, and try to ruin and discredit the ones they cannot buy.

But this is only half of the story, only part of the picture; for as the ambassador from the 23rd century observed, "All things are complex and likely to become more so." Not all of the agencies follow destructive patterns. As a result of our efforts, an increasing number are responding to the call and working with us. Many of our members who have joined the agencies have not sold out but have strengthened their commitment and brought vigor and newness to the task.

There is also another element of complexity. It has to do with the current economic climate and the past behavior of the agencies. In the 1950s the agency establishment had a good reputation and high credibility both with Congress and the Executive Branch of government, but during the past twenty-five years much of that trust has evaporated. There have been too many abuses, too many nonservice-related staff members added, too many unkept promises, too many games played with statistics, too many dollars spent without results, and too much bigness and arrogance and failure to respond. With this heritage the agencies have not fared well under scrutiny in the atmosphere of shrinking dollars and the economic difficulties of the 1980s.

Again, though, there is complexity. Some of the agencies have tightened their belts, looked for ways to increase their efficiency, and sought partnership with the blind in getting Congress and the state legislatures to provide needed funds. Others have tried to continue in the old ways. Instead of partnership they have tried scare tactics. They have attempted to frighten the blind into un-questioning and unconditional support—no reform, no distinction between good and bad programs, and no participation in policy or planning. As I need not remind you, the scare tactics have not worked. We are neither cattle to be herded nor slaves to be driven. It will either be partnership as equals and joint effort, or it will be nothing.

Once upon a time a horse and a man were both being attacked by a wolf. The man said to the horse, "I have hands and skill with weapons. You have speed and strength. Therefore, let us join for-ces to rid ourselves of this menace. Of course, I will have to put a bridle and saddle on you and ride on your back, but if we work together, we can be free."

The horse agreed, and they united and killed the wolf. Then the horse said, "Now we are free. Take off the saddle and bridle, and let us rejoice in our liberty."

To which (as he drove in the spurs) the man answered, "The hell you say! Giddyap, Dobbin." The wolf may stand at the agencies' doors, but this does not mean that we will allow ourselves to be bridled and saddled.

We are not opposed to all agencies, nor do we fail to understand and appreciate the constructive work which many of them have done. We are only saying that all things are complex and likely to become more so. We want partnership and cooperation, not threats and oppression. We will do what we have to do and take what risks we have to take to achieve full citizenship and equal status in society. We have learned our lessons well, and others should also learn; for we know who we are, and we will never go back.

The complexity is not merely with the agencies but also with us. With the strengthening of our movement and growing opportunity we have followed the path of other minorities. Some of us have attempted to hide in the larger sighted community, pretending that we have "made it on our own," and that we have reaped no benefit from the movement and, thus, have no obligation to it. Like some of the blacks of forty years ago, those of us who have taken this road have (figuratively speaking) tried to straighten our hair and lighten our skins—attempting to cross the color line and deny our heritage. But it did not work then, and it will not work now. Either we the blind are equal as a people, or not a single one of us will cross the line to first-class status. This is the message and the truth of our movement—and it cannot and will not be denied. We know who we are, and we will never go back.

Our battle for freedom and recognition parallels to a striking degree that experienced by the blacks, for we are (in every modern sense of the term) a minority. We have our ghettos, our unemployment, our underemployment, and our Uncle Toms. We have our establishment (composed of society as a whole and, particularly, of many of the professionals in the governmental and private agencies). That establishment condescendingly loves us if we stay in our places, and bitterly resents us if we strive for equality. Above all (through our own organization, the National Federation of the Blind) we have discovered our collective conscience and found our true identity. We have learned that it is not our blindness which has put us down and kept us out, but what we and others have thought about our blindness. Yet, they tell us that there is no discrimination and that we are not a minority. We want no strife or confrontation, but we will do what we have to do. We are simply no longer willing to be second-class citizens. We understand the complexity. We know who we are, and we will never go back.

The ambassador from the 23rd century was right: All things are complex and likely to become more so. But the ambassador from the 22nd century was also right, for all things are simple and likely to remain so. Our basic problem in 1940 was society's misconceptions and misunderstanding.

That is still our problem today. The agencies, being part of society, take their attitudes from it (despite their claims of professionalism to the contrary), and when we have reformed society, we will also have reformed the agencies. Likewise, our own attitudes are affected by society—but here there is a difference. In 1940 we were not organized and had not yet developed our philosophy, planned our public education campaigns, worked to eliminate our own false beliefs and misconceptions, or started the slow process of bringing society to new ways of perceiving and understanding. For the blind of the country, the greatest single difference between 1940 and today (and it is a tremendous difference) is the fact of the National Federation of the Blind—our concerted effort, our carefully thought out philosophy, our mutual encouragement and assistance, and our absolute determination to achieve first-class citizenship. Yes, we have learned it the hard way—but we have learned it. We know who we are, and we will never go back.

With respect to public attitudes we still have a long way to go. We can begin with things around the house—like bathing. Sometime ago I received a letter which said:

> Your organization has been recommended as one which may be able to take advantage of a valuable new safety product designed to improve bathing safety for the blind and the handicapped.
>
> The Safety Shower Guard and Safety Tub Guard are low-cost, easily installed products which will stop the flow of water in a bathing area if the temperature becomes too hot for comfort or safety. When the temperature returns to a safe level, flow is automatically allowed to resume.
>
> These products have received the acceptance of the U.S. Department of Housing and Urban Development and conform to ASTM Standard F-444 Consumer Safety Specification for scald- preventing devices.

I must confess that it never occurred to me that looking at the water might keep me from getting burned or that I might have need of a Scald-Preventing Device. I had always thought that when the burned child feared the fire, it was because of touch, not sight.

But let us leave the tub and go to the washing machine. A recent publication of the Maytag Corporation tells of the *advances* the company is making to change their appliances so that, as they put it, their products "can be used by visually disabled persons." The trouble here is the emphasis. I have never in my life known a single blind person who could not learn to use an ordinary washing machine with a minimal amount of effort, and surely it is no great "advance" (worthy of a special announcement) to add a few markings to the dials or the buttons.

But Sears goes Maytag one better. In the summer of 1981 it distributed a colorful flyer with this grabber as a headline: "So the Blind May See." The text that follows is equally dramatic. It reads like this:

> To many people, doing the laundry is a boring chore. And for millions of sight-impaired people operating a washing machine, adjusting an air conditioner, or cooking in a microwave oven can be a difficult chore. This fall, Sears will offer Braille overlays for the controls of several Kenmore appliances, opening new worlds to those with vision impairments.

Again, the problem is with the emphasis and the implication. Braille overlays (which we can easily make for ourselves if we want them) may offer some negligible convenience, but surely they do not open up "new worlds to those with visual impairments." If so, our scope is limited, indeed.

In April of this year the Oster Division of the Sunbeam Corporation wrote me to ask whether it would be (as they put it) "safe" to permit their materials to be transcribed into Braille for use by the blind. Here is what they said:

> Oster, Division of Sunbeam Corporation, manufactures household appliances. We occasionally receive requests from libraries for permission to transcribe our instruction literature into Braille.
>
> We would be pleased to comply with these requests, but we are concerned that a direct transcription of the text may not meet the specific needs of a blind user.

> Since we lack the expertise to make this judgment, we are asking you to review several of our instruction booklets. In determining if the instructions are adequately organized and sufficiently detailed to teach a blind person to safely operate the appliance, please assume that the Braille copy would be a literal transcription of the original.

I responded that blind people throughout the country use power blenders every day without hazard and that it would be perfectly safe to transcribe the instructions (unaltered) into Braille. So far as I know, that settled the weighty matter, and even now the Brailling may be in process.

The public misconceptions about blindness are so bizarre and so much at variance with common sense that they would be laughable if they were not so damaging. Several months ago the Italian Trade Commissioner to this country sent me a press release: "ITALIAN HOUSEHOLD APPLIANCE MADE FOR THE BLIND" it proclaimed. "A leading Italian appliance manufacturer has announced that it has initiated the production of a completely automatic dishwasher and stove specially made for the blind. These appliances are equipped with special devices and acoustic signals which allow the blind to control the machine at any particular moment."

In an accompanying letter the Trade Commissioner said: "We would appreciate receiving a copy of any coverage that will eventually be published in your magazine." Since blind people can use ordinary stoves and dishwashers without difficulty (their only problem usually being having the money to buy such items, a problem partially caused by the false image created by the very kind of press release I have just read), and since I intend to print these remarks in the *Monitor*, I wonder whether the Trade Commissioner would really like to have them. Or would he simply be amazed, angry, and bewildered by it all?

As the ambassador from the 23rd century said, "All things are complex and likely to become more so"; but as the ambassador from the 22nd century observed, "All things are simple." Either way you take it, we know how to operate dishwashers and stoves, and we know how to avoid being scalded or cut by the blender. We also know that eyesight and intelligence have nothing to do with each other, but (unbelievable though it sounds) there are those who apparently do not.

On December 12, 1981, the *Portland* (Oregon) *Daily Journal of Commerce* carried an article headlined "Optometric Business Broadens Its Vision." In view of the text of the article the headline is particularly ironic. The Northwest Congress of Optometry was meeting in Portland, and one of their featured speakers was a man named Allen Pyeatt. This Dr. Pyeatt is clearly no run-of-the-mill person. As the newspaper quotes him: "We're not just people interested in examining eyes and selling glasses."

Well, then, what is he interested in? We are not left in doubt. Under the subheadline "Intellectual Correlation" he tells us:

> In a more general sense, Pyeatt is also involved with the performance of children. But he focuses on recently- formulated premises in the fields of optometry and education that optimal vision capacity is directly related to optimal intellectual capacity.
>
> Pyeatt explains the developments historically covering the evolution of psychological research on intelligence. As the psychological community began to abandon the Stanford-Binet measurement of a presumably constant, unalterable intelligence quotient, the idea that intelligence can be developed and changed emerged.
>
> With that new premise, optometry began to assert its role. "We know vision can be trained," says Pyeatt. "If a person has a vision problem and we improve his vision, it will help him function better intellectually."
>
> The scientific support of such an idea is in the fact that training of any kind increases brain weight. Thus, eye training will generally affect brain capacity, Pyeatt explains.
>
> "It's sort of like weight lifting," Pyeatt says. "You start small and work up."

Broadened vision, indeed! This pseudo-professional double talk is not science but old-fashioned witchcraft straight out of the Middle Ages. All I know to say to it is this: Let Dr. Pyeatt pick a hundred people from his convention, and we will pick a hundred from ours. Then, let the two groups stand head to head in mental contest and intellectual agility, and I think the optometrists will get a new vision. Or, we might simply say to Dr. Pyeatt: "The same to you, brother."

With such misinformation being dispensed in the name of science, it is no wonder that the blind face discrimination in employment. Mary Ann Overbey is a blind teacher with a master's degree in child development. She lives in Boulder, Colorado. In 1979 she applied for a position in a preschool day care center operated by the Boulder YWCA. The State Department of Social Services indicated that they would not license the center if Miss Overbey was employed.

At this stage the Boulder Chapter of the Federation helped Miss Overbey find a lawyer and began to ask questions. As might have been expected, the Department of Social Services (when called to task) tried to shift the blame. They called on the fire department.

And what, one may ask, does the fire department have to do with it? Well, apparently a great deal. Under date of August 13, 1979, Clifford S. Harvey (Assistant Chief of the Boulder Fire Department) wrote to Miss Overbey's lawyer as follows:

This letter is to acknowledge that there are, to the best of my knowledge, no Fire Department policies, Life Safety Code, or Fire Prevention Code requirements prohibiting or restricting the employment of a blind teacher in a day care facility. The concern of the Fire Department is with the adequacy of the structure and associated and/or necessary equipment for a special purpose or occupancy. Any suggestion by this Department that we would take action against a day care center for whomever they employed would have been in error.

However, all involved should understand that, although there is no direct reference in our codes to a blind person being unable to perform a job as a teacher in a day care facility, the Life Safety Code does express concern with exit signs being "readily visible," "distinctive color," "contrast with decorations"; the size of the exit sign "not less than 6 inches high with the principal strokes of letters not less than 3/4 inch wide," and the illumination of the sign "by a reliable light source giving a value of not less than 5 foot candles on the illuminated surface." Emergency lighting is required when the area used is subject to loss of natural and artificial light during hours of supervision. All these requirements are obviously aimed at people who are able to use their sight/vision to react to any emergency.

What a letter! As Alice said in her trip through Wonderland, it all gets curiouser and curiouser. According to the logic of Mr. Harvey blind persons would be prohibited from crossing streets, because the signs and lights are obviously meant for the sighted. Likewise, blind persons could not work in lighted factories, attend lighted schools, or (for that matter) even live in their own homes—assuming that their homes are lighted, which is probably a building code requirement in most localities.

No review of the present condition of the blind would be complete without some discussion of the airlines. Twenty years ago there were relatively few blind passengers, but there were also virtually no problems. Blind people were treated like everybody else. They sat where they chose, kept their canes with them if they liked, and generally traveled without incident.

Then, as an increasing number of us began to find employment and self-confidence, more of us began to travel on airplanes and otherwise participate in the mainstream of daily life. As always happens when a minority moves from dependence toward first-class citizenship, we experienced a certain amount of hostility and resentment. The problem was augmented by the fact that other handicapped groups and minorities were also striving and seeking advancement. Suddenly the airlines became very much aware of the disabled—not just the blind or some other group but all of the disabled. And they went about it in the worst possible way. They seemingly took all of the problems which they conceived each group of the disabled to have and attributed all of them to each of us. The resulting picture was a helpless, pitiable monstrosity.

Seven or eight years ago the Federal Aviation Administration decided to make special rules for us—limiting the number of blind persons who could travel on a single flight, providing that we must sit in certain segregated sections of the plane, and generally restricting our freedom of movement. By letters to Congress, confrontations at airports, and testimony at public hearings throughout the country we opposed these regulations, and they were never put into effect. However, by the late 1970s all sorts of restrictive measures were being *undertaken* by the airlines. It started with insistence that we give up our canes during flight, and it went from there to the bizarre and the ridiculous. Only now are we beginning to prevail in the struggle, but some of the madness still lingers.

In February of this year Frontier Airlines publicly humiliated and verbally abused our Colorado President, Diane McGeorge, because she did not want to move from her assigned seat to the bulkhead area—where, they said, she and her dog Pony would be "more comfortable." They relented only after asking the other passengers in the row whether they objected to having Diane sit by them. In response to a letter from our attorney, Frontier took an injured tone and said that they had led the way in promoting the rights of the blind. They even claimed to have been the ones responsible for getting the Federal Aviation Administration to repeal its regulation prohibiting us from keeping our canes with us at our seats during flight. The way I remember it, we of the National Federation of the Blind filed the lawsuit.

As conclusive proof of their respect for our rights, Frontier pointed to a Braille flight information brochure which they have prepared for blind passengers. The brochure is, indeed, conclusive, but not in the way that Frontier imagines. It says in part:

> You have been seated in an area that will help us make a safe and rapid evacuation. We ask that you *remain seated until the initial flow of passengers has passed you.* By permitting other passengers to evacuate first, we will be in a better position to help you, if necessary.

(Let me interrupt to say that I, for one, don't buy it. If I happen to be on an airplane in time of emergency, I have no intention of sitting there passively until everybody else has left the plane and Frontier's flight personnel have come back to get me. How do I know that they will not panic in the turmoil and give first priority to looking out for themselves...or—even if they don't—that it won't be too late by the time everybody else is off? If there is an emergency, I will take my chance with the rest of the passengers. That is why I keep both my cane and my wits with me when I fly.)

But back to the Frontier brochure. It goes on to say:

> If you have chosen not to fly with your own escort, please understand that the flight attendants are not obligated to extend services beyond that required by all other passengers. In addition, you are responsible for your own lavatory needs; flight attendants are not able to assist.

> Welcome aboard and have a pleasant flight.

What do you suppose they have in mind with respect to assisting with our lavatory needs? As the ambassador from the 23rd century said: All things are complex and likely to become more so.

Southwest Airlines recently issued a "Clarification of Passenger Tariff Rule 10 Refusal To Transport," which says in part:

> Mental or physical conditions such as deaf, blind, mute, or retarded renders [sic] the individual incapable of caring for himself without assistance enroute and definitely would require further attention or assistance from employees of carrier such as, blind could not read instructions, fasten seat belts, signs, change planes unassisted, or help himself in an emergency. Any one of or combination of the above certainly could involve risk to himself or to other persons or to property in the event of any non-routine situation if he became frightened. All personnel must be alert to these situations and use good judgement and tact when having to decline acceptance of these people.

The Station Counter Manual for Pacific Southwest says:

> When accepting unaccompanied blind persons for passage, every effort should be made to determine tactfully the extent of the passenger's helplessness. If the passenger is completely helpless, it should be recommended that he not travel alone. On the other hand, if the passenger seems well-adjusted and experienced in taking care of himself, traveling alone will not be too difficult.

> Arrangements should be made to assist the blind passenger in boarding the airplane, and ensuring that he is seated next to a person of the same sex to take advantage of the latter person's probably voluntary efforts to assist the blind person.

What do you think they expect the person of the same sex to assist the blind person in doing? If they intend for it to stop at the lavatory door, it really won't matter which sex is helping—will it? As the ambassador from the 22nd century said, All things are simple and likely to become more so.

To top it all, an Eastern Airlines Flight Attendant named Claudia recently decided not to bother trying to get the blind passenger to the lavatory at all. She insisted that he sit on a blanket because, as she put it, it is a federal regulation that blind persons have to sit on blankets because they cannot control their bladders. Of course, the blind person refused and pointed out that there is not (and never has been) any such federal regulation, but there was a scene involving public humiliation and embarrassment. There was also the likelihood of a lawsuit. All one can say to such insanity is: Welcome aboard, Claudia, and have a pleasant flight.

And then there is sex. The Andrew Clinic in New York has sent me a letter saying that it provides specialized sex therapy for a number of groups, including the blind, the amputee, and the obese. I often wonder how some of these classifications get made.

At any rate, the letter from the Andrew Clinic begins by saying: "Dear Director of the Federation; Please feel free to disseminate this announcement." Well, all right,—let's disseminate it. It says in part:

> Therapy is conducted either in our OFFICE or at HOME. Therapy modality: empirical. Fees: $250 for 12 sessions for 2 people, $150 for 12 sessions for singles without surrogate, $300 for 12 sessions for singles with an assigned surrogate. Please write or call for detailed information about qualifications, co-therapists, available consultants, or the rules about the assignment of a surrogate. Hoping to hear from you, I remain Cordially yours; Adalbert B. Vajay, M.D. Ph.D.

It has been my observation that we do not need professional therapists to teach us about the basics—or, for that matter, to help us enjoy them—So welcome aboard Adalbert, and have a pleasant flight.

Where does all of this leave us? For one thing (although we treat it with derision) it is not funny. It blights our lives, limits our opportunities, and kills our dreams. It depicts a social climate and a public attitude which bring misery and suffering. It bars us from regular employment and forces us to the degradation and poverty of subminimum wages and sheltered shops.

The state of Utah runs such a shop, and it is notorious. On July 27, 1981, a blind woman wrote to the director of Utah's Services for the Blind:

Dear Dr. Langford: I am writing this letter in protest to tell my complaint about the workshop. At the time I was working there, I was transferred from one job to another from day to day without any explanation as to why, and therefore, I could not pick up good speed.

At the time of my dismissal, Mr. May told me I could work for thirty-eight cents a day. I was deeply hurt and very upset, and I went home and cried for several hours.

The following day my counselor, Dianne Alexander, told me that I could go to ReWall [ReWall is a training facility] on July 6, 1981, for re-evaluation. I did go there. I cooperated on everything they asked me to do, EX-CEPT I would not answer one certain question dealing with my SEX LIFE.

While at ReWall, Diane, Richard, and Bill told me I could work for sixty-eight cents a day. Dianne Alexander—Rehab. Counselor, Bill—ReWall Counselor, Richard—ReWall Instructor.

The next day I confronted Mr. May with this message—of working for sixty-eight cents a day. He just stood there and said nothing. I asked him then if I could return to work. He told me that they were not hiring anybody. Again, I became more upset than ever. I went home and cried and cried and cried. I did not know what to do or who to turn to.

Finally I decided to call my Counselor, Dianne Alexander. I told her what Mr. May had said. She told me to report to work on Monday and Tuesday, July 27 and 28, 1981, at 9:00 a.m. for a period of six weeks, at a $1.55 per hour. I was very grateful to hear this good news, as it will be of some help for our family.

Dr. Langford, I would like to tell you about one of the worst things going on at the Utah Workshop, the foulest language!! The lead man sits there and converses with others in very foul language, where everyone must sit and listen to it. He calls the workers' children "little bastards." When called down on it by the workers, he told us if we didn't like it, we could leave. While I was at ReWall, Bill told me that I would have to put up with it—and not let it bother me. But it does bother me.

While working in the broom shop I sorted better than 200 pounds of corn per day.

Dr. Langford, I would like to know why I have been dismissed. There are several others that were hired after I was, and they are still working there. Dr. Langford, I was at work every day—on time and never late.

My husband and I have 2 small dependent children of school age. Without me working full time, I don't know how we can make it with the high cost of living these days.

Dr. Langford, knowing your position, you might be able to help me get my job back. I would appreciate hearing from you.

Pain and agony come from every line of that letter. It speaks of hurt and misery that cannot be described but only experienced. She is grateful for a $1.55 per hour and is so desperate for help that she begs to be allowed to return to a place where she must constantly hear her two small children referred to as "little bastards." If this were an isolated instance, it would be bad enough, but it is not. It is commonplace—repeated over and over throughout the country. It is no exaggeration to say that many of the blind today live in what can only be called slavery.

But we have learned to fight back, and we are making progress. As a result of our efforts an increasing number of the agencies are adopting new ways and responding to us positively, and so are the members of the public-at-large. It is true that the conditions in the sheltered shops are still unbelievably bad, but it is also true that we have succeeded in getting the National Labor Relations Board to take jurisdiction over the shops and affirm the right of blind workers to organize and bargain collectively. When the Cincinnati Association for the Blind (one of the worst sheltered shops in the country) appealed the NLRB ruling, the federal Court decided in our favor. The Court decision (which was handed down only a few months ago) is as much a testimonial to how far we have come in reforming public attitudes and how successful our educational campaigns have been as it is to the provisions of the law and the enlightenment of the judges. The Cincinnati Association has indicated that it will carry the matter to the Supreme Court of the United States, and it certainly has the money to do it—money wrung from the sweat of exploited blind workers; money extracted from a charitable public, which is only beginning to understand; money gleaned from tax exemptions and federal subsidies. However, even if we should lose the next round of appeals, the fact still remains that even ten years ago the NLRB and federal Court rulings would have been impossible. In a single decade we have made more progress than in all previous history.

Between February and June of this year our Job Opportunities for the Blind program assisted more than fifty people in finding competitive employment at a rate above the minimum wage, and this was done at a time when unemployment among the general public was running at record levels. It is no exaggeration to say that today more blind people are employed at higher wages than ever before in human experience.

And it is not just in employment that we are making gains, but in other areas as well. The airlines are a good example. Bad as the situation is, there are definite signs of progress. Last fall I went to Atlanta at the invitation of Delta to make a training film for its employees, and United (which four or five years ago was one of the most insensitive) recently removed objectionable advertising from radio and television because we asked them to do it.

In every area we are gaining momentum, and tomorrow is bright with promise. As the sighted learn who we are, what we have endured, what we are achieving, and what we can do, they are standing with us in growing numbers. We are capable of living with the sighted, working with the sighted, playing with the sighted, and competing with the sighted on terms of full equality; and the sighted are capable of reciprocating and understanding.

Most important of all, we have found our collective identity and understood what it means to work together as a *movement*. We have made our Federation the strongest force which has ever existed to improve the lot of the blind. Today not only our own members but all of the blind (those who are not part of us, those who have never heard of us, and even those who dislike us) are living better lives and reaching for higher goals than ever before—and they are doing it because of the National Federation of the Blind. No force in the world can now stop our advance to freedom. We understand our heritage, and it gives us strength for the battles ahead. We fight for those who went before us and for those who come after—for the founders of our movement and for the children of the next generation. We also fight for ourselves—for our right to full citizenship and human dignity, for our right to equality under the law, and for our right to work with others and do for ourselves.

My brothers and my sisters, the future is ours. It only remains for us to do the work and make the sacrifice and show the courage to win it. Come! Join me on the barricades, and we will make it all come true!

Chapter 7

Culmination: The Concluding Years of the Second Jernigan Presidency

"Today we are moving with a mighty force," said the President of the National Federation of the Blind in 1983: "For 43 years we have worked and struggled to accelerate our movement and send it in a straight line toward freedom and independence. The efforts of tens of thousands of blind men and women have been spent for almost two generations to reach the current momentum."

"Now," he said, "there is no force on earth that can slow us down or turn us back or change our direction." He went on to declare that the organized blind would wait no longer for equality and opportunity to be granted or handed to them: "Through the centuries we have yearned for acceptance, longed for opportunity, and dreamed of a full life. And too often we have waited. But no more! Never again! The waiting did not work. We have learned our lesson—and learned it well. Equality will not (perhaps cannot) be given to us. If we want it, we must take it. So the waiting is over. The yearning and the longing are at an end. And not just someday or tomorrow—but now! From this day forward it will be action. Let people call us what they will and think what they please. We are simply no longer willing to be second-class citizens. We want no strife or confrontation, but we will do what we have to do. To the extent required we will meet pressure with pressure and force with force. We know who we are, and we will never go back."

It was not so much the message of Kenneth Jernigan's convention speech that was novel in the year 1983; it was rather the tone and spirit that struck a different note from past occasions when the organized blind movement was struggling to survive and embroiled in civil wars or uphill battles against powerful agency forces.

By 1983, when Jernigan spoke of the other half of inertia at the National Convention in Kansas City, the Federation had arrived at a new plateau of peace, prosperity, and progress. Peace came to the movement with the victorious ending of the California lawsuit in that year. The court action against Ammeter and the other members of her faction in Washington state had earlier been concluded, and the lawsuit to confirm by a ruling of the courts the Federation's right to govern the Iowa affiliate and discipline the dissidents in that state in accordance with national policy was (though it would not be finished until 1984) clearly on the way to a favorable decision. But in a deeper sense the Federation's well-being and harmony had not really been achieved through the courts but by a collective act of will on the part of the membership, rallying in convention to cast out the handful of embittered malcontents and to reaffirm support for the democratic structure and progressive goals of the movement. Peace for the National Federation of the Blind was not only the absence of war within—it was also the presence of a new mood and temper throughout the movement, a prevailing self-assurance that spoke of solidarity and quiet strength, of prestige and unprecedented influence in the blindness system and the public at large.

"We have found the other half of inertia," said the President in his banquet speech, "and we are generating the force to make our dreams reality....Yes, we still experience discrimination, denial, and lack of opportunity; but the tide is running the other way. It can be seen in our victories in the sheltered shops; in our radio and television spots, which blanket the nation; and in the jobs which blind people are getting and holding. It can be seen in the hope, the determination, and the zest for the future which blind people now are feeling. It can be seen in the mood and the joy of this convention."

Following is the complete text of President Jernigan's address delivered at the banquet of the 1983 convention in Kansas City, Missouri:

BLINDNESS: THE OTHER HALF OF INERTIA
by Kenneth Jernigan

An essential component of being human is the ability to think; an essential component of the ability to think is the ability to verbalize; and an essential component of the ability to verbalize is a knowledge of the meaning of words. It is not that a knowledge of the meaning of words can make us human or create humanity, but to the extent we lack such knowledge our humanity is diminished. To the extent we have it our humanity is enhanced. And it is not simply the speaking but the understanding of words that counts—the delineation of the subtleties of meaning, the comprehension of definition and connotation, the flow of imagery and association: love...hate...poverty...longing...loneliness...desire...dream....Words—the building blocks of humanity.

There are words for every occasion—words for children, words for scientists, and words for statesmen. There are also words which have special significance for us. Consider, for instance, the word inertia—What does it mean? What does it connote? And why does it have special significance? When most of us think of inertia, we think of something not moving, something inert—and it is not just the physical but also the social. The dictionary tells us that *inertia* means "lack of skill, idleness, laziness."

But this is only half of the meaning. There is the other half. The full definition is this: Things at rest tend to remain at rest, and things in motion tend to remain in motion, at a uniform rate and in a straight line. The only way to change the inertia of an object is by pressure. It is as hard to stop something which is moving as it is to start something which is not.

When the blind came to organize in 1940, the situation was about as bad as it could possibly be. It was almost static. It was worse than static, for there was enough motion to tantalize but not enough to encourage or stimulate hope. At the pace of 1940 it would have taken generations (perhaps centuries) for the blind to

achieve meaningful lives and real opportunity—and a promise
which is measured by centuries is no promise at all. It is only a
shadow and a mockery. More than twenty years ago, in their struggle for recognition and freedom, the blacks (that minority with
whom we have so often compared ourselves) said it all: "If not
now, when?"

Regardless of the future, the world of 1940 held little hope for
the blind—certainly none for the blind of that generation. It was
custody, control, condescension, inferiority, pity, and lack of opportunity.

Then, everything changed. Dr. Jacobus tenBroek and a handful
of others organized the National Federation of the Blind. Suddenly it was not centuries but decades—and, yes, something for the
blind of that generation, something for the blind then alive. In
the beginning the force of inertia worked against us (things at rest
tend to remain at rest); but pressure was applied, and the acceleration was noticeable and immediate. Of course, at first the
progress was slow (it always is). The situation was aggravated by
the mass involved, for with a given pressure the build-up is always
in direct proportion to the mass which has to be moved. And the
mass which we had to move was tremendous. It was all of
society—all of it (including ourselves): society—with its accumulated stereotypes, misconceptions, and prejudices; society—with
its mistaken ideas and "freaky" notions about blindness, going
back to the dawn of history—ideas and notions imbedded in literature, locked in folklore, and sanctified by tradition.

I joined this movement in 1949. I met Dr. tenBroek in 1952, and
I came to my first National Convention the same year. I have
been to every National Convention since—all thirty-two of them;
and I can tell you from firsthand experience that during that time
we have moved an awful lot of mass.

Now, we are in 1983. What is our situation today? Where are we?
How is the state of our inertia? In the first place we should keep
in mind the basic principle: The only way to change the inertia of
an object is by pressure. It is as hard to stop something which is
moving as it is to start something which is not. That is the rule,
and it is as immutable for organizations as for objects. By the
terms of inertia no pressure is ever lost. For forty-three years we
have worked and struggled to accelerate our movement and send
it in a straight line toward freedom and independence. The efforts
of tens of thousands of blind men and women have been spent

for almost two generations to reach the current momentum. Today we are moving with a mighty force. It would take as much pressure and effort to stop our progress and push us back to 1940 as it has taken to get us where we are. I find that a comforting thought, for there is no force on earth that can do it. There is no group (no combination of groups) that can find the nerve, muster the determination, or feel the need. We can summon the strength to resist any conceivable pressure which would slow our acceleration and push us back—for we have experienced pain. We know what it is to hurt. Through the centuries we have yearned for acceptance; longed for opportunity; and dreamed of a full life. And too often we have waited. But no more! Never again. The waiting did not work. We have learned our lesson—and learned it well. Equality will not (perhaps cannot) be given to us. If we want it, we must take it. So the waiting is over. The yearning and the longing are at an end. And not just someday or tomorrow—but now! From this day forward it will be action. Let people call us what they will and think what they please. We are simply no longer willing to be second-class citizens. We want no strife or confrontation, but we will do what we have to do. To the extent required we will meet pressure with pressure and force with force. We know who we are, and we will never go back.

Today we are not in 1940, nor will we ever be there again. Neither have we arrived at our goal. We are in mid-passage. The balances are shifting, and the force of inertia is now more with us than against us. We are moving with accelerating motion in a straight line toward the future, but there are counterpressures—forces of opposition, which seek to slow us down and push us back.

Upon superficial examination it might appear that we are not dealing with one group, but three: the general public, the governmental and private agencies, and ourselves. In a sense this is true, but both the blind and the agencies are part of the larger society, and to the extent we move society as a whole, we also move the component parts. This is so despite the fact that the sheltered shops, the rehabilitation establishment, and the other governmental and private agencies have a heavy investment in the status quo and, thus, a built-in resistance to change. They may come kicking and screaming—but they will come. We the blind are also part of the general public, and even though we are the primary force generating the change and creating the acceleration, we cannot outdistance the inertia we give to the rest of society.

Things at rest tend to remain at rest, but today that half of inertia is not our major concern. The focus is on the other half: things in motion tend to remain in motion. With growing pressure we are accelerating toward the goal of security, equality, and opportunity for the blind. Although our overall momentum is increasing rapidly, the progress is not uniform. In some areas it is steady; in others it is exponential; in still others it is uneven; and in yet others it is hardly noticeable at all.

We have made much progress, but we still have a long way to go. The mistaken notions and ancient stereotypes which people have about blindness are all pervasive. They are so ingrained as to be almost second nature. They go to the central core of our being and permeate every shade of our simplest thought. This is true of the blind as well as the sighted. Sometimes those of us who are blind (even those of us who consciously work on a daily basis to change the status quo) accept the public view of our limitations, without even knowing we are doing it. Sometimes we do it while in the very act of speaking to the contrary.

A few years ago I went to a cafeteria with a sighted associate. We took our trays and moved down the line. When we turned from the cash register and started for the table, an accident occurred. A glass of water fell from the tray and splashed on the floor. "There will be those," I said, "who will see this and think the reason I spilled that glass of water is because I am blind."

"You are right," my sighted associate replied, "for you didn't spill it. I did. It fell from my tray, not yours."

What I have already told you is bad enough, but there is more, and worse. I didn't leave it there: "How did you do that?" I asked.

This time my associate (who is as well versed in our philosophy as the rest of us) responded with more than a touch of acid: "I did it the same way anybody else would," she said. "I tipped my tray. Do you think it is normal for the blind to be clumsy and the sighted to be graceful? Do you think sighted people don't have accidents? Why did you automatically assume that you were the one who spilled the water?"

It was a fair question, and it caused a lot of soul-searching. I reluctantly conclude that (despite all of my philosophy and knowledge to the contrary, despite all of my experience with this very sort of situation dressed out in other forms) I fell into the trap of social conditioning. I hope I won't do it again, but I can't be sure. The force of inertia is powerful, and changes in public attitudes about blindness are hard to set in motion. Things at rest tend to remain at rest.

The blind are like other minorities. Some of us have come a long way on the road to equality; others have only started; and many have not yet begun. The plain truth is that (because of low self-esteem and the role society has taught us to play) a lot of blind people, along with most of the sighted, simply do not believe that it is respectable to be blind. Mainly such people are not in this organization (at least, not actively in it), for we are moving on a different track. We have tested our theories and put them to the proof. The basic tenet of our philosophy can be stated in a single sentence: the average blind person (given reasonable opportunity and an even break) can make the dollars and take the knocks with everybody else.

In April of this year Fred Schroeder, who is one of our upcoming young leaders, represented the Federation at a meeting involving a number of officials from the governmental and private agencies. One of the occurrences which he reported has particular relevance to what we are discussing: "During lunch on Thursday," he said, "I observed an incident which brought into vivid clarity the way in which these folks view themselves as blind people. Mr. Y, who is blind, had joined the group for lunch and was sitting next to Mr. X, who is also blind. I overheard Mr. Y say, 'I have been sitting next to you for ten minutes, and I still don't know whether you are blind or sighted.' With obvious pleasure Mr. X responded, 'Why, thank you very much. I'm blind.'"

What a damning commentary. He thought it was a compliment! This man works with the newly blinded. He serves, if only by example, as a role model of what blind people can do and expect to be. No wonder it has taken us so long to achieve momentum!

Last fall I, too, had occasion to observe Mr. X. He chaired a meeting which I attended, and when it came time for a pause, he said something to this effect: "There are coffee and rolls in the back of the room. We are not going to take a break just yet, but if you like, those of you who can see can go back during the next couple of minutes and get refreshments."

If this attitude of low self-esteem is held by the agency leaders (and it is not just the blind who hold it but often the sighted as well), how do they treat the blind they are employed to help? Many of you in this room do not need documentation to tell you. You know firsthand from painful experience. But the documentation exists. All too frequently, I am sad to say, the agency officials express their feelings of frustration and inadequacy by taking the tack (of course, they do not do it consciously) that if they cannot succeed in business or achieve leadership anywhere else, at least they can bully and dominate the blind.

Consider, for instance, the following letter which I recently received from a blind adult who had attended a camp for the blind in California called Enchanted Hills. "The director and staff," he said, "can stay up as late as they wish—smoke, drink, make noise, and keep the campers up. The campers, on the other hand, can't drink, smoke, or make noise—and we have a curfew. We are adults like they are, and just because we're blind, they think they have the say-so over us."

As you can see, Enchanted Hills is far from idyllic; but it is a model of freedom compared to the Northeastern Association of the Blind at Albany, New York—which (with the help of state and federal funds) operates a rehabilitation training program. Under date of May 17, 1983, our New York president (David Stayer) wrote to the Executive Director of the Northeastern Association as follows:

> Dear Mr. Friedman,
>
> It has been brought to the attention of our organization that you operate a residential facility for blind adults. We have heard that the residents are not treated as adults, and their dignity is nonexistent. As president of our New York affiliate, I am specifically requesting the written policy clearly explaining all the rules and regulations related to your residence, Doc's Motel. I am also requesting the statement of rights that the residents have....
>
> If what we hear is valid, your agency is a disgrace for the way it treats those of us who are blind. It is reported that adults are ordered to bed right after dinner, that specific permission must be obtained before a resident is allowed to leave the motel, and that a ten p.m. curfew exists."

Mr. Friedman responded under date of May 27, 1983. His letter should be studied with care by those who say we exaggerate when we talk about custodialism. He is so out of touch with reality that he does not even know what he is admitting. Yet, his attitudes are closer to the norm than the exception. Here is what he says:

Dear Mr. Stayer:

Your concern about the treatment of blind adults is one that is shared by everyone at this Association. We are concerned that all individuals are treated in a dignified manner. You refer to our operation of a residential facility for blind adults. This is incorrect. Doc's Motel is separate and apart from the area in which certain blind individuals reside. While it is true that the boarding host is the proprietor of a motel, the individuals residing with her live in her home, not in the motel proper. It is also untrue that adults are ordered to bed right after dinner. A 10:00 p.m. curfew exists only in the sense that individuals are expected to respect the rights of others beginning at that time. Quiet hours begin then and usually last until the early morning hours....

In general we expect residents to interact effectively as adults residing in the same situation. However, as a result of experiential deprivation, the existence of other handicapping conditions in addition to legal blindness, and a certain amount of social immaturity, this is not always a realistic expectation. The guidelines were developed to protect the basic rights of the individuals residing at the boarding home, in which are provided clean, comfortable, quiet places to sleep and three meals each day....Access to any other portions of the boarding host's property (aside from common eating areas at appropriate times and bedroom facilities) is on a voluntary basis.

With regard to the imposition of quiet hours, it is reasonable to expect that trainees who are participating in a full-time day training program usually require as a minimum eight hours of sleep per night. Thus, quiet hours are from 10:00 p.m. to 6:30 a.m. on Sunday, Monday, Tuesday, Wednesday, and Thursday nights. Quiet hours of twelve midnight to 8:30 a.m. on Friday and Saturday nights have been established. Should an individual wish to remain outside of his or her bedroom area after 10:00 p.m. on week nights and after twelve p.m. on weekends, the individual is free to do so. How-

ever, the individual is not permitted to return to the
bedroom area until the end of quiet hours. In the case
of week nights, this is 6:30 a.m., and in the case of
weekends this is 8:30 a.m. Thus, no curfew as such exists.
An individual can be required to return to the bedroom
area after the taking of the evening meal. However, as I
have previously mentioned, no individual has ever been
ordered to bed or to sleep at that time....

All current residents are aware of these guidelines and
rules, and each has agreed to sign a copy of the rules and
guidelines when the final draft is completed.

Mr. Stayer, it is unfortunate that an individual who feels
that he or she has been mistreated by our Association
would not seek justice to redress the alleged violations
of his dignity as a human being within the agency that is
providing services to him or her....

For the past seventy-five years the Northeastern Association of the Blind at Albany has worked with members of
the blind community in assisting them to achieve their
maximum potential and independence within the
framework of the services we offer.

I look forward to the time when we all can work con-
structively for the individuals about whom we are rightfully concerned.

Sincerely,
Michael B. Friedman
Executive Director

Remember that this exchange of correspondence is less than two
months old. A young blind woman wants training to be a secretary,
so she goes to the Northeastern Association for help. And what
does she find? The Association is "concerned that all individuals
are treated in a dignified manner." Mr. Friedman tells us so. Furthermore, it is not a residential facility for blind adults—because
Doc's Motel is separate and apart from the area in which certain
blind individuals reside (and besides, they do not live in the motel
proper). A 10:00 p.m. curfew exists only in the sense that individuals are expected to respect the rights of others, beginning
at that time, presumably being free to violate such rights at 9:59
and before. And what is all of this talk about restriction? Residents are not required to be in their rooms by ten on week nights
and twelve on weekends. Well, of course, if they happen to be

late, they can't come back until the next day. They can, one assumes, sleep wherever the party was—or in the park. Probably it
will decrease their "experiential deprivation" and lessen their "social immaturity."

Then, there is the matter of ordering people to their rooms after
dinner. Not true. Well, all right—perhaps they are ordered to
their rooms, but no one has been ordered to bed or to sleep. Can
you believe it? How on earth would you order someone to sleep
if you wanted to? But, not to worry—"For the past seventy-five
years the Northeastern Association of the Blind at Albany has
worked with members of the blind community in assisting them
to achieve their maximum potential and independence within the
framework of the services we offer." In fact, doubly not to worry.
The Northeastern Association of the Blind at Albany is accredited.
By whom? You guessed it—by that advocate of high standards
and quality services, NAC (the National Accreditation Council for
Agencies Serving the Blind and Visually Handicapped). The accreditation is assured until 1986.

And, anyway, the trainees will sign a statement agreeing to the
rules. They have already approved them, even before the final
draft has been written. Mr. Friedman says so. To conclude this
sorry business, let me give you just one brief quote from Mr.
Friedman's rules:

"The resident," the document says, "has the individual right to
occupy his bedroom and store his belongings within the bedroom.
Each individual is also permitted to allow other residents to enter
or exit. If the individual wishes to carry on private and personal
conversations with individuals of his or her choice, he or she may
do so. He or she is not obligated to allow entrance to any other
parties, with the exception of the boarding host or any person
assigned as a *supervisory figure*."

I don't know how all of that strikes you—but I, for one, would
starve before I would take training from that organization. Doc's
Motel is not on the roster of places I intend to visit—unless, of
course, I go there to picket (which, incidentally, I may). The
Northeastern Association of the Blind at Albany is exactly the
kind of organization we intend to reform or put out of action.
Perhaps we can teach them something about the other half of
inertia. Things at rest can be put into rapid motion if you apply
enough force and pour on the pressure. We want no strife or confrontation, but we will do what we have to do—and we don't in-

tend to be sent to our rooms after dinner or kept off the premises until 8:31 on Sunday morning or badgered about our "experiential deprivation." We are simply no longer willing to be second-class citizens. We know who we are, and we will never go back.

Bad as all of this is, we must keep it in perspective. The agencies are not (and cannot be) our principal area of focus. Regardless of their delusions of grandeur and their talk about professionalism and expertise, they do not set the tone. They are merely subordinate parts of the larger society. Their attitudes spring—not from knowledge or "professionalism," as they claim—but from the prejudice and misconceptions of the general public. When we have educated that general public and imparted to it enough momentum to send it accelerating toward first-class status for the blind, the agencies will follow.

And the task we face is formidable. Every day there are letters and articles which cross my desk to prove it. The public attitudes about blindness are straight from the Middle Ages—including witchcraft, superstition, and fear of the dark. There is not a single area of human endeavor which is exempt. The ignorance extends from prison to pulpit, from sex to Sunday school, and from airlines to alcoholism. Do you doubt it?

A journalist from Ohio thinks the blind need special fishing facilities, and he writes me about it: "The U.S. Army Corps of Engineers," he says, "has built thousands of dams throughout the country and plans to build hundreds more. Many of these, such as the Ohio River navigational dams, have tailwaters that, for various reasons, attract millions of fish. These areas offer us a unique opportunity to develop fishing for those previously deprived of the experience by lack of sight or mobility."

A locksmith from Wisconsin believes the blind would benefit from specially shaped door knobs (oval and textured, he thinks), and he is willing to design them. These knobs would warn us of stairs and other so-called "danger areas." A pilot from Pennsylvania thinks we should solve the problems we have with airlines by setting up one of our own: segregated and simple—no more trouble, either for us or the sighted public. A woman from Tennessee thinks her blind daughter is unable to play with sighted children: "Lynn is a smart little girl," she writes, "and makes good grades. Since she can't play with other children, she has turned to books. We call her our little book worm."

Then, there is religion. Many people have enlightened attitudes about it, but a great many do not—and when they do not, the blind come in for very special treatment. First, consider the gentle and compassionate. Not long ago the Augsburg Publishing House distributed a bulletin to the Lutheran Churches. It said in part: "To engage in a lively conversation with someone who is blind as if he is not blind is to honor him." I am sure that the sentiment was kindly meant, but not many of us would feel honored. How do you engage in a conversation with someone who is blind as if he is not blind? It is like engaging in a conversation with someone from Missouri as if he were not from Missouri.

But let us leave this subtle stuff and get to the fire and brimstone. Not long ago a woman from Des Moines wrote me and laid it out.

"I have never heard," she said, "of a Christian family having a blind child. The Lord Jesus Christ looks after His people. People are getting so wicked. God is chastising people for not following Him and doing His ways. Fifty years ago I never heard of blind people. Now there are so many. Hundreds of them. Why don't you all get saved? And then the Lord will heal your eyes if you ask Him to—or go have a minister pray for you."

That puts it on the line. Wouldn't you say? Now, I don't know how you read the scriptures, but that is not the way I read them. If the incidents I am relating were isolated happenings, I would not discuss them—but they are not. They occur on a daily basis, with monotonous frequency. They are the typical, the norm. I deal with hundreds and thousands of them in an ongoing pattern.

Here, for instance, is a letter which Ralph Sanders recently got. It is no less condescending than the one I just quoted, but perhaps it is a bit more secular. "Ralph: to think you have been considered a second-class citizen when you have been required to sit in a certain pew disgusts me. Give the *sighted* some consideration. You count your footsteps and note your directions. Your pew was chosen for you to 'hear' the sermon. It is located where you don't stumble over some sleeping person's feet, and if you happen to really get the spirit during the sermon and forget the footsteps and directions, the person who told you where the best place was for you to sit will be able to identify you and give you companionship as soon as possible."

Yet, they tell us there is no discrimination and that we are not a minority. I have said it before, and I will say it again. We want no strife or confrontation, but we will do what we have to do. To the extent required we will meet pressure with pressure and force with force. We are simply no longer willing to be second-class citizens. We know who we are, and we will never go back.

As I have indicated, there are those who base the claim that we are inferior on religion, but there are also those who base it on science. Here is a case in point: "The blind," the writer declares, "can never be truly equal, because they cannot have any combination of senses to equal vision. For example, they cannot view the lives of microscopic organisms or analyze atomic structures by sight. The key to life itself is left unseen by them."

How many sighted people do you suppose this man thinks have ever seen an atom! And what about electrons and protons and neutrons? To quote Isaac Asimov, "As far as the protons and electrons are concerned, the neutrons can go jump in the lake"— which is about the way I feel about the man who wrote that letter.

Pat Barrett is one of the leaders of the National Federation of the Blind of Idaho. Early this year he wrote me about *Games* magazine. *Games* is published by Playboy Press and has adult crossword puzzles. On the cover of the February, 1983, issue were colloquialisms expressed in the form of pictures. "Holy mackerel" was a fish with holes in it. "Blind as a bat" was a bat carrying a cup of pencils. As Pat said in his letter of protest to Playboy, "the idea that blind persons usually sell pencils on the street corner is outdated and shallow."

The notion that we are inferior is not limited to the everyday world. It penetrates every corner of existence. A prison inmate recently wrote to tell me that he would like to do recording for the blind. As he put it, "If I can help someone less fortunate than I am, I would like to do it."

In a slightly different vein a man wrote me last year to ask for my help concerning a friend who was in the penitentiary. "He is serving three years on theft of property charges stemming from several checks written for over $100.00," the man said. "Prison is no place for a blind person, and I was wondering if you could intervene for an early parole."

A man in Minnesota thinks blind alcoholics cannot benefit from regular programs used by the sighted and suggests segregated services. The *Manchester Union Leader* (one of New Hampshire's most prominent newspapers) says that the governor of the state is so bad that only the deaf, the dumb, and the blind could believe he is competent. Hazel Staley (one of the leaders of our North Carolina affiliate) was denied the right this year to take a tour with her church group through Cannon Mills.

Then, there is the battle which Don Capps had last year with the Hyland Therapeutics Division of Travenol Laboratories of Glendale, California. That organization pays people to participate in its plasmapheresis program. This is a high-toned way of saying that blood is taken from the person, plasma and other components are extracted from the blood, and the remaining portion of the blood is then injected back into the person's body. The laboratory took the position that blind persons were not capable of participating. Don Capps disagreed. "Dear Dr. Rodell," he wrote: "I must conclude from your letter that you know virtually nothing about blindness or blind people....Whether you fully realize it or not, your remarks and the policy they imply are blatantly discriminatory....You subtly imply that blind persons will inhibit or disturb the operation's safety.... You also mention that prospective donors are required to read a detailed Informed Consent Form and then sign it, indicating that the form has been read and understood....If you will think for a moment, you must realize that blind patients undergoing surgery or medical treatment must also sign Informed Consent Forms, as well as a variety of other contracts and legal papers in their lifetimes."

Dr. Rodell didn't like it, but he grudgingly began to give ground. He tried to delay. Under date of October 26, 1981, he wrote: "Since the processing of blind donors requires changes to be made in routine procedures, we are obligated to deny participation until such procedural changes are made in an orderly, thoughtful, and constructive manner. I will instruct my staff to initiate appropriate action in that direction. I sympathize with your concerns relative to problems that are faced by blind persons, but strongly object to and do not agree with your conclusion that we are discriminating against them."

Don was not deterred. He kept at it. When Dr. Rodell (in a letter dated March 23, 1982) finally gave in and said he would accept the blind as donors, he got in as many nasty little licks as he could. In his special rules concerning the blind he said: "On the Donor

Master Form, below the area for allergies, print in red BLIND or
LIMITED-VISION so that the donor's needs are immediately
recognized whenever he presents himself."

All of this gibbering insanity (this talk of blindness as an allergy,
of oval shaped door knobs and segregated fishing facilities, of
Christians not losing their sight, and blind persons not being equal
because of their inability to see atoms) could be chalked up to
madness and soon forgotten—except for this: It translates into
cruelty and pain and deprivation. It means lack of opportunity
and denial of employment. It leads to broken lives and shattered
dreams.

A blind man is denied the right to sell insurance because a company official believes his signature would not be valid. A blind
mother in California has her children taken away from her because she is blind, and we have to go to court and the press to
get them back. Sighted parents from Illinois tell of the treatment
they got when their son became blind:

"Our son is sixteen years old," they write, "and went totally blind
in May of 1980, after he was hit on the head in the hall at school.
Family and friends quietly deserted us. Even now we are that
family with the blind child, and our youngest son has been the
target for ridicule and cruelty because of his 'stupid blind
brother.'"

Sally Prentice is one of our members from Connecticut. She went
to a job fair to seek employment. "In October of 1981," she
writes, "I attended a job fair for the handicapped in Stamford,
Connecticut. It was sponsored by the Easter Seal Center. Attending the fair were representatives of many large corporations,
among them Xerox. Xerox was having its own business problems
and was not hiring at the time. They did, however, take it upon
themselves to offer me advice.

"I went to this job fair in good faith, believing that companies
also sent representatives in good faith to recruit qualified disabled
individuals. I went with my resume in hand (and I have reason to
believe it is well done). I dressed in a skirt and blazer, the kind
of thing anyone would be proud to wear to a job interview. I went
alone, carrying my white cane and portfolio.

"I talked with three representatives from the Xerox personnel office at their booth. After a few moments of conversation, they informed me that they were not hiring and offered the following advice. They said that I was too self-assured, too articulate, and too effective. They advised me that it was obvious from my manner that if anyone were to 'give me a job,' I would not be 'grateful,' but would feel that I deserved it! They said that this attitude would hurt me and that I should, therefore, try to appear more humble.

"It had never before occurred to me that anyone could think I wanted them to 'give me a job.' I was applying to be employed, and I know I have ability worth paying for. A gift can be many things. It can be given out of love or it can be given to the helpless and needy out of charity. I did not want love or charity from the Xerox Corporation. I might have deserved a job if I had received fair consideration. It was clear to me that no blind person could receive fair consideration from these people. They had set different standards for blind job applicants than for sighted ones.

"It may seem surprising, but I was thinking of the interviews I had when I was sighted. I got every job I ever interviewed for. I made a good impression, and employers were pleased to offer me a position. I do not believe that I should change my whole life style because I am blind. It's not good for me. It's not good for employers. It's not good for other blind people. We must find a way to make employers accept us for what we are. I was shaken by this experience, but I was not taken in by it. I am continuing to use the same techniques I have always used to seek employment."

Sally Prentice is a sensitive and intelligent human being. Her letter does more than speak of employment. It tells of a need which cries to be met. It talks of a people born to be free—and a spirit loose in the land. It calls the blind to joint action, and points the way to where we must go. It shows us the past and how far we have traveled. It looks to the future and the distance ahead. It demands and exhorts and encourages. It causes us to think of what we have been through the ages, of what we have become as a movement, and of what we certainly and surely intend to be.

Sally Prentice (and the rest of us like her) cannot be checked in our growing momentum. We have found the other half of inertia, and we are generating the force to make our dreams reality. The very fact of our Federation is the strongest proof of what I have said. Yes, we still experience discrimination, denial, and lack of opportunity; but the tide is running the other way. It can be seen in our victories in the sheltered shops; in our radio and television spots, which blanket the nation; and in the jobs which blind people are getting and holding. It can be seen in the hope, the determination, and the zest for the future which blind people now are feeling. It can be seen in the mood and the joy of this convention.

We have learned the truth of the other half of inertia: things in motion tend to remain in motion—and it is as hard to stop something which is moving as it is to start something which is not. We are moving! We are going with a mighty sweep, straight for equality and first-class status—and no force on earth can slow us down or turn us back or change our direction. My brothers and my sisters, the future is ours. Come! March with me in the quickening pace, and we will make it come true!

The Unfriendly Skies

Although the problem of the airlines did not begin in the concluding years of the second Jernigan presidency, it reached its full climax during that period, so this would seem to be the logical place to discuss it.

Throughout the first half century of the organized blind movement, with all its struggles and humiliations, no event has more vividly or cruelly exposed its status as a minority group than that chapter in its history known to blind people everywhere as the episode of "The Unfriendly Skies." Likewise, no event would more plainly illustrate the fierce determination of this movement of blind Americans not to be treated any longer as inferiors or second-class citizens. Indeed, the dramatic confrontations between the airlines and the blind, individually and collectively, carried resonant echoes of another civil rights struggle—in another era when another minority group, seeking to travel freely, held fast to their seats and refused to move to the back of the bus. ("I'm gonna keep my long white cane, and I'm gonna travel on this here plane!" read a 1980 headline in the *Braille Monitor*.)

The humiliation and harassment of blind passengers in "the wild blue yonder" reached its crescendo in the decade of the eighties as individual airlines and the Federal Aviation Administration somewhat modified their policies or shifted positions in response to increasing protests by blind passengers. By 1984 the incidents of interference by airline personnel with the rights of blind travelers were so frequent as to seem almost commonplace. Accordingly one of the principal items on the agenda of the National Federation of the Blind at its convention that year in Phoenix was the issue of "The Unfriendly Skies." Nearly 2,000 blind people participated in a convention symposium on the subject "Air Travel and the Blind: The Law, the Policy, and the Practice." Chaired by National Federation of the Blind President Kenneth Jernigan, the symposium featured a survey of the issue by Marc Maurer (the future Federation President, who was then a lawyer in private practice), and presentations by a representative of the Federal Aviation Administration, J. E. Murdock III, and an official of Delta Airlines, Foy Phillips. These presentations were followed by questions and comments from the floor, which pointed up the differences of interest and attitude dividing the airline industry and the blind consumers of its service. Here is how some of the discussion went:

Karen Edwards of New Mexico said: "On January 31 of this year I boarded an American Airlines flight in Dallas-Fort Worth destined for El Paso, Texas. After I seated myself, I proceeded to place my cane between the seat and the fuselage of the aircraft. As I buckled my seat belt, a flight attendant approached me and attempted to reach over me to retrieve my cane, saying that it would be necessary to have the cane stored during takeoff because of safety reasons. I informed her that the FAA regulations had been updated so that blind people's rights would be protected and that they could carry their canes at all times with them during the flight. I tried to explain the rationale behind the regulations, but to no avail. The flight attendant left and came back with another person, who said that their inflight manual had these regulations that canes and crutches had to be stored in overhead racks or in an enclosed space. In the meantime most of the passengers had already boarded the aircraft, and the attendants were becoming impatient with me; and finally they presented me with an ultimatum. 'Either you give up your cane now, or you'll have to deplane.' I was not a very experienced person on an aircraft. I'd flown a few times, but I was shaken up by this kind of treatment. I thought my only alternative really was to deplane. I think I could kick myself a few times now for doing it, but I did comply. I was stranded in the Dallas-Fort Worth airport, because there weren't any other flights leaving that night. I didn't know anyone in the city, and having come back from the March on Washington, I only had a few dollars left. My ride had come more than fifty miles to wait for me at the El Paso airport, so he was still waiting there. It took me several phone calls to finally reach someone from the Federation who could make contact with someone in Dallas that I could stay with for the night.

"I ended up having to spend more than sixty dollars in cab fare to get to and from his house. The next day I boarded another American Airlines flight and had no trouble at all. I took my cane with me, and I was expecting trouble—but nothing happened. And I was so curious I had to ask what had taken place. I was informed that their supervisor said that if I wanted to make trouble and my cane became dislodged during flight and injured someone else, I would be liable. Mr. Murdock, I'd like to know first of all, do you approve of such treatment of blind passengers? If not, what can you do to remedy these situations? I can assure you it was extremely humiliating to have to deplane with all the passengers looking on, and I'd like to know if you can do anything. What will you do?"

Mr. Murdock replied: "Let me say first on behalf of the industry which I represent as a government official that I personally apologize to you. I think that's atrocious behavior by American. As to the solution, I think that the ultimate solution (the way to deal with it) is to do what Delta is doing—and I will call Mr. Crandall when I get home (who is the chairman of American Airlines), relate to him the facts—if we can get together and go over the details a little more and indicate to him I think that's pathetic behavior."

President Jernigan said: "Mr. Murdock, we got hold of Mr. Crandall—or tried to. We had letters written on this and other incidents. American sent somebody to my office—a local official, not very high in the hierarchy, to talk to me; and I presume to try to soothe me down. I gave him details of many incidents. American has become one of the most insensitive, and has behaved as badly as anybody could. You've heard one incident. I want quickly to give you some others, and please, all of you, make it go rapidly. Brenda Williams, are you at a mike?"

Brenda Williams said: "On June 29 of this year when I was departing from Baltimore, Maryland, on TWA Airlines, I was going through security; and two guards grabbed me and took my cane from me. I tried to explain to them that the cane would not set the system off; but, anyhow, they said that they did not want to hear that. They just held on to me, refused to turn me loose, and snatched the cane away from me.

Charlie Brown then spoke: "The incident that Marc Maurer referred to about not being able to sit on the upper deck of the 747 occurred to somebody who is well-known to a number of us and had nothing to do with safety, and was pure discrimination. You talk about calling this person or that person. What is it that you will or can actually do? You wouldn't like to get that kind of treatment."

President Jernigan: "What really can you do if you decide something is wrong, Mr. Murdock? In all candor if an airline tells you, 'Look, old buddy, we appreciate your views, but get lost.' What can you do? Anything?"

Mr. Murdock: "The statutory power of the FAA, as I tried to spell out in my speech, is to decide whether things are safe and unsafe. If they are correct in their assumption that something is safe, that the procedure is safe (not safer or closer to an absolute) we're powerless."

President Jernigan: "Look, it's safe to grab Brenda Williams and hold her and take her cane by force from her. That's safe. Yes, it is. And it didn't hurt her. Her pride may be bruised some, but she won't die. Can you do anything about that if you find that's true?"

Mr. Murdock: "We do not have enforcement authority in that kind of behavior."

President Jernigan: "So there really isn't anything you can do about it. Is that so?"

Mr. Murdock: "That's right. That's correct, sir."

Joyce Scanlan of Minnesota said: "I'd like to speak to Mr. Murdock. I do a good bit of traveling, and most of it by air; and I can tell you that that's one of the most unpleasant things that I do. That is because of the treatment that I get from airline personnel all down the line—every step of the way on any trip. I have to worry about these folks descending upon me and custodializing me and making demands of me and so forth. I could give you a whole list of different kinds of things that happen—but one incident, I think, is probably outstanding and that happened with United Airlines when a number of us from Minneapolis were on our way to the 1981 National Convention in Baltimore. We had a stop in Cleveland, Ohio. As we approached the next flight to board, we were confronted by this airline ground person who demanded that we pledge to give up our canes before we would be allowed to get on the airline. Can you imagine that? You know, we need our canes for safety and independence, and this individual insisted that we agree to give up our canes (our safety and our independence) in order to ride that plane. Well, of course, we had a long discussion about it, after which he didn't change his mind; and neither did we. I thought I was among the Nazis. This guy stood there and told us how he was only following orders. He said he was following your orders, Mr. Murdock, from FAA. It was an FAA rule that we had to do all this. So we were refused the right to get on the plane. The only option we had was to go the rest of the way by bus—a twelve-hour ride. I can tell you that wasn't pleasant. But I can tell you that the whole thing was totally unnecessary, and it came about just because of the lack of understanding and the rude, insulting behavior by these airline people. Now, do you support that kind of behavior? And what can you do about it? I guess I'd like to know also what will you do about it."

Mr. Murdock: "Well, as Mr. Maurer already indicated, you are allowed to take your cane on board, and it is to be available to you. That's been done for several years. What we can do in the future is really what Delta has done and several other carriers can do, which is to raise the consciousness of employees. United Airlines employs fifty thousand people. Not all of them are even nearly perfect, and it takes a lot of education by that management to get them to be responsive to your needs and to other travelers' needs."

President Jernigan: "Mr. Murdock, we agree that the FAA did do what you say. It says we can have our canes, and yet a lot of the airline personnel come and straight lie to us and say FAA is now requiring us to do this; and then, they get insulted when we ask to see the regulations—won't show us the regulations, and say you did it and it leads to confrontation. Marc Maurer said: "Dr. Jernigan, the regulation that we have been talking about this morning, 14 CFR 121.586, contains a provision which states that if the administrator finds that in the interest of safety or if, in the public interest, it is necessary to change the airline's regulations, then the Federal Aviation Administrator has that power. I wonder if Mr. Murdock can talk to us about what the FAA will do to change these regulations in the public interest—in our interest to have free and equal access to airlines."

Mr. Murdock: "Public interest is, as Mr. Maurer as a lawyer probably knows, defined in the statute which we have; and unfortunately the Congress in 1938 when it wrote the statute and defined the public interest in Section 102 of the Act, which I'm sure Mr. Maurer has read, does not include the access you're talking about. Now, that doesn't mean I won't try to work for it; but statutorily we have very limited powers, and I'm sure Mr. Maurer knows that."

Mike Hingson of California said: "Mr. Murdock, in September of 1980, I reserved passage and paid for a ticket on Pacific Southwest Airlines to fly from Los Angeles to San Francisco. After arriving at the gate, I was told that most passengers had already boarded the aircraft and I would not be able to fly on that aircraft, because of the fact that I needed to be seated in a bulkhead seat. I was not allowed to fly on that aircraft and attempted to fly on the next scheduled flight on PSA from Los Angeles to San Francisco. I boarded the aircraft in plenty of time; was denied access to the aircraft beyond the bulkhead seat; and had discussions with the flight attendants, the captain of the aircraft, and the supervisor of ground personnel about the situation. I was eventually forcibly ejected from the aircraft. My left arm was bent behind my back. My thumb was injured. My watch was broken off my wrist. Subsequent to all that, we found that PSA's policy was, in fact, that a blind person with a dog guide could sit anywhere on the aircraft they wanted to. There were no bulkhead seating requirements. That policy was carefully researched by a representative from Pacific Southwest Airlines and had been made significantly before the time of my incident. Nevertheless, I was thrown off the aircraft in a very humiliating way. I ask essentially the same questions that have been asked before. Does the FAA support that kind of activity? Is there anything that you can do to prevent that kind of activity from happening in the future? And if so, what will you do about it?"

Mr. Murdock responded: "I sound like I'm repeating myself, but the answer to your first question is no. We do not condone or even accept that kind of behavior. Secondly, what can we do about it? I've outlined for you what I think is the way to go about it.

PSA is liable to you for assault and battery, based on their own procedures. You have lots of legal recourse.

For the next four years the struggle of the blind to achieve equality in air transportation continued and escalated. At the convention of the National Federation of the Blind which occurred in Chicago in the summer of 1988 Kenneth Jernigan described in graphic terms the efforts of airline personnel to deprive blind travelers of basic, essential human rights. By that time the arrests had multiplied. The period of hostility which must be endured before any minority may achieve first-class status had come to be a reality for the blind. Progress was often measured in tiny increments, but the spirit of determination was undaunted, and the mood of the delegates was one of irrepressible confidence in the capacity of the blind to succeed in achieving equality.

Even though the right to fly without intimidation, harassment, and arrest was one of the most hard-fought battles of the Federation during the last decade of its first half-century, and even though at the fifty year mark this struggle had not yet been concluded, it welded the Federation into a unified whole and signaled a new direction. The blind had previously been almost universally ignored by much of society. Certain private agencies and governmental programs had been established to serve the blind, but blindness was almost never considered as a significant factor outside these special entities. Without understanding the implications, airline officials promulgated a set of rules for the treatment of the blind. It is not astonishing that these rules discriminated. However, blind people insisted on equal treatment. The organized blind movement declared that the entire airline industry must come to admit that it had no useful information about blindness. Airline officials, said the Federation, must learn to treat blind people as equals, and the teaching would be done by the blind. This is the message Kenneth Jernigan presented in his address delivered on July 6, 1988, at the convention of the National Federation of the Blind in Chicago:

AIR TRAVEL AND THE BLIND
THE STRUGGLE FOR EQUALITY
by Kenneth Jernigan

When we met for our convention last year in Phoenix, the problems which blind persons are having with the airlines were a major topic of discussion. During the past twelve months the discrimination and abuse have grown worse. Today the situation is such that no blind person anywhere in the country can board a plane without fear of harassment, public humiliation, and possibly arrest and bodily injury.

The incidents involve almost every aspect of air travel—insistence that blind passengers pre-board, insistence that we post-board, demands that we demonstrate our capacity to fasten or unfasten a seat belt, requirements that we sit (or not sit) in various sections of the plane, and even attempts to take our small children from us when we are boarding or leaving the aircraft. But the item which has unquestionably created the most heat and publicity centers around exit row seating. It is not that blind passengers have asked to be assigned to these seats but that airline personnel have repeatedly put us there and then insisted (with great public commotion) that we move. In these confrontations the word "safety" is always trotted out and made the excuse for every unreasonable and illegal act which anybody cares to perpetrate.

In May of 1987 Joseph Sontag and Nancy Kruger were arrested on a Simmons Airlines plane. Members of the Simmons flight crew insisted that Sontag and Kruger give up their canes instead of being allowed to keep them at their seats as permitted by federal regulations, and when Sontag and Kruger refused, the police were called. We filed a complaint with the federal Department of Transportation, and although almost a year has passed, nothing has been done about it—and there is no indication that anything will be done about it.

In October of 1987 Bill Meeker (a blind employee of the U. S. Department of Labor's Office of Federal Contract Compliance Programs) was traveling on official business. He experienced what has almost come to be the standard airline treatment. He boarded a Midwest Express airplane for Milwaukee and took his assigned seat. He learned that it was an exit row, and almost immediately thereafter he was confronted and ordered to move, being told that he was violating a federal regulation. When he said that he knew the law, that no such regulation existed, and that he would not move under such circumstances, he was arrested. As is typical in these cases, the charges were later dropped.

Last November Robert Greenberg was refused transportation by American Airlines. He was assigned a seat (an assignment he had not requested) near an emergency exit and was then publicly and abusively ordered to move. When he refused, the flight was canceled and the passengers were told to leave the plane. Everybody but Greenberg was then reboarded. Not only was he not permitted to reboard, but he was also told that he could never ride another American Airlines plane again at any time in the future. He was also denied a refund on his ticket. Once more, we filed a complaint with the federal Department of Transportation—and again nothing has happened.

In January of this year Congressman James A. Traficant introduced H.R. 3883, the Air Travel Rights for Blind Individuals Act. There are now 110 cosponsors of that bill, which is pending in the House of Representatives. In February Senator Ernest F. Hollings introduced the same bill, S. 2098. That bill now has twenty-four senate cosponsors. These bills by Senator Hollings and Congressman Traficant prohibit any special seating restrictions for blind air passengers.

Shortly before last year's convention we got a ruling from the Maryland Attorney General that it was unlawful for airlines to apply special seating restrictions to the blind. The effectiveness of that ruling was proved when Sharon Gold, who was flying from Baltimore to California, showed it to the American Airlines crew who were trying to make her move from her assigned seat before takeoff. She did not move, and she was not arrested or taken off the plane. As you will remember, we brought copies of the Maryland ruling to last year's convention and asked all of you to move quickly and firmly to set up meetings with every state attorney general in the nation, and with the manager of every airport. At that time I said to you: "Show them the Maryland ruling, and remind them that their state has a white cane law, which has the same provisions that the Maryland law has. Get a ruling from your attorney general. Get an agreement from your airport manager. Once you get the ruling, make many copies of it, and see that every blind person who flies has one in his or her pocket."

Today the attorneys general of ten states have made such rulings, and since Chicago is a central transfer point for air travel, the ruling by Illinois Attorney General Neil Hartigan has special significance. Attorney General Hartigan is here today, and not only the blind but all others who believe in the rule of law instead of whim and special privilege owe him a debt of gratitude.

If we were really dealing with a question of safety, no one (blind or sighted) would object, but we are not. Consider, for instance, the opinion of an airline pilot. In an affidavit made in 1985, he says in part:

> I, Jared Haas, being first duly sworn, depose and state: I have been a pilot for many years. I currently fly 727 aircraft, and I have been employed to do so since June of 1974.
>
> I am familiar with a number of blind people, and I am generally familiar with the capacities of the blind. In an emergency situation there are circumstances in which it would be helpful to have an able-bodied blind person seated in an emergency exit row with a sighted person. In those cases in which there is smoke in the cabin, an able-bodied blind person, being used to handling situations without sight, would be able to assist with more facility in the evacuation. An able-bodied blind person would not hinder an emergency evacuation.

That is what a pilot says, and he is not just talking theory. I am aware of at least one case where it was put to the test. Everybody in this organization knows who the late Lawrence (Muzzy) Marcelino was. In the early 1980s he was flying home from Baltimore to California, and when the plane got ready to land in San Francisco, there was a problem. The landing gear wouldn't come down. The plane landed on foam, and the lights went out. An emergency evacuation occurred. It was night, and there was near panic. It was Muzzy who got to the exit and helped the sighted passengers find it.

So far as I have been able to determine, there is not a case on record in which a blind person has been involved in the blocking of an exit or the slowing of traffic in an airline emergency, and as I have just told you, I know of at least one instance (the one involving Muzzy) in which blindness was a positive asset. Yet, the airlines keep prattling to us about safety while, at the same time, knowingly doing things which diminish safety. I refer to the serving of liquor to passengers in exit rows and the practice of permitting excess carry-on luggage to be stowed with passengers at their seats. For that matter, serving liquor at all on a plane in flight probably reduces the safety margins, and so does smoking. I am not saying that these things should be eliminated but only that the treatment of the blind should be seen in perspective.

When I was participating in the regulatory negotiation process last summer to persuade the Department of Transportation to come up with rules to prevent discrimination against the blind in air travel, I personally heard officials of the Flight Standards Administration of the Federal Aviation Administration repeatedly say that they felt there was no safety question involved in blind persons' sitting in exit rows on planes. They said that if they had felt there was a safety question, they would long since have made appropriate regulations. The Flight Standards Administration is that branch of FAA which is responsible for determining questions of safety in air travel. Only when FAA attorneys began to apply pressure did the nature of the comments by Flight Standards officials change. Rather than oppose the airlines, the FAA apparently finds it easier to duck behind the safety issue.

The problem with the arguments being advanced by the FAA and the airlines is that those arguments are based on the false premise that sighted persons (excluding the elderly, the frail, the pregnant, and children) are uniformly capable and alert. The blind person (with whatever limitations and strengths he or she may possess) is compared with the ideal sighted person—a person who in most cases does not exist. Last fall when Senator Dole promised to help deal with the airline problem, he said that it would not occur to anybody to suggest that he should not be allowed to sit in an exit row. Yet (because of his physical handicap), he would not, he said, be able to open the exit.

Several years ago when we were taking both sighted and blind people to the Baltimore airport to make a test evacuation of a World Airways plane, we had to eliminate from consideration many of the sighted that we might have chosen. One had back problems; another had foot problems; and still another had difficulties with heart and blood pressure. In the real world of everyday commercial air travel none of these people would have been excluded from the exit row. Why, then, should the blind be held to a different standard from the sighted?

The truth is that if you consider the scarcity of accidents in proportion to the number of miles which are flown and the relatively small number of blind people who are likely to be on a given flight at a given time, the potential risk would almost be zero—

even if all of the claims by the airlines about the unsafeness of the blind were true. The serving of liquor to passengers, the permitting of smoking, the carry-on luggage, the undetected emotional and physical problems of the average passenger, and a hundred other things are much more real as problems than the minimal risk potentially posed by the blind—plus the fact, as I have already said, that in certain circumstances the blind would have an advantage in helping themselves and others. Nevertheless, the airlines persist in their phony game of "It is all a matter of safety," and the FAA bows to the pressure and seeks to take the easy way out.

In truth and in fact we are not dealing with a safety issue at all but a matter of civil rights, and we simply will not be bullied and intimidated into submission. We will speak to the public and the Congress until we get results. And make no mistake about it—we *will* be heard, and we *will* be heeded.

Two incidents this spring graphically illustrate the unreasonableness of the treatment which we are receiving from the airlines. On a Midway Airlines flight from Baltimore to Des Moines Peggy Pinder (the Second Vice President of the National Federation of the Blind and the President of the National Federation of the Blind of Iowa) was arrested for refusing to move to a seat near an emergency exit; and only a few days later Jim Gashel (our Director of Governmental Affairs) was arrested and removed from a United Airlines flight for almost the exact opposite reason. He was sitting in his assigned seat (one he had not requested) in an exit row and refused to move. In Peggy's case the facts are thoroughly documented and particularly vicious and ugly, not to mention ironic.

She was going home to Iowa from Washington after a day of testifying before the Republican National Committee on ways of increasing participation of blind persons in the mainstream of American life and of eliminating discrimination against the blind. When she arrived at the airport, she was ordered to pre-board the plane. She declined but was told that she would either pre-board or not be permitted to travel. She submitted and did as she was ordered. The plane had open seating, so she went to the back and took a seat in the smoking section. She said she did not need a special briefing, but when she was publicly and abusively ordered to take one, she did it. Then, when she refused to change her seat (which was not in an exit row), she was arrested and bodily carried from the plane in a particularly offensive manner. In her own words:

> The officer lifted me from my seat and physically moved me into the aisle. At this point I stood up and waited for the officer's next action. The officer positioned himself behind me and lifted me from the floor. He accomplished this by reaching his arms around me from behind and placing his hands on my breasts. From this position he lifted me from the floor and carried me off the plane, at one point saying, "Jesus Christ."

> While asserting my legal rights on board the airplane, I maintained a posture of calmness. I found the personal confrontation emotionally upsetting. I was also upset by being physically carried from the plane and having my breasts grasped. I did nothing to provoke this physical abuse and violation of my person; yet, the officer took control over my body.

The fact that Peggy Pinder was arrested for not moving to another seat is confirmed by statements made by Midway officials in the *New York Times*. The *Times* article, dated April 3, 1988, says in part:

> A Midway Airlines spokeswoman, Sandra Allen, said it is the airline's policy to seat all handicapped people in the first row of the plane near where they can be easily evacuated. According to both the spokeswoman and Miss Pinder, after she refused to switch seats the airport police were called to remove her from the plane.

Not only the *New York Times* but also radio, television, and other newspapers throughout the land discussed the matter. Overwhelmingly the editorial comment was favorable to our cause. Apparently Midway thought it had better change its story. Maybe where Peggy was sitting had nothing to do with it. Maybe she had violated a federal regulation in some other way. Maybe she had refused to listen to a briefing about safety features of the airplane. Never mind that sighted passengers are not required to look at the demonstrations which flight attendants give and that Peggy can hear what the flight attendants say during those demonstrations as well as anybody else.

Under date of April 15, 1988, David Armstrong (Midway's Secretary and Vice President for Legal Affairs) wrote a letter to

Matthew Scocozza, Assistant Secretary for Policy and International Affairs of the federal Department of Transportation. He began by very chummily scratching out "Dear Mr. Scocozza" and replacing it with "Dear Mat." The story Mr. Armstrong told was one of virtue, long-suffering patience, and saintly behavior by Midway personnel. Peggy Pinder was not ordered to pre-board but politely asked to do so. She unreasonably declined and then was permitted to board with the regular passengers. In Mr. Armstrong's words: "Ms. Pinder boarded the aircraft with the first passengers on the regular boarding queue."

Mr. Armstrong went on to portray Miss Pinder as unreasonable, petulant, and immature. In his words: "Ms. Pinder indicated that she did not wish to be briefed because she 'had flown several times.'" Mr. Armstrong went on to say that flight attendants continued (at least four more times) to try to get Miss Pinder to consent to be briefed but that she persisted in her refusal—thus violating the federal law, endangering every passenger on the plane, and compelling the pilot to call the police.

This matter of a "briefing" is made to sound like a divine mystery instead of the routine speech and demonstration which it is. Passengers rarely pay attention to it. They do not stop their conversations or put aside their magazines, newspapers, books, earphones, or calculators—especially after their first few flights; and nobody tries to force them or put them under arrest for their inattention.

But let us put this to one side and deal with the more basic question of the contradictory statements. Who is telling the truth—Mr. Armstrong, or Miss Pinder? If Midway's statements to the press at the time of the occurrence are not sufficient, perhaps the police report will suffice. In his official statement the arresting officer said: "I along with Officer M. Young responded to the dispute. We approached the suspect with flight attendant Freitag. Flight attendant Freitag again asked the suspect to listen to the handicap briefing. The suspect at this time listened to the briefing. The flight attendant then asked the suspect to move to the appropriate seat which is in accordance with Midway policy. The suspect refused. Officer Young and myself asked the suspect to move to the other seat. The suspect refused. Officer Young then assisted the suspect off the plane per order of the captain."

Peggy Pinder was, if you can believe it, arrested on charges of "criminal trespass"; but as is typical in these cases, the charges were dropped. Why? Out of kindness? Don't you believe it. Midway was wrong—and they know they were wrong. Sooner or later there had to be a court case to put a stop to this kind of vicious abuse, and this seems about as good a one as any. We hereby serve notice on Midway Airlines that they should ready their defenses and prepare to justify their behavior before a jury. They have tried to forestall the problem by filing a lengthy petition asking the federal Department of Transportation to rule that what they did was in accordance with Department rules and that (take note, Attorney General Hartigan) the states are preempted in the matter by the federal government.

As to the Department of Transportation, it has now indicated that it will (at long last) make the rules which the Air Carrier Access Act of 1986 required it to issue over a year ago. The proposed rules are a classic example of federal double talk and deceit. They say very piously and forthrightly that air carriers may not discriminate against any blind person in seating arrangements except in instances where the Federal Aviation Administration requires it for safety, but they will establish a list of required functions. With a straight face the chief counsel of the Federal Aviation Administration recently told me that no blind person could be excluded from an exit row seat but that if a person could not see, he or she might be excluded from such a seat. It is all a matter of function, he said, not blindness. And these are the people who are writing the rules and protecting the public.

As we consider what to do about our problems with the airlines, I want to remind you of some of the things which have been said about liberty and freedom. "They that give up essential liberty," said Benjamin Franklin, "to obtain a little temporary safety deserve neither liberty nor safety." "Freedom," said Max Stirner, "cannot be granted. It must be taken."

We hear, and we understand. We know what we must do, and we have counted the cost. Is freedom meant only for the sighted, or is it meant for us, too? Is it all right (even praiseworthy) for sighted Americans to resist coercion and fight for their rights but not all right for the blind? Can blind people hope to be free Americans? We gave our answer to that question almost fifty years ago. We formed the National Federation of the Blind—and it is still here, stronger and more active today than ever before in its history.

The battle lines are now drawn on the issue of freedom in air travel for the blind, and we could not withdraw from the fight even if we would. We will either win or lose. We did not seek this fight, but we have no intention of running from it—and we certainly have no intention of being beaten into the ground. We have taken our case to the Congress, and we will also take it to the public and the courts—and we intend to prevail. We want no strife or confrontation, but we will do what we have to do. We are simply no longer willing to be second-class citizens.

Less than a year after this convention appearance Jernigan struck the same theme in testimony before the Subcommittee on Aviation of the Senate Committee on Commerce, Science, and Transportation. He was appearing in his role as Executive Director of the National Federation of the Blind—and as the long-time leader of the organized blind of America. His testimony was a summation of years of experience with the airlines and a distillation of decades of experience with discrimination and prejudice. It is reprinted here as an appropriate commentary on the drama—unfortunately still unfinished—of the organized blind in the unfriendly skies.

Testimony: March 14, 1989

Mr. Chairman, I am Kenneth Jernigan, Executive Director of the National Federation of the Blind. This hearing concerns the Air Travel Rights for Blind Individuals Act (S. 341), introduced by Senator Hollings and others last month. We are pleased, Mr. Chairman, that you and Senator McCain are original co-sponsors of the bill. The Air Travel Rights for Blind Individuals Act is necessary legislation. The blind, who have come here this morning from throughout the United States, can tell you from personal experience that this is so.

Today the situation is such that no blind person in this country can board a plane without fear of harassment, public humiliation, and possibly arrest and bodily injury. I have been riding on airplanes for more than thirty-five years, and I can say from firsthand knowledge that it was not always like this. Prior to the 1970s blind people almost never experienced problems in air travel. We bought our tickets, went to the airport, boarded the plane, traveled to our destination, got off, and went about our business just like everybody else. If one of us wanted help in boarding a plane or making a connection, the assistance was requested and given without a thought.

Then, things began to change. Ironically the problem was caused by the 1973 amendments to the federal Rehabilitation Act and the growing emphasis on affirmative action and prohibition of discrimination against the handicapped. One would have thought these things would have been positive steps, but they were not—at least, not for the blind. Airline personnel and federal regulators didn't become knowledgeable overnight or lose their prejudices just because somebody told them to engage in affirmative action and nondiscrimination. Mostly with respect to air travel the blind didn't need any affirmative action. We were doing just fine as it was. But the airlines and the federal regulators wouldn't have it that way.

They began by lumping all of what they perceived to be the handicapped together—wheelchair users, the blind, the deaf, the quadriplegic, the cerebral palsied, and everybody else—including, very often, small children. Next they catalogued what they believed to be the problems, needs, and characteristics of these groups and then assumed that each item on the list applied to every member of every group they had included. The resulting mythical composite was a monstrosity, totally helpless, totally in need of custody, and totally nonexistent except in the minds of airline officials and federal regulators.

When we objected and insisted on our right to the same freedom of travel that other Americans enjoy, the airline officials and federal regulators reacted with anger and resentment. Since nobody wants to admit to prejudice and ignorance, they said their treatment of us was based on safety. After all, who can fight safety!

In 1986 Congress passed a law specifically prohibiting discrimination on the basis of handicap in air travel, and even that law has now been twisted into the exact opposite of what Congress intended. Today we are faced with a proposed regulation by the Federal Aviation Administration in response to the 1986 law, and it is not by accident that the regulation was published just prior to this hearing. Of course, the regulation is made in the name of safety, but it is not a question of safety at all but of human rights and the freedom to travel. More specifically the regulation prohibits blind persons from sitting in exit rows on airplanes, but much more than exit row seating is involved. If the Air Travel

Rights for Blind Individuals Act is adopted, a signal will be sent to the airlines and the Federal Aviation Administration. If the legislation is not passed and the FAA rule is allowed to stand, a signal will also be sent—that the blind are fair game for any kind of treatment the airlines and the FAA wish to give us, as long as it is done in the name of safety.

If the abuse we are taking from the airlines had anything to do with safety, we wouldn't object, but it doesn't. The truth is that we are being made victims of a misdirected and misapplied federal policy that has irrationally gone wild. Let me give you examples and show you what I mean.

In early February of this year the blind were in Washington to talk to Congress about (among other things) the unreasonable treatment we are receiving from the airlines. Going home from that meeting Verla Kirsch, a blind woman from Iowa, was assaulted and publicly humiliated by Midway Airlines flight personnel. Even though Mrs. Kirsch's white cane was on the floor in the approved FAA manner, the flight attendant (over her protest) took it from her, returning it after takeoff. On the descent into Chicago two Midway flight attendants sneaked up on Mrs. Kirsch, hunkered down, grabbed and lifted her legs, (yes, I literally mean that) and in her words, "yanked the cane from under my feet, bending the cane and nearly breaking it."

On the trip from Chicago to Des Moines (still on Midway) Mrs. Kirsch found that the word had gone ahead of her, but this time she was prepared and refused to be caught off guard. After publicly harassing her, flight personnel found in their own manual that Mrs. Kirsch was in the right and that blind persons (according to Midway's own policies) may keep their canes at their seats. But the damage was done. Imagine the spectacle, the embarrassment, and the public humiliation! This (and not just exit row seating) is what is really at stake with the proposed FAA rule, this hearing, and the passage of the Air Travel Rights for Blind Individuals Act.

Is it safe for blind persons to sit in exit rows? Are there, in fact, times when it would be a plus? Here is the sworn statement of a pilot:

> I, Jared Haas, being first duly sworn, depose and state:
> I have been a pilot for many years. I currently fly 727

aircraft, and I have been employed to do so since June of 1974.

I am familiar with a number of blind people, and I am generally familiar with the capacities of the blind. In an emergency situation there are circumstances in which it would be helpful to have an able-bodied blind person seated in an emergency exit row with a sighted person. In those cases in which there is smoke in the cabin, an able-bodied blind person, being used to handling situations without sight, would be able to assist with more facility in the evacuation. An able-bodied blind person would not hinder an emergency evacuation.

That is what a pilot says, and he is not just talking theory. I am aware of at least one case in which it was put to the test. In the early 1980s Lawrence Marcelino, a member of the board of directors of the National Federation of the Blind, was flying home from Baltimore to California; and when the plane got ready to land in San Francisco, there was a problem. The landing gear wouldn't come down. The plane landed on foam, and the lights went out. An emergency evacuation occurred. It was night, and there was near panic. It was Marcelino who got to the exit and helped the sighted passengers find it.

So far as I have been able to determine, there is not a case on record in which a blind person has been involved in the blocking of an exit or the slowing of traffic in an emergency, and as I have just told you, I know of at least one instance (the one involving Marcelino) in which blindness was a positive asset. Yet, the FAA and the airlines keep prattling to us about safety.

What evidence do they have? I have carefully studied the FAA's proposed rule, and they rely heavily on tests made in 1973 by the Civil Aeromedical Institute (CAMI). The FAA's own words discredit the CAMI tests.

In their report CAMI said that blind passengers caused a slight slowing of the evacuation of an airplane. However, for the critical portion of the tests they did not use real blind persons but sighted persons who pretended to be blind. These sighted pretenders would have no experience in the techniques used by the blind, nor would they have the background to know how to function with skill and speed under blindfold. The real blind persons were not allowed to open the emergency exits or to go down the evacuation slides. It was a matter of safety, done for their own protection. They were allowed to walk from their seats to the emergency exits.

Moreover, the selection of the people who were to be tested is interesting. The sighted (the so-called nonhandicapped) were FAA employees or people recruited through the University of Oklahoma's Office of Research Administration. The blind (not the simulated but the real) were recruited from the Oklahoma League for the Blind, which operates a sheltered workshop. FAA employees are likely to be familiar with aircraft and probably are frequent flyers. In short, the sighted who participated in the test were selected for maximum success.

Federal statistics tell us that a large percentage of sheltered workshop employees are multiply handicapped. In addition, their low wages and limited opportunities make it unlikely that they are regular air travelers. In short, the blind participants (even when they were real and not simulated) were selected for poor performance. I am not suggesting that all of this was consciously done. Nevertheless, it was done. It is not very difficult to see what the results would have been if blind frequent air travelers had been tested against sighted sheltered workshop employees—or, for that matter, against the FAA personnel who were actually used.

But we do not have to speculate about the competence of blind persons to perform in emergency evacuations of airplanes. On April 3, 1985, members of the National Federation of the Blind took part in the evacuation of an airplane at the Baltimore airport. The airplane was real, and the blind persons were real. They were not simulated, and they did not simply walk from their seats to the exits but went all of the way—opening the emergency exit, deploying the evacuation slide, and jumping out. I know, for I was there. I jumped out of that airplane twice.

The test made by the National Federation of the Blind was much more realistic than the one performed by CAMI. We wanted approximately equal numbers of blind and sighted persons so that we could see whether there was any difference in their speed and efficiency. Our first problem was to find competent sighted participants. One person had back problems; another had a bad heart; another had foot problems; and so it went. But in the real world of everyday flying every one of these people would have qualified for exit row seating, without a question or a thought.

We videotaped that test evacuation, and I have the tape here with me today to submit as part of the record. If you run it once through at normal speed, you will see passengers seated in a plane, then moving to the exit, and going down the slide. Mostly you will not be able to tell the difference between the sighted and the blind. They move with equal ease.

When you run the tape slowly (stopping at critical points to study it), what it tells you is damning to the FAA's case. The airline personnel said we should move quickly in a double line, but a flight attendant was standing at the exit partially blocking it. I know, for I had to go around her. In a real emergency I would not have been slowed as I was in the test. I would have simply picked her up, placed her gently but firmly on the slide, and followed her.

Standing beside the flight attendant, you will see a male airline employee. He slows the flow of traffic by peeking around the flight attendant to look down the slide to see whether the blind are making it. The flight attendant also takes time out to peek, further blocking the exit.

You will observe that one of the passengers has a dog guide. He was moving quickly to go down the evacuation slide but was slowed by the male flight attendant, who insisted on trying to tell him how to do it. The female flight attendant kept reaching her arm back into the flow of traffic, presumably trying to help but in reality impeding the evacuation. In one instance it can be seen that she locks elbows with a female evacuee and then grabs at her, causing the passenger to lose balance. Nevertheless, the descent was made safely. As I have already said, in the real world the airline personnel would probably not have had the opportunity to slow the evacuation. In any case the tape speaks for itself.

Last week I had occasion to fly from Denver to Washington, and what happened to me is illustrative of the problem we are facing. Although on many other trips I have been harassed and threatened, nothing like that happened on this one. Everybody was friendly and good-tempered, and I am sure the flight attendants were not even aware that their actions were noteworthy. But you be the judge. Put yourself in my place.

I was traveling with my sighted wife. Shortly after we took our seats, a flight attendant came and very pleasantly and politely said that she must give me a special briefing. She asked me to feel the oxygen mask and then said that she would like me to fasten and unfasten my seat belt for her. Sighted persons are neither required to look at nor listen to briefings, and certainly they are not asked publicly to demonstrate that they are capable of fastening and unfastening a seat belt. Nevertheless, I complied with good temper and without protest.

But, you may say, what's the big deal? Such treatment doesn't really mean that you are being treated like a child, or thought of as one. Perhaps—but a few minutes later a second flight attendant (again, a most pleasant individual) came to my seat and said to my wife: "Has he had his special briefing yet?"

I smiled and replied: "Yes, he has had his briefing."

The flight attendant gave a small embarrassed laugh, and the rest of the flight proceeded without incident—but what I have just told you has far more significance than superficial appearance would indicate. It translates into a general public feeling that the blind are incompetent and unable to compete. Put to one side the damage it does to the self-image of the blind who are still in doubt of their own worth—or, for that matter, what it would do to any of us, whether blind or sighted—especially, if the occurrence is not isolated but part of an everyday pattern.

This simple incident which seems so innocent and unimportant is the very essence of our problem. It translates into unemployment, lack of acceptance, low self-esteem, and second-class citizenship. Is it all right (even praiseworthy) for other Americans to insist on their rights but not all right for the blind to do it? Are human dignity and freedom meant for everybody else in this country but not for the blind? Is the American dream exclusively the property of the sighted—or is it meant for the blind, too? I believe it is meant for all of us, and I think Congress and the public think so, too. I believe that as you learn the facts, you will not permit the airlines and the FAA to continue what they are doing to the blind.

Yes, we are talking about safety, but not the kind contemplated by the FAA in its discriminatory rule. That is why we are asking for your help. That is why we are asking you to pass (and pass quickly) the Air Travel Rights for Blind Individuals Act.

To Braille or Not to Braille

The decade of the eighties found the organized blind facing a new and complex issue—one which brought the movement into conflict and debate with some of the educators and teachers of blind children. The issue was the use of Braille in the school curriculum, particularly in connection with students having some residual vision. On one side of the debate were those educators who regarded Braille as generally obsolete and not competitive with other reading methods; on the other side were some of the educators and the majority of blind people who regarded Braille as the essential means to literacy for blind persons.

The intensity of the debate over the teaching of Braille during this decade might seem puzzling to those unfamiliar with the subject and without the personal associations of memory and tradition which it calls up for many who are blind. As a preface to more systematic examination of the issue, here is an impressionistic narrative of one blind youth's encounter with the world of Braille, books, and boarding schools. Written by Kenneth Jernigan, the article appeared in the June-July, 1987, *Braille Monitor*:

OF BRAILLE AND MEMORIES AND THE *MATILDA ZIEGLER*
by Kenneth Jernigan

When I was a boy growing up in Tennessee, Braille was hard to come by. At the Tennessee School for the Blind (where I spent nine months of each year) Braille was rationed. In the first grade we were allowed to read a book only during certain hours of the day, and we were not permitted to take books to our rooms at night or on weekends. Looking back, I suppose the school didn't have many books, and they probably thought (perhaps correctly) that those they did have would be used more as missiles than instruments of learning if they let us take them out. When we advanced to the second grade, we were allowed (yes, allowed) to come down for thirty minutes each night to study hall. This was what "big boys" did. In the first grade we had been ignominiously sent to bed at seven o'clock while our elders (the second and third graders and those beyond) were permitted to go to that mysterious place called study hall. The first graders (the "little boys") had no such status or privilege.

When we got to the third grade, we were still not permitted to take books to our rooms, but we were allowed to increase our study hall time. We could actually spend a whole hour at it each night Monday through Friday. It was the pinnacle of status for the primary grades.

When we got to the "intermediate" department (the fourth, fifth, and sixth grades) we were really "growing up," and our status and prestige increased accordingly. We were allowed (I use the word advisedly—"allowed," not "forced") to go for an hour each night Monday through Friday to study hall, and during that time we could read books and magazines to our hearts' content. True, the choice was not great—but such as there was, we could read it. Of course, we could not take books to our rooms during the week, but on Friday night each boy (I presume the girls had the same privilege) could take one Braille volume to his room for the weekend.

Before I go further, perhaps I had better explain that comment about the girls. The girls sat on one side of the room, and the boys sat on the other; and woe to the member of one sex who tried to speak or write notes to a member of the other. Girls, like Braille books, were difficult to get at—and all the more desirable for the imagining. But back to the main thread.

As I say, each boy in the "intermediate" department could check out one Braille volume on Friday night. Now, as every good Braille reader knows, Braille is bulkier than print; and at least four or five Braille volumes (sometimes more) are required to make a book. It is also a matter of common knowledge that people in general and boys in particular (yes, and maybe girls, too) are constantly on the lookout to "beat the system." What system? Any system.

So on Friday nights we boys formed what would today be called a consortium. One of us would check out volume one of a book; the next, volume two; the next, volume three; et cetera. With our treasures hugged to our bosoms we would head to our rooms and begin reading. If you got volume three (the middle of the book), that's where you started. You would get to the beginning by and by.

Now, girls and Braille books were not the only items that were strictly regulated in the environment I am describing. The hours of the day and night fell into the same category. Study hall ended at 8:00, and you were expected to be in your room and in bed by 9:40, the time when the "silence bell" rang. You were also expected to be trying to go to sleep, not reading.

But as I have said, people like to beat the system; and to us boys, starved for reading during the week, the hours between Friday night and Monday morning were not to be wasted. (Incidentally, I should say here that there were usually no radios around and that we were strictly forbidden—on pain of expulsion, and God knows what else—to leave the campus except for a brief period on Saturday afternoon—after we got big enough, that is, and assuming we had no violations on our record which required erasure by penalty.) In other words the campus of the Tennessee School for the Blind was what one might call a closed ecology. We found our entertainment where we could.

Well, back to Friday night and the problem of the books. Rules are rules, but Braille can be read under the cover as well as anywhere else; and when the lights are out and the sounds of approaching footsteps are easy to detect, it is virtually impossible to prohibit reading and make the prohibition stick. The night watchman was regular in his rounds and methodical in his movements. He came through the halls every sixty minutes on the hour, and we could tell the time by his measured tread. (I suppose I need not add that we had no clocks or watches.)

After the watchman had left our vicinity, we would meet in the bathroom (there was one for all twenty-six of us) and discuss what we had been reading. We also used the occasion to keep ourselves awake and exchange Braille volumes as we finished them. It made for an interesting way to read a book, but we got there—and instead of feeling deprived or abused, we felt elated. We were beating the system; we had books to read, something the little boys didn't have; and we were engaged in joint clandestine activity. Sometimes as the night advanced, one of us would go to sleep and fail to keep the hourly rendezvous, but these were minor aberrations—and the weekend was only beginning.

After breakfast on Saturday mornings most of us (not all) would continue reading—usually aloud in a group. We kept at it as long as we could, nodding off when we couldn't take it any more. Then, we went at it again. Let me be clear. I am talking about a general pattern, not a rigid routine. It did not happen every weekend, and even when it did, the pace was not uniform or the schedule precise. We took time for such pleasantries as running, playing, and occasional rock fights. We also engaged in certain organized games, and as we grew older, we occasionally slipped off campus at night and prowled the town. Nevertheless, the reading pattern was a dominant theme.

Time, of course, is inexorable; and the day inevitably came when we outgrew the intermediate department and advanced to "high school"—seventh through twelfth grades. Again, it meant a change in status—a change in everything, of course, but especially reading. Not only could we come to study hall for an hour each night Monday through Friday and take a Braille volume to our room during weekends, but we could also check out Braille books whenever we liked, and (within reason) we could take as many as we wanted.

Let me now go back once more to the early childhood years. Before I was six, I had an isolated existence. My mother and father, my older brother, and I lived on a farm about fifty miles out of Nashville. We had no radio, no telephone, and no substantial contact with anybody except our immediate neighbors. My father had very little formal education, and my mother had left school just prior to graduating from the eighth grade. Books were not an important part of our family routine. Most of the time we did not have a newspaper. There were two reasons: Our orientation was not toward reading, and money was scarce. It was the early thirties. Hogs (when we had any) brought two cents a pound; and anything else we had to sell was priced proportionately.

I did a lot of thinking in those preschool days, and every time I could, I got somebody to read to me. Read what? Anything—anything I could get. I would nag and pester anybody I could find to read me anything that was available—the Bible, an agriculture yearbook, a part of a newspaper, or the *Sears Roebuck Catalog.* It didn't matter. Reading was magic. It opened up new worlds.

I remember the joy—a joy which almost amounted to reverence and awe—which I felt during those times I was allowed to visit an aunt who had books in her home. It was from her daughter (my cousin) that I first heard the fairy stories from *The Book of Knowledge*, a treasure which many of today's children have unfortunately missed. My cousin loved to read and was long-suffering and kind, but I know that I tried her patience with my insatiable appetite. It was not possible for me to get enough, and I always dreaded going home, finding every excuse I could to stay as long as my parents would let me. I loved my aunt; I was fascinated by the radio she had; and I delighted in her superb cooking—but the key attraction was the reading. My aunt is long since dead, and of course I never told her. For that matter, maybe I never really sorted it out in my own mind, but there it was—no doubt about it.

As I have already said, I started school at six—and when I say six, I mean six. As you might imagine, I wanted to go as soon as I could, and I made no secret about it. I was six in November of 1932. However, school started in September, and six meant six. I was not allowed to begin until the next quarter—January of 1933.

You can understand that after I had been in school for a few weeks, I contemplated with mixed feelings the summer vacation which would be coming. I loved my family, but I had been away from home and found stimulation and new experiences. I did not look forward to three months of renewed confinement in the four-room farm house with nothing to do.

Then, I learned that I was going to be sent a Braille magazine during the summer months. Each month's issue was sixty Braille pages. I would get one in June, one in July, and one in August. What joy! I was six, but I had learned what boredom meant—and I had also learned to plan. So I rationed the Braille and read two pages each day. This gave me something new for tomorrow. Of course, I went back and read and re-read it again, but the two new pages were always there for tomorrow.

As the school years came and went I got other magazines, learned about the Library of Congress Braille and talking book collection, and got a talking book machine. By the time I was in the seventh grade I was receiving a number of Braille magazines and ordering books from three separate regional libraries during the summer. Often I would read twenty hours a day—not every day, of course, but often. I read *Gone With the Wind, War and Peace,* Zane Grey, Rafael Sabatini, James Oliver Curwood, and hundreds of others. I read whatever the libraries sent me, every word of it; and I often took notes. By then it was clear to me that books would be my release from the prison of the farm and inactivity. It was also clear to me that college was part of that program and that somehow I was going to get there. But it was not just escape from confinement or hope for a broader horizon or something to be gained. It was also a deep, ingrained love of reading.

The background I have described conditioned me. I did not feel about reading the way I see most people viewing it today. Many of today's children seem to have the attitude that they are "forced," not "permitted," to go to school—that they are "required," not "given the privilege and honor," to study. They are inundated with reading matter. It is not scarce but a veritable clutter, not something to strive for but to take for granted. I don't want children or the general public to be deprived of reading matter, but I sometimes think that a scald is as bad as a freeze. Is it worse to be deprived of books until you feel starved for them or to be so overwhelmed with them that you become blasé about it? I don't know, and I don't know that it will do me any good to speculate. All I know is that I not only delight in reading but believe it to be a much neglected joy and a principal passport to success, perspective, civilization, and possibly the survival of the species. I am of that group which deplores the illiteracy which characterizes much of our society and distinguishes many of its would-be leaders and role models. I am extremely glad I have had the opportunity and incentive to read as broadly as I have, and I believe my life is so much better for the experience that it borders on the difference between living and existence.

It is interesting to contemplate how a particular train of thought can be set in motion. The memories and reflections I have been recounting were called to mind by a press release which recently crossed my desk. I want to share it with you and then make a few comments about it. Here it is:

Free Magazine For Blind Completes 80 Years

New York, March, 1987—With its March issue, The *Matilda Ziegler Magazine for the Blind* completes eighty years as a free general interest magazine for blind and visually impaired persons. The *Ziegler*, as it is affectionately known by readers, was founded in 1907 by Electa Matilda Ziegler, wealthy widow of William Ziegler, founder of the Royal Baking Powder Company. The *Ziegler* has no print edition—its ten issues per year are in Braille and on recorded flexible disc.

Since one of the main difficulties faced by blind people is lack of easy access to the thousands of print magazines and books published every year, the *Ziegler* gives its readers an informative, stimulating, and entertaining selection from these print materials. It reprints articles from newspapers and magazines, and includes short stories, poetry, and humor. While the *Ziegler* is not *about* blindness, it does devote space to news and information of special interest to people with vision problems. In "Reader's Forum," readers have an opportunity to "sound off" on any subject and to discuss solutions to problems caused by lack of, or poor, sight. The *Ziegler's* highly popular "Pen Pals" section enables blind and visually impaired persons worldwide to get in touch.

It was a highly improbable sequence of events that led to the founding of the *Ziegler*. In 1906 Walter Holmes, a Tennessee newspaperman, was on a business trip to New York City, when he came across a newspaper description of a large bequest to charity. Irritated by the fact that no money was left to benefit blind people, he dashed off a note to the paper, pointing out how desperately blind people needed books that they could read with their fingers. Few books, he noted, were transcribed into a form that could be read by touch, and those few were far too expensive. The then popular *Ben Hur,* for example, cost only $1 in print, but an embossed version cost all of $30!

Walter Holmes' letter was published, and he received a response from one E. M. Ziegler, who asked to meet him. E. M. Ziegler turned out to be a woman, Electa Matilda Ziegler, and at their meeting she agreed to pay for a magazine for the blind, if Holmes would run it. To this serendipitous meeting the *Ziegler Magazine* traces its origins. Why was Mrs. Ziegler so interested in blind people? What was Mr. Holmes' interest? She had a blind son, and he had a blind brother.

True to her word, Mrs. Ziegler paid the expenses (some $20,000 per year) from her own pocket until 1928, when she set up an endowment. It is this carefully invested fund that has underwritten the magazine ever since.

The *Ziegler's* first issue in March, 1907, was greeted with enormous enthusiasm by blind and sighted people alike. Blind and deaf Helen Keller, then twenty-six years old, wrote to Mrs. Ziegler, "I must send you my glad thanks for the pleasure and the facilities which you have placed within our reach. I have waited many years for such a magazine."

Mark Twain wrote: "I think this is one of the noblest benefactions that has been conferred upon a worthy object by any purse during the long stretch of my seventy-one years."

Eighty years later readers are still full of praise and gratitude for the magazine. One old lady, who has been a reader since that first issue, recently asked to have her subscription changed from Braille to recorded disc since, at her advanced age, she could no longer read Braille as quickly as she would like, but she did not want to miss a single issue.

To mark the completion of eighty years, the *Ziegler* asked its readers to submit essays to a contest on the subject, "An Unforgettable Journey." First prize was won by a reader in Jerusalem, Siranoosh A. Ketchejian, who described a 1909 journey as a small girl from her home in Armenia to a school for blind children in Jerusalem.

The second prize went to Virginia A. Reagan of Rogersville, Missouri. Her essay describes her continuing journey toward independence despite total blindness and orthopedic problems that oblige her to use a wheelchair. She points out, however, that her biggest battles were with the discouraging attitudes of doctors and others who believed she would never be capable of living independently.

James R. Stell of Glasgow, Kentucky, won third prize for his vivid recollection of a journey he made to New York City thirty years ago with the band of the Alabama School for the Blind. The band played at an international Lions convention.

By printing this press release I do not mean to imply that the *Matilda Ziegler Magazine* is (or ever was) the greatest thing since sliced bread or even that I think it is unusually well done. I have not read or even seen a copy of it for years, and I have often heard it snidely called the "Lydia Pinkham" magazine—an epithet which may elude some of the members of the younger generation. Be that as it may, the *Ziegler* was one of those early Braille magazines that I had the opportunity to get my hands on when I was searching for anything that I could find to read. Along with the *Search Light*, the *Weekly*, the *Children's Friend*, *Discovery*, the *Reader's Digest*, and a host of other Braille magazines, it provided me with both pleasure and information at a time when I most urgently needed them—and it was one of the first. I must confess that the *Ziegler* was not my favorite, but I read it—and I am not putting it down.

It was one of the early Braille magazines, which was freely made available to anybody who requested it, and I am sure that through the years it has brought countless hours of pleasure to a great many people. Because of the progress of the National Library Service for the Blind and Physically Handicapped, the advent of the computer, the Braille and recorded magazines now available, the number of volunteer transcribers who are willing to produce material, and the accumulation of Braille and recorded books scattered throughout the country, the blind children and adults of today will hopefully never have to repeat the experiences I have described. Yet, the hunger for Braille, the isolation and loneliness, and the early magazines like the *Ziegler* are an important part of our heritage as blind people—a heritage we should not forget and from which we should continue to profit and learn.

The explosive growth of new procedures and technology, notably in the area of communication skills, caused the *Braille Monitor* to devote an entire issue (May, 1982) to the subject of Braille and its alternatives. The lead article was a comprehensive summary and assessment by the NFB's President, which explained much of the controversy and raised many of the issues which were to gain attention during the decade:

BRAILLE: CHANGING ATTITUDES,
CHANGING TECHNOLOGY
by Kenneth Jernigan

On rare occasions we devote an entire issue of the *Monitor* to a single topic. That is what we are doing in the present instance. The topic is Braille. Braille is so central in the lives of the blind and so much is happening in the way of new attitudes and new technology that an overview is needed—a bringing together of facts, an attempt at perspective.

Before the time of Louis Braille, blind persons had very little opportunity to read at all. Of course, because of the low literacy rate, many of the sighted were in the same boat. Nevertheless, the blind were at a distinct disadvantage. Through the years there had been attempts to develop this or that sort of tactile system, but it was Louis Braille who made the breakthrough in 1825.

However, his invention was only a beginning. Throughout the remainder of the nineteenth century Braille was the center of controversy and opposing views. Different systems and configurations of dots to form the alphabet coexisted side by side, and each had its advocates. The disputes continued into the twentieth century, and, for that matter, are still taking place. Even now, the Braille Authority of North America is debating new rules and contemplating changes.

When I entered the Tennessee School for the Blind as a boy of six in the early 1930s, I was exposed to New York Point, American Braille, Grade One, Grade One and One-Half, Grade Two, Moon Type, and some sort of unfathomable raised print, the name of which I either never heard or soon forgot. I hasten to add that nobody even attempted to teach me all of these various systems. I was merely exposed to them and told of their numerous virtues or shortcomings by whichever advocate happened to be speaking at the moment. In the first grade I was taught (or, at least, an attempt was made in that direction) both to read and write Grade One Braille. The writing was done on a board slate, and I have always been glad that I learned the use of the slate before being introduced to the Brailler (the equivalent of a typewriter). Incidentally, although I can now read Braille with perfect ease at several hundred words a minute and can write it with speed and accuracy on slate or Brailler, I flunked both Braille reading and Braille writing in the first grade, necessitating going through the first grade again the following year. Yes, it was a different world.

As I progressed through high school and college, I became acquainted with the British system of writing Braille, which had a number of differences from what I was accustomed to. For instance, the first time I realized that the British used the letters JC for Jesus Christ, I thought it a bit familiar and not at all in keeping with what my history books had taught me about the conservative and stodgy nature of the inhabitants of that part of the world.

Even so, by the early 1940s everybody who could read Braille very well at all could get along with almost anything that was floating around. New York Point was not being produced anymore, and American Braille was about in the same situation. Moon Type (which was a series of curved lines invented by an Englishman named Dr. Moon for the purpose of making it easier for older blind persons to read) was almost nonexistent, a few volumes being kept at most of the residential schools for the blind as conversation pieces and to impress visitors.

In the early 1940s most blind children went to residential schools, and Braille was pretty much the standard medium for teaching. Large print (or sightsaving material—a term with curious connotations since it does nothing of the sort) was discussed now and again, but mostly it was still waiting in the wings. Students who were blind enough to go to the residential school but who had some remaining eyesight ("partials" they were called—and some of them were quite high "partials") learned to read Braille with their eyes, and they stubbornly and persistently took every opportunity to do it despite the scoldings and objections of their teachers. In fact, there was quite an art to the rapid reading of Braille visually. As I understand it, the dots were not read directly. Instead, the page was so held that the dots cast shadows, and these were read. Be that as it may, a constant state of war always seemed to exist between the teachers and the "partials," doubtless honing wits of both groups and building character into the bargain. The teachers developed a large cloth apron-type affair (known as a "blindfold," which it wasn't) and insisted that the partials wear it while reading or writing Braille. A loop fitted over the neck and the cloth "blindfold" was draped over the Braille material. The student was expected to put his or her hands underneath the cloth and do the reading or writing. The "partials" countered by trying to hold the top of the "blindfold" away from the body and peeking under it. Of course, when the teacher's back was turned, the "blindfold" was pushed aside altogether.

In some of the schools the teachers stepped up the warfare by turning off all of the lights in the night study hall sessions—leaving sighted teachers (most of them were sighted at that time), "partials," and the totally blind all in the dark together. Of course, in such a situation the totally blind were at a considerable advantage, and the sighted teachers (having usually learned very few if any of the techniques of blindness) labored under a severe handicap. The "partials" were somewhere between, depending on how well they had learned to function as blind people.

I was called on to supervise such a night study hall in the late forties and early fifties when I was a teacher of English at the Tennessee School for the Blind, and the maintenance of discipline posed unique problems. It takes a bit of practice and skill to follow the trajectory of a thrown object back to its point of origin, but the science can be mastered—not to mention which the teacher tends to have certain inherent advantages in such warfare. At least, such was the case in the climate of discipline and practice which prevailed at that particular time in our history. Let me simply say that the outcome was not always certain and that the situation was turbulent, but it provided a certain amount of stimulation and was both challenging and do-able.

In the meantime another element was beginning to come into play, one that would have a far-reaching impact on the future of Braille. In the 1930s the talking book machine began to be increasingly available and popular. At first its impact on the teaching of Braille (especially, in the residential schools—and that is where most of the teaching was done) was minimal. Because of the politics of the federal legislation authorizing library services for the blind, talking books, which were a principal component of the library services, were not supposed to be available to children. The talking book machines and records were not used in most of the residential schools until after the mid-forties and even then at a very slowly accelerating pace.

In view of the fact that blind adults (people somewhere in the neighborhood of sixteen or thereabouts) were entitled to borrow from the libraries around the country; in view of the fact that the definition of the word "adult," as well as the way of figuring one's age can be variously interpreted, depending upon the exigencies of the situation; and in view of the further fact that many of the libraries were in states far removed from their borrowers and could do little to test the veracity of the information provided to them by those borrowers, talking book machines and records began to make their appearance in the schools with increasing frequency.

However, they were not generally used in the classrooms or the school study halls but in the bedrooms of the students and in their homes during vacations. The early talking book machines were heavy and cumbersome, and the records would only play about fifteen minutes to the side. *War and Peace*, for instance, came in eight large containers comprising 160 records, and *Gone With The Wind* was on 80 records. Nevertheless, the quality of the reading was excellent, and one could do other things with the hands while listening. Before the advent of the talking book, Braille was the only "game in town." If you were blind and if you wanted to read, you learned Braille, but now there was an alternative.

When the wave of retrolental fibroplasia spread throughout the population in the forties and fifties, leaving thousands of children blind, the residential schools could not have handled (even if they had wanted to) the massive influx of students. Before retrolental fibroplasia, most state residential schools for the blind had somewhere between one hundred and two hundred students. Now, in the late forties and fifties, the number of blind children needing education was several times that much in many of the states. There were not enough trained teachers to meet the need, and the American Foundation for the Blind got into the act, helping promote teacher-training courses in a number of colleges and universities. Many felt that the American Foundation added a negative element to the problem by its constant discussion of which was the better setting for educating the blind child, the residential school or the local public school. Of course, the debate was largely meaningless since the residential schools could not possibly have met all of the need and since many of the local public schools were also unable to do an adequate and meaningful job. Be this as it may, the American Foundation filled a gap which no one else was prepared to fill and, thereby, performed a positive service. The philosophy was usually not the best, and there were often power plays; but the alternative to the American Foundation's stepping into the breach would undoubtedly have been that many blind children who got at least a fair degree of education would likely have had none at all.

In the pre-retrolental fibroplasia days, when the great majority of blind children and most of the newly blind adults who received instruction in Braille got it in the residential schools, classes were relatively small, and a good deal of individual attention could be given. Moreover, most (not all but most) of the Braille teachers were really expert at Braille. They knew Braille, and they could read and write it.

With the new wave of blind children coming into the schools, there were bound to be changes—and not only changes but also a loss of quality in certain areas—the kind of thing which always characterizes "crash programs." Many of the new teachers were not expert in Braille, and they were not as sure of its centrality and necessity as their predecessors had been.

The talking book machines were now lighter and smaller than they had been, and the records were beginning to be lighter and longer playing. As compared with the heavy thirty-three and one-third rpm, fifteen minutes to the side, disc of the 1930s, for instance, today's talking book record is a paper thin, lightweight, floppy disc, which runs at eight and one-third rpm and plays an hour to the side. Other things have also come to compete with Braille. First came the open reel tape, and today it is the cassette. The cassette player and the books recorded on cassette are much more portable and easier to get from place to place than Braille. In the schools today talking books and cassettes are often used early on, and this necessarily means less reliance on Braille.

Then, there is the matter of large print (the "sightsaving" material of old) and various electronic and manually operated magnification systems for blind children who have some remaining residual vision. This is not merely a matter of new facts and techniques but often of philosophy as well. I have sometimes told the story of going into a classroom and having a teacher say to me in the presence of two young children, one totally blind and one with some remaining vision, "This little girl can read print. This little girl has to read Braille." Of course, the words "can" and "has to" were the key to the matter. Undoubtedly without consciously knowing that she was doing it or meaning to do it, the teacher was "putting down" Braille and making it less attractive and pleasant to read. She may have been helping to cause the totally blind child to be a poor Braille reader, or virtually a non-Braille reader. She was teaching both children that it is not respectable to be blind and that, if you are blind, you cannot expect to compete on terms of equality. After all, the girl with some residual vision had only about ten percent of her eyesight, and if you are capable in proportion to your ability to see, ten percent of a person is not much.

This is not to say that some of the magnification devices and other visual aids have not been of help to those with residual vision, for they have. Rather, it is to make the obvious point that such devices have led (at least, to some degree) to a de-emphasis of Braille. If visual aids are seen in context and used with reason, they can be positive (whether for children or adults), but if their use is pushed to the extreme (as has been the case in some of the schools and adult training programs), the results can be very nearly disasters. For example, I know a number of people who wanted to learn Braille when they were children in school and were not permitted to do it, being told that the "normal" thing to do was to read print and use their remaining vision. They were compelled to do this despite the fact that their prognosis was for continuing deterioration of sight and despite the fact that their vision was so poor that they could not read print (even large print) with comfort and fluency. Many of those people are now totally blind, and no small number of them deeply resent the way they were treated. They are either poor Braille readers or have had to expend a great deal of time and effort to learn the skills they could easily have been taught in school.

There are other developments which have impacted upon Braille—the thermoform machine, for instance. When it was announced, the thermoform seemed such a positive thing. It allowed an individual to take a regular sheet of Braille, place it on a platform, and draw a piece of heated, thin plastic down over it to reproduce the Braille dots. It was a veritable copy machine for the blind. It made it possible to duplicate single copies of individual Braille paper, or for that matter, short-run multiple copies. If it had been used for program agendas, throw away information, or making copies of Braille letters—in other words if it had been used as print copy machines are used, it would have been an unmixed blessing. It would have strengthened the use of Braille.

But such was not to be the case. Over the years a great many books have been hand-transcribed by sighted volunteers. More and more, with the advent of the thermoform machine, the original paper Braille copy of the book has been kept on file by the transcribing group or the library as a "master," and thermoform duplicates have been sent out to fill requests. In my opinion (and that opinion is shared by most Braille readers with whom I talk) this has done a great deal to discourage the use of Braille.

For my part I find prolonged reading of thermoform extremely unpleasant. The plastic sheets tend to stick to the hands, and the fingers tend to be irritated after a time. Moreover, I cannot read thermoform nearly as rapidly as I can read Braille produced on paper. Certainly I cannot read it as pleasantly.

I suspect that if print were so produced that it hurt the eyes of sighted people who read it, far less reading would be done by the sighted than is the case today. I further suggest that the alternative to print (television) would—assuming that such is possible—be even more popular than it is today. This is not to blame anyone, nor is it to shrug off the problems (economic and otherwise). It is simply to state facts as I see them and to hope that we can find solutions.

The last few years have brought still other developments in technology. There is the Kurzweil Reading Machine, which scans a print page and translates it into spoken words. This machine has achieved some positive results, but it still has a ways to go to fulfill the initial hopes which people had for it. It is too costly for the individual blind person to afford; it still has certain technical problems; it is not easily portable; and it is not clear whether enough capital will continue to be put into its development to make it an ongoing major factor in the total mix of reading for the blind.

Then, there is the Optacon—a scanning system which translates what the camera sees on the printed page into a pattern of vibrating, closely packed reeds which can be felt with one finger. Again, there have been certain positive results with the Optacon, but there are also severe limitations—and when exaggerated claims are made concerning its usefulness and performance, the minuses quickly outstrip the plusses. By and large, reading with the Optacon is quite slow, and a great deal of training is required for its skillful use. Moreover, expense is again a factor, but not as much as in the case of the Kurzweil machine.

By no means all (but a great deal) of the Braille produced in this country is purchased through the program of the National Library Service for the Blind and Physically Handicapped of the Library of Congress (NLS). The same is true of recorded and other reading material available to the blind. Thus, NLS has a major voice in determining what kind of reading material will be available to the blind, and in what form that reading material will be.

In the early days of the library program the service was limited to the blind, and Braille received a major emphasis (incidentally, the restriction against serving blind children has, to the satisfaction of everybody, long since been abolished). In the 1960s pressure began to be brought to open up the library service for the blind to other physically handicapped groups. The NLS was not opposed to this because it would broaden its mission and, presumably, strengthen its power base. Further, since the other groups of the handicapped have never been as strongly organized as the blind, it would presumably water down the political impact on policy matters by making us a smaller part of the total constituency. To say that these political considerations undoubtedly figured in the Library's policy decision is not to say that the Library may not also have felt that the other groups needed service and that NLS could fill that need.

When the legislation to add other groups to the library service was introduced, we opposed. We said that we favored providing library service to the other groups but that we felt it should be done through another division of the Library of Congress. We said that since these groups did not use Braille, their inclusion would mean a proportionately smaller amount of resources devoted to the production of Braille. We further expressed concerns that all phases of service to the blind would suffer by adding the larger constituency as opposed to establishing for it a separate program. Nevertheless, when the legislation was introduced into the next session of Congress, we agreed to its passage provided safeguards could be established and assurances could be given that our concerns could be satisfied.

Within recent years there has seemed to come a recognition that Braille must again receive an increased emphasis. Valuable as the other means of communication may be, there are certain areas in which there is simply no substitute for Braille for the blind person. Taking notes and writing can be done more efficiently in Braille than by recording—assuming, of course, that the person using the Braille is skilled. Intensive study is more easily done by Braille than from a recording, and there is no adequate substitute for Braille in delivering a public speech, verbatim or from notes. There is also the pleasure of reading aloud to others or to oneself, but this admittedly gets into the realm of the subjective. However, it is highly doubtful whether the majority of the sighted population would consider for a moment giving up all print in favor of recorded material—or, even for that matter, television.

As we move into this present decade, there are several hopeful signs. In the first place let it be said that the NLS and all other groups involved with the blind would like (if a feasible way can be found to do it) to have plentiful and readily available Braille at low cost for the blind. The question is how to do it. Some of the recent developments in the production of Braille by computer are extremely hopeful and could serve as the subject for an entire article themselves. There is increasing hope that the computer can provide breakthroughs which will make possible a greatly increased quantity of Braille at a much reduced cost.

However, unless those of us in the field recognize the importance of Braille and train people to read it and rely on it, it will become a dying skill regardless of its cheapness or availability. Furthermore, unless we make Braille available in a form and in a texture which allows for rapid and pleasant reading, its use will diminish.

Braille is one of the most useful tools which the blind have, and we must extract from it its maximum potential.

This brings me to one of the most revolutionary concepts in the production, cost, portability, and usability of Braille which has ever been contemplated. I refer to what has been called "cassette" or "paperless" Braille. The idea is that a large quantity of Braille could be stored on a very small cassette and could be displayed through small pins that could be raised to form the Braille dots. There are several such machines in the offing, and the National Library Service is considering purchasing one of them—or a hybrid of the best features of as many of them as it can put together. If the effort is successful, NLS would probably look toward eventually replacing regular Braille volumes in its collection with the cassette-Braille machines. I have personally examined two of these machines—an earlier model of the Elinfa and TSI's Versabrailler. I have not examined the Rose Reader, but if it can do what its inventors claim, it may hold the key to the future. Of course, the "if" must be kept in mind. The problem with the Elinfa and the Versabrailler is that they display only one line at a time—and not a very long line at that. I think this would mean that the fast Braille reader would be slowed down, but we will have to see. When I tried the Versabrailler (and I must emphasize that I only used it for a few minutes on one occasion), I could read Braille on it very nearly as fast as I could talk. However, I can read ordinary Braille on a regular paper page much more rapidly than that. Of course, I do not know what I could do if I spent time training on the Versabrailler, but since I use both hands and read on two lines at once in reading ordinary Braille, common sense tells me that if I have access to only one short line at the time I will necessarily be slowed down.

When I tried the Elinfa, I thought it was totally worthless. However, I cannot emphasize too strongly that I saw it only once, that it was an early model, and that it probably still had bugs to be worked out of it. Since it displays only a single short line at the time, some of my comments about the Versabrailler would also be applicable.

As I have said, I have not examined the Rose Reader, but its inventor claims that it will display an entire Braille page at once. I should think that this would be a tremendous advantage.

The National Library Service has recently been making tests involving cassette Braille. It has also found itself in a controversy

with some of the manufacturers of the machines—particularly
with Mr. Leonard Rose, one of the inventors of the Rose
Reader....

Five years after the publication of that article, the controversy surrounding the teaching of Braille had heated up around the country—and particularly, in the National Federation's "home" state of Maryland. There, on many occasions, leaders of the organized blind, such as Kenneth Jernigan and Mary Ellen Reihing (at that time, president of the Baltimore Chapter of the National Federation of the Blind) found themselves engaging in debate or contentious correspondence with Dr. Richard Welsh, Superintendent of the Maryland School for the Blind. Two such episodes, typical of many others, were discussed by Jernigan in what might be described as a delicious commentary, entitled "A Taste of Rarebit," published in the *Braille Monitor* in August, 1987. The essay follows:

A TASTE OF RAREBIT
by Kenneth Jernigan

Before I came to Maryland in 1978, I had never had the pleasure of meeting Dr. Richard Welsh, the Superintendent of the Maryland School for the Blind. That deficiency in my social experience has now been remedied, for on more than one occasion during the past nine years Dr. Welsh and I have occupied the same platform, sat in the same room at meetings, and shared with one another such wisdom as each of us possessed.

Last fall at the convention of the National Federation of the Blind of Maryland Dr. Welsh was a speaker. He did not come willingly or with good temper but only after a number of contacts had been made with members of his board to suggest that it was inappropriate for the superintendent of the state school for the blind to refuse to attend. After all, the NFB of Maryland is the largest organization of blind people in the state, and the School has (or should have) a certain degree of accountability.

Dr. Welsh's segment of the agenda was not characterized by placidity. In fact, one might call it tempestuous. He said, among other things, that it might be a bad thing for a growing child to try to learn both print and Braille since it might slow both processes. I got the impression that he was saying that a child had a certain amount of reading capacity and that if you split it between print and Braille, you would probably come out with around fifty percent efficiency in each. It was certainly a novel theory, but novelty was about all that it had to recommend it.

When some of us pointed out to him that children sometimes learn two languages simultaneously and seem to have increased proficiency in each because of the experience of having learned the other, he only answered with emotion instead of logic. He seemed to feel that Braille was vastly inferior to print and that a child should, if possible, read print at all costs, even if Braille would be faster and more efficient. I got the definite impression that Dr. Welsh felt that print was "normal" and that Braille was subnormal.

He said that if a family really felt that their child should learn Braille, that this should be taken into consideration, but it was made very clear that the School would discourage it. He also made a great point of the fact that all children are different and that they should not be treated alike or fitted into a rigid mold. It sounds good, but what does it mean? To Dr. Welsh it meant that blind children should not be (as he put it) pressured or forced to learn Braille. We asked him whether sighted children should be put into a rigid mold and forced to learn print. He thought this was different. It is "normal" to read print.

In the circumstances it is not surprising that Dr. Welsh did not believe that teachers of blind children (even those who teach reading) should be required to have proficiency in Braille. We asked him whether a teacher of French should be required to know French. He thought this was not relevant. We asked him whether a teacher of math should be required to know math. He didn't think that was relevant either. Certain legislators who were present thought it was extremely relevant. Dr. Welsh was not happy. Federationists are troublemakers. They are militant, too.

Not surprisingly, a bill was introduced into the Maryland legislature early this year to require that Braille be made available to every blind and severely visually impaired child in the state. Also not surprisingly, the special education teachers and Dr. Welsh (some of the very people who certainly should and often don't know Braille) came out in force to oppose the bill. Dr. Welsh's performance was not only in poor taste but also possibly even worse than that. He brought small children and their parents to the legislature to talk about how terrible it would be if they were forced into the rigid mold. It was enough to make one cry, and a number of people did—some for one reason, and some for another. Temporarily Dr. Welsh got his way. For another year blind children in Maryland will not be "forced" to learn to read. They will avoid the evils of literacy. But the battle is only beginning.

Under date of April 15, 1987, a letter from Mary Ellen Reihing, president of the Baltimore Chapter of the National Federation of the Blind of Maryland, appeared in the *Baltimore Sun*:

Literacy Crisis for the Blind

Editor: A whole generation of blind children in Maryland is in grave danger of becoming functionally illiterate. Special education teachers certified to teach blind children, both at the School for the Blind and in public school programs, are discouraging their students from learning Braille. Of the 120 children in academic programs at the Maryland School for the Blind, the school reports that only 33 are learning Braille.

Why? Poor teacher training programs account for part of the problem. It is possible to become certified to teach blind students in Maryland without being able to read Braille fluently. Volunteer Braille transcribers, who often do not have college degrees and are not accorded "professional" status, must demonstrate a knowledge of Braille to be certified which is greater than that required of a teacher of the visually impaired seeking a master's degree.

The root of the literacy crisis for blind children goes beyond the poor quality of teacher preparation. At its heart is the notion that the techniques used by blind people are inferior to those used by the sighted. It is "normal" to read print. It is "abnormal" to read Braille. Therefore, a blind child with residual vision, no matter how poor that vision may be, is taught to read print even when Braille would be more efficient.

Joe can see well out of the corner of his eye, but he can't focus on any detail work. He can't read the banner headlines in a newspaper. If he uses a closed circuit television system, he can read print that is so enlarged that four or five letters will fit on a twelve-inch television screen. Since he has not learned Braille, he has no way to read any of the notes he has written until he can return home to use his closed circuit television.

Jane was born with cataracts which were removed when she was a baby. She also had a condition that caused her eyes to jump uncontrollably. Focusing caused her pain, but she could read regular print very effectively—for about ten minutes. If she tried to read longer, tears rolled down her face, and she was unable to focus on anything at all for several hours. Her teachers told her she was being lazy when she said that she couldn't read any more. As she got older, and reading demands increased, she fell farther and farther behind. Jane became convinced that she was stupid and dropped out of high school. Jane has come to understand that her reading problems are visual, not mental. Even so her attitudes about reading are fixed. Though she could read books that have been recorded on tape, she structured her life to avoid books in any form.

Lynn read large print when she was a child. She had friends who were totally blind, and she wanted to learn Braille so she could write letters to them, but her teachers refused to help her learn it. In fact, they punished her for trying to read Braille because she wasn't "blind." Shortly after she graduated from high school, Lynn lost the rest of her vision. She had to quit her job as a secretary to learn Braille. Fortunately for Lynn, she was able to find another secretarial job after her training. If she had known Braille from the beginning, she would not have had to interrupt her career.

Expense has been given as a reason for denying literacy to blind children. No one is suggesting that regular classroom teachers become proficient in Braille. The only teachers who would be involved are the special education instructors who are already supposed to be fluent in Braille. The Library of Congress offers a free course to anyone who wants to learn Braille transcription. Those who talk about expense should think about the life-long cost of illiteracy and noncompetitive functioning for blind people.

Administrators say that many blind students at the Maryland School for the Blind see too well to need Braille. One is left to wonder what such students are doing in a specialized program for blind children if they really do not need any of the techniques of blindness. Perhaps the real problem is that those charged with the responsibility of teaching our blind children really do not believe that blindness is respectable.

Mary Ellen Reihing, Baltimore.

Under date of April 25, 1987, Dr. Welsh replied. He said that it was perfectly proper for blind children in Maryland not to know Braille since blind children in the rest of the country don't know it either. If only fifteen percent of the blind youngsters in the country can read Braille, Maryland's thirteen percent is only two percentage points worse. In other words illiteracy is all right if you can just prove that other people are almost as uneducated as you are. One has to wonder if Dr. Welsh really understands the implications of what he is saying.

He went on to say that some ninety-five percent of the students at his school had other handicaps besides blindness, from which one was presumably meant to reason that it is all right to push a multiply handicapped child toward reading print but not all right to push him or her toward reading Braille. Besides, the argument about multiple handicaps is always trotted out by anybody and everybody with a weak case—the sheltered workshops, which don't want to pay decent wages; the airlines, which don't want to let blind persons sit in exit rows; the schools, which don't want to teach Braille.

Next Dr. Welsh said that current state and federal laws require that the program for a handicapped child's education must be based on an assessment of that particular child's individual needs and abilities. He jumped from this to the conclusion that blind children need not be taught Braille. He then threw in a few words about his rigid mold and topped it off with some comments about how bad it was that the schools of twenty years ago taught visually impaired students under blindfold. Twenty years ago is always bad. Blindfolds are bad. By implication, Braille is bad.

In the rest of his letter Dr. Welsh talks about the damage which was done to the blind children of a generation ago who were forced to learn Braille. I know a great many of those people, and my observation contradicts Dr. Welsh's theories. I believe the people to whom he refers were neither educationally nor psychologically damaged by being taught Braille. Dr. Welsh says:

"Respect for blind people begins with the recognition that each blind person is an individual, and each should be treated as such."

"Bravo!" one cries. But what does this have to do with learning to read? I favor the flag and the Bill of Rights. Does this mean that sighted children should not be taught to read print? I have always thought that freedom and literacy went hand in hand, that liberty and education were almost synonymous. Apparently Dr. Welsh thinks otherwise. But let him speak for himself. Here is his letter:

Braille Isn't For All Sight-Impaired Kids

Editor: On April 15 you published a letter from Mary Ellen Reihing, President of the local chapter of the National Federation of the Blind, which pointed out that most visually impaired students in Maryland do not use Braille. The writer concluded that the reasons for this are that teachers are poorly trained, that it is too expensive to teach Braille and that administrators do not believe that blindness is "respectable"; therefore, the techniques used by blind people are considered to be inferior, and are not taught.

The 1986 report of the American Printing House for the Blind indicates that only fifteen percent of all visually impaired children in the United States use Braille. This is very close to the thirteen percent of the students at the Maryland School for the Blind who use Braille. But the reasons for these facts are very different than those suggested by Ms. Reihing.

First, ninety-five percent of the children who attend the Maryland School for the Blind have additional handicaps to their visual impairment. Forty percent have severe and profound developmental disabilities which make them incapable of reading, regardless of the medium they are using. Many have orthopedic or neurological impairments which make it impossible to read Braille. Most have some degree of usable vision which they can use efficiently to read print.

We have many teachers who are proficient in reading and teaching Braille, and we capably provide this instruction when it is needed. We also teach other special techniques and adaptations which are used by blind people, not only for academic learning but also for independent mobility, vocational training, daily living skills and leisure activities.

Current state and federal laws require the educational program provided each handicapped child to be based on an assessment of that child's needs and abilities and to be approved by the child's parents. This is an improvement over past educational practices, which were influenced by general theories about what was best for all children in a particular category, regardless of the needs of the individual child. Fortunately, most schools do not operate that way anymore.

Thirty years ago, it was the general belief that all visually impaired children should learn Braille, whether they needed it or not. Children who had enough vision to learn to read print were blindfolded and forced to read Braille with their fingers.

The vast majority of these children never used Braille again in any functional way, and many had to teach themselves how to read print after they left school. It is the position of the Maryland School for the Blind and most educators that, in general, if a child has the cognitive ability required for reading and is able to recognize print symbols, then strong consideration is given to print as the reading medium for that child. Print is the more common communication system used in the community, and more information is available in print than in any other medium.

If a child is unable to use print as an efficient reading medium then Braille, along with auditory and/or multiple media, is considered as a possible reading and learning mode. In some cases, a child whose primary medium is either print or Braille may also be taught to read in one or more of the other media, when that child's visual prognosis or personal interest suggests that learning to read in multiple media may be of value. This is particularly true when the child is clearly going to lose all useful vision.

During each of the last two legislative sessions, the National Federation of the Blind has requested that legislation be introduced which would change state law to reflect their philosophy on the use of Braille. Both times, the responses of visually impaired students and their parents, blind adults and educators who are trained in this specialty have led to the defeat of this proposed legislation.

We cannot return to the practice of treating all people in a given category as if they are the same. We do not educate children without handicaps in this manner, and we should not allow it for handicapped children. Respect for blind people begins with the recognition that each blind person is an individual, and each should be treated as such.

Richard L. Welsh, Baltimore.

As one reads Dr. Welsh's letter, various emotions compete for ascendancy. Perhaps the only appropriate response is a piece of doggerel: A kiss is dry without a squeeze; So is a rarebit without some cheese.

One of the most instructive and authoritative articles yet to appear on the educational role of Braille was published in the *Braille Monitor* in August, 1988, under the title "Braille: Pedagogy, Prejudice, and the Banner of Equality." The author was Fred Schroeder, president of the National Association of Blind Educators, and a member of the Board of Directors of the National Federation of the Blind. Schroeder, who had been an elementary schoolteacher and later an orientation and mobility instructor, was also formerly the coordinator of Low Incidence Programs for the Albuquerque Public Schools. His article, which combines first-hand experience with professional expertise, was given as a paper in Toronto, Canada, on June 1, 1988, at a conference sponsored by the Canadian National Institute for the Blind, the theme of which was "Braille: Future Directions." Schroeder became Director of the New Mexico Commission for the Blind in July of 1986:

BRAILLE: PEDAGOGY, PREJUDICE, AND THE BANNER OF EQUALITY
by Fred Schroeder

When speaking generally about Braille, it can be said without controversy that Braille represents the means to literacy for the blind. On its face it seems self-evident that for the blind to be literate we must have a tactile method of reading and writing. As with most truths that appear self-evident, our particular beliefs and attitudes color our perception and affect the way in which our beliefs are put into action. Although we flatter ourselves with the belief that we are rational beings, we cannot ignore the impact of prejudice on our behavior. For this reason a discussion of Braille must necessarily encompass a discussion of societal beliefs about blindness, as well as our own beliefs as blind people about blindness.

When I was seven years old, I lost the majority of my eyesight. While not totally blind, I was no longer able to function competitively using my sight. At that time in my life I did not regard myself as a blind person and if asked would have fiercely resisted viewing myself as blind. The intensity of my aversion to thinking of myself as blind was directly tied to my fear of blindness. While recognizing that I was no longer fully sighted, I would not think of myself as a blind person since for me blindness conjured up images of hopelessness and helplessness. I did not know what had shaped my beliefs up to that time, but looking back I can identify many of the events which helped strengthen my negative beliefs about blindness. I was one of four children, and as in most families various household chores were divided up among us. While never explicitly stated, the chores I was assigned were those in which my poor vision would cause me the least difficulty. Both my family and I assumed that the tasks around the house routinely involving sight necessarily required sight and, therefore, none of us sought alternative methods for me to do other jobs. Rather than promoting confidence by giving me a belief that I could contribute, this practice led me to the conclusion that I could function competitively only by means of my remaining vision. When I returned to school, the same pattern continued. If I could not see well enough to do a particular thing, I was either excused from the assignment or paired off with a partner who generally did the majority of the work. Whichever way it went, the belief persisted that to see was to be competent and not to see was to be incompetent.

During the time I grew up, it was believed that the more a person used his or her remaining eyesight the sooner it would deteriorate. For this reason I was not encouraged to use print for fear that it would cause a further decrease in my vision. Since I was not using print, there seemed little need to teach me to spell. As you can imagine, the effect on my academic training of not reading was widespread and damaging. My mother, realizing that I would not be using print and recognizing the need for me to become literate, arranged for me to receive instruction in Braille. It was at this point that my beliefs about blindness began to surface in a tangible way. I resisted learning Braille and applied great quantities of effort to insuring that I would never learn it. I would read dots with my remaining sight and not by touch. I would refuse to practice between lessons, hide my book before lessons, and in every way possible avoid contact with Braille. I would argue with my mother that I did not need to know Braille since more and more material was being recorded on tape. In short, my beliefs about blindness were governing my attitude toward Braille. By not wanting to think of myself as a blind person, I resisted learning the skills I needed to function competitively. My fear of being less capable prevented me from learning the very skill which would have enabled me to function on a par with my sighted peers.

Now that the "sight-saving" era is behind us, I often wonder what would have happened to me in today's educational system. Would I have been taught Braille, or would I have been encouraged to read print with a closed circuit television or other similar device? Unfortunately the answer is all too easy to predict. The modern-day educational system does not encourage teachers of blind children to concentrate on Braille as a primary reading system for other than the totally blind. Children with any remaining eyesight are pressed to read print long past the point of reason and common sense.

In my professional life I started as a teacher of blind children. I have observed children using print in situations and under conditions which defy reason. In particular I can vividly remember watching a child being instructed in print using a CCTV at full magnification. To complicate matters this child could not see well if there was any glare in the room, so before he started reading, the blinds were closed. To complicate matters further, this child could not read letters that were at all stylized. Therefore, the teacher would first retype all of the child's material, using a sans serif large print typewriter which made very plain typewritten letters. After the teacher had retyped the child's material, closed the venetian blinds, and turned the CCTV to full magnification, this child was able to read a few letters at a time with excruciating slowness. Nevertheless, I was told that she was not being taught Braille because her parents wished her to read print. When this child became my student, I set about teaching her Braille and found that her parents came to value her ability to read and take pride in her newfound literacy. I firmly believe that their reluctance to allow her to learn Braille was directly tied to their desire

not to think of their child as blind rather than to a belief that
print represented a more efficient means of reading for her. I also
believe that their negative attitudes were shaped by the negative
attitudes of the teacher.

When I first determined to become a teacher of blind children, I
took it for granted that Braille reading and writing would be
stressed. My teacher preparation program required a one-
semester course in Braille with an optional semester course in
Braille math and music notation. This limited amount of training
in Braille is disturbing enough. However, my program was, at that
time, regarded as placing more emphasis on Braille than most
other programs throughout the nation. Quantity of Braille instruction alone was not the problem. Prospective teachers completing
the Braille course had only marginal reading and writing ability,
and if the course was taken early in their program, they might not
use Braille for several years before becoming certified as teachers
of blind children.

When I was student teaching, I needed to have large quantities
of material transcribed into Braille. To assist me I hired a woman
who had just taken the Braille course the previous semester. She
had received an "A" in the course and, therefore, would (I assumed) be reasonably facile with Braille. The material she first
transcribed for me averaged sixteen Braille errors per page. I was
having this woman transcribe my material on eight-and-a-half by
eleven-inch paper. Figuring two to two-and-a-half Braille pages
for each print page, this is analogous to hiring a typist who had
just completed a typing course with an "A" grade who averages
thirty to forty errors per typewritten page. I believe it is fair to
say that many teachers of blind children are not skilled in Braille
and, therefore, seek alternatives to Braille in working with their
students. I remember when the Optacon was first introduced. The
manufacturer claimed that the Optacon would make Braille obsolete. The manufacturer, in cooperation with leading professionals in the field, developed a reading program adapted for the
Optacon. This was not a program to teach a child who was already
a skilled reader to transfer that skill to the Optacon. Rather, this
was a program intended to teach children the skill of reading by
means of the Optacon. If this belief were limited only to the wild
exaggerations of the manufacturer, it could be more easily dismissed. Unfortunately, while going through my teacher training,
I had friends who seriously proposed eliminating Braille as a requirement from the teacher preparation curriculum since it would
soon be obsolete.

Lack of use of Braille by the teachers compounds the problem. I was once told by a leading professional that it is not uncommon for an itinerant teacher to have periods of seven to ten years without a single Braille student. I would argue that this would not be the case if all children who should be taught Braille were taught Braille. Nevertheless, if it is the practice, it is easy to see how a teacher's proficiency could easily deteriorate—assuming, of course, that the teacher had such proficiency in the first place.

A fundamental question which must be asked is this: Which children should be taught to read Braille, and which children should be taught to read print? In my professional work I developed a set of criteria which I used to answer this question. I believe that if a child can read standard sized print (holding it at a normal reading distance) and if that child can read for a sustained period of time without eye strain, then it is reasonable for that child to read print. In other words, if a child can function as a normally sighted person, then it can be reasonably expected that the child will be able to function competitively as a print reader. If the child suffers eye strain and cannot read for sustained periods of time, then it is reasonable for that child to learn Braille. All children must have a reading method which allows them to be fully literate. I believe the criteria I have listed are really nothing more than a functional definition of literacy. While no one would argue against literacy, the fact of teachers not receiving adequate training in Braille (coupled with new technology, such as CCTVs) has steered educational practice away from Braille and away from literacy.

Four or five years ago a leading professional organization in the United States circulated a proposed position paper asking for comments from the field. This position paper was intended to establish working criteria to settle once and for all the question of which children should read print and which children should read Braille. I was astonished when I read that one of the criteria seriously being proposed was that a child who was able to read print at ten words per minute should continue to be a print reader and not be taught Braille. To the best of my knowledge this position paper was never formally adopted. However, I was dumbfounded that a leading professional would even propose such a criterion.

I believe that there exists a prejudice against Braille and that, as with most prejudice, it is not deliberately intended or, for that matter, even recognized by those who feel it most deeply. I believe the source of the prejudice is nothing deeper or more mysterious than the public misunderstanding and misconceptions about blindness. Dr. Kenneth Jernigan, Executive Director of the National Federation of the Blind, tells of visiting a classroom of blind children and being told by the teacher: "This little girl reads print. This little girl *has to* read Braille." It is human nature that prejudice (while irrational) is defended by seemingly rational explanations. This is certainly true with the prejudice against Braille. We are told that Braille is too bulky and too expensive to produce—that it is limited in quantity and that, therefore, to teach a child Braille is to limit what the child will be able to read. We are told that it is better to teach a child print, thereby making available great quantities (virtually endless quantities) of reading material to the child. Never mind that the child may be only able to read at ten words per minute. Never mind that the child may suffer eye strain and only be able to read for a brief time. While Braille is too expensive, never mind the cost of Optacons, talking computers, or CCTVs. While Braille is too bulky, never mind the size and awkwardness of many low vision aids.

Several years ago I attended a professional conference and saw a presentation on the mainstreaming of blind children into a regular public school. One of the slides showed a child with a CCTV mounted on a cart, which he wheeled with him from class to class. Yet, Braille is too bulky, too expensive, and too limited. As an educator, I have seen low vision children with smudges on their noses from trying to read their own handwriting—their own handwriting which was done with a soft lead pencil or felt tip pen. Yet, somehow many of the professionals who shape the thinking of society cling to the belief that to read print is inherently better than to read Braille—inherently "normal."

Young blind children must be instructed in the skill of Braille writing, not only by means of the Braille writer but with the slate and stylus as well. Earlier in this century Braille writers were in scarce supply, and generations of blind children grew up learning to write with the slate and stylus from the time they entered the first grade. Now we are told that young blind children lack the fine motor control to use the slate and stylus and, therefore, that this skill should not be taught until middle school. When a child is in middle school, he or she must already have a reliable means of taking notes. It is too late to be introducing a notetaking system. Even though the slate has represented an efficient notetaking system for generations of blind people, modern day pedagogy suggests that the slate is too slow and causes too much confusion to be a useful tool because it teaches children to "write backward." Many teacher preparation programs introduce the slate as little more than a relic of bygone days. Instead of being taught an efficient writing method, far too many children are given soft lead pencils or felt tip pens and are taught to handwrite notes which they can only decipher with great difficulty if at all. How will these children compete in today's society? How will they obtain a college education when they are not able easily to read their own handwriting? How will they make a class presentation or deliver a speech without being able easily to read from a printed text? The answer (Braille) seems obvious, and it is certainly available—but this simple truth seems to elude many of today's "professionals" in the field.

What we need and must have is an understanding in ourselves and in society that, as blind people, we must be able to compete on terms of equality with the sighted. To compete we must be literate, and to be literate we must be able to read and write Braille. We must promote a belief and an attitude that it is respectable to be blind and that there is no inherent inferiority or second-class status in the methods associated with blindness. As a child, when I resisted learning Braille, I was resisting conceiving of myself as a blind person. I automatically assumed that to be blind was to be inferior and, therefore, that to use the tools of blindness was an acceptance of inferiority. By rejecting blindness (and with it Braille) I was rejecting the very skill which would have allowed me to compete on an equal footing with my peers.

We cannot allow our attitudes and the attitudes of society to rob us of our right to first-class status. We must press for greater emphasis on Braille among our school children. We must press for greater availability of Braille. Perhaps the greatest gift of our high tech age is computer production of Braille, reducing both cost and transcription time. But above all, we must press for an understanding that the tools we use as blind people are not the badge of second-class status, but rather the banner of equality.

A Study in Scholarship

Almost from its inception the National Federation of the Blind sought ways to fund and award scholarships for deserving blind students. In 1984 the NFB was able to expand its existing program of awards into a broad scholarship system directed to blind post-secondary students. Beginning in that year more than

$50,000 was devoted annually to these scholarships, which by 1990 had grown in number to a total of twenty-six. Of these the smallest award was in the amount of $2,000, and the largest was $10,000. When President Jernigan first outlined the new program, he was concerned not only with recognizing the achievements of outstanding blind students and helping with their educational expenses but also with assembling every year a portfolio of blind individuals whose accomplishments would explode the myth that blind persons cannot excel at the entire panoply of "higher learning." All of these worthy goals could, of course, have been accommodated simply by announcing the scholarship winners and mailing them their checks. But Jernigan had an additional goal in mind, one more important perhaps than all the rest. He proposed to bring blind students, the brightest and the best, to the National Convention for a week of communion with the Federation in its characteristic activity—during which the students might learn more about themselves, about blindness, and about the organized blind in ways that no amount of formal learning could duplicate. The unique bond of the Federation, after all, was ultimately the bond of community, of deeply shared personal commitment one to another, and could only be taught and learned in live association. For that reason the scholarship program was designed to require attendance at the convention as a condition of eligibility.

From the first year of the expanded program, it was clear that making it possible for scholarship recipients to attend the National Convention was appropriate and constructive. The number of winners each year matched the number of scholarships available; thus before the scholarship committee made its final decisions on the awards, there was opportunity to meet and get to know the students to a degree that few other award-granting institutions could approximate. And there was something more to be bestowed than the monetary awards; there was the gift of the Federation itself. That was the thrust of remarks made at the 1989 convention by the committee chairman, Peggy Pinder (who was also the NFB's Second Vice President), in the course of her scholarship presentations:

> Now that we have bestowed the 1989 scholarships, I want to say
> a final word to each of you who is a winner this year. We have

given to you of our treasure, of our hard-earned income; but we have also given to you something else. We consider our scholarships to you only secondary to this. We have given you another and greater gift as through the week we have spent time with you, attended meetings with you, dined with you, played poker with you, talked with you, laughed with you, danced with you, debated and discussed with you. Through our common experiences we have shown to you that which is most important of all to you, the most precious thing we have, and the thing we now offer to you— our organization, the National Federation of the Blind.

We blind people first felt the need ourselves to establish an organization because we did not have a common philosophy, a structure through which to implement that philosophy, or the policies that brought it into life. We have made that philosophy, that organization, and those policies, and we now offer them to you. But we ask you to recognize with us that a philosophy, a structure, and policies in common do not make the National Federation of the Blind. They are merely the building above the ground. Underneath it is our feeling for one another. We do love one another. We do hurt when one of us is hurt. We do comfort one another when hurt occurs. We do fight for one another when one of us is wronged. We do defend one another. We rejoice with one another when achievements occur because they are the achievements of each of us, not in some verbal sense, but really truly ours because we do love one another and feel that strength of attachment for one another on which our philosophy, our structure, and our policies are built. We offer all of these to you, but particularly the love. You have shown great achievement and shown that you can give as well. We give our movement to you, and ask you to love it as we have loved it, ask you to nurture it as we have nurtured it, ask you to make it grow as we have made it grow. We are proud of it just as we are proud of you.

Scholarship winners, congratulations! Let's work together to make all our futures come true!

In the first year of the scholarship program, one of the winners was a high school senior who had lost his sight a few years before. He was tentative during his convention appearance about his career plans and about his ability to navigate independently. Five years later, this same student was confidently exercising the skills first learned in the Federation as he attended Yale Law School and simultaneously led America's blind students as their elected chief. In another case, a scholarship winner had intended to pursue a career in college teaching; but as he came to learn about the Federation, he also learned that he had selected that career to minimize his contacts with the general public—whose attitudes were so often painful to encounter. Working with Federationists, he discovered that he had a liking for social action and public mingling, after all, and he subsequently became a management trainee with IBM.

The week-long experience of the NFB convention itself was typically an inspiration for the scholarship winners. While committee members and others took on the responsibility of teaching the students how to use a long white cane effectively, more important than this instruction was the graphic example all around them of hundreds of other blind persons speeding about, both at work and play, on schedules and travel routes that were part of the routine day. Of course, it was then common enough for blind persons somewhere along the way in their lives to be taught a little about the white cane; but it was equally common for the instructor to be sighted and for the student to conclude that getting around must be a terrible burden for the blind—simply because there were no role models of confident, self-possessed blind persons included in the cane curriculum. At the Federation conventions, on the other hand, hundreds of such positive role models were encountered in the daily round of activities; no one could be a part of that for many days without getting the point and learning the lesson of independent mobility.

The effects of the program were dramatic. Not only were blind students encouraged to seek higher education, but the brightest among them came to understand a new philosophy of blindness. State programs of rehabilitation (although they were established to assist blind students to obtain proper training) often failed to provide inspiration, talented instruction, or the resources for securing educational opportunity. All of these were available at the convention of the National Federation of the Blind. Perhaps the most significant was the encouragement and the spirit which were engendered: "If they can do it, so can I."

Train Up a Child

As the Federation grew through the 1970s and into the 1980s, more and more of its members realized that the Federation message was simply not reaching people quickly enough. Some blind people lost their sight as adults. but many of them were children, some of whom did not hear of the Federation until they had reached adulthood. Why, Federation leaders thought, not make available to blind children and their parents the same message that was being disseminated to blind adults?

The Federation began by establishing a Committee on Parental Concerns. Then, in 1982 the first seminar for parents of blind children was held at the National Convention, and it immediately became an annual event. These seminars attracted parents of blind children from throughout the country. The parents themselves planned the program and met throughout the convention week, sometimes in formal sessions on topics specific to the education of their children and sometimes informally to share frustrations and successes. The blind children, too, came to the National Convention, along with their brothers and sisters who were not blind. Specific programs were organized for the blind children to meet and get to know young blind adults with whom they might form friendships. Since blindness occurs randomly in the population, most blind children do not have blind parents. Therefore, it was felt to be important to make sure that the children had as role models a variety of blind adults to help them envision themselves growing up into competent, responsible citizens.

The parents and children alike were given the chance to learn the same thing that the scholarship winners were learning— the efficiency of the long white cane, the broad array of jobs being successfully handled by the blind, and a sensible perspective on blindness. The reaction of parents to the Federation message was often relief mixed with anger—relief that they had finally found someone who talked sensibly about their blind children as normal people, combined with anger that no "professional" had told them about the Federation. And all of the family members—parents, blind children, and sighted siblings—left the convention feeling that they had met hundreds of blind people who would happily serve as continuing resources in the years to come.

By 1981 the Federation was publishing *Future Reflections,* the most widely circulated and respected magazine in the field dealing with the concerns and problems of parents of blind children. The Federation had also established a parents division, which was actively working throughout the country as a resource and support group. Barbara Cheadle, president of the Parents of Blind Children Division, was editor of *Future Reflections,* and she and her husband John were devoting substantial energy to contacting and organizing parents. Although both of the Cheadles were sighted, they were dedicated to the Federation and gave it a high priority in their lives. One reason for this devotion was undoubtedly the fact that the Cheadles had an adopted blind child of their own. Barbara Cheadle wrote an article which appeared in the March, 1985, *Braille Monitor,* which talked about the establishment and progress of *Future Reflections:*

FUTURE REFLECTIONS
by Barbara Cheadle

In July, 1981, at the annual meeting of the NFB Parental Concerns Committee a motion was made and carried to start a newsletter for parents of blind children. Under the leadership of Susan Ford and others the committee was alive with excitement. All kinds of creative ideas and projects were being discussed and proposed. The newsletter was one of them.

Later that summer I—as the new volunteer editor of this venture—pulled out paper and pens, sat down at the kitchen table, and started to put together our first issue. We mailed out 368 copies of a 15-page newsletter that November of 1981. John's parents came to see us the weekend that we were right in the middle of folding, stapling, labeling, and trying to puzzle out the postal regulations for bundling all those papers. We put John's parents to work, too. Before they left, they even "paid" for the privilege of helping. They left us a check as a donation to the National Federation of the Blind. It had taken us all weekend to get the job done.

This month—November, 1984, three years later—we had 7,000 issues of a 32-page magazine (now called *Future Reflections*) printed for circulation. This time we didn't assemble and label them in my living room. We did that on the dining room table at Frank and Glenda Smith's home. (Frank Smith is the first vice president of the NFB Parents of Blind Children Division. Glenda handles the mailing list on her home computer. They also have six children, and a *big* table.) Our NFB Western Chapter president was there to help, too. Between telephone calls, sick kids, and babies with runny noses, we had the issue ready to mail in two days.

From November, 1981, to November, 1984, the circulation of *Future Reflections* has increased almost 2,000 percent. Originally a project of the NFB Parental Concerns Committee, it is now published (like the *Braille Monitor*) by our National Office. Currently, we are the largest publication for parents of blind children in the nation. We are also the only magazine for parents of blind children. There are two other national publications for parents of blind children. One is a four-page quarterly newsletter put out by the International Institute for the Visually Handicapped, 0-7, Inc. This group deals exclusively with pre-school children. We have reprinted articles from this newsletter from time to time in *Future Reflections*. The other newsletter is published by the National Association of Parents of the Visually Impaired (NAPVI). This is the American Foundation for the Blind parent group. Typically, the content reflects the AFB attitudes about blindness. I have had parents tell me that there is no comparison between *Future Reflections* and *Awareness*, the NAPVI newsletter. *Future Reflections* is read from cover to cover and kept for reference. The NAPVI newsletter gets a glance and is tossed aside.

Remarks about reading *Future Reflections* from "cover to cover" are common. Some young mothers report locking themselves in the bathroom to read it as soon as the issue arrives. (If you think that seems like a strange thing to do, then you've never been a young mother. The bathroom is the only place I've found where you can get a little privacy when you have small children in the house.)

The comment that best describes most parents' reactions came from a California mother. She said, "This is the first time I have read your newsletter, and I am delighted and excited to know it exists...I found a wealth of information THAT I CAN USE!"

Fathers read *Future Reflections*, too. "I gain so much from your publication," was the brief—but very much to the point—note from one busy father. Another parent from Hawaii wrote saying, "I am writing to you to ask if you could send me your magazine, *Future Reflections*. I saw a copy of your magazine and was really impressed by it. I have a son who is blind. Your magazine really gave me some ideas on how to work with him, how to cope with future problems I may have, and how to deal with Chris as a person. Also, it could be used as a reference to more information I may need. I really feel comfortable with your information." Parents aren't the only ones who read and benefit from *Future Reflections*. Teachers frequently write requesting subscriptions or expressing their appreciation. One teacher wrote in the spring of 1984 saying, "As a teacher of visually impaired children, I was very impressed with your new publication. Keep up the good work." Another teacher from Georgia wrote, "As an educator, I do appreciate and learn from your publication, *Future Reflections*. Thanks for a job well done." Other teachers have commented on our "professional" quality.

It's very important that we continue to reach these teachers. Often, the teacher for the visually impaired is the only contact parents have with someone who has any knowledge about blindness at all. Parents and their blind child can become very attached to and dependent upon this teacher. There are obviously problems with that. Even some of the best teachers have little contact with blind adults in general, and even less with the organized blind movement. Needless to say, that seriously limits their understanding of blindness.

Colleges, universities, libraries, pre-school programs, schools for the blind, hospitals, eye clinics, churches, and agencies for the blind are just some of the institutions that subscribe to *Future Reflections*. Special education professors distribute copies to their students. An ophthalmologist in California keeps copies in his patients' waiting room. Our magazine is distributed and used in college programs for preparation of teachers of the visually impaired. Agencies for the blind, such as the Vision Foundation in Massachusetts, keep multiple copies on hand to distribute in information packets to parents. *Future Reflections* is quoted and used as a reference by educators, and top educational administrators recommend and praise it to teachers and parents alike. The executive director of the Royer-Greares School for the Blind in Pennsylvania sent us this year a "letter of appreciation...on behalf of the teachers of this school for multihandicapped blind boys and girls." Other representatives of institutions have expressed similar feelings.

Future Reflections is also becoming known outside the United States. We have a growing number of subscriptions from Canada. A teacher from the Hollywood School, Metro Day Program for the Blind in Canada, called it an "excellent magazine." A teacher with the school for the blind in Gambia, West Africa, says that parents especially respond to the NFB's "approaches to blindness."

We often like to say in the Federation that "it is respectable to be blind." One of the most exciting things about the magazine is that it is helping to make that statement a reality for thousands of blind children. Most of the time we will never know what impact an article or issue will have on any individual parent, child, or teacher. But we do know this: *Future Reflections* is respected and valued by thousands of parents and teachers nationally. Since *Future Reflections* is published by the National Federation of the Blind—by BLIND people—it is only logical and inevitable that these parents and teachers now have more respect for blind people than they had three years ago. And you don't discriminate against, coddle, or treat as inferiors those you respect.

There is another aspect to the influence of *Future Reflections* that reminds me of the nursery rhyme, "The House that Jack Built." The rhyme links all kinds of events and relationships together. A rat is killed, a cow tramples a dog, a maiden is kissed and wed, and a farmer sows his corn—violence, murder, romance, and rebirth—all because Jack built a house!

Future Reflections did not arise out of a vacuum. Long before the magazine became a reality we had Doris Willoughby demonstrating how Federation philosophy can work in the education of blind children. Susan Ford was an early leader in the formation of the parental concerns committee. She is the current president of the Parents of Blind Children Division and sets an example for other parents with her own down to earth wisdom and savvy about rearing children. Marc Maurer in the Student Division helped demonstrate how dynamic our national divisions and committees can be. The NFB has accumulated over the years a library of literature and information that provides the best, most accurate insights about blindness anywhere in the nation, or world for that matter. And it all goes back to 1940 when Dr. Jacobus tenBroek and blind representatives from seven states met and laid the philosophical and organizational foundation for our "house"—the NFB.

The philosophical foundations are, of course, the reason we succeed where the American Council of the Blind cannot. We were not the first to attempt to publish a newsletter for parents of blind children. The ACB tried to but their circulation never reached beyond about 300 and finally their newsletter folded. Unlike the NFB, the ACB does not have a unifying goal, philosophy, and purpose. That's why we succeed where they fail.

Just as the success of *Future Reflections* has been influenced by the work of Federationists in years past, so has the magazine been influencing the growth of the Federation in some rather surprising and unlikely ways. Here's an example.

Shortly after we started publication, I began collecting names and addresses of visually impaired teachers from the various states. (We now have such lists from over two-thirds of the fifty states plus D.C. We would like to get the other one-third also, so write and let us know if you would like to help in that effort.)

One state president was really on the ball and was among the first to get such a list from her department of education. A year later that state president called me and said, "Guess what? *Future Reflections* just helped us set up a new NFB chapter." She and an organizing team had gone into a new community to organize a chapter but weren't having much success finding blind folks. She did have the name of a teacher of the visually impaired, so she called her. The teacher was ecstatic when she heard that they were with the NFB. "I just got my latest issue of your magazine for parents of blind children this morning," she said. "I read it from cover to cover. It's a wonderful magazine. Of course, I'll help you." The town soon had a new chapter, and that teacher was one of its charter members.

There are so many possibilities. We can use *Future Reflections* to educate, to increase membership, to raise funds, to improve job opportunities for the blind, and more. But it can be effective only if WE promote it and use it. Marc Maurer recently used *Future Reflections* to get a donation for the NFB from a service club. It wasn't hard to do. People are happy to donate their money when they know it is going to be helping blind children right in their own communities. But how many of us have thought to do that? Time and priorities surely have something to do with it, and perhaps simply a lack of knowledge about the effectiveness of *Future Reflections*—a problem I hope this article will help take care of.

There is an interesting phenomenon about the reactions of sighted members of the public and blind Federationists after they have read their first issue. Both are often surprised. About two years ago a high school journalism teacher (who was going to do some volunteer typing for us) took her first look at an issue and exclaimed, "Hey, this ain't no rag." At first I thought it was because of me. Maybe no one expected a homemaker and mother working out of her own home to be the editor of a first-class publication. But as incident after incident occurred, I wondered if it wasn't something else.

Not long ago a Federationist, who had just read an issue, remarked to my husband with shock in his voice, "It was really good!" This came just after I had had a talk with a Federation leader who wanted me to speak at a state NFB seminar for parents of blind children. It didn't look as if I could go, and she was worried. She didn't think she knew enough about raising and educating blind children. "Well," I said, "Why do you think I know more than you? I'm the parent of a blind child. Do you think that makes me more qualified than you?"

"Well, no," she said.

"All right," I said. "I have completed one half of a college education program for the preparation of teachers of the visually impaired. Does that make me more knowledgeable than you?"

She laughed (she knew what college I was talking about). "No!" she said.

"You're a mother," I said. "You were a blind child, and even more important, you're a knowledgeable member and leader of the NFB. Where do you think I learned about blindness? From you and from the thousands of other Federationists who have directly or indirectly taught me everything I know. You're the real 'experts' about blindness."

I wonder how many of us still secretly believe that the "professionals" know something that we don't.

Future Reflections is a first-class publication. It's first-class because the National Federation of the Blind is first-class; because blind people are first-class. Let's use it, distribute it, and promote it with pride.

Passport to Freedom

"An increasing number of us are living our Federationism on a daily basis, knowing it to be our passport to freedom....We must finish our march to acceptance and full membership in society. Our heritage requires it; our purpose proclaims it; our humanity demands it. This cause of ours is a sacred trust. It is worthy of all that we have or can ever hope to be—and we shall not fail."

So spoke the President of the National Federation of the Blind at the banquet of the National Convention in Phoenix, Arizona, in 1984. The twelve months just ended had been one of the most successful times in the organization's history, and the convention was a celebration of that fact—but it was more. It was a time to review the problems and triumphs of the past year and to chart the course for the year ahead. In his report to the members at the convention President Jernigan said:

One way to measure our progress during the past year is by the increasing amount of recognition we have received from public officials throughout the country. This year more governors declared National Federation of the Blind Month, Week, or Day in their states than ever before in history. Last year a number of us went to Vice President Bush's office to talk with him about issues affecting the blind. This year we met with President Reagan in the Oval Office at the White House.

During the past year, President Jernigan continued, we have made greater progress than ever before in getting our message to the public through the media. The October 1, 1983, issue of *Vital Speeches* carried the 1983 banquet speech—"Blindness: The Other Half of Inertia." *Vital Speeches* goes to every college and university in the country and to many of the nation's high schools. Our spots now saturate the airwaves. Not only are our messages used on local stations but they are also carried by most of the networks. On November 30 Peggy Pinder and Barbara Pierce appeared for an eight-minute segment on the television program *Hour Magazine*. Used by 160 television stations, this is one of the most popular daytime TV shows in the country. On April 13 of this year we were featured on the *Today* show. We had eleven minutes to tell our story to one of the largest television audiences in the nation.

In the rest of his 1984 report President Jernigan detailed a variety of problems and triumphs. Then, he said in conclusion: "When you look back over the past year, you cannot help but feel joy and satisfaction at what we have accomplished. Yes, there have been problems and battles, but what an absolutely wonderful year we have had! We have kept the faith with Dr. tenBroek and the other founders of our movement, and we have kept the faith with ourselves. We have lived the dream and fulfilled the promise."

As always, the banquet was the climax of the convention; and when President Jernigan rose to make his banquet address, he talked of the damage which sophistry had done to the blind:

The clever and plausible but false and misleading arguments (the propositions which put us down and keep us out) are temptingly easy to accept and believe, he said. With respect to the blind the message is clear and uncomplicated: The blind lack eyesight. Other people have it. Sight is important. Therefore, the blind are inferior. We are unable to compete. We must be taken care of. We cannot hold jobs—not, that is, unless the work is very simple, very repetitive, and very subsidized. We cannot raise children, travel independently, or manage our own lives....This is the traditional norm, the time-honored belief; and if it is true, we should face it, not fight or deny it. But, of course, this is *not* the way it is, he said to a roaring response from his audience; and no sophistry on earth can make it that way.

The text of the 1984 banquet speech follows:

BLINDNESS: THE CIRCLE OF SOPHISTRY
by Kenneth Jernigan

Sophistry, we are told, is an argument or option which is clever and plausible, but false and misleading. To illustrate let as consider color. We learn from the dictionary that color is: "The property of reflecting light of a particular wavelength." In other words if an object is green, the color (or wavelength) green is reflected back, and all other colors (or wavelengths) are absorbed. White, as everyone knows, is the absence of color, and black is the opposite. Yet, what we call black reflects no light waves at all and is, thus, the absence of color—white what we call white (again to quote the dictionary) is: "The reflection of all the rays that produce color." Therefore, the logic is inevitable: black is white, and white is black.

I wish I could say that the linguistic sleight-of-hand which I have just performed is symbolic of nothing more vicious than verbal gymnastics or a pleasant game, but that is not the way of it. Sophistry is no toy. It is one of the most deadly weapons in the arsenal of tyranny. It has bedeviled and bedazzled humanity since the beginning of history. If (as the saying goes) hypocrisy is the tribute which vice pays to virtue, then sophistry is the tribute which lies pay to the truth.

Sophistry takes its name from the sophists of ancient Athens. It was the principal instrument which they used first to discredit, then to imprison, and finally to execute Socrates. It was big in the middle ages with the Inquisition and the burning of witches. It flourishes today in the twentieth century. All we need do to understand the power of clever and plausible but false and misleading words is to remember the twisted rhetoric of Joseph Goebels and Adolph Hitler. Except for the glitter and hypnotic lure of sophistry the Nazi tanks might never have rolled, and the death and destruction of the Second World War might never have been.

And what sophistry has done to society as a whole it has done to the component parts—especially and particularly to disadvantaged minorities. And of all the minorities, none has experienced more cruelly and bitterly the blight of sophistry than those of us who are blind. It has been our greatest stumbling block, our heaviest burden. It remains so today.

The clever and plausible but false and misleading arguments (the propositions which put us down and keep us out) are temptingly easy to accept and believe. With respect to the blind the message is clear and uncomplicated: the blind lack eyesight. Other people have it. Sight is important. Therefore, the blind are inferior. We are unable to compete. We must be taken care of. We cannot hold jobs—not, that is, unless the work is very simple, very repetitive, and very subsidized. We cannot raise children, travel independently, or manage our own lives. When one of us makes an achievement of obvious excellence, we are told that it means we have special genius, special talents, or unusual powers. Our other senses have grown keener to compensate. We are marvels, freaks, conversation pieces, and objects of pity—and often all at the same time and by the same person. According to this line of thought, whatever you call it and however you cut it, we are not (and can never hope to be) everyday, normal people—laughing, crying, working, playing, succeeding, failing, hoping, and dreaming like those around us. We are blind. That is sufficient. It is a matter of simple logic and common sense.

This is the traditional norm, the time-honored belief; and if it is true, we should face it, not fight or deny it. And we should face it not angrily or bitterly but with acceptance and humility, with gratitude for the charity we receive and the sufferance we are given. Moreover, if (as we are repeatedly told) this is really how it is, we should disband the National Federation of the Blind and confront our troubles alone—drawing whatever comfort we can from doctor, social worker, or priest; for there will be little purpose in collective action. If our problems are inherent in our blindness (if they are truly innate and not externally imposed), then our whole organizational existence has been not only a tragic mistake but a cruel detriment, for we have kindled hopes which can never be realized and conjured dreams which can never come true.

But, of course, this is not the way it is; and no carefully spun sophistry can make it that way. The arguments and propositions which hold that we are inferior are clever and plausible, but they are false and misleading. To put it bluntly, they are just plain lies. The fact is that the average blind person can compete on terms of equality with the average sighted person—in whatever line of endeavor you care to mention: work, play, criminal conduct, saintliness, immorality, rectitude, ill-temper, gentle behavior, laziness, or creativity. Then, why (one reasonably may ask) do seventy percent of the blind of employable years not have jobs? And even when we do get jobs, why are so many of us relegated to the sheltered shops and paid less than the minimum wage? Why (if what I am saying is the truth) are we told where we can sit on airplanes, denied insurance on equal terms with others, custodialized in the home by our families, condescended to on the streets by strangers, and treated in general as if we were children or freaks?

The answer is easy to give but hard (at least at the emotional level) for the average person to accept. In primitive societies light (whether firelight or daylight) meant safety and survival. Darkness meant danger and fear. Light and the ability to see were equated, and they were thought of as good and pure. Blindness was considered synonymous with darkness, and darkness meant evil and inferiority.

The blind were not good at hunting or dodging a spear, so they were regarded as a drag on the tribe, a burden and a hindrance. They were treated and thought of as second-class, and they doubtless accepted the public view of their limitations, with a great many feelings of guilt and shame thrown in for good measure.

We no longer live in the hunting culture of primitive times, but we often act as if we do. The myths and prejudices of those times still dominate our feelings and control our subconscious. In today's society there is very little premium on killing a saber-tooth tiger or dodging a spear, but when you dig beneath the surface and get to where we live, our attitudes indicate otherwise. The cave-man culture is gone, but the cave-man values remain. At the core of our being we fear the dark; we shiver at the roar of the saber-tooth tiger; and we feel that the blind are a burden to the tribe.

How (in the face of irrefutable evidence to the contrary) are all of these myths maintained? How (with blind persons successfully doing every conceivable kind of job, having families and raising children as effectively as anybody else, and participating fully in the political and social life of the community) can the false assumptions and second-class treatment survive? The answer can be given in a single word—sophistry. It is not, for the most part, that the average citizen on the street wants to do us harm or deprive us of opportunity. It is not (except when their jobs or their vested interests or their egos are involved) that the employees of the governmental and private agencies doing work with the blind wish us ill. Certainly it is not that we ourselves seek to sell ourselves short and limit our horizons. Yet, the myths about blindness remain, bolstered and reinforced by clever and plausible but false and misleading arguments and propositions.

The mistaken beliefs and false concepts are almost universally accepted by the general public, and when people lose their eyesight, they carry with them into blindness the erroneous ideas which they held when they were sighted. They then live the part they are expected to play and feed back to society the conceptions which it gave them in the first place. Likewise, those who are born blind are taught their roles from the beginning, and unless they are given counterbalancing information, they live as they are expected to live. They think as they are expected to think.

To make matters worse the employees (whether blind or sighted) of the governmental and private agencies established to give service to the blind are also (with notable exceptions) part of the negative process. The urge to feel important is very nearly irresistible. Therefore, when these "experts" tell the blind that they must adjust to a very limited existence and when they tell the sighted that their work is so difficult and complex as to approach the mysterious, they are generally believed. This is so even though what they are dispensing is not "professional" knowledge or the results of research or new truth but simply old ideas and the fear of the dark, which they absorbed as children. Thus, the circle is complete, with each component giving feedback and reinforcement to the rest of the loop.

Yet, despite the sophistry and the widespread belief that we are inferior, we have made gains. In fact, during the past four decades there has been such an upsurge of progress and achievement as to constitute a veritable revolution. The new element (the root cause) is represented by those of us here tonight. You know what it is as well as I do. It is the National Federation of the Blind.

When Dr. Jacobus tenBroek and the rest of that handful of founders met in Wilkes-Barre, Pennsylvania, in 1940 to organize our movement, they understood what they were doing and what it would mean. The Federation was to be the vehicle for concerted action by the blind. It was to be the circuit breaker to stop the flow of clever and plausible but false and misleading ideas which went in a seemingly endless circle from the sighted public to the agencies serving the blind to the blind themselves and back again.

That is what the National Federation of the Blind was created to do, and that is what it has done. We have done it in the past; we are doing it now; and we intend to keep on doing it in the future—regardless of who dislikes it or how much they resent it. Established patterns are comfortable. They require no mental effort, and they give money and power and prestige to various groups and individuals. But we are simply no longer willing to be second-class citizens. We want no strife or confrontation, but we will do what we have to do; and we are absolutely determined to break the circle of destructive sophistry which blights our lives and limits our opportunities. We know who we are, and we will never go back.

One of our problems is the tendency of the general public to try (regardless of the truth of the matter) to make us conform to their notions of what we are. When the facts are at variance with their preconceptions, they tend to forget the facts and cling to their preconceptions. No one is worse at this "don't bother me with the facts; I know how it is" attitude than the members of the media.

The July 24, 1981, edition of the *Tribune* of Tacoma, Washington, carried a feature article about Glen Latham. Glen, who is totally blind and a staunch Federationist, is a Vietnam veteran. He is also a home owner in Tacoma. The newspaper reporter (a Ms. Willene Anderson) said that she wanted to write an article to help remove the stereotypes and misconceptions about the blind. She came to Glen's house and talked with him at length. You can determine from the letter which Glen wrote to Ms. Anderson's boss whether she told it like it was or simply liked it the way she told it:

> The purpose of my letter, [Glen wrote,] is two-fold. The first is concerned with me personally. The second is concerned with the blind in general and the stereotyped view that Ms. Anderson's article encourages.
>
> Ms. Anderson has me quoted as saying, "Our sight is one of many things we take for granted. When it is gone, we must start our lives all over again, just as children learning—only this time in the dark." I do not recall making such a statement. Children learn to walk and talk. They do not have to be taught to see. I did not have to learn to walk or talk again.
>
> I recall mentioning to Ms. Anderson that my mother had died. Ms. Anderson made no inquiries as to when my mother died or if I lived with her. I made no statement which could even possibly have implied that I lived with my mother after my return from the war. When I came back from Vietnam in February of 1968, I spent 50 months in Balboa Naval Hospital in San Diego, six months in rehabilitation in Palo Alto, then six months back in the hospital for further operations. My mother died a month after my release from the hospital. Had Ms. Anderson asked, she would have known this.
>
> Ms. Anderson leads her readers to believe that after I recovered from my wounds, I went to live with my mother. Then she died, leaving me all alone to pick up the pieces of my life once again. Stating that I lived with my mother is a complete falsehood.

Ms. Anderson has me quoted as saying, "It used to be so important to me, the outdoors—things I could see. I had always dreamed of living in this area." This is false. During the interview, Ms. Anderson said, and I quote, "Glen, you are very athletic. What do you think about the handicapped climbers of Mt. Rainier?" Ms. Anderson assumed that I am athletic; I am not. I made no mention of liking the outdoors or of being athletically inclined. I did not tell her that I had "always dreamed of living in this area." I stated that I had always *liked* living in this area. There is a big difference between "liking" and "dreaming."

When I was looking for a home to purchase, Ms. Anderson implies that I had to take into account numerous special considerations. She states that "many homebuyers are looking for things that are aesthetically pleasing." This implies that I was not. Why wouldn't I want a home that is aesthetically pleasing? Of course it was an important factor!

Ms. Anderson states that the house doesn't have any "extra barriers, like steep stairs or sharp corners." Whose house did she look at? From the street it is obvious that the house has a second floor. She made no inquiries concerning the architectural design of the place. But how could she have missed the upstairs, even if she missed the basement? There are, in fact, two flights of what are considered "steep" stairs in my home. One flight leads to the second floor, and the other leads to the basement, where I spend most of my time working at my desk. My home could not be considered small. I have 2,400 square feet of living space. The previous owners of the house were not visually impaired or physically disabled in any way, and the house remains structurally and architecturally the same as it was when I bought it.

Ms. Anderson also states that I "get help in mowing my lawn and other outside work." She made no inquiries concerning yard work. The fact of the matter is that I have hired a professional lawn service. The lawn service I use serves over 90 homes in the Tacoma area, and very few of these homes are occupied by the disabled or the elderly. The hiring of the lawn service does not mean that I cannot do the work myself. Why do the other homeowners have the same service?

Ms. Anderson states that my relatives help me. My cousin and her son live with me. I am helping her go to college. We have a living arrangement that is helpful to both of us. She has lived with me for the past year. Prior to that she lived in California, and for almost five years I lived alone. I was not, and am still not, dependent on my relatives.

Ms. Anderson states that my furnishings are simple. I think this is a commentary on her taste and not my furniture. She states that "furniture in the middle of the room would be bothersome." Bothersome to whom? Perhaps she didn't see the coffee table that stands in front of the ten foot sofa that she was sitting on during the interview. Perhaps she didn't see the large ottoman which sits in front of the large round swivel chair that I was sitting in.

Ms. Anderson made no inquiries as to who does the grocery shopping. Yet, she says in her article that I rely on my relatives to do it. Sometimes I shop with them; sometimes I don't. My cousin and I usually shop for groceries once a month as a matter of convenience because of our busy schedules. We buy large quantities, requiring the use of a car—which, I may add, I own.

Ms. Anderson also stated that "house cleaning chores are mostly done by relatives." How does she know this? She certainly didn't ask. If she had, she would have found that we all share equally in the housework. Everyone keeps their own room clean, including my cousin's seven-year-old son. We all share in keeping the rest of the house clean. She has me quoted as saying that I can cook, iron clothes, and do household chores. However, she turns right around and states that "house-cleaning chores are mostly done by relatives."

I am sure Ms. Anderson felt she was doing a great service to me and the blind community. I also realize that for a newspaper to attract its readers, it must have "good copy," and that in many cases a story must be dramatized to emphasize a point. However, this article is so distorted and false that I feel it has done more damage than good. The attitudes she expresses are more sophisticated than the stereotyped sob story of the blind man selling pencils on the street corner, but the fundamentals are the same.

This is Glen Latham's letter, and it sums up an entire system—the clever and plausible but false and misleading ideas and beliefs which have blocked our progress and blighted our lives through the centuries. The reporter's intentions were doubtless good and her motives the best, but the damage is no less severe and the hurt no easier to bear—not to mention which a lot of us are getting tired of having our road to hell paved with other people's good intentions. More often than not, such people act shocked if we try to set them straight and feel angry if we are not grateful for the efforts they have made. Our conduct is at variance with the humility they expect us to demonstrate. We do not wish to be arrogant or turbulent, but we are not prepared to sit passively by and be pictured as what we are not. Let people think what they will and call us what they please. We are simply no longer willing to be second-class citizens. We have learned the truth about ourselves and our blindness, and (regardless of the consequences) we intend to live that truth. We know who we are, and we will never go back.

If the Glen Latham story were an isolated instance, it would be regrettable but not worth making much noise about. However, it is not isolated but typical. The Jaycees of Sioux Falls, South Dakota, encouraged the blind of the area to become members. With no further details one would applaud the action. However, the Jaycees established a segregated chapter for the blind—and what do you suppose the chapter was named? It was called the Deadeye Chapter. If the name was meant to be funny, it is sick. If it was not, it is sicker. Ben Mayry and our other South Dakota members are fighting hard to combat such madness, and we are making progress; but the road stretches far ahead.

The United States Association for Blind Athletes is relatively non-controversial, but in 1979 a seemingly innocent event concerning that organization occurred which demonstrates why the sophistries about blindness are so attractive to the members of the sighted public. Jeff Hopper is vice president of marketing and administration for a savings and loan association in the Puget Sound area. He is also volunteer president of the Northwest Chapter of the United States Association for Blind Athletes. In a magazine column he wrote as follows:

> The concept of winning has long been taught through athletic competition. It is a priority in our society and most people who would be considered "successful" can relate to some form of athletic competition.

Until recently, however, blind and visually impaired persons in the United States have been excluded from athletic participation. More importantly, the lack of athletic participation for the visually handicapped has restricted their learning of the winning process.

I am sure that Mr. Hopper is both generous and sincere, and at first glance there would seem to be nothing wrong with his statement. But look again. Is it really necessary for the blind (or, for that matter, the sighted) to engage in athletics to learn the concept of winning or understand how to be successful? If it is, and if the blind never had the opportunity to participate in athletics before the establishment of the United States Association for Blind Athletes, then how very much more important and significant is Mr. Hopper's volunteer work than it would be if he were simply performing a run-of-the-mill civic or community project. Of course, the whole proposition is nothing but nonsense and sophistry. A great many of the most successful people the world has ever known have not had the slightest interest in athletics; and as we know from personal experience, there are (and always have been) plenty of ways for the blind to learn the concept of winning without engaging in athletics. This is not to take anything away from the United States Association for Blind Athletes or Mr. Hopper. It is only to point out one of the reasons why sophistries about the blind are so attractive. They permit sighted people with feelings of inferiority to feel important.

Even though the actions of the newspaper reporter, the Jaycees, and Mr. Hopper do us harm, there may be some excuse for their behavior. They are not constantly dealing with blind people, and they do not have the opportunity on a daily basis to observe the problems created by the misconceptions and wrong ideas which they help to promote. For the most part they do not claim to be experts.

Unfortunately the same cannot be said for the employees of the governmental and private agencies established to give service to the blind. Their much vaunted "professionalism," their very rationale for being, rests upon the premise that they know what blindness is about and how to deal with it. In the manner of doctors dealing with medical matters, they hold themselves out as the possessors of correct information, and they say they can teach that information not only to the public but also to those of us who are blind.

Yet, much of the literature which comes from these agencies is worse than what we get from the public. As an example, I call your attention to a book published by the American Foundation for the Blind in 1974 and reissued in 1978. It was written by a person with impressive credentials named Anne Yeadon, and it is entitled *Toward Independence—The Use of Instructional Objectives in Teaching Daily Living Skills to the Blind.* If there was ever a case of destructive sophistry and just plain drivel, this book is it. If what it teaches represents all we can expect in the way of independence, who can wonder at the fear people have about blindness and the low esteem in which we are so often held!

This treatise on "independence" has sections on: table behavior, domestic tasks, kitchen equipment, and cooking. Let us look at the section on table behavior. It contains these subparts:

Seating Self at a Table
The Locating Technique
An Informal Place Setting
Exploring Contents of a Plate of Food
Use of a Knife and Fork to Cut Food
Placing Knife on Plate When Not in Use
Checking for Food Dropped from Plate
Placing of Knife and Fork at Close of Meal
Differentiating Pepper and Salt
Applying Pepper and Salt
Pouring Cold Liquids
Adding Sugar to a Drink
Use of the Spoon for Stirring
Obtaining Food From a Relish Dish
Boning a Fish
Serving Self at the Table
Pouring of Hot Liquids
Carrying Containers of Food/Liquid
Drinking Soup With the Aid of a Spoon
"Scooping" Food With the Aid of a Fork
The "Buffer" Technique
Buttering a Piece of Bread
Cutting Salad With a Knife and Fork
Use of a Fork to Eat Desserts
Handling and Eating Dry Foods
Cutting Fried Eggs With the Aid of a Knife and Fork
Cutting a Piece of Pie/Cake
Lighting a Cigarette
Using an Ash Tray

I think we can get the tone of the book by examining two of these items. First, let us see what it says about "Placing Knife on Plate When Not in Use":

TITLE: Demonstrating the placing of the knife on the plate.

OBJECTS: During the course of a meal the student will demonstrate the ability to place the knife on the top right hand side of the plate. This will be done in accordance with the following criteria:

1. With the handle of the knife over-lapping the edge of the plate;

2. Without the knife being pushed over or into the plate;

3. Ensuring ease in relocating knife by using same position each time.

TECHNIQUE (Manual Dexterity): The student, during the course of a meal, may decide he does not need the use of the knife. In order to relocate the knife easily, it is suggested that it be placed in the same position on the plate each time, e.g. across the top right-hand corner of the plate, between a 12 o'clock and 3 o'clock position. [I might inject here that most of the plates I deal with do not have corners...but back to the text.]

In order to achieve the above, the student will bring his right hand to the right side edge of the plate-but will not allow the knife to touch the table. The thumb will locate an approximate 3 o'clock position. The handle of the knife will be placed in this position, with the tip of the hand slightly overlapping the edge of the plate—this allows the student to relocate the knife by running his fingers along the outer edge of the plate and not placing his hand into the plate.

Safety Awareness: The student will attempt to retain a mental picture of the position of the knife, as the fork, when being used, may inadvertently push the knife from the plate.

That is what it says, and for the life of me I cannot understand the comment about safety. Moreover, one gets the distinct impression that the author is speaking to a child, programming a robot, or talking to a person who has never had contact with civilization. When an individual becomes blind, that individual does not automatically lose all of the knowledge and abilities that he or she ever possessed; nor does the person become retarded.

But back to the book. What is said about the knife is no worse than what is said about the spoon:

TITLE: Demonstrating the use of a spoon for stirring.

OBJECTIVE: When presented with a container of liquid and a spoon the student will demonstrate the ability to use the spoon to stir the liquid. This will be done in accordance with the following criteria:

1. By placing the spoon into the container without causing the container to overturn or overflow;

2. By introducing the "stirring motion" without the liquid overflowing;

3. By replacing the spoon in its original position without disturbing other items.

TECHNIQUE (Manual Dexterity): The student will hold the spoon in the same manner as a soup spoon, except that it will be held with the inner bowl facing the student's body and in a vertical position when placed in the container. [I interrupt to wonder how else except in a vertical position one could hold the spoon if the container has any depth and if it is in an upright position with its bottom on the table—but back to the learned text.]

If the container has a handle the student will grasp it firmly. If the container does not have a handle the student will place the thumb of the free hand over the top, side edge and the remaining fingers will lie just below the thumb along the side of the bowl. The spoon will be brought to the container and the bowl of the spoon placed to the liquid.

Finger Manipulation and Safety Awareness: The spoon will be turned, usually clockwise motion, around the circumference of the container, by a gentle circular motion of the wrist without scraping the sides or bottom of the container. The spoon will then be returned to its original position. If, however, the liquid is thick, the handle of the spoon should be lightly tapped on the side of the container—to remove excess—before returning to its original position.

NOTE: The instructor will hold her hand over the student's and vice versa, and demonstrate the smoothness of the task. A student low on concepts will probably require extensive practice to achieve successful results.

I find myself very nearly overwhelmed—and also beset by a number of questions. What if the she is a he? What if I don't want to move the spoon in a clock-wise direction? What if I don't want to grasp the handle of the container or drape my fingers over the top side edge? It is enough to drive one to drink—after, of course, the spoon has been removed as a matter of safety.

Remember that there is an entire book full of this idiocy and that this is not an isolated but a typical example of what we are getting from the agencies. Is it any wonder that the public is reinforced in its misconceptions and that the blind (especially blind children who grow up in the system or newly blind persons who fall into its clutches) come to doubt their worth and belittle their abilities!

With this sort of madness coming not just from the public but also from the agencies it is no wonder that blind persons (especially those not having the perspective which is gained by the information, the shared experiences, and the reinforcement which come from membership in the National Federation of the Blind) often develop offbeat and unrealistic devices for trying to gain prestige and for not appearing to be like other blind people. There is the Uncle Remus technique of pretending to be crafty and possessed of special powers, which is typified by a quote attributed to a blind man who was formerly in the Maryland legislature. In the article concerning his death in the July 31, 1979, *Baltimore Sun,* this passage appears: "As a legislator, he maintained that his blindness was an aid as well as a handicap. He once told a reporter that he developed an increased sense of hearing because of his loss of sight, which he said allowed him to pick up word of political deals being made far down a hall or across a committee room."

Of course, we know that such claims are utter nonsense, playing on the credibility of the public and reinforcing and feeding back to the sighted their own superstitions. Or perhaps the man didn't say it at all. Maybe it was simply made up by the reporter as a good line and a plausible story. Whichever way it happened, this sort of thing does not achieve the objective of making the blind seem more capable. It harms us and increases the general notion of our abnormality.

Then, there is another technique. In the May 10, 1984, *Washington Post* there is an article headlined "Blind Student Seizes Challenges." The article details the accomplishments of a blind student—president of the student body, floor president of his dormitory, administrative assistant to the College Democrats, and a lot more of the same. In the midst of it all, this passage occurs: "Schroeder lives in a house off campus with three other students. He usually walks the 20 minutes from home to campus alone. No dog, no cane, no guide. Using any of these aids would mean 'admitting that he is blind,' said Andrew Sherman, a good friend. 'And he doesn't envision himself as a blind person. He sees himself as a person who is blind.'"

This is not independence. It is pathetic self-deception. Again, it does not elevate the image or improve the standing of the blind—not even of the student in question. The very article we are discussing proves the point by talking about how the student gets lost and spends hours trying to find his way home, and how he is very proud of not having to ask for help.

So the circle is complete—the misconceptions of the public, the acceptance and strengthening of those misconceptions by the agencies, the passthrough to the blind, and the feedback once more to the public: each component reinforcing the myths and false beliefs of the other and each using the other as authority. In such circumstances is it any wonder that I recently received a letter from an inventor who said that he had constructed a special toilet paper holder for the blind and that he would like us to help him market it? Is it any wonder that another inventor thinks the blind cannot clean themselves at all and should only use toilet paper for drying after being washed by the special spray he has constructed? In his letter of October 25, 1983, the inventor says: "The blind will really appreciate the use of the Hygeia cleaning because the designed spray cleans quickly and thoroughly. Drying is complete by only using a few sheets of tissue or a small cloth."

Is it any wonder that a man wrote to me a few months ago saying that he would rather be dead than blind! In his own words: "I have just been told I have the narrow type glaucoma that might lead to an emergency. I'm scared. Please send any prevention data. Couldn't live without eyesight. Wouldn't want to."

So what does it mean—all of this analyzing of the circle of sophistry about blindness, all of this talk about where we are and where we have been? What is our present situation, and what lies ahead? In the first place let us recognize that, with all of our problems, we have it better today than we have ever had it before in all of our history. In ancient times we were exposed to die on the hillsides as babies. In the middle ages we were dressed in donkey ears and forced to fight each other at country fairs for public sport. In the early years of the present century we were treated with more apparent kindness, but as we know, appearances are not always what they seem. We were no longer put out to die on the hillsides or forced to fight each other for the entertainment of our neighbors, but the substance of public attitudes remained the same. There were no jobs, no opportunities, and no hope.

I know from personal experience (and so do many of the rest of you) the pain and despair of continued isolation and nothing to do. Some of us broke free. The rest remained captive—some for a lifetime, and some still existing. There comes a time when the spirit dies and the body lives on. It is a close question as to whether it is better to die as a child or continue to exist year after year in the living death which many of the blind have endured. Yes, I know the implications of the question; and no, I am not exaggerating. I mean exactly and literally what I say.

But, of course, our answer to the question is simple: we are no longer willing to accept either one of these alternatives. We have learned to be free, and we intend to keep it that way. We have eaten at the table of liberty, and we will never again settle for the crumbs on the floor.

As our movement continues to strengthen, the circle of sophistry weakens. There is much good will toward the blind, and while it is true that some people resent our progress, most do not. As they learn who we are and what we are, the majority join with us. With the work of the Federation in South Dakota the Deadeye Chapter of the Jaycees lasted for less than a year. Our television and radio announcements blanket the airwaves, and we have had major network coverage in recent months. We confront the airlines when they try to make us take segregated seating. We find new jobs in expanded areas of employment. Above all, an increasing number of us are living our Federationism on a daily basis, knowing it to be our passport to freedom. In the days ahead our task will not be easy. We know it, and we are prepared. Whatever the sacrifice, we will make it. Whatever the price, we will pay it. We must finish our march to acceptance and full membership in society. Our heritage requires it; our purpose proclaims it; our humanity demands it. This cause of ours is a sacred trust. It is worthy of all that we have or can ever hope to be—and we shall not fail. My brothers and my sisters, the future is ours. Come! Join me in the battle, and we will make it all come true!

Philosophy in Action

In 1985 at the annual convention banquet Kenneth Jernigan delivered what was to be his penultimate address as the Federation's President. Speaking on the topic, "Blindness: The Pattern of Freedom," Jernigan drew the attention of his audience to the parallels between the civil rights struggle of the 1960s, involving the rising demands of blacks for freedom, and the civil rights battle of the eighties, involving the rising demands of the blind for freedom. It was, he said, in both cases, the same pattern of freedom. With regard to the black movement, "As long as the law made it impossible for them to buy or rent certain property, required them to attend segregated schools, made them ride at the back of the bus, and even said they must use separate water fountains and toilets, all of the self-belief and public education in the world would not be sufficient. They had to change the laws and the interpretation of the laws, and they did change them."

And Jernigan went on to declare: "Our situation is parallel. We must fight in the courts and the Congress. Judges order children to be taken from blind parents on the ground that the blind cannot raise them; airline officials tell us we cannot occupy exit row seats and that we must sit on blankets for fear we cannot control our bladders; insurance companies deny us coverage; amusement parks refuse to let us ride; health clubs decline to let us in; and employers routinely discriminate. Unless we can move toward equal treatment under the law, self-belief and public education will not be sufficient and cannot be sustained." And he pointed out that the changes in the law could not be accomplished without confrontation.

President Jernigan's banquet address spelled out the full context—legal, moral, and political—within which certain basic rights were then being debated and would be decided: the right to fly, the right to a chance for a decent education, the right to bear and raise children, the right to receive training with the special tools and techniques needed by the blind, the right to equal opportunity to employment, and the right to be recognized and accepted as normal human beings. It was truly a civil rights speech—in the great tradition of such orations—and in that sense it evoked and embodied the essential keynote of the organized blind movement. It summarized the philosophy of freedom in practical terms—delineating the steps essential to the integration of a minority into the broader society. It called for action, and demanded that the philosophy of equality be made real. The keynote was *freedom*—and not merely in theory. Freedom means power to do specific things—power to be left alone, power to travel, power to sit where one chooses, and power to become an element within the overall pattern of freedom.

Following is the text of the 1985 convention banquet address:

BLINDNESS: THE PATTERN OF FREEDOM
by Kenneth Jernigan

When the playful dawn came down to the sea,
I ruffled its hair with gladness.
I saw the waves and flexed my soul in freedom.
Humanity comes through the optic nerve,
And justice lives in the eye.
Not creed or law or politics
But curvature and the nature of light.
The blind man yearns in a land apart,
Slave though richest king.
Not for him the full broad sweep of mind and spirit—
Dark the channel, nerve and tissue;
Long eternal through the night.
Day comes down to touch the ocean,
And I stand up to look and live.
Books of science unromantic—freedom's passport to the soul.[1]

When I first read that poem, I thought how literate, how polished, how skillfully written—how absolutely gross and totally false. Poetry is the art of saying so much in so few words that prose will not work as a means of expression. It does for language what the computer does for science and what the aerial photograph does for a landscape. On nothing more than a sheet of paper you can do any calculation which the most up-to-date computer can do, but if the problem is complex, you will do it more slowly—so much so that you will never live to finish it. You will not understand the patterns and relationships—or, for that matter, even know they exist. They will be buried in minutiae and lost in delay. Likewise, you can walk the earth and map a continent, but you can never see its patterns and perspectives. There is too much detail, and it will take too long to put it together.

Poetry (properly used) cuts through verbiage and speaks to the soul. Like the computer and the aerial photograph, it condenses time and repeats patterns. But we must not be bamboozled. There is no magic in sophisticated tools. They are only as good as our understanding. Ancient astronomy predicted quite accurately the course of the stars and the date of eclipses, but it was based on the mistaken notion that the earth is flat and the center of the universe. In the absence of understanding a computer would not have brought enlightenment. It would only have reinforced the misconceptions. Aerial photographs are equally subject to misinterpretation. They give us data but not the wisdom to comprehend it.

Poetry is the same. It does not live in a vacuum but is built on a frame of accepted values and assumed truths. Therefore, when the poet tells us that humanity comes through the optic nerve and justice lives in the eye—when he speaks of freedom as a product of sight—he is not proclaiming new discoveries but repeating old superstitions: our common heritage—man's ancient fear of the dark, the equation of sight with light and light with good. He is doing what the perceptive poet always does. He is resolving contradictions and distilling (whether true or false) the essence of cultural consensus. He is going to the core of our inner being and making us face what we truly believe.

But, of course, an increasing number of us do not believe it. In fact, it is not a question of belief. As we go about our business from hour to hour and minute to minute, we know from personal experience that it is false. Blindness does not mean dehumanization. In our homes and our offices, in factories and laboratories, on farms and in universities, in places of recreation and forums of civic accomplishment we live the refutation of it every day. While it is true that seventy percent of us do not have jobs and that all of us are routinely treated like children and wards, it is equally true that thirty percent of us have jobs and that all of us are coming to realize that the problem is not blindness but mistaken attitudes. If even one of us can be a scientist (and many of us are), that does not prove that if an individual is blind he or she can be a scientist, but it does prove that blindness will not prevent a person from being a scientist. In short, it proves that blindness is not the barrier.

Sight is enjoyable; it is useful; it is convenient. But that is all that it is—enjoyable, useful, and convenient. Except in imagination and mythology it is not more than that. It does not have mysterious psychological implications; and it is not the single key to happiness, the road to knowledge, or the window to the soul. Like the other senses, it is a channel of communication, a source of pleasure, and a tool—nothing less, nothing more. It is alternative, not exclusive. It is certainly not the essential component of human freedom. The urge to liberty and the need to be free are commodities of the spirit, not the senses. They divide civilization from savagery and human beings from animals.

Liberty has been the focal point of more study and comment than perhaps any other idea which has ever troubled, motivated, and inspired mankind. It is the stuff of dreams, not optic nerves and eyeballs. The effort is always to understand and, by so doing, make life better and more in tune with ultimate reality—a combination of bread and the prayer book, food for the body and food for the soul.

Liberty and freedom. Two words, one concept. Always noble, always imposing—ever the dream, ever the mover of nations. And while we cannot capture freedom in a rigid cage, we can describe it, seek it, and recognize its transcendent power.

Harold Laski said: "We acquiesce in the loss of freedom every time we are silent in the face of injustice."

Daniel Webster said: "God grants liberty only to those who love it, and are always ready to guard and defend it."

Benjamin Franklin said: "They that give up essential liberty to obtain a little temporary safety deserve neither liberty nor safety."

Samuel Adams said: "If you love wealth better than liberty, the tranquillity of servitude better than the animating contest of freedom, go home from us in peace."

John Dewey said: "Liberty is not just an idea, an abstract principle. It is power, effective power to do specific things. There is no such thing as liberty in general; liberty, so to speak, at large."

Cicero said: "Freedom is participation in power."

Herbert J. Muller said: "Freedom is the condition of being able to choose and to carry out purpose."

Herbert Spencer said: "No one can be perfectly free until all are free. No one can be perfectly moral until all are moral."

The nineteenth-century German writer Max Stirner said: "Freedom cannot be granted. It must be taken."

Walter Lippmann said: "Men cannot be made free by laws unless they are in fact free because no man can buy and no man can coerce them. That is why the Englishman's belief that his home is his castle and that the king cannot enter it, like the American's conviction that he must be able to look any man in the eye and tell him to go to hell, are the very essence of the free man's way of life."

So the tapestry of freedom is constantly being woven, and we are part of the fabric; but there is something beyond. There always is. Each minority has its separate pattern, its road to freedom, its task to be done. And for the blind that task is monumental. It is nothing less than the total redirection of society's effort and perception—for we are not patients, and (contrary to popular belief) our problem is not lack of eyesight or inability to perform.

What we need most is not, as the professionals would have it, medical help or psychological counseling but admission to the main channels of daily life and citizenship, not custody and care but understanding and acceptance. Above all, what we need is not more government programs or private charitable efforts. Instead, we want jobs, opportunity, and full participation in society. Give us that, and we will do the rest for ourselves. Give us jobs, equal treatment, and a solid economic base; and we will do without the counseling, the sheltered workshops, and the social programs. We will not need them. We have the same medical, vocational, social, and recreational needs as others; but our blindness does not create those needs, and it does not magnify or enlarge them. It does not make them special or different. We are neither more nor less than normal people who cannot see, and that is how we intend to be treated. We want no strife or confrontation, but we have learned the power of collective action, and we will do what we have to do to achieve first-class status. We are simply no longer willing to be second-class citizens.

When the National Federation of the Blind came into being in 1940, the means were limited and the numbers few, but the goal was clear. Today (almost fifty years later—when we have tens of thousands of members and are the strongest presence in the affairs of the blind) the purpose is unchanged. It is exactly what it was in 1940. It can be told in a sentence. We want freedom—jobs, homes, the chance to succeed or fail on our own merit, access to places of public accommodation, interdependence with our neighbors, and full participation in society. The words are easy, but the fact has been long delayed. From the dawn of history blind men and women have worked and hoped and waited, but only in recent years (only with the coming of the National Federation of the Blind) has our dream approached reality. And now the waiting is over. Yes, we have waited—oh, God, how we have waited!—but never again! No more! In this generation our time has finally come—for we are determined at long last to live the truth of what we are, and not what others think we are or try to make us become or believe. As Cicero said: "Freedom is participation in power." And as Max Stirner said: "Freedom cannot be granted. It must be taken."

There are four essential elements in the pattern of our freedom. Each has a different part to play, and each is necessary. They blend to form a tapestry, which can never be finished without the composite.

The first and most important of these elements is internal. It is what we believe and become within ourselves. The second is public education. The third is the law. The fourth is confrontation. Other people tend to treat and value us as we treat and value ourselves. In matters of the spirit, before a thing can become reality, we must believe it; and before we can believe it, we must say we believe it.

We say we are as good as the sighted, able to compete with them on terms of equality. We say that we deserve all of the privileges and responsibilities of citizenship and that we are capable of exercising them. We say that it is respectable to be blind. When the time comes that a majority of us know for a certainty within ourselves that these things are true (know it so surely that we act and live it every day and do not even need to think about it or question it), our battle will largely be won.

Walter Stromer is a blind professor. He lives in a small town in Iowa and teaches at the local college. He is thought of by his colleagues and students as successful, quite successful—and he doubtless shares that opinion. But do his associates think of him as successful measured by others on the campus, or only by the standard of what they think a blind person can do and can be expected to do? Which standard does Dr. Stromer use? For that matter, does he even know that there are different standards? Does he perhaps enjoy being thought of as remarkable, unusual, inspiring, and brave—failing to realize that he has made a bad bargain and that the eye is not freedom's passport to the soul?

A number of years ago Stromer appeared on a panel to discuss the meaning of blindness, and as a result he published a paper entitled "One Day In The Life of Me." Speaking of his early morning radio listening, he says: "Fortunately the station I listen to most is near the end of the dial. Finding stations in the middle of the dial can be a problem unless you know exactly what program to listen for."

Progressing to the time of departure for work, he says: "Just before I leave for class I remember I forgot to have my wife record the grades for the speeches made yesterday. I could do it in Braille, but it would be most tedious and time-consuming."

In further reference to Braille he says: "Looking for one sheet of paper in a stack is not bad when you can see; it's maddeningly slow when you have to run your fingers over the first dots of every sheet to figure out what it is."

As he leaves the house, he says: "But finally I'm off to school, after pausing in the door for a minute to try to remember if I've got everything. Others do that, too, but they can see things lying on the chair or table, to remind them to take along; with me it has to be a more conscious mental effort. Which explains of course why I'm so alert, because I have to use my brain more, which is what keeps it sharp, or wears it to a frazzle."

His thoughts as he goes from home to campus are in the same vein: "Walking to school is fairly relaxing," he says. "At least once

a week I try to remember to be grateful for not having to fight
the noise and congestion of the city." What a melodramatic piece
of self-pity! Many people prefer small towns to cities, but I
wonder how many of them are able to work blindness and pathos
into it. After all, the city has advantages, too—and you could
probably get blindness into that as well if you put your mind to
it.

And how does Stromer feel about his teaching? He says: "In a
few minutes I'm in class. After twenty-two years I'm fairly comfortable."

After all of this tension and heavy introspection, it is only natural
that Stromer feels tense and a little weary. A counteractant might
be in order. "Home to lunch now," he says. "Just a good eight-
minute walk, downhill all the way. A small glass of wine, a short
nap, maybe only five minutes, and then lunch and I'm ready for
the afternoon....I stretch out for a nap before supper. I wonder
if all blind people need those naps as much as I do. I think I'm
fairly relaxed, but I'm sure an average day takes more nervous
energy out of me than it does out of somebody with good vision,
because so many things that sighted people can do without thinking, I have to do with a good bit of conscious effort."

Stromer is not a phony. He believes it—and his associates believe
it. But it is false to the core. It is what I call "The Stromer
Syndrome." His neighbors think (within the limits, of course, of
common sense and what they believe a blind person can do) that
he is wonderful. They make of him a conversation piece. They tell
him, each other, and anybody else who will listen that he is witty,
accomplished, and inspiring. He uses the same words we use—independence, understanding, realistic approach to blindness, full
participation in society, and all of the rest—but he does not mean
what we mean. In his daily life and thinking he exemplifies almost
every misconception about the inferiority and helplessness of the
blind that I have ever heard: Blind people have difficulty tuning
in radio stations. Braille is tedious and ineffective. It cannot be
scanned. Blind people have more trouble than others remembering what to take to work. This makes their minds alert. They meet
their problems with humor. They are grateful to live in a small
town to avoid the congestion of cities. After twenty-two years they
are fairly comfortable teaching. They have more tensions than
others and, therefore, require more naps, and a little wine.

Stromer undoubtedly feels that his attitudes and behavior are a plus in the struggle of the blind for advancement, but every day his influence is negative. Society (knowing nothing about blindness) has made him what he is and taught him its values. Now, he returns the compliment. He reinforces the misconceptions and teaches society. If his situation was unique (if the "Stromer Syndrome" was personal to the man), it would hardly be worth our attention. We would simply turn our heads in pity and embarrassment and let it go at that. But it is not personal. It is endemic and generic. It has dogged the heels of every minority that has ever walked the road to freedom. How many blacks in the early part of this century tried to straighten their hair and look white? How many laughed, shuffled their feet, and played Amos and Andy to fit the mold of the times? Even more to the point, how many secretly thought the role they were given was just and proper? All of them some of the time, and some of them all of the time. The incentive to believe was overwhelming. Every day they were rewarded for conforming and punished for objecting. Believing, they lived the myth and helped it come true—and both they and society were diminished accordingly. As Herbert Spencer said: "No one can be perfectly free until all are free. No one can be perfectly moral until all are moral." Only when a majority of the blacks came to realize that no imagined advantage, no immediate gain, and no avoidance of punishment could take the place of the privileges and, for that matter, the pains and responsibilities of first-class status did they begin to experience fulfillment—and, then, the world changed.

As it was with the blacks, so it is with the blind. We are part of the general culture, and the pressure to believe and conform is constantly with us. It all comes together in a single sentence in a letter I recently received from a man in Ohio. After telling me that he was losing his sight, he said: "I believe I would rather be dead than blind." Consider the capacity for enjoyment and productive work and the level of daily activity of the average member of the National Federation of the Blind, and ask yourself whether you believe this man's opinion results from dire predicament or cultural conditioning.

Sometimes, of course, the blind person's acceptance of the stereotype is not just conditioning but an attempt (whether conscious or otherwise) to use it for advantage. Phillip Mangold is a blind man who lives in California. In 1980 he wrote a booklet called: *The Pleasure of Eating for Those Who Are Visually Impaired*. We do not have to go beyond the title to find the problem.

There is pleasure in eating, and those who are blind eat; but to imply that there is a connection is a distortion and a disservice. It plays upon the notion that the blind are mysteriously different from the sighted and that we require expert help (presumably from Mr. Mangold) to do the simplest task. His appeal to the public's fears and misconceptions may sell his booklet and promote his employment, but (whether he knows it or not) the price is too high and the bargain bad. When we consider public education (the second of the four essential components in our pattern of freedom), we are reminded again that none of the four stands alone. They overlap and interweave to form a composite. What the blind believe about themselves, they teach to the public; and what the public believes conditions the blind. Not only individuals but also organizations may have negative impact and mistaken attitudes. The American Council of the Blind is a prime example.

Its state affiliate, the Missouri Council of the Blind, plans to hold its 1985 convention in St. Joseph. Carolyn Anderson, secretary-treasurer of the local chapter of the Missouri Council of the Blind, talked to the *St. Joseph News-Press* about the matter last fall. In an article appearing October 28, 1984, she says: "We have a commitment from Boy Scouts who are working on merit badges to serve as volunteer guides when needed by a delegate. Free transportation from both bus stations to the hotel has been arranged. And, since there is no day or night for the blind, the hotel is even providing for food service in case someone decides it's breakfast time at 2 in the morning."

If we did not know the philosophy of the American Council of the Blind, we might be astonished. As it is, we accept this statement as standard procedure—simply another obstacle to overcome on our road to freedom. In an article captioned "Blind But Not Dumb" which appeared in the *St. Joseph News-Press* of November 20, 1984, Beryl Gordon (our local NFB president) tried to mitigate the damage. He said:

> Often I am asked, 'Why can't organizations of and for the blind get together? They are all working toward the same thing, aren't they?' This is a very hard question to answer in one short sentence, and until you see something in the newspaper such as I have recently read you don't even try.
>
> A member of the Missouri Council of the Blind was quoted as saying that since there is no day or night for

the blind, the hotel where they will be holding their 1985 convention will be providing food service in case one of them would decide it was breakfast time at 2:00 a.m.

Can you just imagine what life would be like for the blind if all of us believed something this ignorant? Can you imagine what potential employers might think when reading something this degrading about blind persons' intelligence?

It's no wonder we can't find jobs. It is no wonder public facilities do not want us to come in. It is no wonder others have the attitude that we need to be taken care of.

In case you think Ms. Anderson was misquoted by the reporter, listen to her answer in the *News-Press* of November 29, 1984. She says: "As usual, the National Federation of the Blind misinterprets and twists things for their own purposes. We believe the NFB confronts everything with rudeness, abruptness and single-mindedness. Such negative reactions make it more difficult for those of us trying to work in a positive way. We try to deal with local businesses, officials and the public without considering them to be our enemies. Focusing our efforts on the good and the positive and remembering with gratitude the help we get from the sighted in our community, we have improved our outlook. We try to keep a sense of humor and look at life's inconveniences with some amount of laughter. Perhaps the NFB should try this and not be critical of other people and their efforts."

Whatever else may be said, Carolyn Anderson and Beryl Gordon are not working for the same thing. In one sense, of course, she is right: We could laugh at ourselves, be grateful for whatever we get, and accept the stereotype—but the price is too high. Such conduct translates into exclusion from employment, custodial treatment, and second-class status; and it also blights the spirit and shrivels the soul—for whatever we live and believe, that we surely become.

And we are not just dealing with generalities. It is not simply a matter of being nice or saving feelings. To the extent that we fail to find a way to educate the public, lack the courage to provide that education even in the face of hostility, or are unable to understand our true potential, we and all other blind people suffer. I recently received a letter from the sighted mother of an adopted blind child expressing appreciation for our literature and encouragement: "My daughter Shelly," she said, "is now eleven years old. She is fully integrated in a local school and has learned to read and write Braille.

"Six years ago, when we adopted her, she was a 'potential unknown,' high-risk adoption case. We took her out of a small institution, where she had lived all of her life. She had spent most of her time confined to a large hospital-sized crib, with no stimulation and little human contact. She was in diapers and ate only pureed baby food, which had to be fed to her. In the past six years this same child has become bilingual, is in her third year of piano lessons, skates, swims, rides a double bike, reads and writes, and is no longer a 'potential unknown' but rather a child of great potential."

So writes this sighted mother, and her words give us perspective. It is not pleasant to disagree with others and take public stands, but sometimes the alternative is worse. We do not regard our neighbors as enemies, but this does not mean that we are willing to submit to diapers and pureed baby food. It does not mean that we are willing to accept slavery—even if the slavery is gently offered, kindly meant, and well-intentioned. As John Dewey said: "Liberty is not just an idea, an abstract principle. It is power, effective power to do specific things." And as Benjamin Franklin said: "They that give up essential liberty to obtain a little temporary safety deserve neither liberty nor safety." We want no strife or confrontation, but we are not willing to give up essential liberty to obtain a little temporary safety. We have learned the power of collective action, and we will do what we have to do. We are simply no longer willing to be second-class citizens.

The need for public education is everywhere apparent. The fact is typified by an article appearing in the *Omaha World-Herald* of December 5, 1984. Headlined "Donations Pay for Glasses for Needy During the Year," the article says: "Detecting and solving vision problems are important in the proper development of children, said Dr. Matilda McIntire, director of community pediatrics at Creighton University. That is why the cooperative effort of The *World-Herald* Good Fellows and Creighton is valuable to the community," she said. "We feel very strongly that a child cannot learn if he cannot see."

To which we reply, thousands of us grew up as blind children and have achieved a moderate degree of literacy and success. If Dr. McIntire is right, I wonder how we did it.

Early this year I received a letter from one P. F. Membrey, who described himself as the director of CAPEX, a product consulting and export firm from London, England. He said, concerning a new Braille-Writer which he wished to sell: "Following its recent introduction to the United Kingdom market, CAPEX have been appointed sole distribution agents for this unique product. Accordingly, we are now able to supply the BRAILLEWRITER to those institutions or individuals who work with or have care of blind or partially sighted people." Mr. Membrey, Carolyn Anderson, and Dr. Stromer would probably say we are nit-picking, but people usually say what they mean even if they do not mean to say what they say. The orientation which (whether inadvertently or not) leads to talk of selling a product to "institutions or individuals who have care of blind or partially sighted people" is destructive and damaging. We must observe it, reject it, and attack it—not only for public enlightenment but for our own self-respect. As Harold Laski said: "We acquiesce in the loss of freedom every time we are silent in the face of injustice." We want no strife or confrontation, but we are simply no longer willing to be second-class citizens.

The need for public education about blindness is repeatedly demonstrated. Emotional newspaper articles appear telling about sighted people who blindfold themselves to know what it is like to be blind; the *National Geographic* talks about an inchworm "groping along slowly, reminiscent of a blind man with a cane,"[2] and in a descriptive brochure Ewing Mays (the founder of Mays Mission for the Handicapped) says: "Every day there are handicapped people here training handicapped people...one amputee working with another amputee, one deaf person training another deaf person, and even a blind person guiding another blind person." The operative word, of course, is "even." Why "even"? In that one word is summed up the prejudice of centuries—a way of life and a system we are determined to change.

And we are changing the system. We are heightening our own self-awareness and conducting extensive campaigns of public education—but this is not enough. We must deal with the legal system and the law. Again, let us consider the blacks. Before they could begin to achieve equality, they had to build an image within themselves. That was the first and most important thing. Then, they had to educate the public, for they could not exist in a vacuum or live what the culture would not accept. But they also had to do something else. As long as the law made it impossible for them to buy or rent certain property, required them to attend segregated schools, made them ride in the back of the bus, and even said they must use separate water fountains and bathrooms, all of the self-belief and public education in the world would not be sufficient. They had to change the laws and the interpretation of the laws, and they did change them.

Our situation is parallel. We must fight in the courts and the Congress. Judges order children to be taken from blind parents on the ground that the blind cannot raise them; airline officials tell us we cannot occupy exit row seating and that we must sit on blankets for fear we cannot control our bladders; insurance companies deny us coverage; amusement parks refuse to let us ride; health clubs decline to let us in; and employers routinely discriminate. Unless we can move toward equal treatment under the law, self-belief and public education will not be sufficient and cannot be sustained. And, of course, we are making headway. Through court action we have repeatedly restored blind children to their parents. We have persuaded Congress and the state legislatures to expand opportunities and remove discrimination—and we currently have at least a dozen lawsuits under way.

Let anyone who believes we can live with the law as it is presently written consider the following section of the Tennessee Code: "Section 22-1-102. Incompetent persons.—Persons convicted of certain infamous offenses specially designated in this code, persons of unsound mind, persons not in the full possession of their senses of hearing and seeing, and habitual drunkards are incompetent to act as jurors."

That section of the Code is the law in Tennessee at this very moment. John Robb, a blind Tennessean, served on a jury in Nashville last year, but he did it on sufferance and at the whim of the judge. The Tennessee jury law is not only degrading—it is false in its premises. Today we are striking down such laws in state after state, and an increasing number of us are proving their absurdity by serving on juries. I did it myself last year.

As we make progress in reforming the law and getting new interpretations by the courts, we strengthen our self-belief and educate the public. Self-belief, public education, and the law—these three elements intertwine and overlap. But something else is required— the fourth element, confrontation. What minority has ever gone from second-class status to first-class citizenship without it? What minority could? As we come to feel that we deserve equality, we increasingly resist coercion. But it goes beyond that. Unless we are willing to be absolutely docile and totally self-effacing, confrontation is inevitable. In this connection our experience with the airlines is instructive. They deal with us in an arbitrary, capricious, and custodial manner. If we are willing to be humiliated publicly and handled like children, airline personnel will generally treat us fairly well. Otherwise, we are likely to be subjected to anything from a tongue lashing to a trip off the plane with the police.

A few months ago a blind woman in the state of Washington was plopped down on a blanket in an airplane seat, told by airline personnel that she must sit there, and loudly and publicly informed by the flight attendant that, as the attendant put it, it was not because she might "wet" her "pants" but so that in case of emergency she could be quickly lifted onto the evacuation slide. Explaining that she was quite mobile and unwilling to endure such treatment, the blind woman vocally refused to sit on the blanket and pushed it onto the floor. Later she brought a legal action against the airline and was given monetary damages and an apology. But if she had meekly followed orders, the lawsuit would never have been filed. She would have been humiliated and "put down," and her self-esteem and the public image would have suffered accordingly. But in objecting she created hostility and might have been arrested. If we intend to stand up for our rights at all, we can simply not avoid a certain amount of confrontation.

Mike Uribes is one of our members in Fresno, California. Not long ago his chapter president had occasion to write the following letter to a Fresno business establishment:

> On December 19, Mr. Michael Uribes, a blind Fresno resident, while shopping in your mall, was approached by one of your security employees, Mr. Tim Levinson.
>
> Mr. Levinson asked Mr. Uribes if he needed any assistance. Mr. Uribes responded that he did not. However, Mr. Levinson proceeded to follow Mr. Uribes through the mall and a couple of times even put his hand on Mr. Uribes's arm. Again, Mr. Uribes stated that he really did not need any assistance and thanked Mr. Levinson for his offer. Mr. Levinson walked away indignantly saying, "Those damned blind people! They sure are arrogant."
>
> If Mr. Uribes had been a sighted person, this incident would not have happened.

> Mr. Uribes has lived in Fresno all of his life and has been shopping without aid in your mall for at least twelve years. He travels independently.
>
> Mr. Uribes is a member of the National Federation of the Blind of Fresno, which is affiliated with a state and national organization of the same name. Blind persons have the same rights and responsibilities as the sighted and wish to be treated as first-class citizens.

In writing that letter our Fresno president undoubtedly created hostility, but what was she to do? For that matter, what was Mike Uribes to do? He could have avoided confrontation by meekly doing as he was told and allowing himself to be led around the store at Mr. Levinson's whim. By taking Mr. Uribes's arm when he was asked not to do so, Mr. Levinson committed a battery and violated the law; but public sentiment being what it is, he was probably never in danger of being prosecuted. However, what if Mr. Uribes had responded in kind? What if he had shown as much bad temper as Mr. Levinson did? Can we always be sure that the blind person will be cool, polite, level-headed, long-suffering, and patient—even if the sighted person is not? In fact, is that what we want?

As Walter Lippman said: "Men cannot be made free by laws unless they are in fact free because no man can buy and no man can coerce them. That is why the Englishman's belief that his home is his castle and that the king cannot enter it, like the American's conviction that he must be able to look any man in the eye and tell him to go to hell, are the very essence of the free man's way of life."

Is that sort of thing all right (in fact, praiseworthy) for the sighted but not all right for the blind? And what does Lippman mean when he says that no man can coerce you if you are truly free? Does he mean that it is all right for the sighted to resist coercion—even if it means looking somebody in the eye and telling him to go to hell—even if it means using necessary force—but that it is not all right for the blind? Is Lippman's pronouncement meant only for everybody else—or does it include us, too? Can blind people hope to be free Americans? We gave our answer to that question almost fifty years ago. We formed the National Federation of the Blind—and it is still here, stronger and more active today than every before in its history.

It is not only the "Stromer Syndrome" which is arrayed against us. It is also the "be grateful and do as I tell you, or I'll call you militant" syndrome. Let those who oppose our march to freedom call us what they please and say what they like. We will not grovel; we will not pretend that right is wrong; and we will not turn back from the course we have set. No, we do not want strife and confrontation—and yes, we prefer peace and reason. But we know the power of collective action, and we will do what we have to do. We are simply no longer willing to be second-class citizens.

Self-belief, public education, the law, and confrontation—these are the elements in the pattern of our freedom, and each is necessary. They overlap and interweave, and if anyone of them is omitted, all of the rest become meaningless and impossible. Because of the work of the National Federation of the Blind, we who are blind have it better today than ever before in our history, and the hostility we face is not a cause for dejection but an omen of victory; for until a minority is close to its goal, confrontation is neither achievable nor useful. Earlier it is impossible, and later it is unnecessary.

The beginning strands of the pattern of freedom are always woven by slaves, and we have known slavery. Some of us still endure it, and none of us has totally escaped it. A few of us are so immersed in it that we even say we like it and do not know another way exists. But the National Federation of the Blind is abroad in the land, and the blind are learning new ways. We hear the statements of freedom, and they call to our souls and quicken our dreams:

"If," said Samuel Adams, "you love wealth better than liberty, the tranquility of servitude better than the animating contest of freedom, go home from us in peace."

"They that give up essential liberty," said Benjamin Franklin, "to obtain a little temporary safety deserve neither liberty nor safety."

"Freedom," said Max Stirner, "cannot be granted. It must be taken."

We hear, and we understand. We know what we must do, and we have counted the cost. We fight not only for ourselves but also for those who went before us, for Dr. tenBroek and the other founders of our movement—and for those who come after, the blind of the next generation, the children and the children to be.

And we will not fail. The stakes are too high and the alternative too terrible. Tomorrow is bright with promise. We go to meet it with gladness: And we take with us all that we have—our hopes and our dreams, our will to work and our knowledge of deprivation, our faith and our purpose, and our heritage of slavery. And this also we take—our trust in ourselves, our love for each other, and our belief in the ultimate goodness of people. My brothers and my sisters, the future is ours! Come, join me!—and we will march together to freedom!

FOOTNOTES

1. This poem was copied from a wall in New York City in 1985.

2. *National Geographic*, August, 1983, p. 222.

Departure and the Coming of the Third Generation

Presidential terms are for two years in the National Federation of the Blind. In 1984 President Jernigan had told the delegates that while he intended to stand for election that year, he would definitely not be a candidate in 1990. He left open the question as to whether he would stand for election in 1988 or even 1986. In 1985 he told the convention that he would not be a candidate in 1986. He said he felt that many organizations destroyed themselves by not planning for an orderly succession to their top offices and, particularly, by not allowing for a long enough period of transition in the change of executives.

This was a subject which Jernigan had been discussing at the leadership seminars from the time of the mid-seventies. He felt that he should step aside as President some time during the mideighties and then assist in the training of a new leader. The membership repeatedly and overwhelmingly expressed its wish that he continue as President, but in 1985 he announced that a new President must be elected in 1986.

He told the convention delegates that he intended to support Marc Maurer for the presidency in 1986 and that he was making his feelings known so that anyone who had other ideas would have time and opportunity to promote other candidates. In 1986 Maurer was unanimously elected, and the Jernigan presidency ended. Shortly thereafter, Jernigan accepted the unsalaried position of Executive Director of the Federation, working through the remainder of the decade to assist the new President in the duties of the office.

At the 1986 convention, one year after describing the "Pattern of Freedom," Kenneth Jernigan made his final banquet speech as President to the convention of the National Federation of the Blind. This final summation, entitled, "Blindness: The Coming of the Third Generation," spoke of the urgent need for self expression of the blind in the context of the fourth dimension—time. The striving of blind people to make themselves heard through the organized blind movement had been proceeding for forty-six years. How could the spirit of independence and the urgency and immediacy of the need be kept alive and poignant for the decades ahead? What could be expected to be built on the solid and substantial foundation of philosophy and practice developed in the Federation from its beginning? These questions were central to the final banquet address of the Jernigan presidency, delivered in Kansas City, Missouri, on July 3, 1986.

Many organizations (and some countries) have ceased to be significant because their leaders have failed to consider the effects of time. But in the Federation plans had been made for the third generation, the fourth generation, and the fourth dimension. The maturity of the organized blind movement can be seen by the degree of care that it gave in planning for the decades to come. As Jernigan said: "The progress of a people toward civilization can probably best be measured by the degree to which it is concerned with time." The 1986 banquet speech follows:

BLINDNESS: THE COMING OF THE THIRD GENERATION
by Kenneth Jernigan

"Go, sir," said Napoleon to an aide. "Gallop! And don't forget that the world was made in six days. You can ask me for anything you like except time."

Time [said Sir Walter Scott] *will rust the sharpest sword,*
Time will consume the strongest cord;
That which molders hemp and steel,
Mortal arm and nerve must feel.

T. S. Eliot said: "Time present and time past are both perhaps present in time future, and time future is contained in time past."

Plato said, "Time is the image of eternity"; and Pythagoras said, "Time is the soul of the world."

Sir Francis Bacon said, "What we call the age of antiquity is, in reality, the *youth* of the world. *These* times are the ancient times, when the *world* is ancient, and not those which we call ancient by a computation backward from ourselves."

The progress of a people toward civilization can probably best be measured by the degree to which it is concerned with time. Primitive cultures treat time casually, day slipping into day and season into season with grand imprecision; but when the calendar comes, medicine and mathematics come—and soon come poetry, art, and compassion.

Mathematics and concepts of time are, of course, involved in the making of terrible weapons and vicious systems of torture and control, but the urge to kill and the compulsion to maim are not products of science and learning. Exactly the opposite. They come from earlier times and are softened by technology and civilization. While it is true that Adolph Hitler tortured Jews, it is equally true that Good King Richard in Medieval England did likewise. His agents, on one occasion, rounded up all the Jews they could find, locked them in a large building, set it on fire, and burned it. Yet, King Richard was regarded as good and universally admired, while Hitler was regarded as evil and universally condemned. The difference can be found in the culture. In the Middle Ages King Richard's behavior was so commonplace as to go without remark; in the twentieth century, only 700 years later, Hitler's behavior (in many respects the same behavior) was so noteworthy as to provoke worldwide outrage and revulsion.

Time is not only a yardstick of civilization but also a dimension of intelligence. Viewed in the present, intelligence is three-dimensional. To the extent one can change the environment, to the extent (when this is not possible) one can adapt to the environment, and to the extent one knows when to do which—to that extent one is intelligent. When time is added, we have the fourth dimension, and we call it maturity. To the extent one ranges backward in time to understand the causes of present conditions, and to the extent one ranges forward to anticipate future consequences of present acts, one is mature. Maturity is intelligence in depth.

The National Federation of the Blind was founded in 1940. I joined in 1949, during the first decade of the movement. In the 1950s (the second decade of the movement) I became a state president and a national board member. In the 1960s (the third decade of the movement) our founder, Dr. tenBroek, died; and I was elected President. In the 1970s (the fourth decade of the movement) I began conducting regular leadership seminars; we achieved the goal of having chapters and affiliates in every state; and I moved from Des Moines to Baltimore to establish the National Center for the Blind. In the 1980s (the fifth decade of the movement) I was present with many of you at a convention (the one last year in Louisville) attended by over 2,000 registered delegates. It was the largest gathering of blind people ever held in the history of the world. At the present convention (in 1986) I cease being President. Let me, then, from the vantage of the years, talk to you about our movement.

I attended my first National Federation of the Blind convention in 1952. I have never missed one since, so this is my thirty-fifth consecutive convention. What shall I say to you on this last night of my presidency—what that I have not already said many times before? Perhaps we should test the fourth dimension of our intelligence by ranging backward and forward in time. This is 1986. The Federation is forty-six years old. Let us divide that time into two twenty-three-year periods and consider each of them. Let us also consider the next twenty-three years. What will it be like for the blind and for this organization in the year 2009? What will the new century bring?

When the National Federation of the Blind came into being in 1940, the situation was about as bleak as it could possibly be. It was good enough to make the blind hope, and bad enough to kill the hope. Those few who broke out of the system to gain recognition and success did not, for the most part, really break out of the system at all. Their failure can be summarized in a single false concept: "I have made it on my own, without any help from anybody." They shunned other blind people—pretending not to think about blindness at all and dismissing the subject (when they could not avoid it) with so-called "humor" or embarrassment. They made an outward show (reinforced by family and friends) of being superior and not like other blind people. Simultaneously they had an inner fear (in fact, at times a certainty) that they were

exactly like other blind people—at least, exactly like what they
thought blind people were like-just as inferior, just as dependent,
and just as inadequate. They felt complimented when a sighted
person said: "You do things so well that I forget you are blind
and think of you as being just like the rest of us." I say this not
to condemn those blind people (indeed, some of them are still
with us) but to catalog their behavior. Not censure but understanding is required.

Most of the apparently "successful" pre-1940 blind people were
taken over by the agencies and placed in positions of high
visibility, either on the staff or the board. If their function had
been to guide or oversee, the results could have been healthy and
constructive, but the time was not right, the perspective not sufficient, the culture not ready. As it was, the "successful" blind of
that day were (for the most part) fronts and puppets for the agencies. Those who did not join the agencies tended to shun their
fellow blind. That some of them neither succumbed to the agencies nor tried to hide in sighted society is a greater testimonial to
their spirit and maturity than has usually been recognized.

From the ranks of such as these came the founders of our movement. When Dr. Jacobus tenBroek and the handful who joined
with him organized the National Federation of the Blind in 1940,
they did what every minority does on its road to freedom. They
shifted emphasis from the few to the many, from enhancement to
basics. In the pre-1940 era those who thought about blindness at
all (the blind as well as the sighted) put their major effort into
helping the gifted and promoting the exceptional. The Federation
took a different course. It started with the premise that until there
are food, decent clothing, and adequate shelter, there can be no
meaningful rehabilitation, real opportunity, or human dignity. It
was not that the few or the superior were to be neglected but
rather a recognition that none can be free as long as any are
enslaved. The Federation's top priority in the early 1940s was to
get (not as charity but as a right) sufficient public assistance to
provide a basic standard of living for the blind who had no way
to provide for themselves.

There was something else: The Federation said that the blind had
the right to speak for themselves through their own organization
and that no other group or individual (regardless of how well-intentioned) could do it for them—whether public agency, private
charity, blind person prominent in the community, or blind person
heading an agency. The right was exclusive, and only those elected

by the blind could speak for the blind. The test was not blindness, and it was certainly not connection with an agency. Instead, it was representative democracy and self-determination. That is what we stood for in 1940; that is what we stand for today; and that is what we will stand for in the year 2009. From the beginning there has been opposition to this concept—from members of the general public, who have feared and misunderstood blindness; from some of the blind themselves, who have clung to the security of custody and care; and especially from many of the governmental and private agencies, who have felt a vested interest in keeping us passive and seeing that we remain dependent. But on this principle there can be no compromise. It is the bedrock of Federationism. We want no strife or confrontation, but we will do what we have to do. We are simply no longer willing to be second-class citizens.

As the decade of the 1940s advanced and drew to a close, the blind in growing numbers joined the Federation and learned to work together for common good. As the 1950s came and went, we were well on the way to realizing our goal of basic support for the blind who had neither the means nor the opportunity to do for themselves. By 1963 (the end of the first twenty-three years) rehabilitation and job opportunities were emerging as the top priority. The ranks of the first generation of Federationists were thinning, and the blind of the second generation were advancing through the lines to take up the banner and carry it forward.

In the 1940s, when the National Federation of the Blind was young and weak, and when the agencies still hoped to subvert or ignore it, there was relatively little conflict. By the 1950s the situation was different. The agencies launched an all-out attack in an effort completely to destroy our movement and discredit its leaders. By the 1960s the agencies were in full line of battle, and the blind of the second generation stood forth to meet them. It need only be said that we did not die and that we are stronger today than we have ever been. We have never wanted strife or confrontation, but we will do what we have to do. We are simply no longer willing to be second-class citizens.

In 1963 we were still concerned with securing subsistence for needy blind persons (as, indeed, we are today), but that battle was well on the way to being won. Our focus now broadened to include a prime emphasis on rehabilitation. We sought education, training, jobs, and career advancement—and not just through govern-

ment but through private means and, increasingly, through our
own initiative.

As the 1960s advanced and the 1970s and the early 1980s came
and went, our focus again broadened, and our emphasis once
more shifted. Now, in 1986, we are still concerned with adequate
subsistence and with jobs commensurate with ability, but the agencies are no longer as important in our lives as they once were,
and we are devoting increasing attention to the civil rights and
full realization of citizenship which the founders of our movement
originally envisioned as the long range goal. We who are blind are
like all of the rest. When we are hungry, we want to eat; and until
that need is satisfied, we have difficulty thinking about very much
else. But food is not enough. As I have said, we are like all of
the rest. After we have eaten, we want jobs and useful occupation—just like the rest. And after food and jobs, we want equal
participation and human dignity—just like the rest. It was the task
of the first generation of our movement to deal with hunger; it
has been the task of the second generation to deal with jobs; it
will be the task of the third generation to deal with civil rights.

As we survey our situation in 1986, looking back to the founding
and forward to the new century, how far have we come and what
still remains to be done? My first response is that we have come
a long way, probably farther than any of us would have thought
possible in the time we have had to do it. My second response is
that we still have a long way to go. It is as simple and as complex
as a conversation I recently had while riding a train. The sleeping
car attendant was a woman, and she was neither as tall nor as
physically strong as I. She was having trouble reaching high
enough and at the same time applying pressure enough to turn a
lock to move a partition. I asked her to give me the wrench, and
I turned it for her. She was willing to accept the assistance and
seemed grateful to have it, but as she was leaving, she asked if I
wanted a wheelchair when we got to the station. Twenty-three
years ago she would probably not have been permitted to have
the job, and I would probably not have been permitted to help
with the wall.

Twenty-three years ago the battle we are having today with the
airlines would have been unthinkable—and in 2009 (twenty-three
years in the future) I believe it will be equally unthinkable. In the
early 1960s comparatively few blind people were traveling, and
the battle for civil rights was still largely ahead—at least for the
rank and file, for the average blind person. Twenty-three years in

the future (unless we and the blind of the third generation totally default on our responsibilities) the airline battle will long since have been won.

It is not just workers in the transportation industry who misunderstand or block our progress. As we have learned to our cost, our battle for freedom and first-class status is not helped but made more difficult by the actions of many of the governmental and private agencies established to give us service. Earlier this year a top official of the American Printing House for the Blind answered an inquiry concerning the Braille edition of the Lutheran Book of Worship. He said: "The only source for this book which I know of is the Fortress Church Supply Store of Philadelphia, Pennsylvania. We produce the Lutheran Book of Worship for Fortress Press. The reason for the handwritten ink numbers is so that sighted people can pull the pages which are going to be used in a particular worship service so that the blind reader does not have to search through the book for the pages."

The picture which this conjures up is not very hopeful. One would think that the blind person who is able to read the hymn from the Braille page might also have the dexterity and initiative to read the number from the Braille page—and might prefer to do it. The scene is not hard to imagine. The custodialism is virtually total. The sighted keeper opens the book to the appropriate page, places it on the blind person's lap, and says: "Here it is. Sing it." The interchange would probably make most of us in this room feel more like swearing than praying.

But bad as this is, it fades into insignificance when compared with the behavior of Guide Dogs for the Blind, Incorporated, of San Rafael, California. Toni Gardiner is a mature, self-sufficient adult, who holds a responsible job and leads a busy life. When she applied to the San Rafael school for a guide dog, she was (to say the least) not pleased with the response she got. It was not that they rejected her application, for they did not. It was the proposed contract and accompanying material which caused the trouble. Perhaps the best way to demonstrate the nature of the problem is to review with you a document entitled: "Suggested List of Items You Will Need for Your Four-Week Stay With Us." You will have no trouble understanding why Toni Gardiner was unhappy. Here is what Guide Dogs for the Blind sent her:

CLOTHING

low-heeled walking shoes (not new)
slacks, jeans, skirts or dresses
shorts (warm weather)
tops or blouses
dress or pantsuit for graduation and Sundays
shoes for graduation and Sundays
heavy sweater or jacket
heavy coat, optional
scarf or warm hat
gloves
slip
bras
underpants
girdle
pantyhose
socks or knee highs
pajamas or nightgown
robe and slippers
raincoat and rainhat (Oct.-April classes)
rainboots (Oct.-April classes)
swimming suit and cap (May-Nov. classes)

OTHER ESSENTIALS:

comb
brush (for hair and clothes)
toothbrush
toothpaste
shampoo and conditioner
deodorant
hair spray
sanitary pads
usual medicines (aspirin, laxatives, prescriptions, etc.)
shower cap (we have showers only)
Diabetics only: one month supply of insulin, needles,
syringes. Do not pre-measure insulin.
stationery (some addressed envelopes)
For smokers: two-week supply of cigarettes
MEDICAL COVERAGE CARD OR PAPERS

All I can say is this: Maybe the arrangements are made by the
same people who find the appropriate page of the hymn book and
say: "Here it is. Sing it." Maybe the guide dog officials say: "Here
it is. Wear it." Be that as it may, Toni Gardiner wasn't having

any. In a letter to me she said: "I have never been an agency person and resent many of the clauses in the San Rafael contract."

Her letter to the school was straight to the point. It said:

This is to inform you that I am withdrawing my application for a guide dog from Guide Dogs for the Blind, Inc....

I have been a guide dog user for the past seventeen years and have had only two dogs during that time. Both worked until death claimed them....

...Your school's custodial attitude is revealed and reflected in your suggested clothing list. Guide Dogs for the Blind, Inc., is providing a service for adult blind people. Your clothing list is so patronizing as to list sanitary napkins as a necessary item for the month's stay. Do you presume that blind women need such specific information?

I have purchased a Golden Retriever and am paying an ex-Guiding Eyes trainer to train her for me. Although this is a costly proposition, it frees me from having to deal with an institution that assumes that I am a mentally deficient blind person who must be cared for by the "professionals" in the field of guide dog work. Guide Dogs for the Blind, Inc., has a good reputation for turning out well-trained dogs. The time has come to modernize your condescending thinking and to realize that you are providing a service for blind adults who do not require custodial care.

The attitude of Guide Dogs for the Blind of San Rafael is not unique, and it is not limited to the agencies which work with the blind. It is widely pervasive throughout society. Under date of July 1, 1985, the project coordinator for the National Council of Teachers of English wrote to me asking that I send material about blindness so that English teachers throughout the country could help their students learn proper attitudes. Naturally I was pleased. However, my enthusiasm was considerably dampened when she went on to say that she felt it was important for the children to learn compassion while they were young.

Then, there is a booklet which came to me last summer in which the author (a woman who is partially blind) described her limitations. She said: "Everything takes more time and effort, plus five pairs of glasses in a flower pot—a small price for independence. Some things I can't do, like distinguishing traffic lights, cutting my toenails, or recognizing a face except when close up. I've learned to accept limitations."

The problem, of course, is the mixture of fact and foolishness. She is right: She cannot visually recognize a face, but if she listens, she can determine the flow of traffic and, therefore, know when the traffic light changes. As to cutting her toenails, most of us (including the totally blind) have done it since we were children. The overall message attempts to be witty, comes off as only "cute," and is totally false.

In September of 1985 members of the Baltimore Chapter of the National Federation of the Blind went to a local TV station to take part in an audience participation talk show. They wanted to make an announcement about our annual walk-a-thon. In order to make such announcements an organization must bring at least twenty people so that there will be a large audience. On this particular day the guests were a pilot, a flight attendant, and a fired air traffic controller. Questions from the audience were encouraged. Therefore, since the topic was air safety, one of our members raised her hand. The producer approached a sighted member of the group to ask whether he or some other sighted person could speak for the blind and present their questions. The producer was referred to Patricia Maurer, who insisted that the blind be allowed to speak for themselves and ask their own questions. The producer said he was afraid to have a blind person walk to the microphone, and (despite protests from the group) he refused to let them speak. During the program the cameras showed the faces of other sections of the audience but only the backs of the blind. Finally the producer undertook to ask the question for the blind himself. I probably do not need to tell you that the question was watered down and poorly stated. In such an atmosphere our public service announcement was a mockery.

The occurrences I have cited are not isolated but typical. They happen every day. A random list from the last few months makes the point. A woman writes to say that she has devised a way for the blind to play bingo without stress. An inventor wants us to promote a special stair rail for the blind. A corporation writes to ask what kind of hotels should be built for the blind. A court takes a baby from its blind mother and refuses to give it back unless she will agree to feed it in a highchair instead of on her lap, the argument being that the highchair will foster independence while the lap will be messy. A blind woman in the District of Columbia, being arrested for disorderly conduct while under the influence, is taken not to the local jail but to the local mental hospital. A pamphlet on diseases of the eye says that people with macular degeneration cannot safely boil an egg. A prosecutor tells a judge in Missouri that the accused is obviously lying about being blind since his neighbors have observed him playing cards, mowing his lawn, and repairing his porch. A Sioux City blood bank refuses to let a blind man sell his blood, claiming that U. S. Department of Agriculture regulations prevent it. And, then, there is the letter I received from a man from Colorado. He said he was facing a moral dilemma. He had made a contribution to our organization to help disseminate information to the blind, but now he was having second thoughts. He wondered whether he had done the right thing. Maybe, he said, the day's news should be withheld from the blind in their own best interest.

What a dismal catalog! Yet, with all of the discrimination and lack of opportunity, the blind have never had it so good. We are better off today than we have ever been—and the best is still ahead. I have a faith amounting to certainty that during the next generation we will go most of the rest of the way to full participation and equal status in society.

But in view of the fact that the National Federation of the Blind is forty-six years old and that the problems I have discussed still exist in such massive proportion, how can I feel such confidence? Here is where we need the fourth dimension of our intelligence. Progress always begins slowly. It takes time to create an organizational structure, train leaders, and recruit members. That groundwork is now behind us. We have an organizational structure second to none in the world, and we have leaders to match it. We have tens of thousands of knowledgeable members who know what they want and what they must do to get it. The reason we now hear more about the problems I have discussed than we did earlier in the century is not because there is more repression or exclusion at the present time than there was forty-six or twenty-three years ago. There is far less. It is simply that we are more aware of it and more prepared and able to do something about it.

Today we are winning on virtually every front. A little over a month ago forty-four United States Senators sent a letter on our behalf to Secretary of Transportation Elizabeth Dole concerning the airline problem—and this is not remarkable but symptomatic.

We are receiving favorable press coverage; blind persons are finding new jobs; and our members are increasingly participating in public affairs and running for elective office.

But there is something else—something even more basic—something which causes the optimism, gladdens the heart and quickens the spirit for the battles ahead. It is the underlying reason for the confidence and certainty. It is contained in what I said to you at last year's banquet. It is this:

> We say we are as good as the sighted, able to compete with them on terms of equality. We say that we deserve all of the privileges and responsibilities of citizenship and that we are capable of exercising them. We say that it is respectable to be blind. When the time comes that a majority of us know for a certainty within ourselves that these things are true (know it so surely that we act and live it every day and do not even need to think about it or question it), our battle will largely be won.

That is what I said to you last year, and there is mounting evidence that the time I spoke of is at hand. The long years of struggle and preparation are bearing fruit. At first our philosophy was only understood by a few of the leaders, and it seemed to have little application in the daily lives of the rank and file—but year after year, on an ever-widening basis, it was discussed, assimilated, and internalized. Now, Federationism is an integral part of the bodies and souls of tens of thousands of blind Americans. It is personal, compelling, and alive.

A few weeks ago a Federationist from Pennsylvania wrote a letter which brings it all together. He is Terry McManus, who is at this convention. Terry is a quiet man. He does not seek confrontation, but when he was faced with decision, he found that it was easier to endure abuse and public humiliation than to go back to custodialism and second-class status. As you listen to Terry's letter, remember that (though he was in a crowd) he was alone. Nobody would have known if he had ducked the issue or betrayed his principles—but he would have known. He had done it before, but this time he could not. Without ever being aware of it he had crossed an invisible line to become irreversibly a new person. This is what we mean when we say: We know who we are, and we will never go back.

In what happened to Terry, and in his reaction to it, liberation takes tangible form. Diane McGeorge, Mike Hingson, Judy Sanders, Russell Anderson, and numerous other Federationists faced incidents of harassment and bullying on airplanes; and they resisted as best they could—sometimes standing their ground, sometimes ultimately bowing to the pressure, but always undergoing attack and humiliation. We wrote about their experiences in the *Braille Monitor;* and (at national conventions, at state and local meetings, and individually) we discussed what was happening to them. Each of us wondered what we would do if our time came—and the process of internalization continued. Going home from last year's convention (fresh from the discussions and the reinforcement) Steve and Nadine Jacobson found it better to go to jail (with all of the accompanying indignities) than to bend the knee and behave like slaves or wards. Their experience was written about and discussed—and Jim Moynihan, Mary Ellen Reihing, Jacquilyn Billey, Ramona Walhof, Peggy Pinder, Marc Maurer, Steve Hastalis, and countless others listened and thought and took courage. And when their time came, they remembered and were strengthened—and they, in their turn, gave example and courage to others.

When Terry McManus rode on a city bus and the driver and the other passengers tried to make him play the part of the helpless blind man, he remembered—and refused. Here is his letter:

I am writing to relate a blatant incident of discrimination which occurred against me on Tuesday, January 14, 1986. I think you will find it strikingly similar to the outrages blind people have experienced at the hands of airline officials.

On that afternoon at about 5:15 I boarded a standing-room-only Port Authority Transit Bus. Just as I stepped through the door, the driver shouted, "Handicapped passenger; give him a seat." I explained to him that blindness did not in any way limit my ability to stand, that I had good balance and preferred to stand. At this he became quite irate and proclaimed that if I didn't immediately take a seat, he would not move the bus. I calmly told him that I would continue to stand. He began apologizing to the passengers for the inconvenience I was causing them. Then, he spotted a supervisor on the street and got off to consult with him. Meanwhile, the other passengers began bitterly attacking me, calling me "crazy," "inconsiderate," "ignorant," "arrogant," and a few other things which are not printable. One man sarcastically said that he hoped I would sleep well that night. I tried to explain to them that it was not I, but the driver, who was inconveniencing them, and that it was a matter of discrimination and a violation of my civil rights that was involved. They didn't want to listen and grew angrier. I was frightened but knew that I had to continue standing.

You see, this was not the first time I had been harassed by a bus driver in this manner. It had happened a number of times in the past, and on each occasion I sat down after a violent argument. Each time I was embarrassed and humiliated and felt that I had sold out my blind brothers and sisters, who were courageously battling similar discriminatory actions. The last time it happened I promised myself that it would never happen again.

The driver returned with the supervisor, who said he concurred with the driver's decision not to move the bus if I didn't sit. I told him I would stand. He said the seats in the front of the bus were reserved for handicapped persons. I told him I was not handicapped in my ability to stand. I said that if I was breaking some law, he should have me arrested and that if I was not, he should order the driver to move the bus. He obviously knew that I wasn't doing anything wrong because he did not call the police. He said there was an empty bus behind the one I was on and that I could get on that one and sit without feeling that I was being discriminated against. I said I would stay where I was. The driver and the supervisor conferred a bit longer and then decided to take all of the other passengers off the bus and put them on the one behind. They all filed past me, continuing to pour out abuse and make disparaging comments, until only an elderly woman and I remained on board. She explained that she was not able to stand on the other bus. The driver went to see if there was space and returned to report that there was room but that he didn't want to inconvenience the passengers by asking one of them to stand for her. How ironic! He created a major incident by harassing a blind person who was perfectly capable of standing but would not ask passengers to stand for someone with a legitimate reason for requiring a seat. Finally, another bus came, and the elderly woman left.

The supervisor returned, and he and the driver continued to badger me with excuses for their actions:

Since, as the supervisor put it, I didn't have the "privilege of seeing," I wouldn't know when people wanted to get past me and thus would create an obstruction. (They obviously had no trouble filing past me to get to the other bus.)

People are crazy and might knock me down. (I weigh close to 200 pounds, so that is not likely.)

I was standing too close to the driver and obstructing his view. (Other people were standing as close to him as I was, and I would have been happy to move; but the bus was jammed, and there was nowhere to go.)

I had been standing there for about thirty minutes and was beginning to fear that I would spend the rest of the evening on that bus, being badgered to sit—or something even worse. Finally, believe it or not, they decided to take the bus out of service for the general public and drive me to my stop. In retrospect I guess that this is no more unbelievable than cancelling a flight to get rid of a blind passenger. Of course, I continued to stand as we drove to my stop.

The driver went on harassing me about what an ignorant and inconsiderate person I was. I again repeated that it was a question of civil rights. I explained that this was just a small part of a large pattern of discrimination faced by blind people every day. He said that, as a black man, he had been facing discrimination for four hundred years—but of course this was different since sitting down would have in no way prevented me from reaching my destination. I explained that this was precisely the argument used against blacks who dared to object to being forced to sit at the back of the bus, but he refused to see my point. I told him that all of the employers, landlords, insurance carriers, airline officials, and other service providers who practice discrimination feel that their situations are also "different." He informed me that if he ever saw me waiting for a bus again, he would pass me up, and he hoped and anticipated that other drivers would do the same. He further stated that I might have "signed my own death warrant," because the passengers I had inconvenienced would remember me and take action against me on the street. I asked for his bus number, and he sarcastically replied that I should "go out and look at it." Finally, we reached the stop, and I bade him good day. He said I had already ruined it.

As I began walking up the hill toward my home, the shock began to take full effect, and I felt badly shaken by the brutal and dehumanizing treatment I had just received. At the same time I was grateful that my involvement in the National Federation of the Blind had given me the courage to endure such an experience—not only for myself but for all blind people. I was also grateful for the hard work of the members of the National Federation of the Blind of Pennsylvania in securing passage of the amendments to our state's human relations act, which outlaws this type of behavior. I determined to file complaints with both the city and state human relations commissions, requesting the following relief: 1) The Port Authority be required to issue a clear policy statement indicating that its drivers may not order blind passengers to be seated on buses when no seats are available and when other passengers are permitted to stand, and that drivers may not in any way treat blind passengers differently from others; 2) the driver be required to publish in the newspaper a public apology for his abusive behavior; and 3) the Port Authority be required to pay me fifteen hundred dollars in personal damages.

I also decided to bring the matter to the attention of the media. The story received coverage on radio, television, and in the press with varying degrees of support. At first the Port Authority refused to comment, saying that I had threatened legal action. (I never made such a statement to them.) Later they began to claim that I had refused to stand anywhere but in the front of the bus and that I was obstructing the driver's view. (As I have already said, this is not the truth.) The company refused to have a representative appear on camera, but they issued a written statement to the media which claimed that their policy was that elderly and handicapped passengers could stand on buses, provided that they did not interfere with the operation of the bus. In the opinion of the driver, I had done just that. Later, on a call-in talk show, the president of their board of directors indicated that it was the company's policy that handicapped passengers be required to sit. This further demonstrates the need for a clear policy statement. About two weeks later their director of public relations appeared on a talk show, gave a total fabrication of the incident, and poked fun at me.

Thus far, the pain I have suffered has borne some fruit. I have been on several buses since then where the drivers have allowed me to stand. They may have learned something.

People with whom I have discussed this matter are surprised that I was willing to pay such a large price for such a small privilege. One friend observed that I was "all alone on that bus." I explained to him that I was not alone, that there were more than 50,000 people standing shoulder to shoulder with me as I bore the indignities—people like Judy Sanders, Russell Anderson, the Jacobsons, and Mike Hingson—and I was with them when they faced their ordeals. As I read the recent account of what happened to Jim Moynihan, I heard once again the ridicule of the passengers ringing in my ears. We all continue to derive strength from the collective pain, and love is our motivating force. My sympathy goes out to those blind people who have not had the courage and perception to stand with us. By daring to stand and fight together, we insure eventual triumph. Some day all of this will be a thing of the past.

Yours in Federationism,
Terry McManus

To me this letter symbolizes the coming together of the second and the third generations of our movement. As we range backward in time to understand the causes of today's conditions, and as we range forward to anticipate the consequences of our present acts, the experience of Terry McManus and all of the others I have mentioned is pivotal. We have assimilated and internalized the philosophy of our movement, and no force on earth can stay our progress.

I leave the presidency of this organization knowing that our movement has come of age and is fully mature. Make no mistake: We will go the rest of the way to freedom. I know it as surely as I know that the blind are as competent as others. I know it as surely as I know that the sighted are capable of accepting us as the equals we are. We of the second generation of the movement have kept faith with the first generation. We have treasured the heritage, expanded the opportunities, resisted custodialism, fought where we could with the weapons we have had to advance the cause, supported each other, nurtured our fellow blind, and sacrificed and planned for the future. We have also kept faith with our children, the third generation. We have transmitted to them a powerful movement. We have trained them in the ways of freedom. We have shared with them our beliefs and our understanding. We have wanted better for them than we have had for ourselves. And, above all, we have loved them. We do not seek to make them like us, for in our strongest imaginings we cannot go to the house of their ultimate tomorrow. We seek only to go with them as far as we can on the way.

At this convention we have elected a new President. Marc Maurer will make a good President. He will lead with a firm hand, and he will lead with love and maturity. My brothers and my sisters, come! Let us move together into the third generation of the movement.

Chapter 8

The Third Generation and the Maurer Presidency

"It was the task of the first generation of our movement to deal with hunger; it has been the task of the second generation to deal with jobs; it will be the task of the third generation to deal with civil rights."

Those were the words of Kenneth Jernigan in his final convention address as President of the National Federation of the Blind. His 1986 banquet speech dealt with the successive passing of the torch—first from the generation of the founders (epitomized by Jacobus tenBroek) to the second generation of the builders (led by Kenneth Jernigan), and now from these in turn to the emerging third generation of the "defenders" (symbolized by the new President, Marc Maurer). Each generation has had its appointed task, its special mission in the world, said the outgoing President; and as he defined them one by one he had in mind the original and overarching mission of the organized blind movement—the ultimate goals long since proclaimed by the NFB motto and logo which had resounded through the generations and would surely echo down the corridors of future time. Those goals, as every Federationist of each generation had known well, were three: *Security* (dealing with hunger); *Opportunity* (dealing with jobs), and *Equality* (dealing with rights).

For President Jernigan to declare that it would be the task of the third generation to deal with civil rights was, even as he spoke, not just a prophecy but a statement of fact. In the concluding years of his own presidency, the agenda of the movement was already heavily committed to the establishment and defense of the civil rights of blind persons. The battle in the "unfriendly skies," for one thing, was being fought out in terms of civil rights: the rights particularly of equal treatment, of mobility, and of access—and more generally of personal liberty and social equality. Civil rights were also at the center of Federation lawsuits targeting discrimination and prejudice against blind persons.

Like his predecessor in the presidency, Marc Maurer was thoroughly committed to the cause of civil rights well before his election to the leadership. As an attorney representing the NFB, he had for years been instrumentally involved in its civil rights litigation. An early harbinger of Maurer's commitment might be found in a speech delivered at the 1983 convention of the NFB in Kansas City, Missouri, under the title "To Establish Justice: The Law and the Organized Blind Movement." His address was a comprehensive overview of the legal history (and more precisely the civil rights history) of the organized blind movement. Among other things it related the civil service story, the dark history of the sheltered sweatshops, the agony of the airlines, the cruel episodes of blind parents threatened with losing custody of their children, the denial of licenses to blind doctors, and much more. In this illuminating speech Maurer gave an early demonstration to Federationists of the qualities of mind and will which he would later bring to the presidency—and in particular of his determined commitment to establishing justice and protecting civil rights for the blind. Here is what he had to say:

TO ESTABLISH JUSTICE: THE LAW
AND THE ORGANIZED BLIND MOVEMENT
by Marc Maurer

One of the most widespread criticisms of the law is that it is deadly dull. H. L. Mencken said, "One may think of the Supreme Court as a theater of dullness so heavy that the very cat's-paws drowse, and of imbecility so vast that even Congress is shamed and made to hang its head. Nevertheless, I have heard in that very chamber arguments that stimulated me like the bouquet of a fine Moselle, or a smile of a princess of the blood, or an unexpected kick in the pantaloons." The law has its dull moments, but it also has passion, danger, and hope. In any law matter of consequence there will be uncertainty and fear.

Certainly that is true of the legal matters with which we deal. No one knows how any particular case may come out. A negative precedent may be established which will cripple the prospects for blind people for decades to come. However, there is also the possibility of triumph. We proceed with the faith that a proper and thorough presentation of our case will show that logic and reason are the bedrock on which we make our complaint. We trust the promise that justice will not be denied. The truth will come out and be seen for what it is. The proof of ability will be more important than prejudice. The normality of blind people and the thirst of the blind for full and equal partnership in the grand experiment of life is far more important than man's ancient fear of the dark.

The statute books and the administrative codes do not speak of the crying, compelling need of the blind to be recognized as productive, able, intensely human creatures who must be woven into the mosaic which is our culture—but we do. The law contains the rules and judgments that gird us round. They can rein us in and hold us back, but they can also help to set us free. In large part it depends on what we do to shape this thing called law.

Almost a hundred years ago a band of enterprising entrepreneurs decided to put on a show, which would consist of a magnificent train wreck. Two engines faced each other from the crests of opposite hills. They were raced at full speed into the valley between. The showmen sold tickets to the great event. Printed on each ticket was the statement that the people running the show would not be responsible for any injuries to the spectators. Lemonade was sold, and everyone had a jolly good time—they did, that is, until the great moment.

The two engines collided. The steam boilers blew up. Red hot slivers of steel arced into the air and rained on the spectators, and hundreds of people were maimed or killed.

In the argument which followed, the showmen said that no person was authorized to be in the area unless he or she had a ticket. Each ticket was a contract. Each ticket specifically provided that the spectator, not the showmen, was responsible for all injuries. The showmen said that they could not be held liable for injuries to spectators.

Today (a hundred years later) no matter what the ticket said, the showmen could not escape responsibility. The law has changed. It would not permit the avoidance of responsibility for such danger.

In 1980, only three years ago, Michael Hingson was ejected from a plane because he would not sit where airline officials had decided the blind should sit. He would not give up his right to full equality and first-class citizenship. He would not knuckle under to airline officials when they told him that he was second-rate. In 1980 the airline told Mike Hingson that there was a government regulation which required the airline to segregate him from the rest of the passengers. Mike Hingson (with his dog guide Holland) must sit in the first row of seats.

In 1983 the airline changed its story and said that it had insisted that Mike Hingson sit in the front seat because it would be safer. After all, they said, Mike would be closer to the door of the plane. It would be easier for airline personnel to help him get off if he were in the front seat. The National Federation of the Blind had filed a lawsuit in 1981 to protest this discriminatory treatment. Shortly thereafter, an airline official for the defendant, Pacific Southwest Airlines, said that the airline had made a mistake. This official testified under oath that the airline had violated its own policies in enforcing this segregation.

Nevertheless, a federal court would not permit us to present this evidence. The court ruled in favor of the airline. The judge said that if airline officials had safety matters in the back of their minds, they could present their concerns to the court. With such a ruling in hand airline officials, of course, remembered thinking of hundreds of ways in which the blind could be injured—caught in a burning flame, maimed in the breakup of the aircraft, or otherwise dismembered or done in.

Between 1980 and 1983 the airline had three years to remember all of the circumstances which could cause personal injury. Although the airline had never mentioned all of this to Mike Hingson, the memories of airline officials were graphic when called upon to describe air crashes. The fear of blindness was evident in the testimony of these officials. Because they did not know what they would do if they were blind, because they were afraid they would be helpless as blind people, because they are sure that they would be second class if they became blind, they insisted that we are second class.

The court ruled against us, but we are appealing. We cannot let it stand. We are reaching out for our dignity and our self-worth. They are trying to snatch those birthrights from us. And make no mistake, it is not just Mike Hingson or Pacific Southwest Airlines that is on trial—it is every one of us in this room: all of us—those here, those in the rest of the country, and those who are still children.

But the laws change. The National Federation of the Blind has been in existence for only a short time. Already a mighty labor has been accomplished. It is just the beginning, but what a beginning it is!

Back in 1940, when Dr. tenBroek brought the blind of seven states together to form the National Federation of the Blind, there was little legal protection for the blind. The Randolph-Sheppard Act had been passed, but very few vending stands were in operation. There was no Rehabilitation Act to provide services to the blind. There was no protection against discrimination. The Social Security Act had been adopted, which provided a little welfare money; but there was no Supplemental Security Income program and no Disability Insurance as we now know it. There was no right to work in the federal civil service, and no right to work for federal contractors. The Wagner-O'Day Act had been passed, but it did more for the workshop bosses than for us. It stimulated and expanded the sheltered workshop system, in which the blind have so often received less than the minimum wage. The books for the blind program had begun, and free mailing privileges for this program had been established. That was all. A few books; a little welfare; (perhaps, if you were very lucky) a vending stand.

By the mid-1960s Dr. tenBroek could argue that it was the policy of the nation that the blind be integrated into society as full and equal partners. Such an argument was a declaration of belief—belief in the capacity of the blind. Furthermore, it was a statement of faith that the courts would recognize that capacity, that society would understand it, and that understanding would bring acceptance. By the mid-1960s, we had gained the right to work in the civil service. There were many blind vendors, and aid to the blind programs had been liberalized so that there was at least some money available.

Many of the problems faced by the blind in the 1960s are foreign to us now. We never hear of them. They don't even stir our memories. The Kirschner case, for example. That landmark (tried in the 1960s) declared that the blind could not be denied aid to the blind (now replaced by Supplemental Security Income) on the grounds that there might be relatives financially able to care for their needs. The Parrish case held that night raids against blind welfare recipients were an invasion of privacy and unconstitutional.

Today, these problems are so removed from our daily lives that they seem as fantastic as the old sumptuary laws, which decreed that there could be no more than two courses at a meal. They are as outmoded as the English statute which created trial by combat as one method for settling disputes. Before the Parrish case some governmental officials thought that night raids against aid to the blind recipients were reasonable. Today, that thought is outrageous. With time and effort the laws change.

In the early 1960s the raids involved aid to the blind recipients. In the 1980s the raids are different—and more ominous. The problem began with the question of whether blind persons are competent to adopt children. Some adoption agencies thought that blind parents could not raise children. Their requests to adopt children were denied. We fought this prejudice, and the adoption agencies backed down. But this was only the beginning. In several cases in recent years blind parents have been told by social welfare agencies that they may not raise their *own* children. The homes of these blind people have been invaded. The children of blind parents have been taken. Often it has been done in secret. The blind parent leaves home in the morning (for the office or to go shopping) and returns home to discover that his or her own child is gone—vanished—taken by the whim of a social worker or a judge (no prior notice, no hearing, no due process—simply gone). The courts and the social welfare agencies do it in the name of protecting the children. They claim that the blind parents are not fit: that the children will not be safe. In the ordinary case involving ordinary human beings this sort of thing does not happen. There must be extraordinary evidence to permit the invasion of a home. To justify breaking up a family the court must find that there is danger to the children. There must be evidence of child abuse, or a strong reason to believe that, without court intervention, there will be child abuse. The court must find that there is an emergency which requires immediate and drastic action. That standard is very difficult to meet. Nevertheless, the courts have decided to take the children from blind parents in several states.

In one case the court ruled that the blind mother could keep her children only if she put locks on all the drawers in the house and gates in front of stairways. The judge thought that the children might fall down the stairs. Maybe they would get into the drawers and find dangerous objects such as knives and scissors. This may be called the "gates and locks" test for safety. If the home of blind parents is so constructed that a child cannot fall, and if the objects in the home are locked away so that the child could not be hurt, then the court will grudgingly permit the child to live with its own parents. The court did not say whether the couch in the living room must be so constructed that the child could not fall off of it.

Of course, this is the very sort of thing which makes it necessary to have a National Federation of the Blind. In the case in point we went both to the court and the press—and I am pleased to tell you that we were successful. The children are once more at home with their mother, and they are doing quite nicely—no terrible accidents, no pressing danger, no psychological trauma or ruin—only the normal bumps and bruises of childhood—and of course, the love and tenderness which only a mother can provide.

In another case the court removed the child from a blind mother because the child had fallen and bruised its face. The mother took her child to the doctor. Otherwise, the court would never have known that the accident had occurred. The doctor reported the injury to the authorities, and the authorities took the child. The doctor, as it was put, "knew" when he saw the child that it was in danger. This is the "know it when you see it" test for safety. If any person (doctor, minister, social worker, neighbor down the street, or stranger passing through) reports that the child is in danger, and if the parent is blind, the court, by this doctrine, may invade the home and destroy the security of the family. Of course, we could not let these cases stand. We fought them, and we won.

Beginning in the late 1960s, the Federation began to take an ever more active role in the courts. In almost every case we were seeking to preserve, protect, and defend the civil rights of the blind. For almost two decades we have had ongoing cases dealing with the right of blind people to teach in the public schools. The names of the people involved call up memories of discrimination, organized action, battle in the courts, and a succession of triumphs: Evelyn Weckerly...Pauline Fucinari...Judy (Miller) Sanders... Linda Garshwiler...Joanne Walker...Judy Gurmankin... Ellen Schumann...and Virginia Reagan. The National Federation of the Blind relied on the law and went to court, and the teachers got the jobs. To many who hear these words, some of these names will be only that—names—but each constitutes a personal account of rejection, hope, and achievement; and each constitutes a milestone on the long road to freedom which the blind as a people are traveling.

Then there is the civil service. The organized blind has been fighting with civil service officials for so long that it has almost come to be a way of life. The first case in this area ever taken by the Federation started back in 1950. It involved the right of a blind person to take a civil service examination and be put on the register for a job with a federal agency. We lost that fight because the agency abolished the register. The court said the case was moot. The court could not rule that the blind person should be put on the register because no register existed on which to do the putting. However, as a result of the court action, the Congressional pressure, the widespread publicity, and the all-around general uproar, the civil service officials were forced to open at least a few jobs to blind applicants. For the first time in history blind persons could compete for government jobs.

But this was just the beginning. When the city of Chicago refused to permit blind people to take certain civil service examinations, we brought a lawsuit. The blind can now take those tests. When the state of Minnesota refused to hire a blind computer programmer, we brought a lawsuit. The programmer got the job. In 1980 (30 years after the first civil service case) we of the Federation found ourselves in another action involving federal employment. An economist for the Labor Department, Al Saille, had no trouble getting a job. He had been working as an economist for the federal government for almost fifteen years. The problem was he could not get fair treatment in gaining a promotion. In other words, we could get in the door, but we were to be kept in the outer room. We had reached a new stage in the battle. The blind were no longer fighting simply to get into the federal civil service. The new fight was not whether we could enter the federal civil service but whether we could get equal treatment once we got in. It is not enough that blind people get jobs at the entry level. There must be pay increases, advancement in rank, and promotion to higher levels as well. In other words, the same kind of treatment that others get. Discrimination does not occur solely during the interview and hiring processes. It can also happen in the course of an ongoing job. It happened to Al Saille. But we fought—and we won. Al Saille got the job.

The decade of the 1970s brought a change to the Federation. For the first time we had the money and the capacity to make widespread use of the courts as one of the principal instruments to help us gain equality and first-class status. In the beginning (a decade ago) we took two or three lawsuits a year. Today, we count them in dozens.

Through these lawsuits the Federation has demanded that the blind be treated with fairness and respect. We insist that private employers do not discriminate against the blind. Through such cases as Jesse Nash, the Tennessee vendors, and a score of others going back through the years, we have secured the right of blind vendors to work free of unlawful restrictions and to receive the money due them.

Throughout the country in recent years we have battled the medical licensing boards when they have tried to deny licenses to blind doctors on the ground, not that they were not competent, but that they were blind. We have fought with the schools when they would not let blind students attend law school or participate in chemistry labs. We took the Federal Aviation Administration to court when it told us that we could not keep our canes on airplanes. We sued the agencies (the Cleveland Society for the Blind, the Minneapolis Society for the Blind, and others) to bring reform and to insure that blind people receive proper services.

We gained the right to organize in the Chicago Lighthouse for the Blind, the Cincinnati Association for the Blind, and the Houston Lighthouse for the Blind. We insisted that blind people have a right to equal treatment in renting apartments. The cases go on and on.

The first civil rights cases concentrated on the necessities. Are blind people getting the government benefits to which they are entitled? Do the blind have a right to equal treatment when seeking a place to live? Do blind people get jobs without facing discrimination so that the money is there to pay the bills? These were the questions addressed by the courts when we began to use the lawsuit as a tool to gain equality. Today, we have gone beyond those bare necessities. We have begun asserting our independence in other ways.

Donna Yates wanted to take a Caribbean Cruise. The cruise line told her that, because she was blind, she must stay at home. They were afraid that someone would be required to care for her. Besides, the accommodations on the cruise would be for double occupancy. The clear implication of the cruise line officials was that Donna's cabin mate might find her offensive because she is blind. We fought this unreasonable discrimination, and earlier this year Donna took the cruise.

In an automobile, power is measured in horsepower. In a rocket, it is measured in pounds of thrust. In the Federation, one way to measure power is by the reaction of our opponents. Laws change—and not just for us. Each change shapes not just our rights, but the rights of those around us. When a sheltered shop is organized, the bosses who run it find themselves living in a new and different world. As our power grows, the responses from our opponents become more desperate. The increasing level of conflict to which we are subjected is one of the strongest indications of our growth.

In 1981 a member of the Federation, Dean Stanzel, was fired from his job at the Rehabilitation Services Administration because of his work with the Federation to protect the rights of the blind. The firing was brought about by a complaint from the Iowa Commission for the Blind. This action invited a lawsuit. We accepted the invitation, but before we got to the hearing, the government capitulated. Dean Stanzel got his job back.

In 1978 Bob Acosta decided to ignore democracy in the California affiliate of the Federation. When the California board of directors voted to accept his resignation as president, Bob decided only those votes which favored him should count. With this principle clearly in mind, he went to the chapters and shouted down any opposition. This incident brought on a lawsuit. In the ordinary course of things it would have been a brief and unremarkable footnote in the history of the Federation. However, our reactionary agency opponents were running scared. They needed to divert attention from their own unethical behavior, and they wanted to cause dissension in the Federation. There is every evidence they poured money into the lawsuit to keep it alive. Every legal technicality was used to delay and prolong the case. It took five years, but we do not enter lawsuits lightly. You know the story. We prevailed.

A few weeks ago in Morristown, Tennessee, a chapter of the National Federation of the Blind came into being. Many of its members work at the sheltered shop in Morristown. Shop management came and told these workers that they could not join the Federation. If they joined, or if they wrote to their Congressman about the workshop, they would be fired. This is a direct attack upon the Federation and the rights of blind people to work collectively. It is an attack upon the freedom of speech and the freedom of association. It cannot be permitted. The Federation has gone to Morristown, supported the workers, and brought legal action to stop this outrage.

These three cases (the Dean Stanzel case, the California lawsuit, and the Morristown sheltered shop case) illustrate a pattern. The agencies that oppose the Federation have become increasingly desperate, as they have seen their grip on the lives of blind people loosen. They have attacked the right of blind people to have an organization of their own choosing, governed by the democratic vote of the blind. They have tried to intimidate us when they could. They have tried to control or ruin the Federation when intimidation failed. We won the Dean Stanzel case; we won the California lawsuit; and we will win the Morristown sheltered shop case.

What is in the future for us in the National Federation of the Blind? As I have examined our civil rights cases, I have observed at least two patterns. First, there is the matter of safety. The airlines speak to us of safety, as they segregate us to the first row of seats and take our canes. The courts talk of safety, as they deprive blind parents of their children. Universities tell us safety is the reason that blind people cannot work in chemistry labs. We have come a long way on the road to full equality and first-class citizenship, but there is still much to do. We must meet and defeat that unreasoning fear of blindness which is so often manifested as a concern for safety. In other words, we must use the law to help us abolish the "safety" test.

The second pattern that emerges is the effort by the opponents of the Federation to use the courts as a vehicle for attack. The attacks may be direct, as in the California lawsuit; or they may be indirect, as in Morristown. In either case, we must meet and defeat them as we have in the past, and as we certainly shall in the battles to come.

In the future we must expand and strengthen the base of our rights—and the starting point must be the law. We do not have the scope of legal protection that we need to live secure as equal partners with others in society. We must gain that protection, even if only a step at a time. We must gain it through campaigns of public education; we must gain it through mutual encouragement and heightened conscience; but we must also gain it in the statute books and the courtrooms. There is no final safety (no lasting security or real equality) until we have enshrined it in the law.

The history of our movement tells us one thing clearly. The law does change, and we are the agents of change. It is not the legislatures that do it. It is not the courts. We cause it to happen. The dream of full, joyous, unhampered participation takes shape and finds reality in the hearts and the minds of the blind. We—we are the ones who do it. We seek out the legislators. We go before the judges. We talk to the governors, and the officials, and the public-at-large—and when we are through, the laws have changed. The world is a different place. The blind have taken one more step toward freedom. This is the power and importance of the law.

The Training of a Leader

It is no accident that the Federation's third generation should have found its spokesman in Marc Maurer. He came to the movement while still in his teens, learned the creed of Federationism as a student and apprentice of Kenneth Jernigan, and thereafter remained at the center of the fray. It could be said of Maurer that in him the third generation found its reflection, its embodiment, and its voice.

The relationship began when the young Maurer, a native Iowan blind from infancy, went to Des Moines as a high school student to visit the Iowa Commission for the Blind. It was then that he met its director, Kenneth Jernigan, and it was there that he would return after graduation to enroll at the Commission's Orientation and Adjustment Center. In those days in Iowa it was possible for young people like Marc Maurer to stay for several months at the center learning to live "the Federation way"—i.e., independently, energetically, and proudly—and Maurer took full advantage of the opportunity. He came to realize among other things that he had been held back all his life not only by the low expectations of others but by his own poor self-esteem—and that each of these negatives fed the other. Around him at the Iowa Center was all the positive evidence he needed, and all the support he sought.

While still in training Maurer was given the opportunity to attend NFB conventions in other states—among them South Carolina, where he was taken in hand by a leader of unusual ability, Don Capps—thereby witnessing both the diffusion of Federationism and the singularity of the Iowa experience under the inspired tutelage of Kenneth Jernigan.

It was Jernigan who recommended to Maurer that he drop his plans to attend a college comfortably near home and instead venture out to a distant institution of higher learning—namely, the University of Notre Dame. So he did—not only completing the undergraduate curriculum (with honors) but going on to obtain a law degree from Indiana University. All this he did while supporting himself with entrepreneurial endeavors and building his movement by such activities as organizing for the NFB's Student Division. In the end he served three terms as president of that division, and meanwhile was elected president of the NFB of Indiana at the age of 22. While matriculating at the law school, with all its notorious demands on the time of students, Maurer continued to devote hours of his time daily—and days of his time monthly—to the Federation. It might have been said of his curriculum then that he had a dual major: the law and the Federation. But that would be to assume that the two were separate and equal; of course they were not. One was the means to an end; the other was the end itself. The study of law meant for young Maurer a key for the admission of the blind to the corridors of power, a map across the legal wastelands and quicksands of judicial process and administrative procedure, a tool with which to change the structure of society which had for centuries assigned the blind to a limited and secondary role—in short, a means to the end of turning around those obstacles written into the statute books and enshrined in case law which confronted the blind as an insurmountable barrier for so many generations. Jacobus tenBroek, the movement's founding father, had been a scholar and philosopher of the law; Marc Maurer determined to be a practitioner and master of it.

Later, as an attorney for the Civil Aeronautics Board in Washington, D.C., Maurer held down a secure position with challenges enough to suit most young and ambitious members of the bar. But he found himself chafing uncomfortably in his official assignments, looking forward to the free time when he could get back to work on his Federation projects. Still later on, in private practice, Maurer found himself more and more often representing blind persons in court; although the remuneration was certainly no better than for other clients, the rewards were somehow greater and more lasting. By this time in his career, Maurer knew with a certainty that he had found his calling. It was not in the law, though he might continue his practice. It was not in politics, though he might undertake a campaign for elective office. His calling was to be in the thick of the movement of the organized blind.

When he was elected to the presidency of the National Federation of the Blind in 1986, Maurer rose to say these words:

> The presidency of the National Federation of the Blind is a sacred trust. It carries with it both great honor and tremendous responsibility. When I joined this organization in 1969, Dr. Jernigan was our President. My first convention was dynamic and exciting. Like Dr. tenBroek before him, Dr. Jernigan stayed on the cutting edge. He combined hard decision making with great compassion. Dr. Jernigan's presidency has been characterized by imagination, enthusiasm, love for others, and the drive for success. And there are other things: We never lose because we never quit. Sometimes there are minor and temporary setbacks—but that is just what they are, minor and temporary. If one approach doesn't work, we think up another. If the first effort isn't successful, we alter the strategy and try again. Our problems are solved because we never leave them until they *are* solved. This is what Dr. Jernigan's presidency has meant. This is our heritage—the responsibilities which you as members and I as President are pledged to meet.
>
> In the National Federation of the Blind we give our Presidents great power. We expect them to use it wisely and well. But use it they must—making plans, taking risks, and making progress. I am glad that I have been a part of our movement while Dr. Jer-

nigan was President. It goes without saying that I am also extremely glad that he will continue to be an integral part of and a moving
force in the presidency which is about to begin. This organization
is the single most important factor in the struggle by the blind for
equality and independence. I intend that we shall go forward
without interruption. In a word, under this presidency we must
continue to be the National Federation of the Blind.

The Jernigan presidency had been powerful and dynamic. Although there had been problems aplenty, the decisiveness, in-
genuity, and forcefulness of the response had been more than
adequate to meet every contingency. There were those who
wondered what would be the character of the Maurer term of office. At the 1987 convention in Phoenix, the wondering came to
an end. President Maurer came before the convention to deliver
his first report as President. The events summarized in the
Presidential Report indicated that the Federation was as vital as
ever. This is how President Maurer put it:

I was elected to the presidency of the National Federation of the
Blind one year ago. During the past twelve months I have come
to have a greater understanding of the spirit of our movement
than ever before. It has been a year of real unity and tremendous
growth. I have worked closely with Dr. Jernigan, who (shortly
after last year's convention) agreed to serve as the unpaid Executive Director of the Federation; and, of course, I have worked
with you the members concerning state and local problems
throughout the nation. Although I have been a member of this
organization for almost twenty years, and although I have served
in a number of capacities, I have come during the past twelve
months to appreciate in a different way the scope of our activities,
the complexity of the work we do, and the depth and breadth of
leadership we have. If anyone doubts the level of our commitment
or the unity of our purpose, let that person come here today and
see the blind in our thousands at this convention.

This year has been one of the busiest we have ever had. Our position as a leader in affairs of the blind has become ever more widely recognized. The Xerox Corporation held a training session last
November for its district personnel managers. The meeting took
place in the secluded Xerox Corporation Training Center at Lees-
burg, Virginia. Only one organization involved with the blind (and,
for that matter, only one dealing with the handicapped) was invited to come and speak. The invitation was extended to the Na-

tional Federation of the Blind. Our message was clear and
strong—blind people want work, and we are good employees. I
am confident that our November meeting with Xerox and the contacts since then will result in more and better jobs for blind
workers.

After delineating a variety of activities of the Federation in
dealing with problems involving the airlines, questions regarding
the eligibility of blind persons to receive Social Security benefits,
and disputes surrounding the right of certain blind people to
operate vending facilities on state and federal property, President
Maurer summarized quickly a variety of civil rights concerns. He
said:

> Last September Kevan and Debbie Worley and their two children
> went to the Trailways Bus Station in downtown St. Louis. They
> were planning an outing for the day. Little did they know that
> their proposed trip would become an incident focusing national
> attention on the need to protect the rights of blind people to
> travel without unreasonable interference.
>
> Kevan wanted to buy bus tickets for his family to travel to Festus,
> Missouri, about 40 miles south of St. Louis. The agent at the bus
> station refused to sell the tickets. She said that Kevan and Debbie
> would need to present a letter from a doctor. They explained that
> they only wanted to buy bus tickets to Festus and that they wanted
> to pay the regular fare. They did not want a handicapped ticket
> or a reduced fare, so no doctor's statement would be needed. But
> the agent persisted in refusing to sell them tickets.
>
> You know the rest of the story. The police came and arrested
> Kevan. He was the victim of physical violence and verbal abuse.
> Even so, he (not the police officer) was charged with disturbance
> of the peace. Kevan did not violate the law, however. We
> demonstrated that in the courts. There was no disturbance of the
> peace caused by Kevan. Within hours of the incident the blind of
> the nation were rallying for a public protest. We made signs, and
> we picketed the bus station at the very spot where Kevan had
> been thrown to the pavement by the police. The press came in
> force. Even the police came, and grew increasingly friendly—as
> well they should. The Kevan Worley case is behind us, but we
> must not forget its lessons. That, too, is why we have the National
> Federation of the Blind.

Connie Leblond, one of our leaders in Maine, filed a complaint against Head Start when she was told that her blind son could attend classes only when the regular teacher was present. When the regular teacher was sick or absent, Connie's son Seth must stay home. Our complaint against this kind of unreasonable treatment was filed, and the decision was made last fall. The Office for Civil Rights ruled that this behavior of the Head Start Program is discrimination and that it must be stopped.

This spring we got a decision in the Carol Coulter case. Carol is a Federationist from Missouri, who wanted to operate a day care center to keep small children. She was denied an unrestricted license solely on grounds of blindness. The Missouri Division of Family Services tried to require her to have a sighted person present with the children at all times, but Carol Coulter (with our help) fought back. The ruling on her civil rights complaint has been made, and the unrestricted license will be granted.

Then, there is Debra Duncan. She was denied a day care license in California because of blindness despite the fact that she cares for two children of her own. Her case will go to a hearing before the California State Department of Social Services later this month. Debra will not be alone. We will be with her, and we expect to get the license.

When Sheila Killian and a sighted friend tried to patronize a Raspberries Ice Cream Parlor in California, they were not served because of the presence of Sheila's dog guide. After a law suit, which we backed, the Raspberries Ice Cream Parlor had to pay Sheila $3,900. That was an expensive lesson. It is one that should be learned by anyone in the country who tries to deny the rights of the blind. Expensive or not, we will continue to teach—and when we do, we will expect service with a smile.

Geerat Vermeij is a blind marine biologist at the University of Maryland. He was scheduled to participate in a research cruise to the Aleutian Islands; but a professor at the University of Alaska (the institution which operates the ship) raised objections to his going. The reason—need I tell you?—was concerned with safety. Dr. Vermeij is prominent in his field and has traveled throughout the world doing research. Nine years ago, in fact, he went on a research cruise on the very ship in question. In the resolution of this case you can see the Federation at work. Jim Omvig (from his headquarters in Alaska) and I (working from the National Center in Maryland) collaborated. The matter has been resolved.

Geerat Vermeij will participate in all activities of the research project (from ship to shore and otherwise), and there will be no discrimination—but there probably would have been if it had not been for the National Federation of the Blind.

In the banquet speech at last year's National Convention Dr. Jernigan described the details of the Terry McManus case. A bus driver told Terry that he would have to sit in a seat for the handicapped when there was only standing room on the bus. Terry said he preferred to stand, and he did. Rather than driving the bus, the operator asked all of the other passengers to leave. Terry stayed, and he stood. The rest of the story you know. The bus was driven on its route with Terry still standing—and all alone. This spring the Pennsylvania Human Relations Commission ruled that the Port Authority of Pittsburgh had violated the law. Our determination no longer to be second-class citizens was vindicated once again.

Last year Mary Freeman of Maryland sought a job with the Internal Revenue Service of the United States. She applied in the usual manner. She took a competitive civil service test, and she passed it with an excellent grade. But the Baltimore District Office of the IRS still refused to hire her. Had she been sighted, Mary Freeman would have had a job at IRS without difficulty. But Mary Freeman is blind.

When Mary applied for the job, she was told that she would need to be trained by Arkansas Enterprises for the Blind. Sighted people are trained by IRS. They are paid during their training. But IRS told Mary Freeman that she would be responsible for obtaining her own training from Arkansas Enterprises for the Blind, and that she would not be paid while she was doing it. No job would be guaranteed even if she successfully passed all of the required tests.

This was discrimination. As part of our assistance to Mary we contacted the appropriate IRS official in Washington. Significantly, he had attended last year's convention in Kansas City. Sometimes I am asked what good it does to have government officials here to speak to us. The next time I get such a question I think I may simply say, "Mary Freeman." The matter was settled quickly. On March 9th of this year, Mary started her training at the IRS District Office in Baltimore. She was not required to go to the Arkansas Enterprises for the Blind, and she was paid from the day her training began. She is now working every day as a taxpayer service representative and is being considered for promotion. This is another example of what we can achieve through collective action and organized effort—in other words, the National Federation of the Blind.

Ben Rushton is a blind father living with his children in South Carolina. Several years ago, when he was blinded in an automobile accident, his former wife brought legal action to remove the children from his custody on the grounds that a blind father could not exercise proper parental supervision. Don Capps and other Federationists assisted with this case, and the decision has now been reached. This spring the court agreed with us and said that blindness is not grounds for withdrawing child custody. This is one more case in which the rights of blind parents have been protected by the know-how and determination of the organized blind.

Again this year there are more and better scholarships than ever before. You will meet the students who are receiving them at this convention. Past results demonstrate that the Scholarship Program has been an unqualified success. Our Scholarship Program has been widely publicized—being mentioned in *Seventeen Magazine*, newsletters from Congressional offices, and student aid publications. As a result of our effort, blind students have better opportunity than ever before, and we are also reaching people we have never reached.

The current round of remodeling and renovation at the National Center for the Blind is almost finished. The Records Management Center, recording studios, new offices, dining facilities, and other renovations at the National Center for the Blind are nearly ready for use. Beyond a doubt our National Center is the most productive and the finest facility of its kind in the nation. With this resource goes responsibility. We must ship specialized aids, appliances, and materials to state and local affiliates throughout the nation and to others who need them, and the figures show that we are doing it. During the past year we have duplicated and distributed 7,000 presidential releases, and we have sent out more than a million pieces of literature. The volume of material we are handling has increased more than twenty percent over what we were doing a year ago; and this does not include circulation of the *Monitor*, which is also up substantially and accelerating. As you know, we began making the *Monitor* available on cassette a few months ago, and this means still wider circulation to come. Two years ago, when we were producing 18,000 issues of the *Monitor* each month, I thought we were close to the saturation point; but the rate of increase during the intervening time has been faster than ever before in our history. Today we are producing almost 26,000 copies per month—and still growing.

Our aids, appliances, and materials have been moved to new quarters, occupying more than 14,000 feet of shelf space, and this does not include the more than 28,000 boxes of material stored at the ground floor level in the Barney Street Wing. We have now computerized the operation, and this should increase efficiency and result in even better service.

We now distribute the *American Bar Association Journal* on tape, and we are publishing *Future Reflections* (the magazine for parents of blind children) and also *The Voice of the Diabetic* (the newsletter of our Diabetics Division). The circulation of these publications is increasing at a rapid rate, and there are others— the *Blind Educator*, the newsletter of the National Association to Promote the Use of Braille, *Slate and Style* (the magazine of the Writers Division), *The Brief* (which as you would imagine is published by the National Association of Blind Lawyers), the newsletter of the Merchants Division, and the magazines and newsletters of other divisions and local affiliates.

The Job Opportunities for the Blind (JOB) Program is still one of the most successful efforts we have ever undertaken. This year alone we have distributed 14,000 *JOB Bulletins* to blind applicants, and we have provided information to 6,000 employers. More than 2,000 blind job seekers have been assisted by the program since our last report, and the number of blind people who have been employed (which is, after all, the figure that counts) has topped the 700 mark since the beginning of the program.

During the past year guests from a number of foreign countries and many agencies doing work with the blind have visited the National Center for the Blind. Last fall the chairman of the Royal National Institute for the Blind came from England to examine our programs and learn about our success. This spring an industrialist who manufactures products for the blind in India came to the Center and talked with us about the future of technology. Shortly after last year's convention a representative from one of the organizations for the blind in Israel toured the Center and sought advice about methods for promoting self-organization for the blind in that country, and there have been more—many more.

All of the things I have been discussing with you can be summarized in a very few words: hope, opportunity, information, and the belief that it is respectable to be blind. Recently a letter came to me which illustrates what we are, how we are perceived, where we are going, and what we must do. The letter came not from some other country or California or Tennessee or New Mexico but from Baltimore. This is what it said:

> I am a young mother at the age of nineteen. My son is eleven months old and his name is David. David is blind.
>
> I received a packet of information through the mail from your organization. I can't send money, but I would greatly appreciate your help.
>
> I was scared from the start about being a mother, but now raising a blind child terrifies me. I want to be the best mother for David that I can, and I want him to lead a normal childhood.
>
> I have heard relatives refer to David as poor blind David and I don't want that. I want them to think of David first, not his blindness.
>
> I am so happy to have found your organization. If it would not be any trouble, could you send me information about your organization?
>
> Sincerely,

How can we respond to that letter? This blind boy and his mother urgently need our help, and of course they will get it. The circumstances surrounding their situation (our educational mail campaigns; the confusion of the parents of blind children and their need for help; our accumulated resources of literature and know-how; our members who have achieved success and who still recognize the importance of participating in the movement and continue to draw strength and knowledge from it while serving as role models; our capacity to care; and our strength to make the caring count)—all of these bring together in a single composite what we are and what we must remain.

During the past twelve months we have grown mightily, but we have not diluted our commitment or our personal intimacy of relationship to each other or the people who seek our help. We are stronger today and better organized than we have ever been, but with all of our accomplishments much still remains to be done. As I look back through the year just ended, I am proud of what

we have achieved together—you as members and I as President—
and I am extremely grateful to each of you for the support and
trust which you have given to me, your new President. I have tried
to merit that support and trust, and I shall continue to try to
merit it. Regardless of the accomplishments I make in the years
ahead (and hopefully there will be some) or the mistakes (and
certainly there will be many), I will need to count on your continued understanding and backing. In this, the first year of my
presidency, I find that I do not know as much as I would like to
know, but there is one thing of which I am absolutely certain. The
letter from the young mother with the eleven-month-old son
named David strikes home to me. I myself have a son named
David. He is three years old, and so far as I know, he has normal
sight. When my son David and that other David (the blind eleven-
month-old child of the nineteen-year-old mother) come to manhood, they must find a better world for the blind than we have
today. That is my job. That is your job. That is our job as members of the National Federation of the Blind—and we must not
fail to accomplish it. We do it for the leaders who laid the foundation of this movement and pioneered its development—leaders
like Muzzy Marcelino, who died last fall; we do it for ourselves
and the blind of today; and we do it for the blind of tomorrow,
the children who are now too young to do it for themselves—the
blind children and also the sighted children, who will live fuller
lives if the blind are not degraded as subhumans and written off
as second-class citizens. In the tradition of Dr. tenBroek, who
brought our Federation into being in 1940, and of Dr. Jernigan,
who is here today as the living symbol of our achievements and
our battle for freedom, we must continue to build and look to the
future. We in the National Federation of the Blind are dreamers
and planners and builders. The past year (with all of its problems)
has been good, because we have worked to make it good. The
coming year (again, with all of its problems) can be even better;
and I believe it will be, because we will work to make it better.
This is my commitment; this is my pledge; and this is my report
to you.

The Movement, the Members, the Memories

It was at that 1987 National Convention in Phoenix that
Marc Maurer delivered his inaugural banquet address as President
of the National Federation of the Blind. For him it was, in the
full sense of the phrase, a "moment of truth." Although he had
been elected to the presidency a year before, that was only a

preliminary. This was the real hour of consummation—the Federation's own ceremonial investiture: the annual presidential address. It was important to be eloquent, to be effective; but as he awaited the occasion Maurer felt it was more essential to be strictly honest with his fellow Federationists, to speak simply and openly of his own path to the present and of his vision for the future. He could be philosophical as well (that was a part of himself); he would surely be political (in the Federationist way); he might even be humorous at times (that came naturally). But the thrust of his talk would be personal, stemming from his experience and flowing from his heart.

And the banquet audience—nearly 1,500 of the Federation family—was there for him, waiting and welcoming and even a little worrying. Most of them already knew Marc Maurer, some very well, through the nearly twenty years of his youth and maturity in the movement. To the members of the Third Generation in particular he was an esteemed peer and companion, one of their own. They all wished him well; but when he rose to speak, at this unaccustomed podium in this unfamiliar role, he was on his own. He had never felt so alone in his life.

It lasted only for a moment—a sentence or two. Then he was into the speech, his own composition, carried along by its cadences and absorbed by its messages. He had given it an unusual title: "Back to Notre Dame." The reference would become clear in the course of the address, as he came to speak of his own schooling and apprenticing as a Federationist. But he began on a different note, observing that the greatest changes in history and society are often the least dramatic—making their impact felt slowly and quietly over time. "The process of quiet but dramatic change is an integral part of being human," he said. "It is also the very essence of the National Federation of the Blind." And he went on to recall the obscurity and indifference which attended the founding of the organized blind movement:

> In 1940 Dr. Jacobus tenBroek and a handful of others formed the National Federation of the Blind. Only later was it fully recognized that these pioneers had done something so dramatic that the lives of the blind throughout the world would never again be the same. The spirit which came into being at our founding in Wilkes-Barre, Pennsylvania, took root quietly. There was no roll

of drums, no clap of thunder, no blazing fire to celebrate the event—only Dr. tenBroek and the small group who gathered with him to dream and plan for the future and take the first steps toward making it happen....They could not have imagined that from that humble beginning would spring the powerful fifty-thousand-member National Federation of the Blind which we have become and now are. Still, they believed—that a future could be created, that the years would not slip away with only emptiness for the blind, that it was possible for the blind to build and grow and come together in one great family. That dream, that faith, has partly been realized—but the road stretches far ahead, and the rest is for us to do. And we will do it. We will do it by education and unspectacular change if we can. We will do it by more dramatic means if we must—but we will do it. As Dr. Jernigan has so often said, we are simply no longer willing to be second-class citizens.

That was how the new President began this banquet address. It was only a beginning, as far as the speech was concerned; but it was also conclusive, as far as the audience was concerned. For with that ringing declaration, Marc Maurer ended all doubts as to his leadership capacity and presidential stature. The Federation audience knew that, when push came to shove, their President would not only expound their view but exclaim it from the housetops; he would exhort; he would expostulate; he would expose. In short, he would lead.

Following is the complete text of that 1987 banquet address:

BACK TO NOTRE DAME
by Marc Maurer

Once in a great while there comes a dramatic change—an event so striking in its effect that forever after a new direction is inevitable. But more often, change does not have the appearance of drama. Instead, there is a slight shift in emphasis—an alteration of mood. Often the change that tips the scale is so slight that (at the time it occurs) it is completely unrecognized. Only later, with the long view of history, can it be seen that this was the particular moment, the watershed, the critical juncture.

Today, the world (whether Christian or non-Christian) counts time from the birth of Christ; but twenty centuries ago, at the time the event occurred, the vast majority of Roman citizens were totally unaware of it. Even if they had known, it would have seemed of no significance.

Fire is generally regarded as the essence of drama. Flames shoot dozens (even hundreds) of feet into the air, but fire is merely oxidation at a rapid rate. Although it is momentarily spectacular, its consequences are far less significant than those of other forms of oxidation. In the total range of rust, rot, leaf mold, and metabolism fire is (so to speak) only a flash in the pan, a momentary aberration. Of vastly more importance to the people of the world are the slow, unspectacular chemical changes which take place every day—the oxidation of millions of tons of matter, occurring so slowly as to pass without comment.

This does not mean that drama is unimportant, that fire can be dismissed with a shrug and a yawn. Nor does it mean that the actions of everyday life have no effect or drama. The events which cause hope and despair, joy and depression, are of tremendous significance even when they pass unnoticed and without remark. The process of quiet but dramatic change is an integral part of being human. It is also the very essence of the National Federation of the Blind. The cumulative effect of the drama without fanfare which is reflected in the growth of our movement and the lives of its members is perhaps more spectacular than any other single event which the decades have brought, regardless of how pivotal and far-reaching that event may have seemed at the moment.

In 1940 Dr. Jacobus tenBroek and a handful of others formed the National Federation of the Blind. Only later was it fully recognized that these pioneers had done something so dramatic that the lives of the blind throughout the world would never again be the same. The spirit which came into being at our founding in Wilkes-Barre, Pennsylvania, took root quietly. There was no roll of drums, no clap of thunder, no blazing fire to celebrate the event—only Dr. tenBroek and the small group who gathered with him to dream and plan for the future and take the first steps toward making it happen. They did not—indeed, could not—know what the final outcome would be. They were people of discernment and tremendous insight, but they could not have imagined that from that humble beginning would spring the organized blind movement of today—the powerful fifty thousand-member National Federation of the Blind which we have become and now are. Still, they believed—that a future could be created, that the years would not slip away with only emptiness for the blind, that it was possible for the blind to build and grow and come together in one great family. That dream, that faith, has partly been realized—but the road stretches far ahead, and the rest is for us to do. And we will do it. We will do it by education and unspectacular change if we can. We will do it by more dramatic means if we must—but we will do it. As Dr. Jernigan has so often said: We are simply no longer willing to be second-class citizens.

For forty-seven years we have been working quietly (and sometimes not so quietly) to win our way to first-class status in society. There have, of course, been public demonstrations, dramatic confrontations, and historic documents; but these have not been the primary vehicles of change and accomplishment. Instead, the individual hopes and dreams of blind people—the cumulative effect of their unspectacular daily decisions and actions—have come together to create the positive and powerful force which is represented here tonight. No one who is in this room or who is in any way connected with affairs of the blind needs to be told what that force is. It is the National Federation of the Blind.

When I joined the Federation in 1969, there had already been twenty-nine years of hard, dedicated work; and the results were plain. The Federation had built a solid record of accomplishment. There was a body of literature about blindness which undergirded and gave direction to our efforts. The ideas and basic assumptions contained in the writings of Dr. tenBroek and Dr. Jernigan had been put to the test. There was no doubt that blind people could compete successfully in business or the professions. The programs of the Federation had demonstrated that this was not speculation but fact. The theories worked. Blind people got jobs. The question was not if or whether but how and when. The problem of 1969 was to expand the scope of our activities. We needed more than a demonstration. We needed opportunity, and not just for a few.

In 1969, as I came to be part of the movement, I did not know that these things were true. Only in retrospect did I know it. In one sense I did not (when I joined this movement) understand the organization at all, but even in my ignorance, the Federation spoke to me with quiet force. For the first time in my life what I thought made a difference. It was absolutely astonishing to me that this was so—that anyone would do something because I, a blind person, wanted it done. I did not understand the reason for such unusual behavior, or appreciate its significance; and although

I was fascinated with the Federation, I must confess that I did not think it would change my life—at least, not very much.

As I was growing up, I (like all others, blind and sighted alike) was conditioned by my culture and society. I hoped that there would be something interesting or important for me to do, but I was afraid that blindness might keep me from it. When I came to the Federation, I found blind people working and making substantive contributions. I was told that blindness need not be a terrible limitation. I hoped that the Federation was right, but I had doubts. Nevertheless, I said that I believed, and I tried to act as though I did. It was only later that I realized (with something of a shock) that the belief had come to be a reality in my life—and a good while before I recognized it.

Dr. Jernigan taught me about blindness and the organized blind movement—and there were others. I talked with blind people who were lawyers, teachers, factory workers, and farmers. At Federation meetings blind leaders spoke of the power of collective action. Soon I began to repeat what those around me were saying: that blindness could be reduced to the level of a physical nuisance, that with proper training and opportunity the average blind person could do the average job in the average place of business—in short that it was respectable to be blind.

Then, I went to college at Notre Dame—and it was a sudden plunge into ice water. On a campus with six thousand other students, I found myself completely isolated and alone. I could not find a single other person who understood what I thought I understood or believed what I said I believed, the simple truth that blind people had capacity and could compete. I met no one else who thought it was respectable to be blind. The coach in the athletic department told me that I should not take any gym classes because I might get hurt. When signing up for an accounting course, I was praised by the professor for my great courage. Then (without even changing gears) the professor promised me a good grade. I got the idea that I did not have to earn it, that just being there and being courageous would be enough. I worked hard to deserve that grade, and I worked hard for the other grades I got, too. It was an unforgettable experience; and although I have physically returned to that campus only once since graduation, I have (sociologically speaking) been back to Notre Dame many times through the years.

That first semester I learned with real force (I might say with dramatic force) that blindness could not stop me, but I also learned that prejudice and misunderstanding might. Something had to be done. The situation was intolerable. All of those professors and students had to be told. I needed help. I needed the National Federation of the Blind. As the years at the university passed, I became increasingly active in our movement. My priorities crystalized and became clear.

After college I did graduate work, and in 1977 I finished law school. In 1978, with the help of Federation members, I got a job in the office of the General Counsel at the Civil Aeronautics Board. With my philosophy and idealism in hand, I went to that job willing and anxious to work. I wanted to give of my time, my effort, and my energy. I wanted to advance myself and the cause of the blind. The Civil Aeronautics Board made United States civil aviation policy. Here, I thought, is an opportunity for me to do something really useful. However, I soon discovered that a pattern existed—a pattern which reminded me of the professor who told me that I was courageous, and promised me a good grade. I felt right at home. It was just like being back at Notre Dame.

My assignments were almost always routine. If there was a trip to London for an international negotiation, somebody else was asked to go. If a hearing officer needed to take testimony in a small town to determine the feasibility of air service, I was never sent. These assignments (calculated to vary the routine) were highly prized and much sought after. Others went while I stayed home— and was courageous. Sometimes there was not enough routine work to fill my day. So I was left to occupy my time as I chose. My superiors would have been content if I had spent my time listening to the radio or reading. They would have been content— but I would not have been content. I did not want the rest of my life to be a sham and a deception, a guaranteed succession of endless raises and lack of meaningful work. Discrimination is not necessarily confined to the job interview or the entry level. It can also happen after employment is permanent and safe.

My job with the federal government was absolutely secure. It would have lasted until retirement through a long and rustful life. There was something else: we all tend to be conditioned by our environment. I knew that if I stayed long enough and my salary became high enough, I might begin to succumb to temptation and rationalize. I might become accustomed to the lack of useful activity and gradually lose my initiative, my sense of values, my perspective, my willingness to leave, and my soul.

Not only had the Federation taught me about blindness but also about self-examination, objectivity, and perspective. In 1981 I left the Civil Aeronautics Board to start my own law practice. I knew that I might starve, but I also knew that if I starved, it would be a starvation of the body and not of the soul. I knew that I would be free, and not a token or a cipher. Slavery does not have to be a matter of chains and whips. It can also be a captivity of the mind and a shackling of the spirit. Every person in this room can give testimony to that. We in the Federation have cut our teeth on it, and we never stop learning it. On a daily basis we continue to teach it to ourselves and each other, and we give it in strong doses to new recruits. This is why some, who do not understand our philosophy, call us militant.

In the practice of law my dream that I might do something worthwhile and useful came true. Again, Federation members and leaders helped and encouraged me. As part of my practice I frequently found myself representing blind persons. The textbooks tell us that American law is based on fairness and justice regardless of who is involved or what the circumstances may be. My job was to help make this principle applicable to the blind as well as the sighted.

When I represented blind people, my opponents were often major employers, airlines, departments of government, or agencies doing work with the blind. Although the approaches of these different entities might vary, their opinions about blindness usually did not. Whether it was an airline, an employer, a department of government, or a service agency for the blind, what they said about blindness was always just about the same. I felt right at home. It was exactly like being back at Notre Dame. The blind are courageous; they will get a good grade; no need to work; and plenty of meaningless assignments. Of course, when I insisted on equal treatment for my clients, attitudes hardened. Those across the table now thought the blind (and that included me) were ungrateful, unreasonable, and unrealistic—not courageous at all but just plain radical and militant.

If (after my experiences at Notre Dame and the Civil Aeronautics Board) anything else was needed to confirm me in my opinion that the National Federation of the Blind was not only needed but necessary, I found it in the practice of law. It is not that people mean to be unreasonable or that they are deliberately cruel. Rather, it is that they have the ancient fear of the dark and that they equate blindness with darkness, and darkness with evil and lack of ability to perform. Despite the progress we have made (and we have made a great deal of it), regressive attitudes about blindness are unfortunately still the norm.

The director of sales for Elsafe Hawaii, Incorporated (a company that markets safes), writes to say that he is selling a special safe for the blind. He says:

> I would like to take this opportunity to acquaint you with this product, as it seems to be particularly well suited to the needs of the blind. This safe is operated by means of a combination that is entered via a keypad identical to a standard telephone keypad. There are no keys required for normal operation—and, therefore, nothing to lose. I would like to make the members of your organization aware of this product.

The conclusion is inevitable. This man believes that the blind, incompetent as we are, cannot keep track of the simplest objects—including keys. To help the unfortunate blind he wants to sell us special safes, but one wonders if he understands the implications of his own letter. If blind people cannot manage keys, how can we collect anything of sufficient value to put into his safe?

A radio commercial from the Corning Glass company for Corlon lenses opens with a man speaking to a coat rack. He does not possess Corlon lenses, so he mistakes the coat rack for an assistant in the eye doctor's office. As the commercial proceeds, the man causes a stir by almost sitting (inadvertently) on the lap of a lady in the waiting room. Without the lenses he cannot see her. Finally, this poor unfortunate (blinded by the absence of Corlon lenses) attempts to leave the office through a closet and becomes completely befuddled. Sight, according to this advertisement, is required to prevent a person from mistaking a coat rack for a human, from becoming lost in a closet, and from social blunders such as sitting in other people's laps. The inescapable conclusion is that blindness means almost total helplessness with a dash of buffoonery thrown in for good measure. I cannot recall having spoken recently to a coat rack, and I doubt that you can; nor do I think the reason why blind people sit in laps is usually that they do not know what they are doing. We are frequently exploited by companies which take advantage of the stereotypes about us to sell products, regardless of the truth of their claims or the harm they do.

The Konica Medical Corporation of Wayne, New Jersey, provides darkroom equipment to hospitals. Not long ago, Konica became aware of two blind people working as darkroom technicians in a Florida medical center. As a gesture of good will, Konica issued a press release about the valuable work of these two blind employees. The release said in part, "Visually Impaired Technicians Find Rewarding Careers at Medical Center." The article went on to say, "Imagine, if you can, what it would be like to live without the ability to see the world around you. Simple tasks like walking, eating, and reading would take on a whole new complexity."

As I studied this press release, I felt conflicting emotions. The headline tells us that blind people are at work in rewarding careers at a hospital; and even though I think blind people are often pushed toward the darkroom in the mistaken belief that the absence of ordinary light makes this job especially suitable for them, I recognize that darkroom work is a useful activity in a competitive occupation. But the body of the release ruins the headline and takes it all away. It declares that the blind have trouble with the most mundane tasks. Is it really so hard for us to walk? And how about eating? We don't seem to have had much trouble at this banquet. Of course, reading requires the use of alternative techniques such as Braille, recordings, sighted readers, and the like; but even here the situation is more a matter of coping than crying.

The message of the companies in private industry is based on a common theme. They say that blind people are different and less able than others. Even when these companies attempt to be positive and offer commendation, they say that we cannot do anything as well as the sighted and that we are very limited, very special, very deprived, very brave, and very subnormal. People with this kind of attitude refer to the blind and other groups as "handicapable" and "physically challenged," and they use other such cutesy euphemisms—euphemisms which are uncalled for, unhealthy, unhelpful, unconvincing, and unbecoming.

But if private industry is uninformed, having relatively little exposure to the blind and facts about blindness, surely the agencies doing work with the blind are more enlightened. One would think so, but as we have learned to our cost, the exact opposite is often the case. Consider, for instance, the South Carolina Commission for the Blind. That agency was brought into being in the mid-1960s through the efforts of Don Capps and the other leaders of the National Federation of the Blind of South Carolina. There was also assistance from beyond the borders of the state. Dr. Jernigan went to South Carolina to testify before the committee which the legislature had established to study the matter, and a leading South Carolina legislator came to Iowa to examine the programs which Dr. Jernigan was operating at the state Commission for the Blind. Justifiably the blind of South Carolina regard the Commission for the Blind as theirs.

Imagine, then, how they feel (and how responsible staff members at the South Carolina Commission feel) when an official publication of the Commission embodies the worst of the harmful stereotypes about blindness and is massively circulated throughout the state. They are understandably outraged. But let the brochure speak for itself. It consists of fifty-eight so- called "helpful suggestions for families and friends of blind persons," grouped under six headings as follows: "General," "With People," "In the House," "Traveling," "Guiding," and "At the Table." You may have thought that the proposition in the Konica news release (that eating for a blind person takes on special complexity) was simply to be dismissed as the chatter of a well-intentioned kook.

Listen, then, to the experts. Here is what the South Carolina brochure says about eating. Twelve "helpful suggestions" are listed under the heading "At the Table." I can do no better than give them to you as they come, word for word from the brochure. Here they are:

> 1. Maintain usual standards. 2. Tell him what is in the dish or on the plate which is being passed. 3. Don't pass things across in front of the blind person. Expect him to share in the passing of food. 4. Address the blind person directly so that he will know that he is being asked to pass something. 5. Mention what is on his plate so that he will know how to handle the food. 6. At first, if he wishes it, cut meat, and butter the bread. 7. Get in the habit of placing the meat to the front of his plate. It is easier to cut there. 8. Use good-sized napkins. 9. Don't make unnecessary comments when food is spilled. 10. If food is spilled on clothing, mention it casually so that it can be removed at once. 11. Ask the individual if he wants sugar or cream as these are difficult for him to

serve himself unless the sugar is in lump form and the cream in individual pitchers. 12. When serving food, mention where it has been placed so the individual will not accidentally knock over a glass, paper cup, sherbert (sic), cup and saucer, etc.

Although these "helpful suggestions for family and friends" cannot, by any stretch of the imagination, be called subtle, the pamphlet does not say precisely what it means. Let me offer the writers at the South Carolina Commission for the Blind some "helpful suggestions" of my own. Let me say in clear statements what their pamphlet necessarily implies, and what (though they might deny it) I think they really mean. Keep in mind that they are talking about you and me. Here, then, is the truthful rewrite:

"Maintain usual standards." You do not need to be sloppy just because a blind person (who will undoubtedly be sloppy) is at the table.

"Don't pass things across in front of the blind person. Expect him to share in the passing of food." The blind person, just like a three-year-old, will be flattered if you let him help. If he isn't motivated by the flattery, you may have to prod him a little.

"Mention what is on his plate so that he will know how to handle the food." The blind person is probably not accustomed to eating in polite society and will likely not be able to identify food without your help. In any case, it is your responsibility, not the blind person's.

"Use good-sized napkins." Of course, the blind person will be messy and spill things, and you must look out for him or her. After all, it is your responsibility. Certainly the blind person is not in charge. You are.

"Ask the individual if he wants sugar or cream as these are difficult for him to serve himself unless the sugar is in lump form and the cream in individual pitchers." After all, the blind person can't ask for what he wants. You must take the initiative and take care of him.

When I first came across this brochure, I felt that I had gone back to Notre Dame, for it deals with something much more far-reaching than table talk. It embodies a whole way of life, an entire philosophy, and a complete cultural tradition. Through every line is the implicit assumption that somebody else is in charge and that even if the home and the table belong to the blind person, he or she is no longer in control, no longer the host, no longer an equal among equals. If you are still not convinced after all you have heard, consider these other samples from the pamphlet. Here they are exactly as they appear:

> Talk and act naturally when with a blind person. Be frank. If he needs to shine his shoes, tell him so. Do not needlessly hurry a blind person. He will appreciate a calm approach to the matter in hand. Let him do everything possible for himself. In helping a blind person, do not make him conspicuous by the way you do things. Read his mail promptly and refrain from commenting on the content of the letter unless requested to do so. A second reading is often appreciated. Refrain from uncouthness in the presence of a blind person; he can hear you picking your teeth. Be alert but restrained; do not startle a blind person needlessly. Don't let a blind person's hand dangle in the air. If obviously it is his purpose to shake hands, grasp his hand and greet him. Don't limit your knowledge and interest in the blind generally to the blind mendicant who is sometimes a social parasite from choice. Do not patronize blind persons; they're 'just regular people' more than you realize. In conversation, address the blind person by name if he is the one expected to reply. Otherwise, he may not know the remark is being directed to him. Leave the possessions of a blind person where they have placed them unless you indicate specifically where they may find them. When traveling, describe interesting and beautiful scenes. Comment casually on sensations which blind persons can enjoy such as pleasant odors, a cooling breeze, the tinkle of a brook, etc. When taking an individual into a restroom indicate position of toilet, paper, washbowl, soap, and towels. When walking with a blind person, mention familiar landmarks so that he can get his bearings. Don't push a blind person ahead of you. Walk straight across the street. To do so diagonally may cause the blind person to trip when reaching the curb.

There you have in summation the philosophy of the South Carolina Commission for the Blind, and I believe that I have never in all of my life seen such a concentrated dose of distortion and false notions. Is it any wonder that the blind of the state are at war with the agency? How could it be otherwise? I have no doubt that Don Capps and the other Federationists in South Carolina will teach the Commission a new way of looking at blindness. Our role may not be as limited or our temperament as passive as the South Carolina custodians think.

And, of course, it is not just South Carolina. There are other agencies in other states. Consider, for instance, the Mary Bryant Home for Blind Men and Women, located in Springfield, Illinois. Keep in mind, as I describe this facility to you, that it is not a place exclusively designed for the elderly. It is meant for the young as well. I feel it necessary to make this point since otherwise you might have difficulty believing what you are about to hear.

Therefore, I offer in evidence a letter dated March 23rd, 1987, to directors of rehabilitation agencies in a number of Midwestern states. The letter is signed by the Administrator of the Mary Bryant Home, who has the rather intriguing name of Frances Trees. The letter says:

Dear Director:

As you are aware, there comes a time in the lives of many visually impaired persons when they are unable to live independently. Some younger persons return to their homes following their education from a school for the visually impaired. In many cases, these young men and women are returning to homes where both parents are employed outside the home, and find themselves staying alone all day with nothing to do.

Some older persons no longer have a support system to aid and assist them to live independently. Many are sent inappropriately to nursing homes, where they are often endangered by not being able to protect themselves.

The Mary Bryant Home is a resource I wish you would consider when it comes to assisting individuals or families to deal with the issue of placement....Currently our residents range in age from 24 to 96 years of age....

Sincerely,
Frances J. Trees
Administrator

As we examine what the Mary Bryant Home says about itself, remember that some of the residents are as young as twenty-four and that they are at the Mary Bryant facility because, as Administrator Trees says, "these young men and women are returning to homes where both parents are employed outside the home, and find themselves staying alone all day with nothing to do." Here are direct quotes from the packet of literature sent by Administrator Trees to the rehabilitation directors:

> The building is rectangular in shape, which allows the residents to walk in a circular pattern for exercise—especially during inclement weather....The home is arranged for convenience, on one level—no stairs....Hand rails are installed throughout the home....Our full and part-time staff provide round-the-clock service to the residents seeing to their health, safety, nutritional, recreational and emotional needs....Leave of absence may be taken by residents for a short period of time providing the person taking the resident out sign a release of responsibility for injuries, accidents, or illnesses which might occur during the time they are away from the Mary Bryant Home....Personal property, other than clothing, may be brought to the home only with the prior approval of the Administrator....Food is prohibited in the resident rooms. BEER, WINE, AND OTHER INTOXICATING LIQUOR: Only when approved by the resident's physician please, and all items of this nature are to be kept at the Medicine Room, not in resident's room....Incoming calls for residents may be received on the house phones, but it would cause less confusion and less interruption if these calls were to be made between the hours of 1:00 p.m. and 4:30 p.m....Visiting hours are from 10:00 a.m. to 8:00 p.m. Visits will be restricted when adversely indicated in the opinion of the resident's physician and so documented in the resident's clinical record....Smoking in resident rooms is prohibited for both residents and visitors. Residents who are capable of handling smoking supplies with safety may smoke in the activity room, and we request visitors to smoke only in these areas also....

There is more, much more—but I think I have given you enough to make the point. Any self-respecting blind person faced with such an outrageous conglomeration of insulting rules, directives, requirements, and restrictions would walk out the door three minutes after arriving. Of course, most blind people that I know would resist going to such a facility in the first place. With all of the work we have done to change public attitudes, many people still feel that the blind should live in segregated homes, or sometimes nursing homes. In this connection I recently received the following letter:

Dear Sir:

My mother has been legally blind for about twenty years. During all that time she has been in a nursing home in Rochester, Indiana, and she is only forty-three years old. She has not in all that time had any training that the blind need, such as how to read Braille. The nursing home has been her only world because of her inability to get around. I feel my mother desperately needs help. She needs to be taught the things the blind need to function in society. She is much too young to be in a nursing home.

I wonder if the National Federation of the Blind can help in this matter. I don't have money or the know-how to assist her, and I was told maybe you could help. She's wanting to get out of the nursing home.

Sincerely yours,

Twenty years of a person's life is a long time—and for this woman (and many others like her) those twenty years are a bleak memory of twisted hell—of desolation, pain, and lack of opportunity. We in the National Federation of the Blind are organized to make it absolutely certain that brochures like the one issued by the South Carolina Commission for the Blind stop being written, that facilities like the Mary Bryant Home either change their philosophy or go out of business, and that blind men and women have something better to do with their lives than go into nursing homes in their twenties. We are committed to changing public attitudes so that manufacturers will not believe that we cannot keep track of our keys, so that companies can no longer get away with picturing us as helpless and pathetic unless we have eyeglasses, and so that the public will no longer tolerate advertisements which exploit the concept that we are especially suited to work in the dark. We are determined to educate not merely the public at large but also our fellow blind and ourselves—and, of course, we are doing it.

On Saturday, May 23rd, of this year I did not physically leave Baltimore—but on that day (as I have so often done) I went back to Notre Dame. I was in a clothing store, trying on the very suit I am wearing tonight. At a critical juncture in the fitting, the salesman said to the sighted person who was with me: "Can you take off his shoes?" I suppose I don't need to tell you that I did not walk barefooted to Notre Dame. I removed my own shoes.

The changes we are making in public attitudes often seem slow and long in coming, but (like oxidation) they remove more trash and debris than the flames of spectacular conflagration. Since our founding in 1940 we have removed a tremendous amount of garbage—some by conflagration, and a great deal more by steady oxidation. We also (even those of us who have never been to Indiana) continue to return to Notre Dame—but (thankfully) the visits are becoming fewer and farther between.

For those of us who are blind, the world holds more promise today than ever before in history. It is not that incidents of the kind I have described are more numerous now than they formerly were. Rather, it is that we are more aware of them and more prepared to take appropriate action. Once they were universal. Now, they are only usual. But since 1940 there has been a new element, a new force which has changed the balances. You know what it is as well as I do. It is the National Federation of the Blind. As everyone in this room knows, we are thoroughly organized, fully aware of where we have been and where we are going, and absolutely unstoppable.

No power on earth can now send us back or keep us from going the rest of the way to freedom and first-class citizenship. We know it; our opponents know it; and the public at large is beginning to learn it. As we approach the end of the twentieth century, our mood is optimistic, and our hearts are joyous. My brothers and my sisters, let us march to the future together!

Back to Harvard

Like Kenneth Jernigan before him, President Maurer found himself called upon to meet with and speak before a wide variety of groups, inside and outside the movement, as a standard part of his leadership responsibility. Some of these encounters were largely ceremonial; a few were confrontational; and others were, in one way or another, broadly educational. Maurer especially welcomed opportunities to convey the philosophy of Federationism—the doctrine of equality—to public audiences unfamiliar with the organized blind movement and potentially valuable as friends and allies. Such an opportunity arrived with an invitation to address the faculty and students of Harvard University's John F. Kennedy School of Government at a symposium in December, 1987. Many of the faculty members in that audience were either statesmen or the advisors of statesmen; many of the students would become future leaders. It was a rare opportunity to influence the influential; and the Federation's chief spokesman made the most of it. He entitled his short speech "The Cost of a Gift," and he spoke of the nature of charity and the price it exacted. His message, carefully reasoned and quietly articulated, was that the blind were no longer content with the gift of charity but demanded instead the harder bargain of equality. And the warmth of his reception by the Harvard audience demonstrated that the message was no less cogent and persuasive in the groves of academe than it was in the meeting halls of the National Federation of the Blind.

Here is the Harvard speech:

THE COST OF A GIFT
by Marc Maurer

The blind, the halt, and the lame have traditionally been objects of pity and charity. This has meant a certain degree of kindness, but the generosity has always been a mixed blessing. In physics it is said that for any action there is an equal and opposite reaction. In social affairs the same concept applies. There is no such thing as a free lunch. Those who receive charity are (contrary to the popular belief) always obliged to pay for it.

One of the greatest problems faced by the blind today is that we are the objects of charity. The society at large feels that it will be called upon to give something to the blind. There is no law which requires equal treatment for the sighted. Such a law is unnecessary. However, there is a law which demands that the handicapped shall not be subjected to discrimination—at least part of the time. This law is mostly ineffective. The general public is expected to give equality to a class of persons which it regards as not being entitled to it.

How do we pay for charity? What can be offered in return for the "gifts" we receive? How are the scales balanced? What is taken from the blind (or, for that matter, from other groups) in order to reach equilibrium? To answer this question contrast the position in our culture maintained by the local banker or entrepreneur with that customarily associated with the blind. As I have already said, nondiscrimination laws apply to the blind. They don't apply to the banker. Reasonable accommodation is required for the blind. It is not for the banker. Charitable fund drives are conducted for the blind. It is inconceivable that they would be for the banker. Generosity and pity are felt for the blind. The banker gets something else. For the banker there is sometimes a little envy, occasionally a touch of fear, and almost always a substantial measure of respect. The reason for the difference is that the banker has something that most people in society want. The blind are not regarded in the same way.

What pays for the charity? For a large segment of the population the income tax deduction is insufficient to induce a gift. Instead, there has to be another reason. Charity salves the conscience. It is a tangible reminder for those who have done something which they regard as less than good that their lives are not without redeeming features. But there is something even more powerful than the need to compensate for past misdeeds. It is the wish to feel secure in the knowledge that the donor is helping those less fortunate. This, of course, may be restated. If I can regard you as an object of pity and charity, I am in a position superior to yours. Therefore, if I make you a gift from charitable motives, I am necessarily your superior. The blind and handicapped pay for the charity. The gift necessarily connotes inequality. This means that one of the most serious problems faced by the handicapped today is that we are the objects of charity. If we permit these circumstances to continue, we give tacit consent to the two-class system.

In a relatively free society when two parties transact business, one sets the price, and the other determines the quantity. It never happens that one party decides both price and quantity. If the buyer says that fifty items are required, the seller will establish the price. If the seller indicates that the price for a specific commodity will be one hundred dollars, the purchaser will determine the number to be bought. The number may be zero or some quantity higher than that. If, on the other hand, the purchaser says that the price of the commodity will be not a hundred dollars but fifty, the seller may decide to take the merchandise and go home. In other words the quantity may be zero.

The blind (just like others) have always needed certain basic commodities. Food, shelter, and clothing are essential. In the past governmental institutions, charitable organizations, or benevolent individuals have provided these necessities. But price and quantity are never controlled by the same party. The blind demanded a certain quantity; those who made the gifts controlled the price. Only when blind people began to have sufficient resources to meet basic needs, did these circumstances begin to change. If a group of individuals within society never has the opportunity to choose whether it will determine price or quantity, it lacks the essentials for freedom. Until fairly recently, the blind have been in this position. Blind people determined quantity, and someone else set the price. Because blind people were not regarded as having any trading stock—goods or services that could be sold—payment had to be made in other coin, and the price was always high.

Blacks in America constitute a minority. As this group began to move from second-class status to full equality, it faced almost the same economic circumstances that now confront the blind. But there was one significant difference. Blacks were regarded as having the capacity for manual labor. The blind are ordinarily not considered suitable to perform the ordinary job in the ordinary place of business. Therefore, in the effort to become a fully integrated part of our society, blind people are at a greater disadvantage than blacks have ever been. This is true despite the absence of blind slavery. The difference is that the blind are thought of as having nothing to offer. Not only are the skills and talents possessed by the blind not sought in the job market, but often those blind persons who volunteer to give their time without cost find their offer rejected. In the minds of many the final summation for blindness is: nothing to sell and nothing that will be accepted as a gift—complete worthlessness.

Of course, this understanding of blindness is completely false. The blind represent a cross section of the general population. All of the talent and all of the virtue that can be found among ordinary human beings is possessed by the blind. All of the abilities that others possess (except the ability to see) are possessed by the blind. The blind people I know are as bright, as energetic, as willing to give without counting the cost, as anxious to do a good job, and as trustworthy as anyone else in society. They are also as dull, as boring, as willing to take without giving, and as lazy. In other words blind people have all of the characteristics of the general population, except one—sight. The problem is that blindness has been regarded as the only meaningful attribute. After it has become clear that the individual in question is blind, nothing else matters. In the minds of many this one factor is the final summation.

Do I state the case too strongly? Recently a blind man in St. Louis, Missouri, approached the ticket counter in a Trailways bus depot. He wanted to buy a full-fare bus ticket. The ticket agent told him that he must produce a doctor's certificate because this was necessary for a "handifare" ticket. A "handifare" ticket costs less than the ordinary bus ticket. The blind man (a member of the National Federation of the Blind) responded that a "handifare" ticket was not needed. He wanted to pay full fare for an ordinary ticket. Nevertheless, the agent refused to sell him one. When the blind man insisted on his right to pay full fare, and when he refused to leave the counter until such a ticket was issued to him, personnel at the Trailways bus station called the police and had him arrested. The language used by the police and their behavior at the depot is reminiscent of the ugly confrontations in the black civil rights movement.

Last March a blind man in Washington State bought a ticket to ride on an Amtrak train. After boarding, he tried to ascend the stairs to the upper level of the observation car. The conductor told him that blind people were not permitted on the upper level. Amtrak (just like Trailways) sells tickets to the handicapped at a reduced rate.

What should we do to promote a more realistic approach? I do not recommend that all charity come to an end. Nor do I recommend that the blind stop accepting all gifts. Instead, I urge all of us to try to understand the nature of what we do. For all human beings everywhere there are times that demand charity. However, there also comes a time when responsibility must be accepted. Full participation in society will produce more and cost less than dependence upon charity. If we, as a culture, systematically refuse to permit a group of people to reach its potential, then we have set the stage for conflict. Such behavior creates an inferior class. When the group that is regarded as inferior discovers that the two-class system is a lie, it will insist upon its rights. When this happens, there will be confrontation.

The blind of this nation (organized in the National Federation of the Blind) are committed to achieving equality and first-class citizenship. We regret that there is apparently a certain amount of conflict built into the transition from second- to first-class status. But we know that blind individuals, blind people as a group, and our entire society will benefit if the worth we represent is recognized and given its proper place. We are appreciative of the kind words, the good wishes, and the donations of those who have joined us to ensure that our struggle for freedom comes to fruition. But we are also committed to ending forever the philosophy which says that the proper role of the blind person is the recipient of someone else's charity. The proper role for the blind is the same as it is for the sighted. There should be charity given and received on both sides. There should also be responsibility and opportunity.

Unconventional Convention

The 1988 National Convention in Chicago broke precedent in more than one way. In sheer size it was the largest in Federation history; well over three thousand conventioneers filled three hotels (as Barbara Pierce was to report in the *Monitor*'s convention roundup), and just under 2,500 of them registered formally as attendees. Some fourteen special divisions and committees held their own meetings—ranging from the Merchants Division of the NFB, among the oldest, to the newly created National Association of Dog Guide Users.

One of the highlights of the convention was the appearance Thursday afternoon, July 7, of radio celebrity Paul Harvey. In the past some of Harvey's remarks (see 1976 banquet address, "Blindness: Of Visions and Vultures") had drawn criticism from the blind, but Harvey demonstrated by what he said at the 1988 convention that he had read and understood the Federation's message. His reception by the delegates was tumultuously enthusiastic.

No less than twenty-six scholarships were presented at the banquet, topped off by the $10,000 Ezra B. Davis Memorial Scholarship of the American Brotherhood for the Blind. And the banquet itself was presided over—for the first time in two decades—by Master of Ceremonies Kenneth Jernigan, the Federation's former President and current Executive Director, who was plainly enjoying his old role as much as the overflow audience enjoyed him in it.

The banquet had always been the culminating event and dramatic climax of the National Convention—a celebration of community and a renewal of commitment, a time for recognition and praise, a chorus of voices raised in song, a great family feast. But none of these things was the true highlight of the evening; that had always been, and in the minds of Federationists could only be, the banquet address by the President. This annual speech in this distinctive setting was somehow set apart by the conventioneers from all other talks and utterances; it had a special place in their hearts and made a deeper impact on their sensibilities. Down the years and decades of these National Conventions—from the era of the eloquent prophet Jacobus tenBroek through the long distinguished tenure of the brilliant Kenneth Jernigan to the new unfolding age, alive with promise, of the Maurer Presidency—the banquet address had registered, year by year, the mind and will and vaulting aspiration of the movement and its people. It was the peak experience of the convention week and the lasting memorial of the Federation year.

So it was to be again in 1988, at the banquet of the Chicago convention. President Maurer outlined a perspective at once historical and philosophical within which the long upward struggle of the blind could best be understood. "We who are blind, organized throughout the land, have the strength and purpose to change the course of history, at least our own history," he said. "We believe it is our responsibility to make it happen, and we accept the challenge with the full knowledge that the moving force is and must necessarily be the National Federation of the Blind." Maurer's address, entitled "Preparation and the Critical Nudge," is reprinted in full below.

PREPARATION AND THE CRITICAL NUDGE
by Marc Maurer

Lord Bolingbroke once said that history is the teaching of philosophy by examples. Each historical figure is remembered for expressing in action a certain philosophy. The important moments in time have become significant because of actions taken by individuals which have represented specific points of view. However, those events which have helped shape the course of history have had more than one element. There are competing philosophies—each seeking ascendancy. The educator Lewis Mumford wrote that in human experience there are singular moments when the merest nudge can move mountains and change the course of history. These points in time are critical, because it is only then that the balances between compelling, competing ideas—alternate philosophies—can be changed by concerted effort or individual acts of courage. At such times, as Andrew Jackson observed, one human being with courage makes a majority.

These critical points in history do not occur by happenstance. They must be created deliberately, and with strenuous effort. A philosophy which has guided a government or shaped the mental processes of a social order cannot be fundamentally altered easily or simply. Regardless of the seeming spontaneity and suddenness of an event, no philosophy which competes with the established norm can be fixed in the hearts and minds of a society without an accumulation of advance preparation. Only with such preconditioning can a new social balance be reached. But after the old order has been sufficiently challenged that a new equilibrium has almost been achieved, a small choice (a simple decision—or the lack of it) may determine the course of a life or the destiny of a people. Change ordinarily evolves over hundreds of years, but when a fundamental difference in the way we view the world comes quickly (even though necessarily with a considerable amount of advance preparation), the shift in our thinking is called revolution.

These principles apply not only to societies and governments but also to individuals and social movements as well. A change in direction often takes place not because the governing institutions have had a change of heart, but because the pressure brought to bear by individuals organized for collective action has added the necessary impetus. The critical point for the reordering of basic values is (regardless of appearances) never reached individually or spontaneously. The times are right for revolution only when individuals have organized to create the social climate which will permit it. Even when events follow one another with such rapidity that a fundamental alteration is made in a relatively short time, the causes can be found much earlier. Slavery was legal in the United States in 1861. Four years later, after a war had been fought, the Thirteenth Amendment (prohibiting slavery) had been ratified. However, the seeds of the change are discernible almost a hundred years earlier in the slavery provisions of the Constitution, adopted in 1787.

We express (each and every one of us) our philosophy in the actions of our daily lives. As a movement we declare our principles not only in the words we use but also in the steps we take to put those words into practice. The individual act contributes to the totality. The philosophy of a movement is a composite. It is the combined hopes and dreams of thousands of individuals—but it is more than that. It is a shared ambition, a collective determination.

The philosophy of the National Federation of the Blind is simple—and (at least we are sometimes told) revolutionary. We believe that blind people, organized throughout the land, have the strength and purpose to change the course of history—at least their own history. We believe it is our responsibility to make it happen—and we accept the challenge, with the full knowledge that the moving force is, and must necessarily be, the National Federation of the Blind.

The conviction that we the blind have not only the ability to determine our own future but also the right to do it—the right to be the principal architects of the programs and activities which affect our lives—is the very essence of our movement. It is the central thread which has run through the Federation from the day of its beginning. When the National Federation of the Blind came into being in 1940 under the leadership of Dr. Jacobus tenBroek, the doctrine of self-determination was an unquestioned given. This same spirit of independence has been the prime factor in the building of the Federation from the forties to the present. The faith (in fact, the certainty) that our own actions can dramatically change the opportunities available to us—a faith and a certainty so eloquently proclaimed in the speeches of Dr. Kenneth Jernigan—originally brought us together, sustains us today as a movement, and will give us the strength we need for the battles of the future. Without this unshakable core of belief and knowledge, we would cease to be the powerful movement which we are and simply become one among the many who attempt in this way or that to assist the blind. As it is, we are unique—the strongest force in the affairs of the blind today. We are the National Federation of the Blind.

Implied in the thesis that we are responsible for our own destiny is an alteration in the traditional role of the blind. All segments of society—the blind, agencies serving the blind, and the public as a whole—are involved; and when we have completed our work, each of us (and each component of the social order) will be different.

Some time ago I received a letter from a disabled graduate student who asked that I provide him with incidents involving disability and humor for a college research paper. His request said in part:

> I am a graduate student at Arizona State University. At present I am involved in a research project and would appreciate your assistance. I am looking at the dynamics involved in humor and disability. I am seeking jokes, cartoons, or personal accounts about the experience of being disabled.
>
> Part of my interest in humor and disability stems from the fact that I have been disabled for twelve years. During this time I have found numerous situations in which humor has turned possible disaster into something I could put behind me. I feel that I cannot be the only one to use humor in such a manner and am asking others to share their experiences with me.

Perhaps the writer of this letter does not believe that the blind are a minority. One phenomenon associated with many minority groups is that the individuals comprising those groups often become the objects of humor. There are ethnic stories and racial slurs. There are also jokes about the blind. However, the humor is not really humor, and it demeans both the teller and the listener—both the majority and the minority. It is always a put-down, and often an excuse.

There are some who will argue that raising an objection to a little humor is overreacting. "Surely," they will say, "you would not want to be oversensitive. Those who are unable to find humor in a situation take themselves too seriously. Being able to laugh at yourself demonstrates a sense of inner security. Those who cannot do this are touchy, insecure, and without a sense of humor."

To which I say, nonsense! Let those who say that a little innocent fun at the expense of the blind is harmless (and perhaps even admirable) consider the program "Saturday Night Live." On March 5th, 1988, this comedy show carried a skit depicting a blind man being interviewed about his blindness on a television talk show. This ostensibly humorous routine contains one of the most dismal and dreary accounts of blindness I have ever heard. Blindness is the overwhelming characteristic in the man's life. Nothing else really matters. Notice that in the midst of the gloom and the twisted mockery there is yet the positive language of hope—which only makes matters worse. In the Middle Ages it was considered amusing to decorate blind men's heads with donkey ears and make them fight at county fairs. The ears are absent, but the jeering and public ridicule are still with us—on "Saturday Night Live." Here are excerpts from the broadcast. The dialogue begins with the talk show hostess:

"You've still had a fulfilling life, right?"

"Doing what," the blind man replies, "listening? Listening to a sunset? Didn't they tell you, Honey, I'm blind. Okay? Hello? Blind. Where are you? Can't see you."

"I understand that. But given everything, isn't blindness just one more obstacle to overcome?"

"Yeah, right. I'll tell you what. Why don't you try it for about a day and a half?"

"I'm sure it's very challenging, but what about the positives? Your other senses are heightened, aren't they?"

"Oh yeah, yeah. They're great. I can smell a little better now. That really comes in handy on the subway every day. Not to mention the hearing, of course. Yeah. So let's figure this one out. Let's see, I can hear crickets chirping a little louder than you can, and you can see? Yeah, that sounds fair. That's a fair trade-off. Thanks, God!"

"You're a little bitter, Hal. No doubt about it. But you haven't let this stop you from leading a normal life."

"Well, yeah, I'm pretty much dead in the water, I'd say. Mostly I just hang around the house and drink a lot of beer. That's about it."

"You know something? You're a horrible man. Do you know that? A few weeks ago we had a blind horseshoe pitcher, and he was just wonderful. [Here the talk show hostess breaks into tears.] And then we had a blind sky diver, and he always managed to adapt, and he got out there in the world—"

"Well they're insane. Okay, honey? They've got no grip on reality. Guys, you're blind, okay? Calm down. Stop embarrassing the rest of us. I don't understand it. What do you people want from us, anyway? Do you want us to perform for you! Is that it? I'll tell you what. Why don't I just do a little dance for you! Blind man dancing. Okay, is that good? All right. I'm sorry. I'll think of something to say that's nice for blind people. Okay? Something like, okay, if you go blind, it's not so bad. You get a nice tax thing, a little deduction there, and oh yeah, you can look right at an eclipse. That's no problem."

That is what millions of people heard and saw less than six months ago on "Saturday Night Live"; and far from being funny, it is disgusting; it is sick; and it is a straight-out lie. Blind people (we are told) get a tax deduction. We drink a lot of beer—and sit at home. Even those of us who are successful (a success, it should be noted, which betokens insanity) have only been able to succeed by engaging in some sort of recreational pursuit. The responsibilities of citizenship, the participation in community activities, and the holding of a job are not even considered. If this is what passes for humor, forget it. If this is what we are supposed to cultivate to prove we are adjusting, we will remain unadjusted—and write a new script. We don't control the air waves; but we recognize a lie when we meet one, and we also know enough to avoid being conned into being satisfied with second-class status on the grounds that we have a duty to demonstrate a so-called sense of humor. Again I say, forget it! We have put behind us the donkey ears of the Middle Ages and the donkey tails of "Saturday Night Live." We have thrown off the pathos and bitterness, the dejection and gloom, and the passive docility which have traditionally been expected of us. Instead, our mood is one of hope, accomplishment, and the joy of discovery. We know that with reasonable opportunity we can compete on terms of full equality in society, and we also know that with reasonable opportunity the sighted can come to accept us for what we are.

What is required is a redirection of public attitudes and beliefs— and remarkable as it may seem, one of our principal areas of effort must be with the very governmental and private agencies which have been established to help us do the job. The sad truth is that the agencies often have worse attitudes about us than do the members of the general public. They portray us as helpless and inept. An issue of the *Journal*, a District of Columbia newspaper, tells of a teen-age girl who wanted to help the blind. Influenced perhaps by the attitudes of those who work at the agency where she volunteered, she decided to write a cookbook for the blind. Sometimes misconceptions about blindness are veiled and hidden, but not this time. This is the way the article describes her work:

> Cooking hurts when you're blind. It is a vexing daily chore for America's eleven and one-half million blind and visually impaired populations, according to the American Foundation for the Blind. For many of them, it is a frustrating and defeating stumble around the kitchen for sustenance conducted dimly or in total darkness by people who long to be as self-sufficient as the rest of sighted America.

> That's why seventeen-year-old Elizabeth Warshawsky plucks our heart strings with the recent publication of her Braille and large-print cookbooks for the blind.

> The high-school student from Shaker Heights, Ohio, took two years to write and design her cookbook, only part of a busy schedule of study and volunteer work at her local Society for the Blind.

> [The article continues with quotes from the student.] "I couldn't get *The Miracle Worker* out of my mind," said the high school senior, in a telephone interview. "I saw the movie in the second grade, and it changed me. It made me see how we could help the blind by just taking some time to think about them, to work with them a little.

> "So [the article continues] in ninth grade this idea comes to me," she explained. "I saw how the blind people I volunteered for had such a terrible time with food. It's so frustrating and dangerous in the kitchen for them; they solve the problem of eating by getting into a rut, sticking to apples, lunch meats, and sandwiches; and malnutrition is a real problem for many of them.

> "But what really excited me," she recalled, "was all this new food that can be easily prepared, food that is nutritious and hot, the kind of foods blind people once had—when they could see."

So the article says, and it is hard to know how to respond to such a messy mishmash of misinformation. Has this student really met blind people? What influences were brought to bear to teach her that the ordinary kitchen is for the blind a dangerous and frustrating place, a veritable minefield of terror and booby traps? How did she conclude that malnutrition is a serious problem for those of us who are blind? Did the local agency for the blind (reinforced by the American Foundation for the Blind) give her the impression that blind people stumble around the kitchen, feeling defeated? No matter how it came to be, the misunderstanding of blindness has now been learned. A book has been written containing the most blatant misrepresentations about blindness. Opportunities which might have been available will never be, and it has all been done in the name of helping the blind. Instead of this half-baked collection of underdone ideas, we prefer reality and a more positive view of our prospects and possibilities. We reject this gloomy assessment, along with the bitterness and blight traditionally associated with blindness. Rather, our mood is one of hope, accomplishment, and the joy of discovery. We believe that we who are blind, organized throughout the land, have the strength and purpose to change the course of history—at least our own history. We believe it is our responsibility to make it happen—and we accept the challenge, with the full knowledge that the moving force is, and must necessarily be, the National Federation of the Blind.

A company calling itself Safe-E-Scape of Tampa, Florida, writes to tell us that it has devised a set of burglar bars, which are most appropriate for the blind. These bars, which fit on the inside of the window, have a locking mechanism which is opened without a key. In writing to me Safe-E-Scape says: "We feel that this product can be very important to blind people everywhere and of every economic and social level. We are, of course, a for-profit concern and are first seeking customers who (we feel) most need and will best accept our product."

That is what they say, and I ask you: Why are these burglar bars particularly appropriate for the blind? Why more for us than for others? Are we less able to protect our property than the ordinary sighted citizen? Is there a concerted effort by criminals to seek out the homes of the blind? As far as I know, the property of blind people is not more valuable than the property of the sighted. Or, is the reason for selling this product to the blind contained in the fact that there is no key? If the blind are more helpless than others, there is a need for greater protection. But the very helplessness of blind people contains inherent disadvantages. Those who are helpless may misplace a key (or worse still) may not be able to use it even if it is not lost. These notions are all contained in the advertisement for the special burglar bars for the blind.

And they are also contained in a bill considered by the House of Delegates of the 1988 Maryland General Assembly. The bill (which embodies the inherent assumption that the blind and other so-called "vulnerable groups" need special, segregated laws to protect them) was entitled "An Act Concerning Crimes Against the Elderly and Vulnerable." The language of this legislative measure leaves no doubt as to what is meant by those who are "vulnerable." It says, in part:

> The maximum sentence allowed by law for commission of any crime of violence may be doubled for commission of that crime of violence against a person who is: (1) 60 years old or older; (2) Blind; (3) Paraplegic; or (4) Quadriplegic.

According to this bill, if you are blind, you are more vulnerable (in fact, twice as vulnerable) to crimes of violence than other people are. But our experience teaches us otherwise. Blindness does not mean that keyless burglar bars or extra legal protection is required. We are able to live in the world as it is. I am pleased to say that the bill for the vulnerable died in the Maryland legislature. The views of the Federation helped kill it, and we hope that the misunderstandings about blindness which it represented are also on the way to being killed.

In our organizational efforts and our daily activity our mood is one of hope, accomplishment, and the joy of discovery. We believe that we who are blind, organized throughout the land, have the strength and purpose to change the course of history—at least our own history. We believe it is our responsibility to make it happen—and we accept the challenge, with the full knowledge that the moving force is, and must necessarily be, the National Federation of the Blind.

Traditionally those who seek to tell the story of blindness exaggerate and distort. They tell us that blindness alters the mental processes—that we who are blind are characterized by heightened sensitivity, extreme joy, and deep gloom. There is, for instance, the report some time back in *People* Magazine concerning a blind child who became so depressed while attending a school for the blind that he forgot how to smile. He had to be taught how to move his face.

However, as we know from our own personal experience, blindness and depression are not necessarily synonymous. Nor (as we can testify) does blindness carry with it some of the other peculiar results, weird side effects, and odd-ball associated characteristics which some have claimed. In the book *And There Was Light* by the blind author Jacques Lusseyran, we find this astonishing passage: "Shortly after I became blind, I felt indescribable relief, and happiness so great it almost made me laugh. Confidence and gratitude came as if a prayer had been answered. I found light and joy at the same moment, and I can say without hesitation that from that time on, light and joy have never been separated in my experience."

To which one is tempted to respond: Yuk! One blind person could not move his face; the other felt relief and happiness. The only way I know to reply to such fantasy is by calling on the poets. If memory serves me, James Russell Lowell said something to this effect:

> Here comes Mr. Poe with his raven,
> Like Barnaby Rudge;
> Three-fifths of him genius,
> And two-fifths sheer fudge.

I would agree with Lowell, but I would change the ratio.

National Industries for the Blind, the agency which distributes millions of dollars' worth of government contracts to sheltered workshops for the blind, has recommended that a special sandpaper-type material be attached to the floor in buildings where blind people walk. The blind (or so National Industries for the Blind apparently believes) cannot effectively get around by any other method and should follow the sandpaper to find their way.

Then, there is the opinion of a researcher into low vision, reprinted some time ago in an issue of the *Architectural Record*. As you might expect, the findings of this researcher are couched in terms of architectural barriers. However, the conclusion reached is, to say the least, astonishing.

One of the most difficult architectural barriers faced by partially sighted persons [the publication says] is locating a rest room in a public building and determining whether it is for men or for women. This problem can be easily solved by affixing panels to rest room doors in such a way that visually impaired persons can readily identify the facilities. Those on men's rest room doors should be an equilateral triangle with a vertex pointing upward, and those on women's rest room doors should be a circle. The edges of the triangle should be one foot long, as should be the diameter of the circle, and all panels should be one-quarter inch thick. The color and gray value of these geometric figures should be distinct from the color and gray value of the doors. [I interrupt to ask you to disregard the hidden Freudian pornographic symbolism contained in this treatise and to say that there are other (possibly even better) ways of determining which bathroom is which. But back to the article.]

If this were done [it continues] even the totally blind could touch the edge of a panel and easily determine whether it is straight or curved.

As I ponder this report, I confess to a certain curiosity. Are the geometric shapes intended to represent the people involved—men triangular with straight edges, vertex pointing upward; and women circles with lots of curves? It is embarrassingly suggestive. Let me simply leave it at this: although it is often important to find a bathroom, most blind people seem to manage; and I believe it is a foolish and overdramatic exaggeration to describe the matter as one of the most important problems faced by the blind.

Shortly before last summer's National Federation of the Blind convention an item appeared in the *Honolulu Advertiser* which declared that there are characteristics of blindness which are advantageous in marriage. Here is the item in full:

> Marriages among blind people last longer statistically than marriages among people with good eyesight. Or, so our Love and War man has been informed. He doesn't doubt it. It's common knowledge that the blind tend to be better lovers than the sighted. For two reasons: 1. It's quite comfortable for them to communicate with their hands. 2. And, they make love with inner visions of each other, which remain forever as they so desire.

So there you have it. You may have been under the impression that blind people were just like everybody else except that we can't see. Not so! We have the ability to communicate with our hands—and besides, there is that special inner vision which we conjure up when making love. When reading this piece of so-called news from the *Honolulu Advertiser*, I wondered where the reporter got his information. In my experience with thousands of blind people (some of whom have attended conventions of the National Federation of the Blind), I have reached the conclusion that the mating patterns of the blind do not vary substantially from those of the larger society. Let any reporter interested in field testing come to this gathering of blind people from throughout the nation. I suspect that the research will show that we have about the same experience (and the same attributes) as others—just as loving, just as bad, just as wonderful.

The Queen's University of Belfast has a program for teaching the blind about dentistry and oral hygiene. There is even a kit with models and tape recordings. The brochure has this to say about the course:

> The Queen's University of Belfast Touch Tooth Kit has been developed by the Department of Pediatric and Preventive Dentistry within the University.
>
> It is a complete dental health programme for the visually impaired.
>
> It includes the smells and sounds of the dental surgery, large models for the student to feel what he is learning, and a complete set of Teachers' Notes to lead them through an up-to-date programme of dental health education.

Why anyone would want to experience the smells of dentistry without being compelled to do so is something I can't understand. Why a university should think that blind people need the sound of the dentist's drill, the spicy aroma of tooth decay, and the feel of a deteriorating molar is beyond comprehension. Perhaps the designers of this course have concluded that the psychological stresses for blind people have been too great. Consequently, they may have decided that the blind are abnormally interested in the bizarre. How else can the existence of this dental education program for the blind be explained? Why is the ordinary dental hygiene program not enough? Most of the blind people I know have teeth, and the toothbrush is not an unknown quantity. I venture to say that blind people are as aware of dental hygiene as the sighted are. If the message were not so destructive, it would be amusing. The basic assumption is that blindness necessarily means diminished ability, that we do not have the capacity to learn with the ordinary tools in the usual way. As with so much else, we reject this assessment. Rather, our mood is one of hope, accomplishment, and the joy of discovery. We believe that we who are blind, organized throughout the land, have the strength and purpose to change the course of history—at least our own history. We believe it is our responsibility to make it happen—and we accept the challenge, with the full knowledge that the moving force is, and must necessarily be, the National Federation of the Blind.

Agencies for the blind have been established to provide services to blind people. However, the actions of the officials of some of these agencies frequently represent the most difficult problems that we face. It is unfortunately too often true that the agencies established to serve the blind create more problems than they solve—more than would have existed if they had never been there at all.

Last year a supervisor in the vending program of the Division of Eye Care of the Department of Human Services of the State of Maine sent a written directive to all blind vendors in the state expressing her opinion that the blind are not only incompetent but at least as immature as small children. Here, in part, is what she said:

> It has come to my attention recently that some of you are not aware of the guidelines for operators regarding dress and hygiene. Although this is not a formal dress code, excessive deviations deemed by the program supervisor to be detrimental to the image which we want to convey of viable small business people in the community will be noted and may become part of a corrective action procedure. [I interrupt to say that this portion of the document seems clear enough. There is no formal dress code. However, if you do not follow the informal dress code, action will be taken against you. But back to the text.]
>
> Jeans are permissible as long as they are in one piece, clean, and fit properly. [Again, I ask: Why were such instructions given? In the vending program, blind vendors are supposedly operators of independent small businesses. Is it proper for a state official to send a memorandum to licensed vendors telling them to wash their jeans? What does it mean if a state official thinks it is necessary to instruct an entire class of people that the pants they wear should be in one piece? These are the directions ordinarily reserved for small children or the mentally defective. However, this is not all that the state of Maine

thinks should be addressed to independent blind vendors in its program.]

Clothes should, of course, [the document continues] be clean and complimentary. Beyond that, the clothes you are wearing should not be provocative in any way, by this I mean that there should not be a lot of bare skin showing (shoulders, low necklines, et cetera), fit should be good without being tight, proper undergarments should be worn, midriffs should not be bare. We are operating public businesses, not the bar at the country club.

I already mentioned [this official continues] that clean hair (washed several times each week) is essential. Hair style should be attractive and neat, whether long or short. This means that regular hair cuts are expected, no matter what style you've chosen. Facial hair is acceptable as long as beards and mustaches are trimmed and clean. Men should shave every morning unless they can demonstrate that their facial hair growth is not visible over longer periods.

In order to eliminate unpleasant body odors, [this supervisor's letter goes on] a shower or bath each day and the use of deodorants is imperative. Hands should be washed with soap and water frequently and fingernails must be clean. Most people need to wash their hair at least every other day, especially in this type of environment.

Remember that this state official is talking to people who are supposedly operating their own businesses. Although much of the substance of her directive is objectionable, the primary problem is in the tone and the spirit. Of course, one should wash one's hands and wear clean underwear, but the condescending tone of the order is intolerable. Is it any wonder that the blind of the state rose in condemnation of such statements? Within a few weeks the directive of the vending supervisor was rescinded. The reason for the change is not hard to find. The members of the National Federation of the Blind of Maine had taken concerted action and had said, "Enough!" The result is indicative of what is happening throughout the country. Our mood is one of hope, accomplishment, and the joy of discovery. We believe that we who are blind, organized throughout the land, have the strength and purpose to change the course of history—at least our own history. We believe it is our responsibility to make it happen—and we accept the challenge, with the full knowledge that the moving force is, and must necessarily be, the National Federation of the Blind.

Sometimes there are incidents which underscore with dramatic force the urgency of the work we do and the magnitude of the task still left for us to accomplish. Recently a person flying from Baltimore to Indianapolis on USAir, found a paper attached to his ticket. It said "unaccompanied child." Written across the face of the document was the word "blind." There were spaces on the form to indicate who would be responsible for the traveler, both at the origin and destination of the flight. The person flying that day was the president of the National Federation of the Blind. I was that person. I had been classified automatically in the same category as small unaccompanied children.

Less than two months ago a totally blind woman, Shelia Marque, called to ask for the help of the Federation. She has been blind for less than a year. Her husband is a custodian at the First United Methodist Church in Chanute, Kansas. The Marques live in the country with their three children, and Mrs. Marque is a student, studying elementary education, at a nearby college. Although she has qualified for student teaching, there has been no placement. Faculty members at the university tell her that it is not possible to find a teacher willing to work with her.

Sometimes Mrs. Marque rides into town with her husband. While he performs custodial duties at the church, she explores the town and practices with her cane. When the travel is finished, she returns to the church to wait for her husband to complete his tasks. Mrs. Marque called because of what happened to her when she wanted to attend a funeral in the church. She was told by officials of the church that she should not be in the building because it was bad publicity to have a blind person on the grounds. She called us to ask if someone could do something about this discrimination. As she said, "I have been blind for less than a year, and all I have faced are setbacks." And where, one wonders, shall the blind worship if not at church? Where, indeed!

What a picture! The blind are ridiculed on "Saturday Night Live." We need separate burglar bars and cookbooks. There should be special laws to protect us. We forget how to smile and must be taught to move our faces—or alternatively, we smile constantly and are surrounded by light. We must have sandpaper on the floor to guide us, and circles and triangles on the bathroom doors to intrigue and inform us. We must be told when to change our underwear and wash our hands. We need to be taught the smells of the dentist's office. We make good lovers because we know how to use our hands and have inner visions. And finally, we are not even permitted to come to the church. Is this a picture of gloom and despair? Not at all.

We are better off today than we have ever been before. We recognize the prejudices and misconceptions which we face, and we are organized to do something about them. The fact that we understand and catalog does not mean that we feel bitterness, defeat, or despair. When we identify these injustices and bring them into the open, the very fact of doing so begins the process of change and improvement. Yes, many of the governmental and private agencies are negative in their outlook and are still mired in the past, but others (a growing number) are working with us in progress and partnership. And increasingly throughout the country we are establishing training programs of our own to serve as models and touchstones.

Likewise, although the media and the public at large are still characterized by outworn notions and lack of information about the true nature of blindness, the progress toward enlightenment and change has been amazingly rapid, and it continues at an accelerating pace. More people today are with us than against us, and the balances are constantly shifting in our favor. Invariably when the press and the public understand, they are with us.

But we do not need to rely on logic and statistics to see what we are achieving. Look about you! Never before in the history of the world has such an assemblage as we have in this room tonight been brought together. In the presence of this determined, united multitude, can you doubt our ultimate success? In the final analysis our future will be what we determine it to be—what we are willing to work, plan, and sacrifice to make it be. We can ask for no more, and we can accept no less.

There are critical times for a nation, a social order, an individual, or a movement—times when a nudge or a single act can make the difference. But no such critical time has ever occurred without extensive advance preparation. The final act may precipitate the event, but the act cannot occur without all of the others which went before it. Which step is more important—the first or the last? The answer, of course, is that neither is more important. Both must be taken for either to be significant or at all memorable. And there are also the steps between—the ones we are taking now—and have been taking through all of the years since the National Federation of the Blind was established. Changes in the social fabric can only be made after individual effort has created the climate and prepared the way, and in the complexity of present society individual effort is lost unless it is joined in concerted action. This is a lesson we have learned well—and we have also learned the value of the first step, and patience, and the long view. And something more! We have come to understand the importance (indeed, the necessity) of knowing when to refuse to wait, when to reject patience, when to say no to delay—the courage and judgment to insist that freedom and opportunity must be now, not tomorrow! All of this comes with the maturing of a movement, and every movement must either mature or die. We have no intention of dying. Rather, our mood is one of hope, accomplishment, and the joy of discovery. We believe that we who are blind, organized throughout the land, have the strength and purpose to change the course of history—at least our own history. We believe it is our responsibility to make it happen—and we accept the challenge, with the full knowledge that the moving force is, and must necessarily be, the National Federation of the Blind.

The philosophy of our movement is expressed in the individual actions of each of us—and make no mistake! Act we will! Our prospects have never been as bright; our determination has never been as strong; and our goal has never been as clear. My brothers and my sisters, let us march together to the future!

1989: An End and a Beginning

The last year of the decade was also the final year of the first half century—the formative fifty years—of the organized blind movement in the United States. And, as it happened, 1989 was itself a year of decision and a harbinger of hope. By the time of the Denver convention in July, the National Federation of the Blind was clearly turning a page of its history and on the point of turning what Kenneth Jernigan had called "the corner of time."

This sense of simultaneous arrival and departure found expression in the ferment and excitement of convention activity at Denver, both in the formal events of the business agenda and in the spontaneous happenings characteristic of this massive gathering of the clans. During the week there was joy and there was sorrow; it was all in the family. The undercurrent of joy was sufficiently strong to be identified by Barbara Pierce, Associate Editor of the *Monitor,* as the defining mood of the convention. "It was joy," she wrote in her follow-up report on the event, "the quiet joy one sometimes stumbles upon in the midst of hard work and challenge, a momentary pause in the frantic rush of activity, during which one savors the contentment of a job well in hand and the love of colleagues who share a dream."

And the sorrow arose from the successive passing, only weeks before the convention, of two beloved Federationists, Jim Walker of Nebraska and Connie McCraw of Maryland. There was sorrow as well in the illnesses of several delegates during the course of the convention, at the involuntary absence of others for reasons of health, at the memory of comrades-in-arms who had fallen. And there was sorrow of another kind—more chronic and hard- edged—at the persisting folly of all those agencies and institutions of the blindness system still clinging to the superstitions of the Stone Age. But this was a sorrow that issued not in silence but in resounding condemnation punctuated by satire—as in the new Federation song that sprang from the camaraderie of a post-banquet gathering around the grand piano at the Hyatt Regency Denver, commemorating the struggle against exclusionary practices by the U.S. State Department. In part the song went like this (to the tune of "Yankee Doodle"):

The State Department keeps us out;
They say that we're not able;
They won't let our readers in
To read their secret cables.

(Refrain):
State Department let us in;
We want to serve our nation;
We will fight until we win,
'Cause we're the Federation.

At this 1989 convention, and most notably at the banquet, there was a pervasive sense of transition that gave an additional charge to the always electric atmosphere of the annual meetings. And the banquet this year let no one down—and left no one out.

"The banquet was again," wrote Barbara Pierce, "what the banquet always is for the Federation—the apex of the convention, the high point of the Federation year, the very touchstone of our movement." Balloons (courtesy of the Cambridge Chapter of the Massachusetts affiliate) festooned the banquet hall, and TVs with giant speakers broadcast the festivities to an enthusiastic overflow crowd outside the hall. The master of ceremonies, to everyone's delight, was the Federation's President Emeritus and current Executive Director, Kenneth Jernigan, who announced at one point toward the end of the program: "Let me now tell you what's next on this evening's agenda. We'll do these things. We will present the scholarships; we will recognize some other people from the head table; we will ask the hotel personnel to take a few minutes to clear the tables; and we will then begin the morning session."

What some in the banquet audience were already calling the "spirit of '89" found its appropriate expression in an address of singular power and resonance delivered by President Marc Maurer. His speech, entitled "Language and the Future of the Blind," was subsequently published in *Vital Speeches of the Day* and came to be widely admired beyond the boundaries of the organized blind movement. Taking as his theme the interconnection of speech and behavior, Maurer called for a sweeping change in the "bad habits" of ordinary speech as a means to the changing of minds and the reform of attitudes. In order "to change a pattern of behavior," he declared, "we must change the habit of speech." Does blindness mean darkness and despair? Many people have thought so, he said: But the Federation proposes to refute that myth, alter that perception, and change that meaning. His speech was an eloquent first step in that direction.

Following is the text of the 1989 banquet address:

LANGUAGE AND THE FUTURE OF THE BLIND
by Marc Maurer

One of the most powerful instruments for determining the prospects of an individual, the future of a social movement, or the development of a culture is language—the expression in writing or speech of human thought. However, there is at least one theory which maintains that language possesses its power because the relationship between thought and speech is very often misunderstood. According to this thesis these two (thought and speech) are not separate entities at all. They are one. Thoughts cannot occur without being verbalized (either physically or in the mind), and words cannot be spoken or imagined without expressing thought. The words and the thought are the same.

The historian and essayist Thomas Carlyle once noted that language is not the garment of thought but the body of it. Modern anthropologists have advanced the Whorf-Sapir hypothesis, which declares that all of human culture is fabricated by language. The poet Percy Bysshe Shelley said that man was given speech, "and speech created thought." Samuel Taylor Coleridge observed that "language is the armory of the human mind, and at once contains the trophies of its past and the weapons of its future conquests." Socrates asserted that language is the guiding spirit of all human endeavor. "Such as thy words are," he said, "such will thine affections be; and such as thine affections will be thy deeds; and such as thy deeds will be thy life." If the language is modified, the thought is also altered. If the thought is shifted, the deed cannot remain the same. Therefore, to change a pattern of behavior, we must change the habit of speech.

If this theory is true, patterns of speech are at least as important to the future of the blind as the buildings possessed by the agencies, or the money appropriated for rehabilitation, or the gadgetry designed to lighten the burden of life for us. The policy statements, the laws, the public pronouncements in print and on television, the scholarly papers of those conducting so-called "research" into the nature of blindness, the thought processes of employers and the public-at-large (sometimes expressed in words but more often simply internalized without being uttered), and our own words and thoughts—these will determine the future for the blind. If the language is positive, our prospects will be correspondingly bright. If the words used to describe the condition of the blind are dismal, we will find that our chances for equality are equally bleak. However, this is not a matter to be left to fate. For thousands of years false and downbeat words have been forced upon the blind—words like *wretched, purposeless, unfortunate*. But we are no longer willing to abide such labels. We are not inarticulate. We will write our own story and use our own words. Our thoughts will be the dreams of tomorrow, and the language will say: success, independence, freedom!

In 1940, as the National Federation of the Blind was brought into being, there was almost nothing in the language to combat the erroneous but generally accepted view that blindness meant ignorance and inability. Dr. Jacobus tenBroek, the founder and first President of the National Federation of the Blind, and the handful who worked with him to pioneer our movement had to commence the process of altering the patterns of thought by correcting the language. He and those others had to begin to create a literature of independence and freedom for the blind. In the 1950s Dr. Kenneth Jernigan, one of the most powerful writers ever to consider the subject of blindness, joined Dr. tenBroek in building a climate of understanding that would permit the blind to achieve equality. A new language began to appear with new adjectives for the blind. The words employed by Dr. tenBroek and Dr. Jernigan were upbeat, shot-through with vitality, and suffused with confidence. This new method of expression carried with it an innovative pattern of thought, and the altered mental process brought action. No longer were the old words permitted to stand alone. No longer were the limitations of those words accepted without challenge. We came to understand that it is with the blind as it has been with other minorities: the liberation of lives begins with the liberation of language.

Today, at our forty-ninth convention, *blindness* does not mean what it did when the Federation was established. The word itself has changed because the thoughts associated with it have changed. In 1940 the dictionary definition was the only readily available explanation of blindness, and the dictionary was entirely negative. In 1989 there is a substantial body of literature which indicates that the dictionary is wrong. Blindness does not mean helplessness, lack of purpose, inferiority, or absence of intelligence. The dictionary definition will not stand close examination, and we are not willing to let it serve as the definitive statement of our hopes and aspirations. We are the blind, with our own story and our own words—and we intend to speak for ourselves.

Recently an advertisement appeared from the Carrollton Corporation, a manufacturer of mobile homes. Apparently the Carrollton Corporation was facing fierce competition from other mobile home builders, who were selling their products at a lower price. Consequently, the Carrollton Corporation wanted to show that its higher priced units were superior. In an attempt to convey this impression, the company depicted the blind as sloppy and incompetent. Its advertisement said in part: "Some manufacturers put out low-end products. But they are either as ugly as three miles of bad road, or they have so many defects—crumpled metal, dangling moldings, damaged carpet—that they look like they were built at some school for the blind." What a description! There is the ugliness of three miles of bad road, or crumpled metal, dangling moldings, and damaged carpet. The slipshod work is all attributed to the incompetence of the blind. It is not a portrayal calculated to inspire confidence or likely to assist blind people to find employment. However, the work that we in the Federation are doing is paying dividends. When it was called to the attention of company executives that the advertisement was negative and harmful, they apologized for its publication and withdrew it. The manufacturer changed its public representation because of the protest of the organized blind movement.

It is not hard to imagine why a manufacturing company might misunderstand the nature of blindness. Such companies do not have routine association with us. Although their misrepresentation of the abilities of blind people must be brought forcibly to their attention, it is reasonable to suppose that the ignorance they sometimes display stems from lack of information. The same cannot be said of agencies for the blind. They hold themselves out as knowledgeable about blindness and thoroughly familiar with every aspect of our lives and behavior. It is, therefore, ironic that some of the most false and damaging literature written about blindness comes directly from these agencies.

The Delaware Center for Vision Rehabilitation distributes a brochure called *Images*. This flier leaves no doubt about the opinion of the Delaware Center regarding the ability of the blind. The grammatical construction is that of the agency. Here is a portion of the language used: "The eyes and vision are priceless parts of every person, shaping their attitudes, experiences, expectations, and physical and mental capabilities." As I read this statement, I wondered if they could really believe it. Do our attitudes differ from those of the sighted? Do our physical and mental powers change with the loss of sight? If our mental capabilities are altered, do they get better—or worse? The brochure from Delaware does not say, but the context leaves no doubt as to what they think.

On the other hand, an article appearing in the *Columbus* [Ohio] *Register* about two years ago answers this question differently. The headline says: "Nearsighted found to have higher IQs." The article goes on to say: "While the nearsighted may need glasses, their lack of perfect vision could be a sign of high intelligence, say researchers who studied myopic Israeli teen-agers. Doctors tested 157,748 Israeli military recruits, ages 17 to 19, and discovered a link between nearsightedness and high IQs. 'There can be no doubt about the reality of the correlation between myopia and intellectual performance,' wrote Drs. Mordechai Rosner and Michael Belkin. Still, they wrote, the 'cause and effect relationship is not clear.'"

This is what the article says—and of course, it does not go on to claim that the more restricted your vision becomes, the more intelligent you get—until at total blindness you arrive at total genius. But it does suggest that there may be a correlation. Did the learned doctors construct a faulty test? Did they make a mistake in the way they administered it? Or did they simply fall victim to the ancient stereotype that the blind are peculiar and possessed of mysterious powers? Who knows—and in a very real sense who cares? We who are blind are neither specially blessed nor specially cursed, and one misconception is as bad as the other. Regardless of that and the claims of the doctors, there has not been, so far as I know, a rush of employers to hire the blind because of our superior intelligence. Even if we were smarter than the sighted (and I don't believe for a minute that we are), the public attitudes about blindness would likely remain just about where they are—a lot of superstition, growing enlightenment, and a long pull ahead.

A reporter from the *Chicago Tribune* recently said categorically and unequivocally that: "A sighted person with the IQ of a genius would be hard-pressed to make tuna salad while blindfolded." In other words, even if those who are blind have greater intelligence, it doesn't really matter. Sight is essential. Those who lack it cannot even get around their kitchens to make tuna salad.

The National Aeronautics and Space Administration (NASA) recently issued a tech brief on its newly developed "Public-Facilities Locator for the Blind." This is a device intended to help the blind become more independent in daily travel. The document describing the new aid is suitably couched in technical terms. It says in part: "A proposed coded infrared transmit/receive scheme would enable a blind person in a building to detect and locate specific 'landmarks', such as elevators, water fountains, restrooms, and emergency exits. A synthesized voice would announce a landmark. Each landmark (the document continues) has a code. A pulse code modulation (PCM) scheme transmits each one, the code being the binary grey code (a one chip encode/one chip decode). The transmitter gives out a burst of two identifications; for example, 'men's room—men's room,' and repeats it continuously at an even cadence." That is what the tech brief says, and there is more of this high-flown technological jargon in the NASA report. Computer signals have been devised for the stairwell, the lady's bathroom, the escalator, and the telephone. When we tell these space technologists that their legerdemain is not only unnecessary but harmful to the blind, they will probably say that we are super-sensitive and that they are only trying to help. They will not understand that the presence of such gadgetry will encourage both the blind and the sighted to believe that we need complex adaptations of the environment for the simplest acts of our daily lives and that those who work in such modified buildings will be quietly and inevitably indoctrinated to the conclusion that blindness means abnormality and incompetence. Of course, there are dozens of ways in which technology can serve our needs. However, if it is truly to be useful to us, its designers must recognize the fundamental capacity of the blind for full integration into society on the basis of equality. Specialized aids and appliances must enhance independence, not stand as a declaration that the blind are so lacking in intelligence that we cannot even find the bathroom or the telephone. How often we have been told that one of the major problems of blindness is being able to find the bathroom.

One thing is certain—the mickey mouse contraptions and the prejudice against blindness that they represent must go! We will no longer permit the scientists and engineers to imply that we are somehow peculiar and strange. If necessary we will build the equipment we need for ourselves. We the blind are abroad in the land, and we will not remain silent while the technocrats combine antiquated fantasy and modern science to form a spurious portrait of the helpless blind. We have found our voice, and we know how to use it. They cannot tell us how it is for the blind. For we (as was said on another occasion) have been to the mountaintop, and we know how it is for the blind. The technologists can work with us if they will. But we know what we want and how to get it. And we intend to speak for ourselves.

One of the oldest and tiredest jokes about the blind is that the Braille system works better on a date. Now, there is a company that has decided to try to capitalize on that sick so-called sense of humor. An outfit calling itself Valley Enterprises prints T-shirts with easily feelable raised dots. The name they give to this printing is so predictable as to be both inevitable and totally disgusting—

they call it "Body Braille." There are six preprinted messages available on the back of their T-shirts or sweat shirts. They will also print them on the front, if you like. Blind people across the country have heard these messages over and over again. Here are the six: "Out of Sight," "Keep in Touch," "Touch of Class," "Hands on Experience," "Feeling Good," and "Handle with Care." According to the maker of these shirts, the purpose of the company is not merely to raise money for its owners. Instead, they say: "'Body Braille' clothing is a unique means of communicating self-awareness and self-expression for individuals who are visually impaired, a means to raise the consciousness of the sighted public, and an avenue for all people to demonstrate their support of the visually impaired."

To which I reply: "Yuk and double yuk." Why is it that this company (and so many other people) feel that they have to offer a socially acceptable justification for poking fun at the blind? Blind people do not make a practice of feeling one another up, and we are unwilling for any other group to assume that we do—or, for that matter, that it would be all right if we did, or that it is all right for them to do so with us as an excuse. Furthermore, I, for one, am tired of the slightly off-colored humor that is so often claimed to be funny. The blind are like others. We will find the times and the places when intimacy is appropriate. Otherwise, leave it alone, and do not talk or act as if we (like the slaves of a bygone time) are generally available.

There is a well-known theory which holds that all blind people require psychological counseling and adjustment. This bald proposition has been given sufficient credence by certain agencies for the blind that they have permanent psychologists on staff to minister to the needs of their clients. Blind people seeking assistance from these agencies are not asked whether they want psychological services. It is simply assumed that all who are blind need them. Often those who try to avoid the psychologist are informed that the ministrations of this specialist are part of the package if they want help in learning the skills of blindness (such as Braille and mobility), securing financial aid for college tuition, or gaining assistance in locating a job. If the blind hope to receive any service at all, they may have to endure the testing, the questioning, and the probing into every corner of daily life and personal behavior.

Perhaps you imagine that this psychological review is of the standard sort. Don't you believe it. Some of the agencies (no doubt employing their years of experience and so-called research tools) have decided that the usual tests are insufficient. After all, the standard psychological examinations are designed for the sighted. The blind are different. They are blind. Therefore, an alternative series of tests (special tests just for the blind) has been designed and is now in use.

The American Foundation for the Blind has produced a special psychological test called "The Anxiety Scale for the Blind." Apparently the putative experts believe that there is a need to measure psychological stress in the blind and that no ordinary analysis will do. Here is a sample of what the test designers say: "Although there are a number of general anxiety measures available, counselors and psychologists working with blind clients may question the use with the blind of instruments that have been constructed for the sighted. The purpose of research on the Anxiety Scale for the Blind (ASB) was," they go on to say, "to provide a measure of manifest anxiety which could be standardized on populations of blind persons and which later could have wide applicability in the field of work for the blind." There you have it. It is necessary to test the anxieties of blind people, and this is no ordinary task. The anxiety felt by the blind is special. It is certainly not the same as the anxiety felt by the sighted. And these are the people who are charged with providing services to the blind. We have many hundreds of blind people meeting and enjoying themselves at this banquet tonight. Forget your good spirits for a moment, and ask yourself whether you have special anxiety. Do you feel it? Well, I don't either. And what kinds of services do you suppose will likely be offered with this anxiety scale as a background?

The next revelation of these so-called experts (from the American Foundation for the Blind) is that they intend to test us all. Psychological examinations have traditionally been given in this country to select groups to achieve specific purposes. They have not been given to entire populations for nonspecific reasons. However, the designers of the Anxiety Scale for the Blind tell us that its use is to be much broader. Although the authors developed this test with students attending schools for the blind, they say: "Local norms should be established for blind persons in various environmental settings such as the home, the sheltered workshop, and the competitive work situation." But this is not all. They go on to recommend that there be, in their words: "a study of the effects of manifest anxiety on the academic achievement of blind students; a study of the effect of anxiety on learning mobility skills; a study of manifest anxiety in relation to social behavior in courtship and other social situations; a study of the effects of anxiety on success in the competitive work environment; and a study of manifest anxiety in leadership potential among blind persons."

The environment of George Orwell's *1984* has, I am glad to say, not yet been fully imposed upon the general population, and we are not going to have it for the blind either. We don't need special testing beyond that given to others in our education, our jobs, or our social lives. If we have reasonable opportunity and a fair chance to compete for jobs on equal terms with others, we will hold our own as well as the next person. We are not freaks; we are not basket cases; and we are not so fragile that we will break. Our problems are more in the area of civil rights and vocational exclusion than maladjustment and the need for counseling—and don't you forget it.

But back to the testers and the anxiety scale. After informing us that there is virtually no aspect of the daily lives of blind people that should not be subjected to the rigors of this mental measuring stick, the testers list seventy-eight statements. The person being examined is expected either to agree or disagree. Here is a sample from the seventy-eight. As you consider these statements, ask yourself how much confidence is inspired by the language employed.

Statement number two: "I almost always trust the people who guide me."

That statement assumes that the blind need guidance, that this need causes dependency, and that the lack of freedom of movement results in anxiety. The implication is that the blind person cannot function without the superior knowledge or judgment of somebody else and that a degree of decision-making power and control will necessarily be surrendered. All people require guidance from time to time. This is as true of the blind as it is of the sighted. However, hidden in this statement is the insinuation of an innate helplessness by the blind. If this is what they believe, they are not well acquainted with the energy, the resourcefulness, and the self-reliance of blind people. One is tempted to reply with an answer like this: "I do almost always trust the people who guide me, except when the guidance comes from the people who designed this test." But back to the psychological examination. The statements go on. Here are some of the others. Ask yourself what is meant by each and how you might respond.

Number six: "I am uncomfortable when I must eat with sighted persons."

Number ten: "I would say that blindness has completely ruined my life."

Number fifteen: "I refuse to carry a cane because it makes me appear helpless."

Number nineteen: "I would say that in most cases blind people should marry other blind people."

Number thirty: "I don't worry about being blind."

I interrupt to ask how could one help it when the psychologists are trying to ram it down our throats? But there is more to the test.

Number thirty-one: "I would not date a sighted person."

Number thirty-seven: "I would say that I often feel unwanted when with my blind friends."

Number thirty-eight: "Sighted people rarely make me feel useless."

Number forty-one: "I often find it difficult to express my ideas when in the company of sighted people."

Number forty-nine: "Frequently, when I am with sighted persons I have trouble with my words."

Number fifty-one: "In familiar surroundings, I sometimes have a feeling of being absolutely lost."

Number fifty-five: "I have about the same number or fewer fears than my blind friends."

Number fifty-six: "I have to be cautious in the company of sighted people."

Number fifty-seven: "Because I cannot see, life is a constant state of stress."

Number sixty: "I constantly think and often talk about being able to see well."

Number sixty-four: "I am more irritable when I am with sighted people than when I am with blind people."

Number sixty-five: "I frequently feel uneasy about competing with sighted people."

Number sixty-eight: "I am overly sensitive about my physical condition."

Number seventy: "Frequently, I feel that a familiar room has changed shape."

Number seventy-three: "I do not mind asking sighted people for help."

Number seventy-four: "I often worry about looking ridiculous to sighted people."

Number seventy-five: "Often I am not polite to sighted people."

There is one statement among the seventy-eight which exemplifies the approach of the whole miserable examination. It reads: "I often feel under strain because I must stay alert." Now, I ask you, why is it necessary for the blind to be more alert than others? Are blind people more likely to get into trouble? Are we more accident-prone? Is there something about the blind that makes us miss factual information if we do not concentrate more diligently than others? What could possibly be the need for this extraordinary vigilance? Have the testers really met the blind and worked with us on a daily basis? Can they truly understand our fundamental ability, our wishes, and our aspirations? There must have been some reason for including this novel suggestion. Perhaps the explanation is contained in statement twenty-nine. It says: "I would say that blindness is a personal punishment." Did these psychological experts learn their scientific principles from ancient mythology or venerable lore? Blindness, a punishment? From whom does the retribution come? Such a statement, in a supposedly even-handed psychological test, puts one in mind of the old Middle Eastern proverb: "When you see a blind man, kick him. Why should you be kinder to him than God has been?"

Dependence, rejection, uncertainty, frustration—these are the words associated with the portrayal of the blind in this test. The Anxiety Scale for the Blind is certainly not a document that will engender peace of mind. The set of idiotic statements is well named. It will certainly cause anxiety in the blind, in those, at least, who are gullible, inexperienced, or beaten down enough to take it seriously. And it will also cause anxiety in the rest of us—an anxiety to eradicate such misbegotten notions as those advocated by the test.

The blind are not less secure or more sensitive than others. It is not reasonable to suppose that lack of sight indicates mental imbalance. The experience of tens of thousands of us shows that it is not so. This so-called scientific test is not really based on evidence at all. It is a sham dressed up in the jargon of science, and its image is harmful to the blind. Its symbolism is the archaic language of deprivation and fear. We reject this prejudicial, ridiculous document because it does not represent blindness as it is. We will not permit it to stultify our hopes and curtail our opportunities. Instead, we will build our own images and use our own words. The language will be ours, and we will say it like it is. For the blind there will be—success, independence, freedom!

So often those who consider the subject of blindness focus on the dining table. Everyone must eat, and the blind are no exception. One company, Liblan, Incorporated, of Wheeling, Illinois, has designed and patented a special dish and spoon for the blind. In a letter to me Liblan's president says that his company has developed a special "Plastic food container and utensil construction designed for manipulation by the sense of touch only." I was asked to send letters of endorsement to major manufacturers so that they would produce this special bowl and spoon for the blind. I leave it to you to determine whether I did.

A report in the *Tulsa* (Oklahoma) *World* states that a nonprofit organization called New View, Incorporated, has established a program to encourage awareness of blindness by inviting public officials to breakfast and insisting that they eat blindfolded. The results are predictable. All the misconceptions of blindness are enhanced and reinforced by the brief experience. Why are supposedly knowledgeable people willing to believe that blindness can be understood within half an hour? The alternative techniques required for a blind person to function (not to mention the philosophical implications of blindness) are far more complex than the skills required for perhaps a hundred other tasks. Nevertheless, it is assumed that blindfolding a group of public officials for an hour or less will teach them about blindness. These same public officials know that it takes longer than that to learn how to drive a car or shoe a horse. Still, they are urged to think that they know all about blindness with absolutely no training. Here is the way it appeared in the *Tulsa World*:

> If you want a lifetime appreciation of sight, try life without it for half an hour.
>
> A dinner fork becomes a spear when you can't see it coming toward your face. Rich foods make you thirsty, but you don't drink. A glass is a water tower. A reach through the darkness could be a spill and flood everyone's meal.
>
> Coffee is drunk with hesitation. A sip can become a gulp. A gulp can become a scald.
>
> You make a lot of noise with eating utensils when you're blind. You stick your fork heavily onto empty china, and with your increased sense of hearing, it sounds as if you're beating drums to everyone's annoyance.
>
> You don't talk as much during a meal when you're blind. The loss of one sense amplifies the others.
>
> You hear more, and restaurant background music becomes blaring. You think you're shouting just to speak above it.
>
> You eat less when you can't see. To hunt for food is to push it off your plate, onto the table, onto your lap. Scambled eggs can burn like a brand.
>
> One napkin isn't enough when you're newly blind. You wipe food onto the napkin, then you wipe it back onto your face.
>
> You know you're blind and suspect you're bothersome.
>
> People who involuntarily lose their sight have a problem with sorrow about what they can't do. People who voluntarily lose it have trouble with guilt about what they can. When you're blind you no longer care that the Russians boycotted the Olympics.

> You can't even cut your food. Yet the real blind people
> shave and brush their teeth. You finally think more about
> their braveness and bravura than your own blindness.

The newspaper reporter tells us that the blind are brave for shaving; that blind people cannot cut their food; that one napkin is not enough for the newly blinded; that blind people eat less, talk less, and make more noise than the sighted; that the loss of sight heightens the other senses; that the blind are full of grief, and the sighted full of guilt. All of this occurred because an agency for the blind wanted to impress (and doubtless get money from) public officials by frightening them into believing that it was dealing with a catastrophic situation. The inevitable result is that the agency will receive deference and (no doubt) more sympathy for its fund-raising efforts. But what will the blind receive? More public misconceptions to overcome; more difficulty in finding jobs; and more problems in having the opportunity to live normal, ordinary, everyday lives.

If these misstatements, false notions, and devastating descriptions were not so serious, they might be downright funny. However, they have a dramatic impact on the lives of each of us. With this kind of public perception about blindness the job market is closed. The professors at educational institutions may not turn us away, but they will not regard us as serious students. Service in positions of responsibility in government or the private sector will not be available. However, the article in the *Tulsa World*, with its mistaken notions about blindness, is only one of the public utterances about the blind. There are many others. Our work in the Federation has continued for forty-nine years, and there are measurable changes.

For a number of years one of the problems facing the blind was that we were banned from jury service because of blindness. Indeed, in some states the laws still specifically restrict us from being selected. However, the work of the Federation is bringing change. In many states the laws now say that the blind cannot be categorically excluded from jury service. One indicator of our progress is shown by a poll conducted recently by radio station WBZ in Boston. Ninety-five percent of those questioned said that blind people should be allowed to serve on juries. One word, one image, one symbol, one thought at a time—we are changing what it means to be blind. One word, one image, one symbol, one thought at a time—we are achieving independence, self-sufficiency, and equality. The day when the blind can no longer be excluded from jury service is not a dream for the distant future. It is within our reach. First, jury service. Then, other rights—the right to employment on terms with others, the right to live peacefully in our homes without unwanted interference from government officials, the right to travel without harassment or intimidation—the right to participate fully in all the activities of daily life.

The psychological tests, the blindfolded public officials, the patented dishes and spoons for the blind—all of these have an impact on our personal lives. Shortly after last year's convention I received a letter which describes eloquently in unadorned prose the problems we face. The Federationist who sent it knows disappointment and frustration first-hand. The letter contains an exceptional poignancy, more for what it does not say than for what it does. Here it is:

September 30, 1988

Dear President Maurer:

Two years ago I decided to move back home for convenience reasons. In the past few months I have been treated worse by my mother than by airline personnel or a stranger on the street. Let me give you a few examples. I was asked to take a pot of coffee from the house to my father's machine shop, which was only about a four minute walk either by the road or through the trail in the woods. Well, by the time mother had the coffee ready, and I was ready to go, she changed her mind and said I might fall down with it and hurt myself. Mr. Maurer, I have never fallen down on my way from the house to the machine shop.

Another incident: every time food is served at the table, whether it be spaghetti or hamburger meat, it comes to me in a bowl. Not only that, but with a spoon. I asked once, why the spoon? She replied, "I thought you could handle it better that way."

The other night was better than that. I was served soup with several sheets of newspaper under the bowl. I wanted to say something about this, but we would both just get mad and have a fight. I threw a spoon at her one time. And then, of course, I felt embarrassed and humiliated afterward.

I am tired of my mother's negative remarks toward me as to what I can and can't do as a blind person. It seems like, after 37 years, she ought to know damn well what I can and cannot do. Just what can I do to change her attitude about blindness?

Well, tonight for dinner fried fish was served with tartar sauce. Then, I noticed she was laying paper down before she served the plate. I asked my father, "Where is your paper for your plate?" He explained he didn't need paper. So, I just got up and walked away.

What can I say to this Federationist? How can I answer his letter? It is bad enough that the agencies promote negative attitudes about us, that the advertisers belittle us in order to sell their products, and that the newspapers misunderstand and compound the problem. But it is even worse when the members of our own families (conditioned by the words and thoughts of society) do the same. It makes little difference that more often than not the members of our families put us down and treat us like children for motives of love. The tragedy, the pain, and the loss hurt no less for the lack of malice.

Sometimes, in our humiliation and frustration, we may think the first best step is to leave the table hungry for a night—but this is no answer, no remedy, no solution to the problem. There must be concerted action and coordinated effort to change public attitudes and improve the social climate. And we are taking those actions. We are making those efforts. The members of our families are part of the general public, and so are the agencies and their psychologists. For that matter, so are we.

For thousands of years we who are blind have been regarded as incompetent, and for the most part we have accepted the legends we have been taught. But that time is at an end. It is true that some still tell us that we cannot perform in the factory or workshop; that we have an altered mentality; that we are unable to handle routine tasks in the kitchen; that we require extraordinary technological devices to help us find the bathroom; that we need raised dot T-shirts to enhance our self-awareness; that we suffer from special anxiety; that we cannot use ordinary tableware; that, when we finally get to the table, we will eat less, talk less, and make more noise than others; and that our lives are filled with grief.

But it is equally true that these are not any longer the predominant elements of our lives. In 1940 we organized to speak for ourselves through the National Federation of the Blind, and in the intervening half century the blind have achieved more progress than ever before in all previous recorded history. We have replaced the ancient terms of negativism with a new language of hope, and society has increasingly come to accept us for what we are—normal people with normal aspirations and normal abilities.

More and more the words (and therefore, the thoughts and the deeds) of the work place and the home, the school and the church, the street and the playground reflect this new mood. And underlying it all, fueling the change and focusing the progress, is (as it has been for the past half century) the National Federation of the Blind. With all of the problems and all of the work we still have to do, we come to this meeting tonight with a feeling of hope and a mood of gladness. We come with a joy and a certainty of triumph. At long last we know who we are and what we must do. We are organized, confident, and prepared for what lies ahead—and no force on earth can turn us back. Our words, our thoughts, and our dreams reach for a tomorrow which is bright with promise, and the heart of that promise is the individual determination of each of us and the unshakeable power of our vehicle for collective action—the National Federation of the Blind. The past has belonged to others, but the future belongs to us. Let us speak, think, and act in support of each other—and we will make it all come true!

Chapter 9

Global Vision: The Federation on the World Scene

"I propose to you tonight that a new and grand objective be added to our established goals and purposes: namely, the inauguration of a World Federation of the Blind."

Those words of Jacobus tenBroek, spoken during a banquet address at the NFB's 1964 convention in Phoenix, drew an immediate and widespread response of affirmation both in America and abroad. Directly following that convention banquet, leaders of the NFB met with some fifteen distinguished foreign visitors from eight countries to lay the cornerstone of what was to be the International Federation of the Blind—the first independent global association of blind people in history. The decision to inaugurate the International Federation came as the climax of a series of events which blatantly exposed the voiceless and powerless status of the blind in the world at large. For many years the NFB had been represented by a delegate in the World Council for the Welfare of the Blind, the only international organization in the field. Formed and controlled by agencies for the blind (predominantly in Western Europe and North America), the WCWB faithfully reflected its managerial character in the narrow scope and quality of its operations. All efforts to improve this situation, by the NFB and the few other national organizations represented in the World Council, were rebuffed by its agency leadership.

The exclusion of the organized blind from this international blindness cartel was completed in 1962 with the official ouster of the NFB's delegate (Jacobus tenBroek) from his established seat on the World Council's executive committee. That peremptory action followed a stormy summer meeting in Hanover, Germany, where Dr. tenBroek was denied an official hearing and barred from the seat to which the National Federation of the Blind had been democratically elected for a five-year term just three years before. In a subsequent report, Dr. tenBroek declared that the tight control over the world organization exercised by a handful of American and British agencies raised a critical question for blind people everywhere: "Should a world organization of the blind themselves now be created to meet the needs not being met by the WCWB?"

The organized blind of America had already shown their readiness to sail into uncharted international waters through a resolution passed in the 1962 convention of the NFB in Detroit, which was forthright and unequivocal in support of a world federation:

WHEREAS, the blind people of the world at present have no effective world agency or instrumentality through which they may represent themselves or take effective collective action for the improvement of their lot, the discussion of their experiences, and the formulation of solutions to their problems; and

WHEREAS, the World Council for the Welfare of the Blind is dominated by agencies for the blind rather than representatives of organizations of the blind and is in any event largely ineffective and inactive; and

WHEREAS, even that minimal and inequitable representation possessed by the blind of the United States in the World Council for the Welfare of the Blind and upon its Executive Committee seems about to be further curtailed by improper and unconstitutional actions of the officials of the WCWB: Now therefore,

BE IT RESOLVED by the National Federation of the Blind in convention assembled at the Statler Hotel in Detroit, Michigan, this seventh day of July, 1962, that this organization herewith declare the urgent desirability and imperative necessity of a world organization of the blind themselves for purposes of self-expression and self-improvement. We declare it as our policy henceforth to encourage and stimulate the development of such an organization. We instruct our President, our delegate to the WCWB, and our Executive Committee to take all such actions in such manner and in such times as seems to them most meet and feasible and supported by such resources as are available to bring about the establishment of such an organization.

The National Federation of the Blind continued to direct a drumbeat of critical fire at the agency-dominated World Council during the following year, with the most formidable onslaught reserved for the occasion of the 1963 National Convention in Philadelphia. In that "Cradle of Liberty," on Independence Day (July 4), Jacobus tenBroek delivered an address which many in his audience regarded as a "veritable declaration of independence" for the blind people of all nations *from* the World Council for the Welfare of the Blind. Addressing the question "Whither the World Council?" Dr. tenBroek sought first to set forth the expectations that blind people might reasonably have regarding the role and responsibility of the world organization which purported to be acting in their name and for their well-being.

"Most of all," tenBroek said, "we can expect and demand of that leadership a reach of rhetoric to match the depth of its dedication: a bold capacity for fresh and eloquent expression of the high goals of social evolution—the emancipating goals of opportunity and equality, of independence and integration to which any world organization for the welfare of the blind must surely be devoted." He continued:

> We cannot expect immediate solutions to the global terrors of fear and hunger which torment the blind; but we can expect an impassioned proclamation of their urgency and devastation. We cannot expect a cure-all for the cultural and social blights that stunt the growth of countless blind youths and condemn them to lives of futile desperation; but we can expect a resounding manifesto against the defeatism and indifference that permit these things to rage unchecked. We cannot expect a social revolution overnight; but we can expect a full and fearless revelation. We cannot expect, from the labors of the World Council, an instant conferral upon the world's blind of the epaulets of dignity and the credentials of acceptance; but we can expect, and we can demand,

a Universal Declaration of the Rights of Blind Persons, a declaration paralleling and enlarging the two great pronouncements already promulgated by the United Nations: the Universal
Declaration of Human Rights, and the Universal Declaration of
the Rights of the Child.

The Federation leader went on to assert that the World
Council had failed both in its proclaimed purpose and its performance: "It has avoided offending any vested interests in the su-
perannuated agencies of the world. It has placed its stamp of
approval upon sheltered workshops and other mouldering ar-
tifacts of custodial caretaking. It has gone through the motions
of a live body, but has placed no substantial matter in motion. In
general, and in effect, it has tended to let ill enough alone.

The deepest failure of the World Council, tenBroek said,
could be simply stated: "It has shown itself to be lacking in vision.
It has been unable to prevent its own blindness. Confronted with
the grave social and human issues facing blind people everywhere,
it has chosen to look away. It has shed no light and generated no
heat." All that the WCWB had generated, tenBroek maintained,
was conflict—with the very people, the blind populations of the
world, whom it claimed to serve and to represent. "The conflict
between the National Federation and the reigning officialdom of
the Council is less significant in itself than as a symbol of the
severe malady from which this global agency is suffering. It is a
disease of unsympathetic atrophy, whose symptoms are paralysis
of the will, morbid sensitivity to illumination, and a fear of open
places—accompanied by fits of pique and delusions of grandeur."

TenBroek concluded his speech to the NFB convention with
these words: "The founding fathers of the World Council were of
the agencies. Its representative members, by constitutional fiat,
are of the agencies. Its ruling directorate of titular and non-
titular heads are of the agencies. We may say of the World Council, in summary, that the voice it affects is the voice of the blind
man—but the hand is still the hand of the custodian."

At the same time as it was becoming apparent that organizations of the blind themselves could not hope to gain an effective
voice in the WCWB, pioneering efforts were set in motion in a
variety of new and old nations of Asia, Africa, and Latin America

toward the formation of independent blind associations. A notable instance was Pakistan, where the NFB's "goodwill ambassador," Dr. Isabelle Grant of California, instilled the spirit of Federationism into an adventurous band of men and women. (More will be said about this globetrotting gentleperson in later pages.) The Pakistan Association of the Blind, under the leadership of Dr. Fatima Shah, took its place in the early sixties in the vanguard of independent national organizations of blind persons which were arising in parallel with the newly won independence of their countries.

It was in order to further and facilitate this "revolution of rising expectations" on the part of the world's blind people, as well as to counteract the paternalistic and custodial character of the World Council for the Welfare of the Blind, that organized blind leaders from several continents merged their efforts and aspirations in the year 1964 in the common cause of an International Federation of the Blind. The nature of that common cause—the spirit of Federationism among the blind at home and abroad—was powerfully articulated by Jacobus tenBroek, in a banquet address delivered at the NFB's Phoenix convention in 1964. His speech—entitled "The Parliament of Man, the Federation of the World"—was at once a summation of the American success story of the National Federation of the Blind and a new definition of Federationism expressed in universal terms. This is what he said:

THE PARLIAMENT OF MAN, THE FEDERATION
OF THE WORLD
by Jacobus tenBroek

One score and four years ago, a little group of willful men from thirteen states met in Convention Hall in Pennsylvania in order to form a more perfect union. If you find an historic analogy in that, so be it.

The union we formed on that distant day in Wilkes-Barre was far from perfect. It is imperfect still. But it has met the test of time and turmoil, trouble and tribulation; it has not perished from the earth.

The National Federation of the Blind is still standing—but it is not standing still. It is on the move once more, as it was in its first years of wrath and rebellion—more united than ever and more confident of its power, stronger in its faith, and richer by its experience—an older movement and wiser one, now revitalized and recharged by an astonishing vision, an idea even more fantastic than that which lured the handful of founders to the Pennsylvania cradle of Federationism.

The vision which moves us now is nothing less than the image of world federation. I propose to you tonight that a new and grand objective be added to our established goals and purposes: namely, the inauguration of a World Federation of the Blind.

And why not? Our own National Federation of the Blind has blazed the trail and shown the way. We have demonstrated what blind men and women can do in freedom and in concert, through independence and interdependence. We have proved, in the fires of battle, our right to organize, to speak for ourselves, and to be heard. We have established beyond gainsaying our capacity to take the leadership in our own cause. We have slowly and steadily won recognition in the halls of government, in the agencies of welfare, and in the public mind. Through our deeds and programs, by argument and example, in action and philosophy, we have earned respect for ourselves and our fellow blind, the respect of free men and of equals.

All this, and more, Federationism has done for blind Americans. All this it can do for others. It is time that we shared these fruits of struggle and victory with our brothers in other lands. Let the word go out from this convention that we of the National Federation stand ready to lend our efforts and energies to the building of world unity among the blind. Let the liberating principle of federation—the spirit of democratic association and collective self-direction—catch fire among the blind people of Asia, of Europe, of Africa, of Latin America—as it caught fire and blazed forth in the hearts of blind Americans twenty years ago, and still sustains them by its warmth.

What is this peculiar potent spirit which we call Federationism? What are its explosive ingredients? What does it have to offer to the blind of all nations which they do not have and cannot obtain from their governments, their private agencies, and public corporations?

Federationism is many things to many men. First of all it is an indispensable means of collective self-expression, a megaphone through which the blind may speak their minds and voice their demands—and be assured of a hearing.

Federationism is a source of comradeship, the symbol of a common bond, an invitation to commingling and communion—in a word, to brotherhood among the blind.

Federationism is a tool of political and social action, an anvil on which to hammer out the programs and policies, projects and platforms, that will advance the mutual welfare and security of the blind as a group.

Federationism is the expression of competences and confidence, the sophisticated construction of able men and women—not a retreat for the lost and foundered. It is a home of the brave and a landmark of the free.

Federationism is the synonym of independence—the antonym of custodialism and dependency. It is the blind leading themselves, standing on their own feet, walking in their own paths at their own pace by their own command. It is the restoration of pride, the bestowal of dignity, and the achievement of identity.

Federationism is an agency of orientation—a school for the sightless—an incomparable method of personal rehabilitation and adjustment to the unpopular condition of being blind.

Federationism is a dedication—a commitment of the mind and heart, an act of faith, and an adventure of the spirit which issues a call to greatness and a summons to service on the part of all who volunteer to enter its ranks.

Federationism is a spearhead of revolution, bespeaking a rising tide of expectation on the part of the once "helpless blind"—a blunt repudiation of time-dishonored stereotypes and an organized demand for the conferral of rights too long withheld and hopes too long deferred.

These are some—by no means all—of the features and faces of Federationism which are a familiar part of the experience of organized blind Americans. There is nothing about them that is exclusive to Americans or prohibited to others. They are not contraband but common currency. They are as universal as the claims of democracy. Federationism, like blindness, is no respecter of persons or peoples. For purposes of democratic self-organization among us there is neither black nor white, Jew nor Greek, Christian nor Brahman—they are all one within the universal community of the blind....

A few years before the outbreak of World War II, Franklin Delano Roosevelt declared prophetically that his generation of Americans had a rendezvous with destiny. They did indeed. They kept that rendezvous, and all mankind is thankful that they arrived on time for the appointment. I am convinced that this generation of blind Americans now has a rendezvous with destiny: that we are the advance guard of a movement destined in time to transform the lives and fortunes of the blind people of the world. That transformation will not be accomplished in the first year or in the first decade or even in the first generation. But, in the well-remembered words of another President, let us begin. Let us reason together—to compare our experiences, to pool our resources and to combine our strengths. Let us act together, to build our common foundations and to erect our platforms. Let us march together, against the ubiquitous foes of ignorance and folly, prejudice and pride, which stand across our paths the world over.

Above all, let us begin.

The convention banquet at which Dr. tenBroek delivered his address on the spirit of Federationism came as the capstone to a day-long international program featuring the NFB's distinguished guests from around the globe. Presided over by Kenneth Jernigan as master of ceremonies, the banquet also witnessed the conferral of the Newel Perry Award upon Dr. Isabelle Grant in honor of her years of tireless globetrotting in the interests of blind welfare and education. Immediately following the banquet, as the night grew late, the international visitors and leaders of the NFB met to lay the cornerstone of the world organization; and they left their labors in the early hours of the morning with the certain anticipation of a new day dawning for the international movement of the organized blind.

That day of judgment and decision came less than a month later, on July 30, 1964, in New York City, when the International Federation of the Blind was officially inaugurated at a charter meeting of delegates and prospective members. Dr. Jacobus ten-Broek was unanimously elected president; Rienzi Alagiyawanna of Ceylon was chosen first vice president; and Dr. Fatima Shah of Pakistan was named second vice president. The goals and purposes of the IFB were set forth in the preamble to its constitution adopted by the delegates at the New York meeting:

The International Federation of the Blind is the blind people of the world speaking for themselves—acting in concert for their mutual advancement and more effective participation in the affairs of their respective nations.

The International Federation of the Blind is an organization of the blind of all nations, operated by the blind of all nations, for the blind of all nations. It is an educational and fraternal association, nonprofit and nonpolitical in character, dedicated solely to serving the common needs and aspirations of blind men and women everywhere in the world.

We join in this common cause to:

Cooperate with the World Council for the Welfare of the Blind in achieving its objective, providing the means of consultation between organizations of and for the blind in different countries.

Encourage self-organization and self-determination by blind people in all countries through their own voluntary associations, joined together in turn by membership in the International Federation.

Serve as a world assembly for meetings, communication, and interchange among blind persons of all nationalities, toward the end of reinforcing their confidence in themselves, in each other, and in their common cause.

Provide a forum for collective self-expression and discussion by the blind of the world, and to act as the articulate voice for their joint decisions and common objectives.

Work for the progressive improvement and modernization, throughout the world, of public policies and practices governing the education, health, welfare, rehabilitation, and employment of the blind.

Disseminate accurate information, increase knowledge, and promote enlightened attitudes on the part of the peoples of the world toward blind persons.

Solicit the support of national governments everywhere for the programs and policies of the organized world blind, and advise and assist those governments in their implementation.

Furnish a beacon for the underprivileged and disadvantaged blind people of the earth—and create a potent symbol through which blind people everywhere seek the rights and opportunities that are the birthright of all men.

Stand as living proof to the essential normality, equality, and capability of blind men and women as first-class citizens of the world as well as of their individual nations.

Slightly over a decade after this inaugural event, Kenneth Jernigan—who had meanwhile succeeded tenBroek as President of the National Federation of the Blind—recalled the bright beginning and high promise of the International Federation in an address prepared for delivery at the World Congress of the Jewish Blind held in Jerusalem in August, 1975. After reviewing the in-auguration of the IFB in the mid-sixties, Jernigan spoke of its mission and its further progress:

Thus was the spirit of Federationism transformed into a worldwide liberation movement. Emboldened by visions of self-realization and achievement, the International Federation has since penetrated the farthest corners of the earth. Its ambassadors and missionaries have traveled tirelessly by airplane, steamship, and white cane to scores of countries—carrying the gospel of hope, of unity, and above all of collective self-determination. It has not been a placid journey; the road to equality and inter-dependence for the blind people of the world is strewn with stum-bling-blocks. Some are unrelated directly to blindness: poverty, ignorance, and powerlessness. But even these can be reduced and reformed by measures planned to aid and rehabilitate the blind. It is not by accident that most of the blind are poor, and that many of the poor are blind. It is not by accident that the blind nearly everywhere have been kept in ignorance—untrained, unlet-tered, and undeveloped. Ignorance is no more than the state of being ignored. That state has ended for the blind in America; it is ending in Europe; it will be ended, step by step and country by country, through the determination and self-determination of blind people themselves.

There have been three identifiable stages in the social history of the blind in the Western world: those of persecution, protection, and participation. For many millennia blindness was regarded as a fate worse than death, and accordingly the blind were consigned to a fate akin to death. Later, through the conscience of the Judeo-Christian heritage and the consciousness of the Greco-Roman, the blind became objects of charity, philanthropy, and welfare. In our own time the third stage has become a reality for some and a possibility for all: the ultimate stage of integration and independence, of participation and power. In summary, it might be said that during the first stage of their existence the blind were people *to* whom things were done; in the second stage they were people *for* whom things were done; and in the third stage we are people who are doing for ourselves.

That is the essential message of Federationism—and the word that I would bring to you from your fellow blind around the world.

Through the early decades of international activity, there was one person in particular—one very particular personality—who, in company with Jacobus tenBroek and Kenneth Jernigan, led the way for the National Federation of the Blind onto the world scene. Dr. Isabelle Grant (a retired Los Angeles educator, who was born in Scotland) seemed an unlikely candidate for the role of world traveler and trailblazer when she first entered the field: recently blinded, physically slight, culturally sheltered much of her life, she might have stepped out of the pages of Mark Twain's *Innocents Abroad*. But appearances were deceiving; this frail Scotswoman, accompanied only by her inseparable companion—a white cane named "Oscar"—girdled the globe again and again over a quarter of a century in the cause of welfare, health (and above all, education) for the blind masses of the world. Something of her unique accomplishment, and of its relation to the international activities of the National Federation of the Blind, was eloquently reviewed by Hazel tenBroek in a 1979 article published by the *Braille Monitor*. Following is a portion of her commentary.

Dr. Grant's interest in education for the blind grew as she met successful blind people in this country and elsewhere. It became obvious that training and education—and self-help organizations—were the roads to salvation for the blind. She attended a meeting in Oslo, Norway, in 1957 on the Education of Blind Youth and came home imbued with the crusader's zeal to spread the benefits of training and organizing. Dr. Grant decided that it was time to take her sabbatical leave since regulations required that she teach for at least two years after returning, and her normal retirement date was fast approaching. Urged by this and spurred by her curiosity and desire to help, she determined to travel. Pakistan, she concluded, would be her major goal and as many other of the surrounding nations as she could manage.

Typewriter, Brailler, paper, stylus and slate strapped about her, one hand free for her white cane, lugging the rest of her baggage as best she might, Dr. Grant took off on a plane Pakistan-bound, though she was so exhilarated that she might easily have carried herself away. She was in Pakistan for six months—September, 1959, to February, 1960. During that time she turned the thoughts of the blind of that country away from their despair and custodialism and helped to move toward self-governance.

There she found Dr. Fatima Shah, a well-educated, highly placed physician who had lost her sight in 1957 and who—as is common among the sighted—regarded blindness as just one step better than being dead. The greatest shock to Dr. Shah, however, was the realization that "others had given her up and regarded her blindness as termination of her active life." With Dr. Grant urging her on, Dr. Shah discovered that her life and her training need only be redirected. She helped to found the Pakistan Association of the Blind. That organization has grown in size and influence. Dr. Shah, its first president, is now the president of the International Federation of the Blind.

Dr. Grant did travel to other countries surrounding the subcontinent and made frequent stops on her road to and returning from those places. She made hundreds of contacts with blind people. When she returned to the United States and her teaching duties, it was with the determination to travel again as soon as she could to learn more about the blind and especially about blind children. She kept up a flow of correspondence with those she had met, exhorting them to take action. Appalled at the absence of the barest means of communicating and learning, Dr. Grant began her own recycling projects. She scrounged slates, styluses, paper, watches, Braille books, typewriters, Braille writers, and anything else she thought might be useful, and sent them off to anyone in those far and foreign parts who could write and ask. Though the NFB organized fundraising and the gathering and mailing of books and materials on a regular basis, Dr. Grant continued her personal projects along these lines.

Dr. Grant was looking forward to her retirement—and more travel. That event occurred at the end of the school year in June, 1962. The occasion was marked by many events and the bestowing of many honors. The greatest of these was a Fulbright Fellowship. This was supplemented by a grant from the National Federation of the Blind, and Dr. Grant once again made travel plans. Main target—Africa.

She started her travels by accompanying the tenBroeks to a meeting of the executive committee of the World Council for the Welfare of the Blind, in Hanover, Germany. The NFB wanted to talk with those worthies about how the NFB representation in the WCWB was being exploited and outright denied in something other than an above-board fashion. The NFB spokesmen were given a very chilly reception, were otherwise gratuitously insulted, and were not permitted to attend the committee's sessions though the NFB was, at the least, a dues-paying member.

Dr. Grant and Dr. tenBroek sat having tea and toast in a small neighborhood guesthouse after the sessions had adjourned and bemoaned the domination of a worldwide organization dealing with the blind by the American Foundation for the Blind and other agencies. Dr. tenBroek had been in contact with some of the leaders of organizations of the blind in Europe. As he and Dr. Grant talked, it became obvious that if the blind were to be properly represented and were to govern their own affairs, sooner or later they would have to organize on something larger than national scopes.

Dr. Grant made her way east. She developed a technique for finding blind people and for managing to see ministers high in the governing ranks of many countries—not infrequently, the heads of state. To all of them she talked of organization, of teaching, of training. Sometimes Dr. Grant had to stamp her foot or shake a finger in anger when discussing the conditions of the blind with these plenipotentiaries, but those actions were rarely taken amiss. Occasionally these officials caught her fervor for the necessity of educating blind youth to get them out of the deep and unending poverty that was their lot. In some countries she was permitted to conduct seminars for teachers of the blind on proper methods of instruction. In other countries, she was able to persuade governments to institute educational programs or other measures for the rehabilitation and training of the large blind populations, especially the young. In all countries she encouraged the blind to organize for their own improvement after the model of the National Federation of the Blind.

Dr. Grant's expressed goal was an international student division organized to feed trained people into new national organizations of the blind. Every country had some sort of agency *for* the blind, but only in Europe, the United States, Australia, and New Zealand were there organizations *of* the blind which were independent of the agencies. She saw the students as the future leaders of those oppressed millions of blind people in other countries, who would lead them out of their bondage of poverty to the independence which was every man's birthright.

The leaders of the Federation, however, felt the time was ripe to create an international unit more comprehensive than a student division. With Dr. Grant's enthusiastic participation, plans were set afoot for the formation of a worldwide organization. The 1964 NFB convention in Phoenix was the convention, as it turned out, of the International Federation of the Blind. One whole day was devoted to the presentations of foreign dignitaries. Representatives of seven countries were present, and a number of others sent papers about conditions and programs in their nations. As reported in the 1964 Convention Roundup:

> The visitors came to Phoenix with varying points of view on programs for the blind, from countries with widely divergent needs of the blind, and in different stages of readiness for world organization of the blind. To a man, however, they recognized the need for organization of the blind themselves on a world basis, the necessary major features of such an organization, the common aspirations of the blind everywhere for independence and integration, the common goals to be achieved by organization, and the common functions to be performed.

Preliminary meetings were held at Phoenix and later in New York. All saw their dreams brought to fruition when, with a constitution drawn by Kenneth Jernigan, and under the leadership of Dr. Jacobus tenBroek, the International Federation of the Blind became a reality. Professor tenBroek's banquet address, "The Parliament of Man: The Federation of the World," set forth the problems and the solutions.

But the fitting climax to that convention, and to these early years of Isabelle Grant's involvement with the organized blind movement in the United States and around the world, was the conferral upon her of the Newel Perry Award by NFB President Russell Kletzing. In presenting the award, President Kletzing made the following remarks, which serve as a fitting summation of the career of a most courageous and far-seeing woman:

> If we of the National Federation honor Isabelle tonight, it is because she has been doing us honor for many years. To blind people everywhere she has become the gracious and dynamic symbol of Federationism—of voluntary self-organization and self-advancement. We have long since dubbed Isabelle our "ambassador without portfolio"; and indeed she needs no portfolio since she carries the message and spirit of our movement in her heart and expresses it in her work.

> Isabelle Grant is of course more than that—more than our ambassador and chief missionary overseas. In her own right she is a leader of the blind, a skillful educator, a tireless promoter, and an astonishing example of the triumph of mind and will over physical limitation. Everyone here knows of her fabled travels around the world, accompanied only by her faithful, understanding, and sustaining companion—a white cane named "Oscar." And we all know what these travels have been like: not the leisurely excursion of a tourist but the hard road of the crusader—seeking not ease but hardship, and concentrating in particular upon those newly emerging, poverty-stricken lands whose teeming populations of blind people are both the largest and neediest in the world.

> Nor do I need to dwell at length upon the social miracles achieved by Dr. Grant over the past six years for the blind of Pakistan. She has inspired them with faith, a faith once undreamed of, in their powers and their collective future. She has stimulated their voluntary organization and worked with them to build a strong foundation of Federationism. She has pushed, prodded, and pestered the government of Pakistan into sponsoring a full-fledged

revolution in its attitudes surrounding the education of
blind children and the training of teachers for them.

But no list of specifics can convey the full scope of this
gentlewoman's teaching. By her deeds, by her words, and by her
enlightened example, Dr. Grant has truly educated us all.

During the later seventies and into the next decade, to the
dismay of the organized blind in America and elsewhere in the
world, the International Federation of the Blind fell victim to
what came to be seen as a tragic irony. Although it had been
founded explicitly in order to secure the independence of the
blind from the agency-controlled World Council, it began to appear that the divorce had never become final and that the party
of the second part—the IFB—was again being seduced and com-
promised by the powers of the World Council. Specifically, it was
sought to bring about a merger of the two organizations and
thereby effectively to co-opt the IFB and absorb it once again
within the global network of the blindness system.

During this period the National Federation of the Blind persistently worked to hold the IFB to its original principles and to
carry the progressive philosophy of Federationism, "American
style," to the world at large. In this spirit Rami Rabby, the NFB's
representative on the executive committee of the International
Federation, attended the third general convention of the IFB held
in Antwerp in 1979, where he found broad support among the
generality of delegates (as distinguished from the official leadership) for the approach of the National Federation. The prevailing
atmosphere at the IFB convention was conveyed in a subsequent
report on the event, which appeared in the *Braille Monitor*
(December, 1979):

> The National Federation of the Blind of the United States was
> represented at the Third General Assembly of IFB by Rami
> Rabby and Harold Snider. Since Dr. Jernigan was not in a position
> to travel to Belgium, Rami Rabby (a member of the executive
> committee of IFB) carried out two official duties on his behalf.
> On Thursday morning, July 26, he chaired a convention session
> on the subject of legislation for the blind. Earlier in the week (on
> Tuesday morning, July 24) he presented a paper entitled "Or-
> ganization of the Blind," which explained in some detail the need

for an organization which is truly *of* the blind, national in scope, and structured in the form of a federation united under a centralized administration. He described typical activities carried out by the NFB at the chapter, state, and national levels.

The presentation was well received, and the questions and comments which followed it reflected, to a much greater extent than was the case at the 1974 IFB General Assembly, a community of interest between the blind of the United States and the blind of other nations, both industrialized and developing, and the similarity between agency-consumer relationships in America and elsewhere in the world. Here are just two examples of question-and-answer exchanges that took place following Rabby's presentation:

Question from the delegate from Greece:

"Do you in the United States have a situation like we do in Greece, where our organization is the true organization of the blind, but the agencies and the government have set up their own puppet organizations of the blind, and they always say that *they* speak for the blind, and that *we* don't? Do you have something like that?"

Rabby's Answer:

"You bet we do! We are very familiar with that kind of situation. Isn't it amazing how agencies behave in the same way from one country to the next? Yes, in the United States, the puppet organization of the blind is sometimes called the American Council of the Blind, and other times, it may be called the Independent Blind of Illinois, and the agencies are always trotting them out in front of the press and financing their publications and telling everybody that *they* are the real blind and that *we* are not; whereas, in reality, these puppet organizations speak only for the agencies."

Question from the delegate from Pakistan:

"Do you have problems in the United States with blind people who have had a good education and who have succeeded in their jobs, and so they forget about all the other blind and do not want to join our organization?"

Rabby's Answer:

"Yes, unfortunately, we do know that problem very well. We know blind people who feel and act that way, and we try to make them realize that it is mainly because of the National Federation of the Blind that they were offered the opportunity of a good education and a good job in the first place and that it is now their responsibility to fight with us so that others may have the same opportunity."

The effort by the American leaders of the organized blind to keep the International Federation independently on track continued in the next year (1980) with an invitation to the newly elected president of the IFB, Dr. Franz Sonntag of Germany, to address the NFB's 1980 convention in Minneapolis. Dr. Sonntag began his speech with a pertinent recollection: "It is hardly possible," he said, "to speak about the IFB without commemorating Dr. Jacobus tenBroek, who took the initiative in establishing the International Federation of the Blind. I remember very well the day of the founding assembly in New York in 1964 when Dr. tenBroek succeeded in drawing up this fascinating picture of a strong world-wide organization of all the blind."

In the course of his speech Dr. Sonntag made a revealing observation concerning the respective weight and authority of the IFB and its agency counterpart, the World Council. "As to the relation between the IFB and the World Council for the Welfare of the Blind," he pointed out, "there are certain difficulties. First of all, some facts: The World Council for the Welfare of the Blind has an annual budget of approximately $160,000; whereas, the International Federation of the Blind has an annual budget of approximately $40,000." Nevertheless he told the convention that he could not imagine any future amalgamation of the IFB with the World Council because of the determination of the IFB to keep its independence and its commitment. He concluded by speaking in English for the first time: "We know who we are," he said, "and we can never go back."

Unfortunately, the events of the next few years were to prove the IFB president wrong on all counts. Whether or not the leaders of the International Federation knew who they were, they could and did go back—to their old condition as minions of the World Council. By 1984—a date with ominous overtones in science fiction and in the international blind movement—the National Federation judged the situation to have deteriorated to such a point as to preclude its continued participation in the IFB. After a full score of years, in which it had successively inspired and nurtured the fledgling international organization to its present maturity, the National Federation of the Blind of the United States felt compelled to withdraw from membership and to express its displeasure in no uncertain terms. National Federation of the Blind President Kenneth Jernigan, in a letter to President Sonntag of the IFB, noted the mandate given him by the 1984 convention and summarized the principal causes leading to the NFB's decision to withdraw:

Baltimore, Maryland
September 25, 1984

Dr. Franz Sonntag, President
International Federation
of the Blind
Federal Republic of Germany

Dear Dr. Sonntag:

At the annual convention of the National Federation of the Blind held in Phoenix, Arizona, in July of 1984, the delegates passed a resolution directing that our organization withdraw from the International Federation of the Blind unless (at the discretion of the Board of Directors) it could be determined before the beginning of the proposed meeting in Saudi Arabia in October of this year that the International Federation of the Blind had begun to move again toward the achievement of the goals for which it was originally founded. No such movement has occurred. The IFB was established to provide a vehicle for concerted action by organizations *of* the blind throughout the world. By the most generous interpretation that can possibly be made it no longer meets that standard. In fact, the International Federation of the Blind is now largely controlled not by independent organizations of the blind but by government agencies, blind people who represent nobody except themselves, and (most especially) by the agencies and individuals who dominate the World Council for the Welfare of the Blind. The fact that some of the principal actors in this drama are blind has nothing to do with what I am saying. It is one thing to be blind and quite another to be elected by other blind people to represent them.

Moreover, the International Federation of the Blind no longer has any meaningful program but simply parrots the actions of the WCWB. Under the circumstances it is understandable why talk about merging the two organizations seems logical instead of ludicrous, as it would have seemed when the first meeting of the IFB occurred in New York City in 1964. I was there; I drafted the original IFB Constitution; so I ought to know what the mood and the intent were.

We are not withdrawing from the WCWB, for it does not claim to be an organization *of* the blind, representing the blind. It claims to be a mixture of agencies and organizations of the blind, and I think it more nearly meets its stated purposes than does IFB.

In the circumstances it is not surprising that IFB has chosen to hold its convention in a city which excludes one of the members of its own Executive Committee, that it no longer represents rank and file blind people of the world, and that it bends the knee to the WCWB.

This letter constitutes official notice that the National Federation of the Blind of the United States (the founding member of the IFB) is no longer a member of IFB effective at the beginning of the first official meeting of the membership or Executive Committee of IFB to be held in Saudi Arabia in October. This letter also constitutes official notice that Harold Snider and Avraham Rabby are no longer members of the Executive Committee of IFB effective at the beginning of the first meeting of either the Executive Committee of IFB or the delegates of IFB at the meeting to be held in Saudi Arabia in October.

There is, we think, an organization in the United States of America which more nearly accords with the current behavior and philosophy of IFB than we do. We refer to the American Council of the Blind. We recommend that you admit them to membership since, according to our observation, they move in the orbit of the more regressive agencies in this country, do not represent rank and file blind people, and do not aggressively fight for the interests of blind people. We feel certain that you and they will find such a marriage both convenient and congenial.

It is our current plan to initiate action to work directly with independent organizations of the blind in other countries to establish an international vehicle for the expression of the collective will of the blind of the world and to further the goals for which the IFB was originally established. The National Federation of the Blind of the United States of America formally and officially asks that this letter be read to the opening session of the delegate assembly of the International Federation of the Blind in Saudi Arabia and that it also be read at the first meeting of the IFB Executive Committee to be held in Saudi Arabia.

Very truly yours,
Kenneth Jernigan, President
National Federation of the Blind

As it happened, 1984 would turn out to be a watershed year for the cause of international organization and representation—not only negatively, with the National Federation's withdrawal from the IFB, but positively as well. For in that year a new global framework was inaugurated, under the name of the World Blind Union, resulting from the merger of the IFB and the World Council for the Welfare of the Blind. Since the National Federation had retained its membership in the WCWB, it was positioned to play an instrumental role in the new World Blind Union should there be reasonable grounds for optimism regarding its potential capacity to serve the needs of blind people. Putting reservations aside in an act of faith and good will, the National Federation accepted a seat on the WBU's executive committee and commenced to build its involvement and influence—which culminated in 1987 with the election of Kenneth Jernigan to the presidency of the combined North America/Caribbean Region (to which he was re-elected in 1988 for a four-year term). In his Regional Report to the World Blind Union at its convention in Madrid, Spain, in 1988, Jernigan (who was in attendance as part of a large American delegation) summed up the organizational activity of the preceding four years and gave his assessment of the prospects and problems facing the WBU and its global constituency. The text of his report follows:

In 1984 the International Federation of the Blind and the World Council for the Welfare of the Blind met in Saudi Arabia to merge and become the World Blind Union. This coming together was not achieved without difficulty. Many (including my own organization, the National Federation of the Blind of the United States) had serious misgivings about the merger, but we decided to go forward with a positive attitude to participate in the newly established world body.

That was 1984, and we now meet in Madrid in 1988 to take stock of the past four years and chart the course for the quadrennium ahead. The numbers attending this General Assembly and the hope and enthusiasm which pervade its deliberations make it clear that the sanguine expectations of 1984 were well founded. The World Blind Union is a functioning reality, already possessing the beginnings of a tradition and the framework of a protocol of operation.

An integral part of that protocol is the regional structure of the Union. Shortly after the Assembly in Riyadh in 1984, the delegates of the then North America Region met in Washington to elect officers and make plans. There were (and are) six delegates from the United States. Three of these (the delegate from the American Council of the Blind, the delegate from the Blinded Veterans Association, and the delegate from the National Federation of the Blind) represent organizations *of* the blind. Three (the delegate from the Association for Education and Rehabilitation of the Blind and Visually Impaired, the delegate from the American Foundation for the Blind, and the delegate from the National Library Service for the Blind and Physically Handicapped) represent organizations *for* the blind. Of the four delegates from Canada two represent the Canadian National Institute for the Blind, and two represent the Canadian Council of the Blind. At that initial meeting in Washington in the fall of 1984 we were seeking a basis for joint action and a means of personal understanding and cooperation. Since that time we have held seven meetings, one each spring and one each fall, and we have had a continuous exchange of correspondence and individual visits.

When we look back over the past four years, the accomplishments of the North America/Caribbean Region have been, by any standard, impressive. Under the leadership of Dr. Euclid Herie, Managing Director of the Canadian National Institute for the Blind, our region has raised $30,000.00 to endow the Louis Braille Museum at Coupvray, France; and we are now in the process of making additional substantial contributions. In cooperation with Mr. Andre Nicole and others we intend to raise enough money throughout the world to insure the permanent financial security of the Louis Braille Museum and to make certain that this monument to one of the principal benefactors of the blind continues in perpetuity. Braille is a significant part of our heritage, and one of the principal yardsticks for measuring the vitality and validity of a civilization or culture is the degree to which it shows respect and reverence for the ancestors who brought it into being. Working with Mr. Nicole and his colleagues, we in the North America/Caribbean Region intend to place the Louis Braille Museum on a firm and enduring foundation.

In New York in the fall of 1986 our region hosted the meeting of the World Blind Union Executive Committee. It was the occasion for constructive interaction with the United Nations and increased public awareness of the needs and aspirations of the blind.

Our region has now been enlarged to encompass the Caribbean Council for the Blind, and two representatives from that organization currently serve as delegates—so that our regional structure now consists of twelve delegates: six from the United States, four from Canada, and two from the Caribbean. Acting through the regional structure, Canada and the United States have provided material and technical assistance to the Caribbean area, and there is every prospect that such assistance will continue.

We have established a regional Committee on the Status of Blind Women, and that committee is functioning actively. The Committee met during the time of our regional meeting in Toronto in May of this year and presented a proposed plan of action to the full delegation. The plan was adopted and is now being put into effect.

At the World Blind Union Executive Committee meeting in New York in the fall of 1986 our region presented a resolution to require that all meetings of the WBU officers, Executive Committee, and other committees be open for any member of the organization to attend. We also sponsored a resolution to require that WBU meetings be held in countries which would not exclude for political, cultural, philosophical, or religious reasons individuals, delegations, or representatives of the blind from any place on earth. Both of these resolutions were adopted by the WBU Executive Committee, and we feel that the organization is strengthened (both politically and morally) as a result.

Meeting in Toronto in the spring of 1988, the North America/Caribbean Region adopted for recommendation to this Assembly a resolution to require that the World Blind Union not blur its distinctive role by participating in coalitions with other disability groups. As you consider our proposal during the meetings of this Assembly, we ask that you read it carefully, both for what it says and what it does not say. We would not prohibit (where appropriate) cooperation with other groups of the disabled, but we would preserve with unmistakable clarity the concept that the primary purpose of this organization is to deal with problems of the blind, not the disabled as a whole.

So far, I have talked to you about tangible achievements which we have made in our region during the past four years, but our most important accomplishment has not been tangible. It has been attitudinal and spiritual. The World Blind Union has been the means of bringing us together to work cooperatively as a team. There are, of course, still philosophical differences which divide certain ones of us on particular issues, but those differences have not been emphasized in our deliberations. In fact, they have receded in prominence and have gradually been replaced by an atmosphere of joint effort to reach common goals. And this sense of increasing closeness and community of purpose is spreading beyond the narrow confines of the formality of the regional structure to every aspect of our organizational functioning and our personal and professional relationships.

Let me specify. In June of this year I went to Kingston, Ontario, to speak at the convention of the Canadian Council of the Blind; and in July Dr. Herie, managing director of the Canadian National Institute for the Blind, and Mrs. Braak, president of the Canadian Council of the Blind, came to Chicago to participate in the convention of the National Federation of the Blind. Plans are already under way for future exchanges, and the resulting shared information and strengthened bonds of friendship give a new dimension to what we are doing.

Last July (and I think this is clearly the result of our WBU regional contacts) a program of truly historic significance occurred in Montreal at the meeting of the Association for Education and Rehabilitation of the Blind and Visually Impaired. Geraldine Braak, Canadian Council of the Blind; Oral Miller, American Council of the Blind; Susan Spungin, American Foundation for the Blind; Euclid Herie, Canadian National Institute for the Blind; and I, National Federation of the Blind, participated in a two-hour panel discussion. The very fact that such a panel could take place at all (particularly, considering the participants) is noteworthy. It could not have happened four years ago. Moreover, the tone of the discussion was friendly and constructive, and positive developments resulted.

It was agreed that the five organizations involved would meet next year at the National Center for the Blind in Baltimore for a detailed exploration of common concerns and possible programs of joint action. The meeting will be hosted by the National Federation of the Blind and may (if all the participants agree) be expanded to include the Association for Education and Rehabilitation of the Blind and Visually Impaired, and possibly others. This, indeed, is progress.

One other item should be mentioned in this report. The North America/Caribbean Region comes to Madrid unanimously urging the General Assembly to elect Dr. Euclid Herie as treasurer of the World Blind Union. As in so many other things during the past four years, we are unanimous in this action. We know Dr. Herie; we like him; and we respect him. Moreover, his competence and experience particularly suit him for the position. He administers a program with a large budget; yet, he finds time to deal compassionately and sensitively with the problems of individuals.

I would like to conclude this report by making these observations: In a very real sense every day of our lives is a new crossroad, requiring decisions which inevitably lead to advancement or failure, but not all days are equally important. Some stand out above others, representing times of crucial significance in the history of a person or a social movement. Madrid in 1988 constitutes one of these landmark times. What we do here during this brief period may well determine the course of the affairs of the blind of the world for generations to come.

There are certain issues with which we must deal, both wisely and decisively. We must decide how we will allocate the resources we have, and what we will do to increase those resources. We must deal with the problems of the blind of the developing countries, and must do it in such a way that we do not give the impression (either to ourselves or others) that there are two classes of blind people in the world, the inferior and the superior. We must recognize that we are brothers and sisters, and our actions must suit our words. Above all, we must understand and support the concept that we who are blind intend to have the major voice in determining our own destiny. Through the centuries others have made our decisions and settled our fate, but that time is at an end. We are determined that it will be at an end. We will have no more of it. The World Blind Union can and should be the vehicle for the emancipation of the blind. Otherwise, we default on our responsibility. If this organization simply becomes another forum for meaningless talk and learned professional papers, it will be one of the tragic lost opportunities of history. The World Blind Union (approached in good faith and properly utilized) can be the key to open the door of first-class status for the blind of the world. My brothers and my sisters, let us work together to make it come true.

"The blind of the world have waited long, but the waiting must now end." With these words, Kenneth Jernigan, in his role as regional president, summed up the essential message of a major address which he delivered in September, 1988, before this Second General Assembly of the World Blind Union in Madrid. In the address, entitled "Fighting Discrimination and Promoting Equality of Opportunity," he called upon the WBU and its delegates from all parts of the world to make of their organization a society of equals—"members of a family, sharing and working throughout the world in a common effort for the salvation of each other, and the salvation of all of us." This trenchant address, presented to an international audience of his peers, might stand as a fitting testament to the arrival of the National Federation of the Blind and of its long-time leader to a position of major influence in the field of blindness, not only in America but in the field at large. Here are excerpts from his address:

FIGHTING DISCRIMINATION
AND PROMOTING EQUALITY OF OPPORTUNITY
by Kenneth Jernigan

When the World Blind Union came into being four years ago in Saudi Arabia, the question facing the delegates was not purpose or method but whether the organization should be established. Today the question is not whether, but why and how. Four years ago the General Assembly was concerned with organizational structure, political viability, and worldwide acceptance. Today it is concerned with the means of achieving its objectives and a clear definition of what those objectives should be.

Of course, our Constitution has a statement of purpose. It says in Section 1 of Article II: "The purposes of the World Blind Union shall be to work for the prevention of blindness and towards the advancement of the well-being of blind and visually impaired people, with the goal of equalization of opportunities and full participation in society, if necessary by special, legal, or administrative measures; to strengthen the self-awareness of blind persons, to develop their personality, self-respect, and sense of responsibility; and to provide an international forum for the exchange of knowledge and experience in the field of blindness."

That is what the Constitution says, and the first statement of purpose ("to work toward the prevention of blindness") and the last ("to provide an international forum for the exchange of knowledge and experience in the field of blindness") are clear and unmistakable. But what about the rest of it—in some ways the very heart and soul of it?

No one would minimize the importance of preventing blindness, but this is largely a medical problem; and the World Blind Union will not (and, indeed, should not) ever be the prime mover in this area. As to providing "an international forum for the exchange of knowledge and experience in the field of blindness," that is certainly important, but in and of itself it is not enough. It is a means rather than an end. If we are to get at the real problem of blindness, we must (as our Constitution says) find a way to advance the well-being of blind and visually impaired people by equalizing their opportunities; helping them achieve full participation in society; and making it possible for them to have self-respect, self-awareness, and a sense of responsibility.

But how shall we do it? First of all, we must be (and, moreover, must regard ourselves as being) an organization of equals. This means that the primary purpose of the World Blind Union cannot be merely to serve as a vehicle for channeling money from those who have it to those who don't. It will be easy for me to be misunderstood on this point, for it is a sensitive area. I am not saying that the members of a family should not share what they have with each other; nor am I saying that the blind of the world should not regard themselves as a family, for they should. Rather, I am saying that the members of a family should first *be* members of the family and that as a consequence sharing should follow— and not just sharing of material things but also of spiritual and intellectual things as well. It cannot be the other way around. We cannot (because of urgent need, feelings of guilt, superiority, or a sense of duty) create an organization for the primary purpose of the one-way flow of money from more fortunate to less fortunate people. We cannot because it will be detrimental to both the givers and the receivers, because it will create acrimony instead of harmony, and because it will not lead to a permanent solution of the problem. Moreover, if the giving of money is the primary purpose and everything else is incidental, there are better and more effective ways of doing it than through the World Blind Union.

If we are to succeed in our efforts, we must carry out the purpose clause of our Constitution. We must help the blind of the world achieve equality of opportunity, self-awareness, and self-respect. Of course, this necessarily means the provision of resources (more resources than have ever before been provided); but it means more than that. It means opportunity as a matter of right, not charity; and it means opportunity stimulated and provided from within each country as well as from external sources. It means that we who are blind must be members of a family (equals), sharing and working throughout the world in a common effort for the salvation of each other, and the salvation of all of us. It means action, not just words. It means recognition of the fact that we who are blind are brothers and sisters—facing a common problem, which requires a common solution achieved through joint action.

There is something else. We must not try to impose our own political systems or cultural values upon each other. Societal norms are different in almost every part of the world, and if we wish to change them, this is not the forum for doing it. Instead, we must strive to see that the blind of every country have the same opportunity, economic base, social recognition, and civic responsibility as others in their culture. This means more than money, but it means that, too.

If we are to deal with each other as equals and work together to solve our problems, we must understand that those problems are essentially the same for all of us—whether we live in the East or the West, the industrialized or the unindustrialized, the developed or the underdeveloped countries. There are, of course, individuals who are exceptions; but as a general rule, the blind of every nation on earth (the most developed as well as the least developed) are—when compared with others in their culture—economically and socially disadvantaged....

So what must we do as a World Blind Union? How shall we achieve our objectives of equal opportunity and first-class status? For answer let me call on the experience of the organization I represent. When Dr. Jacobus tenBroek and those who joined with him organized the National Federation of the Blind of the United States in 1940, they did what every minority does on its road to freedom. They shifted emphasis from the few to the many, from enhancement to basics. In our country in the pre-1940 era those who thought about blindness at all (the blind as well as the sighted) put their major effort into helping the gifted and promoting the exceptional. We of the National Federation of the Blind took a different course. We started with the premise that until there are food, decent clothing, and adequate shelter, there can be no meaningful rehabilitation, real opportunity, or human dignity. It was not that the few or the superior were to be neglected but rather a recognition that none can be free as long as any are enslaved. The Federation's top priority in the early 1940s was to get (not as charity but as a right) sufficient governmental assistance to provide a basic standard of living for the blind who had no way to provide for themselves.

There was something else: The Federation said that the blind had the right to speak for themselves through their own organization and that no other group or individual (regardless of how well-intentioned) could do it for us—whether public agency, private charity, blind person prominent in the community, or blind person heading an agency. The right was exclusive, and only those elected by the blind could speak for the blind. The test was not blindness, and it was not connection with an agency. Instead, it was self-determination. That is what the National Federation of the Blind of the United States stood for in 1940; that is what it stands for today; and that is what I believe the World Blind Union must stand for, now and in the years to come. The blind of the world are a distinguishable minority with identifiable problems which can only be solved through collective action. Therefore, the blind must have the right of self-determination, the right to speak for themselves with their own voice.

It is true that the World Blind Union not only consists of organizations *of* the blind but also organizations and agencies *for* the blind, but it is also true that many of these organizations and agencies for the blind are controlled by the blind and that their leaders are chosen by the blind. We must deal with substance instead of form, reality instead of shadow, and fact instead of terminology. The World Blind Union must either be truly representative of the will of the blind themselves, or it cannot long survive. That is not to say that we should not have sighted members or agency members representing only themselves or their programs. Rather, it is to say that the organization must be controlled by the blind and representative of the blind. This can be determined not only by its structure but also by its programs and behavior.

If the World Blind Union is to be meaningful, it must deal with basics. It must address the needs of both body and soul. We who are blind are like all of the rest. When we are hungry, we want to eat; and until that need is satisfied, we have difficulty thinking about very much else. But food is not enough. As I have said, we are like all of the rest. After we have eaten, we want meaningful jobs and useful occupation—just like the rest. And after food and jobs, we want equal participation and human dignity—just like the rest.

The blind of the world have waited long, but the waiting must now end. Yesterday and tomorrow meet in this present time, and we who are assembled here in Madrid (we who are blind and those of you who are sighted and have committed yourselves to work with us) have an unavoidable responsibility and an unparalleled opportunity. What we do in this Second General Assembly will have consequences for decades to come. Our task will not be easy, but we must make this organization succeed. The stakes are too high and the alternatives too unacceptable to allow it to be otherwise. If we fail to meet the challenge, the present favorable circumstances may not come again for another generation.

If the blind of the world are to have meaningful opportunity and if discrimination is successfully to be resisted, we must have a world mechanism to focus the energy and muster the resources to make it happen, and the World Blind Union is the only mechanism we have. To build another would be difficult at best. If all of us who are here today come to the task with good faith, true commitment, and real determination, tomorrow will be bright with promise. Let us put the past behind us and work together to make it come true.

Chapter 10

Sheltered Workshops
and Blind Alleys

I n 1971 the leader of the organized blind movement in the United States sent a message to the agencies serving the blind. This is what he said:

> If you tell us that you are important and necessary to our lives, we reply: It is true. But tear down every agency for the blind in the nation, destroy every workshop, and burn every professional journal; and we can build them all back if they are needed. But take away the blind, and your journals will go dusty on the shelves. Your counselors will walk the streets for work, and your broomcorn will mold and rot in your sheltered shops. Yes, we need you; but you need us, too. We intend to have a voice in your operation and your decisions since what you do affects our lives. We intend to have representation on your boards, and we intend for you to recognize our organizations and treat us as equals. We are not your wards, and there is no way for you to make us your wards. The only question left to be answered is whether you will accept the new conditions and work with us in peace and partnership or whether we must drag you kicking and screaming into the new era. But enter the new era you will, like it or not.

When Kenneth Jernigan delivered that emphatic message at the 1971 convention of the National Federation of the Blind, the struggle to reform the agencies and "rehabilitate" the nation's workshops for the blind was still being waged. And nearly twenty years later, as the National Federation of the Blind celebrated its Golden Anniversary, that struggle had not yet ended. But much had changed in half a century—including the character and dimensions of the struggle. The movement itself, embodied in the National Federation of the Blind, had grown astonishingly in size and strength to become a dominant player in the blindness system and a critical factor in the shaping of public policy toward the blind. And the agency establishment in its turn—influenced by the Federation and infiltrated by Federationists—had matured substantially over the years and even mellowed somewhat in its relations with the movement. Nevertheless, there remained deep pockets of resistance and resentment within the blindness system, most notably in those notorious backwaters of custodial control which represented the residual remains of the Victorian almshouses and workhouses—namely, the sheltered workshops.

The story of the sheltered workshops as institutions for the blind has its origin in the poor laws of the Dark Ages. (Some would say that today's workshops are living relics of the Dark Ages.) In their American incarnation the sheltered shops grew up during the nineteenth century in connection with both the workhouses for the poor and the early schools for the blind. The effect which these ancestral influences had upon the course of the workshop movement—and upon its hapless blind participants—was delineated in an extraordinarily meticulous analysis of state statutes and other data governing the programs which was prepared by Jacobus tenBroek and published in two versions—complete account with full references (*Braille Monitor*, June, 1960) and a shorter version with notes and references removed (*Blind American*, May, 1962). Professor tenBroek's scholarly study concluded on the hard evidence of the statutes that "the sheltered workshop as it exists within the states today is a welfare 'catch-all' which means all things to all men," and therefore that it "has become an anachronism which America, if it is to practice successfully the democratic welfare philosophy it professes, can ill afford to perpetuate."

The abridged version of Dr. tenBroek's classic paper follows:

THE CHARACTER AND FUNCTION OF SHELTERED WORKSHOPS
by Jacobus tenBroek

The institution of the sheltered workshop, for over a century an inconspicuous feature of the American welfare scene, has recently emerged from its obscurity to become the storm center of one of the liveliest controversies in the entire field of social work and public welfare. At the heart of the controversy is a fundamental disagreement over the proper function and future role of the sheltered shop. One viewpoint holds that a proper role of the shops is that of providing work evaluation, determination of abilities, and the development of work tolerance on the part of disabled persons—along with vocational training itself—as part of the process of vocational rehabilitation. More recently, doctors and health officials have begun to campaign for the use of the workshop as a medical facility for restorative, adjustive, and prevocational services, centering around the principle of work therapy. Finally, the oldest and perhaps still the most widely held viewpoint is that which regards the workshop as a place of remunerative employment for disabled individuals.

Two of these approaches to the sheltered workshop find support for their arguments in federal law and administrative rulings. The proponents of the vocational adjustment and training function point out that, since the passage of the Vocational Rehabilitation Act in 1954, sheltered workshops have been recognized as a legitimate training adjunct of the federal-state vocational rehabilitation program; and in addition they may now cite the majority ruling of the National Labor Relations Board, handed down in March of this year (1960), that rehabilitation is *the* essential function of the workshop.

The defenders of the employment status of the workshop may demonstrate that, even with the Vocational Rehabilitation Act, "sheltered workshop" is defined as primarily a place which provides remunerative employment, and that in fact rehabilitation administrators frequently regard the placement of their clients in such shops as sufficient to meet the remunerative placement requirements which are the ultimate objective of vocational rehabilitation programs. Moreover, the employment argument finds further support in the fact that the very exemption of sheltered workshops from the minimum wage provisions of the Fair Labor Standards Act was granted on the premise that they are places of employment.

To some extent the issues raised by these differences of viewpoint are theoretical in nature, involving such questions as: What are the proper goals of workshops? What is their greatest usefulness as instruments of welfare?

To a larger extent, perhaps, the issues are practical. What in actual fact are the functions of such shops? What are the prevailing conditions of training, work, and release?

On both the theoretical and practical levels, disagreement is widespread and often acrimonious. Insofar as they are theoretical, the questions raised by the workshop can only be settled by reference to policies and goals. Insofar as they are practical, such questions can only be answered by reference to fact.

Unfortunately, some of those who are in a position to assemble and disseminate the facts have not done so. For example, the Sheltered Workshop Committee within the Department of Labor has not chosen to fulfill its duties in these areas.

One important source of information concerning sheltered workshops, however, is available to all. It consists of the statutes of the various states governing their publicly operated sheltered shops. Anyone with access to a law library can look at these statutes. No doubt they yield their information by means of complicated sentences and technical language, but they do yield it. That information is, in large measure, the content of the pages to follow.

In particular, we shall seek to identify the salient characteristics and purposes of the workshops as specified in these laws—with reference to the objectives they purport to serve, the nature of their opportunities and undertakings, the attitudes they reflect toward those who participate in them, and their working conditions and social atmosphere.

The principal question to keep in mind through these pages is: What light do they shed upon the basic issue of the proper role and function of sheltered workshops within a system of welfare? Do they distinguish among—or do they merely confuse and commingle—the separate functions of (1) a vocational evaluation, adjustment, and training center; (2) a therapeutic facility; and (3) a place of remunerative employment?

General Background

Sheltered workshops, as such, first arose in America over a century ago as an outgrowth of the special schools for the blind whose curricula concentrated upon the provision of simple forms of vocational training—in such limited and manual skills as weaving, knitting, and chair caning, as well as in music and similar arts. At first it was the hope of the educators that "the blind, with proper instruction, will be able to maintain themselves free of charge from their friends or the state." Unfortunately, however, nothing had been done to persuade society of the capacities of these blind trainees; and before long, as one report put it, "Our graduates began to return to us, representing the embarrassment of their condition abroad, and soliciting employment at our hands." Thus were born the sheltered workshops—as segregated places of permanent employment for those regarded by society (if not by themselves and their protectors) as "unemployable."

Although sheltered workshops emerged in their modern form a century ago, their ancestry may be traced at least to the Middle Ages. It is possible to distinguish four separate historical associations from which the contemporary workshops derive: namely, those of the workhouse, the church, the hospital, and the school. Since the traces of this long and complicated heritage are still to be seen in many sheltered workshops of today, it is instructive to glance briefly at the sources and character of these various influences.

The oldest influence of all is that which had its origin in religious protection of the disabled. "Since the Church was the first charitable organization," a federal official has written, "inevitably some lines of the workshop movement have strong religious ties. When the indigent, the physically disabled, and the mentally different were herded into the asylums of the 1700s, they were being brought together not to ameliorate their condition but simply to get them off the street." A primary concern of the church for its disabled and indigent wards was with their souls as well as with their bodies—with spiritual redemption and moral uplift perhaps more than with vocational rehabilitation and physical restoration as understood today. Among many privately operated workshops today, such as those of the Salvation Army and the Society of St. Vincent de Paul, these are still the principal goals of workshop activity. The Volunteers of America (an offshoot of the Salvation Army) currently sponsors at least 70 such workshops; while perhaps the most successful of all the mission or church-sponsored workshop chains is that of the Goodwill Industries, founded by a Methodist minister in 1905, which by 1957 controlled 120 shops throughout the country.

A corollary line of development from which the contemporary workshop has emerged is that of the medieval and early modern hospital which, like the asylum, was generally under church auspices, but may be distinguished in terms of its specific function. European hospitals of the early sixteenth century were described by one observer as "those places where the sick are fed and cared for, where a certain number of paupers are supported, where boys and girls are reared, where abandoned infants are nourished, where the insane are confined, and where the blind dwell." The purpose of the hospital was primarily to care for the sick and totally disabled, but in the bedlam created by its motley population there were also the rudiments of school, nursery, almshouse, and insane asylum. Those present-day workshops which incorporate the provision of medical and therapeutic services therefore may be seen as the outcome of a line of development reaching back to the medieval hospital and extending through the American county hospitals of more recent times—institutions which also sought to fulfill the "double function" of healing the sick and employing the handicapped.

Another significant precursor of the sheltered workshop was the workhouse, or almshouse, which evolved as an institution of work relief accompanying the Poor Laws of the sixteenth and seventeenth centuries. For present purposes the chief importance of the workhouse was that it was designed, not primarily for the ill or handicapped, but for the able-bodied poor. The workhouse provided an institutionalized form of poor-relief; and in keeping with Elizabethan assumptions of the characterological causes of poverty, it was made as disagreeable as possible and its wages held to a bare minimum above starvation so that not many would willingly seek admission or contentedly remain. The gospel of work as the means of salvation (and, conversely, of idleness as the route to damnation) virtually converted the almshouse into a forced-labor camp; indeed, the distinction between workhouse and jailhouse was often difficult to discern.

Finally, as indicated above, the sheltered workshops grew up as adjuncts of the special schools for the blind established in the nineteenth century. However, it is significant that these schools soon deliberately severed their connection with the shops they had themselves created, as it became apparent that the functions of education and employment could not feasibly be mixed within the same program. Thereafter, the workshops came to be operated independently of educational and custodial institutions.

The historical development of modern welfare philosophy has been one of increasing recognition of the necessary distinctions and incompatibilities among these several emphases and approaches to the problem of disability. Some among them—notably that of the workhouse and almshouse, and possibly also to some extent that of the religious mission—have come to be recognized as anachronisms. Others, such as the vocational training emphasis of the early schools and the sheltered employment conception which succeeded it, still retain some support in welfare theory and policy. But it is clear that the direction of progress has been completely away from the primitive notion of an encompassing "bedlam" in which all the sick and disabled, rejected and despised members of society would be thrown together—and in which the various and dissimilar functions of the church, the school, the factory, the hospital, and the prison would be simultaneously carried on.

It remains to be seen whether the statutes of the states governing their publicly operated sheltered workshops have kept pace with this clear direction of progress.

Conditions of Labor

State employees generally are excluded from compulsory coverage of unemployment compensation under the Internal Revenue Code of 1954. The Code also exempts charitable organizations, including privately operated workshops, from compulsory coverage. Such states as Oregon, California, Washington, and Wisconsin have taken legislative and administrative steps to extend the coverage of unemployment compensation to some or all of the workers in their state-operated sheltered workshops. With respect to privately operated workshops, Hawaii is the only one of thirty-two states having such shops to take legislative action changing their status. It did so by dropping the exemptions of charitable organizations from unemployment compensation coverage. In short, the vast majority of employees of sheltered workshops (both public and private) throughout the country are without the protection of unemployment compensation laws.

The workers in sheltered shops face an additional deprivation. The Labor Management Relations Act excludes the states and their political subdivisions from the definition of "employer" for purposes of collective bargaining. A recent ruling of the National Labor Relations Board withheld the collective bargaining provisions of the Act from privately operated sheltered shops. This ruling was handed down in the case of *Sheltered Workshops of San Diego, Inc. vs. United Association of Handicapped*. By a majority decision of three to two, the National Labor Relations Board refused to assert jurisdiction. The ground taken was that "the Workshop's purposes are directed entirely toward rehabilitation of unemployable persons" and that "its commercial activities should be viewed only as a means to that end." The chief arguments against this ruling were forcefully stated by the dissenting opinion of the two minority members of the National Labor Relations Board: "Why then does the majority find that it would not effectuate the purposes of the Act to assert jurisdiction here? It does so because the Workshop's rehabilitation work benefits the entire community. We do not, of course, deny that this is so, but we reject the implicit corollary that a non-profit organization engaging in socially beneficial activities therefore owes its employees less than other employers do. The right of employees to select a representative and to bargain with their employer concerning their grievances and work conditions should not be so lightly disregarded. The majority has balanced the Workshop's commercial activities against its rehabilitation program and has decided that the latter outweighs the former. We would balance the Workshop's total program, commercial and rehabilitative, against the rights of these unfortunate and disabled employees, and would find that the latter is equally important."

The greatest deprivation to workers in sheltered workshops is the exemption of these shops from the minimum wage provisions of the Fair Labor Standards Act. With reference to the blind alone, at least 85 of the more than 100 sheltered shops primarily employing sightless workers hold certificates of exemption issued by the Department of Labor under Section 214 of the Act. The average minimum of such exemptions (1960) is 53 cents per hour—as opposed to the national minimum wage of $1.00 per hour for industrial labor. About 100 blind workers in sheltered shops receive a minimum wage below 40 cents per hour. Given the generally acknowledged fact that blind persons have special additional expenses incident to their blindness, exemption from minimum wage guarantees is thus a fact of vital significance to workers in sheltered shops.

It is such considerations as these which have led a special subcommittee of the House Committee on Ways and Means—reporting in March of this year (1960) on the Social Security Program of Disability Insurance—to question whether employment in sheltered workshops should properly be regarded as substantial gainful activity. The subcommittee concluded that wage conditions in the shops were generally so deplorable that it should be a rare case in which an employee of a sheltered workshop may be considered to be engaged in substantial gainful activity and thus held ineligible for disability insurance payments. (*Administration of So-*

cial Security Disability Program, Preliminary Report to the Committee on Ways and Means, submitted by the Subcommittee on the Administration of the Social Security Laws, March 11, 1960, page 22.)

With but few exceptions, it may be said in summary, the employees of sheltered workshops, both publicly and privately operated, (1) do not possess the benefits of unemployment compensation; (2) do not possess the benefits of workmen's compensation; (3) do not possess the benefits of Old Age Survivors and Disability Insurance under the Social Security Program; (4) the privileges of collective bargaining under the National Labor Relations Act are withheld from them; and (5) they are exempted from the minimum wage guarantees of the Fair Labor Standards Act. In such circumstances of enforced poverty, insecurity, and discriminatory withholding of privileges and denial of rights, can it be contended that the sheltered shops rehabilitate or supply remunerative employment for their disabled workers?...

Of the total of 389 workshops holding certificates of exemption from minimum wage laws, 85 primarily serve blind persons. According to the Department of Labor, there were in 1958, 4,700 blind persons employed in these shops (in 1960 the Labor Department statement is "less than 5,000") who were subject to certificates of exemption; there were others who did earn the statutory minimum wage, but statistics relating to them are unavailable. Fifty-seven of these shops presently belong to the National Industries for the Blind, which employed 3,712 blind persons in 1956. The lowest minimum wage approved for these workers in 1958 was 10 cents an hour, the highest minimum wage was 80 cents an hour, and the average minimum wage 53 cents an hour. These figures represent the lowest wage permitted in such shops. In construing the Fair Labor Standards Act, the Department of Labor requires that every worker on piece rates be paid the same wage paid to workers in adjacent private industry for the same work. This is not a very valuable standard, since much of the work done in these shops is not carried on by any appreciable segment of private industry; and in any event this standard is not enforced by the Labor Department.

Conclusion

From this survey of the statutory provisions of the states governing their sheltered workshops, several conclusions clearly emerge. The three distinctive functions of sheltered shops—vocational rehabilitation, medical therapy, and remunerative employment—are rarely distinguished in the statutes. Instead the workshop is commonly conceived as a combination of two, or even all three, of these functions—in effect, as an all-purpose solution to the numerous and varied problems confronted by the blind. In what is perhaps their most characteristic form these statutes simply perpetuate a relic of the past: a vague combination of the workhouse, the almshouse, the factory, and the asylum, carefully segregated from "normal" competitive society and administered by a custodial staff armed with sweeping discretionary authority. In many cases their responsibility for the client of their services is so broad as to appear to embrace the function of nearly all other community agencies and groups. In the administration of moral uplift and regeneration they assume in effect the role of the church; in the provision of intellectual instruction they exercise the function of the schools; in the enforcement of discipline and the power of punishment they resemble a penal institution; and in their emphasis upon group activities of a social, recreational, and cultural nature they take on the characteristics of a service club or voluntary association. Over and above these disparate if not conflicting responsibilities, the assumption of which is surely of doubtful propriety, the sheltered workshop typically furnishes some form of work experience to its participants, generally for wages and often directed toward the objective of self-support. But few state laws differentiate adequately or clearly among the purposes which these activities may be supposed to serve.

On the basis of our study it is not excessive to conclude that the sheltered workshop as it exists within the states today is a welfare "catch-all" which means all things to all men, and therefore possesses no distinctive and specific characteristic upon which all may agree. Indeed, by their failure to distinguish among the three separate functions available to them, the workshops of the states must be adjudged to be failures in all three. The nature and extent of their failure with respect to each of these functions may be briefly stated.

1. *Vocational Rehabilitation.* There are dangers and difficulties involved in the use of sheltered workshops in any program of rehabilitation. Most serious of all are those attending the support of workshops within the public program of vocational rehabilitation (Public Law 565). In their traditional, and still perhaps their most characteristic, role as permanent employment outlets for the disabled, the sheltered shops are incompatible with the purposes and goals of modern vocational rehabilitation. Under no cir-

cumstances should they be utilized as "dumping grounds" for clients of vocational rehabilitation, such as the blind, for whom normal job placement is a difficult but essential prerequisite to proper rehabilitation. Vocational rehabilitation agencies should be discouraged from regarding the option of sheltered employment as a "closure" for their clients, however convenient such a solution may be in terms of economy and rapid turnover of the caseload.

Because of their customary role as sheltered (i.e., segregated, covered, and noncompetitive) employment retreats, the social and psychological environment of the workshops is often not conducive to the paramount objective of vocational rehabilitation: that of restoring the disabled person to a vocational status of normality and equality. Where "feasible" rehabilitants are thrown together with the "non-feasible," where working facilities and methods are geared to outmoded and unproductive handicrafts such as broom making and chair caning, and where the working atmosphere is commonly one of defeatism if not of despair, the overriding purposes of modern vocational rehabilitation cannot be served but only undermined.

Apart from psychological and social factors, the economics of sheltered workshops equally tend to militate against their successful adaptation, as presently constituted, to vocational rehabilitation goals. First, they are in most cases at least partially subsidized and so removed from the normal incentives and competition of ordinary industry. Second, insofar as economic considerations enter, workshop managers are tempted to retain their ablest and most productive workers permanently rather than risk a financial loss by graduating them into normal employment. Finally, the economic and working conditions within sheltered shops are commonly far below those in normal industry. The existence of such conditions strongly argues against the public support of sheltered workshops, under any circumstances, as training centers for vocational rehabilitation clients.

Finally, the historic associations of sheltered workshops with the workhouse, almshouse, asylum, and church of the Middle Ages have left conspicuous traces upon the majority of present-day shops, giving them often the character of agencies for moral redemption rather than that of means to the restoration of productive capacities. Institutions thus motivated are unlikely to be equally qualified or equipped in the mundane areas of vocational guidance, training, and selective placement.

2. *Terminal Employment.* With respect to the function of providing permanent (or "terminal") remunerative employment for the blind and severely disabled, sheltered workshops have failed to fulfill their responsibility to their employees. Indeed, they have for the most part sought to avoid the normal obligations of employers through exemption from the laws fixing minimum standards of employment and working con ditions. Workers in sheltered shops deserve and require the same protection of their rights as do the workers in other industries: specifically, with respect to wages, hours, vacations, sick leave, labor-management relations, and the like. However, blind workshop employees have never received, and do not now receive, such protection. Not only do wages fail to meet the cost of living; they fail to meet the minimum requirements of the Fair Labor Standards Act, from which sheltered shops have in fact been explicitly exempted. Nor can blind workshop employees hope to improve conditions by their own efforts; for one thing, they are not organized into unions, and for another thing (as noted earlier) they have been denied the collective bargaining protection of the National Labor Relations Act. Finally, many of these employees do not have entitlement to workmen's compensation or Social Security privileges, and most are denied the benefits of unemployment compensation. In short, blind workers in sheltered employment are virtually in the position of wards, without legal rights or recourse, and reduced to an abject dependency upon the good will and discretion of their employers. In such circumstances, it is conservative understatement to say that sheltered workshops have failed to meet the conditions of employment to which American workers are entitled and accustomed.

3. *Medical Therapy.* On the basis of our survey of statutory provisions, the least plausible of all claims for sheltered workshops is that they have provided or can provide adequate facilities for medical and therapeutic assistance. For such facilities to be efficient, they should be completely divorced from considerations of remunerative employment on the one hand and of vocational training on the other. The purposes of therapy are, of course, not economic but medical and psychological in character. The very cases for whom such assistance is the primary need—i.e., the multiply and totally disabled—are those incapable of self-sufficient employment, let alone of vocational preparation for return to normal occupations. The statutes which we have examined plainly display the tendency of sheltered shops to become terminal places of employment in which so-called "unemployables" may find a drudge's niche at the workbench. It goes without saying that some-

thing more than the stereotyped "blind trades" of weaving and chair caning is required to serve a genuine therapeutic purpose and furnish healthy incentives to personal adjustment. The clinging heritage of the almshouse and asylum, into which the supposed derelicts of society were dumped and forgotten, remains sufficiently in evidence in present-day workshops to vitiate the prospect of their constructive uses for medical and therapeutic purposes. What the severely disabled clients of such services most clearly and urgently need is a form of productive endeavor carefully adjusted to their unique individual circumstances and individually designed to make constructive use of their enforced leisure. Such a therapeutic enterprise must be in the fullest sense "client-centered" rather than geared to industrial markets, economic consideration, or the convenience of traditional trades and handicrafts.

This is not to say, of course, that the three separate functions which sheltered workshops have purported to serve—those of vocational rehabilitation, of employment, and of therapy—have no place in modern programs of health and welfare. For the blind and other disabled persons in the productive years of life, vocational rehabilitation is the essential and overriding need; but its purposes of occupational guidance, training, and com petitive job placement cannot be met by the sheltered workshop. If, either within or outside the vocational rehabilitation process, there is need for "vocational adjustment" or therapeutic centers, that need should be met not by the sheltered shop but by special rehabilitation facilities such as those authorized by Public Law 565 (where they are carefully distinguished from workshops). "Rehabilitation facility," the law states, "means a facility operated for the primary purpose of assisting in the rehabilitation of disabled persons—(1) which provides one or more of the following types of services: (A) testing, fitting, or training in the use of prosthetic devices; (B) prevocational or conditioning therapy; (C) physical or occupational therapy; (D) adjustment training; or (E) evaluation or control of special disabilities; or (2) through which is provided an integrated program of medical, psychological, social, and vocational evaluation and services under competent professional supervision...." Finally, there is no doubt that a genuine need exists for permanent noncompetitive employment of certain categories of the severely handicapped, but that need also (as we have seen above) is not met by sheltered workshops of the type described by the governing statutes of the states.

In summary, the fundamental failure of sheltered workshops for the blind and disabled lies in their indiscriminate intermingling of functions and purposes which are demonstrably incompatible if not mutually exclusive. It is not too much to conclude, on the basis of the statutory evidence, that the sheltered workshop has become an anachronism which America, if it is to practice successfully the democratic welfare philosophy it professes, can ill afford to perpetuate.

"Gimme Shelter"

There is an irony in the history of the sheltered workshops that is illustrated by the operative term "sheltered." Originally it was the employment itself, reserved for the blind or disabled, that was "sheltered" from competition by the able-bodied; in that sense, for an earlier era in which the blind as a class were regarded as unemployable, the concept of a "work shelter" could appear as positive and constructive. In those protected and segregated shops the blind were given work to do (however menial); they were taught a trade (however trivial); they were paid a wage (however marginal); and they were rescued from the vice of idleness. In the Depression decade of the 1930s, when the original legislation now known as the Javits-Wagner-O'Day Act was passed, that must have seemed a substantial step forward for the blind. The new law sheltered them from competition in the setting of the workshop; but it was not only the blind workers who were sheltered by the law—it was the enterprise itself. The Javits-Wagner-O'Day Act provided a shelter for the workshop industry and its management from the harsh reality of the minimum wage. The shops were legislatively gifted with the windfall of a "wage shelter"—something even better than a tax shelter—exempting them from the requirements of all other federal laws governing wages and hours, working conditions, and fair labor standards. In their special field of employment, with regard to their own pool of workers, the sheltered shops were able at a stroke to repeal half a century of humanitarian reforms on the part of organized labor and the federal government. Everywhere else laboring men and women—let alone children—were legislatively protected from exploitation in the workplace; everywhere else workers had acquired a legal shelter. But not here. In the sheltered workshop alone the blind workers were unsheltered.

It was a principal goal of the organized blind movement, virtually from the beginning, to change all that: to reform the sheltered workshops, enforce the minimum wage, and generally defend blind shopworkers from exploitation and harassment. During the first decade of the Federation, to be sure, the plight of the sheltered broom maker and basket weaver seemed less critical to the movement's leaders than the predicament of other blind people who had no work at all and no security other than that which the Federation itself was gradually carving out of the nearly impervious hide of government. But in the second decade of the Federation, the fifties—largely through the efforts of the organized blind themselves—the new issues of opportunity, competitive jobs, and new careers were taking precedence over the problems of security and subsistence on the agenda of Federationists. In this altered context the sheltered workshops took on a role not of diminished but of greater prominence; now the issue was one of worker rights, of the minimum wage, and of vocational rehabilitation—changes which would move workers out of the shelters and into the mainstream.

Unionizing and the Minimum Wage

During the fifties and sixties the Federation became actively involved in defending the rights of blind shop workers to organize collectively, to express grievances, and to seek a living wage. These efforts led to the establishment in 1971 of a Sheltered Workshop Division within the National Federation of the Blind.

The struggle of the organized blind to reform the sheltered workshops was fought out through the years not only in the press and in the workplace but also in the courts. In the late 1970s and early eighties the Federation brought before the National Labor Relations Board a series of cases involving the right of blind shop workers to organize. The earlier opinions of the Board that the blind were not really employees at all but only rehabilitation clients were now repudiated; in each instance the NLRB affirmed the right of blind workers to join unions and bargain collectively. Several of these cases were appealed by the shop management to the courts. In both the Fifth Circuit Court of Appeals and the Sixth Circuit Court of Appeals, the right to organize was upheld. However, the Court of Appeals for the Eighth Circuit refused to follow the recommendation of the labor board; instead, it held that the blind inmates of the sheltered shops, whatever in fact they were, could not be regarded as employees.

The first of the workshop cases which the Federation took to the NLRB was the one involving the Chicago Lighthouse for the Blind. This was in 1975, and it was to be a nasty fight. Federation leader James Omvig (a blind attorney uniquely suited to the task, being both a former shopworker at the Chicago Lighthouse and a former hearing officer for the National Labor Relations Board) played an important role in shaping the Federation's long drive to win collective bargaining rights for the blind in sheltered workshops. He served as an officer in the Sheltered Workshop Division; he contacted workers in the shops and did organizing; and he wrote the brief in the Chicago Lighthouse case—a pivotal document which resulted on June 28, 1976, in the reversal by the National Labor Relations Board of its long-standing policy not to take jurisdiction over the nation's sheltered workshops.

In an address delivered at the National Warehouse Conference of the International Brotherhood of Teamsters in Toronto, Canada, on August 15, 1978, Kenneth Jernigan summed up the situation in Chicago and a number of other workshops. Here, in part, is what he said:

> I am here today to tell you something about our organization. More particularly, I am here because you the Teamsters have helped us start on the road to organize the workers in the so-called "sheltered shops" for the blind. Let me tell you something about these shops. In the first place most blind persons could work in regular business and industry on equal terms with others (just as productive and just as competitive) if they had the training and the opportunity. But they don't, so they work in the sheltered shops.
>
> Some of these shops are run by state government. Many of them are private organizations set up by a few prominent citizens in the community, who get publicity and satisfaction from serving on the board and having their names connected with a worthwhile cause but who really know very little about what goes on in the day-to-day operation. The real control is usually exercised by the paid (highly paid) director and other management staff.

The managers of the workshops have had a good thing of it. They have had prestige and respect in the community; they have raised money in the name of helping the blind; and very few questions have been asked, because it has been thought they were doing such noble work in helping unfortunate people. They have told the Congress that the blind are not capable of real productivity, and so they have been permitted to pay less than the minimum wage (sometimes as little as fifty cents an hour) on the theory that the activity in the shops is not actually real work as much as it is therapy, that it is rehabilitation *training* to prepare the workers to go into competitive employment, and that the shops will go broke (have you heard that before?) if they pay the workers decent wages and fringe benefits. Yet, they have enough money to pay salaries often running to more than $50,000 a year to their top management. They can afford fancy offices, a lot of travel to conferences in expensive hotels, and a very thorough package of fringe benefits for supervisors and other professional staff. Blind workers can be laid off or fired at will; and they often have no sick leave, no vacation, and no say about working conditions.

The songs people sing tell a great deal about their lives. In the National Federation of the Blind we have several songs about sheltered shops. One of these is sung to the tune of the religious song "Bringing in the Sheaves," but it is titled "Bringing in the *Thieves*." The chorus goes like this:

> *Bringing in the thieves,*
> *Bringing in the thieves,*
> *The workshops come rejoicing,*
> *Bringing in the thieves.*

As you might imagine, the thieves to which the reference is made are not the workers. Another song is done to the tune of "I've Been Workin' on the Railroad." It is called "I've Been Workin' in the Workshop," and goes like this:

> *I've been workin' in the workshop,*
> *All the livelong day,*
> *And with the wages that they pay me,*
> *It's just to pass my time away.*

In 1960 the blind workers in the San Diego shop asked the National Labor Relations Board to order an election to permit them to unionize. In a three-to-two split decision the Board refused to take jurisdiction, having been propagandized by management into believing that the prime purpose of the shop was rehabilitative in nature and, therefore, that the blind workers did not need the same rights and protections enjoyed by other Americans in the work force. It was 1976 before we could get this decision reversed. That was the Chicago Lighthouse case. And it was 1978 before we really locked it up. That was when you the Teamsters helped us organize the Cincinnati Association for the Blind.

Since they are either governmental or nonprofit organizations, the workshops pay no taxes. They receive heavy subsidies from the government, and they receive donations from the general public. Federal legislation requires government agencies to buy products from the shops. I am not complaining about all of this. I am only saying that if it is going to happen, I don't want all of the pie to go to management. I want the workers to have a few bites, too.

The workshops have traditionally made brooms, mops, and mattresses. More recently they have received large government contracts to produce a wide variety of items and have subcontracted with private industry....

The Chicago Lighthouse for the Blind operates a sheltered shop. When the workers began to try to organize in 1975, blind persons were being paid less than the minimum wage, and working conditions were bad—no job protection, no rights, and no collective bargaining. Seventy to eighty percent of all workshop contracts were with the Skilcraft Corporation. Skilcraft had no assembly and packaging employees of its own. All assembly and packaging were done by blind employees of the Lighthouse in Skilcraft's own building. None of the individuals was paid the federal minimum wage, and there were no fringe benefits whatsoever. Therefore, in truth and in fact these blind people were employees of Skilcraft, and the Chicago Lighthouse was nothing more than a front for an employer who wanted cheap labor. The workers were not much better off than slaves.

The Chicago Lighthouse tried to explain it by saying that the blind were not "employees" but were "clients," who were in the process of being rehabilitated and trained for outside competitive employment. It was a mighty long period of training. Some of these so-called "clients" had worked for the Lighthouse for from ten to fifteen years. So the Lighthouse had (and for all I know, still has) two classes of workers: one group (all blind) called "clients," and the other group (mostly sighted) called "employees." As the National Federation of the Blind said in its brief to the National

Labor Relations Board in 1976, "Those called 'employees' receive paid vacations, sick leave, paid holidays, personal leave days, hospitalization insurance, life insurance, pension benefits, workmen's compensation benefits, and unemployment insurance; those called 'clients' do not."

"In all other respects," our brief said, "employees and 'clients' receive equal treatment. They are supervised, punch a time clock, work eight-hour days, and observe all of the employer's policies. For instance, the employer has a policy that if an individual is sick for more than two days, he must produce a verifying doctor's statement upon his return to work. Astounding as it may be, the worker who is characterized as a 'client' must follow this policy even though he receives no pay for his time off from work." He must spend his own money in order to get the doctor's statement.

The National Labor Relations Board ordered an election at the Chicago Lighthouse for the Blind in the summer of 1976. Before the election was held, the principal worker engaged in organizing was fired. We lost the election. Shortly afterward, three more leaders of the effort to organize were fired.

The blind of the nation collected what money they could to help feed those fired workers. We are now trying to organize again at the Chicago Lighthouse, and another leading organizer has been fired. We will share what we have with him. To the extent that we have it or can get it, we will see that he has money for food and clothes....

In Massachusetts a few days ago there was a transit strike. State employees were paid for the day on the theory that they could not get to work. Blind workers at the state workshop (also state employees) were not paid for the day—presumably on the theory that they couldn't do anything about it. The Massachusetts workshop is considering a list of factors on which to evaluate its workers. Some of the factors are these: reaction to criticism, reaction to praise, reaction to authority, reaction to co-workers, acceptance of responsibility, posture, sound localization, sense of humor, independent action, worker self-concept, social conduct, motivation, dependability, initiative, work quality, and work quantity. There are other factors on the list, but I think I have given you enough to make the point. The only two things on that list that really ought to be given very much weight are the quantity and the quality of the work the employee does. I am particularly struck by management's intention to evaluate the blind workers

on their sense of humor. It's a bad joke. With conditions what
they are in the sheltered shop there's not a whole lot to laugh
about.

We have a job to do in Massachusetts; and, again, I hope and
believe that you will be at our side. You were with us in Cincinnati
a few weeks ago when the shopworkers voted to be represented
by the Teamsters. I am told that some of the workers in the Cincinnati shop make 58 cents an hour while the director of the organization makes upwards of $50,000 a year. I look forward to
the contract talks, and I suspect you do, too....

Chicago was to be a turning point, for armed with the NLRB
decision that blind shop workers had the right to organize, the
Federation intensified its campaign in shops throughout the
country. The Cincinnati Association for the Blind and the Houston Lighthouse for the Blind were organized—and this time the
elections were not lost, and the workers were not fired. But the
road was long and tortuous. The drama of the situation and the
intensity of the struggle can be seen in an article in the December, 1979, *Braille Monitor*:

TWIN VICTORIES FOR THE BLIND
IN SHELTERED WORKSHOPS:
THE NATIONAL LABOR RELATIONS BOARD RULES
IN OUR FAVOR AGAIN OVER THE PROTESTS OF
THE AFB, NAC, ACB, ALL, AND NIB COMBINE

The battle being waged by the blind to secure a firm and universal
recognition of the fundamental right of blind shop workers to organize and bargain collectively with management through labor
unions has in recent years moved to center stage, occupying the
spotlight as a central issue which divides those of us who are working to rise from second-class status in society from those at the
center of power in the traditional agency structure who desperately want to continue to exercise control over us as inferiors. The
decisions by the National Labor Relations Board (NLRB) over
the past three and one-half years; increased attention by the Congress and the U.S. Department of Labor to our calls for minimum
wage; the investigations of state officials (especially the audits and
legislative reports issued on the workshops in New York State);
and the exposes by investigative reporters for the *Wall Street Journal, U.S. News and World Report*, and the CBS television program
60 Minutes have forced the agency overlords to defend their con-

duct in a public arena where it is increasingly unacceptable to hide behind the cloak of "professionalism" and "all-knowing" expertise.

Now on the heels of these other events comes perhaps the most dramatic and significant single breakthrough to date: two landmark rulings by the NLRB which in the immediate sense affect the workers at both the Cincinnati Association for the Blind and the Houston Lighthouse for the Blind, but in the long run will bring profound and lasting changes in the entire workshop system and in the relationship between the blind (especially the organized blind) and the agencies which have been set up to serve them. The latest "decisions and orders" were handed down by the Labor Board on September 18; they were direct and unequivocal, the basic right of blind sheltered shop workers to form a collective bargaining unit and to designate a labor union to represent them has been upheld in the face of the strongest and best financed opposition possible. There is no question about it now; there is no qualification or wiggling. The NLRB has now taken final and positive action with respect to the Cincinnati Association for the Blind, and the Houston Lighthouse is not far behind.

In the *Braille Monitor* for August-September, 1978, we described the organizing campaign at the Cincinnati Association for the Blind and underscored the significance of the victory which was achieved when, on June 7, 1978, the 79 workers at the Cincinnati Association who were eligible to vote in the union representation election determined, by a vote of 44 to 35, that they would be represented by Local No. 100 of the Truck Drivers, Chauffeurs, and Helpers Union, affiliated with the International Brotherhood of Teamsters, Chauffeurs, Warehousemen, and Helpers of America. On June 15, 1978, the Regional Director of the NLRB certified the election of Teamster's Local 100 as the "exclusive representative" of the employees (including those which are often referred to as "clients") at the Cincinnati Association. This was a truly historic event, the strongest affirmation ever of the right of the blind to organize and bargain collectively, but little did most of us know that the toughest battle had just begun.

The first indications that we were still in for a long, hard fight came during the summer of 1978 when the Teamsters contacted the Cincinnati Association to initiate the collective bargaining process. Several good-faith attempts were made to bring the Association to the bargaining table, but to no avail—rulings of the NLRB seemed to make no difference, the Cincinnati Association would not negotiate a contract. We are well accustomed to hearing the agency overlords speak of themselves and their "expertise" in the loftiest of terms usually reserved only for the highest ministers of state, so we were not overly astonished when Milton Jahoda, executive director of the Cincinnati Association, refused to comply with federal labor law by failing to recognize a duly authorized and officially certified collective bargaining unit representing his workers. By late August it became clear to all of us, and to officials of the NLRB as well, that the Cincinnati Association would not bargain with the blind through the Teamsters Union unless forced to do so by an authority higher than the Labor Board, perhaps a Federal Court.

On August 31, 1978, the General Counsel of the NLRB commenced the actions necessary to compel the Cincinnati Association to come to the bargaining table and negotiate an agreement with the workers through the Union. This action took the form of an "unfair labor practice" charge leveled against the Cincinnati Association by the General Counsel of the NLRB and filed with the Board itself for a determination. The Association, as expected, denied the charge, arguing that there were no valid grounds for the Labor Board to order a union election in the first place, so now that a union had been voted in it should not have to comply with the demands for collective bargaining. This amounted to a full-blown appeal of the Labor Board's original decision handed down in May of 1978 ordering the election for union representation.

That the case of the Cincinnati Association goes far beyond the confines of that single workshop is (or ought to be) readily apparent, but in case there are any doubts, consider what happened next in the proceedings before the NLRB—enter, National Industries for the Blind (NIB), intervener, defending the actions of Respondent, Cincinnati Association for the Blind, and calling for repudiation of the Labor Board's original decision in the Cincinnati Case. NIB is the well-financed and federally designated coordinating agency responsible for allocating federal government and other contracts to its affiliated workshops throughout the country, and in turn (for its "services") NIB receives a percentage (four percent for most non-military, and ten percent for most military, contracts) of the gross sales under these contracts. During the fiscal year ending September 30, 1978, there were gross sales in the NIB system exceeding $120,000,000. Many of NIB's executives are former military top brass, retired on taxpayer-funded pensions. At last report, in the spring of 1979, the organization had no blind employees in a work force of approximately 60. Total salaries and pension contributions in the year ended June, 1977, exceeded $1 million, and you can be sure that no one on NIB's staff earns less than minimum wage.

NIB, then, is an organization which primarily coordinates workshop contracting; hence virtually its only source of revenue is the percentage it receives on each contract, which, in turn, is paid for out of the proceeds generated by production activity in the workshops, all of which means that the blind who work in the workshops (many on less than minimum wage) contribute substantially toward paying the salaries of NIB's well compensated executives, many of whom also dip into the federal coffers for their not so meager military retirement pensions. But this is only part of the financial arrangement—it also follows that since NIB's income is primarily generated by the productivity of the blind workers in the workshops, any actions which NIB takes, such as intervening on behalf of the Cincinnati Association for the Blind before the NLRB, will be financed by the sweat from the blind workers' brows as well. And so this is how it is with NIB. The blind workers should be proud—you never go second-class when you go with NIB, unless, of course, you are the one who is really doing the work to bring home the money to pay the bills; but even so, the blind workers will be proud to know that through their collective efforts they managed to provide NIB with enough income to hire what is generally regarded as the most prestigious (and the most expensive) law firm in Washington, D.C. (the firm of Covington and Burling), to argue the NIB case against the blind before the Labor Board.

In terms of the longer view, the appeal by the Cincinnati Association for the Blind, backed by the NIB with its historic and continuing ties to the rest of the AFB, NAC, ACB, and ALL combine, has to be seen as just one more in a series of preplanned tactics to break the back of the Union by disregarding the will of the blind as expressed by their democratic vote. There was really no substantive issue left for the NLRB to decide, and the Cincinnati Association knew this, but perhaps it was the feeling that, with the money of NIB and the prestige of its high-priced law firm, the original decision just might be overturned, and even if it was not, look what could be gained; another year of paying less than minimum wage, another year with few or no benefits for the workers, another year with no "show-up pay," and another year without having to bargain with the Labor Union.

So the appeal went forward at the Labor Board, and along the way the Federation intervened on behalf of the blind and the local Teamsters Union; briefs were filed; the months went by, while the workers inside the workshop did their best to keep their spirits and their hopes up with the encouragement of NFB leaders and members from throughout the country. Then, on September 18, the waiting was over—the decision was issued—we had come face-to-face with the power and the money of the agencies, and we had won again. The decision which came down is an important one, for it establishes more firmly than ever before our right to organize and bargain collectively and finds that, by blocking the exercise of this right by the blind workers in Cincinnati, the Cincinnati Association for the Blind is guilty of "unfair labor practices" which are prohibited by the National Labor Relations Act. Better yet, the Association is now "ordered" by the Labor Board to "cease and desist" from further committing these unfair labor practices and to initiate collective bargaining with its employees through the Teamsters Union. The "decision and order" by the Board reads in part as follows (references to the "Act" mean the National Labor Relations Act, as amended):

Conclusions of Law

1. Cincinnati Association for the Blind is an employer engaged in commerce within the meaning of Section 2(6) and (7) of the Act.

2. Truck Drivers, Chauffeurs, and Helpers Local Union No. 100, affiliated with the International Brotherhood of Teamsters, Chauffeurs, Warehousemen, and Helpers of America, is a labor organization within the meaning of Section 2(5) of the Act.

3. All production and maintenance employees and clients, including shipping and receiving employees, of Respondent's workshop located at 2045 Gilbert Avenue, Cincinnati, Ohio, excluding office clerical employees, professional employees, guards and supervisors as defined in the Act, constitute a unit appropriate for the purposes of collective bargaining within the meaning of Section 9(b) of the Act.

4. Since June 15, 1978, the above-named labor organization has been and now is the certified and exclusive representative of all employees in the aforesaid appropriate unit for the purpose of collective bargaining within the meaning of Section 9(a) of the Act.

5. By refusing on or about August 25, 1978, and at all times thereafter, to bargain collectively with the above- named labor organization as the exclusive bargaining representative of all the employees of Respondent in the appropriate unit, Respondent has engaged in and is engaging in unfair labor practices within the meaning of Section 8(a)(5) of the Act.

6. By the aforesaid refusal to bargain, Respondent has interfered with, restrained, and coerced, and is interfering with, restraining, and coercing, employees in the exercise of the rights guaranteed them in Section 7 of the Act, and thereby has engaged in and is engaging in unfair labor practices within the meaning of Section 8(a)(1) of the Act.

7. The aforesaid unfair labor practices are unfair labor practices affecting commerce within the meaning of Section 2(6) and (7) of the Act.

ORDER

Pursuant to Section 10(c) of the National Labor Relations Act, as amended, the National Labor Relations Board hereby orders that the Respondent, Cincinnati Association for the Blind, Cincinnati, Ohio, its officers, agents, successors, and assigns, shall:

1. Cease and desist from:

(a) Refusing to bargain collectively concerning rates of pay, wages, hours, and other terms and conditions of employment with Truck Drivers, Chauffeurs, and Helpers Local Union No. 100, affiliated with the International Brotherhood of Teamsters, Chauffeurs, Warehousemen and Helpers of America, as the exclusive bargaining representative of its employees.

(b) In any like or related manner interfering with, restraining, or coercing employees in the exercise of the rights guaranteed them in Section 7 of the Act.

2. Take the following affirmative action which the Board finds will effectuate the policies of the Act:

(a) Upon request, bargain with the above-named labor organization as the exclusive representative of all employees in the aforesaid appropriate unit with respect to rates of pay, wages, hours, and other terms and conditions of employment, and, if an understanding is reached, embody such understanding in a signed agreement.

(b) Post at 2045 Gilbert Avenue, Cincinnati, Ohio, copies of the attached notice marked "Appendix." Copies of said notice, on forms provided by the Regional Director for Region 9, after being duly signed by Respondent's representative, shall be posted by Respondent immediately upon receipt thereof, and be maintained by it for 60 consecutive days thereafter, in conspicuous places, including all places where notices to employees are customarily posted. Reasonable steps shall be taken by Respondent to insure that said notices are not altered, defaced, or covered by any other material.

(c) Notify the Regional Director for Region 9, in writing, within 20 days from the date of this Order, what steps have been taken to comply herewith.

Dated, Washington, D.C., September 18, 1979

By any standard this is a resounding victory and one which has not been handed to us on a silver platter. There have been expensive legal bills together with much ground-work and educating of the Teamsters, and Federationists and their friends by the thousands have all had a part in bringing this great day about. Of course, it goes without saying that the battle continues; orders of the National Labor Relations Board are not self-enforcing, and you can be sure that the Cincinnati Association, having firmly established its course of non-negotiation will not willingly retreat. The notice referred to as an Appendix to the Labor Board's Order amounts to an affirmation that the Cincinnati Association will recognize its obligation to come to the bargaining table and enter into an agreement with its workers, but as expected, the Association refuses to sign or post the notice and has instead filed a petition with the Federal Court of Appeals for the Sixth Circuit, asking to have the decision and order of the NLRB reviewed and set aside.

Thus the battle in Cincinnati now moves from the National Labor Relations Board to the Federal Courts. More time will be taken; there will be more delays; more briefs, oral arguments will be scheduled, and the months will go by while the blind workers inside the workshop at the Cincinnati Association will try to keep their spirits up, hoping for a swift and satisfactory conclusion of the next steps in this series of classic maneuvers to establish the right to organize and bargain collectively. As the months spread before us all, the strength and resolve of all Federationists will be needed to see the battle in Cincinnati through to its ultimate conclusion. Our energy, our time, our strong and confident voice, along with especially our money and our collective will must be available as never before. Yes, the battle grows long in Cincinnati, but even so, all blind people have more dignity and a better status in society today because of it.

Meanwhile at the Houston Lighthouse, events, similar to those which had occurred before the election for Union representation in Cincinnati, were taking place. In the *Braille Monitor* for April, 1979, we reported the decision of the Regional Director for the National Labor Relations Board in Houston who, exercising his own authority, ordered an election at the Houston Lighthouse. The Lighthouse, as we reported in April, appealed to the National Board in Washington, and the Board decided that it would review the Regional Director's decision, while temporarily upholding the order for an election and impounding the ballot box pending the outcome of the review.

In a way, while it was somewhat disappointing (and certainly served to delay matters) for the full Board to review the Regional Director's decision, the fact that the original decision was made at all at the Regional level was heartening for it shows that a clearer precedent has been established as the result of Cincinnati and the earlier case in Chicago. In both Cincinnati and Chicago it will be remembered that the NLRB Regional Directors declined to rule on the petitions for election, passing the cases along for full Board action in Washington. Now, with the Labor Board's firm orders in Cincinnati and Houston, we can expect more decisive and positive action at the Regional level as future cases are brought to the NLRB.

Again, in Houston, the months went by as attorneys for the respective parties and our attorneys (the Federation had been admitted into the case as an "intervener") filed their briefs and made their arguments. Not surprisingly, the issues were identical to those in the Cincinnati case: Are blind workers to be considered employees under the National Labor Relations Act? Is the Lighthouse substantially engaged in business activity and commercial enterprise? Would it "effectuate the purposes" of the National Labor Relations Act for the Labor Board to assert jurisdiction? The Board had already decided the Cincinnati Case in 1978 on these and related questions, so it now remained to determine whether Houston was similar enough to invoke the Cincinnati precedent. The Board determined that it was. The "decision on review" reads in part (the "employer" referred to in the decision is the Houston Lighthouse for the Blind):

> The fifth department within the Employer's operations is the Industrial Division which is the one involved herein. This division generates almost 90 percent of the Employer's annual revenues. The Industrial Division produces felt-tipped pens, mops, and commercial scrub brushes; bottles disinfectants and detergents; and performs subcontracting work. In 1977 the Industrial Division manufactured 40,539,744 felt-tipped pens, 250,000 mops, and 300,000 brushes. In addition it produced 145,000 gallons of disinfectant and 30,000 gallons of detergents. Items such as the mops and brushes manufactured by Workshop A of the Industrial Division are sold in market outlets in Harris County and Houston, Texas. Pursuant to contracts with the U.S. General Services Administration (GSA), many of the felt-tipped pens, as well as the detergent and the disinfectant, are supplied to the Federal government. The Industrial Division also performs subcontracting work including, *inter alia,* assembling fishing rod holders, performing grease check assembly work, and filling notebook binders with inserts for various companies.

> In 1977 the Industrial Division generated $4,620,000 worth of revenue from sales of the merchandise described above. These revenues netted a profit of $237,000 for the Employer which was utilized in other areas of its operations. The Employer's total revenue income in 1977 was $5,195,000 which included, in addition to the revenue from the Industrial Division, fees from state programs, donations from the United Fund, grants, contributions, and other donations. Expenditures by the Employer in 1977 included $3,631,000 for materials and goods, $752,000 for labor costs and other industrial operations, $644,000 for rehabilitation, and $123,000 for general administrative expenses. The balance of these totals reveals that the Employer netted a profit of $45,000.

> The Employer also contends that the Board should decline jurisdiction on discretionary grounds. In this regard, the Employer maintains that its commercial activity is "merely ancillary" to its purpose of providing

rehabilitation to handicapped persons and that the impact of the Employer's operations on interstate commerce is not sufficient to warrant the Board's assertion of jurisdiction. We do not agree.

Although the Employer contends that but for the grants from charities such as the United Way and moneys received from the Federal Government for experimental purposes, it would have lost $244,000 in 1977, the record amply demonstrates the impact and nature of the Employer's industrial operations with respect to commerce. Thus, as noted above, the Employer enters into contracts with the General Services Administration of the United States Government as well as other employers in the Houston area to manufacture and distribute products. The Employer's merchandising sales from its Industrial Division accounted for approximately 88.5 percent of the total revenues received by the Employer in 1977. A similar percentage was expended toward the operations of the Industrial Division. The production figures noted above, including the manufacture of 40 million pens and various other items, indicates to us that, contrary to its assertions, the Employer's substantial production and distribution of items by its Industrial Division attest to the commercial nature of the Employer's operations. Further, it is clear that the Employer endeavors to increase its manufacturing output, broaden its markets, and essentially operates as would a private employer. For these reasons we find no basis for exercising our discretion to decline jurisdiction, but rather conclude that it will effectuate the purposes of the Act to assert jurisdiction over the Employer.

II.

The Employer further contends that its handicapped workers in Workshop A, who are the subject of the instant petition, are not employees within the meaning of Section 2(3) of the Act. The Employer argues that the relationship between the Employer and its "clients" is one of rehabilitation. Both the Petitioner and the Federation assert that the persons in the petitioned-for unit are statutory employees and that the Employer's operations are commercial in nature.

The record in the instant case shows that the Employer operates Workshop A under normal business conditions and that Workshop A employees are treated essentially as are regular employees in the private sector. Employees in Workshop A are paid at least the minimum wage, the range being from $2.89 to $3.40 per hour based on performance. These employees are paid overtime rates when working more than 8 hours a day. Moreover, they are eligible to receive merit raises based on productivity, and these merit raises are subject to rescission if the employee does not demonstrate that this productivity can be sustained at that level. Employees in Workshop A receive a retirement program, vacations, and health benefits. They are covered under workmen's compensation and unemployment compensation. They punch a timeclock. They have nine paid holidays per year. Social Security deductions are made from their paychecks. While the Employer maintains that its relationship to a person in Workshop A is one primarily of rehabilitation, the record shows, for example, that with respect to discipline the Employer resolves these problems using normal economic and business considerations. Thus, there is undisputed evidence that employees have been terminated and suspended for, among other things, fighting, insubordination, low production, refusal to work, excessive tardiness, and excessive absenteeism. Moreover, although the Employer attempts to place employees in private industry, the record shows that many of these employees returned to the Industrial Division Workshop A. We also note that a large proportion of the employee complement of Workshop A has worked for Employer for at least 10 years and some for as many as 20 years.

These facts lead us to agree with the observation of one of the Employer's witnesses at the hearing in this case that the Industrial Division "operates like any manufacturing operation." It is clear from these facts and the facts as recited by the Regional Director that the Employer's relationship with its Workshop A "clients" is guided "to a great extent by business considerations." We therefore conclude that the employees in Workshop A of the Employer's Industrial Division are employees within the meaning of Section 2(3) of the Act. Accordingly, we affirm the Regional Director's Decision and Direction of Election and direct that the ballots which had been impounded be opened and counted by the Regional Director and that thereafter he take such further appropriate action as required by Section 102.69 of the Board's Rules and Regulations, Series 8, as amended.

Dated, Washington, D.C., September 18, 1979

On September 24, pursuant to the Board's order, the ballots cast by the workers at the Houston Lighthouse were opened by the Regional Director of the NLRB, and, by an affirmative vote of 47 to 17, they became the second group of sheltered shop employees to designate a labor union (once again the Teamsters) to represent them for purposes of collective bargaining. At this writing, in late September, the process of officially certifying the union's election is going forward, and you can be sure that there will be as many appeals as possible until the matter, as in the case of Cincinnati, reaches the Federal Courts.

We have traveled a very long road from the days when the right to organize and bargain collectively was a dream and a hope expressed in our resolutions and public statements to the point where this right is now recognized by the National Labor Relations Board, but this is where the latest rulings by the NLRB have placed us. No one should think that the battle is over, however, for there will be many more delays, more appeals, more briefs, and more rulings. The course of the future is clear, though, and we are firmly resolved to follow it through. In doing so we confront money, prestige, and all the power of the traditional agency establishment in work with the blind, because one thing it cannot tolerate is recognizing the essential right which blind people have to speak, think, and act for themselves through their chosen representatives, whether the representative selected is a Labor Union or the National Federation of the Blind.

In a very real sense, this is the most significant message transmitted by the most recent events in the battle to bring organized labor into the sheltered workshops. We have often said that they do not want us to speak for ourselves, and if there was ever need for proof of this truism, here it is in the cases of Houston and Cincinnati. The field of work with the blind is full of people who are determined to carve out our destiny for us, and they firmly intend to do it, using any tactic which they can find, never mind considerations of right and wrong, morality, or even matters of legality.

One almost wonders, with the rulings of the National Labor Relations Board, if the agency overlords will now begin to say that the members of the Board are surely bad and corrupt people, probably as bad and corrupt, they will likely say, as that "dogmatic" and "abrasive" National Federation of the Blind and its "irrational President, Kenneth Jernigan." Perhaps the members of the Board will become the subject of personal attack and abuse in the pages of the *Des Moines Register*. Likely as not Chairman Fanning (chairman of the National Labor Relations Board) will be charged with "megalomania." "How dare him order a workshop for the blind to listen and respond to the blind people; shame, shame." And who can tell, maybe, just maybe, the *Register* will discover that the windows of the building occupied by the NLRB in Washington are made of a mysterious substance known as Lexan.

No question about it, the recent developments on the workshop organizing front must be seen in the context of the broader struggle of the blind to achieve equality and first-class status in the face of the stubborn and often mulish resistance of the very agencies which some might say practice fraud upon the general public by holding themselves out as the "helpers of the blind" while actually subjecting the blind to the worst forms of slavery ever known. And it is significant, as in the case of the minorities who have gone before us, that we have only ourselves to count on for support and strength.

There is much to be said about this; we have often asked, where is the American Council of the Blind, and the inevitable answer comes back: "Down in the barnyard with the agencies, slinging mud at the blind who have the nerve to stand up and make decisions for themselves." And what about this outfit called ALL (the Affiliated Leadership League of and for the Blind)? It purports to work on behalf of "all those of and for the blind." Where was it when the Labor Board ruled? Nowhere to be found; ALL gone, if you will.

But we know where we were, we were on the barricades in Cincinnati, and we were fighting in the trenches in Houston. This we did, and this we must continue to do. The twin victories of Cincinnati and Houston have opened up vast new possibilities for the blind who work in other workshops throughout this country, and for all of us they have provided a new sense of personal dignity and a resounding affirmation of the absolute necessity to maintain a strong and truly independent organized blind movement through the National Federation of the Blind. It is one more answer to the question "Why the National Federation of the Blind." It is another way of underlying our battle cry of recent years (a battle cry which is not a necessary slogan but a way of life and a statement of faith—in ourselves, in society, and in the future). The battle cry is increasingly repeated and increasingly understood: We know who we are, and we will never go back.

The early and mid-1980s were to see a series of skirmishes and battles between the blind and the workshops throughout the country. In Cincinnati and Houston shop management appealed to the courts, and both of them ultimately lost. The Cincinnati administrators sought to have the United States Supreme Court review their case, but the court declined. Unions were established in Cincinnati and Houston, and efforts were made in North Carolina, Arkansas, and elsewhere. In Arkansas the vote to unionize the Lighthouse for the Blind was lost in the heat of a furious conflict, but the National Labor Relations Board ruled that there had been such flagrant abuse and so many unfair labor practices that a union should be established despite the election. Management then appealed to the Eighth Circuit Court, and contrary to the rulings of both the Fifth and Sixth Circuits, the Eighth Circuit ruled in favor of the shop in 1988.

In 1986 Congress, at the urging of the National Federation of the Blind, amended the Fair Labor Standards Act. It was a landmark amendment. From the beginning the blind employees of sheltered shops had been excluded from the minimum-wage provisions of the act; and those who believed they were being paid unfairly had no effective way of protesting. The 1986 amendments changed all that; no longer were blind workers powerless to seek justice and secure their rights. The full significance of the legal change, and its consequences for blind workers, were spelled out in an article by Kenneth Jernigan appearing in the November, 1989, issue of the *Braille Monitor:*

THE DILEMMA OF THE SHELTERED SHOP WORKER
by Kenneth Jernigan

It is common knowledge that most of the workshops for the blind in the United States have substandard working conditions and pay shamefully low wages to their blind employees. They can get away with this because of a provision in the federal Fair Labor Standards Act which says that blind shop workers may be paid less than the minimum wage if they cannot produce as much as a sighted worker similarly situated in private industry. Of course, sighted workers in private industry cannot be paid less than the minimum wage regardless of their productive capacity. And then there is also the question of how productive capacity is measured and who is similarly situated.

Presumably tests are made, but we have repeatedly demonstrated that many of those tests are rigged. What would happen to the average factory worker in the United States if there were no federal labor laws, no unions, and no governmental mechanisms for inspection? All we have to do for an answer is to look at what happened during the last century. But with the blind it is even worse. Nobody believes that the average sighted person is incapable of working competitively, but the traditional wisdom is that the blind are substandard and only able to work if they are given charity and special consideration. Attitudes are changing, but the outmoded notions are still far too prevalent.

In the circumstances it is not surprising that sheltered workshop managers take advantage of the situation and exploit. It would be remarkable if they did not. There are budgets to meet, administrative salaries to pay, and little likelihood that the managers will have to pay penalties (and certainly not personal penalties) if they stretch the law or cheat. Therefore, they say that their employees are not really workers at all but just trainees, that most of them are multiply handicapped, and that the workers (no, "trainees") like the conditions at the shop, and wouldn't have them otherwise.

So what do you do if you are a blind employee in a sheltered shop in the United States today? If you complain, try to help form a union, or contact government authorities, you are likely to get fired, have your wages cut, or be told that there just isn't enough work to keep you on a full-time basis. It may be done with big words and professional terminology. It may even be documented and supported by studies—but it hurts just as much, and the message is just as clear. On the other hand, if you remain silent, you are likely to continue with starvation wages and substandard conditions for the rest of your life. It is not easy, and it is not pleasant; but it is the everyday experience of many blind shop workers throughout the country.

Here is where the National Federation of the Blind comes in. Unlike labor unions, we are knowledgeable about the Fair Labor

Standards dodge and the ways of the professionals, and we cannot be bamboozled. Moreover, we are strong enough to resist pressure, and we cannot be intimidated. Through our division for shop workers (the Blind Industrial Workers of America) and through local chapters, workshop employees are joining the Federation in growing numbers. They are beginning to have heightened expectations and to feel their strength.

President Maurer recently received a letter from an NFB chapter officer concerning conditions in the local workshop. The letter and President Maurer's response are indicative of what is beginning to happen in the shops, and I want to share them with you. For obvious reasons the name and locality are being omitted. These letters should cause each of us to do soul-searching and to ask ourselves what action we can take to help the shop workers in our local areas. Regardless of our financial situation or social position, each of us has a stake in what happens to the shop workers. Their struggle is our struggle; their hope is our hope; their dream is our dream. Here is the correspondence:

Dear President Maurer:

At our last chapter meeting we discussed at length the workshop for the blind here in our city. As I am sure you know, this is a sheltered workshop that employs many handicapped persons, including a few blind, and some of our chapter members. Most of these people, including myself, are paid less than the minimum wage. Last July there was a ruling by the board of directors of the shop that they were going to pay each worker what he or she produced and no longer have any make-up pay. In the past each person was guaranteed a base rate and also received more than that if his piece rate was above this rate.

Since only about fifteen percent are blind, it is next to impossible to get a union in there. Many of the workers are slow learners and would not understand the benefits of the union. Often we are put on jobs where we do not make close to the minimum wage, and the shop management assures us that soon new time studies will be made—but they never are. The employees are hesitant to file a complaint with the Labor Board because we are fearful that if a hearing were held, we would still not get the higher wages.

It was mentioned at our last chapter meeting that the Federationists who are working at the shop should sign a petition, stating the complaints, and circulating it to the suppliers of contracts for the shop, thus making them aware of the problem.

Our chapter is wanting to help in any way it can, but we do not want to do the wrong thing. We have thought of going to the press or the news media, but the local stations have been doing advertising for the workshop. Any advice you can give is appreciated by all of us.

Sincerely yours,

————————

Baltimore, Maryland

Dear ——:

I have your recent letter describing problems of blind workers at your local workshop. In 1986 a law was adopted by Congress at the urging of the National Federation of the Blind. This law said that any person working in a sheltered workshop for the blind who was being paid less than the minimum wage had the right to file an appeal with the Department of labor. The Department of Labor is responsible for conducting a hearing to determine whether the wages paid to the blind employee are proper. The employer must demonstrate that the wages are fair. If the employer fails to do this, the blind worker is entitled to receive at least the minimum wage. The burden of proof is on the employer. The employee does not have to show that the wages paid are unfair. Subminimum wages are presumed to be unfair unless the sheltered shop administrator can show that they are reasonable.

It is not necessary to establish a union before the complaints are filed with the Department of Labor. The complaints may be filed whether there is a union established or not. If workers want to file such a complaint, the National Office of the Federation is ready to help.

If a workshop is to receive contracts from the federal government through National Industries for the Blind, seventy- five percent (75%) of its direct labor hours must be performed by blind employees. If your local workshop is using very many sighted laborers, it may be in violation of those standards. A complaint may be in order on these grounds as well.

If there are workers who want to raise these questions or others before the Department of Labor, please let me know. Part of the reason for the National Federation of the Blind is to help with problems like these.

Cordially,
Marc Maurer, President
National Federation of the Blind

This is the letter from the local chapter and President Maurer's response. Is it any wonder that the managers of the sheltered shops resent the Federation and call us names? Is it any wonder that they have voted to give up to $200,000 a year to NAC (the National Accreditation Council for Agencies Serving the Blind and Visually Handicapped)? Is it any wonder that NAC is willing to take the money and to accredit these organizations? The answers are obvious, and they speak for themselves.

The pattern of substandard working conditions and sub-minimum wages prevailed in numerous sheltered workshops throughout the decade of the eighties, despite the 1986 amendments and the earlier blistering exposure of these practices in the *Wall Street Journal* in January of 1979. Conditions in the workshops were chillingly described in several hearings before committees of Congress. For example, one employee of a sheltered shop in Utah, Premo Foianini, was beaten with a stick by his supervisor for daring to offer testimony concerning the exploitive wages and sweatshop conditions in his workplace. The report of another situation in the Richmond, Virginia, sheltered shop—known as the Virginia Industries for the Blind—may be taken as typical of many. This is how it appeared in the *Monitor* of May-June, 1988:

THE RICHMOND WORKSHOP:
BAD MANAGEMENT, "QUALITY SERVICES," AND NAC

This article appears in the January, 1988, Newsletter of the National Federation of the Blind of Virginia. As Federationists know, Charlie Brown is NFBV President. The information and statistics revealed in the article should be the occasion for shock and sorrow. The fact that they are not is indicative of the widespread problems which exist in the sheltered workshops for the blind throughout the country.

Moreover, it is not at all surprising that Virginia Industries for the Blind is accredited by NAC (the National Accreditation Council for Agencies Serving the Blind and Visually Handicapped). In view of NAC's history for the past twenty years one would be surprised if it were otherwise. How long must the blind of this nation endure the kind of conditions which are the everyday commonplace in the shops and which are blessed by NAC in the name of professionalism! It is no exaggeration to say that the term "professional," which should be positive and complimentary when applied to employees of programs that are designed to give service to people, has become to the blind of this country a virtual swear word—a bitter term of mockery and disillusionment. Here is Charlie Brown's article.

Some time ago Ed Peay, President of our Richmond Chapter, wrote to George Kogar, Deputy Commissioner of the Department for the Visually Handicapped, and asked him thirty questions about the Virginia Industries for the Blind facility located in Richmond. Mr. Kogar answered Ed's questions in a letter Ed received at the end of November of 1987. We think many of you will be interested in Mr. Kogar's responses to the questions.

According to Mr. Kogar's letter, there are thirty-three blind workers and two trainees employed in the workshop. All of the blind workers are employed in direct labor. All of the supervisors and management personnel are sighted. Only fifteen of the thirty-five blind workers receive the federal minimum wage. All of the sighted production workers, of course, must receive at least the federal minimum wage.

Mr. Kogar also states that "The average annual earnings of a production worker is $6,676.80 per year." Remember that this figure includes the relatively higher earnings of the sighted production workers who must be paid the minimum wage. Mr. Kogar goes on to say that "The average for nonproduction workers is $11,264.26." Again, remember that all of these folks are sighted. One sometimes wonders if the Virginia Department for the Visually Handicapped is operating a sheltered shop for the sighted rather than a sheltered shop for the blind.

There is the additional matter of layoffs. Mr. Kogar informs us that "the industry has laid off blind employees on two occasions over the past three years. No sighted employees were laid off during this time period....The average duration of a layoff for a blind employee would be about eight weeks of intermittent work."

In his cover letter Mr. Kogar, to his credit, concedes, "The Industry has not been managed well for a long period of time. It will be a slow process to correct all of the problems of the past." In this regard the workshop director was let go last year.

Long-time Federationists know that we have been pointing out problems in the workshop for years. Officials have promised us that things would get better. They have not.

During all of this time, anyone who picks up a VDVH brochure or sees the agency letterhead finds proudly displayed the NAC symbol. This symbol proclaims that the agency and its workshop are fully accredited. Everything was deemed to be okay. We the blind are just troublemakers. NAC, everyone was told, would assure that blind people would receive "quality services." Without NAC who knows what might happen to the VDVH programs? Well, for one thing, people might have paid attention to the problems that exist in the Richmond workshop at lot sooner if VDVH had not chosen to hide behind the fictitious NAC shield. But all that is water over the dam. Yet, what are we, the blind of Virginia, to believe when in spite of everything VDVH Commissioner McCann tells us that he is "wedded to NAC?"

When Marc Maurer rose to address the 1989 convention of the National Federation of the Blind in Denver, on the occasion of the annual Presidential Report, he was able to announce a significant victory in the struggle with the workshops—a victory that (like the bloodied effort of Premo Foianini and his fellow shopworkers in Utah) did not come without pain and sacrifice on the part of the blind employees. In short, there was good news and bad news in the dramatic account of events at the Southwest Light-house for the Blind in Lubbock, Texas. Fortunately the good far outweighed the bad; but the shocking nature of that bad news—its ugly note of physical violence—served as a reminder that the fight to organize was still going on for blind people, and that it was still very much a fight. It had become increasingly easy to forget that harsh fact; for although it was known that problems remained in the sheltered shops, they were not thought to include gross abuse and harassment. Few could imagine that, as Glenn Crosby was to reveal, the abuse at the Lubbock workshop was not a rare or isolated occurrence but a practice so common and routine as to be considered normal operating procedure. Crosby, an NFB Board Member who was among the principal organizers of union activity in Lubbock, told the National Convention that there was at least one supervisor in the workshop "who (on a regular basis when frustrated and aggravated) would walk over to blind workers and slap them. It was so common," he added, "that these people didn't even realize that they were being assaulted." He went on to describe what happened when the blind workers did come to realize what was being done to them, not only physically but economically and psychologically:

> The workers in Lubbock called the National Federation of the Blind, and we responded by going out to help. We formed a picket line and were able to get a lot of good press coverage. We took pledges and organized a union. We were able to win a hearing from the Labor Department and are now in the middle of filing complaints. And finally, we have now been able to run off the Director of the shop.

That straightforward summary of the Lubbock situation was amplified and placed in context by Marc Maurer in the course of his Presidential Report to the National Convention. His comments not only underlined the significance of the Texas episode but illustrated the strategic dexterity of Federation leaders in their pursuit of justice and fair play for the blind. This is what he had to say:

> Approximately six thousand blind people are employed in sheltered workshops throughout the country. Very often, working conditions are poor and wages are low. Nowhere is this more dramatically demonstrated than in the Southwest Lighthouse for the Blind in Lubbock, Texas. Last September I went to Lubbock to meet with workers from the Lighthouse. I discovered that most of them were being paid two dollars and five cents an hour. A few were receiving even less—some as little as eighty-five cents. A month earlier, the Lighthouse president had told the workers that the agency was planning to begin deducting money from their pay envelopes for their health insurance coverage. Health insurance had previously been provided by the workshop. Most of

the workers barely had enough for their food and other living expenses. Nevertheless, agency officials insisted that these employees must pay for health insurance or be fired. Instead of handing over a substantial portion of their meager wages, the workers called on the Federation, and the blind took to the streets. The newspaper stories about the injustice in the workshop spread over the nation, and both television and radio carried the news of the exploitation. The Lighthouse president changed his mind. The workers would continue to receive health insurance, and the pay in their envelopes would not be cut. We won the first round.

Before the end of September, we had taken action to begin the next step. We hired a lawyer in Washington, D.C., and helped the Lighthouse workers file complaints with the United States Department of Labor. The minimum wage is three dollars and thirty-five cents an hour. Most sheltered shop workers in Lubbock are receiving two dollars and five cents. Nevertheless, they are expected to work a long day and produce results. The wages are artificially low and shamefully meager. So, we made plans to bring pressure to change them. We submitted complaints to the Department of Labor. These were the first appeals ever filed under the 1986 amendments to the Fair Labor Standards Act, and it will be remembered that they were filed by the National Federation of the Blind. Because of our efforts to educate members of Congress in 1985 and 1986, all blind people receiving subminimum wages have the right to challenge the fairness of their pay. The lawyer we hired once served as the Assistant Secretary of Labor. In that position he learned about the workshops and how they maneuver to violate the law.

In October of last year still another element was added to the battle. With our help, shop employees asked that they be permitted to join a labor union. The Lighthouse challenged their right to organize. By November we were preparing for a full-blown hearing before an officer of the National Labor Relations Board. This hearing was of major importance because several months earlier, a judicial decision had been issued by the eighth circuit Court of Appeals saying that blind workers at the Arkansas Lighthouse for the Blind could not join a union. The right of blind workers in sheltered workshops to organize was being eroded. After the setback in Arkansas, a highly visible public counterstroke was required. We needed to protect shop workers, and Lubbock was the place to do it. Without reviewing all the factors involved, let me just say that the National Federation of the Blind knows about blindness and the law. We are also able to get things done. On December 30, 1988, the workers voted. The question to be answered was: would the workers join a union—or not. By the most overwhelming margin ever recorded in any sheltered workshop election, the workers gave their answer. We won that round, too. There is a union at the Southwest Lighthouse for the Blind in Lubbock, Texas.

Partnership and Progress

The long campaign of the National Federation of the Blind to transform the system of sheltered workshops in America from the blind alleys of the past to modern channels of legitimate employment—a campaign waged continuously through half a century—was afflicted more than most with episodes of crisis, confrontation, and conflict. At virtually every step of the way, as we have seen, the forces of reform were met and countered by forces of reaction determined to retain custodial control over these sweatshop industries which were often (so it was said) as shady as they were sheltered. Progress came slowly, when it came at all; and it almost never came voluntarily, without struggle and recrimination. The sustained conflict often seemed like a non-lethal form of trench warfare, with the battle lines clearly drawn—on one side the insurgent troops of the organized blind, on the other the entrenched mercenaries of the workshop system. No impartial observer looking on at the fray could fail to perceive the values at issue: They were the vested interests of the old order, the *ancien regime*, striving to stay alive, pitted against the democratic interests of the organized blind—of a new world struggling to be born.

Nevertheless, as the first fifty years of Federationism came to a close, the portents of a better day for sheltered shop workers included growing signs of improved relations between the organized blind and numerous workshop management teams across the land. One illustration of such a cooperative relationship, based on the recognition of mutual advantage, was contained in the remarks of the president of Blind Industries and Services of Maryland, Richard J. Brueckner, at the state convention of the NFB of Maryland in 1989. As the Editor of the *Monitor* pointed out in the February 1990 issue, these remarks gained significance in light of past difficulties with the Maryland agency:

"As *Monitor* readers know," the Editor said, "Blind Industries and Services of Maryland (BISM) has not enjoyed an unruffled relationship with the organized blind. Richard Brueckner assumed the presidency of the agency at the beginning of 1989, and early on he began sending signals that he would like to establish constructive relations with the National Federation of the Blind of Maryland." Invited to address the convention of the Maryland affiliate in November of 1989, Brueckner delivered a speech more encouraging than any in recent years from an official of the state agency. He said in part:

> As most of you know, BISM (Blind Industries and Services of Maryland) has existed in one form or another since 1908. I did not come here today to dwell on the past, but rather to talk about the present and future of the new BISM, which started on January 1, 1989. The theme of my speech today can be summarized in two words, *responsibility* and *accountability*.
>
> As President of BISM, I can say that we expect to meet these awesome responsibilities and are perfectly willing to be held accountable for our actions and results. Who are we at BISM accountable to? In response to that question, I list the following: 1) The Governor of the State of Maryland, 2)The Legislature of the State of Maryland, 3) The BISM Board of Trustees, who are appointed by the Governor and ratified by the Legislature, 4) All the blind people in the State of Maryland, 5) The National Federation of the Blind (NFB), 6) The employees of BISM, 7) The vendors in the Maryland Vending Program for the Blind, 8) The Department of Vocational Rehabilitation (DVR), and 9) National Industries for the Blind (NIB).

Commenting on Brueckner's speech, the *Monitor* said: "His message was constructive and sensible. It is too soon to be certain how things will develop, but the early signs are hopeful for a positive relationship with an industries program that employs a number of blind people."

Accordingly, as the movement of the organized blind prepared to enter its second half-century, accordingly, the saga of the sheltered workshops remained as uncertain as it was unfinished. Much had been accomplished over the decades; much was still to be done. The right to organize had been won more than a decade earlier. Minimum wage protection was still not available to blind workers in all states, but the 1986 amendments to the Fair Labor Standards Act offered an appeal procedure for persons victimized by substandard wages. Union contracts were in force at sheltered workshops in Houston, Texas, and Cincinnati, Ohio; and labor representation had been selected by the workers at the Lighthouse for the Blind in Lubbock, Texas. To be sure, not all efforts to organize unions in the workshops had been fruitful; but the success rate of labor organization was increasing, as was the interest in pursuing that course on the part of shop workers throughout the country. Meanwhile, some sheltered workshops were continuing to pay less than the minimum wage to their blind laborers; but a growing number had reached that level and were providing a respectable standard of pay. Thus the many-sided struggle of the blind toward reform of the workshops—for a living wage, for decent working conditions, for protection from abuse, for the right to organize and to bargain collectively—was far from over. But there were hopeful signs of a new spirit which could be the harbinger of a future age of partnership and progress.

And there was something else in the air as well, in the final decade of the century, of still greater portent and promise. There was a change in the climate of opinion, a subtle but definite warming trend in the general atmosphere, which had been brought about by the combined efforts of all the organized blind through the years and decades since 1940. It was the spirit of Federationism abroad in the land—the spirit of a people's movement of irresistible force, of boundless confidence, and of genuine pride. It was not likely that the walls of any sheltered shop, or even of the entire workshop system, could long prevail against this elemental force of consciousness and will—which had long since found its eloquent expression in a few simple lines first spoken at a convention of the early seventies, and thereafter recited year after year by Federationists in a kind of communal chorus:

"We are simply no longer willing to be second-class citizens. We want no strife or confrontation; but we will do what we have to do. We know who we are—and we will never go back."

Chapter 11

Bankruptcy of a System: The Politics of Accreditation

The history of the organized blind movement, according to one of its leaders, might well be seen as a confirmation of the "challenge-and-response" theory of social evolution propounded some decades ago by the British historian Arnold J. Toynbee—which held that the rise and fall of civilizations has corresponded to their ability to meet successive challenges, from without or within, by appropriately vigorous responses. "So long as the response is more energetic than the challenge," said Toynbee, "a civilization may be said to be in the ascendant." "As with societies so with social movements," added Kenneth Jernigan in a presidential speech; "so long as the organized blind remain vigilant against the forces opposed to them, capable of meeting any challenge with an immediate response, for so long will they be a dominant factor within their own sphere of action."

After fifty years of continuous challenge and response, it was clear by 1990 that the National Federation of the Blind was still ascending as a movement and expanding as a force in the special sphere occupied by the blindness system. More and more that system and its constituent agencies had come to recognize this reality and to respect the Federation, if not for its virtue then for its strength. But there were still pockets of resistance in the system (rear-guard elements like those dominating most of the sheltered workshops) which interpreted the progressive philosophy of the NFB as a threat to their very existence. These reactionary elements were neither as numerous nor as formidable as they once had been; but they were as stubborn as ever in their opposition and as determined in their efforts to retain or regain custody over the lives of those they still perceived as their dependent wards.

The present chapter relates the story of one such agency challenge—and of the massive response which was mustered against it. That response, beginning in the sixties, took the form of an aggressive and sustained campaign to reform or retire a self-appointed watchdog group calling itself the National Accreditation Council for Agencies Serving the Blind and Visually Handicapped (NAC). From the time of its origin in the sixties when it was known as the Commission on Standards and Accreditation of Services for the Blind (COMSTAC), NAC operated effectively as a "front" organization for the American Foundation for the Blind and other agencies of the blindness system in their effort to extend control over all those blind persons (numbering in the tens of thousands) who fell within the network of public and private service. While the ostensible purpose of NAC was to provide a neutral and objective arbiter of professional "standards" for the field, its practical intent was to hold a whiphand over service agencies of all kinds through the arbitrary power of accreditation—in other words, to reward its friends (by granting approval) and punish its enemies (by withholding the prize).

The confrontation between the organized blind and the agency known as NAC may be dated from November, 1965, when a national conference was held in New York City by a newly formed group known as the Commission on Standards and Accreditation of Services for the Blind (COMSTAC). The New York conference climaxed two years of elaborate planning on the part of the American Foundation for the Blind, which had conceived the idea of COMSTAC and was its primary source of financial support. (The Foundation initially contributed $225,000 over four years to the project, to which additional funds were later provided by the U.S. Office of Vocational Rehabilitation and, to a much lesser extent, by private foundations.) Some 300 professional workers and administrators took part in the four-day meeting, at which the reports of a dozen technical committees were presented for approval. The announced purpose of the conference, with its massive panoply of professional celebrities and task-force committees, was to "create a new and independent agency to administer an ongoing, voluntary system of accreditation of local and state agencies for the blind on a national basis." The impression sought to be conveyed was one of consensus and harmony on the part of all interests in the field of work for the blind. Most such groups were indeed prominently in attendance: the American Association of Workers for the Blind, the National Rehabilitation Association, National Industries for the Blind, the state commissions, public and private welfare agencies—virtually the entire gamut of professional organizations with an interest in the lives of blind people. The only concerned group which was conspicuous by its almost complete absence—not only in the conference itself but in the numerous preliminary meetings at which standards were initially proposed and formulated—was the organized blind.

The idea of establishing an "independent" accrediting system for all groups doing work with the blind—which led to the formation of COMSTAC and its successor agency, NAC—was not as novel as the conveners of the New York conference pretended to suppose. A decade earlier the American Association of Workers for the Blind had attempted to gain control over the field of services by instituting a "seal of good practices," to be obtained as a reward by agencies conforming to the AAWB's expectations of professional conduct. However, of the several hundred agencies and organizations in the field only 20 or 30 applied for and received the seal; and of those that did, more than a few were regarded by the blind themselves as backward in their philosophy and unproductive in their enterprise. After a short time this counterpart to the "*Good Housekeeping* seal" was quietly shelved by the AAWB.

Apparently profiting from that earlier failure to impose its view of professionalism and its system of control upon the entire field, the American Foundation for the Blind moved prudently to give the impression of independence and autonomy to COMSTAC. The 22 persons named to the commission came from a broad range of professions, many of them outside the field of work with the blind and most of them prestigious. Among the members were public officials, business executives, philanthropists, academicians, and civic leaders. Among them also were appointees of the Foundation from within the field, high-ranking officials of agencies doing work with the blind. Not among them, however, were any representatives of the blind themselves; not a single commissioner came from a membership organization of blind people. Moreover, the paid staff director and moving force of COMSTAC was one of the Foundation's own—Alexander Handel, Foundation insider and employee, who left his job with the Foundation for full-time employment with COMSTAC and later with NAC.

Even before the 1965 conference in New York, the organized blind had reason to be apprehensive concerning the character of the proposed accrediting agency and the quality of its standards. In its preliminary phase COMSTAC was divided into a dozen specialized subcommittees, each involving hundreds of people across the country and further subdivided into smaller groups. While a few spokesmen for organizations of the blind and the many agencies in the field who did not want to be controlled by the American Foundation gained admission to deliberations at the local level, their dissent from the prevailing tone of affirmation went virtually unnoticed. In those rare instances when they were not excluded by the contrived selection process and were in the majority, the blind and the agency dissenters were still effectively neutralized by the heavy-handled tactics and maneuvers of the presiding COMSTAC officials. For example, at the 1965 annual convention of the American Association of Workers for the Blind, where discussion of the COMSTAC standards was invited, only the discussion leaders had copies of the standards, and a concerted attempt on the part of home teachers to seek a vote on standards affecting their specialty—which seemed certain to be negative—was overridden by the chair.

It was for this reason that Jacobus tenBroek, then President of the National Federation of the Blind, emphasized in his 1966 convention address the distinction between what he called "agencies *for* the blind and agencies *against* the blind." "Today in this country there are agencies which choose to work not for the blind but with them—as collaborators, colleagues, and co-equals," he said. "There are agencies that affect toward us a posture of indifference and a mask of neutrality. There are agencies which regard it as their special mission to fight the blind at every turn and with every weapon. There are agencies such as a number of sheltered shops which believe it is their function to control, suppress, and sweat the blind."

"Now comes COMSTAC," tenBroek went on. "The latest, greatest, and most ominous of all agency efforts to dominate the field to the exclusion of the organized blind....COMSTAC's 22 autonomous members—for so they describe themselves—are self-appointed; its tasks are self-assigned; its authority is self-arrogated; its special knowledge is self-proclaimed; its actions are self-serving. The standards it presumes to set for others are misconceived, misdirected, and miserable. Its outlook is paternalistic and condescending. Its interest in the content of programs is incidental if not accidental."

President tenBroek made it clear in this address that his criticism was not directed at the principle of seeking an improvement of services to the blind. "We would and do join in every legitimate effort to improve the qualifications of workers for the blind—that is, to insure that they become more wise, more perceptive, more humane, and more imbued with sympathetic understanding. We would and do join in every reasonable effort to improve programs for the blind—that is, to see to it that they liberate our people from self-imposed and socially imposed restrictions, to restore them to normal lives and normal livelihoods."

TenBroek concluded his speech with the declaration that "For all its bright and shiny newness, COMSTAC in reality is obsolete. Its philosophy of goods and services derives from an earlier age in which the recipients at the end of the line were simply human objects to whom things were done. Those were the good old days, before the revolution in welfare. But the revolution has come—and has brought with it recognition of the recipient not as a passive object of professional manipulation but as a responsible participant in the making of decisions that affect his life and the administering of programs that bear upon his welfare. Of all this COMSTAC is unaware—and uninterested."

In the years following that official assessment of COMSTAC by the leader of the organized blind, a number of events occurred which served both to confuse and to sharpen the issues surrounding the idea of accreditation for agencies in the blindness field. COMSTAC was itself dissolved and immediately reconstituted (or cloned, as someone said) in the form of NAC—which proceeded to declare its autonomy and independence from the network of agencies which had fathered and funded it. Meanwhile the National Federation of the Blind went through its own transition in the late sixties as Kenneth Jernigan succeeded Dr. tenBroek in the presidency; but the succession signaled no change in the NFB's policy of vigilant appraisal of agency activities on the accreditation front. In 1971, five years after Dr. tenBroek's critical address on the subject, President Jernigan submitted a comprehensive "Report to the members of the National Federation of the Blind on COMSTAC and NAC," which reviewed the recent history of developments in the field and concluded with a blistering attack on the integrity, credibility, and viability of the watchdog known as NAC. Under the title "NAC: What Price Accreditation" Jernigan penetrated the screen of professional rhetoric surrounding the role of NAC and exposed the hidden wires and batteries linking it with its parent agencies. He concluded with a warning to Federationists to continue to insist on a voice in the functioning, as well as the accrediting, of any and all programs affecting their lives. The text of his report follows:

NAC: WHAT PRICE ACCREDITATION
A REPORT TO THE MEMBERS OF THE
NATIONAL FEDERATION OF THE BLIND
ON COMSTAC AND NAC
by Kenneth Jernigan

When the Commission on Standards and Accreditation on Services for the Blind (COMSTAC) and its successor organization, the National Accreditation Council for Agencies Serving the Blind and Visually Impaired (NAC), came into being during the 1960s, the leaders of the organized blind movement sounded the alarm. It was pointed out that the American Association of Workers for the Blind had unsuccessfully tried, during the 1950s, to gain control of the field of work for the blind by instituting what it called a "seal of good practices." Of the several hundred agencies and organizations in this country doing work with the blind only twenty or thirty ever applied for and received this "seal." Several of those which did were not regarded by the blind as either very effective or very progressive. As the decade of the '60s approached, the proponents of rigid agency control apparently decided to change tactics. The American Foundation for the Blind and certain other leading agency officials adopted the idea of establishing a so-called "independent" accrediting system for all groups doing work with the blind. Although individual blind persons who were agency officials were involved in the establishment and development of COMSTAC, the blind as a group were not consulted—that is, the representative organizations of the blind were not given a voice, except occasionally as a matter of tokenism. Thus, the consumers of the services were not heard in any meaningful way, and they had no part in developing or promulgating the standards to govern the agencies established to give them assistance.

Profiting by the earlier failure of the AAWB "seal of good practices" experiment, the authors of COMSTAC built more carefully. The American Foundation for the Blind appointed an "independent" commission—the Commission on Standards and Accreditation for Services for the Blind (COMSTAC). The full-time staff consultant for COMSTAC was a staff member of the AFB, on loan to the group, purely as a means of demonstrating the Foundation's concern with the improvement of services for the blind. To add respectability, people of prestige outside of the field of work with the blind were placed on the commission—public officials, business executives, the dean of the Temple Law School, etc. These were people of good will and integrity, but they were not knowledgeable concerning the problems of blindness. Obviously they took their tone and orientation from the Foundation appointees on COMSTAC. All of these appointees, it must be borne in mind, were high-ranking officials doing work with the blind. Not one of them represented the blind themselves. Not one of them came from a membership organization of blind persons.

As its work developed, COMSTAC divided into subcommittees, involving hundreds of people throughout the country, since the subcommittees further subdivided into smaller groups. Again, the pattern was followed. The subcommittees, or the subcommittees of the subcommittees, had, in every instance, at least one of the COMSTAC agency officials as a member, plus people of prestige and ordinary rank and file agency workers or board members. In fact, at the sub-subcommittee level a few members of the organized blind movement were even added.

The American Foundation for the Blind and COMSTAC were later to proclaim with pride that they had sought and achieved a broad consensus throughout the field of work with the blind. However, the method of arriving at that consensus was, to say the least, novel. At Denver in the summer of 1965, for instance, the AAWB convention was largely taken up with a discussion of the COMSTAC standards—to gather opinions and achieve consensus, it was said. Only the discussion leaders had copies of the standards (there had been a delay in mimeographing), and any touchy point which was raised was answered either by the statement that it was covered somewhere else in the COMSTAC standards or that another group was discussing that matter and it was not properly the concern of the group in which it had been raised.

Home teachers from throughout the country were present and were considering the standards affecting their specialty. The overwhelming majority apparently disagreed with a particular item in the COMSTAC document and suggested that a vote be taken to determine the sentiments of the group. They were informed by the discussion leader that a vote certainly would not be taken but that their views would be reported to COMSTAC, which had the sole responsibility for deciding such matters.

Throughout the summer and fall of 1965 promises were repeatedly made that copies of the proposed COMSTAC standards would be made available. They were forthcoming, hundreds of pages of them—three days prior to the final conference in New York City, which brought together hundreds of agency representatives for the announced purpose of arriving at a final consensus. Dr. Jacobus tenBroek and I attended that conference. Again, the democracy and fair play with which it was conducted were novel. One had to indicate in writing ahead of time which particular group discussion he would like to attend. There was no assurance that his choice would be honored. He might be assigned to another group. He could not move from group to group at all. If he had not received a special invitation, he could not attend the meetings. COMSTAC appointees were stationed at the door to check credentials, and I personally witnessed the turning away of one agency director who had been critical of COMSTAC.

It is no wonder that the blind people of the country felt apprehensive. What type of standards were likely to emerge from a commission so appointed and so conducted? Not only the blind but also many of the agencies expressed concern. Many felt that the AFB and federal rehabilitation officials (unwittingly aided by people of prestige in the broader community) would impose a system of rigid controls—which would stifle initiative, foster domination, and take the emphasis off of real service and place it on bureaucracy, red tape, and professional jargon. It was further felt that what purported to begin as a voluntary system would (once firmly established) become mandatory. The AFB and other proponents of COMSTAC and its successor organization, NAC, vigorously denied these assertions. COMSTAC and NAC were to be truly independent. Their very watchword was to be objectivity. They were to be the means of improving services to blind people throughout the country and the vehicle for progressive thought and constructive change.

Readers of the *Braille Monitor* will remember that from 1965 through 1968 a detailed analysis was made of the COMSTAC and NAC reports and activities. The fact that the Federation has not called attention in recent months to COMSTAC and NAC should not lead the blind to believe that the threat has passed or the situation improved. Quite the contrary is the case.

The question of NAC's independence, for example, is no longer a matter for serious debate. The Scriptures tell us that "where a man's treasure is, there will his heart be also." In an official NAC document entitled "Budget Comparison—1968 and 1969," dated April 15, 1968, the following items appear:

> Total approved budget calendar year 1968, $154,034; total projected calendar year 1969, $154,000. Estimated income 1968: grant from American Foundation for the Blind, $70,000; grant from Department of Health, Education, and Welfare, $75,000. Estimated income 1969: grant from American Foundation for the Blind, $70,000; grant from Department of Health, Education, and Welfare, $70,000."

Today (in 1971) the overwhelming majority of NAC's funds still come from HEW and the American Foundation for the Blind. Many of the NAC meetings are held at the AFB building in New York, and the executive director of NAC is a former Foundation staff member, the same one who was on "loan" to COMSTAC. When the first annual NAC awards were given, in 1970, it may be of significance that two recipients were named: Mr. Jansen Noyes, president of the board of directors of the American Foundation for the Blind; and Miss Mary Switzer, the long-time head of rehabilitation in the federal Department of Health, Education, and Welfare. Even more to the point may be Miss Switzer's comments upon that occasion as reported in the NAC minutes of April 24, 1970: "She predicted that difficult times might lie ahead if agencies accept the idea of standards but do nothing about them. The expending or withholding of public money can provide the incentive that is needed."

Thus spoke Miss Switzer, confirming what Federation leaders had predicted and COMSTAC spokesmen had denied a decade ago. The full meaning of Miss Switzer's statement was spelled out by Alexander Handel, executive director of NAC, as reported in the NAC minutes of April 25, 1970: "Mr. Handel reported a new and important step in encouraging accreditation. The Council of State Administrators has passed a resolution that by July 1, 1974, state rehabilitation agencies will require that agencies from which they purchase services be accredited." The use of the word "encouraging" in this context is almost reminiscent of George Orwell's double-think and new-speak of *1984*—only thirteen years away, at that. Perhaps sooner. The "encouraging" of agencies to seek accreditation from NAC will probably be called by some by the ugly name of blackmail. The pressure for conformity and the concentration of power could well be the most serious threat to good programs for the blind in the decade ahead.

Federationists who attended the 1966 Louisville convention will remember that a report on COMSTAC and NAC was given at that time. I had been officially asked to serve on the NAC board. The offer was, of course, tokenism of the most blatant sort; and the question was whether to accept, leaving the Federation open to the charge of approving NAC actions, or to reject, exposing us to the charge of non-cooperation and leaving us with no means of observing and getting information. Federationists will remember that it was decided that I should accept the invitation. Thus, I have been a member of the NAC board since its inception. In the spring of 1970 I was elected to another three-year term. There are more than thirty NAC board members, of whom I am one.

While expressing my minority views, I have tried to be personally congenial and friendly with the NAC board members. Nevertheless, tokenism remains tokenism. The other members of the board not only seemed unconcerned with but unaware of the non-representative character of NAC. It is as if General Motors, Chrysler, Ford, and American Motors should set up a council and put six or seven officials from each of their companies on its board and then ask the UAW to contribute a single representative. What would the unions do in such a situation? What would racial minorities do if their representative organizations were offered such tokenism—in the establishment and promulgation of standards affecting their lives? I think we know what they would do. They would take both political and court action, and they would instigate mass demonstrations. Perhaps the blind should take a leaf from the same book. We cannot and should not exhibit endless patience. We cannot and should not forever tolerate the intolerable. I continue to sit on the NAC board, but I often wonder why. It does not discuss the real problems which face the blind today or the methods of solving those problems. In fact, NAC itself may well be more a part of the problem than the solution. I repeat that tokenism by any other name is still tokenism. In May of 1969, for instance, I received a document from NAC entitled "Statement of Understanding Among National Accreditation Council, National Industries for the Blind, and the General Council of Workshops for the Blind." This document was sent to all NAC board members with the request that they vote to approve or disapprove it. It contained six points, of which one and five are particularly pertinent. They are as follows: "1. By June 30, 1970, all NIB affiliated shops shall have either: a. applied to NAC for accreditation and submitted a self-study guide (or) b. applied to the General Council for a Certificate of Affiliation with NIB and submitted a self-study guide. 5. Certificates of Affiliation with NIB entitle shops to membership in the General Council and to access through NIB to: a. Government business allocated by NIB, b. Commercial business allocated by NIB, c. Consulting services of NIB, d. Any and all other benefits of NIB affiliation." In other words if a workshop for the blind wishes any contracts from the federal government, it had better get into line and "volunteer" for accreditation by NAC. No pressure, of course, merely a system of "voluntary accreditation!" As you might expect, I voted no on the NIB agreement. Along with my ballot, I sent the following comments:

> I do not approve this statement because I do not believe government contracts and other benefits to workshops should be conditioned upon their accreditation by NAC. Rather, receipt of government contracts and other benefits should depend upon the quality of performance of the workshop in question. Does the shop pay at least a minimum wage? Do its workers have the rights associated with collective bargaining? What sort of image of blindness does it present to the public?

"Prior to NAC (in the days of COMSTAC) many of us said that NAC would become a vehicle for blackmail—dressed out nicely, of course, in professional jargon. It would appear that the prophecy is beginning to come true, earlier assurances to the contrary notwithstanding."

As I say, I voted no. What do you suppose the final tally of the ballots indicated? Twenty-seven yes votes and one no vote. How different the results might have been if there had been equal representation of the blind themselves and the agencies! Yes, tokenism is still tokenism.

In order that my position cannot be twisted or misinterpreted I would like to say that the quarrel is not with the concept of accreditation itself. Rather, we object to what is being done in the *name* of accreditation. Proper accreditation by a properly accredited group is a constructive thing. What NAC is doing is something else altogether.

There is, of course, not time here to go into the details of all of the standards originally developed by COMSTAC and how being fostered by NAC, but a brief sample is sufficient to make the point. Federationists will remember that the *Braille Monitor* for February, 1966, carried an analysis of the COMSTAC standards on physical facilities. That analysis said in part:

> The standards [on physical facilities] are perhaps notable chiefly in that they are so vague and minimal as to be equally applicable to office buildings, nursing homes, or universities by the simple substitution of the names of these other facilities....

> Perhaps a brief run-down of the standards themselves would serve as the best and most complete illustration (headings theirs).

> 1. *Overall Suitability*—The total facility is constructed to best serve the needs of the particular agency. It will adequately serve everyone concerned. It will meet the requirements of its governing body, the Department of Health, Education, and Welfare, and the city building code. The physical facilities will be helpful to the program.

> 2. *Location*—The facility is located where it can easily be reached by staff, clients, and others who need to use it. The facility should be close to shopping and other com-

munity interests. The location is reasonably safe, with hazards minimized.

3. *Grounds*—The grounds will be large enough to allow for future expansion. They will be pleasant ("free of undue nuisances and hazards"), with parking areas and roadways. Signs will be posted to help people locate the proper areas.

4. *Activity Area*—The layout of the facility will be efficient. The facility will be designed for the planned activities, will be large enough and well organized (reception rooms next to entries, work areas together, etc.). Sufficient maintenance will be provided for.

5. *Privacy*—People will have as much privacy as individual cases call for. Confidentiality will be maintained.

6. *Health and Safety*—The health and safety codes of the community will be met. Sufficient heat and light will be provided. Sanitary conditions will be as good as possible. Suitable entries will be provided for wheelchairs, etc. Safety features will be related to the level of competence of the occupants, the activities undertaken, and the equipment used. Adequate first aid facilities are provided.

7. *Fire and Disaster Protection*—All buildings will be so designed and equipped as to minimize the danger of fire. The buildings will be inspected by local authorities and/or independent authorities and records of inspection kept. Smoking areas are clearly specified. Proper protection shall be provided the occupants of the facility to minimize danger should fire or disaster occur. Suitable fire extinguishers will be provided. Fire alarms will be installed so as to be heard throughout the facility. Fire drills will be held irregularly. Special provisions will be made for fire warnings to deaf-blind.

8. *Maintenance*—"The condition of the physical facility gives evidence of planful and effective maintenance and housekeeping."

9. *Remodeling*—When remodeling is undertaken, it should be to best suit the needs of the program.

The preceding is an inclusive summary! One can imagine the breadth of interpretation that can result from application of these standards. One can also imagine the range of individual whim and axe-grinding, not to say blackmail and favoritism, that can enter into the proposed accreditation of agencies for the blind based on such vague and capricious requirements. The danger to be anticipated is the possibility of varying application of standards to friends and foes when "accrediting" agencies....

One is tempted to dismiss this entire report of "Standards for Physical Facilities" with the single word, "Blah!" But more intensive study indicates otherwise. Tucked away among the platitudes and the generalities are the age-old misconceptions and stereotypes.

What, for instance, is meant by the requirement that a facility for the blind be located near to shopping and other community interests, and that it be in a location reasonably safe, *with hazards minimized?* The exact words of the committee are, "Where undue hazards cannot be avoided, proper measures are instituted to assure the safety of all persons coming to the agency. (For example, where an agency is on a street with heavy traffic, a light or crosswalk or other means is available for safe crossing by blind persons.)"

If this standard is simply meant to express the general pious platitude that everybody ought to be as safe as possible, then what a farcical and pathetic waste of time and money to assemble a committee to spell out what everybody already knows. On the other hand, if the standard means to imply that the blind are not able to live and compete among the ordinary hazards of the regular workaday world and that they need more shelter and care than others, the implications are not only false but they are insidiously vicious.

Of a similar character is the committee's statement that the grounds must "provide pleasant and appropriate surroundings, and be free of undue nuisances and hazards." Surely we do not need a special commission on standards and accreditation to tell us that people should live in pleasant surroundings that are free of undue hazards, if this is all that is meant. If, however, the committee is saying that the blind require surroundings that are more "pleasant and free from hazards" than the surroundings required by other people, one cannot help but be unhappily reminded of the nineteenth century concept that the blind should be entertained and provided with recreation, that they should be helped in every way possible to "live with their misfortune."

If this type of analysis seems blunt, one can only reply that this is no time for nice words and mousy phrases. The people who were formerly the Commission on Standards, and are now the National Accreditation Council, hold themselves out to the public at large as the qualified experts, the people who have the right to make standards and grant or refuse accreditation to all and sundry. These are not children indulging in the innocent games of childhood. They are adults, playing with the lives of hundreds of people.

Federationists should review the *Braille Monitor* from 1965 through 1968 to study the COMSTAC reports in light of present developments. I have not tried here to analyze the content of those reports. Mostly it is bad, and the standards and rules established by COMSTAC and NAC harmful. Let anyone who doubts this assertion read the COMSTAC reports and the *Monitor* analyses. They speak for themselves.

One final matter requires comment. At a recent meeting of the National Accreditation Council I was telling a new member of the board (a prominent businessman totally uninformed about the problems faced by the blind) that I thought most of the actions of NAC were irrelevant. He seemed surprised and said something to this effect:

"If you think what we are doing here is not relevant, what is relevant?"

To which I said, "Last fall a blind man in Minneapolis (a person who had worked for several years as a computer programmer at Honeywell and was laid off because of the recession) applied to take a civil service examination for computer programmer with the city of Minneapolis. His application was rejected, on the grounds of blindness. The National Federation of the Blind helped him with advice and legal counsel. As a result, he took the examination, and he now has a job with the city of Minneapolis as a computer programmer."

"How many of the people who are on the NAC board," I asked, "are even aware that such an incident occurred? How many of them think it is important?"

"Or," I went on, "consider another incident. A few weeks ago in Ohio a blind high school senior (duly elected by her class) was denied the right to attend the American Legion Girls' State. The story was carried nationwide by United Press, and the matter is still pending. Do you see any of these people here today concerned or excited about this case? Do you see them trying to do anything about it?"

"Well," my companion replied, "your organization seems to be working on matters like this. Maybe NAC is doing good in other areas."

"The difficulty," I told him, "is that the actions of NAC are helping to create the kind of problem situations I have been describing to you."

"How?" he asked me.

"NAC," I said, "accredits workshops, for instance. What kind of standards does it use in determining whether a shop should be approved and presented to the public as a worthy and progressive institution? NAC is concerned about whether the workshop has a good accounting system. It is concerned about good pay and good working conditions for the professional staff (almost all of them sighted). It is concerned with the physical facilities and (perhaps) whether there is a psychologist or psychiatrist available to minister to the blind workers. But what about minimum wages for those same blind workers, or the right of collective bargaining, or grievance committees? On such items NAC is silent. It will accredit a sheltered shop which pays less than fifty cents an hour to its blind workers. By so doing, it puts its stamp of approval on such practices. It helps perpetuate the system that has kept the blind in bondage and made them second-class citizens through the centuries. It helps to slam the door on the computer programmer in Minneapolis and the high school student in Ohio. Worst of all, perhaps, it reinforces and helps to continue the myth that blindness means inferiority, that the blind are unable to compete on terms of equality in regular industry or the professions, that the blind should be grateful for what they have and stay in their places. The workshop example is only that, an example. The same theme is everywhere present in NAC's action and standards—and, for that matter, in its very makeup."

As we talked, my businessman companion seemed shocked that there were sheltered shops paying less than the minimum wage to blind workers. Yet, he is on the NAC board, lending his name to the accreditation. I pointed out to him a variety of other ways in which the work of NAC is helping to promote misconceptions about blindness and add to our problems. I can only hope that the seeds I planted will bear fruit.

To round out the picture we are considering today, one further item might be mentioned. The April 25, 1968, minutes of NAC report as follows:

> Over thirty agencies and schools have indicated, in writing, an interest in applying for accreditation. Official applications have been received from six agencies. Some of these have already paid the application fee. The American Council of the Blind is the first membership association to apply for membership in the National Accreditation Council.

In a letter dated July 11, 1968, from Alexander Handel, executive director of the National Accreditation Council for Agencies Serving the Blind and Visually Handicapped, to members of the NAC Board of Directors an article is discussed which appears in the July, 1968, issue of the *Braille Forum* (the official publication of the American Council of the Blind). The article says in part:

> It should be emphasized, however, that from the first, ACB officers and members actively consulted with the various committees developing the standards, and ACB was the only national organization of the blind which both participated in and financially supported the National Conference on Standards which led to the formation of the National Accreditation Council.

I give you this quotation without comment. It speaks for itself. So do the actions of NAC. I presume all of you have read the exchange of correspondence concerning the appearance of NAC representatives at this meeting today. The contempt and condescension inherent in NAC's bland assumption that it was proper to reject our invitation to appear at this convention because a debate might occur are clear for all to see. Likewise, the agreement just concluded between NAC and the American Foundation for the Blind whereby the Foundation will work with agencies and help prepare them for accreditation is equally revealing.

In any case the one central point which must be repeatedly hammered home is the total irrelevance of NAC as it is now constituted and as it is now performing. What we need today and in the years ahead is not more detailed standards but a real belief in the competence and innate normality of blind people, a willingness on the part of agency officials to help blind people secure meaningful training and competitive employment, a recognition that the blind are able to participate fully in the mainstream of American life. We need acceptance and equality, not shelter and care.

When seen in this light, NAC must be viewed as one of our most serious problems in the decade ahead. The blind of the nation should thoroughly inform themselves about its activities and should insist upon a voice in determining the character of programs affecting their lives. We should insist that state and federal governments not delegate their powers of setting standards for state agencies to a private group, which is not responsive to the needs or views of the consumers of the services. It is true that many of the agencies doing work with the blind need to be reformed and improved, but NAC is not the entity to do it. We the organized blind intend (in the best tradition of American democracy) to have something to say about the scope and direction of the reform and the improvement. We are not children, nor are we psychological cripples. We are free citizens, fully capable of participating in the determination of our own destiny, and we have every right and intention of having something to say about what is done with our lives.

The developments which next occurred, in the period following that report to the membership, amply confirmed the fears of the organized blind concerning the character and purposes of NAC. The events of one day in particular—which happened to fall on December 7, 1971—involved both a confrontation and a conclusion: i.e., a confrontation of the principal antagonists and a conclusion of the first phase of NFB-NAC relations. The drama of that fateful encounter in Manhattan, and the context of events surrounding it, was later narrated in detail by Kenneth Jernigan in a special edition of the *Braille Monitor* (August, 1972) devoted to the NAC controversy. Under the heading, "NAC: Response to Bigotry," the NFB President announced the ending of his personal relationship with NAC and the beginning of a new Federation policy and tactic. Here is the article in its entirety:

NAC: RESPONSE TO BIGOTRY
by Kenneth Jernigan

"December 7, 1941," said Franklin Roosevelt, "is a day that will live in infamy." To the blind of this country December 7, 1971, is also a day that will live in infamy. It was then that the Board of the National Accreditation Council for Agencies Serving the Blind and Visually Handicapped (NAC) met at the Prince George Hotel in New York City and finally and irrevocably showed, for all the world to see, what kind of organization NAC really is.

Members of the organized blind movement will remember the appearance of the NAC representatives at our convention in Houston last July. Mr. Arthur Brandon, president of NAC, and Mr. Alexander Handel, executive director of the organization, spoke to us about NAC's purpose and objectives. Although we were in profound disagreement with the way NAC is structured, its methods of operation, and its basic premises, we treated its representatives with courtesy and respect. There were no personal attacks and no aspersions.

Prior to our Houston convention Mr. Brandon had first accepted the invitation to come and then, when he realized questions would be asked and a discussion would occur, changed his mind on the grounds that he did not wish to engage in debate. After it was pointed out to him that NAC had received hundreds of thousands of tax dollars and thus had some responsibility to appear and give an accounting to the largest group of consumers of its services in the nation, Mr. Brandon again changed his mind and once more agreed to come but only subsequent to considerable publicity. Obviously, he felt embarrassed and ill at ease at having to appear at our convention.

At this stage (apparently judging me by himself and, therefore feeling that I, too, would find a confrontation embarrassing) Mr. Brandon asked me as NFB President to present the views of the organized blind at the December, 1971, NAC Board meeting. He assured me that I would be given courteous treatment and heard with respect. Of course, NAC's exaggerated view of its power to inspire awe is not shared by the Federation, and the prospect was not at all embarrassing. Rather, the invitation should have come when NAC was first established. As Federationists know, I accepted the invitation.

Under date of July 13, 1971, Mr. Brandon wrote to me in a tone and manner that showed he had learned nothing from our convention. He seemed to be saying, "We have all had an opportunity to vent our feelings. Now let's settle back into the old rut of 'NAC-as-usual.'"

Under date of July 20, 1971, I replied to Mr. Brandon, attempting once again to penetrate his bubble of complacency. I said to him in part:

> The tone of your letter (especially that part which says "as we look ahead we must search for ways of working together effectively") indicates a conception of what occurred at Houston and of the attitudes and intentions of the blind not, in my opinion, in accord with the facts. At Houston we did not simply have a friendly little debate which allowed people to "blow off steam." We did not meet before that audience of a thousand people simply to exchange ideas and go back home to business as usual.
>
> What that audience was telling you, and what I have been trying to tell NAC for several years, is simply this: The blind of this nation are not going to allow all of their service programs to come under one uniform system of control with the tune called by the American Foundation for the Blind and the accompaniment played by HEW. The blind are not opposed to reasonable and proper accreditation—far from it. The blind do not oppose good agencies, government or private, which are doing good work. However, the Federation does not believe that NAC is properly constituted, that its standards are reasonable, that it is responsive to the aspirations and desires of consumers, or that it is a positive factor (as now structured) in the field of work with the blind.

Mr. Brandon made no response to my letter, and I prepared to go to New York in December. Under date of November 29, 1971, Dr. Patrick Peppe and Adrienne Asch, members of one of the local New York City affiliates of the Federation, wrote to Mr. Alexander Handel, executive director of NAC, to ask that they and other interested blind persons be permitted to attend the December 7 NAC meeting as observers. Their letter was courteous and respectful. It made no demands or threats; it only requested. The full text of the letter reads:

Dear Mr. Handel:

As consumers of services of agencies serving the blind, we would like to be present at the December 7 meeting of NAC. Since NAC was established to be the accrediting authority for agency service, our lives are vitally affected by its deliberations and actions. Therefore, we ask that we and others—both the organized blind and the unaffiliated but concerned consumers of services—be permitted to observe this meeting to learn more about the current policies and plans of your organization.

We would appreciate hearing from you by letter as soon as possible. Thank you very much for your cooperation.

Yours truly,
Adrienne Asch, Secretary
Patrick V. Peppe, Member, Executive Committee, The Metropolitan Federation of the Blind/Affiliate: The National Federation of the Blind.

Mr. Handel wasted no time in replying. His letter dated December 1, 1971, could serve as a model for insult and condescension. It should be read and re-read by every self-respecting blind person in the land. Its lesson should be learned well and never forgotten. It should be remembered whenever and wherever blind people meet—in private homes or in public gatherings, for business or for recreation.

Mr. Handel wrote to Dr. Peppe and Miss Asch as if they had been small children or mental cripples. He suggested that since the December 7 meeting was to be a "working business session" rather than a meeting at which provision could be made for observers, perhaps Dr. Peppe and Miss Asch might like to meet with him privately at some mutually convenient time so that they could make comments and ask questions. He said that he was "pleased to know" of their interest in NAC, that he would be "glad" to add their names to the mailing list. He said that he would "look forward to hearing" from them and hoped they would telephone him at their convenience. Finally, in a P.S., he explained that the annual meeting of NAC was open to members and invited them to join up.

Lest you think I exaggerate, here is the entire text of Mr. Handel's letter:

Dear Miss Asch and Mr. Peppe:

We are pleased to know of your interest in the work of the National Accreditation Council and we shall be happy to provide you with information about our current policies and plans. If you would like to have your names added to the list of persons who regularly receive our newsletter and other materials, we should be glad to do so.

Meanwhile, since the meeting to which you refer is a working business session of our board rather than a session at which provision can be made for observers, I should like to suggest if you wish to know more about our program that you meet with me at some other mutually agreeable time.

As you know, our standards are available in Braille and recorded. We welcome your comments and suggestions on all or any of these standards. By meeting where a mutual exchange is possible you would be in a position to raise questions and express your views regarding the matters which, as you indicate, are of vital concern to blind persons.

Please telephone for an appointment at your convenience. I look forward to hearing from you.

Sincerely yours,
Alexander F. Handel

P. S. The Annual Meeting of NAC is *open* to its affiliated members. Such affiliation is available to the National Federation of the Blind and is also open to local and state organizations of the blind. (See leaflet.)

Dr. Peppe, Miss Asch, and other blind people in New York City then went to the press. When a reporter called NAC headquarters, Miss Anne New (NAC staff member) revealed more than she realized. She was quoted in the press as follows: "You don't necessarily put a majority of TB patients on the board of a tuberculosis hospital. We know what the patient wants—to be treated as a human being and not some sort of cripple. We stress this in our standards again and again."

If Miss New does not understand why we as blind people object to her statement (and she probably doesn't), she makes our point for us. If Mr. Handel does not understand why we find his letter insulting, condescending, and unresponsive (and, again, he probably doesn't), then he only underscores what we have been saying for years. How could anything better illustrate NAC's total isolation from reality, its complete irrelevance!

It was in this atmosphere and with this background that I went to the Prince George Hotel in New York City late in the afternoon of December 6, 1971. The first event was a cocktail party held in Mr. Brandon's suite. I was met at the door with an air of hostility and resentment.

I think it is pertinent here to call attention once again to the structure of NAC, as well as to the usual format and tenor of its meetings. The American Foundation for the Blind and the Department of Health, Education, and Welfare are, of course, firmly in control. Officials of both have membership on the NAC board; and the executive director, Mr. Handel, is a former Foundation employee. In addition, several other selected agency leaders have membership. To add respectability, people of prestige from outside of the field of work with the blind have been placed on the board—public officials, business executives, university deans, labor leaders, etc. These are people of goodwill and integrity, but they are not knowledgeable concerning the problems of blindness. Obviously they take their tone and orientation from the American Foundation for the Blind and its hard core inner circle.

The atmosphere of the NAC board meetings is invariably snobbish and pretentious—almost pathetically so. The civic and business leaders on the board are made to feel that they have been asked to join an exclusive "private club," a body of national prestige. There is a good deal of socializing and no sense at all of involvement with the "gut" issues facing the blind. There is much gracious, high-toned exchange of compliment and some very businesslike talk about finances. There is considerable discussion about "professionalism" and the maintenance of high standards in work with the blind; but if these people were asked to sit down for serious conversation with a blind welfare recipient or sheltered shop employee or college student or secretary or working man or housewife, they would react with outrage and indignation—if they did not die first of shock, which seems more likely. Here are a group of people who hold themselves out to the public as the setters of standards and the givers or withholders of accreditation but who will not deign to mix with or listen to consumers. In fact, as you will shortly see, they even deny (unbelievable though that is) that the blind *are* consumers.

Under the circumstances it is not surprising that I was greeted with hostility and resentment when I entered Mr. Brandon's suite. Very shortly I was engaged in conversation with Mr. Joseph Jaworski, a lawyer from Houston, Texas. Mr. Jaworski, whose father is a top official of the American Bar Association, was recently added to the NAC board. The reason is fairly obvious. He is a person who evidences no background in or understanding of the problems of blindness but who seems to have many opinions on the subject. He spoke somewhat as follows:

"I have read all of this material about NAC which you sent to the board members, but tell me: What's the *real* complaint?"

I replied that the real complaint was just what we had said—namely, that NAC had been conceived and structured undemocratically. I told him that since the primary function of NAC was to make decisions concerning the lives of blind people, the blind themselves should have a major voice in determining what those decisions would be—and not just individual blind persons, but elected representatives of constituencies. I told him that the blind representation on NAC was only tokenism (six out of thirty-four) and that even the tokenism was largely window dressing since four of the six represented only their agencies or themselves and, by no stretch of the imagination, constituencies of blind people.

He responded in this manner: "There are black people in the city of Houston, and they do not have a majority or equal representation on the city council. Yet, the city council governs them and makes decisions about their lives."

"Yes," I told him, "but the primary purpose of the Houston City Council is not to make decisions concerning blacks, or even the blacks of Houston. Its primary purpose is to make decisions about the *people* of Houston (of whatever color); and, in the proper democratic tradition, the *people* of Houston control it entirely. This is all we are asking of NAC—that the people who are primarily concerned with and affected by its decisions have a major voice in its operation."

Mr. Jaworski did not seem to understand the distinction, nor did two or three others who were listening in. The rest of the cocktail party passed without event, as did the dinner which followed.

After dinner the board began its first business session. The question arose as to what should occur if an agency applied to NAC for accreditation and if the accreditation should be denied. Should the agency have a right to appeal to the entire NAC board, or should the decision of the subcommittee called the Commission on Accreditation be final? I suggested that the NAC board holds itself out to the public as the accrediting body and, therefore, that it cannot properly delegate final accrediting authority to a subcommittee.

At this stage Mr. Fred Storey, a sighted theater owner from Atlanta, took the floor and said: "I think we ought to follow the example of other accrediting bodies in this matter. Since Mr. Jernigan seems to know so much about it, why doesn't he tell us what other groups do?"

I responded that I didn't know what policy other accrediting groups followed. To which Mr. Storey replied: "Then, why don't you be quiet and keep your mouth shut!"

I did not answer in kind but simply told him that as long as I continued to be a member of the board, I would decide when and on what questions I would speak. In fairness let it be said here that not all of the board members approved of Mr. Storey's boorish behavior. Two or three of them came to me privately afterward and expressed apology and regret. However, not one of them stood up in the meeting to call him to task or say a single word of protest; and the Chairman, Mr. Brandon, expressed no disapproval.

After the meeting I went to the front of the room and reminded Mr. Brandon of his promise of courteous treatment and of how he had received no personal abuse but only respect at our Houston convention. His tone was one of petulant fury. He said: "Some of the board members feel that *you* have been abusive to them." He went on to say: "I was never treated so discourteously in my life as at your Houston convention."

"Mr. Brandon," I said, "can you really say that the Federation or I personally did not treat you and Mr. Handel with personal courtesy and respect?"

"Well, no," he said, "but you inflamed the audience with your speech. Besides, I don't have to listen to you, and I can't contro!

how NAC board members treat you when they disapprove of your conduct."

At this, I told Mr. Brandon that I now released him from all of his promises of courtesy and fair treatment and that I would publicize his behavior and that of the board for all to see, which I am now doing. As I walked back through the room, I was accosted by Mr. Storey. He was furiously and childishly belligerent. "I'm Fred Storey," he said, "and I just want to be sure that you know that I'm the one who told you to shut up."

"Look, my friend," I replied—

"I'm not your friend," he said. (To which I could only answer: "I believe that's the truth.") He went on: "You hide behind words like courtesy and fair play. Your real purpose is to create dissension and trouble. You have no business on this board. You are not one of us." This is what he said. I leave it to all who attended the Houston convention or who care to listen to the recordings to determine whether we treated the NAC representatives with respect. I also leave Mr. Storey's loutish behavior to stand as its own commentary, on himself and on NAC.

The next morning the NAC board assembled as usual, behind closed doors. About a dozen local blind persons (representing the organized blind of the area) appeared and sought admission as observers. The request was denied. Apparently fearing to leave these blind people unwatched, NAC stationed a staff member outside of the door to remain with them throughout the day. A delegation of four board members left the meeting to talk with them. It brought back the news that the group would be content if only two of their number could be admitted as observers, pledging to cause no disturbance or say a single word.

I offered a motion to admit the observers. Although the discussion that followed was somewhat characterized by the petty hostility and ill temper of the night before, the substantive question at issue received attention. Dr. Melvin Glasser, director of the Social Security Department of the United Auto Workers Union, said that NAC was only exercising the usual prerogative of any corporation to hold its board meetings behind closed doors. "What about your own organization, the Federation!" he said. "Its board meetings are not open. I couldn't come and attend."

"Ah, but you could!" I told him. "Come on. We would be glad to have you. Our board meetings are open to all, members and non-members alike."

My motion was defeated with only six "yes" votes and twenty "no" votes. It may be interesting to note that four of the six "yes" votes were by blind people, and one of the remaining two was by a black man. In other words two-thirds of the blind members of the board (even the agency representatives) could not bring themselves to vote no, and the black representative of the Urban League also stood to be counted, though he said not a word in defense of the motion and must, therefore, share in the shame of NAC's sorry behavior. In any case the blind were excluded, and the NAC staff member stood guard over them throughout the day. As the NAC minutes admitted, "It should be noted that the demonstrators were peaceful and courteous."

With respect to the matter of closed meetings and secret conduct of affairs, NAC is almost paranoid in its behavior. As a NAC board member, I had great difficulty in even getting a list of the names and addresses of the other members. Finally, under date of May 1, 1971, I received the list; but its form was interesting. On the top line of the first page (printed in capitals, presumably for emphasis) was the word "confidential." Admittedly one might not be proud to have people know he was associated with NAC; but why, in the name of all that is reasonable, should the very names of the NAC board members be kept secret?

Late in the morning I was asked to present the statement which Mr. Brandon had earlier invited me to give. Federationists are too familiar with my views to need them repeated here. They were presented in detail at the Houston convention and in the September, 1971, *Braille Monitor.*

Company unions serve many purposes. In this connection, the arrangement of the NAC agenda is interesting. Immediately following my presentation, Judge Reese Robrahn, president of the American Council of the Blind, delivered a statement. In general he defended NAC and said that while it had some weaknesses and imperfections, ACB supports it since ACB is a "constructive" organization. In an apparent attack upon the NFB for its criticism of NAC and its criticism of some of the so-called "professional" literature about blindness issued by the federal government and the American Foundation for the Blind, Judge Robrahn said: "Anyone with normal intelligence can dissect and distort any standard, sentence or paragraph. This, however, cannot be considered a validation of the attack on a standard, sentence or paragraph."

Judge Robrahn, by implication, defended NAC for not denying accreditation to sheltered shops paying less than the minimum wage to blind workers. Under the circumstances this is not surprising. It dovetails with the fact, which the ACB has failed to publicize, that Mr. Durward McDaniel (ACB Washington representative) now serves as a member of the board of National Industries for the Blind, the infamous organization that controls merchandise orders from the federal government to the sheltered shops. Of course, Judge Robrahn also failed to mention the appearance of Mr. McDaniel in Minnesota last year (with the support of agency officials) to organize an ACB affiliate when the Federation in that state was fighting for the rights of collective bargaining for the workers in the sheltered shop of the Minneapolis Society for the Blind. Many of the blind of the state felt that the ACB affiliate was organized as a company union, fostered by the shop management to divide the workers, break their resistance, and confuse the public.

In this same vein Mississippi agency officials told Federation organizing teams early in 1972 that they would not give lists of names of blind persons to the NFB but that they would give them to the ACB. Later, when the small Mississippi affiliate of the ACB was established, the reports of pressure for membership by agency officials were graphic and widespread.

Judge Robrahn attempted to leave the impression that the ACB is large, growing fast, and about to approach the size of the NFB. The facts, of course, are something else again. Affiliated organizations on paper are not necessarily organizations of actuality or substance.

After Judge Robrahn's presentation there was considerable reaction by the members of the board, particularly to my remarks. Of special interest were the comments of Dr. Melvin Glasser, the United Auto Workers representative. He said that NAC was not properly a social action group but a standard-setting body. I tried to point out to him that NAC could not avoid engaging in social action. By accrediting and giving its stamp of approval to a sheltered shop which pays fifty cents or less per hour to blind workers, NAC helps perpetuate the system. If its standards for determining which shops should be accredited do not take into account the wages of the workers, then those standards are irrelevant; and they constitute a form of social action, keeping the blind down and keeping them out.

What an irony that one should have to explain such matters to a representative of organized labor! Have the unions really become so management-oriented and so out of touch with ordinary people! Obviously Dr. Glasser did not stand at the gates of Ford and General Motors in the 1930s and see the hired thugs beat the workers who tried to organize and improve their condition. Neither did I, but I sat in the NAC meetings of the 1970s and watched the performance of Melvin Glasser. It is a long way from the factory gates of the thirties to the suave manner and condescending behavior of Dr. Glasser in New York, but his shame is none the less for the distance. Those early working men and women who fought and bled to establish his union, who sometimes risked their very lives for the concept of minimum wages and the right to organize, must stir in their troubled graves at the prospect of such behavior by a representative of the UAW.

Dr. Glasser also advanced a novel theory about what a "consumer" really is. He said that, as with hospitals, so with the blind. Consumers of the services of hospitals are not just the "patients" but all of the potential "patients"—therefore, everybody. Thus, the consumers in the field of work with the blind are not merely those who are now blind but also those who may become blind—in other words, everybody. Therefore, he (Dr. Glasser) is as much a consumer and has as much right to representation as you or I. Not only would it appear that the representatives of organized labor support sweatshops and management, but they've also become sophists it would seem.

I wonder how Dr. Glasser would like a dose of his own sophistry. Let us consider his union, for instance. Most people in the country are potential workers in the auto industry. Therefore, they should be eligible for membership in the UAW. They should be able to vote and hold office. After all, it is not only the actual workers but the potential workers as well who must be considered. Even the children will be potential workers someday, and certainly the senior citizens were potential workers once. So the entire American population has equal rights in the UAW. False reasoning? You bet!

Next Mr. Robert Goodpasture, former head of National Industries for the Blind, took the floor. He made a very strongly-worded attack upon me and said that he would move to censure me if a mechanism were available but that, since it was not, he would content himself with his statement. He was particularly incensed that I had made public the vote concerning the link-up between NAC and National Industries for the Blind. Well he might wish to keep that agreement secret in view of its disgraceful implications. I told him that I had never pledged to keep NAC's actions secret and that I had no intention of doing so, now or in the future. I told him that I felt the blind had a right to know what NAC was doing and to have a voice in it.

Then, I moved to have his remarks printed verbatim in the NAC minutes. He and several other board members seemed surprised at this motion and said, "What! Do *you* want what he said printed!"

"Yes," I replied. "His comments make my point better than anything I could say. Let them be printed for all to read."

As you will see, the entire text of the NAC minutes is being reproduced in the *Monitor.*

Most of the rest of the day was taken up with the usual trivia which characterizes NAC. It might be worth noting that Mr. Robert Barnett, director of the American Foundation for the Blind, came back to the meeting after lunch with this comment: "The people outside say that one reason they don't like us is because we have accredited a local New York agency which is anathema to them. Well—I guess we'll just have to change our standards." He said this with a snicker and a smirk as if to dismiss the demonstrators as kooks and nonentities. He might have done better to listen to them.

Their feelings of disgust for him and what he stands for were at least as great as his for them. As one of them later remarked: "The blacks may have their Uncle Toms, but we have our Uncle Bobs." In mid-afternoon I left, feeling that NAC was a total loss— that if anything were to be accomplished, it must be by confrontation, and not in the conference room. We are now left with two questions. What do we do next, and where do we go from here? It is to these questions that we must address ourselves.

In the first place Mr. Storey and Mr. Goodpasture are right. I have no business on the NAC Board. Mr. Storey told me: "You are not one of us!" No, thank God, I am not; and I hope I never will be. I do not see how any blind person or any true friend of the blind can keep his sense of honor and self-respect and serve on the NAC board. Therefore, I am no longer a member of NAC. I do not ask them to accept a resignation or to recognize the fact that I have quit. I simply take this occasion and this means of letting the world know that I am not part of NAC and that I do not want my name associated with it. We will now see if they add to their other faults the bad taste and boorish behavior of trying to expel me after the fact. Let them. We can give their petty action (if they choose to take it) suitable publicity.

Next we must consider NAC's presumptuous behavior in thinking it can hold closed meetings. First we tried reason and persuasion. These were spurned. The blind were not even allowed to have two silent observers in the room. NAC will regret the day. We will now adopt different tactics. NAC will probably try to conceal the time and place of future meetings, (just as it writes "confidential" on the list of the names of its board members), but we will track them down. Wherever they go and whenever they meet, we the blind will go to the doors and demand admission—not only the local blind but as many of us as possible from throughout the country. We will recruit our sighted friends and supporters to swell the numbers, and we will not take "no" for an answer. Whatever is required to make NAC responsive to the needs and problems of the blind, we will do. I have never participated in a demonstration in my life, but enough is enough. This is the time to stand and be counted.

We will send material concerning NAC to federal officials and to every member of the Congress of the United States. Our local and state affiliates and members must follow up with personal contacts and letters. Further, the blind of each state must demand that their state and local agencies not seek accreditation from NAC. If such accreditation is sought, delegations of the blind must call on the governor and go to the press. If an agency has already achieved accreditation, we must demand that the accreditation be repudiated. The blind of each locality must assume responsibility for informing their legislators, governors, public officials, and news media of the threat which NAC poses. When NAC representatives are asked to appear on programs, we must protest and demand equal time.

In short, we must treat NAC like the evil which it is. We must make it behave decently or strangle the life out of it. We must reform it or destroy it. We must have at least equal representation on its board and make it truly serve the blind, or we must kill it. It is that simple. NAC absolutely must not be allowed to take control of the lives of the blind of this country, regardless of the costs or the consequences. If we permit it, we deserve what we get. If we submit meekly while we still have the power to fight, then we are slaves, and justly so.

But, of course, we will not submit, and we will not fail. The right is on our side, and the urge to be free sustains us. December 7, 1971, is a day that will live in infamy, but the stain of that infamy will be cleansed. The shame of that day will be erased. I ask you to think carefully about what I have said. Then, if you will, come and join me on the barricades.

By the seventies the gulf between the blindness agencies supporting NAC and the organized blind themselves led to a breakdown of communication and a systematic effort by the agency coalition to freeze out blind organizations or their representatives from NAC meetings. There resulted a series of dramatic confrontations, organized by the National Federation of the Blind, which soon became a regular annual event held at the time and place of scheduled NAC conferences. In one year—the landmark year 1973—there were actually two such confrontations with NAC, the first one in Chicago attended by 300 blind people, and the second in New York attended by no less than 1,500 blind Americans from all parts of the country. Each of these massive encounters contained a story replete with drama, inspiration, and human interest—as may be seen from the successive reports on the two events published in the *Braille Monitor*. And each of the two NAC confrontations drew broad public attention—symbolized on both occasions by the interview of National Federation of the Blind President Jernigan on nationwide television, first in Chicago and then on NBC's *Today Show* in New York. Following is a collection of brief first-hand reports by participating Federationists as they appeared in the *Monitor*:

INSIDE NAC
by Ralph Sanders

On the Barricades in Chicago: A Preface

I had arrived in Chicago early Tuesday morning to serve, along with John Taylor, as an official observer during the NAC meetings on June 20-21. I was also there to work on the demonstrations by more than three hundred Federationists who had come, by every means imaginable, from throughout the country to let the members of NAC's board know just how the blind of this country feel about their kind of "accreditation without representation."

Tuesday was hectic. We were busily preparing for a press conference for Dr. Jernigan for early Wednesday morning. When the busload of Federationists from California arrived, they all pitched in. As others arrived, things began to fall into place. Finally, Don Morris and I braved the late afternoon Chicago traffic and the outrageously expensive cab fares to venture downtown to finish arrangements for the press conference.

When we returned, materials and signs were ready.

The first feeling of great excitement was apparent when those present met in Don's suite in mid-evening. Following the meeting, a few of us who had not had time earlier sought dinner. As a foreshadowing of the next two days, this was hardly finished when we learned that the Iowans, more than seventy strong, had arrived at the hotel. Again, we met to outline plans.

The next morning, Wednesday, we left a good-sized contingent at the O'Hare Inn to picket as NAC board members arrived, and the rest of us ventured downtown.

The press conference went very well. With Dr. Kenneth Jernigan speaking on behalf of the blind of this country, our position was articulately expressed.

By the time those of us who had attended the press conference arrived at Chicago's Civic Center, picket lines were up on all sides. The public of Chicago heard and read our message. With little time to spare, we finally boarded buses and cars and headed for the O'Hare Inn.

When I disappeared to take up my post as an official observer, I was comforted knowing that some three hundred blind persons manned the barricades in front of the hotel and in the central courtyard.

The Girl Scouts Do It! Why Not NAC?

With the moral support gained from knowing that the boards of directors of such groups as the American Red Cross and the Girl Scouts of America hold closed board meetings, the board of directors of NAC, meeting in Chicago on June 21, 1973, reaffirmed their policy of "openness" with closed meetings.

McCallister Upshaw, board member from Detroit, moved the resolution. Although, in the future, any guests attending a board meeting will have to be there on special invitation from the board of directors, Mr. Upshaw said he didn't feel that the two observers from the National Federation of the Blind should be asked to leave. (One has to wonder what position he would have taken if a representative from *Dialogue* magazine had not also been in attendance.)

The only dissension against the resolution came from our beloved "Uncle Bob," Bob Barnett, from the AFB. No, he wasn't opposing the idea of closed meetings. He simply felt the whole discussion was a waste of time and that NAC ought to get on with the serious items on its agenda.

Based on the quick, unanimous vote in favor of the resolution, one can assume that all of the board members thought consumer participation a waste of time.

A provision of this resolution would allow any group or person who wishes to present to the board a matter dealing with NAC to do so. It is important to note this section of the resolution for it was less than three hours later that NAC, keeping to its true colors, went against its own resolution.

John Taylor had given Peter Salmon copies of a memo from Dr. Jernigan which asked for the minutes of the NAC meeting and asked that the organized blind be permitted two observers at future meetings of the executive committee. John Taylor requested that Mr. Salmon read the memo and distribute copies, which we provided, to the members of the board. Mr. Salmon said that he would do this. Keep in mind that this occurred prior to the adoption of the resolution.

As the NAC meeting was nearing its end, with the members of the board nervously trying to get out to their planes to be jetted home to their agencies and corporations, and the memo still not having been announced, John Taylor addressed the chair to ask that it be done.

Peter Salmon replied, as my notes reflect, that he had discussed the matter with the NAC executive committee; and that it was felt that it was not an appropriate time to present the matter. A number of items in Mr. Salmon's message should raise the blood pressure of the blind of this country: This action contradicted, if not the letter then at least the professed intent of, the provision of the resolution adopted earlier by the NAC board allowing presentations to the board. In addition, there had been no mention of any meeting of the executive committee (perhaps Mr. Salmon gauged the sense of the executive committee by consulting with Uncle Bob). Finally, the sequence of events concerning the NFB memo makes it clear that the resolution barring observers from board meetings only formalized what has been the NAC policy all along—claiming "openness" while operating in secrecy.

These actions should provide final proof to any blind person still having questions about it that NAC intends to continue on its merry way, adopting "professional standards" and methods of self-evaluation despite what the blind themselves think. After all, the members of the board of NAC have devoted years to helping the blind; why shouldn't they know what the blind need?

The annual meeting of NAC took place the previous afternoon, Wednesday, June 20, at Chicago's O'Hare Inn. This was an open membership meeting attended by representatives of agencies accredited by NAC, agencies seeking accreditation, NAC sponsors, NAC board members, and most anyone else who happened along.

The most serious business conducted at this session was the election of board members to fill vacancies created because of deaths or resignations of current board members and because some board members were rotating off and could not, for one reason or another, stand for reelection.

Those elected to the board were: Howard Bleakly, formerly of Pennsylvania, now residing in Illinois, apparently appointed because of personal wealth; William T. Coppage, head of the Virginia State Agency for the Blind; Dr. John Craner, professor of educational psychology at Brigham Young University; Floyd Hammond, co-owner of a lumber company in Phoenix, Arizona, also apparently appointed because of his wealth; Howard Hanson, director of the South Dakota State Agency for the Blind; George Henderson, Jr., vice-president of Burlington Industries, Atlanta, Georgia, again apparently only for his wealth; [?] Morris, member of the Connecticut State Legislature; Bob Riley, Lieutenant Governor of Arkansas; and Lou Rives, Jr., of the Federal Department of HEW, Civil Rights Division.

Following election of board members, there was a report regarding the re-evaluation of agencies which had been accredited by NAC. This discussion led to one regarding how an agency might determine its effectiveness.

Dan Robinson, the newly elected president of NAC and a CPA with the accounting firm of Peat, Marwick, Mitchell, and Company, offered the thought that this depended in large measure on the objectives set by the agency. One must assume that, by Mr. Robinson's standards, if a rehabilitation agency sets as its goal the placement of job-hungry blind persons in a sheltered workshop, and if after a year it is determined that all job placements, regardless of skills, have been made in a workshop, then the agency is highly successful.

At 5:00 p.m. the same day there was a cocktail reception at which John Taylor and I divided in an attempt to visit personally with as many members of NAC's board as possible.

I got an opportunity to talk with many of them, including such notables as Dan Robinson and Morton Pepper. I asked Mr. Robinson to define "consumer." He had barely gotten into some sort of unintelligible definition (it went something like this: a client is not necessarily a consumer of an agency, nor does a consumer have to be a client) when he announced that his boss, presumably from Peat, Marwick, Mitchell, and Company, had arrived, and he danced out of earshot. I had the distinct pleasure of dining with Fred Storey, a millionaire NAC board member from Atlanta, Georgia, with whom all *Monitor* readers should be familiar for his previous outlandish behavior. True to form, he was just as insulting as ever toward our President, and toward the integrity of our movement. Present with us were a number of other board members including Dr. Gerry Scholl, from the University of Michigan; and George Henderson, a new board member from Atlanta. There were others there, but memory fails me.

They were generally as discourteous as they thought they could be, which I assured them was fine. Had I come to Chicago simply to enjoy the company, I would most certainly have been out on the picket lines and not in the lions' den. As with Daniel, God was kind to me, and the dinner session ended early.

The meeting of the board of directors of NAC began at 9:00 a.m. on Thursday. I have already referred to some actions taken by the board. Most of the time was devoted to nice, friendly remarks from Peter Salmon, Dan Robinson, and others, complimenting other members of the board who had either assisted in getting financial gifts from somewhere or who were leaving the board.

I think that there would be general interest in the financial report, however.

It was reported that NAC had started this year with a projected budget of $293,000 but that the budget was now reduced to $278,000—this, it was alleged, because of sound fiscal management by NAC's staff. It was further reported that by June 21, $102,000 had already been spent. Also, an additional $30,000 would have to be raised to reach the $278,000 now projected. The contribution by the Department of HEW has been dropped from $100,000 to $90,000. It was quite obvious from many comments that NAC anticipates this being the last year that federal support is offered. Perhaps they anticipated the power of the Federationists marching outside.

Great attention was given to a donation of approximately $12,000 from a Mrs. Moses and $100,000 from the Goldman Foundation, or some such group. (John Taylor and I did not receive printed copies of the materials that everyone else had before them, so we must rely on our notes.) There was much concern expressed about future sources of financing.

Keep in mind the amount of money NAC needs to operate, and consider that in 1972 fourteen agencies applied for, and eight received, accreditation. Also, remember that the agency seeking accreditation bears a great deal of the cost.

It was reported that NAC has now accredited some fifty agencies. If this sounds impressive, remember that there are more than five hundred agencies in this country.

Other weighty matters discussed included changing NAC's fiscal year from January 1 through December 31 to July 1 through June 30.

The other interesting action taken by the board was the decision to allow the executive committee to determine the time and place of the next NAC meeting.

Sitting through the NAC meetings, I kept asking myself just which of the actions they took did they not want the public to know about? Just what warranted closed, secret meetings? From what are they cowering? Apparently something must have gone on in Chicago that John Taylor and I did not attend and which they wish to keep secret.

They likened themselves unto the Red Cross and the Girl Scouts. It probably never occurred to them that both these organizations operate entirely on private funds, seeking no money from Washington, and that neither of these groups takes actions which determine policies for agencies funded by state and federal tax dollars. But then, they don't care, I'm convinced, about the public's dollars. To them it is simply a question of "professional standards."

I went to Chicago hoping that reason might prevail; that these "distinguished" gentlemen might still be able to appreciate the real importance of consumer participation.

Sitting on the DC-9, winging my way back to Arkansas, homeland of J.M. Woolley and the new NAC Board member, Lieutenant Governor Bob Riley, I recalled the events of June 20 and 21 in Chicago. It is not that these people disagree with us; it is that we speak different languages. Picture Dan Robinson's remark: the word "consumerism" has become so bastardized as to be meaningless. They really don't appreciate what most blind Americans face as a part of daily life. To them a blind American is Peter Salmon, who took occasion to talk about his chauffeur. No, NAC is not going to have a change of heart and reconsider consumer participation. Each of them will try to forget that there were several hundred blind men and women outside, protesting their actions. This they cannot do, however, for they were too aware of our presence. Little was said to acknowledge the demonstration at least—but you could read in their reactions that they were afraid: afraid that things wouldn't be as they had been in the days when the sheltered workshop was considered kind and the agencies' services weren't questioned. A number of them, I am certain, were questioning their participation in NAC. They will do a great deal of thinking in the weeks to come. One should not be too surprised to see a number of resignations in coming months.

It is interesting to note that at least one NAC board member, Bob Buckley, from Iowa, resigned prior to the board meeting. What is particularly enlightening is the fact that neither his name nor his resignation were mentioned during any of the meetings to which John Taylor and I were invited. They are scared: scared of what can happen when a board member copes with personal integrity, and scared to acknowledge resignations. The question we must answer is how scared they will become. The answer lies in our hands.

Following the end of the board meeting, John Taylor and I found our friends in force in the central courtyard, where a dialogue was underway between Don Morris, our ever present and always energetic chairman, and Bob Barnett, "Uncle Bob." But all we got was more evidence that we apparently speak different languages— we "English" and they "NAC-anese." Barnett was finally saved from his embarrassment when two of his friends dragged him from our midst. It seems that Mr. Barnett was about to miss his lunch. Oh well! It was extremely reassuring to sit in the meetings knowing that hundreds of blind friends were outside, braving the sun and fatigue to express the feelings of tens of thousands of blind people from throughout the country, loudly, but peacefully. Our honor, in contrast to NAC's deception, must stand as a symbol: something for all of us to follow in the coming months as we pursue the reformation or disappearance of NAC. Let history record just who it was that failed to meet the issues. NAC, the dirt is on your hands, not on the hands of the Red Cross, the Girl Scouts, or the blind of this country.

"OUR CAUSE GOES MARCHING ON": OUTSIDE NAC
by Don Brown

Glory, glory, Federation;
NAC needs some alteration.
Start with representation—
Our cause goes marching on.

This song, spontaneously created and sung on the Chicago picket lines, captures the spirit and mood of the three hundred

Federationists who came from all over this nation to demonstrate their concern and protest their grievances to the National Accreditation Council for Agencies Serving the Blind and Visually Handicapped. Despite NAC's efforts to keep the time and location of their summer board meeting a secret from the National Federation of the Blind until the last moment; and despite NAC's choice of the O'Hare Inn for their meeting place, a hotel hidden away from the mainstream of Chicago's activity in the airport complex; and despite the choice of the meeting time, June 20th and 21st, in the middle of a work week, the National Federation of the Blind demonstrations against NAC can only be judged an overwhelming success.

I arrived in Chicago in the middle of the afternoon on Tuesday, June 19th, the day before the first NAC meeting, and found a large group of Federationists from several states already busily at work putting together picket signs in the National Federation of the Blind demonstration headquarters located in the O'Hare Inn. The work went cheerfully and quickly, perhaps because we are becoming more proficient in sign assembly with each passing NAC demonstration. The first briefing session took place at nine o'clock that evening. Don Morris urged a standing-room-only crowd that flowed into and down the hall to keep their cool during the demonstrations and to be on our guard against whatever NAC might throw at us. Don pointed out that, based on previous experience, we could expect almost anything from NAC, and he pointed out that we had to maintain restraint at all times.

The next morning, Wednesday, June 20th, Federationists clambered aboard two Greyhound buses; and, leaving a large delegation of demonstrators behind to man picket lines at the front of the hotel, we headed for the downtown Chicago Civic Center. We were greeted there by a large delegation of Illinois Federationists swelling our ranks to well over one hundred enthusiastic demonstrators. We stationed ourselves on the four corners of the block, at the doorways to the Civic Center, with the remainder of us circling the block. All of us carried signs and handed out thousands of handbills to the public. Deep concern and indignation were often expressed by those Chicagoans we had the opportunity to reach that morning. Later that morning President Jernigan arrived from a successful press conference and joined us "at the barricades." Carrying a picket sign, President Jernigan marched around the block. The number and enthusiasm of the Federationists at the Civic Center that morning can be measured by the number of Federationists who attempted to give President

Jernigan and each other handbills. President Jernigan spoke to an interested public by microphone from a platform, eloquently expressing our cause and what they, as concerned citizens, could do to help create an atmosphere in which NAC would be responsive to the needs of the blind.

At noon we boarded the Greyhound buses for the bumper-to-bumper trip back to the O'Hare Inn. Three picket lines were maintained throughout the afternoon and evening of June 20 and the morning of June 21. Two picket lines were at the front of the hotel, one on either side of the hotel's front entrance, while a third group maintained a vigil around the hotel swimming pool. The NAC board meeting room was adjacent to this courtyard area. We walked for hours, singing songs, chanting slogans, and talking to hotel guests.

The Chicago press was on the scene throughout Wednesday afternoon. Newspaper reporters talked to Federationists from all over the country while newspaper photographers captured on film the number of demonstrators for their reading public. Television cameras and microphones were in view that afternoon recording the action and enthusiasm of the festive but disciplined singing and chanting marchers.

The picket lines were disbanded at 9:00 p.m. Wednesday evening, and we returned to the National Federation of the Blind demonstration headquarters for a briefing session at which Don Morris commended the gathered Federationists for their enthusiasm, hard work, and self-discipline.

The next morning at 8:00 a.m., a Greyhound bus carried a group to the airport terminal where they carried signs and gave handbills to the passing public. Thursday morning the press evidenced their interest by their presence, many staying on the scene longer than some of the NAC board members themselves. The bulk of the Federationists were on the three hotel picket lines by 8:00 a.m. Thursday morning. By midmorning the bus had returned from the airport complex and the largest group of Federation demonstrators of the two day meeting began a vigil for the emergence of the NAC board members from their meeting. We all gathered in the inner courtyard adjacent to the NAC board meeting room and softly sang and chanted songs, quietly standing and holding our signs. The NAC board meeting dispersed at 12:30 and the successful National Federation of the Blind demonstration ended at 1:00 p.m. We returned to the National Federation of the Blind demonstration headquarters where we were briefed on the closed NAC board meeting by our two observers.

By any measure, the demonstration was a success. One is moved by the dedication of Federationists who traveled thousands of miles at tremendous personal expense and inconvenience, either individually or in groups, as the National Federation of the Blind of California and the National Federation of the Blind of Iowa did by chartered bus. The solidarity of the group, its self-discipline and enthusiasm were an impressive testimony to those who participated. The impact that we had on Chicago can be measured by the extensive and favorable press coverage that we were given by the local news media. The impact that we had on NAC can be measured by the open hostility that we encountered in many NAC board and staff members. This hostility is witness to our effectiveness for it accurately reflects the feeling of many NACsters that their position of credibility in the eyes of Congress, the blind, and the public has been shaken, and that they are on the run, and that they know that the National Federation of the Blind will continue to track NAC.

REFLECTIONS OF A RANK-AND-FILE PICKETER
by Nancy Smalley

Where does a "Freedom Bus" go? What is a "NACster"? On June 17, 1973, thirty-one California Federationists boarded their bus and left for Chicago. This "Freedom Bus" was chartered by the National Federation of the Blind of California and was financed largely through donations from California's fifty local affiliates. The enthusiastic travelers paid for the rest of the trip out of their own pockets.

The destination of this bus was Chicago's O'Hare Inn, or "NAC-land." NAC, the National Accreditation Council for Agencies Serving the Blind and Visually Handicapped, was holding its semi-annual conference, and Federationists from all over the nation wanted to be present to voice their disapproval of NAC's acts. Giving NAC accreditation to sheltered workshops which pay far below minimum wage standards, for example, is not met with a great deal of acceptance by most blind people. The organized blind have no voice in this so-called accreditation although they are most assuredly affected by it. However, once an agency receives this accreditation it is eligible for federal funds from the Department of HEW. Approximately $600,000 of taxpayers' money has been used to date. Blind people feel that if they, the consumers of the services of these agencies, can voice no opinions regarding these services, then federal funds should not be used for such a program. Thus, hundreds of Federationists felt compelled to personally protest the activities of NAC. The California "Freedom Bus," with its load of weary travelers, pulled into Chicago Tuesday morning, June 19. But these Californians had come to work; and, after a shower, a change of clothes, and a bite to eat, they were busy at work assembling picket signs in the headquarters suite. Phones were capably handled by Judy Boyle [who is multi-handicapped] during most of the Chicago stay. The picket sign assembly line went on into the evening, but finally the last one was completed and stored for easy availability. That night a briefing session was held relating to events for the following day. Californians greeted and mingled with Federationists from other states. Don Brown and Arthur Eick had flown in and joined the group. Mr. Eick, in his eighties, proved there was no generation gap in this high-spirited group which was composed of college students and right on up the ladder of accumulating years.

Wednesday morning found our group back on the "Freedom Bus," but this time only to take the short trip into Chicago's Civic Center Plaza. Hundreds of Federationists carried picket signs and passed out handbills all morning at the Plaza. To further interest and educate the public, Dr. Jernigan and other blind leaders used the Plaza's public-address system to explain our cause. Around noon, picketers, picket signs, and handbills were back on the bus heading toward "NAC-land" where "NACsters" had gathered.

Bob Acosta, ably assisted by Don Brown, was our committee member from California to help coordinate the demonstration. Organized picketing continued throughout Wednesday afternoon and on into late evening while the NAC banquet was in progress. This degree of organization could not have been accomplished without a great deal of hard work on the part of many people. Don Morris, of Iowa, and Ralph Sanders, of Arkansas, were on top of the situation at all times. Dr. Jernigan himself was seen with a picket sign in his hand. Bob received complete cooperation from the Californians, and Bob's own voice could often be heard leading our people in the chant, "NAC, No! Blind Rights, Yes!"

While a majority of people were at the Plaza Wednesday morning, a group remained to cover the O'Hare Inn. This group was most ably organized and overseen by Kathy Northridge and Mary Catalano.

When Thursday morning rolled around the rather tired picketers were back in line, picket signs and handbills in hand, but still enthusiastically singing and chanting. By now most of our people had sunburned faces and blistered feet. Marching on a picket line is no easy task. Braving the elements such as the sun and wind takes a lot of strong will and fortitude.

Federationists were on hand until the final NAC meeting adjourned. But NAC would not talk to us, with the exception of Mr. Talbert, who met briefly with the Californians. John Taylor was not allowed to give his short statement. John and Ralph Sanders surely attended those meetings as silent observers. Bob Barnett, from the American Foundation for the Blind, talked briefly with some of us as he left the meeting but refused to see the seriousness of the matter. Were all our efforts going down the drain? Was NAC completely unfazed by our presence? I think not. They were, indeed, aware of our presence; and they must have realized we are not about to give up the fight. The National Federation of the Blind is going to pursue this matter to the finish.

Thursday afternoon, June 21, the Californians once again boarded their "Freedom Bus" and braced themselves for the long trip back to Los Angeles. Would there be a letdown on the return trip after all the events of the past week? No indeed; there was not. This hearty crew had just begun to fight. Earl Carlson was a mass of bandaids covering the blisters on his feet that he received while acting as messenger throughout the large complex of the O'Hare Inn. Ed Crespin was another who covered the area, assisting people and substituting for picketers needing a break.

A feeling of happiness, success, and togetherness existed throughout the group. Repeated choruses of "Glory, Glory, Federation" could be heard sporadically during the trip. Although the trip was long and tiring, it was relieved with jokes and stories, courtesy of Al Gil and others, singing, and a general good time until the final stop where we parted company.

NAC: CONFRONTATION IN NEW YORK

The Federation's most historic event, aside from its founding, occurred most appropriately on Dr. tenBroek's birthday, Friday, July 6. At about mid-morning a foundation-shaking (American Foundation for the Blind-shaking) rollcall took place. As the President of the National Federation of the Blind called the names of the states, the delegates arose and made their way to their appointed places, secured state standards and picket signs, and marched the half mile, two-by-two, and four-by-four, on "the sidewalks of New York" with dignity, pride, and great decorum, to fill busy Madison Avenue between 27th and 28th Streets, curb to curb, chanting "Fifty thousand blind people/Can't be wrong," and "We can speak/For ourselves." There, before the building which houses NAC, the President of the National Federation of the Blind presided over the hanging of NAC in effigy and its burial in a huge wooden coffin (which had been carried in the line of march by some of the Federation's finest and "heaviest") with such pomp and circumstance as the occasion deserved. President Jernigan addressed the crowd and delivered the following eulogy:

Eulogy for NAC

They came, they said, to help the blind—the poor, unfortunate blind. They came, they said, to help the agencies—the many agencies who help the blind. They came, they said, to establish standards to improve the services provided to the blind—the poor, unfortunate blind.

Instead, they came and they hurt the blind. They came, and they gave sanction to agencies which provide substandard services to the blind. They came, but they came with repression, with bad faith, and with attempts at political control of the blind.

In the beginning there was the American Foundation for the Blind. And the American Foundation begat COMSTAC. And COMSTAC begat NAC. They came from the welfare establishment, and they came from the dens of political power. They came, and they gave us NAC—NAC, which was conceived in sin and born of corruption.

And when we, the blind, saw this NAC and learned of its ways, we came saying, "NAC is not competent to speak for us—at best, it can speak with us."

But they would not listen. NAC would not listen. The American Foundation for the Blind would not listen. When we said, "Let us take part," they closed their doors. When we said, "Let us speak for ourselves," they closed their ears.

Finally we came marching—marching to take part, marching to be heard, marching to be free, marching to be treated like human beings. And when we came marching, they closed their eyes. They locked us out, and they turned us out, but we are here today—because they cannot turn us off. We have tried every channel of communication to bring about reform of NAC. It is not that NAC cannot hear us: They don't want to hear us.

But they will hear us. They will know we are here today—in the largest gathering of blind people ever assembled in the history of the world. And whenever and wherever NAC meets again, we will be there.

NAC is not alone in the harm it has done to the blind, for some of the blame must be shared by officials of the Department of Health, Education, and Welfare, who have given NAC over $600,000 of the taxpayers' money.

We have come too far to forget the American Foundation for the Blind and its role in creating NAC. We have come too far to forget the role of Peat, Marwick, Mitchell, and Company and other wealthy corporations in supporting NAC. We have come too far to forget, for the hurt to blind people has been great.

We have come today to confront NAC. We have come to confront its secrecy and its refusal to talk with us. We have come seeking redress of our grievances and the righting of our wrongs. If NAC will not listen to us, then the Congress will listen; and the public will listen. Our cause is just.

We have come to assert our independence. Hear us, NAC. Hear us clearly. We shall determine our own destinies and be free from you and all that you represent. We have come here to put NAC aside. We have come to put away that which has hurt us and replace it with our own freedom.

The communications media were there in force and in all their forms. The ubiquitous Miss New, NAC's all-around "coverup girl," came as usual to dissuade the press, radio, and TV people from listening to us with her familiar phrase "but it is all a misunderstanding"—on the part of the blind, of course. It would seem that the blind don't appreciate NAC's efforts to run their lives for them. There were many on-the-spot interviews with President Jernigan and other Federationists.

The ceremonies over, most of the marchers returned to the convention. However, several hundred boarded waiting buses for the ride uptown to the headquarters offices of Peat, Marwick, Mitchell, and Company. The huge building on Park Avenue is set well back from the street. It was noon hour, the weather was pleasant, and many people were out on the building's large plaza.

It was obvious that our group was expected. The first Federationists off the bus were greeted by a well-groomed young man who asked seemingly innocent questions spurred by curiosity as he walked the picket line with the marchers. Groups of men in twos or threes approached others with questions about the reason for the picketing, who the marchers were, whom they represented, what the Federation had against NAC, what had Dan Robinson done, and such like. All were answered, politely and in full.

While the pickets marched and chanted in front of the building, a delegation of Federationists, led by Don Morris of Iowa and Ralph Sanders of Arkansas, went up to the offices of Peat, Marwick, Mitchell, and Company to see Mr. Robinson. Needless to say, they were not received by NAC's new president, and his emissary was anything but polite; in fact, he was rude and threatening. But whether there was direct communication or not, NAC got the message.

This great effort to carry our case to NAC and the public would not have been possible without the complete cooperation of New York's public officials and especially its fine police force. The convention expressed its feelings by unanimously adopting the following Resolution:

Resolution 73-15

WHEREAS, the National Federation of the Blind conducted the largest demonstration of blind people in the history of the world to protest against the harmful actions of the National Accreditation Council; and

WHEREAS, this protest demonstration involved the movement of upwards of two thousand demonstrators across midtown Manhattan with attendant disruption of traffic; and

WHEREAS, the complete assistance of the New York City Police Department was rendered with utmost courtesy, efficiency, and friendliness: Now therefore,

BE IT RESOLVED by the National Federation of the Blind in convention assembled this 6th day of July, 1973, in the City of New York, that this organization instruct its President to convey our heartfelt gratitude and deep appreciation for the invaluable services rendered by the Police Department of the City of New York; and

BE IT FURTHER RESOLVED that a special message of thanks be given to Captain Wiener of the New York Police Department who showed more devotion and understanding in two hours than NAC has shown during its entire existence; and

BE IT FURTHER RESOLVED that a copy of this Resolution be delivered to the Honorable John V. Lindsay, Mayor of the City of New York.

WE DID NOT GIVE UP AND GO HOME
by Shirley Lebowitz

The first time I ever carried a picket sign was in December, 1972, when the NAC board of directors held a meeting at the Prince George Hotel in New York City. I joined a small but determined group of Federationists to demonstrate for meaningful consumer representation on the policy-making board of NAC. In spite of the cold, strong, winter winds, we did not put down our picket signs, give up and go home. We spoke then, but NAC did not listen.

Six-and-a-half months later we organized another demonstration. This time there was a longer line of marchers at the O'Hare Inn in Des Plaines, Illinois, and in spite of the blazing hot summer sun, we did not put down our picket signs, give up, and go home. Because of the lack of pedestrian traffic at the O'Hare Inn, we could not speak to the "man on the street" but we came to be heard by NAC, and they did hear us, but once again, they did not listen.

Two weeks later on July 6, 1973, an army of Federationists from every state affiliate joined us as we moved the barricades to the doorstep of the NAC offices at 79 Madison Avenue, New York. Once again, we were seen and heard, and, just as before, NAC did not listen. "When will they ever learn?"

During the seventies, and beyond, the organized blind kept up a drumbeat of activity—marches; confrontations; TV, radio, and press interviews; *Monitor* articles; and more—protesting the policies and practices of NAC and its companion agencies. The persistent campaign was not long in bearing fruit; by the end of the decade NAC had not only lost credibility within the blindness system, it had lost the government funding (provided by Health, Education, and Welfare) and also had lost increasing numbers of agencies no longer interested in its accreditation. Gradually but steadily NAC saw its vaunted power reduced and its authority and reputation put in question. Although it struggled on into the eighties, clinging to its remnant of clients and cursing the name of the organized blind, NAC ceased to be a major impediment in the path of the movement and became instead a minor nuisance.

Among the instrumental factors in the decline of NAC was an authoritative critical analysis of the agency—in the form of "An Open Letter to Directors of Agencies Serving the Blind Concerning N.A.C. and its Accrediting Practices"—which was published in the *Braille Monitor* in 1978 (August-September issue). This comprehensive report, written in scholarly language and painstakingly documented, reviewed the history of NAC with reference particularly to certain key cases which had gained public notoriety during the decade of the seventies (those of NAC-supported sheltered shops in Cleveland and Minneapolis, plus a state agency in Florida). The full text of the *Monitor* report follows:

AN OPEN LETTER TO DIRECTORS OF AGENCIES SERVING THE BLIND CONCERNING N. A. C. AND ITS ACCREDITATION PRACTICES

The purpose of this letter is to provide information about the National Accreditation Council for Agencies Serving the Blind and Visually Handicapped (NAC)—information we hope will cause you to consider seriously whether NAC accreditation is the way to achieve or maintain high standards of service within your agency. The information is presented to you by the National Federation of the Blind, the nation's largest consumer organization of the blind, themselves. Because the Federation has been the collective voice of the blind for nearly 40 years, and because in that time we have been associated with most of the advances in programs and civil rights for the blind, we feel that we can speak about "quality services" with some weight. Yet because we have been at odds with the National Accreditation Council for more than ten years, and because our efforts to reform NAC have led NAC's officers to characterize the Federation, among other things, as the "negative forces of misguided, counterproductive elements," some agency directors have come to regard the National Federation of the Blind as just one side in a political struggle.

Recognizing that this intense controversy has tended to call into question the objectivity of both NAC and the National Federation of the Blind, this letter will rely as little as possible on judgments. It will concentrate on evidence from sources outside of the Federation—from court judgments, from federal investigations, and from people in the field unconnected with the National Federation of the Blind or NAC. This sort of evidence has been piling up for a number of years. We believe there is no longer a question about the worth and purpose of NAC accreditation.

It will be necessary to provide a context for the information we wish to present; and it will be necessary to make a number of judgments in order to do so. These judgments—particularly those relating to events and trends now some ten or more years in the past—could be supported as amply as more recent events. We shall not do so, since one of our purposes here is to state the case briefly. The past, except as a general background, is unnecessary to prove our case. Discount our judgments if you wish to; the events of the last few years speak clearly, and they are verified by evidence that cannot be discounted.

Background

It is generally accepted that the last fifty years have seen a revolution in attitudes toward the blind. Before that— stretching back through history—there was an unquestioned belief that the blind are helpless, suited only for custody in special institutions or, at best, for work in a few handcraft trades (such as chair caning and broom making) or the simple, repetitive tasks performed in the traditional sheltered workshop.

This view of blindness now is recognized by most people as limiting and obsolete. With the development of alternative techniques to overcome a lack of sight, the blind have emerged from their age-old isolation and joined the mainstream of society. The trend toward emphasizing ability rather than disability took some getting used to, but gradually most of those in the field of work with the blind embraced it. Certainly the blind welcomed a philosophy that freed them from their rocking chairs and asylums.

But as happens when any major change in attitudes occurs, there was opposition to the new philosophy of blindness. This was a remarkable thing: Why should those who had devoted their lives to helping the blind resent the progress of the blind toward independence and full participation? The answer is a very common and human one. Some professionals were unable to see beyond their financial and psychological investment in the status quo.

Within the last five years, a questionnaire was distributed to the administrators of sheltered workshops in the country. Near the end appeared the question: "Do you find that your blind clients are less grateful today for what you are doing for them than they were ten years ago?" This is the psychological investment in a nutshell. A few decades ago, an agency director put it a different way when he said: "To dance and sing, to play and act, to swim, bowl and rollerskate, to work creatively in clay, wood, aluminum or tin, to make dresses, to join in group readings or discussions, to have group entertainments and parties, to engage in many other activities of one's own choosing—this is to fill the life of anyone with the things that make life worth living."

In answer to this, Jacobus tenBroek, founder of the National Federation of the Blind, replied: "Are these the vital channels of self-expression for you? Are these the indispensable ingredients that make life worth living? Or are these only the minor and peripheral touches that lend variety to a life well-filled with more substantial things—such as a job, a home, and the rights and responsibilities of citizenship?"

Some professionals understandably felt that the blind were biting the hand that had fed them for centuries. The blind didn't see it this way; they felt that an establishment had grown up that fed on their dependency, that depended on their dependency.

The financial investment of some professionals in the old attitudes is even easier to understand. Work with the blind has long been a place for wealthy philanthropists to direct their contributions and their friends and cousins. Salaries for blindness professionals are high, the emotional rewards are great, the public acclaim for those who enter the field gratifying.

A typical case is the traditional lighthouse or sheltered workshop. Blind workers even today may be paid as little as 25 percent of the minimum wage. Shop managers, on the other hand, are usually paid generous salaries and work with excellent security and in comfortable conditions. Often a good deal of social recognition goes along as an added benefit (if only in the social mixing with the wealthy who support the lighthouses). But when the blind begin to discuss extending minimum wage laws to the shops, or talk about unions, or demand places on the shop board of directors, it is seen by management (and rightly so) as a threat to their traditional perquisites.

This fear of change and resistance to new attitudes was widespread in the 1940s, at the time of the founding of the National Federation of the Blind. But it has largely died away as professionals saw the stunning results of the new ideas. As the blind gained access to education, to the common callings and professions, it became obvious that work with the blind could be a much more positive and truly rewarding endeavor than it had been in the old days of custodialism.

To some, though, this whole trend was a pill so bitter that it could not be swallowed. The agency with the greatest investment—both financially and psychologically—in the old system was the venerable American Foundation for the Blind (AFB), a New York agency that came close to dominating the field in the early part of this century and which had amassed vast financial resources as a result of its pre-eminence. It was involved in some of the early advances in technology for the blind; it virtually owned Helen Keller (it has used her name to raise millions and millions of dollars); in Congress and literally around the world, the AFB was regarded as the ultimate authority on blindness.

As the Federation grew (concurrent with the change in public attitudes toward the handicapped), the American Foundation's domination of the field declined. But unlike most of the other traditional agencies, the Foundation was unwilling to adapt itself to the new situation. It resisted the notion that blind people could speak for themselves; indeed, it labeled their insistence on doing so a form of neurosis growing out of their blindness. Gradually, professionals and agencies in the field who, for whatever reason, found the new independence of the blind inconvenient looked to the Foundation for support. The American Foundation for the Blind became a bastion of the old style custodialism.

The Origins of NAC

This division in the field and the Foundation's waning prestige led to the establishment of the National Accreditation Council.

In the early 1960s, the AFB announced the formation of a Commission on Standards and Accreditation for Services for the Blind (COMSTAC). Later this became the National Accreditation Council. The ostensible reason for COMSTAC and NAC was laudable enough. As expressed in 1976 by Louis Rives, Jr., NAC's current president, this was as follows:

> The standards and accreditation system of which NAC is the voice came from within the field—from the experience of blind people, from government and other suppliers of services to blind people, and from the public which supports agencies and schools for the blind. All agreed there should be some objective way to determine whether an agency or school is doing a good job. In 1967 they joined in creating NAC to provide this objective determination through a voluntary system of accreditation.

The broad consensus Mr. Rives refers to is a public relations fantasy. The American Foundation for the Blind believed it already represented such a consensus; NAC was an attempt to impose the AFB's views on the rest of the field.

There were no open forums to develop standards. Meetings were held that were advertised as having this purpose; but those who attended were handed standards that had been formulated beforehand. Criticisms of this procedure and the standards themselves were ignored. Indeed, those who were thought to be hostile to the AFB were turned away at the door. (In 1973 the National Federation of the Blind prepared three publications documenting the early history of NAC. These are available to anyone who wishes to explore the matter further.)

The origins of NAC, the make-up of its board of directors, and the trading of staff between NAC and the AFB make NAC's claim to represent an objective consensus untenable. Even without all this, NAC's financial history removes all doubt in the matter. In 1968, according to NAC documents, $70,000 out of a projected budget of $154,034 was to come from the AFB; most of the rest came from a $75,000 grant by the U.S. Department of Health,

Education, and Welfare. In succeeding years, particularly after HEW cut off its funding, the AFB increased its contributions to make up for other losses of income. In fiscal 1977 (according to the NAC Annual Report), out of a total income of $301,962, the AFB provided $188,000.

Nor has the Foundation's support been limited to direct grants. When a small band of National Federation of the Blind members broke away in the early 1960s to form the American Council of the Blind (ACB), the Foundation courted the group, spurring it to attack anyone who questioned the value of NAC accreditation. More recently the Foundation began making direct grants to the ACB. Immediately after these grants began, the ACB's magazine, the *Braille Forum*, began printing NAC-originated attacks on the National Federation of the Blind. ACB staff members have been put on the boards of NAC and the Foundation.

During the early years of NAC, despite Mr. Rives's statement about "voluntary" accreditation, the blind witnessed a variety of attempts by the AFB to pass legislation or guidelines at both the state and federal level to condition government funding on NAC accreditation.

Concerning the NAC standards themselves, at first all that could be said was that they placed an overwhelming emphasis on ensuring that agency staff would enjoy job security and their traditional privileges. The standards were also concerned with the details of the agency's bureaucratic structure. The agency's effect on its blind clients—on whether they were being prepared for independent participation in society—was a secondary, and apparently irrelevant, consideration.

Irrelevant as the NAC standards were to the real concerns of blind people, it soon became clear that they were irrelevant for another reason. It became clear that NAC accreditation did not depend on an agency's adhering to the standards. Our reasons for concluding this are discussed later; but there is no reason to doubt that it is so: NAC officials concede the point.

At the NAC annual meeting held in November, 1977, in Phoenix, an observer asked about the discrepancy between the practices of accredited agencies and the language of the standards. Wesley Sprague, chairman of NAC's Commission on Standards, replied that "every agency has—when they're reaccredited or accredited—

has to abide by the standards of the various sections as pertain to them." But then Richard Bleecker, NAC's executive director, interrupted to explain:

> Excuse me, as I may add a postscript to the answer. I want to be complete in responding to Mr. Parker. And I would love nothing more than to concede the correctness. However, I must point out that not every accredited agency is able to meet every standard. And meeting every standard is not a precondition to accreditation. In fact, no accredited agency as yet meets every standard. Accreditation and standards are a direction, and it's a process of improvement. To be accredited, the agency must either meet the standards or have an awareness and commitment to attempt to meet them.

To which we would simply add that if the "precondition" to accreditation is only a "commitment to attempt to meet" the standards, accreditation becomes meaningless.

The Decline of NAC

What must an agency do, then, to gain NAC accreditation? It must give public support to the American Foundation for the Blind and NAC, or some of the agency's directors must also be members of the AFB or NAC boards. To understand why NAC would adopt such a practice (and we believe the fact that it has will not be in question by the end of this letter), we must look at the setbacks NAC has received in the last few years.

At first NAC accomplished a respectable number of accreditations each year. In 1970 (the year NAC had its highest net gain), 16 agencies were added to its list. At that time NAC had high hopes of continuing this rate of growth. According to a 1974 report on NAC by the U.S. General Accounting Office (GAO): "During the SRS team visit in March, 1973, NAC told the team its fiscal year 1978 projected budget was $379,000 and an estimated total of 200 or about 50% of the approximately 400 organizations serving the blind and visually handicapped would by then be accredited."

Yet even when this statement was made, professional and agency support for NAC was dropping away. In fiscal 1975 the net gain was four agencies; in fiscal 1976 it was five; and in fiscal 1977 it was only three. Thus by the end of 1977, instead of nearing its projection of 200, NAC had only 67 accredited agencies. (We use the term "net gains" because during this period several agencies made the decision not to renew their accreditation when it expired.)

Another setback occurred in 1973 when an ad hoc committee of the American Library Association's Round Table on Library Services to the Blind stated: "It is the consensus of the committee members that the NAC standards as they pertain to library service for the blind are no longer relevant." Following this, NAC withdrew its library standards and no longer accredits libraries.

A major setback was the loss of HEW funding, which in the early 1970s accounted for roughly half of NAC's budget. The GAO report discusses the termination of the grant that provided this funding: "The Director, Division of Project Grants Administration, SRS, told us that the NAC grant was recommended for phase-out in 1975 by the Division of Project Grants Administration because of:

"- NAC's poor performance record;

"- Low acceptance of NAC accreditation by blind agencies.

"- A low cost-benefit ratio."*

(*This GAO report, made in response to a request from Congressman John Brademas and published in September 1974, has been talked about widely by NAC and represented as clearing NAC of all the criticisms brought against it. As will be clear from the few portions already quoted, the report simply recounts what GAO investigators were told by the people they talked to. The GAO found no financial malfeasance—which is all that an "accounting office" can determine—but then no financial wrongdoing had been alleged. The problems with NAC have nothing to do with accounting.)

Two other occurrences from this period (1973-1975) are also represented by NAC officials as absolving it from criticism. One is an HEW study done in 1973, the other is a statement inserted in the *Congressional Record* by Congressman Brademas. The HEW study was made by a panel heavily weighted toward NAC. One of the panel members was Louis Rives (now president of NAC and even then a strong partisan of the agency). Another member was Arthur Korn, who had been involved in the organization of COM-STAC, NAC's predecessor.

The circumstances surrounding the Brademas statement speak to NAC's credibility. Speaking in July, 1975, NAC executive director Richard Bleecker said: "You may remember Congressman Brademas as the one who called on the U.S. General Accounting Office, the official investigative arm of the Congress, to make a thorough study of these charges and accusations [against NAC], a study which, as you know, did not sustain them. Since then, Mr. Brademas has been looking with great care at this whole thing to see what the fuss is all about. And, I am pleased to report, he has recently inserted a statement in the *Congressional Record* that uncompromisingly recognizes NAC as a responsible and effective standards-setting, accrediting body."

However, when the Federation contacted Mr. Brademas's office, we learned that the statement in question had been prepared by NAC and that Mr. Brademas inserted it in the *Record* as a courtesy gesture. As Mr. Brademas himself later wrote: "I am troubled to learn that my insertion of a report of NAC's programs has been construed as singling out for recognition of NAC's accreditation process. Rather, I intended my statement and the report of NAC's work to be included in the *Congressional Record* as information for those interested in standards for agencies that serve visually handicapped people."

Finally, NAC relies heavily on the fact that the U.S. Office of Education has NAC on a list of "Nationally Recognized Accrediting Agencies and Associations," a list which includes accrediting bodies for everything from embalming to landscaping. Yet in the summer of 1976, when NAC applied for a grant from the Bureau of Education for the Handicapped—the section of the Office of Education with expertise in blindness—the proposal was rejected. All of these instances show what is generally recognized in any event—that approval or disapproval by the government is a political process and that most government reports have in them something for everyone.

NAC-Accredited Agencies

We now turn to an examination of a few of the agencies determined by NAC to be providing quality services to the blind. Our general thesis is that the test of an accrediting system is not its public statements but the programs it approves. In choosing examples we have focused on agencies whose problems go beyond differences of philosophy.

In 1972, the blind of Florida received services from the NAC-accredited Bureau of Blind Services (this has now been reorganized into the Office of Services for the Blind). It was the state licensing agency for the federal Randolph-Sheppard program (under which blind persons have a priority to operate vending facilities on federal property). As the state licensing agency, the Bureau had responsibility for managing the support services for the vending facilities, a number of which were located at Cape Canaveral.

A state licensing agency may take (or "set aside") a portion of vendors' earnings for certain purposes that are narrowly defined in federal law. These include (1) maintenance and replacement of equipment; (2) purchase of new equipment; (3) management services (in other words, the payment of the salaries of stand supervisors); and (4) assuring a fair minimum return to other operators. The law makes it clear there may be no exceptions to these categories, and it says that the "set-aside" must be "reasonable." In Florida, the Bureau determined that it was reasonable to take 6-1/2 percent of the vendors' gross profits. If a vendor were making a net profit of about 20 percent, this set-aside would amount to one-third of his income.

But in 1972, it emerged that the Bureau of Blind Services was withholding another five percent of gross profits from the vending operations at Cape Canaveral (or about another twenty percent of net profits) and transmitting this money to the recreation fund of the Cape's sighted space workers. When the local newspapers publicized this illegal additional set-aside, the Bureau stopped withholding it. This, however, was just the beginning. The stand supervisor then went to the vendors with a consent form authorizing the Bureau to withhold two percent of gross profits. When one of the vendors refused to sign this, he was told he would lose his vending stand. The vendor, James Parkman, went to court.

At this point the Bureau changed its mind. The suit was dropped after the Secretary of the Department of Health and Rehabilitative Services (of which the Bureau was a part) issued the following directive:

> (A) There shall be no approach of any kind whatsoever to any blind person working in the vending stand program by any employee or agent of the Bureau of Blind Services, including any blind person working in the vending stand program, regarding contributions to the NASA Exchange Council or to any other organization, group, or

fund of any kind except for standard practices such as asking state employees if they would consider contributing to the United Fund or participating in group insurance.

(B) There shall be no action taken by the Bureau of Blind Services, its agents, or employees, including blind persons working in the vending stand program, adverse to the interest of any blind person working in the vending stand program because of his refusal to contribute to any organization, group, or fund, including, but not limited to, the NASA Exchange Council, United Fund, group insurance, nor shall any such refusal be considered in any manner by Bureau of Blind Services with regard to any action adverse to the interests of any blind person working in the vending stand program, including, but not limited to, transfer and termination.

The practice that this directive ended indicated an insensitivity to the rights of the blind vendors. It also, of course, worked a severe financial hardship on them. The blind of Florida considered that it was not an example of "quality service." Whether it was or not, it undoubtedly was a violation of federal law. Throughout this time, the Bureau of Blind Services was accredited by NAC. Despite the Bureau's violation of the law and its coercion of the blind vendors to stifle their complaints, the agency was judged by NAC to be maintaining a high standard of service.

The case of the NAC-accredited Cleveland Society for the Blind is similar to the one discussed, but it goes much further.

In the early 1970s, the Cleveland Society was the so-called "nominee agency" for the Randolph-Sheppard program in Ohio (that is, the state licensing agency contracted with the Society to manage the vending program). Each year the Cleveland Society received a part of its operating budget from the United Torch Services.

The problems with the Society's management of the vending program began to come to light in the fall of 1972, when Cleo Dolan, executive director of the Society, sent a memorandum to the vendors stating that "we are anticipating and expecting the [snack bar] managers to participate in the United Torch Service campaign at the same degree as our regular staff persons....We have tentatively agreed among all of us who are so vitally involved in the United Torch Services campaign this year, that any gifts less than one- half of one percent of the total earnings of a worker would not be an acceptable pledge." Once again, we point out that this 1/2 percent was of gross earnings, or several times that in net earnings.

When the vendors protested the peremptory tone of Mr. Dolan's memo, he wrote back, saying: "We are concerned that we have undoubtedly not provided sufficient strong administrative guidelines and have attempted to involve those who are employed to a greater degree, which apparently has weakened our program."

Mr. Dolan concluded by stating: "Again, I personally doubt that you failed to get the message that we were attempting to communicate, and I think your interpretation was correct. Namely, we do feel strongly about the support of the United Torch Services and we doubt that further elaboration on the reasons should be necessary to this particular group."

Earlier we discussed the amounts that may be "set aside" by an agency administering the Randolph-Sheppard program. Shortly after these memos from Mr. Dolan, the Cleveland Society began deducting an additional set-aside which it called a "service charge." At this point the vendors hired a lawyer and began looking into the Society's management practices. The result was a lawsuit claiming that the Society had, over the years, withheld funds in excess of $1 million "for purposes other than those permitted by the Randolph-Sheppard Vending Stand Act."

This was not the only irregularity found in the Society's management of the vending program. In order to operate a vending facility, a blind person had to sign a contract granting the Society the right to summarily terminate his or her job if the Society decided the vendor had violated any of the contract's terms. These terms covered such matters as diet, dress, bathing habits, use of body deodorants, changes of underwear, and nightly sleep—most of them in such discretionary terms that the vendors were at the complete mercy of Mr. Dolan. Nothing in the Randolph-Sheppard Act gave the Society the authority to require such a contract, and this too was made part of the vendors' lawsuit.

The federal court has yet to rule on the issues in this suit (there have been delays involving jurisdictional matters), but the evidence caused the State of Ohio to terminate its contract with the Society to manage vending stands on state or federal property.

The National Accreditation Council, however, took no action at all. Despite the evidence of illegal conduct and, far worse, gross insensitivity to the human dignity of the blind vendors, NAC continued to regard the Cleveland Society for the Blind as an example of "quality service." It is no coincidence that at that time Cleo Dolan was a member of the board of trustees of the American Foundation for the Blind.

A more blatant example than either of these is the Minneapolis Society for the Blind. As part of its program the Minneapolis Society operates a sheltered workshop for the blind. The Fair Labor Standards Act allows such workshops to pay a blind employee less than the statutory minimum wage if it is shown by a work evaluation that he or she produces less than a sighted worker laboring in the same conditions.

In 1974, a blind man (Lawrence Kettner) was put through such a work evaluation by the Minneapolis Society. The Society did not know that Mr. Kettner had already been hired by a private company at a rate above the minimum wage and was only seeking temporary employment in the Society's workshop until his other job began.

Mr. Kettner was evaluated over a period of 14 days; but time studies were made only on the third, fourth, sixth, and eighth days of the period. His duties were changed—thus it was difficult for him to develop proficiency in any one task. The equipment available to him had breakdowns—although he was being measured against sighted workers using functioning equipment. Finally, there were delays in receiving supplies—yet this was not taken into account by the evaluators. Still, Mr. Kettner's productivity increased markedly between the time studies (from 42% of normal productivity to 79%), stressing the gross unfairness of placing the time studies near the beginning of the evaluation period.

Mr. Kettner was then asked by the Society to sign a minimum-wage waiver indicating that he was capable of only 75% normal productivity. When he resisted, he was told he would sign or receive no pay for the work he had done in the workshop. Needing the money (and with another job already arranged), Mr. Kettner gave in.

This incident was investigated by the U.S. Department of Labor, which issued a finding that the Society had violated the regulations promulgated under the Fair Labor Standards Act.

Once more, here is a violation of the law that is not simply a matter of technical detail. The violation was committed in order to benefit the agency's administration at the cost of tangible damage to blind clients. The matter was brought to NAC; but the Minneapolis Society for the Blind remained an accredited agency.

This was just the beginning. During this same period, the Minneapolis Society decided to build an addition to its workshop. The contract for mechanical work was awarded to a firm owned by the man who was both president of the Society and chairman of the building committee. Although this was widely reported in the Minnesota press, once again NAC took no action to suspend the Society's accreditation.

Reacting to such abuses as the Kettner case, a number of blind persons in Minneapolis decided to seek a voice in the Society's operation. The board of the Minneapolis Society was elected at an annual meeting by the members of the Society. The Society raised funds through mail solicitations, and anyone who donated a dollar or more automatically became a member. So these blind Minnesotans joined the Society.

The Society reacted by expelling all of the members, limiting membership (and thus the privilege of electing the board) to the board members themselves. This action was beyond the board's authority under the articles of incorporation. Not to be stopped by this, the board now came forth with an amendment to the articles which it said had been passed in 1966. This amendment granted the board the power to make further amendments. To be valid, such amendments must be filed with the Secretary of State of Minnesota. The Society board claimed that although their amendment had been passed in 1966, it was not filed with the state until 1972 due to a "clerical oversight."

When the blind persons who had been expelled began discussing a lawsuit, the board members realized they had been too hasty. The board reinstated the membership (although no new members were allowed to join). They also enrolled (without being requested to do so and without collecting any fees) all the members of several large community organizations (the Kiwanis Club, the

Council for Jewish Women, etc.). They then called one last membership meeting to gain approval of their expulsion of the membership. The blind who wanted to join were not even permitted to attend as observers. They went to court instead.

The court, ruling in July, 1977, declared all of the Society's actions to be violations of state law and rescinded them. The judge stated:

> The only reason, therefore, to terminate membership on April 19, 1972, was to eliminate the criticism of the Society by the plaintiff members and to preclude them from increasing their voice in the membership. Membership termination was a subterfuge for expulsion of the plaintiffs without having to comply with reasonable procedures for expulsion.

The judge went further: "At a time when the evidence clearly reflects the need for active and concerned board leadership, the Society blatantly rejected the services of those who had the greatest knowledge of the feelings of the blind and who had progressed the furthest in overcoming the harsh realities of their handicap. In so doing, the defendant violated Minnesota [state law]."

This matter also was brought to NAC's attention. NAC took no action of any kind. It is no coincidence that a member of the Minneapolis Society's board—Raymond Kempf—is also a member of the NAC Board.

Consumer Participation

These examples—the Florida Bureau of Blind Services, the Cleveland Society for the Blind, and the Minneapolis Society for the Blind—speak to the standard of administrative regularity to be expected in a NAC-accredited agency. NAC also asserts that its accredited agencies must have a high degree of consumer participation. (At the 1977 NAC annual meeting, board member Reese Robrahn stated that NAC is unique in the field of accreditation due to this insistence on consumer participation.) Considering that the Minneapolis Society was willing to violate state laws—according to the judge—for the sole purpose of excluding consumer participation, some may wonder how NAC defines the concept.

The NAC concept of consumerism is seen more clearly in the events that occurred at the NAC-accredited Chicago Lighthouse for the Blind. The Chicago Lighthouse manages a large sheltered workshop operation. In 1976, its shops were the subject of a landmark ruling by the National Labor Relations Board (NLRB). Previously, such shops were excluded from the protections of the National Labor Relations Act on the theory that they were rehabilitation programs rather than business operations. In 1976 the NLRB reversed this position (on the simple evidence of the large profits of such "rehabilitation" programs) and ordered a union election at the Lighthouse.

The National Federation of the Blind, reacting to the abuses of the blind workers, had been involved in this NLRB decision. (As an example of the sort of thing we objected to, the Lighthouse created two categories of workers. Sighted workers—who were called "workers"—received the minimum wage and generous fringe benefits. Blind workers—who were called "clients"—received, in general, less than the minimum wage and no fringe benefits. In many cases there was no difference between the duties of "workers" and "clients.")

Although about 85 percent of the shop-workers had signed union pledges before the NLRB ruling, when the election was held the workers voted against a union 68-50. This change of sentiment, it seemed clear to us, was due to the campaign of intimidation carried out by the Lighthouse management. Even before the election was held, the principal union organizer was fired. The management worked to convince the blind workers that a union would mean the end of their jobs and the closing of the shop. (A charge of unfair labor practices brought by several of the workers was not accepted by the NLRB, but it is indisputable that today all of the blind persons who labored to organize a union have been fired or laid off, as have many of those who voted for a union.)

The Federation considers this series of events an indication that the Chicago Lighthouse did not maintain a high standard of service to the blind; but it is brought up here for other reasons: It was one of the first times it became clear that NAC was actively involving itself in the internal affairs of an agency of which it was also purporting to be an objective judge. At the 1976 annual meeting of NAC, Fred McDonald, the executive director of the Lighthouse, made the following statement:

I want to publicly thank Dick [Richard Bleecker, executive director of NAC] and NAC for what they did to help
me in Chicago at a very, very troubled time. As you know,
I took over there as the new director of the Chicago Lighthouse just a year ago the first of December; and at that
time we were under considerable fire from the National
Federation of the Blind and, on top of that, from a labor
union.

Whether or not you feel that blind shopworkers deserve the legal
protections that are extended to sighted workers, it is surely unheard of for an accrediting agency to become directly involved in
the affairs of an agency it accredits. Such a practice destroys even
the semblance of the objectivity that must be the dominant characteristic of accreditation.

Returning to the question of consumer participation, it appears
to have been at the instigation of Richard Bleecker that the
management of the Lighthouse decided to organize its own "consumer organization"—made up of blind Lighthouse staff members. The inference is not farfetched. At the 1976 NAC annual
meeting, Fred McDonald referred to a demonstration planned by
the Federation to protest the firing of the union organizers. He
said:

Our friends downstairs, when they arrive in Chicago on
Friday, are going to have a greeting committee of about
another 100 blind people that are going to be carrying
placards that say "We speak for ourselves; National
Federation of the Blind does not speak for the blind of
this country." And again, the base of this support has
come right from Dick's meeting with our board in
Chicago; and this was very, very important help."

This "consumer group" was formed by the Lighthouse and named,
ironically, the "Independent Blind of Illinois." Its president, Dennis Schreiber, is a Lighthouse staff member. Since then Dennis
Schreiber has been active. To give an example of his activities, a
blind federal employee delivered a speech in California. This blind
man began by stating that his views were his own, and that he was
not speaking for the government. Some days later, the head of
the agency employing this man received a letter from Dennis
Schreiber, writing as president of the Independent Blind although
the letter was on the stationery of the Chicago Lighthouse, and
suggesting that the agency take action against its employee. The

revealing point was that in his speech this blind man had criticized not the Chicago Lighthouse, but the American Foundation for the Blind.

At NAC's 1977 annual meeting, Dennis Schreiber carried this further, suggesting:

> I am asking you to send telegrams to Governor Robert Ray of Iowa and Acting Governor Blair Lee [of Maryland], State Capitol, protesting the harassment, attempts at intimidation, and an attempt at the complete destruction of the National Accreditation Council. If we can get 100 telegrams on the respective desks of these Governors from all over the country, we will make these Governors wonder what is Kenneth Jernigan and Ralph Sanders trying to do.

At the time Ralph Sanders was President of the National Federation of the Blind and an official in Maryland's programs for the blind. Kenneth Jernigan was the immediate past President of the Federation and an Iowa state official.

Perhaps the officers of NAC and the Lighthouse would explain this example of "quality service" by saying that because the National Federation of the Blind has made strong efforts to reform the National Accreditation Council, National Federation of the Blind officers—both present and past—deserve to lose their personal livelihoods. Even if one were to accept such a justification, it seems obvious that NAC has put itself in a position where it is impossible to judge the Lighthouse's program objectively. How could NAC officials take an objective view of activity they themselves had instigated?

Activities Other Than Accreditation

There might be some justification for interference that sought to upgrade the programs of an accredited agency. This was not the case in Chicago. In that instance, and in enough others to form a consistent pattern, NAC began to take retaliatory action against those who were less than whole-hearted in their partisanship. At its last two annual meetings, NAC officials have railed against those they regard as "counter-productive elements," and they announced plans for "dealing decisively with these hostile elements."

This retaliatory activity became the province of a group called the "National Committee for the Advancement of Standards" or NCAS. At the 1977 annual meeting the NAC board elevated the NCAS to the same level as its Commission on Standards and Commission on Accreditation and projected that this new area of activity would be increasing.

Even before the NCAS was formally organized, NAC had been moving in this strange new direction. One of the better documented examples concerns the National Council of State Agencies for the Blind (NCSAB), an organization of directors of state agencies serving the blind.

During 1975, the members of the NCSAB began questioning the organization's official position as a supporter of NAC. Finally the organization voted to withdraw that support pending meaningful reform of NAC.

The next chapter occurred in February, 1976, at a meeting of the Council of State Administrators of Vocational Rehabilitation (CSAVR). A small group of directors of NAC-accredited agencies convened an unauthorized meeting of the NCSAB. Present at the meeting were NAC president Louis Rives and NAC executive director Richard Bleecker. The group voted to declare that this was an official NCSAB meeting. They further voted to declare the office of NCSAB president-elect vacant, and they then chose one of their number (James Carballo) to fill the "vacancy."

Nor did they stop at this. With Richard Bleecker suggesting ways to do it, the group began changing the NCSAB by-laws. At Louis Rives's suggestion, they also voted to resume NCSAB support of NAC. As Robert Pogorelc, the actual president of the NCSAB, later wrote: "If the NAC executive director is responsible for involvement in the 'politics' of private and/or public organizations in the field, in order to further the cause of NAC, I believe that this fact should be published."

In a later letter, to NAC president Rives, Mr. Pogorelc was more definite:

> It is ridiculous for anyone to pretend that NAC has conducted itself in such a manner as to serve as a high model for accuracy, fairness, decency, openness, and propriety. The fact of the matter is that NAC has, in its relations with the NCSAB, frequently conducted itself in a manner

such as to present, at least in my mind, very serious questions as to appropriateness, propriety, and ethics. Perhaps some may wish to deny that NAC has frequently, through covert tactics in which representatives of state agencies have been provided inaccurate and misleading information outside of the spotlight of a public meeting, injected itself into the internal affairs of the NCSAB. I very seriously doubt, though, that those denials would have very much credence with state agency representatives who have witnessed or been exposed to the process.

After this meeting, James Carballo[1] began taking action as "president-elect"; he called yet another unauthorized meeting of the NCSAB. The actual NCSAB sought a judicial restraining order. A Mississippi court (Mr. Carballo lives in Mississippi) granted the order, enjoining "James Carballo from holding himself out as the president-elect or president of the [NCSAB] and further, from representing to members of the National Council of State Agencies for the Blind and other interested persons that the unauthorized alleged annual meeting of the NCSAB scheduled for September 20, 1976, in Hollywood, Florida, is a valid meeting under the bylaws of the NCSAB."

This court order did not deter NAC for long. The next legally constituted NCSAB meeting was scheduled to be an election. The NAC-AFB group let it be known (and this was later publicly admitted at the meeting) that travel expenses were available to NCSAB members who supported NAC. As a result, many who had previously taken no active part in the organization turned up for the election, which—understandably—produced some officers favorable to NAC. The efforts by NAC to dominate the NCSAB have continued unchecked.

The pattern was continued when NAC began to organize attacks against agencies whose only offense was not to seek its accreditation. This came to light when the Youngstown (Ohio) Society for the Blind decided to seek accreditation from the Council on Accreditation of Rehabilitation Facilities (CARF) rather than NAC. Immediately the Youngstown Society found itself under attack.

The Federation first became aware of this when our Washington, D.C., affiliate met with Charles Fegan, the director of the Columbia Lighthouse for the Blind. The Columbia Lighthouse at this time was considering whether to renew its NAC accreditation. Mr. Fegan was explaining to a public meeting that he did not regard himself a partisan of NAC. To illustrate this, he said he had not complied with a request that he write to the director of the Youngstown Society, opposing its decision about NAC. When he was asked who suggested that he write such a letter, Mr. Fegan demurred, perhaps realizing that he had already said too much, considering the consequences that had been visited on others who publicly criticized NAC. In the circumstances, no answer was necessary.

It is important to remember that at this very time the Columbia Lighthouse was weighing the merits of re-accreditation. The request from NAC had the double purpose of harassing the Youngstown Society and reminding the Lighthouse of what would attend a decision not to renew its accreditation.

A month earlier, in March, 1977, Cleo Dolan, executive director of the Cleveland Society for the Blind, wrote a memorandum to one of his subordinates, which read in part:

> As you know, we have long understood that the Youngstown Society for the Blind was planning to be accredited by CARF rather than by NAC because of the pressure from the National Federation of the Blind group. This is in spite of the fact that CARF has never accredited an agency for the blind, nor do they have standards for such areas as mobility and home teaching services. It is further our understanding that the Youngstown Society is proceeding with the approach that CARF standards, as they must be accredited by July to comply with the RSC policies. [sic]
>
> In light of the above, it is our belief that we should start "winding down" our relationship with the Youngstown Society for the Blind. It is recognized that we have funneled the Radio Reading Program state support through the CSB [the Cleveland Society for the Blind] and had planned on several other cooperative working arrangements pertaining to the Radio Reading Service—including sharing a WATS line. However, if they are anticipating "deserting" the field of work with the blind, then it is our belief we should react the way National Federation of the Blind has advised their membership and are causing Youngstown to react accordingly. In other words, if they choose to be accredited under CARF standards, then we will request that no further cooperation or assistance be afforded the Youngstown Society

for the Blind from any of the staff of the Cleveland
Society for the Blind. We will want to sever all communication and relationship in the same manner in which
it has been recommended that they react with accredited
agencies, since they are willing to follow the dictates and
policies of National Federation of the Blind.

For these reasons we would like to have you clean up all
the outstanding obligations they have in relation to the
Radio Reading Service so that all bills can be paid and
we can make a clean break in our relations at the time
their final decision is made with reference to accreditation.

Federation members in Youngstown encouraged the Youngstown
Society's decision. Needless to say, they had no tool of coercion
to equal Mr. Dolan's, nor would they have used it if they had.
Mr. Dolan equates failing to seek NAC accreditation with "desert-
ing the field of work with the blind." For him it is reason enough
to attempt to cripple the radio reading service for blind persons
in that part of the state served by the Youngstown Society.

There are many lesser examples of what NAC calls the "advancement of standards." When the State of California rescinded a
decision to require NAC accreditation of blind agencies doing
business with the state, partly on the advice of a consumer advisory board, NAC went over the heads of state rehabilitation officials to complain to Governor Jerry Brown. Writing to the
Governor's assistant, Richard Bleecker stated: "I am interested in
learning more about the advisory committee's function, composition, representativeness, and decision-making process. Would you
be so kind as to provide me with a statement of the committee's
purpose, the names of the three organizations that are represented, as well as a copy of the minutes or other record which
contains the substance of the committee's discussion of the accreditation issue."

When the board of the Illinois Division of Vocational Rehabilitation (DVR) met to consider a decision by the DVR director to
require NAC accreditation of blind agencies contracting with the
state, NAC brought to the meeting Fred McDonald, executive
director of the Chicago Lighthouse. Mr. McDonald acted as
spokesman for the "Independent Blind of Illinois." He produced
a letter supporting NAC that had 64 names on it. When the letter
was examined, however, it emerged that the names were not

signed but typed. (Since many of the names were of people in Mr. McDonald's employ, even their signatures would have indicated little about the "independence" of their views.)

At this meeting, in response to questions from the DVR board, it was brought out that NAC had never revoked the accreditation of an agency on its list. This appeared to carry great weight with the DVR board, which later voted to rescind the requirement that agencies contracting with the state seek NAC accreditation. NAC was shown to be an accreditation system without teeth, more interested in bolstering its prestige with numbers than enforcing high standards of service.

Shortly after the DVR meeting, NAC revoked the accreditation of one of its agencies. In the circumstances, who would believe that the decision was made on its objective merits. NAC decided it must have an answer the next time such a question was raised.

Conclusion

We began this open letter with the premise that the National Accreditation Council was formed by the American Foundation for the Blind in order to perpetuate its tradition of benevolent custodialism, and further, that this was not a positive development. It is a difficult premise to prove because its validity depends on another premise—that the blind are capable of independence and normal lives.

But over the years the problems with NAC have changed in nature as well as in dimension. This happened because the theory of work with the blind espoused by NAC has lost ground with the field as with the public—it is far more outmoded now than ten years ago. NAC has had to change its thrust simply to remain in existence. It has become the focus for the defensive activities of a very small group of agencies. They are agencies whose directors or programs have been shown by court decisions, or independent studies, or client experience, or federal audits to be substandard. They are agencies whose boards, in general, are interlocking with those of NAC and the American Foundation for the Blind (this has become more the case over the years).

We support—as must all people of sense—the desire of a school or agency to be approved by a reputable accrediting body. But those responsible for making this decision should examine what they are purchasing. NAC accreditation is expensive: it is a commitment of either public tax money or funds contributed by a charitable public. The only valid justification for devoting funds to accreditation is that such accreditation ensures the maintenance of high program standards. With relation to NAC, such a contention becomes absurd in light of NAC's approval of the actions of the Florida agency, the Cleveland Society, the Minneapolis Society, and the Chicago Lighthouse, and its own actions regarding the NCSAB, the Columbia Lighthouse, the Youngstown Society, and the California Department of Rehabilitation.

A majority of agencies and consumers has concluded that NAC accreditation does not ensure high standards of service. It lends an agency no respectability or credibility whatever.

FOOTNOTE

1. James Carballo is the director of Mississippi's Vocational Rehabilitation for the Blind, an agency accredited by NAC. An audit of the agency completed by the Department of Health, Education, and Welfare in late 1977 provides a clear example of what NAC considers "quality service." According to the *Jackson Capitol Reporter* of December 1, 1977:

   The audit, a copy of which was secured by the *Capitol Reporter*, reveals that out of 138 blind rehabilitation clients randomly selected by the HEW auditors, only one had finally been placed in a job in the competitive market. Even then, the audit showed, the one blind person had to take a job as a clerk, whereas she was trained to be a special education teacher.

   Out of 526 blind persons the state agency had shown as rehabilitated in fiscal 1976, the audit shows, almost 85 percent were making less than $2.50 an hour and most were making less than the minimum wage.

   The state agency, according to the audit, violated federal regulations by using Social Security trust funds, Supplemental Security Income funds, income derived in part from use of federal funds, income from vending stands operated by the blind, and "contributions" from vendors paid in part with federal funds to match federal funds.

   Mr. Carballo's part in the NCSAB affair and the results of this HEW audit taken together are a clear paradigm of NAC accreditations: NAC provides its seal of approval to a substandard rehabilitation program; In return the agency publicly supports NAC (or, as in this case, goes a good deal further).

By the mid-1980s it was clear that NAC was disintegrating. As major state programs for the blind dissociated themselves from the organization and rejected its accreditation, NAC moved to recruit smaller and less well-known groups to bolster its numbers. Articles appearing in the *Braille Monitor* in 1986 and 1987 graphically illustrate what was happening. Excerpts and representative headlines follow:

NAC Bites the Dust in Kansas
Braille Monitor, March, 1986

Actually it happened on the last day of 1985, but on January 10, 1986, it became official: Kansas State Services for the Blind renounced NAC's accreditation....

Division of Services for the Blind
Supervisor's Meeting Minutes
January 17, 1986

Present:
Suzannah Erhart
Jayne Frost
Caroline Lauer
Richard Schutz
Robert Sheldon

NAC has been notified that DSB [Division of Services for the Blind] plans to discontinue NAC accreditation. CARF [Commission on Accreditation of Rehabilitation Facilities] accreditation for the rehabilitation center and Kansas Industries for the Blind should be pursued. Richard Schutz will order the necessary CARF materials.

Michigan School for the Blind De-NACs
Braille Monitor, March, 1986

In a brief news release issued in early February the Michigan Department of Education announced that the Michigan School for the Blind (MSB) would not seek re-accreditation by the National Accreditation Council for Agencies Serving the Blind and Visually Handicapped (NAC). The announcement declared that the residential facility could better serve its students by undertaking its own self-study, using an in-state monitoring team. The message was clear—MSB had decided to "de-NAC."

North Carolina Gives NAC the Boot
Braille Monitor, December, 1986

In the March, 1986, *Braille Monitor* we reported that the National Accreditation Council for Agencies Serving the Blind and Visually Handicapped (NAC) had been kicked out of Kansas and Michigan. Now, NAC faces new disasters. North Carolina is joining the parade.

The National Federation of the Blind of North Carolina held its annual convention during the weekend of September 12-14, 1986, in Raleigh. One of the items which was slated to receive attention was the accreditation of the Governor Morehead School for the Blind by NAC. The school had been accredited since 1972, and the blind of the state were determined to bring the nonsense to an end. A resolution had been drafted and was slated for presentation on Sunday morning, September 14; but it never happened. On Saturday afternoon, September 13, Dr. Richard Rideout (drector of the Division of Special Schools for the Blind and Deaf of the Department of Human Resources) announced to the cheering delegates that the Governor Morehead School had decided to end the NAC accreditation.

NAC often talks about the good which it has done and the general public acceptance which it is receiving. However, if any of its board members are at all perceptive or concerned about the way the blind (the people they supposedly do so much to help) feel, they should think long and carefully about the reaction in North Carolina. At the announcement that the Governor Morehead School would de-NAC the blind cheered. When the school gives up its accreditation, no facility working with the blind anywhere in the state will be NAC-accredited. As the joyous delegates chanted: "NC is NAC-Free...."

Memorandum

To: Richard Rideout, Director
Division of Special School for the Blind and Deaf
Department of Human Resources
From: George N. Lee, Superintendent
Governor Morehead School
Re: NAC Accreditation

The Governor Morehead School has just been reaccredited by Southern Association of Colleges and Schools for the next five years. This is important to our school.

The school has also been accredited by the National Accreditation Council for Agencies Serving the Blind and Visually Impaired since 1972....

I do not believe that NAC accreditation has or will have any positive impact on educational programs here at Governor Morehead School. Fact is I can't really think of any real benefits of NAC accreditation....

NAC Thrown Out in Rhode Island
Braille Monitor, December, 1986

The past year has been a time of hardship for NAC (the National Accreditation Council for Agencies Serving the Blind and Visually Handicapped). A few months ago NAC was told it wouldn't be needed anymore in Kansas. At about the same time it got a similar message from Michigan. And these messages didn't come from small, insignificant agencies. They came from the Kansas State Services for the Blind and the Michigan School for the Blind. This fall it was the turn of North Carolina. The Governor Morehead School for the Blind (North Carolina's residential school) decided NAC accreditation was not worth continuing. As the superintendent of the school pointed out, the institution had been accredited for more than a dozen years, so it was in a position to know whether or not NAC accreditation is beneficial.

NAC keeps trying to smile bravely, but the rejection slips keep coming. This time it is Rhode Island. At the annual state convention of the National Federation of the Blind of Rhode Island on September 27, 1986, a representative of the State Services for the Blind announced that NAC accreditation was being dropped at the end of 1986. The blind of the state were overjoyed and greeted the news with cheers....

American Foundation for the Blind Criticizes NAC
Braille Monitor, January, 1987

. . . .

National Braille Association Cuts its Ties With NAC
Braille Monitor, September, 1987

As everybody knows, the last couple of years have been a bad time for NAC (the National Accreditation Council for Agencies Serving the Blind and Visually Handicapped). The North Carolina school for the blind, the Michigan State School for the Blind, Kansas State Services for the Blind, Rhode Island State Services for the Blind, and others decided they had had enough and withdrew. There is an old saying to the effect that nothing wins like success. The reverse of that coin is that nothing loses like failure—and NAC certainly offers graphic testimony to the truth of it all.

One of the latest to leave NAC's sinking ship is NBA (the National Braille Association). Established in 1945, the NBA is described in the 1984 edition of the American Foundation for the Blind *Directory of Agencies Serving the Blind in the U.S.* as follows: "Brings together those interested in production and distribution of Braille, large type, and tape recorded materials for the visually impaired. NBA Braille Book Bank provides thermoform copies of hand-transcribed texts to college students and professional persons; NBA Braille Technical Tables Bank has a collection of over 300 tables which supplement many of the texts; through NBA Reader-Transcriber Registry blind people can obtain vocational daily living material—at below cost; through Braille Transcription Assignment Service requests of college students for Brailled textbooks are filled. Publications to aid transcribers include: *Manual for Large Type Transcribing* and *Tape Recording Manual, 3rd Ed.*, available from LC/DBPH; *Teacher's Manual and Tape Recording Lessons*, from NBA national office; *Guidelines for Administration of Groups Producing Reading Materials for the Visually Handicapped*, from LC/DBPH; *Handbook for Braille Music Transcribers*, from LC/DBPH; and NBA *Bulletin*, issued four times a year to membership, available in print, Braille, or tape.

This is how the National Braille Association is described by the American Foundation for the Blind. Put briefly, it is the nationwide organization of transcribers. It has both prestige and stability. It has been one of NAC's sponsors from the very beginning. Therefore, its withdrawal must be particularly troubling to NAC....

No NAC for Mississippi Industries for the Blind
Braille Monitor, October-November, 1987

. . . .

The foregoing excerpts from the *Braille Monitor* show clearly the pattern of NAC's decline in the eighties. In state after state NAC found itself rejected and on the defensive. By the end of 1989 the American Foundation for the Blind had reduced its long-standing contributions, and agency after agency had withdrawn. The NAC board had been reduced in size, and there was widespread speculation that the demise of the organization was imminent. The majority of the knowledgeable blind of the nation, along with most responsible agencies in the field, were now finding NAC a stumbling block to progress and a hindrance rather than a help.

Chapter 12

On The Record: The Evolution of the Braille Monitor

"According to the dictionary a 'monitor' is a person who 'advises, warns, or cautions.' A Braille monitor is one who carries on this function for the blind, and this is the pledge of the editors of this magazine."

So wrote the first editor of the *Braille Monitor* in the inaugural issue of the monthly journal in July, 1957. Editor George Card's announcement somewhat blurred the significance of the event by presenting the *Monitor* not as a brand new periodical—which in fact it was—but as the continuation under a new name of an already existing publication of a very different kind. That was the *All-Story Braille Magazine*, a publication of the American Brotherhood for the Blind which was reasonably faithful to the promise of its title by publishing mainly short fiction with a limited space reserved for a "Federation News Section." Now all that would be changed, said the editor:

> Beginning with the next monthly issue the name of this magazine will be changed to the *Braille Monitor*. We have been fortunate to be able to return to a monthly [from a quarterly] issue. This is made possible by a subvention from the National Federation of the Blind. The "Federation News Section" has become increasingly popular. Many of our readers have written in to request that more space be devoted to this feature. Program and other developments concerning the blind—many of which are of the utmost importance to the blind men and women of this country—have been emerging in profusion. Even with the return to the monthly issue, a major fraction of the space of this magazine must

be devoted to the coverage of these developments if our people are to continue to be informed.

Before the birth of the *Monitor* in 1957, as that inaugural statement indicates, the organized blind movement lacked a full set of lungs with which to vocalize its message of Security, Opportunity, and Equality. Limited as it was in this respect to the back pages of a fiction magazine, the fledgling Federation found other ways to convey its message during the seventeen years from its founding to the advent of the *Monitor*. The most effective of those ways was also the most basic: the typewriter/mimeograph combination. From the earliest penny-pinched days in 1940 and 1941 when the entire national organization was seemingly contained in a shoe-box flat next door to the University of Chicago, the word of Federationism was spread primarily by means of bulletins, flyers, and broadsides which were devised and dictated by Jacobus tenBroek, typed by Hazel tenBroek, and cranked out by both of them on that granddaddy of Xerox: the mimeograph machine.

But the will to find their own full voice, and the dream that would one day be realized in the form of the *Braille Monitor,* were there from the beginning in the minds of the founders. Almost immediately after the initial National Convention at Wilkes-Barre in 1940, an exchange of letters (which clearly followed earlier discussions) took place between NFB President tenBroek and Perry Sundquist, then the Executive Secretary of the American Brotherhood for the Blind, which published the *All-Story Magazine.* Sundquist opened the exchange with this overture:

> For some time I have been searching for some means by which the American Brotherhood could use its slender resources to a more vital purpose—and the thought has occurred to me that perhaps some arrangement could be made whereby it could publish a monthly bulletin or magazine of the Federation—purely as a service to the Federation in advancing its purposes among the blind of the member states and of other states. As you know, Pennsylvania puts out, quarterly or so, a little paper entitled *We the Blind*—and doubtless this is a potent means of furthering the organization. Well, the Federation could put out a national magazine.

"It certainly would be a godsend," wrote tenBroek in reply, "if the National Federation of the Blind could have at its service a magazine devoted to a discussion of the legislative problems of the blind. Such a magazine would be especially important if it

gave us a monthly contact with our members and if it were directly available to them in Braille." He went on to emphasize the
vital importance of a regular channel of communication with reference to the NFB's social and political objectives: "One of the
immensely difficult problems that the National Federation has to
face is that of communication with the blind throughout the nation, and that communication needs to be fairly frequent if not
constant with respect to the activities of the organization which
will deal almost wholly with legislative and administrative
problems."

That emphatic, no-nonsense stress upon the public agenda
of the Federation as the dominant concern of any magazine it
might initiate reflected the serious, not to say grim, earnestness
of the early leaders in the face of the political and economic ur-
gencies of their time: the grinding poverty of nearly all the adult
blind, the uncomprehending and indifferent attitudes of most
public officials, the blithe complacency of professional workers
for the blind who viewed themselves proudly as the guardians and
caretakers of a hopeless minority doomed to physical immobility,
cultural illiteracy, and economic irrelevance.

Jacobus tenBroek and his colleagues of the first generation
might also have felt grim concerning the prospects of the infant
Federation within a wartime economy in which communications
and travel were severely restricted for all civilian groups and non-
military purposes. It was evidently with some reluctance that
these leaders accepted the compromise arrangement of a Federation supplement in the *All-Story*, which blind readers turned to
less for education than for entertainment. In 1942 Raymond
Henderson, then Executive Director of the Federation, issued a
bulletin to the membership which contained this wistful and even
rueful report on the quest for a journal:

BRAILLE FEDERATION MAGAZINE

The *All-Story Braille Magazine* is continuing to print almost every
month three or four pages on legislation for the blind edited by
Dr. Newel Perry. We need a small magazine devoted to the work
of the Federation. However our finances are still insufficient and
the difficulties in securing metal plates and paper for printing may
delay the establishment of such a magazine. We are informed that
our mimeographed bulletins are read and discussed at the meetings of many of the local clubs of the blind. The Executive Director of the National Federation of the Blind would be interested
in having opinions as to the desirability of such a Braille publica-

tion. However we must again remember that in the present situation it may prove impossible to secure the printing of such a publication even if our finances could stand the strain. In this as in so many other things we must all be patient but we must not allow our interest to flag.

Their interest in a "small magazine devoted to the work of the Federation" certainly did not flag during the remainder of the war years; but even after the war the hopes of the early leaders for a full-fledged independent journal of their own gave way to reluctant acceptance of the status quo (somewhat expanded). In the fall of 1945, less than two months after war's end, Jacobus tenBroek sent a letter to all the blind on his mailing list announcing a significant enlargement of the Federation's section in *All-Story* and urging their subscription to the magazine. He made a point of mentioning that the Federation's pages were under the editorship of the man who was his own mentor and the pioneer of blind self-organization in California: Dr. Newel Perry. His letter follows:

National Federation of the Blind
Office of the President
October 9, 1945

Dear Friend:

A discussion in Braille of national and state legislation affecting the blind and other items of interest to blind persons is now available to all blind readers of grade two. The American Brotherhood for the Blind, publishers of the *All-Story Braille Magazine*, have now enlarged and put upon a systematic basis the section of that magazine dealing with legislation. The magazine is published monthly and may be secured by simply dropping a card to the American Brotherhood for the Blind, 117 West Ninth Street, Los Angeles, California.

The editor of the legislation section is Dr. Newel Perry, 6441-A Colby Street, Oakland 9, California, who is the venerable leader of the blind in California and whose work in the National Federation of the Blind is known to all. Readers of the legislation section are thus assured of an authentic analysis of legislative and other problems of the blind, treated from the viewpoint of the blind themselves.

In the past, the blind have been greatly handicapped in their efforts to improve the conditions under which they live by the absence of adequate means of communication among the blind and between the representatives of the blind and the persons represented. The obvious remedy for this condition is the legislation section of the *All-Story Braille Magazine*. It will serve as a continuous means of contact among the blind, as an instrument for the dissemination of information vitally affecting their welfare, and as a clearing house of their activities in supporting favorable and seeking to defeat harmful legislative or other action.

In the interests of the welfare of the blind, I urge you to apply for and become a regular reader of the *All-Story Braille Magazine* and to send items of interest to Dr. Perry.

Yours sincerely,
Jacobus tenBroek
President

The National Federation continued to speak with that muted voice for another dozen years before it could exercise its full lung power. The title page from a typical monthly issue of *All-Story* (October, 1949) read: *"THE ALL-STORY BRAILLE MAGAZINE with Legislative Supplement; The 'Supplement' is the Official Mouthpiece of the National Federation of the Blind."* And the contents of another issue during that year suggested the low priority given to NFB materials in a journalistic context dominated by fictional romance and melodrama. Here is the contents page of the March, 1949, issue:

Married This Morning, by Irene Kittle Camp (reprinted from the *Good Housekeeping Magazine*)

The Storm, by Laurence Critchell (reprinted from *Collier's*)

Star Boarder, by Libbie Block (reprinted from *McCall's*)

Legislation for the Blind, by Dr. Newel Perry

The transition from *All-Story* to the *Braille Monitor* was preceded by a series of strategic shifts apparently designed to prepare readers for the advent of a "No-Story" Braille magazine devoted exclusively to Federation concerns. In 1955 a "special feature" was announced by *All-Story* Editor George Card which dramatically changed the layout and the character of the venerable journal—for that special issue—from a literary to an organizational purpose. Clearly the editor and his colleagues were testing the waters to ascertain the tolerance of readers for a new kind of magazine: a voice of Federationism that would speak not of fantasy but of truth, and would explore in its pages not the never-never land of imagination but the barren landscape of the here and now—the world of harsh reality (of broomcorn and sawdust, ridicule and rejection) in which the blind must somehow make their way and find their place, by their own exertions, or else fall back upon the charity and pity of their overseers and lighthouse keepers.

That special (February-March, 1955) issue of *All-Story* also introduced a new feature which was destined to become a permanent and integral part of the *Monitor*, continuously upgraded through the years but never altered in format. This is how the innovation was announced:

Editor's Note

Who Are the Blind Who Lead the Blind (Special Feature)

Legislation for the Blind, by Dr. Newel Perry

Editor's Note

We are proud to present in this issue a special feature, "Who are the Blind Who Lead the Blind?" which has just been released by the National Federation of the Blind. This consists of short biographies which undoubtedly will be of great interest to the readers of *"All-Story."* Because of the importance of this feature, it is being included in this issue in the space which would ordinarily be allocated to short stories.

There was another subtle change in the format of the Federation supplement in this premonitory (pre-*Monitor*) period; the title page of the February-March, 1956, issue of *All-Story* reflected a slight but significant expansion of the scope of Federation information; now it was not just legislative and other official material that was carried but "Federation News," suggesting a wider interest in general "news" that was to become more and more prominent over the years in the evolution of the *Braille Monitor*.

The *Monitor* Goes to Press

Under the headline *"All-Story* Gets a New Name," Editor George Card tactfully announced the advent of the *Braille Monitor* in the issue of July, 1957. As noted earlier, he indicated that the change in format and content was responsive to reader demands as well as to a grant from the National Federation of the Blind. And he was careful not to rule out the future inclusion of stories altogether; here is his meticulous circumlocution: "It therefore seems appropriate that we should now change the name of the magazine to one that does not state or imply that all of the contents are stories. Stories will continue to be republished to the extent that space is available."

When the first issue of the *Braille Monitor* under its new name appeared the following month (August, 1957), it was all news and contained no stories. The point had been made; from now on the *Monitor* would be primarily devoted to Federation news—and it would be truly a monitor—"one who advises, warns, or cautions." The leaders of the movement had named their journal well; it was destined to advise the membership, warn the agencies established to give service to the blind, and caution the world. It was not to be all at once everything it could be; that would come in the fullness of time, with growth and maturity. But from the outset the *Braille Monitor* showed its potential; it showed its colors; and it showed its teeth. There would be no truckling to the dominant interests in the field, whether of the government or of the private sector. Thus the July, 1957, issue (announcing the name change) proclaimed on page one that "An attitude of arrogance and hostility was displayed toward the organized blind on the part of the highest officials of the Federal Department of Health, Education, and Welfare" in the course of a Washington conference between NFB and HEW. The unsigned article (clearly reflecting the prose style as well as the sentiments of President Jacobus tenBroek) went on to assert that "the atmosphere of the 'discussion' may be briefly and accurately summarized as chaotic and disorganized; the attitude of the federal officials as intemperate and hostile; the results as wholly negative and discouraging."

The tone set on that opening page with reference to government officialdom was matched the following month in an article (again unsigned but easily identifiable) concerned with actions of the two most powerful private agencies in the blindness system. Headlined "AAWB and AFB Initiate Attacks On Blind Right to Organize Bills," the editorial article struck back vigorously at agency statements in opposition to the Kennedy Bill protecting the right of the blind to organize and to be consulted on programs affecting them. "In its totality," the *Monitor* said of a resolution from the American Association of Workers for the Blind, "this statement adds up to a graphic and unmistakable expression of the anti-democratic custodial philosophy espoused since ancient times by those who have considered themselves the masters of their incompetent blind wards." Again: "...even if this blatantly authoritarian theory of government were to be accepted, a stark factual question would remain of the real extent of 'professional' competence possessed by these antiquarian custodians and lighthouse keepers."

That tone of aggressive defense of the rights of blind persons, and of untiring vigilance against the foes of liberty in all the seats of power, was to remain through the years a defining characteristic of *Monitor* journalism under a succession of editors and leaders. What is striking in retrospect is the remarkable note of confidence—of self-assertion born of self-esteem—expressed by the *Monitor* at a time when the organized blind movement was still in its adolescence and the condition of the blind still shrouded in insecurity and dependence. It was as if (to recall an earlier episode of crisis leadership in the nation) President Jacobus tenBroek of the National Federation of the Blind was announcing to all the blind in all the sheltered shops and blind alleys of America:

"The only thing we have to fear is fear itself."

In order to get the message to that national constituency, however, more was needed than a Braille publication. Some even of the totally blind did not read Braille; most who were partially blind did not. Efforts began immediately to add to the Braille edition an inkprint version of the *Monitor*, and as soon as possible a recorded edition as well. In fact it appears that a tape-recorded version came first, if only in partial form. As early as July of 1957 an NFB Bulletin announced (and the September *Braille Monitor* restated):

NFB TAPE PROGRAM BEGINS

A lending library of tape recordings, designed to give as wide coverage as possible to National Federation news and activities, is presently in process of development. Tapes will be available shortly for a two-week loan period, without charge, to affiliated clubs, chapters, or members of the National Federation of the Blind. The first tape recordings available will cover the 1957 National Convention, either in whole or in part (selected speeches and reports). The Federation News Section of the *Braille Monitor* (formerly the *All-Story* Magazine) will also be available on tape recording. These recordings may also be purchased at two dollars a tape.

Given the difficulties of reel-to-reel tape recording in those pre-cassette days, however, efforts to secure a spoken version of the *Monitor* also took another direction. Following the 1958 Boston convention, the *Monitor* reported that the Executive Committee had adopted a motion by Kenneth Jernigan that "the cost of recording each issue of the *Braille Monitor* on disc records, which could be played on the standard Talking Book machine, be investigated, and that each local affiliate and state organization be informed of this cost, in terms of a twelve-month subscription." The *Monitor* went on to report that: "If 100 subscriptions should be received, with payment in advance, the Federation would then proceed to enter into an arrangement for the regular recording of each monthly issue. Finally, if the required number of paid subscriptions should be received, the first batch of recordings should be sufficiently large so that each state and local affiliate could be sent one sample recording."

Whether the paid subscriptions for this venture fell short of the number required, or for some other reason left unexplained, the disc-recorded edition of the *Monitor* was delayed a full decade and did not make its appearance until July, 1968—in time to record a special memorial issue, "Jacobus tenBroek: The Man and the Movement," and to make it available to the membership at the National Convention in Des Moines that month.

Fortunately the inkprint edition of the *Braille Monitor* was not similarly delayed, although it remained in jeopardy for a time due to the costs it imposed. The first print edition actually produced and distributed was the issue of January, 1958, (although later transcriptions were to give the impression, still retained in bound volumes, of an earlier publication date). Here is the announcement as it appeared in that initial print issue:

BRAILLE MONITOR—INKPRINT EDITION

It has at last become possible to issue an inkprint edition of the *Braille Monitor*. The demand for such a publication has become overwhelming. For the time being, the publication of the inkprint edition will be experimental. Members of the NFB who are now on the mailing list will automatically receive the inkprint edition. Other friends of the Federation and interested persons may have their names placed on the mailing list by writing to NFB Headquarters, 2652 Shasta Road, Berkeley 8, California.

The costs of off-setting and mailing are high. These costs should be met by the readers. The normal way of doing this would be to charge for subscriptions. On the other hand, all Federation members and friends who do not read Braille and who can read or have read the inkprint edition should have an opportunity to gain first-hand acquaintance with Federation news. All readers who wish to do so should send $3.00 to Federation headquarters to help meet expenses. Contributions should be made payable to *Braille Monitor* Inkprint Edition. If not enough people do so, we may have to discontinue the inkprint edition.

For three years, from mid-summer 1957, through December, 1960, the *Monitor* appeared every month without interruption in both Braille and print—with the American Brotherhood for the Blind continuing to function as publisher of the Braille edition while the Federation published the print version. What happened then was as chaotic as it was catastrophic: the abrupt cessation of publishing in any format, the disappearance of the *Monitor* for four and a half years, the emergence and short (four-year) life of the *Blind American*, the travail and departure of the original editor. It is a story of civil war reflected in columns of print. The events of the war itself have been recounted in Chapter Three of this volume; the salient events of the paper war can be briefly summarized.

Monitoring the *Monitor*

When the *Braille Monitor* was born in 1957 its editor was George Card, who was also the First Vice President of the National Federation of the Blind (from 1948) and a veteran field organizer for the movement. Card had previously been the editor of *The All-Story Braille Magazine* and was accustomed to retaining sole control over the contents of his publication; but with the advent of the *Monitor* as the official channel for communication of the full range of Federation activities, this was no longer possible. The center of activity was at the national headquarters, in Berkeley, where the President resided and where the print *Monitor* was to be published; whereas Card lived in far-off Wisconsin, traveled almost continuously on organizing trips, and was no longer on the cutting edge of policy formation or even of major writing efforts. In these circumstances there was bound to be strain, and it began to show almost from the beginning. In the third issue of the *Monitor* (September, 1957), Card openly expressed his displeasure at the new division of editorial labor, while recognizing its necessity and taking care to praise the contributions of President tenBroek. The first item on page one of the September issue read as follows:

SETTING THE RECORD STRAIGHT

As many of you know, I was engaged in field work nearly all of the time between mid-February and late June. This, of course, necessitated my turning over my editorial duties to others. The

May and June issues contained only a few items which were mine. I had no part in the preparation of the July number. Last month I wrote the account of the New Orleans convention, but the rest of the material was prepared by others. Much of the writing during this four-month period was of the highest excellence and I should have been proud to have been its author. The fact remains, however, that I was *not* the author and I think you should know this. I have received a number of letters containing undeserved compliments and a few of the other kind. I have only now had the privilege of reading Dr. tenBroek's brilliant and devastating analysis of the AAWB resolution and the American Foundation attack on our "Right to Organize" bill. If any of you missed this section, for heaven's sake go back and read it right now. It is a superlative bit of writing, and it will make you rejoice if you are a member of an organization which has such a leader and spokesman.

It is my hope that in the future, whenever I am away and others prepare the *Braille Monitor*, they will use their own by-lines.

George Card.

Again in the December, 1957, issue Editor Card prefaced the contents with an entry entitled "Setting the Record Straight." This time he was concerned to identify others who had contributed major articles to the November *Monitor* (but had not followed his counsel to use their own by-lines). "I was absent in the East during the time the November issue was being prepared," wrote Card. "The extremely well written articles—'Was It Really Passed Unanimously' and the two dealing with the support of the Kennedy bill by the Western Conference of Home Teachers, were by Kenneth Jernigan. The 'Bulletins' were the joint product of the Washington and Berkeley offices. I believe Dr. tenBroek wrote or assembled most of the rest of the material. My only contribution was the 'Journal.'"

The next development in this personal/editorial saga came in December of 1958 with a lead article entitled "*Monitor* Editor Resigns NFB Office," carrying the by-line of Jacobus tenBroek. The Federation President announced that George Card had resigned his position as First Vice President due primarily to the stresses of the civil war then raging within the movement. He continued: "George's services will not be wholly lost to us as a result of his decision. As reported elsewhere, the Federation will take over publication of the Braille edition of the *Braille Monitor*. George will now continue his functions as editor of the *Braille Monitor* and as finance director, and will thus be enabled to carry forward much of his invaluable work and contribution to our common cause as a member of the paid staff of the Federation."

In an accompanying letter of resignation, Card wrote in part: "Now that the *Monitor* has become so large and important, it is demanding more and more of my time. I feel it is a part of my job to read all Braille periodicals published in the English-speaking world and to have all inkprint periodicals in our field read to me, so that I can pass on important matters in the columns of the *Monitor*. Each month the volume of correspondence with *Monitor* readers and contributors increases." But he went on to declare that the major reason for his resignation from elective office was the storm and stress of civil war: "The ruthless and lacerating attacks made by a small, disgruntled group during the past fifteen months have taken all the joy out of it for me. Watching the organization which I love so much split into warring factions has made me heartsick."

Despite Card's denunciation of the "small, disgruntled group" of dissidents, and his despair at the Federation's split into "warring factions," he was soon himself to join the dissident faction and to declare his own private war upon the President and the administration of the NFB. That story has been told earlier in these pages (Chapter Three) with reference to the civil war; but it is pertinent here to trace the narrower events which led to the replacement of Card as editor of the *Braille Monitor* and to a new phase (and a new look) in the evolution of the "Voice of Federationism."

In September of 1960 the NFB President Jacobus tenBroek responded to a mounting series of hostile actions on the part of Card by announcing his termination as *Monitor* editor (although tenBroek even then could not bring himself to fire Card outright but merely reduced his workload and placed him on semi-retirement). Thus, wrote the President, "The *Braille Monitor* has been placed under new editorship. We are fortunate that Kenneth Jernigan has consented to undertake this function on a volunteer basis. The September (and possibly the October) issues will again be prepared in the Federation's Berkeley headquarters, but as soon as possible the new editor will take over this responsibility. Therefore all items or material intended for the *Monitor* should be sent in the future to Mr. Jernigan...."

In the subsequent (October) issue of the *Monitor*, two related events were given prominent attention. The first was the bitterly announced resignation of George Card from what was left of his staff position; and the second was a statement by the new *Monitor* editor, Kenneth Jernigan, enunciating his own editorial policy and philosophy. That 1960 declaration was to take on unusual significance in light of Jernigan's future role in directing the evolution of the *Monitor* into the single most influential and widely read periodical in the blindness field. Presented in the form of an "Open Letter to *Monitor* Readers," this was his proclamation of principles:

OPEN LETTER TO *MONITOR* READERS

In assuming the duties of editor I would like to say a few words to all *Monitor* readers. First, this: My success or failure as editor will largely be determined by you. I know that I need not dwell upon the troubled times in which the Federation finds itself or the difficult circumstances under which I assume this task. I also know that the members of the Federation throughout the country will, as they always have, respond to the situation. I will need your comments and criticisms. I will also need material for publication.

This, too, I would like to say: I shall do the best that I can to report to you factually and fairly events as they occur. This does not mean, of course, that I am, or intend to become, a neutral in the civil war which now besets our organization. I believe in the Federation and the principles for which it stands. I believe that our organization is, and that it always has been, democratic and progressive. I believe that our President is a devoted man and not a thief or a scoundrel.

Since I do believe these things, my editorial policies will inevitably be governed accordingly. To say otherwise would be less than honest. Furthermore, I do not believe that it should be the function of the *Monitor* to have no views and no policy at all. Rather, I believe the magazine should follow the policies established democratically by the delegates at Federation conventions. Differing viewpoints have a legitimate place in the magazine but not unfounded charges of slander and vilification, which can only serve to weaken our movement. The purpose of the *Monitor* should be to *build* the Federation, not to destroy it.

Finally, I would like to say this: Even if an editor tries, it is impossible for him not to have an editorial policy. Consider the *Free Press*, for instance. It claims to present all points of view and to be open and unbiased. Yet, almost every article it prints is an attack upon the Federation and its leadership. By the very virtue of what he selects to be printed an editor establishes a policy and espouses a cause.

I pledge to the members of the Federation that I will do my best
to see that they get a factual and fair account of what is occurring
throughout the nation, but I also pledge that I will do everything
possible to strengthen and build the Federation through the pages
of the *Monitor*, keeping the members informed of what the
minority faction is doing and promoting the policies established
by the majority at conventions.

Again I say that I shall need the help of all of you if the task is
to be a success.

Kenneth Jernigan

Almost exactly a score of years after that open letter—in the
June, 1980, issue of the *Monitor*—Kenneth Jernigan published
another "Report to the Members" in which he found himself
reflecting on the twenty-year cycle which had brought him back
once more to the editor's chair. He was now working, he said, "as
a sort of co-editor of the *Monitor*" along with Jim Gashel. "The
last time—at least in an official way—that I had anything to do
with editing the *Monitor* (it was also the first time) was from September through December, 1960. We were in the midst of the
Federation's civil war, and those were troubled times. After four
months of my editorship, the *Monitor* went out of business. (I
hope it was the overall problems of the times and not my editing
that did it.)"

In fact it was not just the overall problems of the times but
the specific problem of the "dearth of finances," as Jacobus ten-
Broek was to put it, that was responsible for the suspension of
Monitor publication at the end of 1960. When it came out again
nearly four years later—with the August, 1964, issue—its editor
was Dr. tenBroek, then the President Emeritus of the Federation.
This is how he described the comeback in that issue:

THE REVIVAL OF THE *BRAILLE MONITOR*

The revival of the *Braille Monitor* comes in the nick of time. The
last issue was published in December, 1960. The suspension was
caused by the dearth of finances which resulted from the internal
warfare of the Federation. During the spring of 1961 the
American Brotherhood for the Blind received a handsome bequest. The Brotherhood, therefore, was able to take over where
the *Monitor* had left off. In August, 1961, the Brotherhood began
the publication of the *Blind American*, in form and content the
replacement of the *Monitor*. These and other heavy drains on the
treasury of the Brotherhood, alas, are now exhausting its reserves.
It had already reduced to a quarterly issue and will now suspend

altogether. The announcement of [NFB] President Kletzing at the NFB Phoenix convention that the income of the Federation would now permit the revival of the *Braille Monitor* thus could not have come at a more opportune moment.

The moment was opportune in more than a fiscal sense, ten-Broek said: "As the *Monitor* suspended at the peak of dissension within the Federation, so it revives with the restoration of harmony, good feeling, and mutual understanding." Thus the rebirth of the *Monitor* coincided with the dawn of an era of good feeling in the movement—compounded of renewed stability, steady growth, and the vitality of an oncoming second generation. All this was to be reflected in its pages in the years to come. But the *Monitor* would also prove to be more than a mirror of the movement; it would become as well a catalyst for change, a learning center, and a kind of monthly "town meeting" for the nationwide community of the organized blind. It would provide a source of comfort and a source of anger; it would alternate philosophy with polemics, education with agitation. In short it would give increased devotion to the commitment implicit in its title of *Monitor*: one that "advises, warns, and cautions."

And it would find a voice—an oral dimension—to supplement the tactile and visual dimensions of Braille and print. Coincident with the revival of the *Monitor* in 1964 came the announcement (carried in the October issue) that a tape edition was now available upon request—the taping through the generosity of the Kansas City Association of the Blind, and the technology by courtesy of Ways and Means of Augusta, Georgia. Meanwhile, as noted earlier, continuing efforts toward a disc-recorded version (widely preferred because of the availability of Talking Book machines) bore fruit finally with the production of the first recorded edition of the *Monitor* in July, 1968. Over the next years the recording process was to be progressively improved and upgraded; and in December, 1970, the recorded edition took on a distinctive sound as Larry McKeever began a long career as the "Voice of the Monitor." McKeever would continue until 1988, when the NFB began recording the *Monitor* in its own studios at the National Center for the Blind in Baltimore. Meanwhile the competitive audio technology of the tape cassette was improving to the point where the Federation could begin producing the *Monitor* on four-track cassettes (as of January, 1987). By the time of the golden anniversary year of 1990—with the multiple editions in Braille and print, on disc and cassette—some 30,000 copies of the *Monitor* were in circulation every month. Unmistakably, the voice of the movement was heard in the land. And the voice was rising.

It had been a steady, if sometimes difficult, ascent to that high plateau of recognition and influence. After the revival of the *Monitor* in 1964, there were to be just four years left of the tenBroek editorship. The death of the founder in early 1968 necessitated a replacement at the helm of the journal no less than at the head of the movement. Kenneth Jernigan, who was elected to succeed Dr. tenBroek in the presidency, moved immediately to fill the vacancy at the *Monitor*, choosing a veteran leader of proven devotion and ability: Perry Sundquist of California. In an "Open Letter to *Monitor* Readers" in the May, 1968, issue, the new President praised Sundquist as "one of Dr. tenBroek's closest associates and oldest friends [who] has always been among the staunchest and most steadfast members of the organized blind movement." He continued: "The *Monitor* will continue to be assembled and printed in the Berkeley office, and Mrs. tenBroek will handle the details of the operation....During Dr. tenBroek's illness her courage and steadfastness were truly tenBroekian. Over the years Dr. tenBroek had been the principal focus of her life, and toward the end she was constantly at his bedside. Yet she found the time and the strength to carry forward the work of the Berkeley office and impart strength to those around her."

That *Monitor* editorial team—made up of Editor Perry Sundquist, Associate Editor Hazel tenBroek, and Publisher Kenneth Jernigan—continued to work together for the next eight years to build the magazine into a journalistic force to be reckoned with. In 1977 the partnership came to an end as both editors retired from their positions (but not from the movement) and the entire editorial operation was shifted from California to the NFB's national headquarters in Des Moines, Iowa. The staff change was announced in an "Open Letter to *Monitor* Readers" from President Jernigan (January, 1977):

> When I became President of the Federation in 1968, two of the key people who formed the team that helped me start my presidency and build for the future were Perry Sundquist and Hazel tenBroek. I asked Perry to serve as editor of the *Monitor* and Hazel to serve as associate editor, as well as manager of the Berkeley office. Both accepted the call to serve, and both have been essential ingredients in the success of our publication, a success unparalleled in the history of periodicals for the blind.

With this issue Perry and Hazel cease their editorial relationship with the *Monitor* but not, of course, their work in the movement or their warm relationship with the President. That is a lifetime involvement.

In a second "Open Letter"—this one to Perry Sundquist and Hazel tenBroek—President Jernigan further summarized the joint accomplishment of the two editors over the years: "I will simply say that with you, Perry, as editor and you, Hazel, as associate editor, the *Braille Monitor* has been tremendously effective and important in improving the lives of the blind. During your tenure we have more than doubled our circulation, increased public awareness, brought changes to the agencies, and stimulated the blind to a greater sense of determination and self-realization than ever before in history. Not bad for eight years." He went on to quote from earlier correspondence with Sundquist in which their professional relationship had come under discussion. In one of those letters the President had written:

This brings me to the question of the relationship of the three of us. As I see it, your function is that of editor—that is, working within the policy laid down by the publisher; to write articles; select and reject material; and plan the overall pattern of publication for the months ahead. Your initiation of the series "Meet Our State President and Our State Affiliate" is a good and constructive example of this. You receive articles, correspond with members and affiliates about the *Monitor*, and stimulate a flow of information. As I see it, my role corresponds to the one ordinarily assumed by the publisher of a newspaper or magazine—that is, I lay down the policy as to the kind of editorial positions we will take. Carrying out this function, I may decide, for instance, that we want to exclude a given type of article or that we want to emphasize a given situation to try to achieve an organizational purpose. From the beginning of time, publishers have also assumed the prerogative (much to the annoyance of editors) of vetoing a given article which they don't like—often on pure whim if they feel like it. Also, publishers have, since the memory of man, insisted on inserting articles which they have taken a fancy to or which they themselves have written—even if such articles have been possessed of no literary merit at all and have upset the plans and the ulcers of the editor. In this respect I call on you to read the history of the stormy relationship existing between Joseph Pulitzer and a whole series of saintly souls. Editor and publisher should serve as a balance wheel to each other. Each must try (as gently as possible) to keep the other from going off the deep end, from damaging the publication with the more obvious madnesses, and from settling into a dull routine....

Having said all this, let me now come back to the specifics of the
articles. I believe that you, Hazel, and I make a good team. The
three of us balance each other quite well. If Hazel had her way
(and she usually does not get it), the *Monitor* would be a learned
tome, full of scholarship and dust, disturbed by nobody. If you
had your way (and you sometimes get it), the magazine would be
a stringing together of popularized human interest stories with a
good sprinkling of generalized welfare articles, read by some but
not getting across the substantial organizational message. If I followed my natural bent (and I very often don't), I would make the
magazine a solid stream of preachments exhorting people to get
in and work in the organization. It would appeal to the hard core
and convert some but lose the value of the audiences that both
you and Hazel would tend to stimulate.

All of these approaches have their problems, but when you put
them together, we have a darned good magazine—the best one I
have seen in the field of work with the blind. The fact of the
success of our editorial policy and teamwork is to be found in the
great organizational upsurge which we are experiencing and in the
growing mailing list of the *Monitor*. I think there is little doubt
that our magazine has more influence than any other periodical
in the field today and that the enthusiasm for it is continuing to
grow.

In another "Open Letter" addressed to *Monitor* readers, Jernigan announced the appointment of a new editor: "He is Don
McConnell, who has been associated for many years with the
Federation and the *Monitor*. He learned his Federationism under
Hazel's tutelage in the Berkeley Office....To Editor McConnell
we say: 'The task you undertake is formidable. You are now editor
of the most influential publication in the field of work with the
blind, but we have confidence that you will bring the *Monitor* to
new heights of excellence. Be aggressive; be sensitive; be resourceful; and never hesitate to tell the truth, regardless of what the
cost may seem to be. The rest will follow.'"

Two and a half years later, President Jernigan found himself
reluctantly addressing another "Open Letter" to *Monitor* readers
in order to announce the resignation of Editor McConnell.
Recalling their years of association, Jernigan wrote: "It was the
beginning of a very successful series of *Monitor* editions. It was
also the beginning of a very productive and harmonious relationship....Mr. McConnell is a good writer; he has editorial capability
and perspective; and he is a knowledgeable and dedicated member
of the movement. His participation in the movement will, of
course, continue, but it will be difficult to find his equal as an

editor." Jernigan went on to note that, pending the employment of a new editor, "Jim Gashel and I will pool our efforts to produce the *Monitor*. I hope this will be a very brief interlude, for the editing of the *Monitor* is a full time and demanding job."

Don McConnell, the retiring editor, penned his own farewell in the form of an "Open Letter to Federationists" which was published in the next issue of the *Monitor* (July-August, 1979). Observing that his years at the national headquarters "were the two most eventful and dramatic years of my life as well as the most rewarding," McConnell presented a thoughtful recollection of the Federation, its members, and its leaders which sought to define and illustrate certain salient characteristics of the movement in its active phase:

OPEN LETTER TO FEDERATIONISTS
by Donald McConnell

As I reflect on my years working for the NFB, a number of characteristics of the organization strike me. The Federation has many faces. If you visit local chapters, it can appear to be an organization of bake sales and committee reports. During the social times at conventions, it is a huge and friendly family. But when the large core of active Federation leaders go into action, the striking feature of the NFB is its cohesiveness and the ability of Federationists to act as a team. Two examples in particular come to mind: the White House Conference on Handicapped Individuals and the FAA demonstration last July. During the ill-starred White House Conference, a group of about three dozen Federationists completely out-maneuvered the Conference staff—expensive consultants and all—and organized a coalition of handicapped consumers that all but took over the Conference. At last July's convention, with fewer than 48 hours' notice, 1,000 Federationists were on the street in front of the Federal Aviation Administration. Even though the day between the decision to demonstrate and the demonstration itself was a national holiday, the pickets carried printed picket signs and even had box lunches on the buses coming over from Baltimore. And we were met in Washington by a massive turnout of the Washington press corps.

After both of these occasions, we were accused of having planned our action weeks in advance. The White House Conference staff told the press that it was obvious we had come to Washington prepared to disrupt the Conference, and they implied we had acted in bad faith. The same complaint came from the FAA. In neither case was it true. They just couldn't believe an organization (and one of blind people at that) could act with such unity and effectiveness.

I have one other reflection on my experience with the Federation, and it concerns a quality of our activity that explains all the rest. It has to do with the kind of people who are in the movement. There are plenty of blind persons who for one reason or another choose not to be part of the Federation. But it is my experience that the best blind people do belong. People call the NFB just one more special interest group, but there is an important difference. Despite the tangible gains we have made for the blind— the liberalization of Social Security rules, for example—the people who benefit are in general not those who put themselves on the line. The blind persons who institute civil rights lawsuits know in advance that whatever the outcome, they will personally bear enormous burdens with little in the way of reward. But they know that the legal principles they establish will help all those who come after. The blind who jeopardize their jobs by demonstrating in front of a repressive lighthouse are in general not the lighthouse employees who will benefit from the action. Many of the most active Federationists have already made it; they could isolate themselves and leave their fellow blind to do the best they can. But they don't do this. Federationists realize that, however it may look, they did not make it on their own; and they acknowledge the responsibility this puts on them. This widespread acknowledgment of responsibility and the obligation to act on it no matter what the personal consequences makes the National Federation of the Blind almost unique in the world. It is what, for me, has made it an honor and a privilege to have been given a chance to have a part in it. Without question the Federation has changed my life and in a way that I will always be grateful for.

Kenneth Jernigan, in his 1979 letter to *Monitor* readers disclosing McConnell's resignation, expressed the hope that his own editorial involvement with the magazine would be "a very brief interlude." That was to turn out to be one of Jernigan's less accurate anticipations; more than a decade later he would still be occupying the editor's chair. In the first year after his assumption of the editorship, Jernigan wrote in a *Monitor* report that: "I am working with Jim Gashel these days as a sort of co-editor of the *Monitor*. It's fun, but it crowds a busy schedule even further." He recalled that following his previous tenure as editor the *Monitor* had gone out of business: "Anyway we didn't start publication again until 1964. This time I have already been at it for more than four months, and there seems to be no indication that we are about to close shop; so I guess that shows progress."

The progress of the *Monitor* then and in the decade to follow was much greater than that diffident remark suggested; and the progress came fast. In his 1983 Presidential Report to the Kansas City convention, Jernigan could say: "We have expanded the distribution of our magazine, the *Braille Monitor*. It now goes to every congressional office and to every agency doing work with the blind in the country. It is beyond question the most influential publication in the field today."

To be sure, not every reader of the *Monitor*—either inside or outside the movement—approved of the way in which the magazine was being run. One fairly new reader (and NFB member) wrote a sternly critical letter to the editor protesting nearly everything he had read in the *Monitor* over the five months he had known of it. Perhaps to his surprise, the letter received a long and thoughtful reply from Co-editor Kenneth Jernigan. Following is that correspondence as published in the December, 1983, *Monitor*:

October 1, 1983

To The Editor of the *Braille Monitor*:

I am writing this letter after five months of reading the *Monitor* in Braille. I wish to comment on the content and the format of the magazine. This letter is not addressed to a specific person, because nowhere in the *Monitor* does it say who the Editor is.

A major problem in producing materials in Braille is the cost. Therefore, it is very disturbing to see how much space is wasted in the *Monitor*. Three of the first six pages of Part I of the August-September issue are blank. Often between articles, an entire page is wasted before the next article begins. I hope this will be corrected.

Sifting through the contents of the *Monitor* makes it apparent that NFB is dealing with important items and doing good work. However, these issues are so buried in NFB rhetoric and biased reporting as to be lost to the reader. Why is it not possible to label editorials as editorials, and separate them from facts and news. Are the people in the National Office viewing the average NFB member as not capable of taking the facts and determining who is right without being led by the nose? This goes against what NFB supposedly stands for. The *Monitor* is read by people in the blindness field who could become friends of the Federation. Some do not because articles in the *Monitor* supposedly reporting on important issues and accomplishments of the Federation, are headed with exceedingly biased headlines, and filled with hateful comments. This hurts the cause of the blind persons in the Federation and those who are potential members.

The *Monitor* is not well organized, in contrast to almost every other magazine I have read. Articles appear in random order with no relationship to one another. In other magazines there are sections in which articles on similar topics or of the same degree of importance are grouped together. Both in the "Monitor Miniatures" (and in the *Monitor* in general) articles just appear one after another with no rhyme or reason. This makes it difficult to read.

I hope you will give my comments serious consideration. They come from someone who is a Federation member and supports what the Federation wants. But I see a lot in the *Monitor* that is confusing, disorganized, and biased. I would like this to change.

Sincerely,

————————

October 24, 1983
Dear Mr.——:

I have your letter of October 1, 1983, and I thank you for it. The reason that certain parts of pages are left blank in the Braille Edition of the *Monitor* is so that the metal plates may be used to make reprints of articles. The American Printing House for the Blind does the formatting, not the people in the National Office of the Federation. The Printing House also Brailles a great many other magazines. Perhaps they could do it more judiciously, but in the circumstances I doubt it.

Let me now turn to your comments about the tone and substance of the *Monitor*. I do not agree with you that the reporting is biased, but my reasons for feeling that way probably spring from the same source as your reasons for feeling that bias exists. In other words I agree (and, of course, I would since I do much of the writing) with what the *Monitor* says. When you find a particular article with which you disagree (especially if the disagreement is strong) you are likely to feel that the article is based on prejudice.

You suggest that editorials should be labeled as such and that news should be reported without comment. If you will reconsider the matter, you may conclude that our practice is more honest than that which many publications claim to follow. It is not possible to publish so-called "facts" without expressing opinion and editorializing. By the very virtue of what you select to print, you create a pattern, editorialize, and exercise censorship.

Once you select the subject, you further editorialize by what facts you print and what you leave out. You editorialize by where you place material in the article and even by the subordination of sentences. Finally, you editorialize by your choice of words: He *"stated"* —he *"alleged"* —he *"declared"* —he *"insisted"*—he *"protested"*—he *"averred"*—etc. All of these verbs might be used interchangeably to express the same action; but oh what a difference in impression. In short, what editorializing! Yet, if you are to write the article at all you must use one or another of these verbs—or something else equally slanted. And this does not even take into account the adjectives and adverbs, which abound and proliferate. Read the average newspaper story or magazine article, and see whether what I am telling you is the truth.

The *Monitor* uses straight language, but I believe that it scrupulously tells the truth. When we make a mistake (as everybody sometimes does), we do not wait for somebody to insist that we print a retraction. We do it immediately and ungrudgingly. Furthermore, we print the retraction as prominently and as fully as the original erroneous statement. I can show you evidence from the pages of the *Monitor* to prove it.

This in no sense takes away from the fact that our language is sometimes quite blunt. We have, for instance, said in a number of cases that this or that individual has been guilty of "stealing" money intended for the blind. Should we have pussyfooted around and said that the individual misappropriated, borrowed, or purloined the money? I think not. In the instances I have in mind the individuals were convicted by courts of law and sent to the penitentiary. I think we would have been editorializing (and in a very dishonest and destructive manner) if we had used any other words than the ones we chose.

To the best of my knowledge no other publication in our field reported these incidents at all. Yet, they knew about them. I have proof that they did. By neglecting to report these stories did these magazines not editorialize? Yes, they did—but they will not be accused of it. They will be regarded as very genteel. I have another word for their conduct, and it is probably one that you would regard as editorializing.

The fact that we report bluntly and truthfully and that we do not avoid controversial topics does not mean, as you suggest, that we demonstrate "hate" (a word, by the way, which itself carries editorial connotations). We do not "hate" the people who exploit the blind, but we certainly do deplore their actions; and we have every intention of exposing such actions and such people for what they are. Let those who like it like it, and let those who dislike it dislike it.

In my opinion the National Federation of the Blind has done more to improve the lives of blind people than any other single entity or force which has existed during the twentieth century, and I think that one of the principal reasons is our willingness (no, our *insistence*) that the truth be told and things be called what they are—regardless of controversy or bitter personal attacks against us or attempts to silence us by trying to destroy our organization. Let us not confuse lack of courage with morality, or blunt truth-telling with hate. I remind you of the words of George Bernard Shaw: "*I* am firm; *you* are stubborn; *he* is pigheaded."

Let me now leave the subject of editorializing and deal with some of the other points you raise. First I would like to comment on the matter of whether Federationists can be "led around by the nose." It cannot be done, whether from inside or outside, whether by friend or foe. The agencies cannot do it; the public cannot do it; you, by the comments in your letter, cannot do it; and, for that matter, I cannot do it. The Federation members are a very sophisticated population, more so than any other group concerned with blindness. They *cannot* be flimflammed or bamboozled—and they *will* not be stampeded. They can distinguish rhetoric from opinion and opinion from fact, and they are not so immature or lacking in self-assurance that they are likely to be disturbed by somebody else's view concerning their method of locomotion.

You say that you are a Federationist and that you have been reading the *Monitor* for five months. This would indicate (and it is clear from the tone of your comments that such is the case) that you have not yet attended one of our National Conventions. Several thousand of us come together for a week of discussion and decision making, and we speak our minds and have our say. The convention is the "supreme authority" of the organization. It makes the policies, and the elected leaders follow those policies. Otherwise, they will stop being the elected leaders, and somebody else will replace them.

One of the most persistent myths which our agency opponents continually try to perpetuate is that the elected leaders of the Federation (and particularly I as President) do not truly speak for the membership and do not accurately reflect their desires and feelings. Not only is this total nonsense but it is also wishful thinking. Let those who doubt it come to the convention and put it to the test. No one steamrollers Federationists into going where they do not wish to go, and they know precisely and exactly what their goals are and how they intend to achieve them.

As an example, the *Monitor* is edited just the way the overwhelming majority of Federationists want it edited. If it were not, there would be changes. The articles are not scattered through the magazines without, as you put it, "rhyme or reason and in random order." There are patterns and purposes. The fact that an individual has not yet perceived or understood those patterns and purposes does not mean that they do not exist.

You say that no one is listed as Editor of the *Monitor*. If you had been in the Federation longer, you would have more background on this point. In 1979 the person who was editing the *Monitor* resigned, and it was announced that James Gashel and I (along with help from a few others) would do the editing until and unless we found someone else to do it. That is still the arrangement; although, it must be said that I have come to do more and more of the work as the months have gone by to the point that, if you have any quarrels with how the magazine is edited, the responsibility is probably mine. I guess I should go on to say that I rather enjoy the job and will probably keep doing it (always keeping in mind what I said about pleasing the majority of the membership or getting kicked out). In the meantime I keep doing the work and finding it fun. Let me deal with one final point. You say that "the *Monitor* is read by people in the blindness field who could become friends of the Federation" and that they do not because of the way the magazine is written. Perhaps this gets at the very heart of what we are discussing. If we were to write the *Monitor* in such a way as to please those people in the blindness field about whom you are talking, most of us would feel the Federation was of little further value. Our movement was not established simply to be one more bland pretense, one more means of living easy and avoiding stepping on toes, one more preacher of pious platitudes. Regardless of the consequences, we have remained true to our purpose, and this is why we are the strongest force in the affairs of the blind today. It is no mere slogan or catch phrase when we say: We know who we are, and we will never go back.

Very truly yours,
Kenneth Jernigan, President
National Federation of the Blind

P. S. How many other organizations or groups in this field do you know that would be willing to print (unedited, unaltered, and without deletion) such a letter from one of their members? Think about it. It will tell you a lot.

Expression, Exposition, and Exposure: The *Monitor* at Maturity

From its maiden issue in the late fifties, the *Braille Monitor* was unapologetically an activist publication, reflecting the urgent social purposes of the movement it served. To the best of their abilities its early editors and writers reported on the hot spots and trouble spots in the field of work with the blind; but of necessity their range was limited and their coverage narrow. For one thing, funds were scarce in those days; for another, the *Monitor* was a different kind of animal, journalistically, and its role and character were not yet clear. There were few precedents for what the National Federation of the Blind was doing in the world; and there were fewer still for what the *Monitor* was seeking to do in its pages. It sought, among other things, to combine the intimacy of a community newsletter with the broad sweep of a national news magazine. It sought also, on one hand, to step back from the fray and reflect philosophically on its meaning, while on the other hand taking the plunge and joining the fight without equivocation. In time these differing purposes would come to be accommodated as complementary rather than contradictory elements in a novel editorial pattern: what might be termed a participative journalism of engagement, "a town meeting on the page." At that future time the *Braille Monitor* would come fully of age.

The stages of journalistic evolution through which the *Monitor* would pass before it reached maturity can be traced in the files of bound volumes stretching from the fifties through the eighties. In the earliest issues the contents were taken up almost exclusively with organizational matters—as witness the table of contents for the edition of September, 1957, which contained a total of seventeen items in a grand total of nineteen pages (small even for that period). The titles, largely self-explanatory, were listed as follows: Setting the Record Straight—Current Developments—Postal Inquiry Dropped—The Helpless Blind—Misconceptions—Bill Taylor Gets the Axe—NFB Pins—A Highly Significant "Clarification"—NFB Tape Program Begins—Illinois' Loss-Nevada's Gain—A Resolution—Financial Support to This Magazine—A Great Loss—Legislative Success in Illinois—Oregon Legislative Report—State Conventions—Here and There.

Apart from the modest size of that *Monitor* issue, it displayed a considerable scope and variety of subject matter, ranging from the political to the personal. The contents demonstrated the range of the Federation's activities, but the major emphasis was on legislative programs and internal matters. Nearly all of the items were brief notices of one or two paragraphs, a format which may have reflected both financial stringency and the exclusively Braille publication of that opening season. Within months the print edition was to make its appearance, and the role of President tenBroek and the Berkeley office to take on greater significance.

The nature of that significance was not to be fully appreciated until the sixties when tenBroek became the primary editor and steadily imposed his own personality and style, as well as his philosophy, upon the *Monitor*. By 1967, a full decade after its inauguration and the final year of tenBroek's career, the NFB's monthly magazine was thoroughly identified with its editor and guiding spirit. Here is the table of contents for a typical issue during that year:

THE BRAILLE MONITOR
AUGUST, 1967
CONTENTS

Convention Roundup
London Blind Workers' Demonstrations End In Victory

IFB Executive Committee Meeting

NFB Testifies In Congressional Hearings
by John Nagle

Tom Joe Goes To Pennsylvania

National Federation of the Blind Student Division News
by Ramona Willoughby

Minnesota Scores Gains

Agencies For The Blind And Tuning
by Stanley Oliver

End Of Social Dislocation Of Leprosy Patients
by O. W. Hasselbled, M.D.

Aloha To Hawaii
by Anthony Mannino

The WCWB Executive Meeting

Blind Student Stereotype Tested

Monitor Miniatures

Are We Equal To The Challenge?
by Jacobus tenBroek

The Blind In Argentina
by Hugo Garcia Garcilazo

The Collecting Box In The Welfare State
by Douglas Houghton

NFB Testifies On Rehabilitation Amendment Of 1967
Statement by John Nagle

What stands out from that 1967 table of contents, as contrasted with the titles of a decade earlier, is the greater range of topics (especially in geographical terms) and the larger size of the edition—52 pages compared with 19 in the 1957 issue. Short items still appear, but the articles have become substantial—even apart from Dr. tenBroek's memorable last banquet address at the Los Angeles convention: "Are We Equal to the Challenge?" There is a distinctive international flavor to the contents (four articles); the Federation's testimony before Congress is reported in two episodes by the Chief of the Washington Office, John Nagle; the Los Angeles convention is covered in both breadth and depth; and there is a noteworthy report of elections in the year-old NFB Student Division, written by a student leader named Ramona Willoughby (who was elected secretary alongside a second vice president named Chuck Walhof, whom she was later to marry).

One decade later, in 1977, successions were occurring both in the presidency of the NFB and in the editorship of the *Monitor*—but the face of the magazine remained unruffled and its contents displayed only continuity and progress. An attentive reader might, however, have noted a new degree of emphasis devoted to the concerns of civil rights. In a typical issue of that year (July, 1977), article after article—virtually without exception—dealt with an array of insults and injuries inflicted upon blind persons in their professional and personal lives, and with the measured responses to all of them undertaken by the National Federation of the Blind. This is how they appeared in the table of contents:

THE BRAILLE MONITOR
JULY, 1977
CONTENTS

Note

The NFB Goes To Court To Defend Blind Vendors:
The Jessie Nash Case

Civil Rights For The Handicapped:
Potentials And Perils For The Blind
by James Gashel

The Light At The End Of The Tunnel:
Another "Invitation" From NAC

With the exception of the last two items in the contents—standard entries both—the entire table consisted of current issues immediately affecting the lives and livelihoods of blind Americans: in their business enterprises (the Jessie Nash case); in the classroom (the Gurmankin case); in the conduct of child care (the Bohrer case); in the sheltered shops (as reported by James Omvig); in the legislature (as reported by James Gashel), and in the continuing campaign against the agency gadfly known as NAC (two articles). This concentration upon civil rights issues affecting the blind was a graphic indication of changing times and oncoming generations in the organized blind movement—of the shift away from traditional problems of subsistence and survival to the concerns of dignity and equality, of opportunity and access, of the rights and immunities of citizens. The *Monitor*, like a social seismograph, registered the tremors emanating from these sources of disturbance; it not only registered but documented them, providing a context and explanatory framework, building a record and preparing a brief. That was what it meant, in 1977, to be a "monitor."

During the decade of the seventies, with the exception of a single year (mid-1977 to mid-1978), Kenneth Jernigan was the President of the Federation. But he was not the editor of the *Monitor* until 1978. Unquestionably his impact, as the leader of the movement, had been felt in the magazine during the seventies; but it was in the following decade that he moved into the foreground and placed the stamp of his personal style and character, directly and unmistakably, upon the *Monitor.*

The signature of the Jernigan style was to be displayed most prominently in two distinctive literary forms: those of investigative reporting and of the personal essay. Neither appeared for the first time in the eighties; the former had been foreshadowed by accounts of discrimination and repression in the days of the fight to organize, and the latter was anticipated by editorial jottings and ruminations in the earliest issues of the magazine. It remained for Jernigan as editor to inaugurate a policy of investigative journalism—and for Jernigan as editorialist to exercise a penchant for the familiar essay.

Both of these journalistic forms, the expressive and the expository, were represented in a typical *Monitor* issue of 1987—a decade after the one last examined above. Once again the table of contents is worthy of reproduction for its evidence of the range of concerns then prevalent in the journal and the movement.

THE BRAILLE MONITOR
JUNE-JULY, 1987
CONTENTS

Of Braille And Memories And The Matilda Ziegler
by Kenneth Jernigan

United Airlines Continues To Harass Blind People

Congressional Momentum In The Airline Controversy Increases

The Future Of A Blind Guy
by Gary Wunder

Building My Piano Business
by Al Sanchez

Payoff Speaks—Nancy Squeaks
by Kenneth Jernigan

The Three Barretts Growing In The Federation
by Ramona Walhof

Jim Moynihan Responds To Professor Eames And Ms. Gardner

Blind Of Milwaukee Produce Television Program

David Stayer
Statement Of Principle

Low Vision As An Alternative Technique
by Richard Mettler

Blood, Signatures, And Safety
by Marc Maurer

On The Nature Of Budgets, Controversy, And Censorship

Another Barrier Falls: Victory In IRS Employment

Monitoradio

The lead article in this richly packed and diversified issue—
"Of Braille and Memories and the *Matilda Ziegler*"—was vintage
Jernigan in his essayist mode. (The complete text of the essay is
reprinted in Chapter Seven of this volume.) The next two articles
were illustrative of the editor, and the Federation, in the "attack"
mode; they presented two contributions in a long-sustained campaign to secure the rights of blind airline passengers. The following two entries, by Gary Wunder and Al Sanchez respectively,
were personal stories in what used to be called the "human interest" vein. The more extended article, "Payoff Speaks—Nancy
Squeaks," by Kenneth Jernigan, exemplified the method of investigative reporting and editorial exposure which was coming more
and more to characterize the journalism of the *Braille Monitor* in
the decade of the eighties. In this instance the topic was a politically inspired appointment to the directorship of the Iowa Commission for the Blind which had become unraveled through the
hard-hitting media coverage of the *Braille Monitor* and TV's
"Sixty Minutes," among others. Something of the flavor of the
Jernigan article may be gleaned from its opening paragraphs:

> In the recent sorry history of the Iowa Commission for the Blind
> no episode has been more grubby than the story of Nancy Nor-
> man. When John Taylor was fired as director in 1982, the
> Governor's office and the Commission board made a great to-do
> about the fact that they were instituting a nationwide search to
> get the best possible candidate. After much fanfare and window
> dressing an unknown named Nancy Norman was given the nod.
> This was done despite the fact that there were qualified applicants
> and that Ms. Norman had no experience at all in the field of work
> with the blind.
>
> As the full scenario began to be revealed, the story was even
> worse than it had first appeared. Ms. Norman's husband was the
> law partner of the man who was then chairman of the Iowa Com-
> mission for the Blind. Moreover, her husband was also a heavy
> contributor to the war chest of Iowa's current Governor, who was

at that time a candidate and running hard. So the much bal-
lyhooed search was simply a disgusting charade, and the appointment was nothing more than a political payoff and (in view of the
law partnership) a sort of secondhand nepotism. Under the circumstances it is not surprising that the results were a failure.

Each of the remaining articles in this representative 1987
issue of the *Monitor* contributed to the overall balance of the contents. Ramona Walhof (nee Willoughby) presented the real-life
domestic drama of a young Federation couple, Pat and Trudy Barrett, and their successful struggle to adopt a child: thus, "The
Three Barretts Growing in the Federation." Indirectly that story
was also about Ramona Walhof and her capacities as a leader and
friend; but this sub-theme had to be read between the lines.
Another very personal, and inspirational, article touching on the
deeper meanings of Federationism in the lives of many members
was "A Statement of Principle," by David Stayer (well-remembered by convention-goers for his ringing tenor delivery of the
invocation in song). A definite shift in perspective from the personal to the professional was provided by a controversial but
authoritative article on "Low Vision as an Alternative Technique," by Richard Mettler. Next, as if to assure an even greater
stretch in the *Monitor's* coverage, there was a lurid-sounding
entry carrying the by-line of NFB President Marc Maurer—
"Blood, Signatures, and Safety"—which turned out to be an account of determined efforts by Federationists in Minnesota, led
by the redoubtable Judy Sanders, to participate in a blood plasma
project despite the prejudice of program professionals. The
NFB's President also reappeared in the contents with a
"patented" Maurer article dealing with Federation involvement
in litigation concerned with the rights of blind persons—in this
case, the right to sue under terms of the 1973 Amendments to
the Vocational Rehabilitation Act. Finally, the June-July issue of
the *Monitor* rounded out its coverage with an astute set of
guidelines, written by Patti Gregory of the NFB of Illinois, for
blind job seekers facing the specter of an employment interview.
There was truly something for everyone in that edition of the
magazine; it fulfilled, with room to spare, the requirements laid
down for a proper "monitor"—to advise, to caution, and to warn.
It also found time, more than once in those seventy pages, to
inspire as well.

Toward the end of the decade the emphasis upon investigative reporting, introduced by Editor Jernigan, became more
prominent and ambitious in its reach. Particularly instrumental

in the implementation of this activist journalism was Barbara Pierce, whose appointment as Associate Editor was announced by Jernigan in the December, 1988, *Monitor*. His introduction was accompanied by these remarks:

> I have been looking for a long time (ten years, to be precise) for an associate editor—and I am pleased to tell you that I have now found her. Beginning with this issue, Barbara Pierce, president of the National Federation of the Blind of Ohio and long-time leader at the national level, joins the *Monitor* staff.
>
> Of course, Barbara is no stranger to Federationists or readers of this publication. She directs our national public relations campaign, participates prominently in National Conventions, and is sometimes seen at NAC demonstrations. She wrote the *Monitor* convention articles for the 1987 and 1988 National Conventions and is a frequent contributor to these pages. I believe she will do an excellent job as associate editor. I suppose I don't need to say that, for if I hadn't believed it, I wouldn't have asked her to serve....
>
> So what will she do in her new position? She will read state and division newsletters to glean items for publication. She will do research on assigned topics for articles. She will think up topics on her own and do original writing. And she will serve as a sounding board, a copy girl, a workhorse, and an ambulatory and auditory adjunct for the Editor. It would now appear that she will spend something like every other week in Baltimore and the remainder of her time working at home. A big order? Yes, but that's how we are.

The increased accent on investigative journalism in the *Monitor* found full and formidable expression early in 1989 with the first of what was to be a series of powerful articles probing and exposing abusive, shabby, and criminal practices in various institutions bearing the NAC seal of approval—most notably and shockingly in the schools for the deaf and blind of Florida and of Alabama. In the March, 1989, issue of the *Monitor*, readers were confronted with an astonishing litany of crimes, misdemeanors, and shoddy practices at the Florida School for the Deaf and the Blind. Here is what they read:

FLORIDA SCHOOL FOR THE DEAF AND THE BLIND:
A DANGEROUS PLACE FOR CHILDREN

The National Accreditation Council for Agencies Serving the Blind and Visually Handicapped (NAC) prides itself on its assertion that the public can count on the NAC seal of approval as an indication of the excellence of the agency displaying it. Twice in recent years the National Federation of the Blind has had occasion to warn Floridians that the NAC seal, far from from being a hallmark of quality, is more often an indication that the institution in question is not serving its constituents well. In the last year the citizens of the state have learned with tragic clarity what we meant.

The Florida School for the Deaf and the Blind (FSDB) enrolls 530 students from as young as four years of age to twenty-one. Roughly 300 are students in the department for the deaf; almost 100 are enrolled in the department for the blind; and the remaining 128 are either deaf-multi-handicapped or blind-multi-handicapped. The number of the multi-handicapped was 129 until October 13, 1988, when Jennifer Driggers, age nine, was scalded to death in the shower room at Vaill Hall, the residence of 39 multi-handicapped children.

On April 26, 1988, a twenty-two-year-old residence supervisor and Boy Scout leader was fired and arrested for sexually assaulting seventeen deaf boys. He is currently standing trial on twenty-four counts of sexual abuse. Four other male staff members (including the father of the man currently standing trial) have been prosecuted for criminal offenses against students of both sexes. One of these four was a teacher in the department for the blind, and his offenses were against blind girls enrolled at the School as students.

Tragedy and abuse have been a way of life at FSDB for several years. In September of 1982, a fourteen-year-old student, Christi Eddleman, fell from her infirmary bed and suffocated in the plastic trash basket liner beneath the bed. She died of complications several months later. About two years ago a blind student, James Thomas, was fatally injured while wrestling with a friend. In addition, at least nine suicide attempts have been made by students at the school during the past year, and abuse of children by other students and staff is widespread.

How could all this have happened in a school with an annual budget of eighteen and a half million dollars and accreditation in good standing for its department for the blind from NAC (the National Accreditation Council for Agencies Serving the Blind and Visually Handicapped)? Is it that the staff members are irresponsible and evil? Is it that the parents are heartless and uncaring? Is it that NAC was too loose with its accreditation and lulled the public and officials of state government with its seal of good standing and its assurance that the school was providing quality services?

With respect to this last question, there can be no doubt, for the sex offenses committed by the teacher in the department for the blind occurred almost a year ago and received publicity in the press. There was a court action with all of the trappings, but the NAC accreditation was not withdrawn. At the time of this writing (January, 1989) NAC accreditation has still not been withdrawn. Only after (as detailed later in this article) the Associate Editor of the *Monitor* called and asked probing questions did NAC indicate that it might consider possibly perhaps taking some sort of undefined action. The Florida School for the Deaf and the Blind (a school riddled with student deaths, suicide attempts, and widespread sex abuse of students by staff) is accredited with NAC's stamp of approval, and that accreditation and approval still continue. Children die; children are subjected to nightmarish unbelievable abuse; yet, NAC accreditation is not withdrawn. If the defense by NAC is that it was unaware of the situation, that is almost as damning as if it had known and failed to act. If the claim is that NAC knew but was powerless, that is equally damning. If NAC (like Pontius Pilate) should try to wash its hands of guilt by saying that the offenses have occurred in the department for the deaf and not in the department for the blind and that, therefore, NAC has no responsibility, that is perhaps most damning of all. Can one department of an institution be pure while the other departments in the overall structure are corrupt? Can a piece of an apple be sound and the rest of it rotten? And what about the sex abuse in the department for the blind?

As we have probed into this house of horrors, we have repeatedly been told of a feeling of despair on the part of the students, a fear to speak out. The revelations are enough to make one weep with outrage, frustration, and sorrow.

The Florida School for the Deaf and the Blind was founded a little over a hundred years ago, and until 1979 it educated students in either the department for the deaf or the department for the blind. That year the school accepted its first multi-handicapped students, and as a result (or, at least, this is the claimed reason), its budget has increased by about thirty-two percent each year since. The 1980 cost for educating each student at the School was reported as $10,944. The cost in 1989 will be $34,943. Yet, each year since 1983 the school has gone to the legislature, warning of dire consequences if it did not receive even larger appropriations than it was given. Despite these predictions of doom, the school (at least, so far as we can determine) has never had to refuse a child because of overcrowding.

When asked, an FSDB official described the institution as being like a private boarding school. Yet, the funding comes from the legislature. A seven-member board of trustees runs the school and answers to the Governor's Cabinet, which is also the State Board of Education. Although the Commissioner of Education is one of the Governor's Cabinet (and is, therefore, a member of the State Board of Education), this is the only connection between the School and the Department of Education (DOE), which has no direct jurisdiction over the School. The School has consistently argued that provisions of Public Law 94-142, the Education of All Handicapped Children Act, do not apply to it.

Both blind and deaf children can qualify for admission to the School only by meeting very specific medical criteria. Multi-handicapped youngsters, on the other hand, are designated as such by parents and FSDB officials and then enrolled. If the staff cannot immediately determine whether a child meets the institution's criteria, the practice has been to enroll him or her for (depending on which official you believe) either thirty or ninety days while conducting an exhaustive evaluation. It is not surprising that the natural inertia of the situation results in the School's deciding to keep students who are already enrolled regardless of the test results. Whether or not the local school district believes that it is able to educate the child, the parent can choose to have a multi-handicapped youngster placed at FSDB if the school agrees.

Those close to the School report that since the passage of P.L. 94-142 and the resulting mainstreaming of many handicapped children, the student body (even in the Departments for the Blind and the Deaf) has changed. For example, about eighty percent of the youngsters currently enrolled in the department for the blind receive counseling of some kind. Relatively few students graduating from the School go on to college.

But the 128 children designated as multi-handicapped are not, for the most part, profoundly disabled. Most are either blind or deaf and, in addition, exhibit a behavioral or emotional disorder. Some are mentally retarded, but the retardation is usually mild.

It is clear from the catastrophic problems FSDB has had in the past several years that supervising the students outside of school hours presents staff with serious difficulties. Roughly 80% of the youngsters' time is spent in their dormitories. We were told that the position of live-in house parent was eliminated shortly after William T. Dawson became president of the institution in the early 1980s. Differing reasons have been given for this action. Some have said that the live-ins wanted to be moved on the campus not for the good of the students but for their own convenience, but others have said that there seemed to be concerns about abuses by staff if they spent long periods of time with the children and that this is why the position of live-in house parent was discontinued. Be this as it may, FSDB has paid a steep price for its decision. The current practice is to have three eight-hour shifts of residential supervisors, and the youngsters have no opportunity to form strong relationships with house parents since every shift brings new supervisors into the dormitory. There are also many more staff members to hire, train, and supervise. According to an official state report, school administration and staff supervision costs have grown until thirty-three percent of salaries are paid to administrators, and twenty-seven percent of all School personnel have no day-to-day contact with children.

Whether as a result of the staff problems or for other reasons, dismaying things have (according to the official report) happened in the dormitories. Deaf-blind students have sometimes spent as much as seven hours without a staff member nearby who could communicate with them. Children have been left for shockingly extended periods of time (up to ten days) in seclusion, and even though the staff-to-student ratio is one to six, children frequently abuse one another without intervention or sometimes even without staff recognition (until later) that injury has taken place.

The residential component of the School's program is not integrated with the two educational departments. So, for example, the principal of the department for the blind has (except tenuously) no involvement with the students in his residential school except when they are engaged in academic pursuits. When we interviewed Dennis Hartenstine (NAC's executive director), he said that NAC could not comment on any part of the School's program which it did not accredit. Presumably, therefore, if dormitory life is not considered part of the department for the blind, NAC (as the accrediting body for the department for the blind) might take the position that it is not involved in what goes on in the dormitory. One can reasonably infer from the comments Hartenstine made in our interview with him that this is the line of defense NAC will use if confronted with its failings in Florida. Not many people would understand or give credence to such hairsplitting distinctions. Most who have considered it at all have undoubtedly assumed that the dormitory arrangements for blind children have been evaluated and accredited along with the academic program in the department for the blind.

Jennifer Driggers was nine years old at the time of her death last October. She was deaf, had some vision problems, and had an IQ of about thirty-five. She functioned at a mental age of between two and three years. She seems also to have had difficulty getting along with other children and staff. She frequently exhibited aggressive behavior although no other student seems to have been injured by her punching, pinching, and hair-pulling.

Jennifer arrived at the school five years ago and caused problems there throughout her short life. In November of 1987 the members of the School staff who worked with her recommended that she be transferred to another facility. Her disabilities, they had concluded, were too profound for FSDB to manage effectively. The administration did not sign this recommendation. In fact, record-keeping procedures at FSDB are so faulty that senior members of the administration apparently did not even know of the recommendation. At least President Dawson is reported to have seemed genuinely shocked when he learned of this assessment at the hearings after Jennifer's death.

Florida School for the Deaf and the Blind officials have been concerned because members of the press have painted their institution in lurid colors. They urged the *Braille Monitor* to be fair and even-handed in its treatment of the story. Here, therefore, is the list of abuses against Jennifer Driggers culled from staff notes in FSDB's own records. They were compiled and printed in the report produced by the Department of Health and Rehabilitative Services:

11-22-85 A handful of Jennifer's hair was pulled out by another student.

11-15-86 Jennifer was hit by another student and found with blood on her face and shirt due to a nose bleed. Also on 11-15-86, she was pushed by another child, causing a bruise on her head.

01-25-87 Jennifer received a cut lip when she was hit by another student.

02-28-87 A blind boy called Jennifer an animal and pushed her.

04-09-87 Another student took Jennifer's clothes off while she was in bed and beat her with a clotheshanger.

04-10-87 Another student hit Jennifer in the head and caused her to bleed.

05-27-87 Jennifer was involved in a fight with a boy—was pushed down—and this resulted in severe bruises on both of her legs.

09-14-87 Jennifer was found to have severe scratches, her arms were bleeding, there was broken glass found by her bed, and another child was thought to be involved.

10-07-87 House parent left Jennifer to continue dressing herself, and when she returned Jennifer was crying—there were marks, bruises and open welts all over her body. These injuries were determined to be inflicted by K.C. by using a shoe and a coat hanger.

02-20-88 Another student hit Jennifer with an umbrella and caused her nose to bleed.

03-26-88 Another student hit Jennifer and caused her to have a bloody nose.

06-06-88 Jennifer was kicked in the clavicle by another student.

09-10-88 Jennifer received a bloody nose after being hit by another student.

09-12-88 Jennifer received a bloody nose after being hit by another student.

09-13-88 Jennifer was bitten on the arm by another student.

09-16-88 Jennifer received a bloody nose after being hit by another student.

09-21-88 Jennifer received a bloody nose after being hit by another student.

Additionally we found the following notes made by staff on the daily comment sheets:

05-29-88 Staff stated, "Can you believe Jennifer had no skills, cannot help herself in any way, and has the nerve to try and be stubborn and hit someone! The nerve of her!"

09-09-88 Jennifer cries a lot. Children are pretty rough.

09-15-88 Staff had to push Jennifer slightly—then she accepted where she had to be led.

09-16-88 Jennifer was pestered by other kids—cried. She is too lonely to be here.

09-20-88 All these girls can hurt her bad if they blow up. She was lucky that I was in every fight.

09-22-88 Jennifer needs closer supervision to prevent other kids from beating her—happens a lot—kids can't stand her.

09-22-88 Jennifer being rejected by kids and staff (most). Getting more and more bruises from kids. Staff member feels sorry for her.

09-23-88 Jennifer is a mess—bumps and bruises—starts when she hits or pulls hair. Other kids hit back. Jennifer looks like a punching bag. Other kids okay.

Based on infirmary records and daily comment sheets, the following are incidents of unexplained injuries to Jennifer:

11-20-84 Jennifer was found to have unexplained marks on her back.

10-15-85 Jennifer was referred to the infirmary for having redness and edema on her face that was unexplained.

10-30-85 Jennifer was seen in the infirmary for a rash and red swollen face.

11-10-85 Jennifer was taken to the infirmary by dorm parent with unexplained bruise on her left shoulder.

01-12-86 Jennifer was found to have an unexplained bruise on her left upper hip. A notation was made that she had wet the bed and smelled bad.

02-13-86 Jennifer was found to have scratches on her face and neck with no explanation.

02-17-86 Jennifer was found bleeding from an unexplained laceration on her head that had to be sutured at Flagler Emergency Room.

05-06-86 Jennifer was found to have abrasions on her arms, shoulders, and around her neck with no explanation for these injuries.

05-20-86 Jennifer was found to have a bruise on her buttocks with scratches. The house parent stated she did not know what happened but felt like she had sat on something or had been jabbed with something. Later that same day she was found to have an unexplained bruise on her cheek.

11-15-86 Dorm parent found an abrasion on Jennifer's elbow, bumps and abrasions to the child's forehead while the dorm parent was giving her a shower.

11-20-86 The dorm parent found a bump and swelling on Jennifer's forehead. Severe enough for the child to be taken to the Flagler Emergency Room with no explanation for the injury.

05-09-87 Jennifer was found to have abrasions on her back. They were diagnosed as rug burns with no explanation.

10-07-87 Jennifer was found to have a bruise on her forearm.

01-08-88 Jennifer was found to have scratch on her forehead with no explanation.

02-12-88 Jennifer was found bleeding from the mouth. A tooth was missing—the tooth could not be located.

02-17-88 Jennifer had abrasions across her abdomen. Doctor diagnosed them as a rug burn.

02-18-88 Jennifer was found to have a black and blue mark on her upper arm with no explanation.

04-21-88 Jennifer was found to be bruised on her buttocks with no explanation.

09-22-88 Jennifer was found to have puffiness on right eye, curved mark on her cheek—school questions whether this may be a belt mark—many bruises on her legs.

09-30-88 Several round marks described as hickies on Jennifer's face and neck and cuts and scratches with no explanation.

10-30-88 Jennifer was found scalded and unconscious in a shower in Vaill Hall, which resulted in her death.

One hardly knows how to react to such a document. Granted, FSDB officials did not have the advantage of reading a tidily written report before this child was fatally injured, but the data were there. The staff knew that serious problems existed. Something is profoundly wrong in a system that has no mechanism for preventing what happened to this child.

Precisely what did happen is not clear. Jennifer suffered from a complicated intestinal problem, to combat which she was to be given a high-fiber diet. She was then to be placed on the toilet in a comfortable position for thirty minutes at a time. She was to have things to amuse her while she sat. The Health and Rehabilitative Services report states that no change was made in her diet. She apparently was placed on the toilet without the use of a footstool for comfort and was given neither toys nor books. The supervisor had to attend to other children who were decorating for Halloween, so she left two mildly retarded girls, ages twelve and seventeen, to supervise Jennifer.

What happened next will never be known. At some point Jennifer vomited, but whether this was while she was still seated or after she was in the shower room seems to be in dispute. She removed her clothes and went (or was taken) into the shower area. One shower head did not have tempered water. All the others were adjusted in such a way that the water could not get too hot. In this one, however, the water temperature was eventually measured at 139 degrees fahrenheit. The staff reported that Jennifer "Had a propensity for turning on the hot water in the showers and tubs." But her mother said that Jennifer was frightened of hot water. The two girls have said that they felt the vibration when Jennifer fell. They looked into the shower area and tried to remove her but could not. They then went for help, and the staff were eventually able to remove the child.

Testimony before the grand jury indicated that the supervisor was away for only about eighteen minutes. But a source close to the situation told the *Braille Monitor* that the medical examiner reported she must have been exposed to the hot water for at least thirty minutes for her flesh to have been as thoroughly cooked as it was.

To one reading the bald facts of this tragedy, it seems incredible that the grand jury found no one at fault or even negligent in this situation. According to one source, the School was able to make its case convincingly that there was simply not enough money to provide adequate supervision. The supervisor on duty did not seem to have broken any rules, and apparently no one was prepared to place blame on the two retarded students.

But even if the grand jury was not willing to find the School negligent, it did make recommendations. Here they are:

Dormitory staff members need training in recognizing and reporting abuse, aggression control and sign language communications.

A central filing system for all injury reports should be maintained.

Appropriate dorm staff-to-student ratios should be established for multi-handicapped students. The grand jury found 10 to 17 multi-handicapped students have routinely been left alone with a single staff member for an entire shift.

Dormitory staff members should get emergency training.

Dormitory teachers should be made aware of the medical condition of each multi-handicapped student in their care.

A position at the school should be established to get parents of students quick information about their children.

Regular reviews of programs at the school should be started.

The 911 emergency system should be updated to pinpoint the exact location of school buildings.

That is what the grand jury recommended, and we wonder again about the NAC accreditation. Is it really conceivable that conditions were this bad in other parts of the School and not bad in the department for the blind? How can one segment of an institution (an institution with the problems of FSDB) be accredited in isolation from the rest of the facility?

The members of the grand jury were not the only ones looking at the Driggers case and offering suggestions. Florida's newspapers have been full of the case for months. On November 13, 1988, the *St. Augustine Record* printed a story that dredged up old memories that the School would, no doubt, have preferred to let rest. Here is what it said:

Driggers Death Mirrors 6-Year-Old D & B Tragedy
by Cynthia Beach

Change the time and place, and the deaths of 14-year-old Christi Eddleman and 9-year-old Jennifer Driggers are all too similar.

Both girls died in bizarre incidents six years apart at the Florida School for the Deaf and the Blind—one in a scalding shower, the other suffocating inside a trash bag.

Both raised questions about supervision at the state school. Each brought conflicting reports of how long the girls were left alone.

Miss Eddleman's case ended with a $125,000 out-of-court settlement. No media attention. No pickets or grand jury. And, according to some, no answers.

"The basis of the suit was negligent supervision," said Tampa attorney Robert Banker, who represented Miss Eddleman's mother, Donna. "I felt some confusion among the people that were supervising the infirmary at the time.

"I felt, yes, there was a lack of supervision in Christi's case," Banker added, "and I was ready to prove it."

During Banker's preparation of the case, FSDB officials were queried about staffing ratios. Banker argued if there had been additional supervision, the brown-haired girl might still be alive.

Miss Eddleman was found unconscious under her infirmary bed by an aide around 10:15 a.m. Sept. 8, 1982. She suffocated from a garbage bag and garbage can covering her head. She was found with her arms crossed over her chest. Suffering from brain damage, the girl remained in a coma until she died on May 2, 1983.

"I was very dissatisfied with the whole situation," Mrs. Eddleman said. "They tried to act like she committed suicide. We really didn't get any answers."

Miss Eddleman, who was blind from birth, slightly retarded, and epileptic, was on medication and feeling nauseated when she checked into the facility.

With one nurse on duty and two other children in the infirmary, Miss Eddleman was left under the supervision of a maid while the nurse was in a separate section of the facility to tend to other children. FSDB officials said, however, the woman was hired as a nurse's aide, in addition to a custodian.

Robert Dawson, president of Florida School for the Deaf and the Blind, testified to Banker that Miss Eddleman was left alone for five minutes. Banker said the time she was left alone was never resolved, but evidence was submitted that she remained alone up to 20 minutes.

Dawson refused an interview about the lawsuit. FSDB public information officer Mary Jane Dillon replied to questions about the case with "He (Dawson) had no recollection of an allegation of neglect."

Yet an attorney for Banker's firm sent a letter to Dawson dated Nov. 17, 1982, saying "an investigation conducted into this matter indicates that Christi's injuries were caused solely by the negligence of employees of the Florida School for the Deaf and the Blind."

Dawson met recently with officials of the state's Office of Risk Management in Tallahassee, the agency which oversees civil lawsuits against state agencies. Said Mrs. Dillon, "In a meeting with an official with risk management in Tallahassee...it was confirmed it was not an issue of neglect."

An attorney representing the state, Bernard McLendon of Jacksonville, responded to the suit in 1984 by placing the blame on the girl. He contended the death was due to "the carelessness and negligence of the deceased."

Nurse Betty Frady, who was on duty at the time of her death, told Banker she was "short-handed" in the infirmary at the time because another nurse who was supposed to be on duty had called in sick. A replacement was not called in.

"Only the maid would keep an eye on the students when she (Ms. Frady) was up in the clinic," testified the infirmary's head nurse, Shirley Harvey.

The staffing standards had been compiled by the FSDB board of trustees, who "had no medical training," said Dawson, except one member who was a dentist.

Banker also questioned why the infirmary staff allowed the child to use the bathroom alone, leaving her unattended with "a tub, sink, shower, and mirror."

But, he added, "My impression of that school was it's a good school. They do wonderful things up there. Through no fault of their own, they probably didn't have enough money to care for the kids."

The death was investigated by the St. Augustine Police Department, who ruled the death accidental after interviewing staff members. Mrs. Eddleman told police she found a large bruise on her daughter's right side.

As a result of her death, changes in the infirmary were implemented, according to Dawson's testimony.

"We immediately took all the plastic bags out of the wastebaskets, and the nurses were told, 'From here on out, you're not going to have coffee together,'" said Dawson, according to court records.

But the death of Miss Driggers has resulted in more than a $125,000 settlement.

The St. Johns County grand jury is investigating, along with probes (ordered by Gov. Bob Martinez) of the

Florida Department of Law Enforcement and Florida Department of Health and Rehabilitative Services. Those reports are expected to be completed by December. Deputy State Attorney Steve Alexander said the jury will reconvene when the Florida Department of Law Enforcement report is completed, and a presentment will follow.

Department of Education Commissioner Betty Castor has allocated approximately $100,000 to the school for immediate additional staffing at Vaill Hall, the dorm where Miss Driggers died.

The jury investigation also could look into requests made by FSDB trustees and allocations given by the Florida Legislature relating to staffing.

"If I don't get answers here," said Miss Driggers' mother, Robin Williams, "I'm not going to stop."

That was the November 13, 1988, story in the *St. Augustine Record*, and it is easy to see why the reporter was reminded of the earlier tragedy as she worked on the Driggers story. It is also clear that tragic lapses in staff supervision of students at FSDB are not recent or isolated occurrences. The Department of Education managed to find $100,000 immediately in order to provide ten more dormitory supervisors for Vaill Hall. Though several months have passed since the allocation was made, our information indicates that no additional personnel have yet been hired. Even if (as some have alleged) the delay is more a matter of bureaucratic inertia than laxness on the part of the School, those involved are still culpable. The Department of Education's response to the School's lament that eighteen and a half million dollars a year is not enough to run the School was the first indication that the funding excuse might be taken seriously as a mitigating circumstance. The grand jury's decision in December of 1988 was the second. But not everyone was prepared to say that the School was blameless.

At FSDB, School officials seem to believe that the press has been unjust to the institution. They say that the School has been the victim of bad luck and that no one set out to harm these children—except, of course, the five male staff members who assaulted students—and, after all, they were fired. The press, however, was not the only body to criticize the School as ultimately responsible for what happened to Jennifer and the others.

The Department of Health and Rehabilitative Services (HRS) was charged with the duty of investigating the School in the wake of the Driggers death. On December 7, 1988, it released an exhaustive study. An independent organization called Therapeutic Concepts, Inc., conducted the actual assessment of the facility, and

HRS officials wrote the final report, including eighty-five recommendations. On December 8, 1988, the *St. Augustine Record* printed two stories about the case, the HRS report, and the FSDB Board of Trustees' reaction. Here are both:

Report Blasts FSDB:
Agency Urges Dismantling of Trustees Board
by Cynthia Beach

Unqualified staff, an "insensitive" administration and excessive physical and mental abuse of students at the Florida School for the Deaf and the Blind were cited in a hypercritical report released late Wednesday by a state health agency.

Sweeping suggestions by the Florida Department of Health and Rehabilitative Services for the state-run school include dismantling the board of trustees and freezing student enrollment.

The school provides residential and academic programs for deaf, blind, and (on an increasing level) multi-handicapped students.

And although a dorm for multi-handicapped students is dangerous for children, the report says, "students are at risk of abuse in all FSDB residential facilities."

In addition to nine suicidal acts by students during the past year, drug abuse and depression "may also be problems among FSDB students," it states.

An administration which receives 33 percent of the school's tax-funded salaries, it says, has been uninvolved in the day-to-day operation of the school. A "general lack of accountability" of school administration coupled with poor management practices also was outlined.

The report calls Vaill Hall, the dorm for multi-handicapped students such as the late Jennifer Driggers, "a poorly staffed, inadequate facility."

The findings and recommendations are part of a 100-page report completed by HRS investigators and a private consulting firm, Therapeutic Concepts, Inc., of Jacksonville. The report was released Wednesday following a press conference by Gov. Bob Martinez.

Martinez called for the probes following the Oct. 13 death of 9-year-old Jennifer Driggers, a deaf, multi-handicapped dorm student. Miss Driggers died after being left unattended in a scalding dorm shower.

HRS officials feel the school "provides excellent overall classroom instruction," but the health and safety of multi-handicapped children and other dorm students have been largely overlooked. The report says about 80 percent of the students' time is spent in dorms, as opposed to 20 percent of time in classrooms.

Aside from staffing inadequacies, HRS officials found poor sanitary conditions for food preparation, fire code violations, a lack of security, inappropriate disciplinary practices, and students who were afraid of reprisal if they reported abuse.

Close to 19 percent of the 530 students reported being abused since 1981, with four abuse cases involving neglect at the school.

Miss Driggers, according to separate reports, had been the subject of physical abuse numerous times while at the school, including being beaten by a coat hanger.

The report says some students appeared traumatized by the death of Miss Driggers, but FSDB "administration and staff appear insensitive to their mental health needs."

The report, without a timetable, recommends:

- A review by the Florida Department of Education on a corrective plan of action by FSDB staff.

- A review of the mission of the school.

- Placement of Vaill Hall under licensed supervision.

- Evaluation of all dorms.

- Establishment of licensing standards by HRS through legislation.

Suggested are the founding of a support program for abused children and improved reviews of students' educational progress.

The report also concludes: adults who have committed sexual abuse on students be tested for AIDS, a building for multi-handicapped students under construction be checked for suitability, criminal history checks and abuse registry checks for dorm staff, and further analysis of FSDB management.

Management, it suggests, faces problems of increased expenses per child and "high ratios of administrative costs to direct service costs."

Administration lacks a "sufficient understanding" at all levels relating to the needs of the multi-handicapped.

HRS also found administration lacking in:

- A system to evaluate residential staff-to-student ratios. The ratios go unchecked with only one supervisor to 25 dorm parents at night.

- Physician review of medical reports.

- Effective detection of potential abuse of students.

- Ongoing review of student services.

- Referrals of students by school districts. Currently, most of the students are enrolled after referrals by organizations for the handicapped, and "friends and relatives."

- Training for residential staff in first aid, sign language, or mental retardation.

- An appropriate boys' dorm staff following the placement of an all-female staff after complaints of sexual abuse.

Other problems found attributed to administration are work orders being signed off by maintenance staff although not completed. "Bottlenecks" in the flow of information of staff have "permit(ted) problems to go undetected or uncorrected...," it says. An increase in the annual cost per student from $10,944 in 1980 to $34,943 in 1989, yet a high ratio of administrative costs needs to be addressed.

Students, the report says, lack proper placement, with some hearing impaired students "appear(ing)" to be placed in multi-handicapped units without clear evidence of handicaps, lack student advocates and suffer from "superficial" contact between staff and parents.

Other problems for students include:

- Inadequate disciplinary practices, namely, students being placed for up to 10 days "in seclusion."

- Menus, room signs, microwave ovens and stoves not Braille labeled.

- A "hopelessness" by students of getting issues resolved because of "staff insensitivity."

- Deaf-blind students left for up to seven hours without staff able to communicate with them.

- A lack of services resulting in approximately 75 percent of students "unduly restricted."

- A lack of privacy. For example, infirmary nurses examine students in a large clinic receiving room without privacy screens.

The condition of school grounds also was criticized. In addition to "numerous" fire code violations and poor security, HRS concerns include:

- Improper access to chemicals or other poisons.

- A lack of training of infirmary nurses.

- Improper discarding of used needles and scalpels in the infirmary.

- Students left unattended in the clinic for short periods with access to unlocked medicine cabinets.

- An infirmary stock of controlled drugs without current registration from the U.S. Drug Enforcement Agency.

- Health and safety problems in Moore Hall and Bloxham Hall, as well as Vaill Hall.

- Unlocked toxic substances in dorm halls.

- Improper food temperatures being maintained and detergent labeled as "pancake and waffle syrup."

FSDB Trustee Charges Report Findings Invalid
by Pete Osborne and Deborah Squires

Gov. Bob Martinez has urged the board of trustees of the Florida School for the Deaf and the Blind and two other state departments "to implement immediate changes" at the school located here.

Martinez urged the changes after accepting a lengthy report Wednesday critical of many aspects of the 102-year-old school.

But the governor's view is not universally shared by the school's trustees.

"In my opinion that report is not valid at all," said board member Celida Grau of Hialeah.

Mrs. Grau, the parent of a recent FSDB graduate, said "the governor has been misinformed about everything," and that investigators sent by his office were ignorant about handicaps.

However, she said the original scope of the school, to educate the blind and the deaf, should be emphasized. The state has pushed for inclusion of multi-handicapped students that should not really be there, Mrs. Grau said.

Trustee chairman Gene Pillot of Sarasota said, "I categorically and strongly disagree with dissolving the board as a governing body. To give the school to the Department of Education is to guarantee that the right kind of attention to governing the school is not going to be given."

Pillot said dissolving the board would be a "patently wrong decision."

Besides the FSDB board of trustees, which meets here Friday, Martinez sent the report and its recommendations to the state Department of Education and back to the Department of Health and Rehabilitative Services. The trustees meeting was scheduled prior to the Oct. 13 scalding death of Jennifer Driggers, 9, of Ruskin.

School President Robert T. Dawson declined Wednesday to comment upon the report or the governor's recommendations, saying he had just received a 35-page summary of the findings and recommendations.

"My priorities are set to prepare for the grand jury and the board," Dawson said. "I need to spend all the time I can preparing for those two meetings," he told *The Record.* "That's why I made the decision not to make myself available to the press until then."

The St. Johns County grand jury today continues its investigation into the death of Miss Driggers, as well as other incidents at the school in recent months. The board of trustees meets at the campus Friday at 9 a.m.

The report given to Martinez detailed a month-long investigation by HRS and contained 85 recommendations prepared by that department and Therapeutic Concepts Inc., a private consulting firm.

Martinez ordered the investigation after Miss Driggers' scalding death in a dormitory shower. Miss Driggers was enrolled in the school's multi-handicapped program.

In his Wednesday press conference in Tallahassee, Martinez said, "dramatic change must occur" at the school to ensure the safety of the 530 students.

In accepting the report, the governor said the school "needs to be changed, overhauled."

The investigation revealed that about 40 students had been reported as abused, and nine suicidal acts by students were recorded in the past year.

Other findings of the report include:

- The number of multi-handicapped students at the school has increased from 35 to 128 since 1985 and now makes up 23 percent of the student enrollment.

- All 39 students in Vaill Hall fit the profile for high or moderate risk of abuse from caretakers or peers.

- Vaill Hall residents have suffered 10 times as many injuries as were found in a representative sample of children in HRS-licensed residential facilities for children with developmental disabilities.

- Thirty-nine students had been reported as abused at the school.

- Costs per student have risen to almost $34,943 a year from $10,944 in 1979, and one-third of the school's salaries are for administrative or supervisory positions.

Saying the state would seek to take governing control of the school operated by the board of trustees, Martinez said, "We need to reduce the level of incidence of injury. There is urgency here," he said.

However, the governor would not answer questions about the safety of students still residing at Vaill Hall, where the Driggers girl died.

School trustee William Proctor of St. Augustine, president of Flagler College, said "I'd have to look at that recommendation," referring to the governor's statements. "It would be premature on my part to make any statement. I would hope the administration would give us some reaction to it, but even tomorrow at the board meeting it would be hard to comment."

Stephen Kiser of Tallahassee joins the board of trustees at its meeting Friday.

"I don't really know at this point what I'm getting into," he said Wednesday night.

"I have no problem conceptually with a single school serving the deaf and blind, and, in addition, serving the multi-handicapped, assuming they have the facility to do that, the staff to do that."

"Lumping together, I don't think is good for either group," he added, saying proper facilities would be separate. "However, if it's going to be a custodial facility, then I certainly think it should meet HRS standards."

Trustees Mike Hannon of Ponte Vedra Beach and Gay Gold, Tampa, contacted by *The Record* Wednesday night, declined to comment on the matter.

But the school's former president, William McClure of St. Augustine, had strong comments:

"I think the problem is that the state has regarded the school as a dumping ground—a place to send children that have no other place to go. When I was president we didn't have to take these children," he said.

"The problem is not with the administration, but with what has been expected of the school in recent years without providing for it. I think Mr. Dawson is a fine administrator. The state has demanded they take these children."

"I don't think the state has provided adequately for this kind of child," McClure said. "The school has asked for a review because that precedes change, and they haven't gotten that from the state."

"In my opinion they (multi-handicapped) shouldn't be there," McClure said in response to Martinez's calls for increased provisions for the multi-handicapped.

"I would say the change needs to be going back to the type of student the school has traditionally had," McClure added.

Trustee Mary Mauldin, Panama City, attends her last meeting tomorrow and will be replaced by Kiser.

"Personally, I think that would be a mistake," she said of the governor's recommendations.

But she said she felt the capable deaf and blind students in the state are being shortchanged under present circumstances. Mrs. Mauldin, who is blind, is an FSDB graduate.

That's what the *St. Augustine Record* paper said about the release of the HRS report, and other news organizations around the state also focused on the same recommendations and the Governor's public reaction to the findings.

The cumulative power of the non-binding recommendations is staggering. There has been wide-spread speculation about whether or not the School would implement any of them. The board met January 14, 1989, to consider its response to the HRS report.

Most of the recommendations would be fairly simple to put into place. Detergent can be removed from containers that say "pancake and waffle syrup," and janitorial and medical supplies can easily be made secure. It should not even be particularly expensive to insure that dishes are washed in sanitary conditions in buildings with a water supply hot enough to scald a child to death. And, as a matter of fact, at its January 14, 1989, meeting the board passed a resolution directing the administration to comply with all of the safety-connected recommendations and to report to the board about how long it would take to complete their implementation.

But there are a handful of recommendations which HRS and the Department of Education view as very important that the board will find more difficult to implement. The HRS recommendation to freeze school admissions immediately until the FSDB house is in order was not carried out immediately by the president. Actually, according to one source, what HRS wanted was to insure that the multi-handicapped population would not increase until it could be certain that those children were receiving proper treatment. According to our information Dawson has not imposed the recommended freeze on multi-handicapped admissions, but as of the beginning of 1989 he has (with the concurrence of the board of trustees) reportedly changed the old procedure of evaluating hard-to-place youngsters after admission. From now on, even if a prolonged assessment is necessary, it will presumably be completed before a child is enrolled.

With respect to the knotty problem of integrating the academic and residential programs for the students at FSDB, the board voted to merge the Individual Educational Plan and the Individual Dormitory Plan for each child into one document. This should enable the right hand to know what the left is doing. How the entire residential program is to be integrated into the two academic departments is more difficult bto determine. But the question is now under study.

The board of trustees is not at all willing to vote itself out of existence, but it is struggling with the problem of accountability. Negotiators have been working on a plan that would, in effect, designate the school as the sixty-eighth school district in the state. The board of trustees would then act as the school board. The school would clearly be subject to Public Law 94-142, and referrals of multi-handicapped students would be made by school districts. The Department of Education would have jurisdiction over the school. We are told that the board's attorney is examining several very real problems associated with this plan.

In the meantime there may be another, simpler way of resolving the accountability issues. Consideration is being given to strengthening an agreement between the school and the Department of Education which would give the department jurisdiction over the school. These reported negotiations may or may not be successful.

According to one source, Betty Caster, Commissioner of Education, has assured the board that she has no intention of going to the Legislature to ask them for clarification on the question of whether or not the School is bound by Public Law 94-142 and the issue of parental choice. In cases of multi-handicapped youngsters this appears to be a deeply held principle at the School, and parents are reportedly adamant about preserving it.

Perhaps a word should be said about the parents' reaction to the the revelations of the past year. One mother withdrew her son from the school in the aftermath of the Driggers death. Another parent testified before the grand jury about her son's treatment at the school before she withdrew him several years ago. She had tried then to make other parents take her warnings about staff abuses seriously, but they were reportedly unwilling to do so. Throughout this past fall, parents have been fiercely loyal to the school. They rallied to protest the efforts of the assistant state's attorney who was pleading Florida's case before the grand jury. They were part of the cheering section in a gathering that took place when the grand jury found the School not guilty of negligence in December of 1988. And they have been lobbying Craig Kiser, the new member of the board of trustees and a blind attorney. These parents are convinced that the school is the best place for their children and that it is being maligned.

Many in the blind community in Florida wonder how much of this support for the school is a direct result of parents' panic at the prospect of having to provide year-round supervision of their children. It is impossible to judge from the outside, but one would feel more confidence in the wisdom of the parents' stand if the general public (parents of blind, deaf, and multi-handicapped children included) were free of ignorance and prejudice concerning such youngsters.

Maybe there is hope for the students at the Florida School for the Deaf and the Blind, but one would have to be powerfully optimistic to believe it. Judging from the amount of distrust, fear, and despair reported among students in the HRS findings, the children are not hopeful about their situation. Perhaps now that state officials have entered the picture, changes for the better will be made at the School. From now on, the institution will presumably be accountable for its actions to outside experts. This, of course, is what one expects as a benefit of accreditation. And on this subject the HRS had an interesting comment:

"There was," its report said, "no evidence of an ongoing self-assessment based on the school's objectives, goals, and organizational framework. There were no effective problem-solving activities, including an ongoing review and evaluation of services provided for the students and procedures for remedial action, as deemed necessary. The School for the Blind had pursued accreditation, but this process was not an internal quality assurance mechanism."

This is what the HRS report says. NAC is the accrediting body referred to, but it is interesting to note with what respect HRS treats the highly touted (by NAC, at any rate) self-study required of member agencies. HRS says that there was no evidence of such "internal quality assurance mechanism."

When the Associate Editor of the *Braille Monitor* asked Dennis Hartenstein, executive director of NAC, for his reaction to the FSDB situation, he said, "I can't comment on any programs that we do not accredit." Many of HRS's findings and recommendations, however, apply to the entire School, and all the children at FSDB are suffering from the School's current crisis.

Hartenstein was asked specifically if NAC would be concerned by an incident in a member agency like the one in which a male FSDB teacher in the Department for the Blind, after plea-bargaining, offered no contest to a charge of battery against a blind female student. Under Florida law, "A person commits battery if he: (a) actually and intentionally touches or strikes another person against the will of the other; or (b) intentionally causes bodily harm to an individual." It is the charge typically brought when authorities are backing off from pressing charges of sexual offenses. Sources have assured the *Braille Monitor* that this case was only the most clear-cut of several brought against the teacher in question by female high school students. Hartenstein replied that NAC certainly would be concerned about such a problem and was only waiting for the report on the incident. Since it occurred in May of 1988, the report seems a little slow in arriving on Mr. Hartenstein's desk. But then there were a lot of problems at the Florida School for the Deaf and the Blind last spring, and record-keeping does not seem to be the administration's long suit.

The problems faced by the Florida School for the Deaf and the Blind are complex and difficult. Every such school is struggling with the question of meeting the needs of multi-handicapped youngsters. Society does not know how to deal with such children, and dumping them into schools for the blind or deaf, when that impairment is one of the child's handicaps, has become the standard solution. In cases like Jennifer Driggers', it is not the correct one, however, and schools and parents should insist on seeing that the proper determination is made. But as so often happens, the schools seem to be eager to insure their continued existence by snapping up every child they are offered, and parents too often are grateful to have any assignment at all made for their children.

But regardless of whether or not a given youngster belongs in a particular school, it must be a fundamental principle that every child should be safe—safe from assault by teachers, staff, and other students; and safe from subhuman care. Even if FSDB officials are correct in their contention that they are trying to do their best for the students enrolled at the school and that no one knowingly set out to injure Jennifer Driggers, the press and public's outrage focused on the school during the past several months has been justified. In fact, the only fault to be found with it is that it did not begin sooner. The board of trustees, or whoever is finally charged with running the Florida School for the Deaf and the Blind, must find and train competent staff, people who can keep accurate records and devise sensible procedures. Recruitment for dormitory staff has already improved with the doubling of the number of references required and the stipulation that the writer have known the applicant for two years. Such changes take no additional funds and very little extra time.

The Florida School for the Deaf and the Blind is not going to go away. There are children living in Florida who need the kind of care provided by such an institution. There are others who will be dumped there because families or local schools cannot or will not keep them at home for their education. The same statements can be made about every residential school in the country. We in the National Federation of the Blind must be vigilant. In a very real way these are our spiritual children. We must fight for their right to a good education in the most constructive environment which can be provided. We must do what we can to guard their safety and well-being. We must also insure that the Florida School for the Deaf and the Blind and its like are no longer dangerous places for children.

Postscript: After completing this article, we received further information. On January 20, 1989, the Associate Editor talked with both Robert Dawson, president of the Florida School for the Deaf and the Blind, and Tuck Tinsley, principal of the Department for the Blind. On January 23, 1989, the Editor talked with Tinsley.

Mr. Dawson said with respect to the live-in house parent question that it had traditionally been the practice at the School to have live-in house parents plus a roving supervisor who circulated through the dormitories throughout the night to see that all was well but that the School became worried about the provisions of the federal Fair Labor Standards Act. The concern was that since the house parents would be expected to be available for emergencies anytime during the night, compensation would have to be paid as if they were on full-time duty. Dawson said that such compensation had not been paid and that, accordingly, the practice of having live-in house parents had been discontinued.

With respect to more staff to supervise activities at Vaill Hall, Dawson said that the promised $100,000 for extra employees has just now (January) been received. He said that immediately after the Driggers tragedy, staff was transferred from a segment of the deaf program to fill the need at Vaill Hall on a temporary basis and that those staff will now be able to return to their former assignments.

Dawson emphasized his conviction that the Florida School for the Deaf and the Blind is deeply committed to the welfare of its students and that both he and the board are behaving accordingly. He says he feels that the HRS recommendations are seriously flawed but that the school will move quickly and decisively to implement those that are valid. In view of the long years of chaos and mismanagement one has to wonder why the Driggers death and the HRS report were needed to make Dawson take action—action which he says will be immediate and thorough.

Dr. Tinsley, who is said by some to be the brightest and most sensitive administrative staff member at the school, has apparently decided to leave. On January 19, 1989, we were informed that Dr. Tinsley had accepted the position of president of the American Printing House for the Blind in Louisville, Kentucky, succeeding Dr. Carson Nolan.

The Associate Editor began her conversation with Dr. Tinsley by alluding to this new appointment. He said that he felt that the problems at the Florida School for the Deaf and the Blind were almost entirely in other areas of the institution and not in the department for the blind. He said that the HRS report commended the staff of the department for the blind for warmth and understanding and the dormitory for being "cheery." In this connection no mention was made of the sex abuse charges.

Dr. Tinsley told the Associate Editor that NAC met in Houston during the weekend of January 14, 1989, and renewed the accreditation of the department for the blind of the Florida School for the Deaf and the Blind for the maximum term. He said that NAC commended the school for its work study program, which brings Flagler College students onto the FSDB campus; its eye health care program; its ear, nose, and throat clinic; its mobility pass program; and its dormitory curriculum. In addition, he said that the Southern Association of Colleges and Secondary Schools has also recently accredited the school with commendation. In this connection it should be kept in mind that outside accrediting bodies such as the Southern Association of Colleges and Secondary Schools tend (this is part of the problem) to rely on NAC accreditation and simply rubber stamp what NAC does. It is to be hoped that the Florida case will go a long way toward changing this.

When Dr. Tinsley talked with the Editor on January 23, he confirmed that there was a sex abuse offense by a staff member in the department for the blind against a blind student some time early last year and another such case of sex abuse by a teacher in the department for the blind in either 1986 or 1987. Dr. Tinsley couldn't remember exactly when. In answer to a question from the Editor Dr. Tinsley said that he believed at least some time was spent in jail by one or the other of the offenders. He said the school was very concerned about such things.

When Dr. Tinsley was asked whether NAC (the National Accreditation Council for Agencies Serving the Blind and Visually Handicapped) had been aware of these problems at the School, he said yes. He said that the NAC team had been on hand last year in the midst of some of the revelations. When he was asked to comment on whether NAC's silence about the problems of the school and its reaccreditation of the school in January of 1989 might not legitimately give rise to questions about NAC's claim that its seal of approval is an assurance of quality services, he remained silent.

Dr. Tinsley said that the Florida School is a good institution and that the charges against it are politically motivated. He gave no explanation as to why anyone would be motivated to attack the school politically, and he confirmed the facts concerning the major abuses we have detailed.

It will be remembered that Dennis Hartenstine, NAC's executive director, told the *Monitor's* Associate Editor that he was waiting for a report concerning the sex abuse incidents in the department for the blind at the school before taking any action. In light of subsequent developments we can reasonably guess what he meant. If Dr. Tinsley's report is accurate, NAC reaccredited the school on the weekend of January 14, 1989, with accolades and commendation. The facts speak for themselves, and neither the blind of the nation nor the self-respecting agencies and schools will forget or remain silent.

There were more such journalistic investigations—and with them more shocking revelations—in the months that followed that initial probe of the Florida School. There were other schools with NAC accreditation (such as Alabama) which turned out to be no less shabby; there were training centers (such as that of Iowa) which were revealed as dens of financial corruption; and there were sheltered workshops (like that of Lubbock, Texas) that were shown to be places of violence and oppression. There would be still more such investigations and revelations in the pages of the *Braille Monitor* in the years to come, following the pattern of fearless inquiry and full disclosure laid down by Editor Kenneth Jernigan. Few if any, however, were likely to be more effective, more expert, or more eloquent than an article directed to the practices of the Alabama Institute for the Deaf and Blind which appeared in the February, 1990, issue of the *Monitor*. It may serve here as an appropriate closing testament to this account of the evolution of the *Braille Monitor*.

OF CHANDELIERS AND SHODDY PRACTICE IN ALABAMA: ANOTHER NAC AGENCY ROCKED BY SCANDAL
by Barbara Pierce

Maybe there is something about work with the blind that attracts disreputable people or encourages the proliferation of despicable human impulses. Maybe, like televangelists, agency personnel in this field are held in such reverence by the public at large that some of them begin to think they are above the law. Or perhaps it is merely the presence in the field of an accrediting body (NAC) that provides protection for virtually any shoddy practice (as long as only the blind are injured), perpetuating a network that inflates or fumigates professional reputations as required. NAC (the National Accreditation Council for Agencies Serving the Blind and Visually Handicapped) may be dying, but it still provides a facade behind which many of its member agencies, and most especially their senior officials, seem to believe they can snuff out the dreams and sometimes the very lives of their clients or students while reaping substantial public commendation and personal financial rewards.

Many of the blind in Alabama feel that Jack Hawkins, Dr. Jack Hawkins (who until July 2, 1989, was the president of the Alabama Institute for the Deaf and Blind at Talladega), is a perfect example of this breed. In the ten years (1979-1989) during which he served as president of this NAC-accredited agency, he severely damaged the Institute's sheltered workshop, using its entire $900,000 nest egg, according to workshop officials, to handle bills the Institute failed to pay after an agency reorganization. His administration consistently invested more funds in the School for the Deaf than the School for the Blind, with such unfairness that even the deaf raised objections. In the opinion of many of the alumni, the AIDB Foundation, which Hawkins established, materially contributed to the increased segregation of both blind and deaf students from the larger community.

The casual hiring practices of Hawkins's administration led, according to many, directly to bringing a man to the Institute who murdered four people associated with the agency. And as if all this were not enough, when in the summer of 1989 he moved out of Talladega to take the position of Chancellor at Alabama's Troy State University, he left behind him police investigations and Ethics Commission probes into two separate matters. He also took with him without authorization thousands of dollars worth of Alabama state property. Last year it was the Florida School for the Deaf and the Blind. Now it is Alabama. What NAC-accredited agency will be next, and what has yet to be uncovered?

But back to Alabama. Has Hawkins's reputation been destroyed by these revelations? It has certainly been tarnished, but astonishingly he continues to serve as a member of the American Foundation for the Blind's board, and he has moved onward and, one presumes, upward to a university presidency. As to the Alabama Institute for the Deaf and Blind, it is not at all astonishing that it continues to enjoy NAC accreditation. After all, what is NAC accreditation for?

The job at the Alabama Institute for the Deaf and Blind which Hawkins left last summer at age forty-four paid him a reported salary of $85,000 a year with an additional expense account of $4,000, and his business travel and entertainment costs were, of course, reimbursed in addition. But there is more: He lived in the President's Mansion (their apt terminology, not ours) at the Institute—a residence which included the services of a maid and gardener, and there is still more: To keep the wolf from scratching the paint from the door of this NAC-accredited mansion the state also reportedly paid for utilities (including phone). But even all of that was apparently not enough. The Hawkinses (as press accounts make painfully clear in minute detail) were permitted to purchase with state funds and to use a mind-boggling array of luxuries. It is hard to believe that the Troy State Chancellorship can be more attractive than what Hawkins had, but why else would he leave the Alabama Institute for the Deaf and Blind, where he had (as the saying goes) the world by the tail with a downhill drag?

The Alabama Institute for the Deaf and Blind (AIDB) in Talladega essentially provides such services as there are for the deaf and the blind of the state. The Institute consists of the industries program (a large sheltered shop, producing an impressive array of products and providing jobs for more than 300 blind and physically handicapped people); the E. H. Gentry Technical School (offering limited rehabilitation and post-secondary training in some fifteen trades); the Helen Keller School (serving deaf-blind and other severely handicapped children from a number of states); the School for the Deaf; and the School for the Blind. The Governor of Alabama appoints a board of trustees to oversee this conglomerate, and the board hires the president of the Institute.

Until the early 1980s the adult programs at the Institute had a more or less autonomous director, who (like the Institute's president) answered directly to the Legislature and prepared and managed a budget separate from that of the rest of the Institute. But all things change, and in September of 1979 thirty-four-year-old Dr. Jack Hawkins, Jr. was appointed president of the Alabama Institute for the Deaf and Blind. He was (according to those who observed him for the past decade) young, energetic, and ambitious—so ambitious that he was not content merely to be president of AIDB. He persuaded his board to give him extra power and responsibility. In addition to the presidency of the Institute they appointed him to be director of Adult Services so that he alone would report to the Legislature and so that only through his office would flow the budget appropriations for the entire conglomerate. Presumably it was argued that this reorganization would result in eliminating duplication and waste, thus increasing the efficiency and cost-effectiveness of the entire administration.

But the financial figures that have now come to light reveal that something else happened instead—something that had drained funds from Adult Services to the great benefit of the School for the Deaf. In 1988 the Alabama Legislature budgeted just under ten million dollars for the Institute's Children and Youth Services, which includes the School for the Blind, the School for the Deaf, the Helen Keller School, and the Parent-Infant Preschool Program. Adult Services received an appropriation of about three and a half million dollars, and the Industries Program got about one and a half million. According to sources close to the Industries Program, this last appropriation is intended to cover the expenses incurred in providing daily transportation for workshop workers and in subsidizing the wages of those workers who cannot work competitively. Though Industries' staff members seem not to have access to the figures that would reveal how much profit or deficit their program is running, they report that Adult Services was expected in 1988 to find almost three quarters of a million dollars as its contribution to what was called Shared Services—the concept here being that each component of the Institute should contribute toward defraying the costs of the services that they all share. With a combined budget of less than half that of the Children and Youth Allocation, Adult Services was suddenly asked to cover sizable new chunks of the Shared Services budget and to do so without any increase in its budget. One is left to conclude that the Industries program must have been showing a profit since Adult Services did manage to produce the funds demanded for shared programs.

According to a confidential document, which was inadvertently released by the Institute, during the first eleven months of the 1988 fiscal year Adult Services contributed the following amounts in several categories of these Shared Services: $47,954 of the

$65,000 salary paid to the vice president whose duties included supervision of the Industries program; $134,000 for health services (according to Industries sources, this bought workers three hours a week of a nurse's time); $44,598, a little more than half of the president's salary; $13,739, about one quarter of the salary of the executive assistant to the president; $147,410, for the business affairs office; $26,583, half of the development officer's salary; $13,062, half of the cost of running the Publications Office; $9,966, about a fifth of the public affairs officer's salary; and $5,424, half of the salary of the president's maid—a salary which, unlike those of the professionals on the staff, would seem to be anything but queenly.

Annualized, Adult Services assessments for shared services for the 1988 fiscal year total $720,000, and Adult Services officials and area legislators reportedly pleaded with the Institute's president and the board to reduce the amount for fiscal 1989. But for whatever reason, the 1989 assessment against Adult Programs was set at $801,000. Also effective in 1989, the board voted to transfer $500,000 from the Adult Programs unrestricted fund—money not provided by the state for specific uses and therefore, almost certainly, profits earned by the blind workers and plowed back into the Industries Program—to be used for "future funding projects," according to a resolution passed at the August, 1988, board of trustees meeting. Apparently the fund transfer will enable the institution to use the money for construction projects on its school campuses.

At the same time all this was happening, the sheltered shop staff was learning the hard way that their bills seemed to be the last ones paid by the Institute, now that the Industries Program was not independently responsible for its own budget and bill-paying. According to those close to the Industries Program, by March of 1988 the shop owed some 1.3 million dollars to suppliers—a revelation which the staffers found astonishing and infuriating. Even National Industries for the Blind made inquiries about when the Alabama shop planned to pay its outstanding bills. Rumor has it, however, that by September of 1989 the amount owed was down to $198,000 and that at the end of the year the slate had been wiped clean. But a decade ago the Industries Program had a nest egg of $900,000 set aside for large equipment purchase and meeting emergencies—a pot of gold which seems to be entirely gone now. Shop workers and management don't usually agree on much at Alabama Industries for the Blind, but the one clear exception is the notion that merging their Program with the rest of the Institute under Dr. Hawkins has been bad for the shop and bad for the state's blind adults.

In the Alabama Code of 1975 the Legislature clearly established the separation between Children and Youth Services and the

Adult Programs, so when Hawkins made his grab, there was a growing restiveness. By the late 1980s concerned citizens encouraged a local legislator (Clarence Haynes) to request the Alabama Attorney General to render an opinion on the legality of the Hawkins reorganization. On February 24, 1989, the Attorney General handed down his opinion, clearly stating that the Hawkins reorganization is illegal. Here is what the Attorney General said:

Don Siegelman
Attorney General
Montgomery, Alabama
February 24, 1989

Honorable Clarence E. Haynes
Member, House of Representatives
Talladega, Alabama

Dear Representative Haynes:

This opinion is issued in response to your request for an opinion from the Attorney General.

Question: Can the department of adult blind and deaf be combined with the Alabama Institute for the Deaf and Blind?

Facts and Analysis: The statute establishing the department of adult blind and deaf is found at *Code of Alabama 1975*, Section 21-1-15. It states:

"There shall be at the Alabama Institute for Deaf and Blind a separate department of adult blind and deaf. Legislative appropriations for the department shall be made separate and apart from the legislative appropriations made for the support and operation of this institute. The department shall have the authority to establish and to operate a library service for blind, visually handicapped, deaf, or severely handicapped persons, and the department is hereby designated as the official agency to operate a regional library for the blind, visually handicapped, deaf, and severely handicapped." [In 1976 then Governor Wallace transferred authority for the library to the State Library.]

The fundamental rule in construing a statute is to ascertain and effectuate legislative intent as expressed in the statute. This intent may be gleaned from the language used, the reason and necessity for the act, and the purpose sought to be obtained. *Shelton v. Wright*, 439 So.2d 55 (Ala.1983).

Section 21-1-15 states that the department of adult blind and deaf is to be a separate department in the Alabama Institute for the Deaf and Blind. According to the statute, legislative appropriations for the department are to be made separate and apart from legislative appropriations made for the support and operation of the institute. These appropriations are to be used solely for the operation of the Adult Deaf and Blind Department. The department is authorized to establish and to operate a library service for blind, visually handicapped, deaf, and severely handicapped persons and is designated as the official agency to operate a regional library for such persons. Therefore, the language used in Section 21-1-15 and the purpose in enacting the statute indicate that it was the intent of the legislature that the department of adult blind and deaf was to be separate from the Alabama Institute for the Deaf and Blind. Furthermore, my research does not reveal any authority that would permit the department to be combined with the Institute for the Deaf and Blind.

Conclusion: The department of adult blind and deaf cannot be combined with the Alabama Institute for the Deaf and Blind.

I hope this sufficiently answers your question. If our office can be of further assistance, please do not hesitate to contact us.

Sincerely,
Don Siegelman
Attorney General

That is what the Attorney General said, but almost a year later it is still not clear what impact the opinion will have on business as usual at the Alabama Institute for the Deaf and Blind. The board is the body that will have to change the institution's course, and forcing that action may require a lawsuit, which several people with whom we talked seem prepared to undertake if necessary.

In the meantime one might be pardoned for hoping that, even if the blind adults in Alabama are suffering because of shared services and mingled funding, blind children, at least, might be benefiting from the skewed system. Alas, this does not seem to be the case. A document circulated to the board of trustees at their August, 1989, meeting indicates that during the past ten years $16,272,000 has been bspent for renovation of existing structures, construction of new buildings, and maintenance of the buildings and grounds. Of this amount $9,569,000 was spent on the School for the Deaf and $2,411,000 on the School for the Blind. In fact, the physical plant of the School for the Deaf received about one and a half times the amount spent on the facilities of all other programs combined. The disproportion has become so lopsided that the Board of Trustees' deaf consumer representative recently recommended that more money be allocated to the School for the Blind, though there is no evidence yet that her plea will be heeded. Parenthetically one might inquire whether the academic programs of these schools are so sound that there really is sixteen million dollars available to lavish on physical plant and presidential luxuries, important as buildings and luxuries may be. Many in the blind community and several in the Alabama Legislature believe that the answer should have been no. But Dr. Hawkins clearly recognized the advantage of heading a facility that looked attractive, whether or not the students were flourishing or, for that matter, safe.

For example, the two vans used by the School for the Blind both have driven, according to the School's principal, more than 200,000 miles. One is a 1975 model; the other was built in 1977. The Institute's director of transportation has said that one of the two is not road-worthy for any extended driving, but as far as is generally known, there are no imminent plans to replace either vehicle.

We are informed that according to a recent furniture bid, the cost of furnishing and equipping the new student center at the School for the Deaf was $198,000 (with $105,000 being spent on furniture alone). On the other hand, the amount spent on furniture in the entire School for the Blind during the decade was $220,000. The new deaf student center contains a conference table, costing a princely $5,500, and 448 stacking chairs, each of which cost $46. During a recent alumni event at the School for the Blind, attendees report that the folding chairs they were using kept collapsing under them. The only other startling expenditures on the furniture bid are a $2,000 desk and several $238 trash baskets. It is puzzling to know how one could manage to spend $238 on a single indoor trash receptacle, but it must be gratifying for the deaf students to know that even their trash is departing in high style.

If the school-age blind population being served in Alabama had been shrinking more rapidly than the deaf population during the past decade, marked differences in the funds expended on the schools might be understandable. But ten years ago 480 deaf students were enrolled at that school, and today there are 240—a decrease of 50 percent. In 1979 140 students attended the School for the Blind; today there are 130—a decrease of less than 10 percent. The Helen Keller School served 135 children in 1979 and enrolls 90 today, 60 of whom are visually impaired. The Parent-Infant Preschool Program works with about 125 blind children and roughly the same number of deaf children. The E. H. Gentry facility has historically served a population, sixty percent of whom are visually impaired, and about two-thirds of the adults working at Alabama Industries for the Blind are blind and about one-third sighted or otherwise handicapped. It is clear from these figures, reported by an Institute official as having been drawn from the Alabama Institute's own annual report, that today a majority of the people served by the institution are blind.

Some observers have worried about what they see as the Institute's increasing tendency under the Hawkins administration to segregate its students from the greater Talladega community. Hawkins' AIDB Foundation—one of those convenient nonprofit reservoirs of money that officials can channel in directions not approved by the legislature—built a chapel that, according to members of the alumni, the students didn't need. These members of the alumni believe that it was preferable for youngsters to attend churches in the town rather than having separate services in a private facility. But the chapel was built to serve the students whether they liked or needed it or not, and as a result, the inmates of the Institute were separated still further from the town.

During the early eighties, apparently as a cost-cutting measure, the Hawkins administration decided to reduce the Institute's security staff. At the same time observers close to the institution report that it was engaging in the kind of sloppy hiring practices that led to such catastrophic results at the Florida School for the Deaf and Blind.

We are told that a man was hired to offer both deaf and blind youngsters at AIDB firsthand experience in artistic expression, without an interview or research into his background. The new employee brought a friend (Daniel Spence) to Talladega with him who had jumped bail in San Francisco and escaped from prison in Nevada, where he had been serving a sentence for stabbing a man to death in a homosexual brawl. This second man, too, began establishing contact with blind and deaf students as a volunteer aide. He described himself around town as working at the Institute, according to sources close to the situation. But again, so far as we can determine, no effort was made to learn anything about the man.

Probably on February 21, 1986 (not all the bodies were discovered for some time), Danny Lee Siebert (also known as Daniel Spence) entered an apartment building housing disabled people and killed two deaf women and the two small sons of one of them. Sometime later in the rampage he also killed his next door neighbor and abandoned her body in a wooded area. Perhaps a routine background check, a face-to-face interview, or the presence of security officers on campus would have done nothing to prevent what happened, but one wonders. NAC, of course, showed no public concern. Whether they were privately concerned, we have no way of knowing. Only one of the deaf women was actually a current Institute student (the other was an alumna), so neither was enrolled in the School for the Blind. The fact that blind Institute students could just as easily have been the ones killed was immaterial. Cavalier hiring practices and cost-cutting in security measures presumably have nothing to do with standards and quality of services in the NAC lexicon.

In May of 1989 Dennis Hartenstine, executive director of NAC, boasted to blind consumers in Michigan: "I assure you, if anything ever occurred and our commission [NAC's Commission on Accreditation] was concerned about the safety of the organization, the safety of the individuals being served and the accredited body did not take action to make changes, the Commission would withdraw accreditation." Viewed in the uncompromising light of Florida and Alabama, NAC's promises, like its standards of excellence, can be seen for what they are—a sham and a mockery.

Apparently everyone in Talladega worked together to hush things up. Only a few people, labeled by the Institute as blind troublemakers, asked difficult questions, and no one in the administration of the Institute or the accrediting body that was supposed to lend it respectability was visibly interested in seeking hard answers.

Hawkins did summarily fire the art instructor, but the instructor was, of course, no longer in touch with the murderer, who had fled the scene of the crime in a car belonging to one of his victims. The murderer was caught eleven months later and is now appealing his sentence to die in the electric chair.

In summary it seems clear that during the years of the Hawkins administration students and clients in general, and the blind in particular, have gotten short shrift at the Alabama Institute. Two things happened in the spring of 1989, however, that suggested a change might be in the wind. In May, Calvin Wooten (one of the two blind Trustees) was elected chairman of the board—the first blind person to be so honored. But according to the blind, he has remained deaf to their concerns. Staff members at the School for the Blind report that he does not visit the school or talk with them about their problems. He does, however, attend some School for the Deaf football games.

As the situation worsened throughout 1989, the blind of Alabama collected about 250 names on a petition asking the state's governor to remove Mr. Wooten from the board. The signers included virtually everyone who could be considered a leader in the blind community in Alabama. Unanimity among the blind has rarely before existed on any issue in the state, but the governor refused seriously to consider either their request or the underlying crisis that the very existence of two hundred-fifty names on such a petition demonstrated. It goes without saying that NAC did not disaccredit the institution or show any visible concern.

Wooten can hardly be blamed for all the difficulties facing the blind at the Institute. After all, he has only chaired the board since May of 1989. Hawkins is clearly much more responsible for the damage to the programs for the blind.

Just about everyone in the blind community was, therefore, delighted to learn that on July 2, 1989, Dr. Hawkins was to resign in order to take the post of Chancellor at Alabama's Troy State University on September 1. In a state with a well-entrenched old-boy network and with an official as tightly tied into that network as Hawkins appears to be, there was no hope of making him accountable for what he had done to damage the Institute or the blind, but at least he would be leaving. Perhaps someone else could be encouraged to assist the blind. So Hawkins was wined and dined. The Alumni Association of the School for the Deaf presented him with a $1,500 set of golf clubs. The AIDB Foundation (the one he had established) bought up the remainder of his country club membership; the new chapel that no one wanted was named after him; and in general he was told what a fine fellow he was and what a wonderful job he had done. The blind, for the most part, remained silent.

Then bits of information began to surface. Alabama has an ethics law with a provision that prevents the president of an institution from influencing the hiring of his wife. It appears, however, to an objective outsider that Hawkins wanted his wife to do some consulting work for the Institute in the Parent-Infant Program. According to some sources, she had been doing the work for years, and it only seemed fair for her to be paid for it. Others maintain that she didn't even begin to earn the salary she was eventually paid. Hawkins apparently dreamed up a scheme which would enable him to funnel some $24,000 of Institute money to his wife through the University of Alabama at Birmingham, an institution with which Mrs. Hawkins had previously been associated. When the story eventually blew open, it was covered by the *Daily Home*, the local Talladega paper. This is the way the *Daily Home* reported the story in late September, 1989:

Preuitt [State Senator]: Hawkins Abused Power as
AIDB President
by Denise Sinclair

Controversy continues to surround former Alabama Institute for Deaf and Blind president Dr. Jack Hawkins, Jr. This time state Senator Jim Preuitt is questioning whether a contract allowing Hawkins' wife Janice to work as a consultant through the University of Alabama at Birmingham is ethical.

Preuitt said Tuesday, "He (Hawkins) primarily contracted with the University of Alabama for $24,350 for a part-time job for Mrs. Hawkins. The money was funneled from AIDB to UAB. It may not be illegal, but it sure sounds unethical."

Preuitt said there is no indication the board approved the contract, which ran from June, 1988, to May, 1989.

The contract was a cooperative agreement between AIDB and UAB for "the exchange of professional and expert services." It involved the AIDB Parent-Infant Program, which provides quality services to the hearing and visually impaired pre-school child.

According to the contract terms, Mrs. Hawkins "developed, promoted, and evaluated" the program.

Under the contract, Mrs. Hawkins received $22,000 for consultant services, $1,350 for travel and $1,000 for materials and supplies.

AIDB reimbursed the University of Alabama for the services at a rate of $2,030 per month under the contract. Also, according to the contract, the services were for a two-thirds position.

Hawkins signed the contract for AIDB. Signatures of Mr. Dudley Pewitt, senior vice president for administration at UAB, and Dr. Keith D. Blayney, dean of the School of Health Related Professions, were also on the contract, which was dated May 17, 1988.

Preuitt pointed out that the contract doesn't say Mrs. Hawkins would be the recipient. "I do know she paid into the Alabama Retirement System for a salary of $22,000 during that period. I think it was cut and dried. It's a cowardly way to put your wife on the local payroll. I questioned Hawkins about this in January in Montgomery as to whether or not his wife was on the payroll. He said I was getting too personal."

The senator said he had the AIDB minutes researched and there is "no authorization by the board" for this contract. "This is another thing where the public will have less confidence in schools. These misuses of funds are reasons the public will not vote on new taxes. Institutions must be accountable."

Preuitt added, "The local legislators have been trying for five years to get redirection of funding at AIDB to children and adults rather than beautification. We did not want to do what we did in Montgomery. But that was the only way we could get Jack Hawkins' attention. We wanted questions answered. Many people thought we were too tough on him at that time.

"We've just scratched the surface. There is so much abuse by this (Hawkins) administration. It got to the point where he thought he was above the law."

Rep. Clarence Haynes said he questions the legality of the contract or agreement. "I understand the contract was typed at AIDB. This is just another example of mismanagement of funds. We have been trying to correct this for a couple of years. It's one of many incidents that are not right. We've (the local legislative delegation) been outgunned and outwritten in the newspapers."

AIDB board member Ralph Gaines said he had no knowledge of the agreement between the Institute and the University of Alabama. "I've been on the board 2-1/2 years. I don't recall any discussion or board action on this contract between UAB and AIDB, particularly Mrs. Hawkins."

Jim Bosarge, assistant director of University Relations at UAB, said, "The consulting agreement was new in 1988. Mrs. Hawkins had maintained a part-time position with UAB since moving to Talladega. She is a long-term employee of UAB since the mid-1970s. The AIDB Field Services Office requested a person for consultation purposes prior to the agreement.

"She had been serving AIDB needs on a voluntary basis for several years. They requested more of her time, which led to the consulting agreement."

Bosarge said the University had information from the Ethics Commission regarding Mrs. Hawkins' employment. "It's my understanding it was OK for her to consult with AIDB in one of her specialties if it occurred through another institution. She was a part-time employee of UAB. There was no reason for her not being hired as a consultant. No one else in the area had the skills to do the work."

AIDB board chairman Calvin Wooten of Anniston declined comment on the agreement.

The *Daily Home* was unable Tuesday afternoon to obtain information from the Ethics Commission in Montgomery regarding the matter.

Preuitt and Haynes both stressed they feel strongly about public institutions' being more accountable for citizens' tax dollars and the recent abuses at AIDB point to this fact.

That's what the newspapers were saying, but that was far from all. Alabama also has a law that prevents anyone from buying state property except at auction. The salary and perquisites—a tax-free expense account and a mansion with maid, gardener, and utilities—bestowed upon Dr. Hawkins by the Alabama Institute for the Deaf and Blind out of funds provided by the state's taxpayers can go a long way in a small southern town, where the cost of living is lower than in most cities; and plenty of people, like the Hawkinses' maid, scrape along on less than $11,000 a year. If the state had provided Dr. Hawkins nothing more, this job would still, by any standard, have been generously (perhaps too generously) remunerative. But apparently Alabama (whether it knew it or not) was prepared to provide the Hawkinses with the use of a kingly array of luxuries in their residence. One state official told the *Braille Monitor* with disgust that Mrs. Hawkins loved wallpaper more than any woman he had ever seen. "Seemed like there was new wallpaper and carpet about every six months."

When the time came to move from Talladega, the Hawkinses apparently couldn't bear to leave behind some of the lovely things the state had purchased. According to Dr. Hawkins, on August 17, 1989, he wrote a check in the amount of $2,781.65 to cover the cost of the items he wished to purchase—no doubt appropriately discounted because they were used merchandise. It is clear that Dr. Hawkins knew about the state prohibition on outright purchasing of Alabama property because he had someone from the Institute call the state's Ethics Commission to inquire how a person could legally buy a desk from the state. Probably assuming that the desk in question was an old and beloved memento of years of service, the state official said that if a check were written for the market value of the piece, it would pass muster, or at least no one would probably bother to ask questions. This is the way the *Daily Home* told the story on September 28, 1989. As you read, ask yourself what happened to the desk in question. Was the initial question asked about a desk simply because it would sound more innocuous that way? Was the desk in question never returned? How many other objects slipped through the cracks? Here is one of the many news stories printed at the time:

Ethics Complaint Filed Against Dr. Hawkins
by Denise Sinclair

An ethics complaint was filed Tuesday against former Alabama Institute for Deaf and Blind president Dr. Jack Hawkins, Jr. for purchasing furniture and china from the president's mansion.

Tom Mills of Tuscaloosa, a 1981 graduate of AIDB's E. H. Gentry Technical Facility, filed the complaint with the state's Ethics Commission. In his complaint to the Commission, Mills said Hawkins improperly used his position to buy the furniture that belonged to the Institute.

Wayne Hall, assistant chief examiner with the state Examiner of Public Accounts Office, said Wednesday afternoon that state law prohibits such a sale.

"State property must be declared surplus property and sold according to the rules and regulations of the Alabama Department of Economic and Community Affairs," Hall said in a telephone interview from Montgomery.

Hawkins resigned from AIDB in the summer to become chancellor of the Troy State University System on September 1.

Before leaving AIDB, Hawkins bought the furniture and china for $2,890. The items had been in the president's home on South Street. The items were a nest of tables, curio cabinet, a set of Lennox China (six place settings), two place settings of Lennox China, a set of queen size bedding, one bed frame, an entertainment center, a butcher block, and one desk.

These items were returned to the mansion Wednesday afternoon, according to an AIDB official, and Hawkins will receive a refund for the items he purchased.

AIDB officials have said they were advised in mid-August by an official of the state examiner of public accounts that the sale would be legal provided Hawkins paid fair market value.

Hall said his office records show the initial contact was made by an AIDB official on Monday. "We received a call on Monday from someone at the school concerning the sale of a desk and the proper procedures. The other items were not mentioned," he said.

Ethics Commission director Melvin Cooper would not comment on the complaint, saying state law prohibits him from doing so.

Mills said, "I'm not accusing Dr. Hawkins of anything. I'm concerned about the public picture statewide regarding presidents of universities and institutions such as this who spend money on lavish lifestyles instead of education. The voters in this state have a right to put their feet down when it comes to boards of trustees around Alabama who buy things like the entertainment center and china. Bibb County next door to me can't afford textbooks. The public should be incensed by this."

Mills said that until this lavish spending is stopped by presidents of institutions, the public will keep saying "no" to any additional tax moneys or funds for education.

"Until these big educational people quit living lavish lifestyles, education in Alabama will suffer," he concluded.

State Representative Clarence Haynes and Senator Jim Preuitt are calling for an investigation concerning other items that were removed from the president's home before Hawkins left office. The items were returned Sunday. Hawkins said the items were inadvertently packed by movers.

Bibb Thompson with Thompson Company, which moved some of the Hawkins' furniture, said, "My company employees only inventory and load what they are told to load by the person or family we are moving."

So said the *Daily Home,* and a careful reading of this article reveals that the entertainment center, nest of tables, Lennox china, etc., is not all that left Talladega with the Hawkinses. In fact, some who lose no love for Dr. Hawkins suggest that the financial transaction on August 17 provided convenient camouflage for the disappearance of a much longer list of items— a list as astonishing for its variety as for its value. But this is only speculation. The facts are clear enough. The Hawkinses have explained and explained that they were both running in and out of the house all day while the movers were there to pack up their possessions. They maintain that they had no idea what was being packed because the movers insisted on wrapping the things they were to move. But the maid reports that Mrs. Hawkins told her to instruct a workman to take down a chandelier for packing, so one suspects that a good deal of planning went into the preparations for moving despite the protestations of the Hawkinses that they never intended to take state property with them.

When the absence of the valuables was noticed, the Hawkinses agreed to return them. Hawkins arranged to bring back the items on a Sunday so that he and members of the board of trustees could go over the inventory list and check off the returned goods. Hawkins just happened to arrive in Talladega Sunday morning instead of Sunday afternoon as agreed. He says he decided to stack the things in the president's mansion just to get them deposited before going to a luncheon engagement. He says he didn't know that the door locks had been changed, which meant that his key (it isn't clear why he still had a key to the mansion at all) didn't fit in the front door. He reports that he then found a side door unlocked, through which he carried the things he was returning. There is now no record of how closely the list of items Hawkins returned resembles the list of those reported as missing—one of the objectives that the Institute should have had in mind when it arranged to have its Trustees present when the goods were returned.

A neighbor, however, had noticed someone carrying goods between a van and the house and apparently concluded that the mansion was being burgled. She called Representative Clarence Haynes, who in turn called the police. [It is worth considering why a citizen, seeing such unusual behavior, would not call the police directly. Could it have been fear of tangling personally with the powerful Alabama Institute? If the observer recognized the ex-president, one can hardly blame her for wishing to avoid being pulled into a legal matter.] In any case, the police dashed to the scene to find the esteemed ex-president of the Institute surreptitiously slipping state property back into the house. Perhaps it really was all an unfortunate mistake—perhaps. But credulity has its limits somewhere. Here is an excerpt from the *Daily Home's* account of the story on September 27, 1989:

Legislators Call for Investigation of AIDB Matter
by Denise Sinclair

TALLADEGA—State Representative Clarence Haynes and Senator Jim Preuitt are calling for a full investigation into an incident in which items, pieces of furniture and silver, were taken from the president's mansion at the Alabama Institute for the Deaf and Blind.

Former AIDB president Dr. Jack Hawkins, Jr. and several others returned Sunday the items, which were discovered missing following an inventory of the mansion. Hawkins assumed the chancellorship at Troy State University on September 1.

Haynes got a phone call Sunday morning from someone who saw a van parked at the mansion, and thought the residence was being burglarized. Haynes reported it to the Talladega Police Department, who on checking found Hawkins there returning the missing items.

Haynes picks up the story from there. "I had zero knowledge of any of this happening before Sunday morning. I received a call that someone had broken into the president's home at AIDB. I don't know who called. I assumed it was someone in the neighborhood who spotted the van. I called the police. The police later called me. I met them there at the home. I was told the Hawkins family had brought some things back from Troy State in a Troy State University van. I understand two weeks ago some AIDB officials had reported a list of items missing from the home after Dr. Hawkins left.

"Through business services and controller's office inventory and with the aid of purchase orders, a list of items was put together that were taken from the home. Hawkins was called and ordered to bring the items back. Had it not been for AIDB board member Ralph Gaines, these items probably would not have been returned."

It was reported by other news agencies in the state and in the *Daily Home* Tuesday afternoon the incident was a misunderstanding according to Gaines and board chairman Calvin Wooten.

In a statement to the *Daily Home* Tuesday afternoon, Gaines said, "The *Daily Home* has reported I have said there was a 'misunderstanding' regarding recent events involving the president's home at AIDB and some of its contents. I have not communicated with anyone at the *Daily Home* until I saw this report in the paper.

"The only misunderstanding I know of was the time and manner certain items which had been removed were to be returned to the home."

Gaines went on to say that Hawkins had done a good job at AIDB and as a board member he hopes no adverse effects on the Institute, its children, and adults would occur because of this issue. "I hope we can continue with the good work that's going on, and I am sorry these things have occurred."

After learning of the incident and not knowing the full story, Haynes asked board Chairman Calvin Wooten, "What's going on?"

Wooten, Haynes noted, said the items had been "inadvertently taken by movers."

Wooten in a telephone conversation Tuesday afternoon called the incident "a comedy of errors." He said, "Everything has been brought back to the mansion. I knew myself he was coming Sunday. I didn't go into any details with him on returning the items and volunteered to help him if he needed assistance. He said he had it under control. It didn't cross my mind the former president would be accused of breaking into his former home. I contend it was no break-in. All the items are inventoried and everything is back in place."

The representative questions why Hawkins returned to Talladega Sunday morning instead of the appointed time of 3:30 p.m. the same day. "He had an appointment with the board at 3:30 Sunday to return the items. I have not talked to him. I do know he and the others went in the house early and put the items back unknown to the current resident, Dr. Erskine Murray. I did not know at the time when I called the police it was Dr. Hawkins. But I want to point out he had no business in that house."

Haynes said that in talking with Wooten, he feels the board chairman wants to "cover up" the matter. "This is the kind of thing that has been going on for years, and this proves what some of us have been trying to point out about the Hawkinses' blatant disregard of the taxpayers' money. I will ask for further investigation by the board into this, and also I want the board to check out the possibility of items bought without purchase orders that are not on the inventory list."

Haynes commended board member Gaines for his effort "to do the right thing." He added, "I only wish the chairman (Wooten) could see things the way Gaines does."

He concluded, "Wooten has tried to shield some of this from the public. It is not right, no matter who it is, to take property that doesn't belong to you. I think people deserve to see the truth—good, bad, or indifferent."

Preuitt echoed Haynes' sentiments and said he will call for a full investigation.

"From all indications the items were taken from the mansion and moved to Troy. The big question is do these items belong to the school, the state, or the taxpayers, and why would they be moved? The merchandise was asked to be returned.

"Hawkins had moved out almost 30 days ago, and he returned with the items Sunday. Why move the items out if they didn't belong to you and then slip them back in? Dr. Murray is living there, and he was not home when this took place. It's wrong. Why take the goods to begin with when they belong to the taxpayers? This warrants a full investigation," Preuitt said.

He, too, thinks a coverup is occurring. "They say the movers got the items by mistake. That will not hold water. Most of the merchandise belonged to the Institute and the taxpayers. The movers were directed to move the items. This is not a mistake on the part of the movers, and it deserves being investigated because it is taxpayers' money."

A list of the items returned to the president's home are: one tea set, one ginger jar with base, one dresser, one lamp globe, two entrance rugs, two small round tables (one with marble top), one brown narrow table, two mirror runners, one octagon mirror, four crystal candle holders, one tea pot with two cups, one large Revere bowl, one soup tureen, two glass decanters, one crystal compote;

One china plate, four figurines, one cup and saucer, three silver wine goblets, 12 small Revere bowls, one large brass planter, one capa de onte planter, Buttercup silver (22 cocktail forks, eight knives, eight forks, six butter spreaders, eight salad forks, seven tablespoons, one sugar spoon, eight teaspoons, and eight soup spoons), 17 silver napkin rings, one lace table cloth;

One casserole dish in silver holder, one silver wire basket, two oblong silver platters, 18 silver coasters with three holders, three silver trays, one set of blue stoneware, one set flatware, two brass lamps, one side table, one soup tureen, three decorative apples, 41 glass serving plates, one waste basket, one gate leg table, one chandelier, one two-drawer file cabinet, one chaise lounge, one padded headboard with bed accessories, one brass floor lamp, one oak desk, one bookcase, one bedside table, one quilt stand, and one VCR.

There it is as it was reported all over the state at the time. And what about the investigation being conducted by the state's Ethics Commission? From the beginning there was next to no chance that the Commission would find against Jack Hawkins. The Old

Boy network in Alabama is alive and well, and the blind are not a part of it. As we go to press in December, the Ethics Commission has found in Hawkins' favor. As one person close to the case, who asked not to be identified said, "He may have broken the law, but not the ethics law, so he is exonerated."

This leaves only the police investigation of the Hawkins' purchase of state-owned goods and his removal and return of still other state property. The District Attorney is not saying what he intends to do. The current grand jury is about to stand down, so he may wish to wait until a new one is impaneled. Maybe justice will yet be done, but the blind of Alabama are understandably skeptical. Why should it begin now?

A new president of the Institute was named on November 9, 1989. He is Thomas Bannister, who was the Superintendent of the Utah School for the Deaf and Blind. He was the only one of the five finalists who had any past experience at all with blindness, so (although as we have seen in the case of Hawkins, experience with blindness is not necessarily a proof of rectitude) perhaps the luck of blind people in Alabama has changed. One can only hope—but may be pardoned for doubting.

With a united voice the blind of Alabama have called for redress. The governor has ignored them, and Legislators James Preuitt and Clarence Haynes (whose blind mother is an active Federationist) have demanded reform of the Institute to no avail. And where was NAC when questions about the quality of services to blind people were being raised and condemnation of the Institute's president was filling virtually every newspaper in the state? In bed with the establishment, of course, where it always wants to be. In May of 1989 Dennis Hartenstein explained with sanctimonious condescension to a group of blind people that NAC's mission is to improve agencies in the field. If accreditation were to be withdrawn or refused, he asked rhetorically, what incentive would there be for that agency to improve its services to the blind? To which one is driven to reply: What impetus is there now? Alabama has never been a good place for blind people, but its attractiveness has been declining during the past decade. Jack Hawkins is clearly the immediate cause of this sorry state of affairs, but the ultimate responsibility must lie at NAC's door. Whether NAC likes it or not, the general public understands the concept of accreditation to be a way for experts to indicate their approval of an agency's actions and policies. NAC must decide whether it would rather claim that the morally bankrupt activities and policies of the Hawkins administration are outside the purview of its standards or that it has simply been looking the other way in an effort (one supposes) to improve the Institute. Both alternatives are damning, and both are probably, to one degree or another, true.

We will say it once again in case we have been misunderstood. We have no quibble with the concept of accreditation. If it were done with commitment to improving the welfare of blind people, if it reflected society's commonly held notions of legality and ethics, if one could ever see a pattern that suggested blind people were flourishing and growing in competence through the work of accredited agencies, then one could embrace NAC accreditation with enthusiasm. The Alabama Institute for the Deaf and Blind, and its checkered history under the leadership of Jack Hawkins, is only the latest chapter in the NAC scandal. The corruption at the Alabama Institute demonstrates once again the true degree of NAC's commitment (or lack thereof) to quality service and high principles. When NAC and its agencies cozy up together and claim to be taking care of the blind, the blind lose every time. We will keep fighting for justice in Alabama, as we have so often done before. Through hard experience we have learned that if we who are blind do not fight for ourselves, no one else will do it for us.

Chapter 13

A People's Movement: Communication, Communion, and Community

The National Federation of the Blind, in the year of its golden anniversary, was irrepressibly a people's movement. The evidence of that was manifest throughout the spacious structure of the organization and the broad reach of its network—stretching from the impressive National Center for the Blind in Baltimore to the farthest outposts of Federationism in Alaska and Hawaii. The people's presence (their sheer vitality and power) was felt most palpably of all at the National Conventions—those summer rites of consecration and initiation, where members of the far-flung clan of "NFB" assembled in their thousands at some appointed urban campsite (Hilton or Hyatt or Sheraton) like the kinfolk of a vast extended family come together in reunion. That might seem only an analogy; in fact from the first convention it was close to the truth. There *was* a kinship of sorts among these people of the Federation; as we have observed more than once in earlier chapters, they were drawn together in their movement not by the physical blindness they had in common (that might as often be an alienating or estranging factor) but by the social vision they shared. From the beginning the organized blind were a visionary community, as someone once said of them; they were not just associated like the frequenters of a club but related to one another in the way of brotherhood and sisterhood. This chapter is about the brothers and the sisters—not all of them, of course, not even a sizable fraction but a representative sample.

A Leader of the People

In 1990 one of the National Federation's largest and strongest affiliates was located in a state of relatively small size and population. The NFB of South Carolina had thirty chapters, three active divisions, and more than a thousand members. Over the years it had persuaded the state legislature to pass some twenty-five major pieces of legislation and had failed with none it favored. The affiliate was known, for the first quarter century, as the Aurora Club—a name to reckon with in the affairs of the state. Although it was to have many good leaders through the years, the secret of its success was primarily due to the the presence of one man: Don Capps.

When young Capps first joined the Aurora Club back in the mid-fifties, he found the range of its endeavors carefully limited to improving what was called the "social and spiritual life" of the blind—and hands off the economic realities of their lives. The first thing he did when he became president of the affiliate in 1956 was to change all that—thereby starting a long uphill struggle against a battery of agencies and authorities clinging to the Stone Age of service to the blind. Before then, as he said in his presidential address that year, "The Club had experienced no real opposition from anyone, undoubtedly due to the fact that its principal activities had been of such a nature that no one in a position of responsibility to the blind felt threatened. However, the fact that we had now become a full-grown state organization with additional goals of an economic nature seemed to create unjustified apprehension and actual fear on the part of some who, in the past, hardly realized we even existed—and cared less."

If Capps had been an ordinary man, he might have backed away from the trouble which his economic and vocational emphasis was stirring up. For one thing, he was an executive with a major insurance company (Colonial Life) and, therefore, especially vulnerable to the influence of pressure and innuendo. But he did not equivocate, and he refused to truckle. His determination to improve the lives of blind South Carolinians did not go unappreciated, then or later. (After his initial election to the state presidency in 1956, he was re-elected to the two-year post nine times and was holding it in 1990.) A veteran member of the Aurora Club expressed the feeling of many in the state when he wrote to Capps in 1958: "Your patient efforts, and the heavy responsibility that you have assumed in the interest of all the blind is so commendable I have no way of expressing and passing on to you the sincere and humble thanks we all owe to you. As I have tried to let you know without saying all I feel, we have needed new blood in the working aims of the blind of this state, and you have more than filled the gap that has been widening over the years. In many ways it will be a thankless task, but I know that your goal has been set, and I know you will keep pushing ahead. More power to you! I know you were hurt badly in recent flare-ups, but one must go forward....Your reward will come in realizing an accomplishment which cannot come about in a month, or even a year; but with determination and faith your effort will not be in vain."

And it was not in vain, as Federationists around the country soon came to know. In addition to his continuing state leadership, Capps quickly moved into prominence at the national level, serving successively as Second Vice President and First Vice President, and remaining on the Board of Directors for the next thirty years. (His career is sketched more fully in Appendix B to this volume: *Who Are the Blind Who Lead the Blind*.) Throughout his long career of service to his fellow blind, no matter how tempestuous the struggle, Don Capps remained a model of courtesy and civility, as well as an immovable rock of stability and integrity. "This," as Kenneth Jernigan once said of him, "is what decency looks like."

The Base of Power

"The Federation has many strengths," wrote the *Monitor* editor in January, 1990, "but one of the greatest is its growing corps of local leaders. They build the chapters, make the telephone calls, and carry on the daily activities. They constitute the base of power, the foundation of strength upon which our movement is built." He then reprinted a profile of one of these local leaders, Ethel Inchausti, which had appeared in *Gem State*

Milestones (the periodical of the National Federation of the Blind of Idaho), adding: "Of such as Ethel Inchausti is the Federation made, and the future is in good hands." Here is the article:

If Ethel had time, she could tell us many stories about Idaho sixty years ago or more. She has been independent and resourceful all her life. At eighty-one she still is. Elected president of the Magic Valley Chapter of the National Federation of the Blind of Idaho last spring, Ethel Inchausti is part of the reason the membership of that chapter has multiplied several times during the last six months. Someone told her she looks younger than she did five years ago, and Ethel wasn't surprised.

Five years ago Ethel was struggling with blindness which seemed almost overwhelming. Cooking, dialing the telephone, and many other activities had become complicated or frightening. Ethel didn't know where to go for help.

One day John Cheadle and Ramona Walhof, part of an organizing team for the NFB in the Magic Valley, knocked on Ethel's door. She told them of her concern, and they told her about the National Federation of the Blind. They also told her of other services. Ethel says that was a turning point for her. Within a few months she had enrolled at the Orientation Center of the Idaho Commission for the Blind. She made friends with blind people who were members of the Federation, and she attended her first National Convention in Denver, Colorado, in 1989.

In 1926 Ethel moved from Norwich, Kansas, to Twin Falls, Idaho, bringing her three-year-old son with her. Since then she has worked as a cook for the Wells Sheep Ranch; she managed the Green Spot Cafe in Castleford, Idaho; and she sorted beans and did a variety of jobs that women did in rural Idaho.

Shortly after arriving in Idaho, Ethel married her husband of more than thirty years (now deceased), who was a farm worker. In addition to her son, Robert, Ethel and her husband had a daughter, Billie Rae. Now Ethel has seven grandchildren, fifteen great grandchildren, and two great great grandchildren.

Ethel remembers when Blue Lakes Boulevard had no businesses, only houses along it. "When you stop to think of it," she says, "it is hard to believe the change! I got lost every time I went to town. Twin Falls was little then. Now I know my way everywhere." And she does. Traveling with a white cane, directing a driver, or catching the bus—Ethel Inchausti goes wherever she wants.

She thinks maybe she talks on the phone as much as anything. "I spend a lot of time talking to blind people. I know what they can do for themselves. I threatened to quit calling one lady if she didn't come out to a meeting, which I knew would be good for her. Of course, I wouldn't have quit calling, but she came and was glad she did."

Ethel Inchausti—local leader, woman of strength.

A Federation Family

Many members of the movement over the years felt that the Federation was like a family—sometimes the only family they knew. But now and then the process also worked the other way; there were real families within the Federation whose warmth and charm became a magnet for the affections of others. John and Connie McCraw were like that; he was the blind partner but they were a unit, inseparable in and out of the Federation; it was natural to both of them to reach out to people, and so people just naturally reached out to them too.

John was already president of the NFB of Maryland when he was elected to the Board of Directors of the National Federation of the Blind in 1977. In June of the following year, an updated version of *Who Are the Blind Who Lead the Blind* said of him that "there was no question in anyone's mind that he should have the job" because "he has long been a favorite of those in the movement who know him." John seemed indefatigable, a man for all seasons and situations: by day he worked as a recreationist, by night he was musical director and band leader for a Baltimore jazz club. In addition to his work with the Federation, he was chairman of the board of Blind Industries and Services of Maryland. Perhaps he gave too much of himself to too many. Two months after the *Monitor's* profile was published, John McCraw was dead of a heart attack.

In his eulogy delivered at a special memorial service, Kenneth Jernigan (then President of the NFB) spoke these words:

John McCraw was a man of great gentleness. He was also a man of great strength and power. He was my brother in the movement to liberate the blind. He was my close, dear friend.

No person who has attended a recent convention of the National Federation of the Blind will ever think of John McCraw without recalling the rumble of that deep voice answering the roll call of the states. It usually brought applause. It always brought an audible murmur of affection, a feeling that can only be described as a surge of love reaching from all parts of the room to touch him. In fact, if one had to describe in a single word the feeling of the blind of the nation for John McCraw, that word would be love. He gave it; he received it; he lived it. And the blind of the nation and the world have better lives as a result.

And it was not just at National Conventions or on special occasions. John was the same every day—at home or in other states, with friends or with strangers, in crowds or in groups of two or three.

When I moved to Maryland a few months ago, John and Connie made it their business to let me know that they wanted to do anything they could to be of service to me. (As it was with John, so was it and so it is with Connie. She worked with John, sharing his activities, his problems, and his triumphs. She belongs to all of us who are blind, and she always will.)

John's trademark was service—and not just occasionally or in major things but on a daily basis—thoughtfully, courteously, and lovingly. During the last week of his life John performed two services for me. He arranged to have some kitchen knives sharpened, and he took a newspaper editor to task who had attacked me. In fact, his handling of the editor was typical of his way of doing business.

When he called to tell me about it, he played the whole thing down and merely said that he thought he had set the man straight on some facts and that we would see better articles in the future. A few days later I learned from a person who was in the room at the time the phone call was being made that John's language and tone were so blunt and earthy that the editor will probably never write another story without making an effort to learn the facts. True to John's prediction, the article of retraction came, and it showed all of the impact of the chastening which had been given.

John did not want credit. He wanted results. He took more pleasure in seeing the rest of us praised than having praise for himself.

In every situation he was an asset. If you were going to a conference, John was a good man to give you level-headed advice. If you were going to a party, John was a good man to help you celebrate. If you were going to a fight, John was a good man to have at your side. He never weaseled; he never chickened out; and he never deserted a friend or a cause. He stuck to the end. He did not try to find a way out by pretending that he was confused or did not understand the issues or had concerns that he could not resolve. He was staunch and steadfast. He was John McCraw.

John, old friend, dear brother, you have made the world a better place for all of us who are blind. You have shown us that gentleness need not be weakness and that love is a natural component of courage, not of cowardice or fear. You have lived your beliefs, and they are reflected in the lives of us all.

Your spirit will march with us in our continuing campaign for the freedom of the blind. Your dedication will strengthen us. Your love will sustain us. When we suffer defeats (and there will be some) or when we achieve victories (and there will be many), we will think of you and make your memory part of our mourning and our rejoicing. No history of the battle of the blind for liberation and first-class citizenship will ever be complete without your name. No story of our journey to independence will fail to include you. Rest in peace! We will keep the movement strong. We will build it and make it reach new heights of achievement and solidarity. We will always remember your deep voice, your abiding dedication, and your great capacity for love. We will keep the faith.

One year later, in its round-up of the 1979 convention in Miami, the *Monitor* included a brief report under the heading, "Connie McCraw Speaks":

One of the most moving moments of the convention came during the banquet when Connie McCraw, widow of the late John Mc-Craw, rose to speak. No member of our movement has ever been more loved or respected than John; and his deep voice, his buoyant enthusiasm, his common sense, and his compassion and sincerity were sorely missed at this year's convention. Connie is also loved and respected, so her remarks carried special emphasis and meaning. She said:

> My Fellow Federationists, this is my first opportunity to meet and greet you collectively since John, your friend and mine, left us last September.
>
> As you all will agree, John's passing left a void in our working lives, and in our hearts and minds that will be hard to fill. I don't mean to presume that no one can do the things he did, but I do say that he was unique in his approach to life in general and his job in particular.
>
> You all, and I do mean all, were so kind and helpful when I needed you, so thoughtful and sincere in that dark hour, so charitable in sharing my grief and sorrow.
>
> Please believe me when I say thank you, for your outpouring of love and friendship, your many, many gifts, and for letting me continue to be one of you.
>
> For John, for myself, for our two beautiful sons, Vince, who is here by my side, and Frank, who left this morning for Fort Bliss, Texas, his first stay in the Army, thank you.

The final installment of this story of two families—the Federation family and the McCraw family—occurred ten years afterward, and was related by Kenneth Jernigan in the *Braille Monitor* (July, 1989):

CONNIE MCCRAW DIES
by Kenneth Jernigan

I was sitting in my office on Thursday morning, June 1, 1989, when I received a call telling me of the death of Connie McCraw. There were no details, just the announcement—the news that she had died.

As her friends know, Connie had not been well for quite some time. Her last years were spent in a retirement home here in Baltimore. Toward the end she was in great pain.

At times like this it is easier to remember than to find the right words. When I came to Baltimore in 1978, John and Connie McCraw were a source of strength to me and a focal point for the warmth and hospitality that I received. John was the leader of the National Federation of the Blind of Maryland, and Connie was always at his side—supporting, loving, and caring. Only a short time after my arrival, John had a sudden heart attack and died. I worked with Connie in planning the funeral and was one of those who delivered a eulogy. Connie grieved at John's death, but she put her sorrow aside to help ease the pain of others. Connie was like that.

As soon as we established the National Center for the Blind, Connie was on hand to help—for many years as a volunteer and for a while as a staff member. Regardless of the job she was doing (and there were many), one factor was always constant. She cared. And everybody knew she cared. It radiated from her in every act.

She was the voice on cassette of the *Braille Spectator*, the newsletter of the National Federation of the Blind of Maryland. In fact, she read every issue except the most recent. Toward the end she was really not well enough to do the reading, but the joy of doing it outweighed the pain. Again, Connie was like that. She was always willing to read or give of her time or do anything else she could to help others.

Big John's booming voice is still remembered and missed at National Federation of the Blind conventions, and Connie's gentle goodness will also be missed. She was ours, and we loved her. We still love her, and our love will be undying.

Connie McCraw—worker, friend, lady, generous helper. We will miss you.

Winning the West

When Sharon Gold, the vigorous president of the NFB of California, was presented in 1983 with the highest award the National Federation can give to one of its own—the Jacobus tenBroek Award—she revealed that one of the things that had brought her into the movement years before was the discriminatory treatment blind people were receiving from the airlines. "It drew me," she said, "because I had been flying since I was ten years old, alone—and I knew that if the airline industry got its way, none of us would fly, and none of us would be free." Three years later Sharon was arrested on a United Airlines plane while enroute home to California from an NFB convention. Her crime was that of occupying her assigned seat (in an exit row, as it happened) and politely declining to leave when told by misinformed flight attendants that she was violating an FAA regulation. Finally, in an episode made ugly by the behavior of airline and airport personnel, Sharon was arrested. She was released shortly thereafter, and charges were quietly dropped—but not before she had made her point and "sat down" for her rights.

That was Sharon Gold: not one to trifle with, but definitely one to be associated with in a crisis. Trained in law and tempered in the school room (she was twenty years a teacher), Sharon never raised her voice or lost her composure; but there was steel in that voice and determination in the bearing. Federationists in California had discovered this for themselves during the mini-civil war, which originated in California in the late seventies and ended in California in the early eighties. It was Sharon Gold who, as the new state president, dug in and hung on through all the flak and buckshot fired off by the furious losers in that fight. It was Sharon Gold who carried through the reorganization of the NFB of California and built up the affiliate to a stature and reputation it had not known since the days of Anthony (Tony) Mannino. She put the state organization on a secure financial basis, and she developed *The Spokesman*, which rapidly became one of the best affiliate newsletters in the country. Gold wasted no time gloating over any of these accomplishments—nor over any of the lawsuits won, the legislation passed, the programs reformed, or the blind people helped by the new NFB of California. She simply did the jobs one by one and got on to the next.

A glimpse into the "private" home life of this dedicated leader of the organized blind was provided for readers of *The Spokesman* in 1980, during the peak of the "late unpleasantness" (as Californians came to call the mini-uprising in their midst). The profile of Sharon Gold was written by Patricia Munson, the capable editor of the newsletter. It is reprinted here in full:

A VISIT WITH OUR PRESIDENT
by Patricia Munson

As Federationists recall, it was in November of 1978 that our affiliate in California was reorganized. At that time Sharon Gold was elected president, and the members gave her the difficult task of providing the strong leadership necessary to build a meaningful, productive unit of the NFB. With the help of all of us, Sharon immediately set to work to begin the rebuilding of the California affiliate of the National Federation of the Blind. Today, we know the degree of our success. The affiliate started with nothing (no money, no office, no supplies). But, we had elected a president with great imagination and foresight; two years later, all has changed.

No organization can be a success if it does not have dedicated members. In California, we have many, many hard working, loyal members. So, with the combination of excellent leadership and fine members how could we fail!

Approximately one year ago, I wrote in *the Spokesman* of my visit to President Gold's home. I told you of how the NFB had invaded not only her life, but also her residence. NFB canes greeted me as I entered the front door; NFB material almost squeezed me off every chair in which I tried to sit; and NFB material met me as I tried to hang up my sweater in the closet. Don't get me wrong, President Gold is a most tidy housekeeper, but what was she to do? As I said, the NFB had moved in. The telephone rang incessantly, for members and non-members always know where to call when assistance is wanted. Her secretary came and went, taking endless dictation. Always President Gold kept asking me for suggestions as to how we could improve the affiliate and how we might progress. I told her that it appeared to me that she was doing exceedingly well on her own.

Some improvements for the affiliate were obvious; it needed money, for with money comes many so-called luxuries such as an office, equipment, and more secretarial help.

Well, the rest is history; Federationists know of the many fundraising projects that have been so successful. Who among us has not sold peanuts, candy, and Knott's Berry Farm products—and which of us has not sold tickets for drawings?

Now let me report to you what I saw during my most recent visit two months ago with our president. Some of those canes still greeted me at her front door; that material still fought me for a free chair; and that closet still looks like a small warehouse for NFB literature—but we now possess a very fine office.

Our new office houses some fine equipment, but now this equipment, too, must also compete with some of those NFB canes and mounds of NFB material. What I am trying to tell you is that our affiliate is growing faster than the speed of light. We have been so successful that we cannot keep up with our own progress. Even when I was there to help, there was never enough time to file and sort all the material that comes in to the affiliate. This is a wonderful predicament. At the height of the Roman Empire, it was said that all roads led to Rome. In California, the progressive blind of this state know that all roads lead to the office of the National Federation of the Blind.

California, indeed, has a very fine affiliate, of which we can all be proud. We certainly have President Gold's leadership abilities to thank for our growth, development, and success.

Of Such as These

"Many younger Federationists have probably never heard of Rudolph and Martha Bjornseth," wrote Kenneth Jernigan in 1986, "and that is a pity, for at a crucial time in Federation history these two played an important (perhaps a crucial) part in saving the movement. It was during the depths of the Federation's civil war, immediately prior to and during the 1961 Kansas City convention."

He went on: "Rudolph and Martha Bjornseth had been Federationists in North Dakota for a long time. I don't know exactly how long, but I came into the movement in 1949, and I have the impression that Rudolph and Martha preceded me. Be that as it may, I remember having contact with them early in my Federation activity. They were quiet people; but they were strong on dedication, belief, and integrity.

"In the election preceding the 1961 convention there was a battle for control of North Dakota," Jernigan recalled. "Out-of-state members of the dissident minority (the group which was later to become the American Council of the Blind), being short on votes and a number of other qualities, came to North Dakota and tried to take over. They insisted that they had the right to vote in the election for state president and (the thing that really motivated them) delegate to the National Convention. Rudolph resisted, and no amount of personal abuse or hoodlum tactics would shake him."

Jernigan continued: "In the election for state president and delegate Rudolph received the majority of the votes of the North Dakota residents attending the state convention—and he *intended* to stand up for his rights and the movement. He came to that stormy 1961 National Convention in Kansas City, and he never wavered. He was subjected to threats, insults, and a variety of other indignities. He was yelled at. It made no difference. He became a rallying point, a symbol of honesty and integrity—almost an embodiment of what we were and must do and be. After the convention Rudolph returned to the quiet life he had led and loved in North Dakota. He and Martha have continued to live and work through the years, supporting the movement as they could and claiming no limelight."

Jernigan wrote that the thing that had brought all this to mind was an article which had appeared in the Bjornseth's local newspaper, the *Fargo Forum* earlier that year, sketching the lives and work of this accomplished couple, both of them blind and now approaching their ninth decade. "I want to share this article with you," wrote the *Monitor* editor. "It is a way of remembering and paying a tribute. The Bjornseths should not be forgotten. Of such as these was the Federation built."

Crossing the Jordan

On a later occasion, in 1989, Kenneth Jernigan wrote another brief introduction in the *Monitor* to an article which had stirred old memories of earlier times and near-forgotten pioneers in the movement of the organized blind. This is how he began:

Recently while I was reading the Fall/Winter, 1988, *Minnesota Bulletin, the publication of the National Federation of the Blind of Minnesota (yes, I got to it late), I read of the death of Torger Lien.*

The article was written by Steve Jacobson, and it caused me to reflect and remember. I am sure that some of my observations and experiences parallel those of Steve.

You see, I knew Torger Lien—and he was stubborn, determined to have his say, and not deterred in the slightest if he found himself in the minority. In fact, he spoke his peace even if he knew that he was a minority of one—and he would be heard. In short, he had the characteristics which a true Federationist most prizes and should possess.

In the later years of his life Torger found himself at odds with the majority of Federationists in his state and was often a thorn in their sides. I myself have felt the sting of his caustic lash. On more than one occasion I was, to say the least, annoyed by Torger's behavior—but all of that has absolutely nothing to do with his sterling qualities and the contributions he made. He was jaggedly honest in his beliefs (even when they were wrong), and he didn't care whether others thought they were wrong or not.

In short, I respected Torger Lien not for what he believed on occasion in his later years but for what he was and for what he did to stimulate a spirit of independence among the blind of Minnesota and (at least to some extent) the blind of the nation. We should not forget the pioneers of our movement, and we should not judge their contributions by the fact that their thinking and philosophy were formed in an earlier day—a day when conditions were different, opportunities for the blind virtually nonexistent, and organized effort by blind people only a hope and a distant dream. If the blind of that day were to make progress, they had to disturb the status quo—and at times that meant being abrasive, stubborn, and just plain muleheaded. Nothing else would work. And Torger Lien fitted the image. As I have already said, he should not be forgotten, and those who did not know him or have never heard of him are poorer for it.

If Torger Lien had been born fifty years later, I believe he would today be one of our strongest and most progressive leaders. But whether he would or not, he would have had opinions, and he would have insisted that they be heard. Whatever the circumstances, he would not have been intimidated or cowed. In the life of Torger Lien there is a lesson for all of us who labor in the vineyards of the Federation today—not only for the leaders but also for the rank and file as well. Who can say whether fifty years from now our **views** and philosophy will fit the mood and the needs of the time? I have no doubt that they will-but, then, perhaps I have a streak of Torger in me. I remember him fondly. Here is Steve Jacobson's article:

Crossing the Jordan: Memories of Torger Lien
by *Steve Jacobson*

"Just keep your tongue straight in your mouth," he would say, as we approached an angled street crossing. Then he might issue what was, to a fourth-grade boy, an awesome threat: "If you get off of the crosswalk, I might have to get one of the girls to find you." Of course, it was not a threat, and those of us in Torger Lien's travel class knew it. It was simply an example of his uniquely gentle way of telling us to concentrate. He would jokingly refer to "crossing the Jordan," but as children, we could not conceive of it happening. When I heard that Torger Lien had passed away, these memories and more came back as clear as if 1960 were yesterday.

As a capable blind teacher, his impact went far beyond the boundaries of the classroom. He was the first person to make me think that I could travel independently. He taught me the importance of developing a good sense of direction, listening for landmarks, and deriving meaningful information from echoes. We would hear what to us were wondrous tales of how Torger Lien rode alone on Twin Cities buses. Of course, he was not the only blind person who did so, but he was someone that we knew personally. It was through him that we learned to dream that some day, as adults, we could do the same.

My first exposure to the theoretical aspects of radio and electricity was accomplished only through the dedication of Torger Lien, and this gift is one that I still carry with me. Besides teaching me some of the theory, he showed me that blind people could wire electrical circuits, make repairs to electrical equipment, and enjoy radio and electronics as a hobby just as sighted people do.

Torger Lien was born in 1898 near Oden in southwestern Minnesota. He would explain that his sense of direction was developed through the crossing of the open fields on his family's farm. He graduated in 1918 from what was then the Minnesota Braille and Sight Saving School in Faribault. After earning a bachelor's degree from the University of Minnesota, and after marrying Jennie

Anderson in 1932, he returned to the Braille school as an instructor in 1934. Torger stressed the importance of one's sense of direction and one's hearing in the development of alternative techniques for independent travel. As a result of his work in this area, he was interviewed by *National Geographic* magazine, certainly not an everyday occurrence.

After retiring from the Braille school in 1962, Torger and Jennie moved to Minneapolis, where he remained active in the alumni association of the Braille school and his church. In addition, he served as president of the Minnesota Organization of the Blind, which later became the NFB of Minnesota.

Torger died of a massive heart attack on October 13, 1988. The death of my father last March should have reminded me how suddenly death can come. I had always intended to explain to Torger that my strong belief in the ability of blind persons to live independent and full lives came from his example. I had intended to tell him that, even with some of our political differences, I had a great deal of respect for him. You could rightfully say, therefore, that I am not writing this entirely as a tribute to him. No, I have a somewhat selfish reason as well. It is my hope that one way or another he will be able to read this on his side of the Jordan.

A Writer's Story

Mary Main lost her sight gradually over the years. By the time she moved to Connecticut and learned of the National Federation of the Blind she was in her seventies, but her dynamic energy and spirit were such that she rapidly became one of the leaders of the state affiliate. She also became known and loved throughout the entire Federation. She was to deliver an address at the National Convention in 1985 at Louisville, but her writings had appeared in the *Braille Monitor* prior to that time. In the January, 1982, edition of the *Monitor* an autobiographical essay of hers was published with these introductory words from the editor:

"As her writing shows, she is a staunch Federationist. As her writing also shows, she is warm and witty and human. Sometimes we are asked, 'What are Federationists like?' Some of them are like Mary Main." Here is her essay:

REFLECTIONS ON LIFE AND BLINDNESS
by Mary Main

I was born in Buenos Aires so long ago that I have no memory of the event. My parents were British. My grandfather, my father and, eventually, my husband came to Argentina to work on the British-owned railways. I was educated at the kind of English boarding school that lay more emphasis on deportment than on scholarship. When I asked if I might learn to type I was told that was not a necessary part of the education of a lady. No one suggested that I should go on to college, much less ever have to earn my own living.

When we were first married my husband and I lived in a railway coach on construction—no paved road, no shops, no human habitation of any sort within leagues. I was the most inexperienced of housewives, and cooking on a tiny wood stove in a railway coach that was periodically shunted back and forth was not the easiest introduction to domesticity.

Just before Pearl Harbor we moved to Toronto, and from then on my husband traveled extensively, building roads, dams, and so forth. My son was in boarding school and I came to New York. New York was the most stimulating and liberating experience of my life. I took an apartment in the Village and began to write. I was triumphant when I sold my first story to a children's magazine for four dollars, but before long I was selling stories to the slick magazines. I had it made—or so I thought.

It was about this time that an ophthalmologist told me I had Retinitis Pigmentosa. I had no idea what that was and it made very little impression on me. He did not mention the word "blind," and he assured me I would always see well enough to read. I was far more troubled by the prospect of divorce.

In 1950 Doubledays suggested that I might write a biography of Eva Peron—I had written a couple of novels which had deservedly died young. I accepted, having no idea of the difficulties that lay ahead.

When I returned to Buenos Aires I soon realized what I had got myself into. The Perons were at the height of their power and Evita did not permit any inquiry into her past—she had published her own idealized version. The interviews I had with people who had known her in her early days had to be conducted in secret. Had it been known they were discussing her they might well have been arrested and perhaps tortured. I, too, ran some risk and I was very glad to get away. *The Woman with the Whip—EVA PERON* was first published in 1952 soon after Evita's early death from cancer. It was written under the pseudonym of Maria Flores for the protection of my friends in Argentina.

I could no longer ignore the fact that my field of vision was diminishing. I went to a number of ophthalmologists who warned me it was not safe for me to be out on the street alone, but did not tell me where I might go for help. One day a taxi rounded a corner in front of me and I walked slap into it. This was the second small accident I had had and my doctor called a friend of mine to warn her I might have others if I was not given help. She sent Ed Lever of the Industrial Home for the Blind in Brooklyn to see me. He was the first blind person I had ever talked to, and I was much encouraged, for he assured me I could continue to live independently—all I needed was a guide dog or a white cane. My failing sight had been a secret I had carefully concealed from my acquaintances. To walk out on the street carrying a white cane was the most difficult thing I have ever had to do. However, once I had taken the plunge, my white cane gave me a wonderful sense of freedom. I felt I could go anywhere, and everyone was so kind. Now, when I bumped into strangers, instead of yelling at me they apologized and offered to help. I wallowed in their sympathy.

My euphoria did not last. I was often sorry for myself but I was outraged to find that others might pity me. I think this was the most difficult period in the process of going blind, when I did not know whether to regard myself as sighted or blind. I could still read perfectly well. I was reading manuscripts for *The Book of the Month Club*. My friend, the one who had sent Ed Lever to me, urged me to go to a school for the blind. I refused, partly because I was afraid I might emerge as apathetic as some of the blind I had seen working at the Lighthouse or the Foundation, but largely, I think, because I didn't want to have anything to do with others who were blind. I felt it would cut me off forever from the sighted world.

In 1960 I bought a house in Provincetown where I lived for the next fourteen years. Fortunately I lived alone so that I had to do cooking, cleaning, writing, gardening, and all the things I had always done, and gradually I learned to do them without my sight. I had been told by a professional that it would be useless for me to learn Braille at my age, but I decided to learn anyway. Braille and touch typing have turned out to be my most useful tools.

My son and his family were living in Paris and I traveled every year to visit them. My sighted friends were astonished at my independence and told me I was wonderful—and I believed them! I still did not know others who were blind.

As my seventieth birthday approached I felt the need to be near my family. My son had returned to this country and when they bought this house in Stamford, I moved into an apartment at the end of the house. I had hoped to take an active part in the community but the house is isolated among the trees and fields, and there is no way of getting anywhere without a car. It was at this point that I had a letter from Howard May (president of the National Federation of the Blind of Connecticut) suggesting that I might call him if I thought I might be interested in the NFB. I knew nothing of the NFB but at that point I was ready to try anything. Howard's voice was so warm and friendly, but when he told me the nearest chapter was in Danbury my heart sank—how could I get there? He suggested I should call the Truehearts who were members. "You'll like them," he said.

I did.

In Danbury I met for the first time with a group of blind people many of whom were much more active and independent than I. I realized how little I knew about the blind: I had not suffered from discrimination, and I had never heard of sheltered workshops, and I understood nothing of the discussion. And, anyway, who was this fellow Jernigan? I felt taken down a peg or two and decided the NFB had nothing to offer me, and refused coffee and doughnuts grumpily.

I joined—begrudgingly to be sure, but I joined. I joined because I loved the Truehearts. I joined because, for all my surliness, the people in Danbury had made me feel welcome; and, little by little, in this miscellaneous group of people who had nothing in common but their lack of sight, I began to find a comradeship I had found nowhere else. I felt deprived when I could not get to a meeting. "I wish we had a chapter in Stamford," I told Howard.

"Well, why don't you start one," he said. And that was how the Stamford Area Chapter of the National Federation of the Blind of Connecticut came into being.

Nothing gives a bigger boost to the ego in old age than a little unexpected success. When the musical *Evita* was first produced in London about three years ago, my book on *Evita* was republished there in paperback, and has sold remarkably well. The new hardback edition brought out by Dodd Mead here has not done so well, but it did bring a flurry of excitement into my life— newspaper and radio interviews, talks, and an appearance on the Charles Kurault Sunday Morning show—all of which I very much enjoyed. However, I think what has most enlivened my old age is my membership in the NFB. It has given me so many new friends and so many new interests, and it has taught me so much. For one thing it has taught me how really independent the blind can be.

Letters and Arts of Leadership

Among the various channels of communication linking people and divisions of the organized blind movement over the years was an elaborate "grapevine" of correspondence between rank-and-file members and elected leaders—a practice especially encouraged and assiduously cultivated by Kenneth Jernigan through several decades. In fact, Jernigan carried on a massive correspondence, not only with insiders but with outsiders as well: agency officials and program administrators, politicians and professors, public celebrities and ordinary citizens. But he devoted particular care and affectionate attention to the letters (thousands of them each year) from members of the Federation. These came in all varieties of expression and shades of opinion— not to mention degrees of coherence and clarity. They also ranged in attitude from warm praise to furious denunciation. An example of the former, typical of countless others, came from a veteran member who wrote in part: "Please let me say that I appreciate your leadership in the *Monitor*, the Federation, and for me personally; for the Federation continues to be one of the three principal influences in my life, along with my family and my church. You were my first teacher in blindness and Federationism, and you have made my life worth living. I feel especially blessed to know you personally and rejoice with all the others with whom you have shared yourself."

On the other hand, there were letters like the following:

To whom it may concern:

In response to Kenneth Jernigan's article...about the treatment of blind people on Airlines:

Mr. Jernigan's statement is causing embarrassment to the blind community who are not members of the N.F.B. of the blind.

I have traveled worldwide on 16 different airlines and have always been treated well by all Airlines personnel. When I travel I take a folding cane with me that fits in the pocket on the seat in front of me. Long canes have to be checked with the stewardess.

I resent the threats that Kenneth Jernigan and the N.F.B. is making about disrupting airline service by running out on runways and causing problems in the terminals.

I was given a pillow and blanket on overnight flights for my own comfort not because I have a loose bladder. They have restrooms on both ends of the plane.

Mr. Jernigan says that he and his members are ready to go to jail if necessary. I hope they do.

If they don't like traveling by plane than they should take a bus.

Sincerely,

——————

Jernigan replied as follows:

Dear Mr.——:

It seems to me that your letter is a bit intemperate. Do you really believe that anyone was questioning whether there are restrooms on airplanes? Perhaps you are not familiar with the circumstances surrounding the experiences of many blind persons who travel on planes. If we wish equal treatment with others, surely it is not reasonable to suggest that our only remedy is to stop flying and ride on buses. If you really wish that a number of your fellow blind citizens will be sent to jail, consider the implications of such a harsh and emotional attitude. Perhaps you would like to know why we have taken the stand we have taken, or perhaps you simply do not wish to be bothered with facts or details. In any case we wish you well and hope only the best for you.

More typical of the generality of letters to which Federation leaders like Jernigan were especially intent on responding was the following:

January 2, 1990

Dear Mr. Jernigan:

I saw your community service announcement on one of my cable stations over the Christmas holiday, and thought that maybe you could help my son.

I am writing this letter on behalf of my son, Bob. Bob is a 32-year-old diabetic with many health problems, including blindness. He recently lost his eyesight, and he is having a difficult time. I have tried to make him as comfortable as possible. However, comfort is not the only important thing. Right now, Bob's life consists of eating and sitting in his chair in his room listening to t.v. I know there has to be more in life for Bob. However, we don't even know where to turn.

I would really appreciate any information you may have regarding schools or anything that will be of help to Bob.

Thank you.

———

January 8, 1990

Dear Mrs.———:

I have your letter of January 2, 1990, and I will do what I can to be of help. In the first place your son needs some training to know how to function as a blind person. He also needs contact with others who are blind—and, particularly, with others who are blind and diabetic. Let me give you some addresses and telephone numbers.

First, let me tell you that you should be in touch with the National Federation of the blind of [name of state]. Therefore, you should contact: [address]. I am sending a copy of your letter and mine to your state president so that he will know about your son's situation.

Also, you should be aware of the Diabetics Division of the National Federation of the Blind. The contact is: Mrs. Karen Mayry, President, Diabetics Division, National Federation of the Blind, 919 Main Street, Suite 15, Rapid City, South Dakota 57701, (605) 342-3885. As with your state president, I am sending a copy of our correspondence to Mrs. Mayry so that she may expect a communication from you or be able to initiate one.

Under separate cover I am sending you and your son material which I think you will find of help. Perhaps Bob has already made contact with the state library for the blind. If he has, he will doubtless have a cassette player which will read four-track slow-speed cassettes. If he has not made this contact, I would suggest that he do it. The address is:——.

The literature I am sending is in print and also on cassette. This means that you can read it and that Bob can also read it for himself. Some of the cassettes will be four-track slow-speed, and some will be normal cassette speed on two tracks. The two-track cassettes will play on any cassette recorder. The important thing to keep in mind as Bob starts to deal with his blindness is this: Blindness need not keep an individual from leading a full and productive life. With reasonable training and opportunity a blind person can compete on equal terms with a sighted person. I know this may not sound reasonable or make sense to you at the present time, but keep it in mind as you read the material and make the contacts. As I have said, we will do what we can to be of help.

Exchanging letters with blind correspondents through the years led Jernigan, on a winter day in 1982, to speculate about the patterns into which these missives tended to fall—and in particular a new pattern which he discerned in the letters of blind persons during recent years. Here is what he had to say about it:

OF LETTERS AND PATTERNS
by Kenneth Jernigan

It is important to recognize the significance of a particular event, but it is even more important to recognize the significance of the pattern which that event implies. Pattern recognition, in the language of computers and sophisticated systems, is one of the most valuable skills that a person may acquire.

If we apply "pattern recognition" to events concerning the blind, we find interesting trends. Forty years ago very few blind people were knowledgeable about the laws affecting them (even when such laws existed, and mostly they didn't). Moreover, the blind had been schooled by society to keep their opinions to themselves—or not to have any.

Even twenty years ago (or ten), the average blind person throughout the country was not likely to be overly concerned with the implications and subtleties of day-to-day life situations as they affected his or her civil rights and responsibilities. The pattern today is quite different. Literally hundreds and thousands of blind Americans all over the nation are "feeling their oats" and expressing their opinions.

It is a heady business, this matter of freedom. It leads to all kinds of diversity of opinion: to views that are thoughtful and sound, and sometimes to expressions that are strident and unreasonable. It leads to error, insight, half truth, oversimplification, precision of analysis, hasty conclusions, and well thought out positions.

But the pattern itself (the overall fact of its shape and existence) is wonderfully positive and filled with promise for the future. For the first time in history the blind are truly coming into their own and experiencing self-recognition and fulfillment.

The evidence of this new pattern is everywhere present. It can be seen in the attitudes and behavior of individuals and in the thrust and direction of the local chapters and state affiliates of our movement. It can also be seen in the letters (the hundreds and thousands of them) that cross my desk on a continuing basis. I want to share two of those letters with you. They are typical of what is happening to the blind.

The first of the letters is from Gertrude Ward of Pennsylvania. She is a senior citizen, outspoken and vocal, with opinions on almost everything. And she never hesitates to express her opinions. She has a lifetime of experience, mixed with sincerity and a touch (but only a touch) of acid. She knows what she thinks, and she intends for others to know it, too.

It goes without saying that I think she misunderstands some of my views and some of those of the Federation, but I suspect she would return the compliment—and do it with vigor. In fact, I have had numerous sharp exchanges with her, and I hope to have many more. On a number of things I think she is absolutely wrong, and on others I think she doesn't have her facts straight, but I think she is thoroughly sincere and ruggedly honest. Moreover, the fact of her expression and the freedom she feels to do it are the strongest possible indicators of how far we have come as a people and how valuable the NFB has been (and continues to be) as a movement. The criticisms made by Gertrude Ward (even when they are wrong or based on faulty information) are not the insidious manifestations of destructiveness and attempted subversion which we have sometimes witnessed but the growing pains of liberty and full citizenship. More power to her, and to her probings and scoldings and compliments and questions and concerns. They are the healthy ebullience of a vital organization, alive and expanding.

The second letter I want to call to your attention is in the same vein as the first. Unlike the letter from Gertrude Ward, it does not turn inward to criticize the organization, but it demands to be heard and insists upon respect. In effect, it says to anyone who cares to contest it: "Yes, I am blind but I have as much right to first-class treatment as you do. You may be sighted or highly educated or rich and powerful, but you stand no taller in today's society than I do. Why? Because I intend to make it that way. I intend to speak for myself and have my rights. I don't demand special treatment, but I do demand equal treatment. The two are not the same. They are sometimes confused, but there is all the difference in the world."

The author of this second letter is William T. Roberts, president of the Ohio Falls Chapter of the NFB of Indiana. Like Gertrude Ward, he reads his *Braille Monitor*. He knows about rights and appeals and courts and such like. He also knows about responsibility and dignity and human values.

As much as anything else, these two letters tell the story of the value of the National Federation of the Blind—the "put downs," the organized effort, the self-awareness, the painful struggle to climb the stairs of freedom, the long road which lies ahead, the pride of self-worth, the confidence which comes from the realization of organizational strength, the hope and the pain and the belief, the spirit to venture, and the wonderful feeling of moving ahead to a better tomorrow. This is the National Federation of the Blind. Let our "pattern recognition" be certain. Let our rememberings and our dreams and our plans be that of a people whose time for a place in the sun has come.

Here are the two letters:

Dunmore, Pennsylvania
September 25, 1981

Dear Mr. Jernigan:

It sounds like a "who done it," except that it scares me as no fiction could. What does? Your report on the break-ins and the paper riffling, etc. I hope you have taken extra precautions against such things; for while I don't always agree with you, I know you are doing what you think is right according to your knowledge and experience. But I do wish NFB people would stop deliberately antagonizing certain people. Why couldn't Mike Hingson [see Chapter Seven] go along with the airline officials! Then, after he got to his destination, he could have brought charges against them. This way he would not have been harmed. A little discretion does pay. What Mike and other guide dog users cannot understand is that it isn't the blind that are being segregated on planes and in restaurants—it is the dogs.

There has been so much opposition to bringing guide dogs into eating places lately that the sighted majority may have a law passed against their use in certain places if the blind don't use more discretion in their use. Besides, dogs are different sizes, and they have different temperaments.

There is no way of predicting how a dog will react to a plane crash if it is injured. I heard that when Gayle Burlingaine died (see article by Harold Bleakley in May, 1981, *Braille Monitor*), his guide dog wouldn't let anyone take away the corpse. This dog was almost the size of a wolf. I saw the dog once in Harrisburg, Pennsylvania. Could a dog that size lay under the seat on a plane? If a blind person chooses to use a guide dog, that is his business, but he has no right to force that dog on other people who do not want it. And any blind person who uses an animal for a guide will have to accept special arrangements for the animal. This is not segregation of the blind, but rather the animal for the protection of the public.

They did not refuse Mike Hingson a seat on the plane, but required that he and his dog sit in a certain place. You may win your case against the airline, but it may spur the public on to outlaw the dogs in certain places. The public has the right to protection, too. Some blind people think only of their own comfort.

Regarding blind teachers: It is a shame and a crying disgrace that children are not taught by their parents to respect their teachers, whether they like the teachers or not. On the other hand, children (by nature) respect only a person who has the upper hand. I think an assertive personality is required for a good teacher. You have to let the students know from the beginning who is the boss in the school room. I felt so angry after reading about the way that blind teacher was treated in Pittsburgh (see *Braille Monitor*, September, 1981) that I would have liked to have thrashed her students within an inch of their lives. That is the only language that brats like that can understand.

The schools will have to crack down on them, or there will be no teachers left, or schools either. It would be a good idea to inspect students at the door of the school for weapons, drugs, etc., and to allow criminally inclined students to be expelled. In other words we need a little more of the old fashioned discipline instead of all this mealy-mouthed permissiveness. Even animals discipline their young. If children know you will discipline them, you seldom have to carry out your threat. My children behaved in school and were never disciplined, because they minded their teachers. No, they were not angels, nor were they hoodlums either.

When I was a small child, my father taught me to print and to do other things before I went to school. My sister, who can see, showed me how to sign my name in longhand on checks when the need arose, and I have been doing it ever since. But I know a person with sight could do better than I. Not that they do better than I in every case, but they should be able to make their lines meet better, etc.

Since it is not the parent who teaches the child in school, I do not think they should have the right to decide where their child should go to school. Some parents overestimate their child's ability. It must be terrible for a teacher in the public school to be confronted with a mentally retarded child, or one that has been shielded so much that it is unable to cope with dressing, etc., even if the child has a right mind.

When I went blind at the age of five, my parents encouraged me to go ahead and do most things just as I had before, and they showed me how to do new things. I think my father's experience of four years in the Spanish-American War and the Philippine Insurrection, along with his experience as a policeman, gave him confidence in the abilities of the blind. My mother was also encouraging.

There are mothers with sight who are not worthy of the name, so I suppose it follows that some blind mothers are in the same boat. Don't authorities need legal grounds for taking children from their parents? Blindness in itself should not constitute legal grounds. Have you ever noticed that some blind people want to have children but do not want to take care of them. The children are just a symbol of their so-called attempt at "normalcy."

Yes, there are all kinds of blind people, and they are not all "independent," etc. You make no allowances for them. It is true that with proper training more blind people could be independent, but there will always be some who (for one reason or another) can never reach complete independence. And that is where you and I part company—because you do not take this into consideration.

How can a deaf-blind person travel if he cannot communicate? The public as a whole cannot understand sign language, and a blind man cannot read lips. This idea of the deaf-blind traveling alone sounds loony. The hard of hearing blind could travel alone with some help. Some deaf-blind people cannot even talk plain.

As you said, NFB has made mistakes but, need it keep on making the *same* mistakes? I'm glad you have started giving resolutions at the National Convention more time and thought. I would like you to make copies of this letter and send it to the different chapters. It will do them good. They need to hear another point of view.

Gertrude Ward

P.S. Ask J. Gashel what a gold card signifies in SSI? What cities in this state have chapters?

New Albany, Indiana
September 20, 1981

U.S. Post Office

Dear Mr. Allen:

Since the summer of 1977 your branch of the post office has been disrupting library service to me.

They have refused to bring my books to me, one such time being when I called it to the attention of former post master Elseworth Hartley in the summer of 1977.

I had to insist that he issue a written order to the foreman of letter carriers that all matter addressed to me (under Public Law 89-522) be delivered to my address of 205 Wainwright Drive.

However, when material was subsequently delivered to me the carrier on route #16 swore at me. The same carrier does not now handle route #16.

Once again, in the fall and winter of 1979-80 the Worldwide Church of God (which distributes *The World Tomorrow* program to hundreds of radio stations, spends thousands of dollars in postage, and also runs a program under Public Law 89-522) reported to me that they were losing so many tapes that they were going to discontinue the program.

I returned what I had on hand to them and explained that some letter carriers and some clerks did not want to handle materials under said law.

Fanning out from the Pasadena, California, post office, with the use of inspectors, they were able to stop the disruption of delivery of their tapes.

Once again, in June of 1981, there was another disruption.

One of your clerks wrote across a magazine "subscriber deceased."

A publication of the Davis Publishing Company, *The Ellery Queen Mystery Magazine*, was returned by your branch and that started a chain action that resulted in the discontinuing of all library services to this address.

I have assumed in the past that said disruptions were due to some misunderstanding or human error, but due to such repeated practices it is clear to me that this is spite action.

Therefore, I am sending copies of this letter to the Louisville Post Office, to the Cincinnati Post Office, to the Davis Publishing Company, to Congressman Lee Hamilton, to the Committee on Postal Affairs of the House and Senate, to the Librarian Kurt Cylke of the Library of Congress-Division for the Blind and Physically Handicapped, and to the Baltimore, Md., office of the National Federation of the Blind.

I hope that matters can be resolved so as not to wind up in Federal Court, but if not then so be it.

Respectfully yours,
William Roberts

Another entry by the redoubtable Gertrude Ward was passed along to *Monitor* readers later in the same year (November, 1982), with an introductory comment by President Jernigan:

COMMENTS WITH A TANG
by Kenneth Jernigan

I get letters of all kinds from all sorts. Sometimes they tell me how good I am, and sometimes they tell me how good it would be if I were gone—long gone. They lecture; they advise; and they preach. They inform; they comfort; and they encourage. I read them all—well, almost all (at least, as many as I can); and I try to learn from them.

And then, there is Gertrude Ward. Her letters are in a category all of their own. She scolds me, gives me a tongue-lashing, tells me what I ought to do, and now and again compliments me. But she is never dull, and she is never wishy-washy. She has definite opinions (on almost everything), and she expresses them. She serves as a check and balance—a touchstone of reality. She helps me keep perspective—and (although my detractors would be shocked at the thought) a touch of humility. If she doesn't like it, she tells you, and you don't have to wonder what she meant.

As you might imagine, we sometimes agree—and we very often don't. It really doesn't matter. She is about as genuine and unphony as anybody I know, and that is sufficient—even if she gets her facts mixed now and again, or tells me mine are mixed. Be that as it may, here is a letter I got from Gertrude in the middle of the summer:

Dear Mr. Jernigan:

It likely has occurred to you that if all the blind employees quit the sheltered shop in a body, the shop would close. If the shop hired other handicapped people in order to stay open, it would violate its charter as a shop for the blind, and would still eventually be closed by the law. For this reason would it not be cheaper to persuade the blind in a shop that abuses them to quit instead of letting themselves be treated like slaves? Such treatment is degrading, to say the least.

So long as the blind are willing to work under such employers, just that long will they be slaves. Even if a few blind people did not follow the majority out of the shop, the shop still could not remain open. In other words, take away their lackeys who earn their bread for them. I suggest you find one shop on which to try out this experiment. Parasites will never change until you deprive them of their prey.

NFB might do better to help blind people find jobs which are easier to obtain first. Then, the faster blind people have jobs, the more they can finance NFB in its fight to obtain better jobs for all of the blind. Let's stop arguing with pig-headed professionals and instead hit them where it hurts—right in their breadbaskets.

Be sure to tell us in the *Braille Monitor* what the Appropriations Committee said about how the National

Library Service has wasted the money that should have been spent on Braille books. Tell NLS we will be double damned if we are going to put up with such waste and deprivation any longer.

Please discuss all of this with the other NFB officers and leaders. I hope you and they will agree to try out my suggestion. NFB must try different methods for bringing certain people to heel.

Gertrude Ward

A Birth of Freedom

"It has often been remarked," wrote the *Monitor* editor in the summer of 1984, "that the National Federation of the Blind is not so much an organization as a people's movement—a cross section of the blind population of America, working together and helping each other. The old, the young; the rich, the poor; the employed, the jobless; the educated, and the unlettered participate. Our conventions know the joys and sorrows of the everyday events of human life.

"On Saturday afternoon, July 7, we had a death in the convention hall. Sam and Gertrude Sitt of Florida have been Federationists and have attended the conventions for many years. Gertrude was seriously ill, but she urgently wanted to attend the Phoenix convention. She came to the sessions and participated as she could. Late Saturday afternoon (just as the convention was drawing to a close) Gertrude went as she would have wanted to do, quietly falling to sleep at the end of a wonderful experience. Sam bore his grief with quiet self-composure, and his fellow Federationists rallied to him for support."

The *Monitor* editor continued: "There was also a birth at the convention. Joanne Fernandes, the energetic and intrepid president of the NFB of Louisiana, was determined to come to the convention. Her baby was past due, but the convention is the convention—and Joanne is a Federationist. At about one o'clock on Wednesday morning, Joanne Fernandes gave birth to Jennica Shanti. (Shanti, incidentally, means peace in Hindustani.) At the Roll Call of States (less than nine hours later) Louisiana was called, and Joanne Fernandes stood up to answer. The audience gave her a roaring ovation. When President Jernigan asked her who would serve on the Nominating Committee from Louisiana that evening, Joanne replied in a matter-of-fact tone: 'I will.' And she did. She worked through the remainder of the convention; and as of this writing, mother and baby are doing well."

A Federationist in Action

In the year 1980 the NFB received a donation that was significant less for its size than for the story it carried with it. Kenneth Jernigan made note of the contribution and its underlying message in a brief article for the *Monitor*, which bore the heading "Gwen Williams—A Dedicated Federationist and a Fighter for the Cause." Here is what he wrote:

Recently Steve Benson, the able president of the National Federation of the Blind of Illinois, sent me a letter, along with a check for $500 from a large corporation. The contribution was secured through the efforts of Gwendolyn Williams, one of our Illinois members. She has neither received nor sought public recognition through the years, but she has worked and lived her Federationism on a daily basis.

The corporate president who sent the check said: "It is with pleasure that we are making this contribution of $500 to your organization which indeed does worthwhile work.

"I became knowledgeable about the work of your organization through Miss Gwen Williams, who I think is a superb representative of your organization as well as a very unusual woman.

"Through our gift, we are not only helping the National Federation of the Blind, we are honoring Miss Williams's outstanding efforts."

Steven Benson wrote to me: "Gwendolyn Williams is ninety years old, but her spirit and her devotion to the philosophy and work of the NFB have no measure in time. She has been, since 1968, one of our strongest and most loyal members. When we picketed the NAC meeting in November, 1978, she was on the line with all the rest of us. She is, indeed, as close to being a front line soldier as anybody can be. The enclosed check is but one small indication of the work she does for us in Illinois and for the organization as a whole. She is a very special lady, a Federationist."

I add my tribute to those of Steve Benson and the corporate executive. As long as we have people like Gwen Williams (people who are willing to work day after day without special recognition, who will raise money for the organization, who will picket NAC, and who will give freely of their spirit and devotion), the Federation will survive and prosper. Gwen, I salute you. The entire movement salutes you. We are stronger and better because you are one of us, and we will keep faith together as we work together toward the achievement of our ideals of true equality and first-class citizenship for the blind.

Wrestling with a Problem

"On Friday, April 14, 1989, a crucial event occurred in the lives of the blind of this country." So said Kenneth Jernigan following the action by the board of the Michigan Commission for the Blind terminating the purchase of services from any organization or agency accredited by the National Accreditation Council for Agencies Serving the Blind and Visually Handicapped (NAC). The force behind this significant move was the Commission's dynamic vice chairman Allen Harris, who was also the president of the NFB of Michigan. The organized blind of the state had long been wrestling with the problem posed by the contradiction between NAC's professed commitment to high standards and its eagerness to grant accreditation to sheltered workshops and other agencies engaged in exploiting blind clients and consumers. Under Allen Harris's leadership the blind of Michigan wrestled with NAC and won—which surprised no one who knew Harris as a champion wrestler in his student days and a winning coach of the sport in his later teaching career.

That Harris's mental toughness matched his physical strength was made evident at a meeting of NAC sympathizers seeking to overturn the action of the Commission for the Blind. As Kenneth Jernigan (himself a winning wrestler in his youth and a fighter all of his life) wrote in summarizing the meeting: "At one point in the discussion Mr. Harris pointed to the Florida School for the Blind and Deaf as an example of NAC's poor performance. Grant Mack (a leader of the American Council of the

Blind) responded by saying that the National Federation of the Blind expects perfection and that this is not reasonable. Referring to the deaths which have been occurring at the Florida School, Mr. Mack said something to this effect: 'Mistakes are made everywhere. Gordon, does anyone ever die at your hospital?' Mr. Harris's response seems particularly apt: We expect people to die in hospitals, but we don't expect our children to die at school— except perhaps in extremely isolated cases. Certainly we don't expect it to happen on a continuing basis and because of mistakes."

Harris had pinned his man down—and clearly won the match on points.

Movement Toward the Center

In the decade of the eighties, after years of discussion and internal debate, the National Federation of the Blind embarked upon an ambitious program of organizing and developing model training centers in a number of states in order to fill a vacuum and provide much needed training for the blind and also in order to establish once again model programs to serve as standard-setters in the field. These centers, which subsequently grew up in four states, took as their own model the enormously successful program of the Iowa Commission for the Blind, which had been administered by Kenneth Jernigan for twenty years, from 1958 to 1978. Taking the lead in translating Federation philosophy into rehabilitation practice were four national leaders of unusual resourcefulness and drive: Joanne Fernandes in Louisiana; Joyce Scanlan in Minnesota; Diane McGeorge in Colorado; and Fred Schroeder in New Mexico.

One of the highlights of the 1988 NFB convention in Chicago was a joint presentation of the accomplishments of the four state training centers. Following is a partial version of the *Monitor*'s report on that event (January, 1989), beginning with remarks by Kenneth Jernigan as chairman of the panel:

STATE TRAINING CENTERS
AND THE ORGANIZED BLIND MOVEMENT

This is an item which is of great concern to us. The National Federation of the Blind is not an agency, governmental or private. It is, as you know, an organization of the blind themselves. Although we have many activities, our prime purpose must never be blurred. That purpose is to serve as a vehicle for collective action. It is to serve, not as a governmental agency, but as a watchdog to see that those agencies do what they are supposed to do—and also, it is a means by which we as blind persons can come together to discuss our problems, and then find a way to do something about those problems,

A number of years ago, as you know, we discussed whether or not, in view of the ineffective training being done by many of the governmental agencies, we should set up some pilot programs of our own to perform this training, so that blind persons might have an opportunity and so that we could also point to those model programs. We have a number of them now in operation in the country, and I want to talk to you a little about them and then introduce the panel members. We want to talk about State Centers and the Organized Blind Movement—Possibilities, Problems, and Challenges.

This is a panel discussion, and we will deal with the different centers around the country which now have the kind of philosophy we are talking about. You can tell from the results how well this philosophy works. You have heard before from the Louisiana Center. This center has now operated long enough to have a track record of success. The capable director of that center is also the president of the National Federation of the Blind of Louisiana. She is Joanne Fernandes.

Joanne Fernandes: The Louisiana Center for the Blind gives to each of its students at their graduation party a plaque, and on the bottom of that plaque it says, "Together We Are Changing What it Means to be Blind." All of our students know that that "together" means every one of you. It means what has been done since 1940. It means the beliefs, the goals, and the dreams of each of you. They know that when they are in the Center, that it's not just the staff, and it's not just the other students or the former students or the Louisiana affiliate. They know that it is the entire National Federation of the Blind. They know that what they accomplish is in your hopes, your beliefs, and your dreams. When they leave the Louisiana Center for the Blind, they know that there is a whole structure in the form of the National Federation of the Blind. And most importantly, they know that they must give back to that structure. They must give back to the National Federation of the Blind and pass on the dreams and the beliefs and the opportunities that they have received at the Louisiana Center for the Blind.

The Louisiana Center for the Blind was started on October 1, 1985. In just two and a half years we have served eighty-four students. We now own our own classroom building and our own apartment complex, which the students live in. We have students now coming to us not only from Louisiana but from seven other states. So what do we do at the Louisiana Center for the Blind?

We teach cane travel, typing, Braille, home economics—the usual courses that are taught in rehabilitation centers. But beyond all that, we teach *genuine* beliefs and hopes and high expectations and confidence to our students. We teach them that they truly can change what it means to be blind.

One of the traditions that we have at the Louisiana Center for the Blind is our bell of freedom. We have a big old school bell (a hand-rung school bell) that sits up in our Braille room. Throughout our short history, whenever a student calls us with some success or some good news, when something very important happens that affects all of us as blind people, we ring the bell of freedom. In the past few months we have rung the bell for George, who called up and said, "I got my first check today from the naval base." We rang the bell when Maria said, "I'm twenty-two years old, but this is the first time I went out and bought a dress for myself."

We rang the bell when John, our young lawyer, came running in. He had graduated from the program: "I haven't called my parents yet. I haven't told my girlfriend yet. I am telling you first. I just got a job as a lawyer."

We rang the bell after two trips down to the state legislature to work on the Braille law. We rang the bell when we found that the Braille law indeed got passed. We rang the bell for Lillian, who received her GED, and for the many other students who received their GEDs. We rang the bell when Nancy and John, two of our former students, got married. We rang the bell when Lina and

Jimmy had their first baby. We rang the bell for our first play on opening night. We rang our bell when the first crop came in from our garden—when we had our first produce as blind people from our very own garden. We rang the bell when all of our nervous and scared students got back from Mardi Gras, an event that they had been dreading for weeks. They got through the crowds. They got through the mobs and proved to themselves inside that they could be successful, capable students.

We rang the bell when Maria was able to cross Bonner Street, a street which she was scared to death to cross with a cane. We rang the bell when a college student (one of our graduates) called in and said, "Hey, I passed a course, and I got a 3.0 average this semester."

We rang the bell when Patty passed her Bar Exam. She is now working as a public defender in Shreveport. We rang the bell when Barry began managing three restaurants in Shreveport, when A.J. got his vending stand, when Joie got his factory job working for Boeing Aircraft, when Connie got a job as a nurse, and when Yvonda successfully finished business school.

We rang our bell when our students successfully prepared and served a meal for forty. We are about ready to ring it again. One of our students is ready to go back to being an elementary school teacher, and another back to being a scientist at Los Alamos Labs in New Mexico. We have another student, who is about ready to graduate and go into child care.

Johnnie Burns, one of our former students, got herself a job teaching blind kids. We now have one of her students, Kim, in our program—successfully learning and advancing, too. She is our first "grandchild." We ring the bell when our students call up and say, "Hey, I was elected president of our local chapter, or vice president," or "I just joined my local chapter." We rang the bell when Zach and Sheena said, "We got Pennsylvania and New Jersey to send us to you. We want good rehabilitation training." We rang the bell when Chris lit her first fire on a camping trip.

Together we are all ringing the bell of freedom and together we are changing what it means to be blind. Thank you.

Dr. Jernigan: Once, long ago in Iowa, Joanne was my student— and, Joanne, you have gone on to do what, in my dreams, I would have hoped that you could and would do. We have said in this organization: First you have to say a thing so that you can believe it, and then you have to believe in it before it can come true. That's part of what a proper training program for the blind is about. And one thing more, the program you have heard about in Louisiana and the others you will hear about, have at least this difference from the governmental agencies. If Joanne were the director of one of those programs, she would be part of a governmental agency, insulated by civil service; and if she didn't do a good job and you didn't like it there wouldn't be anything you could do about it except write memos back and forth. As it is, she is president of a democratic organization of the blind. If she doesn't do what the blind of the state like, they will un-elect her, and that's the way it ought to be.

Let me now introduce to you the director of the second of these centers. This is BLIND, Incorporated. Joyce Scanlan will tell you about it. Joyce Scanlan is the director of BLIND, Incorporated. She is, as you know, also the president of the National Federation of the Blind of Minnesota. The NFB of Minnesota has long and well represented the interests of the blind of that state, and now the Federation in the state is doing training. But keep in mind that the prime purpose of the NFB of Louisiana or the NFB of Minnesota is not to run a training program. That's important, but the prime purpose is to serve as a vehicle by which the blind of these states themselves can speak with their own voice. Seen in that context, the centers in Louisiana, Minnesota, and the other places you will hear about, are tremendous boosts to the self-help of blind people. We are not going to rest in this Federation until each and every blind person in the United States has a chance to work to his or her full potential and to earn his or her own way rather than live at somebody else's whim, and on public assistance. Here is Joyce Scanlan.

Joyce Scanlan: Thank you, Dr. Jernigan. These are very exciting times for blind people across the country, and certainly in Minnesota. Blind people for a long time in Minnesota have wanted an orientation program which would show its belief in blind people, and that is why BLIND, Incorporated, came about. BLIND is an acronym for Blindness: Learning in New Dimensions. We have added a new dimension to our programs in the National Federation of the Blind of Minnesota. We are now able to provide orientation to blindness through training of the kind that Joanne Fernandes has just described as going on in Louisiana.

Let me tell you a little bit of how we determined the name of our program. The name "BLIND" was selected before we decided what words the acronym would mean. The reason for that was that in our state, and I'm sure it's true all over the country, the primary orientation program for the blind (the Minneapolis Society for the Blind) with which everyone here is very familiar, seemed to pride itself on avoiding the word blind and anything to do with blindness. They do low vision aids, and they talk about vision handicaps and visual impairment and low vision, and all kinds of things like that, but they don't want to deal with blindness. They don't want to teach Braille. They don't want to teach cane travel. They really want to skirt the whole issue. We decided that we want to have blindness right up front, so we called our program BLIND. Then we decided that it would mean *Blindness: Learning in New Dimensions*—because we who are blind may not see visually, but we certainly have all kinds of other ways of learning. We get information through other senses. We also felt that our program had a new dimension in that we would deal openly and straightforwardly with the matter of attitudes towards blindness and understanding what blindness means—and, therefore, a new dimension. This decision for Blindness: Learning in New Dimensions was made by three people, Judy Sanders, Peggy Chong, and me, as we were riding on an airplane to New York at the very end of 1986 to attend a NAC demonstration. I think that's a very appropriate situation for the making of such a momentous decision.

BLIND, Incorporated, was incorporated in 1986—on the very last day—so 1987 was a very busy year for us. We had to seek funding for our program from private as well as public sources, resulting in an establishment grant from State Services for the Blind, which covers about sixty-seven percent of our budget, with the remaining portion covered by private sources. We had to find locations for our program. We didn't have an apartment building for our students. We didn't have a center. We had to get those locations. We had to hire a staff.

On January 4, 1988 (the most exciting time for all of us), we opened our doors with staff training, on the very coldest day of the year. Just one week later, January 11, we opened our doors for two very hardy, tough, and tenacious students. It took us six weeks to have five students, and we still have five students (although they are not the same five), but all of our students are at this convention. All of our staff are at this convention as well.

Our early beginnings as a center were in a two-bedroom apartment. We moved from there to a one-bedroom apartment. There was a time when we had a home management class, a typing class, a Braille class, and a travel lesson all going on in one room. We were crowded, and sometimes we were a little on top of each other. But we had a dream, and we had a lot of hope.

Ours is an experiential program in which students learn through real live, normal, experiences. Beginning in January, we started by attending events surrounding the Martin Luther King holiday. We had shopping excursions to buy boots and gloves for the winter. We had dinners out. We had a trip, rather an effort, to go to St. Cloud one night for a spaghetti dinner, but I can tell you that the students didn't quite make it. The van ended up tipped over in the ditch, and the students ended up having dinner at Fudruckers. I said to one of the students, "Was that one of the more exciting or harrowing events you have ever had?"

And she said, "Oh, no." We had a snowball fight. We've attended movies. We have gone strawberry picking. We've had a picnic. We've had many activities, I'm sure, of which I will never be told.

We teach the usual classes. The students go from the apartments down to the Center on the bus. Our students start right out with the bus on the very first day. We learn by doing, as we are at this convention. Learning to deal with crowds, learning to deal with blind people, a couple of thousand strong, learning to be in new surroundings without being upset, staying in a hotel, eating out, meeting new people, reading all kinds of agendas and other materials in Braille—all those are very important learning experiences.

I want to finish by saying just one more thing. I'm sure that many of you have a question as to how we could reconcile the service provider and the advocacy role that we play, and that would be a long discussion. Since I don't have time to undertake that, I just want to say that (consider the alternatives for us) this is the way it has to be done. Therefore, I feel that we are doing the right thing and that we can do it very successfully as long as we keep our perspective and our priorities in the organized blind movement as they have been—our caring for each other, and our love for one another. Thank you.

Dr. Jernigan: The way we reconcile that role, Joyce, is simple. If you do not please the blind of your state, by and large (not one individual person on one individual day but most of the blind most of the time), the blind of the state will have a new president. Now, of course, that wouldn't have anything to do with whether you would be the director of the center immediately, but it probably would over a very short time. So I think we can reconcile the roles without difficulty.

If our organization stands for anything, it stands for the concept that it is respectable to be blind and also that we don't want to be taken care of, but that we want to take care of ourselves. It stands for the fact that we want to be realistic about what we can do, but we don't want someone else with his or her prejudice telling us what realism is. You will find in the July *Monitor* that the lead article has to do with a court case in which a guy sued the Federal Department of Education for not accommodating him reasonably. He argued in the court proceedings that it was not reasonable to expect a blind person to do research unless each and every item was in Braille. He argued that it was not reasonable unless he could have bought for him close to $100,000 worth of equipment. Never mind that blind people all over this country are doing research all of the time and don't have their material in Braille. The government's answer was interesting. They said that they had certainly accommodated him reasonably. They had allowed him to get by (well, they didn't say get by). They had accommodated him by permitting him to do only half the number of letters (now, listen to this) that they expected of their normal employees—twelve letters a week. They only expected six of him. I keep wondering what will happen to the next blind guy who goes in to apply for a job there. That's not reasonable accommodation, and it's not what we are hunting. What we are hunting is a chance to compete on equal terms, and we can cut it on equal terms with others. If we can't, we're not asking for the job, but we are also not asking for someone to determine for us that we can't have a shot at it.

Here is the next of our centers, the Colorado Center for the Blind. Diane McGeorge is the director of that center, and the president of the National Federation of the Blind of Colorado. Diane, tell us about the Colorado Center for the Blind.

Diane McGeorge: Thank you, Dr. Jernigan. In 1985 the NFB of Colorado took a bill to the legislature. That bill would have established the Colorado Center for the Blind had we got the funding. However, the bill didn't pass. We gave then to Joanne Fernandes all of the materials that we had accumulated to prepare the bill. She took it to the governor of Louisiana, and she got it passed—and we were delighted. We were proud that the NFB had a center up and running in the country, but now it's our time in the sun—and we're really proud. We didn't go away and sulk, and we didn't go away and cry and feel bad. What we did was to go away and put together some proposals and put together a little money from here and there and from private fund raising—particularly, a man named Mayer Blinder from the Blinder Robinson Company. We got a little bit of money from this grant, and from that grant and we got the money to start. We opened on January 4 of this year, so we have been up and running for six months.

We have all of our students here today, and I'm going to give you a chance to meet each one of them. I've asked them to be brief. We have our staff here, and I want to introduce them to you. Duncan Larsen is our cane travel teacher; Tom Anderson is our communications teacher; Sheryl Law is our daily living skills and computer teacher; Angie Wood is our clerical help; and we've got the greatest staff you can have anywhere. I'll give you a little background on them. But I'm going to let them tell you about our program. Let me just quickly say to you that during the first week (on the first day we opened, on Monday, January 4) it was fifteen below zero, and it stayed that way for about five weeks. We had two feet of snow on the ground, but the students came on a bus. They did grocery shopping on the first day. They prepared their lists in Braille, made their own grocery lists. We all went to the store on the bus. The other things we did during the first week were to expand on independent travel, and at the end of the first week our students (by themselves) prepared, planned, and served a sit-down dinner for thirty-five people.

Somebody said "What are you going to do for an encore?" For an encore we painted one of the rooms in our center. We couldn't afford to have it done by a professional, so we did it ourselves. We thought it was a great opportunity for our students to learn that you can paint as a blind person. Does that mean that we want them to go out and become painters? I don't care—I just want them to go out and get jobs—and they will. But painting was an excellent lesson in learning what YOU really can do as a blind person. We use sleep shades in all of our training. All center activities (all of them) are done with sleep shades.

You hear about blind and visually impaired. There are very few totally blind people. We don't use the sleep shades so that the students can pretend and find out what it is like to be blind. It's to deal with blindness and how you really feel about yourself. For an encore, besides painting, we went to the Washington Seminar—all of us. We have visited a lot of schools and churches and have spoken. We helped build a float and marched in a parade, but I guess you might say that the tops of all of that is when we started a technical rock climbing class. And I wouldn't be surprised if you hear about that from the students. All of the students and the staff participated in this, and we are talking about real live rock climbing, where you use the ropes and the harnesses. We had a full course of instruction, and when I climbed my first one hundred foot rock, I was proud—and I think all of our students were too. It's an interesting feeling when you are learning to rappel off of the rock and you are about one hundred feet in the air, and your instructor says, "Now, all you do is step backward and lean back."

We have a great program. We challenge our students. Some of our students have called it "boot camp for the blind," and I think that is fairly appropriate. I think one of the most important incidents (and I'm going to tell you quickly because I want you to hear from the students) is this: The students had been in the program for about two and a half weeks, and they were going home from the Center on the bus. The bus driver said, "All you blind people will have to sit down." The bus was crowded, and they were standing. "All of you blind people will have to sit down because the bus won't move until you do." Our students did not sit down.

To walk with pride, to live with dignity, to participate in the community, and to know that through the collective action of the NFB you can give to others—that is the only way to live your life, and I am thinking we are teaching all of that and living all of that at the Colorado Center. Thank you very much.

Dr. Jernigan: Now I want to move directly to the New Mexico Commission for the Blind. Fred Schroeder is the director of the New Mexico Commission for the Blind, and he is also, of course, on our National Board. He has experienced discrimination because he was blind. Even though he had all the credentials required and could have been certified, a group presumed to say that he wasn't qualified to teach travel because he was blind. Fred Schroeder knows what it is to be blind; he knows what it is to face discrimination; but he also knows how to train and teach. Here is Fred Schroeder, the director of the New Mexico Commission for the Blind.

Fred Schroeder: Thank you very much Dr. Jernigan. One of the principles that we have been taught in this organization is that, given proper training and opportunity, we as blind people can compete on terms of equality with the sighted. We have known this for many years. Back in the early 1970s Pauline Gomez, a leader of the National Federation of the Blind of New Mexico, knew that the blind of our state needed training. Blind people didn't have access to orientation and mobility training or Braille or any of the other skills that we need to be competitive, and she and others went to the legislature and had a bill passed that created our orientation center. But that center was placed under the rehabilitation agency, and although the structure then existed, the attitude wasn't right. The attitude that we needed (the attitude that promoted belief in ourselves, the attitude that encouraged us as blind people to go on and do more with our lives) wasn't there. The agency was established. The center was built. It opened its doors, but blind people weren't getting the kind of training that let them go out and become productive citizens. In 1986, the New Mexico Commission for the Blind was established. We are now a separate agency with a three-member board. The board is appointed by the governor. Therefore, if the board doesn't do its job, if it hires a director that isn't working in the best interest of the blind, the board can be replaced. It can be got at easily. We can go to the governor and say, "The board isn't doing its job, and the agency isn't doing what it should to make us productive." I am proud to tell you that in the audience today is the chairman of our board. He is a blind person himself, Mr. Arthur Schreiber. He is the vice president and general manager of the largest radio station in New Mexico, and with his support (and the support of the legislature and governor and blind people throughout the state) we are building an agency that will do right by the blind and assist us in getting the training we need to be productive.

When we took over the agency two years ago, a number of things were said about us. Let me first tell you one. The students were told that I had been hired, and that I was a radical. They were told that I was going to come in and do bad things to them. The first thing that I was going to do was to put blindfolds on their faces, and they wouldn't be able to see. That would be frightening and dangerous, and they would get hurt. They were told that I was mostly a lunatic and that I was going to do this to them. So the students, not knowing better, got together and agreed that on July 1, when I came along and made them blindfold themselves, they would all walk out—and how would I like that? So, July 1 came and went, and I didn't say anything about sleep shades. I came around and talked to people and got to know them. Finally, people said, "Aren't you going to make us wear sleep shades?"

I replied, "No, but if you ask me if it is a good idea, I believe it is—and I will tell you why." And so it went on like that. I talked to people about sleep shades, and in the fall they got with me again and kept pressing me on it. "Aren't you going to make us use sleep shades?"

And I said, "No, probably not. If I do, it will do you more harm than good. If you want to know why I think you should do it, I'll tell you, but I'm not going to make you do it. If you do it with the wrong attitude, it will hurt you, not help you."

And so, in January at a state board meeting, the teachers kind of got me and pressed me even harder as to when I was going to do this. Finally they asked why I wasn't going to do this if it was such a good idea. So I said, "Look, you guys are the teachers. Go back, and if you think it's a good idea, your students will listen to you. They have confidence in you."

"Yes," they said, "but we need a policy."

"No," I said, "I'm not ready to make a policy on it." Well, the administrator of that center retired, and we were looking for someone with the right attitudes, who could lead the center and lead it right, and I found Dick Davis of Iowa. Dick had been trained by Dr. Jernigan, and he'd grown up in the Federation tradition. He understood what rehabilitation services should be. I hired Dick, and during his first week on the job the staff came to him and absolutely demanded of him that he institute a policy requiring sleep shade training. Dick got all of the students together, and they talked about it. He finally had the students vote on it. We now have a policy that says you wear sleep shades in our orientation center. But we don't legislate good attitudes, and we don't beat people into having good attitudes. Rather, we lead them into good attitudes, and that is what we're trying to get done.

There used to be a policy that said you weren't allowed to carry canes inside the building. It strikes me that that is against our state's white cane law, but that was the policy because it was thought that people would trip each other and it would be a problem. So there was a cane rack. I believe there is still a cane rack, but it probably has an inch of dust on it, because people now carry canes in the center.

Many other changes have taken place in the twenty-four months. A year ago we were looking for a new travel teacher and we found Sharon Duffy. Sharon was a blind person who had been teaching travel at the Guild for the Blind in Chicago, and it seemed to me that if you could teach cane travel in Chicago, you could probably teach it in Alamogordo, New Mexico. And so now, blind people are getting the kind of cane travel training they should be getting, and they are getting it under sleep shades. They are getting the right attitudes.

We've started many new programs to help build confidence and help people realize that they can be normal, fully participating citizens. We've instituted an industrial arts program. We have hired a new person by the name of Joseph Pattison, and he is undergoing sleep shade training right now. He is a sighted man. All new staff at the New Mexico Commission for the Blind undergo sleep shade training. Joseph Pattison is with us this week. By the way, he is wearing an NFB pin on his lapel. We will soon have a wood shop program. We decided that we want people to get out and participate in the community and do new things, and so we have a dormitory—and our dormitory serves meals, and we thought that on Friday night people shouldn't sit around the house. And so, Friday night, we don't serve dinner. On Friday night you have a choice. You can go out and find something to eat around the area, or you can get hungry. We found that mostly people don't want to be hungry. They go out and have dinner. They are getting out and finding new restaurants. Now on Saturdays people don't sit around and watch television. They get out and walk. We have a mall (the Alamogordo Mall), which is three and one-half miles away from our center, and we have students walking down there—not the least of whom is a gentleman who is seventy-nine years old.

Mr. Chairman, that is what I want to bring to you about our center. We are promoting the right attitudes about blindness, and with the type of training we are trying to make available, we believe that blind people can go off and participate in society on terms of equality. Thank you.

Dr. Jernigan: We can have these four centers on the platform with pride, and I think it answers the question which some of us had problems with for a while. Newly blinded people would contact me and say, "Where can I go for training?" I couldn't honestly send them anywhere that I knew in the country that gave decent training. I know that the federal government appropriates over a billion dollars each year for rehabilitation, but we couldn't find anywhere to send blind people wanting training. We can now. As you know, I ran a rehabilitation center, or directed it, for some time, and I can tell you something. It was symbolized by an annual ritual. We had a fireplace at the Iowa Center, and each year when it got to be close to winter the students would repeatedly say, "We have a fireplace, and wood needs to be cut. Maybe we should go wood cutting." I would deliberately postpone the wood cutting until the snow was deep and it was cold—and the deeper the snow the better. We could have got somebody to give us the wood, and we could also undoubtedly have got a chain saw to use in cutting it. We didn't. We got two-person crosscut saws and single-person buck saws, and on the coldest, snowiest day you could find, we went out and cut wood. Let me tell you something. Some of the people who came to us (especially, the newly blinded) felt sorry for themselves and down. Put a person on the end of a crosscut saw for a day, and by nighttime that person will not feel sorry for himself or herself. It doesn't happen. Moreover, the person will not come back to the center to worry about blindness. He or she will come back to sleep.

The National Federation of the Blind means many things. It means our scholarship program. It means the training centers that we have helped to develop. It means our Job Opportunities for the Blind program. It means the blind who are working in sheltered shops. It means the blind persons working in vending locations. It means those who are employed in professions (law, teaching, and the ministry). It means the members of this organization who are out trying to do for themselves, and it also means a number of people who are unemployed and who have not been able to find opportunities because of the attitudes of society. Above all, it means that we are truly changing what it means to be blind.

Federationism Is My Life

One of the most energetic and effective leaders of the Federation during the 1980s was Karen Mayry of South Dakota. When she became president of the state affiliate in the late seventies, Federationism in South Dakota was weak and struggling— but that changed almost immediately. Mayry, who was not only diabetic but had also received a kidney transplant, was second to none in dedication, capability, and energy.

In 1985 she spearheaded the establishment of the Diabetics Division of the National Federation of the Blind, which rapidly became one of the rallying points of the movement. By 1990 the Division's newsletter (titled *The Voice of the Diabetic*) was being circulated in print and on cassette throughout the nation. Thirty-five thousand copies were being sent on a quarterly basis to members, hospitals, ophthalmologists, public officials, and interested segments of the general public.

In 1984 at the National Federation's convention banquet in Phoenix, Arizona, Mayry was honored for her contributions to the betterment of the lives of the blind. James Omvig, who presented the award, said in part:

> It is difficult to find a Federationist who has demonstrated more public spirit, more zeal for the cause, or more unselfish dedication to this movement than tonight's recipient. Both in the movement and out this person is a leader with capacity, a citizen with conviction, and a fighter with determination.

> Tonight's recipient first joined the Federation in 1975, and hard work and love paid off with immediate recognition and selection for leadership. By 1977 she was elected to a local chapter presidency and became the state affiliate's president in 1978. She continues in that position today. Since that time, this affiliate has grown tremendously both in numbers and effectiveness. For example, in the past two legislative sessions alone this affiliate has been able to secure the passage of state laws prohibiting discrimination against the blind in employment and in the sale of insurance. This hard-working president also serves on the boards of both the state library for the blind and the state school for the blind. She has received several special governor's citations, and has been one of our most successful membership recruiters.

My brothers and sisters of the National Federation of the Blind, it is a privilege of a very special order for me to present the 1984 Jacobus tenBroek Award to this front-line soldier in the movement, to our distinguished colleague and our friend, Karen Mayry.

In her response Mayry said in part:

"Federationism is my life. I live it every minute of every day. I have to thank Eric Smith and Sharon Monthei Duffy, who found me in South Dakota and taught me that other people thought the same as I thought and that state agencies were not going to keep us down. We have been working hard together—all of us; and I love every one of you."

Women of Strength and Character

From time to time in the seventies and eighties the National Federation of the Blind presented awards of recognition to those who were considered to have made outstanding contributions to the betterment of the lives of the blind. The Newel Perry Award was given to people outside of the movement, and the Jacobus tenBroek Award was presented to Federation members. These awards were not given on an annual basis but only when merit indicated. Indeed, It was unusual for either award to be given in consecutive years, but 1988 and 1989 were exceptions.

The recipient of the 1988 Jacobus tenBroek Award was Jacquilyn Billey, president of the National Federation of the Blind of Connecticut. The recipient in 1989 was Hazel Staley, president of the National Federation of the Blind of North Carolina. Both Billey and Staley were women of remarkable strength and character. Each had built a strong Federation affiliate in her state, and each had conducted extensive campaigns to recruit members to the movement.

Steve Benson, president of the National Federation of the Blind of Illinois and chairman of the Jacobus tenBroek Award Committee, said in his 1988 presentation:

The recipient of this year's award must (as Dr. Jacobus tenBroek did) extend himself or herself beyond the routine and do those things that in the long haul make a significant difference in the lives of blind people. Beyond that, the recipient of this award must love his or her fellow blind people. The Jacobus tenBroek Award Committee for 1988 has selected a person who meets these standards. This year's recipient is a leader—a person who has earned national respect. This person has worked hard to carry our message to the public and to blind people. The 1988 recipient has been involved in the growth and development of local chapters and state affiliates all across the nation. Her (it is a woman) sensitivity, patience, quick wit, and aptness of thought are extraordinary.

She is one of us who was recruited in the 1970s. She takes seriously what she does within and for the NFB. She knows that what happens to blind people in California affects blind people in Louisiana, Minnesota, Florida, and Maine. Tonight's recipient of the Jacobus tenBroek Award sees her work in the Federation with a national perspective. I am speaking about a woman whose background is in education, vocationally, and avocationally. College students acclaim her. State presidents revere her. Members cite her as an example of what a Federationist should aspire to become. The Jacobus tenBroek Award Committee for 1988 has selected as this year's award recipient a person who lives east of the Mississippi and north of the Mason-Dixon Line—whose spirit and work on behalf of all of us transcend political and geographical boundaries.

Tonight I am pleased and privileged to present the 1988 Jacobus tenBroek Award to Jacquilyn Billey, president of the National Federation of the Blind of Connecticut.

In his 1989 presentation Benson said:

It is unusual for this award to be presented in two successive years. However, the committee determined that one individual is so extraordinary that the award should be presented again this year. Our winner has extended herself far beyond the expected to change what it means to be blind. She has built and strengthened chapters, worked to improve educational opportunities for blind children, and begun to reshape the rehabilitation program in her state. A resident of one of the thirteen original states, she exhibits the resilience and determination of the hearty frontier stock from which she comes. Over the past twenty years she has carried the torch of freedom high, in the manner and spirit of Dr. tenBroek. She finds strength in our movement and in her God. Her favorite

Biblical verse is, "I can do all things through Christ, who strengthens me." It gives me great pleasure and genuine honor to present the 1989 Jacobus tenBroek Award to my colleague in the movement, Hazel Staley.

In her response Staley said: "Ever since Don Capps recruited me twenty years ago, the Federation's philosophy and its programs and activities have been top priority with me, and they will continue to be top priority as long as God lets me live."

A Working Politician

As the message of Federationism spread through the blind community and reached out to the general public, more and more members of the movement began to find positions of leadership in civic and political affairs. Peggy Pinder worked as an assistant county prosecutor, ran for state senate, and later served on the city council in her home community. Catherine Horn Randall, one of the leaders of the National Federation of the Blind of Illinois, was elected alderman in Jacksonville. And there were others.

One of the most dynamic of these was Homer Page, a professor in the school of education at the University of Colorado at Boulder. Dr. Page was never content to limit his activities to the classroom. He was interested in politics and people. He was first elected to the Boulder City Council and then to the office of deputy mayor. After that he successfully ran for commissioner; and as the decade of the eighties drew to a close, he was contemplating possible campaigns for state or national office. It was with a mood of enthusiasm and high good humor that Dr. Page spoke at the 1989 NFB convention when it met in Denver, the capital of his home state of Colorado. He talked about his experience in political life and his relationship with the Federation and its members:

THE BLIND IN ELECTIVE OFFICE:
MY EXPERIENCE AS A BOULDER COUNTY COMMISSIONER
by Homer Page

I come before you this morning as a working politician, which leads me into a story about a working politician that I heard the other day. It seems that a loyal supporter of one of my colleagues came to him and said: "Sir, I need to tell you about a problem you've got. There's a fellow up in the northern part of the county who is going around telling a lot of lies about you." So the politician said: "Well, I appreciate that a lot. Your support means a lot to me. But I've got a priority I've got to take care of. There's a fellow down there in the southern part of the county who's telling the truth about me."

Dr. Jernigan said earlier at a meeting at this convention, "Don't apologize and don't brag—just tell it like it is." And I think maybe that's how it is. We'll see.

On January 10, 1989, my life really underwent a significant change. For on that day I was sworn in as a Boulder County Commissioner. In part, my remarks to Diane McGeorge and the students of the Colorado Center for the Blind and other Federationists at the time were these: "This office is at least in part yours." And I want to make that same statement to you because over the years you have supported me—with funds; with your work; and, more importantly, with your faith; and with your encouragement. For that I will always be grateful. I never really thought about running for the office of County Commissioner. I had a job that I enjoyed. I was Deputy Mayor in the city of Boulder. But one day in April of 1988, I started receiving phone calls—first from a County Commissioner; then from the District Attorney; then from the chair of the Boulder County Democratic Party; and, finally, from another Commissioner. All of them asked me if I would consider running for the seat of County Commissioner. The task which I was asked to take on was a difficult one. It involved overturning a seated County Commissioner, who was popular, had not made any mistakes, and was going to have the support of most of the major newspapers in the County.

Marcie and I walked and talked and thought about it, and we decided that it was worth a try—that in fact, if we were to be able to move into a full-time political commitment, this was the best time, and this was the right office. So I ran.

It was a hard race. I did not have the support of the newspapers. They went with the incumbent. However, I did have the support of the news coverage. And the reason that I had that support was that I was able to shape the coverage of the news. News comes from two places: first, it comes from interviews with the candidates written by the reporters, and second, it comes from the speeches and appearances that the candidates make. Throughout the campaign I was able to set the tone, define the issues, and shape the news coverage in a way that I thought would help me win; and it did. It is more important to shape the news than it is to get the editorial endorsements of the news media.

On January 10 I took office. There were a number of issues that concerned both the general public and staff of the county. One of the issues involved reading—getting access to large amounts of material and covering it. I have used readers and a lot of Braille. We have in Boulder what we call the Computer Braille Center, which is run by a good Federationist, Priscilla Simmons. And we've kept Priscilla very busy. I also have an Artic Vision program which gives me access to all internal memos produced by the county. We have to keep up with four major daily newspapers and four weeklies that cover the news in Boulder County. So there's a lot to do. But that hasn't been a major problem.

Each Commissioner also has access to an automobile. We need it because we have to travel extensively throughout the County. The County involves 750 square miles ranging from the Continental Divide far out onto the plains in the eastern part of the state. I contracted with the local cab company instead of having a driver. We found it to be much more efficient. As a matter of fact, the question was raised in the local newspaper about these things. Would it cost more to employ a blind person in the position of Commissioner? My response to them was clear and, I think, correct. From an economic position, the citizens of Boulder County would be much better off if all the Commissioners were blind.

So what is a Commissioner, and what is the job that a Commissioner has to do? Well, we have over a thousand employees and a budget of 75 million dollars. I'm responsible for overseeing that budget and, through those whom I supervise, supervising those one thousand employees. We also meet two days a week in public hearings, considering everything from land use to building subdivisions, from paving roads to issuing fireworks permits on the 4th of July. The County Administration includes the Social Services Department and the Health Department. It administers the JPTA and Headstart programs. We are responsible for all the roads in the county. We administer the jail and the sheriff's office. The District Attorney's office is a part of county government as is the County Clerk's office, which deals with all deeds, marriages, auto licenses, driver's licenses, voting, and voter registration. It really is a major operation. We must perform what I think is probably a very difficult task—to run a county government: not only to make policy, but to direct employees to administer the county government by consensus. There are three members of the Board of Commissioners, and it takes two votes to get anything done. But in fact, if you don't find a way to work together, it really does get very difficult.

Boulder County is made up of some 225,000 people. The assessed value of property in the county is three billion dollars. The major industry there is the University of Colorado and related scientific research facilities. There are a major IBM installation and many other high tech facilities, including biotechnology. We are concerned with the continuing economic health of the county and must be involved throughout the county to ensure that it actually takes place. Over the next three years (and perhaps longer) I need to be concerned, as a working politician, about the next step. What happens? For in politics you really need to move, or you go backward.

A few months ago there was some concern about who would run for Senate on the Democratic side next year. There was some talk that Congressman David Skaggs, who appeared here earlier, might run. Congressman Skaggs is the Representative in my district. One of the things that we needed to consider was whether or not to make a run for that seat if he in fact did relinquish it to run for the Senate. Politics is a game of chance and opportunity and being in the right place at the right time. I enjoy very much being a County Commissioner, and I may be a County Commissioner only one term or the rest of my life. But if the opportunity comes for higher office, I will take it.

There's something about being blind and being in the political arena that I think is important. Political people are leaders. They're recognized as leaders in their communities and in their states, and sometimes it's hard for members of the general public to acknowledge that a blind person is capable of being their leader. Such an idea runs counter to the stereotypes. This fact will always be there, and people will always raise questions. There was a letter to the editor in the local paper, *The Boulder Camera*, a few months ago, some three months after I had taken office. The letter said something like this: "I am really embarrassed by the voters of Boulder County. They have elected an assessor who was just arrested for being in a fight, a sheriff who got drunk and got into a fight, and a District Attorney that lets people off when they should be sent to jail. Now they have elected a blind man who couldn't possibly keep up with the reading. I am really embarrassed by the voters of Boulder County."

Well, a good friend of mine wrote a strong and wonderful letter in response to that—one I did not solicit but that I did appreciate. The point is this. That kind of letter and those kinds of feelings are going to be expressed. Now what I really believe is that my opposition generated that letter to discredit me because they thought that I would be vulnerable along those lines. My public remark was: "To show you how incompetent that campaign really was, they waited until four months after the election to engage in dirty politics." But the truth is that it hurt. I've worked ten years in the public arena to demonstrate that as a blind person I really can do the work. I was elected to the City Council of Boulder, for which candidates run at large. The first time I was the second highest vote-getter. When I ran for re-election, I was the top vote-getter, and in 1988 when I ran for County Commissioner, I overturned a popular incumbent by over 3,500 votes. Yet there are people out there who will write that kind of letter. What one learns in the public arena is that no matter how successful you are or how much you demonstrate that you can do it, for some people you're still just a blind man. That is an important lesson to learn, to hold close, because really what it means is that no matter how much you try to escape from being identified as blind, you can't. But then who would want to?

It is the solidarity I feel with you that allows me to let those kinds of letters and comments roll off my back like water off a duck. On the other hand, I keep winning, so there must be some people out there who believe in me. And if they believe in me, they'll believe in you. And that's what it's all about.

Mother and Child

During the decade of the eighties a mother and daughter team from the state of Nebraska touched the hearts and raised the consciousness of blind people throughout the country. They were Lauren and Lynden Eckery of Omaha. Lauren (Laurie to her friends) was blind, and her daughter Lynden was sighted. During a ten-year period in almost a dozen articles in the *Braille Monitor*, Federationists followed the activities and thinking of the Eckerys.

Laurie wrote of Lynden's experiences in school and with playmates. She examined the attitudes of teachers, neighbors, and other children, and the impact of these attitudes on Lynden's development and growing comprehension. A typical example appeared in the Fall, 1989, *News From Blind Nebraskans*, the publication of the National Federation of the Blind of Nebraska:

WHAT COLOR IS THE SUN?
by Lauren L. Eckery

The burning hot sun of midsummer is shining brightly today as I sit out here on the patio beginning to write. What *color* the sun is is not particularly relevant to me at this moment. I know that for some blind people the color of the sun or, for that matter, what anything looks like visually, seems irrelevant. I do not take this view, however. I am highly interested in my world, including what things look like. There are those who might insist that this could not be so.

Back in 1972, when I was nearing graduation from the University of Nebraska at Lincoln, a sighted male friend and I were discussing my future. This was a friend I very much liked and trusted. However, he knew nothing about the National Federation of the Blind and its positive philosophy of blindness.

I had been approached by the Federation in 1971, had been reading the *Braille Monitor*, but had only begun to assimilate our philosophy on blindness. Therefore, neither of us understood what he was really saying when he remarked: "When you get an apartment of your own, if you have cockroaches, they won't bother you because you won't see them, so you won't even know they are there. Besides, if you don't know what they look like, then you won't know how awful they are." I thought this statement odd and rather gross, and I laughed. I was not aware at that moment that he had indeed epitomized the heartbreaking experience of many of us.

As Pearl S. Buck has written: "There were many ways of breaking a heart. Stories were full of hearts being broken by love, but what really broke a heart was taking away its dream—whatever that dream might be."

My dream, of course, was to be a normal, first-class citizen in our society. My dream, at that particular time, might have included him in that apartment of the future. He had obviously highly respected me as a student, equal to himself, but he really did not respect me as a blind person.

It was only recently, as I began formulating this article, that I remembered his words of seventeen years ago, realizing at once, with my Federation training, what he had really said. I noticed quite a number of attitudinal "cockroaches" in his remarks.

Attitudes like those exemplified in this person's remarks often bring about our being denied opportunities for normal experiences in the world. As far as visual cues are concerned, many such cues about our world are kept from us. As an example: what color something is or where something is located. On the other hand, often we are given far too many details about visual aspects of our world. An example being the clock method on the dinner plate.

Behind all of this thinking are ingrained beliefs similar to those espoused, by implication, by my university friend of 1972. Evidently he assumed that a blind person keeping an apartment by him— or herself would necessarily have cockroaches, since blind people couldn't possibly keep the place clean. (I may not be the best housekeeper, but blindness is not the reason.) If we can see, we automatically notice everything in the world there is to see and we know more about our world because we see it. If we cannot see, we know nothing about the visual qualities of the things in our world—indeed, we know very nearly nothing at all—forget about the use of other senses, and, of course, forget about our ability to reason.

Countless times in our lives we have heard such expressions as: "Out of sight, out of mind," "Seeing is believing," "What you don't know (or see) won't hurt you." These are all suggestions of lack, loss, and inferior capacity for reasoning.

How misinformed was this fine young man, even though he had known me for several years. How misinformed was I to the extent that I was unable to set him straight about blindness, resulting in discouraging him from remaining in a prominent place in my life.

On the other hand, as I began to grow in the Federation, I learned from those who were willing to teach me, and I have also learned from experience (sometimes the hard way) some of the realities of blindness—mainly attitude problems and their impact on our lives and the means for resolving such problems. I have also learned (sometimes the hard way) that standing up strongly against such attitudinal barriers, as a unified collective body, will change these negative attitudes once and for all. Shared individual positive experiences can also help toward exterminating such cockroaches from our lives. Toward this end I relate the following experiences:

When I entered into my course of study at the University of Nebraska at Lincoln, I lived at home. Later I moved to the dorm, thank goodness! Everyday on the way to school we passed a certain building. One day I asked my mother what that particular building looked like. I was startled by her honest answer: "Lauri, we drive past that building every single day. I don't know what it looks like. I haven't really looked at it." Later, of course, she surveyed the building closely, describing it in such detail that if another blind person had asked me what this building looked like, I could have given as accurate a description of the building as my mother had given me.

This is, indeed, a lesson which many people (blind or sighted) fail to learn about sight. Sighted people do not necessarily know more about our world than blind people do. They do not have a constant edge on us simply because they can see and we cannot. Neither are blind people necessarily ignorant about their world simply because they are blind. The blind people I know who are less knowledgeable about their world tend to be those who are bitter about their blindness, refusing to concern themselves with visual factors. This lack of concern may also be noticed in blind people who have not had, or taken, the opportunity to learn alternative techniques of daily living. Or it may be simply that some folks just don't care about those things. Blindness itself does not shut us off from or out of our world.

Another example of this lesson came to me recently. Only several weeks ago my eight-year-old daughter, Lynden, asked: "Mommy, what color is the sun?" She blinks and often sneezes upon looking directly at the sun. Was it possible that she never looked long enough to notice the color of the sun? Was she testing me to see if I knew the color of the sun? What answer did she expect to get from me, the standard "yellow?"

I am totally blind since birth due to congenital glaucoma. I have no vision in the left eye. Before glaucoma took my right eye, I could see light, dark, and blobs of color. I cried the evening before the surgery, panicked a few times immediately thereafter, and that was it. I was not bitter about never seeing another sunset, because I knew that in my mind's eye I could conjure one up easily enough if I wanted to do so. Perhaps this is similar to the manner in which Beethoven was able to write some of his best music when he could no longer hear—he had a good mind, and he used it.

I told Lynden that in the middle of the day the sun is said to be yellow, although it always looked white to me. I explained that toward sunset the color could change from a brighter yellow, becoming more and more orange, sometimes setting in a brilliant red-orange ball with other colors around it (clouds, I surmised). When this occurs, the bright fiery ball on the horizon looks as though it is resting on the ground, quite far away. Eventually it disappears. Sometimes the clouds hide this color. Often the sun does just the opposite at sunrise. Sunrises and sunsets can vary. Artists have painted them; writers have described them in words. Some people often do not notice them at all, but they are there.

"I've never seen the sun change color like that. Why does it change color? Why does it look like the sun is on the ground?" she asked, curiously. Her questions were getting beyond me. I didn't know enough about the physical properties of light, color, refraction, and distance, plus the rotation of the earth, etc., to explain it all to her. Anxiously I said: "Ask your science teacher when school starts again."

With a sigh of relief, I presumed the subject closed, only to hear: "Mommy, could you see rays coming out of the sun?" I told her I couldn't.

"Me neither," she replied. "Then why do people make pictures of the sun with rays coming out all around it?" she continued.

I thought: "Ask your art teacher when school starts again." However, being somewhat more artistic than scientific, I explained that maybe it was an artistic way to show that light and heat were coming from all directions from the yellow circle which represented the sun in the pictures. That was the end of the discussion for the time being.

I believe that, due to stereotypical thinking, Lynden was surprised by the answer she got from a totally blind person. I was equally astonished that a sighted child would bother to ask a totally blind person to describe something visual, taking the answer seriously. I believe we both learned something extremely valuable from this experience.

The knowledge gained and the joy received from this experience were made evident this past weekend as we were riding the bus home from Kansas City to Omaha. Lynden had been sleeping, and I was listening to my Talkman. Suddenly she shouted, with obvious delight, "Mommy, the sun is orange and it is on the ground just like you said." (It looked like it was on the ground.) "It is red-orange, and it's pretty. I've never seen that before."

I was aware that if I had believed all of the stereotypes about blindness, that I would never have done such a normal thing as to get married and have a child—one I was now sharing a sunset with—because I might have believed that a blind person couldn't take care of a child independently. I was thankful for this Federation-influenced blessing. I was also aware at that moment that this sunset might have gone unnoticed by both of us had we not had our previous discussion. Certainly it would not have been a life-or-death disaster to have missed the sunset, but there was a particular joy in our sharing, "What color is the sun?"

New Alignments and the The Winds of Change

Through fifty years and hundreds of pages we have traced in this volume the history of the organized blind movement in the United States. Why, it might be asked, should we include at the end of the final chapter (and, of all things a chapter concerning "A People's Movement") two items about the agencies in the blindness system? The answer is that these two incidents symbolize and typify the mood in the blindness field at the end of the 1980s—the new alignments, the shifting balances of power and influence.

On November 17, 1989, Kenneth Jernigan went to Lancaster, Pennsylvania, to speak to the Penn-Del (Pennsylvania-Delaware) chapter of the AER (the Association for Education and Rehabilitation of the Blind and Visually Impaired). The fact of his invitation, of what he said, and the respect with which it was received had significance far beyond the particular time and place. It was a tacit recognition by all concerned that the National

Federation of the Blind was now a central element in shaping the blindness system. In short the organized blind movement had come to the center of the stage. Here is what Jernigan said:

CONSUMERISM: IMPROVING THE SERVICE DELIVERY SYSTEM
by Kenneth Jernigan

There are those who say that nothing ever changes. I am not one of them. There are those who say that especially nothing ever changes in the blindness field. Again, I am not one of them. I believe that the past half century has brought unprecedented changes, not only in the world at large but also and particularly in the blindness field. Moreover, I think the changes have overwhelmingly been for the good. However, as is almost always the case, with progress has come problems—both in the world at large and in the blindness field.

Today we are talking about consumerism. The fact that we are, along with the popularity and recurrence of the theme, means that there is a felt need and that there are problems. In the summer of 1988 I participated in a panel discussion on this topic at the AER convention in Montreal. Some of the things which I said at that time bear repeating, for they deal with basic questions—matters concerning relationships and performance in our field.

At the National Federation of the Blind convention in Chicago in 1988, 2,443 people registered as attendees. No other group has that kind of attendance. You know it, and I know it. In October of 1989 the National Federation of the Blind distributed (on cassette, on flexible disc, in Braille, and in print) over 29,000 copies of its magazine the *Braille Monitor*. Again, no other publication in our field has that kind of circulation, or anything even approaching it.

At my first NFB convention in 1952 barely 150 people were present, and we had no monthly publication. At that 1952 convention we spent more than fifty percent of our time talking about the rehabilitation system—what it was doing, how to improve it, and what we wanted from it. At our 1988 convention we had twenty-five hours of program content, and we spent a total of forty-five minutes (or three percent of the time) dealing with the rehabilitation system of the United States. Of that forty-five minutes, fifteen minutes was spent hearing from the federal Rehabilitation

Commissioner; fifteen minutes was spent hearing from our Director of Governmental Affairs, who talked about problems blind people were having with the system; and the final fifteen minutes was spent with questions and comments from the audience, indicating their concern with the failure of the system to deliver. In short, only one percent of the program time was used to hear from the rehabilitation system, and none of the time was spent talking about threats to the system or how to save it. Why?

Is it simply, as some have charged, that the members of the Federation (all of the thousands and tens of thousands of them—or, at least, their leaders) are negative and destructive—irresponsible radicals and agency haters? No. Such a thesis cannot be sustained. The facts do not support it. Let us turn again to the statistics of the 1988 NFB convention.

Kurt Cylke, head of the National Library Service for the Blind and Physically Handicapped, was with us for the entire week, and so were several of his staff. Day after day they answered questions, talked with our members, and planned with us for the future. There was an atmosphere of partnership and mutual trust.

Likewise, top officials of the Social Security Administration were present to speak and participate. The Deputy Commissioner for Policy and External Affairs had a forty-minute segment on the program, and other Social Security personnel conducted a seminar and answered questions for most of an afternoon. As with the Library, there was no tension or confrontation—only partnership and a feeling of shared interest and mutual concern. Moreover, with Social Security it must be remembered that many blind people throughout the country experience problems with underpayments, demands for return of overpayments, denial of applications, and similar difficulties; and more often than not, the National Federation of the Blind represents those blind persons in hearings to reverse Social Security's actions. Millions of dollars and numerous professional judgments are repeatedly called into question. Yet, there is no hostility—only friendliness and joint effort. On a continuing basis the National Federation of the Blind and the Social Security Administration share information, exchange ideas, and work together in a spirit of cooperative harmony.

In short, our problems come only with the rehabilitation system, with some of the private agencies which function as part of that system, and with a group of educators. And even here there must be a further narrowing and focusing, for the problem is with the system itself and some of its more vocal spokespersons, not with all of its component parts or personnel. An increasing number of those in the system are beginning to take a new look and work with us. The very fact of our discussion here this morning is an evidence of that trend and the shift in thinking.

This brings me to our topic, "Consumerism." I think blind people must have not an exclusive but a major role in shaping the blindness system. Otherwise, the system will die. Moreover, when I say "blind people," I do not mean just blind individuals. I mean democratic membership organizations *of* the blind. I mean effective participation by the blind, and the only way that can be achieved is through organizations of the blind. In a sense, of course, blind people have always shaped the system, as indeed they do today. In most cases blind persons started (or played a major part in starting) the agencies. There have always been blind agency directors, and individual blind persons prominent in the community have from the beginning served on advisory and policy boards and lent their names and prestige to funding and public support.

Even so, the system has traditionally been custodial in nature and high-handed in dealing with meaningful input from the blind. This is why the system is in trouble. It is in danger of being absorbed into generic programs for the disabled, starving for lack of funds, and losing its position of centrality and perceived importance in the lives of the blind. This would not be the case if the average, thinking, responsible blind adult in this country felt that the system really mattered—excluding, of course, the blind people who work in the system.

Let me be clearly understood. I am not saying that rehabilitation, training in mobility, assistance for the newly blinded, or education are not important—urgently important; for they are. Rather, I am saying that year by year more and more blind persons have come to feel that the system is not effectively providing those things and that it is both unresponsive and irrelevant. Remember that I am talking about the system as a whole, not individual agencies or particular people working in those agencies.

It is not, as a few have claimed, that the organized blind wish to take control of the agencies. It is, from the point of view of the system, far worse than that. It is that more and more blind people are coming to feel that, in the things that count in their daily lives, what the agencies have to offer won't help and doesn't matter.

If I felt that the system was hopeless and that nothing could or should be done to improve it, I would not be here today talking with you. It is late, but if honest evaluation and forthright action occur, I think the system can be saved—and that it is worth saving.

However, certain things must be said without equivocation. As a beginning, the agencies must change their attitudes about criticism and about the role of the organized blind in decision making. The matter of Fred Schroeder is a case in point. As most members of this organization know, Mr. Schroeder is blind. He is currently Director of the New Mexico Commission for the Blind. Before taking that job, he taught mobility professionally, received all of the academic credentials for doing so, and then was denied certification by this organization (the Association for Education and Rehabilitation of the Blind and Visually Impaired). The denial was based on the belief that a blind person cannot safely and competently teach another blind person how to travel—or, if you like, teach another blind person mobility. The National Federation of the Blind as an organization and I as an individual thought you were wrong in that decision, and we were entitled to that opinion. On the other hand, it was perfectly proper for your organization to believe that you were right to attack our position, but it was not proper for the members of your organization to attack us (as some of you did) on irrelevant grounds—denigrating our character and morals because of our beliefs. Of course, the same would obtain for our treatment of you.

Moreover, workers in the blindness system must resist the growing tendency to hide behind the term "professionalism" and must stop treating "professionalism" as if it were a sacred mystery. There is a teachable body of knowledge which can be learned about giving service to the blind; but much of that knowledge is a matter of common sense, good judgment, and experience. Most thinking blind persons (certainly those who have been blind for any length of time and have had any degree of success) know at least as much about what they and other blind people want and need from the system as the professionals do, and it must also be kept in mind that not every act of a "professional" is necessarily a "professional" act or based on "professionalism." Just as in other fields in America today, the professionals in the blindness system must be judged on their behavior and not merely their credentials.

Consider, for instance, the question of whether children with residual vision should be taught Braille. After careful consideration the members of the National Federation of the Blind believe that every such child should at least have the option of being taught to read and write Braille. Some of the educators (especially those who cannot fluently read and write Braille) resist this view. Is their opinion a "professional" judgment, or is it a decision based on vested interest? Whichever it is, the views of the organized blind are entitled to serious consideration and not simply a brush-off, with the statement that the blind don't know what they are talking about and that they probably have bad motives and morals into the bargain.

This brings me back to what I said about Kurt Cylke and the National Library Service for the Blind and Physically Handicapped. The libraries are not in trouble, and (regardless of economic conditions or changing theories) the libraries won't be in trouble. They won't because the blind of this country won't let it happen. And, yes, we have the power to give substance to our feelings. We don't control Kurt Cylke or the libraries. We don't want to—and besides, he wouldn't permit it. Neither does he control us—and for the same reasons. We support the National Library Service for the Blind and Physically Handicapped because we need it, because it gives useful and good service, and because its leaders understand that they *exist* to give us service, and that they have accountability to us. What I have said about the Library is also true of the Social Security Administration and an increasing number of agencies and individuals in the fields of rehabilitation and education.

But the hard core of the blindness system still resists, to its detriment and ours. It tries to say that it speaks for the blind because the head of an agency is blind or because blind people serve on a staff or board. No great intellect is required to understand that in a representative democracy only those elected *by* a group can speak *for* that group; that the heads of agencies can have vested interests which transcend their blindness; and that when an agency can pick and choose individual blind spokespersons from the community, it can get people who will say whatever it wants them to say.

Unless things change, I believe the central core of the blindness system will sink into obscurity and wither away, but I believe this need not happen and should not happen. Blind people (and that means the organized blind) must have a major voice in shaping the blindness system and the programs which operate within it—whether those programs be sheltered shops, residential schools, state agencies, or private nonprofit organizations. It must be a partnership—and not a partnership of dominance and subservience but of consenting equals—a partnership based on trust, respect, and mutuality. Let these things happen, and all else will follow. Let these things happen, and the system will thrive.

If those who work in the public and private agencies want broad support from the blind community, they must be responsive to the concerns which the blind perceive as important. Today there are relatively few major issues which divide the organized blind and the agencies. Twenty years ago it appeared (at least, on the surface) that there was at least one such issue—the National Accreditation Council for Agencies Serving the Blind and Visually Handicapped (NAC). But the problem was more apparent than real. NAC (despite its few remaining vocal supporters) has never been a significant factor in the lives of the nation's blind and is now rapidly becoming a dead letter and a subject only for the historians. It has never been able to get more than twenty or twenty-five percent of the nation's eligible agencies to accept its accreditation, and increasingly as the larger and more prominent agencies have pulled away from it, it has been forced to try to keep its numbers up by accrediting smaller and less well-known organizations. Let the dead be dead, and let the rest of us move on to better things.

The real question we face is not how to resolve controversies between consumers and the agencies but whether consumers can continue to feel that the agencies on balance are relevant enough and important enough for the consumers to nurture and save them—in short, whether there can be common cause, shared purpose, mutual respect, and true partnership. Certainly the problems which face us are formidable and challenging. We still have a long way to go in improving the climate of public opinion so that the blind can have opportunity and full access to the main channels of everyday life. We have made tremendous progress in this area, but much yet remains to be done. All other things being equal, the job can best be handled through joint effort by the blind and the agencies, but handled it must be whether the agencies participate or not.

Likewise, there is a broad spectrum of specific programs and activities, ranging from technology to education to employment, which need urgent and sustained attention—and again (all other things being equal) the job can best be handled by joint effort on the part of the blind community and the agencies. But one way or another, the blind intend to achieve full equality and first-class status in society. The question is what part the agencies will play and what relationship they will have with the increasingly powerful consumer movement.

The story is told that one evening a nightclub patron approached the bandstand and said to the drummer, "Does your dog bite?"

"No," the drummer said, "he doesn't."

The man reached down to pet the dog, and it almost bit his arm off. He leaped back in a fury and said to the drummer, "I thought you said your dog didn't bite."

"He doesn't," the drummer said, "but that isn't my dog."

You see, the man asked the wrong question, so he got an unsatisfactory answer. Let us be sure that in dealing with consumerism in the blindness field we not only try to get the right answers but also ask the right questions. Otherwise, we may lose an arm.

The foregoing address was delivered by Kenneth Jernigan in November of 1989—and significant as it was, something more dramatic was to occur the following month. It involved the American Foundation for the Blind and its director, William Gallagher. Certainly Gallagher (though blind) was no Federationist— and, so far as the author knows, he never had been. Indeed, during the seventies and eighties the Federation often found itself in furious conflict with Gallagher.

Yet, a brief article in the December, 1989, *Braille Monitor* underscored, as nothing else could have, the changes that were occurring in the blindness field. In the early eighties, when Gallagher and Jernigan first began to hold meetings, the atmosphere was anything but cordial. A decade later everything was different. And perhaps it can all be explained by the power of "A People's Movement"—therefore, the appropriateness (even the essential rightness) of this inclusion in our final chapter— Gallagher responding affirmatively to a Federation initiative, and Jernigan apparently congratulating him for doing it, publicly and in the pages of the *Monitor*. Jernigan's article, entitled "The Winds of Change," follows:

THE WINDS OF CHANGE
by Kenneth Jernigan

Most (although certainly not all) of the people who are knowledgeable about such things would agree that today the two strongest forces in the affairs of the blind of this country are the National Federation of the Blind and the American Foundation for the Blind. Consequently, how these two organizations interact is of considerable importance. Sometimes the relationship has been stormy and sometimes quiet, but it has rarely been what one would call close and cordial.

Recently, however, there has been a pronounced change. I suppose it started in the mid-eighties when the Federation and the Foundation began working together in the World Blind Union. It has now spread far beyond that. To begin with, I should say that Bill Gallagher, the Foundation's Executive Director, and I have been meeting on a fairly regular basis for quite some time; and although it is not a controlling factor, I find Bill Gallagher friendly and easy to deal with. In short, I like him as a person. My experience has been that he faces issues and keeps his word. That does not mean that we always agree or that either of us approves of everything the other does. It simply means that it is easier to work with somebody who treats you courteously and shows some responsiveness than with somebody who doesn't.

An incident occurred not long ago which shows what is happening and how the balances are altering. It will be remembered that President Maurer said in his 1989 banquet speech: "The American Foundation for the Blind has produced a special psychological test called the 'Anxiety Scale for the Blind.'" He went on to ridicule the test and tear it to pieces, pointing out how negative it was. Dr. Susan Spungin, one of the Foundation's top officials, was in the audience, having spoken to the Federation convention that afternoon.

Shortly after the conclusion of the NFB convention Bill Gallagher called me to say that he felt it was unfortunate that President Maurer had attacked the Anxiety Scale for the Blind, implying that it was current when in reality it was outdated, having been produced in the late sixties. I told him that it was my understanding that the Anxiety Scale was still being used by the Foundation and that if it was, it didn't matter when it was produced. He said he would look into it.

A few weeks later he called me to say that he had learned that the Foundation was, in fact, still distributing the Anxiety Scale. He said that he had reviewed it and wasn't sure he could pass it himself. He concluded by saying that the document was immediately being withdrawn from circulation and would no longer be used.

This is the sort of responsiveness which can lead to a new climate in the blindness field. I emphasize that the National Federation of the Blind and the American Foundation for the Blind are not going to agree on every issue and that when we believe it is necessary, we will publicly state that we think the Foundation is wrong. But the incident I have just described could not have occurred ten years ago—or, for that matter, even five years ago. Hopefully it may be a sign of things to come.

As the Twig is Bent:
Unto the Fourth
Generation

The first fifty years of the organized blind movement in the United States are now history. At the time of this writing (mid- March, 1990) there seems little doubt as to what direction the second fifty years will take. The details, of course, cannot be predicted; but the vigor, commitment, and continuity seem assured. When (as occurred in 1989) blind children of nine and thirteen join together for collective action in the name of the National Federation of the Blind and blind teen-agers come to the platform at the Federation convention to talk of the movement and its mission, the pattern of the decades ahead seems unmistakable and the road to the future clearly marked. The blind have come of age, determined to speak for themselves and control their own destiny.

The Voice of the Fourth Generation:
Blind Kids Express Their Views
The Braille Monitor, November, 1989

From the Associate Editor: Our opponents are inclined to dismiss the National Federation of the Blind as a bunch of type A overachievers with half-baked notions about how the blind can compete on terms of equality if given an even break. When confronted with the evidence of ordinary blind people successfully living normal, productive lives, they mutter about our philosophy's being nonsense but the training we advocate being sound.

It is not clear how these apologists would explain away the crop of youngsters who are emerging now as products of the NFB's philosophy as expressed and lived by the members of the NFB's Parents of Blind Children Division. Informed and reinforced by the Federation, these parents are demanding that their children receive (often for the first time) appropriate and necessary instruction in Braille, keyboard skills, and cane travel. These parents are coming to understand that their children can live normal, fully productive lives if and only if they learn to believe in themselves and equip themselves with the skills they need to compete with their sighted peers.

Two young men, products of the NFB philosophy so disdained by these experts, took part in a panel discussion during the parents' seminar preceding the 1989 convention of the National Federation of the Blind, sponsored jointly by the Parents of Blind Children Division and the Job Opportunities for the Blind Program. Their remarks are inspiring and highly instructive. As the mother of three sighted youngsters, the youngest of whom is older than these two teen-agers, I am tempted to ask whether most sighted teens could have written and presented talks as interesting, well-constructed, and inspiring as the two reprinted here. Most of us would agree that blindness, while it does not confer special powers, certainly does provide extraordinary opportunities for growth. The remarks that follow illustrate this point.

Dan Ryles, son of Ruby Ryles, first vice president of the Parents of Blind Children Division, is fourteen. He is now a sophomore in high school. Here is what he had to say to parents of blind children when given a chance to tell it like it is. This was his first real public address, and he delivered it from a Braille text:

> Good morning. My family moved to the Seattle area the summer before my eighth grade year. I was, and still am, the only blind kid in my school district, and the teachers and students had little or no experience with blind people before I enrolled. The kids' preconceptions about blindness, along with the normal junior high mentality, made the first semester exceptionally difficult. Not many people spoke to me or had much to do with me. Of course, there were those few who constantly hung around me wanting to know exactly how I did everything. I could live with that, but what hurt me were the times spent getting dressed and undressed for gym class in the locker room. Surely most of you remember what eighth-grade locker

room talk is like. Much of it is obscene and very cruel. My blindness seemed to make me the perfect target for insults and ridicule. I couldn't cry in front of the kids, but I did cry on occasion at home. Even my new girl friend had lots of negative attitudes, which were painful to me.

The science teacher took it upon himself to decide for me what assignments I could and could not do, never considering the possible adaptations I might make. I knew his attitudes were not good when on the first day of class he assumed I would need to tape his lectures instead of Brailling notes with my slate and stylus. Those were hard times, but my mom helped me through them with the philosophy of the National Federation of the Blind. She told me that the things the kids said weren't really true. Junior high kids will find something wrong with everyone, and they will greatly exaggerate it. My blindness was the most obvious characteristic they could see.

I have come a long way since then. The kids have gradually come to accept me. This last year (my ninth-grade year) I took algebra, Spanish, chemistry, American history, English, and symphonic band. I would never have gotten to where I am today if my mom had not had the necessary reading and writing skills to teach me when everyone else was learning them in print. I also learned basic cane skills in first and second grade. That may seem early when compared to some kids' experience, but not as early as I should have been taught it. If I had had a cane in preschool, things would have been a lot easier. The earlier you teach a kid cane skills, the sooner he can travel independently.

Now I can travel as well as anyone and have a daily paper route, which brings in $120 a month. I do the route entirely on my own, including collections, for which I Braille the receipts. I was lucky. I had a mom who didn't overprotect me. I did, and still do, occasionally scrape a knee or bruise an elbow. I once even had stitches in my head, but that's just a natural part of growing up. It has nothing to do with my blindness. What is not natural is for blind kids to have reading and writing skills taught to them later than sighted kids. This may sound a little crude, but if you'll be as mean as my mom, your blind kid will be okay.

Darrell Shandrow, son of Betty Shandrow, President of the Parents of Blind Children Division of Arizona, is a junior in high school. He has taken public speaking, but speech class was never like this. Here is what he had to say:

Good morning, everybody. I have congenital glaucoma. I lost my left eye when I was little, and I have very little usable vision in the other. I was also born deaf, but I have been able to hear since age five. My parents and the National Federation of the Blind are helping me to live independently. My parents felt that it was important that I learn cane travel and other orientation skills at an early age so that I would be independent. By doing so I have been able to participate in public service events and communicate using amateur radio for the last four years. My parents said that I could do anything I set my mind to. I was raised as a normal person who cannot see. I was not over-protected, and this is the major reason I can function normally.

My parents always felt that I should be allowed to function on the same grade level in school as that of the sighted. My mother took classes at the University of Arizona in Grade II Braille, Nemeth Code, abacus, structure and function of the eye, and daily living skills. With this knowledge my mother helped me learn how to read and write and to have a normal life. By tutoring me at home, she made sure that I was not held back. Due to my experiences with amateur radio, my parents felt that I was ready to use high-technology equipment. They got me an Apple II-E computer, an Echo III synthesizer, a printer, a Braille 'n' Speak, and computer software that is written for the blind. This technology makes things go much easier in school. I can take notes on the Braille 'n' Speak at school, and when I get home, I can send the notes to the computer, where they are printed and saved onto a disk.

The National Federation of the Blind has reinforced my independence. I can't help but get that feeling of independence when I'm around people like Jim Omvig, Norm and Bruce Gardner, Ruth Swenson, and the other Federationists. I feel that the NFB promotes independence in many ways. I feel that one of the major ways is through the national convention. It's great to be around so many independent blind people. I also feel that the *Braille Monitor* gives ideas of independence through its informative articles. This is the key to Federation philosophy. We must be independent to fight discrimination. We are the blind speaking for ourselves. That's what makes the National Federation of the Blind unique.

The philosophy of the National Federation of the Blind has caused me to decide that I want to fight against discrimination. The National Federation of the Blind hired Richard Arbach and Ruth Swenson as my attorneys in my case against the Moranna School District to be allowed to attend public school. The case was settled in my favor, and the Moranna School District pays for transportation and tuition for me to attend Pallaverty High School in the Tucson Unified School District. I am now a junior and have a 4.0 grade point average. I would like to thank Ruth Swenson, Richard Arbach, and the National Federation of the Blind for helping me to get into public school. Now I have a famous quote from the *Braille Monitor* that I feel goes along with what I've said about the Federation, and I'm sure you can guess which one it is. It's in the front, I guess on the masthead. It goes like this: "The National Federation of the Blind is not an organization speaking for the blind—it is the blind speaking for themselves," and that's it for me. Thank you.

As The Twig Is Bent
The Braille Monitor, August, 1989

From the Editor: When does a person become mature? At what age does he or she become responsible for helping make the world better, not only for himself or herself but also for others? More to the point (at least, for purposes of this discussion) how old must an individual be to become (in the active, full sense of the word) a Federationist? How about 13? What about 9?

The Associate Editor and I recently received a letter from two students at the Ohio State School for the Blind, which helped me answer the question. I found the letter both delightful and heartwarming. I also found it instructive, for it told me that our message and philosophy are beginning to permeate every segment of the blind population—children, adults, and the elderly; the rich and the poor; the educated and the illiterate. It renewed my faith in the ability of people to act in their own enlightened self-interest and to do it collectively. It underscored something which, at the core of my being, I have never doubted—that the future of the National Federation of the Blind is going to be all right.

Even now the leaders of the fourth generation are developing and reaching for maturity. They are learning their Federation philosophy at an early age and living it on a daily basis. Read the letter from the students at the Ohio State School for the Blind, and you will see what I mean. Here it is:

Columbus, Ohio
April 20, 1989

Dear Dr. Jernigan and Mrs. Pierce:

Our names are Jason Ewell (age 9) and Mike Leiterman (age 13), and we wish to tell you about our coalition—the student alliance coalition (SAC) at the Ohio State School for the Blind. Our committee grew out of a minor student concern, which was soon put on the back burner for a major issue. Therefore, we are writing to tell you about our efforts over the past year concerning totally blind students being discriminated against as dining room workers.

This policy is unjust because only students with high residual vision have been allowed to hold these positions. Collectively we decided to approach the administrator of residential services to share this concern because she oversees the dining room staff and, if persuaded, could use her authority to aid us.

We shared with her our belief that our school should be a discriminatory-free environment, in which we could learn by trying as many things as we wished to attempt. She appreciated our honesty and position. Likewise, she thought that other students should follow our example here at the OSSB. Dorm council was started. Every two weeks we meet for around an hour or so to discuss issues which arise out of living in a residential setting. The dietitian, who acts as immediate supervisor over the dining room staff, came to one of our meetings and agreed to help by restructuring the hiring policy and developing a more efficient training program for all who wish to apply. Weekends and daily after school have been designated as periods for the training sessions. At this time those interested seem to be satisfied with this new procedure.

We feel glad that we were able to work together to end this problem. Even though this issue really only directly pertains to the totally blind, we felt it necessary that those with residual vision be active participants—because what affects one of us, affects us all.

Respectfully,
Jason Ewell and Mike Leiterman

Newel Perry—Teacher of Youth and and Leader of Men

by Jacobus tenBroek

I come before you today—indeed we are all gathered here—to discharge a public duty and to honor a private debt. Newel Perry was a public figure. To us, he was also a personal friend. We can appraise his public contribution. We can only acknowledge our private obligation and personal attachment. We can detail his public record, define his influential role, itemize his accomplishments, recount his deeds, enumerate his statutes, specify his doctrines, disentangle the elements of his social philosophy, identify the general and the institutional fruits of his life's work, analyze and psychoanalyze the personality traits that made him a leader. Upon the life we shared, we can only dwell in memory, sifting through the loose meshes of the mind the hours, the days, the nights, the months, the years of our common experience; the fears, the travails, the aspirations, the laughter that were ours together.

We were his students, his family, his intimates, his comrades on a thousand battlefronts of a social movement. We slept in his house, ate at his table, learned geometry at his desk, walked the streets interminably by his side, moved forward on the strength of his optimism and confidence.

The boundless devotion to him of his wife Lillie (to whom he was married from 1912 until her death in 1935) spilled over onto us to balm our institution-starved spirits, to lighten with gentle affection the bewilderment of our eccentricity and the unnatural confinement of our segregation. Upon a later generation of us, after the death of Lillie, the same bounty was conferred in her turn by his sister Emma Burnham, who lived with Doctor during the last 21 years of his life.

As a forward youngster of 12, who made so bold as to address him as "Doc," I was once thrown out of a class by Doctor with such a lecture as still rings in my ears. As a somewhat older youngster, still forward but now also bored by the slow pace and the unimaginative techniques of high school, I was expelled by him altogether for incorrigible recalcitrance. Eventually, despite these unpromising beginnings, I did graduate from high school. With plenty of ambition but no money, I prepared to enter the University. At that point I was denied state aid to the blind, a program then newly instituted as a result of Doctor's efforts in sponsoring a constitutional amendment and a comprehensive statute. The reason was not that my need was not great. It was that I intended to pursue a higher education while I was being supported by the state. That was too much for the administrative officials. Almost without discussion, Doctor immediately filled the gap. Just as Warring Wilkinson had earlier done for him, he supplied me with tuition and living expenses out of his own pocket for a semester while we all fought to reverse the decision of the state aid officials.

It was ever thus with Doctor. The key to his great influence with blind students was, first of all, the fact that he was blind and therefore understood their problems; and second, that he believed in them and made his faith manifest. He provided the only sure foundation of true rapport: knowledge on our part that he was genuinely interested in our welfare.

Aside from these immediate personal benefactions, there were three habits of life—one might almost say three elements of personality—which I formed out of his teaching and example when I was an adolescent in his charge. First: an attitude towards my blindness, a conception that it is basically unimportant in the important affairs of life. A physical nuisance, yes! A topic of unembarrassed conversation, a subject of loud questions by small children in the street as you pass, certainly. But not something which shapes one's nature, which determines his career, which affects his usefulness or happiness. Second: a basic assumption that sighted people generally have boundless good will towards the blind and an utterly false conception of the consequences of blindness. It is their misconception about its nature which creates the social and economic handicap of blindness. Third: public activity as a rule of life, a sense of responsibility to exert personal effort to improve the lot of others. While I was still a lad in my teens, I was attending meetings and doing work that Doctor assigned me in the blind movement. He was a social reformer. He made me one too. Through participation with him, these attitudes and practices became habits of my life. So deeply instilled were they that they have remained ever after an almost automatic behavioral pattern—potent and often governing factors in my outlook and activity. Mature reflection in later years could only confirm through reason what his influence had so surely wrought in my youth.

It is altogether fitting that we should hold this memorial convocation at the California School for the Blind. It was here that Newel Perry came in 1883 as a ten-year-old boy—penniless, blind, his father dead, his home dissolved. Two years earlier, he had lost his sight and nearly his life as the result of a case of poison oak which caused his eyeballs to swell until they burst and which held him in a coma for a month. It was here at the School that Warring Wilklnson first met and took an interest in him, laying the basis for future years of intimate relationship and mutual endeavor. Warring Wilkinson was the first principal of the California State School for the Deaf and the Blind. He served in that capacity for 44 years, from 1865 to 1909. With his characteristic interest in his charges, he soon saw young Newel's full potentiality. He sent him from here to Berkeley High School to complete his secondary education. It was he who overcame the numerous obstacles to this arrangement, so fruitful in its understanding of education and of the needs of the blind. Newel continued to live here at the School while he attended the University of California from 1892 to 1896. Again admission had to be secured over strong resistance. Again Wllkinson was the pathfinder; Newel his willing and anxious instrument. Wilkinson's role in Newel's life as a youth can hardly be overestimated: father, teacher, guide, supporter—in Newel's own words, "dear Governor."

   As this Institution was not only the school but the home of his boyhood and the foundation of his manhood, so 16 years later, in 1912, at the age of 39, Newel Perry returned here to take up his permanent career as a teacher. He remained in that post until 1947—a third of a century. It was here that his life's work was accomplished. It was from this place as a base that he organized and conducted a movement for social reform. It was here that many of us first met him as his students. It was here that his impact upon us first made itself felt. It was here that our lifelong association with him began. How often in these halls have we heard his footsteps? How often in this chamber, his voice? The sound of those footsteps and that voice have now gone from the world as a physical reality. How often hereafter will they continue to sound in the halls and chambers of our lives!

   In the years between departure from the School in 1896 and return to it in 1912, Newel Perry devoted himself to further education and to the search for an academic job. He took graduate work at the University of California, meanwhile serving successively as an unpaid teaching fellow, a paid assistant and finally as an Instructor in the Department of Mathematics. In 1900, following a general custom of that day, he went to Europe to continue his studies. He did this for a time at the University of Zurich in Switzerland and then at the University of Munich in Germany. From the latter he secured the degree of Doctor of Philosophy in Mathematics, with Highest Honors, in 1901. He lingered in Europe for a time traveling and writing an article on a mathematical topic which was published in a learned journal. He then returned to the United States in 1902, landing in New York where he was to remain until 1912. He had about $80 in capital, a first-class and highly specialized education, and all the physical, mental and personal prerequisites for a productive career, save one, visual acuity.

   During this period, he supported himself precariously as a private coach of university mathematics students. He applied himself, also, to the search for a university position. He had begun the process by mail from Europe even before he secured his Ph.

D. He now continued the process on the ground in New York. He displayed the most relentless energy. He employed every imaginable technique. He wrote letters in profusion. In 1905, he wrote to 500 institutions of every size and character. He distributed his dissertation and published article. He haunted meetings of mathematicians. He visited his friends in the profession. He enlisted the aid of his teachers. He called on everybody and anybody having the remotest connection with his goal.

Everywhere, the outcome was the same. Only the form varied. Some expressed astonishment at what he had accomplished. Some expressed interest. One of these seemed genuine—he had a blind brother-in-law who, he said, was a whiz at math. Some showed in- difference, now and then masked behind polite phrases. Some said there were no vacancies. Some said his application would be filed for future reference. One said—ironically, "as an encouragement to men who labor under disadvantages and who may learn from it how much may be accomplished through resolution and industry." Some averred that he probably could succeed in teaching at somebody else's college. Many said outright that they believed a blind man could not teach mathematics.

Many of these rejections were, of course, perfectly proper. Many were not. Their authors candidly gave the reason as blindness.

We know about this period of Newel Perry's life from reports of contemporaries or near contemporaries such as Hugh Buckingham, a student at the School from 1896 to 1900 during Doctor's absence, who has prepared a manuscript about Doctor's boyhood and youth. We know about it from what Doctor told many of us in later years. But we know about it in all its poignancy, desolation and bleakness, from Newel Perry's own intimate accounts written at the time to his old mentor and true friend, Warring Wilkinson. These accounts, with copies of many of the letters of rejection, have been preserved by the Wilkinson family through the intervening years. In the last two weeks, they have been opened to my inspection by Wilkinson's granddaughter, Florence Richardson Wyckoff, who is here with us today.

I have dwelt on this period and these experiences for several reasons. They reflect, they accurately portray, a phase of all of our lives as blind people. In fact, thirty-five years later, I personally received identical letters from many of these same institutions. It was almost as if a secretary had been set to copying Doctor's file, only changing the signatures and the name of the addressee. Yet great progress has been made. Many of us are now teaching at colleges and universities around the country and filling many other jobs hitherto closed to us.

Doctor Perry's reaction to this decade of defeat and privation was remarkable. He did not break. He did not resign. He did not even become embittered. Discouragement, frustration, a sense of wrong and Injustice, certainly these; but never collapse. He was not licked. We see in these bitter years of hunger and rejection the source of true knowledge about the real problems of the blind and an ineradicable determination to do something about them. Here was a mainspring of social reform, an ever-flowing motivation to redirect public attitudes and actions toward the blind. To this was added the thrust of an active and restless disposition and the wit to perceive remedies and adapt them to the need.

Out of these elements of mind, personality and experience were compounded the public career of Newel Perry; and out of these elements also were constructed the programs the initiation of which made that career publicly significant.

First of all, the distress of poverty must be relieved. The necessities of life must be available. The minimum essentials must be assured. So much in some way had been provided in the Anglo-American system for three centuries before Newel Perry faced near starvation and economic exclusion in New York City. The Elizabethan Poor Laws did it in one way. County direct relief, instituted in California in 1901, did it in another. The almshouse and the county hospital and poor farm did it in still other ways. At the very minimum, it had to be done better. It should be done by a system of cash grants, adequate in amount to maintain standards of decency and health, receivable upon fixed and uniform standards of eligibility, made generally applicable by state participation and control, and expendable by the recipient through a free exercise of self-management and consumption choice. To bring this about, however, prohibitions in the state constitution would have to be removed by the arduous process of a people's amendment, an organic statute would have to be lobbied through the state legislature, faithful administration would somehow have to be secured. Year-by-year and session-by session into the indefinite future, the myriad minor corrections and major improvements made necessary by time and disclosed by experience would have to be worked through the legislature and the administration. And so indeed it came to pass in California.

Secondly, much more had to be done than merely relieve the distress of poverty. Security is a necessity. As an unmixed blessing, however, it is a stultifying concept. An indispensable ingredient of any welfare system is opportunity. One of the objects of public aid must be to stimulate and enable people to become independent of it. Accordingly, their initiative must not be hemmed in. The means of productive activity must not be withdrawn or denied. Independence of action and self-reliance must be encouraged. Legal liability of relatives must be relaxed so as not to spread poverty, increase dependence, and disrupt family life. Economic resources, reasonable amounts of real and personal property, must be devotable to plans for self-support instead of being required to be consumed in meeting daily needs. Incentive to earn must be constructed out of retention of the benefits of earning. And this too presently came to pass in California. The new system took cognizance of the need of the blind for adjustments on the social and psychological as well as the physical level. It permitted and encouraged them to strive to render themselves self-supporting. It applied the democratic principle of individual dignity to an underprivileged class of American citizens. It guaranteed them a fair measure of independence and self-respect in the conduct of their lives. The California system, the Newel Perry system, was thus far in advance of its time. It is still envied and emulated throughout the nation.

Thirdly, the reintegration of the blind into society on a basis of full and equal membership could only be achieved if they had a chance to earn their daily bread as others do in the community. Accordingly, action must be taken to eliminate restrictive barriers and legal discriminations. The main channels of opportunity must be swept clear of artificial and irrational obstructions. The public service, private employment, the common callings, the ordinary trades and occupations, the professions must be rescued from arbitrary exclusions based on blindness when blindness is not a factor bearing on competence and performance. Doctor was a prime mover in securing legal, constitutional and other provisions which: protect the right of the blind to enter a number of professions; forbid arbitrary discriminations against us in the state civil service and in secondary teaching; enable blind college students to pursue their studies with the aid of sighted readers hired by the state; bring the blind in an ever-increasing stream into the colleges and universities of the state and thence into the higher callings.

These achievements—legal, social, economic and political—have been the fruits at once of Doctor Perry's leadership and of the collective self-organization of the blind which that leadership engendered. More than any other person, it was Doctor who implanted and nurtured among the blind of California the sense of common cause, the spirit of collaborative effort in seeking solutions to our problems. More than any other person, it was he who taught us that the blind can and must lead the blind and the sighted, too, when dealing with the problems of the blind. More than any other person, it was he who made us aware that to go on unorganized was to remain disorganized, that only through concerted action can the blind hope to convert and enlist the power of government and to defeat the thoughtless tyranny of public prejudice and opportune ignorance.

Newel Perry was a teacher: a teacher of subject matter and a teacher of men. He taught his specialty of mathematics and taught it very well indeed; but he taught his pupils even better. To be sure, not all the students who came his way during his 35 years on this campus were wholly inspired by him. His personality was vigorous and his standards rigorous. But for many of us who attended the School during those three and a half decades it was Doctor Perry who furnished the impetus and incentive, the goad and the goal, that would light our later lives and nourish our careers. Our bond with him was not broken when our schooldays ended. We went on to become his comrades and colleagues in the cause which was always his true vocation.

Newel Perry was, in short, both a teacher of youth and a leader of men. These two roles were not, however, quite separate. For the secret of his success in both of them lay in this: that his teaching was a kind of leadership, and his leadership a kind of teaching. In his pedagogical method as well as his social purpose Doctor was thoroughly Socratic. His classroom manner was essentially that of the Platonic dialogue: dialectical, inquiring, insistently logical and incessantly prodding.

In this Socratic combination also lies, I think, the secret of Doctor's success as the leader of a social movement. Juet as in the classroom he taught his students by leading them, so as the pioneer of the organized blind movement he led his followers by teaching them. His power, like that of all leaders, rested in the last analysis upon persuasion. His triumphs, however, were not the product of oratorical or literary skill, although he had a notable gift for trenchant and incisive phrasing, the epigrammatic thrust which distills the essence of a complex issue. His persuasive power was not that of the demagogue but of the pedagogue. And It was not only his followers who learned from him. He educated the blind people of the state to an awareness of their capabilities as individuals and of their powers as a group. He educated the legislators in the State Capitol by dint of dogged, relentless, well-nigh incorrigible campaigns of persuasion carried on year after year and decade after decade. He educated the general public by his preachment and his example to regard the blind not in the traditional terms of charity and custody but in the realistic terms of normality and equality.

And most of all, in his role as leader, Newel Perry educated, indoctrinated and persuaded a distinguished group of cohorts to join him in carrying on the struggle and carrying out its goals. Those whom Doctor gathered around him were other blind men and women, mostly former students, whose special talents and professional positions uniquely supplemented his.

Raymond Henderson: by profession an attorney, self-taught, by preoccupation a reformer, with poetry in his soul and literature in his stylus. Born in 1881, he attended this School from 1889 through high school and continued to live here until his graduation from the University of California in 1904. He practiced his profession in Bakersfield, California, from his admission to the Bar until his death in 1945. Raymond came to the organized blind movement in his maturity from a long background of experience in other causes. He brought to it a notable array of personal abilities, a high degree of professional skill, a fine spirit of humanity and the enrichment of wide and intensive activity.

Leslie Schlingheyde: also by profession an attorney, gentle and religious by disposition, practical rather than reflective in frame of mind, with a brilliant academic record and a liberal outlook. He was born in 1893, attended this School from 1906 to 1913, and thus came under Doctor's influence in the year of his graduation. He received a J. D. from the Law School of the University of California in 1920 and from that time until his death in 1957 practiced his profession In Modesto, California, and served the blind movement all over the state.

It was Raymond Henderson and Leslie Schlingheyde who were primarily responsible for handling cases in court, for preparing innumerable legal briefs and arguments, for drafting projected bills and constitutional amendments, for continuous legal counsel during the insurgent and formative years. They were in a real sense the legal arm of the organized blind movement.

Ernest Crowley: again by profession an attorney but distinguished for his service in another arena. He kept a law office open In Fairfield-Suisun from the time of his graduation from the University of California Law School in 1923 until his death in 1952. To him, however, the law was only a necessary and not a particularly attractive means of earning a living. His law office was a cover for his real love and active life—the practice of politics. He was born in 1896 and attended this School from 1910 to 1916. He was thus under Doctor's tutelage as a student for four years. His significant contribution was made as a member of the State Legislature from 1928 to 1952. It was he who introduced and skillfully maneuvered through to passage the memorable bills which are now the statutory landmarks of our movement. In a very real sense, he was the legislative spokesman and arm of the movement.

Perry Sundquist: social worker and public administrator by profession, bringing to his work a sympathetic personality, an unshakable faith in blind people and skillful management of administrative techniques and devices. He was born in 1904 and attended this School from 1918 to 1922. For exactly twenty years now he has been Chief of the Division for the Blind in the State Department of Social Welfare. During those two decades he has translated the principles of the organized blind movement into concrete administrative action, from legislative parchment into practical reality. Under his direction programs for the blind have multiplied and prospered, services have been expanded and their benefits spread. Most important of all, the working philosophy of the movement has been transformed into a working practice. In a very real sense, he has been the effective administrative arm of the movement.

Through the years this little band grew in numbers and evolved in formal structure. It formed the nucleus of the California Council for the Blind, which came into being in 1934 with Doctor Perry as its first president. For 19 productive years, until his retirement in 1953 at the age of 80, Doctor forged and shaped the Council on the anvil of his own will into an instrument larger and more formidable but essentially similar to the informal group from which it originated.

Doctor's social vision in the field of blind welfare outdistanced his time and placed him in the advance guard of thought and planning. His liberality on these matters gains, rather than loses, in significance when it is placed alongside his broader attitudes toward politics and human affairs; for in matters unrelated to the blind, Doctor was fully an heir of the 19th century, conservative, even reactionary, by nature, often inflexible and not without a touch of old-fashioned nationalist imperialism. When it came to the cause to which he was most com mitted, he was far less a Victorian than a Utopian—less a standpatter than a restless progressive in search of new horizons.

How shall we sum up a man's life? How capture the essential quality of a human career? How convey the inward meaning, the im ponderable and intangible qualities of will and heart and spirit? There are the "vital statistics." But they are more statistical than vital. All that they can tell us of a man is that he was born, he lived, he loved, he died. For Newel Perry we must amend the litany at least this much: he lived, and he brought new life to many; he loved, and he was beloved; he died, and he will not be forgotten.

On the day following the death of Franklin Delano Roosevelt, Walter Lippmann wrote some words about him which might also stand as an epitaph to the leader and comrade whom we honor today: "The man must die in his appointed time. He must carry away with him the magic of his presence and that personal mastery of affairs which no man, however gifted by nature, can acquire except in the relentless struggle with evil and blind chance. Then comes the proof of whether his work will endure, and the test of how well he led his people. The final test of a leader is that he leaves behind him in other men the conviction and the will to carry on."

Who Are the Blind
Who Lead the Blind

INTRODUCTION

The National Federation of the Blind has become by far the most significant force in the affairs of the blind today, and its actions have had an impact on many other groups and programs. The Federation's President, Marc Maurer, radiates confidence and persuasiveness. He says, "If I can find twenty people who care about a thing, then we can get it done. And if there are two hundred, two thousand, or twenty thousand—well, that's even better." The National Federation of the Blind is a civil rights movement with all that the term implies.

President Maurer says, "You can't expect to obtain freedom by having somebody else hand it to you. You have to do the job yourself. The French could not have won the American Revolution for us. That would merely have shifted the governing authority from one colonial power to another. So, too, we the blind are the only ones who can win freedom for the blind, which is both frightening and reassuring. If we don't get out and do what we must, there is no one to blame but ourselves. We have control of the essential elements."

Although there are in the United States at the present time many organizations and agencies *for* the blind, there is only one National Federation of the blind. This organization was established in 1940 when the blind of seven states—Minnesota, Wisconsin, Illinois, Ohio, Pennsylvania, Missouri, and California—sent delegates to its first convention at Wilkes-Barre, Pennsylvania. Since that time progress has been rapid and steady. The Federation is recognized by blind men and women throughout the entire country as their primary means of joint expression; and today, with active affiliates in every state and the District of Columbia, it is the primary voice of the nation's blind.

To explain this spectacular growth, three questions must be asked and answered: (1) What are the conditions in the general environment of the blind which have impelled them to organize? (2) What are the purpose, the belief, the philosophy of the National Federation of the Blind? (3) Who are its leaders, and what are their qualifications to understand and solve the problems of blindness? Even a brief answer to these questions is instructive.

When the Federation came into being in 1940, the outlook for the blind was certainly not bright. The nation's welfare system was so discouraging to individual initiative that those who were forced to accept public assistance had little hope of ever achieving self-support again, and those who sought competitive employment in regular industry or the professions found most of the doors barred against them. The universal goodwill expressed toward the blind was not the wholesome goodwill of respect felt toward an equal; it was the misguided goodwill of pity felt toward an inferior. In effect the system said to the blind, "Sit on the sidelines of life. This game is not for you. If you have creative talents, we are sorry, but we cannot use them." The Federation came into being to combat these expressions of discrimination and to promote new ways of thought concerning blindness, and although great progress has been made toward the achievement of these goals, much still remains to be done.

The Federation believes that blind people are essentially normal and that blindness in itself is not a mental or psychological handicap. It can be reduced to the level of a mere physical nuisance. Legal, economic, and social discrimination based upon the false assumption that the blind are somehow different from the sighted must be abolished, and equality of opportunity made available to blind people. Because of their personal experience with blindness, the blind themselves are best qualified to lead the way in solving their own problems, but the general public should be asked to participate in finding solutions. Upon these fundamentals the National Federation of the Blind predicates its philosophy.

As for the leadership of the organization, all of the officers and members of the Board of Directors are blind, and all give generously of their time and resources in promoting the work of the Federation. The Board consists of seventeen elected members, five of whom are the constitutional officers of the organization. These members of the Board of Directors represent a wide cross section of the blind population of the United States. Their backgrounds are different, and their experiences vary widely; but they are drawn together by the common bond of having met blindness individually and successfully in their own lives and by their united desire to see other blind people have the opportunity to do likewise. A profile of the leadership of the organization shows why it is so effective and demonstrates the progress made by blind people during the past half- century—for in the story of the lives of these leaders can be found the greatest test of the Federation's philosophy. The cumulative record of their individual achievements is an overwhelming proof, leading to an inescapable conclusion.

DR. JACOBUS tenBROEK
Author, Jurist, Professor,
Founder of the National Federation of the Blind

The moving force in the founding of the National Federation of the Blind (and its spiritual and intellectual father) was Jacobus tenBroek. Born in 1911, young tenBroek (the son of a prairie homesteader in Canada) lost the sight of one eye as the result of a bow-and-arrow accident at the age of seven. His remaining eyesight deteriorated until at the age of fourteen he was totally blind. Shortly afterward he and his family traveled to Berkeley so that he could attend the California School for the Blind. Within three years he was an active part of the local organization of the blind.

By 1934 he had joined with Dr. Newel Perry and others to form the California Council of the Blind, which later became the the National Federation of the Blind of California. This organization was a prototype for the nationwide federation that tenBroek would form six years later.

Even a cursory glance at his professional career showed the absurdity of the idea that blindness means incapacity. The same year the Federation was founded (1940) Jacobus tenBroek received his doctorate in jurisprudence from the University of California, completed a year as Brandeis Research Fellow at Harvard Law School, and was appointed to the faculty of the University of Chicago Law School.

Two years later he began his teaching career at the University of California at Berkeley, moving steadily up through the ranks to become full professor in 1953 and chairman of the department of speech in 1955. In 1963 he accepted an appointment as professor of political science.

During this period Professor tenBroek published several books and more than fifty articles and monographs in the fields of welfare, government, and law—establishing a reputation as one of the nation's foremost scholars on matters of constitutional law. One of his books, *Prejudice, War, and the Constitution*, won the Woodrow Wilson Award of the American Political Science Association in 1955 as the best book of the year on government and democracy. Other books are *California's Dual System of Family Law* (1964), *Hope Deferred: Public Welfare and the Blind* (1959), and *The Antislavery Origins of the Fourteenth Amendment* (1951)— revised and republished in 1965 as *Equal Under Law*.

In the course of his academic career Professor tenBroek was a fellow at the Center for Advanced Study in the Behavioral Sciences at Palo Alto and was twice the recipient of fellowships from the Guggenheim Foundation. In 1947 he earned the degree of S.J.D. from Harvard Law School. In addition, he was awarded honorary degrees by two institutions of higher learning.

Dr. tenBroek's lifelong companion was his devoted wife Hazel. Together they raised three children and worked inseparably on research, writing, and academic and Federation concerns. Mrs. tenBroek still continues as an active member of the organized blind movement.

In 1950 Dr. tenBroek was made a member of the California State Board of Social Welfare by Governor Earl Warren. Later reappointed to the board three times, he was elected its chairman in 1960 and served in that capacity until 1963.

The brilliance of Jacobus tenBroek's career led some skeptics to suggest that his achievements were beyond the reach of what they called the "ordinary blind person." What tenBroek recognized in himself was not that he was exceptional, but that he was normal—that his blindness had nothing to do with whether he could be a successful husband and father, do scholarly research, write a book, make a speech, guide students engaged in social action movements and causes, or otherwise lead a productive life.

In any case, the skeptics' theory has been refuted by the success of the thousands of blind men and women who have put this philosophy of normality to work in their own lives during the past fifty years.

Jacobus tenBroek died of cancer at the age of fifty-six in 1968. His successor, Kenneth Jernigan, in a memorial address, said truly of him: "The relationship of this man to the organized blind movement, which he brought into being in the United States and around the world, was such that it would be equally accurate to say that the man was the embodiment of the movement or that the movement was the expression of the man.

"For tens of thousands of blind Americans over more than a quarter of a century, he was leader, mentor, spokesman, and philosopher. He gave to the organized blind movement the force of his intellect and the shape of his dreams. He made it the symbol of a cause barely imagined before his coming: the cause of self- expression, self-direction, and self- sufficiency on the part of blind people. Step by step, year by year, action by action, he made that cause succeed."

KENNETH JERNIGAN
Teacher, Writer,
Administrator

Kenneth Jernigan has been a leader in the National Federation of the Blind for more than thirty-five years. He was President (with one brief interruption) from 1968 until July of 1986. Although Jernigan is no longer President of the Federation, he continues to be one of its principal leaders. He works closely with the President, and he continues to be loved and respected by tens of thousands—members and non-members of the Federation, both blind and sighted.

Born in 1926, Kenneth Jernigan grew up on a farm in central Tennessee. He received his elementary and secondary education at the school for the blind in Nashville. After high school Jernigan managed a furniture shop in Beech Grove, Tennessee, making all furniture and operating the business.

In the fall of 1945 Jernigan matriculated at Tennessee Technological University in Cookeville. Active in campus affairs from the outset, he was soon elected to office in his class and to important positions in other student organizations. Jernigan graduated with honors in 1948 with a B.S. degree in Social Science. In 1949 he received a master's degree in English from Peabody College in Nashville, where he subsequently completed additional graduate study. While at Peabody he was a staff writer for the school newspaper, co-founder of an independent literary magazine, and a member of the Writers Club. In 1949 he received the Captain Charles W. Browne Award, at that time presented annually by the American Foundation for the Blind to the nation's outstanding blind student.

Jernigan then spent four years as a teacher of English at the Tennessee School for the Blind. During this period he became active in the Tennessee Association of the Blind (now the National Federation of the Blind of Tennessee). He was elected to the vice presidency of the organization in 1950 and to the presidency in 1951. In that position he planned the 1952 annual convention of the National Federation of the Blind, which was held in Nashville, and he has been planning national conventions for the Federation ever since. It was in 1952 that Jernigan was first elected to the NFB Board of Directors.

In 1953 he was appointed to the faculty of the California Orientation Center for the Blind in Oakland, where he played a major role in developing the best program of its kind then in existence.

From 1958 until 1978, he served as Director of the Iowa State Commission for the Blind. In this capacity he was responsible for administering state programs of rehabilitation, home teaching, home industries, an orientation and adjustment center, and library services for the blind and physically handicapped. The improvements made in services to the blind of Iowa under the Jernigan administration have never before or since been equaled anywhere in the country.

In 1960 the Federation presented Jernigan with its Newel Perry Award for outstanding accomplishment in services for the blind. In 1968 Jernigan was given a Special Citation by the President of the United States. Harold Russell, the chairman of the President's Committee on Employment of the Handicapped, came to Des Moines to present the award. He said: "If a person must be blind, it is better to be blind in Iowa than anywhere else in the nation or in the world. This statement," the citation went on to say, "sums up the story of the Iowa Commission for the Blind during the Jernigan years and more pertinently of its Director, Kenneth Jernigan. That narrative is much more than a success story. It is the story of high aspiration magnificently accomplished—of an impossible dream become reality."

Jernigan has received too many honors and awards to enumerate individually, including honorary doctorates from three institutions of higher education. He has also been asked to serve as a special consultant to or member of numerous boards and advisory bodies. The most notable among these are: member of the National Advisory Committee on Services for the Blind and Physically Handicapped (appointed by the Secretary of Health, Education, and Welfare), special consultant on Services for the Blind (appointed by the Federal Commissioner of Rehabilitation), advisor on museum programs for blind visitors to the Smithsonian Institution, and special advisor to the White House Conference on Library and Information Services (appointed by President Gerald Ford).

Kenneth Jernigan's writings and speeches on blindness are better known and have touched more lives than those of any other individual writing today. On July 23, 1975, he spoke before the National Press Club in Washington, D.C., and his address was broadcast live throughout the nation on National Public Radio. Through the years he has appeared repeatedly on network radio and television interview programs—including the "Today Show," the "Tomorrow Show," and the "Larry King Show."

In 1978 Jernigan moved to Baltimore to become Executive Director of the American Brotherhood for the Blind and Director of the National Center for the Blind. As President of the National Federation of the Blind at that time, he led the organization through the most impressive period of growth in its history. The creation and development of the National Center for the Blind and the expansion of the NFB into the position of being the most influential voice and force in the affairs of the blind stand as the culmination of Kenneth Jernigan's lifework and a tribute to his brilliance and commitment to the blind of this nation.

Jernigan's dynamic wife Mary Ellen is an active member of the Federation. Although sighted, she works with dedication in the movement and is known and loved by thousands of Federationists throughout the country.

Speaking at a convention of the National Federation of the Blind, Jernigan said of the organization and its philosophy (and also of his own philosophy):

As we look ahead, the world holds more hope than gloom for us—and, best of all, the future is in our own hands. For the first time in history we can be our own masters and do with our lives what we will; and the sighted (as they learn who we are and what we are) can and will work with us as equals and partners. In other words we are capable of full membership in society, and the sighted are capable of accepting us as such—and, for the most part, they want to..

We want no Uncle Toms—no sellouts, no apologists, no rationalizers; but we also want no militant hellraisers or unbudging radicals. One will hurt our cause as much as the other. We must win true equality in society, but we must not dehumanize ourselves in the process; and we must not forget the graces and amenities, the compassions and courtesies which comprise civilization itself and distinguish people from animals and life from existence.

Let people call us what they will and say what they please about our motives and our movement. There is only one way for the blind to achieve first-class citizenship and true equality. It must be done through collective action and concerted effort; and that means the National Federation of the Blind. There is no other way, and those who say otherwise are either uninformed or unwilling to face the facts. We are the strongest force in the affairs of the blind today, and we must also recognize the responsibilities of power and the fact that we must build a world that is worth living when the war is over—and, for that matter, while we are fighting it. In short, we must use both love and a club, and we must have sense enough to know when to do which—long on compassion, short on hatred; and, above all, not using our philosophy as a cop-out for cowardice or inaction or rationalization. We know who we are and what we must do—and we will never go back. The public is not against us. Our determination proclaims it; our gains confirm it; our humanity demands it.

MARC MAURER
Attorney and Executive

Born in 1951, Marc Maurer was the second in a family of six children. His blindness was caused by overexposure to oxygen after his premature birth, but he and his parents were determined that this should not prevent him from living a full and normal life.

He began his education at the Iowa Braille and Sight Saving School, where he became an avid Braille reader. In the fifth grade he returned home to Boone, Iowa, where he attended parochial schools. During high school (having taken all the courses in the curriculum) he simultaneously took classes at the junior college.

Maurer ran three different businesses before finishing high school: a paper route, a lawn care business, and an enterprise producing and marketing maternity garter belts designed by his mother. This last venture was so successful that his younger brother took over the business when Maurer left home.

In the summer of 1969, after graduating from high school, Maurer enrolled as a student at the Orientation and Adjustment Center of the Iowa Commission for the Blind and attended his first convention of the NFB. He was delighted to discover in both places that blind people and what they thought mattered. This was a new phenomenon in his experience, and it changed his life. Kenneth Jernigan was Director of the Iowa Commission for the Blind at the time, and Maurer soon grew to admire and respect him. When Maurer expressed an interest in overhauling a car engine, the Commission for the Blind purchased the necessary equipment. Maurer completed that project and actually worked for a time as an automobile mechanic. He believes today that mastering engine repair played an important part in changing his attitudes about blindness.

Maurer graduated cum laude from the University of Notre Dame in 1974. As an undergraduate he took an active part in campus life, including election to the Honor Society. Then he enrolled at the University of Indiana School of Law, where he received his Doctor of Jurisprudence in 1977.

Marc Maurer was elected President of the Student Division of the National Federation of the Blind in 1971 and re-elected in 1973 and 1975. Also in 1971 (at the age of twenty) he was elected Vice President of the National Federation of the Blind of Indiana. He was elected President in 1973 and re- elected in 1975.

During law school Maurer worked summers for the office of the Secretary of State of Indiana. After graduation he moved to Toledo, Ohio, to accept a position as the Director of the Senior Legal Assistance Project operated by ABLE (Advocates for Basic Legal Equality).

In 1978 Maurer moved to Washington, D.C., to become an attorney with the Rates and Routes Division in the office of the General Counsel of the Civil Aeronautics Board. Initially he worked on rates cases but soon advanced to dealing with international matters and then to doing research and writing opinions on constitutional issues and Board action. He wrote opinions for the Chairman and made appearances before the full Board to discuss those opinions.

In 1981 he went into private practice in Baltimore, Maryland, where he specialized in civil litigation and property matters. But increasingly he concentrated on representing blind individuals and groups in the courts. He has now become one of the most experienced and knowledgeable attorneys in the country regarding the laws, precedents, and administrative rulings concerning civil rights and discrimination against the blind. He is a member of the Bar in Indiana, Ohio, Iowa, and Maryland; and he is a member of the Bar of the Supreme Court of the United States.

Maurer has always been active in civic and political affairs, having run for public office in Baltimore and having been elected to the board of directors of the Tenants Association in his apartment complex shortly after his arrival. Later he was elected to the board of his community association when he became a home owner. From 1984 until 1986 he served with distinction as President of the National Federation of the Blind of Maryland.

An important companion in Maurer's activities (and a leader in her own right) is his wife Patricia. The Maurers were married in 1973, and they have two children—David Patrick, born March 10, 1984, and Diana Marie, born July 12, 1987.

At the 1985 convention in Louisville, Kentucky, Dr. Kenneth Jernigan announced that he would not stand for re-election as President of the National Federation of the Blind the following year, and he recommended Marc Maurer as his successor. In Kansas City in 1986, the convention elected Maurer by resounding acclamation, and he has capably served as President ever since.

DIANE MCGEORGE
Medical Secretary and Agency Director

Diane McGeorge was born in 1932 and grew up in Nebraska. She was blinded by meningitis at age two. She says that she was "slightly educated" at the Nebraska School for the Blind. Upon graduating she learned that no blind person—regardless of how well-qualified—has an easy time in the job market. She enrolled in a Denver business college to learn typing and transcribing before going on to the University of Colorado to train as a medical secretary, her profession for a number of years, with time away to raise her family.

McGeorge spent eight years as a full-time homemaker and mother, including stints as den mother, Sunday school teacher, and PTA officer. Throughout these years she was a passive member of the Federation. She served on committees and prepared refreshments, but she did not consider that she had any part in the struggle of the blind against discrimination. Her husband Ray was much more active in the Federation. She ignored or overlooked the instances when she had been turned down by landlords or barred from restaurants because of her dog guide, describing her actions as "looking on the bright side."

However, McGeorge attended the 1973 NFB convention in New York City and discovered for herself the power and commitment that derive from shared experience and determination to alter the status quo. From that moment her life began to change. This is the way she tells it:

"One bitterly cold day in December, Ray and I stopped at a run-down coffee shop. It was the only warm place available, or we wouldn't have set foot in it. We did so, however, and when we did, the proprietor told us we couldn't bring my dog in. I was so furious I almost burst into tears. I walked out, but I thought and thought about that experience—and I said, deep in my heart, that nobody was ever going to make me feel that way again. I had been a coward to let it happen.

"About six months later we attempted to go to a movie, and the manager said we couldn't bring the dog into the theater. I was well-acquainted with Colorado's White Cane Law, so we had what turned out to be a two-hour battle over the issue. I came away from there not feeling cowardly or guilty or as if I were not quite as good as the manager because he could see and I couldn't."

In 1976 Diane McGeorge assumed the state presidency of the NFB of Colorado, and she has been returned to office in every election since. Under her leadership the NFB of Colorado has become one of the strongest state affiliates in the Federation. Recently the NFB of Colorado took a giant step forward in serving the blind of the state. In January of 1988 the Colorado Center for the Blind with Diane McGeorge as Executive Director opened its doors for business. Four students enrolled initially, and the numbers have been growing ever since. These students learn the skills of blindness from teachers who believe in the fundamental competence of the blind. But even more important, they learn positive attitudes about blindness.

In 1977 McGeorge was elected to the Board of Directors of the National Federation of the Blind, and in 1984 she was chosen as the organization's First Vice President. In 1982 Diane and Ray McGeorge were presented with the Jacobus tenBroek Award for their work in improving the lives of the blind of the nation.

McGeorge says of her life since 1973, "These years have been more stimulating and rewarding than any previous period in my life. I don't wish to imply that I was unhappy prior to my becoming active in the Federation—quite the contrary. I was busy, and the things I was doing were important. But they were not as important as the Federation's agenda. Each thing the NFB does affects tens of thousands of people. Part of what I have learned is that what I do matters.

"I suppose," she says, "it is a commentary on the way I used to feel about myself; but until the last few years, it never occurred to me that anyone could do what I am now doing—let alone that *I* could. I would have been astonished to learn that thousands of blind people could and would work together to make real changes that affect all of us profoundly."

PEGGY PINDER
Attorney, City Councilman, Politician

Born in 1953 and raised in Grinnell, Iowa, Peggy Pinder attended regular schools until the middle of the ninth grade. When her eye condition was diagnosed as irreversible decline into total blindness, her father cried for the first and only time in her life—at least, as far as she knows.

Pinder then spent what she characterizes as two and a half unhappy years at the Iowa school for the blind. Academically she learned nothing that she had not already been taught in public schools. The students were discouraged from learning to use the white cane and were never allowed off campus unless they were accompanied by a sighted person. But most soul-destroying of all, the students were discouraged from aspiring to success or from setting themselves challenging goals. Pinder resisted the stifling atmosphere and drew down upon herself the wrath of the school administration, which refused to permit her to complete high school there, forcing her to go back to public school.

Knowing that she was not prepared to make this transition, she and her parents sought help from Dr. Kenneth Jernigan, then Director of the Iowa Commission for the Blind. Pinder enrolled at the Orientation and Adjustment Center, where she mastered the skills of blindness and explored for the first time the healthy and positive philosophy of blindness that has subsequently directed her life.

Pinder went on to Iowa's Cornell College, where she achieved an excellent academic record and edited the *Cornellian*, the school newspaper. She then completed law school at Yale University, receiving her J.D. Degree in 1979.

After graduation from law school, Pinder passed the Iowa Bar in January, 1980. She then began a difficult job search. Although her academic standing at Yale was better than that of most of her classmates, she did not receive a single job offer as a result of the intensive interviewing she had done during her final year of law school. Virtually all Yale-trained attorneys leave the university with offers in hand. The inference was inescapable: employers were discriminating against Pinder because of her blindness. She eventually was hired as Assistant County Attorney for Woodbury County in Sioux City, Iowa, where she prosecuted defendants on behalf of the people.

Pinder's lifetime interest in helping to improve the world around her has been expressed in politics as well as in Federation activity. In 1976 she was a delegate to the Republican National Convention in Kansas City. During the Convention she appeared on national television and in a national news magazine, taking the occasion to acquaint the public with the philosophy of the National Federation of the Blind and the real needs of blind people. At the end of the convention, she was chosen to second the nomination of Senator Robert Dole to be the candidate of the Republican Party for the Vice Presidency of the United States.

In 1986 she completed a campaign for the Iowa State Senate in District 27 (East-Central Iowa) on the Republican ticket. She won the Primary and campaigned hard in a district eighty by thirty miles in size and containing about 60,000 residents, a distinct minority of whom are Republican. From April through November she made hundreds of public appearances and managed an efficient campaign. Like many candidates, Pinder was not elected in her first bid for public office, but she made a very strong showing and is often asked when she will run again. Her interest in participating in her community continues today through her service on the Grinnell City Council and in other community organizations.

Pinder's work in the National Federation of the Blind has been as impressive as her professional career. She held office in the NFB Student Divisions in Iowa and Connecticut, and then served as President of the national Student Division from 1977 to 1979. In 1981 she was elected President of the National Federation of the Blind of Iowa, an office which she continues to hold. Pinder was first elected to serve on the NFB Board of Directors in 1977, and in 1984 she was elected Second Vice President.

For the past several years Pinder, a 1976 winner herself, has chaired the Scholarship Committee of the National Federation of the Blind. Every year approximately twenty- five scholarships, ranging in value from $1,800 to $10,000, are presented to the best blind college students in the nation.

JOYCE SCANLAN
Teacher and Agency Director

Joyce Scanlan was born in Fargo, North Dakota, in 1939. She received her elementary and secondary education at the North Dakota School for the Blind. Having a strong love of reading and theater, she went on to earn a B.A. in English and History and a master's degree in English at the University of North Dakota.

For the next five years she taught these subjects, along with social studies and Latin, in high schools in North Dakota and Montana. Then glaucoma took the rest of her vision, and Scanlan lost her self-confidence. She says, "I quickly fled from the job because I had never known a blind teacher in a public school, and I had had such a struggle those last few weeks in the classroom that I was positive no blind person could ever teach sighted children."

She had trouble finding another job, but as she points out, her own attitudes were as bad as those of her prospective employers. She told a counselor who visited her in the hospital:

"I've never seen a blind person amount to anything yet, so there's no reason to think I can."

In 1970 the National Federation of the Blind convention was in Minneapolis, and Scanlan attended the meeting of the NFB Teachers Division. She says: "I met many teachers there who were blind. In fact, I met blind people from all over the country who were engaged in a great variety of occupations. I learned what the NFB was all about and realized what blind people working together could do." At that convention she also met Tom Scanlan, whom she married four years later.

Joyce Scanlan became active in the NFB in Minnesota. In 1971 she organized a statewide student division. In 1972 she was elected vice president of the NFB of Minnesota and president in 1973. That same year she was appointed to a newly created Minnesota Council on Disabilities—the only representative of a consumer organization on the Commission. Until 1988 she served on the advisory council to State Services for the Blind, a body established in large measure because of the work of the NFB of Minnesota.

The most exciting undertaking of the NFB of Minnesota, however, has been the establishment of its own rehabilitation center for the adult blind, with Joyce Scanlan serving as its executive director. BLIND, Inc. (Blindness: Learning In New Dimensions) admitted its first class, consisting of two students, in January of 1988. This center is establishing a new standard for rehabilitation services in the Midwest. It is easy to understand why the National Federation of the Blind of Minnesota enjoys both respect and prestige. It is also easy to understand why Joyce Scanlan is regarded as able, tough, and determined.

Scanlan was elected to the NFB Board of Directors in 1974 and has continued to serve in that capacity ever since. In 1988 she was elected Secretary of the organization. She says: "The Federation has made a great difference in my life. I still try to spend time attending the theater and reading, but I want to give as much time as possible to working in the NFB. I wish I had known about it before 1970. I want to be sure every blind person

I ever meet hears all about the Federation. If I have any skill as a teacher, I'll use it to benefit the Federation."

ALLEN HARRIS
Teacher and Wrestling Coach

Allen Harris of Dearborn, Michigan, was elected to the Board of Directors of the National Federation of the Blind in 1981. In 1985 he became Secretary, and in 1988 he was elected Treasurer. He says, "I take some satisfaction in many of the things I have accomplished in my life, but nothing has given me more pleasure and reward than my work in the Federation."

Harris may well take satisfaction in his accomplishments. Blind since birth in 1945, he completed high school at the Michigan School for the Blind in Lansing. He says of this period, "The two most valuable things I learned in high school were wrestling and typing. Although I could have used some other things, these two skills have served me well ever since." Allen Harris was a championship wrestler throughout high school and college. He was also a champion debater at Wayne State University and graduated magna cum laude in 1967.

Harris then began looking for a teaching position and enrolled in graduate school. At that time high school teachers were much in demand. He sent out 167 applications and went to 96 interviews without receiving a single job offer. After a year of futile search Harris was depressed, and his friends were outraged. One friend went to a meeting of the school board of the Dearborn Public School System. She spoke openly about the blind applicant for a teaching position who was so well qualified, yet was being ignored by scores of school districts.

The tactic worked. Officials of the school district said that they were unaware of Harris's candidacy although he had submitted an application. He was called for an interview and hired to teach social studies. In addition to a full-time teaching schedule, he coached high school wrestling, as well as swimming and wrestling for boys from age five to fourteen. He has coached at least six high school wrestling teams that have won league championships and one high school state championship team. His age group swimming teams have won five state conference championships, and his age group wrestling teams have won six. Harris also worked for several years in the administration of the age group program, and the Dearborn teams continued to excel.

In 1982 Allen Harris became a social studies teacher at Edsel Ford High School in Dearborn. He became head of the social studies department in 1984. Because of limited time, he gave up the head coaching job and now works only with ninth graders, who have not lost since he has been their coach. In 1985 Harris was selected by the National Council of Social Studies as one of two outstanding teachers of social studies in the state of Michigan.

Harris says that he was aware of some Federation materials at the time he was looking for his first teaching position and that he found them helpful, but his real knowledge of and involvement in the Federation began in 1969 when an organizing team came to his door to pay a visit. They told him there was to be a state convention of the Federation that weekend in Lansing and that he should go. He did, and he was elected secretary of the NFB of Michigan. He served as president of the Detroit chapter of the

NFB from 1970 to 1975 and has been the president of the NFB of Michigan since 1976.

During the years of Allen Harris's presidency, services to the blind in Michigan have been consolidated into a single and separate commission for the blind, a major victory indeed. In 1983 Harris was appointed by the governor to the board of the Michigan Commission for the Blind, and he was reappointed in 1985 and 1988. He serves as Vice Chairman of the Board.

STEPHEN O. BENSON
Teacher, Rehabilitation Specialist,
and Administrator

President of the National Federation of the Blind of Illinois, Stephen O. Benson was born in Kewanee, Illinois, in 1941. Blind from birth, he attended the Chicago Public Schools using large print books through the first four grades. He was not excited about attending Braille classes the next year, but he did so and for the first time in his life learned to read well. He also began to learn the other skills of blindness, which he found more efficient than using sight. In high school Benson was barred from taking physical education although he would have liked to do so. He found this prohibition disturbing and nonsensical since he was permitted to take the Reserve Officers Training Corps (ROTC) course, swimming in the same pool that the physical education classes used. In fact, in Boy Scouts he was able to earn his swimming merit badge and took life saving. Benson found ROTC a positive experience and enjoyed scouting, but he never could understand why regular physical education classes were off limits.

In 1965 Benson graduated from De Paul University with a major in English and a minor in education. Before he decided to specialize in English, he had intended to major in psychology. The state rehabilitation agency for the blind threatened to cut off financial assistance to him because of his change in plans. According to the experts, blind people could not teach in public schools, and as a result, the rehabilitation officials refused to finance such an absurd major. Benson remembers that his attitude at the time was "I dare you to try to stop me!"—and the government agency backed down.

After graduation he prepared himself for the usually difficult task of job-hunting. Surprisingly, he found employment rather quickly, however, as a tenth-grade teacher of honors English at Gordon Technical High School in Chicago. But teaching was not satisfying to Benson. In 1968 he sold insurance while looking for another job. He took one in 1969 with the Veterans Administration Hospital in Hines, Illinois, teaching Braille and techniques of daily living. His title was Rehabilitation Specialist. He continued to work at Hines Blind Rehabilitation Center, Veterans Administration Hospital, until 1983. In 1984 he became assistant director of the Guild for the Blind in Chicago.

Benson married Margaret (Peggy) Gull in 1984. They have one child, Patrick Owen, born in 1985.

Benson first joined the National Federation of the Blind in 1968 when a new affiliate was being formed in Illinois. He was immediately elected to the state board of directors. From 1974 to 1978 he served as President of the Chicago chapter, after which he became President of the NFB of Illinois, a post which he has held ever since. He was first elected to the Board of Directors of the National Federation of the Blind in 1982.

Benson has received many honors and appointments. In 1963 and '64 he was president of Lambda Tau Lambda fraternity. From 1976 to 1981 he served on the governing board of the State Division of Vocational Rehabilitation in Illinois. He has served on the Advisory Board of the Illinois State Library for the Blind and Physically Handicapped and on the Advisory Board to the Attorney General's Advocacy for the Handicapped Division.

"Although I have had good blindness skills for many years," Benson says, "my involvement in the NFB has imbued me with confidence and perspective on life and blindness that have focused my activities and energized my efforts on my own behalf as well as for other blind people."

CHARLES S. BROWN
Attorney and Federal Official

With a Bachelor's Degree from Harvard and a law degree from Northwestern, Charles Brown should have found the job market both exciting and receptive in 1970, a year of expanded economy and bright prospects, but this was not the case. He had impressive credentials and good grades, but he didn't. He was blind. It was not the first time he had observed adverse and extraordinary treatment of the blind, but it was the first time he had personally faced such serious discrimination. It took him an entire year and more than a hundred interviews before he found a job.

In 1971 Brown became a staff attorney for the U.S. Department of Labor (DOL), and he has received regular promotions ever since. Today he is Counsel for Special Legal Services in the Office of the Solicitor at DOL. The Department has presented Brown with achievement awards five times—in 1979, 1985, twice in 1986, and 1987. In 1982 he was presented with the Distinguished Career Service Award, one of DOL's highest honors— often presented at the time of retirement. But Attorney Brown was chosen for this honor after only eleven years of service.

Born blind in 1944 with congenital cataracts, Charlie Brown entered a family that expected success from its members, and he met the expectation. He attended Perkins School for the Blind until the eighth grade. Brown then attended Wellesley Senior High School in Wellesley, Massachusetts, and graduated in 1963, going immediately on to Harvard. When he applied to Northwestern Law School, questions were raised about blindness. He answered them satisfactorily and believes he was one of the first blind law students ever to study there.

During summer jobs in 1966, 1967, and 1968 at agencies serving the blind in Chicago, Brown learned firsthand of the abuses of the sheltered workshop system for the blind in this country. It was also at that time that he met Dr. Kenneth Jernigan and made his initial contact with the National Federation of the Blind. Jernigan was speaking at a national conference, which (among other things) was considering ways of improving methods of instruction and increasing the availability of Braille. After the meeting Brown talked with Jernigan and began to subscribe to the *Braille Monitor*, the Federation's magazine. It was not until 1973, however, when Brown received a personal invitation from a chapter member in Northern Virginia, that he went to a Federation meeting.

Through a chapter in Northern Virginia Brown officially joined the Federation in 1974 and later that year was elected to office. In 1978 he became president of the National Federation of the Blind of Virginia and has been re-elected to that position for successive two-year terms ever since. He was first elected to the Board of Directors of the National Federation of the Blind in 1984.

Brown has always taken an active part in the life of the United Church of Christ. He teaches Sunday school and serves energetically on committees at the Rock Spring Congregational Church and has served generously at the Church's national level. In 1979 he was elected a corporate member of the United Church Board of Homeland Ministries (the body that oversees the missions work of the United Church of Christ). Within two years he was named Chairman of the prestigious Policy and Planning Committee and a member of the Executive Committee, both positions that he filled with distinction for four years.

Brown met his wife Jacqueline during law school, and the couple now has two sons, Richard (born in 1974) and Stephen (born in 1978).

Brown says: "I used to believe that one had to overcome blindness in order to be successful, but I have come to realize that it is respectable to be blind. Our challenge as Federationists is to persuade society of this truth."

DONALD C. CAPPS
Insurance Executive and Civic Leader

Few more compelling examples of personal independence and social contribution can be found among either sighted or blind Americans than Donald C. Capps of Columbia, South Carolina. Since the inception of the National Federation of the Blind of South Carolina in 1956, he has served nine two-year terms as president and presently holds that office. Capps was elected to the second vice presidency of the National Federation of the Blind in 1959 and served in that capacity until 1968. In that year he was elected First Vice President and served with distinction in that position until 1984 when, for health reasons, he asked that his name not be placed in nomination. In 1985 Capps (restored in health) was again enthusiastically and unanimously elected to membership on the Board of Directors of the National Federation of the Blind.

Born in 1928, Capps was educated at the South Carolina School for the Blind and later in public schools. Following his graduation from high school he enrolled in Draughon's Business College in Columbia and, upon receiving his diploma, joined the Colonial Life and Accident Insurance Company of Columbia as a claims examiner trainee. By the time of his retirement, he had risen to the position of Staff Manager of the Claims Department.

Capps first became interested in the organized blind movement in 1953 and by the following year had been elected president of the Columbia Chapter of the Aurora Club of the Blind (now the NFB of South Carolina), which he headed for two years before assuming the presidency of the state organization. Under Capps's energetic leadership the NFB of South Carolina has successfully backed twenty-three pieces of legislation concerning the blind in the state, including establishment of a separate agency serving the blind. Capps edits the *Palmetto Blind,* the quarterly publication of the NFB of South Carolina, articles from which are frequently reprinted in national journals for the blind. In 1960 Capps directed a campaign which led to construction of the National Federation of the Blind of South Carolina's $250,000 education and recreation center, which was expanded in 1970, and again in 1978. He now serves as a member of its Board of Trustees. In this role he has been instrumental in establishing fulltime daily operation of the Federation Center. In addition, Capps has served for more than thirty years as the successful fundraising chairman of the Columbia Chapter. In 1963 Capps was appointed to the Governor's Committee on the Employment of the Physically Handicapped.

In December, 1972, the Colonial Life and Accident Insurance Company presented Capps with an award for "twenty-five years of efficient, faithful, and loyal service" in his managerial capacity. In 1984 Don Capps retired from the Colonial Life and Accident Insurance Company after thirty-eight years of service.

In 1965 Donald Capps was honored as Handicapped Man of the Year, both by his city of Columbia and by his state. In 1967 he was appointed to the Governor's Statewide Planning Committee on Rehabilitation Needs of the Disabled. Capps was elected president of the Rotary Club of Forest Acres of Columbia in 1974. In 1977 he was elected Vice Chairman of the South Carolina Commission for the Blind Consumer Advisory Committee. Also in 1977, at the annual convention of the National Federation of the Blind, Don Capps received the highest honor that can be bestowed by the organized blind movement, the Jacobus tenBroek Award.

Honor and recognition continue to come to Donald Capps. In 1981 he was appointed by the Governor of South Carolina to membership on the Board of Commissioners of the South Carolina School for the Blind, a body on which he now serves as Vice Chairman. In September, 1988, Donald Capps was a member of the NFB delegation to the Second General Assembly of the World Blind Union held in Madrid, Spain.

Betty Capps has been an active Federationist as long as her husband has. The Cappses have two grown children, Craig and Beth, and two grandchildren. Although Donald Capps has retired from business, he continues to be as active and effective as ever in the Federation, exemplifying leadership and confidence. His ongoing dedication to the National Federation of the Blind provides inspiration and encouragement to his many colleagues and friends within and outside the Federation.

GLENN CROSBY
Businessman and Community Leader

The President of the National Federation of the Blind of Texas is Glenn Crosby of Houston. He was first elected to that position in 1968 and served until 1970. He was again elected in 1978. Crosby is a successful restaurant owner and manager, having opened his first snack bar in 1968. During the past twenty years he has owned food service businesses at five separate locations, usually two or three at a time. He has served on the school board of All Saints Elementary Catholic School, been a director of the Houston Heights Little League, and been active in several city and county political campaigns.

On April 15, 1989, Glenn Crosby and Norma Beathard were married. Norma is the capable President of the National Federation of the Blind of Houston.

Born in 1945, Glenn Crosby was blinded at the age of three by an accident. He was educated at the Texas School for the Blind. He says that there were so many restrictive rules at that school that the students learned to defy them. "It was the only way to survive," he says. "We learned (for better or worse) to take risks when we were still young."

The only dating permitted was expeditions to school socials. Students could leave the campus only in groups and only on Saturday afternoons twice a month unless they had specific parental permission for additional trips. Crosby graduated in 1963. The preceding year half the senior class was not graduated because they had left campus a few days before the ceremony for a celebration. The message to the Class of '63 was perhaps not what school officials had intended. The students did not forego their party; they merely took pains to insure that they were not caught. Crosby's assessment of the school's curriculum is that the classes were not bad but that the courses that would have allowed admission to the best colleges and universities were not available. He earned state championships in wrestling and was offered the opportunity to compete for the Olympics in 1964. Crosby believes that blindness was the reason he was not offered a wrestling scholarship at a prestigious school.

Poor as his education was, Crosby is grateful that he was among the relative handful of blind Texans who were educated at all at the time. Many blind youngsters were sent to the school for the blind as teenagers to learn a trade if they could, and most of these people are now employed in the state's thirteen sheltered workshops, frequently earning painfully low wages. It is not hard to understand why Glenn Crosby devotes a large part of his time and energy to the National Federation of the Blind—the consumer organization working to improve the lives and prospects of blind people.

Crosby's first job was with the Poverty Program. The only blind people he knew who earned a decent living worked in food service under the Randolph-Shepherd Program. His parents had been in business and had done some fast food service. Crosby did not want a business run by the state commission for the blind. He believed that he had had enough experience with state bureaucracy at the School for the Blind. Besides, he had learned to take risks young. Crosby does not doubt today that he made the right decision.

"If I had not seen it for myself, it would be hard for me to believe that the blind have made as much progress as we have since I have been a part of the Federation—a little more than twenty years. There are still thousands of blind people in Texas (and I am sure even more throughout the country) who have never had much of an education or much constructive help. The quality of their lives is poor. One day at a time I try to do my part to help improve the quality of life for all of us who are blind."

ROBERT M. ESCHBACH
Clergyman, Social Worker,
and Administrator

In 1932 Robert Eschbach was born in the Philippines, the son of missionary parents. He spent much of his childhood traveling around the world, returning to the United States in 1941 to settle in Michigan. Two years later he lost his sight.

He attended public school in Detroit before entering the Ohio State School for the Blind in the ninth grade. He graduated from Otterbein College in Westerville, Ohio, with majors in theoretical music and English; and in 1958 he received a Master of Divinity degree from United Theological Seminary in Dayton, Ohio.

The Reverend Eschbach served for nine years in the parish ministry. Then, in 1966, he accepted a fellowship in the Division of Religion and Psychology at the Menninger Foundation in Topeka, Kansas. The experience persuaded him to begin a career in social work, and he remained in Topeka to earn an M.S.W. degree at the University of Kansas before returning to Dayton in 1969. Eschbach then accepted a job as a therapist at the Eastway Community Mental Health Center in Dayton. His responsibilities were gradually increased until he became community services director. When the character and scope of the agency changed, Eschbach decided to return to the ministry. He and his wife Pat served two churches before he was appointed in 1985 to the position of assistant director of the Ohio Bureau of Services for the Visually Impaired.

Bob Eschbach became acquainted with the Federation in 1969 when he was invited to join the Dayton Chapter. He immediately concluded that he had discovered an entirely new way of approaching blindness. He became progressively more involved and committed in his local chapter, and in 1972 he attended the NFB convention in Chicago. It was his first exposure to the national movement, and he returned to Dayton feeling he had discovered the place where he wanted to be. He served as president of the NFB of Ohio from 1973 until 1984. During those years the state affiliate made great strides in unity and achieving progress for the blind. Bob Eschbach has served as a member of the NFB Board of Directors since 1974. He has chaired several committees and currently is President of the National Association of Dog Guide Users, the dog guide division of the NFB.

Other appointments include: member of the Consumer Advisory Council to Rehabilitation Services Administration of the State of Ohio; member of the Task Force on Disabilities for the Ohio West Conference of the United Methodist Church; and member of the Disabilities Task Force for the Ohio Council of Churches. Bob Eschbach is also an active member in Lions International, and he and his wife Pat have each participated in the Columbus, Ohio, Area Leadership Program. In 1982 Eschbach chaired the Citizens With Disabilities for Celeste Campaign for Governor.

Eschbach says: "The National Federation of the Blind is an important part of my life. Being part of an organization which is concerned about what happens to blind people has demonstrated to me the way service ought to be given and responsibilities shared. It is an easy and natural follow- through to my personal faith."

JOANNE FERNANDES
Teacher and Agency Director

Born in Chicago, Illinois, in 1946, Joanne Ziehan Fernandes moved with her parents to Webster City, Iowa, when she was seven. When she was 3, doctors had discovered that she had Retinitis Pigmentosa. She remembers everyone's attitude toward her poor eyesight. No one regarded her as blind, but everyone knew her eye condition could lead to blindness, a fact which friends and family did not want to confront. The whispers taught Fernandes that this being "blind" was a dreadful thing. She learned to pretend she could see to avoid the pity that would follow if she could not. And she learned to avoid thinking about blindness. It was too awful. Never once can Fernandes remember discussing blindness with a teacher or friend at school. She never met a single blind person. All she knew was that she did not want to be blind or think about it. Being blind wasn't respectable.

After Fernandes graduated from high school, she enrolled in a junior college. At that time the Iowa Commission for the Blind conducted a career day for blind students, which she attended. For the first time she met blind people. They were confident and capable. She decided that at the end of her second year of junior college she would take time out to attend the Orientation and Adjustment Center. Those nine months she describes as "the most exciting time of my life. I found freedom, and it wasn't always easy."

In 1969 Joanne Fernandes graduated with honor from Iowa State University, where she received a B.S. in Elementary Education. During one quarter she was selected as a Merrill Palmer Scholar to do advanced work in education in Detroit, Michigan.

For the next four years, Fernandes taught elementary school (second and fourth grades) in the Ames, Iowa, public school system. In 1971 she received a Master's degree in Guidance and Counseling. During this time Fernandes helped to organize the North Central Iowa Chapter of the National Federation of the Blind, and she served for several years as its president. From 1977 to 1979 she was first vice president of the National Federation of the Blind of Iowa.

In 1973, Fernandes had stopped teaching to begin a family. She is now the mother of 5 children ages 5 to 15. In 1979 she and her husband moved to Louisiana, and here she continued her Federation work. In 1981, Fernandes led the formation of a new NFB chapter in her hometown of Ruston, Louisiana, and forty people attended the first meeting. It was the eighth chapter in the state. Today in Louisiana there are twenty-one chapters.

Joanne Fernandes was elected President of the NFB of Louisiana in 1983 and has been elected for successive two-year terms ever since. In 1985, Governor Edwin Edwards recommended to the State Legislature that money be appropriated directly to the NFB of Louisiana for a training center for blind adults, and the prestige and reputation of the organization were such that the legislature responded affirmatively.

The Louisiana Center for the Blind opened in October of 1985 with Joanne Fernandes as its director, and the program which has been built is rapidly coming to be recognized throughout the nation as a model. More than a hundred students have now enrolled in the program, and they graduate ready for competition in the mainstream of society—and they graduate not only believing but knowing that it is respectable to be blind.

PRISCILLA FERRIS
Homemaker, Girl Scout Administrator,
and Community Volunteer

In 1938 Priscilla Pacheco Ferris was born in Dighton, Massachusetts. From the time she was a small child, she knew she had weak eyesight, but she and her family did not know that the condition, Retinitis Pigmentosa, would deteriorate into total blindness. During her early school years Ferris used print, but three years later, when her brother (who had the same eye condition) entered school, the staff refused to teach two blind children. So the Pacheco youngsters enrolled in the Perkins School for the Blind in Watertown, Massachusetts.

When Ferris entered Perkins, she was beginning the fourth grade, and she was expected to learn Braille immediately even though she could still read large print. She remembers that it took her about a month. She didn't feel put upon; it was simply a challenge. Today she recalls this when she must deal with debates about whether a blind child should read Braille or print. "Teach both," Ferris says unequivocally. "Low-vision children were not too stupid to learn both when I was a kid, and things haven't changed that much since."

After high school graduation in 1956, Priscilla Pacheco worked in a curtain factory for a year. She would have liked to go to college but did not have the money. Then she worked for five years in a cookie factory, doing whatever needed to be done, including assembly line work, packaging, and packing. She married Jack Ferris in 1961, and in 1963 she resigned to begin a family. The Ferrises now have two grown daughters.

In 1977, Priscilla Ferris finally had an opportunity to attend business school, where she earned a degree and graduated with distinction. Then she found a job as secretary for the Fall River Public Schools. By the time funding cuts eliminated her position, she was too busy with community activities and work for the Federation to look for another job.

Ferris led her first Girl Scout troop while working at the cookie factory in the 1950's. From that time until her own daughters were in Scouts she led troops from time to time. In 1974 she began fourteen years as town Administrator for the Girl Scouts in Somerset, Massachusetts, a job in which she was responsible for the entire scouting program for the city. She quips that, not only can she light a fire in the rain, raise a tent in a storm, and dig a latrine almost anywhere, but she can teach anyone else to. In 1986 she was elected to the Board of Directors of the Girl Scout Council of Plymouth Bay, and she has recently been elected to another three-year term. Ferris's contribution to scouting was recognized by the Council when it presented her with an award as the Outstanding Adult in 1986.

Ferris first heard of the National Federation of the Blind when a new chapter was formed in her area in 1961. She was mildly interested, but she did not join the Federation until 1974, shortly before losing the remainder of her eyesight. In 1976 Ferris was elected president of the Greater Fall River Chapter of the NFB of Massachusetts. She has been re-elected president every year from that time until the present.

In 1977, Ferris was elected second vice president of the NFB of Massachusetts and in 1981 first vice president. In 1985, she was elected President of the National Federation of the Blind of Massachusetts, and she has been re-elected for succeeding two-year terms ever since. She was elected to the Board of Directors of the National Federation of the Blind in July of 1987.

FRANK LEE
Minister

In Huntsville, Alabama, the pastor of Lakeside United Methodist Church is the Reverend Frank Lee. Lakeside claims one of the best-educated congregations of United Methodist churches in Alabama. The Reverend Lee has experienced far more discrimination and misunderstanding within the church and outside it because of his blindness than because of his race. When he first became an ordained minister ready for assignment to a church, the conference leadership planned that he would be a conference evangelist serving without salary. He objected because the church to which he hoped to be assigned was being left without a minister. There was no escaping the conclusion that the conference leaders believed a blind person could not handle the responsibilities of a church pastor. Church members in all but one of the churches to which the Reverend Lee has been assigned have also objected at first to having a blind minister, but Lee has always won their love and respect in short order.

In the United Methodist Church in the mid-seventies it was not customary for the pastor to request a particular church. Rather, the conference bishop and district superintendents conferred with local churches to make assignments. The Reverend Lee found that he must depart from this practice and make the request. As a young minister, he had to challenge the decisions of his superiors, something not calculated ordinarily to gain their confidence and respect, but it was necessary. Winning the trust and affection of church leaders and parishioners has taken time, but Lee has done it.

Frank Lee was born in Semmes, Alabama, in 1942. Soon afterward, his family moved to Dothan. He found himself in the middle of a farm family of fifteen children. When he was six, one eye was injured in an accident. The medicine available to the Lees at the time could not prevent infection from spreading to the other eye, causing total blindness within a few months.

Lee feels fortunate that his family learned about the school for the blind in Talladega, and he went there a year later. He remembers crying when he had to leave home and return to school. He also remembers that it was the only way for him to get an education. The academic curriculum was quite good. Lee participated in many sports, including baseball and volleyball, as well as singing in the choir from elementary through high school.

The school Lee attended was the Alabama Institute for the Deaf and Blind, which consisted of four separate schools: the white deaf, the white blind, the black deaf, and the black blind.

The campus for the black blind was very small, and it was separated from all the others.

Frank Lee remembers things that were exciting opportunities to him at the time. In 1952 he was the first child in his part of the school to use the Perkins Braille Writer. In 1962 he was in the third class to graduate from the black blind school. Prior to 1959 there were so few black blind high school students that they took courses in a public school in Talladega, receiving high school diplomas there. While most schools for the blind in the 1950's and early 1960's were just getting a good start at integrating blind youngsters into public school classes, Lee's school was just getting enough blind students to offer a complete high school curriculum. Integration of the races was still almost a decade away.

Between 1962 and 1966 Frank Lee spent twenty-one months operating a vending facility under the Randolph-Sheppard program, but he wanted to go to college. He had earned good grades, but not until 1966 could he convince the state rehabilitation agency for the blind to help him. In 1970 he earned a bachelor's degree in psychology from Talladega College. During these years Lee worked periodically as a camp counselor and in vending facilities. He was also active in church work. He had been singing in church choirs for years, and in 1962 he preached his first sermon. In 1973 he completed studies at the Interdenominational Theological Center in Atlanta. He also studied at Colgate Rochester Divinity School in Rochester, New York.

In 1976 Frank Lee married Frankie Boyd, whom he met in college.

Lee joined the National Federation of the Blind in 1982 and was elected Treasurer of the NFB of Alabama in 1985. In 1986 he was elected to the National Board of Directors and re-elected in 1988.

BETTY NICELEY
Rehabilitation Instructor
and Outreach Educator

Born in 1934, Betty Niceley was largely raised by her grandparents, who managed a series of country stores in Kentucky. She remembers three of these, each one larger than the one before. The family lived beside the stores, doing whatever needed to be done. It was all part of the family lifestyle—stocking shelves, filling orders, cashiering—and it was good experience for a blind child who might have had trouble finding work elsewhere.

At the age of nine, Betty Niceley left home to attend the Kentucky School for the Blind in Louisville. There she believes she got a reasonably good education. However, she transferred back home to Bell County High School, where she graduated. Her senior class chose her queen and the person most likely to succeed.

Niceley attended Georgetown College in central Kentucky where she received a Bachelor's degree in English and a secondary teaching certificate. It was at this time that she met her husband Charles. The Niceleys now have a daughter and two grandsons.

Her first real job after graduating from college was with the American Printing House for the Blind in Louisville. She did public relations and development work as well as filling in wherever Braille expertise, poise, or common sense were needed. After thirteen years at the Printing House, she changed jobs and began teaching Braille at the Rehabilitation Center operated by the Kentucky Department for the Blind. When the state's Independent Living Center opened in the fall of 1980, she joined the staff and again found herself doing whatever needed to be done. She teaches people of all ages Braille, techniques of daily living, and rudimentary travel skills. She also does virtually all the outreach education for groups who need instruction about blindness and dealing with blind people.

Betty Niceley first joined the Federation in 1968, although she had known about it for a long time without, as she puts it, "finding the time to get involved." Then, she joined and it was not long before her commitment and performance were such that she was elected Secretary of the National Federation of the Blind of Kentucky. At about this time she was also President of the Greater Louisville Chapter, a position she held until 1975. Niceley has served as President of the National Federation of the Blind of Kentucky since 1979.

In 1977 the State of Kentucky created a separate Department for the Blind, responsible directly to the Governor. Niceley points to this as one of the NFB of Kentucky's many accomplishments of which she is especially proud. "When my poor vision worsened and I became totally blind in my senior year of college, I had little trouble adjusting. I had learned to read and write Braille as a child and kept up both skills. That is one of the reasons I have been so excited about the National Association to Promote the Use of Braille (NAPUB)." Betty Niceley was elected its first president, a position which she still holds. She was elected to the Board of Directors of the National Federation of the Blind in 1985 and re-elected in 1987 and 1989.

FRED SCHROEDER
Teacher, Administrator,
and Government Official

Fred Schroeder, the youngest member of the Board of Directors of the National Federation of the Blind, was born in 1957 in Lima, Peru. His parents decided that he and his brother (six years older) would have better opportunities growing up in the United States, so they took steps to make it happen. By the time he was two, Fred had been adopted by Florence Schroeder of Albuquerque, New Mexico.

When he was seven, Schroeder developed an obscure little-known disorder known as Stephens-Johnson's Syndrome, which caused a gradual deterioration of eyesight and other serious physical problems. By the time he was sixteen, he was totally blind.

In order to do his school work during junior high and high school, he used a combination of taped materials, live readers, and simply not doing homework. He was able to take extra courses during these years and still maintain above-average grades. In spite of worsening eyesight, he resisted the idea of learning to read and write Braille. By the time he was a senior in high school, however, he had changed his mind and taught himself to read and write it. He used Braille constantly throughout college.

Schroeder received a bachelor's degree in psychology in 1977 from San Francisco State Universlty. In 1978 he earned a master's in elementary education and qualified for a California teaching certificate. He had then just turned twenty-one.

By 1977 Fred Schroeder had attended several conventions of the National Federation of the Blind of California, and in that year he was elected president of the Student Division in that state. He attended his first national convention in Baltimore during July of 1978. While there, he was offered a job as travel instructor at the Orientation and Adjustment Center in Lincoln, Nebraska. Initially Schroeder turned the job down, preferring to teach children. By the time he received his master's in August, however, he had decided to take the job and move to Nebraska, where he worked for two years. During this time he met Cathlene Nusser, a leader in the NFB of Nebraska, and the two were married in January of 1981.

Also during these Nebraska years, Schroeder took course work at San Francisco State University to strengthen his credentials as an instructor in orientation and mobility.

In September of 1980 Schroeder moved back to Albuquerque, New Mexico, where he became an itinerant teacher of blind children for the Albuquerque Public Schools. He worked for a year in this job before being promoted to the position of Coordinator of Low- Incidence Programs for the Albuquerque Public School System, a job he held with distinction for five years.

In 1986 he was appointed director of the newly-established New Mexico Commission for the Blind. In that position he has earned a nationwide reputation as one of the most dynamic and innovative administrators in the field of work with the blind. Schroeder has completed course work for a Ph.D. in educational administration from the University of New Mexico. He is currently writing his dissertation on teacher evaluation.

Schroeder has served his community and state in a number of positions. He was a member of the Braille Authority of North America from 1982 to 1986 and served as Vice Chairman during part of that time. He served on the governing board of the Registry of Interpreters for the Deaf in New Mexico beginning in 1984. Schroeder represented the Braille Authority of North America and the National Federation of the Blind at the International Conference on English Literary Braille in London, England, in 1988. Since 1987 he has served on the New Mexico Governor's Committee on Concerns of the Handicapped.

In 1980 Schroeder was elected to the Board of Directors of the National Federation of the Blind of New Mexico and in 1982 became the president of the organization, a position he held until 1986. In 1984 Schroeder was elected to the Board of Directors of the National Federation of the Blind. From 1983 to 1989 he served as president of the National Association of Blind Educators.

Schroeder remembers: "In 1978 I was getting a master's degree in the education of blind children, a field in which there was a nationwide shortage. After thirty-five or forty interviews, I didn't have a single job offer. I had to deal first-hand with the very real fact of discrimination against the blind. It is hard to keep an experience like that from eroding your self-confidence. It makes you question whether as a blind person you can compete in society, whether you can get past people's expectations and prejudices to show them what you can really do. The National Federation of the Blind makes the difference. It provides a way for blind people to give each other moral support, encouragement, and meaningful information. It helps people who are coming along to have advantages we didn't—and in the very act of encouraging and supporting others, we sustain and nurture our own morale and self-belief."

RAMONA WALHOF
Business Woman and
Public Relations Executive

Born in 1944, Ramona Willoughby Walhof was the second in a family of three blind children, but the word "blind" was never used when they were small, especially by the ophthalmologists. Nevertheless, even the large print books ordered for the children by the schools did not make reading possible. In the competitive world of the classroom the truth could not be avoided—they were blind. So they were packed up and taken more than two hundred miles away from home to enroll in the Iowa Braille and Sight Saving School. Walhof remembers that her parents found facing this alternative easier than struggling with a public school system that could not find a way to teach three bright youngsters who could not see print. A school for the blind was better than a school that didn't educate.

Walhof remembers learning to lie about what she could see. She didn't think of it as telling falsehoods, but she says, "It made adults happy when they thought I could see things, and at school (even though it was supposedly a school for the blind) one had privileges and responsibilities to the same degree one had usable eyesight."

During the summer following second grade Walhof commandeered her brother's Braille slate and stylus and taught herself to write Braille because the school considered her too young to learn it. She was taught to read using Braille, but she understood from the beginning that reading print (if only she could have managed to decipher it) was better.

In 1962 Ramona Willoughby graduated from high school, valedictorian of her class, but she says "with an extremely limited education and very little experience." Between high school and college, she took a short course of training at the Iowa Commission for the Blind Orientation and Adjustment Center. It was then that she met Kenneth Jernigan, the Commission's Director. She refused to learn much about the NFB although she now says, "The Federation had already begun to have a profound influence on my life." She found college difficult, she says, because her academic background was so weak. Nevertheless, Walhof graduated from Georgetown University in Washington, D.C. in 1967 with a degree in Russian language.

In 1968 Ramona Willoughby married Chuck Walhof of Boise, Idaho. During the next several years she was busy. She and her husband had two children, and she taught two sessions of Headstart and one course in college Russian. She also managed two vending facilities. After the death of her husband in 1972 she returned to Des Moines, Iowa, first as a teacher and then as an assistant director at the Orientation and Adjustment Center of the Iowa Commission for the Blind.

In 1979 Walhof moved to Baltimore, Maryland, to take a position at the National Center for the Blind as the Assistant Director of the Job Opportunities for the Blind Program, operated jointly by the NFB and the U.S. Department of Labor.

In 1982 she returned to Idaho to assume the position of Director of the state Commission for the Blind. Her reputation for innovative approaches and dynamic forthrightness soon reached far beyond the borders of Idaho. In 1984 the blind of the state recognized her achievements by giving her an award in public ceremonies.

Later that year she left government employment to go into private business. Today she operates extensive multi-state public relations and community outreach programs for the blind and other groups.

Ramona Walhof has written widely on topics relating to blindness, including the following books: *Beginning Braille for Adults*, (a teaching manual); *Questions Kids Ask about Blindness; A Handbook for Senior Citizens: Rights, Resources, and Responsibilities*; and *Technical Assistance Guide for Employers*.

In 1988 Walhof became president of the National Federation of the Blind of Idaho and was also elected to membership on the Board of Directors of the National Federation of the Blind.

GARY WUNDER
Senior Programmer Analyst and
Electronics Technologist

Gary Wunder was born three months prematurely in 1955, the oldest of four children. His family lived in Kansas City, Missouri, and Wunder remembers that since he was blind from birth, he managed to persuade everyone in his family except his father to do precisely what he wanted. It would be many years before Wunder could appreciate his father's instinctive understanding that Gary had to learn to do things for himself.

Wunder tells with amusement the story of his dawning awareness of his blindness. When he was two, his home had sliding glass doors separating the living room from the patio. When those doors were closed, he could not hear and therefore did not know what was happening on the other side and assumed that no one else could either. One day he found several soft drink bottles on the patio and broke them. His father then opened the doors and asked if he had broken the bottles. Gary said he had not and that he did not know how they had been broken. His father then astonished him by saying that both his parents had watched him break the bottles and that his mother was now crying because she had thought surely her baby couldn't tell a lie. Gary's response was to say, "Well, she knows better now."

Wunder attended grades one through five at a Kansas City public school. When he was ten, a boy who attended the Missouri School for the Blind persuaded him that he was missing real life by staying at home. At the school, his friend told him kids rode trains and buses. They could bowl and swim and didn't have to listen to parents. As a result, Wunder did some persuading at home and was on hand for sixth grade and some necessary but painful lessons about that real world.

At the close of seventh grade Wunder returned to public schools, having learned several vitally important lessons: He knew the basics of using a white cane; he recognized that his father's demands on him had sprung from strong love and eagerness for his son to succeed; and he understood that people beyond his own family had worth and deserved his respect. But he had also learned that the school for the blind was not the promised land, and he was delighted to be once more in public schools for eighth grade and high school. He was elected to the National Honor Society his senior year but struggled with the mechanics of getting his work done. Braille was not readily available, and readers were hard to recruit without the money to pay them.

Wunder planned to attend the University of Missouri at Kansas City in order to live with his grandmother, but after a taste of freedom at the orientation center in Columbia, Missouri, the summer before college he decided to enroll at the University's Columbia campus, where everyone walked everywhere and where he could contrive as many as three or four dates an evening if he hurried from place to place.

Wunder enjoys recounting the adventure which persuaded him that a blind person should always carry a white cane: "I was having dinner with a young woman who lived near me, so I had not brought my cane, figuring that I wouldn't need it. To my consternation and her distress, my plate of liver and onions slid into my lap. She asked if I wanted her to walk me home so that I could change. I was already so embarrassed that I assured her I would be right back and that I did not need her assistance. The busiest intersection in Columbia lay between me and clean slacks, and after I successfully survived that street crossing, I swore that I would never again be caught without my cane."

Wunder decided to major in political science and philosophy because he felt compelled to avoid the science and math that he loved but feared to take. During his sophomore year he met a professor from Central Missouri State University who suggested that he was ducking the challenge. Together they explored the question of whether or not a blind person could follow schematics and read volt-meters. The answers seemed to be yes, so Wunder transferred to Central Missouri State, where he graduated in 1977 with a degree in electronics technology. He had done well with the courses, but he did not see how he could run a repair shop with its responsibility for mastering hundreds of schematics for appliances. He could teach electronics, but the professors from whom he had learned the most were those who had firsthand experience. He didn't want to be the theory-only kind of teacher.

Wunder looked for interim jobs after graduation while he tried to decide what to do, and he discovered the hard way that blind job- seekers have to be better than the competition in order to be considered at all. He vowed to become so well-trained at doing something that would-be employers could not ignore him. Wunder enrolled in a ten- month course in computer programming offered by the Extension Division of the University of Missouri. No blind person had ever entered the program before, but Wunder completed it successfully and was hired immediately (in the fall of 1978) by the Pathology Department of the University of Missouri Hospital and Clinics in Columbia. Years and promotions later, Wunder is successfully working at the hospital and is now a Senior Programmer Analyst in the Information Services Department.

Wunder first learned about the National Federation of the Blind the summer before his senior year of high school. He says, "In the beginning I thought this talk about discrimination was a pretty good racket. No one did those things to me, and I assumed that all this Federation talk about jobs' being denied and parents' having children taken away from them was an effective way of raising funds. I didn't realize that my father's name and reputation in my hometown were protecting me from the worst of real life. So far I had gotten what I wanted, including a motorcycle to ride on our farm and my own horse. It was some time before I recognized that these talented and committed blind people whom I was getting to know in the Federation were trying to teach me about the world that I was going to inherit. They frightened me a little, but more and more I wanted to be like them."

In late 1973 (several months after Wunder started college in Columbia, Missouri, a Federation organizing team arrived to establish a new chapter, and he took an active part in the preparations. Wunder was elected President, and when he transferred to Central Missouri State two years later, he organized a chapter in Warrensburg. In 1977 Wunder was elected First Vice President of the NFB of Missouri, and in 1979 he became President. Except for one two-year term, he has continued in that post ever since. Wunder was elected to the Board of Directors of the National Federation of the Blind in 1985.

Wunder is a devoted family man. He is married to the former Sue Micich, who was at the time of their marriage President of the NFB of Wisconsin.

Looking back reflectively over the years of his involvement with and commitment to the Federation, Wunder says: "Of all I learned from my parents about honor, responsibility, and the necessity to be competent, what I could never get from them was a sense of where blind people fit in a world composed mostly of sighted people. Friends and loved ones had always told me how wonderful I was (wonderful for a blind person, that is), but until I came to know members of the National Federation of the Blind, no one had the experience or knowledge to say how I could expect to measure up alongside the sighted. The NFB was the first place where I didn't get a round of applause for performing the routine activities of life. If I wanted my Federation colleagues' recognition and admiration, I had to merit this attention. It sounds contradictory, but while I was learning that I wouldn't be applauded for insignificant accomplishments, I was also learning that I didn't have to possess special compensatory senses or talents to make my way in the world. When you think that your only opportunity for success lies in being a musician, when you know that your only musical talent is in listening, and when you suddenly find that you are capable of doing the average job in the average place of business, your sense of freedom, hope, and possibility know no bounds."

Constitution of the National Federation of the Blind, 1940

ARTICLE I THE NAME

The name of this organization is The National Federation of the Blind.

ARTICLE II PURPOSE

The purpose of the National Federation of the Blind is to promote the economic and social welfare of the blind.

ARTICLE III MEMBERSHIP

Section a). The membership of the National Federation of the Blind shall consist of delegations from each of the states of the United States.

Section b). Each state shall have one vote.

Section c). Delegations shall represent organizations of the blind controlled by the blind; but individuals may be admitted to membership with all the privileges and duties of representative members except that they shall not be entitled to vote or hold office.

ARTICLE IV OFFICERS

Section a). The officers of the National Federation of the Blind shall consist of president, first vice-president, second vice-president, secretary and treasurer. They shall be elected biennially.

Section b). The officers shall be elected by majority vote of the states.

Section c). The National Federation of the Blind shall have an Executive Board which shall be composed of the officers plus four members selected in the same way whose regular term shall be four years, but at the first election two shall be elected for two years.

ARTICLE V DUTIES OF OFFICERS

The officers shall have such powers as are usual to their respective offices and they shall be governed by Roberts Rules of Order revised.

ARTICLE VI PROCEEDINGS

Roberts Rules of Order revised shall govern all proceedings.

ARTICLE VII AMENDMENTS

This constitution may be amended at any annual meeting by a two- thirds majority vote of those present and voting.

Adopted and effective from November 16, 1940.

Constitution of the National Federation of the Blind, 1990

ARTICLE I. NAME

The name of this organization is The National Federation of the Blind.

ARTICLE II. PURPOSE

The purpose of the National Federation of the Blind is to serve as a vehicle for collective action by the blind of the nation; to function as a mechanism through which the blind and interested sighted persons can come together in local, state, and national meetings to plan and carry out programs to improve the quality of life for the blind; to provide a means of collective action for parents of blind children; to promote the vocational, cultural, and social advancement of the blind; to achieve the integration of the blind into society on a basis of equality with the sighted; and to take any other action which will improve the overall condition and standard of living of the blind.

ARTICLE III. MEMBERSHIP

Section A. The membership of The National Federation of the Blind shall consist of the members of the state affiliates, the members of divisions, and members at large. Members of divisions and members at large shall have the same rights, privileges, and responsibilities in The National Federation of the Blind as members of state affiliates.

The Board of Directors shall establish procedures for admission of divisions and shall determine the structure of divisions. The divisions shall, with the approval of the Board, adopt constitutions and determine their membership policies. Membership in divisions shall not be conditioned upon membership in state affiliates.

The Board of Directors shall establish procedures for admission of members at large, determine how many classes of such members shall be established, and determine the annual dues to be paid by members of each class.

Section B. Each state or territorial possession of the United States, including the District of Columbia, having an affiliate shall have one vote at the National Convention. These organizations shall be referred to as state affiliates.

Section C. State affiliates shall be organizations of the blind controlled by the blind. No organization shall be recognized as an "organization of the blind controlled by the blind" unless at least a majority of its voting members and a majority of the voting members of each of its local chapters are blind.

Section D. The Board of Directors shall establish procedures for the admission of state affiliates. There shall be only one state affiliate in each state.

Section E. Any member, local chapter, state affiliate, or division of this organization may be suspended, expelled, or otherwise disciplined for misconduct or for activity unbecoming to a member or affiliate of this organization by a two-thirds vote of the Board of Directors or by a simple majority of the states present and voting at a National Convention. If the action is to be taken by the Board, there must be good cause, and a good faith effort must have been made to try to resolve the problem by discussion and negotiation. If the action is to be taken by the Convention, notice must be given on the preceding day at an open Board meeting or a session of the Convention. If a dispute arises as to whether there was "good cause," or whether the Board made a "good faith effort," the National Convention (acting in its capacity as the supreme authority of the Federation) shall have the power to make final disposition of the matter; but until or unless the Board's action is reversed by the National Convention, the ruling of the Board shall continue in effect.

ARTICLE IV.
OFFICERS, BOARD OF DIRECTORS, AND NATIONAL ADVISORY BOARD

Section A. The officers of The National Federation of the Blind shall be: (1) President, (2) First Vice President, (3) Second Vice President, (4) Secretary, and (5) Treasurer. They shall be elected biennially.

Section B. The officers shall be elected by majority vote of the state affiliates present and voting at a National Convention.

Section C. The National Federation of the Blind shall have a Board of Directors, which shall be composed of the five officers and twelve additional members, six of whom shall be elected at the Annual Convention during even numbered years and six of whom shall be elected at the Annual Convention during odd numbered years. The members of the Board of Directors shall serve for two- year terms.

Section D. The Board of Directors may, in its discretion, create a National Advisory Board and determine the duties and qualifications of the members of the National Advisory Board.

ARTICLE V.
POWERS AND DUTIES OF THE CONVENTION, THE BOARD OF DIRECTORS, AND THE PRESIDENT

Section A. Powers and Duties of the Convention. The Convention is the supreme authority of the Federation. It is the legislature of the Federation. As such, it has final authority with respect to all issues of policy. Its decisions shall be made after opportunity has been afforded for full and fair discussion. Delegates and members in attendance may participate in all Convention discussions as a matter of right. Any member of the Federation may make or second motions, propose nominations, and serve on committees; and is eligible for election to office, except that only blind members may be elected to the National Board. Voting and making motions by proxy are prohibited. Consistent with the democratic character of the Federation, Convention meetings shall be so conducted as to prevent parliamentary maneuvers which would have the effect of interfering with the expression of the will of the majority on any question, or with the rights of the minority to full and fair presentation of their views. The Convention is not merely a gathering of representatives of separate state organizations. It is a meeting of the Federation at the national level in its character as a national organization. Committees of the Federation are committees of the national organization. The nominating committee shall consist of one member from each state affiliate represented at the Convention, and each state affiliate shall appoint its member to the committee. From among the members of the committee, the President shall appoint a chairperson.

Section B. Powers and Duties of the Board of Directors. The function of the Board of Directors as the governing body of the Federation between Conventions is to make policies when necessary and not in conflict with the policies adopted by the Convention. Policy decisions which can reasonably be postponed until the next meeting of the National Convention shall not be made by the Board of Directors. The Board of Directors shall serve as a credentials committee. It shall have the power to deal with organizational problems presented to it by any member, local chapter, state affiliate, or division; shall decide appeals regarding the validity of elections in local chapters, state affiliates, or divisions; and shall certify the credentials of delegates when questions regarding the validity of such credentials arise. By a two-thirds vote the Board may suspend one of its members for violation of a policy of the organization or for other action unbecoming to a member of the Federation. By a two-thirds vote the Board may reorganize any local chapter, state affiliate, or division. The Board may not suspend one of its own members or reorganize a local chapter, state affiliate, or division except for good cause and after a good faith effort has been made to try to resolve the problem by discussion and negotiation. If a dispute arises as to whether there was "good cause" or whether the Board made a "good faith effort," the National Convention (acting in its capacity as the supreme authority of the Federation) shall have the power to make final disposition of the matter; but until or unless the Board's action is reversed by the National Convention, the ruling of the Board shall continue in effect. There shall be a standing subcommittee of the Board of Directors which shall consist of three members. The committee shall be known as the Subcommittee on Budget and Finance. It shall, whenever it deems necessary, recommend to the Board of Directors principles of budgeting, accounting procedures, and methods of financing the Federation program; and shall consult with the President on major expenditures.

The Board of Directors shall meet at the time of each National Convention. It shall hold other meetings on the call of the President or on the written request of any five members.

Section C. Powers and Duties of the President. The President is the principal administrative officer of the Federation. In this capacity his or her duties consist of: carrying out the policies adopted by the Convention; conducting the day-to-day management of the affairs of the Federation; authorizing expenditures from the Federation treasury in accordance with and in implementation of the policies established by the Convention; appointing all committees of the Federation except the Nominating Committee; coordinating all activities of the Federation, including the work of other officers and of committees; hiring, supervising, and dismissing staff members and other employees of the Federation, and determining their numbers and compensation; taking all administrative actions necessary and proper to put into effect the programs and accomplish the purposes of the Federation.

The implementation and administration of the interim policies adopted by the Board of Directors are the responsibility of the President as principal administrative officer of the Federation.

ARTICLE VI. STATE AFFILIATES

Any organized group desiring to become a state affiliate of The National Federation of the Blind shall apply for affiliation by submitting to the President of The National Federation of the Blind a copy of its constitution and a list of the names and addresses of its elected officers. Under procedures to be established by the Board of Directors, action shall be taken on the application. If the action is affirmative, The National Federation of the Blind shall issue to the organization a charter of affiliation. Upon request of the National President the state affiliate shall provide to the National President the names and addresses of its members. Copies of all amendments to the constitution and/or bylaws of an affiliate shall be sent without delay to the National President. No organization shall be accepted as an affiliate and no organization shall remain an affiliate unless at least a majority of its voting members are blind. The president, vice president (or vice presidents), and at least a majority of the executive committee or board of directors of the state affiliate and of all of its local chapters must be blind. Affiliates must not merely be social organizations but must formulate programs and actively work to promote the economic and social betterment of the blind. Affiliates and their local chapters must comply with the provisions of the Constitution of the Federation. Policy decisions of the Federation are binding upon all affiliates and local chapters, and the affiliate and its local chapters must participate affirmatively in carrying out such policy decisions. The name *National Federation of the Blind, Federation of the Blind,* or any variant thereof is the property of The National Federation of the Blind; and any affiliate, or local chapter of an affiliate, which ceases to be part of The National Federation of the Blind (for whatever reason) shall forthwith forfeit the right to use the name *National Federation of the Blind, Federation of the Blind,* or any variant thereof.

A general convention of the membership of an affiliate or of the elected delegates of the membership must be held and its principal executive officers must be elected at least once every two years. There can be no closed membership. Proxy voting is prohibited in state affiliates and local chapters. Each affiliate must have a written constitution or bylaws setting forth its structure, the authority of its officers, and the basic procedures which it will follow. No publicly contributed funds may be divided among the membership of an affiliate or local chapter on the basis of membership, and (upon request from the National Office) an affiliate or local chapter must present an accounting of all of its receipts and expenditures. An affiliate or local chapter must not indulge in attacks upon the officers, Board members, leaders, or members of the Federation or upon the organization itself outside of the organization, and must not allow its officers or members to indulge in such attacks. This requirement shall not be interpreted to interfere with the right of an affiliate or local chapter, or its officers or members, to carry on a political campaign inside the Federation for election to office or to achieve policy changes. However, the organization will not sanction or permit deliberate, sustained campaigns of internal organizational destruction by state affiliates, local chapters, or members. No affiliate or local chapter may join or support, or allow its officers or members to join or support, any temporary or permanent organization inside the Federation which has not received the sanction and approval of the Federation.

ARTICLE VII. DISSOLUTION

In the event of dissolution, all assets of the organization shall be given to an organization with similar purposes which has received a 501(c)(3) certification by the Internal Revenue Service.

ARTICLE VIII. AMENDMENTS

This Constitution may be amended at any regular Annual Convention of the Federation by an affirmative vote of two-thirds of the state affiliates registered, present, and voting; provided that the proposed amendment shall have been signed by five state affiliates in good standing and that it shall have been presented to the President the day before final action by the Convention.

National Convention Sites, 1940-1990

1990 - Dallas, Texas
1989 - Denver, Colorado
1988 - Chicago, Illinois
1987 - Phoenix, Arizona
1986 - Kansas City, Missouri
1985 - Louisville, Kentucky
1984 - Phoenix, Arizona
1983 - Kansas City, Missouri
1982 - Minneapolis, Minnesota
1981 - Baltimore, Maryland
1980 - Minneapolis, Minnesota
1979 - Miami, Florida
1978 - Baltimore, Maryland
1977 - New Orleans, Louisiana
1976 - Los Angeles, California
1975 - Chicago, Illinois
1974 - Chicago, Illinois
1973 - New York, New York
1972 - Chicago, Illinois
1971 - Houston, Texas
1970 - Minneapolis, Minnesota
1969 - Columbia, South Carolina
1968 - Des Moines, Iowa
1967 - Los Angeles, California
1966 - Louisville, Kentucky
1965 - Washington, D. C.

1964 - Phoenix, Arizona
1963 - Philadelphia, Pennsylvania
1962 - Detroit, Michigan
1961 - Kansas City, Missouri
1960 - Miami, Florida
1959 - Santa Fe, New Mexico
1958 - Boston, Massachusetts
1957 - New Orleans, Louisiana
1956 - San Francisco, California
1955 - Omaha, Nebraska
1954 - Louisville, Kentucky
1953 - Milwaukee, Wisconsin
1952 - Nashville, Tennessee
1951 - Oklahoma City, Oklahoma
1950 - Chicago, Illinois
1949 - Denver, Colorado
1948 - Baltimore, Maryland
1947 - Minneapolis, Minnesota
1946 - St. Louis, Missouri
1945 - Canceled
1944 - Cleveland, Ohio
1943 - Canceled
1942 - Des Moines, Iowa
1941 - Milwaukee, Wisconsin
1940 - Wilkes-Barre, Pennsylvania

Index

Floyd Matson
"Bio-Bibliography"

Floyd Matson is the author or editor of eleven books in the fields of history and the social sciences. Two of his books were written in collaboration with Jacobus tenBroek, the founder of the National Federation of the Blind; one of those books, Hope Deferred: Public Welfare and the Blind (1959), has acquired the stature of a classic text within the organized blind movement. The other collaboration, Prejudice, War and the Constitution (1954), won the Woodrow Wilson Award of the American Political Science Association. Matson's books—which have been translated into German, Spanish, Italian, and Japanese editions—include The Broken Image (1964), The Idea of Man (1976), The Human Connection (1979), and The Dehumanization of Man (1983). Matson is Professor of American Studies at the University of Hawaii, where he has taught since 1965. Prior to that he was on the faculty of the University of California, Berkeley, where he also earned his Ph.D. in political science. He has lectured widely abroad (including England, Italy, Canada, the Netherlands, Taiwan, and South Korea), and in 1988 he delivered a series of broadcast lectures on American culture to a nationwide television audience in Japan. Among the honors he has received is the Distinguished Humanist Award of the American Humanist Association. He is a past president of the Association for Humanistic Psychology and serves on the editorial boards of three professional journals.